Principles of Computer Security: CompTIA Security+™ and Beyond

Sixth Edition

(Exam SY0-601)

About the Authors

Dr. Wm. Arthur Conklin, CompTIA Security+, CISSP, GICSP, GRID, GCIP, GCFA, GCIA, GCDA, CSSLP, CRISC, is a professor and director at the Center for Information Security Research and Education in the College of Technology at the University of Houston. He is the Dean of the Dragos Academy, the learning arm of Dragos, Inc. He holds two terminal degrees—a PhD in business administration (specializing in information security) from the University of Texas at San Antonio (UTSA) and an Electrical Engineer degree (specializing in space systems engineering) from the Naval Postgraduate School in Monterey, California. He is a fellow of ISSA and $(CS)^2AI$ as well as a senior member of ASQ, IEEE, and ACM. His research interests include the use of systems theory to explore information security, specifically in cyber-physical systems. He has a strong interest in cybersecurity education and is involved with the NSA/DHS Centers of Academic Excellence in Cyber Defense (CAE CD) and the NIST National Initiative for Cybersecurity Education (NICE) Cybersecurity Workforce Framework (NICE Framework). He has coauthored six security books and numerous academic articles associated with information security. He is co-chair of the steering committee for the DHS-sponsored Industrial Control Systems Joint Working Group (ICSJWG) efforts associated with workforce development and cybersecurity aspects of industrial control systems. He has an extensive background in secure coding and has been co-chair of the DHS/DoD Software Assurance Forum Working Group for workforce education, training, and development.

Dr. Gregory White has been involved in computer and network security since 1986. He spent 19 years on active duty with the United States Air Force and 11 years in the Air Force Reserves in a variety of computer and security positions. He obtained his PhD in computer science from Texas A&M University in 1995. His dissertation topic was in the area of computer network intrusion detection, and he continues to conduct research in this area today. He is currently the director for the Center for Infrastructure Assurance and Security (CIAS) and is a professor of computer science at the University of Texas at San Antonio (UTSA). He has written and presented numerous articles and conference papers on security. He is also the coauthor of six textbooks on computer and network security and has written chapters for two other security books. He continues to be active in security research. His current research initiatives include efforts in community incident response, intrusion detection, and secure information sharing.

Chuck Cothren, CISSP, is Manager of Development Operations at Ionic Security, applying over 20 years of information security experience in consulting, research, and enterprise environments. He has assisted clients in a variety of industries, including healthcare, banking, information technology, retail, and manufacturing. He advises clients on topics such as security architecture, penetration testing, training, consultant management, data loss prevention, and encryption. He is coauthor of the books *Voice and Data Security* and *CompTIA Security+ All-in-One Exam Guide, Sixth Edition (Exam SY0-601).*

Roger L. Davis, CISSP, CISM, CISA, is a Senior Customer Success Account Manager for Microsoft supporting enterprise-level companies. He has served as president of the Utah chapter of the Information Systems Security Association (ISSA) and various board positions for the Utah chapter of the Information Systems Audit and Control Association (ISACA). He is a retired Air Force lieutenant colonel with 40 years of military and information systems/security experience. He served on the faculty of Brigham Young University and the Air Force Institute of Technology. He coauthored McGraw Hill's *CompTIA Security+ All-in-One Exam Guide, Sixth Edition (Exam SY0-601)* and *Voice and Data Security*. He holds a master's degree in computer science from George Washington University, a bachelor's degree in computer science from Brigham Young University, and performed postgraduate studies in electrical engineering and computer science at the University of Colorado.

Dwayne Williams, CISSP, CASP, is Associate Director, Technology and Research, for the Center for Infrastructure Assurance and Security at the University of Texas at San Antonio and is Director of the National Collegiate Cyber Defense Competition. He has over 24 years of experience in information systems and network security. His experience includes six years of commissioned military service as a Communications-Computer Information Systems Officer in the United States Air Force, specializing in network security, corporate information protection, intrusion detection systems, incident response, and VPN technology. Prior to joining the CIAS, he served as Director of Consulting for SecureLogix Corporation, where he directed and provided security assessment and integration services to Fortune 100, government, public utility, oil and gas, financial, and technology clients. He graduated in 1993 from Baylor University with a Bachelor of Arts in computer science. He is a coauthor of *Voice and Data Security* and *CompTIA Security+ All-in-One Exam Guide, Sixth Edition (Exam SY0-601).*

About the Technical Editor

Chris Crayton, MCSE, is an author, technical consultant, and trainer. He has worked as a computer technology and networking instructor, information security director, network administrator, network engineer, and PC specialist. Chris has authored several print and online books on PC repair, CompTIA A+, CompTIA Security+, and Microsoft Windows. He has also served as technical editor and content contributor on numerous technical titles for several of the leading publishing companies. He holds numerous industry certifications, has been recognized with many professional teaching awards, and has served as a state-level SkillsUSA competition judge.

Principles of Computer Security: CompTIA Security+™ and Beyond

Sixth Edition

(Exam SY0-601)

Dr. Wm. Arthur Conklin
Dr. Gregory White
Chuck Cothren
Roger Davis
Dwayne Williams

Mc Graw Hill

New York Chicago San Francisco
Athens London Madrid Mexico City
Milan New Delhi Singapore Sydney Toronto

McGraw Hill books are available at special quantity discounts to use as premiums and sales promotions, or for use in corporate training programs. To contact a representative, please visit the Contact Us pages at www.mhprofessional.com.

Principles of Computer Security: CompTIA Security+™ and Beyond, Sixth Edition (Exam SY0-601)

1 2 3 4 5 6 7 8 9 LWI 25 24 23 22 21

Library of Congress Control Number: 2021937295

ISBN 978-1-260-47431-2
MHID 1-260-47431-3

Sponsoring Editor
Tim Green

Editorial Supervisor
Janet Walden

Project Editor
Rachel Fogelberg

Acquisitions Coordinator
Emily Walters

Technical Editor
Chris Crayton

Copy Editor
Bart Reed

Proofreader
Paul Tyler

Indexer
Ted Laux

Production Supervisor
Thomas Somers

Composition
KnowledgeWorks Global Ltd.

Illustration
KnowledgeWorks Global Ltd.

Art Director, Cover
Jeff Weeks

Acknowledgments

We, the authors of *Principles of Computer Security: CompTIA Security+ and Beyond, Sixth Edition (Exam SY0-601)*, have many individuals who we need to acknowledge—individuals without whom this effort would not have been successful.

The list needs to start with those folks at McGraw Hill who worked tirelessly with the project's multiple authors and led us successfully through the minefield that is a book schedule and who took our rough chapters and drawings and turned them into a final, professional product we can be proud of. We thank Emily Walters from the Acquisitions team, Janet Walden from the Editorial Services team, and Tom Somers from the Production team. We also thank the technical editor, Chris Crayton; the project editor, Rachel Fogelberg; the copy editor, Bart Reed; the proofreader, Paul Tyler; and the indexer, Ted Laux, for all their attention to detail that made this a finer work after they finished with it. And to Tim Green, who made these journeys possible.

We also need to acknowledge our current employers who, to our great delight, have seen fit to pay us to work in a career field that we all find exciting and rewarding. There is never a dull moment in security because it is constantly changing.

We would like to thank Art Conklin for again herding the cats on this one.

Finally, we would each like to individually thank those people who—on a personal basis—have provided the core support for us individually. Without these special people in our lives, none of us could have put this work together.

—The Author Team

To my wife, Susan: thank you for your love, support, and patience, and for putting up with me while we lived a year in quarantine!

—Art Conklin

I would like to thank my wife, Charlan, for the tremendous support she has always given me.

—Gregory B. White

Josie, Macon, and Jet: thank you for the love, support, and laughs.

—Chuck Cothren

Geena, all I am is because of you. Thanks for being my greatest support. As always, love to my powerful children and wonderful grandkids!

—Roger L. Davis

To my wife and best friend, Leah, for her love, energy, and support—thank you for always being there. To my kids—this is what Daddy was typing on the computer!

—Dwayne Williams

This book is dedicated to the many cybersecurity professionals who quietly work to ensure the safety of our nation's critical infrastructures. We want to recognize the thousands of dedicated individuals who strive to protect our national assets but who seldom receive praise and often are only noticed when an incident occurs. To you, we say thank you for a job well done!

ABOUT THIS BOOK

Important Technology Skills

Information technology (IT) offers many career paths, and cybersecurity is one of the fastest growing tracks for IT professionals. This book provides coverage of the materials you need to begin your exploration of cybersecurity. In addition to covering all of the CompTIA Security+ exam objectives, this book includes additional material to help you build a solid introductory knowledge of cybersecurity.

***Key Terms**, identified in red, point out important vocabulary and definitions that you need to know.*

***Cross Check** questions develop reasoning skills: ask, compare, contrast, and explain.*

***Tech Tip** sidebars provide inside information from experienced IT professionals.*

***Notes, Tips,** and **Warnings** create a road map for success.*

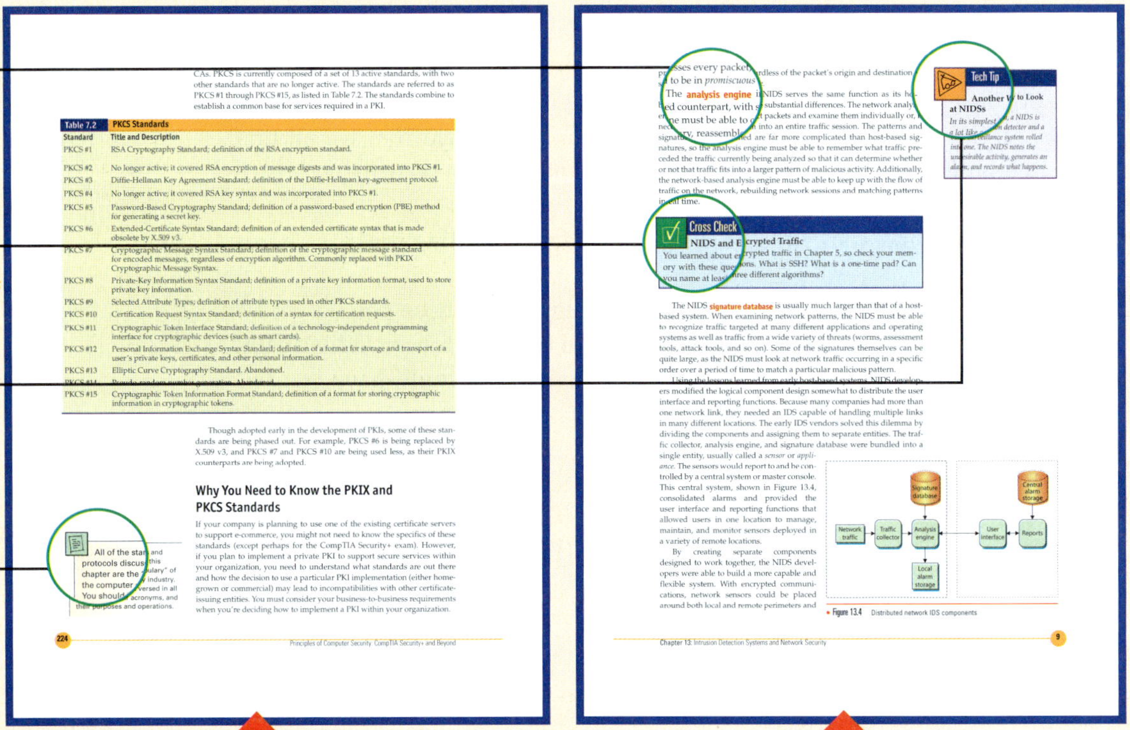

***Engaging and Motivational**— Using a conversational style and proven instructional approach, the authors explain technical concepts in a clear, interesting way using real-world examples.*

***Makes Learning Fun!**— Rich colorful text and enhanced illustrations bring technical subjects to life.*

Proven Learning Method Keeps You on Track

Designed for classroom use and written by instructors for use in their own classes, *Principles of Computer Security* is structured to give you comprehensive knowledge of cybersecurity. The textbook's active learning methodology guides you beyond mere recall and—through thought-provoking activities, labs, and sidebars—helps you develop critical-thinking, diagnostic, and communication skills.

Effective Learning Tools

This feature-rich textbook is designed to make learning easy and enjoyable and to help you develop the skills and critical-thinking abilities that will enable you to adapt to different job situations and to troubleshoot problems. Written by instructors with decades of combined cybersecurity experience, this book conveys even the most complex issues in an accessible, easy-to understand format.

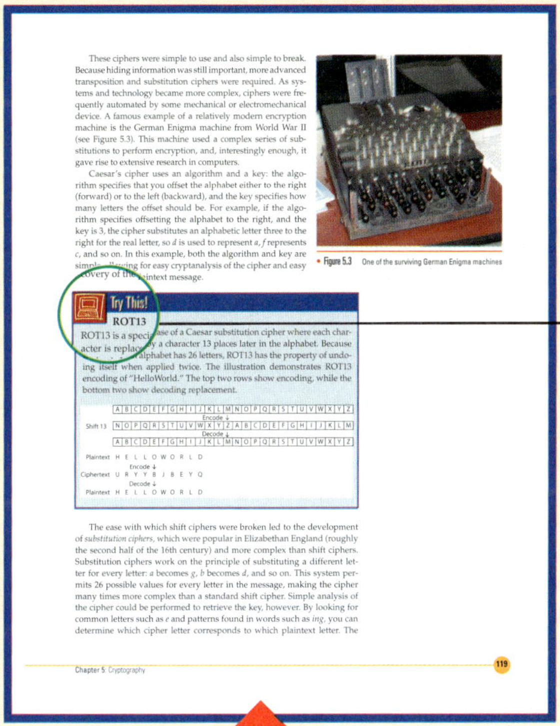

These ciphers were simple to use and also simple to break. Because hiding information was still important, more advanced transposition and substitution ciphers were required. As systems and technology became more complex, ciphers were frequently automated by some mechanical or electromechanical device. A famous example of a relatively modern encryption machine is the German Enigma machine from World War II (see Figure 5.3). This machine used a complex series of substitutions to perform encryption, and, interestingly enough, it gave rise to extensive research in computers.

Caesar's cipher uses an algorithm and a key: the algorithm specifies that you offset the alphabet either to the right (forward) or to the left (backward), and the key specifies how many letters the offset should be. For example, if the algorithm specifies offsetting the alphabet to the right, and the key is 3, the cipher substitutes an alphabetic letter three to the right for the real letter, so *d* is used to represent *a*, *f* represents *c*, and so on. In this example, both the algorithm and key are simp[illegible]wing for easy cryptanalysis of the cipher and easy [illegible]overy of the [illegible]intext message.

• Figure 5.3 One of the surviving German Enigma machines

Try This!

ROT13

ROT13 is a speci[illegible]ase of a Caesar substitution cipher where each character is replac[illegible]y a character 13 places later in the alphabet. Because [illegible] alphabet has 26 letters, ROT13 has the property of undoing itself when applied twice. The illustration demonstrates ROT13 encoding of "HelloWorld." The top two rows show encoding, while the bottom two show decoding replacement.

	A	B	C	D	E	F	G	H	I	J	K	L	M	N	O	P	Q	R	S	T	U	V	W	X	Y	Z
Shift 13	N	O	P	Q	R	S	T	U	V	W	X	Y	Z	A	B	C	D	E	F	G	H	I	J	K	L	M
	A	B	C	D	E	F	G	H	I	J	K	L	M	N	O	P	Q	R	S	T	U	V	W	X	Y	Z

(Encode ↓ between the first two rows; Decode ↓ between the last two rows.)

Plaintext H E L L O W O R L D
Encode ↓
Ciphertext U R Y Y B J B E Y Q
Decode ↓
Plaintext H E L L O W O R L D

The ease with which shift ciphers were broken led to the development of *substitution ciphers*, which were popular in Elizabethan England (roughly the second half of the 16th century) and more complex than shift ciphers. Substitution ciphers work on the principle of substituting a different letter for every letter: *a* becomes *g*, *b* becomes *d*, and so on. This system permits 26 possible values for every letter in the message, making the cipher many times more complex than a standard shift cipher. Simple analysis of the cipher could be performed to retrieve the key, however. By looking for common letters such as *e* and patterns found in words such as *ing*, you can determine which cipher letter corresponds to which plaintext letter. The

Chapter 5: Cryptography 119

Offers Practical Experience—
Tutorials and lab assignments develop essential hands-on skills and put concepts in real-world context.

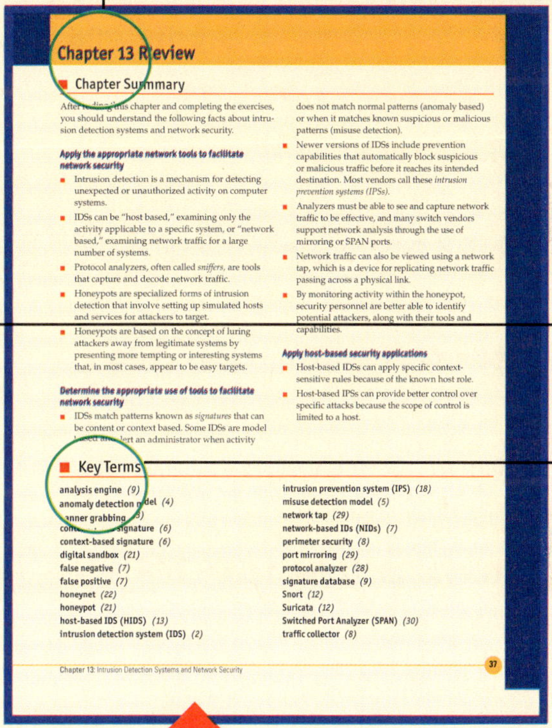

Chapter 13 R[illegible]eview

Chapter Su[illegible]mmary

After [illegible] this chapter and completing the exercises, you should understand the following facts about intrusion detection systems and network security.

Apply the appropriate network tools to facilitate network security

- Intrusion detection is a mechanism for detecting unexpected or unauthorized activity on computer systems.
- IDSs can be "host based," examining only the activity applicable to a specific system, or "network based," examining network traffic for a large number of systems.
- Protocol analyzers, often called *sniffers*, are tools that capture and decode network traffic.
- Honeypots are specialized forms of intrusion detection that involve setting up simulated hosts and services for attackers to target.
- Honeypots are based on the concept of luring attackers away from legitimate systems by presenting more tempting or interesting systems that, in most cases, appear to be easy targets.

Determine the appropriate use of tools to facilitate network security

- IDSs match patterns known as *signatures* that can be content or context based. Some IDSs are model [illegible] [illegible]lert an administrator when activity does not match normal patterns (anomaly based) or when it matches known suspicious or malicious patterns (misuse detection).
- Newer versions of IDSs include prevention capabilities that automatically block suspicious or malicious traffic before it reaches its intended destination. Most vendors call these *intrusion prevention systems (IPSs)*.
- Analyzers must be able to see and capture network traffic to be effective, and many switch vendors support network analysis through the use of mirroring or SPAN ports.
- Network traffic can also be viewed using a network tap, which is a device for replicating network traffic passing across a physical link.
- By monitoring activity within the honeypot, security personnel are better able to identify potential attackers, along with their tools and capabilities.

Apply host-based security applications

- Host-based IDSs can apply specific context-sensitive rules because of the known host role.
- Host-based IPSs can provide better control over specific attacks because the scope of control is limited to a host.

Key Terms

analysis engine *(9)*
anomaly detection [illegible]del *(4)*
[illegible]anner grabbing [illegible]
co[illegible]signature *(6)*
context-based signature *(6)*
digital sandbox *(21)*
false negative *(7)*
false positive *(7)*
honeynet *(22)*
honeypot *(21)*
host-based IDS (HIDS) *(13)*
intrusion detection system (IDS) *(2)*
intrusion prevention system (IPS) *(18)*
misuse detection model *(5)*
network tap *(29)*
network-based IDs (NIDs) *(7)*
perimeter security *(8)*
port mirroring *(29)*
protocol analyzer *(28)*
signature database *(9)*
Snort *(12)*
Suricata *(12)*
Switched Port Analyzer (SPAN) *(30)*
traffic collector *(8)*

Chapter 13: Intrusion Detection Systems and Network Security 37

Robust Learning Tools—
Summaries, key terms lists, quizzes, essay questions, and lab projects help you practice skills and measure progress.

Chapter Review *sections provide concept summaries, key terms lists, and lots of questions and projects.*

Try This! *exercises apply core skills in a new setting.*

Key Terms *presents a list of the important terms identified in the chapter.*

The chapters in this book include the following elements:

- **Learning objectives** that set measurable goals for chapter-by-chapter progress
- **Illustrations** that give you a clear picture of the concepts and technologies
- **Try This!, Cross Check**, and **Tech Tip** sidebars that encourage you to practice and apply concepts in real-world settings
- **Notes, Tips**, and **Warnings** that guide you, and **Exam Tips** that give you advice or provide information specifically related to preparing for the exam
- **Chapter summaries** and **Key Terms lists** that provide you with an easy way to review important concepts and vocabulary
- **Challenging end-of-chapter tests** that include vocabulary-building exercises, multiple-choice questions, essay questions, and on-the-job lab projects

CONTENTS AT A GLANCE

CONTENTS

Chapter 6

Applied Cryptography 148

Chapter 7

Public Key Infrastructure 184

Chapter 15

Types of Attacks and Malicious Software 574

Chapter 21

Business Continuity, Disaster Recovery, and Change Management 800

Chapter 22

Incident Response 836

FOREWORD

Decisions, decisions, decisions—selecting a book for a class is tricky for me. If a book is for personal reading pleasure, I merely decide if I would I like reading it. If the book is for my professional development, I have to decide if it will meet my needs and be a pleasure to read. Finally, if the choice is for my students, I have to decide if it will be a pleasure to read, meet their needs, and be clear and concise.

This new edition of *Principles of Computer Security* passes all three tests with flying colors. I enjoyed reading it. If I needed to pass the CompTIA Security+ or similar practitioner examination, it would prepare me. And finally, based on personal experience, students will like this book and find it to be valuable reading and study material. It even has practice exams for certification and has an e-book for their convenience.

For more than 40 years I have worked in some aspect of computer security. When people ask me what defines my job, I respond with "I don't know until I read the morning newspaper because the security environment changes rapidly." If you want to get into the computer security industry, reading and understanding this book is a great introduction. Now in its sixth edition, *Principles of Computer Security* focuses on a broad spectrum of important topics, across 25 chapters, to prepare you to be a certified computer security practitioner.

Dr. Conklin and his team of coauthors ease you into the meat of the topic by reviewing both security trends and concepts. They then address security from two different perspectives. First, they focus on the organization's need for security, and, second, they focus on the important role of people within the organization. These two perspectives are intertwined; it is essential for a security practitioner to understand the security environment and how the people make it work.

Every practitioner needs to understand the underlying technology and tools of computer security. Some individuals have an idea about security topics but do not have the essential knowledge needed to address them in depth. The authors have provided a series of masterful chapters introducing these key concepts. For example, in a single chapter, they provide the basis for you to deal with security of networks. This chapter provides everything you need to know to address standards and protocols, infrastructure security, remote access and authentication, as well as wireless. The authors integrate these concepts to support public key infrastructure (PKI) and intrusion detection systems for network security without forgetting the importance of physical security in protecting the information system as well as infrastructure.

One of the most debated topics in security is the importance of cryptography. Some would assert that almost all digital security can be accomplished with cryptography—that security and cryptography are inseparable, with cryptography being the cornerstone of securing data in both transmission and storage. However, if computer security were as easy as "encrypt everything," this would be a very short book. Although cryptography is very important and a very complex security measure, it is not a panacea—but it does provide for lively discussions. By discussing applied security and PKI separately, the authors cause you to a focus on the real world. They bring all these components together with a comprehensive chapter on intrusion detection and prevention.

Once you have mastered the basics, the authors address e-mail, malicious software, instant messaging, and web components in such a way that you can apply your knowledge of networks and security fundamentals. You will then be provided with an overview of secure software development. Poorly developed software is one of the biggest cyberthreats—perhaps 90 percent of the threats come through poor software design.

In the final analysis, security is really all about risk management. What is your organization's appetite for risk, and how is that risk managed? The chapters covering risk management lead you through these less technical issues to gain an understanding as to how they impact the organization. Baselines and change management are essential to understanding what assets are being secured and how they are being changed. A reader who learns these skills well will be able to work in incident response, disaster recovery, and business continuity. Understanding these processes and how they work with technical issues expands career opportunities.

The authors conclude their review of the principles of computer security with an examination of privacy, legal issues, and ethics. Although these topics appear at the end of the book, they are crucial issues in the modern world. Remember, as a computer security practitioner, you will have legal access to more data and information than anyone else in the organization.

Although it's not the topic of the last chapter in the book, forensics is covered here last. The authors have done a wonderful job of addressing this complex topic. But why mention it last? Because many times forensics is what one does after computer security fails.

Tonight it is 15 degrees and snowing outside while I sit in my study—warm, dry, and comfortable. My home is my castle. Not bad for mid-winter in Idaho; however, I should not forget that one reason I am comfortable is because certified computer security practitioners are protecting my information and privacy as well as the critical infrastructure that supports it.

For instructors:

I have taught from prior editions of this book for several years. *Principles of Computer Security, Sixth Edition* has instructor materials on a companion website available to adopting instructors. Instructor manuals, including the answers to the end-of-chapter questions, PowerPoint slides, and the test bank of questions for use as quizzes or exams, make preparation a snap.

Corey D. Schou, PhD
Series Editor
University Professor of Informatics
Professor of Computer Science
Director of the National Information Assurance Training and Education Center
Idaho State University

PREFACE

Cybersecurity has moved from the confines of academia to mainstream America in the twenty-first century. Data breaches, information disclosures, and high-profile hacks involving the theft of information and intellectual property seem to be a regular staple of the news. It has become increasingly obvious to everybody that something needs to be done to secure not only our nation's critical infrastructure but also the businesses we deal with on a daily basis. The question is, "Where do we begin?" What can the average information technology professional do to secure the systems they are hired to maintain? One immediate answer is education and training. If we want to secure our computer systems and networks, we need to know how to do this and what security entails.

Our way of life—from commerce to messaging, business communications, and even social media—depends on the proper functioning of our worldwide infrastructure. A common thread throughout the infrastructure is technology—especially technology related to computers and communication. Thus, any individual, organization, or nation-state that wants to cause damage to this nation could attack it, not just with traditional weapons, but with computers through the Internet. Complacency is not an option in today's hostile network environment. The protection of our networks and systems is not the sole domain of the information security professional, but rather the responsibility of all who are involved in the design, development, deployment, and operation of the systems that are nearly ubiquitous in our daily lives. With virtually every system we depend on daily at risk, the attack surface and corresponding risk profile are extremely large. Information security has matured from a series of technical issues to a comprehensive risk management problem, and this book provides the foundational material to engage in the field in a professional manner.

So, where do you, the IT professional seeking more knowledge on security, start your studies? This book offers a comprehensive review of the underlying foundations and technologies associated with securing our systems and networks. The IT world is overflowing with certifications that can be obtained by those attempting to learn more about their chosen profession. The information security sector is no different, and the CompTIA Security+ exam offers a solid introductory level of certification for security. In the pages of this book you will find not only material that can help you prepare for taking the CompTIA Security+ exam but also the basic information you will need in order to understand the issues involved in securing your computer systems and networks today. In no way is this book the final source for learning all about protecting your organization's systems, but it serves as a starting point from which to launch your security studies and career.

One thing is certainly true about this field of study: it never gets boring. It constantly changes as technology itself advances. Something else you will find as you progress in your security studies is that no matter how much technology advances and no matter how many new security devices are developed, at the most basic level, humans are still the weak link in the security chain. If you are looking for an exciting area to delve into, then you have certainly chosen wisely. Cybersecurity offers a challenging blend of technology and people issues. And securing the systems of tomorrow will require everyone to work together—not just security personnel, but developers, operators, and users alike. We, the authors of this book, wish you luck as you embark on an exciting and challenging career path.

Wm. Arthur Conklin, PhD

INTRODUCTION

Cybersecurity has become paramount in enterprises large and small, as the number of security incidents steadily climbs. Not only has the number of incidents increased, but the consequences of the attacks have also increased—in many cases to levels that can threaten a business. Many corporations now spend significant portions of their budget on security hardware, software, services, and personnel. They are spending this money not because it increases sales or enhances the product they provide, but because of the possible consequences should they not take protective actions.

This money is spent on both technology and people to perform security tasks. The people side of the equation includes the security professionals in an organization, but increasingly more and more of the members of the technology team, from developers to testers to management, need an understanding of the security issues, causes, and solutions associated with their technology offerings. This book serves as an introduction to the theories and practices of cybersecurity as it applies to multiple items—from hardware to software, and from equipment that costs less than $25 to enterprise-level systems.

Why Focus on Security?

Security is not something we want to have to pay for; it would be nice if we didn't have to worry about protecting our data from disclosure, modification, or destruction by unauthorized individuals, but that is not the environment we find ourselves in today. Instead, we have seen the cost of recovering from security incidents steadily rise along with the number of incidents themselves. Cyberattacks and information disclosures are occurring so often that one almost ignores them on the news. But with the theft of over 145 million consumers' credit data from Equifax, with the subsequent resignation of the CSO and CEO, and hearings in Congress over the role of legislative oversight with respect to critical records, a new sense of purpose in regard to securing data may be at hand. The multiple $300+ million losses from NotPetya in the summer of 2017 have illustrated the high cost of security failures in business due to security lapses. In 2020, besides a global pandemic that created challenging times for employees and the work-from-home movement, came the SolarWinds incident, a successful attack against thousands of networks. The days of paper reports and corporate "lip service" may be waning, and the time to meet the new challenges of even more sophisticated attackers has arrived. There will never be the last data breach, nor will attackers stop attacking our systems, so our only path forward is to have qualified professionals defending our systems.

A Growing Need for Security Specialists

In order to protect our computer systems and networks, we need a significant number of new security professionals trained in the many aspects of computer and network security. This is not an easy task, as the systems connected to the Internet become increasingly complex, with software whose lines of code number in the millions. Understanding why this is such a difficult problem to solve is not hard if you consider just how many errors might be present in a piece of software that is several million lines long. When you add in the factor of how fast software is being developed—from necessity as the market is constantly changing—then understanding how errors occur is easy.

Not every "bug" in the software will result in a security hole, but it doesn't take many to have a drastic effect on the Internet community. We can't just blame the vendors for this situation, because they are reacting to the demands of government and industry. Many vendors are fairly adept at developing patches for flaws found in their software, and patches are constantly being issued to protect systems from bugs that may introduce security problems. This presents a whole new problem for managers and administrators—patch management. How important this has become is easily illustrated by how many of the most recent security events have occurred as a result of a security bug that was discovered months prior to the security incident, and for which a patch had been available, but the community had not correctly installed the patch, thus making the incident possible. The reasons for these failures are many, but in the end the solution is a matter of trained professionals at multiple levels in an organization working together to resolve these problems.

But the issue of having trained people does not stop with security professionals. Every user, from the boardroom to the mailroom, plays a role in the cybersecurity posture of a firm. Training the non-security professionals in the enterprise to use the proper level of care when interacting with systems will not make the problem go away either, but it will substantially strengthen the posture of the enterprise. Understanding the needed training and making it a reality is another task on the security professional's to-do list.

Because of the need for an increasing number of security professionals who are trained to some minimum level of understanding, certifications such as the CompTIA Security+ have been developed. Prospective employers want to know that the individual they are considering hiring knows what to do in terms of security. The prospective employee, in turn, wants to have a way to demonstrate their level of understanding, which can enhance the candidate's chances of being hired. The community as a whole simply wants more trained security professionals.

Preparing Yourself for the CompTIA Security+ Exam

Principles of Computer Security, Sixth Edition is designed to help prepare you to take the CompTIA Security+ certification exam. When you pass it, you will have demonstrated you have that basic understanding of security that employers are looking for. Passing this certification exam will not be an easy task—you will need to learn many things to acquire that basic understanding of computer and network security.

How This Book Is Organized

The book is divided into chapters that correspond with the objectives of the exam itself. Some of the chapters are more technical than others—reflecting the nature of the security environment where you will be forced to deal with not only technical details but also other issues such as security policies and procedures as well as training and education. Although many individuals involved in computer and network security have advanced degrees in math, computer science, information systems, or computer or electrical engineering, you do not need this technical background to address security effectively in your organization. You do not need to develop your own cryptographic algorithm, for example; you simply need to be able to understand how cryptography is used, along with its strengths and weaknesses. As you progress in your studies, you will learn that many security problems are caused by the human element. The best technology in the world still ends up being placed in an environment where humans have the opportunity to foul things up—and all too often do.

Onward and Upward

At this point, we hope you are excited about the topic of security, even if you weren't in the first place. We wish you luck in your endeavors and welcome you to the exciting field of computer and network security.

INSTRUCTOR WEBSITE

Instructors who have adopted this book for a course can access the support materials identified next. Contact your McGraw Hill sales representative for details on how to access the materials.

Instructor Materials

The *Principles of Computer Security* companion website provides many resources for instructors:

- Answer keys to the end-of-chapter activities in the textbook
- Engaging PowerPoint slides on the lecture topics (including full-color artwork from the book)
- An instructor's manual that includes learning objectives, classroom preparation notes, instructor tips, and a lecture outline for each chapter
- Access to test bank files that allow you to generate a wide array of paper- or network-based tests. The test bank includes:
  - Hundreds of practice questions and a wide variety of question types and difficulty levels, enabling you to customize each test to maximize student progress
  - Blackboard cartridges and other formats may also be available upon request; contact your McGraw Hill sales representative
- The answer keys to the companion text *Principles of Computer Security: CompTIA Security+ and Beyond Lab Manual, Sixth Edition (Exam SY0-601)* (available separately)

chapter 1

Introduction and Security Trends

Experience is merely the name men gave to their mistakes.

—Oscar Wilde, *The Picture of Dorian Gray*

In this chapter, you will learn how to

- **Define computer security**
- **Discuss common threats and recent computer crimes that have been committed**
- **List and discuss recent trends in computer security**
- **Describe common avenues of attacks**
- **Describe approaches to computer security**
- **Discuss the relevant ethical issues associated with computer security**

Why should we be concerned about computer and network security? All you have to do is check your newsfeed to find out about a variety of security problems that affect our nation and the world today. The danger to computers and networks may seem to pale in comparison to the threat of terrorist strikes, but in fact the average citizen is much more likely to be the target of an attack on their own personal computer, or a computer they use at their place of work, than they are to be the direct victim of a terrorist attack. This chapter will introduce you to a number of issues involved in securing your computers and networks from a variety of threats that may utilize any of a number of different attacks.

The Computer Security Problem

Fifty years ago, companies did not conduct business across the Internet. Online banking and shopping were only dreams in science fiction stories. Today, however, millions of people perform online transactions every day. Companies rely on the Internet to operate and conduct business. Vast amounts of money are transferred via networks, in the form of either bank transactions or simple credit card purchases. Wherever there are vast amounts of money, there are those who will try to take advantage of the environment to conduct fraud or theft. There are many different ways to attack computers and networks to take advantage of what has made shopping, banking, investing, and leisure pursuits a simple matter of "dragging and clicking" (or tapping) for many people. Identity theft is so common today that most everyone knows somebody who has been a victim of such a crime, if they haven't been a victim themselves. This is just one type of criminal activity that can be conducted using the Internet. There are many others, and all are on the rise.

Tech Tip

Historical Computer Security

Computer security is an ever-changing issue. Fifty years ago, computer security was mainly concerned with the physical devices that made up the computer. At the time, computers were the high-value items that organizations could not afford to lose. Today, computer equipment is inexpensive compared to the value of the data processed by the computer. Now the high-value item is not the machine, but the information that it stores and processes. This has fundamentally changed the focus of computer security from what it was in the early years. Today, the data stored and processed by computers is almost always more valuable than the hardware.

Definition of Computer Security

Computer security is not a simple concept to define, and it has numerous complexities associated with it. If one is referring to a computer, then it can be considered secure when the computer does what it is supposed to do and *only* what it is supposed to do. But as was noted earlier, the security emphasis has shifted from the computer to the information being processed. Information security is defined by the information being protected from unauthorized access or alteration and yet is available to authorized individuals when required. When one begins considering the aspects of information, it is important to realize that information is stored, processed, and transferred between machines, and all of these different states require appropriate protection schemes. *Information assurance* is a term used to describe not just the protection of information, but a means of knowing the level of protection that has been accomplished.

While *computer security* and *information security* both refer to a state where the hardware and software perform only desired actions and the information is protected from unauthorized access or alteration and is available to authorized users when required, the industry has centered on the term *cybersecurity* for the field.

Historical Security Incidents

By examining some of the computer-related crimes that have been committed over the last 30 or so years, we can better understand the threats and security issues that surround our computer systems and networks. Electronic crime can take a number of different forms, but the ones we examine here fall into one of two basic categories: crimes in which the computer was the target or incidents in which a computer was used to perpetrate the act (for example, there are many different ways to conduct bank fraud, one of which uses computers to access the records that banks process and maintain).

We start our tour of computer crimes with the 1988 Internet worm (Morris worm), one of the first real Internet crime cases. Prior to 1988, criminal activity was chiefly centered on unauthorized access to computer systems and networks owned by the telephone company and companies that provided dial-up access for authorized users. Virus activity also existed prior to 1988, having started in the early 1980s.

> **Tech Tip**
>
> **Intellectual Curiosity**
>
> *In the early days of computer crime, much of the criminal activity centered on gaining unauthorized access to computer systems. In many early cases, the perpetrator of the crime did not intend to cause any damage to the computer but was instead on a quest of "intellectual curiosity"—trying to learn more about computers and networks. Today, the ubiquitous nature of computers and networks has eliminated the perceived need for individuals to break into computers to learn more about them. While there are still those who dabble in hacking for the intellectual challenge, it is more common today for the intellectual curiosity to be replaced by malicious intent. Whatever the reason, today it is considered unacceptable (and illegal) to gain unauthorized access to computer systems and networks.*

The Morris Worm (November 1988)

Robert Morris, then a graduate student at Cornell University, released what has become known as the Internet worm (or the Morris worm). The worm infected roughly 10 percent of the machines then connected to the Internet (which amounted to approximately 6000 infected machines). The worm carried no malicious payload, the program being obviously a "work in progress," but it did wreak havoc because it continually reinfected computer systems until they could no longer run any programs.

Citibank and Vladimir Levin (June–October 1994)

Starting about June of 1994 and continuing until at least October of the same year, a number of bank transfers were made by Vladimir Levin of St. Petersburg, Russia. By the time he and his accomplices were caught, they had transferred an estimated $10 million. Eventually all but about $400,000 was recovered. Levin reportedly accomplished the break-ins by dialing in to Citibank's cash management system. This system allowed clients to initiate their own fund transfers to other banks.

Kevin Mitnick (February 1995)

Kevin Mitnick's computer activities occurred over a number of years during the 1980s and 1990s. Arrested in 1995, he eventually pled guilty to four counts of wire fraud, two counts of computer fraud, and one count of illegally intercepting a wire communication and was sentenced to 46 months in jail. In the plea agreement, Mitnick admitted to having gained unauthorized access to a number of different computer systems belonging to companies such as Motorola, Novell, Fujitsu, and Sun Microsystems. He described using a number of different "tools" and techniques, including social engineering, sniffers, and cloned cellular telephones.

Worcester Airport and "Jester" (March 1997)

In March of 1997, telephone services to the Federal Aviation Administration (FAA) control tower as well as the emergency services at the Worcester Airport and the community of Rutland, Massachusetts, were cut off for a period of six hours. This disruption occurred as a result of an attack on the phone network by a teenage computer "hacker" who went by the name "Jester."

The Melissa Virus (March 1999)

Melissa is the best known of the early macro-type viruses that attach themselves to documents for programs that have limited macro programming capability. The virus, written and released by David Smith, infected about a million computers and caused an estimated $80 million in damages.

The Love Letter Virus (May 2000)

Also known as the "ILOVEYOU" worm and the "Love Bug," the Love Letter virus was written and released by a Philippine student named

Onel de Guzman. The virus was spread via e-mail with the subject line of "ILOVEYOU." Estimates of the number of infected machines worldwide have been as high as 45 million, accompanied by a possible $10 billion in damages (it should be noted that figures like these are extremely hard to verify or calculate).

The Code Red Worm (2001)

On July 19, 2001, in a period of 14 hours, over 350,000 computers connected to the Internet were infected by the Code Red worm. The cost estimate for how much damage the worm caused (including variations of the worm released on later dates) exceeded $2.5 billion. The vulnerability, a buffer-overflow condition in Microsoft's IIS web servers, had been known for a month.

> **Tech Tip**
>
> **Speed of Virus Proliferation**
>
> *The speed at which the Slammer worm spread served as a wakeup call to security professionals. It drove home the point that the Internet could be adversely impacted in a matter of minutes. This in turn caused a number of professionals to rethink how prepared they needed to be in order to respond to virus outbreaks in the future. A good first step is to apply patches to systems and software as soon as possible. This will often eliminate the vulnerabilities that the worms and viruses are designed to target.*

The Slammer Worm (2003)

On Saturday, January 25, 2003, the Slammer worm was released. It exploited a buffer-overflow vulnerability in computers running Microsoft SQL Server or SQL Server Desktop Engine. Like the vulnerability in Code Red, this weakness was not new and, in fact, had been discovered and a patch released in July of 2002. Within the first 24 hours of Slammer's release, the worm had infected at least 120,000 hosts and caused network outages and the disruption of airline flights, elections, and ATMs. At its peak, Slammer-infected hosts were generating a reported 1TB of worm-related traffic *every* second. The worm doubled its number of infected hosts every 8 seconds. It is estimated that it took less than 10 minutes to reach global proportions and infect 90 percent of the possible hosts it could infect.

Cyberwar? (2007)

In May of 2007, the country of Estonia was crippled by a massive denial-of-service (DoS) cyberattack against all of its infrastructure, firms (banks), and government offices. This attack was traced to IP addresses in Russia but was never clearly attributed to a government-sanctioned effort.

Operation Bot Roast (2007)

In 2007, the Federal Bureau of Investigation (FBI) announced that it had conducted Operation Bot Roast, identifying over 1 million botnet crime victims. In the process of dismantling the botnets, the FBI arrested several botnet operators across the United States. Although seemingly a big success, this effort made only a small dent in the vast volume of botnets in operation.

Conficker (2008–2009)

In late 2008 and early 2009, security experts became alarmed when it was discovered that millions of systems attached to the Internet were infected with the Downadup worm. Also known as Conficker, the worm was believed to have originated in Ukraine. Infected systems were not initially damaged beyond having their antivirus solution updates blocked. What alarmed experts was the fact that infected systems could be used in a secondary attack on other systems or networks. Each of these infected systems

> **Tech Tip**
>
> **Software Patches**
>
> *One of the most effective measures security professionals can take to address attacks on their computer systems and networks is to ensure that all software is up to date in terms of vendor-released patches. Many of the outbreaks of viruses and worms would have been much less severe if everybody had applied security updates and patches when they were released. For the operating system that you use, go to your favorite web browser to find what patches exist for the operating system and what vulnerabilities or issues the patches were created to address.*

> **Tech Tip**
>
> **APTs**
>
> *One of the major distinguishing characteristics of APTs is their desire to remain undetected. An APT typically follows these steps:*
>
> - *Infiltrate the network (typically phishing and then malware).*
> - *Use malware to create a communication channel to external servers (command and control, or C2).*
> - *Traverse the network and create multiple accounts/ means of entry.*
> - *Gather credentials and map assets.*
> - *Gather data and exfiltrate it to C2.*
> - *Cover tracks. Rinse and repeat.*
>
> *APTs are the instrument of choice for government hackers, and are used by Russia, China, Iran, and North Korea as means of stealing intellectual property and other information. Common names are applied by industry trade groups.*

was part of what is known as a *bot network* (or *botnet*) and could be used to cause a DoS attack on a target or be used for the forwarding of spam e-mail to millions of users.

U.S. Electric Power Grid (2009)

In April 2009, Homeland Security Secretary Janet Napolitano told reporters that the United States was aware of attempts by both Russia and China to break into the U.S. electric power grid, map it out, and plant destructive programs that could be activated at a later date. She indicated that these attacks were not new and had in fact been going on for years. One article in the *Kansas City Star*, for example, reported that in 1997 the local power company, Kansas City Power and Light, encountered perhaps 10,000 attacks for the entire year. By 2009, the company experienced 30–60 million attacks.

Fiber Cable Cut (2009)

On April 9, 2009, a widespread phone and Internet outage hit the San Jose area in California. This outage was not the result of a group of determined hackers gaining unauthorized access to the computers that operate these networks, but instead occurred as a result of several intentional cuts in the physical cables that carry the signals. The cuts resulted in a loss of all telephone, cell phone, and Internet service for thousands of users in the San Jose area. Emergency services such as 911 were also affected, which could have had severe consequences.

The Current Threat Environment

The threats of the past were smaller, targeted, and in many cases only a nuisance. As time has gone on, more organized elements of cybercrime have entered the picture along with nation-states. From 2009 and beyond, the cyberthreat landscape became considerably more dangerous, with new adversaries out to perform one of two functions: to deny you the use of your computer systems or to use your systems for financial gain, including theft of intellectual property or financial information such as personally identifiable information (PII).

Advanced Persistent Threats

Although there are numerous claims as to when **advanced persistent threats (APTs)** began and who first coined the term, the important issue is to note that APTs represent a new breed of attack pattern. Although specific definitions vary, the three words that comprise the term provide the key elements: advanced, persistent, and threat. *Advanced* refers to the use of advanced techniques, such as spear phishing, as a vector into a target. *Persistent* refers to the attacker's goal of establishing a long-term, hidden position on a system. Many APTs can go on for years without being noticed. *Threat* refers to the other objective: exploitation. If an adversary invests the resources to achieve an APT attack, they are doing it for some form of long-term advantage. APTs are not a specific type of attack, but rather the new means by which highly resourced adversaries target systems.

Tech Tip

Noteworthy APT Groups

In no particular order, here's a list of several noteworthy APT groups:

- ***Lazarus Group (North Korea)*** *Targets U.S. and South Korea. Responsible for Sony hack. Employs ransomware.*
- ***Equation Group (U.S. government)*** *Targets U.S. adversaries. Employs zero-days and EternalBlue.*
- ***APT28/Fancy Bear (Russia)*** *Targets the U.S. and the DNC. Employs spear-phishing.*
- ***Sandworm (Russian military intelligence)*** *Responsible for the Ukrainian grid attacks and the destructive NotPetya.*
- ***APT33/Elfin (Iran)*** *Targets Saudi Arabia. Responsible for Shamoon.*
- ***APT18/Dynamite Panda (China)*** *Targets U.S. Employs trojans, ransomware, and Gh0st RAT.*
- ***APT19/Codoso Group (China)*** *Targets U.S. legal and investment firms.*
- ***APT1/Comment Crew (China)*** *Targets everyone. Known as PLA Unit 61398. Employs spear-phishing.*

For more information, refer to https://www.fireeye.com/current-threats/apt-groups.html.

GhostNet (2009)

In 2009, the Dalai Lama's office contacted security experts to determine if it was being bugged. The investigation revealed it was, and the spy ring that was discovered was eventually shown to be spying on over 100 countries' sensitive missions worldwide. Researchers gave this APT-style spy network the name GhostNet, and although the effort was traced back to China, full attribution was never determined.

Operation Aurora (2009)

Operation Aurora was an APT attack first reported by Google, but it also targeted Adobe, Yahoo!, Juniper Networks, Rackspace, Symantec, and several major U.S. financial and industrial firms. Research analysis pointed to the People's Liberation Army (PLA) of China as the sponsor. The attack ran for most of 2009 and operated on a large scale, with the groups behind the attack consisting of hundreds of hackers working together against the victim firms.

Stuxnet, Duqu, and Flame (2009–2012)

Stuxnet, Duqu, and Flame represent examples of state-sponsored malware. Stuxnet was a malicious worm designed to infiltrate the Iranian uranium enrichment program, to modify the equipment and cause the systems to fail in order to achieve desired results and in some cases even destroy the equipment. Stuxnet was designed to attack a specific model of Siemens programmable logic controller (PLC), which was one of the clues pointing to its objective—the modification of the uranium centrifuges. Although neither the United States nor Israel has admitted to participating in the attack, both have been suggested to have had a role in it.

Duqu (2011) is a piece of malware that appears to be a follow-on of Stuxnet, and has many of the same targets, but rather than being destructive in nature, Duqu is designed to steal information. The malware uses command-and-control (C2) servers across the globe to collect elements such as keystrokes and system information from machines and deliver them to unknown parties.

Flame (2012) is another piece of modular malware that may be a derivative of Stuxnet. Flame is an information collection threat, collecting keystrokes, screenshots, and network traffic. It can record Skype calls and audio signals on a machine. Flame is a large piece of malware with many specific modules, including a kill switch and a means of evading antivirus detection.

Because of the open nature of Stuxnet—its source code is widely available on the Internet—it is impossible to know who is behind Duqu and Flame. In fact, although Duqu and Flame were discovered after Stuxnet, there is growing evidence that they were present before Stuxnet and collected critical intelligence needed to conduct the later attacks. The real story behind these malware items is that they demonstrate the power and capability of nation-state malware.

Sony (2011)

The hacker group LulzSec reportedly hacked Sony, stealing over 70 million user accounts. The resulting outage lasted 23 days and cost Sony in excess of $170 million. One of the biggest issues related to the attack was Sony's poor response, taking more than a week to notify people of the initial attack, and then communicating poorly with its user base during the recovery period. Also notable was that although the credit card data was encrypted on Sony's servers, the rest of the data stolen was not, making it easy pickings for the disclosure of information.

Saudi Aramco (Shamoon, 2012)

In August of 2012, over 30,000 computers were shut down in response to a malware attack (named Shamoon) at Saudi Aramco, an oil firm in Saudi Arabia. The attack hit three out of four machines in the firm, and the damage included data wiping of machines and the uploading of sensitive information to Pastebin. It took 10 days for the firm to clean up the infection and restart its business network.

Data Breaches (2013–Present)

From the end of 2013 through to the time of this writing, data breaches have dominated the security landscape. Target Corporation announced its breach in mid-December 2013, stating that the hack began as early as "Black Friday" (November 29) and continued through December 15. Data thieves captured names, addresses, and debit and credit card details, including numbers, expiration dates, and CVV codes. In the end, a total of 70 million accounts were exposed. Following the Target breach, Home Depot suffered a breach of over 50 million debit and credit card numbers in 2014.

JPMorgan Chase also had a major data breach in 2014, announcing the loss of 77 million account holders' information. Unlike Target and Home Depot, JPMorgan Chase did not lose account numbers or other crucial data elements. JPMorgan Chase also mounted a major PR campaign touting its security program and spending in order to satisfy customers and regulators of its diligence.

At the end of 2014, Sony Pictures Entertainment announced that it had been hacked, with a massive release of internal data. At the time of this writing, hackers have claimed to have stolen as much as 100 terabytes of data, including e-mails, financial documents, intellectual property, personal data, HR information ... in essence, almost everything. Additional reports indicate the destruction of data within Sony; although the extent of the damage is not known, at least one of the elements of malware associated with the attack is known for destroying the master boot record (MBR) of drives. Attribution in the Sony attack is now assigned to the North Korean APT team called the Lazarus Group.

In September of 2016, Yahoo! announced that it had been a victim of a data breach during the 2013–2014 timeframe in which 3 billion user accounts, representing over 500 million users, including real names, e-mail addresses, dates of birth, and telephone numbers, were looted by an apparent nation-state hacking group. This revelation came out during Verizon's acquisition of Yahoo! for $4.4 billion, a figure that was down nearly $400 million as a result of the breach.

> **Tech Tip**
>
> **Data Breaches**
>
> *Are you on one of the following lists?*
>
> - ***Adobe, 2013*** *153 million records*
> - ***Adult Friend Finder, 2016*** *400+ million records*
> - ***eBay, 2014*** *145 million records*
> - ***Equifax, 2017*** *147 million records*
> - ***Heartland Payment Systems, 2008*** *134 million credit cards*
> - ***LinkedIn, 2012/2016*** *165 million accounts*
> - ***Marriott International, 2014–18*** *500 million records*
> - ***My Fitness Pal, 2018*** *150 million accounts*
> - ***MySpace, 2013*** *360 million accounts*
> - ***NetEase, 2015*** *235 million accounts*
> - ***Sina Weibo, 2020*** *538 million accounts*
> - ***Yahoo!, 2013–14*** *3 billion accounts*
> - ***Zynga, 2019*** *218 million accounts*
>
> *Check out https://haveibeenpwned.com/ to see if you are.*

Nation-State Hacking (2013–Present)

Nation-states have become a recognized issue in security—from the Great Firewall of China to modern malware attacks from a wide range of governments. Threat intelligence became more than a buzzword in 2014 as firms such as CrowdStrike exposed sophisticated hacking actors in China, Russia, and other countries. Today, numerous security firms track various APT groups as the attackers go after companies across the globe.

Not all threats are from China. Russia is credited with its own share of malware. Attribution is difficult, and sometimes the only hints are clues, such as the timelines of command-and-control servers for Energetic Bear, an attack on the energy industry in Europe from the Dragonfly Group. The Regin platform, a complete malware platform, possibly in operation for over a decade, has been shown to attack telecom operators, financial institutions, government agencies, and political bodies. Regin is interesting because of its stealth, its complexity, and its ability to hide its command-and-control network from investigators. Although highly suspected to be deployed by a nation-state, its attribution remains unsolved. Russia's military intelligence service has been connected to the hacking group Sandworm, which launched destructive attacks against the Ukrainian electric grid, and with NotPetya, a destructive malware attack that hit across Europe, the U.S., and many other countries.

In 2015, data breaches and nation-state hacking hit new highs with the loss of over 20 million sensitive personnel files from the computers at the U.S. Office of Personnel Management (OPM). This OPM loss, reportedly to China, was extremely damaging in that the data loss consisted of the complete background investigations on peoples who had submitted security clearances. These records detailed extensive personal information on the applicants and their family members, providing an adversary with detailed intelligence knowledge. In the same year it was reported that e-mail systems in the Department of State, the Department of Defense,

Operation Night Dragon was the name given to an intellectual property attack executed against oil, gas, and petrochemical companies in the United States. Using a set of global servers, attackers from China raided global energy companies for proprietary and highly confidential information such as bidding data for leases. The attack shed new light on what constitutes critical data and associated risks.

and the White House had been compromised, possibly by both Russia and China. The sensitive nuclear negotiations in Switzerland between the U.S., its allies, and Iran were also reported to have been subject to electronic eavesdropping by parties yet unknown.

Infrastructure Attacks

From the era of Stuxnet and extending to today, critical infrastructures have been attacked across the globe. The reasons for this are many, but the issues are consistent—critical infrastructures are controlled by computer systems, and these systems are vulnerable to attack. The list of sites is wide, but a couple worthy of mention are the Ukrainian electric grid and the Safety Instrumentation System Attack (TRITON).

Ukraine Electric Grid

On December 23, 2015, Ukraine suffered the first known successful cyberattack against an electric grid. The result was a temporary disruption to customers of three energy distribution companies as well as damaged equipment and operations. Electricity was restored via moving to manual operation of the grid, but full restoration of grid capabilities took more than a year as equipment was damaged, forcing replacement and complete rebuilding of the architecture of the control systems. This attack was not a spur-of-the-moment attack but rather an attack that, after complete analysis, took over nine months, from the initial phishing attack to the turning off of systems. This attack has been attributed to the Russian government, primarily due to the use of the BlackEnergy3 malware from the Sandworm group. Again in 2016, the grid was attacked, again for political reasons, but using different tools and different tactics.

Safety Instrumentation System Attack (TRITON)

In 2017, security technicians discovered a new form of malware in a Saudi Arabian petrochemical plant. This malware targeted the plant's safety instrumentation systems, making this an interesting attack because, on its face, it does nothing. During normal operations, the safety instrumentation system just sits there, but in the event of something going wrong with the plant operations, the safety instrumentation system is there to protect life and property. So this attack is not meant to gather information, or to turn off lights, but rather it is a part of a bigger attack to cause even greater damage. This is less of an attack and more of a test of a larger, more menacing foe—someone who is willing to not just turn things off, but wants to break things, and potentially hurt people.

Ransomware

Ransomware is not a new threat from the theoretical perspective, as the first versions date back to the mid-to-late 1990s. However, its use was virtually nonexistent until recently. Today, ransomware ranks as one of the top threats, having grown steadily since 2012, and now representing a $1 billion a year criminal enterprise. Most current ransomware attacks use a hybrid encrypting scheme, locking the files on a victim's computer until a ransom is paid. In 2017, two major ransomware events occurred.

WannaCry

In May of 2017, WannaCry spread as an encrypting worm, hitting Microsoft Windows systems that had not been patched against a Server Message Block (SMB) vulnerability. Particularly hard hit was the British National Health Service, where more than 150 hospitals and more than 70,000 medical devices were affected over a four-day period. Estimates of the economic impact of WannaCry exceed US$4 billion due to lost time and recovery costs.

NotPetya has been crowned the most damaging malware attack. Total damages were roughly $10 billion, and included firms such as FedEx, Maersk, Merck, and others. A great analysis is available at https://www.wired.com/story/notpetya-cyberattack-ukraine-russia-code-crashed-the-world/.

NotPetya

One of the most destructive major ransomware events was called Petya/NotPetya and occurred in June of 2017, immediately after WannaCry. Petya is a strain of ransomware that dates back to 2016 and utilizes some of the same vulnerabilities that were used by WannaCry. When a new variant of ransomware appeared on the heels of WannaCry, and used the same structures, it was considered by some to be another Petya variant. This version had several differences; most critically there was no recovery option, so Kaspersky Labs dubbed it NotPetya to specifically separate it from Petya. NotPetya was a set of malware deployed in Ukraine by Sandworm and unfortunately spread in the wild, hitting other firms.

Tech Tip

State of Cybersecurity 2020

At the time of writing this edition, midway through 2020, it is interesting to see the current state of cybersecurity. What is the major attack vector used all the time? Phishing. What are the latest threats? Malware, and in many forms, including even Excel macros; in this case disguised as a COVID-19 report from Johns Hopkins. And why do these work? The two major issues are users being tricked into do something, and software that is not patched or kept up to date, providing the vulnerability for the malware. The years have changed, but not the problems.

SolarWinds Attack

In late 2020, the cybersecurity firm FireEye discovered that the SolarWinds product Orion had been compromised by an attacker. Further investigation showed that this attack began earlier in the year, probably in March of 2020, and had been passed to over 18,000 customers including many departments of the federal government. This was a carefully orchestrated supply chain attack that allowed foreign agents a backdoor to systems at these customers.

The attackers used Amazon Web Services cloud hosting to disguise their intrusions as benign network traffic, obfuscating their actions. Additionally, the hackers didn't use the malware planted in SolarWinds' Orion products to breach nearly a third of the victims. Instead they used other hacking techniques, which investigators are still unraveling. Given the time span, the depth of the attack, and the level of skill demonstrated by the attackers, this will be a significant event. The true number of actually compromised systems is still unknown, and this will become one of the biggest and most important attacks in history.

Threats to Security

The incidents described in the previous sections provide a glimpse into the many different threats that administrators face as they attempt to protect their computer systems and networks. There are, of course, the normal natural disasters that organizations have faced for years. In today's highly networked world, however, new threats have developed that we did not have to worry about 50 years ago.

There are a number of ways we can break down the various threats. One way to categorize them is to separate threats that come from outside of the organization from those that are internal. Another is to look at the various levels of sophistication of the attacks—from those by "script kiddies" to those by "elite hackers." A third is to examine the level of organization of the various threats—from unstructured threats to highly structured threats. All of these are valid approaches, and they in fact overlap each other. The following sections examine threats from the perspective of where the attack comes from.

Viruses and Worms

Although your organization may be exposed to viruses and worms as a result of employees not following certain practices or procedures, generally you will not have to worry about your employees writing or releasing viruses and worms. It is important to draw a distinction between the writers of malware and those who release malware. Debates over the ethics of writing viruses permeate the industry, but currently, simply writing them is not considered a criminal activity. A virus is like a baseball bat; the bat itself is not evil, but the inappropriate use of the bat (such as to smash a car's window) falls into the category of criminal activity. (Some may argue that this is not a very good analogy since a baseball bat has a useful purpose—to play ball—whereas viruses have no useful purpose. In general, this is true, but in some limited environments, such as in specialized computer science courses, the study and creation of viruses can be considered a useful learning experience.)

Cross Check

Malware

Viruses and worms are just two types of threats that fall under the general heading of malware. The term *malware* comes from "malicious software," which describes the overall purpose of code that falls into this category of threat. Malware is software that has a nefarious purpose, designed to cause problems to you as an individual (for example, identity theft) or your system. More information on the different types of malware is provided in Chapter 15.

By number, viruses and worms are the most common problem an organization faces because literally thousands of them have been created and released. Fortunately, antivirus software and system patching can eliminate the largest portion of this threat. Viruses and worms generally are also nondiscriminating threats; they are released on the Internet in a general fashion and aren't targeted at a specific organization. They typically are also highly visible once released, so they aren't the best tool to use in highly structured attacks where secrecy is vital.

Intruders

The act of deliberately accessing computer systems and networks without authorization is generally referred to as **hacking**, with individuals who conduct this activity being referred to as **hackers**. The term hacking also applies to the act of exceeding one's authority in a system. This would include authorized users who attempt to gain access to files they aren't permitted to access or who attempt to obtain permissions they have not been granted. While the act of breaking into computer systems and networks has been glorified in the media and movies, the physical act does not live up to the Hollywood hype. Intruders are, if nothing else, extremely patient, since the process to gain access to a system takes persistence and dogged determination. The attacker will conduct many pre-attack activities in order to obtain the information needed to determine which attack will most likely be successful. Typically, by the time an attack is launched, the attacker will have gathered enough information to be very confident that the attack will succeed.

Generally, attacks by an individual or even a small group of attackers fall into the **unstructured threat** category. Attacks at this level generally are conducted over short periods of time (lasting at most a few months), do not involve a large number of individuals, have little financial backing, and are accomplished by insiders or outsiders who do not seek collusion with insiders. Intruders, or those who are attempting to conduct an intrusion, definitely come in many different varieties and have varying degrees of sophistication (see Figure 1.1). At the low end technically are what are generally referred to as **script kiddies**, individuals who do not have the technical expertise to develop scripts or discover new vulnerabilities in software but who have just enough understanding of computer systems to be able to download and run scripts that others have developed. These individuals generally are not interested in attacking specific targets but instead simply want to find any organization that may not have patched a newly discovered vulnerability for which they have located a script to exploit the vulnerability. It is hard to estimate how many of the individuals performing activities such as probing networks or scanning individual systems are part of this group, but it is undoubtedly the fastest growing group, and the vast majority of the "unfriendly" activity occurring on the Internet is probably carried out by these individuals.

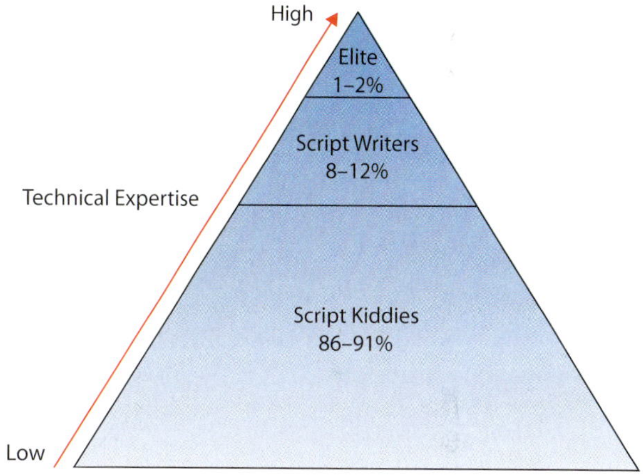

Figure 1.1 Distribution of attacker skill levels

At the next level are those people who are capable of writing scripts to exploit known vulnerabilities. These individuals are much more technically competent than script kiddies and account for an estimated 8 to 12 percent of malicious Internet activity. At the top end of this spectrum are those highly technical individuals, often referred to as **elite hackers**, who not only have the ability to write scripts that exploit vulnerabilities but also are capable of discovering new vulnerabilities. This group is the smallest of the lot, however, and is responsible for, at most, only 1 to 2 percent of intrusive activity.

> Competitors as adversaries? In today's technology-dominated workplace, it should not be a surprise that competitors can be adversaries to your computer systems. Although hacking is an illegal activity, this has not prevented unscrupulous entities from attacking their competition, whether via denial of service, espionage, or fraud.

Insiders

It is generally acknowledged by security professionals that insiders are more dangerous in many respects than outside intruders. The reason for this is simple—insiders have the access and knowledge necessary to cause immediate damage to an organization. Most security is designed to protect against outside intruders and thus lies at the boundary between the organization and the rest of the world. Insiders may actually already have all the access they need to perpetrate criminal activity such as fraud. In addition to unprecedented access, insiders also frequently have knowledge of the security systems in place and are better able to avoid detection. Attacks by insiders are often the result of employees who have become disgruntled with their organization and are looking for ways to disrupt operations. It is also possible that an "attack" by an insider may be an accident and not intended as an attack at all. An example of this might be an employee who deletes a critical file without understanding its critical nature.

Tech Tip

The Inside Threat

One of the hardest threats that security professionals will have to address is that of the insider. Since employees already have access to the organization and its assets, additional mechanisms need to be in place to detect attacks by insiders and to lessen the ability of these attacks to succeed.

As a U.S. Army soldier, Chelsea Manning began funneling classified and sensitive documents to WikiLeaks in 2010, including over a quarter of a million diplomatic cables, and was arrested and eventually convicted. This case illustrates how damaging an insider can be, as the damage done to international relations is still ongoing.

Employees are not the only insiders that organizations need to be concerned about. Often, numerous other individuals have physical access to company facilities. Custodial crews frequently have unescorted access throughout the facility, often when nobody else is around. Other individuals, such as contractors and partners, may have not only physical access to the organization's facilities but also access to computer systems and networks. A contractor involved in U.S. Intelligence computing, Edward Snowden, was charged with espionage in 2013 after he released a wide range of data illustrating the technical capabilities of U.S. Intelligence surveillance systems. He was the ultimate insider, with his name becoming synonymous with the insider threat issue.

Between Manning and Snowden, the United States government and its intelligence agencies have been challenged because of the breadth and depth of the releases. These releases damaged human agent identities, sources, methods, and virtually all types of highly restricted intelligence. And for at least a decade, if not longer, the shadow of these releases continues to mar the U.S. in international relations.

Criminal Organizations

As businesses became increasingly reliant upon computer systems and networks, and as the amount of financial transactions conducted via the Internet increased, it was inevitable that criminal organizations would eventually turn to the electronic world as a new target to exploit. Criminal activity on the Internet at its most basic is no different from criminal activity in the physical world. Fraud, extortion, theft, embezzlement, and forgery all take place in the electronic environment.

One difference between criminal groups and the "average" hacker is the level of organization that criminal elements employ in their attacks. Criminal groups typically have more money to spend on accomplishing the criminal activity and are willing to spend extra time accomplishing the task provided the level of reward at the conclusion is great enough. With the tremendous amount of money that is exchanged via the Internet on a daily basis, the level of reward for a successful attack is high enough to interest criminal elements. Attacks by criminal organizations usually fall into the **structured threat** category, which is characterized by a greater amount of planning, a longer period of time to conduct the activity, more financial backing to accomplish it, and possibly corruption of, or collusion with, insiders.

Nation-States, Terrorists, and Information Warfare

As nations have increasingly become dependent on computer systems and networks, the possibility that these essential elements of society might be targeted by organizations or nations determined to adversely affect another nation has become a reality. Many nations today have developed to some extent the capability to conduct **information warfare**. There are several definitions for information warfare, but a simple one is that it is warfare conducted against the information and information processing equipment used by an adversary. In practice, this is a much more complicated subject, because information not only may be the target of an adversary but also may be used as a weapon. Whatever definition you use, information warfare falls into the **highly structured threat** category. This type of threat is characterized by a much longer period of preparation (years is not uncommon), tremendous financial backing, and a large and organized group of attackers. The threat may include attempts not only to subvert insiders but also to plant individuals inside of a potential target in advance of a planned attack.

Tech Tip

Information Warfare

Once only the concern of governments and the military, information warfare today can involve many other individuals. With the potential to attack the various civilian-controlled critical infrastructures, security professionals in nongovernmental sectors today must also be concerned about defending their systems against attack by agents of foreign governments.

An interesting aspect of information warfare is the list of possible targets available. We have grown accustomed to the idea that, during war, military forces will target opposing military forces but will generally attempt to destroy as little civilian infrastructure as possible. In information warfare, military forces are certainly still a key target, but much has been written about other targets, such as the various infrastructures that a nation relies on for its daily existence. Water, electricity, oil and gas refineries and distribution, banking and finance, telecommunications—these all fall into the category of **critical infrastructures** for a nation. Critical infrastructures are those whose loss would have severe repercussions on the nation. With countries relying so heavily on these infrastructures, it is inevitable that they will be viewed as valid targets during conflict. Given how dependent these infrastructures are on computer systems and networks, it is also inevitable that these same computer systems and networks will be targeted for a cyberattack in an information war.

As demonstrated by the Stuxnet attacks, the cyberattacks in Estonia, and the electric grid attack in Ukraine, the risk of nation-state attacks is real. There have been numerous accusations of intellectual property theft being sponsored by, and in some cases even performed by, nation-**state actors**. In a world where information dominates government, business, and economies, the collection of information is the key to success, and with large rewards, the list of characters willing to spend significant resources is high.

Brand-Name Attacks

By 2015, numerous firms were positioned for selling exploits, exploit kits, vulnerabilities, and other malicious items online. In an effort to develop markets and brands, groups have developed sets of malware, just as other companies build product lines. The Sandworm Group, a group of hackers from Russia, first appeared in 2014 and then disappeared from public view until the Ukrainian electric grid attack in late 2015. All along, Sandworm had been producing and selling malware variants under the BlackEnergy name.

In some cases, the names associated with attacks, groups, or techniques come from the computer security industry, where the firms that discover them give the issue at hand a code name. This can become confusing, as multiple firms assign different names to the same issue, but over time the marketplace adjusts and settles on one name. Here are some of the recent names of interest:

- **Energetic Bear** A group of Russian hackers who used Havex malware in critical infrastructures. Also called Dragonfly.
- **Sandworm** A group of Russian hackers who have brought major issues to Ukraine via numerous attacks over the past couple of years. Also known as Electrum.
- **Shadow Brokers** A team that purportedly leaked NSA hacking tools to the public domain. They released the EternalBlue vulnerability.
- **Equation Group** A team of hackers allegedly linked to the U.S. government.
- **Regin** A team of hackers allegedly associated with the UK's GCHQ.
- **Cozy Bear and Fancy Bear** Hacker groups allegedly tied to Russia and the hacking of the Democratic National Committee (DNC) servers. Fancy Bear, also called Sofacy, is connected to Russia's GRU, and Cozy Bear, also called CozyDuke, is associated with the FSB (the Federal Security Service of the Russian Federation).
- **Vault 7** A list of leaks posted to WikiLeaks claiming to represent CIA cyber-operation methods and tools.
- **Lazarus Group** A group of hackers linked to North Korea and attacks including an $81 million bank robbery and the WannaCry ransomware attacks.
- **Comment Crew** A group of hackers associated with China. Also known as APT1.
- **Anonymous** A group of hackers that use their skills to expose perceived injustices.

Tech Tip

Confessions of a Skilled Hacker

In the summer of 2017, U.S. federal authorities arrested Marcus Hutchins, a 22-year-old UK native who had just been celebrated as the hacker who stopped the WannaCry malware. As a highly skilled hacker and self-taught reverse engineer, he seemingly used his powers for good, single-handedly finding a vulnerability in the WannaCry malware and stopping it in its tracks, worldwide. He was heralded as a hero, but his past caught up with him and he eventually pled guilty in court to writing and using malware. His whole story is worth reading, to see the good and the bad as well as the level of skill and teamwork needed to stop attacks in the current age:

https://www.wired.com/story/confessions-marcus-hutchins-hacker-who-saved-the-internet/

Attributes of Actors

Threat actors can be divided into groups based on abilities, as shown previously in the chapter. Other ways to differentiate the threat actors are by location (internal or external), by level of sophistication, by level of resources, and by intent.

Internal/External

Internal threat actors have one significant advantage over external actors. Internal actors have access to the system, and although it may be limited to user access, it still provides the threat actor the ability to pursue their attack. External actors have an additional step: the establishment of access to the system under attack.

Level of Sophistication

As shown earlier in Figure 1.1, attacker skill or sophistication can be divided into several categories. When examining a group of threat actors, one can consider the individual skills of members of the group. There may well be a mix, with a few highly skilled individuals acting to move larger numbers of less-skilled participants. The greater the skill level, the more an individual will be expected to lead and design the attacks. When it comes to the sophistication level of the attack itself, one notable trend is that as the skill level goes up, so too does the use of minimal methods. Although zero-day attacks widely make the news, true zero-day vulnerabilities are rarely used; they are reserved for the few cases where there are no other options, because once used, they will be patched. Even with highly sophisticated and resourced nation-state teams employing APT methods, there is a surprising number of attacks being performed using old attacks, old vulnerabilities, and simple methods that take advantage of "low-hanging fruit." This is not to say that newer, more advanced methods are not used, but rather that there is an economy of mechanism in the attacks themselves, using just what is needed at each step. There is also a lot of missing data to this picture, as we do not know of the methods that have been used successfully if the threat actor remains undetected.

Resources/Funding

As mentioned earlier, criminal organizations and nation-states have larger budgets, bigger teams, and the ability to pursue campaigns for longer periods of time. Cybersecurity is challenging for attackers as well as defenders, and there are expenses associated with maintaining teams and tools used as threat actors against a system. APTs, with their penchant for long-term attacks (some lasting for years), require significant resources to engage in this type of activity, so there is a need for long-term resources that only major organizations or governments can manage over time.

Intent/Motivation

The intent or motivation behind an attack can be simple or multifold in nature. A script kiddie is just trying to make a technique work. A more skilled threat actor is usually pursuing a specific objective, such as trying to make a point as a hacktivist. At the top of the intent pyramid is the APT threat actor, whose intent or motivation is at least threefold. First is the drive to maintain persistent access mechanisms so that the threat actor has continued access. Second is the drive to remain undetected. In most APT cases that are discovered, the length of intrusion is greater than a year, and it is many times limited by the length of logs. Third is the rationale for the attack in the first place: something of value on the network is going to be stolen. APTs do not go to all the trouble to maintain access and remain invisible just to crash a system or force a rebuild.

Tech Tip

Verizon Data Breach Investigations Report

If a cybersecurity practitioner, an executive, or anyone for that matter, wanted to get a report of the trends that are occurring in today's cybersecurity arena, the Verizon Data Breach Investigations Report is the place to start. While not filled with tons of specific attack details, this document does paint the picture of what is happening to IT systems across tens of thousands of attacks and thousands of breaches—all with an eye to providing top-level guidance on what happened and why. See https://enterprise.verizon.com/resources/reports/dbir for current report.

Security Trends

The biggest change affecting computer security that has occurred over the last 30 years has been the transformation of the computing environment from large mainframes to a highly interconnected network of smaller systems. This interconnection of systems is the Internet, and it now touches virtually all systems. What this has meant for security is a switch from a closed operating environment in which everything was fairly contained to one in which access to a computer can occur from almost anywhere on the planet. This has, for obvious reasons, greatly complicated the job of the security professional.

The type of individual who attacks a computer system or network has also evolved over the last 30 years. As illustrated by the attacks listed previously, the attackers have become more focused on gain over notoriety. Today, computer attacks are used to steal and commit fraud and other crimes in the pursuit of monetary enrichment. Computer crimes are currently big business, not just because it is hard to catch the perpetrators, but because the number of targets is large and the rewards greater than robbing local stores.

In the early days of computers, security was considered to be a binary condition in which your system was either secure or not secure. Efforts were made to achieve a state of security, meaning that the system was secure. Today, the focus has changed. In light of the revelation that a pure state of security is not achievable in the binary sense, the focus has shifted to one of risk management. Today, the question is how much risk your system is exposed to, and from what sources.

Over the past several years, a wide range of computer industry firms have begun issuing annual security reports. Among these firms is Verizon, which has issued its annual Data Breach Investigations Report (DBIR) since 2008. This report has been lauded for its breadth and depth. The 10th edition of the DBIR was published in 2017, and it analyzed more than 42,000 incidents and 1900 confirmed breaches spanning 84 countries and 20 industries. Perhaps the most valuable aspect of the DBIR is its identification of common details that result in a data breach. By the 2020 report, the size had continued to grow to a record total of 157,525 incidents, which after analysis, 3950 were confirmed to be data breaches. The cybersecurity world is not safer.

Targets and Attacks

A particular computer system is generally attacked for one of two reasons: either it is specifically targeted by the attacker or it is an opportunistic target.

Specific Target

In this case, the attacker has chosen the target not because of the hardware or software the organization is running but for another reason—perhaps a political reason. An example of this type of attack would be an individual in one country attacking a government system in another. Alternatively, the attacker may be targeting the organization as part of a **hacktivist** attack. For example, an attacker may deface the website of a company that sells fur coats because the attacker feels that using animals in this way is unethical. Perpetrating some sort of electronic fraud is another reason a specific system might be targeted. Whatever the reason, an attack of this nature is decided upon before the attacker knows what hardware and software the organization has.

> The motive behind most computer attacks falls into one of two categories:
>
> 1. To deprive someone the use of their system
> 2. To use someone else's system to enrich oneself
>
> In some cases, the use of a denial-of-service attack (item 1) precedes the actual heist (item 2).

Opportunistic Target

The second type of attack, an attack against a target of opportunity, is conducted against a site that has software that is vulnerable to a specific exploit. The attackers, in this case, are not targeting the organization; instead, they have learned of a vulnerability and are simply looking for an organization with this vulnerability that they can exploit. This is not to say, however, that an attacker might not be targeting a given sector and looking for a target of opportunity in that sector. For example, an attacker may desire to obtain credit card or other personal information and might search for any exploitable company with credit card information in order to carry out the attack.

Targeted attacks are more difficult and take more time than attacks on a target of opportunity. The latter simply relies on the fact that with any piece of widely distributed software, there will almost always be somebody who either has not patched the system or has not patched it properly.

Minimizing Possible Avenues of Attack

Understanding the steps an attacker will take enables you to limit the exposure of your system and minimize those avenues an attacker might possibly exploit. There are multiple elements to a solid computer defense, but two of the key elements—patching and hardening—involve limiting an attacker's avenues of attack.

The first step an administrator can take to reduce possible attacks is to ensure that all patches for the operating system and applications are installed. Many security problems that we read about, such as viruses and worms, exploit known vulnerabilities for which patches exist. The reason such malware caused so much damage in the past was that administrators did not take the appropriate actions to protect their systems.

The second step an administrator can take is hardening the system, which involves limiting the services that are running on the system. Using only those services that are absolutely needed does two things: it limits the possible avenues of attack (those services with vulnerabilities that can be exploited) and it reduces the number of services the administrator has to worry about patching in the first place. This is one of the important early steps any administrator should take to secure a computer system. System hardening is covered in detail in Chapter 14.

Although there are no iron-clad defenses against attack, or guarantees that an attack won't be successful, you can take steps to reduce the risk of loss. This is the basis for the change in strategy from a defense-based one to one based on risk management. Risk management is covered in detail in Chapter 20.

Approaches to Computer Security

Although much of the discussion of computer security focuses on how systems are attacked, it is equally important to consider the structure of defenses. You have three major considerations when securing a system:

- **Correctness** Ensuring that a system is fully up to date, with all patches installed and proper security controls in place. This goes a long way toward minimizing risk. Correctness begins with a secure development lifecycle (covered in Chapter 19), continues through patching and hardening (Chapters 14 and 21), and culminates in operations (Chapters 3, 4, 20, and 21).
- **Isolation** Protecting a system from unauthorized use, by means of access control and physical security. Isolation begins with infrastructure (covered in Chapters 9 and 10), continues with access control (Chapters 8, 11, and 12), and includes the use of cryptography (Chapters 5, 6, and 7).
- **Obfuscation** Making it difficult for an adversary to know when they have succeeded. Whether accomplished by obscurity, randomization, or obfuscation, increasing the workload of an attacker makes it more difficult for them to succeed in their attack. Obfuscation occurs throughout all topics because it is a built-in element, whether in the form of random numbers in crypto or address space randomizations, stack guards, or pointer encryption at the operating system level.

Each of these approaches has its inherent flaws, but taken together, they can provide a strong means of system defense.

Cybersecurity Kill Chain

One of the newer methods of modeling attacks is via a **cybersecurity kill chain** (see Figure 1.2), a step-by-step process that attacks follow to target and achieve results on victim systems. Originally developed by Lockheed Martin, this framework concept provides a means for the identification and prevention of cyberintrusion activity. The framework identifies the typical steps an adversary must complete in order to achieve their objective. The kill chain concept is important because in many cases the detection of an adversary on your network will be earlier in the kill chain process, giving a firm an opportunity to break the attack pattern before actual damage is done. Modeled after kill chains used to break the lifecycle of other attackers, such as insects, the cybersecurity kill chain gives defenders a means of stopping sophisticated attackers before the damage is done by targeting the attacker's process rather than the victim machine's reaction to the delivery of terminal attack objectives. This enables teams of hunters to go track down attackers and act

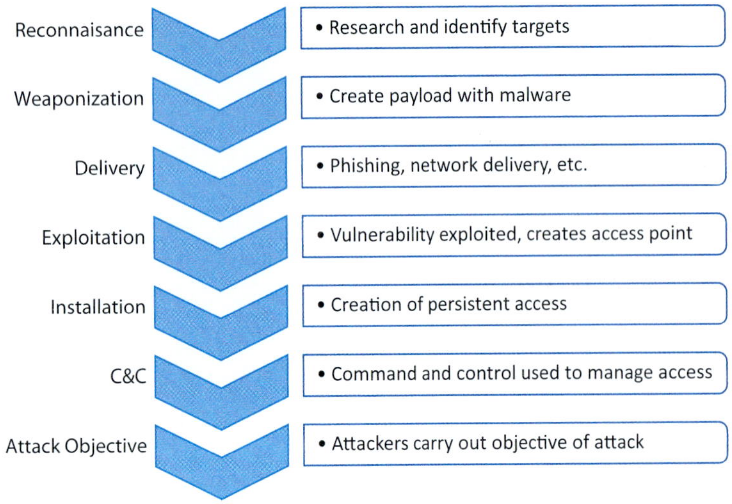

• **Figure 1.2** The cybersecurity kill chain

proactively rather than defending in a reactive mode after an attack has been successful.

Threat Intelligence

Cybersecurity is a game of resource management. No firm has the resources to protect everything against all threats, and even attempting to do so would add complexity that would open up other threat avenues. One of the important decisions is where to apply one's resources in the complex landscape of cyber defense. **Threat intelligence** is a set of actions taken to properly utilize resources to target the actual threats an enterprise is facing. Threat intelligence is the actionable information about malicious actors and their tools, infrastructure, and methods. Threat intelligence includes evidence-based information as to context, mechanisms, indicators, and implications associated with a hazard to a system. It is action-oriented so it can be used to drive responses to the hazard. This is important to security teams because it steers their resources to detect threats in their network and prioritize the response to real threats. Threat intelligence is the basis of understanding adversary **tactics, techniques, and procedures (TTPs)**.

> **Tech Tip**
>
> **Tactics, Techniques, and Procedures (TTPs)**
>
> *The acronym TTP is used to describe how threat agents organize and orchestrate their efforts. Like any other organization, hackers evolve to use repeatable methods that are effective. These methods can be cataloged and understood as attack patterns, enabling defenses to have countering plays developed in advance. TTPs, or the patterns used by adversaries, are a key element of a threat intelligence program.*

Threat intelligence is broken down into three types, with different audiences and objectives for each:

- **Strategic** Broader trends typically meant for a nontechnical audience
- **Tactical** Outlines of the tactics, techniques, and procedures of threat actors for a more technical audience
- **Operational** Technical details about specific attacks and campaigns

Threat intelligence has become a buzzword in the security industry, with numerous firms providing services in this area. Several main forms of threat intelligence are in use today. The biggest and most comprehensive are the **Information Sharing and Analysis Centers (ISACs)** and **Information Sharing and Analysis Organizations (ISAOs)** that have been created to share information across firms. These are typically large-budget operations, with the costs and results shared among members. A second form of threat intelligence is referred to as *open source intelligence*.

In a modern enterprise, threat intelligence is a critical security operation. The information that it gathers can shape policies, operations, vulnerability management, incident response, and risk analysis efforts.

Open Source Intelligence

Open source intelligence (OSINT), sometimes called open source threat intelligence, is the term used to describe the processes used in the collection of threat intelligence information from public sources. There is a wide range of public sources of information concerning current cybersecurity activity. From news articles, to blogs, to government reports, there seems to be a never-ending stream of news concerning what is happening, to whom, and how. This leads to the overall topic of information sharing and the greater topic of threat intelligence (not open source).

Ethics

Any meaningful discussion about operational aspects of information security must include the topic of ethics. *Ethics* is commonly defined as a set of moral principles that guides an individual's or group's behavior. Because information security efforts frequently involve trusting people to keep secrets that could cause harm to the organization if revealed, trust is a foundational element on the people side of security. Also, trust is built on a code of ethics—a norm that allows everyone to understand expectations and responsibilities. Several different ethical frameworks can be applied to making a decision, and these are covered in detail in Chapter 24.

Ethics is a difficult topic; separating right from wrong is easy in many cases, but in other cases it is more difficult. For example, writing a virus that damages a system is clearly bad behavior, but is writing a worm that goes out and patches systems, without the users' permission, right or wrong? Do the ends justify the means? Such questions are the basis of ethical discussions that define the challenges faced by security personnel on a regular basis.

Additional References

http://en.wikipedia.org/wiki/Timeline_of_computer_security_hacker_history

http://www.informationisbeautiful.net/visualizations/worlds-biggest-data-breaches-hacks

https://enterprise.verizon.com/resources/reports/dbir/

Chapter 1 Review

Chapter Summary

After reading this chapter and completing the quizzes, you should understand the following regarding security threats and trends.

Define computer security

- Computer security is defined by a system operating in a manner in which it does what it is supposed to do and only what it is supposed to do.
- Information security is defined by the information being protected from unauthorized access or alteration and yet is available to authorized individuals when required.

Discuss common threats and recent computer crimes that have been committed

- The various threats to security include viruses and worms, intruders, insiders, criminal organizations, terrorists, and information warfare conducted by foreign countries.
- A particular computer system is generally attacked for one of two reasons: it is specifically targeted by the attacker or it is a target of opportunity.
- Targeted attacks are more difficult and take more time than attacks on a target of opportunity.
- The different types of electronic crime fall into two main categories: crimes in which the computer was the target of the attack, and incidents in which the computer was a means of perpetrating a criminal act.
- One significant trend observed over the last several years has been the increase in the number of computer attacks and their effectiveness.

List and discuss recent trends in computer security

- Malicious actors use many different ways to attack computers and networks to take advantage of online shopping, banking, investing, and leisure pursuits, which have become a simple matter of "dragging and clicking" for many people.
- The biggest change that has occurred in security over the last 30 years has been the transformation of the computing environment from large mainframes to a highly interconnected network of much smaller systems.

Describe common avenues of attacks

- An attacker can use a common technique against a wide range of targets in an opportunistic attack, only succeeding where the attack is viable.
- An attacker can employ a variety of techniques against a specific target when it is desired to obtain access to a specific system.

Describe approaches to computer security

- An enterprise can use three main approaches to computer security: one based on correctness, one involving isolation, and one involving obfuscation. The ideal method is to employ all three together.

Discuss the relevant ethical issues associated with computer security

- Ethics is commonly defined as a set of moral principles that guides an individual's or group's behaviors.
- Because information security efforts frequently involve trusting people to keep secrets that could cause harm to the organization if revealed, trust is a foundational element on the people side of security.

Key Terms

advanced persistent threat (APT) *(4)*
computer security *(1)*
critical infrastructure *(13)*
cybersecurity kill chain *(18)*
elite hacker *(11)*
hacker *(10)*
hacking *(10)*
hacktivist *(17)*
highly structured threat *(13)*
Information Sharing and Analysis Center (ISAC) *(19)*
Information Sharing and Analysis Organization (ISAO) *(19)*
information warfare *(13)*
open source intelligence (OSINT) *(19)*
script kiddie *(11)*
state actors *(13)*
structured threat *(12)*
tactics, techniques, and procedures (TTPs) *(19)*
threat intelligence *(19)*
unstructured threat *(11)*

Key Terms Quiz

Use terms from the Key Terms list to complete the sentences that follow. Don't use the same term more than once. Not all terms will be used.

1. A(n) _______________ is characterized by a greater amount of planning, a longer period of time to conduct the activity, more financial backing to accomplish it, and the possible corruption of, or collusion with, insiders.
2. The patterns of activities or methods associated with a specific threat actor or group of threat actors is known as a(n) _______________.
3. A(n) _______________ is one whose loss would have a severe detrimental impact on the nation.
4. _______________ is conducted against the information and information-processing equipment used by an adversary.
5. Actors who deliberately access computer systems and networks without authorization are called _______________.
6. A(n) _______________ is generally short term in nature, does not involve a large group of individuals, does not have significant financial backing, and does not include collusion with insiders.
7. A(n) _______________ is a highly technically competent individual who conducts intrusive activity on the Internet and is capable of not only exploiting known vulnerabilities but also finding new vulnerabilities.
8. Actionable information about malicious actors as well as their tools, infrastructure, and methods is called _______________.
9. A(n) _______________ is an individual who does not have the technical expertise to develop scripts or discover new vulnerabilities in software but who has just enough understanding of computer systems to be able to download and run scripts that others have developed.
10. A(n) _______________ is characterized by a much longer period of preparation (years is not uncommon), tremendous financial backing, and a large and organized group of attackers.

Multiple-Choice Quiz

1. Which threats are characterized by possibly long periods of preparation (years is not uncommon), tremendous financial backing, a large and organized group of attackers, and attempts to subvert insiders or to plant individuals inside a potential target in advance of a planned attack?
   - **A.** Unstructured threats
   - **B.** Structured threats
   - **C.** Highly structured threats
   - **D.** Nation-state information warfare threats
2. In which of the following attacks is an attacker looking for any organization vulnerable to a specific exploit rather than attempting to gain access to a specific organization?
   - **A.** Target of opportunity attack
   - **B.** Targeted attack
   - **C.** Vulnerability scan attack
   - **D.** Information warfare attack
3. The rise of which of the following has greatly increased the number of individuals who probe organizations looking for vulnerabilities to exploit?
   - **A.** Virus writers
   - **B.** Script kiddies
   - **C.** Hackers
   - **D.** Elite hackers
4. For what reason(s) do some security professionals consider insiders more dangerous than outside intruders?
   - **A.** Employees (insiders) are easily corrupted by criminal and other organizations.
   - **B.** Insiders have the access and knowledge necessary to cause immediate damage to the organization.
   - **C.** Insiders have knowledge of the security systems in place and are better able to avoid detection.
   - **D.** Both B and C.
5. Using knowledge associated with an attacker's process to find a weakness in the attack mechanism and then to catch and block the attacker is called what?
   - **A.** Open source intelligence
   - **B.** Cybersecurity kill chain
   - **C.** Active incident response
   - **D.** Defense in depth
6. What is the most common problem/threat an organization faces?
   - **A.** Viruses/worms
   - **B.** Script kiddies
   - **C.** Hackers
   - **D.** Hacktivists

7. Warfare conducted against the information and information-processing equipment used by an adversary is known as what?
   A. Hacking
   B. Cyberterrorism
   C. Information warfare
   D. Network warfare
8. An attacker who feels that using animals to make fur coats is unethical and thus defaces the website of a company that sells fur coats is an example of what?
   A. Information warfare
   B. Hacktivism
   C. Cyber crusading
   D. Elite hacking
9. Criminal organizations would normally be classified as what type of threat?
   A. Unstructured
   B. Unstructured but hostile
   C. Structured
   D. Highly structured
10. Which of the following individuals has the ability to not only write scripts that exploit vulnerabilities but also discover new vulnerabilities?
    A. Elite hacker
    B. Script kiddie
    C. Hacktivist
    D. Insider

Essay Quiz

1. Reread the various examples of computer crimes at the beginning of this chapter. Categorize each as either a crime where the computer was the target of the criminal activity or a crime in which the computer was a tool in accomplishing the criminal activity.
2. A friend of yours has just been hired by an organization as its computer security officer. Your friend is a bit nervous about this new job and has come to you, knowing that you are taking a computer security class, to ask your advice on measures that can be taken that might help prevent an intrusion. What three things can you suggest that are simple but can tremendously help limit the possibility of an attack?
3. Discuss the major difference between a target of opportunity attack and a targeted attack. Which do you believe is the more common one?

Lab Projects

• Lab Project 1.1

A number of different examples of computer crimes were discussed in this chapter. Similar activities seem to happen daily. Do a search on the Internet to see what other examples you can find. Try and obtain the most recent examples possible.

• Lab Project 1.2

Your boss just sent you a copy of the Verizon DBIR, with a note reading, "What does this mean to us?" How would you summarize the DBIR in a presentation with fewer than 10 slides in less than 10 minutes?

chapter 2

General Security Concepts

From one thing, know ten thousand things.

— Miyamoto Musashi

In this chapter, you will learn how to

- Define basic terms associated with computer and information security
- Identify the basic approaches to computer and information security
- Identify the basic principles of computer and information security
- Recognize some of the basic models used to implement security in operating systems

In Chapter 1, you learned about some of the various threats that we, as security professionals, face on a daily basis. In this chapter, you start exploring the field of computer security. Computer security has a series of fundamental concepts that support the discipline. We begin with an examination of security models and concepts and then proceed to see how they are operationally employed.

Basic Security Terminology

The term **hacking** has been used frequently in the media. A hacker was once considered an individual who understood the technical aspects of computer operating systems and networks. Hackers were individuals you turned to when you had a problem and needed extreme technical expertise. Today, primarily as a result of the media, the term is used more often to refer to individuals who attempt to gain unauthorized access to computer systems or networks. While some would prefer to use the terms *cracker* and *cracking* when referring to this nefarious type of activity, the terminology generally accepted by the public is that of hacker and hacking. A related term that may sometimes be seen is **phreaking**, which refers to the "hacking" of the systems and computers used by a telephone company to operate its telephone network.

The field of computer security constantly evolves, frequently introducing new terms that are often coined by the media. Make sure to learn the meaning of terms such as *hacking, phreaking, vishing, phishing, pharming,* and *spear phishing*. Some of these terms have been around for many years (such as hacking), whereas others have appeared only in the last few years (such as spear phishing).

Security Basics

Computer security itself is a term that has many meanings and related terms. Computer security entails the methods used to ensure that a system is secure. Subjects such as authentication and access controls must be addressed in broad terms of computer security. Seldom in today's world are computers not connected to other computers in networks. This then introduces the term *network security* to refer to the protection of the multiple computers and other devices that are connected together. Related to these two terms are two others—*information security* and *information assurance*—that place the focus of the security process not on the hardware and software being used but on the data that is processed by them. Assurance also introduces another concept: that of the availability of the systems and information when we want them. The common press and many professionals have settled on *cybersecurity* as the term to describe the field. Still another term that may be heard in the security world is COMSEC, which stands for *communications security* and deals with the security of telecommunication systems.

Cybersecurity has become regular headline news these days, with reports of break-ins, data breaches, fraud, and a host of other calamities. The general public has become increasingly aware of its dependence on computers and networks and consequently has also become interested in the security of these same computers and networks. As a result of this increased attention by the public, several new terms have become commonplace in conversations and print. Terms such as *hacking, viruses, TCP/IP, encryption,* and *firewalls* are now frequently encountered in mainstream news media and have found their way into casual conversations. What was once the purview of scientists and engineers is now part of our everyday life.

With our increased daily dependence on computers and networks to conduct everything from making purchases at our local grocery store to banking, trading stocks, receiving medical treatment, and driving our children to school, ensuring that computers and networks are secure has become of paramount importance. Computers and the information they manipulate have become a part of virtually every aspect of our lives.

> **Tech Tip**
>
> **CIA of Security**
>
> *While there is no universal agreement on authentication, auditability, and nonrepudiation as additions to the original CIA of security, there is little debate over whether confidentiality, integrity, and availability are basic security principles. Understand these principles, because one or more of them are the reason most security hardware, software, policies, and procedures exist.*

The "CIA" of Security

Almost from its inception, the goal of computer security has been threefold: confidentiality, integrity, and availability—the "CIA" of security. The purpose of **confidentiality** is to ensure that only those individuals who have the authority to view a piece of information may do so. No unauthorized individual should ever be able to view data they are not entitled to access. **Integrity** is a related concept but deals with the generation and modification of data. Only authorized individuals should ever be able to create or change (or delete) information. The goal of **availability** is to ensure that the data, or the system itself, is available for use when the authorized user wants it.

As a result of the increased use of networks for commerce, two additional security goals have been added to the original three in the CIA of security. **Authentication** attempts to ensure that an individual is who they claim to be. The need for this in an online transaction is obvious. Related to this is **nonrepudiation**, which deals with the ability to verify that a message has been sent and received and that the sender can be identified and verified. The requirement for this capability in online transactions should also be readily apparent. Recent emphasis on systems assurance has raised the potential inclusion of the term **auditability**, which refers to whether a control can be verified to be functioning properly. In security, it is imperative that we can track actions to ensure what has or has not been done.

The Fortress Model

The original model for computer security was the **fortress model**—keep the bad out, allow in the good. This was a natural model: build a series of defenses and your system can be secure. This also led to the question "Are we secure?" For this question, a binary yes-or-no answer was expected. However, time has shown that this model is not realistic. A new version of the fortress model, called endpoint security, involves securing of all endpoints in a network are secured from all threats. Not a day goes by in the security industry where some pundit declares that endpoint security is dead. When viewed as the only defense, endpoint security leaves a lot to be desired, but as part of an overall program, endpoint security still plays a valuable role. The fortress model has been shown to not provide sufficient defenses, yet, like endpoint security shows, it is still a valuable component in a modern security program.

The Operational Model of Computer Security

For many years, the focus of security was on prevention. If we could prevent everyone who did not have authorization from gaining access to our computer systems and networks, then we assumed that we had achieved security. Protection was thus equated with prevention. While the basic premise of this is true, it fails to acknowledge the realities of the networked environment our systems are part of. No matter how well we seem to do in prevention technology, somebody always seems to find a way around our safeguards. When this happens, our system is left unprotected. Thus, we need multiple prevention techniques and also technologies to alert us when prevention has failed and to provide ways to address the problem. This results in a modification to our original security equation with the addition of two new

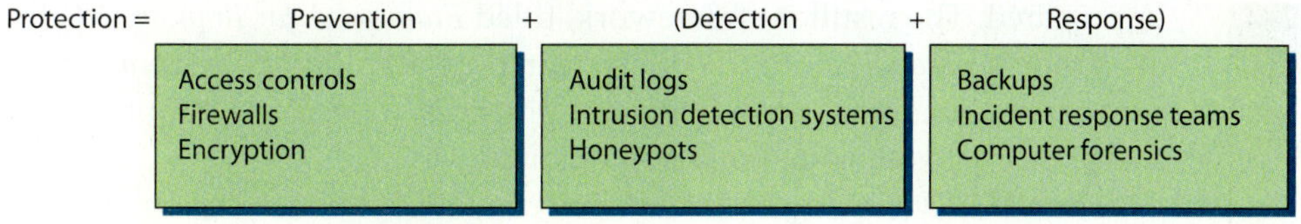

• **Figure 2.1** Sample technologies in the operational model of computer security

elements: detection and response. Our security equation thus becomes the following:

Protection = Prevention + (Detection + Response)

This is known as the **operational model of computer security**. Every security technique and technology falls into at least one of the three elements of the equation. Examples of the types of technologies and techniques that represent each are depicted in Figure 2.1.

Time-Based Security

In 1998, Winn Schwartau published a paper that was clearly ahead of its time. The paper was on the topic of time-based security. Time-based security was not a new concept; in fact, it has been used in physical security for years. Safes are rated in terms of how long they will resist penetration. Bringing the concept of time to the operational security model puts it in line with modern security defense practices. Time-based security allows us to understand the relationship between prevention, detection, and response. The Schwartau paper uses the term *protection* for prevention and the term *reaction* for response. The following is from the Schwartau paper:

> Information security is now a simple affair. You no longer have to build up huge levels of protection. You need to concentrate on the detection and reaction. . . which ultimately determines the amount of effective security you have.

Simply put, the amount of time offered by a protection device, P_t, should be greater than the time it takes to detect the attack, D_t, plus the reaction time of the organization, R_t:

$$P_t > D_t + R_t$$

The remainder of the paper is devoted to the discussion of how to use time-based security to make economic security decisions. One of these key decisions, borne from the arguments in the paper, is whether particularly sensitive information belongs on the network to begin with. "Sometimes, some information has no business being on a network. The cost of protection, versus the downside risk, is just not worth it." This paper describes how we do security today—threat intelligence, kill chains, incident response, and a host of options beyond simple fortress foundations such as firewalls.

Cybersecurity Framework Model

In 2013, President Obama signed an executive order directing the U.S. National Institute of Science and Technology (NIST) to work with industry and develop a cybersecurity framework. This was in response to several significant cybersecurity events where the victim companies appeared to be

Tech Tip

NIST Cybersecurity Framework

The NIST Cybersecurity Framework is a risk-based approach for the implementation of cybersecurity activities in an enterprise. The framework provides a common taxonomy of standards, guidelines, and practices that can be employed to strengthen cybersecurity efforts. To learn more about the NIST Cybersecurity Framework, see https://www.nist.gov/cyberframework.

unprepared. The resultant framework, titled *Framework for Improving Critical Infrastructure Cybersecurity,* was created as a voluntary system, based on existing standards, guidelines, and practices, to facilitate adoption and acceptance across a wide array of industries.

The NIST Cybersecurity Framework provides a common taxonomy and mechanism to assist in aligning management practices with existing standards, guidelines, and practices. Its purpose is to complement and enhance risk management efforts through the following actions:

1. Determining the current cybersecurity posture
2. Documenting the desired target state with respect to cybersecurity
3. Determining and prioritizing improvement and corrective actions
4. Measuring and monitoring progress toward goals
5. Creating a communication mechanism for coordination among stakeholders

The framework is composed of five core functions, as illustrated in Figure 2.2. Two of these core functions, *Identify* and *Protect,* describe actions taken before an incident. *Detect* is the core function associated with intrusion detection or the beginning of an incident response. The last two, *Respond* and *Recover,* detail actions that take place during the post-incident response. Examples of the items under each function are illustrated in the figure. In addition to the five functions, the framework has levels of implementations referred to as *tiers.* These tiers represent the organization's ability, from Partial (Tier 1) to Adaptive (Tier 4).

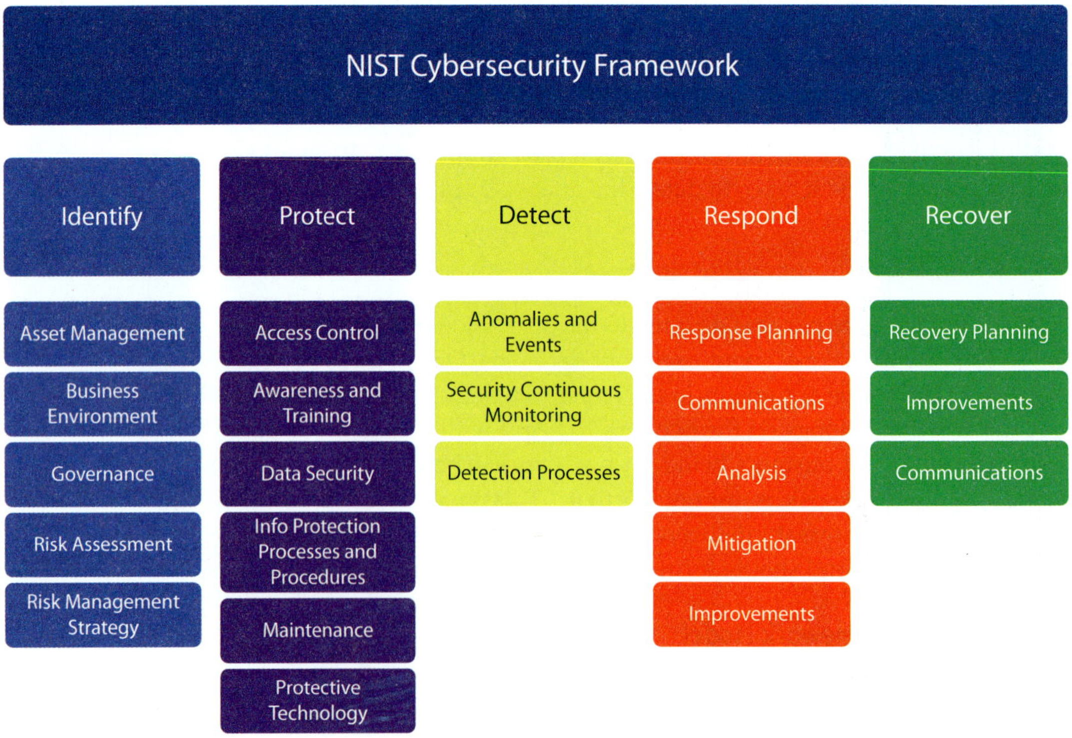

• **Figure 2.2** Cybersecurity Framework core functions

Active Defense Model

A new form of security mode is one based on active defense. While most of the models previously discussed focus on "static" defenses that are enacted to act as a barrier to intruders, active defense goes to the next level, the actual hunting of intruders inside the enterprise. This model capitalizes on elements of both the operational model and time-based security models. It makes the assumption that the static defenses, while necessary, are not sufficient. And as a result, some intruders will succeed in getting into the enterprise. The active defense model is one built around the actions necessary to actively seek out attackers that make it past the defenses. Similar to incident response procedures, but not dependent upon a specific incident, active hunters use their knowledge of baseline conditions for the systems and search for things that are abnormal. When abnormalities are found, they are chased to ground, and if an intruder is found, actions are taken to close the holes used to gain entry.

Security Tenets

In addition to the CIA elements, there are tenets that form a basis for system security. The three operational tenets found in secure deployments are session management, exception management, and configuration management.

> **Tech Tip**
>
> **Session Management Cheat Sheet**
>
> *Session management is a common task for web applications, and the Open Web Application Security Project (OWASP) has a cheat sheet to assist in the correct implementation of session management. See https://www.owasp.org/index.php/Session_Management_Cheat_Sheet.*

Session Management

Session management is the set of activities employed to establish a communication channel between two parties, identifying each in a manner that allows future activity without renewed authentication. Session management allows an application to authenticate once and have subsequent activities ascribed to the authenticated user. Sessions are frequently used in web applications to preserve state and user information between normally stateless clicks.

Sessions are typically identified by an ID that is known to both sides of the conversation. This ID can be used as a token for future identification. If confidentiality is required, then the channel should be secured by an appropriate level of cryptographic protection.

Session management includes all the activities necessary to manage the session—from establishment, during use, and at completion of the conversation. Because the session represents the continuity of a security condition established during authentication, the level of protection that should be afforded to the session ID should be commensurate with the level of security initially established.

Exception Management

Exceptions involve the invocation of conditions that fall outside the normal sequence of operation. Whether by error or malicious action, exceptions are changes to normal processing and need to be managed. The special processing required by conditions that fall outside normal parameters can result in errors either locally or in follow-on processes in a system. The handling of exceptions, referred to as *exception handling,* is an important consideration during software development.

Exception management is more than just exception handling in software development. When the operation of a system encounters an exception, whether it is invoked by a person, process, technology, or combination thereof, the system must effectively handle the condition. This can mean many different things—sometimes even operating outside normal policy limits. Exception management can also be nontechnical in nature: systems or environments that cannot follow organizational security policy, for example, must be documented, exceptions must be approved, and mitigations must be put in place to lower the risk associated with exceptions to policy. The bottom line is simple: either the system must handle the condition and recover or it must fail and be recovered by separate action. Designing exception handling into a system makes it more resilient, because exceptions will happen, and how they are handled is the only unknown outcome.

Configuration Management

Configuration management is key to the proper operation of IT systems. IT systems are first and foremost systems—groups of elements that work together to achieve a desired resultant process. The proper configuration and provisioning of all the components in a system is essential to the proper operation of the system. The design and operation of the elements to ensure the proper functional environment of a system is referred to as *configuration management*. Configuration management is a key operation principle and is thoroughly covered in Chapter 21.

> **Tech Tip**
>
> **Got Network?**
>
> *A classic black T-shirt in the security industry says "got root?" It's a takeoff on the successful ad campaign "got milk?" and indicates the power of root privilege. Similar to "got root?" is "got network?"; if you truly "own" the network, then you have significant control over what passes across it, which can result in information disclosure. To ensure a secure posture, both network and host access levels must be controlled.*

Security Approaches

An organization can take multiple approaches to address the protection of its networks: either ignore security issues, provide host security, provide network-level security, or provide a combination of the latter two. The middle two, host security and network-level security, have prevention as well as detection and response components. Rather than view these two approaches as independent solutions, a mature organization uses both in a complementary fashion.

If an organization decides to ignore security, it has chosen to utilize the minimal amount of security that is provided with its workstations, servers, and devices. No additional security measures will be implemented. Each "out-of-the-box" system has certain security settings that can be configured, and they should be. Actually protecting an entire network, however, requires work in addition to the few protection mechanisms that come with systems by default.

Host Security

Host security takes a granular view of security by focusing on protecting each computer and device individually instead of addressing protection of the network as a whole. When host security is used, each computer is relied upon to protect itself. If an organization decides to implement only host security and does not include network security, there is a high probability of introducing or overlooking vulnerabilities. Most environments are filled with different operating systems (Windows, UNIX, Linux, macOS), different versions of those operating systems, and different types of installed applications. Each operating system has security configurations that differ from those of other systems, and different versions of the same operating system may in fact have configuration variations between them.

Host security is important and should always be addressed. Security, however, should not stop there, as host security is a complementary process to be combined with network security. If individual host computers have vulnerabilities embodied within them, then network security can provide another layer of protection that will, hopefully, stop any intruders who have gotten that far into the environment.

A longtime discussion has centered on whether host- or network-based security is more important. Most security experts now generally agree that a combination of both is needed to adequately address the wide range of possible security threats. Certain attacks are more easily spotted, and some attacks are more easily prevented using tools designed for one or the other of these approaches.

Network Security

In some smaller environments, host security by itself may be an option, but as systems become connected into networks, security should include the actual network itself. In **network security**, an emphasis is placed on controlling access to internal computers from external entities. This control can be through devices such as routers, firewalls, authentication hardware and software, encryption, and intrusion detection systems (IDSs).

Network environments tend to be unique entities because usually no two networks have exactly the same number of computers, the same applications installed, the same number of users, the exact same configurations, or the same available servers. They will not perform the same functions or have the same overall architecture. Since networks have so many variations, there are many different ways in which they can be protected and configured. This chapter covers some foundational approaches to network and host security. Each approach may be implemented in a myriad of ways, but both network and host security need to be addressed for an effective total security program.

Security Principles

In the mid-1970s, two computer scientists from MIT, Jerome Saltzer and Michael Schroeder, published a paper on design principles for a secure computer system. The Saltzer and Schroeder paper, titled "The Protection of Information in Computer Systems," has been hailed as a seminal work in computer security, and the eight design principles in it are as relevant today as they were in 1970s. These principles are useful in secure system design and operation. These eight principles form the foundation for the field. Since they were published, an additional five have been adopted, and this set has stood for decades.

Least Privilege

One of the most fundamental principles in security is **least privilege**. This concept is applicable to many physical environments as well as network and host security. Least privilege means that a subject (which may be a user, application, or process) should have only the necessary rights and privileges to perform its task, with no additional permissions. Limiting an object's privileges limits the amount of harm that can be caused, thus limiting an organization's exposure to damage. Users may have access to the files on their workstations and a select set of files on a file server, but no access to critical data that is held within the database. This rule helps an organization protect its most sensitive resources and helps ensure that whoever is interacting with these resources has a valid reason to do so.

Least privilege means that a subject should have only the necessary rights and privileges to perform its task, with no additional permissions.

Try This!

Examples of the Least Privilege Principle

The security concept of least privilege is not unique to computer security. It has been practiced by organizations such as financial institutions and governments for centuries. Basically, it simply means that individuals are given only the absolute minimum of privileges that are required to accomplish their assigned job. Examine the security policies that your organization has in place and see if you can identify examples of where the principle of least privilege has been used.

The concept of least privilege applies to more network security issues than just providing users with specific rights and permissions. When trust relationships are created, they should not be implemented in such a way that everyone trusts each other simply because it is easier. One domain should trust another for very specific reasons, and the implementers should have a full understanding of what the trust relationship allows between two domains. If one domain trusts another, do all of the users automatically become trusted, and can they thus easily access any and all resources on the other domain? Is this a good idea? Is there a more secure way of providing the same functionality? If a trusted relationship is implemented such that users in one group can access a plotter or printer that is available in only one domain, it might make sense to simply purchase another device so that other, more valuable or sensitive resources are not accessible by the entire group.

Another issue that falls under the least privilege concept is the security context in which an application runs. All applications, scripts, and batch files run in the security context of a specific user on an operating system. They execute with specific permissions as if they were a user. The application may be Microsoft Word and run in the space of a regular user, or it may be a diagnostic program that needs access to more sensitive system files and so must run under an administrative user account, or it may be a program that performs backups and so should operate within the security context of a backup operator. The crux of this issue is that a program should execute only in the security context that is needed for that program to perform its duties successfully. In many environments, people do not really understand how to make programs run under different security contexts, or it may just seem easier to have all programs run under the administrator account. If attackers can compromise a program or service running under the administrator account, they have effectively elevated their access level and have much more control over the system and many more ways to cause damage.

Try This!

Control of Resources

Being able to apply the appropriate security control to file and print resources is an important aspect of the least privilege security principle. How this is implemented varies depending on the operating system the computer runs. Check how the operating system you use provides for the ability to control file and print resources.

Separation of Privilege

Protection mechanisms can be employed to grant access based on a variety of factors. One of the key principles is to base decisions on more than a single piece of information. The principle of **separation of privilege** states that the protection mechanism should be constructed so that it uses more than one piece of information to make access decisions. Applying this principle to the people side of the security function results in the concept of **separation of duties**.

The principle of separation of privilege is applicable to physical environments as well as network and host security. When applied to people's actions, separation of duties specifies that for any given task, more than one individual needs to be involved. The task is broken into different duties, each of which is accomplished by a separate individual. By implementing a task in this manner, no single individual can abuse the system for their own gain. This principle has been implemented in the business world, especially financial institutions, for many years. A simple example is a system in which one individual is required to place an order and a separate person is needed to authorize the purchase.

> Separation of duties specifies that for any given task, more than one individual needs to be involved.

While separation of duties provides a certain level of checks and balances, it is not without its own drawbacks. Chief among these is the cost required to accomplish the task. This cost is manifested in both time and money. More than one individual is required when a single person could accomplish the task, thus potentially increasing the cost of the task. In addition, with more than one individual involved, a certain delay can be expected because the task must proceed through its various steps.

Fail-Safe Defaults

Today, the Internet is no longer the friendly playground of researchers that it once was. This has resulted in different approaches that might at first seem less than friendly but that are required for security purposes. The concept of **fail-safe defaults** is that when something fails, it should do so to a safe state. One approach is that a protection mechanism should deny access by default and should grant access only when explicit permission exists. This is sometimes called **default deny**, and the common operational term for this approach is **implicit deny**.

Frequently in the network world, administrators make many decisions concerning network access. Often a series of rules will be used to determine whether or not to allow access (which is the purpose of a network firewall). If a particular situation is not covered by any of the other rules, the implicit deny approach states that access should not be granted. In other words,

Implicit deny is another fundamental principle of security, and students need to be sure they understand this principle. Similar to least privilege, this principle states that if you haven't specifically been allowed access, it should be denied.

Keep it simple. Another method of looking at the principle of economy of mechanism is that the protection mechanism should be small and simple.

if no rule would allow access, then access should not be granted. Implicit deny applies to situations involving both authorization and access.

The alternative to implicit deny is to allow access unless a specific rule forbids it. Another example of these two approaches is in programs that monitor and block access to certain websites. One approach is to provide a list of specific sites that a user is *not* allowed to access. Access to any site not on the list would be implicitly allowed. The opposite approach (the implicit deny approach) would block all access to sites that are not specifically identified as authorized. As you can imagine, depending on the specific application, one or the other approach will be more appropriate. Which approach you choose depends on the security objectives and policies of your organization.

Economy of Mechanism

The terms *security* and *complexity* are often at odds with each other, because the more complex something is, the harder it is to understand, and you cannot truly secure something if you do not understand it. Another reason complexity is a problem within security is that it usually allows too many opportunities for something to go wrong. If an application has 4000 lines of code, there are a lot fewer places for buffer overflows, for example, than in an application of two million lines of code. The principle of **economy of mechanism** is described as always using simple solutions when available.

An example of this principle concerns the number of services you allow your system to run. Default installations of computer operating systems often leave many services running. The keep-it-simple principle tells us to eliminate or disable those services we don't need. This is also a good idea from a security standpoint because it results in fewer applications that can be exploited and fewer services that the administrator is responsible for securing. The general rule of thumb is to eliminate or disable all nonessential services and protocols. This, of course, leads to the question, how do you determine whether or not a service or protocol is essential? Ideally, you should know what your computer system or network is being used for, and thus you should be able to identify and activate only those elements that are essential. For a variety of reasons, this is not as easy as it sounds. Alternatively, a stringent security approach that one can take is to assume that no service is necessary (which is obviously absurd) and activate services and ports only as they are requested. Whatever approach is taken, there is a never-ending struggle to try to strike a balance between providing functionality and maintaining security.

Complete Mediation

One of the fundamental tenets of a protection system is to check all access requests for permission. Each and every time a subject requests access to an object, the permission must be checked; otherwise, an attacker might gain unauthorized access to an object. **Complete mediation** refers to the concept that each and every request should be verified. When permissions are verified the first time, and the result is cached for subsequent use, performance may be increased, but this also opens the door to permission errors. Should a permission change subsequent to the first use, this change would not be applied to the operations after the initial check.

Complete mediation also refers to ensuring that all operations go through the protection mechanism. When security controls are added after the fact, it is important to make certain that all process flows are covered by the controls, including exceptions and out-of-band requests. If an automated process is checked in one manner, but a manual paper backup process has a separate path, it is important to ensure all checks are still in place. When a system undergoes disaster recovery or business continuity processes, or backup and/or restore processes, these too require complete mediation.

Open Design

The principle of **open design** holds that the protection of an object should not rely upon secrecy of the protection mechanism itself. This principle has been long proven in cryptographic circles, where hiding the algorithm ultimately fails and the true protection relies upon the secrecy and complexity of the keys. The principle does not exclude the idea of using secrecy, but merely states that, on the face of it, secrecy of mechanism is not sufficient for protection.

Another concept in security that should be discussed in this context is the idea of **security through obscurity**. In this case, security is considered effective if the environment and protection mechanisms are confusing or thought to be not generally known. Security through obscurity uses the approach of protecting something by hiding it. Non-computer examples of this concept include hiding your briefcase or purse if you leave it in the car so that it is not in plain view, hiding a house key under a doormat or in a planter, and pushing your favorite ice cream to the back of the freezer so that everyone else thinks it is all gone. The idea is that if something is out of sight, it is out of mind. This approach, however, does not provide actual protection of the object. Someone can still steal the purse by breaking into the car, lift the doormat and find the key, or dig through the items in the freezer to find your favorite ice cream. Security through obscurity may make someone work a little harder to accomplish a task, but it does not prevent anyone from eventually succeeding.

Similar approaches are seen in computer and network security when attempting to hide certain objects. A network administrator may, for instance, move a service from its default port to a different port so that others will not know how to access it as easily, or a firewall may be configured to hide specific information about the internal network in the hope that potential attackers will not obtain the information for use in an attack on the network.

In most security circles, security through obscurity is considered a poor approach, especially if it is the only approach to security. Security through obscurity simply attempts to hide an object; it doesn't implement a security control to protect it. An organization can use security through obscurity measures to try to hide critical assets, but other security measures should also be employed to provide a higher level of protection. For example, if an administrator moves a service from its default port to a more obscure port, an attacker can still actually find this service; thus, a firewall should be used to restrict access to the service. Most people know that even if you do shove your ice cream to the back of the freezer, someone may eventually find it.

Tech Tip

Security Through Obscurity

The principle of open design and the practice of security by obscurity may seem at odds with each other, but in reality they are not. The principle of open design states that secrecy itself cannot be relied upon as a means of protection. The practice of security through obscurity is a proven method of increasing the work factor that an adversary must expend to successfully attack a system. By itself, obscurity is not good protection, but it can complement other controls when both are properly employed.

It often amazes security professionals how frequently individuals rely on security through obscurity as their main line of defense. Relying on some piece of information remaining secret is generally not a good idea. This is especially true in this age of reverse engineering, where individuals analyze the binaries for programs to discover embedded passwords or cryptographic keys. The biggest problem with relying on security through obscurity is that if it fails and the secret becomes known, there often is no easy way to modify the secret to secure it again.

Tech Tip

Sandboxing

Sandboxing separates applications from critical operating systems services and other programs. It adds an extra layer of security to protect critical functions from malware or infected apps.

Least Common Mechanism

The principle of **least common mechanism** states that mechanisms used to access resources should be dedicated and not shared. Sharing of mechanisms allows a potential crossover between channels, resulting in a protection failure mode. For example, if there is a module that enables employees to check their payroll information, a separate module should be employed to change the information, lest a user gain access to change versus read access. Although sharing and reuse are good in one sense, they can represent a security risk in another.

Common examples of the least common mechanism and its isolation principle abound in ordinary systems. *Sandboxing* is a means of separating the operation of an application from the rest of the operating system. Virtual machines (VMs) perform the same task between operating systems on a single piece of hardware. Instantiating shared libraries, in which separate instantiation of local classes enables separate but equal coding, is yet another. The key is to provide a means of isolation between processes so information cannot flow between separate users unless specifically designed to do so.

Psychological Acceptability

Psychological acceptability refers to the users' acceptance of security measures. Another name for psychological acceptability is *least astonishment,* referring to the role that security measures should play with respect to *usability*. Users play a key role in the operation of a system, and if security measures are perceived to be an impediment to the work a user is responsible for, then a natural consequence may be that the user bypasses the control. Although a user may understand that this could result in a security problem, the perception that it does result in their performance failure will present pressure to bypass it.

Psychological acceptability is often overlooked by security professionals focused on technical issues and how they see the threat. They are focused on the threat, which is their professional responsibility, so the focus on security is natural and aligns with their professional responsibilities. This alignment between security and professional work responsibilities does not always translate to other positions in an organization. Security professionals, particularly those designing the security systems, should not only be aware of this concept but should pay particular attention to how security controls will be viewed by workers in the context of their work responsibility, not with respect to security for its own sake.

Defense in Depth

Defense in depth is a principle that is characterized by the use of multiple, different defense mechanisms with a goal of improving the defensive response to an attack. Another term for defense in depth is **layered security**. Single points of failure represent just that—an opportunity to fail. By using multiple defenses that are different, with differing points of failure, a system becomes stronger. While one defense mechanism may not be 100 percent effective, the application of a second defense mechanism to the items that succeed in bypassing the first mechanism provides a stronger response. A couple of different mechanisms can be employed in a defense-in-depth strategy: layered security and diversity of defense. Together these provide a defense-in-depth strategy that is stronger than any single layer of defense.

A bank does not protect the money that it stores only by using a vault. It has one or more security guards as a first defense to watch for suspicious activities and to secure the facility when the bank is closed. It may have monitoring systems that watch various activities that take place in the bank, whether involving customers or employees. The vault is usually located in the center of the facility, and thus there are layers of rooms or walls before arriving at the vault. There is **access control**, which ensures that the people entering the vault have to be given authorization beforehand. And the systems, including manual switches, are connected directly to the police station in case a determined bank robber successfully penetrates any one of these layers of protection.

> Defense in depth can extend beyond simple technical measures. Using different vendors (vendor diversity) provides safeguards against vendor supply issues and vendor-specific technical issues.

Networks should utilize the same type of layered security architecture. There is no "100 percent secure" system, and there is nothing that is foolproof, so a single specific protection mechanism should never be solely relied upon. It is important that every environment have multiple layers of security. These layers may employ a variety of methods, such as routers, firewalls, network segments, IDSs, encryption, authentication software, physical security, and traffic control. The layers need to work together in a coordinated manner so that one does not impede another's functionality and introduce a security hole.

As an example, consider the steps an intruder might have to take to access critical data held within a company's back-end database. The intruder first has to penetrate the firewall and use packets and methods that will not be identified and detected by the IDS (more information on these devices can be found in Chapter 13). The attacker next has to circumvent an internal router performing packet filtering, and then possibly penetrate another firewall used to separate one internal network from another (see Figure 2.3). From there, the intruder must break the access controls that are on the database, which means having to do a dictionary or brute force attack to be able to authenticate to the database software. Once the intruder has gotten this far, the data still needs to be located within the database. This may in turn be complicated by the use of access control lists outlining who can actually view or modify the data. That is a lot of work.

This example illustrates the different layers of security many environments employ. It is important to implement several different layers because if intruders succeed at one layer, you want to be able to stop them at the next. The redundancy of different protection layers ensures that there is no one single point of failure pertaining to security. If a network used only a firewall to protect its assets, an attacker able to penetrate this device successfully would find the rest of the network open and vulnerable.

An example of how different security methods can work against each other is when firewalls encounter encrypted network traffic. An organization may utilize encryption so that an outside customer communicating with a specific web server is assured that sensitive data being exchanged is protected. If this encrypted data is encapsulated within Secure Sockets Layer (SSL) or Transport Layer Security (TLS) packets and then sent through a firewall, the firewall may not be able to read the payload information in the individual packets.

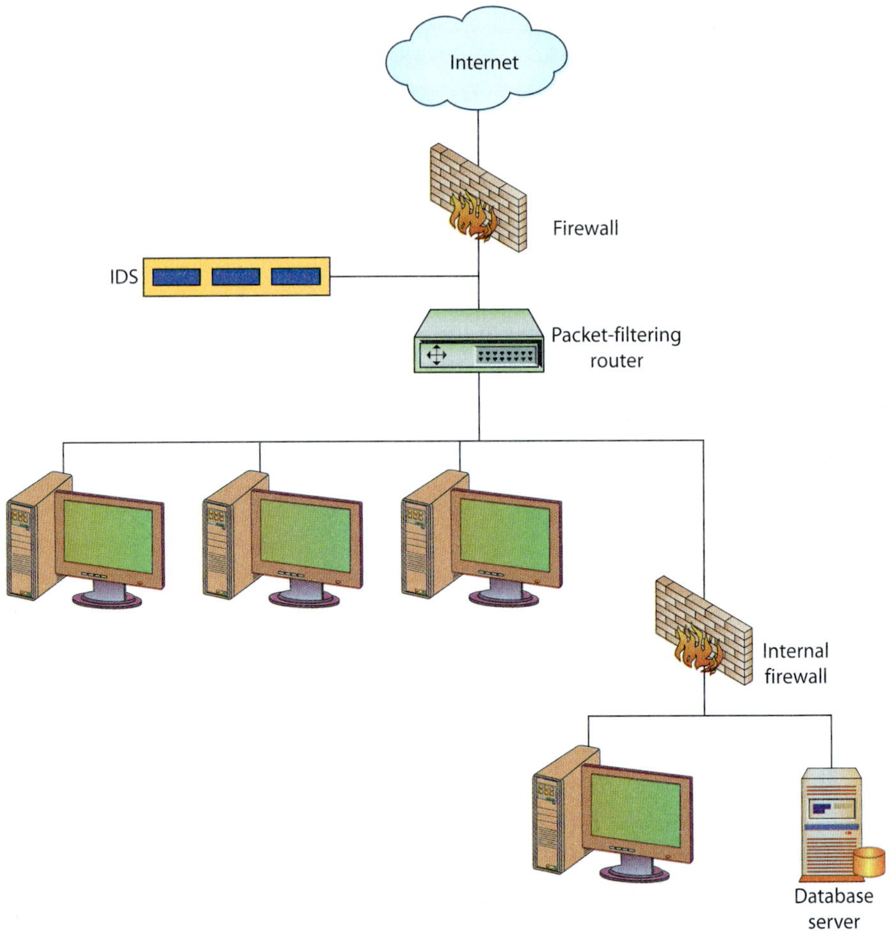

• **Figure 2.3** Layered security

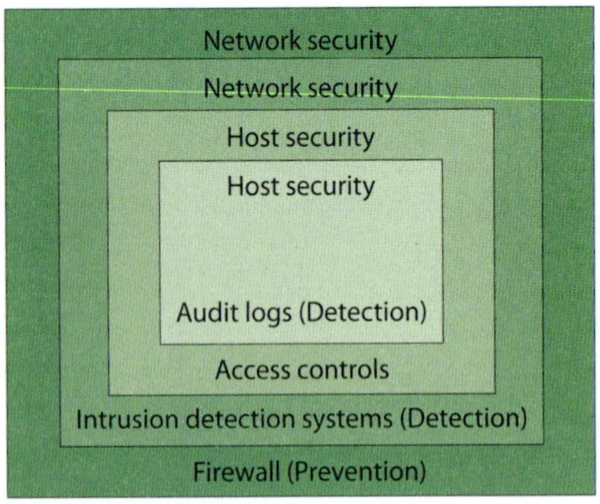

• **Figure 2.4** Various layers of security

The layers usually are depicted starting at the top, with more general types of protection, and progressing downward through each layer, with increasing granularity at each layer as you get closer to the actual resource, as you can see in Figure 2.4. This is because the top-layer protection mechanism is responsible for looking at an enormous amount of traffic, and it would be overwhelming and cause too much of a performance degradation if each aspect of the packet were inspected. Instead, each layer usually digs deeper into the packet and looks for specific items. Layers that are closer to the resource have to deal with only a fraction of the traffic that the top-layer security mechanism does, and thus looking deeper and at more granular aspects of the traffic will not cause as much of a performance hit.

Diversity of Defense

Diversity of defense is a concept that complements the idea of various layers of security. It involves making different layers of security dissimilar so that even if attackers know how to get through a system that comprises one layer, they may not know how to get through a different type of layer that employs a different system for security.

If an environment has two firewalls that form a demilitarized zone (DMZ), for example, one firewall may be placed at the perimeter of the Internet and the DMZ. This firewall analyzes the traffic that is entering through that specific access point and enforces certain types of restrictions. The other firewall may then be placed between the DMZ and the internal network. When applying the diversity-of-defense concept, you should set up these two firewalls to filter for different types of traffic and provide different types of restrictions. The first firewall, for example, may make sure that no FTP, SNMP, or Telnet traffic enters the network but allow SMTP, SSH, HTTP, and SSL traffic through. The second firewall may not allow SSL or SSH through and may interrogate SMTP and HTTP traffic to make sure that certain types of attacks are not part of that traffic.

Encapsulation

The principle of **encapsulation** is used all of the time in protocols. When a higher-level protocol is used to carry a lower protocol, the lower protocol is encapsulated in the data portion of the higher protocol. Think of it like an envelope within an envelope. This simple concept allows separate protocols to work with each other, without interference, and without needing to understand the material being encapsulated. The Open System Interconnection (OSI) and Internet models separating functions into different layers—from the physical layer to the data layer to the network layer, and so on—is an example of encapsulation.

Isolation

Isolation is the concept of separating items so that they cannot interfere with each other. Isolation is common in many functions, both in hardware and software, with the express purpose of preventing interference between the separate processes. Examples of isolation include confinement of a program in a sandbox, or a virtual machine, system call interposition, and software fault isolation.

Trust Relationships

Trust is defined as having an understanding of how a party will react to a given stimulus. In other words, if X happens, what will the party do in response? In this regard, you can trust a scorpion to sting you, even if you rescue him from flood waters. Why? Because that is what scorpions do when handled. Trust is also a key principle in computer security. Will you share resources with another user? The answer depends upon a trust relationship. If you establish a trust relationship between systems, you are granting access to another user or set of resources to perform specific tasks associated with your resources.

Changes in trust occur at **trust boundaries**—logical boundaries that surround specific levels of trust in a system. When outside input is entered into a computer program, it is crossing a trust boundary, and a decision has to be made as to whether or not the input should be trusted. Another name for the boundary around a system where external inputs can interact with a system is referred to as the **attack surface**. A key element in limiting hostile inputs is attack surface minimization, or the limiting of trusting outside information.

Many security failures can be traced to a problem with trust. Social engineering, where someone pretends to be someone they are not, is a trust violation—one that preys on customer service's desire to be helpful. Losing control over internal users, allowing them to have access to more than they need, can create trust issues. Imagine if every user had a building master key—if something ends up missing, then everyone with a key becomes suspect. And to further complicate the issue, one needs to remember that trust can be transitive and shared with other parties. You may trust your assistant with a key, but do you trust everyone they might loan it to? When one applies this line of thinking to the myriad of trust relationships within a data system—developers, customers, third parties, and vendors—these relationships become a challenge. For example, a network trust failure allowed an attacker to get to Target's point-of-sale system via a third-party heating, ventilation, and air conditioning (HVAC) vendor, resulting in a large data breach.

Because of the nature of trust and its high-risk opportunity, the sage advice is to develop and maintain a culture of *reluctance to trust*. For systems to work between parties, trust must be shared, but the sharing should be limited and controlled to only that which is needed for business purposes. Excessive trust only increases risk, without any business benefit.

> **Tech Tip**
>
> **Security Design Principles**
>
> *The eight design principles from Saltzer and Schroeder are listed and paraphrased here:*
>
> - ***Least privilege*** *Use minimum privileges necessary to perform a task.*
> - ***Separation of privilege*** *Access should be based on more than one item.*
> - ***Fail-safe defaults*** *Deny by default (implicit deny) and only grant access with explicit permission.*
> - ***Economy of mechanism*** *Mechanisms should be small and simple.*
> - ***Complete mediation*** *Protection mechanisms should cover every access to every object.*
> - ***Open design*** *Protection mechanisms should not depend on the secrecy of the mechanism itself.*
> - ***Least common mechanism*** *Protection mechanisms should be shared to the least degree possible among users.*
> - ***Psychological acceptability*** *Protection mechanisms should not impact users, but if they do, the impact should be minimal.*
>
> *Reference: J.H. Saltzer and M.D. Schroeder, "The Protection of Information in Computer Systems," Proc. IEEE, vol. 63, no. 9, 1975, pp. 1278–1308.*

Formal Security Models

An important issue when designing the software that will operate and control secure computer systems and networks is the security model that the system or network will be based on. The security model will implement the chosen security policy and enforce those characteristics deemed most important by the system designers. For example, if confidentiality is considered paramount, the model should make certain no data is disclosed to unauthorized individuals. A model enforcing confidentiality may allow unauthorized individuals to modify or delete data, as this would not violate the tenets of the model because the true values for the data would still remain confidential. Of course, this model might not be appropriate for all environments. In some instances, the unauthorized modification of data may be considered a more serious issue than its unauthorized disclosure. In such cases, the model would be responsible for enforcing the integrity of the data instead of its confidentiality. Choosing the model to base the design on is critical if you want to ensure that the resultant system accurately enforces the security policy desired. This, however, is only the starting point, and it does not imply that you have to make a choice between confidentiality and data integrity, as both are important.

Confidentiality Models

Data confidentiality has generally been the chief concern of the military. For instance, the U.S. military encouraged the development of the Bell-LaPadula security model to address data confidentiality in computer operating systems. This model is especially useful in designing multilevel security systems that implement the military's hierarchical security scheme, which includes levels of classification such as Unclassified, Confidential, Secret, and Top Secret. Similar classification schemes can be used in industry, where classifications might include Publicly Releasable, Proprietary, and Company Confidential.

A second confidentiality model, the Brewer-Nash security model, is one defined by controlling read and write access based on conflict of interest rules. This model is also known as the Chinese Wall model, after the concept of separating groups through the use of an impenetrable wall.

Bell-LaPadula Model

The **Bell-LaPadula security model** employs both mandatory and discretionary access control mechanisms when implementing its two basic security principles. The first of these principles is called the **Simple Security Rule**, which states that no subject (such as a user or a program) can read information from an object (such as a file) with a security classification higher than that possessed by the subject itself. This means that the system must prevent a user with only a Secret clearance, for example, from reading a document labeled Top Secret. This rule is often referred to as the "no-read-up" rule.

> The Simple Security Rule is just that: the most basic of security rules. It essentially states that in order for you to see something, you have to be authorized to see it.

The second security principle enforced by the Bell-LaPadula security model is known as the ***-property** (pronounced *star property*). This principle states that a subject can write to an object only if the target's security classification is greater than or equal to the object's security classification. This means that a user with a Secret clearance can write to a file with a Secret or Top Secret classification but cannot write to a file with only an Unclassified classification. This at first may appear to be a bit confusing, since this principle allows users to write to files that they are not allowed to view, thus enabling them to actually destroy files that they don't have the classification to see. This is true, but keep in mind that the Bell-LaPadula model is designed to enforce confidentiality, not integrity. Writing to a file that you don't have the clearance to view is not considered a confidentiality issue; it is an integrity issue.

Whereas the *-property allows a user to write to a file of equal or greater security classification, it doesn't allow a user to write to a file with a lower security classification. This, too, may be confusing at first—after all, shouldn't a user with a Secret clearance, who can view a file marked Unclassified, be allowed to write to that file? The answer to this, from a security perspective, is "no." The reason again relates to wanting to avoid either accidental or deliberate security disclosures. The system is designed to make it impossible (hopefully) for data to be disclosed to those without the appropriate level to view it. As shown in Figure 2.5, if it were possible for a user with a Top Secret clearance to either deliberately or accidentally write Top Secret information and place it in a file marked Confidential, a user with only a Confidential security clearance could then access this file and view the Top Secret information. Thus, data would have been disclosed to an individual not authorized to view it. This is what the system should protect against and is the reason for what is known as the "no-write-down" rule.

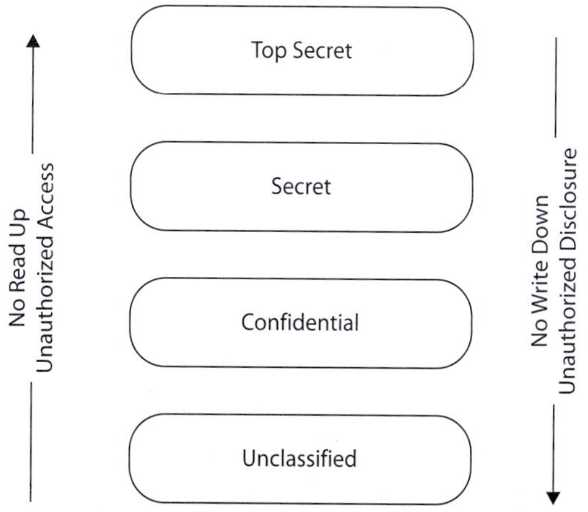

Unclassified users should not access Top Secret material (no read up).
Top Secret files should not be written to Confidential storage (no write down).

• **Figure 2.5** Bell-LaPadula security model

Not all environments are more concerned with confidentiality than integrity. In a financial institution, for example, viewing somebody's bank balance is an issue, but a greater issue would be the ability to actually modify that balance. In environments where integrity is more important, a different model than the Bell-LaPadula security model is needed.

Brewer-Nash Security Model

One of the tenets associated with access is *need to know*. Separate groups within an organization may have differing needs with respect to access to information. A security model that takes into account user conflict-of-interest aspects is the **Brewer-Nash security model**. In this model, information flows are modeled to prevent information from flowing between subjects and objects when a conflict of interest would occur. As previously noted, this model is also known as the Chinese Wall model, after the Great Wall of China, a structure designed to separate groups of people. As shown in Figure 2.6, separate groups are defined and access controls are designed to enforce the separation of the groups.

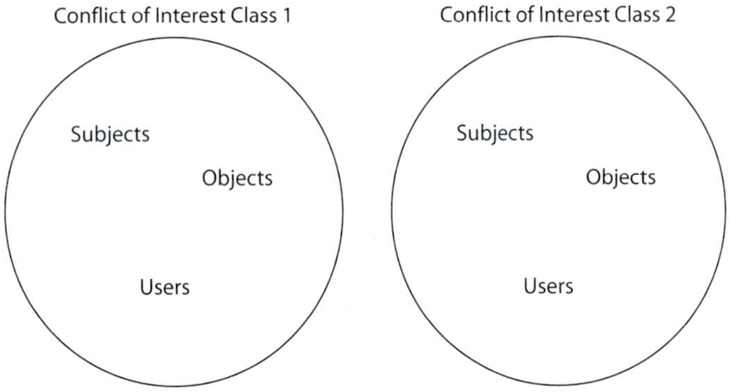

• **Figure 2.6** Brewer-Nash security model

Integrity Models

The Bell-LaPadula model was developed in the early 1970s but was found to be insufficient for all environments. As an alternative, Kenneth Biba studied the integrity issue and developed what is called the Biba security model in the late 1970s. Additional work was performed in the 1980s that led to the Clark-Wilson security model, which also places its emphasis on integrity rather than confidentiality.

The Biba Security Model

In the **Biba security model**, shown in Figure 2.7, instead of security classifications, *integrity levels* are used. A principle of integrity levels is that data with a higher integrity level is believed to be more accurate or reliable than data with a lower integrity level. Integrity levels indicate the amount of "trust" that can be placed in information at the different levels. Integrity levels differ from security levels in another way—they limit the modification of information as opposed to the flow of information.

An initial attempt at implementing an integrity-based model was captured in what is referred to as the **Low-Water-Mark policy**. This policy in many ways is the opposite of the *-property in that it prevents subjects from writing to objects of a higher integrity level. The policy also contains a second rule that states the integrity level of a subject will be lowered if it reads an object of a lower integrity level. The reason for this is that if the subject then uses data from that object, the highest the integrity level can be for a new object created from it is the same level of integrity as the original object. In other words, the level of trust you can place in data formed from data at a specific integrity level cannot be higher than the level of trust you have in the subject creating the new data object, and the level of trust you have in

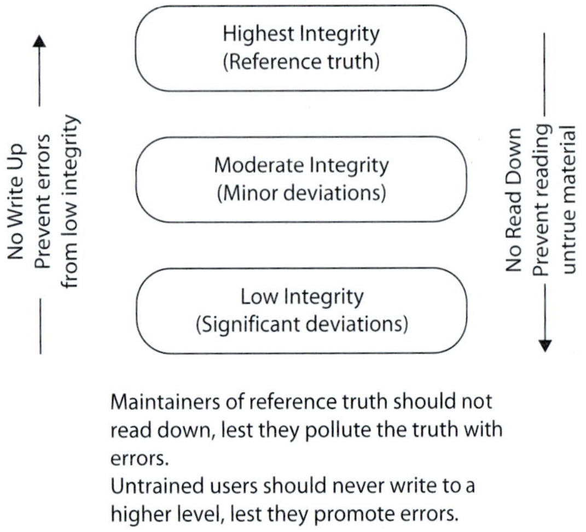

• **Figure 2.7** Biba security model

the subject can only be as high as the level of trust you had in the original data. The final rule contained in the Low-Water-Mark policy states that a subject can execute a program only if the program's integrity level is equal to or less than the integrity level of the subject. This ensures that data modified by a program only has the level of trust (integrity level) that can be placed in the individual who executed the program.

While the Low-Water-Mark policy certainly prevents unauthorized modification of data, it has the unfortunate side effect of eventually lowering the integrity levels of all subjects to the lowest level on the system (unless the subject always views files with the same level of integrity). This is because of the second rule, which lowers the integrity level of the subject after accessing an object of a lower integrity level. There is no way specified in the policy to ever raise the subject's integrity level back to its original value. A second policy, known as the **Ring policy**, addresses this issue by allowing any subject to read any object without regard to the object's level of integrity and without lowering the subject's integrity level. This, unfortunately, can lead to a situation where data created by a subject after reading data of a lower integrity level could end up having a higher level of trust placed upon it than it should.

The Biba security model implements a hybrid of the Ring and Low-Water-Mark policies. Biba's model in many respects is the opposite of the Bell-LaPadula model in that what it enforces are "no-read-down" and "no-write-up" policies. It also implements a third rule that prevents subjects from executing programs of a higher level. The Biba security model thus addresses the problems mentioned with both the Ring and Low-Water-Mark policies.

The Clark-Wilson Security Model

The **Clark-Wilson security model** takes an entirely different approach than the Biba and Bell-LaPadula models, using transactions as the basis for its rules. It defines two levels of integrity only: constrained data items (CDIs) and unconstrained data items (UDIs). CDI data is subject to integrity controls, whereas UDI data is not. The model then defines two types of processes: integrity verification processes (IVPs), which ensure that CDI data meets integrity constraints (to ensure the system is in a valid state), and transformation processes (TPs), which change the state of data from one valid state to another. Data in this model cannot be modified directly by a user; it must be changed by trusted TPs, access to which can be restricted (thus restricting the ability of a user to perform certain activities).

It is useful to return to the prior example of the banking account balance to describe the need for integrity-based models. In the Clark-Wilson model, the account balance would be a CDI because its integrity is a critical function for the bank. A client's color preference for their checkbook is not a critical function and would be considered a UDI. Since the integrity of account balances is of extreme importance, changes to a person's balance must be accomplished through the use of a TP. Ensuring that the balance is correct would be the duty of an IVP. Only certain employees of the bank should have the ability to modify an individual's account, which can be controlled by limiting the number of individuals who have the authority to execute TPs that result in account modification. Certain very critical functions may actually be split into multiple TPs to enforce another important principle: *separation of duties* (introduced earlier in the chapter). This limits the authority any one individual has so that multiple individuals will be required to execute certain critical functions.

Additional References

Saltzer, J.H., and M.D. Schroeder. 1975. "The Protection of Information in Computer Systems." *Proc. IEEE* 63(9): 1278–1308.

Schwartau, W. 1998. "Time-Based Security Explained: Provable Security Models and Formulas for the Practitioner and Vendor." *Computers & Security* 17(8): 693–714.

Chapter 2 Review

Chapter Summary

After reading this chapter and completing the exercises, you should understand the following regarding the basics of security, security terminology, and security models.

Define basic terms associated with computer and information security

- Information assurance and information security place the security focus on the information and not on the hardware or software used to process it.
- The original goal of computer and network security was to provide confidentiality, integrity, and availability—the "CIA" of security.
- Additional elements of security can include authentication, authorization, auditability, and nonrepudiation.
- The operational model of computer security tells us that protection is provided by prevention, detection, and response.

Identify the basic approaches to computer and information security

- Host security focuses on protecting each computer and device individually, whereas network security focuses on addressing protection of the network as a whole.
- For many organizations, a combination of host security and network security is needed to adequately address the wide range of possible security threats.

Identify the basic principles of computer and information security

- The principle of least privilege states that the minimum privileges necessary to perform a task should be used.
- The principle of separation of privilege states that critical items should require multiple parties.
- The principle of fail-safe default states that access decisions should be based on deny by default (implicit deny) with specific exceptions being made via granting access using explicit permissions.
- The principle of economy of mechanism states that protection mechanisms should be small and simple.
- The principle of complete mediation states that protection mechanisms should cover every access to every object and should never be bypassed.
- The principle of open design states that protection mechanisms should not depend on the secrecy of the mechanism itself.
- The principle of least common mechanism states that the protection mechanisms should be shared to the least degree possible among users.
- The principle of psychological acceptability states that protection mechanisms should not impact users, but if they do, the impact should be minimal.
- The principle of defense in depth, or layered security, is that multiple layers of differing, overlapping controls should be employed.
- Diversity of defense is a concept that complements the idea of various layers of security. It means to make the layers dissimilar so that if one layer is penetrated, the next layer can't also be penetrated using the same method.

Recognize some of the basic models used to implement security in operating systems

- Security models enforce the chosen security policy.
- There are two basic categories of models: those that ensure confidentiality and those that ensure integrity.
- Bell-LaPadula is a confidentiality security model whose development was prompted by the demands of the U.S. military and its security clearance scheme. This security model enforces "no-read-up" and "no-write-down" rules to avoid the deliberate or accidental disclosure of information to individuals not authorized to receive it.
- The Brewer-Nash security model (the Chinese Wall model) is a confidentiality model that separates users based on conflicts of interest.
- The Biba security model is an integrity-based model that, in many respects, implements the opposite of what the Bell-LaPadula model does—that is, "no-read-down" and "no-write-up" rules.
- The Clark-Wilson security model is an integrity-based model designed to limit the processes an individual may perform as well as require that critical data be modified only through specific transformation processes.

Key Terms

***-property** *(43)*
access control *(39)*
attack surface *(41)*
auditability *(28)*
authentication *(28)*
availability *(28)*
Bell-LaPadula security model *(43)*
Biba security model *(44)*
Brewer-Nash security model *(44)*
Clark-Wilson security model *(45)*
complete mediation *(36)*
confidentiality *(28)*
default deny *(35)*
defense in depth *(38)*
diversity of defense *(40)*
economy of mechanism *(36)*
encapsulation *(41)*
fail-safe defaults *(35)*
fortress model *(28)*
hacking *(27)*
host security *(32)*
implicit deny *(35)*
integrity *(28)*
isolation *(41)*
layered security *(38)*
least common mechanism *(38)*
least privilege *(33)*
Low-Water-Mark policy *(44)*
network security *(33)*
nonrepudiation *(28)*
open design *(37)*
operational model of computer security *(29)*
phreaking *(27)*
psychological acceptability *(38)*
Ring policy *(45)*
security through obscurity *(37)*
separation of duties *(35)*
separation of privilege *(35)*
Simple Security Rule *(43)*
trust *(41)*
trust boundary *(41)*

Key Terms Quiz

Use terms from the Key Terms list to complete the sentences that follow. Don't use the same term more than once. Not all terms will be used.

1. _______________ is a term used to describe the condition where a user cannot deny that an event has occurred.
2. The _______________ is an integrity-based security model that bases its security on control of the processes that are allowed to modify critical data, referred to as *constrained data items*.
3. The security principle used in the Bell-LaPadula security model that states that no subject can read from an object with a higher security classification is called the _______________.
4. The principle that states that a subject has only the necessary rights and privileges to perform its task, with no additional permissions, is called _______________.
5. _______________ is the principle in security where protection mechanisms should be kept as simple and as small as possible.
6. _______________ is the principle that protection mechanisms should minimize user-level impact.
7. _______________ is the process used to ensure that separate processes do not interfere with each other.
8. The architecture in which multiple methods of security defense are applied to prevent realization of threat-based risks is called _______________.
9. _______________ is the process of using multiple people to perform critical or sensitive tasks.
10. Implicit deny is an operationalization of the principle of _______________.

Multiple-Choice Quiz

1. Which of the following is not a principle of security?
   - **A.** Principle of least privilege
   - **B.** Principle of economy of mechanism
   - **C.** Principle of efficient access
   - **D.** Principle of open access
2. The CIA of security includes which three security goals?
   - **A.** Confidentiality, integrity, authentication
   - **B.** Confidentiality, integrity, availability
   - **C.** Certificates, integrity, availability
   - **D.** Confidentiality, inspection, authentication
3. The security principle used in the Bell-LaPadula security model that states that no subject can read from an object with a higher security classification is known as what?
   - **A.** Simple Security Rule
   - **B.** Ring policy
   - **C.** Mandatory access control
   - **D.** *-property
4. Which of the following concepts requires users and system processes to use the minimal amount of permission necessary to function?
   - **A.** Layer defense
   - **B.** Diversified defense
   - **C.** Simple Security Rule
   - **D.** Least privilege

5. Which security model separates users based on conflict-of-interest issues?
   A. Bell-LaPadula
   B. Brewer-Nash
   C. Biba
   D. Clark-Wilson
6. The Bell-LaPadula security model is an example of a security model that is based on what?
   A. The integrity of the data
   B. The availability of the data
   C. The confidentiality of the data
   D. The authenticity of the data
7. What is the term used to describe the requirement that different portions of a critical process be performed by different people?
   A. Least privilege
   B. Defense in depth
   C. Separation of duties
   D. Job rotation
8. Hiding information to prevent disclosure is an example of what?
   A. Security through obscurity
   B. Certificate-based security
   C. Discretionary data security
   D. Defense in depth
9. What is the problem with the Low-Water-Mark policy?
   A. It's aimed at ensuring confidentiality and not integrity.
   B. It could ultimately result in all subjects having the integrity level of the least-trusted object on the system.
   C. It could result in the unauthorized modification of data.
   D. It does not adequately prevent users from viewing files they are not entitled to view.
10. The concept of blocking an action unless it is specifically authorized is known as what?
   A. Implicit deny
   B. Least privilege
   C. Simple Security Rule
   D. Hierarchical defense model

Essay Quiz

1. Your company has information that must be protected from unauthorized access, and it must also prevent certain business units in certain countries from accessing this information. Which security models apply and how?
2. The new CEO for your company just retired from the military and wants to use some of the same computer systems and security software she used while with the military. Explain to her the reasons that confidentiality-based security models are not adequate for all environments. Provide at least two examples of environments where a confidentiality-based security model is not sufficient.
3. Describe why the concept of "security through obscurity" is generally considered a bad principle to rely on. Provide some real-world examples of where you have seen this principle used.
4. Write a brief essay describing the principle of least privilege and how it can be employed to enhance security. Provide at least two examples of environments in which it can be used for security purposes.

Lab Project

• Lab Project 2.1

In an environment familiar to you (your school or where you work, for example), determine whether the principle of diversity of defense has been employed and list the different layers of security that are employed. Discuss whether you think they are sufficient and whether the principle of defense in depth has also been used.

chapter 3

Operational and Organizational Security

We will bankrupt ourselves in the vain search for absolute security.

—Dwight David Eisenhower

In this chapter, you will learn how to

- Identify various operational aspects to security in your organization
- Identify various policies and procedures in your organization
- Identify the security awareness and training needs of an organization
- Understand the different types of agreements employed in negotiating security requirements

Organizations achieve operational security through policies and procedures that guide users' interactions with data and data-processing systems. Developing and aligning these efforts with the goals of the business are crucial aspects of developing a successful security program. One method of ensuring coverage is to align efforts with the operational security model described in the last chapter. This breaks efforts into groups: prevention, detection, and response elements.

Prevention technologies are designed to keep individuals from being able to gain access to systems or data they are not authorized to use. Originally, this was the sole approach to security. Eventually we learned that in an operational environment, prevention is extremely difficult and relying on prevention technologies alone is not sufficient. This led to the rise of technologies to detect and respond to events that occur when prevention fails. Together, the prevention technologies and the detection and response technologies form the operational model for computer security.

Policies, Procedures, Standards, and Guidelines

The important parts of any organization's approach to implementing security include the policies, procedures, standards, and guidelines that are established to detail what users and administrators should be doing to maintain the security of the systems and network. Collectively, these documents provide the guidance needed to determine how security will be implemented in the organization. Given this guidance, the specific technology and security mechanisms required can be planned for.

Policies are high-level, broad statements of what the organization wants to accomplish. They are made by management when laying out the organization's position on some issue. **Procedures** are the step-by-step instructions on how to implement policies in the organization. They describe exactly how employees are expected to act in a given situation or to accomplish a specific task. **Standards** are mandatory elements regarding the implementation of a policy. They are accepted specifications that provide specific details on how a policy is to be enforced. Some standards are externally driven. Regulations for banking and financial institutions, for example, require certain security measures be taken by law. Other standards may be set by the organization to meet its own security goals. **Guidelines** are recommendations relating to a policy. The key term in this case is *recommendations*—guidelines are not mandatory steps.

Just as the network itself constantly changes, the policies, procedures, standards, and guidelines should be living documents that are periodically evaluated and changed as necessary. The constant monitoring of the network and the periodic review of the relevant documents are part of the process that is the operational model. When applied to policies, this process results in what is known as the *policy lifecycle.* This operational process and policy lifecycle roughly consist of four steps in relation to your security policies and solutions:

1. Plan (adjust) for security in your organization.
2. Implement the plans.
3. Monitor the implementation.
4. Evaluate the effectiveness.

In the first step, you develop the policies, procedures, and guidelines that will be implemented and design the security components that will protect your network. A variety of governing instruments—from standards to compliance rules—will provide boundaries for these documents. Once these documents are designed and developed, you can implement the plans. Part of the implementation of any policy, procedure, or guideline is an instruction period during which those who will be affected by the change or introduction of this new document can learn about its contents. Next, you monitor to ensure that both the hardware and the software, as well as the policies, procedures, and guidelines, are effective in securing your systems. Finally, you evaluate the effectiveness of the security measures you have in place. This step may include a *vulnerability assessment* (an attempt to identify and prioritize the list of vulnerabilities within a system

These documents guide how security will be implemented in the organization:

Policies High-level, broad statements of what the organization wants to accomplish

Procedures Step-by-step instructions on how to implement the policies

Standards Mandatory elements regarding the implementation of a policy

Guidelines Recommendations relating to a policy

or network) and a *penetration test* (a method to check the security of a system by simulating an attack by a malicious individual) of your system to ensure the security is adequate. After evaluating your security posture, you begin again with Step 1, this time adjusting the security mechanisms you have in place, and then continue with this cyclical process.

Regarding security, every organization should have several common policies in place (in addition to those already discussed relative to access control methods). These include, but are not limited to, security policies regarding change management, classification of information, acceptable use, due care and due diligence, due process, need to know, disposal and destruction of data, service level agreements, human resources issues, codes of ethics, and policies governing incident response.

Organizational Policies

The important parts of any organization's approach to implementing security include the policies, procedures, standards, and guidelines that are established to detail what users and administrators should be doing to maintain the security of the systems and network. Collectively, these documents provide the guidance needed to determine how security will be implemented in the organization. Given this guidance, the specific technology and security mechanisms required can be planned for.

Change Management Policy

The purpose of **change management** is to ensure proper procedures are followed when modifications to the IT infrastructure are made. These modifications can be prompted by a number of different events, including new legislation, updated versions of software or hardware, implementation of new software or hardware, and improvements to the infrastructure. The term *management* implies that this process should be controlled in some systematic way, and that is indeed the purpose. Changes to the infrastructure might have a detrimental impact on operations. New versions of operating systems or application software might be incompatible with other software or hardware the organization is using. Without a process to manage the change, an organization might suddenly find itself unable to conduct business. A change management process should include various stages, including a method to request a change to the infrastructure, a review and approval process for the request, an examination of the consequences of the change, resolution (or mitigation) of any detrimental effects the change might incur, implementation of the change, and documentation of the process as it relates to the change.

Change management is about the process of applying change. Change control is about the details of the change itself.

Change Control

Change control is the process of how changes to anything are sourced, analyzed, and managed. Change control is a subset of change management, focused on the details of a change and how it is documented.

Asset Management

Asset management involves the policies and processes used to manage the elements of the system, including hardware, software, and the data contained within them. In order to secure a system, one must have some form of control over these assets, and asset management involves the processes employed to keep the enterprise in positive control over these valuable items. Failures to control hardware can result in rogue network devices or computers accessing systems. Failure to control software can result in system-level vulnerabilities granting attackers free reign over a system and its data. Failure to control the data assets can result in many forms of failure. This makes asset management one of the most important aspects of security, and it is ranked at the top of virtually every standard list of controls.

> **Tech Tip**
>
> **Automation of Policy Enforcement**
>
> *When you're making policies, there are some important questions you need to have answers for: How do you plan to enforce the policy? Should you even have a policy if there's no way to know who isn't following it? Maybe you want the policy just so that you can fire people you happen to catch after the fact (generally a bad idea). The keys to good policies are they support the desired work, they are relatively transparent (they don't impede work), and they are perceived as being fairly enforced. Automation is a key element, because if you know the states, both desired and prohibited, and can measure these with automation, then many of the desired elements can be achieved. Assume that certain functions are not to be used in coding—you can write filters to screen for these on code check-in, thus enforcing compliance with the approved functions policy. If you have something less defined, such as adding security usability tenets to the software development process, this is great as a guideline, but how would you specifically define it or enforce it on projects? The scale could be a problem, there's no way to automate it, and it is subjective—all of which results in uncertain outcomes and uneven enforcement. If you can define a way to automate the policy, this provides a lot of good data on whether it meets many of the goals associated with good policies.*

Security Policies

In keeping with the high-level nature of policies, the **security policy** is a high-level statement produced by senior management that outlines both what security means to the organization and the organization's goals for security. The main security policy can then be broken down into additional policies that cover specific topics. Statements such as "this organization will exercise the principle of least access in its handling of client information" would be an example of a security policy. The security policy can also describe how security is to be handled from an organizational point of view (such as describing which office and corporate officer or manager oversees the organization's security program).

In addition to policies related to access control, the organization's security policy should include the specific policies described in the next sections. All policies should be reviewed on a regular basis and updated as needed. Generally, policies should be updated less frequently than the procedures that implement them, since the high-level goals will not change as often as the environment in which they must be implemented. All policies should be reviewed by the organization's legal counsel, and a plan should be outlined that describes how the organization will ensure that employees will be made aware of the policies. Policies can also be made stronger by including references to the authority who made the policy (whether this policy comes from the CEO or is a department-level policy, for example) and references to any laws or regulations applicable to the specific policy and environment.

Data Policies

System integration with third parties frequently involves the sharing of data. Data can be shared for the purpose of processing or storage. Control over data is a significant issue in third-party relationships. Numerous questions need to be addressed. For example, the question of who owns the data—both the data shared with third parties and subsequent data developed as part of the relationship—is an issue that needs to be established.

Data Ownership

Data requires a data owner. Data ownership roles for all data elements need to be defined in the business. Data ownership is a business function, where the requirements for security, privacy, retention, and other business functions must be established. Not all data requires the same handling restrictions, but all data requires these characteristics to be defined. This is the responsibility of the data owner.

Besides data owners, there are data controllers, processors, and custodians/stewards. Each of these has responsibilities to protect data, and these responsibilities should be guided by policies.

Unauthorized Data Sharing

Unauthorized data sharing can be a significant issue, and in today's world, data has value and is frequently used for secondary purposes. Ensuring that all parties in the relationship understand the data-sharing requirements is an important prerequisite. Equally important is ensuring that all parties understand the security requirements of shared data.

Data Backups

Data ownership requirements include backup responsibilities. Data backup requirements include determining the level of backup, the restore objectives, and the level of protection requirements. These can be defined by the data owner and then executed by operational IT personnel. Determining the backup responsibilities and developing the necessary operational procedures to ensure that adequate backups occur are important security elements.

Classification of Information

A key component of IT security is the protection of the information processed and stored on the computer systems and network. Organizations deal with many different types of information, and they need to recognize that not all information is of equal importance or sensitivity. This requires classification of information into various categories, each with its own requirements for its handling. Factors that affect the classification of specific information include its value to the organization (what will be the impact to the organization if this information is lost?), its age, and laws or regulations that govern its protection. The most widely known system of classification of information is the one implemented by the U.S. government (including the military), which classifies information into categories such as *Confidential*, *Secret*, and *Top Secret*. Businesses have similar desires to protect information and often use categories such as *Publicly Releasable*, *Proprietary*, *Company Confidential*, and *For Internal Use Only*. Each policy for the classification of information should describe how it should be protected, who may have access to it, who has the authority to release it (and how), and how it should be destroyed. All employees of the organization should be trained in the procedures for handling the information they are authorized to access. Discretionary and mandatory access control techniques use classifications as a method to identify who may have access to what resources.

Tech Tip

Data Classification

Information classification categories you should be aware of for the CompTIA Security+ exam include High, Medium, Low, Confidential, Private, and Public.

Data Labeling, Handling, and Disposal

Effective data classification programs include data labeling, which enables personnel working with the data to know whether it is sensitive and to understand the levels of protection required. When the data is inside an information-processing system, the protections should be designed into the system. But when the data leaves this cocoon of protection, whether by printing, downloading, or copying, it becomes necessary to ensure continued protection by other means. This is where data labeling assists users in fulfilling their responsibilities. Training to ensure that labeling occurs and that it is used and followed is important for users whose roles can be impacted by this material.

Training plays an important role in ensuring proper data handling and disposal. Personnel are intimately involved in several specific tasks associated with data handling and data destruction/disposal. If properly trained, they can act as a security control. Untrained or inadequately trained personnel will not be a productive security control and, in fact, can be a source of potential compromise.

Governance

Data *governance* is the process of managing the availability, usability, integrity, and security of the data in enterprise systems. This must be done by policy, as it involves a large number of data owners and users. Data governance should have established data standards and policies that control data usage, security, and retention. Effective governance ensures that data usage is consistent with policies, that data elements are trustworthy, and that data doesn't get misused. The roles and responsibilities of those involved in data governance are covered in Chapter 25.

Retention

Data *retention* is the management of the data lifecycle with an emphasis on when data reaches the end of useful life for an organization. Maintaining old, excess data that no longer serves a business purpose only represents system risk and thus should be removed from the system and properly destroyed. Having a coordinated data retention policy is more than just labeling how long different types of data should be stored. Some types of data, financial records, tax records, and so on have specific regulatory requirements as to how long they must be maintained. The retention policy must also take into account things like legal holds (sometimes referred to as litigation holds) on specific data elements, suspending the destruction of those elements, and other regulatory concerns. Developing a data retention policy is relatively easy, but implementing it in an efficient and effective manner can be significantly more challenging given the diverse nature of data across the enterprise and the challenge presented by item-specific litigation holds.

A legal hold is a court directive to keep all records associated with a subject of a legal proceeding, and this order takes precedence over normal data retention policies.

Need to Know

Another common security principle is that of *need to know,* which goes hand-in-hand with *least privilege.* The guiding factor here is that each individual in the organization is supplied with only the absolute minimum amount of information and privileges they need to perform their work tasks.

The principle of least privilege states that users should only have a level of access permissions necessary to perform their assigned tasks.

To obtain access to any piece of information, the individual must have a justified need to know. A policy spelling out these two principles as guiding philosophies for the organization should be created. The policy should also address who in the organization can grant access to information and who can assign privileges to employees.

Disposal and Destruction Policy

Many potential intruders have learned the value of dumpster diving. An organization must be concerned about not only paper trash and discarded objects but also the information stored on discarded objects such as computers. Several government organizations have been embarrassed when old computers sold to salvagers proved to contain sensitive documents on their hard drives. It is critical for every organization to have a strong *disposal and destruction policy* and related procedures.

Important papers should be shredded, and *important* in this case means anything that might be useful to a potential intruder. It is amazing what intruders can do with what appear to be innocent pieces of information.

Before magnetic storage media (such as disks or tapes) is discarded in the trash or sold for salvage, it should have all files deleted and should be overwritten at least three times with all 1's, all 0's, and then random characters. Commercial products are available to destroy files using this process. It is not sufficient simply to delete all files and leave it at that, because the deletion process affects only the pointers to where the files are stored and doesn't actually get rid of all the bits in the file. This is why it is possible to "undelete" files and recover them after they have been deleted.

A safer method for destroying files from a storage device is to destroy the data magnetically, using a strong magnetic field to *degauss* the media. This effectively destroys all data on the media. Several commercial degaussers are available for this purpose. Another method that can be used on hard drives is to use a file on them (the sort of file you'd find in a hardware store) and actually file off the magnetic material from the surface of the platter. There are many means for storing data externally, from optical drives to USB sticks. In the case of optical discs (CDs, DVDs, and even Blu-ray discs), many paper shredders now have the ability to shred this form of storage media. In some highly secure environments, the only acceptable method of disposing of hard drives and other storage devices is the actual physical destruction of the devices. Matching the security action to the level of risk is important to recognize in this instance. Destroying hard drives that do not have sensitive information is wasteful; proper file scrubbing is probably appropriate. For drives with ultra-sensitive information, physical destruction makes sense. There is no single answer, but as in most things associated with information security, the best practice is to match the action to the level of risk. Data destruction is covered in detail in Chapter 25.

Credential Policies

Credential policies refer to the processes, services, and software used to store, manage, and log the use of user credentials. User-based credential management solutions are typically aimed at assisting end users in managing their growing set of passwords. There are credential management products that provide a secure means of storing user credentials and making them available across a wide range of platforms, from local stores to cloud storage locations. System credential management solutions offer the same advantages to system owners, providing a means to manage who is given access to differing resources across the enterprise.

The key method used to control access to most systems is still one based on passwords. In conjunction with a strongly enforced account policy that prohibits the sharing of passwords and credentials, the use of passwords forms the foundation to support the concept that each user ID should be traceable to a single person's activity. Passwords need to be managed to provide appropriate levels of protection. They need to be strong enough to resist attack, and yet not too difficult for users to remember. An account policy can act to ensure that the necessary steps are taken to enact a secure password solution, both by users and by the password infrastructure system.

Personnel

Users, or *personnel,* require credentials to access specific system resources as part of their job duties. Management of who gets what credentials is part of the access and authorization management system and should be managed via a credential policy. The details behind credentials and policies for access control are covered in Chapter 11.

Third Party

Just as users inside a firm require credentials to access systems, there are situations where third parties also require credentials. Whether credentials for a system or physical access, *third-party* credentials should be managed by policies to ensure they are issued when needed to the correct parties, and when access is no longer needed, they are revoked appropriately.

Devices

Devices are physical items that require access to a network or enterprise system. To have this access, they require credentials just like human users. Unlike human users, devices do not have the ability to change their password, so they are typically enabled with very long passwords to prevent hacking and have longer-than-normal password expiration periods. This makes device accounts natural targets for attackers; while their long passwords may not be crackable, they can be stolen. Device accounts should be controlled by policy and monitored as to scope of use. Mobile device management policies are covered in detail in Chapter 12.

Service Accounts

Service accounts are special accounts that are used to provision permissions for services, or non-human-initiated system activity. Many computer systems have automated services that function as either part of, in addition to, the operating system to enable certain functionalities. These special programs require permissions like all programs that operate, and service accounts are the mechanism used to enable these items to run. Service accounts require auditing and oversight because they run in the background and frequently have significant capabilities. The enterprise needs a policy to determine who can enable and operate these accounts as well as their audit functions.

Because device and service accounts do not have human operators using them, their passwords have special properties, including very long expiration periods. They also commonly are employed to run processes at elevated levels of privilege. This makes them more susceptible to abuse, so their scope and usage should be monitored.

Administrator/Root Accounts

Administrators and root accounts have elevated privileges and require closer scrutiny as to who is issued these credentials and how they are used and monitored. Detailed information concerning the additional safeguards needed for these accounts is detailed in Chapter 11.

Tech Tip

What Makes a Usable Strong Password

New research from the National Institute of Standards and Technology (NIST) indicates that password complexity rules that are designed to force entropy into passwords do so at the risk of other, less-desired password behaviors, such as writing passwords down or versioning them with an increasing number element. The latest guidance is that long passphrases offer the best protection, but for the exam you should know the tried-and-true complexity requirements.

Password and Account Policies

Passwords are as ubiquitous as users; in fact, more so. The average user has more than 20 passwords in today's online environment. It seems that every site you go to wants you to log in and create a password. So if passwords are everywhere, why do we need a policy? Because passwords are important, and improper use and/or control over passwords is a leading cause of account hijacking. Policies can set expectations for the workforce as to what is needed in the form of passwords from a security perspective.

Password Complexity

Passwords must meet the defined *password complexity* requirements in the organization. Typically these requirements specify that the password must be a minimum length and have characters from at least three of the following four groups: English uppercase characters (*A* through *Z*), English lowercase characters (*a* through *z*), numerals (0 through 9), and non-alphabetic special characters (such as !, $, #, and %).

Account Expiration

Account expiration should occur when a user is no longer authorized to use a system. This requires coordination between those who manage the accounts and those who manage the need for access. The best solution is for the managers of the workers requiring access to manage the need—they are close to the situation, understand the need, and are generally the first to know when access is no longer necessary (for example, when an employee transfers or quits). These managers should be the first ones to notify the security team as to any changes in permissions, and human resources (HR) should play a backup role. Having frontline management initiate permissions issues also enables the proper continuation of permissions when a person departs. Who assumes ownership over files the previous person was sole owner of? This is a business decision and best managed by those closest to the business.

In Windows systems, user account expiration is a built-in feature that allows you to create a temporary user account that will expire automatically on the specified dates. Upon reaching the expiration date, the user account is expired and the user is unable to log on to Windows after that date. This can be good for temporary and contract workers.

Account Recovery

Account recovery seems like an esoteric topic until you lose the password on your laptop and have no way back in. This is even more serious if you lose administrator account passwords to key elements of your infrastructure. Having a recovery plan for accounts in case something happens to the people who know the passwords is important in order for the enterprise to continue after the loss of a resource. Rather than focus on all the ways the organization can lose a resource—being fired, leaving on one's own accord, stepping in front of a bus, and so on—focus instead on a simple recovery method like an envelope containing a list of accounts and passwords, put in a safe governed by a different senior executive. Public key infrastructure (PKI) systems have key-recovery mechanisms that are there for a reason—to be used when emergencies happen. Account recovery is no different: you need to have a plan and execute it in order to prepare for an emergency when you need to put the plan into action. If you wait until you need a plan, it is too late to create it.

Account Disablement

Account disablement is the step between the account having access and the account being removed from the system. Whenever an employee leaves a firm, all associated accounts should be disabled to prevent further access. Disabling is preferable to removal because removal might result in permission and ownership problems. Periodic audits of user accounts to ensure they still need access is also a good security measure. Disabling an account is reversible, but it prohibits the account from being used until the issue that resulted in the disabling is resolved. Account disablement can be an automatic response from a security system if there is evidence that the account is under attack (say, from a brute force password attack).

> Accounts have many facets that are governed by both action and policy. Remember, policy directs actions, and the specifics of the question give the context by which you can choose the best answer. There is a lot of detail in this section, and can be relevant in use.

Account Lockout

Account lockout is akin to disablement, although *lockout* typically refers to the ability to log on. If a user mistypes their password a certain number of times, they may be forced to wait a set amount of time while their account is locked before attempting to log in again. These lockouts can be automated on most systems and provide a series of increasing hurdles for an attacker, while minimizing the inconvenience to legitimate users who have credential problems.

Password History

Password history is a reference to previously used passwords by an account. It is good security policy to prohibit the reusing of passwords at least for a set number of previous passwords. In Windows, under Local Group Policy, you can set three elements that work together to manage password history:

- **Enforce password history** Tells the system how many passwords to remember and does not allow a user to reuse an old password.
- **Maximum password age** Specifies the maximum number of days a password may be used before it must be changed.
- **Minimum password age** Specifies the minimum number of days a password must be used before it can be changed again.

The minimum password age is used to prevent a user from changing their password 20 times in a row to recycle back to the previous or current password. Figure 3.1 shows password settings under Local Security Policy in Windows.

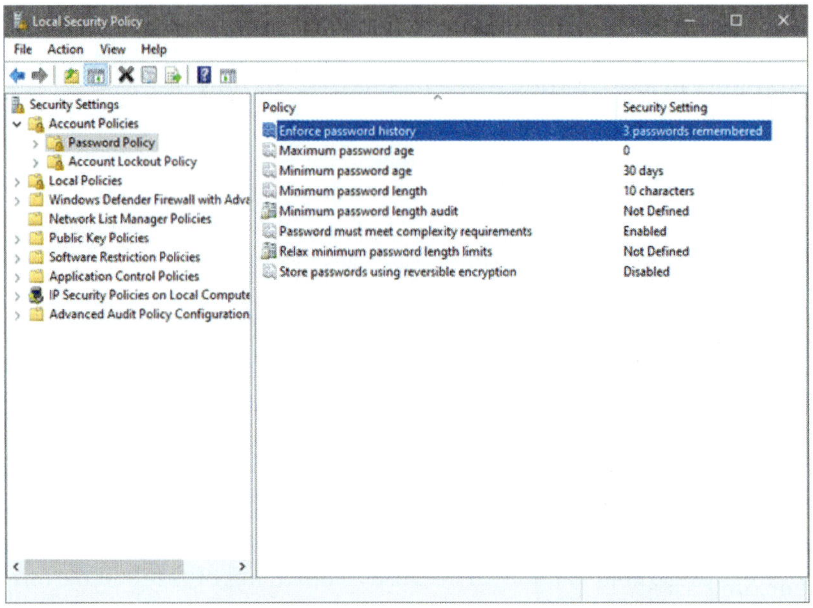

• **Figure 3.1** Password options under Local Security Policy settings in Windows

Password Reuse

Password reuse is a bad idea in that it reopens the organization to exposure from an adversary who has previously obtained a password. Passwords should not be reused for at least a year, and for at least a half dozen changes, whichever comes last. This is to minimize the opportunity for an adversary to take advantage of a reuse case.

Password Length

Password length is critical to password-based security. The true strength of a password lies in its entropy or randomness. The longer the entropy or randomness, the greater the keyspace that must be searched for random matching. Increasing password length and complexity is the easiest way to increase entropy in a password. Recent research has shown that passphrases, 20 characters or more, are easier to remember, are not typically written down, and can provide the required entropy to be effective. The only problem is not all systems take passphrases. That being said, the current standard is at least 10 characters with numbers, mixed-case, and special characters, and a length of 12 characters is preferred.

Protection of Passwords

The policy should stress not writing down passwords where others can find them, not saving passwords and not allowing automated logins, not sharing passwords with other users, and so on. Also, the consequences associated with violation of or noncompliance with the policy, or any part thereof, should be explained.

Human Resources Policies

It has been said that the weakest links in the security chain are humans. Consequently, it is important for organizations to have policies in place relative to their employees. Policies that relate to the hiring of individuals are primarily important. The organization needs to make sure it hires individuals who can be trusted with the organization's data and that of its clients. Once employees are hired, they should be kept from slipping into the category of "disgruntled employee." Finally, policies must be developed to address the inevitable point in the future when an employee leaves the organization—either on their own or with the "encouragement" of the organization itself. Security issues must be considered at each of these points.

> Many organizations overlook the security implications that decisions by HR may have. HR personnel and security personnel should have a close working relationship. Decisions on the hiring and firing of personnel have direct security implications for the organization. As a result, procedures should be in place that specify which actions must be taken when an employee is hired, is terminated, or retires.

Code of Ethics

Numerous professional organizations have established codes of ethics for their members. Each of these describes the expected behavior of their members from a high-level standpoint. Businesses can adopt this idea as well. A code of ethics can set the tone for how employees will be expected to act and conduct business. The code should demand honesty from employees and require that they perform all activities in a professional manner. The code could also address principles of privacy and confidentiality and state how employees should treat client and organizational data. Conflicts of interest can often cause problems, so this could also be covered in the code of ethics.

By outlining a code of ethics, the organization can encourage an environment that is conducive to integrity and high ethical standards. For additional ideas on possible codes of ethics, check professional organizations such as the Institute for Electrical and Electronics Engineers (IEEE), the Association for Computing Machinery (ACM), and the Information Systems Security Association (ISSA).

Job Rotation

An interesting approach to enhancing security that is gaining increased attention is **job rotation**. Organizations often discuss the benefits of rotating individuals through various jobs in an organization's IT department. By rotating through jobs, individuals gain a better perspective on how the various parts of IT can enhance (or hinder) the business. Since security is often a misunderstood aspect of IT, rotating individuals through security positions can result in a much wider understanding throughout the organization about potential security problems. It also can have the side benefit of a company not having to rely on any one individual too heavily for security expertise. If all security tasks are the domain of one employee, and that individual leaves suddenly, security at the organization could suffer. On the other hand, if security tasks are understood by many different individuals, the loss of any one individual has less of an impact on the organization.

> Rotating tasks between users reduces the risk that fraudulent activity can either go undetected or be sustained, and it improves security awareness across various roles in an organization.

Another aspect of the separation of duties principle is that it spreads responsibilities out over an organization so no single individual becomes the indispensable individual with all the "keys to the kingdom" or unique knowledge about how to make everything work. If enough tasks have been distributed, assigning a primary and a backup person for each task will ensure that the loss of any one individual will not have a disastrous impact on the organization.

Separation of Duties

Separation of duties is a principle employed in many organizations to ensure that no single individual has the ability to conduct transactions alone. This means that the level of trust in any one individual is lessened, and the ability for any individual to cause catastrophic damage to the organization is also lessened. An example might be an organization in which one person has the ability to order equipment, but another individual makes the payment. An individual who wants to make an unauthorized purchase for their own personal gain would have to convince another person to go along with the transaction.

Separating duties as a security tool is a good practice, but it is possible to go overboard and break up transactions into too many pieces or require too much oversight. This results in inefficiency and can actually be less secure, since individuals might not scrutinize transactions as thoroughly because they know others will also be reviewing them. The temptation is to hurry something along and assume that somebody else will examine it or has examined it.

Tech Tip

Hiring Hackers

Hiring a skilled hacker may make sense from a technical skills point of view, but an organization also has to consider the broader ethical and business consequences and associated risks. Is the hacker completely reformed or not? How much time is needed to determine this? The real question is not "would you hire a hacker?" but rather "can you fire a hacker once they have had access to your systems?" Trust is an important issue with employees who have system administrator access, and the long-term ramifications need to be considered.

Employee Hiring (Onboarding) and Promotions

It is becoming common for organizations to run background checks on prospective employees and to check the references prospective employees supply. Frequently, organizations require drug testing, check for any past criminal activity, verify claimed educational credentials, and confirm reported work history and even social media behavior. For highly sensitive environments, special security background investigations can also be required. Make sure that your organization hires the most capable and trustworthy employees, and that your policies are designed to ensure this.

After an individual has been hired, your organization needs to minimize the risk that the employee will ignore company rules and affect security. Periodic reviews by supervisory personnel, additional drug checks, and monitoring of activity during work may all be considered by the organization. If the organization chooses to implement any of these reviews, this must be specified in the organization's policies, and prospective employees should be made aware of these policies before being hired. What an organization can do in terms of monitoring and requiring drug tests, for example, can be severely restricted if not spelled out in advance as terms of employment. New hires should be made aware of all pertinent policies, especially those applying to security, and should be asked to sign documents indicating that they have read and understood them.

Tech Tip

Accounts of Former Employees

When conducting security assessments of organizations, security professionals frequently find active accounts for individuals who no longer work for the company. This is especially true for larger organizations, which may lack a clear offboarding process for the personnel office to communicate with the network administrators when an employee leaves the organization. These old accounts, however, are a weak point in the security perimeter for the organization and should be disabled or eliminated.

Occasionally an employee's status will change within the company. If the change can be construed as a negative personnel action (such as a demotion), supervisors should be alerted to watch for changes in behavior that might indicate the employee is contemplating or conducting unauthorized activity. It is likely that the employee will be upset, and whether they act on this to the detriment of the company is something that needs to be guarded against. In the case of a demotion, the individual may also lose certain privileges or access rights, and these changes should be made quickly so as to lessen the likelihood that the employee will destroy previously accessible data if they become disgruntled and decide to take revenge on the organization. On the other hand, if the employee is promoted, privileges may still change, but the need to make the change to access privileges might not be as urgent, though it should still be accomplished as quickly as possible. If the move is a lateral one, changes may also need to take place, and again they should be accomplished as quickly as possible.

A key element when **onboarding** personnel to any position, via hiring and promotions, is to ensure that the personnel are aware of and understand their responsibilities with respect to securing company information and the assets they will be using. Agreements with business partners tend to be fairly specific with respect to terms associated with mutual expectations associated with the process of the business. It should be the same with employees; ensuring the correct security elements are covered during onboarding is essential to setting proper employee expectations. These considerations need to be made prior to the establishment of the relationship, not added at the time that it is coming to an end.

Onboarding policy should include provisions for the handling of data, the disposal of data, acceptable use, and any sanctions that may occur as a result of misuse.

Retirement, Separation, or Termination (Offboarding)

Offboarding refers to the processes and procedures used when an employee leaves an organization. From a security perspective, the offboarding process for personnel is very important. Employee termination needs to be modified to include termination or disablement of all accounts, including those enabled on mobile devices. It's not uncommon to find terminated employees with accounts or even company devices still connecting to the corporate network months after being terminated.

Onboarding and offboarding procedures should be well documented to ensure compliance with legal requirements.

An employee leaving an organization can be either a positive or a negative action. Employees who are retiring by their own choice may announce their planned retirement weeks or even months in advance. Limiting their access to sensitive documents the moment they announce their intention may be the safest thing to do, but it might not be necessary or make business sense. Each situation should be evaluated individually. If the situation is a forced retirement, the organization must determine the risk to its data if the employee becomes disgruntled as a result of the action. In this situation, the wisest choice might be to cut off the employee's access quickly and provide them with some additional vacation time. This might seem like an expensive proposition, but the danger to the company of having a disgruntled employee may justify it. Again, each case should be evaluated individually.

It is better to give a potentially disgruntled employee several weeks of paid vacation than to have them trash sensitive files to which they have access. Because employees typically know the pattern of management behavior with respect to termination, doing the right thing will pay dividends in the future for a firm.

Organizations commonly neglect to have an offboarding policy that mandates the removal of an individual's computer access upon termination. Not only should such a policy exist, but it should also include the procedures to reclaim and "clean" a terminated employee's computer system and accounts.

When an employee decides to leave a company, generally as a result of a new job offer, continued access to sensitive information should be carefully considered. If the employee is leaving as a result of hard feelings toward the company, it might be wise to quickly revoke their access privileges.

If the employee is leaving the organization because they are being terminated, you should assume that they are or will become disgruntled. Although it might not seem the friendliest thing to do, you should immediately revoke their access privileges to sensitive information and facilities in this situation.

Combinations should also be quickly changed once an employee has been informed of their termination. Access cards, keys, and badges should be collected; the employee should be escorted to their desk and watched as they pack personal belongings, and then they should be escorted from the building. E-mail accounts should be disabled promptly as part of the employee termination policy and process. Mobile devices supplied by the company should be collected upon termination. Bring-your-own-device (BYOD) equipment should have its access to corporate resources terminated as part of the offboarding process. Regular audits for old or unterminated accounts should be performed to ensure prompt deletion or disablement of accounts for terminated employees.

Exit Interviews

Exit interviews can be powerful tools for gathering information when people leave a firm. From a security perspective, the offboarding process for personnel is very important. Employee termination needs to be modified to include termination of all accounts, including those enabled on mobile devices. It's not uncommon to find terminated employees with accounts or even company devices still connecting to the corporate network months after being terminated.

Onboarding/Offboarding Business Partners

Don't forget business partners! Onboarding and offboarding business partners should be well documented to ensure compliance with legal requirements.

Just as it is important to manage the on- and offboarding processes of company personnel, it is important to consider the same types of elements when making arrangements with third parties. Agreements with business partners tend to be fairly specific with respect to terms associated with mutual expectations associated with the process of the business. Considerations regarding the onboarding and offboarding processes are important, especially the offboarding. When a contract arrangement with a third party comes to an end, issues as to data retention and destruction by the third party need to be addressed. These considerations need to be made prior to the establishment of the relationship, not added when it is coming to an end.

Adverse Actions

Adverse actions with respect to punishing employees when their behaviors violate policies is always a difficult subject. There are two schools of thought in this area—the first being one of zero tolerance, where "one strike and you're out" is the norm. The defense of this view is that in setting the bar high, you get better performers. The downside is that when an otherwise excellent employee makes a mistake, there is no flexibility to save the employee's career or their future contributions to the firm. In an environment where highly skilled workers are not readily available, this lack of flexibility can lead to staffing and morale issues. The second school of thought is to handle adverse issues using the principle "violations will be punished via a range of HR actions, up to and including termination." The flexibility that this offers makes handling cases more challenging because management must determine the correct level of adverse action, but it also provides the flexibility to retain good workers who have made a mistake. Regardless of which path one takes, the key to being legal and ethical is consistency in practice.

> **Tech Tip**
>
> **Unintentional Consequences**
>
> *You should always consider the possible side effects of a policy. For example, I might want to invoke a policy that says only work-related websites are available to employees, with no personal web browsing. I have ways to enforce this at the proxy, so automation is solved. But now I find that the employees only work 9 to 5 and won't stay late. When employees feel less trusted and feel that the organization doesn't care about them, they are less likely to put in the extra effort when it counts the most. As a result, they end up less productive, with low morale. Simple policies can backfire, and the more regulated a worker feels, the more likely they will lose productivity.*

Mandatory Vacations

Organizations have provided vacation time to their employees for many years. Few, however, force employees to take this time if they don't want to. At some companies, employees are given the choice to either "use or lose" their vacation time; if they do not take all of their vacation time, they lose at least a portion of it. From a security standpoint, an employee who never takes time off might be involved in nefarious activity, such as fraud or embezzlement, and might be afraid that if they leave on vacation, the organization will discover their illicit activities. As a result, requiring employees to use their vacation time through a policy of mandatory vacations can be a security protection mechanism. Using **mandatory vacations** as a tool to detect fraud will require that somebody else also be trained in the functions of the employee who is on vacation. Having a second person familiar with security procedures is also a good policy in case something happens to the primary employee.

Acceptable Use Policy

An **acceptable use policy (AUP)** outlines what the organization considers to be the appropriate use of company resources, such as computer systems, e-mail, Internet access, and networks. Organizations should be concerned about personal use of organizational assets that does not benefit the company.

The goal of the AUP is to ensure employee productivity while limiting organizational liability through inappropriate use of the organization's assets. The AUP should clearly delineate what activities are not allowed. It should address issues such as the use of resources to conduct personal business, installation of hardware or software, remote access to systems and networks, the copying of company-owned software, and the responsibility of users to protect company assets, including data, software, and hardware. Statements regarding possible penalties for ignoring any of the policies (such as termination) should also be included.

Related to appropriate use of the organization's computer systems and networks by employees is the appropriate use by the organization. The most important of such issues is whether the organization considers it appropriate to monitor the employees' use of the systems and network. If monitoring is considered appropriate, the organization should include

In today's highly connected environment, every organization should have an AUP that spells out to all employees what the organization considers appropriate and inappropriate use of its computing and networks resources. Having this policy may be critical should the organization need to take disciplinary actions based on an abuse of its resources.

a statement to this effect in the banner that appears at login. This repeatedly warns employees, and possible intruders, that their actions are subject to monitoring and that any misuse of the system will not be tolerated. Should the organization need to use in a civil or criminal case any information gathered during monitoring, the issue of whether the employee had an expectation of privacy, or whether it was even legal for the organization to be monitoring, is simplified if the organization can point to a statement that is always displayed that instructs users that use of the system constitutes consent to monitoring. Before any monitoring is conducted, or the actual wording on the warning message is created, the organization's legal counsel should be consulted to determine the appropriate way to address this issue in the particular jurisdiction.

Internet Usage Policy

In today's highly connected environment, employee use of and access to the Internet is of particular concern. The goal of the *Internet usage policy* is to ensure maximum employee productivity and to limit potential liability to the organization from inappropriate use of the Internet in a workplace. The Internet provides a tremendous temptation for employees to waste hours as they surf the Web for the scores of games from the previous night, conduct quick online stock transactions, or read the review of the latest blockbuster movie everyone is talking about. In addition, allowing employees to visit sites that may be considered offensive to others (such as pornographic or hate sites) can open the company to accusations of condoning a hostile work environment and result in legal liability.

The Internet usage policy needs to address what sites employees are allowed to visit and what sites they are not allowed to visit. If the company allows them to surf the Web during non-work hours, the policy needs to clearly spell out the acceptable parameters, in terms of when they are allowed to do this and what sites they are still prohibited from visiting (such as potentially offensive sites). The policy should also describe under what circumstances an employee would be allowed to post something from the organization's network on the Web (on a blog, for example). A necessary addition to this policy would be the procedure for an employee to follow to obtain permission to post the object or message.

E-mail Usage Policy

Related to the Internet usage policy is the *e-mail usage policy,* which deals with what the company will allow employees to send in, or as attachments to, e-mail messages. This policy should spell out whether non-work e-mail traffic is allowed at all or is at least severely restricted. It needs to cover the type of message that would be considered inappropriate to send to other employees (for example, no offensive language, no sex-related or ethnic jokes, no harassment, and so on). The policy should also specify any disclaimers that must be attached to an employee's message sent to an individual outside the company. The policy should remind employees of the risks of clicking links in e-mails or opening attachments, as these can be social engineering attacks.

Social Media Analysis

The rise of *social media networks and applications* has changed many aspects of business. Whether used for marketing, communications, customer relations, or some other purpose, social media networks can be considered a form of third party. One of the challenges in working with social media networks and/or applications is their terms of use. While a relationship with a typical third party involves a negotiated set of agreements with respect to requirements, there is no negotiation with social media networks. The only option is to adopt their terms of service, so it is important to understand the implications of these terms with respect to the business use of the social network.

The use of social media sites by employees at work brings in additional risks, in the form of viruses, worms, and spear-phishing data collection. In years past, employers worried about employees using the machines at work to shop on eBay or surf the Web rather than work. Today, the risks are increased beyond just lost time to now include malware introduction to work machines and devices. It is common for firms to use AUPs to restrict employee personal use of things like social media, peer-to-peer (P2P) networking, BitTorrent, and other non-work-related applications.

Clean Desk Policy

Preventing access to information is also important in the work area. Firms with sensitive information should have a *clean desk policy* specifying that sensitive information must not be left unsecured in the work area when the worker is not present to act as custodian. Even leaving the desk area and going to the bathroom can leave information exposed and subject to compromise. The clean desk policy should identify and prohibit things that are not obvious upon first glance, such as passwords on sticky notes under keyboards or mouse pads or in unsecured desk drawers. All of these elements that demonstrate the need for a clean desk are lost if employees do not make them personal. Training for clean desk activities needs to make the issue a personal one, where consequences are understood and the workplace reinforces the positive activity.

Bring-Your-Own-Device (BYOD) Policy

Everyone seems to have a smartphone, a tablet, or other personal Internet device that they use in their personal lives. Bringing these to work is a natural extension of one's normal activities, but this raises the question of what policies are appropriate before a firm allows these devices to connect to the corporate network and access company data. Like with all other policies, planning is needed to define the appropriate pathway to the company objectives. Personal devices offer cost savings and positive user acceptance, and in many cases these factors make allowing BYOD a sensible decision.

The primary purpose of a BYOD policy is to lower the risk associated with connecting a wide array of personal devices to a company's network and accessing sensitive data on them. This places security, in the form of risk management, as a center element of a BYOD policy. Devices need to be maintained in a current, up-to-date software posture, and with certain security features, such as screen locks and passwords, enabled. Remote wipe should also be enabled, and highly sensitive data, especially in aggregate, should not be allowed on the devices. Users should have specific training as to what is allowed and what isn't and should be made aware of the increased responsibility associated with a mobile means of accessing corporate resources.

In some cases it may be necessary to define a policy associated with personally owned devices. This policy will describe the rules and regulations associated with use of personally owned devices with respect to corporate data, network connectivity, and security risks. Policies toward mobile device usage are important, as more data usage is happening on these devices. Mobile device deployment models are covered in Chapter 12.

Privacy Policy

Customers place an enormous amount of trust in organizations to which they provide personal information. These customers expect their information to be kept secure so that unauthorized individuals will not gain access to it and so that authorized users will not use the information in unintended ways. Organizations should have a *privacy policy* that explains what their guiding principles will be in guarding personal data to which they are given access.

A special category of private information that is becoming increasingly important today is *personally identifiable information (PII)*. This category of information includes any data that can be used to uniquely identify an individual. This would include an individual's name, address, driver's license number, and other details. An organization that collects PII on its employees and customers must make sure that it takes all necessary measures to protect the data from compromise.

With the intersection of personnel functions (HR) and medical information, enterprises can end up with personal health information (PHI) as well. This information requires safeguards because disclosure can result in legal actions against the enterprise. PHI and PII are covered in Chapter 25.

> **Cross Check**
>
> **Privacy**
>
> Privacy is an important consideration in today's computing environment. As such, it has been given its own chapter, Chapter 25. Additional details on privacy issues can be found there.

Due Care and Due Diligence

Due care and *due diligence* are terms used in the legal and business community to define reasonable behavior. Basically, the law recognizes the responsibility of an individual or organization to act reasonably relative to another party. If party A alleges that the actions of party B have caused it loss or injury, party A must prove that party B failed to exercise due care or due diligence and that this failure resulted in the loss or injury. These terms often are used synonymously, but **due care** generally refers to the standard of care a reasonable person is expected to exercise in all situations, whereas

due diligence generally refers to the standard of care a business is expected to exercise in preparation for a business transaction. An organization must take reasonable precautions before entering a business transaction or it might be found to have acted irresponsibly. In terms of security, organizations are expected to take reasonable precautions to protect the information that they maintain on individuals. Should a person suffer a loss as a result of negligence on the part of an organization in terms of its security, that person typically can bring a legal suit against the organization.

The standard applied—reasonableness—is extremely subjective and often is determined by a jury. The organization will need to show that it had taken reasonable precautions to protect the information, and that, despite these precautions, an unforeseen security event occurred that caused the injury to the other party. Since this is so subjective, it is hard to describe what would be considered reasonable, but many sectors have a set of "security best practices" for their industry that provides a basis from which organizations in that sector can start. If the organization decides not to follow any of the best practices accepted by the industry, it needs to be prepared to justify its reasons in court should an incident occur. If the sector the organization is in has regulatory requirements, justifying why the mandated security practices were not followed will be much more difficult (if not impossible).

Due Process

Due process is concerned with guaranteeing fundamental fairness, justice, and liberty in relation to an individual's legal rights. In the United States, due process is concerned with the guarantee of an individual's rights as outlined by the Constitution and Bill of Rights. Procedural due process is based on the concept of what is "fair." Also of interest is the recognition by courts of a series of rights that are not explicitly specified by the Constitution but that the courts have decided are implicit in the concepts embodied by the Constitution. An example of this is an individual's right to privacy. From an organization's point of view, due process may come into play during an administrative action that adversely affects an employee. Before an employee is terminated, for example, were all of the employee's rights protected? An actual example pertains to the rights of privacy regarding employees' e-mail messages. As the number of cases involving employers examining employee e-mails grows, case law continues to be established and the courts eventually will settle on what rights an employee can expect. The best thing an employer can do if faced with this sort of situation is to work closely with HR staff to ensure that appropriate policies are followed and that those policies are in keeping with current laws and regulations.

Incident Response Policies and Procedures

No matter how careful an organization is, eventually a security incident of some sort will occur. When it happens, how effectively the organization responds to it will depend greatly on how prepared it is to handle incidents. An **incident response policy** and associated procedures should be developed to outline how the organization will prepare for security incidents and respond to them when they occur. Waiting until an incident happens is not the right time to establish your policies—they need to be designed

Tech Tip

Prudent Person Principle

The concepts of due care and due diligence are connected. Due care addresses whether the organization has a minimal set of policies that provides reasonable assurance of success in maintaining security. Due diligence requires that management actually do something to ensure security, such as implement procedures for testing and review of audit records, internal security controls, and personnel behavior. The standard applied is one of a "prudent person"; for example, would a prudent person find the actions appropriate and sincere? To apply this standard, all one has to do is ask the following question for the issue under consideration: "What would a prudent person do to protect and ensure that the security features and procedures are working or adequate?" Failure of a security feature or procedure doesn't necessarily mean the person acted imprudently.

Due diligence is the application of a specific standard of care. *Due care* is the degree of care that an ordinary person would exercise.

Understanding the differences between due care, due diligence, and due process is important. Due care is having the right policies and procedures, due diligence is checking to see if they are working, and due process is the assurance that all cases go through the appropriate processes.

in advance. The incident response policy should cover five phases: preparation, detection, containment and eradication, recovery, and follow-up actions.

> **Cross Check**
>
> **Incident Response**
>
> Incident response is covered in detail in Chapter 22. This section serves only as an introduction to policy elements associated with the topic. For complete details on incident response, refer to Chapter 22.

Security Awareness and Training

Security awareness and training programs can enhance an organization's security posture in two direct ways. First, they teach personnel how to follow the correct set of actions to perform their duties in a secure manner. Second, they make personnel aware of the indicators and effects of social engineering attacks.

Many tasks that employees perform can have information security ramifications. Properly trained employees are able to perform their duties in a more effective manner, including their duties associated with information security. The extent of information security training will vary depending on the organization's environment and the level of threat, but initial employee security training at the time of being hired is important, as is periodic refresher training. A strong security education and awareness training program can go a long way toward reducing the chance that a social engineering attack will be successful. Security awareness programs and campaigns, which might include seminars, videos, posters, newsletters, and similar materials, are also fairly easy to implement and are not very costly.

Diversity of Training Techniques

Not all people learn in the same fashion: some learn by seeing, some learn better by hearing. Almost everyone learns better by doing, but in some areas, doing a task is not practical or feasible. The bottom line is that there is a wide range of methods of training, and for the best results it is important to match the training methods to the material. Several different training methods, including gamification, capture-the-flag exercises, and simulations, can be effectively used to improve training. There are even more methods to round out a wide diversity of training solutions, including in-person lectures, online content, and practice-based skill development. The key is to match the material to the method and to the learners, and then test outcomes to ensure successful training has been achieved.

Security Policy Training and Procedures

Personnel cannot be expected to perform complex tasks without training with respect to the tasks and expectations. This applies both to the security policy and to operational security details. If employees are going to be expected to comply with the organization's security policy, they must be properly trained in its purpose, meaning, and objectives. Training with respect to the information security policy, individual responsibilities, and expectations is something that requires periodic reinforcement through refresher training.

Because the security policy is a high-level directive that sets the overall support and executive direction with respect to security, it is important that the meaning of this message be translated and supported. Second-level policies such as password, access, information handling, and acceptable use policies also need to be covered. The collection of policies should paint a picture describing the desired security culture of the organization. The training should be designed to ensure that people see and understand the whole picture, not just the elements.

User Training

User training is important to ensure that users are aware of and are following appropriate policies and procedures as part of their workplace activities. As in all personnel-related training, two elements need attention. First, retraining over time is necessary to ensure that personnel keep proper levels of knowledge. Second, as people change jobs, a reassessment of the required training basis is needed, and additional training may be required. Maintaining accurate training records of personnel is the only way this can be managed in any significant enterprise.

Gamification

Gamification is the use of games to facilitate user training. This methodology has several interesting advantages. First, it makes rote learning of training material less boring. Second, it enables a more comprehensive situation-based approach to training, with consequences of bad decisions being shared with those taking the training. Third, it allows for group training by using people's job functions in a manner that facilitates both learning and auditing of the policies and procedures in a nonthreatening environment.

Capture the Flag

A **capture-the-flag** event is hands-on computer skill training where users are tested to see if they can perform specific actions. Should they perform the actions correctly, they will uncover a flag that shows they have completed the test successfully. Many hacking competitions are variations of capture-the-flag events.

Phishing Campaigns

Phishing campaigns are a series of connected phishing attacks against an organization. Since phishing is an operational method of social engineering, the greater the level of institutional, organizational, and personal knowledge one possesses about their target, the greater the chance of success. Phishing campaigns use this common knowledge to increase their odds, rather than just randomly attacking targets. This is why internal communications concerning phishing attempts are important: to alert other users that the system may be under attack and that a heightened sense of awareness toward this form of attack is warranted.

Phishing Simulations

To help users learn and identify phishing attacks, there are methods of running **phishing simulations** against users. A phishing attempt is sent to a user, and should they fall prey to it, the system notifies the user that this was only a drill and that they should be more cautious. This also creates a teachable moment where the user can receive training detailing exactly why they should have spotted the phishing attempt.

Be sure you are familiar with the various user training methods and how they play a role in organizational security. Employ the best method based on circumstances.

Computer-Based Training (CBT)

Computer-based training (CBT) is the use of a computer program to manage training of users. Self-paced modules can facilitate skill development across a wide range of skills, and the flexibility of CBT is very attractive. Not all people learn well under these circumstances, but for those who do, this is a very affordable, scalable training methodology.

Role-Based Training

For training to be effective, it needs to be targeted to the user with regard to their role in the subject of the training. While all employees may need general security awareness training, they also need specific training in areas where they have individual responsibilities. *Role-based training* with regard to information security responsibilities is an important part of information security training.

If a person has job responsibilities that may impact information security, then role-specific training is needed to ensure that the individual understands the responsibilities as they relate to information security. Some roles, such as developer and system administrator, have clearly defined information security responsibilities. The roles of others, such as project manager and purchasing manager, have information security impacts that are less obvious, but these roles require training as well. In fact, the less-obvious but wider-impact roles of middle management can have a large effect on the information security culture, and thus if a specific outcome is desired, training is required.

As in all personnel-related training, two elements need attention. First, retraining over time is necessary to ensure that personnel keep proper levels of knowledge. Second, as people change jobs, a reassessment of the required training basis is needed, and additional training may be required. Maintaining accurate training records of personnel is the only way this can be managed in any significant enterprise.

Data Owner

People who have data responsibilities—whether as a data owner, controller, processor, steward/custodian, or even security specialist—all need specific training in how to respond to these responsibilities. Having training that is targeted to and within the context of a person's responsibilities is easier to assimilate and has better outcomes.

System Administrator

System administrators are administrative users with the responsibility of maintaining a system within its defined requirements. The system owner will define the requirements, such as frequency of backups, whereas the system administrator configures the system to operationally meet these requirements. System administrators have virtually unlimited power over the system—they can control all functions—but what they should not have power over or the responsibility for is the setting of policies for the system. That falls to the system owner.

System Owner

Every system requires a system owner. System ownership is a business function, where the requirements for security, privacy, retention, and other business functions are established. Not all systems require the same policies, but the determination of what the policies for a given system are is the responsibility of the system owner.

User

Normal users need limited access based on their job role and tasks assigned. This is where the principle of least privilege comes into play. Limiting an object's privileges limits the amount of harm that can be caused, thus limiting an organization's exposure to damage. Users may have access to the files on their workstations and a select set of files on a file server, but they have no access to critical data that is held within the database. This rule helps an organization protect its most sensitive resources and helps ensure that whoever is interacting with these resources has a valid reason to do so.

Privileged User

A privileged user has more authority than a standard user. Short of full administrative or root access, a privileged user has permissions to do a wider range of tasks, as their job role may require greater responsibilities. An example would be a database administrator—they would need the equivalent of root access to database functions, but not to all servers or other OS options. Aligning privileges to user responsibilities is good standard policy.

Executive User

Executive users are a special type of user. Their business responsibility may be broad and deep, covering many levels and types of business functions. This work level of responsibilities might not translate directly to their needed computer access. Does the CIO, the highest IT level employee, require all of the permissions of all their subordinates? The true answer is no, because they will not be performing the same level of tasks in their work. And should they on occasion need the access, it can be granted at the time of need.

Limiting the access of executives is not meant to limit their work, but rather limit the range of damage should an account become compromised. Executive users are natural targets for spear phishing attacks, and limiting their system privileges to what is truly needed for them to perform their system-level tasks thus limits the damage a hacker could cause by compromising an executive account.

Continuing Education

Technology and security practices are far from static environments; they advance every year, and relevant skills can become outdated in as little as a couple of years. Maintaining a skilled workforce in security necessitates ongoing training and education. A continuing education program can assist greatly in helping employees keep their skills up to date.

Compliance with Laws, Best Practices, and Standards

A wide array of laws, regulations, contractual requirements, standards, and best practices is associated with information security. Each places its own set of requirements on an organization and its personnel. The only effective way for an organization to address these requirements is to build them into their own policies and procedures. Training to one's own policies and procedures would then translate into coverage of these external requirements.

It is important to note that many of these external requirements impart a specific training and awareness component on the organization. Organizations subject to the requirements of the Payment Card Industry Data Security Standard (PCI DSS), Gramm-Leach-Bliley Act (GLBA), or Health Insurance Portability Accountability Act (HIPAA) are among the many that must maintain a specific information security training program. Other organizations should do so as a matter of best practice.

User Habits

Individual user responsibilities vary between organizations and the type of business each organization is involved in, but there are certain very basic responsibilities that all users should be instructed to adopt:

- Lock the door to your office or workspace, including drawers and cabinets.
- Do not leave sensitive information inside your car unprotected.
- Keep storage media containing sensitive information in a secure storage device (such as a locked cabinet or drawer).
- Shred paper containing organizational information before discarding it.
- Do not divulge sensitive information to individuals (including other employees) who do not have an authorized need to know it.
- Do not discuss sensitive information with family members. (The most common violation of this rule occurs in regard to HR information, as employees, especially supervisors, may complain to their spouse or friends about other employees or about problems occurring at work.)

- Protect laptops and other mobile devices that contain sensitive or important organization information wherever the device may be stored or left. (It's a good idea to ensure that sensitive information is encrypted on the laptop or mobile device so that, should the equipment be lost or stolen, the information remains safe.)
- Be aware of who is around you when discussing sensitive corporate information. Does everybody within earshot have the need to hear this information?
- Enforce corporate access control procedures. Be alert to, and do not allow, piggybacking, shoulder surfing, or access without the proper credentials.
- Be aware of the correct procedures to report suspected or actual violations of security policies.
- Follow procedures established to enforce good password security practices. Passwords are such a critical element that they are frequently the ultimate target of a social engineering attack. Though such password procedures may seem too oppressive or strict, they are often the best line of defense.
- **User habits** are a frontline security tool in engaging the workforce to improve the overall security posture of an organization.

Tech Tip

Reference Frameworks

Industry-standard frameworks and reference architectures are conceptual blueprints that define the structure and operation of the IT systems in the enterprise. Industries under governmental regulation frequently have an approved set of architectures defined by regulatory bodies. Some reference architectures that are neither industry-specific nor regulatory, but rather are technology focused and considered nonregulatory, are the National Institute of Standards and Technology (NIST) Cloud Computing Security Reference Architecture (Special Publication 500-299) and the NIST Framework for Improving Critical Infrastructure Cybersecurity (commonly known as the Cybersecurity Framework, or CSF). It is incumbent on you to understand the appropriate frameworks that apply in the circumstances where you are working.

Training Metrics and Compliance

Training and awareness programs can yield much in the way of an educated and knowledgeable workforce. Many laws, regulations, and best practices have requirements for maintaining a trained workforce. Having a record-keeping system to measure compliance with attendance and to measure the effectiveness of the training is a normal requirement. Simply conducting training is not sufficient. Following up and gathering training metrics to validate compliance and the security posture is an important aspect of security training management.

A number of factors deserve attention when you're managing security training. Because of the diverse nature of role-based requirements, maintaining an active, up-to-date listing of individual training and retraining requirements is one challenge. Monitoring the effectiveness of the training is yet another challenge. Creating an effective training and awareness program when measured by actual impact on employee behavior is a challenging endeavor. Training needs to be current, relevant, and interesting enough to engage employee attention. Simple repetition of the same training material has not proven to be effective, so regularly updating the program is a requirement if it is to remain effective over time.

Tech Tip

Security Training Records

Requirements for both periodic training and retraining drive the need for good training records. Maintaining proper information in security training records is a requirement of several laws and regulations and should be considered a best practice.

Standard Operating Procedures

Procedures are the step-by-step instructions on how to implement policies in the organization. They describe exactly how employees are expected to act in a given situation or to accomplish a specific task. Standards are mandatory elements regarding the implementation of a policy. They are accepted specifications that provide specific details on how a policy is to be enforced. Some standards are externally driven. Regulations for banking and financial institutions, for example, require certain security measures be taken by law. Other standards may be set by the organization to meet its own security goals. **Standard operating procedures** are just that: mandatory step-by-step instructions set by the organization so that in the performance of their duties, employees will meet the stated security objectives of the firm.

Third-Party Risk Management

Every business will have third parties associated with their business operations. Whether these third parties are vendors, suppliers, or business partners, they bring the opportunity for both risk and reward. *Third-party risk management* is a fairly straightforward process. The first step is to recognize that risks are present. You need to inventory and assess these risks and then develop the mitigations necessary to keep them in an acceptable range. The important concept is that risk does not magically vanish because a third party is involved; it still needs to be managed like all other business risks.

Vendors

Vendors are firms or individuals that supply materials or services to a business. These items are purchased as part of a business process and represent some form of a value proposition for the firm purchasing them. But with the value can also come risk. For instance, if an item has embedded code to make it operate, what if the embedded code has vulnerabilities? What if an item that is purchased for a specific purpose fails to meet its specifications? A wide range of risks can be introduced by vendors, and these need to be examined and handled in accordance with standard risk management processes.

Supply Chain

A **supply chain** is a set of firms that operate together to manage the movement of goods and services between firms. If you order a part from a foreign supplier that will become part of your product being manufactured in another country, how do all the parts get to the right place for assembly, at the right time? Supply chains handle the details that make all of this happen. From transportation, to customs and other regulations, to managing schedules, these are all details that are necessary for items to go from one place to another. If a firm only has a single supplier, then this process is fairly simple. However, having multiple suppliers of multiple parts at different stages of your value chain that must work together is where supply chains matter. The pandemic of 2020 illustrated this clearly, as countries closed borders, firms had difficulty operating, factories closed due to sick workers and stay-at-home orders—and none of this was uniform or occurred during the same time period. Global supply chain disruptions caused follow-on effects, where expected parts were delayed because unrelated parts elsewhere were delayed, thus interrupting different supply chains. The need to understand and manage the risks of supply chain functions and their true costs became very evident. It became clear that with extensive supply chain management, lower costs could be achieved, but at the risk of failure when the supply chain had issues.

Business Partners

Business partners are entities that share a relationship with a firm in their business pursuits. Business partners can be enrolled in a business effort for multiple reasons: to share risk, share liability, share costs, leverage specialty expertise, and more. The key to understanding and navigating business partners with respect to cybersecurity and risk is to ensure that the risks and responsibilities on both partners are understood and agreed to before the risk event occurs. With every partnership comes risk and reward; the key is in understanding the level of each and making business decisions with a clear understanding of these elements.

Interoperability Agreements

Many business operations involve actions between many different parties—some within an organization, and some in different organizations. These actions require communication between the parties, defining the responsibilities and expectations of the parties, the business objectives, and the environment within which the objectives will be pursued. To ensure an agreement is understood between the parties, written agreements are used. Numerous forms of legal agreements and contracts are used in business, but with respect to security, some of the most common ones are the service level agreement, business partnership agreement, memorandum of understanding, and interconnection security agreement.

Service Level Agreement (SLA)

A **service level agreement (SLA)** is a negotiated agreement between parties detailing the expectations of the customer and the service provider. SLAs essentially set the requisite level of performance of a given contractual service. SLAs are typically included as part of a service contract and set the level of technical expectations. An SLA can define specific services, the performance level associated with a service, issue management and resolution, and so on. SLAs are negotiated between customer and supplier and represent the agreed-upon terms. Specific security requirements can be specified in an SLA and enforced once both parties agree. Once entered into, the SLA becomes a legally binding document.

Memorandum of Understanding (MOU)

A **memorandum of understanding (MOU)** and memorandum of agreement (MOA) are legal documents used to describe a bilateral agreement between parties. They are written agreements that express a set of intended actions between the parties with respect to some common pursuit or goal. Typically, an MOU has higher-level descriptions, whereas an MOA is more specific; however, the boundary between these two legal terms is blurry and they are often used interchangeably. Both are more formal and detailed than a simple handshake, but they generally lack the binding powers of a contract. MOUs/MOAs are also commonly used between different units within an organization to detail expectations associated with the common business interest, including security requirements.

Measurement Systems Analysis (MSA)

Many security risk management processes rely on measuring things or events. Measurements and measurement systems have to be calibrated to ensure they are evaluating the actual object of interest. **Measurement systems analysis (MSA)** is a field of study that examines measurement systems for accuracy and precision. Before an enterprise relies on measurement systems, it is important to understand whether the chosen measurement system is acceptable for its intended use, to understand the different sources of variation present in it and to identify and understand sources of bias, errors, and factors associated with repeatability and reproducibility. Performing a measurement systems analysis on the measurement systems employed in a security system is the structured process to get to that information and have confidence in the measures developed and used from the system.

Business Partnership Agreement (BPA)

A **business partnership agreement (BPA)** is a legal agreement between partners that establishes the terms, conditions, and expectations of the relationship between the partners. These details can cover a wide range of issues, including typical items such as the sharing of profits and losses, the responsibilities of each partner, the addition or removal of partners, and any other issues. The Uniform Partnership Act (UPA), established by state law and convention, lays out a uniform set of rules associated with partnerships to resolve any partnership terms. The terms in a UPA are designed as "one size fits all" and are not typically in the best interest of any specific partnership. To avoid undesired outcomes that may result from UPA terms, it is best for partnerships to spell out specifics in a BPA.

Be sure you understand the differences between the interoperability agreements SLA, BPA, MOU, and ISA. The differences hinge upon the purpose for each document.

Interconnection Security Agreement (ISA)

An **interconnection security agreement (ISA)** is a specialized agreement between organizations that have interconnected IT systems, the purpose of which is to document the security requirements associated with the interconnection. An ISA can be a part of an MOU detailing the specific technical security aspects of a data interconnection.

NDA

Nondisclosure agreements (NDAs) are standard corporate documents used to explain the boundaries of company secret material—information that control over should be exercised to prevent disclosure to unauthorized parties. NDAs are frequently used to delineate the level and type of information, and with whom it can be shared.

End of Service Life (EOSL)

End of service life (EOSL) is the term used to denote that something has reached the end of its "useful life." When EOSL occurs, the provider of the item or service will typically no longer sell or update it. Sometimes the end of updates will be a specified date in the future. EOSL typically occurs because newer models have been released, replacing the older model. During the EOSL phase, some manufacturers may still offer maintenance options, but usually at a premium price. Old versions of software have had this issue, where critical systems cannot easily be upgraded and instead have contracts with the original vendor to maintain the system past its normal EOSL.

> Do not be confused! End of life (EOL) is the term used to denote that something has reached the end of its "useful life." End of service life (EOSL) or end of support is when service and maintenance for the solution are no longer provided. In most cases, the manufacturer no longer provides maintenance services or security updates.

End of Life (EOL)

End of life (EOL) or end of support is when the manufacturer quits selling an item. In most cases, while security patches may still be offered, the vendor does not provide for new features or continued compatibility. In some cases, this is announced to be a future date, after which support ends. When something enters the EOL phase, it is at the end of its lifecycle and upgrade/replacement needs to be planned and executed.

Chapter 3 Review

Chapter Summary

After reading this chapter and completing the exercises, you should understand the following regarding operational and organizational security.

Identify various operational aspects to security in your organization

- Prevention technologies are designed to keep individuals from being able to gain access to systems or data they are not authorized to use.
- Previously in operational environments, prevention was extremely difficult and relying on prevention technologies alone was not sufficient. This led to the rise of technologies to detect and respond to events that occur when prevention fails.
- An important part of any organization's approach to implementing security is to establish policies, procedures, standards, and guidelines to detail what users and administrators should be doing to maintain the security of the systems and network.

Identify various policies and procedures in your organization

- Policies, procedures, standards, and guidelines are important in establishing a security program within an organization.
- The security policy and supporting policies play an important role in establishing and managing system risk.
- Policies and procedures associated with human resources (HR) functionality include job rotation, mandatory vacations, and hiring (onboarding) and termination (offboarding) policies.

Identify the security awareness and training needs of an organization

- Security training and awareness efforts are vital in engaging the workforce to act within the desired range of conduct with respect to security.
- Security awareness and training are both important in achieving compliance objectives.
- Security awareness and training should be measured and managed as part of a comprehensive security program.

Understand the different types of agreements employed in negotiating security requirements

- The different interoperability agreements, including SLA, MOU, MSA, BPA, and ISA, are used to establish security expectations between various parties.
- NDA agreements assist in sharing of sensitive information with supply chain, business partners, and other parties that need to use the information.

Key Terms

acceptable use policy (AUP) *(67)*
account disablement *(61)*
account lockout *(61)*
business partnership agreement (BPA) *(80)*
capture the flag *(73)*
change control *(54)*
change management *(54)*
due care *(70)*
due diligence *(71)*
end of life *(81)*
end of service life *(81)*
gamification *(73)*
guidelines *(53)*
incident response policy *(71)*
interconnection security agreement (ISA) *(80)*
job rotation *(63)*
mandatory vacations *(67)*
measurement systems analysis (MSA) *(80)*
memorandum of understanding (MOU) *(79)*
nondisclosure agreements (NDAs) *(80)*
offboarding *(65)*

onboarding *(65)*
phishing simulations *(74)*
policies *(53)*
procedures *(53)*
security policy *(55)*
service level agreement (SLA) *(79)*
standard operating procedures *(78)*
standards *(53)*
supply chain *(78)*
user training *(73)*
user habits *(77)*

Key Terms Quiz

Use terms from the Key Terms list to complete the sentences that follow. Don't use the same term more than once. Not all terms will be used.

1. _______________ are high-level statements made by management that lay out the organization's position on some issue.
2. A(n) _______________ describes the requisite level of performance of a given contractual service.
3. Mandatory step-by-step instructions set by the organization so that in the performance of their duties employees will meet the stated security objectives of the firm are called _______________.
4. _______________ are a foundational security tool in engaging the workforce to improve the overall security posture of an organization.
5. _______________ are accepted specifications providing specific details on how a policy is to be enforced.
6. _______________ generally refers to the standard of care a reasonable person is expected to exercise in all situations.
7. A(n) _______________ is a legal document used to describe a bilateral agreement between parties.
8. _______________ is used whenever an employee leaves a firm. All associated accounts should be disabled to prevent further access.
9. _______________ generally refers to the standard of care a business is expected to exercise in preparation for a business transaction.
10. A(n) _______________ is a legal agreement between organizations establishing the terms, conditions, and expectations of the relationship between them.

Multiple-Choice Quiz

1. Which of the following is a description of a business partnership agreement (BPA)?
   - **A.** A negotiated agreement between parties detailing the expectations of the customer and the service provider
   - **B.** A legal agreement between entities establishing the terms, conditions, and expectations of the relationship between the entities
   - **C.** A specialized agreement between organizations that have interconnected IT systems, the purpose of which is to document the security requirements associated with the interconnection
   - **D.** A written agreement expressing a set of intended actions between the parties with respect to some common pursuit or goal

2. What is the name given to mandatory elements regarding the implementation of a policy?
   A. Standards
   B. Guidelines
   C. Regulations
   D. Procedures
3. Which of the following is a contractual agreement between entities that describes specified levels of service that the servicing entity agrees to guarantee for the customer?
   A. Service level agreement
   B. Support level agreement
   C. Memorandum of understanding
   D. Business service agreement
4. During which step of the policy lifecycle does the training of users take place?
   A. Plan for security.
   B. Implement the plans.
   C. Monitor the implementation.
   D. Evaluate for effectiveness.
5. While all employees may need general security awareness training, they also need specific training in areas where they have individual responsibilities. This type of training is referred to as which of the following?
   A. Functional training
   B. User training
   C. Role-based training
   D. Advanced user training
6. Procedures can be described as which of the following?
   A. High-level, broad statements of what the organization wants to accomplish
   B. Step-by-step instructions on how to implement the policies
   C. Mandatory elements regarding the implementation of a policy
   D. Recommendations relating to a policy
7. Which of the following statements are true in regard to a clean desk policy for security? (Select all that apply.)
   A. Although a clean desk policy makes for a pleasant work environment, it actually has very little impact on security.
   B. Sensitive information must not be left unsecured in the work area when the worker is not present to act as custodian.
   C. Even leaving the desk area and going to the bathroom can leave information exposed and subject to compromise.
   D. A clean desk policy should identify and prohibit things that are not obvious upon first glance, such as passwords on sticky notes under keyboards or mouse pads.
8. Key user habits that can improve security efforts include which of the following?
   A. Do not discuss business issues outside of the office.
   B. Never leave laptops or tablets inside your car unattended.
   C. Be alert of people violating physical access rules (piggybacking through doors).
   D. Items B and C.
9. Which of the following is the name typically given to administrative users with the responsibility of maintaining a system within its defined requirements?
   A. System owner
   B. System administrator
   C. Privileged user
   D. Executive user
10. What is the name given to a policy that outlines what an organization considers to be the appropriate use of its resources, such as computer systems, e-mail, Internet, and networks?
   A. Resource usage policy (RUP)
   B. Acceptable use of resources policy (AURP)
   C. Organizational use policy (OUP)
   D. Acceptable use policy (AUP)

Essay Quiz

1. Describe the difference between a BPA and an MOU.
2. Discuss the elements of a good operating procedure.
3. Compare and contrast five HR-related policies with respect to cybersecurity.

Lab Project

• Lab Project 3.1

Describe the four steps of the policy lifecycle. Obtain a policy from your organization (such as an acceptable use policy or Internet usage policy). How are users informed of this policy? How often is it reviewed? How would changes to it be suggested, and who would make decisions on whether the changes were accepted?

chapter 4

The Role of People in Security

We can prescribe actions, but not attitudes, and attitude is the secret sauce of security.

—W. A. Conklin

In this chapter, you will learn how to

- Define basic terminology associated with social engineering
- Describe steps organizations can take to improve their security
- Describe common user actions that may put an organization's information at risk
- Recognize methods attackers may use to gain information about an organization
- Determine ways in which users can aid instead of detract from security
- Recognize the roles training and awareness play in assisting the people side of security

The operational model of computer security discussed in the previous chapter acknowledges that absolute protection of computer systems and networks is not possible and that we need to be prepared to detect and respond to attacks that are able to circumvent our security mechanisms. Another very basic fact that should be recognized is that technology alone will not solve the security problem. No matter how advanced the technology is, it will ultimately be deployed in an environment where humans exist. It is the human element that poses the biggest security challenge. It is hard to compensate for all the possible ways humans can deliberately or accidentally cause security problems or circumvent our security mechanisms. Despite all the technology, despite all the security procedures we have in place, and despite all the security training we may provide, somebody will invariably fail to do what they are supposed to do, or do something they are *not* supposed to do, and create a vulnerability in the organization's security posture. This chapter discusses the human element and the role that people play in security—both the user practices that can aid in securing an organization and the vulnerabilities or holes in security that users can introduce.

People—A Security Problem

The operational model of computer security acknowledges that prevention technologies are not sufficient to protect our computer systems and networks. There are a number of explanations for why this is true; most of them are technical, but one of the biggest reasons that prevention technologies are not sufficient is that every network and computer system has at least one human user, and humans are prone to make mistakes and are often easily misled or fooled.

> **Tech Tip**
>
> **Social Engineering Works!**
>
> *Skilled social engineers set up scenarios where the victim is boxed in by various social/work issues and then makes an exception that enables the social engineer to gain some form of access. The attacker can pretend to be an important party and intimidate a lower-level employee, or he can create a sense of emergency, scarcity, or urgency that moves the victim to act in a manner to reduce the conflict. The attacker can become a "victim," creating a sense of fellowship with the target, creating a false sense of familiarity, and then using that to drive an action. Social engineers can sell ice to Eskimos and make them proud of their purchase, so they are masters at psychological manipulation.*

Social Engineering

Social engineering is the process of an unauthorized individual convincing an authorized individual to provide them with confidential information or access to something that they shouldn't have. It is a technique in which the attacker uses various deceptive practices to convince the targeted person to divulge information they normally would not divulge or to convince the target of the attack to do something they normally wouldn't do. Social engineering is very successful for several reasons. The first is the basic desire of most people to be helpful. When somebody asks a question for which we know the answer, our normal response is not to be suspicious but rather to answer the question. The problem with this is that seemingly innocuous information can be used either directly in an attack or indirectly to build a bigger picture that an attacker can use to create an aura of authenticity during an attack—the more information an individual has about an organization, the easier it will be to convince others that this person is part of the organization and has a right to even sensitive information. An attacker who is attempting to exploit the natural tendency of people to be helpful may take one of several approaches:

- The attacker might simply ask a question, hoping to immediately obtain the desired information. For basic information that is not considered sensitive, this approach generally works. As an example, an attacker might call and ask who the IT manager is.
- The attacker might first attempt to engage the target in conversation and try to evoke sympathy so that the target feels sorry for the individual and is more prone to provide the information. For information that is even slightly sensitive in nature, the request of which could possibly arouse suspicion, this technique may be tried. As an example, an attacker might call and claim to be under some deadline from a supervisor who is upset for some reason. The target, feeling sorry for an alleged fellow worker, might give up the information, thinking they are helping them avoid trouble with the supervisor.
- The attacker might appeal to an individual's ego. As an example, an attacker might call the IT department, claiming to have some sort of problem, and praising them for work they supposedly did to help another worker. After being told how great they are and how much they helped somebody else, the IT department might be tempted to demonstrate that they can supply the same level of help to another individual. This technique may be used to obtain sensitive information, such as having the target's password reset.

The second reason that social engineering is successful is that individuals normally seek to avoid confrontation and trouble. If the attacker attempts to intimidate the target, threatening to call the target's supervisor because of a lack of help, the target may give in and provide the information to avoid confrontation. This variation on the attack is often successful in organizations that have a strict hierarchical structure. In the military, for example, a lower-ranking individual may be coerced into providing information to an individual claiming to be of higher rank or to be working for another individual higher up in the chain of command.

Social engineering can also be accomplished using other means besides direct contact between the target and the attacker. For example, an attacker might send a forged e-mail with a link to a bogus website that has been set up to obtain information from the target or convince the target to perform some action. Again, the goal in social engineering is to convince the target to provide information that they normally wouldn't divulge or to perform some act that they normally would not do. An example of a slightly different attack that is generally still considered social engineering is one in which an attacker replaces the blank deposit slips in a bank's lobby with ones containing his or her own account number but no name. When an unsuspecting customer uses one of the slips, a teller who is not observant could end up crediting the attacker's account with the deposit.

Tools

The tools in a social engineer's toolbox are based on a knowledge of psychology and don't necessarily require a sophisticated knowledge of software or hardware. The social engineer will employ strategies aimed at exploiting people's own biases and beliefs in a manner to momentarily deny them the service of good judgment and the use of standard procedures. Employing social engineering tools is second nature to a social engineer, and with skill they can switch these tools in and out in any particular circumstance, just as a plumber uses various hand tools and a system administrator uses OS commands to achieve complex tasks. When watching any of these professionals work, we may marvel at how they wield their tools, and the same is true for social engineers—except their tools are more subtle, and the target is people and trust. The following sections detail common "techniques" that can be employed in many social engineering attacks.

Principles (Reasons for Effectiveness)

Social engineering is very successful for two general reasons. The first is the basic desire of most people to be helpful. When somebody asks a question for which we know the answer, our normal response is not to be suspicious but rather to answer the question. The problem with this is that seemingly innocuous information can be used either directly in an attack or indirectly to build a bigger picture that an attacker can use to create an aura of authenticity during an attack—the more information an individual has about an organization, the easier it will be to convince others that she is part of the organization and has a right to even sensitive information.

The second reason that social engineering is successful is that individuals normally seek to avoid confrontation and trouble. If the attacker attempts to intimidate the target, threatening to call the target's supervisor because of a lack of help, the target may give in and provide the information to avoid confrontation.

> The effectiveness of social engineering attacks is part technical and part psychological. For an attack to trick most users, psychological hooks are used to make the attacker more effective in getting a user to perform a desired action. Understanding the psychological component of these attacks is important.

Authority

The use of **authority** in social situations can lead to an environment where one party feels at risk in challenging another over an issue. If an attacker can convince a target that he has authority in a particular situation, he can entice the target to act in a particular manner or risk adverse consequences. In short, if you act like a boss when requesting something, people are less likely to withhold it.

The best defense against this and many social engineering attacks is a strong set of policies that has no exceptions. Much like security lines in the airport, when it comes to the point of screening, everyone gets screened, even flight crews, so there is no method of bypassing the critical step.

Intimidation

Intimidation can be either subtle, through perceived power, or more direct, through the use of communications that build an expectation of superiority.

Consensus

Consensus is a group-wide decision. It frequently comes not from a champion, but rather through rounds of group negotiation. These rounds can be manipulated to achieve desired outcomes. The social engineer simply motivates others to achieve her desired outcome.

Scarcity

If something is in short supply and is valued, then arriving with what is needed can bring rewards—and acceptance. "Only *X* widgets left at this price" is an example of this technique. Even if something is not scarce, implied scarcity, or implied future change in availability, can create a perception of scarcity. By giving the impression of **scarcity**, or short supply, of a desirable product, an attacker can motivate a target to make a decision quickly without deliberation.

Familiarity

People do things for people they like or feel connected to. Building this sense of **familiarity** and appeal can lead to misplaced trust. The social engineer can focus the conversation on familiar items, not the differences. Again, by leading with persuasion, a social engineer can convince someone that he has "been there before" or has done something, even if he hasn't, and this perception will lead to the desired familiar feeling on the part of the victim.

Trust

Trust is defined as having an understanding of how something will act under specific conditions. Social engineers can shape the perceptions of a target to where they will apply judgments to the trust equation and come to false conclusions. The whole objective of social engineering is not to force

The key in all social engineering attacks is that you are manipulating a person and their actions by manipulating their perception of a situation. A social engineer preys on people's beliefs, biases, and stereotypes—to the victim's detriment. This is hacking the human side of a system.

people to do things they would not do, but rather to give them a pathway that leads them to feel they are doing the correct thing in the moment.

Urgency

Time can be manipulated to drive a sense of **urgency** and prompt shortcuts that can lead to opportunities for interjection into processes. Limited-time offers should always be viewed as suspect. Perception is the key. Giving the target a reason to believe that they can take advantage of a time situation, whether it really is present or not, achieves the outcome of them acting in a desired manner.

Defenses

A training and awareness program is still the best defense against social engineering attacks.

In all of the cases of impersonation, the best defense is simple—have processes in place that require employees to ask to see a person's ID before engaging with them if the employees do not personally know them. That includes challenging people such as delivery drivers and contract workers. Don't let people in through the door, tailgating/piggybacking, without checking their ID. If this is standard process, then no one becomes offended, and if someone fakes offense, it becomes even more suspicious. Training and awareness do work, as proven by trends such as the diminished effectiveness of pop-up windows. But the key to this defense is to make the training periodic and to tailor it to what is currently being experienced, rather than a generic recitation of best practices.

Phishing, smishing, vishing—these are attacks against users' cognitive state. Using the principles (reasons for effectiveness) discussed earlier in the chapter, one can craft a message that makes falling victim to such an attack more likely. The attack is a combination of a technical element and psychological pressure, and together the user takes the bait and clicks the link.

Attacks

Social engineering attacks target the people portion of your computing environment. Using psychology and technical means, the social engineer attempts to get a user to perform specific actions on a system—actions they normally would not do. These include clicking a link and going to a web page, running a program, saving information, and opening a file. The list is long, and the means of defense is not against the technical but rather against the psychology side of the problem. Training users to think before they click is important.

Impersonation

Impersonation is a common social engineering technique that can be employed in many ways. It can occur in person, over a phone, or online. In the case of an impersonation attack, the attacker assumes a role that is recognized by the person being attacked, and in assuming that role, the attacker uses the potential victim's own biases against their better judgment to follow procedures. Impersonation can take a variety of forms—third parties, help desk operators, vendors, and even online sources.

Third-Party Authorization

Using previously obtained information about a project, deadline, boss, and so on, the attacker (1) arrives with something the victim is somewhat expecting or would see as normal, (2) uses the guise of a project in trouble or some other situation where the attacker will be viewed as helpful or as someone not to upset, and (3) name-drops "Mr. Big," who happens to be out of the office and unreachable at the moment, thus avoiding a reference check. Note that the attacker seldom asks for anything that on the face of it seems unreasonable or is unlikely to be shared based on the circumstances. These actions can create the appearance of a third-party authorization, when in fact there is none.

> Up to this point, social engineering has been discussed in the context of an outsider attempting to gain information about the organization. This does not have to be the case. Insiders may also attempt to gain information they are not authorized to have. In many cases, the insider can be much more successful because they will already have a certain level of information regarding the organization and can therefore better spin a story that might be believable to other employees.

Contractors/Outside Parties

It is common in many organizations to have outside contractors clean the building, water the plants, and perform other routine chores. In many of these situations, without proper safeguards, an attacker can simply put on clothing that matches a contractor's uniform, show up to do the job at a slightly different time than it's usually done, and, if challenged, play on the sympathy of the workers by saying they are filling in for *X* or covering for *Y*. The attacker can then roam the halls unnoticed because they blend in, all the while photographing desks and papers and looking for information.

Help Desk/Tech Support

Calls to or from help desk and tech support units can be used to elicit information. Posing as an employee, a social engineer can get a password reset, details about some system, and other useful information. The call can go the other direction as well, where the social engineer is posing as the help desk or tech support. Then, by calling employees, the attacker can get information on system status and other interesting elements that they can use later.

Online Attacks

Impersonation can be employed in online attacks as well. In these cases, technology plays an intermediary role in the communication chain. Some older forms, such as pop-up windows, tend to be less effective today because users are wary of them. Yet phishing attempts via e-mail and social media scams abound.

Fake Tech Support Pop-up

Phishing

Phishing (pronounced "fishing") is a type of social engineering in which an attacker attempts to obtain sensitive information from users by masquerading as a trusted entity in an e-mail or instant message sent to a large group of often random users. The attacker attempts to obtain information such as usernames, passwords, credit card numbers, and details about the users' bank accounts. The message that is sent often encourages the user to go to a website that appears to be for a reputable entity such as PayPal or eBay, both of which have frequently been used in phishing attempts. The website the user actually visits is not owned by the reputable organization, however, and asks the user to supply information that can be used in a later attack. Often the message sent to the user states that the user's account has been compromised and requests that they, for security purposes, enter their account information to verify the details.

Phishing is now the most common form of social engineering attack related to computer security. The target could be a computer system and access to the information found on it (such as is the case when the phishing attempt asks for a user ID and password), or it could be personal information, generally financial, about an individual (in the case of phishing attempts that ask for an individual's banking information).

In another very common example of phishing, the attacker sends a bulk e-mail, supposedly from a bank, telling the recipients that a security breach has occurred and instructing them to click a link to verify that their account has not been tampered with. If an individual actually clicks the link, they are taken to a site that appears to be owned by the bank but is actually controlled by the attacker. When they supply their account and password for "verification" purposes, they are actually giving it to the attacker.

Smishing

Smishing is a version of a phishing attack using Short Message Service (SMS) on victims' cell phones. It begins with an SMS message directing a user to a URL from which the attacker then can serve up a variety of attack vectors, including forms of malware. This attack works primarily because of the principles of urgency and intimidation, spurred by warnings such as "You are subscribed to XYZ service, which will begin regular billings of $2 a month. Click here to unsubscribe before billing takes place." Then, when the user clicks the URL, the next phase of the attack can begin.

Vishing

A great video showing the use of several social engineering tools can be found at https://www.youtube.com/watch?v=lc7scxvKQOo ("This is how hackers hack you using simple social engineering"). This video demonstrates the use of vishing to steal someone's cell phone credentials.

Vishing is a variation of phishing that uses voice communication technology to obtain the information the attacker is seeking. Vishing takes advantage of the trust that some people place in the telephone network. Users are unaware that attackers can spoof (simulate) calls from legitimate entities using Voice over IP (VoIP) technology. Voice messaging can also be compromised and used in these attempts. This is used to establish a form of trust that is then exploited by the attacker over the phone. Generally, the attackers are hoping to obtain credit card numbers or other information that can be used in identity theft. The user may receive an e-mail asking them to call a number that is answered by a potentially compromised voice message system. Users may also receive a recorded message that appears to come from a legitimate entity. In both cases, the user will be encouraged to respond quickly and provide the sensitive information so that access to their account is not blocked. If a user ever receives a message that claims to be from a reputable entity and asks for sensitive information, the user should not provide it but instead should use the Internet or examine a legitimate account statement to find a phone number that can be used to contact the entity. The user can then verify that the message received was legitimate or report the vishing attempt.

Tech Tip

Beware of Vishing

Vishing (phishing conducted using voice systems) is generally successful because of the trust that individuals place in the telephone system. With caller ID, people believe they can identify who is calling them. They do not understand that, just like many protocols in the TCP/IP protocol suite, caller ID can be spoofed.

Spam

Spam, as just about everybody knows, is bulk unsolicited e-mail. Though not generally considered by many as a social engineering issue, or even a security issue for that matter, spam can still be a security concern. It can be legitimate in the sense that it has been sent by a company advertising a product or service, but it can also be malicious and could include an attachment that contains malicious software designed to harm your system, or a link to a malicious website that may attempt to obtain personal information from you. Because spam is unsolicited, you should always consider the source before clicking any links or directly responding. In this regard, the fact that spam can result in users clicking links, this is a form of social engineering due to altering human behavior.

Spam over Internet Messaging (SPIM)

Though not as well known, a variation on spam is **SPIM**, which is basically spam delivered via an instant messaging application. The purpose of hostile SPIM is the same as that of spam—the delivery of malicious content or links and getting an unsuspecting user to click them, thus initiating the attack.

Spear Phishing

Spear phishing is the term that has been created to refer to a phishing attack that targets a specific group of people or businesses with something in common. Because a specific group is being targeted, such as senior executives, the ratio of successful attacks (that is, the number of responses received) to the total number of e-mails or messages sent usually increases because a targeted attack will seem more plausible than a message sent to users randomly.

Whaling

High-value targets are referred to as whales. A **whaling** attack is thus one where the target is a high-value person, such as a CEO or CFO. Whaling attacks are not performed by attacking multiple targets and hoping for a reply, but rather are custom-built to increase the odds of success. Spear phishing is a common method used against whales, as it is designed to appear to be ordinary business for the target, being crafted to imitate a nonsuspicious communication. Whales can be deceived in the same manner as any other person; the difference is that the target group is limited, hence an attacker cannot rely upon random returns from a wide population of targets.

Pharming

Pharming consists of misdirecting users to fake websites made to look official. Using phishing, attackers target individuals, one by one, by sending out e-mails. To become a victim, the recipient must take an action (for example, respond by providing personal information). In pharming, the user will be directed to the fake website as a result of activity such as DNS poisoning (an attack that changes URLs in a server's domain name table) or modification of local host files (which are used to convert URLs to the appropriate IP address). Once at the fake site, the user might supply personal information, believing that they are connected to the legitimate site.

Tech Tip

Defense Against Social Engineering Attacks

Defending against social engineering attacks, where the technical aspects are beyond your immediate control, as in pharming, seems daunting. Yet, there is a common element to these attacks: the user. Users need to be aware of how social engineers will attack and that they are the social engineers' target. Having users receive periodic training, on a regular basis in very small pieces, has been shown to be effective at improving awareness and detection. Little cues, misspellings, colors, and formats can provide clues that something isn't right. Being asked to do something that is different from the norm, logging in again, and asking for information or actions that are not normal—these are all signs of manipulation. When viewed as someone trying to manipulate you, this can be more noticeable.

Dumpster Diving

The process of going through a target's trash in hopes of finding valuable information that might be used in a penetration attempt is known in the security community as **dumpster diving**. One common place to find information, if the attacker is in the vicinity of the target, is in the target's trash. The attacker might find little bits of information that could be useful for an attack. The tactic is not, however, unique to the computer community; it has been used for many years by others, such as identity thieves, private investigators, and law enforcement personnel, to obtain information about an individual or organization. If the attackers are very lucky, and the target's security procedures are very poor, they may actually find user IDs and passwords.

An attacker may gather a variety of information that can be useful in a social engineering attack. In most locations, trash is no longer considered private property after it has been discarded (and even where dumpster diving is illegal, little enforcement occurs). An organization should have policies about discarding materials. Sensitive information should be shredded, and the organization should consider securing the trash receptacle so that individuals can't forage through it. People should also consider shredding personal or sensitive information that they wish to discard in their own trash. A reasonable quality shredder is inexpensive and well worth the price when compared with the potential loss that could occur as a result of identity theft.

Shoulder Surfing

Shoulder surfing does not necessarily involve direct contact with the target, but instead involves the attacker directly observing the individual entering sensitive information on a form, keypad, or keyboard. The attacker may simply look over the shoulder of the user at work, for example, or may set up a camera or use binoculars to view the user entering sensitive data. The attacker can attempt to obtain information such as a personal identification number (PIN) at an automated teller machine (ATM), an access control entry code at a secure gate or door, or a calling card or credit card number. Many locations now use a privacy screen or filter to surround a keypad so that it is difficult to observe somebody as they enter information. More sophisticated systems can actually scramble the location of the numbers so that the top row at one time includes the numbers 1, 2, and 3 and the next time includes 4, 8, and 0. While this makes it a bit slower for the user to enter information, it thwarts an attacker's attempt to observe what numbers are pressed and then enter the same buttons/pattern, since the location of the numbers constantly changes.

A related, somewhat obvious security precaution is that a person should not use the same PIN for all of their different accounts, gate codes, and so on, because an attacker who learns the PIN for one type of access could then use it for all the other types of access.

Although methods such as adding shields to block the view and having the pad scramble the numbers can help make shoulder surfing more difficult, the best defense is for users to be aware of their surroundings and to not allow individuals to get into a position from which they can observe what the user is entering.

The attacker may attempt to increase the chance of successfully observing the target entering the data by starting a conversation with the target.

This provides an excuse for the attacker to be physically closer to the target. Otherwise, the target could be suspicious if the attacker is standing too close. In this sense, shoulder surfing can be considered a social engineering attack.

Tailgating/Piggybacking

Tailgating (or **piggybacking**) is the simple tactic of following closely behind a person who has just used their own access card or PIN to gain physical access to a room or building. People are often in a hurry and will frequently not follow good physical security practices and procedures. Attackers know this and may attempt to exploit this characteristic in human behavior. An attacker can thus gain access to the facility without having to know the access code or having to acquire an access card. It is similar to shoulder surfing in that it relies on the attacker taking advantage of an authorized user who is not following security procedures. Frequently the attacker may even start a conversation with the target before reaching the door so that the user may be more comfortable with allowing the individual in without challenging them. In this sense, piggybacking is related to social engineering attacks.

Both the piggybacking and shoulder surfing attack techniques rely on the poor security practices of an authorized user in order to be successful. Thus, both techniques can be easily countered by training employees to use simple procedures to ensure nobody follows them too closely or is in a position to observe their actions. A more sophisticated countermeasure to piggybacking is a *mantrap*, which utilizes two doors to gain access to the facility. The second door does not open until the first one is closed, and the doors are closely spaced so that an enclosure is formed that only allows one individual through at a time.

Cross Check

Mantraps, tailgating, and other personal security items related to physical access are covered in Chapter 8. You will find a great picture of a mantrap there as well.

Eliciting Information

Calls to or from help desk and tech support units can be used to *elicit information*. A skilled social engineer can use a wide range of psychological techniques to convince people, whose main job is to help others, to perform tasks resulting in security compromises. Posing as an employee, an attacker can get a password reset, information about some system, or other useful information. The call can go the other direction as well, where the social engineer is posing as the help desk or tech support. Then, by calling employees, the attacker can get information on system status and other interesting elements that they can use later.

Prepending

Prepending is defined as the act of adding something else to the beginning of an item. When used in a social engineering context, prepending is the act of supplying information that another will act upon, frequently before they ask for it, in an attempt to legitimize the actual request, which comes later. Using the psychological constructs of authority, prepending can take the form of the attacker stating that they are sent by someone's boss, or another authority figure, as a means to justify why the victim of the attack should perform a specific action—typically one that, in the absence of the prepend, would not be normal.

Identity Fraud

Identity fraud is the use of fake credentials to achieve an end. This can be a high-risk endeavor, such as pretending to be an official representative of a government agency or a regulator, or it can be lower risk, such as showing up as the person who waters the plants. One could pretend to be a delivery agent, show up with a box—or better yet, a server—and attempt direct delivery to the server room. This works best when the victim is expecting the person, as in the case of a broken server under a repair warranty. Identity fraud can be done online as well, using known information about the person being impersonated (see the "Impersonation" section earlier in the chapter) and deceiving the victim being attacked. Defense against identity fraud is the same as most other social engineering attacks—use strong policies and procedures, without exceptions (for example, all packages must be dropped at the security desk, all visitors who need access must be escorted 100 percent of the time, and so on). Also, there should be no exceptions on disclosure policies, such as resetting passwords and giving a third party access. Doing everything by the rules works. Just look at TSA security—there is no way past their line without being screened first. The accuracy and effectiveness of their screening may be legitimately questioned, but getting around it is not. This is key for stopping most social engineering attacks.

Invoice Scams

Invoice scams are just that—a scam using a fake invoice in an attempt to get a company to pay for things it has not ordered. The premise is simple: send a fake invoice and then get paid. In practice, since most companies have fairly strong accounting controls, the scam involves getting someone outside of the accounting group to initiate the process, thus lending a sense of legitimacy. This all seems like it wouldn't work, yet cybercriminals collect billions of dollars per year using this method. Common items used in these scams are office products such as toner and normal office supplies, cleaning products, organizational memberships, and a wide range of corporate services. Sometimes, to add urgency, the attacker includes a final notice, threatening to involve a collection agency, making a person hesitate before just throwing the bill away.

Credential Harvesting

Credential harvesting is the collection of credential information, such as user IDs, passwords, and so on, thus allowing an attacker a series of passes to the system. A common form of credential harvesting starts with a phishing e-mail that convinces a user to click a link and, in response, brings up a replica of their bank's web page. It looks like the bank's page (and users typically do not check the security settings of their browser connection), and when the user enters their credentials, the credentials (user ID and password) are harvested and stored for later use by the criminal.

The objective of a credential harvest is just that—credentials. Once the criminal has tricked you into providing your credentials, they will either redirect you to the correct website or provide an error and a new connection to the correct website for you to try again. The objective is to make you think everything is working and to mask the fact that they stole your credentials. This attack method has been highly successful, and it is now standard practice for financial firms to follow normal user ID and password with a second factor, such as an out-of-band inquiry, to prevent subsequent use of harvested credentials. While this adds a layer of complexity and inconvenience to the user, it has become an accepted practice and is necessary to prevent harvested credential reuse.

Many of the attacks are designed to get a user's credentials. Any credentials you can share comprise a risk, and to combat this risk, organizations have adopted two-factor authentication. The second factor is a different method of identifying the user and is typically unique and only valid for a limited time. An example is when you log in to your bank, and you get a text message with a code to authorize entry. This code significantly complicates the problem for an attacker if they get your credentials.

Reverse Social Engineering

A slightly different approach to social engineering is called **reverse social engineering**. In this technique, the attacker hopes to convince the target to initiate the contact. This obviously differs from the traditional approach, where the target is the one who is contacted. The reason this attack might be successful is that, because the target is the one initiating the contact, attackers might not have to convince the target of their authenticity. The tricky part of this attack is, of course, convincing the target to make that initial contact. One possible method for accomplishing this involves sending out a spoofed e-mail (a fake e-mail designed to appear authentic) that claims to be from a reputable source and provides another e-mail address or phone number to call for "tech support." Another method might be posting a notice or creating a bogus website for a legitimate company that also claims to provide "tech support." This may be especially successful if timed to coincide with a company's deployment of a new software or hardware platform. Another potential time to target an organization with this sort of attack is when there is a significant change in the organization itself, such as when two companies merge or a smaller company is acquired by a larger one. During these times, employees are not familiar with the new organization or its procedures, and amid the confusion it is easy to conduct either a social engineering or reverse social engineering attack.

Tech Tip

Be Aware of Reverse Social Engineering

Reverse social engineering is not nearly as widely understood as social engineering and is a bit trickier to execute. If the attacker is successful in convincing an individual to make the initial contact, however, the process of convincing that individual of their authenticity is generally much easier than in a social engineering attack.

Reconnaissance

Reconnaissance is a military term used to describe the actions of surveying a battlefield to gain information prior to hostilities. In the field of cybersecurity, the concept is the same—an adversary will examine the systems they intend to attack, using a wide range of methods. Some of these methods do not involve directly engaging the victim—Google searches, public record searches, and so on. But other aspects are involved in directly manipulating people to gain information. Obtaining and then surveying org charts, calling and asking for contact information on people and then building a personnel directory, asking questions about hardware and software via surveys—all of these methods provide information that goes into a description of the system that will be under attack. While most reconnaissance is accepted as inevitable, some of it is helped via items such as press releases telling the world who your security partners are, what products you are employing, and so on. Each of these items of information will be used later as part of the attack process. Known weaknesses against specific products can be employed and are easier to find if the attacker knows what products a company is using. Performing a solid reconnaissance before attacking provides the attacker with key informational elements later when the items are needed.

Hoax

At first glance, it might seem that a **hoax** related to security would be considered a nuisance and not a real security issue. This might be the case for some hoaxes, especially those of the urban legend type, but the reality of the situation is that a *hoax* can be very damaging if it causes users to take some sort of action that weakens security. One real hoax, for example, described a new, highly destructive piece of malicious software. It instructed users to check for the existence of a certain file and to delete it if the file was found. In reality, the file mentioned was an important file used by the operating system, and deleting it caused problems the next time the system was booted. The damage caused by users modifying security settings can be serious. As with other forms of social engineering, training and awareness are the best and first line of defense for both users and administrators. Users should be trained to be suspicious of unusual e-mails and stories, and they should know who to contact in the organization to verify the validity these e-mails if they are received. A hoax e-mail often also advises the user to send it to their friends so that they know about the issue as well—and by doing so, they help spread the hoax. Users need to be suspicious of any e-mail telling them to "spread the word."

Watering Hole Attack

The most commonly recognized attack vectors are those that are direct to a target. Because of their incoming and direct nature, the attack vectors require defenses to be crafted to detect and defend against them. But what if the user "asks" for the attack by visiting a website? Just as a hunter waits near a watering hole for animals to come drink, attackers can plant malware at sites where users are likely to frequent. First identified by RSA, a security firm, a *watering hole attack* involves the infecting of a target website with malware. In some of the cases detected, the infection was constrained to a specific geographical area. These are not simple attacks, yet they can be very effective at delivering malware to a specific groups of end users. Watering hole attacks are complex to achieve and appear to be backed by nation-states and other high-resource attackers. In light of the stakes, the typical attack vector will be a zero-day attack to further avoid detection.

Different threat actors, such as nation-states, and attack vectors are discussed in Chapter 15.

Typo Squatting

Typo squatting is an attack form that involves capitalizing on common typographical errors. If a user mistypes a URL, then the result should be a 404 error, or "resource not found." But if an attacker has registered the mistyped URL, then the user would land on the attacker's page. This attack pattern is also referred to as *URL hijacking, using a fake URL,* or *brandjacking* if the objective is to deceive based on branding.

There are several reasons that an attacker will pursue this avenue of attack. The most obvious is one for a phishing attack. The fake site collects credentials, passing them on to the real site, and then steps out of the conversation to avoid detection once the credentials are obtained. It can also be used to plant drive-by malware on the victim machine. It can also move the packets through an affiliate network, earning click-through revenue based on the typos. There are numerous other forms of attacks that can be perpetrated using a fake URL as a starting point.

Influence Campaigns

Influence campaigns involve the use of collected information and selective publication of material to key individuals in an attempt to alter perceptions and change people's minds on a topic. One can engage in an influence campaign against a single person, but the effect is limited. Influence campaigns are even more powerful when used in conjunction with social media to spread influence through influencer propagation. Influencers are people who have large followings of people who read what they post and, in many cases, act in accordance or agreement. This serves as an amplifying mechanism, where single pieces of disinformation can be rapidly spread to build a following across the Internet. The effects are strong enough that nation-states have used these techniques as a form of conflict, termed **hybrid warfare**, where the information is used to sway people toward a position favored by those spreading it. What makes this effective is the psychological effect of groups—in particular, the bandwagon effect, where when one person leads, and many follow, typically without critically examining the premise they are following. In previous wars, this was called propaganda. Today, with rapid communication worldwide via social media platforms, these methods are even more effective at moving mass belief in groups of populations.

Poor Security Practices

A significant portion of human-created security problems results from poor security practices. These poor practices may be from an individual user not following established security policies or processes, or they may be caused by a lack of security policies, procedures, or training within the user's organization.

Poor password selection is one of the most common of poor security practices, and one of the most dangerous. Numerous studies conducted on password selection have found that, while overall more users are learning to select good passwords, a significant percentage of users still make poor choices. The problem with this, of course, is that a poor password choice can enable an attacker to compromise a computer system or network more easily. Even when users have good passwords, they often resort to another poor security practice—writing their passwords down in an easily located place, which can also lead to system compromise if an attacker gains physical access to the area.

Writing down and hiding passwords doesn't work if someone has physical access. The number of hiding places that are convenient is few, and most security people know them all. Don't write them down—anywhere.

Password Selection

For many years, computer intruders have relied on users' poor selection of passwords to help them in their attempts to gain unauthorized access to systems and networks. If attackers could obtain a list of the users' names, chances were good they could eventually access the system. Users tend to pick passwords that are easy for them to remember, and what easier password could there be than the same sequence of characters that they use for their user ID? If a system has an account with the username *jdoe*, an attacker's reasonable first guess of the account's password would be *jdoe*. If this doesn't work, the attacker would try variations on the same, such as *doej*, *johndoe*, *johnd*, and *eodj*, all of which would be reasonable possibilities.

Organizations have also instituted additional policies and rules relating to password selection to further complicate an attacker's efforts. Organizations, for example, may require users to frequently change their password. This means that if an attacker is able to guess a password, it is only valid for a limited period of time before a new password is selected, after which the attacker is locked out. All is not lost for the attacker, however, because, again, users will select passwords they can remember. For example, password changes often result in a new password that simply incorporates a number at the end of the old one. Thus, a user might select *S3Cr3Tp4$$w0rD12* as a new password, replacing the version that ended in 11. This does not really add security because, if an attacker knew the old one, they can guess the next one.

The complexity of managing passwords has led to the creation of password manager programs. These programs, including the Chrome browser, attempt to make password management easier for users. There are good and bad aspects to these methods. First, if there is any way that a user can recover the password from the system, one must suspect the security. Chrome requires a user's password to return a stored password, but there are utilities that can scrape passwords from the system and display them. This means attackers can as well. Most password managers use encryption to secure their password stores, and this is good. However, once you become beholden to the system, if you lose your master password, you lose everything.

Tech Tip

Harvesting Passwords

In 2014, a vulnerability in the OpenSSL cryptography software library was discovered and given the name Heartbleed because it originated in the heartbeat signal employed by the system. This vulnerability resulted in the potential loss of passwords and other sensitive data across multiple platforms and up to a million web servers and related systems. Heartbleed resulted in random data loss from servers, as 64KB blocks of memory were exfiltrated from the system. Among the items that could be lost in Heartbleed attacks are user credentials, user IDs, and passwords. The discovery of this vulnerability prompted users to change a massive number of passwords across the Web, as users had no knowledge as to the status of their credentials. One of the common pieces of advice to users was to not reuse passwords between systems. This advice is universally good advice, not just for Heartbleed, but for all systems, all the time.

With the proliferation of computers, networks, and users, the password dilemma has gotten worse. Today, the average Internet user probably has at least a half dozen different accounts and passwords to remember. Selecting a different password for each account, following the guidelines mentioned previously regarding character selection and frequency of changes, only aggravates the problem of remembering the passwords. This results in users all too frequently using the same password for all accounts. If a user does this, and then one of the accounts is compromised, all other accounts are subsequently also vulnerable to attack.

The need for good password selection and the protection of passwords also applies to another common feature of today's electronic world: PINs. Most people have at least one PIN associated with their ATM card or a security code to gain physical access to a room. Again, users will invariably select numbers that are easy to remember. Specific numbers, such as the individual's birth date, their spouse's birth date, or the date of some other significant event, are all common numbers to select. Other people will pick patterns that are easy to remember—2580, for example, uses all of the center numbers on a standard numeric pad on a telephone. Attackers know this, and guessing PINs follows the same sort of process that guessing a password does.

Password selection is an individual activity, and ensuring that individuals are making good selections is the realm of the entity's password policy. In order for users make appropriate choices, they need to be aware of the issue and their personal role in securing accounts. An effective password policy conveys both the user's role and responsibility associated with password usage and does so in a simple enough manner that it can be conveyed via screen notes during mandated password change events.

Know the rules for good password selection. Generally, these are to use eight or more characters in your password, include a combination of upper- and lowercase letters, include at least one number and one special character, do not use a common word, phrase, or name, and choose a password you can remember so that you do not need to write it down. Also, don't reuse passwords.

Tech Tip

Passwordless Systems

Microsoft has provided users the option to go passwordless in Windows 10, but how is this secure? You can use a picture, a fingerprint, your face, or a simple PIN to unlock your Windows 10 machine. At first this system seems insecure, but it really isn't passwordless. There are still passwords behind the scenes. Microsoft is simply using a local proxy for the password to allow access to the machine. Any transactions across the network are still done with the same level of security. Your PIN, face, or biometric doesn't leave the machine; it just unlocks your password.

Shoulder Surfing

As discussed earlier, *shoulder surfing* does not involve direct contact with the user, but instead involves the attacker directly observing the target entering sensitive information on a form, keypad, or keyboard. The attacker may simply look over the shoulder of the user at work, watching as a coworker enters their password. Although defensive methods can help make shoulder surfing more difficult, the best defense is for a user to be aware of their surroundings and to not allow individuals to get into a position from which they can observe what the user is entering. A related security comment can be made at this point: a person should not use the same PIN for all of their different accounts, gate codes, and so on, because an attacker who learns the PIN for one could then use it for all the others.

Piggybacking

People are often in a hurry and will frequently not follow good physical security practices and procedures. Attackers know this and may attempt to exploit this characteristic in human behavior. *Piggybacking*, or tailgating, happens because the person is not paying attention to the context of their situation: they are passing a security checkpoint, so security should be their main focus. Frequently the attacker might even start a conversation with the target before reaching the door so that the user is more comfortable with allowing the individual in without challenging them. In this sense, piggybacking is related to social engineering attacks. Both the piggybacking and shoulder surfing attack techniques can be easily countered by using simple procedures to ensure nobody follows you too closely or is in a position to observe your actions. Both techniques rely on the poor security practices of an authorized user to be successful.

Dumpster Diving

As mentioned earlier, attackers need a certain amount of information before launching their attack. One common place to find this information, if the attacker is in the vicinity of the target, is the target's trash. The attacker might find little bits of information that could be useful for an attack. This process of going through a target's trash in hopes of finding valuable information that can be used in a penetration attempt is known in the computer community as *dumpster diving*.

This works because people are lazy and just throw things into the trash without thinking of the risk. Government offices with classified or important paperwork have specially marked "burn bags" where users can place items to be burned. Discipline is the key to avoiding laziness.

There may be a number of individuals who have access to a facility but are not authorized to access the information the systems store and process. We become complacent with the access these individuals have because they often quietly go about their job so as to not draw attention to themselves and to minimize the impact on the operation of the organization. They may also be overlooked because their job does not impact the core function of the organization. A prime example of this is the custodial staff. Becoming complacent about these individuals and not paying attention to what they may have access to, however, could be a big mistake, and users should not believe that everybody who has physical access to the organization has the same level of concern for or interest in the welfare of the organization.

Try This!

Diving into Your Dumpster

The amount of useful information that users throw away in unsecured trash receptacles often amazes security professionals. Hackers know that they can often find manuals, network diagrams, and even user IDs and passwords by rummaging through dumpsters. After coordinating this with your security office, try seeing what you can find that individuals in your organization have discarded (assuming that there is no shredding policy) by either going through your organization's dumpsters or just through the office trash receptacles. What useful information did you find? Is there an obvious suggestion that you might make to enhance the security of your organization?

Installing Unauthorized Hardware and Software

Organizations should have a policy that restricts the ability of normal users to install software and new hardware on their systems. A common example is a user installing unauthorized communication software and a modem to allow them to connect to their machine at work via a modem from their home. Another common example is a user installing a wireless access point so that they can access the organization's network from many different areas. In these examples, the user has set up a backdoor into the network, circumventing all the other security mechanisms in place. The terms *rogue modem* and *rogue access point* may be used to describe these two cases, respectively. A **backdoor** is an avenue that can be used to access a system while circumventing normal security mechanisms and can often be used to install additional executable files that can lead to more ways to access the compromised system. Security professionals can use widely available tools to scan their own systems periodically for either of these rogue devices to ensure that users haven't created a backdoor.

Another common example of unauthorized software that users install on their systems is games. Unfortunately, not all games come in shrink-wrapped packages. Numerous small games can be downloaded from the Internet. The problem with this is that users don't always know where the software originally came from and what may be hidden inside it. Many individuals have unwittingly installed what seemed to be an innocuous game, only to have downloaded a piece of malicious code capable of many things, including opening a backdoor that allows attackers to connect to, and control, the system from across the Internet.

Because of these potential hazards, many organizations do not allow their users to load software or install new hardware without the knowledge and assistance of administrators. Many organizations also screen, and occasionally intercept, e-mail messages with links or attachments that are sent to users. This helps prevent users from, say, unwittingly executing a hostile program that was sent as part of a worm or virus. Consequently, many organizations have their mail servers strip off executable attachments to e-mail so that users can't accidentally cause a security problem.

Data Handling

Understanding the responsibilities of proper data handling associated with one's job is an important training topic. Information can be deceptive in that it is not directly tangible, and people tend to develop bad habits around other job measures … at the expense of security. Employees require training in how to recognize the data classification and handling requirements of the data they are using, and they need to learn how to follow the proper handling processes. If certain data elements require special handling because of contracts, laws, or regulations, there is typically a training clause associated with this requirement. Personnel assigned to these tasks should be specifically trained with regard to the security requirements. The spirit of the training clause is you get what you train, and if security over specific data types is a requirement, then it should be trained. This same principle holds for corporate data-handling responsibilities: you get the behaviors you train and reward.

> Preventing access to information is also important in the work area. Firms with sensitive information should have a "clean desk policy" specifying that sensitive information is not left unsecured in the work area when the worker is not present to protect the material.

Physical Access by Non-Employees

As has been mentioned, if an attacker can gain physical access to a facility, chances are very good that the attacker can obtain enough information to penetrate computer systems and networks. Many organizations require employees to wear identification badges when at work. This is an easy method to quickly spot who has permission to have physical access to the organization and who does not. Although this method is easy to implement and can be a significant deterrent to unauthorized individuals, it also requires that employees actively challenge individuals who are not wearing the required identification badge. This is one area where organizations fail. Combine an attacker who slips in by tailgating off of an authorized

If you work in a place where badges are required for access and you see someone without a badge, you should speak up. Hackers count on you not challenging them and not wanting to become involved. You don't have to make it personal; there is a policy, and policies don't push back. Just politely inquire as to whether they have lost their badge and, if so, escort them to the security desk for a new one.

individual and an environment where employees have not been encouraged to challenge individuals without appropriate credentials and you have a situation where you might as well not have any badges in the first place. Organizations also frequently become complacent when faced with what appears to be a legitimate reason to access the facility, such as when an individual shows up with a warm pizza claiming it was ordered by an employee. It has often been stated by security consultants that it is amazing what you can obtain access to with a pizza box or a vase of flowers.

Another aspect that must be considered is personnel who have legitimate access to a facility but also have the intent to steal intellectual property or otherwise exploit the organization. Physical access provides an easy opportunity for individuals to look for the occasional piece of critical information carelessly left out in the open. With the proliferation of devices such as cell phones with built-in cameras, an individual could easily photograph information without it being obvious to employees. Contractors, consultants, and partners frequently not only have physical access to the facility but may also have network access. Other individuals who typically have unrestricted access to the facility when no one is around are nighttime custodial crewmembers and security guards. Such positions are often contracted out. As a result, hackers have been known to take temporary custodial jobs simply to gain access to facilities.

Clean Desk Policies

Preventing access to information is also important in the work area. Firms with sensitive information should have a "clean desk policy" specifying that sensitive information must not be left unsecured in the work area when the worker is not present to act as custodian. Even leaving the desk area and going to the bathroom can leave information exposed and subject to compromise. The clean desk policy should identify and prohibit certain actions that might not be obvious upon first glance, such as leaving passwords on sticky notes under keyboards or mouse pads or in unsecured desk drawers.

Per the multiple versions of the Verizon Data Breach Investigation Report, introduced in Chapter 1, hacks were discovered more often by internal employees than by outsiders. This means that trained users can be an important part of a security plan.

People as a Security Tool

An interesting paradox when speaking of social engineering attacks is that people are not only the biggest problem and security risk but also the best tool in defending against a social engineering attack. The first step a company should take to fight potential social engineering attacks is to create the policies and procedures that establish the roles and responsibilities for not only security administrators but for all users. What is it that management expects, security-wise, from all employees? What is it that the organization is trying to protect, and what mechanisms are important for that protection?

Security Awareness

Probably the single most effective method to counter potential social engineering attacks, after establishment of the organization's security goals and policies, is an active security awareness program. The extent of the training will vary depending on the organization's environment and the level of threat, but initial employee training on social engineering at the time a person is hired is important, as well as periodic refresher training.

An important element that should be stressed in training about social engineering is the type of information that the organization considers sensitive and may be the target of a social engineering attack. There are undoubtedly signs that the organization could point to as indicative of an attacker attempting to gain access to sensitive corporate information. All employees should be aware of these indicators. The scope of information that an attacker may ask for is very large, and many questions attackers pose might also be legitimate in another context (asking for someone's phone number, for example). Employees should be taught to be cautious about revealing personal information and should especially be alert for questions regarding account information, personally identifiable information, and passwords.

Try This!

Security Awareness Programs

A strong security education and awareness training program can go a long way toward reducing the chance that a social engineering attack will be successful. Awareness programs and campaigns, which might include seminars, videos, posters, newsletters, and similar materials, are also fairly easy to implement and not very costly. There is no reason for an organization to not have an awareness program in place. A lot of information and ideas are available on the Internet. See what you can find that might be usable for your organization that you can obtain at no charge from various organizations on the Internet. (Tip: Check organizations such as NIST and the NSA that have developed numerous security documents and guidelines.)

As a final note on user responsibilities, corporate security officers must cultivate an environment of trust in their office, as well as an understanding of the importance of security. If users feel that security personnel are only there to make their life difficult or to dredge up information that will result in an employee's termination, the atmosphere will quickly turn adversarial and be transformed into an "us-versus-them" situation. Security personnel need the help of all users and should strive to cultivate a team environment in which users, when faced with a questionable situation, will not hesitate to call the security office. In situations like this, security offices should remember the old adage of "don't shoot the messenger."

Social Networking and P2P

With the rise in popularity of social networking sites—notably Facebook, Twitter, and LinkedIn—many people have gotten into a habit of sharing too much information. Using a status of "Returning from sales call to XYZ company" reveals information to people who have no need to know it. Confusing sharing information with friends and sharing business information with those who don't need to know it is a line people are crossing on a regular basis. Don't be the employee who mixes business and personal information and releases information to parties who should not have it, regardless of how innocuous it may seem.

Users also need to understand the importance of not using common programs such as torrents and other peer-to-peer (P2P) file-sharing communication programs in the workplace, as these programs can result in infection mechanisms and data-loss channels. The information security training and awareness program should cover these issues. If the issues are properly explained to employees, their motivation to comply won't simply be to avoid adverse personnel action for violating a policy; they will want to assist in the security of the organization and its mission.

Security Policy Training and Procedures

People in an organization play a significant role in its security posture. As such, training is important because it can provide the basis for awareness of issues such as social engineering and desired employee security habits. These are detailed in Chapter 2.

Chapter 4 Review

Chapter Summary

After reading this chapter and completing the exercises, you should understand the following regarding the role people can play in security.

Define basic terminology associated with social engineering

- Social engineering is a technique in which the attacker uses various deceptive practices to convince the targeted person to divulge information they normally would not divulge, or to convince the target to do something they normally wouldn't do.
- In reverse social engineering, the attacker hopes to convince the target to initiate contact.

Describe steps organizations can take to improve their security

- Organizations should have a policy that restricts the ability of normal users to install new software and hardware on their systems.
- Contractors, consultants, and partners may frequently have not only physical access to the facility but also network access. Other groups that are given unrestricted, and unobserved, access to a facility are nighttime custodial crewmembers and security guards. Both are potential security problems, and organizations should take steps to limit these individuals' access.
- The single most effective method to counter potential social engineering attacks, after establishing the organization's security goals and policies, is an active security awareness program.

Describe common user actions that may put an organization's information at risk

- No matter how advanced security technology is, it will ultimately be deployed in an environment where the human element may be its greatest weakness.
- Attackers know that employees are frequently very busy and don't stop to think about security. They may attempt to exploit this work characteristic through piggybacking or shoulder surfing.

Recognize methods attackers may use to gain information about an organization

- For many years, computer intruders have relied on users' poor selection of passwords to help them in their attempts to gain unauthorized access to a system or network.
- One common way to find useful information (if the attacker is in the vicinity of the target, such as a company office) is to go through the target's trash looking for bits of information that could be useful to a penetration attempt.

Determine ways in which users can aid instead of detract from security

- An interesting paradox of social engineering attacks is that people are not only the biggest problem and security risk but also the best line of defense.
- A significant portion of employee-created security problems arises from poor security practices.
- Users should always be on the watch for attempts by individuals to gain information about the organization and should report suspicious activity to their employer.

Recognize the roles training and awareness play in assisting the people side of security

- Individual users can enhance security of a system through proper execution of their individual actions and responsibilities.
- Training and awareness programs can reinforce user knowledge of desired actions.

Key Terms

authority *(89)*
backdoor *(102)*
consensus *(89)*
credential harvesting *(97)*
dumpster diving *(94)*
familiarity *(89)*
hoax *(98)*
hybrid warfare *(99)*
identity fraud *(96)*
impersonation *(90)*
intimidation *(89)*
invoice scams *(96)*
pharming *(93)*
phishing *(91)*
piggybacking *(95)*
prepending *(96)*
reconnaissance *(97)*
reverse social engineering *(97)*
scarcity *(89)*
shoulder surfing *(94)*
social engineering *(87)*
smishing *(92)*
spam *(92)*
spam over Internet messaging (SPIM) *(93)*
spear phishing *(93)*
tailgating *(95)*
trust *(89)*
urgency *(90)*
vishing *(92)*
whaling *(93)*

Key Terms Quiz

Use terms from the Key Terms list to complete the sentences that follow. Don't use the same term more than once. Not all terms will be used.

1. A(n) _______________ is an avenue that can be used to access a system while circumventing normal security mechanisms.
2. _______________ is a procedure in which attackers position themselves in such a way as to be able to observe an authorized user entering the correct access code.
3. The process of going through a target's trash searching for information that can be used in an attack, or to gain knowledge about a system or network, is known as _______________.
4. _______________ is the simple tactic of following closely behind a person who has just used their access card or PIN to gain physical access to a room or building.
5. In _______________, the attacker hopes to convince the target to initiate contact.
6. _______________ is a variation of _______________ that uses voice communication technology to obtain the information the attacker is seeking.
7. Social engineers will use psychological tools to mislead users into trusting them. Examples of these techniques include _____________, ____________, and __________.

Multiple-Choice Quiz

1. Which of the following is considered a good practice for password security?
   - **A.** Using a combination of upper- and lowercase characters, a number, and a special character in the password itself.
   - **B.** Not writing the password down.
   - **C.** Changing the password on a regular basis.
   - **D.** All of the above.
2. The password dilemma refers to which fact?
   - **A.** Passwords that are easy for users to remember are also easy for attackers to guess.
   - **B.** The more difficult we make it for attackers to guess our passwords, and the more frequently we force password changes, the more difficult the passwords are for authorized users to remember and the more likely they are to write them down.
   - **C.** Users will invariably attempt to select passwords that are words they can remember. This means they may select things closely associated with them, such as their spouse's or child's name, a beloved sports team, or a favorite model of car.
   - **D.** Passwords assigned by administrators are usually better and more secure, but are often harder for users to remember.
3. The simple tactic of following closely behind a person who has just used their own access card or PIN to gain physical access to a room or building is called what?
   - **A.** Shoulder surfing
   - **B.** Tagging-along
   - **C.** Piggybacking
   - **D.** Access drafting
4. The process of going through a target's trash in hopes of finding valuable information that might be used in a penetration attempt is known as what?
   - **A.** Dumpster diving
   - **B.** Trash trolling
   - **C.** Garbage gathering
   - **D.** Refuse rolling
5. Which of the following is a type of social engineering attack in which an attacker attempts to obtain sensitive information from a user by masquerading as a trusted entity in an e-mail?
   - **A.** Spam
   - **B.** SPIM
   - **C.** Phishing
   - **D.** Vishing
6. Reverse social engineering involves which of the following?
   - **A.** Contacting the target, eliciting some sensitive information, and convincing them that nothing out of the ordinary has occurred
   - **B.** Contacting the target in an attempt to obtain information that can be used in a second attempt with a different individual
   - **C.** An individual lower in the chain of command convincing somebody at a higher level to divulge information that the attacker is not authorized to have
   - **D.** An attacker attempting to somehow convince the target to initiate contact in order to avoid questions about authenticity

7. Which of the following is a reason for not allowing users to install new hardware or software without the knowledge of security administrators?
   A. They might not complete the installation correctly, and the administrator will have to do more work, taking them away from more important security tasks.
   B. They might inadvertently install more than just the hardware or software; they could accidentally install a backdoor into the network.
   C. They may not have paid for it and thus could be exposing the organization to civil penalties.
   D. Unauthorized hardware and software are usually for leisure purposes and will distract employees from the job they were hired to perform.
8. Once an organization's security policies have been established, what is the single most effective method of countering potential social engineering attacks?
   A. An active security awareness program
   B. A separate physical access control mechanism for each department in the organization
   C. Frequent testing of both the organization's physical security procedures and employee telephone practices
   D. Implementing access control cards and wearing security identification badges
9. Which of the following types of attacks utilizes instant messaging services?
   A. Spam
   B. SPIM
   C. Phishing
   D. Vishing
10. Which of the following are psychological tools used by social engineers to create false trust with users?
   A. Impersonation
   B. Familiarity
   C. Creating a sense of scarcity or urgency
   D. All of the above

Essay Quiz

1. Explain the difference between social engineering and reverse social engineering.
2. Discuss how a security-related hoax might become a security issue.
3. How might shoulder surfing be a threat in your school or work environment? What can be done to make this sort of activity more difficult?
4. For an environment familiar to you (such as work or school), describe the different non-employees who might have access to facilities that could contain sensitive information.
5. Describe some of the user security responsibilities you feel are most important for users to remember.

Lab Projects

• Lab Project 4.1

If possible, at either your place of employment or your school, attempt to determine how easy it would be to perform dumpster diving to gain access to information at the site. Are trash receptacles easy to gain access to? Are documents shredded before being discarded? Are areas where trash is stored easily accessible?

• Lab Project 4.2

Perform a search on the Web for articles and stories about social engineering attacks or reverse social engineering attacks. Choose and read five or six articles. How many of the attacks were successful? How many failed and why? How could those that may have initially succeeded been prevented?

• Lab Project 4.3

Similar to Lab Project 4.2, perform a search on the Web for articles and stories about phishing attacks. Choose and read five or six articles. How many of the attacks were successful? How many failed and why? How might the successful attacks have been mitigated or successfully accomplished?

chapter 5

Cryptography

If you are designing cryptosystems, you've got to think about long-term applications. You've got to try to figure out how to build something that is secure against technology in the next century that you cannot even imagine.

—Whitfield Diffie

In this chapter, you will learn how to

- **Understand the fundamentals of cryptography**
- **Identify and describe the three types of cryptography**
- **List and describe current cryptographic algorithms**
- **Explain how cryptography is applied for security**

Cryptography is the science of *encrypting*, or hiding, information—something people have sought to do since they began using language. Although language allowed people to communicate with one another, those in power attempted to hide information by controlling who was taught to read and write. Eventually, more complicated methods of concealing information by shifting letters around to make the text unreadable were developed. These complicated methods are cryptographic algorithms, also known as *ciphers*. The word *cipher* comes from the Arabic word *sifr*, meaning empty or zero.

When material, called plaintext, needs to be protected from unauthorized interception or alteration, it is encrypted into ciphertext. This is done using an algorithm and a key, and the rise of digital computers has provided a wide array of algorithms and increasingly complex keys. The choice of a specific algorithm depends on several factors, which will be examined in this chapter.

Cryptanalysis, the process of analyzing available information in an attempt to return the encrypted message to its original form, required advances in computer technology for complex encryption methods. The birth of the computer made it possible to easily execute the calculations required by more complex encryption algorithms. Today, the computer almost exclusively powers how encryption is performed. Computer technology has also aided cryptanalysis, allowing new methods to be developed, such as linear and differential cryptanalysis. **Differential cryptanalysis** is done by comparing the input plaintext to the output ciphertext to try and determine the key used to encrypt the information. **Linear cryptanalysis** is similar in that it uses both plaintext and ciphertext, but it puts the plaintext through a simplified cipher to try and deduce what the key is likely to be in the full version of the cipher.

Cryptography in Practice

Although cryptography may be a science, it performs critical functions in the enabling of trust across computer networks both in business and at home. Before we dig deep into the technical nature of cryptographic practices, an overview of current capabilities is useful. Examining cryptography from a high level reveals several relevant points today.

Cryptography has been a long-running event of advances both on the side of cryptography and the side of breaking it via analysis. With the advent of digital cryptography, the advantage has clearly swung to the side of cryptography. Modern computers have also increased the need for, and lowered the cost of, employing cryptography to secure information. In the past, the effectiveness rested in the secrecy of the algorithm, but with modern digital cryptography, the strength is based on sheer complexity. The power of networks and modern algorithms has also been employed in automatic key management.

Cryptography has many uses besides just enabling confidentiality in communication channels. Cryptographic functions are used in a wide range of applications, including, but not limited to, hiding data, resisting forgery, resisting unauthorized change, resisting repudiation, enforcing policy, and exchanging keys. In spite of the strengths of modern cryptography, it still fails due to other issues; known plaintext attacks, poorly protected keys, and repeated passphrases are examples of how strong cryptography is rendered weak via implementation mistakes.

Modern cryptographic algorithms are far stronger than needed given the state of cryptanalysis. The weaknesses in cryptosystems come from the system surrounding the algorithm, implementation, and operationalization details. Adi Shamir—the *S* in RSA—states it clearly: "Attackers do not break crypto; they bypass it."

Over time, weaknesses and errors, as well as shortcuts, are found in algorithms. When an algorithm is reported as "broken," the term can have many meanings. It could mean that the algorithm is of no further use, or it could mean that it has weaknesses that may someday be employed to break it, or anything between these extremes. As all methods can be broken with brute force, one question is how much effort is required, and at what cost, when compared to the value of the asset under protection.

Cryptography is much more than encryption. Cryptographic methods enable data protection, data hiding, integrity checks, nonrepudiation services, policy enforcement, key management and exchange, and many more elements used in modern computing. If you used the Web today, odds are you used cryptography without even knowing it.

When you're examining the strength of a cryptosystem, it is worth examining the following types of levels of protection:

1. The mechanism is no longer useful for any purpose.
2. The cost of recovering the clear text without benefit of the key has fallen to a low level.
3. The cost has fallen to equal to or less than the value of the data or the next least-cost attack.
4. The cost has fallen to within several orders of magnitudes of the cost of encryption or the value of the data.
5. The elapsed time of attack has fallen to within magnitudes of the life of the data, regardless of the cost thereof.
6. The cost has fallen to less than the cost of a brute force attack against the key.
7. Someone has recovered one key or one message.

This list of conditions shows the risks/benefits in descending order, where conditions 6 and 7 are regular occurrences in cryptographic systems and are generally not worth worrying about at all. In fact, it is not until the fourth condition that one has to have real concerns. With all this said, most organizations consider replacement between conditions 5 and 6. If any of the first three are positive, the organization seriously needs to consider changing its cryptographic methods.

Fundamental Methods

Modern cryptographic operations are performed using both an algorithm and a key. The choice of algorithm depends on the type of cryptographic operation that is desired. The subsequent choice of key is then tied to the specific algorithm. Cryptographic operations include encryption (for the protection of confidentiality), hashing (for the protection of integrity), digital signatures (to manage nonrepudiation), and a bevy of specialty operations such as key exchanges.

The methods used to encrypt information are based on two separate operations: substitution and transposition. **Substitution** is the replacement of an item with a different item. **Transposition** is the changing of the order of items. Pig Latin, a child's cipher, employs both operations in simplistic form and is thus easy to decipher. These operations can be done on words, characters, and, in the digital world, bits. What makes a system secure is the complexity of the changes employed. To make a system reversible (so you can reliably decrypt it), there needs to be a basis for the pattern of changes. Historical ciphers used relatively simple patterns, and ones that required significant knowledge (at the time) to break.

Assurance is a specific term in security that means that something is not only true but can be proven to be so to some specific level of certainty.

Modern cryptography is built around complex mathematical functions. These functions have specific properties that make them resistant to reversing or solving by means other than the application of the algorithm and key.

While the mathematical specifics of these operations can be very complex and are beyond the scope of this level of material, the knowledge to properly employ them is not. Cryptographic operations are characterized by the quantity and type of data as well as the level and type of protection sought. Integrity protection operations are characterized by the level of assurance desired. Data can be characterized by its state: data in transit, data at rest, or data in use. It is also characterized in how it is used, either in block form or stream form.

Comparative Strengths and Performance of Algorithms

Several factors play a role in determining the strength of a cryptographic algorithm. First and most obvious is the size of the key and the resulting keyspace. The **keyspace** is defined as a set of possible key values. One method of attack is to simply try all the possible keys in a brute force attack. The other factor is referred to as *work factor,* which is a subjective measurement of the time and effort needed to perform operations. If the work factor is low, then the rate at which keys can be tested is high, meaning that larger keyspaces are needed. Work factor also plays a role in protecting systems such as password hashes, where having a higher work factor can be part of the security mechanism.

A larger keyspace allows the use of keys of greater complexity, and thus more security, assuming the algorithm is well designed. It is easy to see how key complexity affects an algorithm when you look at some of the encryption algorithms that have been broken. The Data Encryption Standard (DES) uses a 56-bit key, allowing 72,000,000,000,000,000 possible values, but it has been broken by modern computers. The modern implementation of DES, Triple DES (3DES), uses three 56-bit keys, for a total key length of 168 bits (although for technical reasons the effective key length is 112 bits), or 340,000,000,000,000,000,000,000,000,000,000,000,000 possible values.

When an algorithm lists a certain number of bits as a key, it is defining the keyspace. Some algorithms have key lengths of 8192 bits or more, resulting in very large keyspaces, even by digital computer standards.

Modern computers have also challenged work factor elements, as algorithms can be rendered very quickly by specialized hardware such as high-end graphic chips. To defeat this, many algorithms have repeated cycles to add to the work and reduce the ability to parallelize operations inside processor chips. This is done to increase the inefficiency of a calculation, but in a manner that still results in suitable performance when given the key and still complicates matters when done in a brute force manner with all keys.

> **Tech Tip**
>
> **Keyspace Comparisons**
>
> *Because the keyspace is a numeric value, it is very important to ensure that comparisons are done using similar key types. Comparing a key made of 1 bit (two possible values) and a key made of 1 letter (26 possible values) would not yield accurate results. Fortunately, the widespread use of computers has made almost all algorithms state their keyspace values in terms of bits.*

Key Length

The strength of a cryptographic function typically depends on the strength of a key—a larger key has more entropy and adds more strength to an encryption. Because different algorithms use different methods with a key, direct comparison of key strength between different algorithms is not easily done. Some cryptographic systems have fixed key lengths, such as 3DES, while others, such as AES, have multiple lengths (for example, AES-128, AES-192, and AES-256).

Some algorithms have choices, and as a general rule longer is more secure, but also will take longer to compute. With regard to the tradeoff of security versus usability, there are some recommended minimum key lengths:

- Symmetric key lengths of at least 80–112 bits.
- Elliptic curve key lengths of at least 160–224 bits.
- RSA key lengths of at least 2048 bits. In particular, the CA/Browser Forum Extended Validation (EV) Guidelines require a minimum key length of 2048 bits.
- DSA key lengths of at least 2048 bits.

Cryptographic Objectives

Cryptographic methods exist for a purpose: to protect the integrity and confidentiality of data. There are many associated elements with this protection to enable a system-wide solution. Elements such as perfect forward secrecy, nonrepudiation, and others enable successful cryptographic implementations.

Diffusion

Diffusion is the principle that the statistical analysis of plaintext and ciphertext results in a form of dispersion rendering one structurally independent of the other. In plain terms, a change in one character of plaintext should result in multiple changes in the ciphertext in a manner that changes in ciphertext do not reveal information as to the structure of the plaintext.

Confusion

Confusion is a principle that affects the randomness of an output. The concept is operationalized by ensuring that each character of ciphertext depends on several parts of the key. Confusion places a constraint on the relationship between the ciphertext and the key employed, forcing an effect that increases entropy.

Obfuscation

Obfuscation is the masking of an item to render it unreadable, yet still usable. Take a source code example: if the source code is written in a manner that it is easily understood, then its functions can be easily recognized and copied. Code obfuscation is the process of making the code unreadable because of the complexity invoked at the time of creation. This "mangling" of code makes it impossible to easily understand, copy, fix, or maintain. Using cryptographic functions to obfuscate materials is more secure in that it is not reversible without the secret element, but this also renders the code unusable until it is decoded.

Program obfuscation can be achieved in many forms, from tangled C functions with recursion and other indirect references that make reverse engineering difficult, to proper encryption of secret elements. Storing secret elements directly in source code does not really obfuscate them because numerous methods can be used to find hard-coded secrets in code. Proper obfuscation requires the use of cryptographic functions against a nonreversible element. An example is the storing of password hashes—if the original password is hashed with the addition of a salt, reversing the stored hash is practically not feasible, making the key information, the password, obfuscated.

Perfect Forward Secrecy

Perfect forward secrecy (PFS) is a property of a public key system in which a key derived from another key is not compromised even if the originating key is compromised in the future. This is especially important in session key generation, where the compromise of future communication sessions may become compromised; if perfect forward secrecy were not in place, then past messages that had been recorded could be decrypted.

> Perfect forward secrecy gives assurance that session keys will not be compromised.

Security Through Obscurity

Security via **obscurity** alone has never been a valid method of protecting secrets. This has been known for centuries. However, this does not mean obscurity has no role in security. Naming servers after a progressive set of objects, like Greek gods, planets, and so on, provides an attacker an easier path once they start obtaining names. Obscurity has a role, making it hard for an attacker to easily guess critical pieces of information, but it should not be relied upon as a singular method of protection.

Historical Perspectives

Cryptography is as old as secrets. Humans have been designing secret communication systems for as long they've needed to keep communication private. The Spartans of ancient Greece would write on a ribbon wrapped around a cylinder with a specific diameter (called a *scytale*). When the ribbon was unwrapped, it revealed a strange string of letters. The message could be read only when the ribbon was wrapped around a cylinder of the same diameter. This is an example of a **transposition cipher**, where the same letters are used but the order is changed. In all these cipher systems, the unencrypted input text is known as **plaintext** and the encrypted output is known as **ciphertext**.

Algorithms

Every current encryption scheme is based on an **algorithm**, a step-by-step, recursive computational procedure for solving a problem in a finite number of steps. A cryptographic algorithm—what is commonly called an *encryption algorithm* or *cipher*—is made up of mathematical steps for encrypting and decrypting information. The following illustration shows a diagram of the encryption and decryption process and its parts. Three types of encryption algorithms are commonly used: hashing, symmetric, and asymmetric. Hashing is a very special type of encryption algorithm that takes an input and mathematically reduces it to a unique number known as a *hash*, which

> **Tech Tip**
>
> **XOR**
>
> *A popular function in cryptography is* **eXclusive OR (XOR)***, which is a bitwise function applied to data. The XOR function is the key element of most stream ciphers, as it is the operation between the key and the data resulting in the stream cipher. When you apply a key to data using XOR, then a second application undoes the first operation. This makes for speedy encryption/decryption but also makes the system totally dependent on the secrecy of the key.*

is not reversible. Symmetric algorithms are also known as *shared secret algorithms,* as the same key is used for encryption and decryption. Finally, asymmetric algorithms use a very different process by employing two keys, a public key and a private key, making up what is known as a *key pair.*

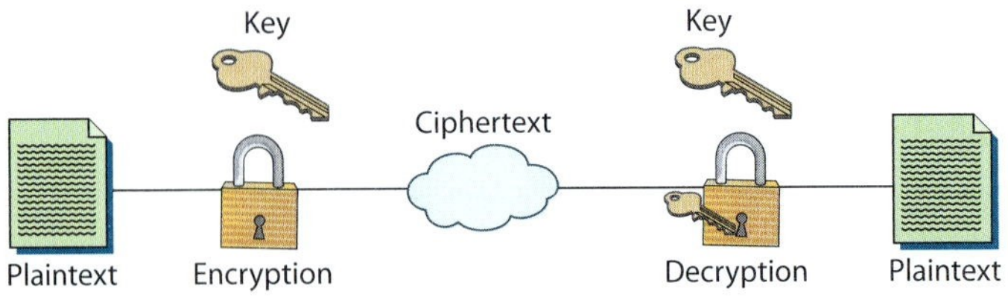

A **key** is a special piece of data used in both the encryption and decryption processes. The algorithms stay the same in every implementation, but a different key is used for each, which ensures that even if someone knows the algorithm you use to protect your data, they cannot break your security. The key in cryptography is analogous to a key in a common door lock, as shown in Figure 5.1.

Comparing the strength of two different algorithms can be mathematically very challenging; fortunately for the layperson, there is a rough guide. Most current algorithms are listed with their key size in bits, e.g., AES256. Unless a specific algorithm has been shown to be flawed, in general, the greater number of bits will yield a more secure system. This works well for a given algorithm but is meaningless for comparing different algorithms. The good news is that most modern cryptography is more than strong enough for all but technical uses, and for those uses experts can determine appropriate algorithms and key lengths to provide the necessary protections.

Substitution Ciphers

The Romans typically used a different method known as a **shift cipher**. In this case, one letter of the alphabet is shifted a set number of places in the alphabet for another letter. A common modern-day example of this is the ROT13 cipher, in which every letter is rotated 13 positions in the alphabet: *n* is written instead of *a*, *o* instead of *b*, and so on. These types of ciphers are commonly encoded on an alphabet wheel, as shown in Figure 5.2.

• **Figure 5.1** While everyone knows how to use a knob to open a door, without the key to unlock the deadbolt, that knowledge is useless.

• **Figure 5.2** Any shift cipher can easily be encoded and decoded on a wheel of two pieces of paper with the alphabet set as a ring; by moving one circle the specified number in the shift, you can translate the characters.

These ciphers were simple to use and also simple to break. Because hiding information was still important, more advanced transposition and substitution ciphers were required. As systems and technology became more complex, ciphers were frequently automated by some mechanical or electromechanical device. A famous example of a relatively modern encryption machine is the German Enigma machine from World War II (see Figure 5.3). This machine used a complex series of substitutions to perform encryption, and, interestingly enough, it gave rise to extensive research in computers.

Caesar's cipher uses an algorithm and a key: the algorithm specifies that you offset the alphabet either to the right (forward) or to the left (backward), and the key specifies how many letters the offset should be. For example, if the algorithm specifies offsetting the alphabet to the right, and the key is 3, the cipher substitutes an alphabetic letter three to the right for the real letter, so *d* is used to represent *a*, *f* represents *c*, and so on. In this example, both the algorithm and key are simple, allowing for easy cryptanalysis of the cipher and easy recovery of the plaintext message.

• **Figure 5.3** One of the surviving German Enigma machines

Try This!

ROT13

ROT13 is a special case of a Caesar substitution cipher where each character is replaced by a character 13 places later in the alphabet. Because the basic Latin alphabet has 26 letters, ROT13 has the property of undoing itself when applied twice. The illustration demonstrates ROT13 encoding of "HelloWorld." The top two rows show encoding, while the bottom two show decoding replacement.

	A	B	C	D	E	F	G	H	I	J	K	L	M	N	O	P	Q	R	S	T	U	V	W	X	Y	Z
Shift 13	N	O	P	Q	R	S	T	U	V	W	X	Y	Z	A	B	C	D	E	F	G	H	I	J	K	L	M
	A	B	C	D	E	F	G	H	I	J	K	L	M	N	O	P	Q	R	S	T	U	V	W	X	Y	Z

(Encode ↓ between the first two rows; Decode ↓ between the last two rows)

Plaintext H E L L O W O R L D

Encode ↓

Ciphertext U R Y Y B J B E Y Q

Decode ↓

Plaintext H E L L O W O R L D

The ease with which shift ciphers were broken led to the development of *substitution ciphers*, which were popular in Elizabethan England (roughly the second half of the 16th century) and more complex than shift ciphers. Substitution ciphers work on the principle of substituting a different letter for every letter: *a* becomes *g*, *b* becomes *d*, and so on. This system permits 26 possible values for every letter in the message, making the cipher many times more complex than a standard shift cipher. Simple analysis of the cipher could be performed to retrieve the key, however. By looking for common letters such as *e* and patterns found in words such as *ing*, you can determine which cipher letter corresponds to which plaintext letter. The

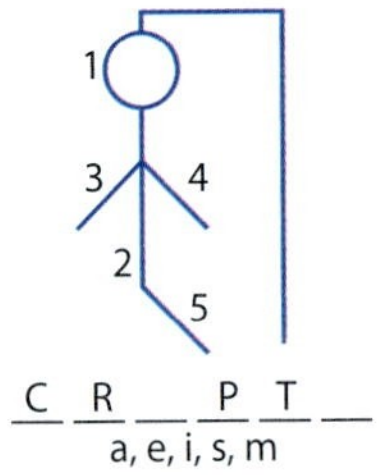

• **Figure 5.4** Making educated guesses is much like playing hangman—correct guesses can lead to more or all of the key being revealed.

examination of ciphertext for frequent letters is known as *frequency analysis*. Making educated guesses about words will eventually allow you to determine the system's key value (see Figure 5.4).

To correct this problem, more complexity had to be added to the system. The **Vigenère cipher** works as a *polyalphabetic substitution cipher* that depends on a password. This is done by setting up a substitution table like the one in Figure 5.5.

Then the password is matched up to the text it is meant to encipher. If the password is not long enough, the password is repeated until one character of the password is matched up with each character of the plaintext. For example, if the plaintext is *A Sample plaintext* and the password is *secretkey,* Figure 5.5 illustrates the encryption and decryption process.

The cipher letter is determined by use of the grid, matching the plaintext character's row with the password character's column, resulting in a single ciphertext character where the two meet. Consider the first letters, *A (from plaintext—rows)* and *S (from keystream—columns)*: when plugged into the grid they output a ciphertext character of *S*. This is shown in yellow on Figure 5.5. The second letter is highlighted in green, and the fourth letter in blue. This process is repeated for every letter of the message. Once the rest of the letters are processed, the output is SWCDTEOTJSMPKIQD.

In this example, the key in the encryption system is the password. The example also illustrates that an algorithm can be simple and still provide strong security. If someone knows about the table, they can determine

Plaintext \ Keystream	A	B	C	D	E	F	G	H	I	J	K	L	M	N	O	P	Q	R	S	T	U	V	W	X	Y	Z
A	A	B	C	D	E	F	G	H	I	J	K	L	M	N	O	P	Q	R	S	T	U	V	W	X	Y	Z
B	B	C	D	E	F	G	H	I	J	K	L	M	N	O	P	Q	R	S	T	U	V	W	X	Y	Z	A
C	C	D	E	F	G	H	I	J	K	L	M	N	O	P	Q	R	S	T	U	V	W	X	Y	Z	A	B
D	D	E	F	G	H	I	J	K	L	M	N	O	P	Q	R	S	T	U	V	W	X	Y	Z	A	B	C
E	E	F	G	H	I	J	K	L	M	N	O	P	Q	R	S	T	U	V	W	X	Y	Z	A	B	C	D
F	F	G	H	I	J	K	L	M	N	O	P	Q	R	S	T	U	V	W	X	Y	Z	A	B	C	D	E
G	G	H	I	J	K	L	M	N	O	P	Q	R	S	T	U	V	W	X	Y	Z	A	B	C	D	E	F
H	H	I	J	K	L	M	N	O	P	Q	R	S	T	U	V	W	X	Y	Z	A	B	C	D	E	F	G
I	I	J	K	L	M	N	O	P	Q	R	S	T	U	V	W	X	Y	Z	A	B	C	D	E	F	G	H
J	J	K	L	M	N	O	P	Q	R	S	T	U	V	W	X	Y	Z	A	B	C	D	E	F	G	H	I
K	K	L	M	N	O	P	Q	R	S	T	U	V	W	X	Y	Z	A	B	C	D	E	F	G	H	I	J
L	L	M	N	O	P	Q	R	S	T	U	V	W	X	Y	Z	A	B	C	D	E	F	G	H	I	J	K
M	M	N	O	P	Q	R	S	T	U	V	W	X	Y	Z	A	B	C	D	E	F	G	H	I	J	K	L
N	N	O	P	Q	R	S	T	U	V	W	X	Y	Z	A	B	C	D	E	F	G	H	I	J	K	L	M
O	O	P	Q	R	S	T	U	V	W	X	Y	Z	A	B	C	D	E	F	G	H	I	J	K	L	M	N
P	P	Q	R	S	T	U	V	W	X	Y	Z	A	B	C	D	E	F	G	H	I	J	K	L	M	N	O
Q	Q	R	S	T	U	V	W	X	Y	Z	A	B	C	D	E	F	G	H	I	J	K	L	M	N	O	P
R	R	S	T	U	V	W	X	Y	Z	A	B	C	D	E	F	G	H	I	J	K	L	M	N	O	P	Q
S	S	T	U	V	W	X	Y	Z	A	B	C	D	E	F	G	H	I	J	K	L	M	N	O	P	Q	R
T	T	U	V	W	X	Y	Z	A	B	C	D	E	F	G	H	I	J	K	L	M	N	O	P	Q	R	S
U	U	V	W	X	Y	Z	A	B	C	D	E	F	G	H	I	J	K	L	M	N	O	P	Q	R	S	T
V	V	W	X	Y	Z	A	B	C	D	E	F	G	H	I	J	K	L	M	N	O	P	Q	R	S	T	U
W	W	X	Y	Z	A	B	C	D	E	F	G	H	I	J	K	L	M	N	O	P	Q	R	S	T	U	V
X	X	Y	Z	A	B	C	D	E	F	G	H	I	J	K	L	M	N	O	P	Q	R	S	T	U	V	W
Y	Y	Z	A	B	C	D	E	F	G	H	I	J	K	L	M	N	O	P	Q	R	S	T	U	V	W	X
Z	Z	A	B	C	D	E	F	G	H	I	J	K	L	M	N	O	P	Q	R	S	T	U	V	W	X	Y

Plaintext	a	s	a	m	p	l	e	p	l	a	i	n	t	e	x	t
Keystream	s	e	c	r	e	t	k	e	y	s	e	c	r	e	t	k
CIPHERTEXT	S	W	C	D	T	E	O	T	J	S	M	P	K	I	Q	D

• **Figure 5.5** Polyalphabetic substitution cipher

how the encryption was performed, but they still will not know the key to decrypting the message. This example also shows what happens with a bad password—that is, one with a lot of common letters, such as A, as this would reveal a lot of the message. Try using the grid and the keystream "AB" and see what happens.

Try This!

Vigenère Cipher

Make a simple message that's about two sentences long and then choose two passwords: one that's short and one that's long. Then, using the substitution table presented in this section, perform simple encryption on the message. Compare the two ciphertexts; since you have the plaintext and the ciphertext, you should be able to see a pattern of matching characters. Knowing the algorithm used, see if you can determine the key used to encrypt the message.

The more complex the key, the greater the security of the system. The Vigenère cipher system and systems like it make the algorithms rather simple but the key rather complex, with the best keys comprising very long and very random data. Key complexity is achieved by giving the key a large number of possible values.

Atbash Cipher

The Atbash cipher is a specific form of a monoalphabetic substitution cipher. The cipher is formed by taking the characters of the alphabet and mapping to them in reverse order. The first letter becomes the last letter, the second letter becomes the second-to-last letter, and so on. Historically, the Atbash cipher traces back to the time of the Bible and the Hebrew language. Because of its simple form, it can be used with any language or character set. Figure 5.6 shows an Atbash cipher for the standard ASCII character set of letters.

> One-time pads are examples of perfect ciphers from a mathematical point of view. But when put into practice, the implementation creates weaknesses that result in less-than-perfect security. This is an important reminder that perfect ciphers from a mathematical point of view do not create perfect security in practice because of the limitations associated with the implementation.

One-Time Pads

One-time pads are an interesting form of encryption in that they theoretically are perfect and unbreakable. The key is the same size or larger than the material being encrypted. The plaintext is XORed against the key producing the ciphertext. What makes the one-time pad "perfect" is the size of the key. If you use a keyspace full of keys, you will decrypt every possible message of the same length as the original, with no way to discriminate which one is correct. This makes a one-time pad unable to be broken by even brute force methods, provided that the key is not reused. This makes a one-time pad less than practical for any mass use.

Plaintext	A	B	C	D	E	F	G	H	I	J	K	L	M	N	O	P	Q	R	S	T	U	V	W	X	Y	Z
Ciphertext	Z	Y	X	W	V	U	T	S	R	Q	P	O	N	M	L	K	J	I	H	G	F	E	D	C	B	A

• **Figure 5.6** Atbash cipher

Key Management

Because the security of the algorithms relies on the key, **key management** is of critical concern. Key management includes anything having to do with the exchange, storage, safeguarding, and revocation of keys. It is most commonly associated with asymmetric encryption because asymmetric encryption uses both public and private keys. To be used properly for authentication, a key must be current and verified. If you have an old or compromised key, you need a way to check to see that the key has been revoked.

Key management is also important for symmetric encryption, because symmetric encryption relies on both parties having the same key for the algorithm to work. Since these parties are usually physically separate, key management is critical to ensure keys are shared and exchanged easily. They must also be securely stored to provide appropriate confidentiality of the encrypted information. There are many different approaches to the secure storage of keys, such as putting them on a USB flash drive or smart card. While keys can be stored in many different ways, new PC hardware often includes the Trusted Platform Module (TPM), which provides a hardware-based key storage location that is used by many applications. (More specific information about the management of keys is provided later in this chapter and in Chapters 6 and 7.)

> **Tech Tip**
>
> **Randomness Issues**
>
> *The importance of proper random number generation in cryptosystems cannot be underestimated. Recent reports by the* Guardian *and the* New York Times *assert that the U.S. National Security Agency (NSA) has put a backdoor into the Cryptographically Secure Random Number Generator (CSPRNG) algorithms described in NIST SP 800-90A, particularly the Dual_EC_DRBG algorithm. Further allegations are that the NSA paid RSA $10 million to use the resulting standard in its product line.*

Random Numbers

Many digital cryptographic algorithms have a need for a random number to act as a seed and provide true randomness. One of the strengths of computers is that they can do a task over and over again in the exact same manner—no noise or randomness. This is great for most tasks, but in generating a random sequence of values, it presents challenges. Software libraries have pseudo-random number generators—functions that produce a series of numbers that statistically appear random. But these random number generators are deterministic in that, given the sequence, you can calculate future values. This makes them inappropriate for use in cryptographic situations.

> The level or amount of randomness is referred to as entropy.

The level or amount of randomness is referred to as **entropy**. Entropy is the measure of uncertainty associated with a series of values. Perfect entropy equates to complete randomness, such that given any string of bits, there is no computation to improve guessing the next bit in the sequence. A simple "measure" of entropy is in bits, where the bits are the power of 2 that represents the number of choices. So if there are 2048 options, then this would represent 11 bits of entropy. In this fashion, one can calculate the entropy of passwords and measure how "hard they are to guess."

To resolve the problem of appropriate randomness, there are systems to create cryptographic random numbers. The level of complexity of the system is dependent on the level of pure randomness needed. For some functions, such as master keys, the only true solution is a hardware-based random number generator that can use physical properties to derive entropy. In other, less demanding cases, a cryptographic library call can provide the necessary entropy. While the theoretical strength of the cryptosystem depends on the algorithm, the strength of the implementation in practice can depend on issues such as the key. This is a very important issue, and mistakes made in implementation can invalidate even the strongest algorithms in practice.

Salting

To provide sufficient entry for low entropy inputs to hash functions, the addition of a high entropy piece of data concatenated with the material being hashed can be used. The term *salt* refers to this initial data piece. Salts are particularly useful when the material being hashed is short and low in entropy. The addition of a high entropy (say, a 30-character) salt to a 3-character password greatly increases the entropy of the stored hash.

Another term used in this regard is *initialization vector,* or *IV,* and this is used in several ciphers, particularly in the wireless space, to achieve randomness even with normally deterministic inputs. IVs can add randomness and are used in block ciphers to initiate modes of operation.

A *nonce* is a number used only once, and is similar to a salt, or an IV, but it is only used once, and if needed again, a different value is used. Nonces provide random, nondeterministic entropy to cryptographic functions and are commonly used in stream ciphers to break stateful properties when the key is reused.

Tech Tip

Salts and Password Hashes

Passwords are stored in the form of a hash, making them unrecoverable, but exposing a separate problem: if multiple users have the same hash, then their passwords are the same. A salt adds additional entropy, or randomness, to the encryption key, specifically providing separation between equal inputs such as identical passwords on different accounts.

Hashing Functions

Hashing functions are commonly used encryption methods. A *hashing function* or *hash function* is a special mathematical function that performs a *one-way function,* which means that once the algorithm is processed, there is no feasible way to use the ciphertext to retrieve the plaintext that was used to generate it. Also, ideally, there is no feasible way to generate two different plaintexts that compute to the same **hash** value. The hash value is the output of the hashing algorithm for a specific input. The following illustration shows the one-way nature of these functions:

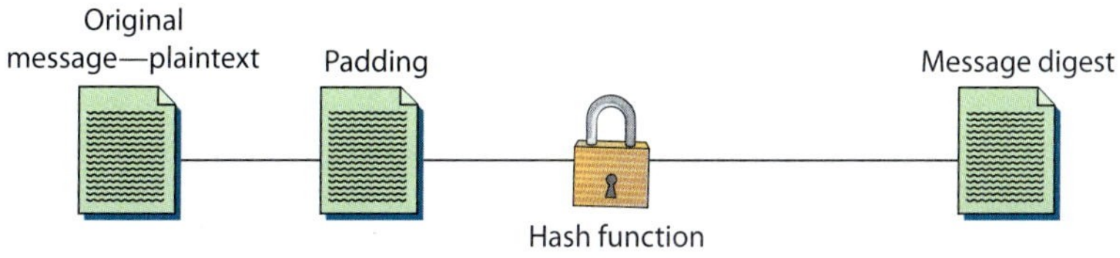

Common uses of hashing algorithms are to store computer passwords and to ensure message integrity. The idea is that hashing can produce a unique value that corresponds to the data entered, but the hash value is also reproducible by anyone else running the same algorithm against the same data. So you could hash a message to get a message authentication code (MAC), and the computational number of the message would show that no intermediary has modified the message. This process works because hashing algorithms are typically public, and anyone can hash data using the specified algorithm. It is computationally simple to generate the hash, so it is simple to check the validity or integrity of something by matching the given hash to one that is locally generated. Several programs can compute hash values for an input file, as shown in Figure 5.7. Hash-based message authentication code (HMAC) is a special subset of hashing technology. It is a hash algorithm applied to a message to make a MAC, but it is done with a previously shared secret. So the HMAC can provide integrity simultaneously with authentication. HMAC-MD5 is used in the NT LAN Manager version 2 challenge/response protocol.

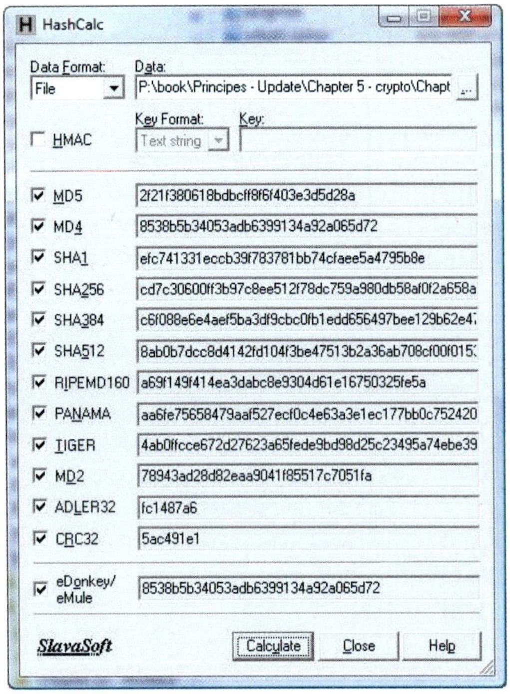

• **Figure 5.7** Several programs are available that accept an input and produce a hash value, letting you independently verify the integrity of downloaded content.

A hash algorithm can be compromised with what is called a **collision attack**, in which an attacker finds two different messages that hash to the same value. This type of attack is very difficult and requires generating a separate algorithm that attempts to find a text that will hash to the same value of a known hash. This must occur faster than simply editing characters until you hash to the same value, which is a brute force type of attack. The consequence of a hash function that suffers from collisions is a loss of integrity. If an attacker can make two different inputs purposefully hash to the same value, they might trick people into running malicious code and cause other problems. Popular hash algorithms are the Secure Hash Algorithm (SHA) series, ChaCha20, the RIPEMD algorithms, and the Message Digest (MD) hash of varying versions (MD2, MD4, and MD5). Because of weaknesses and collision attack vulnerabilities, many hash functions are now considered to be insecure, including MD2, MD4, and MD5 as well as the SHA series shorter than 384 bits.

Hashing functions are very common and play an important role in the way information, such as passwords, is stored securely and the way in which messages can be signed. By computing a digest of the message, less data needs to be signed by the more complex asymmetric encryption, and this still maintains assurances about message integrity. This is the primary purpose for which the protocols were designed, and their success will allow greater trust in electronic protocols and digital signatures.

Tech Tip

Why Hashes and Not CRC-32?

CRC-32 is a 32-bit error detection algorithm. You can use it to determine small errors during transmission of small items. However, cyclic redundancy checks (CRCs) can be tricked; by modifying any four consecutive bytes in a file, you can change the file's CRC to any value you choose. This technique demonstrates that the CRC-32 function is extremely malleable and unsuitable for protecting a file from intentional modifications.

Tech Tip

Warning on Deprecated Hashing Algorithms

The hashing algorithms in common use are MD2, MD4, and MD5 as well as SHA-1, SHA-256, SHA-384, SHA-512, and SHA-3. Because of potential collisions, MD2, MD4, and MD5, as well as SHA-1 and SHA-256, have been deprecated by many groups; although not considered secure, they are still found in use—a testament to the slow adoption of better security. Going forward, only SHA-384, SHA-512, and SHA-3 should be used.

Message Digest

Message Digest (MD) is the generic version of one of several algorithms designed to create a message digest or hash from data input into the algorithm. MD algorithms work in the same manner as SHA in that they use a secure method to compress the file and generate a computed output of a specified number of bits. The MD algorithms were all developed by Ronald L. Rivest of MIT.

MD2

MD2 was developed in 1989 and is in some ways an early version of the later MD5 algorithm. It takes a data input of any length and produces a hash output of 128 bits. It is different from MD4 and MD5 in that MD2 is optimized for 8-bit machines, whereas the other two are optimized for 32-bit machines.

MD4

MD4 was developed in 1990 and is optimized for 32-bit computers. It is a fast algorithm, but it is subject to more attacks than more secure algorithms such as MD5. An extended version of MD4 computes the message in parallel and produces two 128-bit outputs—effectively a 256-bit hash.

MD5

MD5 creates a 128-bit hash of a message of any length.

MD5 was developed in 1991 and is structured after MD4, but with additional security to overcome the problems in MD4. Therefore, it is very similar to the MD4 algorithm, only slightly slower and more secure.

Czech cryptographer Vlastimil Klíma published work showing that MD5 collisions can be computed in about eight hours on a standard home PC. In November 2007, researchers published results showing the ability to have two entirely different Win32 executables with different functionality but the same MD5 hash. This discovery has obvious implications for the development of malware. The combination of these problems with MD5 has pushed people to adopt a strong SHA version for security reasons.

SHA

Secure Hash Algorithm (SHA) refers to a set of hash algorithms designed and published by the National Institute of Standards and Technology (NIST) and the National Security Agency (NSA). These algorithms are included in the SHA standard Federal Information Processing Standards (FIPS) 180-2 and 180-3. The individual standards are named SHA-1, SHA-224, SHA-256, SHA-384, and SHA-512. The latter three variants are occasionally referred to collectively as SHA-2. The newest version is known as SHA-3, which is specified in FIPS 202.

Tech Tip

Block Mode in Hashing

Most hash algorithms use block mode to process; that is, they process all input in set blocks of data such as 512-bit blocks. The final hash is typically generated by adding the output blocks together to form the final output string of 160 or 512 bits.

SHA-1

SHA-1, developed in 1993, was designed as the algorithm to be used for secure hashing in the U.S. Digital Signature Standard (DSS). It is modeled on the MD4 algorithm and implements fixes in that algorithm discovered by the NSA. It creates message digests 160 bits long that can be used by the Digital Signature Algorithm (DSA), which can then compute the signature of the message. This is computationally simpler, as the message digest is typically much smaller than the actual message—smaller message, less work.

SHA-1 works, as do all hashing functions, by applying a compression function to the data input. It accepts an input of up to 2^{64} bits or less and then compresses down to a hash of 160 bits. SHA-1 works in block mode, separating the data into words first, and then grouping the words into blocks. The words are 32-bit strings converted to hex; grouped together as

Try to keep attacks on cryptosystems in perspective. While the theory of attacking hashing through collisions is solid, finding a collision still takes enormous amounts of effort. In the case of attacking SHA-1, the collision is able to be found faster than a pure brute force method, but by most estimates will still take several years.

16 words, they make up a 512-bit block. If the data that is input to SHA-1 is not a multiple of 512, the message is padded with zeros and an integer describing the original length of the message. Once the message has been formatted for processing, the actual hash can be generated. The 512-bit blocks are taken in order until the entire message has been processed.

At one time, SHA-1 was one of the more secure hash functions, but it has been found to be vulnerable to a collision attack. The longer versions (SHA-256, SHA-384, and SHA-512) all have longer hash results, making them more difficult to attack successfully. The added security and resistance to attack in SHA-2 does require more processing power to compute the hash.

SHA-2

SHA-2 is a collective name for SHA-224, SHA-256, SHA-384, and SHA-512. SHA-256 is similar to SHA-1 in that it also accepts input of less than 2^{64} bits and reduces that input to a hash. This algorithm reduces to 256 bits instead of SHA-1's 160. Defined in FIPS 180-2 in 2002, SHA-256 is listed as an update to the original FIPS 180 that defined SHA. Similar to SHA-1, SHA-256 uses 32-bit words and 512-bit blocks. Padding is added until the entire message is a multiple of 512. SHA-256 uses sixty-four 32-bit words, eight working variables, and results in a hash value of eight 32-bit words, hence 256 bits. SHA-224 is a truncated version of the SHA-256 algorithm that results in a 224-bit hash value. There are no known collision attacks against SHA-256; however, an attack on reduced-round SHA-256 is possible.

SHA-512 is also similar to SHA-1, but it handles larger sets of data. SHA-512 accepts 2^{128} bits of input, which it pads until it has several blocks of data in 1024-bit blocks. SHA-512 also uses 64-bit words instead of SHA-1's 32-bit words. It uses eight 64-bit words to produce the 512-bit hash value. SHA-384 is a truncated version of SHA-512 that uses six 64-bit words to produce a 384-bit hash.

Although SHA-2 is not as common as SHA-1, more applications are starting to utilize it after SHA-1 was shown to be potentially vulnerable to a collision attack.

The SHA-2 and SHA-3 series are currently approved for use. SHA-1 has been deprecated and its use discontinued in many strong cipher suites.

SHA-3

SHA-3 is the name for the SHA-2 replacement. In 2012, the Keccak hash function won the NIST competition and was chosen as the basis for the SHA-3 method. Because the algorithm is completely different from the previous SHA series, it has proved to be more resistant to attacks that are successful against them. SHA-3 is not commonly used, but is approved in U.S. FIPS Pub 202.

RIPEMD

RACE Integrity Primitives Evaluation Message Digest (RIPEMD) is a hashing function developed by the RACE Integrity Primitives Evaluation (RIPE) consortium. It originally provided a 128-bit hash and was later shown to have problems with collisions. RIPEMD was strengthened to a 160-bit hash known as RIPEMD-160 by Hans Dobbertin, Antoon Bosselaers, and Bart

Preneel. There are also 256-and 320-bit versions of the algorithm known as RIPEMD-256 and RIPEMD-320.

RIPEMD-160

RIPEMD-160 is an algorithm based on MD4, but it uses two parallel channels with five rounds. The output consists of five 32-bit words to make a 160-bit hash. There are also larger output extensions of the RIPEMD-160 algorithm. These extensions, RIPEMD-256 and RIPEMD-320, offer outputs of 256 bits and 320 bits, respectively. While these offer larger output sizes, this does not make the hash function inherently stronger.

Hashing Summary

Hashing functions are very common, and they play an important role in the way information, such as passwords, is stored securely and the way in which messages can be signed. By computing a digest of the message, less data needs to be signed by the more complex asymmetric encryption, and this still maintains assurances about message integrity. This is the primary purpose for which the protocols were designed, and their success will allow greater trust in electronic protocols and digital signatures. The following illustration shows hash calculations in (a) Linux, (b) Windows 10, and (c) Microsoft PowerShell:

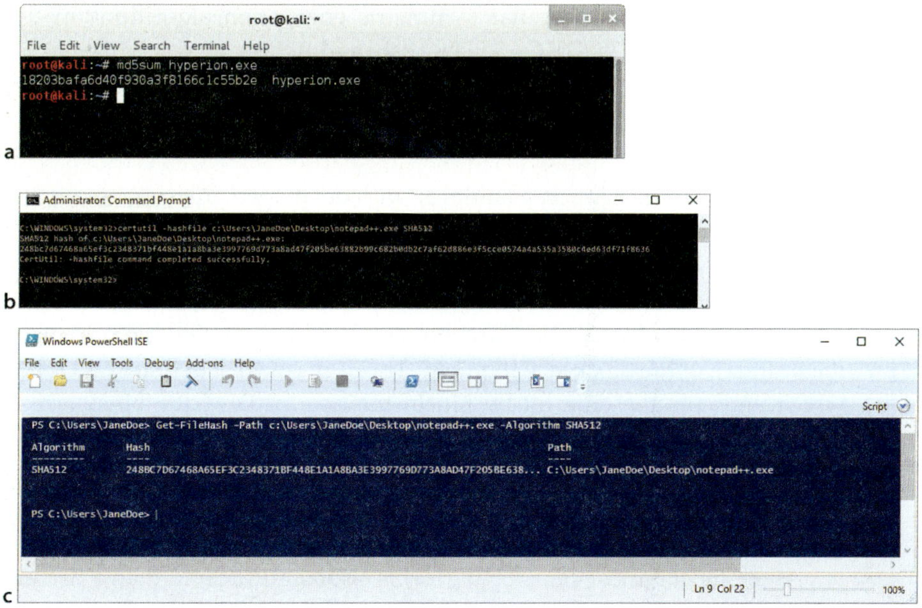

Symmetric Encryption

Symmetric encryption is the older and simpler method of encrypting information. The basis of symmetric encryption is that both the sender and the receiver of the message have previously obtained the same key. This is, in fact, the basis for even the oldest ciphers—the Spartans needed the exact same size cylinder, making the cylinder the "key" to the message, and in shift ciphers both parties need to know the direction and amount of shift being performed. All symmetric algorithms are based on this **shared secret** principle, including the unbreakable one-time pad method.

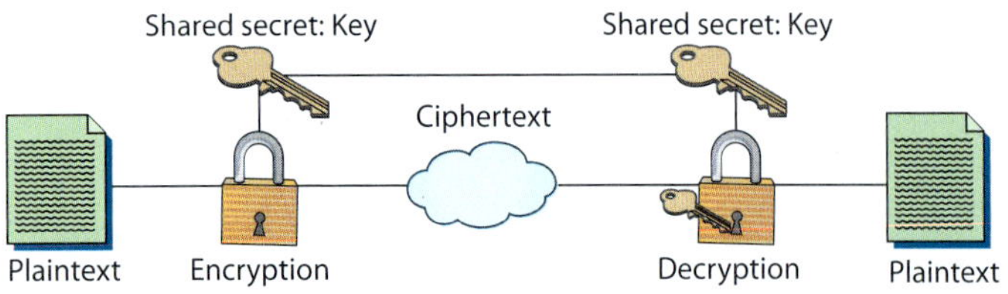

• **Figure 5.8** Layout of a symmetric algorithm

Figure 5.8 is a simple diagram showing the process that a symmetric algorithm goes through to provide encryption from plaintext to ciphertext. This ciphertext message is, presumably, transmitted to the message recipient, who goes through the process to decrypt the message using the same key that was used to encrypt the message. Figure 5.8 shows the keys to the algorithm, which are the same value in the case of symmetric encryption.

Unlike with hash functions, a cryptographic key is involved in symmetric encryption, so there must be a mechanism for *key management* (discussed earlier in the chapter). Managing the cryptographic keys is critically important in symmetric algorithms because the key unlocks the data that is being protected. However, the key also needs to be known by, or transmitted in a confidential way to, the party with which you wish to communicate. A key must be managed at all stages, which requires securing it on the local computer, securing it on the remote one, protecting it from data corruption, protecting it from loss, and, probably the most important step, protecting it while it is transmitted between the two parties. Later in the chapter we will look at public key cryptography, which greatly eases the key management issue, but for symmetric algorithms the most important lesson is to store and send the key only by known secure means.

Some of the more popular symmetric encryption algorithms in use today are AES, ChaCha20, CAST, Twofish, and IDEA.

Tech Tip

How Many Keys Do You Need?

*Since the same key is used for encryption and decryption in a symmetric scheme, the number of keys needed for a group to communicate secretly depends on whether or not individual messages are to be kept secret from members of the group. If you have K members in your group, and your only desire is to communicate secretly with respect to people outside of the K members, then one key is all that is needed. But then all K members of the group can read every message. If you desire to have protected communications in the group, then K * (K – 1)/2 keys are needed to manage all pairwise communications in the group. If the group has 10 members, this is 45 keys. If the group has 100 members, it is 4950 keys, and for 1000 members it is 499,500! Clearly there is a scale issue. One of the advantages of asymmetric encryption is that the pairwise number is K—clearly a huge scale advantage.*

DES

DES, the Data Encryption Standard, was developed in response to the National Bureau of Standards (NBS), now known as the National Institute of Standards and Technology (NIST), and was adopted as a federal standard in 1976. DES is what is known as a **block cipher**; it segments the input data into blocks of a specified size, typically padding the last block to make it a multiple of the block size required. This is in contrast to a stream cipher, which encrypts the data bit by bit. In the case of DES, the block size is 64 bits, which means DES takes a 64-bit input and outputs 64 bits of ciphertext. This process is repeated for all 64-bit blocks in the message. DES uses a key length of 56 bits, and all security rests within the key. The same algorithm and key are used for both encryption and decryption.

At the most basic level, DES performs a substitution and then a permutation (a form of transposition) on the input, based on the key. This action is called a *round*, and DES performs this 16 times on every 64-bit block. The algorithm goes step by step, producing 64-bit blocks of ciphertext for each plaintext block. This is carried on until the entire message has been encrypted with DES. As mentioned, the same algorithm and key are used to decrypt and encrypt with DES. The only difference is that the sequence of key permutations is used in reverse order.

Over the years that DES has been a cryptographic standard, a lot of cryptanalysis has occurred, and while the algorithm has held up very well, some problems have been encountered. *Weak keys* are keys that are less secure than the majority of keys allowed in the keyspace of the algorithm. In the case of DES, because of the way the initial key is modified to get the subkey, certain keys are weak keys. The weak keys equate in binary to having all 1's or all 0's, like those shown in Figure 5.9, or to having half the key all 1's and the other half all 0's.

Key
0000000 0000000
0000000 FFFFFFF
FFFFFFF 0000000
FFFFFFF FFFFFFF

• **Figure 5.9** Weak DES keys

Semi-weak keys, where two keys will encrypt plaintext to identical ciphertext, also exist, meaning that either key will decrypt the ciphertext. The total number of possibly weak keys is 64, which is very small relative to the 2^{56} possible keys in DES. With 16 rounds and not using a weak key, DES was found to be reasonably secure and, amazingly, has been for more than two decades. In 1999, a distributed effort consisting of a supercomputer and 100,000 PCs over the Internet was made to break a 56-bit DES key. By attempting more than 240 billion keys per second, the effort was able to retrieve the key in less than a day. This demonstrates an incredible resistance to cracking the then 20-year-old algorithm, but it also demonstrates that more stringent algorithms are needed to protect data today.

3DES

Triple DES (3DES) is a variant of DES. Depending on the specific variant, it uses either two or three keys instead of the single key that DES uses. It also spins through the DES algorithm three times via what's called **multiple encryption**. This significantly improves the strength.

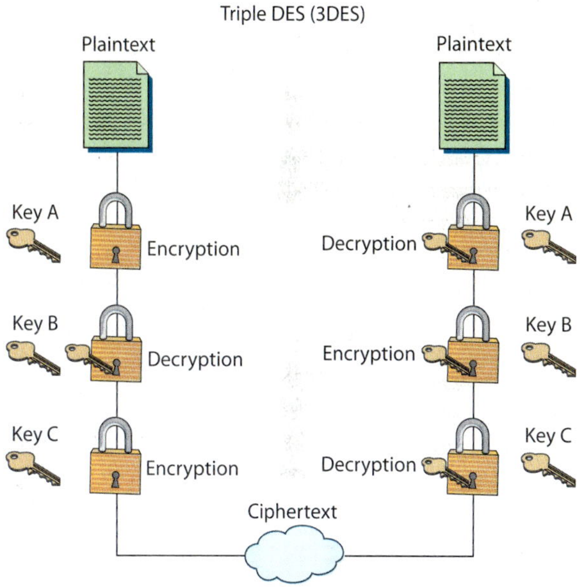

• **Figure 5.10** Diagram of 3DES

Multiple encryption can be performed in several different ways. The simplest method of multiple encryption is just to stack algorithms on top of each other—taking plaintext, encrypting it with DES, then encrypting the first ciphertext with a different key, and then encrypting the second ciphertext with a third key. In reality, this technique is less effective than the technique that 3DES uses. One of the modes of 3DES (EDE mode) is to encrypt with one key, then decrypt with a second, and then encrypt with a third, as shown in Figure 5.10.

This greatly increases the number of attempts needed to retrieve the key and is a significant enhancement of security. The additional security comes at a price, however. It can take up to three times longer to compute 3DES than to compute DES. However, the advances in memory and processing power in today's electronics make this problem irrelevant in all devices except for very small low-power handhelds.

The only weaknesses of 3DES are those that already exist in DES. However, due to the use of different keys in the same algorithm, which results in a longer key length by adding the first keyspace to the second keyspace, and the greater resistance to brute forcing, 3DES has less actual weakness. While 3DES continues to be popular and is still widely supported, AES has taken over as the symmetric encryption standard.

AES

The current gold standard for symmetric encryption is the AES algorithm. In response to a worldwide call in the late 1990s for a new symmetric

> **Tech Tip**
>
> **AES in Depth**
>
> *AES is a 128-bit block cipher, and its blocks are represented as 4×4 arrays of bytes that are called a "state." The AES key sizes refer to the number of "rounds" that the plaintext will be put through as it's encrypted:*
>
> - *128-bit key = 10 rounds*
> - *192-bit key = 12 rounds*
> - *256-bit key = 14 rounds*
>
> *Each round the "state" undergoes includes substitutions from a lookup table, rows shifted cyclically, and a linear mixing operation that combines the 4 bytes in each column. For decryption, a set of reverse rounds is performed. For a more in-depth description of AES, see the NIST document http://csrc.nist.gov/publications/fips/fips197/fips-197.pdf.*

cipher, a group of Dutch researchers submitted a method called Rijndael (pronounced *rain doll*).

In the fall of 2000, NIST picked Rijndael to be the new AES. It was chosen for its overall security as well as its good performance on limited-capacity devices. Rijndael cipher can also be configured to use blocks of 192 or 256 bits, but AES has standardized on 128-bit blocks. AES can have key sizes of 128, 192, and 256 bits, with the size of the key affecting the number of rounds used in the algorithm. Longer key versions are known as AES-192 and AES-256, respectively.

The Rijndael/AES algorithm has been well tested and has a suitable key length to provide security for many years to come. Currently, no attack methods are known to exist against AES. AES as a block cipher is operated using modes, and using Galois Counter Mode (GCM) it can support Authenticated Encryption with Associated Data (AEAD) and is the most widely used block cipher in TLS 1.2 and 1.3. When run in GCM and CCM (Counter with CBC_MAC) mode, AES provides a stream cipher function to support message authentication for TLS 1.3, making it an AEAD as opposed to a plain block cipher.

CAST

CAST is an encryption algorithm that is similar to DES in its structure. It was designed by Carlisle Adams and Stafford Tavares. CAST uses a 64-bit block size for 64- and 128-bit key versions, and a 128-bit block size for the 256-bit key version. Like DES, it divides the plaintext block into a left half and a right half. The right half is then put through function *f* and then is XORed with the left half. This value becomes the new right half, and the original right half becomes the new left half. This is repeated for eight rounds for a 64-bit key, and the left and right outputs are concatenated to form the ciphertext block. The algorithm in CAST-256 form was submitted for the AES standard but was not chosen. CAST has undergone thorough analysis, with only minor weaknesses discovered that are dependent on low numbers of rounds. Currently, no better way is known to break high-round CAST than by brute forcing the key, meaning that with a sufficient key length, CAST should be placed with other trusted algorithms.

RC

RC is a general term for several ciphers all designed by Ron Rivest—RC officially stands for *Rivest Cipher*. RC1, RC2, RC3, RC4, RC5, and RC6 are all ciphers in the series. RC1 and RC3 never made it to release, but RC2, RC4, RC5, and RC6 are all working algorithms.

RC2

RC2 was designed as a DES replacement, and it is a variable-key-size block-mode cipher. The key size can be from 8 bits to 1024 bits, with the block size being fixed at 64 bits. RC2 breaks up the input blocks into four 16-bit words and then puts them through 18 rounds of either mix or mash operations, outputting 64 bits of ciphertext for 64 bits of plaintext.

According to RSA, RC2 is up to three times faster than DES. RSA maintained RC2 as a trade secret for a long time, with the source code eventually being illegally posted on the Internet. The ability of RC2 to accept different key lengths is one of the larger vulnerabilities in the algorithm. Any key length below 64 bits can be easily retrieved by modern computational power. Additionally, there is a related key attack that needs 234 chosen plaintexts to work. Considering these weaknesses, RC2 is not recommended as a strong cipher.

RC5

RC5 is a block cipher written in 1994. It has multiple variable elements, numbers of rounds, key sizes, and block sizes. This algorithm is relatively unproven, but if configured to run enough rounds, RC5 seems to provide adequate security for current brute forcing technology. Rivest recommends using at least 12 rounds. With 12 rounds in the algorithm, cryptanalysis in a linear fashion proves less effective than brute-force against RC5, and differential analysis fails for 15 or more rounds. A newer algorithm is RC6.

RC6

RC6 is based on the design of RC5. It uses a 128-bit block size, separated into four words of 32 bits each. It uses a round count of 20 to provide security, and it has three possible key sizes: 128, 192, and 256 bits. RC6 is a modern algorithm that runs well on 32-bit computers. With a sufficient number of rounds, the algorithm makes both linear and differential cryptanalysis infeasible. The available key lengths make brute force attacks extremely time-consuming. RC6 should provide adequate security for some time to come.

RC4

RC4 was created before RC5 and RC6, and it differs in operation. RC4 is a **stream cipher**, whereas all the symmetric ciphers we have looked at so far have been block ciphers. A stream cipher works by enciphering the plaintext in a stream, usually bit by bit. This makes stream ciphers faster than block-mode ciphers. Stream ciphers accomplish this by performing a bitwise XOR with the plaintext stream and a generated keystream.

RC4 operates in this manner. It was developed in 1987 and remained a trade secret of RSA until it was posted to the Internet in 1994. RC4 can use a key length of 8 to 2048 bits, though the most common versions use 128-bit keys. The key is used to initialize a 256-byte state table. This table is used to generate the pseudo-random stream that is XORed with the plaintext to generate the ciphertext. Alternatively, the stream is XORed with the ciphertext to produce the plaintext.

RC4 finally fell to various vulnerabilities and was removed from supported versions of TLS by most trusted browsers by 2019.

Tech Tip

RC4 Deprecated

RC4 is considered to be no longer secure and has been deprecated by all the major players in the security industry. It is replaced by using AES with GCM and CCM in a pseudo-stream-generation mode or by newer stream ciphers like ChaCha20.

Blowfish

Blowfish was designed in 1994 by Bruce Schneier. It is a block-mode cipher using 64-bit blocks and a variable key length from 32 to 448 bits. It was designed to run quickly on 32-bit microprocessors and is optimized for

> **Tech Tip**
>
> **S-Boxes**
>
> *S-boxes, or substitution boxes, are a method used to provide confusion, a separation of the relationship between the key bits and the ciphertext bits. Used in most symmetric schemes, they perform a form of substitution and can provide significant strengthening of an algorithm against certain forms of attack. They can be in the form of lookup tables, either static like DES or dynamic (based on the key) in other forms such as Twofish.*

situations with few key changes. Encryption is done by separating the 64-bit input block into two 32-bit words, and then a function is executed every round. Blowfish has 16 rounds; once the rounds are completed, the two words are then recombined to form the 64-bit output ciphertext. The only successful cryptanalysis to date against Blowfish has been against variants that used a reduced number of rounds. There does not seem to be a weakness in the full 16-round version.

Twofish

Twofish was developed by Bruce Schneier, David Wagner, Chris Hall, Niels Ferguson, John Kelsey, and Doug Whiting. Twofish was one of the five finalists for the AES competition. Like other AES entrants, it is a block cipher, utilizing 128-bit blocks with a variable-length key of up to 256 bits. It uses 16 rounds and splits the key material into two sets—one to perform the actual encryption and the other to load into the algorithm's S-boxes. This algorithm is available for public use and has proven to be secure.

IDEA

IDEA (International Data Encryption Algorithm) started out as PES, or Proposed Encryption Cipher, in 1990, and it was modified to improve its resistance to differential cryptanalysis and its name was changed to IDEA in 1992. It is a block-mode cipher using a 64-bit block size and a 128-bit key. The input plaintext is split into four 16-bit segments: *A*, *B*, *C*, and *D*. The process uses eight rounds, with a final four-step process. The output of the last four steps is then concatenated to form the ciphertext.

All current cryptanalysis on full, eight-round IDEA shows that the most efficient attack would be to brute force the key. The 128-bit key would prevent this attack being accomplished, given current computer technology. The only known issue is that IDEA is susceptible to a weak key—like a key that is made of all 0's. This weak key condition is easy to check for, and the weakness is simple to mitigate.

ChaCha20

ChaCha20 is a relatively new stream cipher, developed by Daniel Bernstein as a follow-on to Salsa20. ChaCha20 uses a 256-bit key and a 96-bit nonce and uses 20 rounds. It is considered to be highly efficient in software implementations and can be significantly faster than AES. ChaCha20 was adopted as an option for TLS 1.3 because when it is used with the Poly1305 authenticator, it can replace RC4 and act as a crucial component to Authenticated Encryption with Associated Data (AEAD) implementations.

ChaCha20 also uses the current recommended construction for combining encryption and authentication. It's built using an Authenticated Encryption with Associated Data (AEAD) construction. AEAD is a way of combining a cipher and an authenticator together to get the combined properties of encryption and authentication. AEAD is covered in more detail later in the chapter.

Cipher Modes

In symmetric or block algorithms, there is a need to deal with multiple blocks of identical data to prevent multiple blocks of cyphertext that would identify the blocks of identical input data. There are multiple methods of dealing with this, called *modes of operation*. Descriptions of the common modes ECB, CBC, CTM, and GCM are provided in the following sections.

> ECB is not recommended for use in any cryptographic protocol because it does not provide protection against input patterns or known blocks.

ECB

Electronic Codebook (ECB) is the simplest mode operation of all. The message to be encrypted is divided into blocks, and each block is encrypted separately. This has several major issues; the most notable is that identical blocks yield identical encrypted blocks, telling the attacker that the blocks are identical. ECB is not recommended for use in cryptographic protocols.

CBC

Cipher Block Chaining (CBC) is defined as a block mode where each block is XORed with the previous ciphertext block before being encrypted. An example is in AES-CBC which is the used of CBC with the AES algorithm. To obfuscate the first block, an initialization vector (IV) is XORed with the first block before encryption. CBC is one of the most common modes used, but it has two major weaknesses. First, because there is a dependence on previous blocks, the algorithm cannot be parallelized for speed and efficiency. Second, because of the nature of the chaining, a plaintext block can be recovered from two adjacent blocks of ciphertext. An example of this is in the POODLE (Padding Oracle On Downgraded Legacy Encryption) attack. This type of padding attack works because a 1-bit change to the ciphertext causes complete corruption of the corresponding block of plaintext as well as inverts the corresponding bit in the following block of plaintext, but the rest of the blocks remain intact.

Counter

Counter Mode (CTM) uses a "counter" function to generate a nonce that is used for each block encryption. Different blocks have different nonces, enabling parallelization of processing and substantial speed improvements. The sequence of operations is to take the counter function value (nonce), encrypt using the key, and then XOR with plaintext. Each block can be done independently, resulting in the ability to multithread the processing. CTM is also abbreviated CTR in some circles.

CCM is a mode of operation involving CBC (Cipher Block Chaining, described previously) with a MAC, or CBC-MAC. This method was designed for block ciphers with a length of 128 bits, and the length of the message and any associated data must be known in advance. This means it is not an "online" form of AEAD, which is characterized as allowing any length of input.

Galois Counter Mode (GCM) is an extension of CTM via the addition of a Galois mode of authentication. This adds an authentication function to the cipher mode, and the Galois field used in the process can be parallelized, providing efficient operations. GCM is employed in many international standards, including IEEE 802.1ad and 802.1AE. NIST has recognized

> **Tech Tip**
>
> **Authenticated Encryption**
>
> *Why do you need authenticated encryption? To protect block ciphers against a wide range of chosen ciphertext attacks, such as POODLE, one needs a second layer of protection, using a MAC implementation such as HMAC-SHA. This is done as follows:*
>
> 1. *Computing the MAC on the ciphertext, not the plaintext*
> 2. *Use of different keys—one for encryption and a different one for the MAC*
>
> *This specific, yet generic prescription adds steps and complications for developers. To resolve this, special modes for block ciphers called Authenticated Encryption (AE) or Authenticated Encryption with Associated Data (AEAD) were devised. These provide the same protection as the block cipher–MAC combination, but in a single function with a single key. AE(AD) modes were developed to make solutions easier for implementations, but adoptions have been slow. Use of AEAD is one of the significant improvements in TLS 1.3.*

• **Figure 5.11** Symmetric keys must match exactly to encrypt and decrypt the message.

AES-GCM as well as GCM and GMAC. AES-GCM cipher suites for TLS are described in IETF RFC 5288.

Authenticated Encryption with Associated Data (AEAD)

Authenticated Encryption with Associated Data (AEAD) is a form of encryption designed to provide both confidentiality and authenticity services. A wide range of authenticated modes are available for developers, including GCM, OCB, and EAX.

OCB is Offset Codebook Mode, a patented implementation that offers the highest performance, but because of patents, it is not included in any international standards. EAX solves the patent problem, but likewise has not been adopted by any international standards. This leaves GCM, which was described in the previous section.

Block vs. Stream

When encryption operations are performed on data, there are two primary modes of operation: block and stream. Block operations are performed on blocks of data, enabling both transposition and substitution operations. This is possible when large pieces of data are present for the operations. Stream data has become more common with audio and video across the Web. The primary characteristic of stream data is that it is not available in large chunks, but either bit by bit or byte by byte—pieces too small for block operations. Stream ciphers operate using substitution only and therefore offer less robust protection than block ciphers. Table 5.1 compares and contrasts block and stream ciphers.

Table 5.1 Comparison of Block and Stream Ciphers

Block Ciphers	Stream Ciphers
Require more memory to process	Faster than block ciphers in operation
Stronger	More difficult to implement correctly
High diffusion	Low diffusion
Resistant to insertions/modifications	Susceptible to insertions and/or modifications
Susceptible to error propagation	Low error propagation
Can provide for authentication and integrity verification	Cannot provide integrity or authentication protections
Common algorithms: 3DES and AES	Common algorithms: A5 and RC4

Symmetric Encryption Summary

Symmetric algorithms are important because they are comparatively fast and have few computational requirements. Their main weakness is that two geographically distant parties both need to have a key that matches the other key exactly (see Figure 5.11).

Asymmetric Encryption

Asymmetric encryption is more commonly known as public key cryptography. Asymmetric encryption is in many ways completely different from symmetric encryption. While both are used to keep data from being seen by unauthorized users, asymmetric cryptography uses two keys instead of one. It was invented by Whitfield Diffie and Martin Hellman in 1975. The system uses a pair of keys: a private key that is kept secret and a public key that can be sent to anyone. The system's security relies on resistance to deducing one key, given the other, and thus retrieving the plaintext from the ciphertext.

Asymmetric encryption creates the possibility of digital signatures and also addresses the main weakness of symmetric cryptography. The ability to send messages securely without senders and receivers having had prior contact has become one of the basic concerns with secure communication. Digital signatures will enable faster and more efficient exchange of all kinds of documents, including legal documents. With strong algorithms and good key lengths, security can be ensured.

Asymmetric encryption involves two separate but mathematically related keys. The keys are used in an opposing fashion. One key undoes the actions of the other, and vice versa. So, as shown in Figure 5.12, if you encrypt a message with one key, the other key is used to decrypt the message. In the top example, Alice wishes to send a private message to Bob, so she uses Bob's public key to encrypt the message. Then, because only Bob's private key can decrypt the message, only Bob can read it. In the lower example, Bob wishes to send a message, with proof that it is from him. By encrypting it with his private key, anyone who decrypts it with his public key knows the message came from Bob.

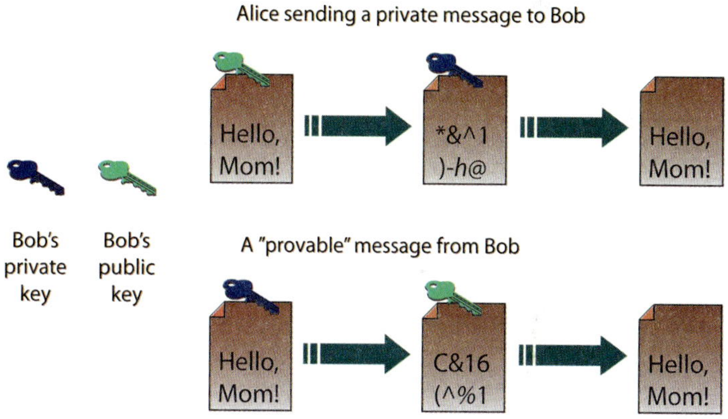

• **Figure 5.12** Using an asymmetric algorithm

Asymmetric keys are distributed using certificates. A digital certificate contains information about the association of the public key to an entity, along with additional information that can be used to verify the current validity of the certificate and the key. When keys are exchanged between machines, such as during an SSL/TLS handshake, the exchange is done by passing certificates.

Public key systems typically work by using hard math problems. One of the more common methods relies on the difficulty of factoring large numbers. These functions are often called **trapdoor functions**, as they are difficult to process without the key but easy to process when you have the key—the trapdoor through the function. For example, given a prime number (say, 293) and another prime (such as 307), it is an easy function to multiply them together to get 89,951. Given 89,951, it is not simple to find the factors 293 and 307 unless you know one of them already. Computers can easily multiply very large primes with hundreds or thousands of digits but cannot easily factor the product.

The strength of these functions is very important: because an attacker is likely to have access to the public key, they can run tests of known plaintext

Tech Tip

Key Pairs

Public key cryptography always involves two keys—a public key and a private key—that together are known as a key pair. *The public key is made widely available to anyone who may need it, while the private key is closely safeguarded and shared with no one.*

Asymmetric methods are significantly slower than symmetric methods and therefore are typically not suitable for bulk encryption.

and produce ciphertext. This allows instant checking of guesses that are made about the keys of the algorithm. Public key systems, because of their design, also form the basis for **digital signatures**, a cryptographic method for securely identifying people. RSA, Diffie-Hellman, elliptic curve cryptography (ECC), and ElGamal are all popular asymmetric protocols. We will look at all of them and their suitability for different functions.

> **Cross Check**
>
> **Digital Certificates**
>
> In Chapter 7 you will learn more about digital certificates and how encryption is important to a public key infrastructure. Why is an asymmetric algorithm so important to digital signatures?

Diffie-Hellman

The **Diffie-Hellman (DH)** algorithm was created in 1976 by Whitfield Diffie and Martin Hellman. This protocol is one of the most common encryption protocols in use today. Diffie-Hellman is important because it enables the sharing of a secret key between two people who have not contacted each other before. It plays a role in the electronic key exchange method of Transport Layer Security (TLS), Secure Shell (SSH), and IP Security (IPSec) protocols.

The protocol, like RSA, uses large prime numbers to work. Two users agree to two numbers, P and G, with P being a sufficiently large prime number and G being the generator. Both users pick a secret number, a and b. Then both users compute their public number:

User 1 $X = Ga \bmod P$, with X being the public number
User 2 $Y = Gb \bmod P$, with Y being the public number

The users then exchange public numbers. User 1 knows P, G, a, X, and Y.

User 1 Computes $Ka = Y^a \bmod P$
User 2 Computes $Kb = X^b \bmod P$

With $Ka = Kb = K$, now both users know the new shared secret, K.

This is the basic algorithm, and although methods have been created to strengthen it, Diffie-Hellman is still in wide use. It remains very effective because of the nature of what it is protecting—a temporary, automatically generated secret key that is good only for a single communication session.

Variations of Diffie-Hellman include Diffie-Hellman Ephemeral (DHE), Elliptic Curve Diffie-Hellman (ECDH), and Elliptic Curve Diffie-Hellman Ephemeral (ECDHE).

> Diffie-Hellman is the gold standard for key exchange, and for the CompTIA Security+ exam, you should understand the subtle differences between the different forms: DH, DHE, ECDH, and ECDHE.

Groups

Diffie-Hellman (DH) groups determine the strength of the key used in the key exchange process. Higher group numbers are more secure, but require additional time to compute the key. DH group 1 consists of a 768-bit key, group 2 consists of a 1024-bit key, and group 5 comes with a 1536-bit key. Higher number groups are also supported, with correspondingly longer keys.

DHE

There are several variants of the Diffie-Hellman key exchange. **Diffie-Hellman Ephemeral (DHE)** is a variant where a temporary key is used in the key exchange rather than the same key being reused over and over. An **ephemeral key** is a key that is not reused, but rather is only used once, thus improving security by reducing the amount of material that can be analyzed via cryptanalysis to break the cipher.

Ephemeral keys improve security. They are cryptographic keys that are used only once after generation.

ECDHE

Elliptic Curve Diffie-Hellman (ECDH) is a variant of the Diffie-Hellman protocol that uses elliptic curve cryptography. ECDH can also be used with ephemeral keys, becoming **Elliptic Curve Diffie-Hellman Ephemeral (ECDHE)**, to enable perfect forward security.

RSA Algorithm

The *RSA algorithm* is one of the first public key cryptosystems ever invented. It can be used for both encryption and digital signatures. RSA is named after its inventors, Ron Rivest, Adi Shamir, and Leonard Adleman, and was first published in 1977.

This algorithm uses the product of two very large prime numbers and works on the principle of difficulty in factoring such large numbers. It's best to choose large prime numbers that are from 100 to 200 digits in length and are equal in length. These two primes will be P and Q. Randomly choose an encryption key, E, so that E is greater than 1, is less than $P * Q$, and is odd. E must also be relatively prime to $(P - 1)$ and $(Q - 1)$. Then compute the decryption key D:

$$D = E^{-1} \bmod ((P - 1)(Q - 1))$$

Now that the encryption key and decryption key have been generated, the two prime numbers can be discarded, but they should not be revealed.

To encrypt a message, it should be divided into blocks less than the product of P and Q. Then

$$C_i = M_i^E \bmod (P * Q)$$

C is the output block of ciphertext matching the block length of the input message, M. To decrypt a message, take ciphertext, C, and use this function:

$$M_i = C_i^D \bmod (P * Q)$$

The use of the second key retrieves the plaintext of the message.

This is a simple function, but its security has withstood the test of more than 20 years of analysis. Considering the effectiveness of RSA's security and the ability to have two keys, why are symmetric encryption algorithms needed at all? The answer is speed. RSA in software can be 100 times slower than DES, and in hardware it can be even slower.

RSA can be used to perform both regular encryption and digital signatures. Digital signatures try to duplicate the functionality of a physical signature on a document using encryption. Typically, RSA and the other public key systems are used in conjunction with symmetric key cryptography. Public key, the slower protocol, is used to exchange the symmetric key (or shared secret), and then the communication uses the faster symmetric key protocol. This process is known as *electronic key exchange.*

Because the security of RSA is based on the supposed difficulty of factoring large numbers, the main weaknesses are in the implementations of the protocol. Until recently, RSA was a patented algorithm, but it was a de facto standard for many years.

ElGamal

ElGamal can be used for both encryption and digital signatures. Taher Elgamal designed the system in the early 1980s. This system was never patented and is free for use. It is used as the U.S. government standard for digital signatures.

The system is based on the difficulty of calculating discrete logarithms in a finite field. Three numbers are needed to generate a key pair. User 1 chooses a prime, P, and two random numbers, F and D. F and D should both be less than P. Then user 1 can calculate the public key A like so:

$$A = D^F \bmod P$$

Then A, D, and P are shared with the second user, with F being the private key. To encrypt a message, M, a random key, k, is chosen that is relatively prime to $P - 1$. Then

$$C_1 = D^k \bmod P$$
$$C_2 = A^k M \bmod P$$

C_1 and C_2 make up the ciphertext. Decryption is done by

$$M = C_2/C_1^F \bmod P$$

ElGamal uses a different function for digital signatures. To sign a message, M, once again choose a random value, k, that is relatively prime to $P - 1$. Then

$$C_1 = D^k \bmod P$$
$$C_2 = (M - C_1 * F)/k \pmod{P - 1}$$

C_1 concatenated to C_2 is the digital signature.

ElGamal is an effective algorithm and has been in use for some time. It is used primarily for digital signatures. Like all asymmetric cryptography, it is slower than symmetric cryptography.

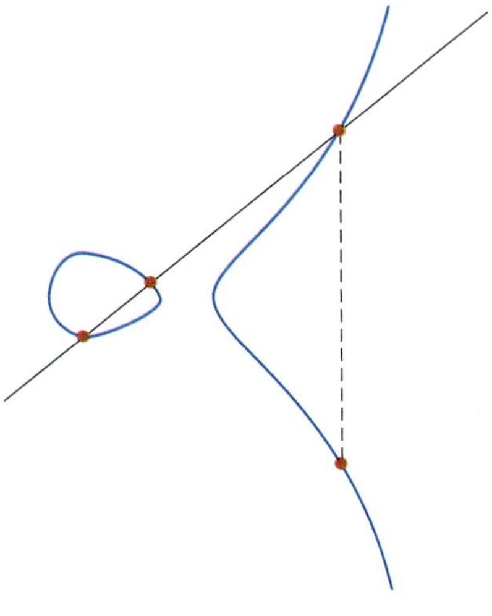

ECC

Elliptic curve cryptography (ECC) works on the basis of elliptic curves. An elliptic curve is a simple function that is drawn as a gently looping curve on the X,Y plane. Elliptic curves are defined by this equation:

$$y^2 = x^3 + ax^2 + b$$

Elliptic curves work because they have a special property—you can add two points on the curve together and get a third point on the curve, as shown in the illustration.

For cryptography, the elliptic curve works as a public key algorithm. Users agree on an elliptic curve and a fixed curve point. This information is not a shared secret, and these points can be made public without compromising the security of the system. User 1 then chooses a secret random number, K_1, and computes a public key based on a point on the curve:

$$P_1 = K_1 * F$$

User 2 performs the same function and generates P_2. Now user 1 can send user 2 a message by generating a shared secret:

$$S = K_1 * P_2$$

User 2 can generate the same shared secret independently:

$$S = K_2 * P_1$$

This is true because

$$K_1 * P_2 = K_1 * (K_2 * F) = (K_1 * K_2) * F = K_2 * (K_1 * F) = K_2 * P_1$$

The security of elliptic curve systems has been questioned, mostly because of lack of analysis. However, all public key systems rely on the difficulty of certain math problems. It would take a breakthrough in math for any of the mentioned systems to be weakened dramatically, but research has been done about the problems and has shown that the elliptic curve problem has been more resistant to incremental advances. Again, as with all cryptography algorithms, only time will tell how secure they really are. The big benefit to ECC systems is that they require less computing power for a given bit strength. This makes ECC ideal for use in low-power mobile devices. The surge in mobile connectivity has led to secure voice, e-mail, and text applications that use ECC and AES algorithms to protect a user's data.

Elliptic curve functions can be used as part of a Diffie-Hellman key exchange, in which case the method is referred to as Elliptic Curve Diffie-Hellman (ECDH). This technique can provide the advantages of elliptic curve and the functionality of Diffie-Hellman.

Tech Tip

Curve25519 and Curve448

Elliptic curve cryptography has several standard curves that can be used. ECDH uses a curve; most software uses the standard NIST curve P-256. Two of the newer curves, Curve25519 and Curve448, offer faster computation for a given security level. Curve448 can offer stronger protections, but at the cost of increased computations. These are both implemented in TLS 1.3, and when a signature algorithm is based on elliptic curves, then it's ECDSA for P-256 or Ed25519 for Curve25519.

Asymmetric Encryption Summary

Asymmetric encryption creates the possibility of digital signatures and also corrects the main weakness of symmetric cryptography. The ability to send messages securely without senders and receivers having had prior contact has become one of the basic concerns with secure communication. Digital signatures will enable faster and more efficient exchange of all kinds of documents, including legal documents. With strong algorithms and good key lengths, security can be ensured.

Symmetric vs. Asymmetric

Both symmetric and asymmetric encryption methods have advantages and disadvantages. Symmetric encryption tends to be faster, is less computationally involved, and is better for bulk transfers. But it suffers from a key management problem in that keys must be protected from unauthorized parties. Asymmetric methods resolve the key secrecy issue with public keys, but add significant computational complexity that makes them less suited for bulk encryption.

Bulk encryption can be done using the best of both systems, by using asymmetric encryption to pass a symmetric key. By adding in ephemeral key exchange, you can achieve perfect forward secrecy, discussed earlier in the chapter. Digital signatures, a highly useful tool, are not practical without asymmetric methods.

Quantum Cryptography

Cryptography is traditionally a very conservative branch of information technology. It relies on proven technologies and does its best to resist change. A big new topic in recent years has been quantum cryptography. *Quantum cryptography* is based on quantum mechanics—principally superposition and entanglement. A discussion of quantum mechanics is beyond the scope of this text, but the principle we are most concerned with in regard to cryptography is that in quantum mechanics, the measuring of data disturbs the data. What this means to cryptographers is that it is easy to tell if a message has been eavesdropped on in transit, allowing people to exchange key data while knowing that the data was not intercepted in transit. This use of quantum cryptography is called *quantum key distribution.* This is currently the only commercial use of quantum cryptography, and although there are several methods for sending the key, they all adhere to the same principle. Key bits are sent and then checked at the remote end for interception, and then more key bits are sent using the same process. Once an entire key has been sent securely, symmetric encryption can then be used.

> Quantum computing will make changes in both computing and communications. In computing, quantum methods promise solutions to currently unsolvable problems. In communications, quantum methods offer new means of security, including key distribution, which is already available via quantum key distribution.

Quantum computing is one of the frontiers of computing and involves the creation of a whole new type of computer. Quantum computers use a new structure called *qubits,* which allow information to be represented differently than just on or off as binary bits do. In a fashion, qubits enable multiple paths of a problem to be computed simultaneously. Quantum computing is more than just hardware; it involves new forms of software, and there is significant development in this area as well. Recently scientists have claimed to surpass conventional computing power with a quantum machine, but before you get all excited, this was not a general-purpose machine, but one dedicated to solving only a single, specific problem. In spite of all of the current limitations, quantum computing will bring significant breakthroughs in computing in the future.

The other field of research involving quantum mechanics and cryptography is quantum cryptanalysis. A quantum computer is capable of factoring large primes exponentially faster than a normal computer, potentially making the RSA algorithm, and any system based on factoring prime numbers, insecure. This has led to research in cryptosystems that are not vulnerable to quantum computations—a field known as *post-quantum cryptography.*

Post-Quantum

As quantum computing presents a challenge for many of today's cryptographic algorithms, significantly reducing their strength, there is a movement to develop algorithms that are not easily solved via quantum methods. This is not a theoretical exercise, as government agencies and others have been working on practical solutions to have answers and substitute algorithms should any existing algorithm fail, whether by quantum computing or some other problem.

Currently, several cryptographic algorithms have been developed in response to quantum methods and are believed to be resistant to quantum computing–based decryption methods to a reasonable level. These methods use different mathematical properties, thus making simultaneous solution sets not as effective and limiting the power of quantum computing in solving this type of problem. As with all systems, there are tradeoffs, and in this case the newer methods tend to use longer keys and require more computational power to employ.

Lightweight Cryptography

In a world where computing devices gain power with every iteration of CPU, it is hard to imagine the need for less compute-intensive cryptography, but enter the world of the Internet of Things (IoT), where small, portable, and energy- and compute-resource-constrained devices abound. These devices are small, cheap, and number in the hundreds of millions to billions. And they have a need to communicate securely and manage functions such as authentication. *Lightweight cryptography* is a specialized suite of cryptographic algorithms designed to operate in this resource-constrained environment.

Entire suites of lightweight algorithms, designed for 8-bit processors, have been developed, including hash functions, block and stream ciphers, and even asymmetric and signing functions. There has been significant research in recent years driven by NIST, and an ISO/IEC standard series, ISO/IEC 29192, covers the methods and details.

For lightweight cryptography, the main constraints we have are typically related to power requirements, gate equivalents (GEs), and timing. GEs are a means of measuring how much area on an application-specific integrated circuit is needed to hardwire a solution. An example of the savings can be seen by comparing GEs for different algorithms; for instance, SHA-256 needs around 15,000 gates, while Chaskey, a lightweight protocol, requires about 3300 to do the same tasks.

Homomorphic Encryption

One of the primary purposes of cryptography is to prevent unauthorized access to data. This is important for data at rest and data in transit, but can be an issue for data in use as well. Data that is encrypted while stored or being moved is protected from observation or alteration by unauthorized parties. But this also forces authorized parties to perform decryption steps before performing computations, followed by additional re-encryption steps after computations, which represents a significant penalty for use. Enter the world of homomorphic encryption. **Homomorphic encryption** is a set of algorithms that allow operations to be conducted on encrypted data, without decrypting and re-encrypting. The concept is simple: create a system that allows operations on ciphertext that, when decrypted, will have the same result as if the operation was performed on plaintext.

Most of the operations associated with homomorphic encrypted data involve work on numbers—specifically integers in the form of addition. While this may seem to be a limitation, this is a huge advance because much of the data that is "changed" in systems is in fact numbers and values in databases. What's more, if the number can be added to, then with multiple rounds of addition, multiplication can be achieved, and by using negative numbers, subtraction can be achieved. This makes the use of homomorphic methods valuable for many transactional-based systems.

For More Information

Applied Cryptography, Second Edition, Bruce Schneier (1996, John Wiley & Sons)

Cryptool: https://www.cryptool.org

Bruce Schneier's blog: https://www.schneier.com/cryptography.html

Chapter 5 Review

Chapter Summary

After reading this chapter and completing the exercises, you should understand the following about cryptography.

Understand the fundamentals of cryptography

- Understand the fundamental methods.
- Understand how to compare the strengths and performance of algorithms.
- Have an appreciation of the historical aspects of cryptography.

Identify and describe the three types of cryptography

- Symmetric cryptography is based on the concept of a shared secret or key.
- Asymmetric cryptography is based on a key that can be made openly available to the public, yet still provide security.
- One-way (hashing) cryptography takes data and enciphers it. However, there is no way to decipher it and no key.
- Proper random number generation is essential for cryptographic use, as the strength of the implementation frequently depends on it being truly random and unknown.

List and describe current cryptographic algorithms

- Hashing is the use of a one-way function to generate a message summary for data integrity.
- Hashing algorithms include SHA (Secure Hash Algorithm) and MD (Message Digest).
- Symmetric encryption is a shared secret form of encrypting data for confidentiality; it is fast and reliable, but needs secure key management.
- Symmetric algorithms include DES (Data Encryption Standard), 3DES, AES (Advanced Encryption Standard), ChaCha20, CAST, Blowfish, IDEA, and RC (Rivest Cipher) variants.
- Asymmetric encryption is a public/private keypair encryption used for authentication, nonrepudiation, and confidentiality.
- Asymmetric algorithms include RSA, Diffie-Hellman, ElGamal, and ECC.
- Lightweight cryptographic methods extend cryptographic functionality to low-power and resource-constrained devices.
- Homomorphic algorithms are unique in that they enable specific operations on encrypted data without the need to decrypt the data and re-encrypt afterwards.

Explain how cryptography is applied for security

- Confidentiality is gained because encryption is very good at scrambling information to make it look like random noise, when in fact a key can decipher the message and return it to its original state.
- Integrity is gained because hashing algorithms are specifically designed to check integrity. They can reduce a message to a mathematical value that can be independently calculated, guaranteeing that any message alteration would change the mathematical value.

- Nonrepudiation is the property of not being able to claim that you did not send the data. This property is gained because of the properties of private keys.
- Authentication, or being able to prove you are you, is achieved through the private keys involved in digital signatures.
- Key-generation methods, such as the use of ephemeral keys, are important tools in the implementation of strong cryptosystems.
- Digital signatures, combining multiple types of encryption, provide an authentication method verified by a third party, allowing you to use them as if you were actually signing the document with your regular signature.
- The principle of perfect forward secrecy protects future messages from previous message key disclosures.
- Proven cryptographic technologies are important because most cryptographic systems fail, and only a few stand the test of time. Homebrew systems are ripe for failure.

Key Terms

algorithm *(117)*
Authenticated Encryption with Associated Data (AEAD) *(134)*
block cipher *(128)*
Cipher Block Chaining (CBC) *(133)*
ciphertext *(117)*
collision attack *(124)*
confusion *(116)*
Counter Mode (CTM/CTR) *(133)*
cryptanalysis *(112)*
cryptography *(112)*
differential cryptanalysis *(113)*
Diffie-Hellman (DH) *(136)*
Diffie-Hellman Ephemeral (DHE) *(137)*
Diffie-Hellman groups *(136)*
diffusion *(116)*
digital signature *(136)*
Electronic Codebook (ECB) *(133)*
elliptic curve cryptography *(138)*
Elliptic Curve Diffie-Hellman Ephemeral (ECDHE) *(137)*
entropy *(122)*
ephemeral keys *(137)*
eXclusive OR (XOR) *(118)*
Galois Counter Mode (GCM) *(133)*
hash *(123)*
homomorphic encryption *(141)*
key *(118)*
key management *(122)*
keyspace *(115)*
linear cryptanalysis *(113)*
multiple encryption *(129)*
obfuscation *(116)*
obscurity *(117)*
perfect forward secrecy (PFS) *(117)*
plaintext *(117)*
shared secret *(127)*
shift cipher *(118)*
stream cipher *(131)*
substitution *(114)*
transposition *(114)*
transposition cipher *(117)*
trapdoor function *(135)*
Vigenère cipher *(120)*

Key Terms Quiz

Use terms from the Key Terms list to complete the sentences that follow. Don't use the same term more than once. Not all terms will be used.

1. Making two inputs result in the exact same cryptographic hash is called a(n) _______________.
2. A simple way to hide information, the _______________ moves a letter a set number of places down the alphabet.
3. To provide for perfect forward security, one should use _______________.
4. _______________ is required for symmetric encryption.
5. _______________ is the evaluation of a cryptosystem to test its security.
6. _______________ refers to every possible value for a cryptographic key.
7. _______________ is the function most commonly seen in cryptography, a "bitwise exclusive" or.
8. The measure of randomness in a data stream is called _______________.
9. Cryptographic methods that enable specific manipulation of encrypted fields are called _______________.
10. The basis for symmetric cryptography is the principle of a(n) _______________.

Multiple-Choice Quiz

1. When a message is sent, no matter what its format, why do we care about its integrity?
   - **A.** To ensure proper formatting
   - **B.** To show that the encryption keys are undamaged
   - **C.** To show that the message has not been edited in transit
   - **D.** To show that no one has viewed the message
2. How is 3DES different from many other types of encryption described in this chapter?
   - **A.** It only encrypts the hash.
   - **B.** It hashes the message before encryption.
   - **C.** It uses three keys and multiple encryption and/or decryption sets.
   - **D.** It can display the key publicly.
3. If a message has a hash, how does the hash protect the message in transit?
   - **A.** If the message is edited, the hash will no longer match.
   - **B.** Hashing destroys the message so that it cannot be read by anyone.
   - **C.** Hashing encrypts the message so that only the private key holder can read it.
   - **D.** The hash makes the message uneditable.
4. What is the biggest drawback to symmetric encryption?
   - **A.** It is too easily broken.
   - **B.** It is too slow to be easily used on mobile devices.
   - **C.** It requires a key to be securely shared.
   - **D.** It is available only on UNIX.

5. What is Diffie-Hellman most commonly used for?
   - **A.** Symmetric encryption key exchange
   - **B.** Signing digital contracts
   - **C.** Secure e-mail
   - **D.** Storing encrypted passwords
6. What is public key cryptography a more common name for?
   - **A.** Asymmetric encryption
   - **B.** SHA
   - **C.** Symmetric encryption
   - **D.** Hashing
7. What algorithm can be used to provide for bulk encryption of data?
   - **A.** AES
   - **B.** RC4
   - **C.** RIPEMD
   - **D.** ElGamal
8. A good hash function is resistant to what?
   - **A.** Brute forcing
   - **B.** Rainbow tables
   - **C.** Interception
   - **D.** Collisions
9. Which of the following is an approved stream cipher for TLS 1.3?
   - **A.** RC4
   - **B.** A5
   - **C.** ChaCha20
   - **D.** AES_CBC
10. What is the best kind of key to have?
   - **A.** Easy to remember
   - **B.** Long and random
   - **C.** Long and predictable
   - **D.** Short

Essay Quiz

1. Describe how polyalphabetic substitution works.
2. Explain why asymmetric encryption is called public key encryption.
3. Describe cryptanalysis.

Lab Projects

• Lab Project 5.1

Using a utility program, demonstrate how single-character changes can make substantial changes to hash values.

• Lab Project 5.2

Create a keyset and use it to transfer a file securely.

• Lab Project 5.3

Take a given file and compute a series of hash values using the native OS functionality in Linux, Windows, and PowerShell. Compute the CRC-32. Make a copy of an .exe file and change something like the copyright in the file using a hex editor. Note the changes to the values for CRC and hashes. Then using Python or some other language, manipulate bytes to force the CRC to its original value. Again, compare the hashes and CRCs. Hint: You can find scripts on the Web to force CRC values.

Chapter 6 Applied Cryptography

There are two types of encryption: one that will prevent your sister from reading your diary and one that will prevent your government.

—Bruce Schneier

In this chapter, you will learn how to

- Correctly use the elements of cryptography
- Examine cipher suites and common uses
- Identify cryptographic attack methods

None of the still steadily growing Internet commerce would be possible without the use of standards and protocols that provide a common, interoperable environment for exchanging information securely. Due to the wide distribution of Internet users and businesses, the most practical solution to date has been the commercial implementation of public key infrastructures.

Cryptography Use

The use of cryptography grows every day. More and more information becomes digitally encoded and placed online, and all of this data needs to be secured. The best way to do that with current technology is to use encryption. This section considers some of the tasks cryptographic algorithms accomplish and those for which they are best suited. Security is typically defined as a product of five components: confidentiality, integrity, availability, authentication, and nonrepudiation. Encryption addresses all of these components except availability. Key escrow will be one of the most important topics as information becomes universally encrypted; otherwise, everyone may be left with useless data. Digital rights management and intellectual property protection are also places where encryption algorithms are heavily used. Digital signatures combine several algorithms to provide reliable identification in a digital form.

Confidentiality

Confidentiality typically comes to mind when the term *security* is brought up. Confidentiality is the ability to keep some piece of data a secret. In the digital world, encryption excels at providing confidentiality. In most cases, symmetric encryption is favored because of its speed and because some asymmetric algorithms can significantly increase the size of the object being encrypted. Asymmetric cryptography also can be used to protect confidentiality, but its size and speed make it more efficient at protecting the confidentiality of small units for tasks such as electronic key exchange. In all cases, the strength of the algorithms and the length of the keys ensure the secrecy of the data in question.

Integrity

Integrity, better known as **message integrity**, is a crucial component of message security. When a message is sent, both the sender and recipient need to know that the message was not altered in transmission. This is especially important for legal contracts—recipients need to know that the contracts have not been altered. Signers also need a way to validate that a contract they sign will not be altered in the future.

Integrity is provided via one-way hash functions and digital signatures. The hash functions compute the message digests, and this guarantees the integrity of the message by allowing easy testing to determine whether any part of the message has been changed. The message now has a computed function (the hash value) to tell the users to resend the message if it was intercepted and interfered with. This hash value is combined with asymmetric cryptography by taking the message's hash value and encrypting it with the user's private key. This lets anyone with the user's public key decrypt the hash and compare it to the locally computed hash, not only ensuring the integrity of the message but positively identifying the sender.

> Message integrity has become increasingly important as more commerce is conducted digitally. The ability to independently make sure that a document has not been tampered with is very important to commerce. More importantly, once the document is "signed" with a digital signature, it cannot be refuted that the person in question signed it.

Authentication

Authentication is the matching of a user to an account through previously shared credentials. This information must be protected, and a combination of cryptographic methods is commonly employed. From hashing to key stretching to encryption and digital signatures, multiple techniques are used as part of the operations involved in authentication.

> **Try This!**
>
> **Document Integrity**
>
> Download a hash calculator that works on your operating system, such as SlavaSoft HashCalc, available at www.slavasoft.com/hashcalc/index.htm. Then create a simple document file with any text you prefer. Save it, and then use the hashing program to generate the hash and save the hash value. Now edit the file, even by simply inserting a single blank space, and resave it. Recalculate the hash and compare.

> **Tech Tip**
>
> **HOTP and TOTP**
>
> *An* **HMAC-based One-Time Password (HOTP)** *algorithm is a key component of the Open Authentication Initiative (OATH). YubiKey is a hardware implementation of HOTP that has significant use. Because of how it is implemented, an HOTP offers greater security than simple passwords, as they are no longer valid after use. A Time-based One-Time Password (TOTP) algorithm offers even more protection as it expires after a given interval, whether used or not.*

Nonrepudiation

An item of some confusion, the concept of nonrepudiation is actually fairly simple. Nonrepudiation means that the message sender cannot later deny that they sent the message. This is important in electronic exchanges of data because of the lack of face-to-face meetings. Nonrepudiation is based on public key cryptography and the principle of only you knowing your private key. The presence of a message signed by you, using your private key, which nobody else should know, is an example of nonrepudiation. When a third party can check your signature using your public key, that disproves any claim that you were not the one who actually sent the message. Nonrepudiation is tied to asymmetric cryptography and cannot be implemented with symmetric algorithms.

> Digital signatures provide a means of verifying the authenticity and integrity of a message: you know both who the sender is and that the message has not been altered. By itself, a digital signature does not protect the contents from unauthorized reading.

Digital Signatures

Digital signatures have been touted as the key to truly paperless document flow, and they do have promise for improving the system. Digital signatures are based on both hashing functions and asymmetric cryptography. Both encryption methods play an important role in signing digital documents. Unprotected digital documents are very easy for anyone to change. If a document is edited after an individual signs it, it is important that any modification can be detected. To protect against document editing, hashing functions are used to create a digest of the message that is unique and easily reproducible by both parties. This ensures that the message integrity is complete.

A **digital signature** is a cryptographic implementation designed to demonstrate authenticity and identity associated with a message. Using public key cryptography, a digital signature allows traceability to the person signing the message through the use of their private key. The addition of hash codes allows for the assurance of the integrity of the message as well. The operation of a digital signature is a combination of cryptographic elements to achieve a desired outcome. The steps involved in digital signature generation and use are illustrated in Figure 6.1. The message to be signed is hashed, and the hash is encrypted using the sender's private key. Upon receipt, the recipient can decrypt the hash using the sender's public key. If a subsequent hashing of the message reveals an identical value, two things are known: First, the message has not been altered. Second, the sender possessed the private key of the named sender and therefore is presumably the sender him- or herself.

A digital signature does not by itself protect the contents of the message from interception. The message is still sent in the clear, so if confidentiality of the message is a requirement, additional steps must be taken to secure the message from eavesdropping. This can be done by encrypting the message itself, or by encrypting the channel over which it is transmitted.

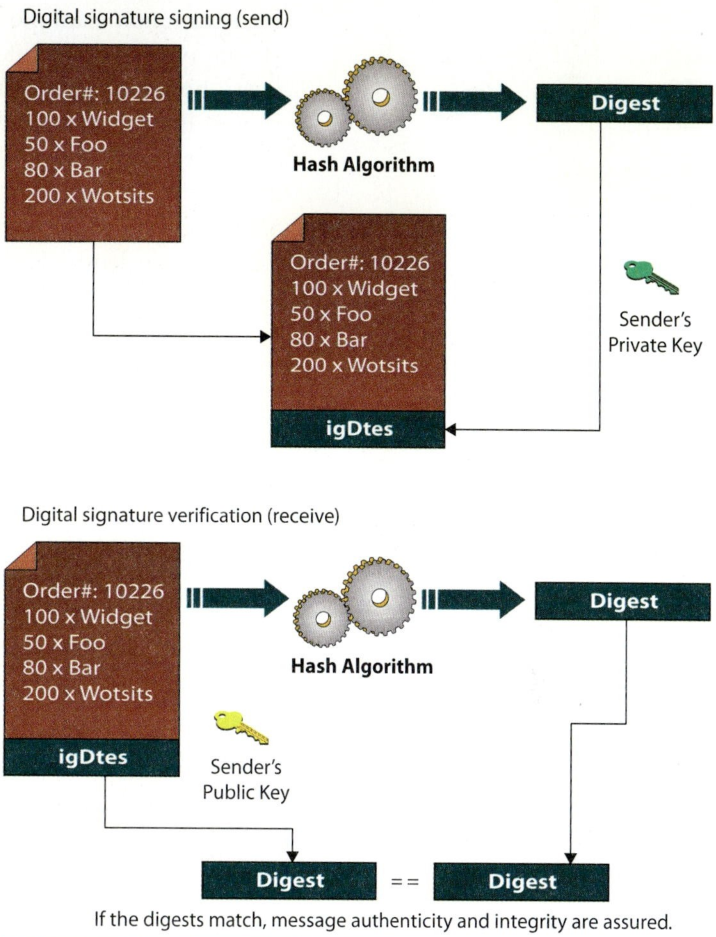

• **Figure 6.1** Digital signature operation

Digital Rights Management

Digital rights management (DRM) is the process for protecting intellectual property from unauthorized use. This is a broad area, but the most concentrated focus is on preventing piracy of software or digital content. Before easy access to computers, or the "digital revolution," the content we came in contact with was analog or print based. Although it was possible to copy this content, it was difficult and time consuming to do so, and usually resulted in a loss of quality. It was also much more difficult to send 1000 pages of a handwritten copy of a book to Europe, for example. Computers and the Internet have made such tasks trivial, and now it is very easy to copy a document, music, or video and quickly send it thousands of miles away.

Cryptography has entered the fray as a solution to protect digital rights, though it is currently better known for its failures than its successes. The DVD Content Scramble System (CSS) was an attempt to make DVDs impossible to copy by computer. CSS used an encryption algorithm that was licensed to every DVD player; however, creative programmers were able to retrieve the key to this algorithm by disassembling a software-based DVD player. CSS has been replaced by the Advanced Access Content System (AACS), which is used on the next-generation Blu-ray discs. This system encrypts video content via the symmetric AES algorithm with one or more keys. Several decryption keys have been cracked and released to the Internet, allowing pirates to freely copy the protected content. The music and computer game industries have also attempted several different DRM applications, but nearly all of these have eventually been cracked, allowing piracy.

A common example of DRM that is mostly successful is the broadcast stream of digital satellite TV. Because the signal is beamed from space to every home in North America, the satellite TV provider must be able to protect the signal so that it can charge people to receive it. Smart cards are employed to securely hold the decryption keys that allow access to some or all of the content in the stream. This system has been cracked several times, allowing a subset of users free access to the content; however, the satellite TV providers learned from their early mistakes and upgraded to new smart cards to correct the old problems.

DRM will also become very important in the industry of Software as a Service (SaaS). Similar to companies that provide satellite TV service, companies that provide SaaS rely on a subscription basis for profitability. If someone could pay for a single license and then distribute that to hundreds of employees, the provider would soon go out of business. Many systems in the past have been cracked because the key was housed inside the software.

Cryptographic Applications

A few applications can be used to encrypt data conveniently on your personal computer. *Pretty Good Privacy (PGP)* is mentioned later in this chapter because it is a useful protocol suite and has historical significance. One of the unique features of PGP is its ability to use both symmetric and asymmetric encryption methods, accessing the strengths of each method and avoiding the weaknesses of each as well. Symmetric keys are used for bulk encryption, taking advantage of the speed and efficiency of symmetric encryption. The symmetric keys are passed using asymmetric methods, capitalizing on the flexibility of this method. PGP-based technology is now sold as part of a commercial application, with home and corporate versions.

Filesystem Encryption

Filesystem encryption is becoming a standard means of protecting data while in storage. Even hard drives are available with built-in AES encryption. Microsoft expanded its Encrypting File System (EFS), available since the Windows 2000 operating system, with BitLocker, a boot-sector encryption method that protects data that was introduced with the Windows Vista operating system. BitLocker is also used in Windows Server 2019 and Windows 10 operating systems. BitLocker utilizes AES encryption to encrypt every file on the hard drive automatically. All encryption occurs in the background, and decryption occurs seamlessly when data is requested. The decryption key can be stored in the Trusted Platform Module (TPM) or on a USB key.

Database Encryption

Due partly to increased regulatory concerns and partly to more targeted attacks, databases have begun to offer native support for encryption. Protecting data at rest in the enterprise frequently involves data stored in databases. Building data protection mechanisms into the database systems is not new (it has been around for a long time), but enterprise adoption of this functionality has been slow. Symmetric encryption algorithms such as 3DES and AES are used to encrypt data internally in the database. Protection mechanisms that can be managed by row and by column are included in most major database applications; the challenge is in convincing organizations to use this proven protection methodology. It does add complexity to the system, but in today's environment of data breaches and corporate espionage, the complexity is easier to manage than the effects of a data loss.

Blockchain

Blockchains are lists of records, where each addition to the list is done by a cryptographic algorithm. While this may seem complex, it serves an important purpose: records in a blockchain are resistant to modification. This permits a distributed ledger that can record transactions and have both verification of additions and protection with respect to integrity. The strength of the integrity comes from both the signing of records and the distributed nature of the blockchain. While a record can be altered, it would require all records after it to also be altered, and thus would be detectable across the copies on the distributed storage of the chain. So, while records are technically alterable, in practicality the system is provably secure.

Blockchain is the record-keeping technology behind Bitcoin. It is a distributed and decentralized public record.

The concept of blockchains was invented to create the public transaction ledger of cryptocurrencies. A cryptocurrency is a currency system built on a finite set of "rare" numbers that are mined and then "created." As there is no central authority, numbers when mined are entered into the distributed ledger, marking their creation. All transactions are also entered into the ledger, preventing double-spending of the tokens. The use of the distributed public ledger provides the protections that physical tokens provide—only one person can control a given currency token at any given time, and all transactions are immutable.

Tech Tip

Public Ledgers

While cryptocurrencies like Bitcoin get the headlines, the true winner in blockchains has been the implementation of distributed public ledgers. Public ledgers *have been used to resolve many challenging problems in tracking financial transactions, supply chains, and other ledger-based issues. Applications for items such as music royalties, DNS systems, and tracking food from farm to table are all examples of blockchain technology solutions under development.*

Use of Proven Technologies

When you're setting up a cryptographic scheme, it is important to use proven technologies. Proven cryptographic libraries and proven cryptographically correct random-number generators are the foundational elements associated with a solid program. Homegrown or custom elements in these areas can greatly increase risk associated with a broken system. Developing your own cryptographic algorithms is beyond the abilities of most groups. Algorithms are complex and difficult to create. Any algorithm that has not had public review can have weaknesses in it. Most good algorithms are approved for use only after a lengthy test and public review phase.

Cipher Suites

In many applications, the use of cryptography occurs as a collection of functions. Different algorithms can be used for authentication, encryption/decryption, digital signatures, and hashing. The term **cipher suite** refers to an arranged group of algorithms. For instance, Transport Layer Security (TLS) has a published TLS Cipher Suite Registry at www.iana.org/assignments/tls-parameters/tls-parameters.xhtml.

Tech Tip

TLS Cipher Suite Example

A cipher suite is the combination of algorithms used during the following stages:

- *Key Agreement*
- *Authentication*
- *Symmetric Cipher and Key Size*
- *Hash Algorithm for Message Authentication*

The choice of algorithms is made by selecting rows from the TLS cipher suite registry during the TLS handshake. It is important to pick algorithms of sufficient strength and avoid older, deprecated ones. The list of cipher suites follows the format shown in the following image.

Cipher ID = 0x00C02B

TLS_ECDHE_ECDSA_WITH_AES_128_GCM_SHA256

TLS – protocol is TLS
ECDHE – Key agreement - Elliptic Curve Diffie-Hellman Ephemeral
ECDSA – Authentication - Elliptic Curve Digital Signature Algorithm
With – placeholder for readability
AES_128_GCM – Symmetric cipher
SHA256 – Hash for message authentication

Tech Tip

Disabling SSL

Because all versions of SSL, including v3, have exploitable vulnerabilities that make the protocol no longer considered secure, users should not rely on it for security. Google Chrome no longer uses SSL. For Internet Explorer, you need to uncheck the SSL boxes under Internet Options.

Strong vs. Weak Ciphers

There is a wide range of ciphers—some old and some new—each with its own strengths and weaknesses. Over time, new methods and computational capabilities change the viability of ciphers. The concept of strong versus weak ciphers is an acknowledgment that, over time, ciphers can become vulnerable to attacks. The application or selection of ciphers should take into consideration that not all ciphers are still strong. When you're selecting a cipher for use, it is important to make an appropriate choice. For example, if a server offers Secure Sockets Layer (SSL) v3 and TLS, you should choose TLS only, as SSL v3 has been shown to be vulnerable.

As new computing platforms become available, cloud-based GPUs, AI machines, quantum computers, and cryptography will be some of the things that are aimed at by attackers. This has led to a continuation of the cryptographic arms race, where cryptographers are inventing new algorithms, typically specifically designed for either performance considerations, such as lightweight systems, or resistance to mass computational brute force. Significant advancements have been achieved, such as the release of authenticated encryption with associated data (AEAD) systems, TLS v1.3, lightweight cryptographic systems, newer elliptical curves, new hash functions, and new stream ciphers.

Weak/Deprecated Algorithms

Over time, cryptographic algorithms fall to different attacks or just the raw power of computation. The challenge with these algorithms is understanding which ones have fallen to attacks, even though they may still be available for use in software libraries, resulting in their inappropriate application in use. Although this list will continue to grow, it is important to consider this topic because old habits die hard. Hash algorithms, such as MD5, should be considered inappropriate, as manufactured collisions have been achieved. Even newer hash functions have issues, such as SHA-1, and soon SHA-256. The Data Encryption Standard (DES) and its commonly used stronger form, 3DES, have fallen from favor. The good news is that new forms of these functions are widely available, and in many cases, such as AES, they are computationally efficient, providing better performance.

Secret Algorithms

Algorithms can be broken into two types—those with published details and those where the steps are kept secret. Secrecy has its uses in security. Keeping your password secret, for instance, is an essential element in its proper functionality. Secrecy in how to apply security elements can assist in thwarting reverse engineering. An example of this is the use of multiple rounds of multiple hash functions to provide password security. How many rounds, as well as the order of algorithmic application, is important with respect to the application but is not needed for normal use because it is encoded into the application itself. Keeping this secret can enhance security because it makes reverse engineering difficult, if not impossible.

Secret cryptographic algorithms lead to another issue. Yes, keeping an algorithm secret can impose challenges to those wishing to explore methods of breaking it, but it also reduces the testing of an algorithm by cryptographers attacking it. The most secure algorithms are those that have survived over time the onslaught of cryptographic researchers attacking them.

The best algorithms are always public algorithms that have been published for peer review by other cryptographic and mathematical experts. Publication is important, as any flaws in the system can be revealed by others before actual use of the system. This process greatly encourages the use of proven technologies. Several proprietary algorithms have been reverse-engineered, exposing the confidential data the algorithms try to protect. Examples of this include the decryption of Nikon's proprietary RAW format, white-balance encryption, and the cracking of the ExxonMobil Speedpass RFID encryption. The use of a proprietary system can actually be less secure than using a published system. Whereas proprietary systems are not made available to be tested by potential crackers, public systems are made public for precisely this purpose.

> One of the most common cryptographic failures is the creation of your own encryption scheme. Rolling your own cryptography, whether in creating algorithms or implementation of existing algorithms yourself, is a recipe for failure. Always use approved algorithms and always use approved crypto libraries to implement them.

A system that maintains its security after public testing can be reasonably trusted to be secure. A public algorithm can be more secure because good systems rely on the *encryption key* to provide security, not the algorithm itself. The actual steps for encrypting data can be published, because without the key, the protected information cannot be accessed.

Key Exchange

Cryptographic mechanisms use both an algorithm and a key, with the key requiring communication between parties. In symmetric encryption, the secrecy depends on the secrecy of the key, so insecure transport of the key can lead to failure to protect the information encrypted using the key. **Key exchange** is the central foundational element of a secure symmetric encryption system. Maintaining the secrecy of the symmetric key is the basis of secret communications. In asymmetric systems, the key exchange problem is one of key publication. Because public keys are designed to be shared, the problem is reversed from one of secrecy to one of publicity.

Early key exchanges were performed by trusted couriers. People carried the keys from senders to receivers. One could consider this form of key exchange to be the ultimate in *out-of-band* communication. With the advent of digital methods and some mathematical algorithms, it is possible to pass keys in a secure fashion. This can occur even when all packets are subject to interception. The Diffie-Hellman key exchange is one example of this type of secure key exchange. The Diffie-Hellman key exchange depends on two random numbers, each chosen by one of the parties, and kept secret. Diffie-Hellman key exchanges can be performed *in band*, and even under external observation, as the secret random numbers are never exposed to outside parties.

> **Tech Tip**
>
> **Man-in-the-Middle Attack**
>
> *A man-in-the-middle attack is designed to defeat proper key exchange by intercepting the remote party's key and replacing it with the attacker's key in both directions. If done properly, only the attacker knows that the encrypted traffic is not secure and can be read by the attacker.*

Key Escrow

The impressive growth of the use of encryption technology has led to new methods for handling keys. Encryption is adept at hiding all kinds of information, and with privacy and identity protection becoming more of a concern, more information is encrypted. The loss of a key can happen for a multitude of reasons: it might simply be lost, the key holder might be incapacitated or dead, software or hardware might fail, and so on. In many cases, that information is locked up until the cryptography can be broken, and, as you have read, that could be millennia. This has raised the topic of **key escrow**, or keeping a copy of the encryption key with a trusted third party. Theoretically, this third party would only release your key to you or your official designate on the event of your being unable to get the key yourself. However, just as the old saying from Benjamin Franklin goes, "Three may keep a secret if two of them are dead." Any time more than one copy of the key exists, the security of the system is broken. The extent of the insecurity of key escrow is a subject open to debate and will be hotly contested in the years to come.

> **Tech Tip**
>
> **Key Escrow Has Benefits and Hazards**
>
> *Key escrow can solve many of the problems that result when a key is lost or becomes inaccessible, allowing access to data that otherwise would be impossible to access without key escrow, but it can open up private information to unauthorized access.*

Key escrow can negatively impact the security provided by encryption, because the government requires a huge, complex infrastructure of systems to hold every escrowed key, and the security of those systems is less efficient than the security of your memorizing the key. However, there are two sides to the key escrow coin. Without a practical way to recover a key if or when it is lost or the key holder dies, for example, some important information will be lost forever. Such issues will affect the design and security of encryption technologies for the foreseeable future.

Session Keys

A **session key** is a symmetric key used for encrypting messages during a communication session. It is generated from random seeds and is used for the duration of a communication session. When correctly generated and propagated during session setup, a session key provides significant levels of protection during the communication session and also can afford perfect forward secrecy. Session keys offer the advantages of symmetric encryption, speed, strength, simplicity, and, with key exchanges possible via digital methods, significant levels of automated security.

Ephemeral Keys

Ephemeral keys are cryptographic keys that are used only once after they are generated. When an ephemeral key is used as part of the Diffie-Hellman scheme, it forms an Ephemeral Diffie-Hellman (EDH) key exchange. An EDH mechanism generates a temporary key for each connection, never using the same key twice. This provides for perfect forward secrecy. If the Diffie-Hellman scheme involves the use of elliptic curves, it is called Elliptic Curve Diffie-Hellman Ephemeral (ECDHE).

Key Stretching

Key stretching is a mechanism that takes what would be weak keys and "stretches" them to make the system more secure against brute force attacks. A typical methodology used for key stretching involves increasing the computational complexity by adding iterative rounds of computations. To extend a password to a longer length of key, you can run it through multiple rounds of variable-length hashing, each increasing the output by bits over time. This may take hundreds or thousands of rounds, but for single-use computations, the time is not significant. When one wants to use a brute force attack, the increase in computational workload becomes significant when done billions of times, making this form of attack much more expensive.

The common forms of key stretching employed in use today include Password-Based Key Derivation Function 2 (PBKDF2) and Bcrypt.

> Key stretching is a mechanism that takes what would be weak keys and "stretches" them. This increases the workload, making the passwords take longer to compute but also much harder to brute force.

PBKDF2

Password-Based Key Derivation Function 2 (PBKDF2) is a key-derivation function designed to produce a key derived from a password. This function uses a password or passphrase and a salt and then applies an HMAC to the input thousands of times. The repetition makes brute force attacks computationally unfeasible.

Bcrypt

Bcrypt is a key-stretching mechanism that uses the Blowfish cipher and salting and then adds an adaptive function to increase the number of iterations. The result is the same as other key-stretching mechanisms (single use is computationally feasible), but when an attempt is made to brute force the function, the billions of attempts make it computationally unfeasible.

Transport Encryption

Transport encryption is used to protect data that is in motion. When data is being transported across a network, it is at risk of interception. An examination of the Open Systems Interconnection (OSI) networking model shows a layer dedicated to transport, and this abstraction can be used to manage end-to-end cryptographic functions for a communication channel. When

Secure Sockets Layer (SSL) was the original transport layer protocol but has since fallen to vulnerabilities and should no longer be used. Transport Layer Security (TLS) is the current cryptographic protocol used to provide data integrity and security over networks by encrypting network connections at the transport layer. In many cases, people use the term SSL even when TLS is in fact the protocol being used.

the TCP/IP protocol is used, TLS is the preferred method of managing the security at the transport level.

Transport Layer Security (TLS) provides the most common means of interacting with a public key infrastructure (PKI) and certificates. This protocol provides for secure connections between the client and server and subsequent exchange of information. TLS can also provide server authentication (and optionally, client authentication) and confidentiality of information transfers. See Chapter 17 for a detailed explanation of the web-based security implementations.

The Internet Engineering Task Force (IETF) established the TLS working group in 1996 to develop a standard transport layer security protocol. The working group began with SSL version 3.0 as its basis and released RFC 2246, "The TLS Protocol Version 1.0," in 1999 as a proposed standard. The working group also published RFC 2712, "Addition of Kerberos Cipher Suites to Transport Layer Security (TLS)," as a proposed standard, and two RFCs on the use of TLS with HTTP. Like its predecessor SSL, TLS is a protocol that ensures privacy between communicating applications and their users on the Internet. When a server and client communicate, TLS ensures that no third party can eavesdrop or tamper with any message.

Tech Tip

Proper TLS Configuration

Protocols:

- *Deactivate SSLv2 and SSLv3, TLSv1.1.*
- *Activate TLSv1.2 and TLSv1.3.*

Configuration:

- *Deactivate client-initiated renegotiation (to prevent a specific form of DOS against TLS).*
- *Deactivate TLS compression, to prevent the attack known as CRIME (CVE-2012-4929).*
- *Activate support for forward secrecy.*

Cipher suites:

- *Deactivate cipher suites with keys that are shorter than 128 bit.*
- *Deactivate cipher suite RC4, to prevent attacks against RC4 (CVE-2013-2566).*

Certificates:

- *Certificates must include hostnames and domains in the CN and SAN fields.*
- *Use hash-algorithm SHA-256 instead of MD5 and SHA-1 for certificates.*

TLS is composed of two parts: the TLS Record Protocol and the TLS Handshake Protocol. The TLS Record Protocol provides connection security by using supported encryption methods. The TLS Record Protocol can also be used without encryption. The TLS Handshake Protocol allows the server and client to authenticate each other and to negotiate a session encryption algorithm and cryptographic keys before data is exchanged.

Though TLS is based on SSL and is sometimes referred to as SSL, they are not interoperable. However, the TLS protocol does contain a mechanism that allows a TLS implementation to back down to SSL 3.0. The difference between the two is the way they perform key expansion and message authentication computations. The TLS Record Protocol is a layered protocol. At each layer, messages may include fields for length, description, and content. The Record Protocol takes messages to be transmitted, fragments the data into manageable blocks, optionally compresses the data, applies a message authentication code (HMAC) to the data, encrypts it, and transmits the result. Received data is decrypted, verified, decompressed, and reassembled and then delivered to higher-level clients.

The TLS Handshake Protocol involves the following steps, which are summarized in Figure 6.2:

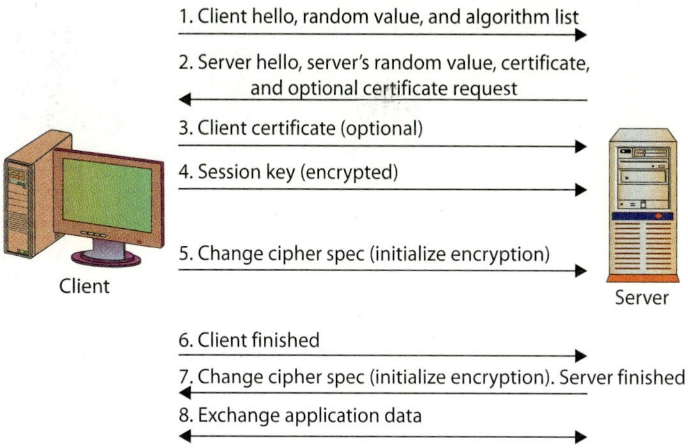

• **Figure 6.2** TLS Handshake Protocol

1. Client sends hello message, containing supported TLS options.
2. Server responds with a hello message selecting the TLS options. Then server sends its certificate.
3. Client sends client certificate (optional).
4. Client generates master secret and sends encrypted session key.
5. Client initializes encryption.
6. Client sends finished message to verify that key exchange was successful.
7. Server initializes encryption and sends message that it is ready for data.
8. Encrypted session begins.

Though it has been designed to minimize this risk, TLS still has potential vulnerabilities to a man-in-the-middle attack. A highly skilled and well-placed attacker can force TLS to operate at lower security levels. Regardless, through the use of validated and trusted certificates, a secure cipher suite can be selected for the exchange of data.

Once established, a TLS session remains active as long as data is being exchanged. If sufficient inactive time has elapsed for the secure connection to time out, it can be reinitiated.

TLS v1.3

TLS version 1.3 is a complete update to the TLS standard and is designed to address performance and security issues. TLS removed a lot of primitives and features that have contributed to weaknesses in previous versions. The cipher suites supported under TLS v1.3 are limited to AEAD ciphers, primarily to ward off a series of attacks against block ciphers. TLS v1.3 has other security enhancements to specifically protect against weak configurations and common vulnerabilities exploited by the attacks employed in DROWN, Vaudenay, Lucky 13, POODLE, SLOTH, and CRIME.

On the performance front, TLS v1.3 has made improvements in the handshake process, through the combination of steps, going from seven steps down to five. Additionally, TLS supports zero round-trip time resumption (0-RTT), a method by which if a client and server have previously negotiated a TLS v1.3 connection, a reconnection can be achieved with one fewer round trip. While the elimination of round trips may seem like a small gain, the number of times these events happen behind the scenes is a lot, and these improvements can be noticeable especially on devices suffering from increased latency on each round trip.

Data in Transit/Motion

Transport encryption is used to protect **data in transit**, or data that is in motion. When data is being transported across a network, it is at risk of interception. An examination of the OSI networking model shows a layer dedicated to transport, and this abstraction can be used to manage end-to-end cryptographic functions for a communication channel. When the TCP/IP protocol is being used, TLS is one specific method of managing the security at the transport level. SSL is another example of transport layer security. Managing a secure layer of communications is an essential element in many forms of computer operations.

Data at Rest

Protecting **data at rest** is the most prominent use of encryption and is typically referred to as data encryption. Whole disk encryption of laptop data to provide security in the event of device loss is an example of data-at-rest protection. The same concept applies to data being stored in the cloud, where encryption can protect against unauthorized reading.

Data in Use/Processing

> *Data in transit, data at rest,* and *data in use* are terms commonly used to describe states of data in a computing system. Understanding how to differentiate these terms based on their similarities and differences when it comes to cryptography is a very testable item.

Data in use is the term used to describe data that is stored in a nonpersistent state of either RAM, CPU caches, or CPU registers. Data in use is of increasing concern to security professionals as attacks such as RAM-scraping malware are occurring. Data in use is still data that requires protection, and in modern secure systems, this data can be encrypted. New techniques, such as Intel's SGX, promise a future where sensitive data can be protected from all other processes on a system, even those with higher levels of authority, such as root.

Implementation vs. Algorithm Selection

When using cryptography for protection of data, you need to include several factors in the implementation plan. One of the first decisions is in algorithm selection. Not only should you avoid deprecated algorithms, but you also need to match the algorithm to the intended use.

Cryptographic Service Provider

A **cryptographic service provider (CSP)** is a software library that implements cryptographic functions. CSPs implement encoding and decoding functions, which computer application programs may use, for example, to implement strong user authentication or for secure e-mail. In Microsoft Windows, the Microsoft CryptoAPI (CAPI) is a CSP for all processes that need specific cryptographic functions. This provides a standard implementation of a complex set of processes.

Crypto Modules

A cryptographic module is a hardware or software device or component that performs cryptographic operations securely within a physical or logical boundary. **Crypto modules** use a hardware, software, or hybrid cryptographic engine contained within the boundary as well as cryptographic keys that do not leave the boundary, maintaining a level of security. Maintaining all secrets within a specified protected boundary has been a foundational element of a secure cryptographic solution.

Common Use Cases

Cryptographic services are being employed in more and more systems, and there are many common use cases associated with them. Examples include implementations to support situations such as low power, low latency, and high resiliency, as well as supporting functions such as confidentiality, integrity, and nonrepudiation.

Low-Power Devices

Low-power devices such as mobile phones and portable electronics are commonplace and have need for cryptographic functions. Cryptographic functions tend to take significant computational power, and special cryptographic functions, such as elliptic curve cryptography (ECC), are well suited for low-power applications.

Low Latency

Some use cases involve low-latency operations. This makes specialized cryptographic functions needed to support operations that have extreme time constraints. Stream ciphers are examples of low-latency operations.

High Resiliency

High-resiliency systems are characterized by functions that have the ability to resume normal operational conditions after an external disruption. The use of cryptographic modules can support resiliency through a standardized implementation of cryptographic flexibility.

Supporting Confidentiality

Protecting data from unauthorized reading is the definition of confidentiality. Cryptography is the primary means of protecting data confidentiality, data at rest, data in transit, and data in use.

Supporting Integrity

Times arise where the integrity of data is needed, such as during transfers. Integrity can demonstrate that data has not been altered. Message authentication codes (MACs) supported by hash functions are an example of cryptographic services supporting integrity.

Supporting Obfuscation

There are times when information needs to be obfuscated (that is, protected from casual observation). In the case of a program, obfuscation can protect the code from observation by unauthorized parties.

Supporting Authentication

Authentication is a property that deals with the identity of a party—be it a user, a program, or piece of hardware. Cryptographic functions can be employed to demonstrate authentication, such as the validation that an entity has a specific private key that's associated with a presented public key, thus proving identity.

Supporting Nonrepudiation

Nonrepudiation is a property that deals with the ability to verify that a message has been sent and received so that the sender (or receiver) cannot refute sending (or receiving) the information. An example of this in action is seen with the private key holder relationship. It is assumed that the private key never leaves the possession of the private key holder. Should this occur, it is the responsibility of the holder to revoke the key. Thus, if the private key is used, as evidenced by the success of the public key, then it is assumed that the message was sent by the private key holder. Therefore, actions that are signed cannot be repudiated by the holder.

Resource vs. Security Constraints

Cryptographic functions require system resources. Using the proper cryptographic functions for a particular functionality is important for both performance and resource reasons. Determining the correct set of security and resource constraints is an essential beginning step when planning a cryptographic implementation.

The commonly used hash functions in HMAC are MD5, SHA-1, and SHA-256. Although MD5 has been deprecated because of collision attacks, when it's used in the HMAC function, the attack methodology is not present and the hash function still stands as useful.

HMAC

HMAC is an acronym for keyed-*hash message authentication code,* a special form of message authentication code. Message authentication codes are used to determine whether a message has changed during transmission. Using a hash function for message integrity is common practice for many communications. When you add a secret key and crypto function, then the MAC becomes an HMAC, and you also have the ability to determine authenticity in addition to integrity.

S/MIME

In early 1996, the Internet Mail Consortium (IMC) was formed as a technical trade association pursuing cooperative use and enhancement of Internet electronic mail and messaging. An early goal of the IMC was to bring together the Department of Defense (DoD), along with its vendor community, and the commercial industry in order to devise a standard security protocol acceptable to both. The Secure/Multipurpose Internet Mail Extensions (S/MIME) message specification is an extension to the MIME standard that provides a way to send and receive signed and encrypted MIME data. RSA Security created the first version of the S/MIME standard, using the RSA encryption algorithm and the Public Key Cryptography Standards (PKCS) series. The second version dates from 1998 but had a number of serious restrictions, including the restriction to 40-bit Data Encryption Standard (DES). The current version of the IETF standard is dated July 2004 and requires the use of Advanced Encryption Standard (AES).

Cross Check

E-mail Encryption

Want to understand e-mail encryption? Flip ahead to Chapter 17, which is on the Web, e-mail, and instant messaging, for more details on e-mail encryption. Then answer these questions:

- Why is it important to encrypt e-mail?
- What impacts can malicious code have on a business?
- Why is instant messaging a higher risk than e-mail?

The changes in the S/MIME standard have been so frequent that the standard has become difficult to implement until v3. Far from having a stable standard for several years that product manufacturers could have time to gain experience with, there were many changes to the encryption algorithms being used. Just as importantly, and not immediately clear from the IETF documents, the standard places reliance on more than one other standard for it to function. Key among these is the format of a public key certificate as expressed in the X.509 standard.

IETF S/MIME History

The S/MIME v2 specifications outline a basic strategy for providing security services for e-mail but lack many security features required by the DoD for use by the military. Shortly after the decision was made to revise the S/MIME v2 specifications, the DoD, its vendor community, and commercial industry met to begin development of the enhanced specifications. These new specifications would be known as S/MIME v3. Participants agreed that backward compatibility between S/MIME v3 and v2 should be preserved; otherwise, S/MIME v3–compatible applications would not be able to work with older S/MIME v2–compatible applications.

A minimum set of cryptographic algorithms was mandated so that different implementations of the new S/MIME v3 set of specifications could be interoperable. This minimum set must be implemented in an application for it to be considered "S/MIME compliant." Applications can implement additional cryptographic algorithms to meet their customers' needs, but the minimum set must also be present in the applications for interoperability with other S/MIME applications. Thus, users are not forced to use S/MIME-specified algorithms; they can choose their own. However, if the application is to be considered S/MIME compliant, the standard algorithms must also be present.

IETF S/MIME v3 Specifications

> **Tech Tip**
>
> **S/MIME in a Nutshell**
>
> *S/MIME provides two security services to e-mail: digital signatures and message encryption. Digital signatures verify sender identity, and encryption can keep contents private during transmission. These services can be used independently of each other and provide the foundational basis for message security.*

Building on the original work by the IMC-organized group, the IETF has worked hard to enhance the S/MIME v3 specifications. The ultimate goal is to have the S/MIME v3 specifications receive recognition as an Internet standard. The current IETF S/MIME v3 set of specifications includes the following:

- Cryptographic Message Syntax (CMS)
- S/MIME v3 message specification
- S/MIME v3 certificate-handling specification
- Enhanced security services (ESS) for S/MIME

The CMS defines a standard syntax for transmitting cryptographic information about the contents of a protected message. Originally based on the PKCS #7 version 1.5 specification, the CMS specification was enhanced by the IETF S/MIME working group to include optional security components. Just as S/MIME v3 provides backward compatibility with v2, CMS provides backward compatibility with PKCS #7, so applications will be interoperable even if the new components are not implemented in a specific application.

Integrity, authentication, and nonrepudiation security features are provided by using digital signatures using the SignedData syntax described by the CMS. CMS also describes what is known as the EnvelopedData syntax to provide confidentiality of the message's content through the use of encryption. The PKCS #7 specification supports key encryption algorithms such as RSA. Algorithm independence is promoted through the addition of several fields to the EnvelopedData syntax in CMS, which is the major difference between the PKCS #7 and CMS specifications. The goal was to be able to support specific algorithms such as Diffie-Hellman and the Key Exchange Algorithm (KEA), which is implemented on the Fortezza Crypto Card developed for the DoD. One final significant change to the original specifications is the ability to include X.509 Attribute Certificates in the SignedData and EnvelopedData syntaxes for CMS.

An interesting feature of CMS is the ability to nest security envelopes to provide a combination of security features. As an example, a CMS triple-encapsulated message can be created in which the original content and associated attributes are signed and encapsulated within the inner SignedData object. The inner SignedData object is in turn encrypted and encapsulated within an EnvelopedData object. The resulting EnvelopedData object is then also signed and finally encapsulated within a second SignedData object, the outer SignedData object. Usually the inner SignedData object is signed by the original user and the outer SignedData object is signed by another entity, such as a firewall or a mail list agent, thus providing an additional level of security.

This triple encapsulation is not required of every CMS object. All that is required is a single SignedData object created by the user to sign a message or an EnvelopedData object if the user desired to encrypt a message.

PGP

Pretty Good Privacy (PGP) is a popular program that is used to encrypt and decrypt e-mail and files. It also provides the ability to digitally sign a message so the receiver can be certain of the sender's identity. Taken together, encrypting and signing a message allows the receiver to be assured of who sent the message and to know that it was not modified during transmission. Public-domain versions of PGP have been available for years, as have inexpensive commercial versions.

PGP was one of the most widely used programs and was frequently used by both individuals and businesses to ensure data and e-mail privacy. It was developed by Philip R. Zimmermann in 1991 and quickly became a de facto standard for e-mail security. The popularity of PGP lead to the OpenPGP Internet standard, RFC 4880, and open source solutions. GNU Privacy Guard (GPG) is a common alternative to PGP in use today. What PGP started is now done in numerous apps, both free and commercial, protecting communications on a wide range of platforms from mobile devices to PCs.

OpenPGP is a widely used e-mail encryption standard. A nonproprietary protocol for encrypting e-mail using public key cryptography, it is based on PGP, as originally developed by Phil Zimmermann, and is defined by the OpenPGP working group of the IETF proposed standard RFC 4880.

How PGP Works

PGP uses a variation of the standard public key encryption process. In public key encryption, an individual (here called the *creator*) uses the encryption program to create a pair of keys. One key is known as the *public key* and is designed to be given freely to others. The other key is called the *private key* and is designed to be known only by the creator. Individuals who want to send a private message to the creator encrypt the message using the creator's public key. The algorithm is designed such that only the private key can decrypt the message, so only the creator will be able to decrypt it.

This method, known as *public key* or *asymmetric encryption,* is time consuming. *Symmetric encryption* uses only a single key and is generally faster. It is because of this that PGP is designed the way it is. PGP uses a symmetric encryption algorithm to encrypt the message to be sent. It then encrypts the symmetric key used to encrypt this message with the public key of the intended recipient. Both the encrypted key and message are then sent. The receiver's version of PGP first decrypts the symmetric key with the private key supplied by the recipient and then uses the resulting decrypted key to decrypt the rest of the message.

PGP can use two different public key algorithms: Rivest-Shamir-Adleman (RSA) and Diffie-Hellman. The RSA version uses the International Data Encryption Algorithm (IDEA) and a short symmetric key to encrypt the message, and then uses RSA to encrypt the short IDEA key using the recipient's public key. The Diffie-Hellman version uses the Carlisle Adams and Stafford Tavares (CAST) algorithm to encrypt the message and the Diffie-Hellman algorithm to encrypt the CAST key. To decrypt the message, the reverse is performed. The recipient uses their private key to decrypt the IDEA or CAST key and then uses that decrypted key to decrypt the message. These are both illustrated in Figure 6.3.

To generate a digital signature, PGP takes advantage of another property of public key encryption schemes. Normally, the sender encrypts

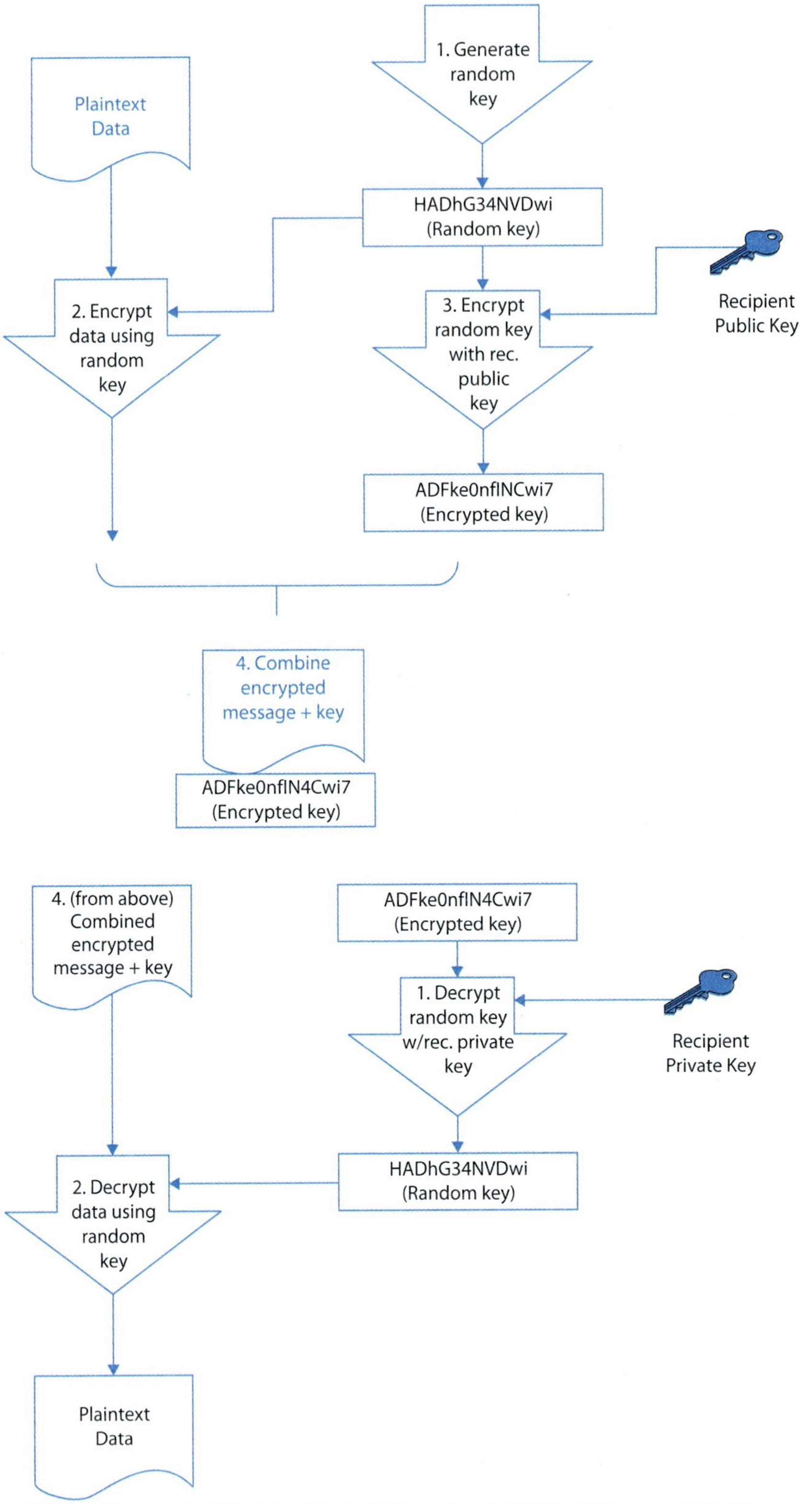

• **Figure 6.3** How PGP works for encryption

using the receiver's public key and the message is decrypted at the other end using the receiver's private key. The process can be reversed so that the sender encrypts (signs) with their own private key. The receiver then decrypts the message with the sender's public key. Because the sender is the only individual who has a key that will correctly be decrypted with the sender's public key, the receiver knows that the message was created by the sender who claims to have sent it. The way PGP accomplishes this task is to generate a hash value from the user's name and other signature information. This hash value is then encrypted with the sender's private key known only by the sender. The receiver uses the sender's public key, which is available to everyone, to decrypt the hash value. If the decrypted hash value matches the hash value sent as the digital signature for the message, then the receiver is assured that the message was sent by the sender who claims to have sent it.

Typically, versions of PGP contain a user interface that works with common e-mail programs such as Microsoft Outlook. If you want others to be able to send you an encrypted message, you need to register your public key, generated by your PGP program, with a PGP public key server. Alternatively, you have to either send your public key to all those who want to send you an encrypted message or post your key to some location from which they can download it, such as your web page. Note that using a public key server is the better method, for all the reasons of trust described in the discussion of PKIs in Chapter 7.

Tech Tip

Where Can You Use PGP?

For many years the U.S. government waged a fight over the exportation of PGP technology, and for many years its exportation was illegal. Today, however, PGP-encrypted e-mail can be exchanged with most users outside the United States, and many versions of PGP are available from numerous international sites. Of course, being able to exchange PGP-encrypted e-mail requires that the individuals on both sides of the communication have valid versions of PGP. Interestingly, international versions of PGP are just as secure as domestic versions—a feature that is not true of other encryption products. It should be noted that the freeware versions of PGP are not licensed for commercial purposes.

Steganography

Steganography, an offshoot of cryptography technology, gets its meaning from the Greek word *steganos*, meaning covered. Invisible ink placed on a document hidden by innocuous text is an example of a steganographic message. Another example is a tattoo placed on the top of a person's head, visible only when the person's hair is shaved off.

Steganography is a technique used to hide secret data within non-secret data in order to avoid detection.

Hidden writing in the computer age relies on a program to hide data inside other data. The most common application is the concealing of a text message in a picture file. The Internet contains multiple billions of image files, allowing a hidden message to be located almost anywhere without being discovered. Because not all detection programs can detect every kind of steganography, trying to find the message in an Internet image is akin to attempting to find a needle in a haystack the size of the Pacific Ocean; even a Google search for steganography returns thousands of images:

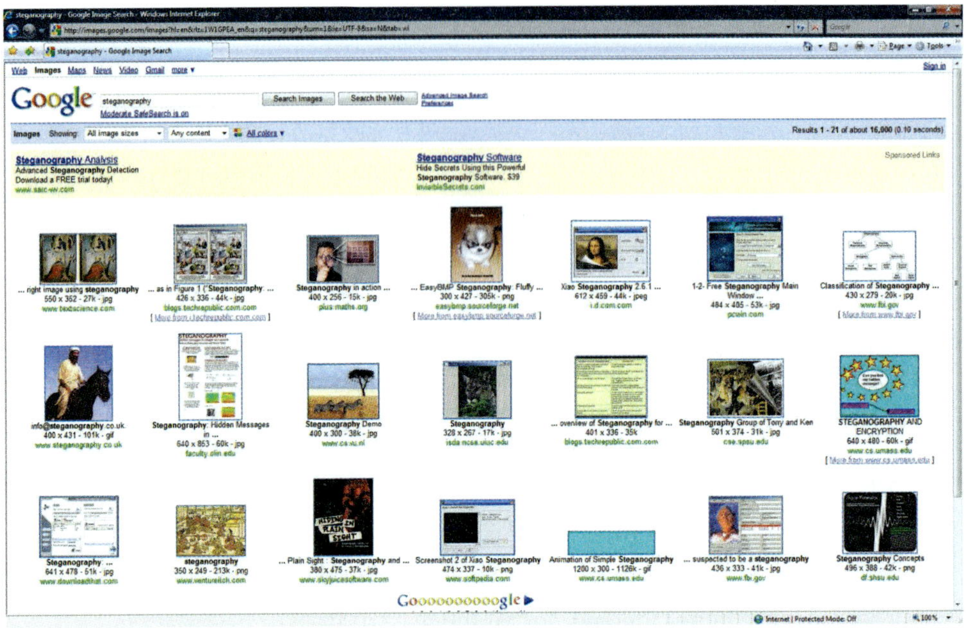

The nature of the image files also makes a hidden message difficult to detect. Although it is most common to hide messages inside images, they can also be hidden in video and audio files.

The advantage to steganography over the use of encryption alone is that the messages do not attract attention, and this difficulty in detecting the hidden message provides an additional barrier to analysis. The data that is hidden in a steganographic message is frequently also encrypted so that if it is discovered, the message will remain secure. Steganography has many uses, but the most publicized uses are to hide illegal material, often pornography, or allegedly for covert communication by terrorist networks.

Steganographic encoding can be used in many ways and through many different media. Covering them all is beyond the scope for this book, but we will discuss one of the most common ways to encode into an image file: LSB encoding. LSB, or *least significant bit,* is a method of encoding information into an image while altering the actual visual image as little as possible. A computer image is made up of thousands or millions of pixels, all defined by 1's and 0's. If an image is composed of Red Green Blue (RGB) values, each pixel has an RGB value represented numerically from 0 to 255. For example, 0,0,0 is black, and 255,255,255 is white, which can also be represented as 00000000, 00000000, 00000000 for black and 11111111, 11111111, 11111111 for white. Given a white pixel, editing the least significant bit of the pixel to 11111110, 11111110, 11111110 changes the color. The change in color is undetectable to the human eye, but in an image with a million pixels, this creates a 125KB area in which to store a message.

Some popular steganography detection tools include Stegdetect, StegSecret, StegSpy, and the family of SARC (Steganography Analysis and Research Center) tools. All of these tools use detection techniques based on the same principle: pattern detection. By looking for known steganographic encoding schemes or artifacts, they can potentially detect embedded data. Additionally, steganography insertion tools can be used to attempt to decode images with suspected hidden messages. Invisible Ink is a small program for steganographic insertion of messages and then the extraction of those messages, as illustrated here:

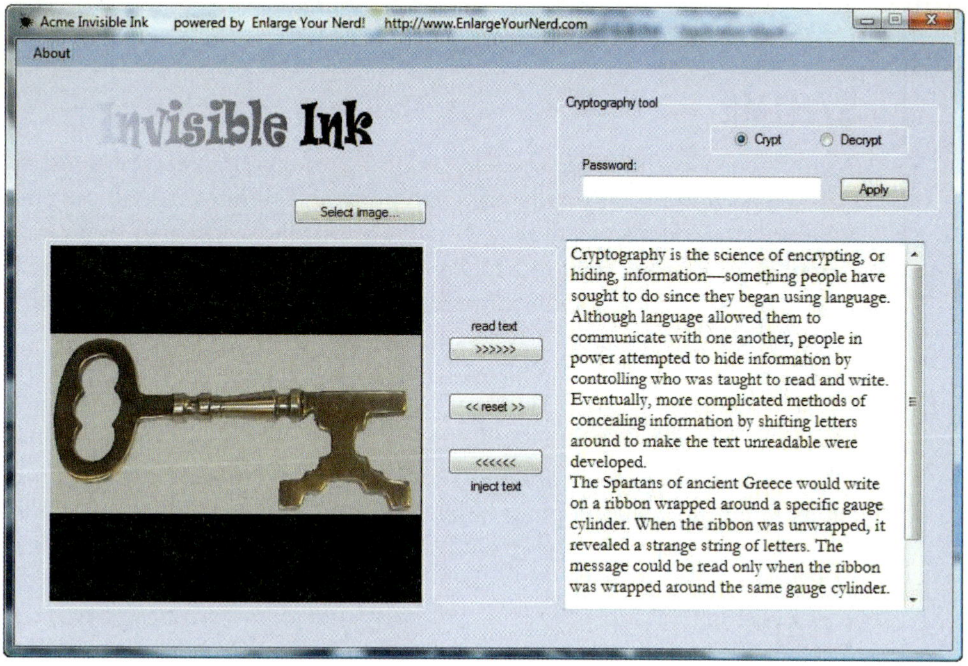

Secure Protocols

Protocols act as a common language, allowing different components to talk using a common, known set of commands. Many different protocols exist, all of which are used to achieve specific communication goals.

DNSSEC

The Domain Name Service (DNS) is a protocol for the translation of names into IP addresses. When users enter a name such as www.example.com, the DNS system converts this name into the actual numerical IP address. DNS records are also used for e-mail delivery. The DNS protocol uses UDP over port 53 for standard queries, although TCP can be used for large transfers such as zone transfers. DNS is a hierarchical system of servers, from local copies of records, up through Internet providers to root-level servers. DNS is one of the primary underlying protocols used on the Internet and is involved in almost all addressing lookups. The problem with DNS is that requests and replies are sent in plaintext and are subject to spoofing.

DNSSEC is a set of extensions to the DNS protocol, which through the use of cryptography enables origin authentication of DNS data, authenticated denial of existence, and data integrity, but not does not extend to availability or confidentiality. DNSSEC records are signed so that all DNSSEC responses are authenticated but not encrypted. This prevents unauthorized DNS responses from being interpreted as correct.

> **Tech Tip**
>
> **Common Ports**
>
> | | |
> |---|---|
> | *SSH* | *TCP 22* |
> | *LDAPS* | *TCP 636 or 3269* |
> | *FTPS* | *TCP 989 and 990* |
> | *SFTP* | *TCP 22 (SSH)* |
> | *SNMP* | *UDP 161 and 162 or TCP 161 and 162* |
> | *HTTPS* | *TCP 443* |
> | *Secure POP* | *TCP 995* |
> | *Secure IMAP* | *TCP 993* |
> | *Secure SMTP* | *TCP 465* |

SSH

The **Secure Shell (SSH)** protocol is an encrypted remote terminal connection program used for remote connections to a server. SSH uses asymmetric encryption but generally requires an independent source of trust with a server, such as manually receiving a server key, to operate. SSH uses TCP port 22 as its default port.

S/MIME

As previously mentioned, **S/MIME (Secure/Multipurpose Internet Mail Extensions)** is a standard for public key encryption and signing of Multipurpose Internet Mail Extensions data in e-mails. S/MIME is designed to provide cryptographic protections to e-mails and is built into the majority of modern e-mail software to facilitate interoperability.

SRTP

The **Secure Real-time Transport Protocol (SRTP)** is a network protocol for securely delivering audio and video over IP networks. SRTP uses cryptography to provide encryption, message authentication, and integrity, as well as replay protection to the RTP data.

LDAPS

By default, LDAP traffic is transmitted insecurely. You can make LDAP traffic secure by using it with SSL/TLS. Commonly, LDAP is enabled over SSL (LDAPS) by using a certificate from a trusted certificate authority (CA). **Lightweight Directory Access Protocol Secure (LDAPS)** involves the use of an SSL tunnel to connect LDAP services. Technically, this method was retired with LDAPv2 and replaced with Simple Authentication and Security Layer (SASL) in LDAPv3. SASL is a standard method of using TLS to secure services across the Internet. LDAP is the primary protocol for transmitting directory information. Directory services may provide any organized set of records, often with a hierarchical structure, and are used in a wide variety of situations, including Active Directory data sets. LDAPS communication occurs over TCP port 636. LDAPS communication to a global catalog server occurs over TCP 3269. When connecting to port 636 or 3269, SSL/TLS is negotiated before any LDAP traffic is exchanged.

FTPS

FTPS is the implementation of FTP over an SSL/TLS secured channel. This supports complete FTP compatibility, yet provides the encryption protections enabled by SSL/TLS. FTPS uses TCP ports 989 and 990.

SFTP

SFTP involves the use of FTP over an SSH channel. This leverages the encryption protections of SSH to secure FTP transfers. Because of its reliance on SSH, it uses TCP port 22.

SNMPv3

The **Simple Network Management Protocol version 3 (SNMPv3)** is a standard for managing devices on IP-based networks. SNMPv3 was developed to specifically address the security concerns and vulnerabilities of SNMPv1 and SNMPv2. SNMP is an application layer protocol, part of the IP suite of protocols, and can be used to manage and monitor devices, including network devices, computers, and other devices connected to the IP network. All versions of SNMP require ports 161 and 162 to be open on a firewall. Most SNMP systems use UDP, but TCP can be used as well.

TLS

As previously mentioned, **Transport Layer Security (TLS)** is an IETF standard for the employment of encryption technology and replaces SSL. Using the same basic principles, TLS updates the mechanisms employed by SSL. Although sometimes referred to as SSL, TLS is a separate standard. The standard port for TLS is undefined because it depends on what the protocol being protected uses—for example, HTTP (port 80) becomes port 443 when it is HTTPS. The current versions of TLS are 1.2 and 1.3.

HTTPS

Most web activity occurs using the Hypertext Transfer Protocol (HTTP), but this protocol is prone to interception. **HTTP Secure (HTTPS)** uses either SSL or TLS to secure the communication channel. Originally developed by Netscape Communications and implemented in its browser, HTTPS has since been incorporated into most common browsers. HTTPS uses the standard TCP port 443 for TCP/IP communications rather than the standard port 80 used for HTTP. As previously discussed, because of vulnerabilities in SSL, only TLS is recommended for HTTPS today.

> IMAP uses port 143, but SSL/TLS-encrypted IMAP uses port 993. POP uses port 110, but SSL/TLS-encrypted POP uses port 995. SMTP uses port 25, but SSL/TLS-encrypted SMTP uses port 465.

Secure POP/IMAP

Secure POP3 and **Secure IMAP** are basically POP3 and IMAP, respectively, over an SSL/TLS session. Secure POP3 utilizes TCP port 995 and Secure IMAP uses TCP port 993. Encrypted data from the e-mail client is sent to the e-mail server over an SSL/TLS session. With the deprecation of SSL, TLS is the preferred protocol today. If e-mail connections are started in nonsecure mode, the STARTTLS directive tells the clients to change to the secure ports.

IPSec

IP Security (IPSec) is a collection of IP security features designed to introduce security at the network or packet-processing layer in network communication. Other approaches have attempted to incorporate security at higher levels of the TCP/IP suite, such as at the level where applications reside. IPSec is designed to provide secure IP communications over the Internet. In essence, IPSec provides a secure version of the IP by introducing authentication and encryption to protect Layer 4 protocols. IPSec is optional for

IPv4 but is required for IPv6. Obviously, both ends of the communication need to use IPSec for the encryption/decryption process to occur.

IPSec provides two types of security service to ensure authentication and confidentiality for either the data alone (referred to as IPSec *transport mode*) or for both the data and header (referred to as *tunnel mode*). See Chapter 11 for more detail on tunneling and IPSec operation. IPSec introduces several new protocols, including the Authentication Header (AH), which basically provides authentication of the sender, and the Encapsulating Security Payload (ESP), which adds encryption of the data to ensure confidentiality. IPSec also provides for payload compression before encryption using the IP Payload Compression Protocol (IPcomp). Frequently, encryption negatively impacts the ability of compression algorithms to fully compress data for transmission. By providing the ability to compress the data before encryption, IPSec addresses this issue.

IPSec is a secure network protocol suite that is used to authenticate and encrypt data packets sent between systems. It provides authentication, integrity, and confidentiality.

Secure Protocol Use Cases

Protocols are used to allow parties to have a common understanding of how communications will be handled, and they define the expectations for each party. Because different use cases have different communication needs, different protocols will be used by different use cases. Work has been afoot to standardize some general-purpose security protocols, ones that can be reused over and over instead of new ones being invented for each use case. The Simple Authentication and Security Layer (SASL) effort is an example of that—it's a standardized method of invoking a TLS tunnel to secure a communication channel. This method is shown to work with a wide range of services—currently more than 15, and increasing.

The remainder of this section examines some common secure protocol use cases and the associated secure protocols used in them. Although the protocols have been discussed earlier, these are the use cases.

Voice and Video

Voice and video are frequently streaming media and, as such, have their own protocols for the encoding of data streams. The *Secure Real-time Transport Protocol (SRTP)* can be used for securely delivering audio and video over IP networks. SRTP is covered in RFC 3711 (https://tools.ietf.org/html/rfc3711).

Time Synchronization

NTP (Network Time Protocol) is the standard for time synchronization across servers and clients. NTP has no assurance against a man-in-the-middle attack, and although this has raised concerns over the implications, to date, nothing has been done to secure NTP directly or to engineer an out-of-band security check. If an organization is hypersensitive to this risk, it could enclose all time communications using a TLS tunnel, although this is not an industry practice.

E-mail and Web

E-mail and the Web are both native plaintext-based systems. With the need for secure web connections, SSL and TLS are available, as denoted by the HTTPS protocol. The use of SSL/TLS is widespread and common. Also, it is worth remembering that SSL is no longer considered secure. E-mail is a bit more complicated to secure, and the best option is to use S/MIME, as discussed previously in this chapter.

File Transfer

Secure file transfer can be accomplished via a wide range of methods, ensuring the confidentiality and integrity of file transfers across networks. FTP is not secure, but as previously discussed, secure alternatives such as SFTP and FTPS exist and can be used.

Directory Services

Directory services use LDAP as the primary protocol. When security is required, LDAPS is a common option, as described previously. Directory services are frequently found behind the scenes with respect to logon information.

Remote Access

Remote access is the means by which users can access computer resources across a network. Securing remote access can be done via many means; some for securing the authentication process, and others for the actual data access itself. As with many situations requiring securing communication channels, or data in transit, SSL/TLS is commonly employed.

Domain Name Resolution

Domain name resolution is performed primarily by the DNS protocol. DNS is a plaintext protocol, and the secure version, DNSSEC, is not widely deployed globally as yet. For local deployments, DNSSEC has been available in Windows Active Directory domains since 2012.

Routing and Switching

Routing and switching are the backbone functions of networking in a system. Managing the data associated with networking is the province of SNMPv3. SNMPv3 enables applications to manage data associated with networking and devices.

Network Address Allocation

Managing network address allocation functions in a network requires multiple decision criteria, including the reduction of complexity and the management of device names and locations. SNMPv3 has many functions that can be employed to manage the data flows of this information to management applications that can assist administrators in network assignments.

IP addresses can be allocated either statically (with a manual, fixed IP to each device solution) or via Dynamic Host Configuration Protocol (DHCP, which allows the automation of assigning IP addresses). In some cases, a mix of static and DHCP is used. IP address allocation is part of proper network design, which is crucial to the performance and expandability of a network. Learn how to properly allocate IP addresses for a new network—and learn your options if you run out of IP addresses.

Subscription Services

Subscription services involve the management of data flows to and from a system based on either a push (publish) or pull (subscribe) model. Managing what data elements are needed by which nodes is a problem that can be tackled using directory services such as LDAP. Another use of subscription services is the Software as a Service (SaaS) model, where software is licensed on a subscription basis. The actual software is hosted centrally (commonly in the cloud), and user access is based on subscriptions. This is becoming a common software business model.

Cryptographic Attacks

Attacks against the cryptographic system are referred to as *cryptographic attacks.* These attacks are designed to take advantage of two specific weaknesses. The first is on the side of a user. Users widely view cryptography as magic, or otherwise incomprehensible stuff, leading them to trust without valid reasons. The second factor is aimed at algorithmic weaknesses that can be exploited. Although understood by computer scientists, they are frequently overlooked by developers. A variant and much more likely algorithmic weakness is in the actual implementation of the algorithm in code. Errors in coding encryption algorithms can result in systems that appear to work, but in reality are weak or incorrect implementations. As we will explore in Chapter 19, during software development it is important to use vetted libraries for cryptographic functions and proven algorithms.

There is a wide array of known cryptographic attack mechanisms. From known-plaintext attacks to chosen-plaintext attacks, ciphertext-only attacks, chosen-ciphertext attacks (both CCA1 and CCA2), chosen-key attacks, and meet-in-the-middle attacks, the list of things a crypto-developer needs to be aware of and protect against can be intimidating. This is one of the reasons one should only use approved crypto libraries, where implementations are vetted and have specific protections against common modes of attack. There are implementation-based attack methods, such as man-in-the-middle attacks, the KRACK attack against WPA2, replay attacks, and side-channel attacks, that also require consideration and protection. At the end of the day, the very complexity that enables the functions of modern cryptography can obscure and enable these attack vectors.

Birthday

The **birthday attack** is a special type of brute force attack that gets its name from something known as the birthday paradox, which states that in a group of at least 23 people, the chance that two individuals will have the same birthday is greater than 50 percent. Mathematically, we can use the equation $1.25k^{1/2}$ (with k equaling the size of the set of possible values), and in the birthday paradox, k would be equal to 365 (the number of possible birthdays). This same phenomenon applies to passwords, with k (number of passwords) being quite a bit larger. This is the result of having many combinations of two items from a large group, making the number of potential matching states higher. The key to the birthday attack is not to search for a match to a specific item, but rather to find any two items with the same key.

> **Tech Tip**
>
> **Weak Keys**
>
> *Keys are instrumental in the functioning of the algorithm, and there are cases where a key can be considered a weak key because it forces the algorithm output to an undesired path, resulting in an encrypted version that is easily broken. Weak rotor combinations led to weak encryption with Enigma machines in WWII. Another example is in Triple DES, where certain key patterns can lead to weak results. For instance, the DES key is broken into 16 subkeys in use. If the key creates 16 identical subkeys, this will result in weaker-than-normal results. Another example is in Blowfish, where S-boxes are key dependent and certain keys can create weak S-boxes. The verification of proper keys for an algorithm needs to be one of the functions of the key-generation mechanism; otherwise, real-life operation may result in failure.*

Known Plaintext/Ciphertext

If an attacker has the original plaintext and ciphertext for a message, they can determine the key used through brute force attempts through the keyspace. *Known plaintext/ciphertext* attacks can be difficult to mitigate, as some messages are particularly prone to this problem. In the event of having known messages, such as the German weather reports, it was possible using cryptanalysis techniques to eventually determine the Enigma machine rotor combinations, leading to the breakdown of that system (see Tech Tip "Weak Keys"). Modern cryptographic algorithms have protections included in the implementations to guard against this form of attack. One is the use of large keyspaces, making the brute force spanning of the keyspace, or even a significant portion of it, no longer possible.

Chosen Cipher Text Attack

A common attack methodology used against encryption schemes is the chosen cipher text attack. In this attack, an attacker presents a chosen cipher text to the system and, using the information from a series of these decryption efforts, can perform cryptanalysis to attempt to determine the key. If blocks are padded as part of the process, then by playing with the padding, information can be recovered. Although these attacks are highly technical and can require significant resources to interpret, the scale of web-based systems can result in millions of these messages being sent and received, providing significant information for an attacker to use in key discovery. One of the primary drivers of AEAD was its resistance to this type of attack.

> **Tech Tip**
>
> **Chosen Plain Text Attack**
>
> *If you can get your adversary to send a known message (chosen plaintext), then this can assist in breaking the key. This was done in several cases in WWII both against the Germans to break Enigma keys (using weather reports) and against Japan (using a fake set of intelligence about broken equipment).*

Weak Implementations

Weak implementations are another problem associated with backward compatibility. The best example of this is SSL. SSL, in all of its versions, has now fallen to attackers. TLS, an equivalent methodology that does not suffer from these weaknesses, is the obvious solution; yet many sites still employ SSL. Cryptography has long been described as an arms race between attackers and defenders, with multiple versions and improvements over the years. Whenever an older version is allowed, there is a risk associated with weaker implementations.

Meet-in-the-Middle Attacks

The **meet-in-the-middle attack** involves attacking the problem from two directions and looking for the match. The plaintext is encrypted with every possible key in one direction. The cryptographic message is decrypted with every possible key in the other direction. The result of the comparison can help to discover which algorithm is used and the secret key that was used.

Replay

Replay attacks work against cryptographic systems like they do against other systems. If one can record a series of packets and then replay them, what was valid before may well be valid again. There are a wide range of defenses against replay attacks, and therefore this should not be an issue. However, developers who do not follow best practices can create implementations that lack replay protections, enabling this attack path to persist.

Downgrade

As part of a TLS/SSL setup, there is a specification of the cipher suite to be employed. This is done to enable the highest form of encryption that both the server and browser can support. In a **downgrade attack**, the attacker takes advantage of a commonly employed principle to support backward compatibility, to downgrade the security to a lower or nonexistent state.

> **Tech Tip**
>
> **Password Defenses**
>
> *There are two players in password defenses: the system designer and the user.*
>
> *A system designer needs to ensure that a password system does the proper handling, storage (of the salted hash only) of passwords, and logging of activity. The designer also needs to invoke lockouts if incorrect passwords are entered. Failure to lock out incorrect choices allows unlimited attempts on the part of an attacker.*
>
> *Users need to be trained in good password hygiene: how to create a good password, not to share passwords between accounts, and to watch for phishing attempts that try to obtain their password.*
>
> *Passwords are still useful for security, but they need to be instantiated and used properly.*

Collision

A **collision attack** is where two different inputs yield the same output of a hash function. Through making "invisible to the user" changes to a digital file and creating many copies, then using the birthday attack to find a collision between any two of the many versions, one has a chance to create a file with changed visible content but identical hashes.

Password Attacks

The most common form of authentication is the user ID and password combination. Although it is not inherently a poor mechanism for authentication, the combination can be attacked in several ways. All too often, these attacks yield favorable results for the attacker—not as a result of a weakness in the scheme, but usually due to the user not following good password procedures.

Poor Password Choices

The least technical of the various password-attack techniques consists of the attacker simply attempting to guess the password of an authorized user of the system or network. It is surprising how often this simple method works, and the reason it does is because people are notorious for picking poor passwords. Users need to select a password that they can remember, so they create simple passwords, such as their birthday, their mother's maiden name, the name of their spouse or one of their children, or even simply their user ID itself. All it takes is for the attacker to obtain a valid user ID (often a simple matter, because organizations tend to use an individual's names in some combination—first letter of their first name combined with their last name, for example) and a little bit of information about the user before guessing can begin. Organizations sometimes make it even easier for attackers to obtain this sort of information by posting the names of their "management team" and other individuals, sometimes with short biographies, on their websites.

Even if a person doesn't use some personal detail as their password, the attacker may still get lucky because many people use a common word for their password. Attackers can obtain lists of common passwords—a number of such lists exist on the Internet. Words such as "password" and "secret" have often been used as passwords. Names of favorite sports teams also often find their way onto lists of commonly used passwords.

Tech Tip

Rainbow Tables

Rainbow tables *are precomputed hash tables that enable looking up small text entries via their hash values. This makes hashed passwords "reversible." The use of rainbow tables works for small passwords (fewer than 10 characters) and is very fast. Salting passwords is one of the defenses against these tables.*

Rainbow Tables

Rainbow tables are precomputed tables or hash values associated with passwords. This can change the search for a password from a computational problem to a lookup problem. This can tremendously reduce the level of work needed to crack a given password. The best defense against rainbow tables is the use of salted hashes, as the addition of a salt value increases the complexity of the problem by making the precomputing process not replicable between systems.

Dictionary

Another method of determining passwords is to use a password-cracking program that uses a list of dictionary words to try to guess the password, hence the name *dictionary attack*. The words can be used by themselves, or two or more smaller words can be combined to form a single possible password. A number of commercial and public domain password-cracking programs employ a variety of methods to crack passwords, including using variations on the user ID.

These programs often permit the attacker to create various rules that tell the program how to combine words to form new possible passwords. Users commonly substitute certain numbers for specific letters. If the user wanted to use the word *secret* for a password, for example, the letter *e* could be replaced with the number 3, yielding *s3cr3t*. This password will not be found in the dictionary, so a pure dictionary attack would not crack it, but the password is still easy for the user to remember. If a rule were created that tried all words in the dictionary and then tried the same words substituting the number 3 for the letter *e*, however, the password would be cracked.

Rules can also be defined so that the cracking program will substitute special characters for other characters or combine words. The ability of the attacker to crack passwords is directly related to the method the user employs to create the password in the first place, as well as the dictionary and rules used.

Brute Force

If the user has selected a password that is not found in a dictionary, even if various numbers or special characters are substituted for letters, the only way the password can be cracked is for an attacker to attempt a *brute force attack,* in which the password-cracking program attempts all possible password combinations.

The length of the password and the size of the set of possible characters in the password will greatly affect the time a brute force attack will take. A few years ago, this method of attack was very time consuming, since it took considerable time to generate all possible combinations. With the increase in computer speed, however, generating password combinations is much faster, making it more feasible to launch brute force attacks against certain computer systems and networks.

A brute force attack on a password can take place at two levels: it can attack a system where the attacker is attempting to guess the password at a login prompt, or it can attack against the list of password hashes contained in a password file. The first attack can be made more difficult if the account locks after a few failed login attempts. The second attack can be thwarted if the password file is securely maintained so that others cannot obtain a copy of it.

Online vs. Offline

When the brute force attack occurs in real time against a system, it is frequently being done to attack a single account with multiple examples of passwords. Success or failure is determined by the system under attack: either you get in or you don't. Online brute force attacks tend to be very noisy and easy to see by network security monitoring. They are also limited by system response time and bandwidth.

Offline, brute force can be employed to perform hash comparisons against a stolen password file. This has the challenge of stealing the password file, but if accomplished, it is possible to use high-performance, GPU-based, parallel machines to try passwords at very high rates and against multiple accounts at the same time.

Hybrid Attack

A *hybrid* password attack is a system that combines the preceding methods. Most cracking tools have this option built in, first attempting a dictionary attack and then moving to brute force methods.

Password Spraying Attacks

Password *spraying* is an attack that uses a limited number of commonly used passwords and applies them to a large number of accounts. Traditional brute force attacks attempt to gain unauthorized access to a single account by guessing the password. Spraying is the reverse of this, using a limited number of passwords and trying them against all the accounts. This is a useful attack when you don't care which account you get, and it's fairly successful when given a large set of accounts. Defending against this attack is important in organizations because if one account is breached, it is the foothold that is needed to gain entry.

Plaintext/Unencrypted

Passwords that are stored are subject to retrieval. Any time a system can send you a copy of your password, there is a security issue. Plaintext password attacks are those taken against these specific issues. Lest anyone think that this is only a problem from rogue systems or programs, even mainstream systems can fall prey to this trap. Microsoft allows administrators to push out passwords for local accounts via group policy preferences. To protect the passwords, they are encrypted using Advanced Encryption Standard (AES). For reasons of compatibility with other systems, Microsoft published the AES key. See the problem?

In Microsoft Windows systems, Mimikatz is a security tool that can extract Kerberos tickets from memory, and it also possesses the ability to extract plaintext passwords from process dumps of the LSASS process. This means that by using the security tools ProcDump and Mimikatz, one can harvest plaintext passwords from a system.

Other Standards

Many additional standards are associated with information security that are not specifically or solely associated with PKI and/or cryptography. The remainder of the chapter introduces these standards and protocols.

FIPS

The **Federal Information Processing Standards Publications (FIPS PUBS, or simply FIPS)** describe various standards for data communication issues. These documents are issued by the U.S. government through the National Institute of Standards and Technology (NIST), which is tasked with their development. NIST creates these publications when a compelling government need requires a standard for use in areas such as security or system interoperability and no recognized industry standard exists. Three categories of FIPS PUBS are currently maintained by NIST:

- Hardware and software standards/guidelines
- Data standards/guidelines
- Computer security standards/guidelines

These documents require that products sold to the U.S. government comply with one (or more) of the FIPS standards. The standards can be obtained from www.nist.gov/itl/fips.cfm.

FIPS 140-2 relates to specific cryptographic standards for the validation of components used in U.S. government systems. Systems can be accredited to the FIPS 140-2 standard to demonstrate levels of security from "approved algorithms" to higher levels that include additional protections up to and including physical security and tamperproof mechanisms.

Common Criteria

The Common Criteria (CC) for Information Technology Security is the result of an effort to develop a joint set of security processes and standards that can be used by the international community. The major contributors to the CC are the governments of the United States, Canada, France, Germany, the Netherlands, and the United Kingdom. The CC also provides a listing of laboratories that apply the criteria in testing security products. Products that are evaluated by one of the approved laboratories receive an Evaluation Assurance Level of EAL1 through EAL7 (EAL7 is the highest level), with EAL4, for example, designed for environments requiring a moderate to high level of independently assured security, and EAL1 being designed for environments in which some confidence in the correct operation of the system is required but where the threats to the system are not considered serious. The CC also provides a listing of products by function that have performed at a specific EAL.

ISO/IEC 27002 (Formerly ISO 17799)

ISO/IEC 27002 is a very popular and detailed standard for creating and implementing security policies. ISO/IEC 27002 was formerly ISO 17799, which was based on version 2 of the British Standard 7799 (BS7799), published in May 1999. With the increased emphasis placed on security in both the government and industry in recent years, many organizations are now training their audit personnel to evaluate their organizations against the ISO/IEC 27002 standard. The standard is divided into 12 sections, each containing more detailed statements describing what is involved for that topic:

- **Risk assessment** Determine the impact of risks
- **Security policy** Guidance and policy provided by management
- **Organization of information security** Governance structure to implement security policy
- **Asset management** Inventory and classification of assets
- **Human resources security** Policies and procedures addressing security for employees, including hires, changes, and departures
- **Physical and environmental security** Protection of the computer facilities
- **Communications and operations management** Management of technical security controls in systems and networks
- **Access control** Restriction of access rights to networks, systems, applications, functions, and data
- **Information systems acquisition, development, and maintenance** Building security into applications
- **Information security incident management** Anticipating and responding appropriately to information security breaches
- **Business continuity management** Protecting, maintaining, and recovering business-critical processes and systems
- **Compliance** Ensuring conformance with information security policies, standards, laws, and regulations

Chapter 6 Review

Chapter Summary

After reading this chapter and completing the exercises, you should understand the following about applied cryptography.

Learn the elements involved in the correct use of cryptography

- Cryptography is used to ensure confidentiality, integrity, authentication, and nonrepudiation.
- How common cryptographic applications, including digital signatures, digital rights management, and file and database encryption systems, are used to secure information in systems and during communications.

Examine cipher suites and common uses

- Understand algorithm selection and use to implement secret communications and key exchanges.
- The common use cases of low-power devices, low latency, high resiliency, and supporting confidentiality, integrity, obfuscation, and authentication.
- Encryption for transport, including data in transit, data at rest, and data in use.

Learn cryptographic attack methods

- Common attack methods, including birthday, collision, downgrade, known-plaintext, and meet-in-the-middle attacks.
- An examination of password attacks, including poor password choices, rainbow tables, dictionary, brute force, and hybrid attacks.
- Digital rights management (DRM) uses some form of asymmetric encryption that allows an application to determine if you are an authorized user of the digital content you are trying to access. For example, DVDs and certain digital music formats such as AACS use DRM.
- Cipher suites provide information to assist developers in choosing the correct methods to achieve desired levels of protection.

Key Terms

Bcrypt *(157)*
birthday attack *(175)*
cipher suite *(153)*
collison attack *(176)*
cryptographic service provider (CSP) *(160)*
crypto modules *(161)*
data at rest *(160)*
data in transit *(160)*
data in use *(160)*
digital rights management (DRM) *(151)*
digital signature *(150)*
DNSSEC *(169)*
downgrade attack *(176)*
ephemeral keys *(157)*
Federal Information Processing Standards Publications (FIPS PUBS or simply FIPS) *(179)*
FTPS *(170)*
HMAC-based one-time password (HOTP) *(150)*
Hypertext Transfer Protocol Secure (HTTPS) *(171)*
IPSec *(171)*
key escrow *(156)*
key exchange *(155)*
key stretching *(157)*
Lightweight Directory Access Protocol Secure (LDAPS) *(170)*
meet-in-the-middle attack *(176)*
message integrity *(149)*
Password-Based Key Derivation Function 2 (PBKDF2) *(157)*
Pretty Good Privacy (PGP) *(165)*
rainbow tables *(177)*
replay attack *(176)*
Secure IMAP *(171)*
Secure POP3 *(171)*
Secure/Multipurpose Internet Mail Extensions (S/MIME) *(170)*
Secure Real-time Transport Protocol (SRTP) *(170)*
Secure Shell (SSH) *(170)*
session key *(156)*

SFTP *(170)*

Simple Network Management Protocol version 3 (SNMPv3) *(171)*

steganography *(167)*

transport encryption *(157)*

Transport Layer Security (TLS) *(171)*

Key Terms Quiz

Use terms from the Key Terms list to complete the sentences that follow. Don't use the same term more than once. Not all terms will be used.

1. _______________ is a protocol used to secure DNS packets during transmission across a network.
2. A common encryption method designed to encrypt above the network layer, enabling secure sessions between hosts, is called _______________.
3. _______________ is the use of special encoding to hide messages within other messages.
4. ____________ provide precomputed answers to a problem.
5. A _______________ is a software library that implements cryptographic functions.
6. E-mails and their attachments can be secured using _______________.
7. The use of multiple nearly identical messages can lead to the _______________ cryptographic attack method.
8. The _______________ is a network protocol for securely delivering audio and video over IP networks.
9. Reusing previous user input to bypass security is an example of a(n) _______________ attack.
10. _______________ is a popular encryption program that has the ability to encrypt and digitally sign e-mail and files.

Multiple-Choice Quiz

1. Which of the following is used to strengthen passwords from brute force attacks?
   - A. Bcrypt2
   - B. PBKDF2
   - C. DNSSEC
   - D. SSH-enabled logins
2. Why is LSB encoding the preferred method for steganography?
   - A. It uses much stronger encryption.
   - B. It applies a digital signature to the message.
   - C. It alters the picture the least amount possible.
   - D. It adds no additional entropy.
3. Transport Layer Security consists of which two protocols?
   - A. The TLS Record Protocol and TLS Handshake Protocol
   - B. The TLS Record Protocol and TLS Certificate Protocol
   - C. The TLS Certificate Protocol and TLS Handshake Protocol
   - D. The TLS Key Protocol and TLS Handshake Protocol
4. What is the advantage of using a crypto module?
   - A. Custom hardware adds key entropy.
   - B. It performs operations and maintains the key material in a physical or logical boundary.
   - C. It performs encryption much faster than general-purpose computing devices.
   - D. None of the above.
5. Which of the following is a detailed standard for creating and implementing security policies?
   - A. PKIX
   - B. ISO/IEC 27002
   - C. FIPS
   - D. X.509
6. Why does ECC work well on low-power devices?
   - A. Less entropy is needed for a given key strength.
   - B. Less computational power is needed for a given key strength.
   - C. Less memory is needed for a given key strength.
   - D. None of the above.

7. What makes a digitally signed message different from an encrypted message?
   A. The digitally signed message has encryption protections for integrity and nonrepudiation.
   B. A digitally signed message uses much stronger encryption and is harder to break.
   C. The encrypted message only uses symmetric encryption.
   D. There is no difference.
8. Which of the following is a secure e-mail standard?
   A. POP3
   B. IMAP
   C. SMTP
   D. S/MIME
9. Which of the following is not an advantage of TLS v1.3 over TLS v1.2 and earlier?
   A. Removal of RC4
   B. Reduction in round trips during handshakes
   C. Use of AES
   D. Restriction to AEAD ciphers
10. Transport Layer Security for HTTP uses what port to communicate?
   A. 53
   B. 80
   C. 143
   D. 443

Essay Quiz

1. Imagine you are a web developer for a small, locally owned business. Explain when using HTTP would be satisfactory, and why, and explain when you should use HTTPS, and why.
2. Explain in your own words how, by applying both asymmetric and symmetric encryption, your browser uses TLS to protect the privacy of the information passing between your browser and a web server.
3. It is well understood that asymmetric encryption consumes more computing resources than symmetric encryption. Explain how PGP uses both asymmetric and symmetric encryption to be both secure and efficient.

Lab Projects

Note that for these lab projects, it would be best to have a partner so that you can each have your own pair of public/private keys to confirm the operation of PGP.

• Lab Project 6.1

Load either a trial version of PGP or Gnu Privacy Guard (GPG). Install it and create a public/private key pair for yourself. Create a document using a word processor and encrypt it using the receiver's public key. Send it to a partner (or yourself), and then decrypt it using the corresponding private key.

• Lab Project 6.2

Create another document different from the one used in Lab Project 6.1. This time use your private key to digitally sign the document and send it to a partner (or yourself), who can then use the public key to confirm that it really is from you, the indicated sender.

chapter 7

Public Key Infrastructure

Without trust, there is nothing.

—Anonymous

In this chapter, you will learn how to

- Implement the basics of public key infrastructures
- Describe the roles of certificate authorities and certificate repositories
- Explain the relationship between trust and certificate verification
- Identify centralized and decentralized infrastructures
- Understand the lifecycle of certificates
- Describe public and in-house certificate authorities
- Identify the standards involved in establishing an interoperable Internet PKI
- Explain interoperability issues with PKI standards
- Describe how the common Internet protocols implement the PKI standards

Public key infrastructures (PKIs) are becoming a central security foundation for managing identity credentials in many companies. The technology manages the issue of binding public keys and identities across multiple applications. The other approach, without PKIs, is to implement many different security solutions and hope for interoperability and equal levels of protection.

PKIs comprise several components, including certificates, registration and certificate authorities, and a standard process for verification. PKIs are about managing the sharing of trust and using a third party to vouch for the trustworthiness of a claim of ownership over a credential document, called a **certificate**.

The Basics of Public Key Infrastructures

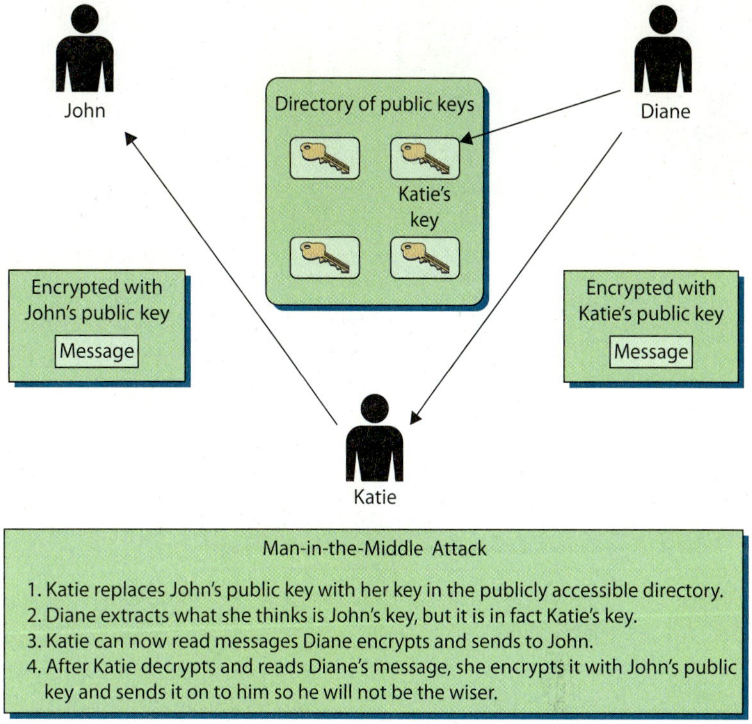

• **Figure 7.1** Without PKIs, individuals could spoof others' identities.

A **public key infrastructure (PKI)** provides all the components necessary for different types of users and entities to be able to communicate securely and in a predictable manner. A PKI is made up of hardware, applications, policies, services, programming interfaces, cryptographic algorithms, protocols, users, and utilities. These components work together to allow communication to take place using public key cryptography and symmetric keys for digital signatures, data encryption, and integrity.

Although many different applications and protocols can provide the same type of functionality, constructing and implementing a PKI boils down to establishing a level of trust. If, for example, John and Diane want to communicate securely, John can generate his own public/private key pair and send his public key to Diane, or he can place his public key in a directory that is available to everyone. If Diane receives John's public key, either from him or from a public directory, how does she know the key really came from John? Maybe another individual, Katie, is masquerading as John and has replaced John's public key with her own, as shown in Figure 7.1 (referred to as a man-in-the-middle attack). If this took place, Diane would believe that her messages could be read only by John and that the replies were actually from him. However, she would actually be communicating with Katie. What is needed is a way to verify an individual's identity, to ensure that a person's public key is bound to their identity and thus ensure that the previous scenario (and others) cannot take place.

> **Tech Tip**
>
> **Public and Private Keys**
>
> *Recall from Chapter 5 that the public key is the one you give to others and that the private key never leaves your possession. Anything one key does, the other undoes, so if you encrypt something with the public key, only the holder of the private key can decrypt it. If you encrypt something with the private key, then everyone who uses the public key knows that the holder of the private key did the encryption. Certificates do not alter any of this; they only offer a standard means of transferring keys.*

In PKI environments, entities called registration authorities (RAs) and certificate authorities (CAs) provide services similar to those of the Department of Motor Vehicles (DMV). When John goes to register for a driver's license, he has to prove his identity to the DMV by providing his passport, birth certificate, or other identification documentation. If the DMV is satisfied with the proof John provides (and John passes a driving test), the DMV will create a driver's license that can then be used by John to prove his identity. Whenever John needs to identify himself, he can show his driver's license. Although many people may not trust John to identify himself truthfully, they do trust the third party, the DMV.

In the PKI context, while some variations exist in specific products, the RA will require proof of identity from the individual requesting a certificate and will validate this information. The RA will then advise the CA to generate a certificate, which is analogous to a driver's license. The CA will digitally sign the certificate using its private key. The use of the private key ensures to the recipient that the certificate came from the CA. When Diane receives John's certificate and verifies that it was actually digitally signed

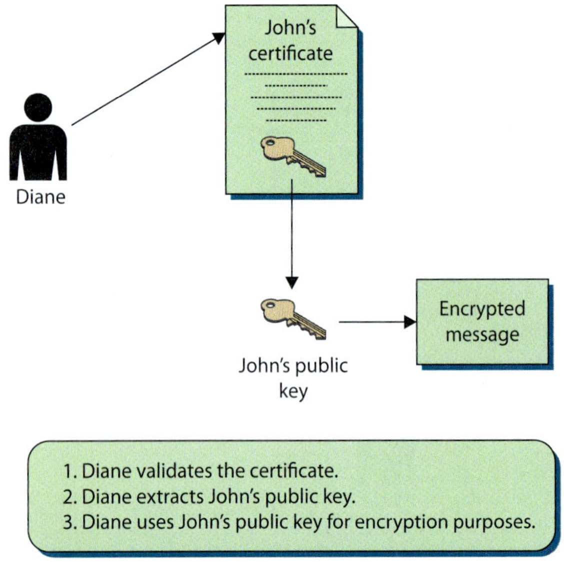

• **Figure 7.2** Public keys are components of digital certificates.

by a CA that she trusts, she will believe that the certificate is actually John's—not because she trusts John, but because she trusts the entity that is vouching for his identity (the CA).

This is commonly referred to as a *third-party trust model*. Public keys are components of digital certificates, so when Diane verifies the CA's digital signature, this verifies that the certificate is truly John's and that the public key the certificate contains is also John's. This is how John's identity is bound to his public key.

This process allows John to authenticate himself to Diane and others. Using the third-party certificate, John can communicate with Diane, using public key encryption, without prior communication or a preexisting relationship.

Once Diane is convinced of the legitimacy of John's public key, she can use it to encrypt messages between herself and John, as illustrated in Figure 7.2.

Numerous applications and protocols can generate public/private key pairs and provide functionality similar to what a PKI provides, but no trusted third party is available for both of the communicating parties. For each party to choose to communicate this way without a third party vouching for the other's identity, the two must choose to trust each other and the communication channel they are using. In many situations, it is impractical and dangerous to arbitrarily trust an individual you do not know, and this is when the components of a PKI must fall into place—to provide the necessary level of trust you cannot, or choose not to, provide on your own.

PKIs are composed of several elements:

- Certificates (containing keys)
- Certificate authorities (CAs)
- Registration authorities (RAs)
- Certificate revocation lists (CRLs)
- Trust models

What does the "infrastructure" in public key infrastructure really mean? An infrastructure provides a sustaining groundwork upon which other things can be built. So an infrastructure works at a low level to provide a predictable and uniform environment that allows other, higher-level technologies to work together through uniform access points. The environment that the infrastructure provides allows these higher-level applications to communicate with each other and gives them the underlying tools to carry out their tasks.

Certificate Authorities

A **certificate authority (CA)** is a trusted authority that certifies individuals' identities and creates electronic documents indicating that individuals are who they say they are. The electronic document is referred to as a **digital certificate**, and it establishes an association between the subject's identity and a public key. The private key that is paired with the public key in the certificate is stored separately.

A CA is more than just a piece of software, however; it is actually made up of the software, hardware, procedures, policies, and people who are involved in validating individuals' identities and generating the certificates. This means that if one of these components is compromised, it can negatively affect the CA overall and can threaten the integrity of the certificates it produces.

> **Cross Check**
>
> **Certificates Stored on a Client PC**
>
> Certificates are stored on user PCs. Chapter 17 covers the use of the Internet and associated materials, including the use of certificates by web browsers. Take a moment to explore the certificates stored on your PC by your browser. To understand the details behind how certificates are stored and managed, see the details in Chapter 17.

Every CA should have a **certification practices statement (CPS)** that outlines how identities are verified; the steps the CA follows to generate, maintain, and transmit certificates; and why the CA can be trusted to fulfill its responsibilities.

The CPS describes how keys are secured, what data is placed within a digital certificate, and how revocations will be handled. If a company is going to use and depend on a public CA, the company's security officers, administrators, and legal department should review the CA's entire CPS to ensure that it will properly meet the company's needs, and to make sure that the level of security claimed by the CA is high enough for their use and environment. A critical aspect of a PKI is the trust between the users and the CA, so the CPS should be reviewed and understood to ensure that this level of trust is warranted.

The **certificate server** is the actual service that issues certificates based on the data provided during the initial registration process. The server constructs and populates the digital certificate with the necessary information and combines the user's public key with the resulting certificate. The certificate is then digitally signed with the CA's private key.

> **Tech Tip**
>
> **Trusting CAs**
>
> *The question of whether a CA can be trusted is part of the continuing debate on how much security PKIs actually provide. Overall, people put a lot of faith in CAs. If a CA was compromised or did not follow through on its various responsibilities, word would get out and it would quickly lose customers and business. CAs work diligently to ensure that the reputation of their products and services remains good by implementing very secure facilities, methods, procedures, and trained personnel. But it is up to the company or individual to determine what degree of trust can actually be given and what level of risk is acceptable.*

Registration Authorities

A **registration authority (RA)** is the PKI component that accepts a request for a digital certificate and performs the necessary steps of registering and authenticating the person requesting the certificate. The authentication requirements differ depending on the type of certificate being requested. Most CAs offer a series of classes of certificates with increasing trust by class. The specific classes are described later in the section titled "Certificate Classes."

Each higher class of certificate can carry out more powerful and critical tasks than the one below it. This is why the different classes have different requirements for proof of identity. If you want to receive a Class 1 certificate, you may only be asked to provide your name, e-mail address, and physical address. For a Class 2 certification, you may need to provide the RA with more data, such as your driver's license, passport, and company information that can be verified. To obtain a Class 3 certificate, you will be asked to provide even more information and most likely will need to go to the RA's office for a face-to-face meeting. Each CA will outline the certification classes it provides and the identification requirements that must be met to acquire each type of certificate.

Local Registration Authorities

A **local registration authority (LRA)** performs the same functions as an RA, but the LRA is closer to the end users. This component is usually implemented in companies that have their own internal PKIs and have distributed sites. Each site has users that need RA services, so instead of requiring them to communicate with one central RA, each site can have its own LRA. This reduces the amount of traffic that would be created by several users making requests across wide area network (WAN) lines. The LRA performs identification, verification, and registration functions. It then sends the request, along with the user's public key, to a centralized CA so that the certificate can be generated. It acts as an interface between the users and the CA. LRAs simplify the RA/CA process for entities that desire certificates only for in-house use.

Public Certificate Authorities

An individual or company might decide to rely on a CA that is already established and being used by many other individuals and companies—a public CA. Alternatively, the company might decide it needs its own CA for internal use, which gives the company more control over the certificate registration and generation process and allows it to configure items specifically for its own needs. This second type of CA is referred to as a *private CA* (or *in-house CA*), discussed in the next section.

> Users can remove CAs from their browser list if they want to have more control over whom their system trusts and doesn't trust. Unfortunately, system updates can restore the CAs, thus requiring regular certificate store maintenance on the part of the users.

A public CA specializes in verifying individual identities and creating and maintaining their certificates. These companies issue certificates that are not bound to specific companies or intracompany departments. Instead, their services are to be used by a larger and more diversified group of people and organizations. If a company uses a public CA, the company will pay the CA organization for individual certificates and for the service of maintaining these certificates. Some examples of public CAs are VeriSign (including GeoTrust and Thawte), Entrust, and GoDaddy.

One advantage of using a public CA is that it is usually well known and easily accessible to many people. Most web browsers have a list of public CAs installed and configured by default, along with their corresponding root certificates. This means that if you install a web browser on your computer, it is already configured to trust certain CAs, even though you might have never heard of them before. So, if you receive a certificate from Bob, and his certificate was digitally signed by a CA listed in your browser, you automatically trust the CA and can easily walk through the process of verifying Bob's certificate. This has raised some eyebrows among security professionals, however, since trust is installed by default, but the industry has deemed this is a necessary approach that provides users with transparency and increased functionality.

The *certificate policy (CP)* allows users to decide what certification classes are acceptable and how they will be used within the organization. This is different from the CPS, which explains how the CA verifies entities, generates certificates, and maintains these certificates. The CP is generated and owned by an individual company that uses an external CA, and it allows the company to enforce *its* security decisions and control how certificates are used with its applications.

In-house Certificate Authorities

An *in-house CA* is implemented, maintained, and controlled by the company that implemented it. This type of CA can be used to create certificates for internal employees, devices, applications, partners, and customers. This approach gives the company complete control over how individuals are identified, what certification classifications are created, who can and cannot have access to the CA, and how the certifications can be used.

Choosing Between a Public CA and an In-house CA

When deciding between an in-house CA and public CA, you need to identify and account for various factors. Setting up your own PKI takes significant resources, especially skilled personnel. Several companies have started on a PKI implementation, only to quit halfway through, resulting in wasted time and money, with nothing to show for it except heaps of frustration and many ulcers.

In some situations, it is better for a company to use a public CA, since public CAs already have the necessary equipment, skills, and technologies. In other situations, companies may decide it is a better business decision to take on these efforts themselves. This is not always a strictly monetary decision—a specific level of security might be required. Some companies do not believe they can trust an outside authority to generate and maintain their users' and company's certificates. In this situation, the scale may tip toward an in-house CA.

Each company is unique, with various goals, security requirements, functionality needs, budgetary restraints, and ideologies. The decision of whether to use a private CA or an in-house CA depends on the expansiveness of the PKI within the organization, how integrated it will be with different business needs and goals, its interoperability with the company's current technologies, the number of individuals who will be participating, and how it will work with outside entities. This could be quite a large undertaking that ties up staff, resources, and funds, so a lot of strategic planning is required, and what will and won't be gained from a PKI should be fully understood before the first dollar is spent on the implementation.

Outsourced Certificate Authorities

The last available option for using PKI components within a company is to outsource different parts of it to a specific service provider. Usually, the more complex parts are outsourced, such as the CA, RA, CRL, and key recovery mechanisms. This occurs if a company does not have the necessary skills to implement and carry out a full PKI environment.

Although outsourced services might be easier for your company to implement, you need to review several factors before making this type of

Tech Tip

Why In-house CAs?

In-house CAs provide more flexibility for companies, which often integrate them into current infrastructures and into applications for authentication, encryption, and nonrepudiation purposes. If the CA is going to be used over an extended period of time, this can be a cheaper method of generating and using certificates than having to purchase them through a public CA. Setting up in-house certificate servers is relatively easy and can be done with simple software that targets both Windows and Linux servers.

Certificate authorities come in many types: public, in-house, and outsourced. All of them perform the same functions, with the only difference being an organizational one. This can have a bearing on trust relationships, as one is more likely to trust in-house CAs over others for which there is arguably less control.

Tech Tip

Outsourced CA vs. Public CA

An outsourced CA is different from a public CA in that it provides dedicated services, and possibly equipment, to an individual company. A public CA, in contrast, can be used by hundreds or thousands of companies—the CA doesn't maintain specific servers and infrastructures for individual companies.

commitment. You need to determine what level of trust the company is willing to give to the service provider and what level of risk it is willing to accept. Often a PKI and its components serve as large security components within a company's enterprise, and allowing a third party to maintain the PKI can introduce too many risks and liabilities that your company is not willing to undertake. The liabilities the service provider is willing to accept, the security precautions and procedures the outsourced CAs provide, and the surrounding legal issues need to be examined before this type of agreement is made.

Some large vertical markets have their own outsourced PKI environments set up because they share similar needs and usually have the same requirements for certification types and uses. This allows several companies within the same market to split the costs of the necessary equipment, and it allows for industry-specific standards to be drawn up and followed. For example, although many medical facilities work differently and have different environments, they have a lot of the same functionality and security needs. If several of them came together, purchased the necessary equipment to provide CA, RA, and CRL functionality, employed one person to maintain it, and then each connected its different sites to the centralized components, the medical facilities could save a lot of money and resources. In this case, not every facility would need to strategically plan its own full PKI, and each would not need to purchase redundant equipment or employ redundant staff members. Figure 7.3 illustrates how one outsourced service provider

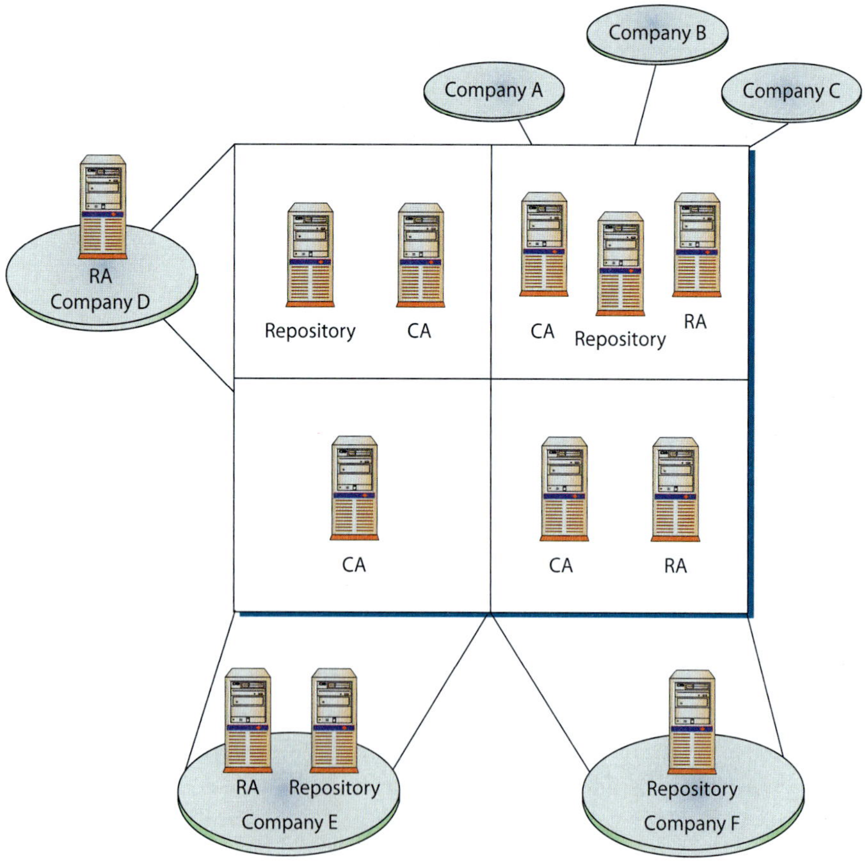

• **Figure 7.3** A PKI service provider (represented by the four boxes) can offer different PKI components to companies.

can offer different PKI components and services to different companies, and how companies within one vertical market can share the same resources.

A set of standards can be drawn up about how each different facility should integrate its own infrastructure and how it should integrate with the centralized PKI components. This also allows for less-complicated intercommunication to take place between the different medical facilities, which will ease information-sharing attempts.

Online vs. Offline CA

Certification servers must be online to provide certification services, so why would one have an offline server? The primary reason is security. For a given certificate authority that is only used for periodic functions, such as the signing of specific certificates that are rarely reissued or signed, keeping the server offline except when needed provides a significant level of security to the signing process. Other CA requests, such as CRL and validation requests, can be moved to a validation authority approved by the CA. **Offline CAs** are immune from many forms of attack and serve a valuable function as a backup data reference, while **online CAs** handle normal transactional work.

Stapling

Stapling is the process of combining related items to reduce communication steps. As an example, when someone requests a certificate, the stapling process sends both the certificate and Online Certificate Status Protocol (OCSP) responder information in the same request to avoid the additional fetches the client should perform during path validations.

Pinning

When a certificate is presented for a host, either identifying the host or providing a public key, this information can be saved in an act called **pinning**, which is the process of associating a host with a previously provided X.509 certificate or public key. This can be important for mobile applications that move between networks frequently and are much more likely to be associated with hostile networks where levels of trust are low and the risk of malicious data is high. Pinning assists in security through the avoidance of the use of DNS and its inherent risks when on less-than-secure networks.

The process of reusing a certificate or public key is called *key continuity*. This provides protection from an attacker, provided that the attacker was not in position to attack on the initial pinning. If an attacker is able to intercept and taint the initial contact, then the pinning will preserve the attack. You should pin any time you want to be relatively certain of the remote host's identity, relying on your home network security, and are likely to be operating at a later time in a hostile environment. If you choose to pin, you have two options: you can either pin the certificate or pin the public key.

> **Tech Tip**
>
> **Trust Models**
>
> *Several forms of trust models are associated with certificates. Hierarchical, peer-to-peer, and hybrid are the primary forms, with the web of trust being a form of hybrid. Each of these models has a useful place in the PKI architecture under different circumstances.*

Trust Models

Potential scenarios exist other than just having more than one CA—each of the companies or each department of an enterprise can actually represent a trust domain itself. A *trust domain* is a construct of systems, personnel, applications, protocols, technologies, and policies that work together to provide a certain level of protection. All of these components can work together seamlessly within the same trust domain because they are known to the other components within the domain and are trusted to some degree. Different trust domains are usually managed by different groups of administrators, have different security policies, and restrict outsiders from privileged access.

Most trust domains (whether individual companies or departments) usually are not islands cut off from the world—they need to communicate with other, less-trusted domains. The trick is to figure out how much two different domains should trust each other as well as how to implement and configure an infrastructure that would allow these two domains to communicate in a way that will not allow security compromises or breaches. This can be more difficult than it sounds.

In the nondigital world, it is difficult to figure out whom to trust, how to carry out legitimate business functions, and how to ensure that one is not being taken advantage of or lied to. Jump into the digital world and add protocols, services, encryption, CAs, RAs, CRLs, and differing technologies and applications, and the business risks can become overwhelming and confusing. So start with a basic question: what criteria will we use to determine whom we trust and to what degree?

One example of trust considered earlier in the chapter is the driver's license issued by the DMV. Suppose, for example, that Bob is buying a lamp from Carol and he wants to pay by check. Since Carol does not know Bob, she does not know if she can trust him or have much faith in his check. But if Bob shows Carol his driver's license, she can compare the name to what appears on the check, and she can choose to accept it. The *trust anchor* (the agreed-upon trusted third party) in this scenario is the DMV because both Carol and Bob trust it more than they trust each other. Bob had to provide documentation to the DMV to prove his identity, and that organization trusted him enough to generate a license. Because Carol trusts the DMV, she decides to trust Bob's check.

Consider another example of a trust anchor. If Joe and Stacy need to communicate through e-mail and would like to use encryption and digital signatures, they will not trust each other's certificate alone. But when each receives the other's certificate and sees that it has been digitally signed by an entity they both do trust—the CA—they have a deeper level of trust in each other. The trust anchor here is the CA. This is easy enough, but when we need to establish trust anchors between different CAs and PKI environments, it gets a little more complicated.

If two companies need to communicate using their individual PKIs, or if two departments within the same company use different CAs, two separate trust domains are involved. The users and devices from these different trust domains need to communicate with each other, and they need to exchange certificates and public keys, which means that trust anchors need to be identified and a communication channel must be constructed and maintained.

A trust relationship must be established between two issuing authorities (CAs). This happens when one or both of the CAs issue a certificate for the other CA's public key, as shown in Figure 7.4. This means that each CA registers for a certificate and public key from the other CA. Each CA validates the other CA's identification information and generates a certificate containing a public key for that CA to use. This establishes a trust path between the two entities that can then be used when users need to verify other users' certificates that fall within the different trust domains. The trust path can be unidirectional or bidirectional, so either the two CAs trust each other (bidirectional) or only one trusts the other (unidirectional).

Three forms of **trust models** are commonly found in PKIs:

- Hierarchical
- Peer-to-peer
- Hybrid

As illustrated in Figure 7.4, all the users and devices in trust domain 1 trust their own CA, CA 1, which is their trust anchor. All users and devices in trust domain 2 have their own trust anchor, CA 2. The two CAs have exchanged certificates and trust each other, but they do not have a common trust anchor between them.

The trust models describe and outline the trust relationships between the different CAs and different environments, which will indicate where the trust paths reside. The trust models and paths need to be thought out before implementation to restrict and control access properly and to ensure that as few trust paths as possible are used. Several different trust models can be used: the hierarchical, peer-to-peer, and hybrid models are discussed later in the chapter.

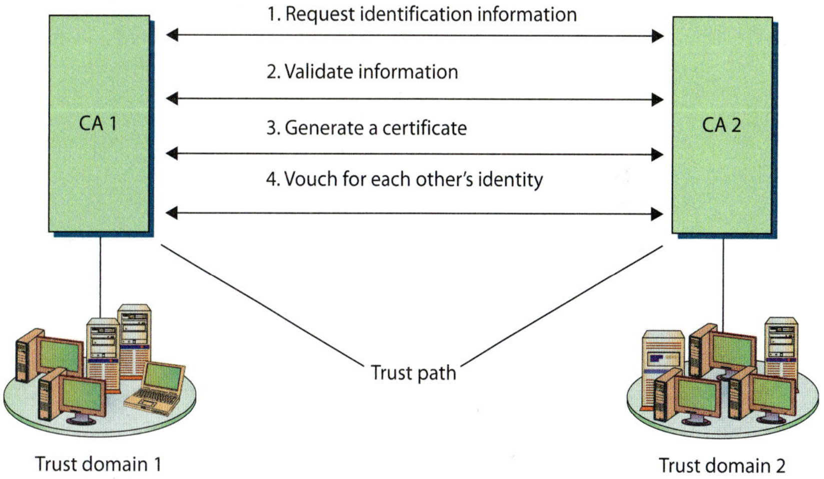

• **Figure 7.4** A trust relationship can be built between two trust domains to set up a communication channel.

Certificate Chaining

Certificates are used to convey identity and public key pairs to users, but this raises the question, why trust the certificate? The answer lies in the certificate chain, a chain of trust from one certificate to another, based on signing by an issuer, until the chain ends with a certificate that the user trusts. This conveys the trust from the trusted certificate to the certificate that is being used. Examining Figure 7.5, we can look at the ordered list of certificates from the one presented to the one that is trusted.

Certificates that sit between the presented certificate and the root certificate are called *chain* or **intermediate certificates**. The intermediate certificate is the signer/issuer of the presented certificate, indicating that it trusts the certificate. The root CA certificate is the signer/issuer of the intermediate certificate, indicating that it trusts the intermediate certificate. The **certificate chaining** is a manner of passing trust down from a trusted root certificate. The chain terminates with a root CA certificate. The root CA certificate is always signed by the CA itself. The signatures of all certificates in the chain must be verified up to the root CA certificate.

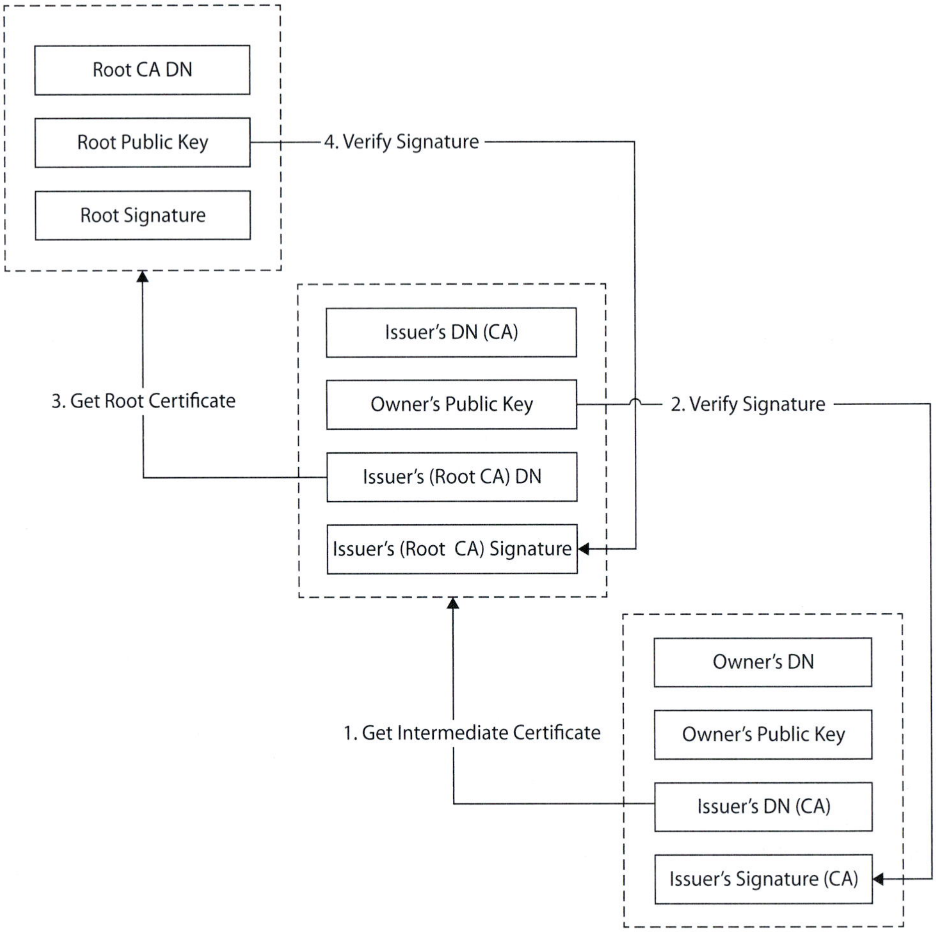

• **Figure 7.5** Certificate chaining

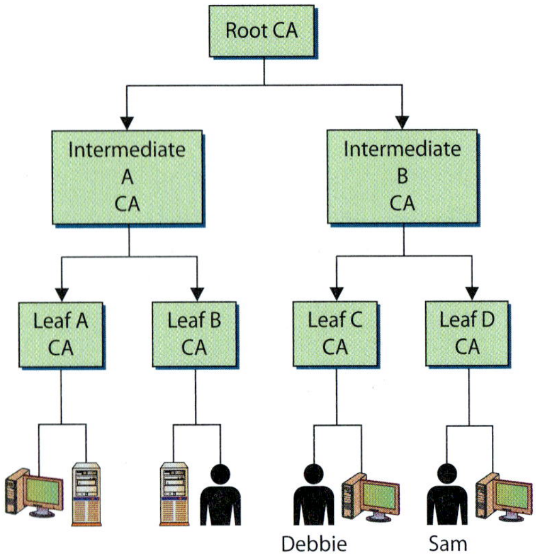

• **Figure 7.6** The hierarchical trust model outlines trust paths.

Hierarchical Trust Model

The **hierarchical trust model** is a basic hierarchical structure that contains a root CA, intermediate CAs, leaf CAs, and end-entities. The configuration is that of an inverted tree, as shown in Figure 7.5. The root CA is the ultimate trust anchor for all other entities in this infrastructure, and it generates certificates for the intermediate CAs, which in turn generate certificates for the leaf CAs, and the leaf CAs generate certificates for the end-entities (users, network devices, and applications).

Intermediate CAs function to transfer trust between different CAs. These CAs are referred to as *subordinate CAs* because they are subordinate to the CA they reference. The path of trust is walked up from the subordinate CA to the higher-level CA; in essence, the subordinate CA is using the higher-level CA as a reference.

As shown in Figure 7.6, no bidirectional trusts exist—they are all unidirectional trusts, as indicated by the one-way arrows. Because no other entity can certify and generate certificates for the root CA, it creates a *self-signed certificate*. This means that the certificate's Issuer and Subject fields hold the same information, both representing the root CA, and the root CA's public key will be used to verify this certificate when that time comes. This root CA certificate and public key are distributed to all entities within this trust model.

Peer-to-Peer Model

In a **peer-to-peer trust model**, one CA is not subordinate to another CA, and no established trusted anchor between the CAs is involved. The end-entities will look to their issuing CA as their trusted anchor, but the different CAs will not have a common anchor.

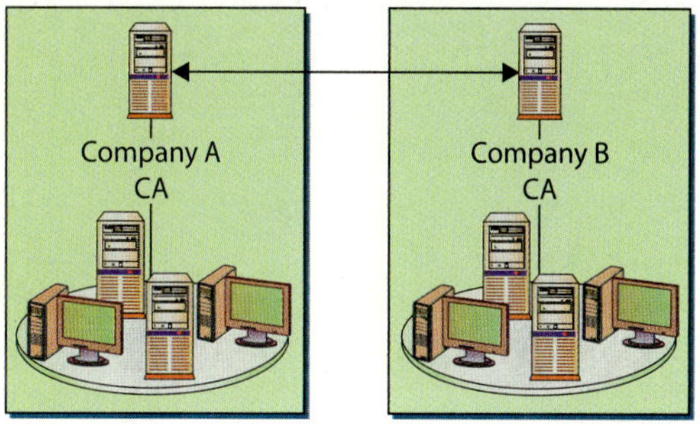

Figure 7.7 Cross-certification creates a peer-to-peer PKI model.

Figure 7.7 illustrates this type of trust model. The two different CAs will certify the public key for each other, which creates a bidirectional trust. This is referred to as *cross-certification* because the CAs are not receiving their certificates and public keys from a superior CA, but instead are creating them for each other.

One of the main drawbacks to this model is scalability. Each CA must certify every other CA that is participating, and a bidirectional trust path must be implemented, as shown in Figure 7.8. If one root CA were certifying all the intermediate CAs, scalability would not be as much of an issue.

Figure 7.8 represents a fully connected *mesh architecture,* meaning that each CA is directly connected to and has a bidirectional trust relationship with every other CA. As you can see in this figure, the complexity of this setup can become overwhelming.

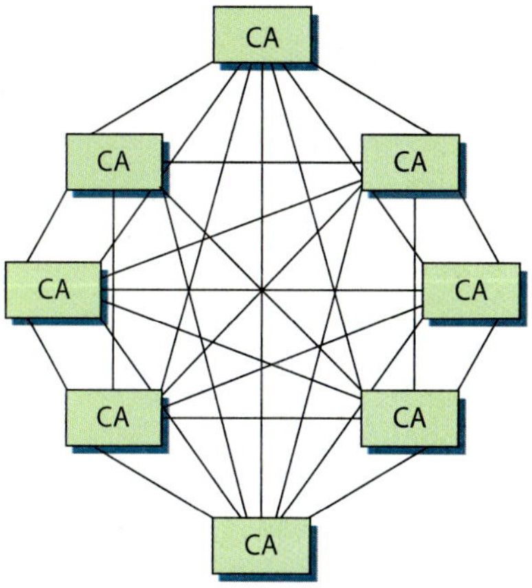

Figure 7.8 Scalability is a drawback in cross-certification models.

In any network model, fully connected mesh architectures are wasteful and expensive. In trust-transfer models, the extra level of redundancy is just that: redundant and unnecessary.

Hybrid Trust Model

A company can be internally complex, and when the need arises to communicate properly with outside partners, suppliers, and customers in an authorized and secured manner, this complexity can make sticking to either the hierarchical or peer-to-peer trust model difficult, if not impossible. In many implementations, the different model types have to be combined to provide the necessary communication lines and levels of trust. In a **hybrid trust model**, the two companies have their own internal hierarchical models and are connected through a peer-to-peer model using cross-certification.

Another option in this hybrid configuration is to implement a bridge CA. Figure 7.9 illustrates the role a bridge CA could play—it is responsible for issuing cross-certificates for all connected CAs and trust domains. The bridge is not considered a root or trust anchor, but merely the entity that generates and maintains the cross-certification for the connected environments.

Three trust models exist: hierarchical, peer-to-peer, and hybrid. Hierarchical trust is like an upside-down tree, peer-to-peer is a lateral series of references, and hybrid is a combination of hierarchical and peer-to-peer trust.

Walking the Certificate Path

When a user in one trust domain needs to communicate with a user in another trust domain, one user will need to validate the other's certificate. This sounds simple enough, but what it really means is that each certificate for each CA, all the way up to a shared trusted anchor, also must

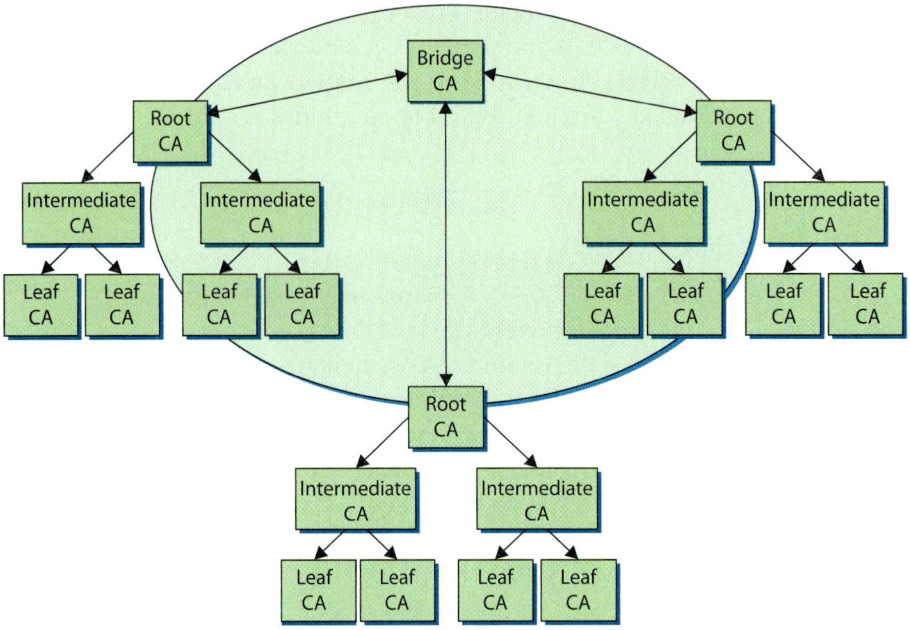

• **Figure 7.9** A bridge CA can control the cross-certification procedures.

> **Tech Tip**
>
> **Root CA**
>
> *If the root CA's private key were ever compromised, all entities within the hierarchical trust model would be drastically affected, because this is their sole trust anchor. The root CA usually has a small amount of interaction with the intermediate CAs and end-entities, and can therefore be taken offline much of the time. This provides a greater degree of protection for the root CA, because when it is offline it is basically inaccessible.*

be validated. If Debbie needs to validate Sam's certificate, as shown in Figure 7.10, she actually also needs to validate the Leaf D CA and Intermediate B CA certificates, as well as Sam's.

So in Figure 7.10, we have a user, Sam, who digitally signs a message and sends it and his certificate to Debbie. Debbie needs to validate this certificate before she can trust Sam's digital signature. Included in Sam's certificate is an Issuer field, which indicates that the certificate was issued by Leaf D CA. Debbie has to obtain Leaf D CA's digital certificate and public key to validate Sam's certificate. Remember that Debbie validates the certificate by verifying its digital signature. The digital signature was created by the certificate issuer using its private key, so Debbie needs to verify the signature using the issuer's public key.

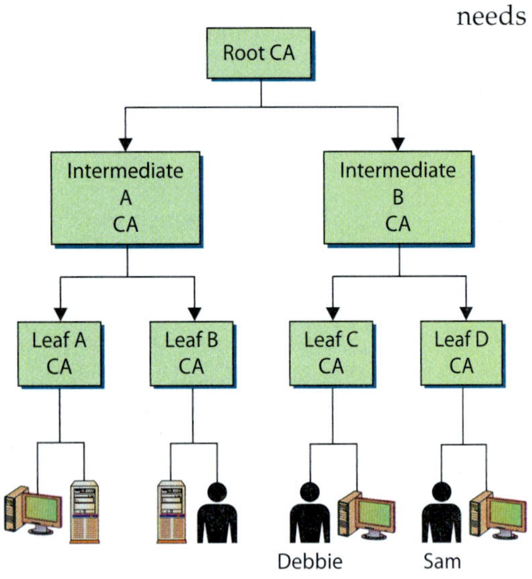

• **Figure 7.10** Verifying each certificate in a certificate path

Debbie tracks down Leaf D CA's certificate and public key, but she now needs to verify this CA's certificate, so she looks at the Issuer field, which indicates that Leaf D CA's certificate was issued by Intermediate B CA. Debbie now needs to get Intermediate B CA's certificate and public key.

Debbie's client software tracks this down and sees that the issuer for Intermediate B CA is the root CA, for which she already has a certificate and public key. So Debbie's client software had to follow the **certificate path**, meaning it had to continue to track down and collect certificates until it came upon a self-signed certificate. A self-signed certificate indicates that it was signed by a root CA, and Debbie's software has been configured to trust this entity as her trust anchor, so she can stop there. Figure 7.10 illustrates the steps Debbie's software had to carry out just to be able to verify Sam's certificate.

This type of simplistic trust model works well within an enterprise that easily follows a hierarchical organizational chart, but many companies cannot use this type of trust model because different departments or offices require their own trust anchors. These demands can be derived from direct business needs or from inter-organizational politics. This hierarchical model might not be possible when two or more companies need to communicate with each other. Neither company will let the other's CA be the root CA, because each does not necessarily trust the other entity to that degree. In these situations, the CAs will need to work in a peer-to-peer relationship instead of in a hierarchical relationship.

Digital Certificates

A digital certificate binds an individual's identity to a public key, and it contains all the information a receiver needs to be assured of the identity of the public key owner. After an RA verifies an individual's identity, the CA generates the digital certificate, but how does the CA know what type of data to insert into the certificate?

The certificates are created and formatted based on the **X.509 standard**, which outlines the necessary fields of a certificate and the possible values that can be inserted into the fields. As of this writing, X.509 version 3 is the most current version of the standard. X.509 is a standard of the International Telecommunication Union (www.itu.int). The IETF's Public Key Infrastructure (X.509) working group, or PKIX working group, has adapted the X.509 standard to the more flexible organization of the Internet, as specified in RFC 5280, and is commonly referred to as PKIX for Public Key Infrastructure X.509.

Table 7.1 lists and describes the fields in an X.509 certificate.

Figure 7.11 shows the actual values of the different certificate fields for a particular certificate in Internet Explorer. The version of this certificate is v3 (X.509 v3) and the serial number is also listed—this number is unique for each certificate that is created by a specific CA. The CA used the SHA-1 hashing algorithm to create the message digest value and then signed it using the CA's private key using the RSA algorithm. The actual CA that issued the certificate is Symantec Class 2 Shared Intermediate Certificate Authority, and the valid dates indicate how long this certificate is valid. The subject is Art Conklin, University of Houston, which is the entity that registered this certificate and that is bound to the embedded public key. The actual public key is shown in the lower window and is represented in hexadecimal.

The subject of a certificate is commonly a person, but it does not have to be. The subject can also be a network device (router, web server, firewall, and so on), an application, a department, or a company. Another example used in Table 7.1 is "CN = *.google.com, O = Google LLC, L = Mountain View, S = California, C = US." Each certificate has its own identity that needs to be verified and proven to another entity before secure, trusted communication can be initiated. If a network device is using a certificate for authentication, the certificate may contain the identity of that device. This allows a user of the device to verify its authenticity based on the signed certificate and trust in the signing authority. This trust can be transferred to the identity of the device, indicating authenticity.

Table 7.1 X.509 Certificate Fields

Field Name	Field Description
Certificate Version	X.509 version used for this certificate: Version 1 = 0 Version 2 = 1 Version 3 = 2
Serial Number	A nonnegative integer assigned by the certificate issuer that must be unique to the certificate.
Signature Algorithm Parameters (optional)	The algorithm identifier for the algorithm used by the CA to sign the certificate. The optional Parameters field is used to provide the cryptographic algorithm parameters used in generating the signature.
Issuer	Identification for the entity that signed and issued the certificate. This must be a Distinguished Name within the hierarchy of CAs.
Validity Not valid before time Not valid after time	Specifies a period of time during which the certificate is valid, using a "not valid before" time and a "not valid after" time (expressed in UTC or in a generalized time).
Subject	The Distinguished Name for the certificate owner. This can contain the Common Name and other elements, such as Organization, Location, State and Country: CN = *.google.com, O = Google LLC, L = Mountain View, S = California, C = US.
Subject Public Key Info	An encryption algorithm identifier followed by a bit string for the public key.
Issuer Unique ID	Optional for versions 2 and 3. This is a unique bit-string identifier for the CA that issued the certificate.
Subject Unique ID	Optional for versions 2 and 3. This is a unique bit-string identifier for the subject of the certificate.
Extensions Extension ID Critical Extension Value	Optional for version 3. The extensions area consists of a sequence of extension fields containing an extension identifier, a Boolean field indicating whether the extension is critical, and an octet string representing the value of the extension. Extensions can be defined in standards or defined and registered by organizations or communities.
Thumbprint Algorithm Algorithm Parameters (optional)	Identifies the algorithm used by the CA to sign this certificate. This field must match the algorithm identified in the Signature Algorithm field.
Thumbprint	The signature is the bit-string hash value obtained when the CA signed the certificate. The signature certifies the contents of the certificate, binding the public key to the subject.

Certificate Classes

The types of certificates available can vary between different CAs, but usually at least three different types are available, and they are referred to as classes:

- **Class 1** A Class 1 certificate is generally used to verify an individual's identity through e-mail. A person who receives a Class 1 certificate can use his public/private key pair to digitally sign e-mail and encrypt message contents.
- **Class 2** A Class 2 certificate can be used for software signing. A software vendor would register for this type of certificate so that it could digitally sign its software. This provides integrity for the software after it is developed and released, and it allows the receiver of the software to verify from where the software actually came.
- **Class 3** A Class 3 certificate can be used by a company to set up its own CA, which will allow it to carry out its own identification verification and generate certificates internally.

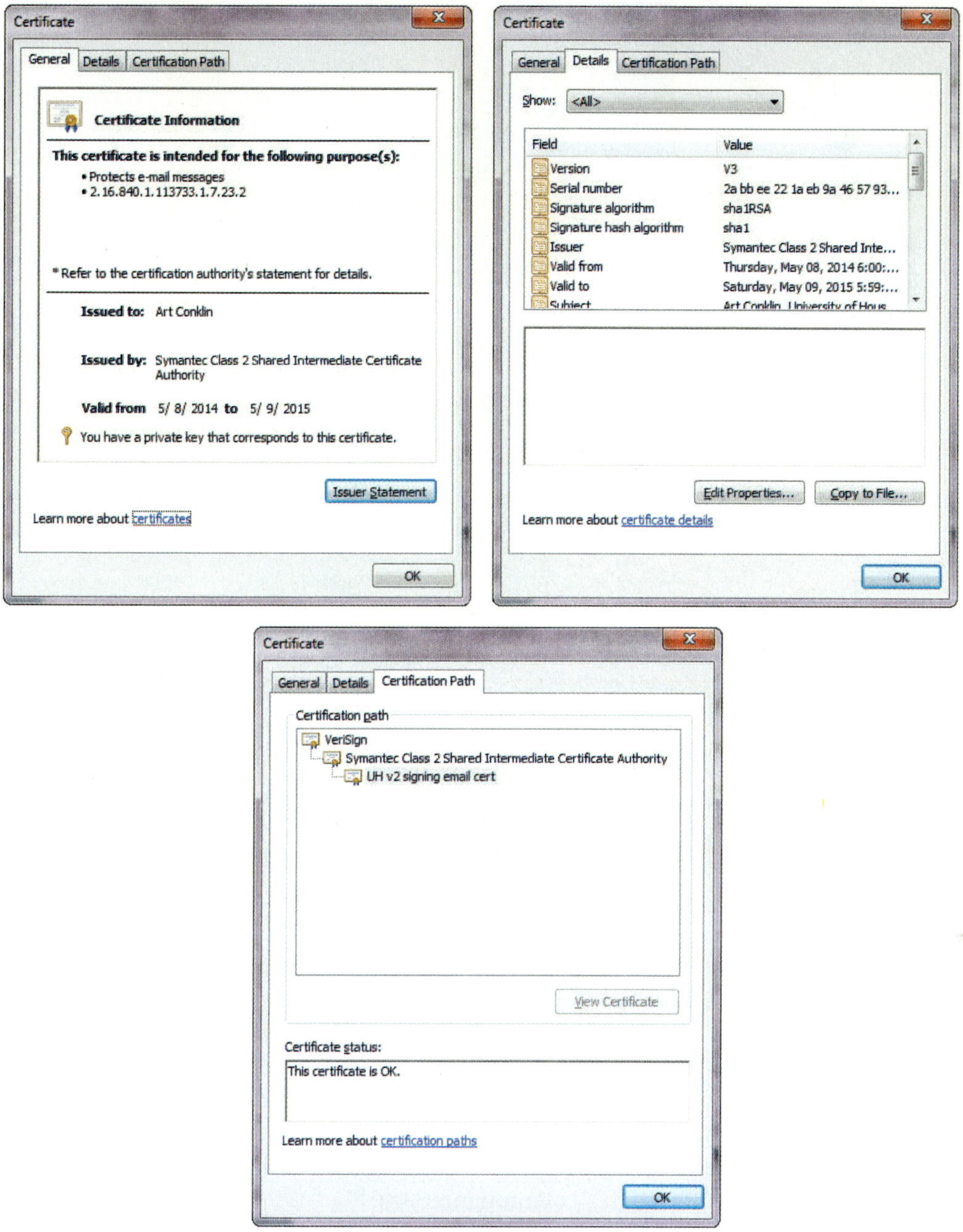

• **Figure 7.11** Fields within a digital certificate

In most situations, when a user requests a Class 1 certificate, the registration process will require the user to enter specific information into a web-based form. The web page will have a section that accepts the user's public key, or it will step the user through creating a public/private key pair, which will allow the user to choose the size of the keys to be created. Once these steps have been completed, the public key is attached to the certificate registration form and both are forwarded to the RA for processing. The RA is responsible only for the registration process and cannot actually generate a certificate. Once the RA is finished processing the request and verifying the individual's identity, the RA sends the request to the CA. The CA uses the RA-provided information to generate a digital certificate, integrates the

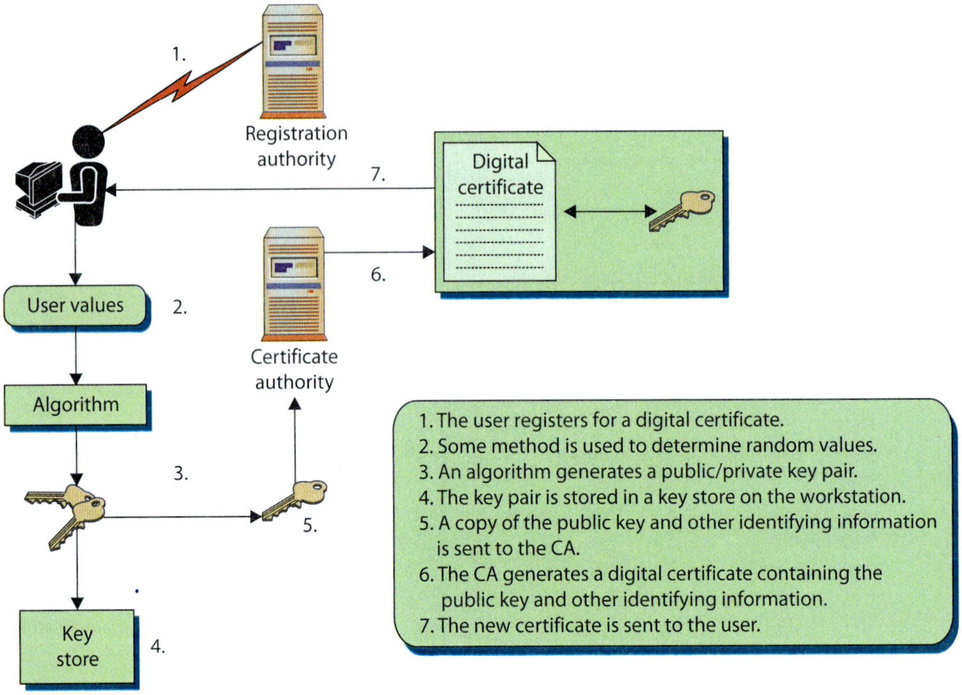

• **Figure 7.12** Steps for obtaining a digital certificate

necessary data into the certificate fields (user identification information, public key, validity dates, proper use for the key and certificate, and so on), and sends a copy of the certificate to the user. These steps are shown in Figure 7.12. The certificate may also be posted to a publicly accessible directory so that others can access it.

Note that a 1:1 correspondence does not necessarily exist between identities and certificates. An entity can have multiple key pairs, using separate public keys for separate purposes. Thus, an entity can have multiple certificates, each attesting to separate public key ownership. It is also possible to have different classes of certificates, again with different keys. This flexibility allows entities total discretion in how they manage their keys, and the PKI manages the complexity by using a unified process that allows key verification through a common interface.

If an application creates a key store that can be accessed by other applications, it will provide a standardized interface, called the *application programming interface (API)*. As an example, Figure 7.13 shows that Application A went through the process of registering a certificate and generating a key pair. It created a key store that provides an interface to allow other applications to communicate with it and use the items held within the store.

The RA verifies the identity of the certificate requestor on behalf of the CA. The CA generates the certificate using information forwarded by the RA.

Certificate Extensions

Certificate extensions allow for further information to be inserted within the certificate, which can be used to provide more functionality in a PKI implementation. Certificate extensions can be standard or private. *Standard certificate extensions* are implemented for every PKI implementation. *Private certificate extensions* are defined for specific organizations (or domains

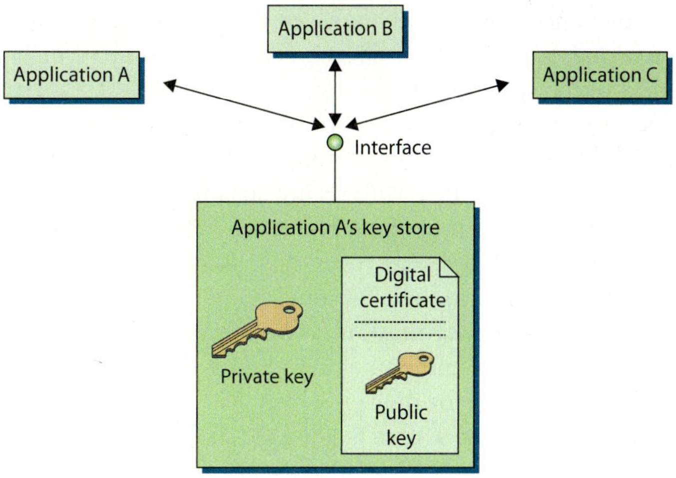

• **Figure 7.13** Some key stores can be shared by different applications.

within one organization), and they allow companies to further define different, specific uses for digital certificates to best fit their business needs.

Tech Tip

X.509 Digital Certificate Extensions

Following are some key examples of certificate extensions:

- ***DigitalSignature*** *The key used to verify a digital signature.*
- ***KeyEncipherment*** *The key used to encrypt other keys used for secure key distribution.*
- ***DataEncipherment*** *The key used to encrypt data, which cannot be used to encrypt other keys.*
- ***CRLSign*** *The key used to verify a CA signature on a CRL.*
- ***KeyCertSign*** *The key used to verify CA signatures on certificates.*
- ***NonRepudiation*** *The key used when a nonrepudiation service is being provided.*

Several different extensions can be implemented, one being *key usage extensions,* which dictate how the public key that is held within the certificate can be used. Remember that public keys can be used for different functions: symmetric key encryption, data encryption, verifying digital signatures, and more.

A nonrepudiation service can be provided by a third-party notary. In this situation, the sender's digital signature is verified and then signed by the notary so that the sender cannot later deny signing and sending the message. This is basically the same function performed by a traditional notary using paper—validate the sender's identity and validate the time and date of an item being signed and sent. This is required when the receiver needs to be *really* sure of the sender's identity and wants to be legally protected against possible fraud or forgery.

> **Tech Tip**
>
> **Critical Flag and Certificate Usage**
>
> *When an extension is marked as critical, it means that the CA is certifying the key for only that specific purpose. If Joe receives a certificate with a* DigitalSignature *key usage extension and the critical flag is set, Joe can use the public key only within that certificate to validate digital signatures, and no more. If the extension was marked as noncritical, the key can be used for purposes outside of those listed in the extensions, so in this case it is up to Joe (and his applications) to decide how the key will be used.*

If a company needs to be sure that accountable nonrepudiation services will be provided, a trusted time source needs to be used, which can be a trusted third party called a *timestamp authority (TSA)*. Using a trusted time source gives users a higher level of confidence as to *when* specific messages were digitally signed. For example, suppose Barry sends Ron a message and digitally signs it, and Ron later civilly sues Barry over a dispute. This digitally signed message may be submitted by Ron as evidence pertaining to an earlier agreement that Barry now is not fulfilling. If a trusted time source was not used in their PKI environment, Barry could claim that his private key had been compromised before that message was sent. If a trusted time source was implemented, then it could be shown that the message was signed *before* the date on which Barry claims his key was compromised. If a trusted time source is not used, no activity that was carried out within a PKI environment can be truly proven because it is so easy to change system and software time settings.

Critical and Noncritical Extensions

Certificate extensions are considered either *critical* or *noncritical*, which is indicated by a specific flag within the certificate itself. When this flag is set to critical, it means that the extension *must* be understood and processed by the receiver. If the receiver is not configured to understand a particular extension marked as critical, and thus cannot process it properly, the certificate cannot be used for its proposed purpose. If the flag does not indicate that the extension is critical, the certificate can be used for the intended purpose, even if the receiver does not process the appended extension.

Object Identifiers (OID)

Each extension to a certificate has its own ID, expressed as an object identifier, which is a set of values, together with either a critical or noncritical indication. The system using a certificate must reject the certificate if it encounters a critical extension that it does not recognize, or that contains information it cannot process. A noncritical extension may be ignored if it is not recognized but must be processed if it is recognized.

Certificate Attributes

Four main types of certificates are used:

- End-entity certificates
- CA certificates
- Cross-certification certificates
- Policy certificates

End-entity certificates are issued by a CA to a specific subject, such as Joyce, the Accounting department, or a firewall, as illustrated in Figure 7.14. An end-entity certificate is the identity document provided by PKI implementations.

A **CA certificate** can be self-signed, in the case of a standalone or root CA, or it can be issued by a superior CA within a hierarchical model. In the

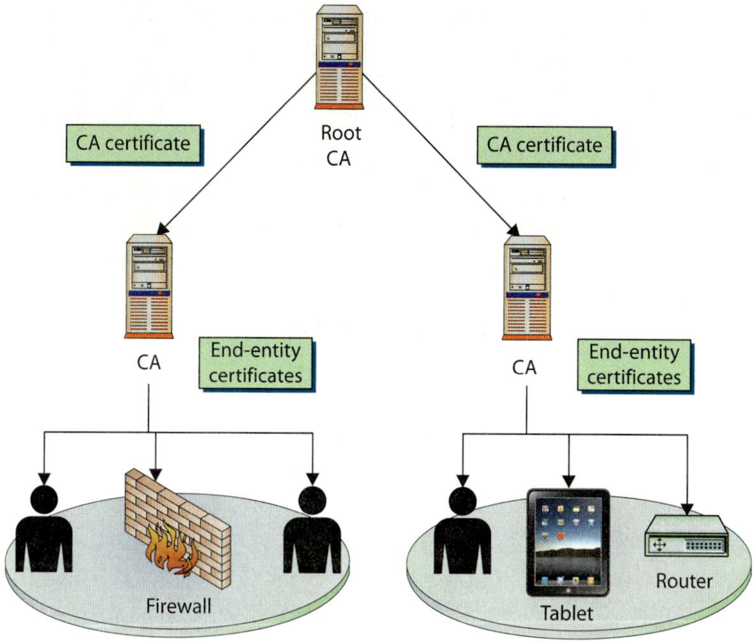

• **Figure 7.14** End-entity and CA certificates

model in Figure 7.14, the superior CA gives the authority and allows the subordinate CA to accept certificate requests and generate the individual certificates itself. This may be necessary when a company needs to have multiple internal CAs, and different departments within an organization need to have their own CAs servicing their specific end-entities in their sections. In these situations, a representative from each department requiring a CA registers with the higher trusted CA and requests a Certificate Authority certificate. (Public and private CAs are discussed in the "Public Certificate Authorities" and "In-house Certificate Authorities" sections earlier in this chapter, as are the different trust models that are available for companies.)

A **cross-certification certificate**, or *cross-certificate,* is used when independent CAs establish peer-to-peer trust relationships. Simply put, cross-certificates are a mechanism through which one CA can issue a certificate allowing its users to trust another CA.

Within sophisticated CAs used for high-security applications, a mechanism is required to provide centrally controlled policy information to PKI clients. This is often done by placing the policy information in a **policy certificate**.

Wildcard

Certificates can be issued to an entity such as example.com. But what if there are multiple entities under example.com that need certificates? In this case, you can either issue distinct certificates for each specific address or use wildcard certificates. **Wildcard certificates** work exactly as one would expect. A certificate issued for *.example.com, for instance, would be valid for both one.example.com and two.example.com.

CN

The **Common Name (CN)** field is represented in the Subject field of the certificate and is the fully qualified domain name (FQDN) for which the certificate is valid. A common representation in the subject line of a certificate may read as follows: CN = *.google.com, O = Google LLC, L = Mountain View, S = California, C = US. The CN is Common Name, O is Organization, L is Location, S is State, and C is Country.

A Distinguished Name (DN) is a term that describes the identifying information in a certificate and is part of the certificate itself. A certificate contains DN information for both the owner or requestor of the certificate (called the Subject DN) and the CA that issues the certificate (called the Issuer DN).

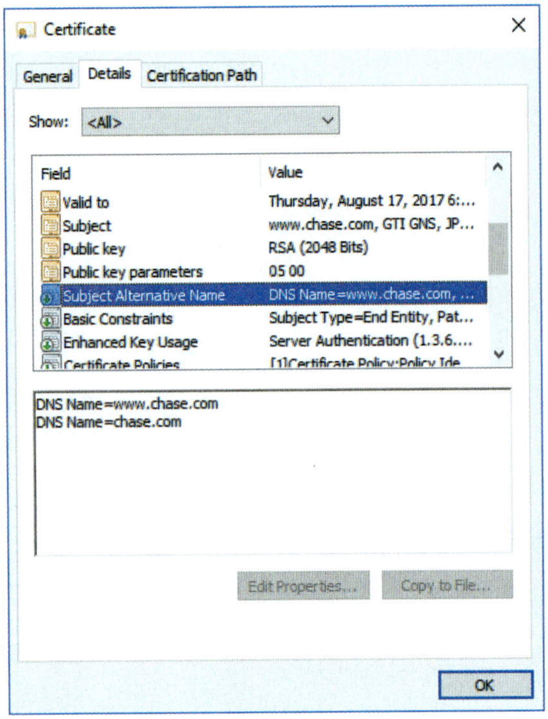

• **Figure 7.15** Subject Alternative Name

> SAN certificates allow you to secure a primary domain and then add more domains to the Subject Alternative Name field of the certificate. For example, you can secure all these domains with a single SAN certificate:
>
> - www.example.com
> - email.example.com
> - intranet.example.com
> - www.example.net

SAN

Subject Alternative Name (SAN) is a field (extension) in a certificate that has several uses. In certificates for machines, it can represent the fully qualified domain name (FQDN) of the machine. For users, it can be the user principal name (UPN), or in the case of an SSL certificate it can indicate multiple domains across which the certificate is valid. Figure 7.15 shows the multiple domains covered by the certificate in the box below the field details. SAN is an extension that is used to a significant degree, as it has become a standard method used in a variety of circumstances.

Code Signing

Certificates can be designated for specific purposes, such as code signing. This is to enable the flexibility of managing certificates for specific functions and reducing the risk in the event of compromise. Code-signing certificates are designated as such in the certificate itself, and the application that uses the certificate adheres to this policy restriction to ensure proper certificate usage.

Self-Signed

Certificates are signed by a higher-level CA, providing a root of trust. As with all chains, there is a final node of trust, the root node. Not all certificates have to have the same root node. A company can create its own certificate chain for use inside the company, and thus it creates its own root node. This certificate must be self-signed, as there is no other "higher" node of trust. What prevents one from signing their own certificates? The trust chain would begin and end with the certificate, and the user would be presented with the dilemma as whether or not to trust the certificate. In the end, all a certificate does is detail a chain of trust to some entity that an end user trusts.

Machine/Computer

Certificates bind identities to keys and provide a means of authentication, which at times is needed for computers. Active Directory Domain Services (AD DS) can keep track of machines in a system via machines identifying themselves using machine certificates. When a user logs in, the system can use either the machine certificate, identifying the machine, or the user certificate, identifying the user—whichever is appropriate for the desired operation.

E-mail

Digital certificates can be used with e-mail systems for items such as digital signatures associated with e-mails. Just as other specialized functions, such as code signing, have their own certificate, it is common for a separate certificate to be used for identity associated with e-mail.

User certificates are used by users for Encrypting File System (EFS), e-mail, and client authentications, whereas computer certificates help computers to authenticate to the network.

User

User certificates are just that—certificates that identify a user.

Root

Root certificate is the name given to a certificate that forms the initial basis of trust in a trust chain. All certificates are signed by the CA that issues them, and these CAs can be chained together in a trust structure. Following the chain, one climbs the tree of trust until they find a self-signed certificate, indicating it is a root certificate. What determines whether a system trusts a root certificate is whether or not it is in the system's store of trusted certificates. Different vendors such as Microsoft and Apple have trusted root certificate programs where they have determined by corporate policy which CAs they will label as trusted.

Tech Tip

Certificate Issues

Certificates are a foundational element in establishing trust, and errors in their configuration, implementation, and use can result in improper trust. A certificate that is trusted when it shouldn't be, by whatever means, results in an incorrect assumption of trust. There is no such thing as minor or insignificant issues when it comes to establishing trust. Throughout the text many examples of trust violations can be seen as part of an attack vector.

Domain Validation

Domain validation is a low-trust means of validation based on control over Transport Layer Security (TLS), where the applicant has been validated by proving some level of control over a Domain Name Service (DNS) domain. This can be automated via checks against a DNS record. A domain validation–based certificate, typically free, offers very little in assurance against a legal entity because the applicant need not supply that information. Domain validation scales well and can be automated with little to no real interaction between an applicant and the CA, but in return it offers little assurance. Domain validation is indicated differently in different browsers, primarily to differentiate it from extended validation certificates.

Extended Validation

Extended validation (EV) certificates are used for HTTPS websites and software to provide a high level of assurance as to the originator's identity. EV certificates use the same methods of encryption to protect certificate integrity as do domain- and organization-validated certificates. The difference in assurance comes from the processes used by a CA to validate an entity's legal identity before issuance. Because of the additional information used during the validation, EV certificates display the legal identity and other legal information as part of the certificate. EV certificates support multiple domains, but do not support wildcards.

To assist users in identifying EV certificates and their enhanced trust, several additional visual clues are provided when EVs are employed. When an EV is implemented in a browser, the legal entity name is displayed, in addition to the URL and a lock symbol, and in most instances the entire URL bar is green. All major browser vendors provide this support, and because the information is included in the certificate itself, this function is web server agnostic.

Certificate Formats

Digital certificates are defined in RFC 5280, "Internet X.509 Public Key Infrastructure Certificate and Certificate Revocation List (CRL) Profile." This RFC describes the X.509 v3 digital certificate format in detail. There are numerous ways to encode the information in a certificate before instantiation as a file, and the different methods result in different file extensions. Common extensions include .der, .pem, .crt, .cer, .pfx, .p12, and .p7b. Although they all can contain certificate information, they are not all directly interchangeable.

DER

Distinguished encoding rules (DER) is one of the Abstract Syntax Notation One (ASN.1) encoding rules that can be used to encode any data object into a binary file. With respect to certificates, the data associated with the certificate, a series of name-value pairs, needs to be converted to a consistent format for digital signing. DER offers a consistent mechanism for this task. A .der file contains binary data and can be used for a single certificate.

PEM

Privacy Enhanced Mail (PEM) is the most common format used by certificate authorities when issuing certificates. PEM comes from RFC 1422, which defined the specification for Privacy Enhanced Mail in 1993 and is a Base64-encoded ASCII file that begins with "-----BEGIN CERTIFICATE-----", followed by the Base64 data, and closes with "-----END CERTIFICATE-----". A .pem file supports multiple digital certificates, including a certificate chain. This file can contain multiple entries, one after another, and can include both public and private keys. Most platforms, however, such as web servers, expect the certificates and private keys to be in separate files. The PEM format for certificate data is used in multiple file types, including .pem, .cer, .crt, and .key files.

> If you need to transmit multiple certificates, or a certificate chain, use .pem for encoding. PEM encoding can carry multiple certificates, whereas DER can only carry a single certificate.

> The only time CRT and CER can safely be interchanged is when the encoding type is identical (for example, PEM encoded CRT = PEM encoded CER). The latter (.cer) is a file extension for an SSL certificate file format used by web servers to help verify the identity and security of the site in question.

CER

The **.cer** file extension is used to denote an alternative form, from Microsoft, of .crt files. The .cer/.crt extension is used for certificates and may be encoded as binary DER or as ASCII PEM. The .cer and .crt extensions are nearly synonymous. Again, .cer is most commonly associated with Microsoft Windows systems, whereas .crt is associated with UNIX systems.

KEY

A KEY file (denoted by the file extension .key) can be used both for public and private PKCS#8 keys. The keys may be encoded as binary DER or as ASCII PEM.

PFX

A PKCS#12 file is a portable file format with a .pfx extension. It is a binary format for storing the server certificate, intermediate certificates, and the private key in one file. **Personal Information Exchange (PFX)** files are typically used on Windows machines to import and export certificates and private keys.

P12

P12 is an alternative file extension for a PKCS#12 file format, a binary format for storing the server certificate, intermediate certificates, and the private key in one encrypted file. These files usually have an extension such as .pfx or .p12. They are typically used on Windows machines to import and export certificates and private keys.

P7B

The PKCS#7 or **P7B** format is stored in Base64 ASCII format and has a file extension of .p7b or .p7c. A P7B file begins with "-----BEGIN PKCS7-----" and only contains certificates and chain certificates (intermediate CAs), not the private key. The most common platforms that support P7B files are Microsoft Windows and Java Tomcat.

Certificate Lifecycles

Keys and certificates should have lifetime settings that force the user to register for a new certificate after a certain amount of time. Determining the proper length of these lifetimes is a tradeoff: shorter lifetimes limit the ability of attackers to crack them, but longer lifetimes lower system overhead. More-sophisticated PKI implementations perform automated and often transparent key updates to avoid the time and expense of having users register for new certificates when old ones expire.

This means that the certificate and key pair have a lifecycle that must be managed. Certificate management involves administrating and managing each of these phases, including registration, certificate and key generation, renewal, and revocation. Additional management functions include CRL distribution, certificate suspension, and key destruction.

Setting certificate lifetimes way into the future and using them for long periods of time provides attackers with extended windows to attack the cryptography. As stated in Chapter 5, cryptography merely buys time against an attacker; it is never an absolute guarantee.

Registration and Generation

A key pair (public and private keys) can be generated locally by an application and stored in a local key store on the user's workstation. The key pair can also be created by a central key-generation server, which will require secure transmission of the keys to the user. The key pair that is created on the centralized server can be stored on the user's workstation or on the user's smart card, which will allow for more flexibility and mobility.

The act of verifying that an individual indeed has the corresponding private key for a given public key is referred to as *proof of possession*. Not all public/private key pairs can be used for digital signatures, so asking the individual to sign a message and return it to prove that they have the necessary private key will not always work. If a key pair is used for encryption, the RA can send a challenge value to the individual, who, in turn, can use their private key to encrypt that value and return it to the RA. If the RA can successfully decrypt this value with the public key that was provided earlier, the RA can be confident that the individual has the necessary private key and can continue through the rest of the registration phase.

Key regeneration and replacement is usually done to protect against these types of threats, although as the processing power of computers increases

Good key management and proper key replacement intervals protect keys from being compromised through human error. Choosing a large key size makes a brute force attack more difficult.

Tech Tip

Centralized vs. Local Key Generation

In most modern PKI implementations, users have two key pairs. One key pair is often generated by a central server and used for encryption and key transfers. This allows the corporate PKI to retain a copy of the encryption key pair for recovery, if necessary. The second key pair, a digital signature key pair, is usually generated by the user to make sure that they are the only one with a copy of the private key. Nonrepudiation can be challenged if there is any doubt about someone else obtaining a copy of an individual's signature private key. If the key pair was created on a centralized server, that could weaken the case that the individual was the only one who had a copy of their private key. If a copy of a user's signature private key is stored anywhere other than in their possession, or if there is a possibility of someone obtaining the user's key, then true nonrepudiation cannot be provided.

and our knowledge of cryptography and new possible cryptanalysis-based attacks expands, key lifetimes may drastically decrease. As with everything within the security field, it is better to be safe now than to be surprised later and sorry.

The PKI administrator usually configures the minimum required key size that users must use to have a key generated for the first time, and then for each renewal. Most applications provide a drop-down list of possible algorithms to choose from, as well as possible key sizes. The key size should provide the necessary level of security for the current environment. The lifetime of the key should be long enough that continual renewal will not negatively affect productivity, but short enough to ensure that the key cannot be successfully compromised.

CSR

A **certificate signing request (CSR)** is the actual request to a CA containing a public key and the requisite information needed to generate a certificate. The CSR contains all the identifying information that is to be bound to the key by the certificate-generation process.

Renewal

The certificate itself has its own lifetime, which can be different from the key pair's lifetime. The certificate's lifetime is specified by the validity dates inserted into the digital certificate. These are beginning and ending dates indicating the time period during which the certificate is valid. The certificate cannot be used before the start date, and once the end date is met, the certificate is expired and a new certificate will need to be issued.

A renewal process is different from the registration phase in that the RA assumes that the individual has already successfully completed one registration round. If the certificate has not actually been revoked, the original keys and certificate can be used to provide the necessary authentication information and proof of identity for the renewal phase.

The certificate may or may not need to change during the renewal process; this usually depends on why the renewal is taking place. If the certificate just expired and the keys will still be used for the same purpose, a new certificate can be generated with new validity dates. If, however, the key pair functionality needs to be expanded or restricted, new attributes and extensions might need to be integrated into the new certificate. These new functionalities may require more information to be gathered from the individual renewing the certificate, especially if the class changes or the new key uses allow for more powerful abilities.

This renewal process is required when the certificate has fulfilled its lifetime and its end validity date has been met.

Suspension

When the owner of a certificate wishes to mark a certificate as no longer valid prior to its natural expiration, two choices exist: revocation and suspension. Revocation, discussed in the next section, is an action with a permanent outcome. Instead of being revoked, a certificate can be *suspended*, meaning it is temporarily put on hold. If, for example, Bob is taking an extended vacation and wants to ensure that his certificate will not be compromised or used during that time, he can make a suspension request to the CA. The CRL would list this certificate and its serial number, and in the field that describes why the certificate is revoked, it would instead indicate a hold state. Once Bob returns to work, he can make a request to the CA to remove his certificate from the list.

Another reason to suspend a certificate is if an administrator is suspicious that a private key might have been compromised. While the issue is under investigation, the certificate can be suspended to ensure that it cannot be used.

A certificate suspension can be a useful process tool while investigating whether or not a certificate should be considered valid.

Relying on an expiration date on a certificate to "destroy" the utility of a key will not work. A new certificate can be issued with an "extended date." To end the use of a key set, an entry in a CRL is the only sure way to prevent reissuance and re-dating of a certificate.

Certificate Revocation

A certificate can be revoked when its validity needs to be ended before its actual expiration date is met, and this can occur for many reasons: for example, a user may have lost a laptop or a smart card that stored a private key; an improper software implementation may have been uncovered that directly affected the security of a private key; a user may have fallen victim to a social engineering attack and inadvertently given up a private key; data held within the certificate might no longer apply to the specified individual; or perhaps an employee left a company and should not be identified as a member of an in-house PKI any longer. In the last instance, the certificate, which was bound to the user's key pair, identified the user as an employee of the company, and the administrator would want to ensure that the key pair could not be used in the future to validate this person's affiliation with the company. Revoking the certificate does this.

Once revoked, a certificate cannot be reinstated. This is to prevent an unauthorized reinstatement by someone who has unauthorized access to the key(s). A key pair can be reinstated for use by issuing a new certificate if at a later time the keys are found to be secure. The old certificate would still be void, but the new one would be valid.

If any of these things happens, a user's private key has been compromised or should no longer be mapped to the owner's identity. A different individual may have access to that user's private key and could use it to impersonate and authenticate as the original user. If the impersonator used the key to digitally sign a message, the receiver would verify the authenticity of the sender by verifying the signature using the original user's public key, and the verification would go through perfectly—the receiver would believe it came from the proper sender and not the impersonator. If receivers could look at a list of certificates that had been revoked before verifying the digital signature, however, they would know not to trust the digital signatures on the list. Because of issues associated with the private key being compromised, revocation is permanent and final—once revoked, a certificate cannot be reinstated. If reinstatement was allowed and a user revoked their certificate, then the unauthorized holder of the private key could use it to restore the certificate validity.

A certificate should never be assumed to be valid without checking for revocation before each use.

Certificate Revocation List

The CA provides protection against impersonation and similar fraud by maintaining a **certificate revocation list (CRL)**, a list of serial numbers of certificates that have been revoked. The CRL also contains a statement indicating why the individual certificates were revoked and a date when the revocation took place. The list usually contains all certificates that have been revoked within the lifetime of the CA. Certificates that have expired are not the same as those that have been revoked. If a certificate has expired, it means that its end validity date was reached. The format of the CRL message is also defined by X.509. The list is signed, to prevent tampering, and contains information on certificates that have been revoked and the reasons for their revocation. These lists can grow quite long, and as such, there are provisions for date and time stamping the list and for issuing delta lists, which show changes since the last list was issued.

The CA is the entity responsible for the status of the certificates it generates; it needs to be told of a revocation, and it must provide this information to others. The CA is responsible for maintaining the CRL and posting it in a publicly available directory.

We need to have some system in place to make sure people cannot arbitrarily have others' certificates revoked, whether for revenge or for malicious purposes. When a revocation request is submitted, the individual submitting the request must be authenticated. Otherwise, this could permit a type of denial-of-service attack, in which someone has another person's certificate revoked. The authentication can involve an agreed-upon password that was created during the registration process, but authentication should not be based on the individual proving that they have the corresponding private key, because it may have been stolen, and the CA would be authenticating an imposter.

The CRL's integrity needs to be protected to ensure that attackers cannot modify data pertaining to a revoked certification on the list. If this were allowed to take place, anyone who stole a private key could just delete that key from the CRL and continue to use the private key fraudulently. The integrity of the list also needs to be protected to ensure that bogus data is not added to it. Otherwise, anyone could add another person's certificate to the list and effectively revoke that person's certificate. The only entity that should be able to modify any information on the CRL is the CA.

The mechanism used to protect the integrity of a CRL is a *digital signature*. The CA's revocation service creates a digital signature for the CRL, as shown in Figure 7.16. To validate a certificate, the user accesses the directory where the CRL is posted, downloads the list, and verifies the CA's digital signature to ensure that the proper authority signed the list and to ensure that the list was not modified in an unauthorized manner. The user

Tech Tip

CRL Reason Codes

Per the X.509 v2 CRL standard, the following reasons are used for revocation:

Reason Code	***Reason***
0	*Unspecified.*
1	*All keys compromised; indicates compromise or suspected compromise.*
2	*CA compromised; used only to revoke CA keys.*
3	*Affiliation changed; indicates a change of affiliation on the certificate.*
4	*Superseded; the certificate has been replaced by a more current one.*
5	*Cessation; the certificate is no longer needed, but no reason exists to suspect it has been compromised.*
6	*Certificate hold; indicates the certificate will not be issued at this point in time.*
7	*Remove from CRL; used with a delta CRL to indicate a CRL entry should be removed.*

The certificate revocation list is an essential item to ensure a certificate is still valid. CAs post CRLs in publicly available directories to permit automated checking of certificates against the list before certificate use by a client. A user should never trust a certificate that has not been checked against the appropriate CRL.

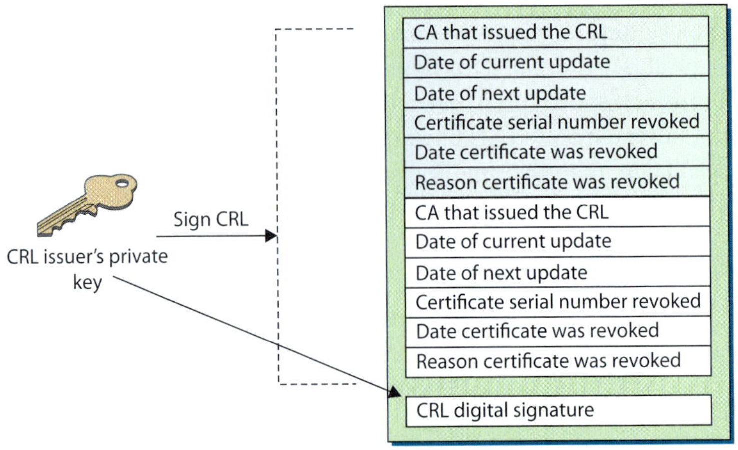

• **Figure 7.16** The CA digitally signs the CRL to protect its integrity.

then looks through the list to determine whether the serial number of the certificate they are trying to validate is listed. If the serial number is on the list, the private key should no longer be trusted, and the public key should no longer be used. This can be a cumbersome process, so it has been automated in several ways, which are described in the next section.

One concern is how up to date the CRL is—how often is it updated and does it actually reflect *all* the certificates currently revoked? The actual frequency with which the list is updated depends on the CA and its certification practices statement (CPS). It is important that the list is updated in a timely manner so that anyone using the list has the most current information.

CRL Distribution

CRL files can be requested by individuals who need to verify and validate a newly received certificate, or the files can be periodically pushed down (sent) to all users participating within a specific PKI. This means the CRL can be pulled (downloaded) by individual users when needed or pushed down to all users within the PKI on a timed interval.

The actual CRL file can grow substantially and transmitting this file and requiring PKI client software on each workstation to save and maintain it can use a lot of resources. Therefore, the smaller the CRL is, the better. It is also possible to first push down the full CRL and subsequently push down only *delta* CRLs, which contain only the changes to the original or base CRL. This can greatly reduce the amount of bandwidth consumed when CRLs are updated.

In implementations where the CRLs are not pushed down to individual systems, the users' PKI software needs to know where to look for the posted CRL that relates to the certificate it is trying to validate. The certificate might have an extension that points the validating user to the necessary *CRL distribution point*. The network administrator sets up the distribution points, and one or more points can exist for a particular PKI. The distribution point holds one or more lists containing the serial numbers of revoked certificates, and the user's PKI software scans the list(s) for the serial number of the certificate the user is attempting to validate. If the serial number is not present, the user is assured that it has not been revoked. This approach helps point users to the right resource and also reduces the amount of information that needs to be scanned when checking that a certificate has not been revoked.

> **Tech Tip**
>
> **Authority Revocation Lists**
>
> *In some PKI implementations, a separate revocation list is maintained for CA keys that have been compromised or should no longer be trusted. This list is known as an* **authority revocation list (ARL)**. *In the event that a CA's private key is compromised or a cross-certification is cancelled, the relevant certificate's serial number is included in the ARL. A client can review an ARL to make sure the CA's public key can still be trusted.*

Online Certificate Status Protocol (OCSP)

One last option for checking distributed CRLs is an *online service*. When a client user needs to validate a certificate and ensure that it has not been revoked, they can communicate with an online service that will query the necessary CRLs available within the environment. This service can query the lists for the client instead of pushing down the full CRL to each and every system. So if Joe receives a certificate from Stacy, he can contact an online service and send to it the serial number listed in the certificate Stacy sent. The online service would query the necessary CRLs and respond to Joe, indicating whether or not that serial number was listed as being revoked.

One of the protocols used for online revocation services is the **Online Certificate Status Protocol (OCSP)**, a request and response protocol that obtains the serial number of the certificate that is being validated and

Certificate revocation checks are done either by examining the CRL or by using OCSP to see if a certificate has been revoked.

Tech Tip

Historical Retention of Certificates

Note that in modern PKIs, encryption key pairs usually must be retained long after they expire so that users can decrypt information that was encrypted with the old keys. For example, if Bob encrypts a document using his current key and the keys are updated three months later, Bob's software must maintain a copy of the old key so he can still decrypt the document. In the PKI world, this issue is referred to as key history maintenance.

reviews revocation lists for the client. The protocol has a responder service that reports the status of the certificate back to the client, indicating whether it has been revoked, is valid, or has an unknown status. This protocol and service saves the client from having to find, download, and process the right lists.

The goal is to make sure that no one can gain access to a key after its lifetime has ended and use that key for malicious purposes. An attacker might use the key to digitally sign or encrypt a message with the hopes of tricking someone else about their identity (this would be an example of a man-in-the middle attack). Also, if the attacker is performing some type of brute force attack on your cryptosystem, trying to figure out specific keys that were used for encryption processes, obtaining an old key could give the attacker more insight into how your cryptosystem generates keys. The less information you supply to potential hackers, the better.

Key Destruction

Key pairs and certificates have set *lifetimes*, meaning that they will expire at some specified time. It is important that the certificates and keys are properly destroyed when that time comes, wherever the keys are stored (on users' workstations, centralized key servers, USB token devices, smart cards, and so on).

Certificate Repositories

Once the requestor's identity has been proven, a certificate is registered with the public side of the key pair provided by the requestor. Public keys must be available to anybody who requires them to communicate within a PKI environment. These keys, and their corresponding certificates, are usually held in a publicly available repository. **Certificate repository** is a general term that describes a centralized directory that can be accessed by a subset of individuals. The directories are usually LDAP-compliant, meaning that they can be accessed and searched via a Lightweight Directory Access Protocol (LDAP) query from an LDAP client.

When an individual initializes communication with another, the sender can send their certificate and public key to the receiver, which will allow the receiver to communicate with the sender using encryption or digital signatures (or both) without needing to track down the necessary public key in a certificate repository. This is equivalent to the sender saying, "If you would like to encrypt any future messages you send to me, or if you would like the ability to verify my digital signature, here are the necessary components." But if a person wants to encrypt the first message sent to the receiver, the sender needs to find the receiver's public key in a certificate repository.

A certificate repository is a holding place for individuals' certificates and public keys that are participating in a particular PKI environment. The security requirements for repositories themselves are not as high as those needed for actual CAs and for the equipment and software used to carry out CA functions. Since each certificate is digitally signed by the CA, if a certificate stored in the certificate repository is modified, the recipient will be able to detect this change and know not to accept the certificate as valid.

Sharing Key Stores

Different applications from the same vendor may share key stores. Microsoft applications keep user keys and certificates in a Registry entry within that user's profile. The applications can then save and retrieve them from this single location or key store. Other applications could also use the same keys if they knew where they were stored by using Registry API calls.

The local key store is just one location where these items can be held. Often, the digital certificate and public key are also stored in a certificate repository (as discussed earlier in the "Certificate Repositories" section of this chapter) so that they are available to a subset of individuals.

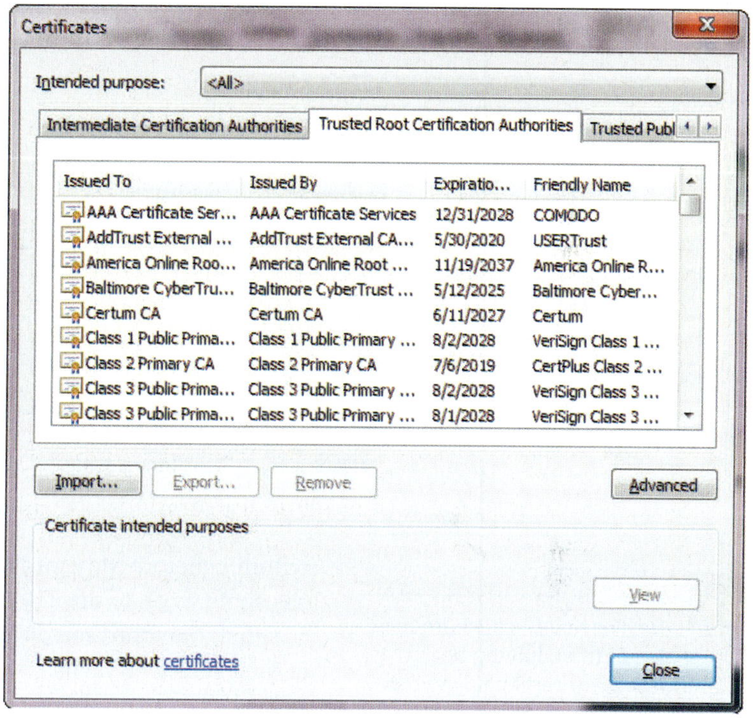

• **Figure 7.17** Browsers have a long list of CAs configured to be trusted by default.

Trust and Certificate Verification

We need to use a PKI if we do not automatically trust individuals we do not know. Security is about being suspicious and being safe, so we need a third party that we *do* trust to vouch for the other individual before confidence can be instilled and sensitive communication can take place. But what does it mean that we trust a CA, and how can we use this to our advantage?

When a user chooses to trust a CA, they will download that CA's digital certificate and public key, which will be stored on their local computer. Most browsers have a list of CAs configured to be trusted by default, so when a user installs a new web browser, several of the most well-known and most trusted CAs will be trusted without any change of settings. An example of this listing is shown in Figure 7.17.

In the Microsoft CAPI (Cryptographic Application Programming Interface) environment, the user can add and remove CAs from this list as needed. In production environments that require a higher degree of protection, this list will be pruned, and possibly the only CAs listed will be the company's *internal* CAs. This ensures that digitally signed software will be automatically installed only if it was signed by the company's CA. Other products, such as Entrust, use centrally controlled policies to determine which CAs are to be trusted, instead of expecting the user to make these critical decisions.

A number of steps are involved in checking the validity of a message. Suppose, for example, that Maynard receives a digitally signed message from Joyce, whom he does not know or trust. Joyce has also included her digital certificate with her message, which has her public key embedded

Tech Tip

Distinguished Names

A Distinguished Name is a label that follows the X.500 standard. This standard defines a naming convention that can be employed so that each subject within an organization has a unique name. An example is {Country = US, Organization = Real Secure, Organizational Unit = R&D, Location = Washington}. CAs use Distinguished Names to identify the owners of specific certificates.

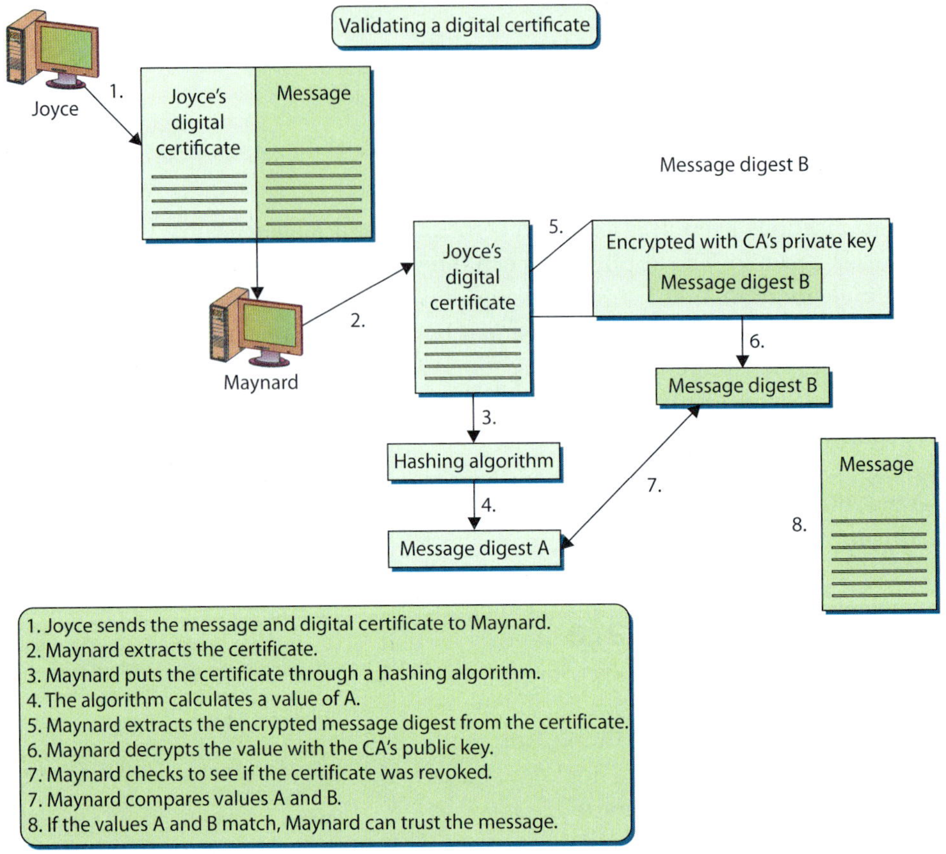

Figure 7.18 Steps for verifying the authenticity and integrity of a certificate

> Because certificates produce chains of trust, having an unnecessary certificate in your certificate store could lead to trust problems. Best practices indicate that you should understand the certificates in your store as well as the need for each. When in doubt, remove it. If the certificate is needed, you can add it back later.

within it. Before Maynard can be sure of the authenticity of this message, he has some work to do. The steps are illustrated in Figure 7.18.

First, Maynard sees which CA signed Joyce's certificate and compares it to the list of CAs he has configured within his computer. He trusts the CAs in his list and no others. (If the certificate was signed by a CA that he does not have in the list, he would not accept the certificate as being valid, and thus he could not be sure that this message was actually sent from Joyce or that the attached key was actually her public key.)

Maynard sees that the CA that signed Joyce's certificate is indeed in his list of trusted CAs, so he now needs to verify that the certificate has not been altered. Using the CA's public key and the digest of the certificate, Maynard can verify the integrity of the certificate. Then Maynard can be assured that this CA did actually create the certificate, so he can now trust the origin of Joyce's certificate. The use of digital signatures allows certificates to be saved in public directories without concern for them being accidentally or intentionally altered. If a user extracts a certificate from a repository and creates a message digest value that does not match the digital signature embedded within the certificate itself, that user will know that the certificate has been modified by someone other than the CA and will know not to accept the validity of the corresponding public key. Similarly, an attacker could not create a new message digest, encrypt it, and embed it within the certificate because they would not have access to the CA's private key.

But Maynard is not done yet. He needs to be sure that the issuing CA has not revoked this certificate. The certificate also has start and stop dates, indicating a time during which the certificate is valid. If the start date hasn't happened yet or the stop date has been passed, the certificate is not valid. Maynard reviews these dates to make sure the certificate is still deemed valid.

Another step Maynard may go through is to check whether this certificate has been revoked for any reason. To do so, he will refer to the *certificate revocation list (CRL)* to see if Joyce's certificate is listed. He could check the CRL directly with the CA that issued the certificate, or he could use a specialized online service that supports the Online Certificate Status Protocol (OCSP). (Certificate revocation and list distribution were explained in the "Certificate Lifecycles" section, earlier in this chapter.)

Maynard now trusts that this certificate is legitimate and that it belongs to Joyce. Now what does he need to do? The certificate holds Joyce's public key, which he needs to validate the digital signature she appended to her message, so Maynard extracts Joyce's public key from her certificate, runs her message through a hashing algorithm, and calculates a message digest value of X. He then uses Joyce's public key to decrypt her digital signature (remember that a digital signature is just a message digest encrypted with a private key). This decryption process provides him with another message digest of value Y. Maynard compares values X and Y, and if they are the same, he is assured that the message has not been modified during transmission. Thus, he has confidence in the integrity of the message. But how does Maynard know that the message actually came from Joyce? Because he can decrypt the digital signature using her public key, which indicates that only the associated private key could have been used. There is a miniscule risk that someone could create an identical key pair, but given the enormous keyspace for public keys, this is impractical. The public key can only decrypt something that was encrypted with the related private key, and only the owner of the private key is supposed to have access to it. Maynard can be sure that this message came from Joyce.

After all of this, he reads her message, which says, "Hi. How are you?" All of that work just for this message? Maynard's blood pressure would surely go through the roof if he had to do all of this work only to end up with a short and not very useful message. Fortunately, all of this PKI work is performed without user intervention and happens behind the scenes. Maynard didn't have to exert any energy. He simply replies, "Fine. How are you?"

Tech Tip

Validating a Certificate

The following steps are required for validating a certificate:

1. *Compare the CA that digitally signed the certificate to a list of CAs that have already been loaded into the receiver's computer.*
2. *Calculate a message digest for the certificate.*
3. *Use the CA's public key to decrypt the digital signature and recover what is claimed to be the original message digest embedded within the certificate (validating the digital signature).*
4. *Compare the two resulting message digest values to ensure the integrity of the certificate.*
5. *Review the identification information within the certificate, such as the e-mail address.*
6. *Review the validity dates.*
7. *Check a revocation list to see if the certificate has been revoked.*

Centralized and Decentralized Infrastructures

Keys used for authentication and encryption within a PKI environment can be generated in a centralized or decentralized manner. In a *decentralized* approach, software on individual computers generates and stores cryptographic keys local to the systems themselves. In a *centralized* infrastructure, the keys are generated and stored on a central server, and the keys are transmitted to the individual systems as needed. You might choose one type over the other for several reasons.

If a company uses an asymmetric algorithm that is resource-intensive to generate the public/private key pair, and if large (and resource-intensive) key sizes are needed, then the individual computers might not have the necessary processing power to produce the keys in an acceptable fashion. In this situation, the company can choose a centralized approach in which a very high-end server with powerful processing capabilities is used, probably along with a hardware-based random number generator.

Central key generation and storage offer other benefits as well. For example, it is much easier to back up the keys and implement key recovery procedures with central storage than with a decentralized approach. Implementing a key recovery procedure on each and every computer holding one or more key pairs is difficult, and many applications that generate their own key pairs do not usually interface well with a centralized archive system. This means that if a company chooses to allow its individual users to create and maintain their own key pairs on their separate workstations, no real key recovery procedure can be put in place. This puts the company at risk. If an employee leaves the organization or is unavailable for one reason or another, the company may not be able to access its own business information that was encrypted by that employee.

So a centralized approach seems like the best approach, right? Well, the centralized method has some drawbacks to consider, too. Secure key distribution is a tricky event. This can be more difficult than it sounds. A technology needs to be employed that will send the keys in an encrypted manner, ensure the keys' integrity, and make sure that only the intended users are receiving the keys.

Also, the server that centrally stores the keys needs to be highly available and is a potential single point of failure, so some type of fault tolerance or redundancy mechanism might need to be put into place. If that one server goes down, users will not be able to access their keys, which might prevent them from properly authenticating to the network, resources, and applications. Also, since all the keys are in one place, the server is a prime target for an attacker—if the central key server is compromised, the whole environment is compromised.

One other issue pertains to how the keys will actually be used. If a public/private key pair is being generated for digital signatures, and if the company wants to ensure that this key pair can be used to provide *true* authenticity and nonrepudiation, the keys should not be generated at a centralized server. This would introduce doubt that only the one person had access to a specific private key. It is better to generate end-user keys on a local machine to eliminate doubt about who did the work and "owns" the keys.

If a company uses smart cards to hold users' private keys, each private key often has to be generated on the card itself and cannot be copied for archiving purposes. This is a disadvantage of the centralized approach. In addition, some types of applications have been developed to create their own public/private key pairs and do not allow other keys to be imported and used. This means the keys would have to be created locally by these applications, and keys from a central server could not be used. These are just some of the considerations that need to be evaluated before any decision is made and implementation begins.

Hardware Security Modules

PKIs can be constructed in software without special cryptographic hardware, and this is perfectly suitable for many environments. But software can be vulnerable to viruses, hackers, and hacking. If a company requires a higher level of protection than a purely software-based solution can provide, several hardware-based solutions are available. A **hardware security module (HSM)** is a physical device that safeguards cryptographic keys. HSMs enable a higher level of security for the use of keys, including generation and authentication.

In most situations, HSM solutions are used only for the most critical and sensitive keys, which are the root key and possibly the intermediate CA private keys. If those keys are compromised, the whole security of the PKI is gravely threatened. If a person obtained a root CA private key, they could digitally sign any certificate, and that certificate would be quickly accepted by all entities within the environment. Such an attacker might be able to create a certificate that has extremely high privileges, perhaps allowing them to modify bank account information in a financial institution, and no alerts or warnings would be initiated because the ultimate CA, the root CA, signed it.

Tech Tip

Storing Critical Keys

HSMs take many different forms, including embedded cards, network-attached devices, and even USB flash drives. HSMs assist in the use of cryptographic keys across the lifecycle. They can provide dedicated support for centralized lifecycle management, from generation to distribution, storage, termination, archiving, and recordkeeping. HSMs can increase the efficiency of cryptographic operations and assist in compliance efforts. Common uses include use in PCI DSS solutions, DNSSEC, signing operations (including certificates, code, documents, and e-mail), and large-scale data encryption efforts.

Private Key Protection

Although a PKI implementation can be complex, with many different components and options, a critical concept common to all PKIs must be understood and enforced: the private key needs to stay private. A digital signature is created solely for the purpose of proving who sent a particular message by using a private key. This rests on the assumption that only one person has access to this private key. If an imposter obtains a user's private key, authenticity and nonrepudiation can no longer be claimed or proven.

When a private key is generated for the first time, it must be stored somewhere for future use. This storage area is referred to as a *key store*, and it is usually created by the application registering for a certificate, such as a web browser, smart card software, or other application. In most implementations, the application will prompt the user for a password, which will be used to create an encryption key that protects the key store. So, for example, if Cheryl used her web browser to register for a certificate, her private key would be generated and stored in the key store. Cheryl would then be prompted for a password, which the software would use to create a key that will encrypt the key store. When Cheryl needs to access this private key later that day, she will be prompted for the same password, which will decrypt the key store and allow her access to her private key.

The security associated with the use of public key cryptography revolves around the security of the private key. Nonrepudiation depends on the principle that the private key is only accessible to the holder of the key. If another person has access to the private key, they can impersonate the proper key holder.

Unfortunately, many applications do not require that a strong password be created to protect the key store, and in some implementations the user can choose not to provide a password at all. The user still has a private key available, and it is bound to the user's identity, so why is a password even necessary? If, for example, Cheryl decided not to use a password, and another person sat down at her computer, he could use her web browser and her private key and digitally sign a message that contains a nasty virus. If Cheryl's coworker Cliff received this message, he would think it came from Cheryl, open the message, and download the virus. The moral to this story is that users should be required to provide some type of authentication information (password, smart card, PIN, or the like) before being able to use private keys. Otherwise, the keys could be used by other individuals or imposters, and authentication and nonrepudiation would be of no use.

Because a private key is a crucial component of any PKI implementation, the key itself should contain the necessary characteristics and be protected at each stage of its life. The following list sums up the characteristics and requirements of proper private key use:

- The key size should provide the necessary level of protection for the environment.
- The lifetime of the key should correspond with how often it is used and the sensitivity of the data it is protecting.
- The key should be changed at the end of its lifetime and not used past its allowed lifetime.
- Where appropriate, the key should be properly destroyed at the end of its lifetime.
- The key should never be exposed in clear text.
- No copies of the private key should be made if it is being used for digital signatures.
- The key should not be shared.
- The key should be stored securely.
- Authentication should be required before the key can be used.
- The key should be transported securely.
- Software implementations that store and use the key should be evaluated to ensure they provide the necessary level of protection.

If digital signatures will be used for legal purposes, these points and others may need to be audited to ensure that true authenticity and nonrepudiation are provided.

> The most sensitive and critical public/private key pairs are those used by CAs to digitally sign certificates. These need to be highly protected because if they were ever compromised, the trust relationship between the CA and all of the end-entities would be threatened. In high-security environments, these keys are often kept in a tamperproof hardware encryption store, such as an HSM, and are accessible only to individuals with a need to know.

Key Recovery

One individual could have one, two, or many key pairs that are tied to their identity. That is because users may have different needs and requirements for public/private key pairs. As mentioned earlier, certificates can have specific attributes and usage requirements dictating how their corresponding keys can and cannot be used. For example, David can have one key pair he uses to encrypt and transmit symmetric keys, another key pair that allows him to encrypt data, and yet another key pair to perform digital signatures. David can also have a digital signature key pair for his work-related activities and another key pair for personal activities, such as e-mailing his friends. These key pairs need to be used only for their intended purposes, and this is enforced through certificate attributes and usage values.

If a company is going to perform key recovery and maintain a key-recovery system, it will generally back up only the key pair used to encrypt data, not the key pairs that are used to generate digital signatures. The reason that a company archives keys is to ensure that if a person leaves the company, falls off a cliff, or for some reason is unavailable to decrypt important company information, the company can still get to its company-owned data. This is just a matter of the organization protecting itself. A company would not need to be able to recover a key pair that is used for digital signatures, since those keys are to be used only to prove the authenticity of the individual who sent a message. A company would not benefit from having access to those keys and really should not have access to them because they are tied to one individual for a specific purpose.

Key archiving is the process of storing a set of keys to be used as a backup should something happen to the original set. *Key recovery* is the process of using the backup keys.

Two systems are important for backing up and restoring cryptographic keys: key archiving and key recovery. **Key archiving** is a way of backing up keys and securely storing them in a repository; **key recovery** is the process of restoring lost keys to the users or the company.

If keys are backed up and stored in a centralized computer, this system must be tightly controlled, because if it were compromised, an attacker would have access to all keys for the entire infrastructure. Also, it is usually unwise to authorize a single person to be able to recover all the keys within the environment, because that person could use this power for evil purposes instead of just recovering keys when they are needed for legitimate purposes. In security systems, it is best not to fully trust anyone.

Recovery agent is the term for an entity that is given a public key certificate for recovering user data that is encrypted. This is the most common type of recovery policy used in PKI, but it adds the risk of the recovery agent having access to secured information.

Dual control can be used as part of a system to back up and archive data encryption keys. PKI systems can be configured to require multiple individuals to be involved in any key recovery process. When key recovery is required, at least two people can be required to authenticate using the key recovery software before the recovery procedure is performed. This enforces *separation of duties,* which means that one person cannot complete a critical task alone. Requiring two individuals to recover a lost key together is called **dual control**, which simply means that two people have to be present to carry out a specific task.

Tech Tip

Keysplitting

Secret splitting using m *of* n *authentication schemes can improve security by requiring that multiple people perform critical functions, preventing a single party from compromising a secret.*

This approach to key recovery is referred to as "*m* of *n* authentication," where *n* number of people can be involved in the key recovery process, but at least *m* (which is a smaller number than *n*) *must* be involved before the task can be completed. The goal is to minimize fraudulent or improper use of access and permissions. A company would not require all possible individuals to be involved in the recovery process, because getting all the people together at the same time could be impossible considering meetings, vacations, sick time, and travel. At least some of all possible individuals must be available to participate, and this is the subset *m* of the number *n*. This form of secret splitting can increase security by requiring multiple people to perform a specific function. Requiring too many people for the *m* subset increases issues associated with availability, whereas requiring too few increases the risk of a small number of people colluding to compromise a secret.

All key recovery procedures should be highly audited. The audit logs should capture at least what keys were recovered, who was involved in the process, and the time and date. Keys are an integral piece of any encryption cryptosystem and are critical to a PKI environment, so you need to track who does what with them.

Key recovery is a process that allows for lost keys to be recovered. *Key escrow* is a process of giving keys to a third party so that they can decrypt and read sensitive information when this need arises.

Key Escrow

Key recovery and *key escrow* are terms that are often used interchangeably, but they actually describe two different things. You should not use them interchangeably after you have read this section.

Key escrow, allowing another trusted party to hold a copy of a key, has long been a controversial topic. This essential business process provides continuity should the authorized key-holding party leave an organization without disclosing keys. The security of the escrowed key is a concern, and it needs to be managed at the same security level as for the original key.

Key escrow is the process of giving keys to a third party so that they can decrypt and read sensitive information if the need arises. Key escrow almost always pertains to handing over encryption keys to the government, or to another higher authority, so that the keys can be used to collect evidence during investigations. A key pair used in a person's place of work may be required to be escrowed by the employer for two reasons. First, the keys are property of the company, issued to the worker for use. Second, the company may have need for them after an employee leaves the firm.

Several movements, supported by parts of the U.S. government, would require all or many people residing in the United States to hand over copies of the keys they use to encrypt communication channels. The movement in the late 1990s behind the Clipper chip is the most well-known effort to implement this requirement and procedure. It was suggested that all American-made communication devices should have a hardware encryption chip within them. The chip could be used to encrypt data going back and forth between two individuals, but if a government agency decided that it should be able to eavesdrop on this dialogue, it would just need to obtain a court order. If the court order was approved, a law enforcement agent would take the order to two escrow agencies, each of which would have a piece of the key that was necessary to decrypt this communication information. The agent would obtain both pieces of the key and combine them, which would allow the agent to listen in on the encrypted communication outlined in the court order.

The Clipper chip standard never saw the light of day because it seemed too "Big Brother" to many American citizens. But the idea was that the encryption keys would be escrowed to two agencies, meaning that each agency would hold one piece of the key. One agency could not hold the whole key, because it could then use this key to wiretap people's conversations illegally. Splitting up the key is an example of separation of duties, put into place to try and prevent fraudulent activities. The current issue of governments demanding access to keys to decrypt information is covered in Chapter 24.

Certificate-Based Threats

Although certificates bring much capability to security through practical management of trust, they also can present threats. Because much of the actual work is done behind the scenes, without direct user involvement, a false sense of security might ensue. End users might assume that if an HTTPS connection was made with a server, they are securely connected to the proper server. Spoofing, phishing, pharming, and a wide range of sophisticated attacks prey on this assumption. Today, the industry has responded with a high-assurance certificate that is signed and recognized by browsers. Using this example, we can examine how an attacker might prey on a user's trust in software getting things correct.

If a hacker wishes to have something recognized as legitimate, they may have to obtain a certificate that proves this point to the end-user machine. One avenue would be to forge a false certificate, but this is challenging because of the public key signing of certificates by CAs. To overcome this problem, the hacker needs to install a false, self-signed root certificate on the end-user PC. This false key can then be used to validate malicious software as coming from a trusted source. This attack preys on the fact that end users do not know the contents of their root certificate store, nor do they have a means to validate changes. In an enterprise environment, this attack can be thwarted by locking down the certificate store and validating changes against a white list. This option really is not very practical for end users outside of an enterprise.

Stolen Certificates

Certificates act as a form of trusted ID and are typically handled without end-user intervention. To ensure the veracity of a certificate, a series of cryptographic controls is employed, including digital signatures to provide proof of authenticity. This statement aside, stolen certificates have been used in multiple cases of computer intrusions/system attacks. Specially crafted malware has been designed to steal both private keys and digital certificates from machines. One of the most infamous malware programs, the Zeus bot, has functionality to perform this task.

> A stolen certificate and/or private key can be used to bypass many security measures. Concern over stolen SSL/TLS credentials led to the creation of high-assurance certificates, which are discussed in Chapter 17.

Stolen certificates have been implemented in a wide range of attacks. Malware designed to imitate antivirus software has been found dating back to 2009. The Stuxnet attack on the Iranian nuclear production facility used stolen certificates from third parties that were not involved in any way other than the unwitting contribution of a passkey in the form of a certificate. In less than a month after the Sony Pictures Entertainment attack became public in 2014, malware using Sony certificates appeared. Whether the certificates came from the break-in or one of the previous Sony hacks is unknown, but the result is the same.

PKIX and PKCS

Two main standards have evolved over time to implement PKIs on a practical level on the Internet. Both are based on the X.509 certificate standard (discussed earlier in the "X.509" material) and establish complementary standards for implementing PKIs. PKIX and PKCS intertwine to define the most commonly used set of standards.

PKIX was produced by the Internet Engineering Task Force (IETF) and defines standards for interactions and operations for four component types: the user (end-entity), certificate authority (CA), registration authority (RA), and the repository for certificates and certificate revocation lists (CRLs). PKCS defines many of the lower-level standards for message syntax, cryptographic algorithms, and the like. The PKCS set of standards is a product of RSA Security.

The PKIX working group was formed in 1995 to develop the standards necessary to support PKIs. At the time, the X.509 Public Key Certificate (PKC) format was proposed as the basis for a PKI. X.509 includes information regarding data formats and procedures used for CA-signed PKCs, but it doesn't specify values or formats for many of the fields within the PKC. PKIX provides standards for extending and using X.509 v3 certificates and

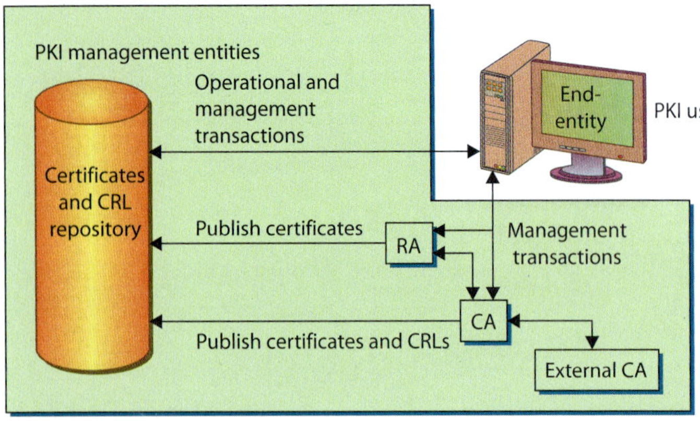

• **Figure 7.19** The PKIX model

> **Tech Tip**
>
> **PKI Essentials**
>
> *A PKI brings together policies, procedures, hardware, software, and end users to create, manage, store, distribute, and revoke digital certificates.*

for managing them, enabling interoperability between PKIs following the standards.

PKIX uses the model shown in Figure 7.19 for representing the components and users of a PKI. The user, called an *end-entity*, is not part of the PKI, but end-entities are either users of the PKI certificates, the subject of a certificate (an entity identified by it), or both. The *certificate authority (CA)* is responsible for issuing, storing, and revoking certificates—both PKCs and Attribute Certificates (ACs). The RA is responsible for management activities designated by the CA. The RA can, in fact, be a component of the CA rather than a separate component. The final component of the PKIX model is the repository, a system or group of distributed systems that provides certificates and CRLs to the end-entities. The *certificate revocation list (CRL)* is a digitally signed object that lists all the current but revoked certificates issued by a CA.

PKIX Standards

Now that we have looked at how PKIX is organized, let's take a look at what PKIX does. Using X.509 v3, the PKIX working group addresses five major areas:

- PKIX outlines certificate extensions and content not covered by X.509 v3 and the format of version 2 CRLs, thus providing compatibility standards for sharing certificates and CRLs between CAs and end-entities in different PKIs. The PKIX profile of the X.509 v3 PKC describes the contents, required extensions, optional extensions, and extensions that need not be implemented. The PKIX profile suggests a range of values for many extensions. In addition, PKIX provides a profile for version 2 CRLs, allowing different PKIs to share revocation information.
- PKIX provides certificate management message formats and protocols, defining the data structures, management messages, and management functions for PKIs. The working group also addresses the assumptions and restrictions of their protocols. This standard identifies the protocols necessary to support online interactions between entities in the PKIX model. The management protocols support functions for entity registration, initialization of the certificate (possibly key-pair generation), issuance of the certificate, key-pair update, certificate revocation, cross-certification (between CAs), and key-pair recovery if available.
- PKIX outlines certificate policies and certification practice statements (CPSs), establishing the relationship between policies and CPSs. A policy is a set of rules that helps determine the applicability of a certificate to an end-entity. For example, a certificate for handling routine information would probably have a policy on creation, storage, and management of key pairs quite different from a policy for certificates used in financial transactions, due to the sensitivity of

the financial information. A CPS explains the practices used by a CA to issue certificates. In other words, the CPS is the method used to get the certificate, whereas the policy defines some characteristics of the certificate and how it will be handled and used.

- PKIX specifies operational protocols, defining the protocols for certificate handling. In particular, protocol definitions are specified for using File Transfer Protocol (FTP) and Hypertext Transfer Protocol (HTTP) to retrieve certificates from repositories. These are the most common protocols for applications to use when retrieving certificates.
- PKIX includes timestamping and data certification and validation services, which are areas of interest to the PKIX working group, and which will probably grow in use over time. A timestamp authority (TSA) certifies that a particular entity existed at a particular time. A Data Validation and Certification Server (DVCS) certifies the validity of signed documents, PKCs, and the possession or existence of data. These capabilities support nonrepudiation requirements and are considered building blocks for a nonrepudiation service.

PKCs are the most commonly used certificates, but the PKIX working group has been working on two other types of certificates: Attribute Certificates and Qualified Certificates. An Attribute Certificate (AC) is used to grant permissions using rule-based, role-based, and rank-based access controls. ACs are used to implement a privilege management infrastructure (PMI). In a PMI, an entity (user, program, system, and so on) is typically identified as a client to a server using a PKC. There are then two possibilities: either the identified client pushes an AC to the server, or the server can query a trusted repository to retrieve the attributes of the client. This situation is modeled in Figure 7.20.

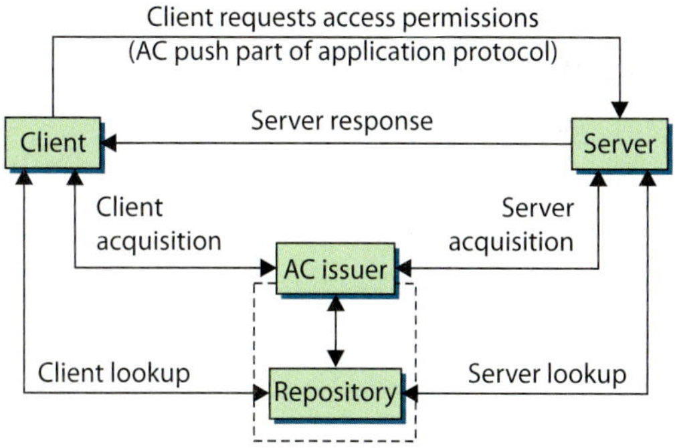

• **Figure 7.20** The PKIX PMI model

The client push of the AC has the effect of improving performance, but no independent verification of the client's permissions is initiated by the server. The alternative is to have the server pull the information from an AC issuer or a repository. This method is preferable from a security standpoint, because the server or server's domain determines the client's access rights. The pull method has the added benefit of requiring no changes to the client software.

The Qualified Certificate (QC) is based on the term used within the European Commission to identify certificates with specific legislative uses. This concept is generalized in the PKIX QC profile to indicate a certificate used to identify a specific individual (a single human rather than the *entity* of the PKC) with a high level of assurance in a nonrepudiation service. There are dozens of IETF Requests for Comment (RFCs) that have been produced by the PKIX working group for each of these five areas.

PKCS

RSA Laboratories created the **Public Key Cryptography Standards (PKCS)** to fill some of the gaps in the standards that existed in PKI implementation. As they have with the PKIX standards, PKI developers have adopted many of these standards as a basis for achieving interoperability between different

CAs. PKCS is currently composed of a set of 13 active standards, with two other standards that are no longer active. The standards are referred to as PKCS #1 through PKCS #15, as listed in Table 7.2. The standards combine to establish a common base for services required in a PKI.

Table 7.2 PKCS Standards

Standard	Title and Description
PKCS #1	RSA Cryptography Standard; definition of the RSA encryption standard.
PKCS #2	No longer active; it covered RSA encryption of message digests and was incorporated into PKCS #1.
PKCS #3	Diffie-Hellman Key Agreement Standard; definition of the Diffie-Hellman key-agreement protocol.
PKCS #4	No longer active; it covered RSA key syntax and was incorporated into PKCS #1.
PKCS #5	Password-Based Cryptography Standard; definition of a password-based encryption (PBE) method for generating a secret key.
PKCS #6	Extended-Certificate Syntax Standard; definition of an extended certificate syntax that is made obsolete by X.509 v3.
PKCS #7	Cryptographic Message Syntax Standard; definition of the cryptographic message standard for encoded messages, regardless of encryption algorithm. Commonly replaced with PKIX Cryptographic Message Syntax.
PKCS #8	Private-Key Information Syntax Standard; definition of a private key information format, used to store private key information.
PKCS #9	Selected Attribute Types; definition of attribute types used in other PKCS standards.
PKCS #10	Certification Request Syntax Standard; definition of a syntax for certification requests.
PKCS #11	Cryptographic Token Interface Standard; definition of a technology-independent programming interface for cryptographic devices (such as smart cards).
PKCS #12	Personal Information Exchange Syntax Standard; definition of a format for storage and transport of a user's private keys, certificates, and other personal information.
PKCS #13	Elliptic Curve Cryptography Standard. Abandoned.
PKCS #14	Pseudo-random number generation. Abandoned.
PKCS #15	Cryptographic Token Information Format Standard; definition of a format for storing cryptographic information in cryptographic tokens.

Though adopted early in the development of PKIs, some of these standards are being phased out. For example, PKCS #6 is being replaced by X.509 v3, and PKCS #7 and PKCS #10 are being used less, as their PKIX counterparts are being adopted.

Why You Need to Know the PKIX and PKCS Standards

If your company is planning to use one of the existing certificate servers to support e-commerce, you might not need to know the specifics of these standards (except perhaps for the CompTIA Security+ exam). However, if you plan to implement a private PKI to support secure services within your organization, you need to understand what standards are out there and how the decision to use a particular PKI implementation (either homegrown or commercial) may lead to incompatibilities with other certificate-issuing entities. You must consider your business-to-business requirements when you're deciding how to implement a PKI within your organization.

All of the standards and protocols discussed in this chapter are the "vocabulary" of the computer security industry. You should be well versed in all these titles, their acronyms, and their purposes and operations.

ISAKMP

The **Internet Security Association and Key Management Protocol (ISAKMP)** provides a method for implementing a key exchange protocol and for negotiating a security policy. It defines procedures and packet formats to negotiate, establish, modify, and delete security associates. Because it is a framework, it doesn't define implementation-specific protocols, such as the key exchange protocol or hash functions. Examples of ISAKMP are the Internet Key Exchange (IKE) protocol and IP Security (IPSec), which are used widely throughout the industry.

An important definition for understanding ISAKMP is that of the term *security association*. A security association (SA) is a relationship in which two or more entities define how they will communicate securely. ISAKMP is intended to support SAs at all layers of the network stack. For this reason, ISAKMP can be implemented on the transport layer using TCP or User Datagram Protocol (UDP), or it can be implemented on IP directly.

Negotiation of an SA between servers occurs in two stages. First, the entities agree on how to secure negotiation messages (the ISAKMP SA). Once the entities have secured their negotiation traffic, they then determine the SAs for the protocols used for the remainder of their communications. Figure 7.21 shows the structure of the ISAKMP header. This header is used during both parts of the ISAKMP negotiation.

The Initiator Cookie is set by the entity requesting the SA, and the responder sets the Responder Cookie. The Payload byte indicates the type of the first payload to be encapsulated. Payload types include security associations, proposals, key transforms, key exchanges, vendor identities, and other things. The Major and Minor Revision fields refer to the major version number and minor version number for the ISAKMP, respectively. The Exchange Type helps determine the order of messages and payloads. The Flags bits indicate options for the ISAKMP exchange, including whether the payload is encrypted, whether the initiator and responder have "committed" to the SA, and whether the packet is to be authenticated only (and is not encrypted). The final fields of the ISAKMP header indicate the Message Identifier and a Message Length. Payloads encapsulated within ISAKMP use a generic header, and each payload has its own header format.

Once the ISAKMP SA is established, multiple protocol SAs can be established using the single ISAKMP SA. This feature is valuable due to the overhead associated with the two-stage negotiation. SAs are valid for specific

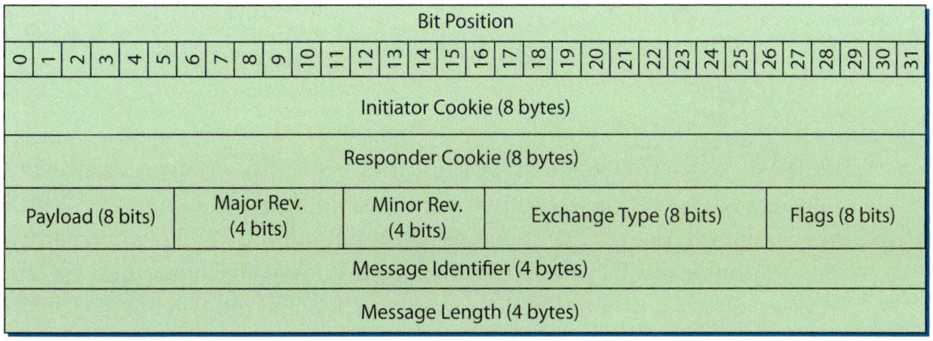

• **Figure 7.21** ISAKMP header format

periods of time, and once the time expires, the SA must be renegotiated. Many resources are also available for specific implementations of ISAKMP within the IPSec protocol.

CMP

> **Tech Tip**
>
> **CMP Summarized**
>
> *CMP is a protocol to obtain X.509 certificates in a PKI.*

The PKIX Certificate Management Protocol (CMP) is specified in RFC 4210. This protocol defines the messages and operations required to provide certificate management services within the PKIX model. Though part of the IETF PKIX effort, CMP provides a framework that works well with other standards, such as PKCS #7 and PKCS #10.

CMP provides for the following certificate operations:

- CA establishment, including creation of the initial CRL and export of the public key for the CA
- Certification of an end-entity, including the following:
    - Initial registration and certification of the end-entity (registration, certificate issuance, and placement of the certificate in a repository)
    - Updates to the key pair for end-entities, required periodically and when a key pair is compromised or keys cannot be recovered
    - End-entity certificate updates, required when a certificate expires
    - Periodic CA key-pair updates, similar to end-entity key-pair updates
    - Cross-certification requests, placed by other CAs
    - Certificate and CRL publication, performed under the appropriate conditions of certificate issuance and certificate revocation
    - Key-pair recovery, a service to restore key-pair information for an end-entity; for example, if a certificate password is lost or the certificate file is lost
    - Revocation requests, supporting requests by authorized entities to revoke a certificate

CMP also defines mechanisms for performing these operations, either online or offline using files, e-mail, tokens, or web operations.

XKMS

The XML Key Management Specification (XKMS) defines services to manage PKI operations within the Extensible Markup Language (XML) environment. These services are provided for handling PKI keys and certificates automatically. Developed by the World Wide Web Consortium (W3C), XKMS is intended to simplify integration of PKIs and management of certificates in applications. As well as responding to problems of authentication and verification of electronic signatures, XKMS also allows certificates to be managed, registered, or revoked.

XKMS services reside on a separate server that interacts with an established PKI. The services are accessible via a simple XML protocol. Developers can rely on the XKMS services, making it less complex to interface with the PKI. The services provide for key information retrieval (owner, key value, key issuer, and the like) and key management (such as key registration and revocation).

Retrieval operations rely on the XML signature for the necessary information. Three tiers of service are based on the client requests and application requirements. Tier 0 provides a means of retrieving key information by embedding references to the key within the XML signature. The signature contains an element called a *retrieval method* that indicates ways to resolve the key. In this case, the client sends a request, using the retrieval method, to obtain the desired key information. For example, if the verification key contains a long chain of X.509 v3 certificates, a retrieval method could be included to avoid sending the certificates with the document. The client would use the retrieval method to obtain the chain of certificates. For tier 0, the server indicated in the retrieval method responds directly to the request for the key, possibly bypassing the XKMS server. The tier 0 process is shown in Figure 7.22.

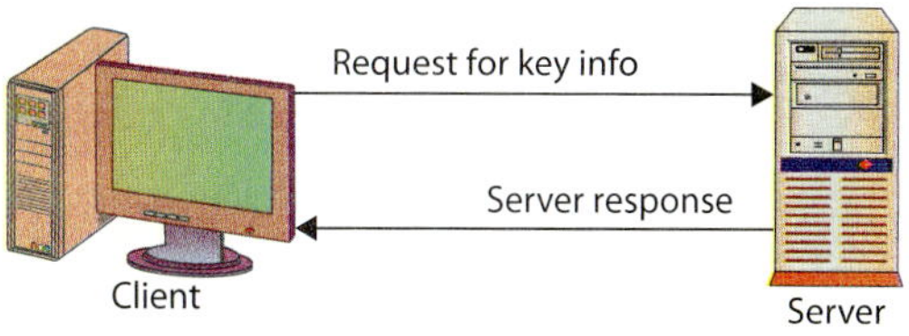

Figure 7.22 XKMS tier 0 retrieval

With tier 1 operations, the client forwards the key-information portions of the XML signature to the XKMS server, relying on the server to perform the retrieval of the desired key information. The desired information can be local to the XKMS server, or it can reside on an external PKI system. The XKMS server provides no additional validation of the key information, such as checking whether the certificate has been revoked or is still valid. Just as in tier 0, the client performs final validation of the document. Tier 1 is called the *locate service* because it locates the appropriate key information for the client, as shown in Figure 7.23.

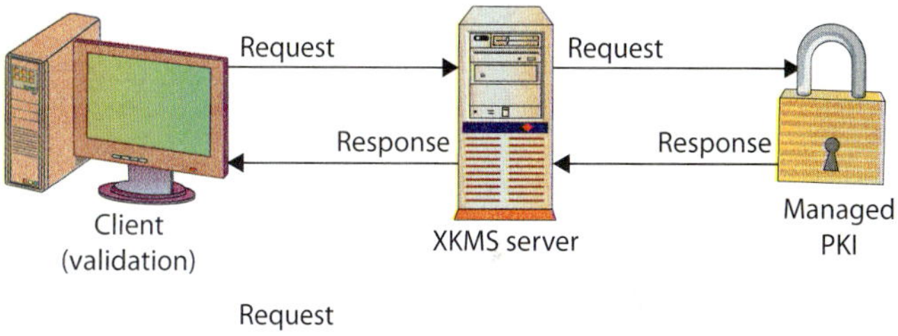

Figure 7.23 XKMS tier 1 locate service

Tier 2 is called the *validate service* and is illustrated in Figure 7.24. In this case, just as in tier 1, the client relies on the XKMS service to retrieve the relevant key information from the external PKI. The XKMS server also performs data validation on a portion of the key information provided by the client for this purpose. This validation verifies the binding of the key information with the data indicated by the key information contained in the XML signature.

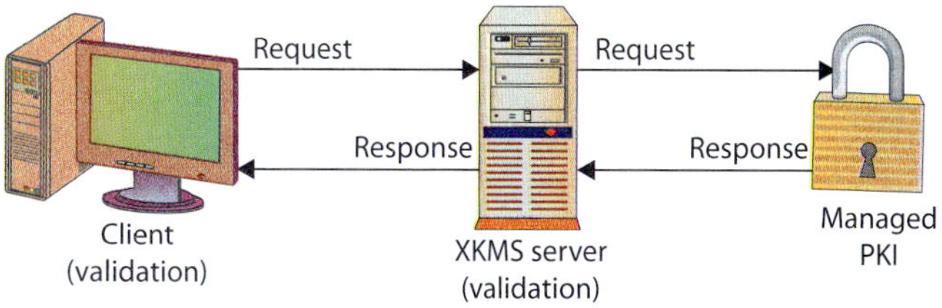

Figure 7.24 XKMS tier 2 validate service

The primary difference between tier 1 and tier 2 is the level of involvement of the XKMS server. In tier 1, it can serve only as a relay or gateway between the client and the PKI. In tier 2, the XKMS server is actively involved in verifying the relation between the PKI information and the document containing the XML signature.

XKMS relies on the client or underlying communications mechanism to provide for the security of the communications with the XKMS server. The specification suggests using one of three methods for ensuring server authentication, response integrity, and relevance of the response to the request: digitally signed correspondence, a transport layer security protocol (such as SSL, TLS, or Wireless TLS), or a packet layer security protocol (such as IPSec). Obviously, digitally signed correspondence introduces its own issues regarding validation of the signature, which is the purpose of XKMS.

It is possible to define other tiers of service. Tiers 3 and 4, an *assertion service* and an *assertion status service,* respectively, are mentioned in the defining XKMS specification, but they are not defined. The specification states they "could" be defined in other documents.

XKMS also provides services for key registration, key revocation, and key recovery. Authentication for these actions is based on a password or passphrase, which is provided when the keys are registered and when they must be recovered.

CEP

Certificate Enrollment Protocol (CEP) was originally developed by VeriSign for Cisco Systems. It was designed to support certificate issuance, distribution, and revocation using existing technologies. Its use has grown in client and CA applications. The operations supported include CA and RA public key distribution, certificate enrollment, certificate revocation, certificate query, and CRL query.

One of the key goals of CEP was to use existing technology whenever possible. It uses both PKCS #7 (Cryptographic Message Syntax Standard) and PKCS #10 (Certification Request Syntax Standard) to define a common message syntax. It supports access to certificates and CRLs using either the Lightweight Directory Access Protocol (LDAP) or the CEP-defined certificate query.

Chapter 7 Review

Chapter Summary

After reading this chapter and completing the exercises, you should understand the following about public key infrastructures.

Implement the basics of public key infrastructures

- PKI solutions include certificate authorities (CAs) and registration authorities (RAs).
- PKIs form the central management functionality used to enable encryption technologies.
- The steps a user performs to obtain a certificate for use are listed in the text and are important to memorize.

Describe the roles of certificate authorities and certificate repositories

- CAs create certificates for identified entities and maintain records of their issuance and revocation.
- CRLs provide a means of letting users know when certificates have been revoked before their end-of-life date.

Explain the relationship between trust and certificate verification

- Trust is based on an understanding of the needs of the user and what the item being trusted offers.
- Certificate verification provides assurance that the data in the certificate is valid, not whether it meets the needs of the user.

Identify centralized and decentralized infrastructures

- The three different CA architectures are hierarchical, peer-to-peer, and hybrid.
- Multiple CAs can be used together to create a web of trust.

Understand the lifecycle of certificates

- Certificates are generated, registered, and historically verified by the originating CA.
- The two main mechanisms to manage the revocation of a certificate are CRL and OCSP.
- Keys, and hence certificates, have a lifecycle; they are created, used for a defined period of time, and then destroyed.
- Certificates are handled via a certificate server and client software.
- The three classes of certificates have the following typical uses:
  - **Class 1** Personal e-mail use
  - **Class 2** Software signing
  - **Class 3** Setting up a CA

Describe public and in-house certificate authorities

- Public CAs exist as a service that allows entities to obtain certificates from a trusted third party.
- In-house certificates provide certificates that allow a firm the means to use certificates within company borders.

Identify the standards involved in establishing an interoperable Internet PKI

- PKIX and PKCS define the most commonly used PKI standards.
- PKIX, PKCS, X.509, ISAKMP, XKMS, and CMP combine to implement PKI.
- SSL/TLS, S/MIME, HTTPS, and IPSec are protocols that use PKI.

Explain interoperability issues with PKI standards

- Standards and protocols are important because they define the basis for how communication will take place.
- The use of standards and protocols provides a common, interoperable environment for securely exchanging information.
- Without these standards and protocols, two entities may independently develop their own method to implement the various components for a PKI, and the two will not be compatible.
- On the Internet, not being compatible and not being able to communicate are not options.

Describe how the common Internet protocols implement the PKI standards

- Three main standards have evolved over time to implement PKIs on the Internet.
- Two of the main standards are based on a third standard, the X.509 standard, and establish complementary standards for implementing PKIs. These two standards are Public Key Infrastructure X.509 (PKIX) and Public Key Cryptography Standards (PKCS).
- PKIX defines standards for interactions and operations for four component types: the user (end-entity), certificate authority (CA), registration authority (RA), and the repository for certificates and certificate revocation lists (CRLs).
- PKCS defines many of the lower-level standards for message syntax, cryptographic algorithms, and the like.
- There are other protocols and standards that help define the management and operation of the PKI and related services, such as ISAKMP, XKMS, and CMP.

Key Terms

.cer *(206)*
authority revocation list (ARL) *(211)*
CA certificate *(202)*
certificate *(184)*
certificate authority (CA) *(186)*
certificate chaining *(193)*
certificate path *(196)*
certificate repository *(212)*
certificate revocation list (CRL) *(209)*
certificate server *(187)*
certificate signing request (CSR) *(208)*
certification practices statement (CPS) *(187)*
Common Name (CN) *(203)*
cross-certification certificate *(203)*
digital certificate *(186)*
distinguished encoding rules (DER) *(206)*
dual control *(219)*
end-entity certificate *(202)*
hardware security module (HSM) *(217)*
hierarchical trust model *(194)*
hybrid trust model *(195)*
intermediate certificate *(193)*
Internet Security Association and Key Management Protocol (ISAKMP) *(225)*
key archiving *(219)*
key escrow *(220)*
key recovery *(219)*
local registration authority (LRA) *(188)*
offline CA *(191)*
Online Certificate Status Protocol (OCSP) *(211)*
online CA *(191)*
P12 *(207)*
P7B *(207)*
peer-to-peer trust model *(195)*
Personal Information Exchange (PFX) *(206)*
pinning *(191)*
policy certificate *(203)*
Privacy Enhanced Mail (PEM) *(206)*
Public Key Cryptography Standards (PKCS) *(223)*
public key infrastructure (PKI) *(185)*
registration authority (RA) *(187)*
stapling *(191)*
Subject Alternative Name (SAN) *(204)*
trust model *(193)*
wildcard certificates *(203)*
X.509 *(197)*

Key Terms Quiz

Use terms from the Key Terms list to complete the sentences that follow. Don't use the same term more than once. Not all terms will be used.

1. The _______________ is the trusted authority for certifying individuals' identities and creating an electronic document indicating that individuals are who they say they are.
2. A(n) _______________ is the actual request to a CA containing a public key and the requisite information needed to generate a certificate.
3. The _______________ is a method of determining whether a certificate has been revoked that does not require local machine storage of CRLs.
4. The _______________ is the actual service that issues certificates based on the data provided during the initial registration process.
5. A physical device that safeguards cryptographic keys is called a(n) _______________.
6. A(n) _______________ is a holding place for individuals' certificates and public keys that are participating in a particular PKI environment.
7. A(n) _______________ is used when independent CAs establish peer-to-peer trust relationships.
8. A(n) _______________ is a structure that provides all the necessary components for different types of users and entities to be able to communicate securely and in a predictable manner.
9. _______________ is the process of giving keys to a third party so that they can decrypt and read sensitive information if the need arises.
10. In a(n) _______________, one CA is not subordinate to another CA, and there is no established trust anchor between the CAs involved.

Multiple-Choice Quiz

1. When a user wants to participate in a PKI, what component do they need to obtain, and how does that happen?

   A. The user submits a certificate request to the CA.

   B. The user submits a key-pair request to the CRL.

   C. The user submits a certificate request to the RA.

   D. The user submits proof of identification to the CA.

2. How does a user validate a digital certificate that is received from another user?

   A. The user first sees whether their system has been configured to trust the CA that digitally signed the other user's certificate and then validates that CA's digital signature.

   B. The user calculates a message digest and compares it to the one attached to the message.

   C. The user first sees whether their system has been configured to trust the CA that digitally signed the certificate and then validates the public key that is embedded within the certificate.

   D. The user validates the sender's digital signature on the message.

3. What is the purpose of a digital certificate?

   A. It binds a CA to a user's identity.

   B. It binds a CA's identity to the correct RA.

   C. It binds an individual identity to an RA.

   D. It binds an individual identity to a public key.

4. What steps does a user's software take to validate a CA's digital signature on a digital certificate?
   - **A.** The user's software creates a message digest for the digital certificate and decrypts the encrypted message digest included within the digital certificate. If the decryption performs properly and the message digest values are the same, the certificate is validated.
   - **B.** The user's software creates a message digest for the digital signature and encrypts the message digest included within the digital certificate. If the encryption performs properly and the message digest values are the same, the certificate is validated.
   - **C.** The user's software creates a message digest for the digital certificate and decrypts the encrypted message digest included within the digital certificate. If the user can encrypt the message digest properly with the CA's private key and the message digest values are the same, the certificate is validated.
   - **D.** The user's software creates a message digest for the digital signature and encrypts the message digest with its private key. If the decryption performs properly and the message digest values are the same, the certificate is validated.

5. Why would a company implement a key archiving and recovery system within the organization?
   - **A.** To make sure all data encryption keys are available for the company if and when it needs them
   - **B.** To make sure all digital signature keys are available for the company if and when it needs them
   - **C.** To create session keys for users to be able to access when they need to encrypt bulk data
   - **D.** To back up the RA's private key for retrieval purposes

6. Within a PKI environment, where does the majority of the trust actually lie?
   - **A.** All users and devices within an environment trust the RA, which allows them to indirectly trust each other.
   - **B.** All users and devices within an environment trust the CA, which allows them to indirectly trust each other.
   - **C.** All users and devices within an environment trust the CRL, which allows them to indirectly trust each other.
   - **D.** All users and devices within an environment trust the CPS, which allows them to indirectly trust each other.

7. Which of the following properly describes what a public key infrastructure (PKI) actually is?
   - **A.** A protocol written to work with a large subset of algorithms, applications, and protocols
   - **B.** An algorithm that creates public/private key pairs
   - **C.** A framework that outlines specific technologies and algorithms that must be used
   - **D.** A framework that does not specify any technologies but provides a foundation for confidentiality, integrity, and availability services

8. Once an individual validates another individual's certificate, what is the use of the public key that is extracted from this digital certificate?
   - **A.** The public key is now available to use to create digital signatures.
   - **B.** The user can now encrypt session keys and messages with this public key and can validate the sender's digital signatures.
   - **C.** The public key is now available to encrypt future digital certificates that need to be validated.
   - **D.** The user can now encrypt private keys that need to be transmitted securely.

9. Why would a digital certificate be added to a certificate revocation list (CRL)?
   A. If the public key had become compromised in a public repository
   B. If the private key had become compromised
   C. If a new employee joined the company and received a new certificate
   D. If the certificate expired

10. How can users have faith that the CRL was not modified to present incorrect information?
   A. The CRL is digitally signed by the CA.
   B. The CRL is encrypted by the CA.
   C. The CRL is open for anyone to post certificate information to.
   D. The CRL is accessible only to the CA.

Essay Quiz

1. You are the Information Security Officer at a medium-sized company (1500 employees). The CIO has asked you to explain why you recommend using commercial PKIs rather than implementing such a capability in-house with the software developers you already have. Write three succinct sentences that would get your point across and address three key issues.
2. Describe the pros and cons of establishing a key archiving system program for a small- to medium-sized business.
3. Why would a small- to medium-sized firm implement a PKI solution? What business benefits would ensue from such a course of action?
4. Describe the steps involved in verifying a certificate's validity.
5. Describe the steps in obtaining a certificate.
6. Compare and contrast the hierarchical trust model, peer-to-peer trust model, and hybrid trust model.

Lab Projects

• Lab Project 7.1

Investigate the process of obtaining a personal certificate or digital ID for e-mail usage. What information is needed, what are the costs, and what protection is afforded based on the vendor?

• Lab Project 7.2

Determine what certificates are registered with the browser instance on your computer.

chapter 8

Physical Security

Fully secure systems don't exist today and they won't exist in the future.

—Adi Shamir

In this chapter, you will learn how to

- Describe how physical security directly affects computer and network security
- Discuss steps that can be taken to help mitigate risks
- Describe the physical security components that can protect your computers and network
- Identify environmental factors that can affect security
- Identify the different types of fires and the various fire suppression systems designed to limit the damage caused by fires
- Explain electronic access controls and the principles of convergence
- Prevent disclosure through electronic emanations

Physical security consists of all mechanisms used to ensure that physical access to the computer systems and networks is restricted to only authorized users. Additional physical security mechanisms may be used to provide increased security for especially sensitive systems such as servers as well as devices such as routers, firewalls, and intrusion detection systems. When considering physical security, you should take into account access from all six sides—not only should the security of obvious points of entry be examined, such as doors and windows, but the walls themselves as well as the floor and ceiling should also be considered. Questions such as the following should be addressed:

- Is there a false ceiling with tiles that can be easily removed?
- Do the walls extend to the actual ceiling or only to a false ceiling?
- Is there a raised floor?
- Do the walls extend to the actual floor, or do they stop at a raised floor?
- How are important systems situated?
- Do the monitors face away from windows, or could the activity of somebody at a system be monitored from outside?
- Who has access to the facility?

- What type of access control is there, and are there any guards?
- Who is allowed unsupervised access to the facility?
- Is there an alarm system or security camera that covers the area?
- What procedures govern the monitoring of the alarm system or security camera as well as the response should unauthorized activity be detected?

These are just some of the numerous questions that need to be asked when you're examining the physical security surrounding a system.

> **Tech Tip**
>
> **Physical Security Is Also Important to Computer Security**
>
> *Computer security professionals recognize that they cannot rely only on computer security mechanisms to keep their systems safe. Physical security must be maintained as well, because in many cases, if an attacker gains physical access, they can steal data and destroy the system.*

The Security Problem

The problem that faces professionals charged with securing a company's network can be stated rather simply: physical access negates all other security measures. No matter how impenetrable the firewall and intrusion detection system (IDS), if an attacker can find a way to walk up to and touch a server, they can break into it.

Consider that most network security measures are, from necessity, directed at protecting a company from Internet-based threats. Consequently, a lot of companies allow any kind of traffic on the local area network (LAN). So if an attacker attempts to gain access to a server over the Internet and fails, they may be able to gain physical access to the receptionist's machine and, by quickly compromising it, use it as a remotely controlled zombie to attack what they are really after. Figure 8.1 illustrates the use of a lower-privilege machine to obtain sensitive information. Physically securing information assets doesn't mean just the servers; it means protecting physical access to all the organization's computers and its entire network infrastructure.

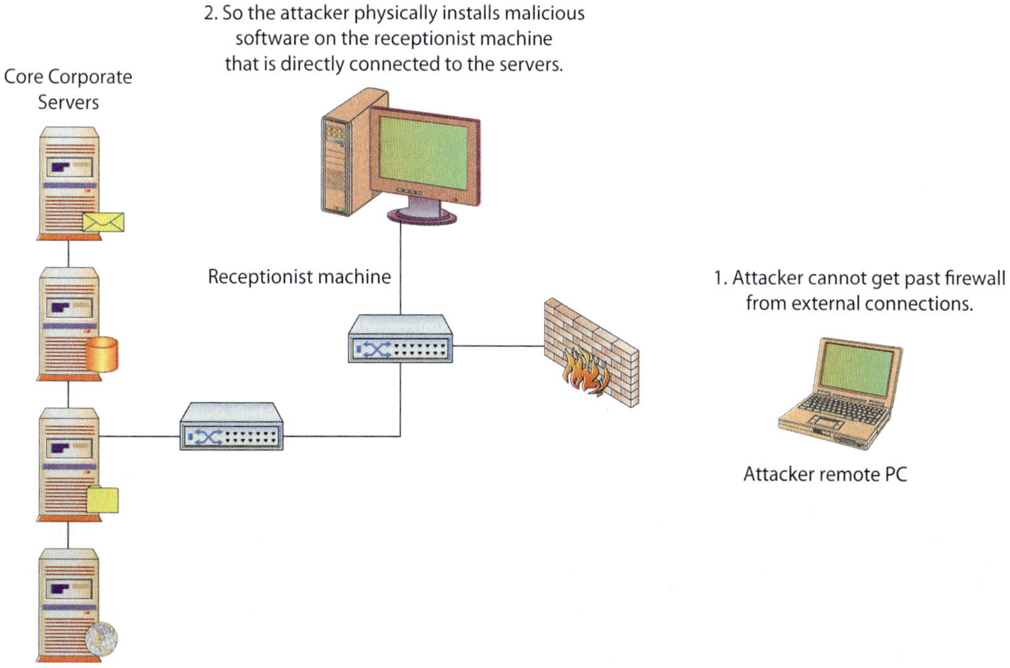

• **Figure 8.1** Using a lower-privilege machine to get at sensitive information

Physical access to a corporation's systems can allow an attacker to perform a number of interesting activities, starting with simply plugging into an open Ethernet jack. The advent of handheld devices with the ability to run operating systems with full networking support has made this attack scenario even more feasible. Prior to handheld devices, the attacker would have to work in a secluded area with dedicated access to the Ethernet for a time. The attacker would sit down with a laptop and run a variety of tools against the network, and working internally typically put the attacker inside the firewall and IDS. Today's capable mobile devices can assist these efforts by allowing attackers to place the small device onto the network to act as a *wireless bridge*, as shown in Figure 8.2.

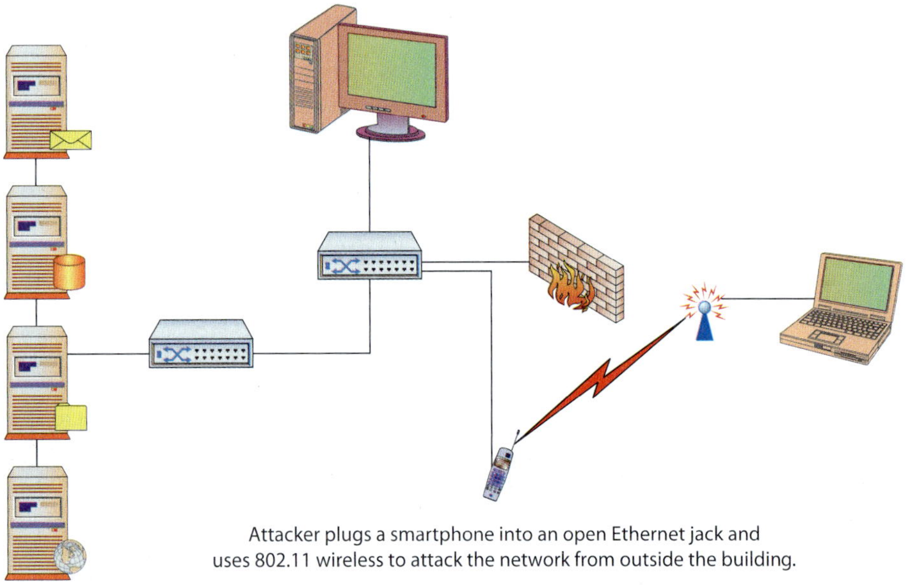

• **Figure 8.2** A wireless bridge can allow remote access.

The attacker can then use a laptop to attack a network remotely via the bridge from outside the building. If power is available near the Ethernet jack, this type of attack can also be accomplished with an off-the-shelf access point. The attacker's only challenge is finding an Ethernet jack that isn't blocked by furniture or some other obstruction.

Another simple attack that can be used when an attacker has physical access is called a **bootdisk**. Any media used to boot a computer into an operating system that is not the native OS on its hard drive could be classified as a bootdisk. This can be in the form of a CD, DVD, or a USB flash drive. A boot source can contain a number of programs, but the most typical ones would be NTFSDOS or a Linux distribution that can be used to perform a number of tasks, including mounting the hard drives and performing at least read operations, all done via script. Once an attacker is able to read a hard drive, the password file can be copied off the machine for offline password-cracking attacks. If write access to the drive is obtained, the attacker could alter the password file or place a remote-control program to be executed automatically upon the next boot, guaranteeing continued access to the machine. The most obvious mitigation is to tell the BIOS not to boot from removable media, but this too has issues.

When you're booting from any external media, the veracity of the media is important because, with today's capacities, entire systems can easily be on a small device like a thumb drive, and the changes they can impart to a system can be critical.

Tech Tip

Secure Boot

A traditional BIOS will boot any software, so it's possible for malware, such as a rootkit, to replace your boot loader. The rootkit could load your normal operating system with no indication anything was wrong, staying completely invisible and undetectable on your system. The BIOS doesn't know the difference between malware and a trusted boot loader—it just boots whatever it finds on the boot device. Microsoft's Secure Boot is a component of the Windows operating system that helps prevent malicious software applications and "unauthorized" operating systems from loading during the system start-up process. Secure Boot relies on the Unified Extensible Firmware Interface (UEFI) specification's secure boot functionality and uses a digital signature check that allows other authorized OSs, such as Linux, to boot. This makes it only somewhat effective against someone using an external media, as a signed copy of Linux with hacker tools can boot. Keeping attackers from physically accessing machines is important even with advanced measures like Secure Boot.

There are operating system distributions specifically designed to run the entire machine from an optical disc without using the hard drive. These are commonly referred to as LiveCDs. A **LiveCD** contains a bootable version of an entire operating system, typically a variant of Linux, complete with drivers for most devices. LiveCDs give an attacker a greater array of tools than could be loaded onto a floppy disk, such as scanners, sniffers, vulnerability exploits, forensic tools, drive imagers, password crackers, and so on. These sets of tools are too numerous to list here (and the list changes every day). The best resource is to search the Internet for popular LiveCD distributions such as Kali (formerly BackTrack), Knoppix, and PHLAK. A sample collection of LiveCDs is shown in Figure 8.3.

• **Figure 8.3** A collection of sample LiveCDs

Try This!

Create a Bootdisk

Bootdisks allow you to boot a computer to the disk rather than the OS that is on the hard drive. Create a bootdisk for your own personal computer. The steps differ between different OSs and depend on the media you wish to make bootable. Perform a little research to determine the correct procedure for your OS and give it a try. Also, try making a bootable USB flash drive.

Drive imaging is a threat because all existing access controls to data can be bypassed and all the data stored on the drive can be read from the image.

A USB data blocker prevents attackers from infecting a device with malware or stealing data. Also remember that turning off the AutoPlay setting in the operating system will prevent malicious code from automatically running when you plug in a USB or other external media device.

For example, with a LiveCD or bootable USB, an attacker would likely have access to the hard disk and also to an operational network interface that allows them to send the drive data over the Internet if properly connected. These bootable operating systems could also be custom-built to contain any tool that runs under Linux, allowing an attacker to build a standard bootable attack image or a standard bootable forensic image, or something customized for the tools they like to use. Bootable USB flash drives emulate the function of a CD-ROM and provide a device that is both physically smaller and logically larger.

These types of devices have spawned a new kind of attack in which a flash drive is left in an opportunistic place where members of a target organization may pick it up and use it. This flash drive is typically loaded with malware and is referred to as a *road apple*. The attack relies on curious people plugging the device into their work computer to see what's on it. Occasionally the attacker may also try to tempt the passerby with enticing descriptions like "Employee Salaries" or even something as simple as "Confidential." Once a user loads the flash drive, the malware will attempt to infect the machine.

Physical access is the most common way of imaging a drive, and the biggest benefit for the attacker is that drive imaging leaves absolutely no trace of the crime. Besides physically securing access to your computers, you can do very little to prevent drive imaging, but you can minimize its impact. The use of encryption even for a few important files provides protection. Full encryption of the drive protects all files stored on it. Alternatively, placing files on a centralized file server keeps them from being imaged from an individual machine, but if an attacker is able to image the file server, the data will be copied.

Tech Tip

Encryption to TPM-Based Keys

Many computers now come with a security chip that follows the Trusted Platform Module (TPM) standard. This TPM chip allows for the creation and storage of encryption keys. One of the strengths associated with this level of security is that if a copy of a drive, or even the drive itself, is stolen, the contents are unusable without the key. Having this key locked in hardware prevents hackers from stealing a copy of the key from a memory location.

Cross Check

Forensic Images

When you're taking a forensic-based image, it is important to follow proper forensic procedures to ensure the evidence is properly secured. Forensic processes and procedures are covered in detail in Chapter 23.

A denial-of-service (DoS) attack can also be performed with physical access. Physical access to the computers can be much more effective than a network-based DoS attack. Stealing a computer, using a bootdisk to erase all data on the drives, or simply unplugging computers are all effective DoS attacks. Depending on the company's frequency of backing up critical systems, as well as the quality of those backups, a DoS attack using these methods can have lasting effects.

Physical access can negate almost all the security that the network attempts to provide. Considering this, you must determine the level of physical access that attackers might obtain. Of special consideration are persons with authorized access to the building who are not authorized users of the systems. Janitorial personnel and others have authorized access to many areas, but they do not have authorized system access. An attacker could pose as one of these individuals or attempt to gain access to the facilities through them.

Physical Security Safeguards

Although it is difficult, if not impossible, to make an organization's computer systems totally secure, many steps can be taken to mitigate the risk to information systems from a physical threat. The following sections discuss access control methods and physical security policies and procedures that should be implemented.

Walls and Guards

The primary defense against a majority of physical attacks is the barriers between the assets and a potential attacker—walls, fences, gates, and doors. Some organizations also employ full- or part-time private security staff to attempt to protect their assets. These barriers provide the foundation upon which all other security initiatives are based, but the security must be designed carefully, as an attacker has to find only a single gap to gain access.

All entry points to server rooms and wiring closets should be closely controlled, and, if possible, access should be logged through an access control system. This includes access from the outside via windows.

Walls may have been one of the first inventions of man. Once he learned to use natural obstacles such as mountains to separate him from his enemy, he next learned to build his *own* mountain for the same purpose. Hadrian's Wall in England, the Great Wall of China, and the Berlin Wall are all famous examples of such basic physical defenses. The walls of any building serve the same purpose, but on a smaller scale: they provide barriers to physical access to company assets. *Bollards* are small and round concrete pillars that are constructed and placed around a building to protect it from being damaged by someone driving a vehicle into the side of the building, or getting close and using a car bomb.

To protect the physical servers, you must look in all directions: Doors and windows should be safeguarded, and a minimum number of each should be used in a server room. Less obvious entry points should also be considered: Is a drop ceiling used in the server room? Do the interior walls extend to the actual roof, raised floors, or crawlspaces? Access to the server room should be limited to the people who need access, not to all employees of the organization. If you are going to use a wall to protect an asset, make sure no obvious holes appear in that wall.

Guards

Guards provide an excellent security measure because they are a visible presence with direct responsibility for security. Other employees expect security guards to behave a certain way with regard to securing the facility. Guards typically monitor entrances and exits and can maintain access logs of who has entered and departed the building. In many organizations, everyone who passes through security as a visitor must sign the log, which can be useful in tracing who was at what location and when.

Security personnel are helpful in physically securing the machines on which information assets reside, but for an organization to get the most benefit from their presence, they must be trained to take a holistic approach to security. The value of data typically can be many times that of the machines on which the data is stored. Security guards typically are not computer

The bigger challenge associated with capturing surveillance activities or other attempted break-in efforts is their clandestine nature. These efforts are designed to be as low profile and nonobvious as possible to increase the chances of success. Training and awareness are necessary not just for security personnel but for all personnel. If an employee hears multiple extensions all start ringing in the middle of the night, do they know whom to notify? If a security guard notes such activity, how does this information get reported to the correct team?

Tech Tip

Fence Types

Fences come in a variety of types and heights. The following table assists you in choosing the correct size based on need:

Height	*Protection*
1 meter / 3–4 feet	*Deters casual trespassers*
2 meter / 6–7 feet	*Too high to climb easily*
2.4 meter / 8 feet (with top guard)	*Deters determined intruder*

Bollards are sturdy posts often made of concrete or galvanized or stainless steel. They are used to protect entry ways and prevent unauthorized entry or vehicle ramming attacks.

security experts, so they need to be educated about the value of the data and be trained in network security as well as physical security involving users. They are the company's eyes and ears for suspicious activity, so the network security department needs to train them to notice suspicious network activity as well. Multiple extensions ringing in sequence during the night, computers rebooting all at once, or strange people parked in the parking lot with laptop computers are all indicators of a network attack that might be missed without proper training.

Many traditional physical security tools such as access controls and closed-circuit television (CCTV) camera systems are transitioning from closed hardwired systems to Ethernet- and IP-based systems. This transition opens up the devices to network attacks traditionally performed on computers. With physical security systems being implemented using the IP network, everyone in physical security must become smarter about network security.

Robot Sentries

Guard duty is by and large boring work, and although guards aren't highly paid over time, having a number of guards can be expensive. Robot technology has progressed to the point where robots can now perform many simple tasks, and guard duty can be one of these tasks. **Robot sentries** can patrol empty buildings and, using sensors, can detect the presence of unauthorized people. Robot sentries can then report the issue to a manned station that can alert the proper authorities for a response.

Fences

Outside of the building's walls, many organizations prefer to have a perimeter fence as a physical first layer of defense. Chain-link fencing is most commonly used, and it can be enhanced with barbed wire. Anti-scale fencing, which looks like very tall vertical poles placed close together to form a fence, is used for high-security implementations that require additional scale and tamper resistance.

To increase security against physical intrusion, higher fences can be employed. A fence that is three to four feet in height will deter casual or accidental trespassers. Six to seven feet will deter a general intruder. To deter more determined intruders, a minimum height of eight feet is recommended, with the addition of barbed wire or razor wire on top for extreme levels of deterrence.

Barricades/Bollards

Barricades provide the foundation upon which all other physical security initiatives are based. Barricades can also be used to control vehicular access to (or near) a building or structure. A simple post-type barricade that prevents a vehicle from passing but allows people to walk past it is called a **bollard**. Bollards also act to prevent some forms of physical entry but, like a window, do not obscure vision as a wall or fence might. Physical security elements must be designed and deployed carefully, as an attacker has to find only a single gap to gain access.

Lights and Signage

Having the appropriate visual cues or, in some cases, the lack thereof is an important part of physical security. So, if you want to be seen, add lights; if you don't want to be seen, try industrial camouflage. Signs to alert people to boundaries and rules as well as alarms to indicate specific conditions are part of an overall physical security program.

Lighting

Proper **lighting** is essential for physical security. Unlit or dimly lit areas allow intruders to lurk and conduct unauthorized activities without a significant risk of observation by guards or other personnel. External building lighting is important to ensure that unauthorized activities cannot occur without being observed and responded to. Internal lighting is equally important because it enables more people to observe activities and see conditions that are not correct. Similarly, windows can play an important role in assisting the observation of the premises. Having sensitive areas well lit and open to observation through windows prevents activities that would otherwise take place in secret. Unauthorized parties in server rooms are more likely to be detected if the servers are centrally located, surrounded in windows, and well lit.

> **Tech Tip**
>
> **Lighting Types**
>
> *Lighting not only provides a deterrent to intruders but also assists other access control systems.*
>
> *Types of lighting systems:*
>
> - ***Continuous lighting*** *A series of fixed lights arranged to flood a given area continuously*
> - ***Trip lighting*** *Activated when an intruder crosses a sensor*
> - ***Standby lighting*** *Similar to continuous lighting, except lights are not continuously lit*
> - ***Emergency lighting*** *Activated in emergency events (for example, a power failure or fire)*
>
> *Specific types of lighting:*
>
> - ***Glare projection lighting*** *Used to light a specific area and deter intruder actions*
> - ***Floodlight*** *Used to light a large area to facilitate security monitoring*

Signs

Signs (or **signage**) act as informational devices and can be used in a variety of ways to assist in physical security. Signs can provide information as to areas that are restricted, or they can indicate where specific precautions, such as keeping doors locked, are required. A common use of signs in high-security facilities is to delineate where visitor are allowed versus secured areas where escorts are required. Visual security clues can assist in alerting users to the need for specific security precautions. Visual clues as to the types of protection required can take the form of different color name badges that dictate the level of access, visible lanyards that indicate visitors, colored folders, and so forth.

Alarms

Alarms serve to alert operators to abnormal conditions. Physical security can involve numerous sensors, intrusion alarms, motion detectors, switches that alert to doors being opened, video and audio surveillance, and more. Each of these systems can gather useful information, but it is only truly useful if it is acted upon. When one of these systems has information that can be of use to operational personnel, an alarm is the easiest method of alerting personnel to the condition. Alarms are not simple; if there are too many alarm conditions, especially false alarms, then the operators will not react to these conditions as desired. Tuning alarms so that they provide useful, accurate, and actionable information is important if you want them to be effective.

There are many types of alarm systems. Local alarm systems ring only locally. A central station system is one where alarms (and CCTV) are monitored by a central station. Many alarms will have auxiliary or secondary reporting functions to local police or fire departments. Alarms work by alerting personnel to the triggering of specific monitoring controls. Typical controls include the following:

- Dry contact switches use metallic foil tape as a contact detector to detect whether a door or window is opened.
- Electro-mechanical detection systems detect a change or break in a circuit. They can be used as a contact detector to detect whether a door or window is opened.
- Vibration detection systems detect movement on walls, ceiling, floors, and so forth, by vibration.
- Pressure mats detect whether someone is stepping on the mat.
- Photoelectric or photometric detection systems emit a beam of light and monitor the beam to detect for motion and break-in.
- Wave pattern motion detectors generate microwave or ultrasonic wave and monitor the emitted waves to detect for motion.
- Passive infrared detection systems detect changes of heat waves generated by an intruder.
- Audio or acoustical-seismic detection systems listen for changes in noise levels.
- Proximity detectors or capacitance detectors emit a magnetic field and monitor the field to detect any interruption.

• **Figure 8.4** A neighborhood substation in plain sight

Industrial Camouflage

Camouflage is the specific act of rendering an item so it is not readily observable. Considered by many to be a military thing, it began in nature, where insects and animals would have patterns making them seem to be different than they really are. This same principle is used all the time to make things hide in plain sight. **Industrial camouflage** is a term used to describe the use of these techniques to make infrastructure items less visible to ordinary observers. Cell phone towers built to look like trees make them less conspicuous, and generally improve the visual surroundings. In response to physical acts against electrical substations, many utilities have put walls around the substations, making the internal equipment no longer visible and less of a target. Figure 8.4 shows a small house that is actually a substation.

Try This!

Want to see some industrial camouflage in action? Use Street View in Google Maps and look at these locations:

58 Joralemon Street, New York City. This is a ventilation shaft and emergency access to the New York subway.

640 Millwood Road, Toronto, Canada is an electrical substation, one of 250 in the city.

51 W. Ontario Street, Chicago, Illinois, is another substation—this one by Commonwealth Edison. On this substation, the doors are fake and don't open, and the windows are actually vents.

Physical Access Controls and Monitoring

Physical access control means control of doors and entry points. The design and construction of all types of access control systems, as well as the physical barriers to which they are most complementary, are fully discussed in other texts. Here, we explore a few important points to help you safeguard the information infrastructure, especially where it meets with the physical access control system. This section talks about physical locks, layered access systems, and electronic access control systems. It also discusses closed-circuit television (CCTV) systems and the implications of different CCTV system types.

• **Figure 8.5** Contactless access cards act as modern keys to a building.

Layered Access

Layered access is an important concept in security. It is often mentioned in conversations about network security perimeters, but in this chapter it relates to the concept of physical security perimeters. To help prevent an attacker from gaining access to important assets, these assets should be placed inside multiple perimeters. Servers should be placed in a separate secure area, ideally with a separate authentication mechanism. For example, if an organization has an electronic door control system using **contactless access cards** (such as the example shown in Figure 8.5) as well as a keypad, a combination of the card and a separate PIN code would be required to open the door to the server room.

Access to the server room should be limited to staff with a legitimate need to work on the servers. To layer the protection, the area surrounding the server room should also be limited to people who need to work in that area.

Locks

Locks have been discussed as a primary element of security. Although locks have been used for hundreds of years, their design has not changed much: a metal "token" is used to align pins in a mechanical device. As all mechanical devices have tolerances, it is possible to sneak through these tolerances by "picking" the lock. Most locks can be easily picked with simple tools, some of which are shown in Figure 8.6.

• **Figure 8.6** Lockpicking tools

As we humans are always trying to build a better mousetrap, high-security locks, such as the one shown in Figure 8.7, have been designed to defeat attacks; these locks are more sophisticated than a standard home deadbolt system. Typically found in commercial applications that require high security, these locks are made to resist picking and drilling, as well as other common attacks such as simply pounding the lock through the door. Another common feature of high-security locks is *key control*, which refers to the restrictions placed on making a copy of the key. For most residential locks, a trip to the hardware store will allow you to make a copy of the key. Key control locks use patented keyways that can only be copied at a locksmith, who will keep records on authorized users of a particular key.

• **Figure 8.7** A high-security lock and its key

High-end lock security is more important now that attacks such as "bump keys" are well known and widely available. A *bump key* is a key cut with all notches to the maximum depth, also known as "all nines." This key uses a technique that has been around a long time, but has recently gained a lot of popularity. The key is inserted into the lock and then sharply struck, bouncing the lock pins up above the shear line and allowing the lock to open. High-security locks attempt to prevent this type of attack through various mechanical means such as nontraditional pin layout, sidebars, and even magnetic keys.

Layered access is a form of defense in depth, a principle component of any strong security solution.

Other physical locks include programmable or cipher locks, locks with a keypad that require a combination of keys to open the lock, and locks with a reader that require an access card to open the lock. These may have special options such as a hostage alarm (which supports a key combination to trigger an alarm). Master-keying (which supports key combinations to change the access code and configure the functions of the lock) and key-override functions (which support key combinations to override the usual procedures) are also options on high-end programmable locks.

Device locks are used to lock a device to a physical restraint, preventing its removal. Another method of securing laptops and mobile devices is a cable trap, which allows a user to affix a cable lock to a secure structure.

A *fail-soft* (or *fail-safe*) lock is unlocked in a power interruption, meaning the door defaults to being unlocked. A *fail-secure* lock is locked in a power interruption, meaning the door defaults to being locked.

Doors

Doors to secured areas should have characteristics to make them less obvious. They should have similar appearance to the other doors to avoid catching the attention of intruders. Security doors should be self-closing and have no hold-open feature. They should trigger alarms if they are forcibly opened or have been held open for a long period.

Door systems, like many systems, have two design methodologies: fail-safe and fail-secure. While *fail-safe* is a common enough phrase to have entered the lexicon, think about what it really means—being safe when a system fails. In the case of these electronic door systems, fail-safe means that the door is unlocked should power fail. *Fail-secure*, on the other hand, means that the system will lock the door when power is lost. This can also apply when door systems are manually bypassed. It is important to know how each door will react to a system failure, not only for security but also for fire code compliance, as fail-secure is not allowed for certain doors in a building.

A mantrap/turnstile door arrangement can prevent unauthorized people from following authorized users through an access-controlled door, which is also known as *tailgating*.

Mantraps and Turnstiles

The implementation of a **mantrap** is one way to combat tailgating. A mantrap is composed of two doors closely spaced that require the user to card through one and then the other sequentially. Mantraps make it nearly impossible to trail through a doorway undetected—if you happen to catch the first door, you will be trapped in by the second door.

As shown here, a **turnstile** is a physical gated barrier that allows only one person at a time to pass. Turnstiles can also be used for exits, allowing only a single direction of traffic.

Reception Areas

Reception areas are used as buffer zones between different areas of a facility, segmenting the building into separate zones. Having a visitor check-in desk allows for control over visitors; it enables functions like logging visitors, managing deliveries, and assigning escorts for visitors. In lower security environments, this reception area may simply be someone at a desk, with no physical barrier. In more secure facilities, the receptionist is not only the gatekeeper for logs, access badges, and notifying escorts, but also controls the door that you would go through. In very highly controlled environments, the actual door control is done remotely from the other side of the door, so you can't force your way past the receptionist.

Cameras

Closed-circuit television (CCTV) cameras are similar to the door control systems—they can be very effective, but how they are implemented is an important consideration. The use of CCTV cameras for surveillance purposes dates back to at least 1961, when cameras were installed in a London Transport train station. The development of smaller and more sophisticated camera components and decreasing prices for the cameras have caused a boom in the CCTV industry since then.

CCTV cameras are used to monitor a workplace for security purposes. These systems are commonplace in banks and jewelry stores, places with high-value merchandise that is attractive to thieves. As the expense of these systems dropped, they became practical for many more industry segments. Traditional cameras are analog and require a video multiplexer to combine all the signals and make multiple views appear on a monitor. IP-based cameras have changed that, as most of them are standalone units viewable through a web browser, such as the camera shown in Figure 8.8.

• **Figure 8.8** IP-based cameras leverage existing IP networks instead of needing a proprietary CCTV cable.

These IP-based systems add useful functionality, such as the ability to check on the building from the Internet. This network functionality, however, makes the cameras subject to normal IP-based network attacks. A DoS attack launched at the CCTV system just as a break-in is occurring is the last thing anyone would want (other than the criminals). For this reason, IP-based CCTV cameras should be placed on their own separate network that can be accessed only by security personnel. The same physical separation applies to any IP-based camera infrastructure.

If you depend on the CCTV system to protect your organization's assets, carefully consider camera placement and the type of cameras used. Different iris types, focal lengths, and color or infrared capabilities are all options that make one camera superior to another in a specific location.

> **Tech Tip**
>
> **PTZ Cameras**
>
> *Pan-tilt-zoom (PTZ) cameras are ones that have the functionality to enable camera movement along multiple axes, as well as the ability to zoom in on an item. These cameras provide additional capability, especially in situations where the video is monitored and the monitoring station can maneuver the camera.*

Infrared Detection

Infrared (IR) radiation is not visible to the human eye, but it can be used just like a light source to detect a range of things. Motion from living creatures can be seen because of the heat signatures of their bodies. *Infrared detection* is a technical means of looking for things that otherwise might not be noticed. At night, when it is dark, someone can hide in the shadows, but infrared light can point them out to IR-sensing cameras.

Motion Detection

When an area is being monitored for unauthorized activity, one potentially useful tool is a **motion detection**. In areas where there is little or no expected traffic, a motion detector can alert an operator to activity in an area. Motion detectors come in a variety of types, but most are based on infrared radiation

It is interesting to note that today many of the "events" taking place across cities during protests in 2020 are also being recorded. Those caught on surveillance systems vandalizing and looting may be held legally accountable as a result of being detected by motion and object detection camera sensors. In several high-profile cases, these sensors provide police critical details to act upon as leads—like a unique shirt from Etsy that was eventually traced to an arsonist.

(heat) and can detect the changes of a warm body moving. They can be tuned for size, ignoring smaller movement such as small animals in outdoor settings. Although not useful in busy office buildings during normal daily use, motion detectors can be useful during off-hours, when traffic is minimal. Motion detectors can be used to trigger video systems, so they do not record large amounts of "empty" activity. Video monitoring of the loading dock area in the back of the building can be triggered in this fashion, using the motion detector to turn on cameras whenever activity is occurring.

Object Detection

Modern surveillance video systems come with some impressive software. Even cameras sold to homeowners can scan video for movement and detect people, cars, and other designated objects such as packages left on a porch. The use of video software for **object detection** does not replace a human, but it significantly enhances a guard's ability to effectively use large banks of cameras to cover a facility. The city-wide video surveillance system in London was the primary source of evidence that identified the terrorists who set off a series of bombs across the city in 2005.

Noise Detection

Noise detection is a sensor method that listens for specific sounds. Ordinary things can have different sounds, and each has a spectral signature that can be used to hear some items while ignoring others. Glass breakage has a specific sound, and sensors can be tuned to "hear" glass breakage and provide an alert when it occurs. The use of sensors that target events such as this and provide the information to a central alarm panel can greatly increase the effectiveness of security personnel in monitoring a larger facility.

Proximity Reader

Proximity readers are sensors that provide a signal at a specified distance. The most common application of these are card readers that are connected to doors; you "swipe" your card by placing it near the reader, and if the codes are correct, you are granted access. However, these devices have much greater utility. Having a series of proximity readers scattered throughout a facility can act as a reporting sensor, monitoring guards as they traverse their appointed rounds. Guards can check in to each point by interacting with the proximity reader, typically by swiping a card near the device, and the device records their presence at that spot at that time. With near field communications (NFC) and advanced Bluetooth becoming a utility via smartphones, the uses of proximity readers beyond just paying for things is growing exponentially. For example, proximity devices in bus stops allow you to get an updated bus schedule on your smartphone. The ability to sense and communicate over short distances has almost endless possibilities.

Moisture Detection

Moisture (or in other words, water) can have significant detrimental effects on things. *Moisture detection* sensors provide a remote means of monitoring everything from water leaks to humidity problems. As with all sensors, the objective is to provide better "eyes and ears" for the security personnel, allowing 24/7 coverage of issues, many times in remote areas, for conditions that may require attention.

Safes

Safes are physical storage devices meant to increase the work factor for unauthorized personnel attempting to access the protected contents within. Safes come in a wide variety of shapes, sizes, and costs. The higher the level of protection from the physical environment, the better the level of protection against unauthorized access. Safes are not perfect; in fact, they are rated in terms of how long they can be expected to protect their contents from theft and/or fire. The better the rating, the more expensive the safe.

Secure Cabinets/Enclosures

There are times when using a safe is overkill—when it provides better levels of security than really needed. A simpler solution is to use a *secure cabinet* or *enclosure*. Secure cabinets and enclosures provide system owners a place to park an asset until it's needed. Most secure cabinets/enclosures do not offer all the levels of protection that one gets with a safe, but they can be useful, especially when the volume of secure storage is large.

Protected Distribution/Protected Cabling

Cable runs between systems need to be protected from physical damage to the cables and subsequent communication failures. This is accomplished by *protected distribution/protected cabling* during the cable installation. This may be something as simple as metal tubes or as complex as concrete pipes to run buried cables. The objective is to prevent any physical damage to the physical layer portion of the system.

Air Gap

Air gap is a term used to describe a network that is not physically connected to other networks. This separation was designed to prevent unauthorized data transfers to and from the network. The flaw in this logic is that users will move data by other means in order to get their work done. Frequently called *sneakernet,* this unauthorized bypassing of the air gap, although ostensibly for the purpose of mission accomplishment, increases system risk because it also bypasses checks, logging, and other processes important in development and deployment.

Faraday Cage

A **Faraday cage**, or Faraday shield, is an enclosure of conductive, grounded material designed to provide shielding against electromagnetic interference (EMI). These can be room-sized or built into a building's construction; the critical element is that there is no significant gap in the enclosure material. These measures can help shield EMI, especially in high-radio-frequency environments.

EMI can plague any type of electronics, but the density of circuitry in the typical data center can make it a haven for EMI. EMI is defined as the disturbance on an electrical circuit caused by that circuit's reception of electromagnetic radiation. Magnetic radiation enters the circuit by induction, where magnetic waves create a charge on the circuit. The amount of sensitivity to this magnetic field depends on a number of factors, including the length of the circuit, which can act like an antenna. EMI is grouped into two general types: narrowband and broadband. Narrowband is, by its nature, electromagnetic energy with a small frequency band and, therefore, is typically sourced from a device that is purposefully transmitting in the specified band. Broadband covers a wider array of frequencies and is typically caused by some type of general electrical power use such as power lines or electric motors. More information on EMI is provided in the section "Electromagnetic Environment" later in the chapter.

In the United States, the Federal Communications Commission (FCC) has responsibility for regulating products that produce EMI and has developed a program for equipment manufacturers to adhere to standards for EMI immunity. Modern circuitry is designed to resist EMI. Cabling is a good example; the twists in unshielded twisted pair (UTP) cable—or Category 5e, 6, 6a, and 7 cable—is there to prevent EMI. EMI is also controlled by metal computer cases that are grounded; by providing an easy path to ground, the case acts as an EMI shield. Shielding can be important for network cabling. It is important not to run lengths of network cabling in parallel with power cables. Twisted pair offers some degree of protection, but in electrically noisy environments such as industrial facilities, shielded twisted pair (STP) may be necessary.

Cable Locks

Portable equipment has a principal feature of being moveable, but this can also be a problem because portable equipment, laptops, projectors, and the like can be easily removed or stolen. **Cable locks** provide a simple means of securing portable equipment to the furniture in the room where it resides. Cable locks can be used by road warriors to secure laptops from casual theft. They also can be used in open areas such as conference centers, or rooms where portable equipment is exposed to a wide range of visitors.

Screen Filters

Shoulder surfing is the process of looking over someone's shoulder while they are typing, usually to read passwords or other sensitive information. Given the close physical spacing on today's aircraft and other public conveyances, if one is going to use a laptop, others are going to have access to see the screen. *Screen filters* are optical filters that limit the angle of viewability to a very narrow range, making it difficult for others to visually eavesdrop. Screen filters have a wide range of uses—for road warrior laptops, kiosks, reception desks, as well as places where sensitive data is displayed, such as medical data in medical environments.

Key Management

Physical locks have physical keys, and keeping track of who has what keys can be a chore. Add in master keys and maintaining a list of who has physical access to each space can quickly become a task requiring a software solution. *Key management* is the process of keeping track of where the keys are and who has access to what. A physical security environment that does not have a means of key management is living on borrowed time. Key management will be essential when something goes wrong and the question arises of who has keys that can give them access.

Logs

Physical security logs provide the same utility that computer logs do for a security investigation. They act as a record of what was observed at specific points in time. Having roving guards check in at various places across a shift via a log entry provides a record of the actual surveillance. Logs of visitors going in and out and equipment going in and out, as well as other types of log entries, serve as a record of the physical happenings in a facility.

Cameras, IR detection, motion detection, and logs are all methods associated with detection—and frequently after-the-fact detection at that. These devices and methods provide valuable attribution fact patterns, even after an actual event.

Electronic Access Control Systems

Access tokens are defined as "something you have." An access token is a physical object that identifies specific access rights. Access tokens are frequently used for physical access solutions, just as your house key is a basic physical access token that allows you access into your home. Although keys have been used to unlock devices for centuries, they do have several limitations. Keys are paired exclusively with a lock or a set of locks, and they are not easily changed. It is easy to add an authorized user by giving the user a copy of the key, but it is far more difficult to give that user selective access unless that specified area is already set up as a separate key. It is also difficult to take access away from a single key or key holder, which usually requires a rekey of the whole system.

Tech Tip

Master Keys

Mechanical keying systems with industrial-grade locks have provisions for multiple master keys. This allows individual master keys to be designated by floor, by department, for the whole building, and so forth. This provides tremendous flexibility, although if a master key is lost, significant rekeying will be required.

Tokens/Cards

Physical access to a facility can be via a door, but who keeps random visitors from using that door? For some doors, a physical key can be used to unlock them. For facilities with larger numbers of people coming and going, a badging system using either tokens or cards that can be tied to automated ID checks, in addition to the logging of entry/exit, can provide much greater detail in tracking who is in the facility and when they have come and gone. Tokens and cards can be enabled to provide a serialized ID for each user, thus enabling user-specific logging. Originally designed to augment payroll time cards, these electronic IDs have improved security through the logging of employees' in and out times.

In many businesses, physical access authentication has moved to contactless radio frequency cards and proximity readers. When passed near a card reader, the card sends out a code using radio waves. The reader picks up this code and transmits it to the control panel. The control panel checks the code against the reader from which it is being read and the type of access the card has in its database. One of the advantages of this kind of token-based system is that any card can be deleted from the system without affecting any other card or the rest of the system. The RFID-based contactless entry card shown in Figure 8.9 is a common form of this token device employed for door controls and is frequently put behind an employee badge. In addition, all doors connected to the system can be segmented

• **Figure 8.9** Smart cards have an internal chip as well as multiple external contacts for interfacing with a smart card reader.

in any form or fashion to create multiple access areas, with different permissions for each one. The tokens themselves can also be grouped in multiple ways to provide different access levels to different groups of people. All of the access levels or segmentation of doors can be modified quickly and easily if the building space is repurposed. Newer technologies are adding capabilities to the standard token-based systems.

The advent of **smart cards** (cards that contain integrated circuits capable of generating and storing cryptographic keys) has enabled cryptographic types of authentication. Smart card technology has proven reliable enough that it is now part of a governmental standard for physical and logical authentication. Known as *personal identity verification (PIV)* cards, these smart cards adhere to the FIPS 201 standard. They include a cryptographic chip and connector as well as a contactless proximity card circuit. They also have standards for a photo and name printed on the front. Biometric data can be stored on the cards, providing an additional authentication factor, and if the PIV standard is followed, several forms of identification are needed in order to get a card.

The primary drawback of token-based authentication is that only the token is being authenticated. Therefore, the theft of the token could grant anyone who possesses the token access to what the system protects. The risk of theft of the token can be offset by the use of multiple-factor authentication. One of the ways that people have tried to achieve multiple-factor authentication is to add a biometric factor to the system.

Tech Tip

Personnel ID Badges

Having personnel wear a visible ID **badge** *with their picture is a common form of physical security. If everyone is supposed to wear a badge visibly, then anyone who sees someone without a badge can ask them who they are, and why they are there. This greatly increases the number of eyes watching for intruders in large, publicly accessible facilities.*

Biometrics

Biometrics uses the measurements of certain biological factors to identify one specific person from others. These factors are based on parts of the human body that are unique. The most well-known of these unique biological factors is the fingerprint. Fingerprint readers have been available for several years in laptops—and more recently in smartphones. These come in a variety of form factors, such as the example shown in Figure 8.10, and as standalone USB devices.

• **Figure 8.10** Newer laptop computers often include a fingerprint reader.

Convergence

There is a trend toward converging elements of physical and information security in order to improve identification of unauthorized activity on networks. For example, if an access control system is asked to approve access to an insider using an outside address, yet the physical security system identifies them as being inside the building, then an anomaly exists and should be investigated. This trend of **convergence** can significantly improve defenses against cloned credentials.

Policies and Procedures

A policy's effectiveness depends on the culture of an organization, so all the policies mentioned here should be followed up by functional procedures that are designed to implement them. Physical security **policies and procedures** relate to two distinct areas: those that affect the computers themselves and those that affect users.

To mitigate the risk to computers, physical security needs to be extended to the computers themselves. To combat the threat of bootdisks, begin by removing or disabling the ability of a system to automatically play connected devices, such as USB flash drives. Other activities that typically require physical presence should be protected, such as access to a system's BIOS at bootup.

BIOS

A safeguard that can be employed is the removal of removable media devices from the boot sequence in the computer's BIOS (basic input/output system). The specifics of this operation depend on the BIOS software of the individual machine. A related step that must be taken is to set a BIOS password. Nearly all BIOS software will support password protection that allows you to boot the machine but requires a password to edit any BIOS settings. Although disabling the optical drive and setting a BIOS password are both good measures, do not depend on this strategy exclusively because, in some cases, BIOS manufacturers will have a default BIOS password that still works.

> Depending on BIOS passwords is also not a guaranteed security measure. For many machines, it is trivial to remove and then replace the BIOS battery, which will reset the BIOS to the "no password" or default password state.

Try This!

Exploring Your BIOS Settings

Next time you boot your PC, explore the BIOS settings. Usually, pressing the F2 key immediately upon powering up will allow you to enter the BIOS setup screens. Most PCs will also have a brief time when they prompt for "Setup" and give a key to press, most commonly F2 or F12. Explore elements such as the boot order for devices, options for adding passwords, and other options. For safety, do not save changes unless you are absolutely certain that you want to make those changes and are aware of the consequences. To prevent an attacker from editing the boot order, you should set **BIOS passwords**.

UEFI

Unified Extensible Firmware Interface (UEFI) is a standard firmware interface for PCs, designed to replace BIOS. Supported by macOS, Linux (later versions), and Windows 8 and beyond, UEFI offers some significant security advantages. UEFI has a functionality known as Secure Boot, which allows only digitally signed drivers and OS loaders to be used during the boot process, preventing bootkit attacks. As UEFI is replacing BIOS, and provides additional characteristics, it is important to keep policies and procedures current with the advancement of technology.

> USB devices can be used to inject malicious code into any machine to which they are attached. They can be used to transport malicious code from machine to machine without using the network.

USB

USB ports have greatly expanded users' ability to connect devices to their computers. USB ports automatically recognize a device being plugged into the system and usually work without the user needing to add drivers or configure software. This has spawned a legion of **USB devices**, from MP3 players to CD burners.

The most interesting of these, for security purposes, are the USB flash memory–based storage devices. USB drive keys, which are basically flash memory with a USB interface in a device typically about the size of your thumb, provide a way to move files easily from computer to computer. When plugged into a USB port, these devices automount and behave like any other drive attached to the computer. Their small size and relatively large capacity, coupled with instant read-write capability, present security problems. They can easily be used by an individual with malicious intent to conceal the removal of files or data from the building or to bring malicious files into the building and onto the company network.

In addition, well-intentioned users could accidentally introduce malicious code from a USB device by using it on an infected home machine and then bringing the infected device to the office, allowing the malware to bypass perimeter protections and possibly infect the organization. If USB devices are allowed, aggressive virus scanning should be implemented throughout the organization. The devices can be disallowed via Active Directory policy settings or with a Windows Registry key entry. USB can also be completely disabled, either through BIOS settings or by unloading and disabling the USB drivers from users' machines, either of which will stop all USB devices from working. However, doing this can create more trouble if users have USB keyboards and mice. There are two common ways to disable USB support in a Windows system. On older systems, editing the Registry key is probably the most effective solution for users who are not authorized to use these devices. On newer systems, the best way is through Group Policy in a domain or through the Local Security Policy MMC on a standalone box.

Laptops and tablets are popular targets for thieves and should be locked inside a desk when not in use or secured with special computer lockdown cables. If desktop towers are used, use computer desks that provide a space in which to lock the computer. All of these measures can improve the physical security of the computers themselves, but most of them can be defeated by attackers if users are not knowledgeable about the security program and do not follow it.

AutoPlay

Another boot device to consider is the CD/DVD drive. This device can probably also be removed from or disabled on a number of machines. A DVD not only can be used as a boot device, but also can be exploited via the **AutoPlay** feature that some operating systems support. AutoPlay was designed as a convenience for users, so that when a CD/DVD or USB containing an application is inserted, the computer instantly prompts for input versus requiring the user to explore the device file system and find the executable file. Unfortunately, because the AutoPlay functionality runs an executable, it can be programmed to do anything an attacker wants. If an AutoPlay executable is malicious, it could allow an attacker to gain remote control of the machine. Figure 8.11 illustrates an AutoPlay message prompt in Windows, giving a user at least minimal control over whether to run an item or not.

• **Figure 8.11** AutoPlay on a Windows system

Since the optical drive can be used as a boot device, a DVD loaded with its own operating system (called a *LiveCD*, introduced earlier in the chapter) could be used to boot the computer with malicious system code (see Figure 8.12). This separate operating system will bypass any passwords on the host machine and can access locally stored files.

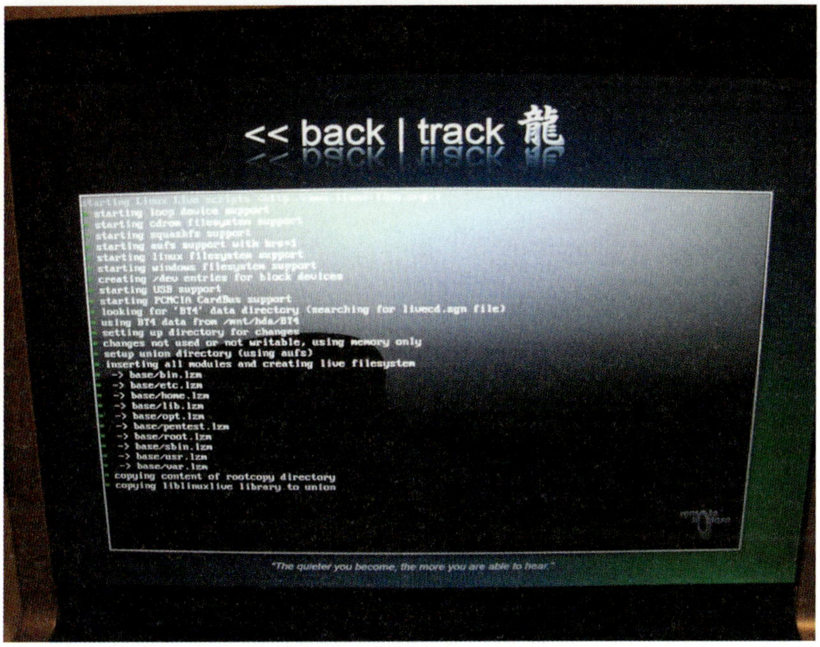

• **Figure 8.12** A LiveCD boots its own OS and bypasses any built-in security of the native operating system.

Tech Tip

Disabling the AutoPlay Feature in Windows

Disabling the AutoPlay feature is an easy task using Local Group Policy Editor in Windows. Simply launch the Local Group Policy Editor (gpedit.msc) and navigate to this location:

Computer Configuration | Administrative Templates | Windows Components | AutoPlay Policies

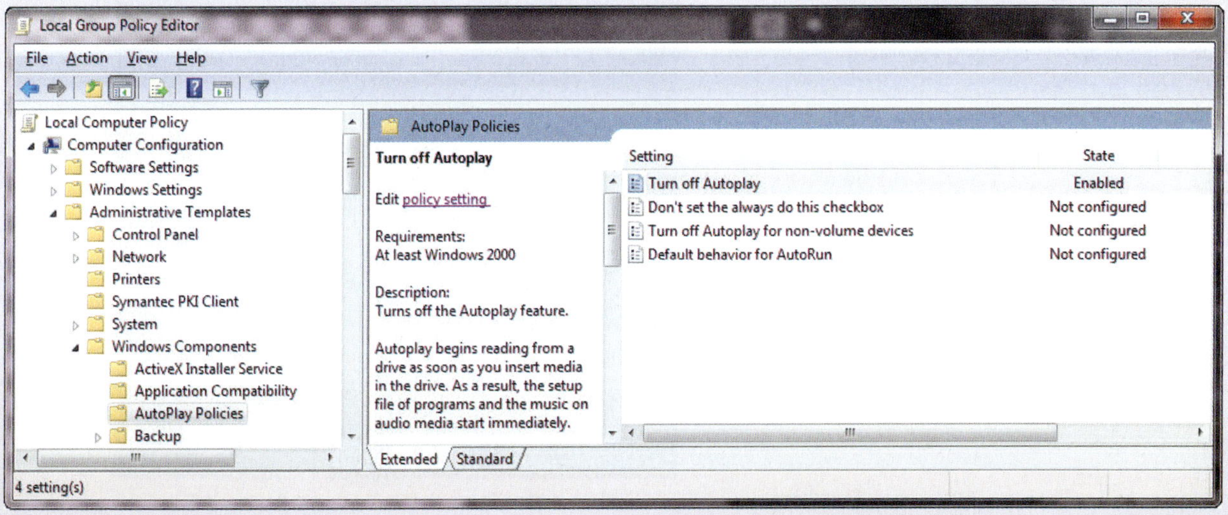

Device Theft

The outright theft of a computer is a simple physical attack. This attack can be mitigated in a number of ways, but the most effective method is to lock up equipment that contains important data. Insurance can cover

> ⚠ Mobile device thefts from cars and other locations can occur in seconds. Thieves have been caught taking mobile devices from security screening areas at airports while the owner was distracted in screening. Snatch-and-grab attacks occur in restaurants, bars, and cafes. Tablets and smartphones have significant value, and physical precautions should be taken at all times.

the loss of the physical equipment, but this can do little to get a business up and running again quickly after a theft. Therefore, implementing special access controls for server rooms and simply locking the rack cabinets when maintenance is not being performed are good ways to secure an area. From a data standpoint, mission-critical or high-value information should be stored on a server only. This can mitigate the risk of a desktop or laptop being stolen for the data it contains. Loss of laptops has been a common cause of information breaches.

> **Cross Check**
>
> **Mobile Device Security**
>
> Mobile device security is covered in depth in Chapter 12. For a more detailed analysis of safeguards unique to mobile devices, refer to that chapter.

Users can perform one of the simplest, yet important, information security tasks: locking their workstation immediately before they step away from it.

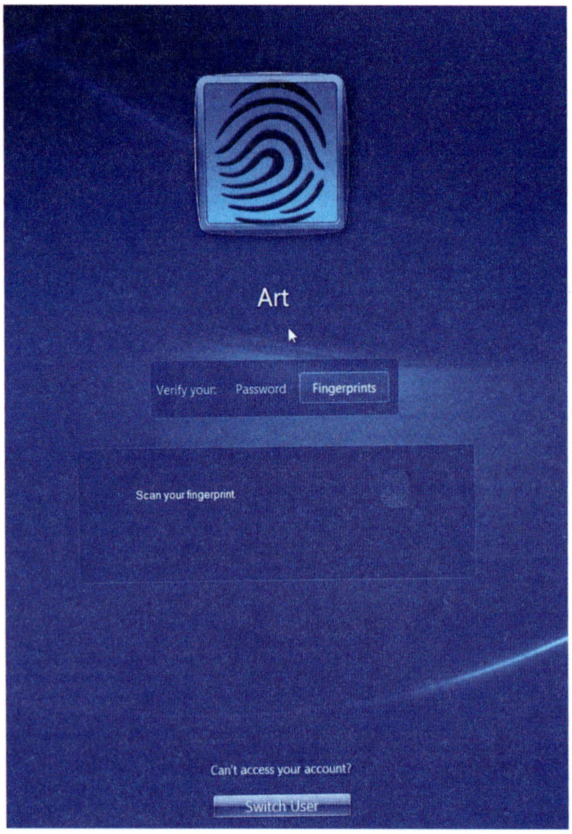

Although use of a self-locking screensaver is a good policy, setting it to lock at any point less than 10 to 15 minutes after becoming idle is often considered a nuisance and counterproductive to active use of the computer on the job because the computer will often lock while the employee is still actively using it. Thus, computers typically sit idle for at least 15 minutes before automatically locking under this type of policy. Users should manually lock their workstations, as an attacker only needs to be lucky enough to catch a machine that has been left alone for five minutes.

Environmental Controls

While the confidentiality of information is important, so is its availability. Sophisticated environmental controls are needed for current data centers. Servers can generate large levels of heat, and managing the heat is the job of the environmental control.

BTU stands for *British thermal unit.* A single BTU is defined as the amount of energy required to raise the temperature of one pound of liquid water one degree Fahrenheit.

Controlling a data center's temperature and humidity is important to keeping servers running. Heating, ventilating, and air conditioning (HVAC) systems are critical for keeping data centers cool, because typical servers put out between 1000 and 2000 BTUs of heat. The temperature of a data center should be maintained between 70 and 74 degrees Fahrenheit (°F). If the temperature is too low, it may cause mechanisms to slow down. If the temperature is too high, it may cause equipment damage. The temperature-damaging points of different products are as follows:

- Magnetic media: 100°F
- Computer hardware: 175°F
- Paper products: 350°F

It should be noted that these are temperatures of the materials; the surrounding air is frequently cooler. Temperature measurements should be obtained on equipment itself to ensure appropriate protection.

Multiple servers in a confined area can create conditions too hot for the machines to continue to operate. This problem is made worse with the advent of blade-style computing systems and with many other devices shrinking in size. Although physically smaller, they tend to still expel the same amount of heat. This is known as *increased data center density*—more servers and devices per rack, putting a greater load on the cooling systems. This encourages the use of a hot aisle/cold aisle layout. A data center that is arranged into hot and cold aisles dictates that all the intake fans on all equipment face the cold aisle, and the exhaust fans all face the opposite aisle. The HVAC system is then designed to push cool air underneath the raised floor and up through perforated tiles on the cold aisle. Hot air from the hot aisle is captured by return air ducts for the HVAC system. The use of this layout is designed to control airflow, with the purpose being never to mix the hot and cold air. This requires the use of blocking plates and side plates to close open rack slots. The benefits of this arrangement are that cooling is more efficient and can handle higher density. The failure of HVAC systems for any reason is cause for concern. Rising copper prices have made HVAC systems the targets for thieves, and general vandalism can result in costly downtime. Properly securing these systems is important in helping prevent an attacker from performing a physical DoS attack on your servers.

Understanding airflow allows you to understand hot and cold aisles. Cold air is produced by the HVAC equipment, and this cold air is sent to servers. The servers shed their heat, making air hot, which is removed. The aisles keep the hot air from mixing with the cold air, thus keeping the cooling efficient. You wouldn't leave a door open in summer with the air conditioning on, would you?

Tech Tip

Environment and Fires

Although it may at first seem to the security professional that environmental controls and natural disasters such as fires don't have anything to do with computer security, think of it in terms of availability. If the goal of the attacker is not information but rather to deny an organization the use of its resources, environmental factors and disasters such as fires can be used to deny the target the use of its own computing resources. This, then, becomes a security issue as well as an operational issue.

Hot and Cold Aisles

The trend toward smaller, denser servers means more servers and devices per rack, putting a greater load on the cooling systems. This encourages the use of a hot aisle/cold aisle layout. A data center that is arranged into **hot and cold aisles** dictates that all the intake fans on all equipment face the cold aisle, and the exhaust fans all face the opposite aisle. The HVAC system is then designed to push cool air underneath the raised floor and up through perforated tiles on the cold aisle. Hot air from the hot aisle is captured by return air ducts for the HVAC system. The use of this layout is designed to control airflow, with the purpose being never to mix the hot and cold air. This requires the use of blocking plates and side plates to close open rack slots. The benefits of this arrangement are that cooling is more efficient and can handle higher density.

Fire Suppression

According to the Fire Suppression Systems Association (www.fsaa.net), 43 percent of businesses that close as a result of a significant fire never reopen. An additional 29 percent fail within three years of the event. The ability to respond to a fire quickly and effectively is thus critical to the long-term success of any organization. Addressing potential fire hazards and vulnerabilities has long been a concern of organizations in their risk analysis process. The goal obviously should be never to have a fire, but in the event that one does occur, it is important that mechanisms are in place to limit the damage the fire can cause.

Water-Based Fire Suppression Systems

Water-based fire suppression systems have long been, and still are today, the primary tool to address and control structural fires. Considering the amount of electrical equipment found in today's office environment and the fact that, for obvious reasons, this equipment does not react well to large applications of water, it is important to know what to do with equipment if it does become subjected to a water-based sprinkler system. The National Fire Protection Association's NFPA 75, "Standard for the Protection of Information Technology Equipment," from 2013, outlines measures that can be taken to minimize the damage to electronic equipment exposed to water. This guidance includes these suggestions:

- Open cabinet doors, remove side panels and covers, and pull out chassis drawers to allow water to run out of equipment.
- Set up fans to move room-temperature air through the equipment for general drying. Move portable equipment to dry, air-conditioned areas.
- Use compressed air at no higher than 50 psi to blow out trapped water.
- Use handheld dryers on lowest setting to dry connectors, backplane wire wraps, and printed circuit cards.
- Use cotton-tipped swabs for hard-to-reach places. Lightly dab the surfaces to remove residual moisture.

Even if these guidelines are followed, damage to the systems may have already occurred. Because water is so destructive to electronic equipment, not only because of the immediate problems of electronic shorts to the system but also because of longer-term corrosive damage water can cause, alternative fire suppression methods have been sought.

Halon-Based Fire Suppression Systems

A fire needs fuel, oxygen, and high temperatures for the chemical combustion to occur. If you remove any of one these elements, the fire will not continue. Halon interferes with the chemical combustion present in a fire. Even though halon production was banned in 1994, a number of these systems still exist today. They were originally popular because halon will mix quickly with the air in a room and will not cause harm to computer systems. Halon is, however, dangerous to humans, especially when subjected to extremely hot temperatures (such as might be found during a fire), when it can degrade into other toxic chemicals. As a result of these dangers, and also because it has been linked with the issue of ozone depletion, halon is banned in new fire suppression systems. It is important to note that under the Environmental Protection Agency (EPA) rules that mandated no further production of halon, existing systems were not required to be destroyed. Replacing the halon in a discharged system, however, will be a problem, since only existing stockpiles of halon may be used and the cost is becoming prohibitive. For this reason, many organizations are switching to alternative solutions.

> **Tech Tip**
>
> **Drills**
>
> *In the event of an emergency, people will be challenged to perform correct actions when stressed by the emergency. The use of drills, plans, and testing will ensure that escape plans and escape routes are known and effective and that people are familiar with their use. The time to practice is before the problem, and repeating practice over time builds confidence and strengthens familiarity.*

Clean-Agent Fire Suppression Systems

These alternatives are known as *clean-agent fire suppression systems,* because they not only provide fire suppression capabilities but also protect the contents of the room, including people, documents, and electronic equipment. Examples of clean agents include carbon dioxide, argon, Inergen, and FM-200 (heptafluoropropane). Carbon dioxide (CO_2) has been used as a fire suppression agent for a long time. The Bell Telephone Company used portable CO_2 extinguishers in the early part of the 20th century. Carbon dioxide extinguishers attack all three necessary elements for a fire to occur. CO_2 displaces oxygen so that the amount of oxygen remaining is insufficient to sustain the fire. It also provides some cooling in the fire zone and reduces the concentration of "gasified" fuel. Argon extinguishes fire by lowering the oxygen concentration below the 15 percent level required for combustible items to burn. Argon systems are designed to reduce the oxygen content to about 12.5 percent, which is below the 15 percent needed for the fire but is still above the 10 percent required by the EPA for human safety.

Handheld Fire Extinguishers

Automatic fire suppression systems designed to discharge when a fire is detected are not the only systems you should be aware of. If a fire can be caught and contained before the automatic systems discharge, it can mean significant savings to the organization in terms of both time and equipment

The type of fire distinguishes the type of extinguisher that should be used to suppress it. Remember that the most common type is the ABC fire extinguisher, which is designed to handle all types of fires except flammable-metal fires, which are rare.

costs (including the recharging of the automatic system). Handheld extinguishers are common in offices, but the correct use of them must be understood or else disaster can occur. There are four different types of fire, as shown in Table 8.1. Each type of fire has its own fuel source and method for extinguishing it. Type A systems, for example, are designed to extinguish fires with normal combustible material as the fire's source. Water can be used in an extinguisher of this sort because it is effective against fires of this type. Water, as we've discussed, is not appropriate for fires involving wiring or electrical equipment. Using a type A extinguisher against an electrical fire will not only be ineffective but can result in additional damage. Some extinguishers are designed to be effective against more than one type of fire, such as the common ABC fire extinguishers. This is probably the best type of system to have in a data processing facility. All fire extinguishers should be easily accessible and should be clearly marked. Before anybody uses an extinguisher, they should know what type of extinguisher it is and what the source of the fire is. When in doubt, evacuate and let the fire department handle the situation.

Table 8.1 Types of Fire and Suppression Methods

Class of Fire	Type of Fire	Examples of Combustible Materials	Example Suppression Method
A	Common combustibles	Wood, paper, cloth, plastics	Water or dry chemical
B	Combustible liquids	Petroleum products, organic solvents	CO_2 or dry chemical
C	Electrical	Electrical wiring and equipment, power tools	CO_2 or dry chemical
D	Flammable metals	Magnesium, titanium	Copper metal or sodium chloride

Try This!

Handheld Fire Extinguishers

Computer security professionals typically do not have much influence over the type of fire suppression system that their office includes. It is, however, important that they are aware of what type has been installed, what they should do in case of an emergency, and what needs to be done to recover after the release of the system. One area that they can influence, however, is the type of handheld fire extinguisher located in their area. Check your facility to see what type of fire suppression system is installed. Also check to see where the fire extinguishers are in your office and what type of fires they are designed to handle.

Fire Detection Devices

An essential complement to fire suppression systems and devices are fire detection devices (fire detectors). Detectors may be able to detect a fire in its very early stages, before a fire suppression system is activated, and sound a warning that potentially enables employees to address the fire before it becomes serious enough for the fire suppression equipment to kick in.

There are several different types of fire detectors. One type, of which there are two varieties, is activated by smoke. The two varieties of smoke detector are ionization and photoelectric. A photoelectric detector is good for potentially providing advance warning of a smoldering fire. This type of device monitors an internal beam of light. If something degrades the light (for example, by obstructing it), the detector assumes it is something like smoke and the alarm sounds. An ionization style of detector uses an ionization chamber and a small radioactive source to detect fast-burning fires. Shown in Figure 8.13, the chamber consists of two plates—one with a positive charge and one with a negative charge. Oxygen and nitrogen particles in the air become "ionized" (an ion is freed from the molecule). The freed ion, which has a negative charge, is attracted to the positive plate, and the remaining part of the molecule, now with a positive charge, is attracted to the negative plate. This movement of particles creates a very small electric current that the device measures. Smoke inhibits this process, and the detector will detect the resulting drop in current and sound an alarm. Both of these devices are often referred to generically as smoke detectors, and combinations of both varieties are possible.

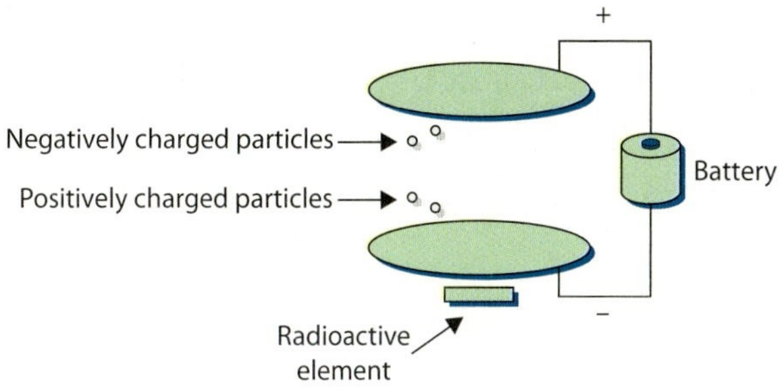

• **Figure 8.13** An ionization chamber for an ionization type of smoke detector

> **Tech Tip**
>
> **Testing Controls**
>
> *Because of the importance of their protection, safety controls should be periodically tested for proper operation and alerting. This should be a system-level test, not a device-level test, to ensure the entire control system performs in the intended manner.*

Another type of fire detector is activated by heat. These devices also come in two varieties. Fixed-temperature or fixed-point devices activate if the temperature in the area ever exceeds some predefined level. Rate-of-rise or rate-of-increase temperature devices activate when there is a sudden increase in local temperature that may indicate the beginning stages of a fire. Rate-of-rise sensors can provide an earlier warning but are also responsible for more false warnings.

A third type of detector is flame activated. This type of device relies on the flames from the fire to provide a change in the infrared energy that can be detected. Flame-activated devices are generally more expensive than the other two types but can frequently detect a fire sooner.

Electromagnetic Environment

In 1985, a paper by Wim van Eck of the Netherlands described what became known as the *van Eck phenomenon*. In the paper, van Eck described how eavesdropping on what was being displayed on monitors could be accomplished by picking up and then decoding the electromagnetic interference produced by the monitors. With the appropriate equipment, the exact image of what is being displayed can be re-created some distance away. While the original paper discussed emanations as they applied to video display units (monitors), the same phenomenon applies to other devices such as printers and computers.

This phenomenon had actually been known about for quite some time before van Eck published his paper. The U.S. Department of Defense used the term **TEMPEST** (referred to by some as the *Transient ElectroMagnetic Pulse Emanation STandard*) to describe both a program in the military to control these electronic emanations from electrical equipment and the actual process for controlling the emanations. There are three basic ways to prevent these emanations from being picked up by an attacker:

- Put the equipment beyond the point that the emanations can be picked up.
- Provide shielding for the equipment itself.
- Provide a shielded enclosure (such as a room) to put the equipment in.

One of the challenges in security is determining how much to spend on security without spending too much. Security spending should be based on likely threats to your systems and network. While electronic emanations can be monitored, the likelihood of this taking place in most situations is remote, which makes spending on items to protect against it at best a low priority.

One of the simplest ways to protect against equipment being monitored in this fashion is to put enough distance between the target and the attacker. The emanations can be picked up from only a limited distance. If the physical security for the facility is sufficient to put enough space between the equipment and publicly accessible areas that the signals cannot be picked up, then the organization doesn't have to take any additional measures to ensure security.

Distance is not the only way to protect against eavesdropping on electronic emanations. Devices can be shielded so their emanations are blocked. Acquiring enough property to provide the necessary distance needed to protect against an eavesdropper may be possible if the facility is in the country with lots of available land surrounding it. Indeed, for smaller organizations that occupy only a few offices or floors in a large office building, it would be impossible to acquire enough space. In this case, the organization may resort to purchasing shielded equipment. A "TEMPEST approved" computer will cost significantly more than what a normal computer would cost. Shielding a room (for example, using a Faraday cage) is also an extremely expensive endeavor.

Tech Tip

Modern Eavesdropping

Not just electromagnetic information can be used to carry information out of a system to an adversary. Recent advances have demonstrated the feasibility of using the webcams and microphones on systems to spy on users, recording keystrokes and other activities. There are even devices built to intercept the wireless signals between wireless keyboards and mice and transmit them over another channel to an adversary. USB-based keyloggers can be placed in the back of machines, because in many cases the back of a machine is unguarded or facing the public (watch for this the next time you see a receptionist's machine).

A natural question to ask is, how prevalent is this form of attack? The equipment needed to perform electromagnetic eavesdropping is not readily available, but it would not cost an inordinate amount of money to produce it. The cost could certainly be afforded by any large corporation, and industrial espionage using such a device is a possibility. Although there are no public records of this sort of activity being conducted, it is reasonable to assume that it does take place in large corporations and the government, especially in foreign countries.

Power Protection

Computer systems require clean electrical power, and for critical systems, uninterrupted power can be important as well. Several elements are used to manage the power to systems, including uninterruptible power supplies and backup power systems.

UPS

An uninterruptible power supply (UPS) is used to protect against short-duration power failures. There are two types of UPS: online and standby. An online UPS is in continuous use because the primary power source goes through it to the equipment. It uses AC line voltage to charge a bank of batteries. When the primary power source fails, an inverter in the UPS will change the DC of the batteries into AC. A standby UPS has sensors to detect power failures. If there is a power failure, the load will be switched to the UPS. It stays inactive before a power failure, and it takes more time than an online UPS to provide power when the primary source fails.

Backup Power and Cable Shielding

A *backup power source,* such as a motor generator or another electrical substation, is used to protect against a long-duration power failure. A voltage regulator and line conditioner are used to protect against unstable power supply and spikes. Proper grounding is essential for all electrical devices to protect against short circuits and static electricity.

In more sensitive areas, cable shielding can be employed to avoid interference. Power line monitoring can be used to detect changes in frequency and voltage amplitude, warning of brownouts or spikes. An *emergency power-off (EPO) switch* can be installed to allow for the quick shutdown of power when required. To prevent electromagnetic interference and voltage spikes, electrical cables should be placed away from powerful electrical motors and lighting. Another source of power-induced interference can be fluorescent lighting, which can cause radio frequency interference.

Tech Tip

UPS Attributes

UPS systems have several attributes to consider:

- *The electrical load they can support (measured in kVA)*
- *The length of time they can support the load*
- *The speed of providing power when there is a power failure*
- *The physical space they occupy*

Generator

Backup generators are used to provide power when normal sources of electricity are lost. The power for these devices is either natural gas or diesel, and they produce sufficient electrical power to cover the desired services during a power outage. Generators come with a host of requirements, including maintenance and testing, and they require significant electrical architecture work to isolate the desired circuits. The objective typically isn't to provide power to everything that the normal power source supplies, as the scale of generation can be costly in some instances. The circuits energized by the backup generator are separate circuits that provide power to the desired components. Sizing of the backup generator is done with respect to the load, and because of the physical infrastructure, it is not easy or cost efficient to continuously resize the backup power. The other issue is that when long-term use happens in the case of diesel generators, a resupply of fuel needs to be managed. As these systems are typically used during natural disasters, having contracts in place that function during the disaster are important for refueling and maintenance operations.

Dual Supply

Individual pieces of equipment have power supplies in them to convert the line power in the facility to the voltages and currents used by the devices. The individual power supplies are one of the weakest links in a piece of equipment, as they tend to fail at a much higher rate than the lower-voltage equipment that they supply power to; hence, a plan needs to be in place for these when they fail. In cases where a minor outage is okay, having spare power supplies that can be replaced offline works.

For servers and other pieces of critical infrastructure, however, having a redundant, dual-supply system is essential. A dual supply is a system where two independent power supply units, either capable of handling the load, are used. In the event that either supply is lost, the other continues to carry the load. Typically, these devices are also made to be hot swappable, so in the event of a failure, the bad supply can be replaced without powering down the unit.

Managed Power Distribution Units (PDUs)

A managed power distribution unit (PDU) is a device designed to handle the electrical power for server racks. A fully populated server rack can use as much as 30kVA, or 10 times the amount of electricity for a typical home. This is why server rooms need special HVAC to handle the heat distribution, and they use managed power distribution units to efficiently handle the electrical side. A PDU can take three-phase 440/240VAC power in and convert it to either single-phase 110VAC or 48VDC power. The objective of a PDU is to efficiently convert the power, and manage the heat from the conversion, while producing a power flow that is conditioned from spikes and over/under voltage conditions. Most PDUs offer extensive monitoring capability, so entire racks of servers can have their power remotely monitored for conditions that might cause issues.

Drones/UAVs

Drones and **unmanned aerial vehicles (UAVs)** have become a common thing in the past couple of years. From home/hobbyist models that can carry a small camera, to larger industrial rigs that can carry larger cameras for longer periods, these devices have revolutionized remote viewing of items. From drones used by railroads to inspect tracks, to drones used by electric companies to inspect lines, the ability to go almost anywhere and visually inspect things is a great resource. These offer interesting use cases for both offense and defense in cybersecurity because they can be used to surveil physical facilities remotely, providing eyes on demand to a variety of places you might not want a person to go to, or in a timeframe that can't be met any other way.

Chapter 8 Review

Chapter Summary

After reading this chapter and completing the exercises, you should understand the following facts about how physical security impacts network security.

Describe how physical security directly affects computer and network security

- Physical access defeats all network security protections.
- Bootdisks allow file system access.
- Drive imaging is simple to accomplish with physical access.
- Access to the internal network is simple with physical access.
- Theft of hardware can be an attack in and of itself.

Discuss steps that can be taken to help mitigate risks

- Disabling media drives when they are unnecessary can help mitigate bootdisk attacks.
- Removal of CD-ROM devices also makes physical access attacks more difficult.
- BIOS passwords should be used to protect the boot sequence.
- USB devices are a threat; if possible, USB drivers should be removed.
- All users need security training.
- Authentication systems should use multiple factors when feasible.

Describe the physical security components that can protect your computers and network

- Physical security consists of all mechanisms used to ensure that physical access to the computer systems and networks is restricted to only authorized users.
- The purpose of physical access controls is the same as that of computer and network access controls—to restrict access to only those who are authorized to have it.
- The careful placement of equipment can provide security for known security problems exhibited by wireless devices and that arise due to electronic emanations.

Identify environmental factors that can affect security

- Environmental issues are important to security because they can affect the availability of a computer system or network.
- Loss of HVAC systems can lead to overheating problems that can affect electronic equipment, including security-related devices.
- Fires are a common problem for organizations. Two general approaches to addressing this problem are fire detection and fire suppression.

Identify the different types of fires and the various fire suppression systems designed to limit the damage caused by fires

- Fires can be caused by and can consume a number of different materials. It is important to recognize what type of fire is occurring, because the extinguisher to use depends on the type of fire.
- The ABC fire extinguisher is the most common type and is designed to handle most types of fires. The only type of fire it is not designed to address is one with combustible metals.

Explain electronic access controls and the principles of convergence

- Access controls should have layered areas and electronic access control systems.
- Electronic physical security systems need to be protected from network-based attacks.

Prevent disclosure through electronic emanations

- With the appropriate equipment, the exact image of what is being displayed on a computer monitor can be re-created some distance away, allowing eavesdroppers to view what you are doing.
- Providing a lot of distance between the system you wish to protect and the closest place an eavesdropper could be is one way to protect against eavesdropping on electronic emanations. Devices can also be shielded so that their emanations are blocked.

Key Terms

access tokens *(249)*
alarms *(241)*
AutoPlay *(252)*
badges *(250)*
biometrics *(250)*
BIOS passwords *(251)*
bollards/barricades *(240)*
bootdisk *(236)*
cable locks *(248)*
closed-circuit television (CCTV) *(245)*
cold aisle *(256)*
contactless access cards *(243)*
convergence *(250)*
drones/UAVs *(262)*
Faraday cage *(247)*
hot aisle *(256)*
industrial camouflage *(242)*
layered access *(243)*
lighting *(241)*
LiveCD *(237)*
mantrap *(244)*
motion detection *(245)*
noise detection *(246)*
object detection *(246)*
physical access control *(243)*
policies and procedures *(250)*
proximity reader *(246)*
robot sentries *(240)*
signage *(241)*
smart cards *(250)*
TEMPEST *(259)*
turnstile *(244)*
Unified Extensible Firmware Interface (UEFI) *(251)*
USB devices *(251)*

Key Terms Quiz

Use terms from the Key Terms list to complete the sentences that follow. Don't use the same term more than once. Not all terms will be used.

1. A door system designed to only allow a single person through is called a(n) _______________.
2. _______________ include MP3 players and flash drives.
3. _______________ is the program to control the electronic emanations from electrical equipment.
4. Removable media from which a computer can be booted is called a(n) _______________.
5. _______________ forces a user to authenticate again when entering a more secure area.
6. Items carried by the user to allow them to be authenticated are called _______________.
7. _______________ is the measurement of unique biological properties such as the fingerprint.
8. _______________ prevent an attacker from making a machine boot off its DVD drive.
9. _______________ is a system where the camera and monitor are directly linked.
10. Continuous, standby, trip, and emergency are all types of _______________.

Multiple-Choice Quiz

1. What is the most common example of an access token?
   A. Smart card
   B. Handwriting sample
   C. Air gap
   D. Key
2. What is used in data centers for fire extinguishers?
   A. CO_2 fire extinguishers
   B. Water sprinklers
   C. Dry agent extinguishers
   D. Special nonconductive foam agents
3. Probably the simplest physical attack on the computer system is which of the following?
   A. Accessing an Ethernet jack to attack the network
   B. Using an imitation to fool a biometric authenticator
   C. Installing a virus on the CCTV system
   D. Outright theft of a computer
4. What is a common threat to token-based access controls?
   A. The key
   B. Demagnetization of the strip
   C. A system crash
   D. Loss or theft of the token
5. Why can USB flash drives be a threat?
   A. They use too much power.
   B. They can bring malicious code past other security mechanisms.
   C. They can be stolen.
   D. They can be encrypted.
6. Why is HVAC important to computer security?
   A. Sabotage of the AC unit could take out the electrical power.
   B. Sabotage of the AC unit would make the computers overheat and shut down.
   C. The AC units could be connected to the network.
   D. HVAC is not important to security.
7. Why should security guards get cross-training in network security?
   A. They are the eyes and ears of the corporation when it comes to security.
   B. They are the only people in the building at night.
   C. They are more qualified to know what a security threat is.
   D. They have the authority to detain violators.
8. Emergency exit doors for manned security sensitive spaces should be what type of door?
   A. Fail-secure
   B. Fail-safe
   C. Unlocked at all times
   D. Locked unless monitored

9. Why is physical security so important to good network security?
   A. Because encryption is not involved
   B. Because physical access defeats nearly all network security measures
   C. Because an attacker can steal biometric identities
   D. Authentication

10. How high should a fence be to deter casual climbing?
   A. Five feet if the fence is monitored visually
   B. Ten feet
   C. Seven feet
   D. Eight feet or higher with barbed wire

Essay Questions

1. You have been asked to report on the feasibility of installing an IP CCTV camera system at your organization. Detail the pros and cons of an IP CCTV system and how you would implement the system.
2. Write a memo justifying layered access for devices in an organization.
3. Write a memo justifying more user education about physical security.
4. Write a sample policy regarding the use of USB devices in an organization.

Lab Projects

• Lab Project 8.1

Create a Kali bootable USB and then mount it on your machine and examine the tools it provides. (You will need a bootable 16GB USB for this lab.) Here are the steps to follow:

1. Download a copy of Kali Linux. A good site from which to obtain this is www.kali.org/downloads/.
2. Build your USB per www.kali.org/docs/usb/kali-linux-live-usb-install/.
3. Reboot the machine, allowing the USB to start the machine in Linux.
4. Once Kali Linux is running, open a terminal window and type **wireshark**.
5. With Wireshark open as a sniffing program, record the traffic to and from your computer by following these steps:
   - A. Open Capture | Options.
   - B. Select Start on your Ethernet interface (usually eth0).
   - C. Stop packet capture by selecting Capture | Stop.
   - D. Click any packet listed to view the analysis.
6. View the other tools on the USB under KDE | Kali.

• Lab Project 8.2

Disable AutoPlay on your system for several types of media. For this lab, you will need the following materials:

- A computer with Windows
- A USB flash drive that is set to be bootable
- A CD/DVD with an AutoPlay file

Here are the steps to follow:

1. Insert the CD/DVD and verify that AutoPlay is on and working.
2. Follow this chapter's instructions for disabling AutoPlay.
3. Reinsert the CD/DVD and verify that AutoPlay is disabled—nothing should appear when the CD/DVD is inserted now.
4. Insert the USB flash drive and see if AutoPlay works for it; if it does, disable it using the same method.

Chapter 9 Network Fundamentals

The value of a communications network is proportional to the square of the number of its users.

—Metcalfe's Law

In this chapter, you will learn how to

- Identify the basic network architectures
- Examine segregation, segmentation, and isolation with respect to network architectures
- Classify security zones
- Explain routing and address translation
- Examine the Internet Protocol in depth
- Define the basic network protocols
- Explore additional elements of networking

By the simplest definition in the data world, a **network** is a means to connect two or more computers together for the purposes of sharing information. The term *network* has different meanings depending on the context and usage. A network can be a group of friends and associates, a series of interconnected tunnels, or, from a computer-oriented perspective, a collection of interconnected devices. Network sizes and shapes vary drastically, ranging from two personal computers connected with a crossover cable or wireless router all the way up to the Internet, encircling the globe and linking together untold numbers of individual, distributed systems. Though data networks vary widely in size and scope, they are generally defined in terms of their architecture, topology, and protocols.

Network Architectures

Every network has an architecture—whether by design or by accident. Defining or describing a specific network's architecture involves identifying the network's physical configuration, logical operation, structure, procedures, data formats, protocols, and other components. For the sake of simplicity and categorization, people tend to divide network architectures into two main categories: LANs and WANs. A **local area network (LAN)** typically is smaller in terms of size and geographic coverage and consists of two or more connected devices. Home networks and most small office networks can be classified as LANs. A **wide area network (WAN)** tends to be larger, covering more geographic area, and consists of two or more systems in geographically separated areas connected by any of a variety of methods such as leased lines, radio waves, satellite relays, microwaves, or even dial-up connections. With the advent of wireless networking as well as optical and cellular technology, the lines between LAN and WAN models may seem to blur, but in practice the two categories merge seamlessly into a single network entity. For example, most corporations have multiple LANs within each office location that all connect to a WAN that provides intercompany connectivity. Figure 9.1 shows an example of a corporate network. Each office location will typically have one or more LANs, which are connected to the other offices and the company headquarters through a corporate WAN.

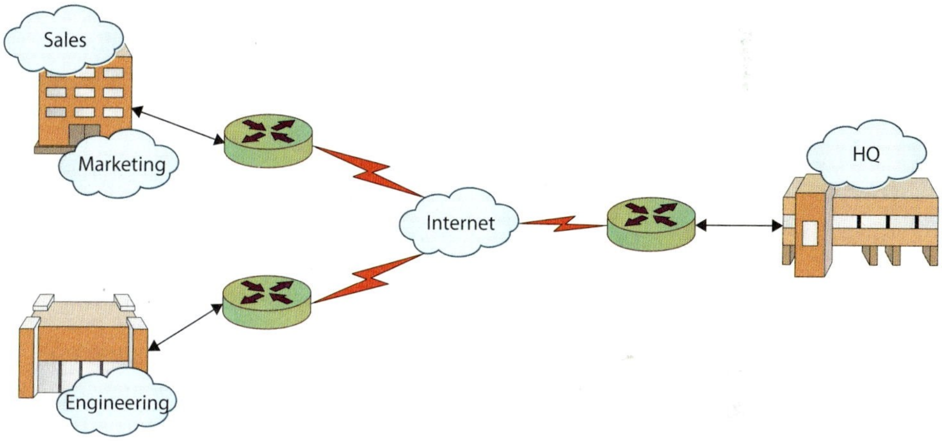

• **Figure 9.1** Corporate WAN connecting multiple offices

Over time, as networks have grown, diversified, and multiplied, the line between LAN and WAN has become blurred. To better describe emerging, specialized network structures, new terms have been coined to classify networks based on size and use:

> A LAN is a local area network—an office building, home network, and so on. A WAN is a wide area network—a corporate network connecting offices in Dallas, New York, and San Jose, for example.

- **Campus area network (CAN)** A network connecting any number of buildings in an office or university complex (also referred to as a *campus wide area network*).
- **Intranet** A "private" network that is accessible only to authorized users. Many large corporations host an intranet to facilitate information sharing within their organization.
- **Internet** The "global network" connecting hundreds of millions of systems and users.
- **Metropolitan area network (MAN)** A network designed for a specific geographic locality such as a town or a city.
- **Storage area network (SAN)** A high-speed network connecting a variety of storage devices such as tape systems, RAID arrays, optical drives, file servers, and others.

- **Virtual local area network (VLAN)** A logical network allowing systems on different physical networks to interact as if they were connected to the same physical network.
- **Client/server** A network in which powerful, dedicated systems called *servers* provide resources to individual workstations, or *clients*.
- **Peer-to-peer** A network in which every system is treated as an equal, such as a home network.
- **Software-defined network** A network where the routing and switching functions are under separate software control.

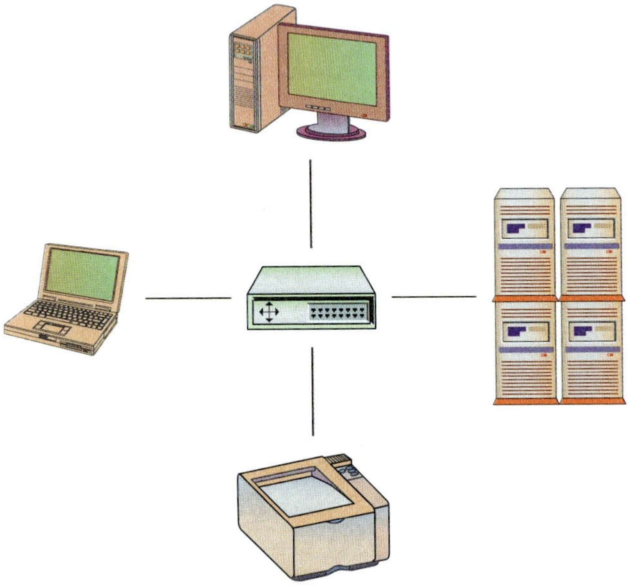

• **Figure 9.2** Star topology

Network Topology

One major component of every network's architecture is the network's topology. Network **topology** is how the network components are physically or logically arranged. Terms to classify a network's topology have been developed, often reflecting the physical layout of the network. The main classes of network topologies are star, bus, ring, and mixed:

- **Star topology** Network components are connected to a central point (see Figure 9.2).
- **Bus topology** Network components are connected to the same cable, often called "the bus" or "the backbone" (see Figure 9.3).
- **Ring topology** Network components are connected to each other in a closed loop, with each device directly connected to two other devices (see Figure 9.4).
- **Mixed topology** Larger networks, such as those inside an office complex, may use more than one topology at the same time. For example, an office complex may have a large ring topology that

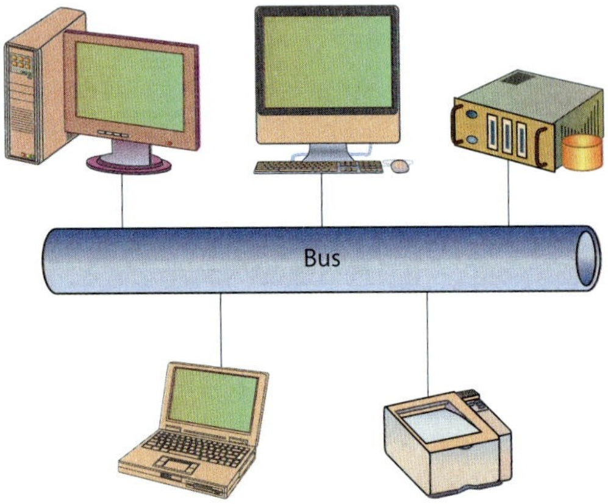

• **Figure 9.3** Bus topology

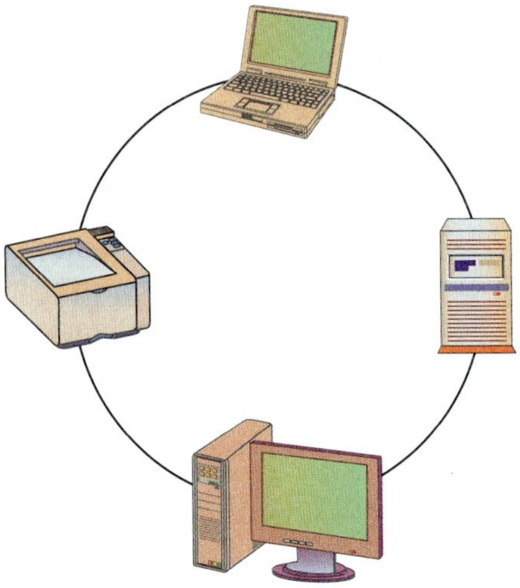

• **Figure 9.4** Ring topology

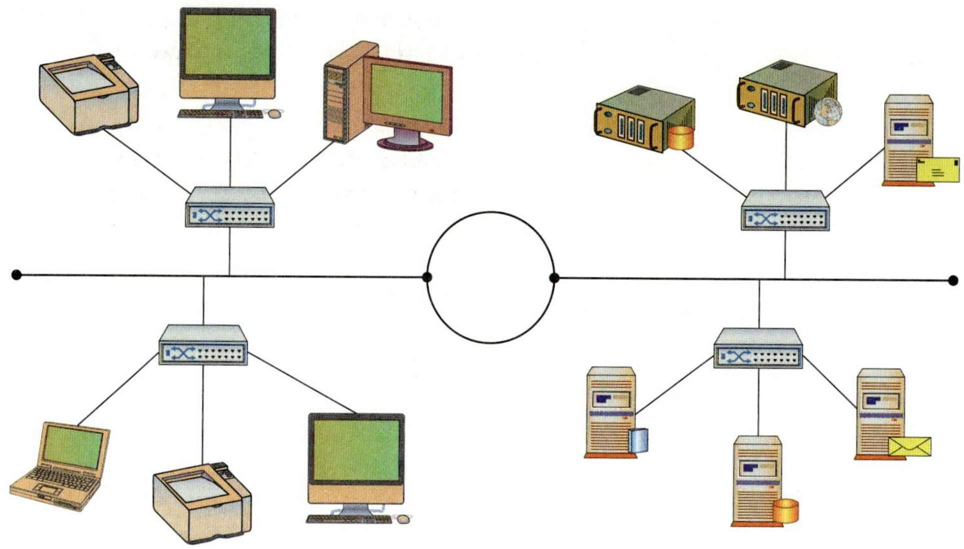

• **Figure 9.5** Mixed topology

interconnects all the buildings in the complex. Each building may have a large bus topology to interconnect star topologies located on each floor of the building. This is called a *mixed* or *hybrid* topology (see Figure 9.5).

With recent advances in technology, these topology definitions often break down. While a network consisting of five computers connected to the same coaxial cable is easily classified as a bus topology, what about those same computers connected to a switch using Cat-6 cables? With a switch, each computer is connected to a central node, much like a star topology, but the backplane of the switch is essentially a shared medium. With a switch, each computer has its own exclusive connection to the switch like a star topology but has to share the switch's communications backbone with all the other computers, much like a bus topology. To avoid this type of confusion, many people use topology definitions only to identify the physical layout of the network, focusing on how the devices are connected to the network. If we apply this line of thinking to our example, the five-computer network becomes a star topology whether we use a hub or a switch.

Wireless networks use radio waves as their medium to transmit packets, and those radio waves don't stop at the walls of your house or your organization. Anyone within range can "see" those radio waves and attempt to either sniff your traffic or connect to your network. Encryption, MAC address filtering, and suppression of beacon frames are all security mechanisms to consider when using wireless networks. Wireless networks, because of the signal propagation, can easily assume a mesh structure.

Wireless

Wireless networking is the transmission of packetized data by means of a physical topology that does not use direct physical links. This definition can be narrowed to apply to networks that use radio waves to carry the signals over either public or private bands, instead of using standard network cabling.

The topology of a wireless network is either a hub-and-spoke model or mesh. In the hub-and-spoke model, the wireless access point is the hub and is connected to the wired network. Wireless clients then connect to this access point via wireless, forming the spokes. In most enterprises, multiple wireless access points are deployed, forming an overlapping set of radio signals allowing clients to connect to the stronger signals. With tuning and proper antenna alignment and placement of the access points, the desired areas of coverage can be achieved and interference minimized.

The other topology supported by wireless is a mesh topology. In a mesh topology, the wireless units talk directly to each other, without a central access point. This is a form of ad hoc networking and is discussed in more detail in the next section. A new breed of wireless access points has emerged on the market that combines both of these characteristics. These wireless access points talk to each other in a mesh network method, and then once they have established a background network, where at least one station is connected to the wired network, wireless clients can connect to any of the access points as if the access points were normal access points. But instead of the signal going from wireless client to access point to wired network, the signal is carried across the wireless network from access point to access point until it reaches the master device that is wired to the outside network.

Ad Hoc

An **ad hoc** network is one where the systems on the network direct packets to and from their source and target locations without using a central router or switch. Windows supports ad hoc networking, although it is best to keep the number of systems relatively small. A common source of ad hoc networks is in the wireless space. From Zigbee devices that form ad hoc networks to Wi-Fi Direct, a wireless ad hoc network is one where the devices talk to each other, without the benefit of an access point or a central switch to manage traffic.

Ad hoc networks have several advantages. Without the need for access points, ad hoc networks provide an easy and cheap means of direct client-to-client communication. Ad hoc wireless networks can be easy to configure and provide a simple way to communicate with nearby devices when running cable is not an option.

Ad hoc networks have disadvantages as well. In enterprise environments, managing an ad hoc network is difficult because there isn't a central device through which all traffic flows. This means there isn't a single place to visit for traffic stats, security implementations, and so on. This also makes monitoring ad hoc networks more difficult.

Segregation/Segmentation/Isolation

Network segmentation is where you have configured the network devices to limit traffic access across different parts of a network. This can be done to prevent access to sensitive machines, but it also aids in network traffic management. A group of database servers that never need direct connection to the Internet can be located on a network segment where routing rules will not allow direct connection from outside of the protected enclave. Dividing a network into segments generally does not take more equipment, but rather is done in how the networking equipment is configured to communicate across the defined segments. A DMZ is an example of a segment—one that is accessible from the Internet, and from the internal network, but cannot be crossed directly.

Physical Separation

Physical separation is where you have separate physical equipment for the packets to use: separate switches, separate routers, and separate cables. This is the most secure method of separating traffic, but also the most expensive. Having separate physical paths is common in enterprises in the outermost sections of the network where connections to the Internet are made. This is mostly for redundancy, but it also acts to separate the traffic.

There are contractual times where physical separation may be called for, such as in the Payment Card Industry Data Security Standards (PCI DSS). Under PCI DSS, if an organization wishes to have a set of assets be considered out of scope with respect to the security audit for card number processing systems, then it must be physically separated. Enclaves (discussed next) are an example of physical separation.

Enclaves

Modern networks, with their increasingly complex connections, result in systems where navigation can become complex between nodes. Just as a DMZ-based architecture allows for differing levels of trust, the isolation of specific pieces of the network using security rules can provide differing trust environments. Several terms are used to describe the resulting architecture from network segmentation: segregation, isolation, and enclaves. **Enclaves** is the most commonly used term to describe sections of a network that are logically isolated by networking protocol. The concept of breaking a network into enclaves can create areas of trust where special protections can be employed and traffic from outside the enclave is limited or properly screened before admission.

Enclaves are not diametrically opposed to the concept of a flat network structure; they are just carved-out areas, like gated neighborhoods, where one needs special credentials to enter. A variety of security mechanisms can be employed to create a secure enclave. Layer 2 addressing (subnetting) can be employed, making direct addressability an issue. Firewalls, routers, and application-level proxies can be employed to screen packets before entry or exit from the enclave. Even the people side of the system can be restricted through the use of a special set of sysadmins to manage the systems.

Enclaves are an important tool in modern secure network design. Figure 9.6 shows a network design with a standard two-firewall implementation of a DMZ. On the internal side of the network, multiple firewalls can be seen, carving off individual security enclaves, zones where the same security rules apply. Common enclaves include those for high-security databases, low-security users (call centers), public-facing kiosks, and the management interfaces to servers and network devices. Having each of these in its own zone provides for more security control. On the management layer, using a nonroutable IP address scheme for all of the interfaces prevents them from being directly accessed from the Internet.

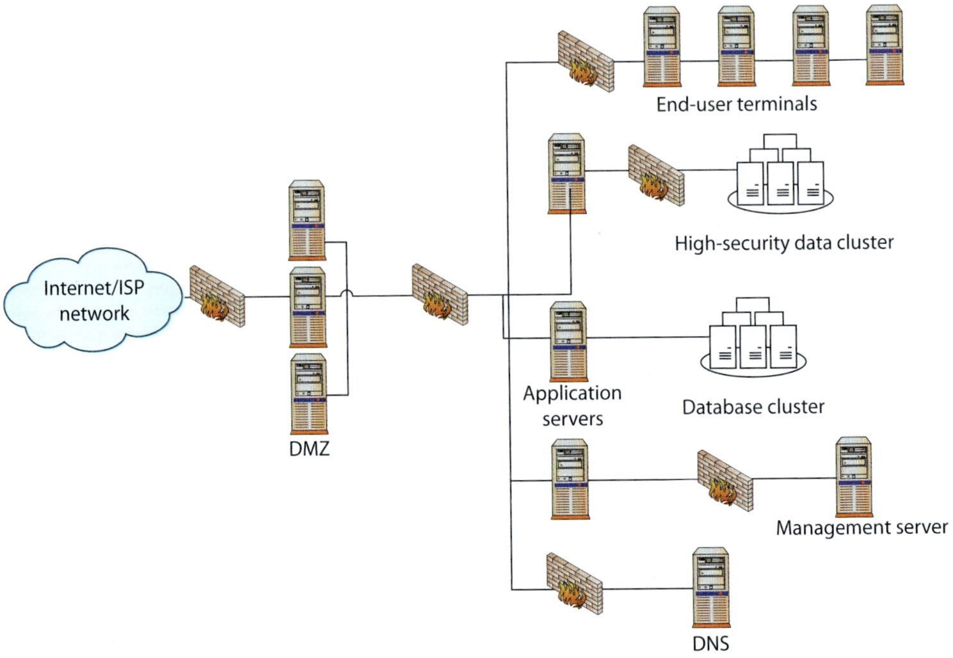

• **Figure 9.6** Secure enclaves

Logical (VLAN)

A LAN is a set of devices with similar functionality and similar communication needs, typically co-located and operated off a single switch. This is the lowest level of a network hierarchy and defines the domain for certain protocols at the data link layer for communication. A virtual LAN (VLAN) is a logical implementation of a LAN and allows computers connected to different physical networks to act and communicate as if they were on the same physical network. A VLAN has many of the same characteristic attributes of a LAN and behaves much like a physical LAN but is implemented using switches and software. This very powerful technique allows significant network flexibility, scalability, and performance and allows administrators to perform network reconfigurations without having to physically relocate or re-cable systems.

A *broadcast domain* is a logical division of a computer network. Systems connected to a broadcast domain can communicate with each other as if they were connected to the same physical network, even when they are not.

Trunking is the process of spanning a single VLAN across multiple switches. A trunk-based connection between switches allows packets from a single VLAN to travel between switches, as shown in Figure 9.7. Two trunks are shown in the figure: VLAN 10 is implemented with one trunk, and VLAN 20 is implemented with the other. Hosts on different VLANs cannot communicate using trunks and thus are switched across the switch network. Trunks enable network administrators to set up VLANs across multiple switches with minimal effort. With a combination of trunks and VLANs, network administrators can subnet a network by user functionality without regard to host location on the network or the need to re-cable machines.

Physical separation requires creating two or more physical networks, each with its own servers, switches, and routers. Logical separation uses one physical network with firewalls and/or routers separating and facilitating communication between the logical networks.

Security Implications

VLANs are used to divide a single network into multiple subnets based on functionality. This permits accounting and marketing, for example, to

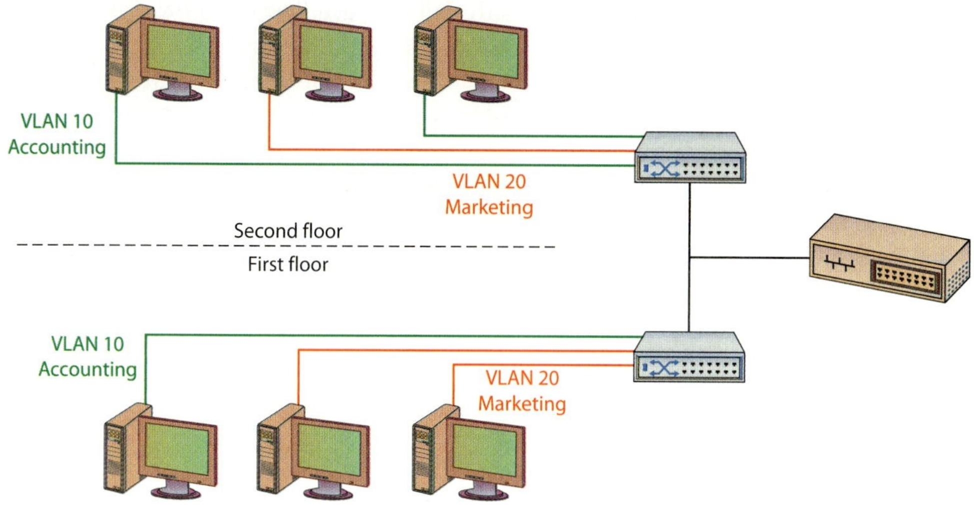

• **Figure 9.7** VLANs and trunks

share a switch because of proximity, yet still have separate traffic domains. The physical placement of equipment and cables is logically and programmatically separated so that adjacent ports on a switch can reference separate subnets. This prevents unauthorized use of physically close devices through separate subnets that are on the same equipment. VLANs also allow a network administrator to define a VLAN that has no users and map all of the unused ports to this VLAN (some managed switches allow administrators to simply disable unused ports as well). Then, if an unauthorized user should gain access to the equipment, that user will be unable to use unused ports, as those ports will be securely defined to nothing. Both a purpose and a security strength of VLANs is that systems on separate VLANs cannot directly communicate with each other.

Trunks and VLANs have security implications that you need to heed so that firewalls and other segmentation devices are not breached through their use. You also need to understand how to use trunks and VLANs to prevent an unauthorized user from reconfiguring them to gain undetected access to secure portions of a network.

Virtualization

Virtualization offers server isolation logically while still enabling physical hosting. Virtual machines allow you to run multiple servers on a single piece of hardware, enabling the use of more powerful machines in the enterprise at higher rates of utilization. By definition, a virtual machine provides a certain level of isolation from the underlying hardware, operating through a hypervisor layer. If a single piece of hardware has multiple virtual machines running, they are isolated from each other by the hypervisor layer as well.

Airgaps

Airgap is the term used to describe when two networks are not connected in any way except via a physical gap between them. Physically or logically, there is no direct path between them. Airgaps are considered by some to be a security measure, but this topology fails for several reasons. First, sooner or later, some form of data transfer is needed between airgapped systems. When this happens, administrators transfer files via USB-connected external media—and there no longer is an airgap.

Airgaps as a security measure fail because people can move files and information between the systems with external devices, and because of the false sense of security imparted by the airgap, these transfers are not subject to serious security checks. About the only thing that airgaps can prevent are automated connections such as reverse shells and other connections used to contact servers outside the network from within.

Zones and Conduits

The terms **zones** and *conduits* have specialized meaning in control system networks. **Control systems** are the computers used to control physical processes, ranging from traffic lights to refineries, manufacturing plants, critical infrastructure, and more. These networks are now being attached to enterprise networks, and this will result in the inclusion of control system network terminology into IT/network/security operations terminology. A term commonly used in control system networks is *zone*, which is a grouping of elements that share common security requirements. A conduit is defined as the path for the flow of data between zones.

Zones are similar to enclaves in that they have a defined set of common security requirements that differ from outside the zone. The zone is marked on a diagram, indicating the boundary between what is in and outside the zone. All data flows in or out of a zone must be via a defined conduit. The conduit allows a means to focus the security function on the data flows, ensuring the appropriate conditions are met before data enters or leaves a zone. Conduits are ideal locations for security solutions such as firewalls and network sensors. More details on network segregation in control networks is presented in Chapter 14.

Zero Trust

Traditional IT network security is based on the castle-and-moat model. In the castle-and-moat model, it is hard to obtain access from outside the network because of walls and the moat, with the only access being the gate where IDs are checked. Once you're inside, trust is conveyed by the fact you passed the gate check. This approach has been used for years because it is simple to implement, but the problem with this approach is that once an attacker gains access to the network, they have access to everything inside.

Zero trust is a security model centered on the belief that you should not trust any request without verifying authentication and authorization. Zero trust implementations require strict identity verification for every account trying to access resources, regardless of their location. Zero trust security requires a holistic approach to security that incorporates several additional layers of defense and technologies.

Security Zones

The first aspect of security is a layered defense. Just as a castle has a moat, an outside wall, an inside wall, and even a keep, so too does a modern secure network have different layers of protection. Different zones are designed to provide layers of defense, with the outermost layers providing basic protection and the innermost layers providing the highest level of protection. A constant issue is that accessibility tends to be inversely related to level of protection, so it is more difficult to provide complete protection and unfettered access at the same time. Tradeoffs between access and security are handled through zones, with successive zones guarded by firewalls enforcing ever-increasingly strict security policies. The outermost zone is the Internet, a free area, beyond any specific controls. Between the inner, secure corporate network and the Internet is an area where machines are considered at risk. This zone has come to be called the DMZ, after its military counterpart, the demilitarized zone, where neither side has any specific controls. Once inside the inner, secure network, separate branches are frequently carved out to provide specific functionality.

DMZ

DMZ is a military term for ground separating two opposing forces, by agreement and for the purpose of acting as a buffer between the two sides. A DMZ in a computer network is used in the same way: it acts as a buffer zone between the Internet, where no controls exist, and the inner, secure network, where an organization has security policies in place (see Figure 9.8). To demarcate the zones and enforce separation, a firewall is used on each side of the DMZ. The area between these firewalls is accessible from either the inner, secure network or the Internet. Figure 9.8 illustrates these zones as caused by firewall placement. The firewalls are specifically designed to prevent access across the DMZ directly, from the Internet to the inner, secure network. It is important to note that typically only filtered Internet traffic is allowed into the DMZ. For example, an organization hosting a web server and an FTP server in its DMZ may want the public to be able to "see" those services but nothing else. In that case, the firewall may allow FTP, HTTP, and HTTPS traffic into the DMZ from the Internet and then filter out everything else.

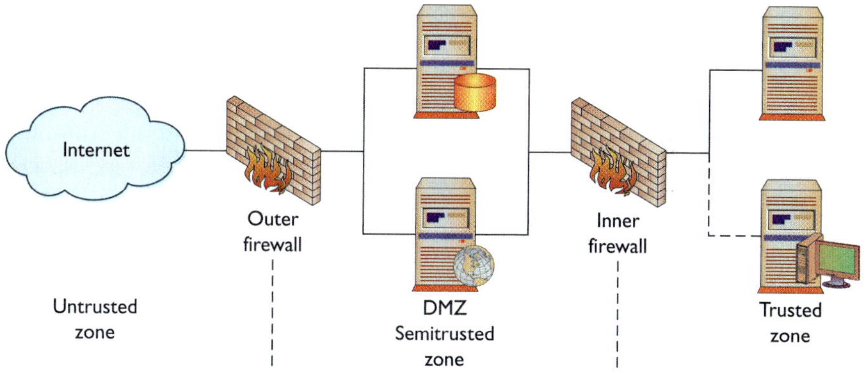

• **Figure 9.8** The DMZ and zones of trust

Special attention should be paid to the security settings of network devices placed in the DMZ, and they should be considered at all times to be at risk for compromise by unauthorized use. A common industry term, **hardened operating system**, applies to machines whose functionality is locked down to preserve security—unnecessary services and software are removed or disabled, functions are limited, and so on. This approach needs to be applied to the machines in the DMZ, and although it means that their functionality is limited, such precautions ensure that the machines will work properly in a less-secure environment.

Many types of servers belong in this area, including web servers that are serving content to Internet users, as well as remote access servers and external e-mail servers. In general, any server directly accessed from the outside, untrusted Internet zone needs to be in the DMZ. Other servers should not be placed in the DMZ. Domain name servers for your inner, trusted network and database servers that house corporate databases should not be accessible from the outside. Application servers, file servers, print servers—all of the standard servers used in the trusted network—should be behind both firewalls and the routers and switches used to connect these machines.

The idea behind the use of the DMZ topology is to provide publicly visible services without allowing untrusted users access to your internal network. If the outside user makes a request for a resource from the trusted network, such as a data element from an internal database that is accessed via a publicly visible web page in the DMZ, then this request needs to follow this scenario:

1. A user from the untrusted network (the Internet) requests data via a web page from a web server in the DMZ.
2. The web server in the DMZ requests the data from the application server, which can be in the DMZ or in the inner, trusted network.
3. The application server requests the data from the database server in the trusted network.
4. The database server returns the data to the requesting application server.
5. The application server returns the data to the requesting web server.
6. The web server returns the data to the requesting user from the untrusted network.

DMZs (CompTIA now refers to them as *screened subnets*) act as a buffer zone between unprotected areas of a network (the Internet) and protected areas (sensitive company data stores), allowing for the monitoring and regulation of traffic between these two zones.

This separation accomplishes two specific, independent tasks. First, the user is separated from the request for data on a secure network. By having intermediaries do the requesting, this layered approach allows significant security levels to be enforced. Users do not have direct access or control over their requests, and this filtering process can put controls in place. Second, scalability is more easily realized. The multiple-server solution can be made to be very scalable, literally to millions of users, without slowing down any particular layer.

Internet

The Internet is a worldwide connection of networks and is used to transport e-mail, files, financial records, remote access—you name it—from one network to another. The Internet is not a single network but a series of interconnected networks that allows protocols to operate and enables data to flow across it. This means that even if your network doesn't have direct contact with a resource, as long as a neighbor, or a neighbor's neighbor, and so on, can get there, so can you. This large web allows users almost infinite ability to communicate between systems.

Because everything and everyone can access this interconnected web and it is outside of your control and ability to enforce security policies, the Internet should be considered an untrusted network. A firewall should exist at any connection between your trusted network and the Internet. This is not to imply that the Internet is a bad thing—it is a great resource for all networks and adds significant functionality to our computing environments.

The term World Wide Web (WWW) is frequently used synonymously to represent the Internet, but the WWW is actually just one set of services available via the Internet. WWW or "the Web" is more specifically the Hypertext Transfer Protocol–based services that are made available over the Internet. This can include a variety of actual services and content, including text files, pictures, streaming audio and video, and even viruses and worms.

East-West Traffic

Data flows in an enterprise can be described in patterns, such as north-south and east-west. Data flowing in to and out of a data center or enterprise is called north-south traffic. **East-west traffic** is the data flow pattern between devices within a portion of the enterprise (that is, between functionally related boxes to support north-south traffic). The levels of east-west traffic are important to network engineers, as the networking infrastructure must be able to sustain operational loads.

East-west traffic refers to network data flows within an enterprise network. *North-south traffic* refers to data flowing between the enterprise network or data center and the outside of the network.

Intranet

An **intranet** describes a network that has the same functionality as the Internet for users but lies completely inside the trusted area of a network and is under the security control of the system and network administrators. Typically referred to as campus or corporate networks, intranets are used every day in companies around the world. An intranet allows a developer and a user the full set of protocols—HTTP(S), FTP(S), instant messaging, and so on—that is offered on the Internet, but with the added advantage of trust from the network security. Content on intranet web servers is not available over the Internet to untrusted users. This layer of security offers a significant amount of control and regulation, allowing users to fulfill business functionality while security is ensured.

An *intranet* is a private, internal network that uses common network technologies—HTTP(S), FTP(S), and so on—to share information and provide resources to organizational users.

Two methods can be used to make information available to outside users: Duplication of information onto machines in the DMZ can make it available to other users. Proper security checks and controls should be made prior to duplicating the material to ensure security policies concerning specific data availability are being followed. Alternatively, *extranets* (discussed in the next section) can be used to publish material to trusted partners.

Should users inside the intranet require access to information from the Internet, a proxy server can be used to mask the requestor's location. This helps secure the intranet from outside mapping of its actual topology. All Internet requests go to the proxy server. If a request passes filtering requirements, the proxy server, assuming it is also a cache server, looks in its local cache of previously downloaded web pages. If it finds the page in its cache, it returns the page to the requestor without needing to send the request to the Internet. If the page is not in the cache, the proxy server, acting as a client on behalf of the user, uses one of its own IP addresses to request the page from the Internet. When the page is returned, the proxy server relates it to the original request and forwards it on to the user. This masks the user's IP address from the Internet. Proxy servers can perform several functions for a firm; for example, they can monitor traffic requests, eliminating improper requests such as inappropriate content for work. They can also act as a cache server, cutting down on outside network requests for the same object. Finally, proxy servers protect the identity of internal IP addresses using Network Address Translation (NAT), although this function can also be accomplished through a router or firewall using NAT as well. NAT is further detailed later in the chapter.

Extranet

An **extranet** is an extension of a selected portion of a company's intranet to external partners. This allows a business to share information with customers, suppliers, partners, and other trusted groups while using a common set of Internet protocols to facilitate operations. Extranets can use public networks to extend their reach beyond a company's own internal network, and some form of security, typically VPN, is used to secure this channel. The use of the term *extranet* implies both privacy and security. Privacy is required for many communications, and security is needed to prevent unauthorized use and events from occurring. Both of these functions can be achieved through the use of technologies described in this chapter and other chapters in this book. Proper firewall management, remote access, encryption, authentication, and secure tunnels across public networks are all methods used to ensure privacy and security for extranets.

An *extranet* is a semiprivate network that uses common network technologies—HTTP(S), FTP(S), and so on—to share information and provide resources to business partners. Extranets can be accessed by more than one company because they share information between organizations.

Wireless

Because wireless networks have a different security perspective than physical networks, it is good practice to have them in a separate zone. Isolating the traffic to allow inspection before allowing it to interact with more critical resources is a best practice.

Guest

A **guest** zone is a network segment that is isolated from systems that guests would never need to access. This is very common in wireless networks, where a guest network can be established logically with the same hardware but providing separate access to separate resources based on login credentials.

Honeynets

A **honeynet** is a network designed to look like a corporate network but is made attractive to attackers. A honeynet is a collection of honeypots. It looks like the corporate network, but because it is known to be a false copy, all of the traffic is assumed to be illegitimate. This makes it easy to characterize the attacker's traffic and also to understand where attacks are coming from. A **honeypot** is a server designed to act like the real server on a corporate network, but rather than having the real data, the data it possesses is fake. Honeypots serve as attractive targets to attackers. A honeypot acts as a trap for attackers, as traffic in the honeypot can be assumed to be malicious.

Honeynets are networks composed of fake machines and used to catch attackers. A similar entity, a *honeyfile,* is a file composed of false data that is there to lure an attacker into looking at it or trying to take it out of the enterprise. Honeyfiles can be placed in honeynets or even among other files on the legit network.

Flat Networks

As networks have become more complex, with multiple layers of tiers and interconnections, a problem can arise in connectivity. One of the limitations of the Spanning Tree Protocol (STP) is its inability to manage layer 2 traffic efficiently across highly complex networks. STP was created to prevent loops in layer 2 networks and has been improved to the current version of Rapid Spanning Tree Protocol (RSTP). RSTP creates a spanning tree within the network of layer 2 switches, disabling links that are not part of the spanning tree. RSTP (IEEE 802.1w) provides a more rapid convergence to a new spanning tree solution after topology changes are detected. The problem with the spanning tree algorithms is that the network traffic is interrupted while the system recalculates and reconfigures. These disruptions can cause problems in network efficiencies and have led to a push for **flat network** designs, which avoid packet-looping issues through an architecture that does not have tiers.

One name associated with flat network topologies is *network fabric*, a term meant to describe a flat, depthless network. These types of networks are becoming increasingly popular in data centers and other areas of high-traffic density, as they can offer increased throughput and lower levels of network jitter and other disruptions. Although this is good for the efficiency of network operations, this "everyone can talk to everyone" idea is problematic with respect to security.

> Throughout this chapter and the whole book, you'll see numerous references to protocols such as HTTP, FTP, and others that are no longer considered secure and have encrypted variants (such as HTTPS and FTPS) to secure them. The choice to call them by their original name and not specifically the secure version is an editorial decision. When implementing a system, you should always opt for the secure versions of the protocols. With this in mind, when you see HTTP in this book, consider it standing for HTTP and HTTPS. The same goes for other protocols.

Network Protocols

How do all these interconnected devices communicate? What makes a PC in China able to view web pages on a server in Brazil? When engineers first started to connect computers together via networks, they quickly realized they needed a commonly accepted method for communicating—a protocol.

Protocols

A **protocol** is an agreed-upon format for exchanging or transmitting data between systems. A protocol defines a number of agreed-upon parameters, such as the data compression method, the type of error checking to use, and mechanisms for systems to signal when they have finished either receiving or transmitting data. There is a wide variety of protocols, each designed with certain benefits and uses in mind. Some of the more common protocols that have been used in networking are listed next. Today, most networks are dominated by Ethernet and Internet Protocol.

- **Asynchronous Transfer Mode (ATM)** A protocol based on transferring data in fixed-size packets. The fixed packet sizes help ensure that no single data type monopolizes the available bandwidth.
- **Ethernet** The LAN protocol developed jointly by Xerox, DEC, and Intel—the most widely implemented LAN standard.
- **Fiber Distributed Data Interface (FDDI)** The protocol for sending digital data over fiber-optic cabling.

- **Internet Protocol (IP)** The Internet Protocol encompasses a suite of protocols for managing and transmitting data between packet-switched computer networks, originally developed for the Department of Defense. Most users are familiar with IP protocols such as e-mail, File Transfer Protocol (FTP), Telnet, and Hypertext Transfer Protocol (HTTP).
- **Signaling System 7 (SS7)** The telecommunications protocol used between private branch exchanges (PBXs) to handle tasks such as call setup, routing, and teardown.
- **Systems Network Architecture (SNA)** A set of network protocols developed by IBM, originally used to connect IBM's mainframe systems, now carried over IP.
- **Token Ring** A LAN protocol developed by IBM that requires systems to possess the network "token" before transmitting data. Token Ring lost the network marketing war to Ethernet in 2001.
- **Transmission Control Protocol/Internet Protocol (TCP/IP)** The collection of communications protocols used to connect hosts on the Internet. TCP/IP is by far the most commonly used network protocol and is a combination of the TCP and IP protocols.
- **X.25A protocol** Developed by the Comité Consultatif International Téléphonique et Télégraphique (CCITT, now ITU-T) for use in packet-switched networks. This was the original packet-switched data networking protocol and predates IP.

In most cases, communications protocols were developed around the Open Systems Interconnection (OSI) model. The OSI model, or OSI Reference Model, is an International Organization for Standardization (ISO) standard for worldwide communications that defines a framework for implementing protocols and networking components in seven distinct layers. Within the OSI model, control is passed from one layer to another (top-down) before it exits one system and enters another system, where control is passed bottom-up to complete the communications cycle. It is important to note that most protocols only loosely follow the OSI model; several protocols combine one or more layers into a single function. The OSI model also provides a certain level of abstraction and isolation for each layer, which only needs to know how to interact with the layers above and below it. The application layer, for example, only needs to know how to communicate with the presentation layer—it does not need to talk directly to the physical layer. Figure 9.9 shows the different layers of the OSI model.

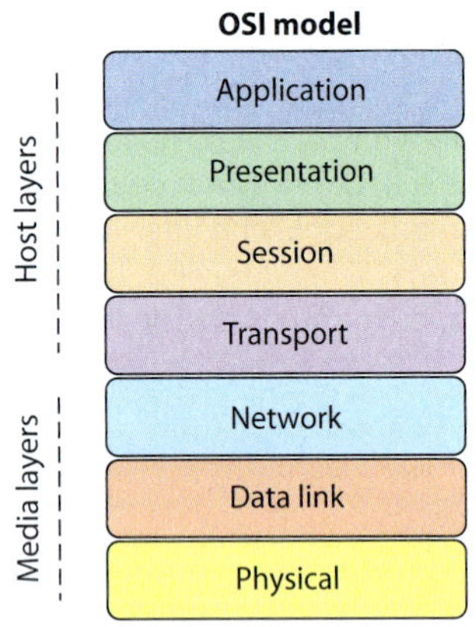

Figure 9.9 The OSI Reference Model

Packets

Networks are built to share information and resources, but like other forms of communication, networks and the protocols they use have limits and rules that must be followed for effective communication. For example, large chunks of data must typically be broken up into smaller, more manageable chunks before they are transmitted from one computer to another. Breaking the data up has advantages—you can more effectively share bandwidth with other systems and you don't have to retransmit the entire dataset if there is a problem in transmission. When data is broken up into smaller pieces for transmission, each of the smaller pieces is typically called a **packet**. Each protocol has its own definition of a packet—dictating how much data can be carried, what information is stored where, how the packet should be interpreted by another system, and so on.

A standard packet structure is a crucial element in a protocol definition. Without a standard packet structure, systems would not be able to interpret the information coming to them from other systems. Packet-based communication systems have other unique characteristics, such as size, that need to be addressed. This is done via a defined maximum and by fragmenting packets that are too big, as shown in the next sections.

The concept of breaking a message into pieces before sending it is as old as networking. The terms used to describe these pieces can vary from protocol to protocol. Frame Relay and Ethernet both use the term *frame*. ATM calls them *cells*. Many protocols use the generic term *packet*. In the OSI model, the term *datagram* is used. At the end of the day, regardless of what it is called, these pieces are protocol-defined, formatted structures used to carry information.

Maximum Transmission Unit

When packets are transmitted across a network, there are many intervening protocols and pieces of equipment, each with its own set of limitations. The **maximum transmission unit (MTU)** is the largest packet that can be carried across a network channel. One of the factors used to determine how many packets a message must be broken into is the MTU. The value of the MTU is used by TCP to prevent packet fragmentation at intervening devices. **Packet fragmentation** is the splitting of a packet while in transit into two packets so that they fit past an MTU bottleneck.

Packet Fragmentation

Built into the Internet Protocol is a mechanism for the handling of packets that are larger than allowed across a hop. Under ICMP v4, a router has two options when it encounters a packet that is too large for the next hop: break the packet into two fragments, sending each separately, or drop the packet and send an ICMP message back to the originator, indicating that the packet is too big. When a fragmented packet arrives at the receiving host, it must be reunited with the other packet fragments and reassembled. One of the problems with fragmentation is that it can cause excessive levels of packet retransmission because TCP must retransmit an entire packet for the loss of a single fragment. In IPv6, to avoid fragmentation, hosts are required to determine the minimal-path MTU before the transmission of packets to avoid fragmentation en route. Any fragmentation requirements in IPv6 are resolved at the origin, and if fragmentation is required, it occurs before sending.

IP fragmentation can be exploited in a variety of ways to bypass security measures. Packets can be purposefully constructed to split exploit code into multiple fragments to avoid detection by an intrusion detection system (IDS). Because the reassembly of fragments is dependent on data in the fragments, it is possible to manipulate the fragments to result in datagrams that exceed the 64KB limit, resulting in denial of service.

Tech Tip

IPv6 and Fragmentation

IPv6 systems calculate the MTU and then adhere to that from host to host. This prevents fragmentation en route. Instead, all fragmentation is done by the originating host to fit under the MTU limit.

Internet Protocol

The **Internet Protocol (IP)** is not a single protocol but a suite of protocols. The relationship between some of the IP suite and the OSI model is shown in Figure 9.10. As you can see, there are differences between the two versions of the protocol in use (that is, v4 and v6). The protocol elements and their security implications are covered in the next sections of this chapter. One of these differences is the replacement of the Internet Group Management Protocol (IGMP) with the Internet Control Message Protocol (ICMP) and Multicast Listener Discovery (MLD) in IPv6.

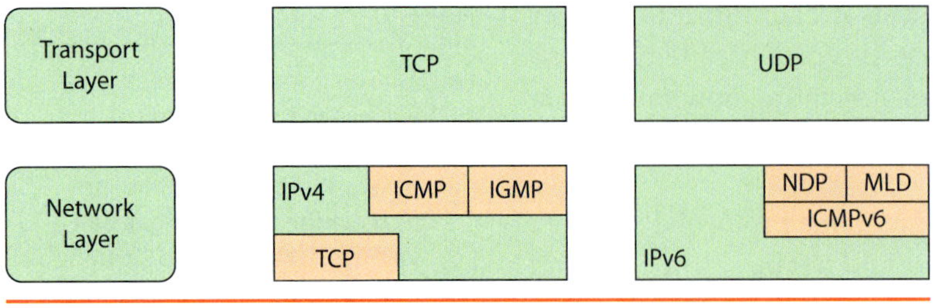

• **Figure 9.10** Internet Protocol suite components

IP Packets

To better understand packet structure, let's examine the packet structure defined by the IP protocol. An IP packet, often called a **datagram**, has two main sections: the header and the data section (sometimes called the *payload*). The header section contains all of the information needed to describe the packet (see Figure 9.11).

In IPv4, there are common fields to describe the following options:

- What kind of packet it is (protocol version number).
- How large the header of the packet is (packet header length).
- How to process this packet (type of service telling the network whether or not to use options such as minimize delay, maximize throughput, maximize reliability, and minimize cost).
- How large the entire packet is (the overall length of packet). Because this is a 16-bit field, the maximum size of an IP packet is 65,535 bytes, but in practice most packets are around 1500 bytes.
- A unique identifier so that this packet can be distinguished from other packets.

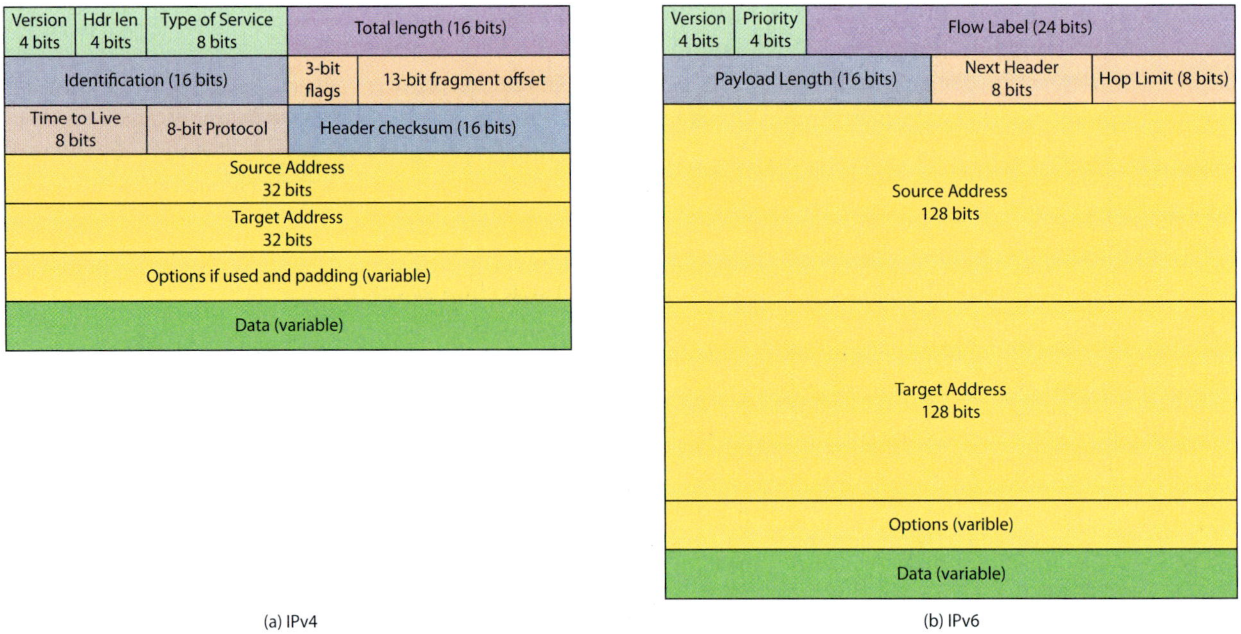

• **Figure 9.11** Logical layout of an IP packet: (a) IPv4, (b) IPv6

- Whether or not this packet is part of a longer data stream and should be handled relative to other packets.
- Flags that indicate whether or not special handling of this packet is necessary.
- A description of where this packet fits into the data stream as compared to other packets (the fragment offset).
- A "time to live" field that indicates the packet should be discarded if the value is zero.
- A protocol field that describes the encapsulated protocol.
- A checksum of the packet header (to minimize the potential for data corruption during transmission).
- Where the packet is from (source IP address, such as 10.10.10.5).
- Where the packet is going (destination IP address, such as 10.10.10.10).
- Option flags that govern security and handling restrictions, whether or not to record the route this packet has taken, whether or not to record timestamps, and so on.
- The data this packet carries.

In IPv6, the source and destination addresses take up much greater room, and for equipment and packet-handling reasons, most of the informational options have been moved to the optional area after the addresses. This series of optional extension headers allows the efficient use of the header in processing the routing information during packet-routing operations.

One of the most common options is the IPSec extension, which is used to establish IPSec connections. IPSec uses encryption to provide a variety of protections to packets. IPSec is fully covered in Chapter 6.

As you can see, this standard packet definition allows systems to communicate. Without this type of "common language," the global connectivity we enjoy today would be impossible—the IP protocol is the primary means for transmitting information across the Internet.

Tech Tip

The Importance of Understanding TCP/IP Protocols

A security professional must understand how the various TCP/IP protocols operate. For example, if you're looking at a packet capture of a suspected port scan, you need to know how "normal" TCP and UDP traffic works so you will be able to spot "abnormal" traffic. This chapter provides a very basic overview of the most popular protocols: TCP, UDP, and ICMP.

TCP vs. UDP

Protocols are typically developed to enable a certain type of communication or solve a specific problem. Over the years, this approach has led to the development of many different protocols, each critical to the function or process it supports. However, there are two protocols that have grown so much in popularity and use that, without them, the Internet as we know it would cease to exist. These two protocols, the **Transmission Control Protocol (TCP)** and **User Datagram Protocol (UDP)**, are ones that run on top of the IP network protocol. As separate protocols, each has its own packet definitions, capabilities, and advantages, but the most important difference between TCP and UDP is the concept of "guaranteed" reliability and delivery.

TCP is a "connection-oriented" protocol and offers reliability and guaranteed delivery of packets. UDP is a "connectionless" protocol with no guarantees of delivery.

UDP is known as a "connectionless" protocol because it has very few error-recovery services and no guarantee of packet delivery. With UDP, packets are created and sent on their way. The sender has no idea whether the packets were successfully received or whether they were received in order. In that respect, UDP packets are much like postcards—you address them and drop them in the mailbox, not really knowing if, when, or how the postcards reach your intended audience. Even though packet loss and corruption are relatively rare on modern networks, UDP is considered to be an unreliable protocol and is often only used for network services that are not greatly affected by the occasional lost or dropped packet. Time-synchronization requests, name lookups, and streaming audio are good examples of network services based on UDP. UDP also happens to be a fairly "efficient" protocol in terms of content delivery versus overhead. With UDP, more time and space are dedicated to content (data) delivery than with other protocols such as TCP. This makes UDP a good candidate for streaming protocols, as more of the available bandwidth and resources are used for data delivery than with other protocols.

Think of the three-way handshake as being similar to a phone call. You place a call to your friend—that's the SYN. Your friend answers the phone and says "hello"—that's the SYN/ACK. Then you say "Hi, it's me"—that's the ACK. Your connection is established, and you can start your conversation.

TCP is a "connection-oriented" protocol and was specifically designed to provide a reliable connection between two hosts exchanging data. TCP was also designed to ensure that packets are processed in the same order in which they were sent. As part of TCP, each packet has a sequence number to show where that packet fits into the overall conversation. With the sequence numbers, packets can arrive in any order and at different times, and the receiving system will still know the correct order for processing them. The sequence numbers also let the receiving system know if packets are missing—receiving packets 1, 2, 4, and 7 tells us that packets 3, 5, and 6 are missing and needed as part of this conversation. The receiving system can then request retransmission of packets from the sender to fill in any gaps.

The "guaranteed and reliable" aspect of TCP makes it very popular for many network applications and services such as HTTP, FTP, and Telnet. As part of the connection, TCP requires that systems follow a specific pattern when establishing communications. This pattern, often called the **three-way handshake** (shown in Figure 9.12), is a sequence of very specific steps:

1. The originating host (usually called the *client*) sends a SYN (synchronize) packet to the destination host (usually called the *server*). The SYN packet tells the server what port the client wants to connect to and the initial packet sequence number of the client.
2. The server sends a SYN/ACK packet back to the client. This SYN/ACK (synchronize/acknowledge) tells the client "I received your request" and also contains the server's initial packet sequence number.
3. The client responds to the server with an ACK packet to complete the connection establishment process.

Tech Tip

Encapsulation and Security

A packet is created by aggregation. Working down the OSI stack, the entire datagram becomes the data segment for the next layer, getting a new header. When the TCP header is added, one of the elements is the TCP handshake, which is added to the first packet. The handshake is done by setting bits in the TCP header. This does not prevent data from being transmitted in the first packet, and this has been used by hackers to avoid detection by some security tools. The reason is that many applications wait until the handshake is complete before processing data, but this is not correct because even data on the SYN packet should be processed. The important lesson is to understand how information is embedded in the encapsulation process, both in the header and datagram.

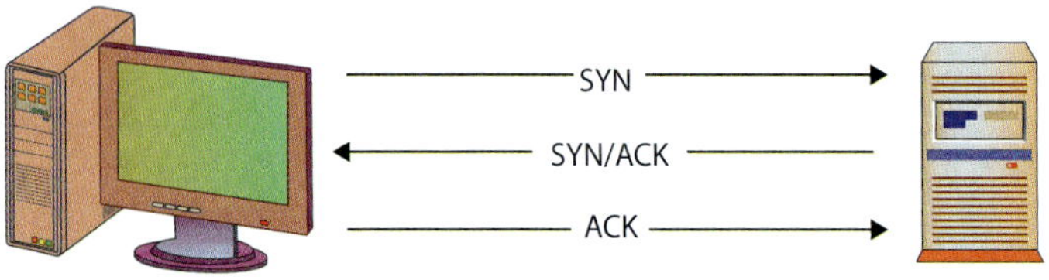

Figure 9.12 TCP's three-way handshake

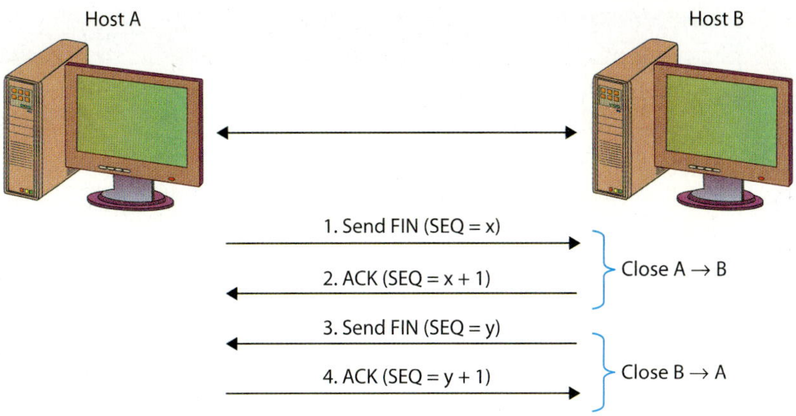

• **Figure 9.13** TCP termination process

Tearing down a TCP connection can be done in two manners. The first is the transmission of a TCP reset message. This can be done by sending a packet with the TSP RST flag set. The second method is to perform a handshake terminating the connection. The termination handshake is a four-way handshake, as shown in Figure 9.13. If machine A wishes to terminate the connection, it sends a TCP FIN packet to machine B. Machine B acknowledges the request by sending an ACK, including the sequence number +1. Machine B also sends a TCP FIN packet with its own sequence number to A. A then acknowledges the FIN with an acknowledgment of B's packet +1.

1. One computer sends a FIN packet to the other computer, including an ACK for the last data received (N).
2. The other computer sends an ACK number of N+1.
3. It also sends a FIN with the sequence number of X.
4. The originating computer sends a packet with an ACK number of N+1

ICMP

While TCP and UDP are arguably the most common protocols, the **Internet Control Message Protocol (ICMP)** is probably the third most commonly used protocol. During the early development of large networks, it was quickly discovered that there needed to be some mechanism for managing the overall infrastructure—handling connection status, traffic flow, availability, and errors. This mechanism is ICMP. ICMP is a control and information protocol and is used by network devices to determine such things as a remote network's availability, the length of time to reach a remote network, and the best route for packets to take when traveling to that remote network (using ICMP redirect messages, for example). ICMP can also be used to handle the flow of traffic, telling other network devices to "slow down" transmission speeds if packets are coming in too fast.

Tech Tip

TCP Packet Flags

TCP packets contain flags—dedicated fields that are used to help the TCP protocol control and manage the TCP session. There are eight different flags in a TCP packet, and when a flag is "set," it has a value of 1. The eight different flags are as follows:

- ***CWR (Congestion Window Reduced)*** *Set by a host to indicate that it received a packet with the ECE flag set and is taking action to help reduce congestion.*
- ***ECE (ECN-Echo)*** *Indicates that the TCP peer is ECN capable when used during the three-way handshake. During normal traffic, this flag means that a packet with a Congestion Experienced flag in its IP header was received by the host sending this packet.*
- ***URG (Urgent)*** *When set, the urgent pointer in the packets should be read as valid and followed for additional data.*
- ***ACK (Acknowledgment)*** *Indicates that the data in the ACK field should be processed.*
- ***PSH (Push)*** *Indicates that data delivery should start immediately rather than waiting for buffers to fill up first.*
- ***RST (Reset)*** *Resets the current connection. This is a start-over feature often used by IPS/IDS devices to interrupt sessions.*
- ***SYN (Synchronize)*** *Used to help synchronize sequence numbers.*
- ***FIN (Finish)*** *Indicates the sender is finished and has no more data to send.*

ICMP, like UDP, is a connectionless protocol. ICMP was designed to carry small messages quickly with minimal overhead or impact to bandwidth. ICMP packets are sent using the same header structure as IP packets, with the protocol field set to 1 to indicate that it is an ICMP packet. ICMP packets also have their own header, which follows the IP header and contains type, code, checksum, sequence number, identifier, and data fields. The "type" field indicates what type of ICMP message it is, and the "code" field tells us what the message really means. For example, an ICMP packet with a type of 3 and a code of 2 would tell us this is a "destination unreachable" message and, more specifically, a "host unreachable" message—usually indicating that we are unable to communicate with the intended destination. Because ICMP messages in IPv6 can use IPSec, ICMP v6 messages can have significant protections from alteration.

Unfortunately, ICMP has been greatly abused by attackers over the last few years to execute **denial of service (DoS)** attacks. Because ICMP packets are very small and connectionless, thousands and thousands of ICMP packets can be generated by a single system in a very short period of time. Attackers have developed methods to trick many systems into generating thousands of ICMP packets with a common destination—the attacker's target. This creates a literal flood of traffic that the target—and in most cases the network the target sits on—is incapable of dealing with. The ICMP flood drowns out any other legitimate traffic and prevents the target from

Tech Tip

ICMP Message Codes

With ICMP packets, the real message of the packet is contained in the "type and code" fields, not the data field. Following are some of the more commonly seen ICMP type codes. Note that ICMP v6 has broken the listing into two types: error messages (0–127) and informational messages (128–255, presented in the latter half of the table).

IPv6 introduced many new protocols, two of which will have significant implications: the Neighbor Discovery Protocol (NDP), which manages the interactions between neighboring IPv6 nodes, and Multicast Listener Discovery (MLD), which manages IPv6 multicast groups.

Type	ICMP v4	ICMP v6 Error Messages (0–127)
0	Echo reply	Reserved
1	Reserved	Destination unreachable
2	Reserved	Packet too big
3	Destination unreachable	Time exceeded
4	Source quench (deprecated)	Parameter problem
5	Redirect	Reserved
8	Echo request	Reserved
11	Time exceeded	Reserved
13	Timestamp	Reserved
30	Traceroute (deprecated)	Reserved
Type		**ICMP v6 Informational Messages (128–255)**
128		Echo request
129		Echo reply
130		Multicast Listener Query
131		Multicast Listener Report
132		Multicast Listener Done
133		Router Solicitation (NDP)
134		Router Advertisement (NDP)
135		Neighbor Solicitation (NDP)
136		Neighbor Advertisement (NDP)
137		Redirect Message (NDP)
138		Router Renumbering
139		ICMP Node Information Query
140		ICMP Node Information Response
141		Inverse Neighbor Discovery Solicitation Message
142		Inverse Neighbor Discovery Advertisement Message
143		Multicast Listener Discovery (MLD v2) reports (RFC 3810)
144		Home Agent Address Discovery Request Message
145		Home Agent Address Discovery Reply Message
146		Mobile Prefix Solicitation
147		Mobile Prefix Advertisement
148		Certification Path Solicitation (SEND)
149		Certification Path Advertisement (SEND)
151		Multicast Router Advertisement (MRD)
152		Multicast Router Solicitation (MRD)
153		Multicast Router Termination (MRD)
155		RPL Control Message
255		Reserved for expansion of ICMP v6 informational messages

Tech Tip

ICMPv4 Type 3 Message Codes

Many of the ICMP messages have associated code values that make the message more specific. For example, ICMP v4 messages with a type of 3 can have any of the following codes:

Code	Name/Description
1	Net unreachable.
2	Host unreachable.
3	Protocol unreachable.
4	Port unreachable.
5	Fragmentation needed and DF bit set.
6	Source route failed.
7	Destination network unknown.
8	Destination host unknown.
9	Source host isolated.
10	Communication with destination network is administratively prohibited.
11	Communication with destination host is administratively prohibited.
12	Destination network unreachable for TOS.
13	Destination host unreachable for TOS.

accomplishing its normal duties, thus denying access to the service the target normally provides. This has led to many organizations blocking all external ICMP traffic at their perimeter.

Tech Tip

Should You Block ICMP?

ICMP is a protocol used for troubleshooting, error reporting, and a wide variety of associated functionality. This functionality expands in ICMP v6 into multicasting. ICMP got a bad name primarily because of issues associated with the ***ping*** *and* ***traceroute*** *commands, but these represent a tiny minority of the protocol functionality. There are numerous, important uses associated with ICMP, and blocking it in its entirety is a bad practice. Blocking specific commands and specific sources makes sense; blanket blocking is a poor practice that will lead to network inefficiencies. Blocking ICMP v6 in its entirety will block a lot of IPv6 functionality because ICMP is now an integral part of the protocol suite.*

IPv4 vs. IPv6

The most common version of IP in use is IPv4, but the release of IPv6, spurred by the depletion of the IPv4 address space, has begun a typical logarithmic adoption curve. IPv6 has many similarities to the previous version, but it also has significant new enhancements, many of which have significant security implications.

Expanded Address Space

The expansion of the address space from 32 bits to 128 bits is a significant change. Whereas IPv4 did not have enough addresses for each person on the planet, IPv6 has over 1500 addresses per square meter of Earth's entire surface. This has one immediate implication: whereas you could use a scanner to search all addresses for responses in IPv4, doing the same in IPv6 will take significantly longer. A one-millisecond scan in IPv4 equates to a 2.5-billion-year scan in IPv6. In theory, the 128 bits of IPv6 address space will allow for 3.4×10^{38} possible nodes. The IPv6 addressing protocol has been designed to allow for a hierarchal division of the address space into several layers of subnets, to assist in the maintaining of both efficient and logical address allocations. One example is the embedding of the IPv4 address space in the IPv6 space. This also has an intentional effect of simplifying the backbone routing infrastructures by reducing the routing table size.

There is more than just an expanded address space in size. Each interface has three addresses: link-local, unique-local, and global. Link-local addresses are used for a variety of communications, including mandatory addresses for communication between two IPv6 devices (like ARP but at layer 3). Link-local addresses begin with FE80::. Unique-local addresses are not routable on the Internet and are used for local communications. They are identified by FC00:: at the beginning of the address. Global addresses are good globally and are structured hierarchically.

IPv6 no longer uses the concept of a broadcast message. There are three types of messages:

Unicast Address of a single interface. One-to-one delivery to single interface.

Multicast Address of a set of interfaces. One-to-many delivery to all interfaces in the set.

Anycast Address of a set of interfaces. One-to-one-of-many delivery to a single interface in the set that is closest.

As is becoming readily apparent, IPv6 is substantially more complicated than IPv4, and is much more capable. Further details would require an entire book, and if you will be doing a lot of network-intensive security work, you will need more knowledge in the intricacies of IPv6.

> **Tech Tip**
>
> **IPv6 Address Notation**
>
> *IPv6 addresses are 128 bits long, and a new shorthand has been developed to allow for simple notation of these addresses. The addresses are specified as eight groups of four hexadecimal characters separated by colons. Leading zeroes in any group may be suppressed, and consecutive groups of zeroes may be represented by two colons (::) once in an address. Thus, the IPv6 address of 2001:0ced:7738:0000:0000:0000:00df:1234 can be shortened to 2001:ced:7738::df:1234.*
>
> *Your local loopback address (which was 127.0.0.1) is now 0:0:0:0:0:0:0:1, or simply ::1. The address 0:0:0:0:0:0:0:0 (or simply ::) is unspecified and is used as a placeholder in messages that need the fields filled but that have no meaning.*

Neighbor Discovery

IPv6 introduces the Neighbor Discovery Protocol (NDP), which is useful for auto-configuration of networks. NDP can enable a variety of interception and interruption threat modes. A malevolent router can attach itself to a network and then reroute or interrupt traffic flows. In IPv6, there is no longer an Address Resolution Protocol (ARP) function. The function of ARP is replaced in IPv6 by Neighbor Solicitation (NS) messages.

Figure 9.14 shows the results of an IPv4 **arp** command on a Windows system, which results in the dumping of the local cache to the screen. Figure 9.15 shows the equivalent request on a Windows IPv6 system, where the command results in an ICMPv6 Neighbor Solicitation request (code = 135), which gets an ICMPv6 Neighbor Advertisement (code = 136) response. DHCPv6 has undergone a similar rework so that it can interface with NDP and allow auto-configuration of devices.

> **Tech Tip**
>
> **IPv6 Top Security Concerns**
>
> *There are numerous IPv6 security concerns—some technical, some operational. Here are some of the top security concerns:*
>
> - *Lack of IPv6 security training/education.*
> - *Security device bypass via IPv6.*
> - *Poor IPv6 security policies.*
> - *Address notation makes grepping through logs difficult, if not impossible.*
> - *IPv6 complexity increases operational challenges for correct deployment.*

Benefits of IPv6

Change is always a difficult task, and when the change will touch virtually everything in your system, this makes it even more difficult. Changing from IPv4 to IPv6 is not a simple task because it will have an effect on every networked resource. The good news is that this is not a sudden or surprise process; vendors have been making IPv6-capable products for almost a decade. By this point, virtually all the network equipment you rely on will be dual-stack capable, meaning that it can operate in both IPv4 and IPv6 networks. This provides a method for an orderly transfer from IPv4 to IPv6.

```
Administrator: Command Prompt

C:\WINDOWS\system32>arp -a

Interface: 192.168.86.217 --- 0x5
  Internet Address      Physical Address      Type
  192.168.86.1          70-3a-cb-60-c9-b8     dynamic
  192.168.86.23         14-91-82-06-2a-95     dynamic
  192.168.86.24         14-91-82-46-76-f1     dynamic
  192.168.86.25         14-91-82-4a-5a-dd     dynamic
  192.168.86.26         14-91-82-48-62-89     dynamic
  192.168.86.27         14-91-82-4d-11-f9     dynamic
  192.168.86.28         14-91-82-45-dc-39     dynamic
  192.168.86.29         14-91-82-4f-7d-35     dynamic
```

• **Figure 9.14** IPv4 **arp** command in Windows

```
Administrator: Command Prompt

C:\WINDOWS\system32>netsh int ipv6 show neigh | more

Interface 5: Wireless Network Connection


Internet Address                              Physical Address   Type
--------------------------------------------  -----------------  -----------
fe80::25:c37b:1d24:4034                       00-00-00-00-00-00  Unreachable
fe80::26:8efe:bed6:5f8e                       00-00-00-00-00-00  Unreachable
fe80::420:4e00:3313:fd64                      00-00-00-00-00-00  Unreachable
fe80::38cc:73ff:fe54:a22                      70-3a-cb-60-c9-b8  Stale
fe80::8a71:e5ff:fe8e:6071                     00-00-00-00-00-00  Unreachable
fe80::8a71:e5ff:fe8e:a299                     00-00-00-00-00-00  Unreachable
fe80::8a71:e5ff:fed9:256                      00-00-00-00-00-00  Unreachable
fe80::8a71:e5ff:fef3:ae09                     00-00-00-00-00-00  Unreachable
ff02::1                                       33-33-00-00-00-01  Permanent
ff02::2                                       33-33-00-00-00-02  Permanent
ff02::c                                       33-33-00-00-00-0c  Permanent
ff02::16                                      33-33-00-00-00-16  Permanent
ff02::fb                                      33-33-00-00-00-fb  Permanent
ff02::1:2                                     33-33-00-01-00-02  Permanent
ff02::1:3                                     33-33-00-01-00-03  Permanent
ff02::1:ff0c:aeae                             33-33-ff-0c-ae-ae  Permanent
```

• **Figure 9.15** IPv6 NS request in Windows

IPv6 has many useful benefits and ultimately will be more secure because it has many security features built into the base protocol series. IPv6 has a simplified packet header and new addressing scheme. This can lead to more efficient routing through smaller routing tables and faster packet processing. IPv6 was designed to incorporate multicasting flows natively, which allows bandwidth-intensive multimedia streams to be sent simultaneously to multiple destinations. IPv6 has a host of new services, from auto-configuration to mobile device addressing, as well as service enhancements to improve the robustness of quality of service (QoS) and Voice over IP (VoIP) functions.

The security model of IPv6 is baked into the protocol and is significantly enhanced from the nonexistent one in IPv4. IPv6 is designed to be secure from sender to receiver, with IPSec available natively across the protocol. This will significantly improve communication-level security, but it has also drawn a lot of attention. The use of IPSec will change the way security functions are performed across the enterprise. Old IPv4 methods, such as NAT and packet inspection methods of IDS, will need to be adjusted to the new model. Security appliances will have to adapt to the new protocol and its enhanced nature.

Packet Delivery

Protocols are designed to help information get from one place to another, but in order to deliver a packet, we have to know where it is going. Packet delivery can be divided into two sections: local and remote. Ethernet is common for local delivery, whereas IP works for remote delivery. Local packet delivery applies to packets being sent out on a local network, whereas remote packet delivery applies to packets being delivered to a remote system, such as across the Internet. Ultimately, packets may follow a "local delivery–remote delivery–local delivery" pattern before reaching their intended destination. The biggest difference in local versus remote delivery is how packets are addressed. Network systems have addresses, not unlike office numbers or street addresses, and before a packet can be successfully delivered, the sender needs to know the address of the destination system.

Tech Tip

MAC Addresses

Every network device should have a unique MAC address. Manufacturers of network cards and network chipsets have blocks of MAC addresses assigned to them, so you can often tell what type of equipment is sending packets by looking at the first three pairs of hexadecimal digits in a MAC address. For example, "00-00-0C" would indicate the network device was built by Cisco Systems.

Ethernet

Ethernet is the most widely implemented Layer 2 protocol. Ethernet is standardized under IEEE 802.3. Ethernet works by forwarding packets on a hop-to-hop basis using MAC addresses. Layer 2 addressing can have numerous security implications. Layer 2 addresses can be poisoned, spanning tree algorithms can be attacked, VLANs can be hopped, and more. Because of its near ubiquity, Ethernet is a common attack vector. It has many elements that make it useful from a networking point of view, such as its broadcast nature and its ability to run over a wide range of media. But these can also act against security concerns. Wireless connections are frequently considered to be weak from a security point of view, but so should Ethernet—unless you own the network, you should consider the network to be at risk.

Local Packet Delivery

Packets delivered on a network, such as an office LAN, are usually sent using the destination system's hardware address, or **Media Access Control (MAC) address**. Each network card or network device is supposed to have a unique hardware address so that it can be specifically addressed for network traffic. MAC addresses are assigned to a device or network card by the manufacturer, and each manufacturer is assigned a specific block of MAC addresses to prevent two devices from sharing the same MAC address. MAC addresses are usually expressed as six pairs of hexadecimal digits, such as 00:07:e9:7c:c8:aa. In order for a system to send data to another system on the network, it must first find out the destination system's MAC address.

> **Try This!**
>
> **Finding MAC Addresses on Windows Systems**
>
> Open a command prompt on a Windows system. Type the command **ipconfig /all** and find your system's MAC address. (Hint: It should be listed under "Physical Address" on your network adapters.) Now type the command **arp –a** and press ENTER. What information does this display? Can you find the MAC address of your default gateway?

> MAC addresses can be "spoofed," or faked. Some operating systems allow users with administrator-level privileges to explicitly set the MAC address for their network card(s). For example, in Linux operating systems you can use the **ifconfig** command to change a network adapter's MAC address. The command **ifconfig eth0 hw ether 00:07:e9:7c:c8:aa** will set the MAC address of adapter eth0 to 00:07:e9:7c:c8:aa. Also, a number of software utilities allow you to do this through a GUI, such as the GNU MAC Changer. GUI utilities to change MAC addresses on Windows systems are also available.

Maintaining a list of every local system's MAC address is both costly and time consuming, and although a system may store MAC addresses temporarily for convenience, in many cases the sender must find the destination MAC address before sending any packets. To find another system's MAC address, the **Address Resolution Protocol (ARP)** is used. Essentially, this is the computer's way of finding out "who owns the blue convertible with license number 123JAK." In most cases, systems know the IP address they wish to send to, but not the MAC address. Using an ARP request, the sending system will send out a query: Who is 10.1.1.140? This broadcast query is examined by every system on the local network, but only the system whose IP address is 10.1.1.140 will respond. That system will send back a response that says, "I'm 10.1.1.140 and my MAC address is 00:07:e9:7c:c8:aa." The sending system will then format the packet for delivery and drop it on the network media, stamped with the MAC address of the destination workstation.

> **Cross Check**
>
> **Mandatory Access Control vs. Media Access Control**
>
> In Chapter 11 you will learn about a different acronym: MAC, for mandatory access control. What is the difference between mandatory access control and Media Access Control? What is each used for? When using acronyms, it can be critical to ensure all parties are aware of the context of their usage.

> **Tech Tip**
>
> **Rogue Device Detection**
>
> *There is always a risk of a rogue (unauthorized) device being inserted into the network. Maintaining a list of all authorized MAC addresses can help detect these devices. Although MACs can be copied and spoofed, this would also set up a conflict if the original device was present. Monitoring for these conditions can detect the insertion of a rogue device.*

ARP Attacks

Address Resolution Protocol (ARP) operates in a simplistic and efficient manner—a broadcast request followed by a unicast reply. This method leaves ARP open to attack, which in turn can result in the loss of integrity, confidentiality, and availability. Because ARP serves to establish communication channels, failures at this level can lead to significant system compromises. There is a wide range of ARP-specific attacks, but one can classify them into types based on effect.

ARP can be a vector employed to achieve a man-in-the-middle (on-path) attack. There are many specific ways to create false entries in a machine's ARP cache, but the effect is the same: communications will be routed to an attacker. This type of attack is called *ARP poisoning*. The attacker can use this method to inject himself into the middle of a communication, hijack a session, sniff traffic to obtain passwords or other sensitive items, or block the flow of data, creating a denial of service.

Although ARP is not secure, all is not lost with many ARP-based attacks. Higher-level packet protections such as IPSec can be employed so that the packets are unreadable by interlopers. This is one of the security gains associated with IPv6, because when security is employed at the IPSec level, packets are protected below the IP level, making Layer 2 attacks less successful.

Remote Packet Delivery

While packet delivery on a LAN is usually accomplished with MAC addresses, packet delivery to a distant system is usually accomplished using Internet Protocol (IP) addresses. IP addresses are 32-bit numbers that usually are expressed as a group of four numbers (such as 10.1.1.132). In order to send a packet to a specific system on the other side of the world, you have to know the remote system's IP address. Storing large numbers of IP addresses on every PC is far too costly, and most humans are not good at remembering collections of numbers. However, humans are good at remembering names, so the **Domain Name System (DNS)** protocol was created.

DNS

DNS translates names into IP addresses. When you enter the name of your favorite website into the location bar of your web browser and press ENTER, the computer has to figure out what IP address belongs to that name. Your computer takes the entered name and sends a query to a local DNS server. Essentially, your computer asks the DNS server, "What IP address goes with www.myfavoritesite.com?" The DNS server, whose main purpose in life is to handle DNS queries, looks in its local records to see if it knows the answer. If it doesn't, the DNS server queries another, higher-level domain server. That server checks its records and queries the server above it, and so on, until a match is found. That name-to-IP-address matching is passed back down to your computer so it can create the web request, stamp it with the right destination IP address, and send it.

> The Domain Name System is critical to the operation of the Internet—if your computer can't translate www.espn.com into 68.71.212.159, then your web browser won't be able to access the latest scores. (Because DNS is a dynamic system, the IP address may change for www.espn.com; you can check with the **tracert** command.)

Before sending the packet, your system will first determine if the destination IP address is on a local or remote network. In most cases, it will be on a remote network and your system will not know how to reach that remote network. Again, it would not be practical for your system to know how to directly reach every other system on the Internet, so your system will forward the packet to a network gateway. Network gateways, usually called *routers*, are devices that are used to interconnect networks and move packets from one network to another. That process of moving packets from one network to another is called **routing** and is critical to the flow of information across the Internet. To accomplish this task, routers use forwarding tables to determine where a packet should go. When a packet reaches a router, the router looks at the destination address to determine where to send the packet. If the router's forwarding tables indicate where the packet should go, the router sends the packet out along the appropriate route. If the router does not know where the destination network is, it forwards the packet to its defined gateway, which repeats the same process. Eventually, after traversing various networks and being passed through various routers, your packet arrives at the router serving the network with the website you are trying to reach. This router determines the appropriate MAC address of the destination system and forwards the packet accordingly.

A request to a DNS server can return a significant amount of information in the form of records. There are several record types, as shown in Table 9.1.

Table 9.1 A Sample of DNS Record Types

Record Name	Use
A	IPv4 address
AAAA	IPv6 address
MX	Specifies the mail exchange server for a DNS domain name
TXT	Holds arbitrary text, such as SPF for e-mail verification
CNAME	Canonical name record for aliases
NS	Specifies an authoritative name server for given host
PTR	Used to look up domain names based on an IP address
SOA	Specifies core information about a DNS zone
RRSIG	DNSSEC signature

There are many more record types used for specific purposes. The total number of types is over 40.

DNSSEC

Because of the critical function DNS performs and the security implications of DNS, a cryptographically signed version of DNS was created. **DNSSEC** (short for DNS Security Extensions) is an extension of the original DNS specification, making it trustworthy. DNS is one of the pillars of authority associated with the Internet—it provides the addresses used by machines for communications. Lack of trust in DNS and the inability to authenticate DNS messages drove the need for and creation of DNSSEC. The DNSSEC specification was formally published in 2005, but system-wide adoption has been slow. In 2008, Dan Kaminsky introduced a method of DNS cache poisoning, demonstrating the need for DNSSEC adoption. Although Kaminsky worked with virtually all major vendors and was behind one of the most coordinated patch rollouts ever, the need for DNSSEC still remains, and enterprises are slow to adopt the new methods. One of the reasons for slow adoption is complexity. Having DNS requests and replies digitally signed requires significantly more work, and the increase in complexity goes against the stability desires of network engineers.

DNSSEC was designed to protect DNS client resolvers from accepting forged DNS data, such as sent in a DNS cache poisoning attack. DNS answers in DNSSEC are digitally signed, providing a means of verifying integrity. DNSSEC adds new records to the DNS protocol, as well as new header flags. The records are Resource Record Signature (RRSIG), DNS Public Key (DNSKEY), Delegation Signer (DS), and Next Secure (NSEC/NSEC2).

The new flags are Checking Disabled (CD) and Authenticated Data (AD). When a DNS request is received, DNS provides a signed response, enabling the receiver of the response to have trust that the answer came from a reliable source.

Tech Tip

How DNS Works

DNS is a hierarchical distributed database structure of names and addresses. This system is delegated from root servers to other DNS servers that each manage local requests for information. The top level of authorities, referred to as authoritative sources, *maintain the correct authoritative record. As records change, they are pushed out among the DNS servers, so records can be maintained in as near a current fashion as possible. Transfers of DNS records between DNS servers are called DNS zone transfers. Because these can result in massive poisoning attacks, zone transfers need to be tightly controlled between trusted parties.*

To avoid request congestion, DNS responses are handled by a myriad of lower name servers, referred to as resolvers. *Resolvers have a counter that refreshes their record after a time limit has been reached. Under normal operation, the DNS function is a two-step process:*

1. *The client requests a DNS record.*
2. *The resolver replies with a DNS reply.*

If the resolver is out of date, the steps expand:

1. *The client requests a DNS record.*
2. *The recursive resolver queries the authoritative server.*
3. *The authoritative server replies to the recursive resolver.*
4. *The recursive resolver replies with a DNS response to client.*

DNS was designed in the 1980s when the threat model was substantially different than today. The Internet today, and its use for all kinds of critical communications, needs a trustworthy addressing mechanism. DNSSEC is that mechanism, and as it rolls out, it will significantly increase the level of trust associated with addresses. Although certificate-based digital signatures are not perfect, the level of effort to compromise this type of protection mechanism changes the nature of the attack game, making it out of reach to all but the most resourced players. The coupled nature of the trust chains in DNS also serves to alert to any intervening attacks, making attacks much harder to hide.

DNS over HTTPS (DoH)

Domain Name System (DNS) over Hypertext Transfer Protocol using Transport Layer Security (HTTPS) is referred to as **DNS over HTTPS (DoH)**. DoH is useful in preventing eavesdropping and manipulation of DNS traffic, as it encrypts DNS requests to provide privacy, integrity, and source authentication for DNS transactions with a client's DNS resolver. While DoH is useful to protect DNS information transfers from attackers, it can cause issues with enterprise monitoring of DNS traffic. These monitoring issues can be overcome, but the main risk is in connecting to external DNS providers using DoH—connections that would be difficult to monitor and control at the edge of the network.

Tech Tip

DNS in the Enterprise Environment

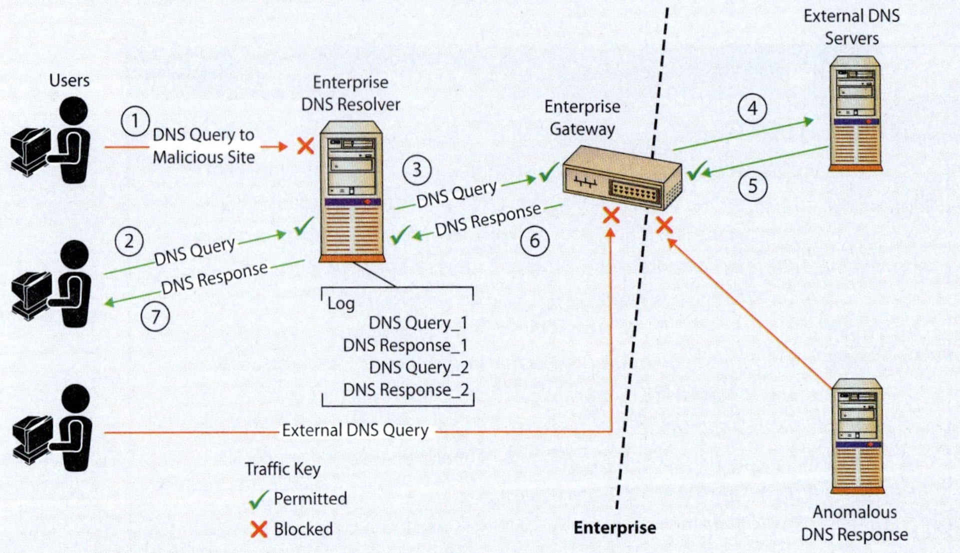

1. *The user wants to visit a website they do not know is malicious and types the domain name into the web browser. The enterprise DNS resolver blocks the request.*
2. *The request for the domain name is sent to the enterprise DNS resolver with a plaintext packet on port 53. Queries that violate DNS monitoring policies should generate alerts and/or be blocked.*
3. *If the IP address for the domain is not in the enterprise DNS resolver's cache of domains and the domain is not filtered, a DNS query will be sent through the enterprise gateway.*
4. *The enterprise gateway forwards the plaintext DNS request to an external DNS server. It also blocks DNS requests not from the enterprise DNS resolver.*
5. *The response to the query with the IP address of the domain, the address of another DNS server with more information, or an error is returned in plaintext back through the enterprise gateway.*
6. *The enterprise gateway forwards the response back to the enterprise DNS resolver. Steps 3–6 repeat until either the IP address for the requested domain name is found or there is an error.*
7. *The DNS resolver returns the response back to the user's web browser, which then requests the web page from the IP address in the response.*

Source: "Adopting Encrypted DNS in Enterprise Environments." National Security Agency. https://media.defense.gov/2021/Jan/14/2002564889/-1/-1/0/CSI_ADOPTING_ENCRYPTED_DNS_U_OO_102904_21.PDF

Dynamic Host Configuration Protocol

When an administrator sets up a network, they usually assign IP addresses to systems in one of two ways: statically or through DHCP. A static IP address assignment is fairly simple; the administrator decides what IP address to assign to a server or PC, and that IP address stays assigned to that system until the administrator decides to change it. The other popular method is through the **Dynamic Host Configuration Protocol (DHCP)**. Under DHCP, when a system boots up or is connected to the network, it sends out a query looking for a DHCP server. If a DHCP server is available on the network, it answers the new system and temporarily assigns to the new system an IP address from a pool of dedicated, available addresses. DHCP is an "as available" protocol—if the server has already allocated all the available IP addresses in the DHCP pool, the new system will not receive an IP address and will not be able to connect to the network. Another key feature of DHCP is the ability to limit how long a system may keep its DHCP-assigned IP address. DHCP addresses have a limited lifespan, and once that time period expires, the system using that IP address must either renew use of that address or request another address from the DHCP server. The requesting system either may end up with the same IP address or may be assigned a completely new address, depending on how the DHCP server is configured and on the current demand for available addresses. DHCP is very popular in large user environments where the cost of assigning and tracking IP addresses among hundreds or thousands of user systems is extremely high.

IP Addresses and Subnetting

As you'll recall from earlier in the chapter, IPv4 addresses are 32-bit numbers. Those 32 bits are represented as four groups of 8 bits each (called *octets*). You will usually see IP addresses expressed as four sets of decimal numbers in dotted-decimal notation (10.120.102.15, for example). Of those 32 bits in an IP address, some are used for the network portion of the address (the network ID), and some are used for the host portion of the address (the host ID). **Subnetting** is the process that is used to divide those 32 bits in an IP address and tell you how many of the 32 bits are being used for the network ID and how many are being used for the host ID. As you can guess, where and how you divide the 32 bits determines how many networks and how many host addresses you may have. To interpret the 32-bit space correctly, we must use a **subnet mask**, which tells us exactly how much of the space is the network portion and how much is the host portion. Let's look at an example using the IP address 10.10.10.101 with a subnet mask of 255.255.255.0.

First, we must convert the address and subnet mask to their binary representations:

Subnet mask: 11111111.11111111.11111111.00000000
IP address: 00001010.00001010.00001010.01100101

Then, we perform a bitwise AND operation to get the network address. The bitwise AND operation examines each set of matching bits from the binary representation of the subnet mask and the binary representation of the IP address. For each set where both the mask and address bits are 1, the result of the AND operation is a 1. Otherwise, if either bit is a 0, the result is a 0. So, for our example we get

Subnet mask: 11111111.11111111.11111111.00000000
IP address: 00001010.00001010.00001010.01100101
Network address: 00001010.00001010.00001010.00000000

which in decimal is 10.10.10.0, the network ID of our IP network address (translate the binary representation to decimal). Note how the fourth octet of 00000000 in the mask in effect removes the last octet of the IP address, converting it to all zeroes.

> **Tech Tip**
>
> **RFC 1918: Private Address Spaces**
>
> *RFC 1918 is the technical specification for private address space. RFC stands for Request for Comment, and there are RFCs for just about everything to do with the Internet—protocols, routing, how to handle e-mail, and so on. You can find RFCs at www.ietf .org/rfc.html.*

The network ID and subnet mask together tell us that the first three octets of our address are network related (10.10.10.), which means that the last octet of our address is the host portion (101 in this case). In our example, the network portion of the address is 10.10.10 and the host portion is 101. Another shortcut in identifying which of the 32 bits is being used in the network ID is to look at the subnet mask after it has been converted to its binary representation. If there's a 1 in the subnet mask, the corresponding bit in the binary representation of the IP address is being used as part of the network ID. In the preceding example, the subnet mask of 255.255.255.0 in binary representation is 11111111.11111111.11111111.00000000. We can see that there's a 1 in the first 24 spots, which means that the first 24 bits of the IP address are being used as the network ID (which is the first three octets of 255.255.255).

Network address spaces are usually divided into one of three classes:

- **Class A** Supports 16,777,214 hosts on each network, with a default subnet mask of 255.0.0.0. Subnets: 0.0.0.0 to 126.255.255.255 (127.0.0.0 to 127.255.255.255 is reserved for loopback).
- **Class B** Supports 65,534 hosts on each network, with a default subnet mask of 255.255.0.0. Subnets: 128.0.0.0 to 191.255.255.255.
- **Class C** Supports 253 hosts on each network, with a default subnet mask of 255.255.255.0 (see Figure 9.16). Subnets: 192.0.0.0 to 223.255.255.255.

Everything above 224.0.0.0 is reserved for either multicasting or future use.

In addition, certain subnets are reserved for private use and are not routed across public networks such as the Internet:

- 10.0.0.0 to 10.255.255.255
- 172.16.0.0 to 172.31.255.255
- 192.168.0.0 to 192.168.255.255
- 169.254.0.0 to 169.254.255.255 (Automatic Private IP Addressing)

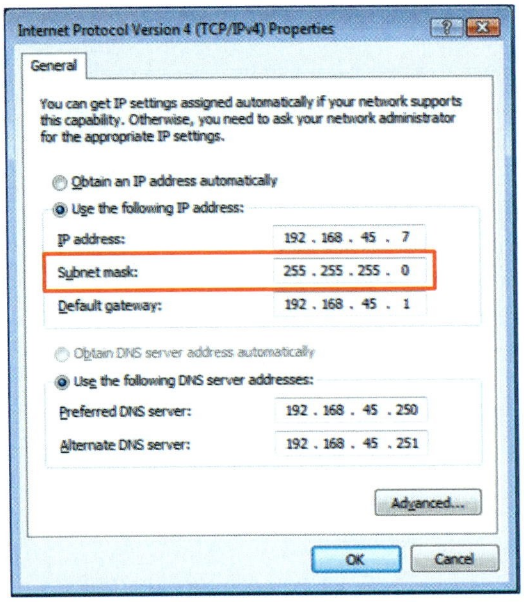

• **Figure 9.16** A subnet mask of 255.255.255.0 indicates this is a Class C address space.

Finally, when determining the valid hosts that can be placed on a particular subnet, you have to keep in mind that the "all 0's" address of the host portion is reserved for the network address, and the "all 1's" address of the host portion is reserved for the broadcast address of that particular subnet. Again from our earlier example:

Subnet network address:
10.10.10.0
00001010.00001010.00001010.00000000

Broadcast address:
10.10.10.255
00001010.00001010.00001010.11111111

In their forwarding tables, routers maintain lists of networks and the accompanying subnet mask. With these two pieces, the router can examine the destination address of each packet and then forward the packet on to the appropriate destination.

As mentioned earlier, subnetting allows us to divide networks into smaller logical units, and we use subnet masks to do this. But how does this work? Remember that the subnet mask tells us how many bits are being used to describe the network ID—adjusting the subnet mask (and the number of bits used to describe the network ID) allows us to divide an address space into multiple, smaller logical networks. Let's say you have a single address space of 192.168.45.0 that you need to divide into multiple networks. The default subnet mask is 255.255.255.0, which means you're using 24 bits as the network ID and 8 bits as the host ID. This gives you 254 different host addresses. But what if you need more networks and don't need as many host addresses? You can simply adjust your subnet mask to borrow some of the host bits and use them as network bits. If you use a subnet mask of 255.255.255.224, you are essentially "borrowing" the first 3 bits from the space you were using to describe host IDs and using them to describe the network ID. This gives you more space to create different networks but means that each network will now have fewer available host IDs. With a 255.255.255.224 subnet mask, you can create six different subnets, but each subnet can only have 30 unique host IDs. If you borrow 6 bits from the host ID portion and use a subnet mask of 255.255.255.252, you can create 62 different networks, but each of them can only have two unique host IDs.

> **Try This!**
>
> **Calculating Subnets and Hosts**
>
> Given a network ID of 192.168.10.X and a subnet mask of 255.255.255.224, you should be able to create eight networks with space for 30 hosts on each network. Calculate the network address, the first usable IP address in that subnet, and the last usable IP address in that subnet. (Hint: The first network will be 192.168.10.0. The first usable IP address in that subnet is 192.168.10.1, and the last usable IP address in that subnet is 192.168.10.30.)

Network Address Translation

If you're thinking that a 32-bit address space that's chopped up and subnetted isn't enough to handle all the systems in the world, you're right. While IPv4 address blocks are assigned to organizations such as companies and universities, there usually aren't enough Internet-visible IP addresses to assign to every system on the planet a unique, Internet-routable IP address. To compensate for this lack of available IP address space, we use **Network Address Translation (NAT)**. NAT translates private (nonroutable) IP addresses into public (routable) IP addresses.

From our discussions earlier in this chapter, you may remember that certain IP address blocks are reserved for "private use," and you'd probably agree that not every system in an organization needs a direct, Internet-routable IP address. Actually, for security reasons, it's much better if most of an organization's systems are hidden from direct Internet access. Most organizations build their internal networks using the private IP address ranges (such as 10.1.1.X) to prevent outsiders from directly accessing those internal networks. However, in many cases those systems still need to be able to reach the Internet. This is accomplished by using a NAT device (typically a firewall or router) that translates the many internal IP addresses into one of a small number of public IP addresses.

For example, consider a fictitious company, ACME.com. ACME has several thousand internal systems using private IP addresses in the 10.X.X.X range. To allow those IPs to communicate with the outside world, ACME leases an Internet connection and a few public IP addresses, and it deploys a NAT-capable device. ACME administrators configure all their internal hosts to use the NAT device as their default gateway. When internal hosts need to send packets outside the company, they send them to the NAT device. The NAT device removes the internal source IP address out of the outbound packets and replaces it with the NAT device's public, routable address and then sends the packets on their way. When response packets are received from outside sources, the device performs NAT in reverse, stripping off the external, public IP address in the destination address field and replacing it with the correct internal, private IP address in the destination address field before sending it on into the private ACME.com network. Figure 9.17 illustrates this NAT process.

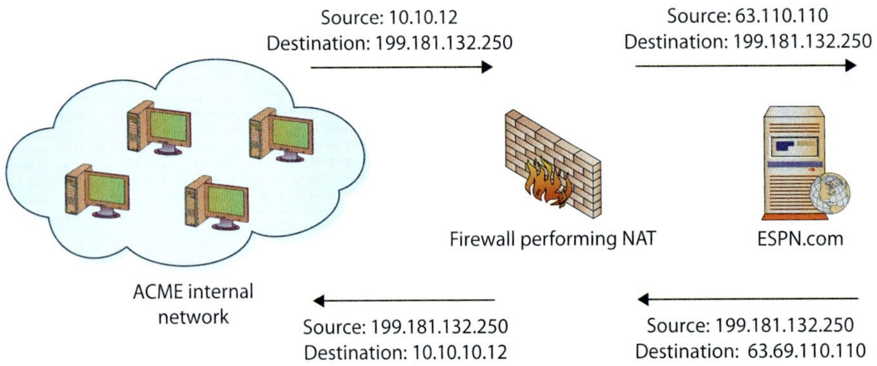

• **Figure 9.17** Logical depiction of NAT

Tech Tip

Different Approaches for Implementing NAT

Although the concept of NAT remains the same, there are actually several different approaches to implementing it:

- ***Static NAT*** *Maps an internal, private address to an external, public address. The same public address is always used for that private address. This technique is often used when hosting something you wish the public to be able to get to, such as a web server behind a firewall.*
- ***Dynamic NAT*** *Maps an internal, private IP address to a public IP address selected from a pool of registered (public) IP addresses. This technique is often used when translating addresses for end-user workstations and the NAT device must keep track of internal/external address mappings.*
- ***Port Address Translation (PAT)*** *Allows many different internal, private addresses to share a single external IP address. Devices performing PAT replace the source IP address with the NAT IP address and replace the source port field with a port from an available connection pool. PAT devices keep a translation table to track which internal hosts are using which ports so that subsequent packets can be stamped with the same port number. When response packets are received, the PAT device reverses the process and forwards the packet to the correct internal host. PAT is a very popular NAT technique and is in use at many organizations.*

In Figure 9.17, we see an example of NAT being performed. An internal workstation (10.10.10.12) wants to visit the ESPN website at www.espn.com (68.71.212.159). When the packet reaches the NAT device, the device translates the 10.10.10.12 source address to the globally routable 63.69.110.110 address, the IP address of the device's externally visible interface. When the ESPN website responds, it responds to the device's address, just as if the NAT device had originally requested the information. The NAT device must then remember which internal workstation requested the information and route the packet to the appropriate destination.

Inter-Networking

The Internet is viewed by many as a single large network, but it is in reality a series of interconnected networks. These systems are called **autonomous systems (ASs)**, and they have their own standard protocol methods of communications. The **Border Gateway Protocol (BGP)** is used to manage routing and reachability information between adjoining ASs. There are tens of thousands of ASs, from individual campus networks, to ISPs, to major corporations and government agencies. The routing of information between these ASs is done using BGP—specifically, external BGP, or eBGP.

BGP can have a huge effect on global traffic if it is incorrectly configured. On more than one occasion, a communications provider has provided bad information to the BGP system. The effect can be to capture or block Internet traffic. In 2004, a Turkish ISP improperly coded a BGP route, forcing all of the Internet to try and route through the ISP. In a separate instance in 2008, a Pakistani ISP put a BGP route in place to block Pakistani users from being able to access YouTube. The result ended up as a near worldwide block as the route moved from AS to AS.

BGP can be hijacked as well, and because of its widespread implementation, it is difficult to change, as this act would require coordination between virtually every AS for a simultaneous switching of the protocol specifics.

MPLS

Multi-protocol label switching (MPLS) is an underlay technology; specifically, it's a network that sits beneath the network infrastructure and provides connectivity. Because MPLS operates across switched telecommunication circuits, it has a performance advantage over the packet-switched Internet, with reduced jitter and latency. MPLS is a high-performance telecommunications data-carrying technique used to connect multiple sites and can carry multiple different types of traffic, including VoIP, video conferencing, and virtual/remote desktop operations. MPLS operates by placing labels onto the packets and moving them via switching as opposed to routing. MPLS operates at layer 2 instead of layer 3, providing increased performance between defined nodes. MPLS offers higher, guaranteed performance, but at a higher cost due to the use of private networks as opposed to the public-based Internet.

Software-Defined Networking (SDN)

Software-defined networking (SDN) is a network architecture where the control plane and the data plane are separated. This allows for networking hardware to be under programmatic control, even while processing data.

Traditional network architectures have the data plane and the control plane coexisting, and one of the results is the reduced flexibility of changing the network. This comes as a result of the scope of communications with respect to data. Where a data stream doesn't go has only limited programmability options. With SDN, a complete network programming stack exists, separate from data flows and programmable across the entire network. This provides significant flexibility and programmability in SDN networks, although at the cost of complexity. A key element of SDN is network function virtualization (NFV). NFV is an architecture that virtualizes network services, such as routers, firewalls, and load balancers, as opposed to running them on dedicated, specific hardware. Together, SDN and NFV create a fully functional network under the Infrastructure as Code architectural model.

From a security perspective, SDN adds advantages and disadvantages. In today's virtualized server world, servers can be spun up and moved with simple commands from orchestration software. This makes server deployment from model (that is, secure) exemplars fast and easy. SDN promises the same for network function deployment, such as firewalls. Network function virtualization (NFV) offers many of the same advantages that server virtualization offers. Preconfigured firewalls can be moved into traffic patterns with the simple command of the orchestration software. On the disadvantage side, the actual SDN software itself can increase the attack surface, and there are currently no good tools to monitor the SDN software for misuse or corruption.

A specific subset of SDN is software-defined wide area networking (SD-WAN). SD-WAN refers to the use of software to implement and manage a wide area network. This includes virtualizing network functions such as routers and firewalls, as well as network centralization. There are firms that have created specific SD-WAN implementations as an alternative to MPLS network technologies. Unlike MPLS, which is an underlay technology, SD-WAN is an overlay technology. SD-WAN technology uses software to create layers of network abstraction that can be used to run multiple discrete virtualized network layers over the physical layer. This makes SD-WAN implementations still subject to the underlying jitter and latency issues associated with the Internet.

Software-Defined Visibility (SDV)

For a network device to operate on data, it must see the data flow. Firewalls can't manage data they don't see, so firewalls are physically positioned throughout the network in line with the system's physical architecture. Just as software-defined networking has changed how networks are managed, *software-defined visibility (SDV)* is an extension of this Infrastructure as Code idea for the network visibility problem. Rather than the next-generation firewall (NGFW) being positioned strategically in line with data flows physically, it is done via code through the SDN fabric. This allows flexibility in design and the ability to reconfigure networks on the fly, including the security components.

Quality of Service (QoS)

Quality of service (QoS) is the use of specific technologies on a network to guarantee its ability to manage traffic based on a variety of indicators. High-bandwidth, real-time traffic, such as Voice over IP (VoIP), video conferencing, and video-on-demand, has a high sensitivity to network issues such as latency and jitter. QoS technologies are used to manage network conditions such as bandwidth (throughput), latency (delay), jitter (variance in latency), and error rates. They do this by providing differentiated handling and capacity allocation to specific flows based on packet type and source. QoS enables network administrators to assign the priority in which packets are handled as well as the amount of bandwidth afforded to that application or traffic flow.

Traffic Engineering

Traffic engineering is the set of processes and procedures used by network operators to efficiently deal with large amounts of data flowing through their networks. Traffic engineering involves manipulating the network to relieve congestion and balance loads more evenly across paths. While the protocols used in networking may operate independently of outside influence, they do not always work to optimal efficiencies, especially with heavy traffic loads. Traffic engineering deals with creating efficient network routes that reduce issues such as jitter and latency.

Route Security

Routing is the basis of interconnecting networks that comprise the Internet. Packets cross the networks to move information from source to destination. Depending on where the source and destination are with respect to each other, the route a packet takes can be wide ranging, from simple and short to complex and long. The protocols used to connect the various networks range from simple, like the Internet Protocol (IP), to more complex, such as BGP, IS-IS, OSPF, EIGRP, and RIPv2. Maintaining route security is part of the function of each of these protocols, and each serves to fulfill a specific needed functionality in connecting networks. From a Security+ perspective, the details behind each of these protocols is out of scope for this book, but understanding that they work together both to enable network functionality and secure packet transfers is important.

For More Information

Networking *CompTIA Network+ Certification All-in-One Exam Guide, Seventh Edition*, McGraw Hill, 2018

The Internet Engineering Task Force www.ietf.org

Chapter 9 Review

Chapter Summary

After reading this chapter and completing the exercises, you should understand the following about networks.

Identify the basic network architectures

- The two broad categories of networks are LANs and WANs.
- The physical arrangement of a network is typically called the network's *topology*.
- The four main types of network topologies are ring, bus, star, and mixed.
- Additional architectures include wireless and ad hoc.

Examine segregation, segmentation, and isolation with respect to network architectures

- Understand both physical and logical structures, and their differences.
- The use of airgaps, zones, and conduits in control system architectures is a key element of their network security architecture.
- Enclaves act as local segregation entities.
- Using zero trust for the authentication model changes the old perimeter security model of networks.

Classify security zones

- A *DMZ* is a buffer zone between networks with different trust levels. Companies often place public resources in a DMZ so that Internet users and internal users may access those resources without exposing the internal company network to the Internet.
- An *intranet* is a private, internal network that uses common network technologies (HTTP, FTP, and so on) to share information and provide resources to organizational users.
- An *extranet* is a semiprivate network that uses common network technologies (HTTP, FTP, and so on) to share information and provide resources to business partners.
- An *enclave* is a specialized security zone with common security requirements.
- A *VLAN* (or *virtual LAN*) is a group of ports on a switch configured to create a logical network of computers that appear to be connected to the same network, even if they are located on different physical network segments. Systems on a VLAN can communicate with each other but cannot communicate directly with systems on other VLANs.
- *Trunking* is the process of spanning a single VLAN across multiple switches.

Explain routing and address translation

- The process of moving packets from one end device to another through different networks is called *routing*.
- *Subnetting* is the process of dividing a network address space into smaller networks.
- DHCP allows network devices to be automatically configured on a network and temporarily assigned an IP address.
- Network Address Translation (NAT) converts private, internal IP addresses to public, routable IP addresses, and vice versa.

Examine the Internet Protocol in depth

- IP packets provide the method of moving data, with headers defining the type of packet.
- Different packet types, TCP and UDP, have different levels of overhead and delivery guarantees.
- ICMP packets manage errors and diagnostic issues.
- IPv6 is a complete overhaul of the IP protocol, not just an expanded address space.

Define the basic network protocols

- Protocols, agreed-upon formats for exchanging or transmitting data between systems, enable computers to communicate.
- When data is transmitted over a network, it is usually broken up into smaller pieces called *packets*.
- Most protocols define the types and format for the packets used in them.

- TCP is connection oriented, requires the three-way handshake to initiate a connection, and provides guaranteed and reliable data delivery.
- UDP is connectionless, lightweight, and provides limited error checking and no delivery guarantee.
- Each network device has a unique hardware address known as a *MAC address*. The MAC address is used for packet delivery.
- Network devices are also typically assigned a 32-bit number known as an *IP address*.
- The Domain Name Service (DNS) translates names like www.cnn.com into IP addresses.

Explore additional elements of networking

- Internetworking covers how different networks are connected using BGP and other protocols.
- MPLS covers how packets can traverse telecom networks with switching to guarantee performance.
- Software-defined networks (SDNs) separate the data and management planes to gain flexibility and capability.
- Quality of service (QoS) recognizes that not all packets need the same level of technical timing and allow for flexibility in capacity.
- Traffic engineering comprises the steps to achieve quality of service and performance metrics.
- Route security examines the concepts of end-to-end protection of communications.

Key Terms

ad hoc *(272)*
Address Resolution Protocol (ARP) *(294)*
airgap *(275)*
autonomous systems (ASs) *(303)*
Border Gateway Protocol (BGP) *(303)*
bus topology *(270)*
control systems *(276)*
datagram *(284)*
denial of service (DOS) *(288)*
DMZ *(277)*
DNS over HTTPS (DoH) *(297)*
DNSSEC *(296)*
Domain Name System (DNS) *(295)*
Dynamic Host Configuration Protocol (DHCP) *(298)*
east-west traffic *(279)*
enclave *(273)*
Ethernet *(293)*
extranet *(280)*
flat network *(281)*
guest *(280)*
hardened operating system *(277)*
honeynet *(280)*
honeypot *(280)*
Internet Control Message Protocol (ICMP) *(287)*
Internet Protocol (IP) *(283)*
intranet *(279)*
local area network (LAN) *(269)*
maximum transmission unit (MTU) *(283)*
Media Access Control (MAC) address *(293)*
mixed topology *(270)*
multi-protocol label switching (MPLS) *(303)*
network *(268)*
Network Address Translation (NAT) *(301)*
network segmentation *(272)*
packet *(283)*
packet fragmentation *(283)*
physical separation *(273)*
protocol *(281)*
quality of service (QoS) *(305)*
ring topology *(270)*
routing *(295)*
software-defined networking *(303)*
star topology *(270)*
storage area network (SAN) *(269)*
subnet mask *(299)*
subnetting *(299)*
three-way handshake *(286)*
topology *(270)*
Transmission Control Protocol (TCP) *(285)*
trunking *(274)*
User Datagram Protocol (UDP) *(285)*
virtual local area network (VLAN) *(270)*
virtualization *(275)*
wide area network (WAN) *(269)*
wireless *(271)*
zero trust *(276)*
zones *(276)*

Key Terms Quiz

Use terms from the Key Terms list to complete the sentences that follow. Don't use the same term more than once. Not all terms will be used.

1. A(n) _______________ is a group of two or more devices linked together to share data.
2. A packet in an IP network is sometimes called a(n) _______________.
3. Moving packets from source to destination across multiple networks is called _____________.
4. The _______________ is the hardware address used to uniquely identify each device on a network.
5. A(n) _______________ tells you what portion of a 32-bit IP address is being used as the network ID and what portion is being used as the host ID.
6. The shape or arrangement of a network, such as bus, star, ring, or mixed, is known as the _______________ of the network.
7. A small, typically local network covering a relatively small area such as a single floor of an office building is called a(n) _______________.
8. A(n) _______________ is an agreed-upon format for exchanging information between systems.
9. The packet exchange sequence (SYN, SYN/ACK, ACK) that initiates a TCP connection is called the _______________.
10. _______________ is the protocol that allows the use of private, internal IP addresses for internal traffic and public IP addresses for external traffic.

Multiple-Choice Quiz

1. What is Layer 1 of the OSI model called?
   - **A.** The physical layer
   - **B.** The network layer
   - **C.** The initial layer
   - **D.** The presentation layer
2. Which of the following statements best describes the User Datagram Protocol (UDP)?
   - **A.** It provides excellent error-checking algorithms.
   - **B.** It is a connectionless protocol.
   - **C.** It guarantees delivery of packets.
   - **D.** It requires a permanent connection between the source and destination.
3. What is the process that dynamically assigns an IP address to a network device called?
   - **A.** NAT
   - **B.** DNS
   - **C.** DHCP
   - **D.** Routing
4. What is the three-way handshake sequence used to initiate TCP connections?
   - **A.** ACK, SYN/ACK, ACK
   - **B.** SYN, SYN/ACK, ACK
   - **C.** SYN, SYN, ACK/ACK
   - **D.** ACK, SYN/ACK, SYN
5. Which of the following is a control and information protocol used by network devices to determine such things as a remote network's availability and the length of time required to reach a remote network?
   - **A.** UDP
   - **B.** NAT
   - **C.** TCP
   - **D.** ICMP
6. What is the name of the protocol that translates names into IP addresses?
   - **A.** TCP
   - **B.** DNS
   - **C.** ICMP
   - **D.** DHCP

7. Dividing a network address space into smaller, separate networks is called what?
   A. Translating
   B. Network configuration
   C. Subnetting
   D. Address translation
8. Which protocol translates private (nonroutable) IP addresses into public (routable) IP addresses?
   A. NAT
   B. DHCP
   C. DNS
   D. ICMP
9. Which of the following statements best describes the Transmission Control Protocol (TCP)?
   A. It is connectionless.
   B. It provides no error checking.
   C. It allows for packets to be processed in the order they were sent.
   D. It has no overhead.
10. Which of the following would be a valid MAC address?
   A. 00:07:e9
   B. 00:07:e9:7c:c8
   C. 00:07:e9:7c:c8:aa
   D. 00:07:e9:7c:c8:aa:ba

Essay Quiz

1. A developer in your company is building a new application and has asked you if she should use TCP- or UDP-based communications. Provide her with a brief discussion of the advantages and disadvantages of each protocol.
2. Your boss wants to know if DHCP is appropriate for both server and PC environments. Provide her with your opinion and be sure to include a discussion of how DHCP works.
3. Describe three basic types of network topologies and provide a sample diagram of each type.
4. Describe the three-way handshake process used to initiate TCP connections.
5. Your boss wants to know how subnetting works. Provide her with a brief description and be sure to include an example to illustrate how subnetting works.

Lab Projects

• Lab Project 9.1

A client of yours only has five external, routable IP addresses but has over 50 systems that they want to be able to reach the Internet for web surfing, e-mail, and so on. Design a network solution for the client that addresses their immediate needs but will still let them grow in the future.

• Lab Project 9.2

Your boss wants you to learn how to use the **arp** and **nslookup** commands. Find a Windows system and open a command/DOS prompt. Type in **arp** and press ENTER to see the options for the **arp** command. Use the **arp** command to find the MAC address of your system and at least five other systems on your network. When you are finished with **arp**, type in **nslookup** and press ENTER. At the prompt, type in the name of your favorite website, such as www.cnn.com. The **nslookup** command will return the IP addresses that match that domain name. Find the IP addresses of at least five different websites.

chapter 10

Infrastructure Security

The higher your structure is to be, the deeper must be its foundation.

—SAINT AUGUSTINE

In this chapter, you will learn how to

- Construct networks using different types of network devices
- Understand virtualization concepts
- Use basic terminology associated with network functions related to information security
- Understand security devices employed in a network
- Enhance security using security devices
- Understand the placement of security devices
- Identify the different types of media used to carry network signals
- Describe the different types of storage media, including the cloud, used to store information

Infrastructure security begins with the design of the infrastructure itself. The proper use of components improves not only performance but security as well. Network components are not isolated from the computing environment and are an essential aspect of a total computing environment. From the routers, switches, and cables that connect the devices, to the firewalls and gateways that manage communication, from the network design, to the protocols that are employed—all these items play essential roles in both performance and security.

Devices

A complete network computer solution in today's business environment consists of more than just client computers and servers. *Devices* are needed to connect the clients and servers and to regulate the traffic between them. Devices are also needed to expand this network beyond simple client computers and servers to include yet other devices, such as wireless and handheld systems. Devices come in many forms and with many functions—from hubs and switches, to routers, wireless access points, to special-purpose devices such as virtual private network (VPN) devices. Each device has a specific network function and plays a role in maintaining network infrastructure security.

Cross Check

The Importance of Availability

In Chapter 2 we examined the *CIA* of security: confidentiality, integrity, and availability. Unfortunately, the availability component is often overlooked, even though availability is what has moved computing into the modern networked framework and plays a significant role in security.

Security failures can occur in two ways. First, a failure can allow unauthorized users access to resources and data they are not authorized to use, thus compromising information security. Second, a failure can prevent a user from accessing resources and data the user is authorized to use. This second failure is often overlooked, but it can be as serious as the first. The primary goal of network infrastructure security is to allow all authorized use and deny all unauthorized use of resources.

Workstations

Most users are familiar with the client computers used in the client/server model called workstation devices. The **workstation** is the machine that sits on the desktop and is used every day for sending and reading e-mail, creating spreadsheets, writing reports in a word processing program, and playing games. If a workstation is connected to a network, it is an important part of the security solution for the network. Many threats to information security can start at a workstation, but much can be done in a few simple steps to provide protection from many of these threats.

Cross Check

Workstations and Servers

Servers and workstations are key nodes on networks. The specifics for securing these devices are covered in Chapter 14.

Servers

Servers are the computers in a network that host applications and data for everyone to share. Servers come in many sizes—from small single-CPU boxes that may be less powerful than a workstation, to multiple-CPU monsters, up to and including mainframes. The operating systems used by servers range from Windows Server, to Linux, to Multiple Virtual Storage (MVS) and other mainframe operating systems. The OS on a server tends to be more robust than the OS on a workstation system and is designed to service multiple users over a network at the same time. Servers can host a variety of applications, including web servers, databases, e-mail servers, file servers, print servers, and servers for middleware applications.

Mobile Devices

Mobile devices such as laptops, tablets, and mobile phones are the latest devices to join the corporate network. Mobile devices can create a major security gap, as a user may access separate e-mail accounts—one personal, without anti-malware protection, and the other corporate. Mobile devices are covered in detail in Chapter 12.

Device Security, Common Concerns

> **Tech Tip**
>
> **Default Accounts**
>
> *Always reconfigure all default accounts on all devices before exposing them to external traffic. This is to prevent others from reconfiguring your devices based on known access settings.*

As more and more interactive devices (that is, devices you can interact with programmatically) are being designed, a new threat source has appeared. In an attempt to build security into devices, typically, a default account and password must be entered to enable the user to access and configure the device remotely. These default accounts and passwords are well known in the hacker community, so one of the first steps you must take to secure such devices is to change the default credentials. Anyone who has purchased a home office router knows the default configuration settings and can check to see if another user has changed theirs. If they have not, this is a huge security hole, allowing outsiders to "reconfigure" their network devices.

Network-Attached Storage

Because of the speed of today's Ethernet networks, it is possible to manage data storage across the network. This has led to a type of storage known as **network-attached storage (NAS)**. The combination of inexpensive hard drives, fast networks, and simple application-based servers has made NAS devices in the terabyte range affordable for even home users. Because of the large size of video files, this has become popular for some users as a method of storing TV and video libraries. Because NAS is a network device, it is susceptible to various attacks, including sniffing of credentials and a variety of brute force attacks to obtain access to the data.

Removable Storage

Because removable devices can move data outside of the corporate-controlled environment, their security needs must be addressed. Removable devices can bring unprotected or corrupted data into the corporate environment. All removable devices should be scanned by antivirus software upon connection to the corporate environment. Corporate policies should address the copying of data to removable devices. Many mobile devices can be connected via USB to a system and used to store data—and in some cases vast quantities of data. This capability can be used to avoid some implementations of data loss prevention (DLP) mechanisms.

Virtualization

Virtualization technology is used to allow a computer to have more than one OS present and, in many cases, operating at the same time. **Virtualization** is an abstraction of the OS layer, creating the ability to host multiple OSs on a single piece of hardware. One of the major advantages of virtualization is the separation of the software and the hardware, creating a barrier that can improve many system functions, including security. The underlying hardware is referred to as the host machine, and on it is a host OS. Either the host OS has built-in hypervisor capability or an application is needed to provide the hypervisor function to manage the virtual machines (VMs). The virtual machines are typically referred to as the guest OSs.

Newer OSs are designed to natively incorporate virtualization hooks, enabling virtual machines to be employed with greater ease. There are several common virtualization solutions, including Microsoft Hyper-V, VMware, Oracle VM VirtualBox, Parallels, and Citrix Xen. It is important to distinguish between virtualization and boot loaders that allow different OSs to boot on hardware. Apple's Boot Camp allows you to boot into Microsoft Windows on Apple hardware. This is different from Parallels, a product with complete virtualization capability for Apple hardware.

Virtualization offers much in terms of host-based management of a system. From snapshots that allow easy rollback to previous states, faster system deployment via preconfigured images, ease of backup, and the ability to test systems, virtualization offers many advantages to system owners. The separation of the operational software layer from the hardware layer can offer many improvements in the management of systems.

Hypervisor

To enable virtualization, a *hypervisor* is employed. A **hypervisor** is a low-level program that allows multiple operating systems to run concurrently on a single host computer. Hypervisors use a thin layer of code to allocate resources in real time. The hypervisor acts as the traffic cop that controls I/O and memory management. Two types of hypervisors exist: Type 1 and Type 2.

A *hypervisor* is the interface between a virtual machine and the host machine hardware. Hypervisors are the layer that enables virtualization.

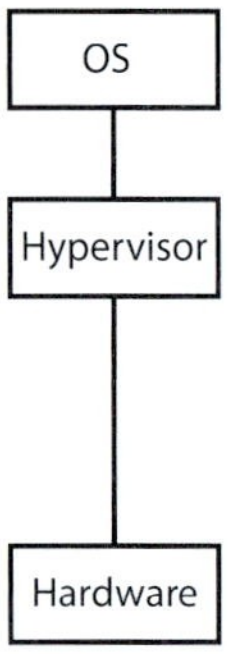

Type 1 Hypervisor

Type 1

Type 1 hypervisors run directly on the system hardware. They are referred to as a native, bare-metal, or embedded hypervisors in typical vendor literature. Type 1 hypervisors are designed for speed and efficiency, as they do not have to operate through another OS layer. Examples of Type 1 hypervisors include KVM (Kernel-based Virtual Machine, a Linux implementation), Xen (Citrix Linux implementation), Microsoft Windows Server Hyper-V (a headless version of the Windows OS core), and VMware's vSphere/ESXi platforms. All of these are designed for the high-end server market in enterprises and allow multiple VMs on a single set of server hardware. These platforms come with management toolsets to facilitate VM management in the enterprise.

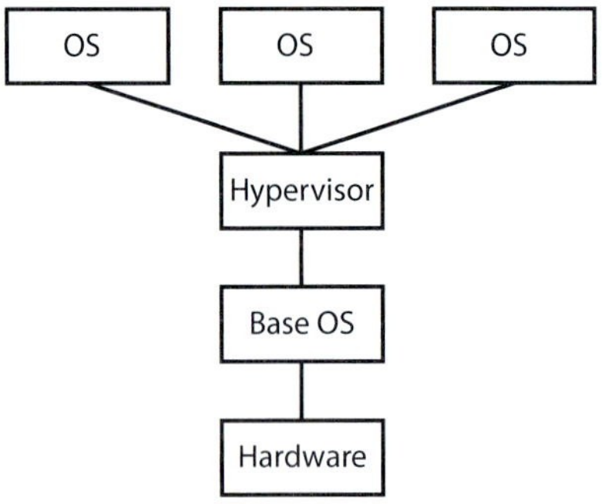

Type 2 Hypervisor

Type 2

Type 2 hypervisors run on top of a host operating system. In the beginning of the virtualization movement, Type 2 hypervisors were the most popular. Administrators could buy the VM software and install it on a server they already had running. Typical Type 2 hypervisors include Oracle's VirtualBox and VMware's VMware Workstation Player. These are designed for limited numbers of VMs, typically in a desktop or small server environment.

Application Cells/Containers

A hypervisor-based virtualization system enables multiple OS instances to coexist on a single hardware platform. *Application cells/containers* are the same idea, but rather than having multiple independent OSs, a container holds the portions of an OS that it needs separate from the kernel. In essence, multiple containers can share an OS, yet have separate memory, CPU, and storage threads, thus guaranteeing that they will not interact with other containers. This allows multiple instances of an application or different applications to share a host OS with virtually no overhead. This also allows portability of the application to a degree separate from the OS stack. There are multiple major container platforms in existence, and the industry has coalesced around a standard form called the Open Container Initiative, designed to enable standardization and the market stability of the container marketplace.

One can think of containers as the evolution of the VM concept into the application space. A container consists of an entire runtime environment—an application, plus all the dependencies, libraries and other binaries, and configuration files needed to run it, all bundled into one package. This eliminates the differences between the development, test, and production environments because the differences are in the container as a standard solution. Because the application platform, including its dependencies, is containerized, any differences in OS distributions, libraries, and underlying infrastructure are abstracted away and rendered moot.

VM Sprawl Avoidance

VM sprawl is the uncontrolled spreading of disorganization caused by a lack of an organizational structure when many similar elements require management. Just as you can lose a file or an e-mail and have to go hunt for it, virtual machines can suffer from being misplaced. When you only have a few files, sprawl isn't a problem, but when you have hundreds of files, developed over a long period of time, and not necessarily in an organized manner, sprawl does become a problem. The same is happening to virtual machines in the enterprise. In the end, a virtual machine is a file that contains a copy of a working machine's disk and memory structures. If an enterprise only has a couple of virtual machines, then keeping track of them is relatively easy. But as the number grows, sprawl can set in. VM sprawl is a symptom of a disorganized structure. If the servers in a server farm could move between racks at random, there would be an issue finding the correct machine when you needed to go physically find it. The same effect occurs with VM sprawl. As virtual machines are moved around, finding the one you want in a timely manner can be an issue. *VM sprawl avoidance* is a real thing and needs to be implemented via policy. You can fight VM sprawl by using naming conventions and proper storage architectures so that the files are in the correct directories, thus making finding a specific VM easy and efficient. But like any filing system, it is only good if it is followed; therefore, policies and procedures need to ensure that proper VM naming and filing are done on a regular basis.

VM Escape Protection

When multiple VMs are operating on a single hardware platform, one concern is *VM escape*. This occurs when software (typically malware) or an attacker escapes from one VM to the underlying OS and then resurfaces in a different VM. When you examine the problem from a logical point of view, you see that both VMs use the same RAM, the same processors, and so on; therefore, the difference is one of timing and specific combinations of elements within the VM environment. The VM system is designed to provide protection, but as with all things of larger scale, the devil is in the details. Large-scale VM environments have specific modules designed to detect escape and provide *VM escape protection* to other modules.

> Virtual environments have several specific topics that may be asked on the exam. Understand the difference between Type 1 and Type 2 hypervisors, and where you would use each. Understand the differences between VM sprawl and VM escape as well as the effects of each.

Snapshots

A **snapshot** is a point-in-time saving of the state of a virtual machine. Snapshots have great utility because they are like a savepoint for an entire system. Snapshots can be used to roll a system back to a previous point in time, undo operations, or provide a quick means of recovery from a complex, system-altering change that has gone awry. Snapshots act as a form of backup and are typically much faster than normal system backup and recovery operations.

Patch Compatibility

Having an OS operate in a virtual environment does not change the need for security associated with the OS. Patches are still needed and should be applied, independent of the virtualization status. Because of the nature of a virtual environment, it should have no effect on the utility of patching because the patch is for the guest OS.

Host Availability/Elasticity

When you set up a virtualization environment, protecting the host OS and hypervisor level is critical for system stability. The best practice is to avoid the installation of any applications on the host-level machine. All apps should be housed and run in a virtual environment. This aids in the system stability by providing separation between the application and the host OS. The term *elasticity* refers to the ability of a system to expand/contract as system requirements dictate. One of the advantages of virtualization is that a virtual machine can be moved to a larger or smaller environment based on need. If a VM needs more processing power, then migrating the VM to a new hardware system with greater CPU capacity allows the system to expand without you having to rebuild it.

Security Control Testing

When applying security controls to a system to manage security operations, you need to test the controls to ensure they are providing the desired results. Putting a system into a VM does not change this requirement. In fact, it may complicate it because of the nature of the relationship between the guest OS and the hypervisor. It is essential to specifically test all security controls inside the virtual environment to ensure their behavior is still effective.

Sandboxing

Sandboxing refers to the quarantining or isolation of a system from its surroundings. Virtualization can be used as a form of sandboxing with respect to an entire system. You can build a VM, test something inside the VM, and, based on the results, make a decision with regard to stability or whatever concern was present.

Networking

Networks are used to connect devices together. Networks are composed of components that perform networking functions to move data between devices. Networks begin with network interface cards and then continue in layers of switches and routers. Specialized networking devices are used for specific purposes, such as security and traffic management.

Network Interface Cards

To connect a server or workstation to a network, a device known as a **network interface card (NIC)** is used. A NIC is a card with a connector port for a particular type of network connection, either Ethernet or Token Ring.

The most common network type in use for LANs is the Ethernet protocol, and the most common connector is the RJ-45 connector. While the term *card* is retained in the name, most network interfaces are built into the motherboard of a system. Only in servers with the need for multiple network connections is one likely to find an actual card for network connectivity.

A NIC is the physical connection between a computer and the network. The purpose of a NIC is to provide lower-level protocol functionality from the OSI (Open Systems Interconnection) model. Because the NIC defines the type of physical layer connection, different NICs are used for different physical protocols. NICs come in single-port and multiport varieties, and most workstations use only a single-port NIC, as only a single network connection is needed. For servers, multiport NICs are used to increase the number of network connections, thus increasing the data throughput to and from the network.

Each NIC port is serialized with a unique code, 48 bits long, referred to as a Media Access Control (MAC) address. These are created by the manufacturer, with 24 bits representing the manufacturer and 24 bits being a serial number, guaranteeing uniqueness. MAC addresses are used in the addressing and delivery of network packets to the correct machine and in a variety of security situations. Unfortunately, these addresses can be changed, or "spoofed," rather easily. In fact, it is common for personal routers to clone a MAC address to allow users to use multiple devices over a network connection that expects a single MAC.

Tech Tip

Device/OSI Level Interaction

Different network devices operate using different levels of the OSI networking model to move packets from device to device, as detailed in the following table:

Device	OSI Layer
Hub	Layer 1, physical layer
Bridge	Layer 2, data link layer
Switch	Layer 2, data link layer
Router	Layer 3, network layer

Hubs

A **hub** is networking equipment that connects devices that use the same protocol at the physical layer of the OSI model. A hub allows multiple machines in an area to be connected together in a star configuration, with the hub as the center. This configuration can save significant amounts of cable and is an efficient method of configuring an Ethernet backbone. All connections on a hub share a single **collision domain**, a small cluster in a network where collisions occur. As network traffic increases, it can become limited by collisions. The collision issue has made hubs obsolete in newer, higher-performance networks, with inexpensive switches and switched Ethernet keeping costs low and usable bandwidth high. Hubs also create a security weakness in that all connected devices see all traffic, enabling sniffing and eavesdropping to occur. In today's networks, hubs have all but disappeared, being replaced by low-cost switches.

Bridges

Bridges are networking equipment that connect devices using the same protocol at the data link layer of the OSI model. A **bridge** operates at the data link layer, filtering traffic based on MAC addresses. Bridges can reduce collisions by separating pieces of a network into two separate collision domains, but this only cuts the collision problem in half. Although bridges are useful, a better solution is to use switches for network connections.

Switches

A **switch** forms the basis for connections in most Ethernet-based LANs. Although hubs and bridges still exist, in today's high-performance network environment, switches have replaced both. A switch has separate collision domains for each port. This means that for each port, two collision domains exist: one from the port to the client on the downstream side, and one from the switch to the network upstream. When *full duplex* is employed, collisions are virtually eliminated from the two nodes: host and client.

MAC filtering can be employed on switches, permitting only specified MACs to connect to them. This can be bypassed if an attacker can learn an allowed MAC because they can clone the permitted MAC onto their own NIC and spoof the switch. To filter edge connections, IEEE 802.1X is more secure (it's covered in Chapter 11). This can also be referred to as *MAC limiting.* Be careful to pay attention to context on the exam, however, because MAC limiting also can refer to preventing flooding attacks on switches by limiting the number of MAC addresses that can be "learned" by a switch.

Switches operate at the data link layer, while routers act at the network layer. For intranets, switches have become what routers are on the Internet—the device of choice for connecting machines. As switches have become the primary network connectivity device, additional functionality has been added to them. A switch is usually a Layer 2 device, but Layer 3 switches incorporate routing functionality.

Hubs have been replaced by switches because switches perform a number of features that hubs cannot perform. For example, the switch improves network performance by filtering traffic. It filters traffic by only sending the data to the port on the switch where the destination system resides. The switch knows what port each system is connected to and sends the data only to that port. The switch also provides security features, such as the option to disable a port so that it cannot be used without authorization. The switch also supports a feature called *port security,* which allows the administrator to control which systems can send data to each of the ports. The switch uses the MAC address of the systems to incorporate traffic-filtering and port security features, which is why it is considered a Layer 2 device.

Port Security

Switches can perform a variety of security functions. Switches work by moving packets from inbound connections to outbound connections. While moving the packets, it is possible for switches to inspect the packet headers and enforce security policies. *Port security* is a capability provided by switches that enables you to control which devices and how many of them are allowed to connect via each port on a switch. Port security operates through the use of MAC addresses. Although not perfect—MAC addresses can be spoofed—port security can provide useful network security functionality.

Port address security based on Media Access Control (MAC) addresses can determine whether a packet is allowed or blocked from a connection. This is the very function that a firewall uses for its determination, and this same functionality is what allows an 802.1X device to act as an "edge device."

Port security has three variants:

- **Static learning** A specific MAC address is assigned to a port. This is useful for fixed, dedicated hardware connections. The disadvantage is that the MAC addresses need to be known and programmed in advance, making this good for defined connections but not good for visiting connections.

- **Dynamic learning** Allows the switch to learn MAC addresses when they connect. Dynamic learning is useful when you expect a small, limited number of machines to connect to a port.
- **Sticky learning** Also allows multiple devices to a port, but also stores the information in memory that persists through reboots. This prevents the attacker from changing settings through power cycling the switch.

Broadcast Storm Prevention

One form of attack is a flood. There are numerous types of flooding attacks: ping floods, SYN floods, ICMP floods (Smurf attacks), and traffic flooding. Flooding attacks are used as a form of denial of service (DoS) to a network or system. Detecting flooding attacks is relatively easy, but there is a difference between detecting the attack and mitigating the attack. Flooding can be actively managed through dropping connections or managing traffic. *Flood guards* act by managing traffic flows. By monitoring the traffic rate and percentage of bandwidth occupied by broadcast, multicast, and unicast traffic, a flood guard can detect when to block traffic to manage flooding.

> Flood guards are commonly implemented in firewalls and IDS/IPS solutions to prevent DoS and DDoS attacks.

Bridge Protocol Data Unit (BPDU) Guard

To manage the Spanning Tree Protocol (STP), devices and switches can use Bridge Protocol Data Unit (BPDU) packets. These are specially crafted messages with frames that contain information about the Spanning Tree Protocol. The issue with BPDU packets is, while necessary in some circumstances, their use results in a recalculation of the STP, and this consumes resources. An attacker can issue multiple BPDU packets to a system to force multiple recalculations that serve as a network denial-of-service attack. To prevent this form of attack, edge devices can be configured with *Bridge Protocol Data Unit (BPDU) guards* that detect and drop these packets. While this eliminates the use of this functionality from some locations, the resultant protection is worth the minor loss of functionality.

Loop Prevention

Switches operate at layer 2 of the OSI reference model, and at this level there is no countdown mechanism to kill packets that get caught in loops or on paths that will never resolve. This means that a mechanism is needed for *loop prevention*. On layer 3, a time-to-live (TTL) counter is used, but there is no equivalent on layer 2. The layer 2 space acts as a mesh, where potentially the addition of a new device can create loops in the existing device interconnections. Open Shortest Path First (OSPF) is a link-state routing protocol that is commonly used between gateways in a single autonomous system. To prevent loops, a technology called spanning trees is employed by virtually all switches. STP allows for multiple, redundant paths, while breaking loops to ensure a proper broadcast pattern. STP is a data link layer protocol and is approved in IEEE standards 802.1D, 802.1w, 802.1s, and 802.1Q. It acts by trimming connections that are not part of the spanning tree connecting all of the nodes. STP messages are carried in BPDU frames described in the previous section.

> BPDU guards, MAC filtering, and loop detection are all mechanisms used to provide port security. Understand the differences in their actions. MAC filtering verifies MAC addresses before allowing a connection, BPDU guards prevent tampering with BPDU packets, and loop detection finds loops in local networks.

Dynamic Host Configuration Protocol (DHCP) Snooping

When an administrator sets up a network, they usually assign IP addresses to systems in one of two ways: statically or dynamically through DHCP. A static IP address assignment is fairly simple: the administrator decides what IP address to assign to a server or PC, and that IP address stays assigned to that system until the administrator decides to change it. The other popular method is through the **Dynamic Host Configuration Protocol (DHCP)**. Under DHCP, when a system boots up or is connected to the network, it sends out a broadcast query looking for a DHCP server. All available DHCP servers reply to this request. Should there be more than one active DHCP server within the network, the client uses the one whose answer reaches them first. From this DHCP server, the client then receives the address assignment. DHCP is very popular in large user environments where the cost of assigning and tracking IP addresses among hundreds or thousands of user systems is extremely high.

The weakness of using the first response received allows a rogue DNS server to reconfigure the network. A rogue DHCP server can route the client to a different gateway, an attack known as DHCP spoofing. Attackers can use a fake gateway to record data transfers, obtaining sensitive information, before sending data on to its intended destination, which is known as a man-in-the-middle attack. Incorrect addresses can lead to a DoS attack blocking key network services. *Dynamic Host Configuration Protocol (DHCP) snooping* is a defensive measure against an attacker that attempts to use a rogue DHCP device. DHCP snooping prevents malicious DHCP servers from establishing contact by examining DHCP responses at the switch level and not sending those from unauthorized DHCP servers. This method is detailed in RFC 7513, co-authored by Cisco and adopted by many switch vendors.

> MAC filtering can be employed on wireless access points but can be bypassed by attackers observing allowed MAC addresses and spoofing the allowed MAC address for the wireless card.

Media Access Control (MAC) Filtering

MAC filtering is the selective admission of packets based on a list of approved Media Access Control (MAC) addresses. Employed on switches, this method is used to provide a means of machine authentication. In wired networks, this enjoys the protection afforded by the wires, making interception of signals to determine their MAC addresses difficult. In wireless networks, this same mechanism suffers from the fact that an attacker can see the MAC addresses of all traffic to and from the access point and then can spoof the MAC addresses that are permitted to communicate via the access point.

> Network traffic segregation by switches can also act as a security mechanism, preventing access to some devices from other devices. This can prevent someone from accessing critical data servers from a machine in a public area.

Port address security based on MAC addresses can determine whether a packet is allowed or blocked from a connection. This is the very function that a firewall uses for its determination, and this same functionality is what allows an 802.1X device to act as an "edge device."

One of the security concerns with switches is that, like routers, they are intelligent network devices and are therefore subject to hijacking by hackers. Should a hacker break into a switch and change its parameters, they might be able to eavesdrop on specific or all communications, virtually undetected. Switches are commonly administered using the Simple Network Management Protocol (SNMP) and Telnet protocol, both of which have a serious weakness in that they send passwords across the network in cleartext. A hacker armed with a sniffer that observes maintenance on a switch can capture the administrative password. This allows the hacker to come back to the switch later and configure it as an administrator. An additional problem is that switches are shipped with default passwords, and if these are not changed when the switch is set up, they offer an unlocked door to a hacker.

Switches are also subject to electronic attacks, such as ARP poisoning and MAC flooding. *ARP poisoning* is when a device spoofs the MAC address of another device, attempting to change the ARP tables through spoofed traffic and the ARP table-update mechanism. *MAC flooding* is when a switch is bombarded with packets from different MAC addresses, flooding the switch table and forcing the device to respond by opening all ports and acting as a hub. This enables devices on other segments to sniff traffic.

> To secure a switch, you should disable all access protocols other than a secure serial line or a secure protocol such as Secure Shell (SSH). Using only secure methods to access a switch will limit the exposure to hackers and malicious users. Maintaining secure network switches is even more important than securing individual boxes because the span of control to intercept data is much wider on a switch, especially if it's reprogrammed by a hacker.

Routers

A **router** is a network traffic management device used to connect different network segments together. Routers operate at the network layer (Layer 3) of the OSI model, using the network address (typically an IP address) to route traffic and using routing protocols to determine optimal routing paths across a network. Routers form the backbone of the Internet, moving traffic from network to network, inspecting packets from every communication as they move traffic in optimal paths.

Routers operate by examining each packet, looking at the destination address, and using algorithms and tables to determine where to send the packet next. This process of examining the header to determine the next hop can be done in quick fashion.

> Access control lists (ACLs) can require significant effort to establish and maintain. Creating them is a straightforward task, but their judicious use will yield security benefits with a limited amount of maintenance at scale.

Routers use access control lists (ACLs) as a method of deciding whether a packet is allowed to enter the network. With ACLs, it is also possible to examine the source address and determine whether or not to allow a packet to pass. This allows routers equipped with ACLs to drop packets according to rules built into the ACLs. This can be a cumbersome process to set up and maintain, and as the ACL grows in size, routing efficiency can be decreased. It is also possible to configure some routers to act as quasi–application gateways, performing stateful packet inspection and using contents as well as IP addresses to determine whether or not to permit a packet to pass. This can tremendously increase the time for a router to pass traffic and can significantly decrease router throughput. Configuring ACLs and other aspects of setting up routers for this type of use are beyond the scope of this book.

One serious security concern regarding router operation is limiting who has access to the router and control of its internal functions. Like a switch, a router can be accessed using SNMP and Telnet and programmed remotely. Because of the geographic separation of routers, this can become a necessity because many routers in the world of the Internet can be hundreds of miles apart, in separate locked structures. Physical control over a router is absolutely necessary because if any device—be it a server, switch, or router—is physically accessed by a hacker, it should be considered compromised. Therefore, such access must be prevented. As with switches, it is important to ensure that the administrator password is never passed in the clear, that only secure mechanisms are used to access the router, and that all of the default passwords are reset to strong passwords.

As with switches, the most ensured point of access for router management control is via the serial control interface port. This allows

• **Figure 10.1** A small home office router for cable modem/DSL

access to the control aspects of the router without having to deal with traffic-related issues. For internal company networks, where the geographic dispersion of routers may be limited, third-party solutions to allow out-of-band remote management exist. This allows complete control over the router in a secure fashion, even from a remote location, although additional hardware is required.

Routers are available from numerous vendors and come in sizes big and small. A typical small home office router for use with cable modem/DSL service is shown in Figure 10.1. Larger routers can handle traffic of up to tens of gigabytes per second per channel, using fiber-optic inputs and moving tens of thousands of concurrent Internet connections across the network. These routers, which can cost hundreds of thousands of dollars, form an essential part of e-commerce infrastructure, enabling large enterprises such as Amazon and eBay to serve many customers' use concurrently.

Security Devices

A range of devices can be employed at the network layer to instantiate security functionality. Devices can be used for intrusion detection, network access control, and a wide range of other security functions. Each device has a specific network function and plays a role in maintaining network infrastructure security.

> A firewall is a network device (hardware, software, or combination of the two) that enforces a security policy. All network traffic passing through the firewall is examined; traffic that does not meet the specified security criteria or violates the firewall policy is blocked.

Firewalls

A **firewall** is a network device—hardware, software, or a combination thereof—whose purpose is to enforce a security policy across its connections by allowing or denying traffic to pass into or out of the network. A firewall is a lot like a gate guard at a secure facility. The guard examines all the traffic trying to enter the facility—cars with the correct sticker or delivery trucks with the appropriate paperwork are allowed in; everyone else is turned away (see Figure 10.2).

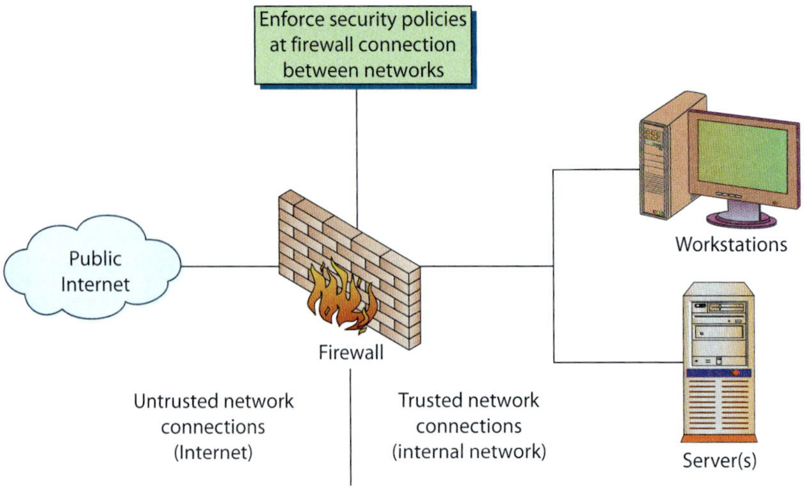

• **Figure 10.2** How a firewall works

The heart of a firewall is the set of security policies that it enforces. Management determines what is allowed in the form of network traffic between devices, and these policies are used to build rule sets for the firewall devices used to filter traffic across the network.

Firewall security policies are a series of rules that defines what traffic is permissible and what traffic is to be blocked or denied. These are not universal rules, and there are many different sets of rules for a single company with multiple connections. A web server connected to the Internet may be configured only to allow traffic on ports 80 (HTTP) and 443 (HTTPS) and have all other ports blocked. An e-mail server may have only necessary ports for e-mail open, with others blocked. A key to security policies for firewalls is the same as has been seen for other security policies—the principle of least access. Only allow the necessary access for a function; block or deny all unneeded functionality. How an organization deploys its firewalls determines what is needed for security policies for each firewall. You may even have a small office/home office (SOHO) firewall at your house, such as the RVS4000 shown in Figure 10.3. This device from Linksys provides both routing and firewall functions.

The security topology determines what network devices are employed at what points in a network. At a minimum, the corporate connection to the Internet should pass through a firewall, as shown in Figure 10.4. This firewall should block all network traffic except that specifically authorized

Tech Tip

Firewall Rules

Firewalls are in reality policy enforcement devices. Each rule in a firewall should have a policy behind it, as this is the only manner of managing firewall rule sets over time. The steps for successful firewall management begin and end with maintaining a policy list by firewall of the traffic restrictions to be imposed. Managing this list via a configuration-management process is important to prevent network instabilities from faulty rule sets or unknown "left-over" rules.

Orphan or *left-over rules* are rules that were created for a special purpose (testing, emergency, visitor or vendor, and so on) and then forgotten about and not removed after their use ended. These rules can clutter up a firewall and result in unintended challenges to the network security team.

• **Figure 10.3** Linksys RVS4000 SOHO firewall

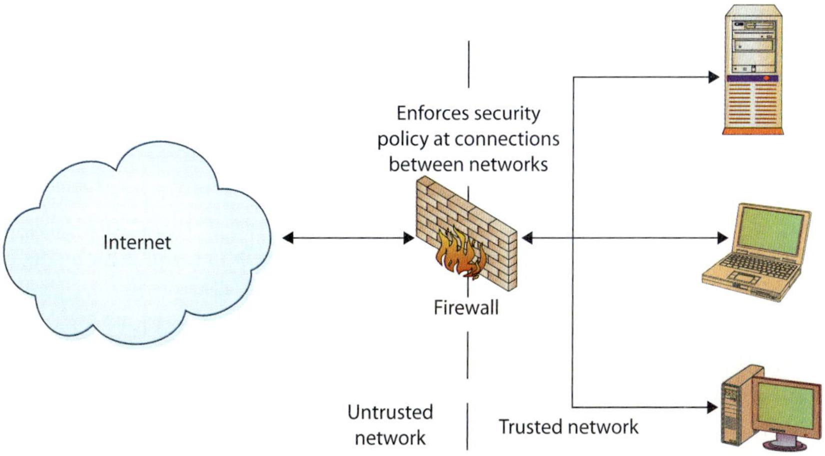

• **Figure 10.4** Logical depiction of a firewall protecting an organization from the Internet by the security policy. This is actually easy to do: blocking communications on a port is simply a matter of telling the firewall to close the port. The issue comes in deciding what services are needed and by whom, and thus which ports should be open and which should be closed. This is what makes a security policy useful but, in some cases, difficult to maintain.

The perfect firewall policy is one that the end user never sees and one that never allows even a single unauthorized packet to enter the network. As with any other perfect item, it is rare to find the perfect security policy for a firewall.

To develop a complete and comprehensive security policy, it is first necessary to have a complete and comprehensive understanding of your network resources and their uses. Once you know what your network will be used for, you will have an idea of what to permit. Also, once you understand what you need to protect, you will have an idea of what to block. Firewalls are designed to block attacks before they get to a target machine. Common targets are web servers, e-mail servers, DNS servers, FTP services, and databases. Each of these has separate functionality, and each of these has separate vulnerabilities. Once you have decided who should receive what type of traffic and what types should be blocked, you can administer this through the firewall.

Stateless vs. Stateful

The typical network firewall operates on IP addresses and ports, in essence a *stateless* interaction with the traffic. The most basic firewalls simply shut off either ports or IP addresses, dropping those packets upon arrival. While useful, they are limited in their abilities, as many services can have differing IP addresses, and maintaining the list of allowed IP addresses is time consuming and, in many cases, not practical. But for internal systems (say, a database server) that have no need to connect to a myriad of other servers, having a simple IP-based firewall in front can limit access to the desired set of machines.

A *stateful* packet inspection firewall can act upon the state condition of a conversation—is this a new conversation or a continuation of a conversation, and did it originate inside or outside the firewall? This provides greater capability, but at a processing cost that has scalability implications. To look at all packets and determine the need for each and its data requires stateful packet filtering. Stateful means that the firewall maintains, or knows, the context of a conversation. In many cases, rules depend on the context of a specific communications connection. For instance, traffic from an outside server to an inside server may be allowed if it is requested but blocked if it is not. A common example is a request for a web page. This request is actually a series of requests to multiple servers, each of which can be allowed or blocked. As many communications will be transferred to high ports (above 1023), stateful monitoring will enable the system to determine which sets of high-port communications are permissible and which should be blocked. A disadvantage of stateful monitoring is that it takes significant resources and processing to perform this type of monitoring, and this reduces efficiency and requires more robust and expensive hardware.

How Do Firewalls Work?

Firewalls enforce the established security policies. They can do this through a variety of mechanisms, including the following:

- **Network Address Translation (NAT)** As you may remember from Chapter 9, NAT translates private (nonroutable) IP addresses into public (routable) IP addresses.
- **Basic packet filtering** **Basic packet filtering** looks at each packet entering or leaving the network and then either accepts the packet or rejects the packet based on user-defined rules. Each packet is examined separately.
- **Stateful packet filtering** Stateful packet filtering also looks at each packet, but it can examine the packet in its relation to other packets. Stateful firewalls keep track of network connections and can apply slightly different rule sets based on whether or not the packet is part of an established session.
- **Access control lists (ACLs)** ACLs are simple rule sets applied to port numbers and IP addresses. They can be configured for inbound and outbound traffic and are most commonly used on routers and switches.
- **Application layer proxies** An application layer proxy can examine the content of the traffic as well as the ports and IP addresses. For example, an application layer has the ability to look inside a user's web traffic, detect a malicious website attempting to download malware to the user's system, and block the malware.

NAT is the process of modifying network address information in datagram packet headers while in transit across a traffic-routing device, such as a router or firewall, for the purpose of remapping a given address space into another. See Chapter 9 for a more detailed discussion on NAT.

One of the most basic security functions provided by a firewall is NAT. This service allows you to mask significant amounts of information from outside of the network. This allows an outside entity to communicate with an entity inside the firewall without truly knowing its address.

Basic packet filtering, also known as *stateless packet inspection*, involves looking at packets, their protocols and destinations, and checking that information against the security policy. Telnet and FTP connections may be prohibited from being established to a mail or database server, but they may be allowed for the respective service servers. This is a fairly simple method of filtering based on information in each packet header, like IP addresses and TCP/UDP ports. This will not detect and catch all undesired packets, but it is fast and efficient.

To look at all packets, determining the need for each and its data, requires stateful packet filtering. Advanced firewalls employ stateful packet filtering to prevent several types of undesired communications. Should a packet come from outside the network, in an attempt to pretend that it is a response to a message from inside the network, the firewall will have no record of it being requested and can discard it, blocking access. As many communications will be transferred to high ports (above 1023), stateful monitoring will enable the system to determine which sets of high-port communications are permissible and which should be blocked. The disadvantage to stateful monitoring is that it takes significant resources and processing to do this type of monitoring, and this reduces efficiency and requires more robust and expensive hardware. However, this type of monitoring is essential in today's comprehensive networks, particularly given the variety of remotely accessible services.

As they are in routers, switches, servers, and other network devices, ACLs are a cornerstone of security in firewalls. Just as you must protect the device from physical access, ACLs do the same task for electronic access. Firewalls can extend the concept of ACLs by enforcing them at a packet level when packet-level stateful filtering is performed. This can add an extra layer of protection, making it more difficult for an outside hacker to breach a firewall.

Some high-security firewalls also employ application layer proxies. As the name implies, packets are not allowed to traverse the firewall, but data instead flows up to an application that in turn decides what to do with it. For example, an SMTP proxy may accept inbound mail from the Internet and forward it to the internal corporate mail server, as depicted in Figure 10.5. While proxies provide a high level of security by making it very difficult for an attacker to manipulate the actual packets arriving at the destination, and while they provide the opportunity for an application to interpret the data prior to forwarding it to the destination, they generally are not capable of the same throughput as stateful packet-inspection firewalls. The tradeoff between performance and speed is a common one and must be evaluated with respect to security needs and performance requirements.

Firewalls can also act as network traffic regulators in that they can be configured to mitigate specific types of network-based attacks. In denial-of-service (DoS) and distributed denial-of-service (DDoS) attacks, an attacker can attempt to flood a network with traffic. Firewalls can be tuned to detect these types of attacks and act as flood guards, mitigating the effect on the network.

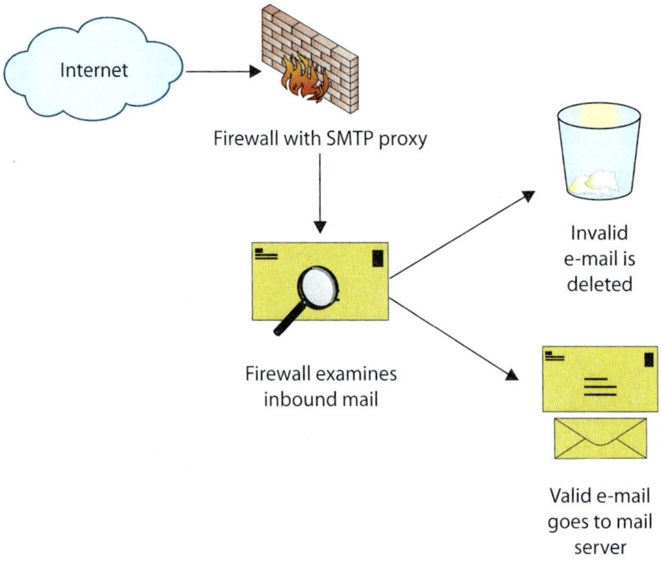

• **Figure 10.5** Firewall with SMTP application layer proxy

Tech Tip

Firewalls and Access Control Lists

Many firewalls read firewall and ACL rules from top to bottom and apply the rules in sequential order to the packets they are inspecting. Typically they will stop processing rules when they find a rule that matches the packet they are examining. If the first line in your rule set reads "allow all traffic," then the firewall will pass any network traffic coming into or leaving the firewall—ignoring the rest of your rules below that line. Many firewalls have an implied "deny all" line as part of their rule sets. This means that any traffic that is not specifically allowed by a rule will get blocked by default.

Many firewalls contain, by default, an *implicit deny* at the end of every ACL or firewall rule set. This simply means that any traffic not specifically permitted by a previous rule in the rule set is denied.

Tech Tip

Firewall Operations

Application layer firewalls such as proxy servers can analyze information in the header and data portion of the packet, whereas packet-filtering firewalls can analyze only the header of a packet.

Firewalls can act as flood guards, detecting and mitigating specific types of DoS/DDoS attacks.

Next-Generation Firewall (NGFW)

Firewalls operate by inspecting packets and by using rules associated with IP addresses and ports. A **next-generation firewall (NGFW)** has significantly more capability and is characterized by these features:

- Deep packet inspection
- A move beyond port/protocol inspection and blocking
- Added application-level inspection
- Added intrusion prevention
- Bringing intelligence from outside the firewall

A next-generation firewall is more than just a firewall and IDS coupled together; it offers a deeper look at what the network traffic represents. In a legacy firewall, with port 80 open, all web traffic is allowed to pass. Using a next-generation firewall, traffic over port 80 can be separated by website, or even activity on a website (for example, allow Facebook, but not games on Facebook). Because of the deeper packet inspection and the ability to create rules based on content, traffic can be managed based on content, not merely site or URL.

Firewall Placement

Firewalls at their base level are policy-enforcement engines that determine whether or not traffic can pass, based on a set of rules. Regardless of the type of firewall, the placement is easy—firewalls must be inline with the traffic they are regulating. If there are two paths for data to get to a server farm, then either the firewall must have both paths go through it or two firewalls are necessary. One place for firewalls is on the edge of the network—a perimeter defense. The challenge to this is simple: an enterprise network can have many different types of traffic, and trying to sort/filter at the edge is not efficient.

Firewalls are commonly placed between network segments, thereby examining traffic that enters or leaves a segment. This allows them the ability to isolate a segment while avoiding the cost or overhead of doing this on each and every system. A firewall placed directly in front of a set of database servers only has to manage database connections, not all the different traffic types found on the network as a whole. Firewalls are governed by the rules they enforce, and the more limited the traffic types, the simpler the rule set. Simple rule sets are harder to bypass; in the example of the database servers previously mentioned, there is no need for web traffic, so all web traffic can be excluded. This leads to easier-to-maintain and better security in these instances.

Web Application Firewalls (WAFs) vs. Network Firewalls

Increasingly, the term *firewall* is getting attached to any device or software package that is used to control the flow of packets or data into or out of an organization. For example, *web application firewall (WAF)* is the term given to any software package, appliance, or filter that applies a rule set to HTTP/HTTPS traffic. Web application firewalls shape web traffic and can be used to filter out SQL injection attacks, malware, cross-site scripting (XSS), and so on. By contrast, a *network firewall* is a hardware or software package that controls the flow of packets into and out of a network. Web application firewalls operate on traffic at a much higher level than network firewalls, as web application firewalls must be able to decode the web traffic to determine whether or not it is malicious. Network firewalls operate on much simpler aspects of network traffic such as source/destination port and source/destination address.

Open Source vs. Proprietary

Firewalls come in many forms and types, and one method of differentiating them is to separate them into *open source* and *proprietary* (commercial) solutions. Open source firewalls are exemplified by iptables, a built-in functionality in Linux systems. Iptables and other open source solutions have the cost advantage of being free, but the initial cost of a firewall solution is not the only factor. Ease of maintenance and rule management are the key drivers for long-term use, and many proprietary solutions have worked to increase the utility of their offerings through improving these interfaces.

One of the most common firewalls employed is Microsoft Windows Defender Firewall, a proprietary firewall built into the Windows OS.

Hardware vs. Software

Firewalls can be physical devices, hardware, or a set of software services running on a system. For use on a host, a software solution like Microsoft Windows Defender Firewall or iptables on a Linux host may well fit the bill. For use in an enterprise setting at a network level, with a need to separate different security zones, a dedicated hardware device is more efficient and economical.

Appliance vs. Host Based vs. Virtual

Firewalls can be located on a host, either as a separate application or part of the operating system itself. In software-defined networking (SDN) networks, firewalls can be instantiated as virtual network functions, providing all of the features under a virtual software solution. Firewalls can also be instantiated via an appliance, acting as a network segregation device, separating portions of a network based on firewall rules.

VPN Concentrator

Network devices called **concentrators** act as traffic-management devices, managing flows from multiple points into single streams. Concentrators typically act as endpoints for a particular protocol, such as SSL/TLS or VPN. The use of specialized hardware can enable hardware-based encryption and provide a higher level of specific service than a general-purpose server. This provides both architectural and functional efficiencies.

A virtual private network (VPN) is a construct used to provide a secure communication channel between users across public networks such as the Internet. A **VPN concentrator** is a special endpoint inside a network designed to accept multiple VPN connections and integrate these independent connections into the network in a scalable fashion. The most common implementation of VPN is via IPSec, a protocol for IP security. IPSec is mandated in IPv6 and is optional in IPv4. IPSec can be implemented in hardware, software, or a combination of both, and it's used to encrypt all IP traffic. In Chapter 11, a variety of techniques are described that can be employed to instantiate a VPN connection. The use of encryption technologies allows either the data in a packet to be encrypted or the entire packet to be encrypted. If the data is encrypted, the packet header can still be sniffed and observed between source and destination, but the encryption protects the contents of the packet from inspection. If the entire packet is encrypted, it is then placed into another packet and sent via a tunnel across the public network. Tunneling can protect even the identity of the communicating parties.

A VPN concentrator is a hardware device designed to act as a VPN endpoint, managing VPN connections to an enterprise.

A **VPN concentrator** takes multiple individual VPN connections and terminates them into a single network point. This single endpoint is what should define where the VPN concentrator is located in the network. The VPN side of the concentrator is typically outward facing, exposed to the Internet. The inward-facing side of the device should terminate in a network segment where you would allow all of the VPN users to connect their machines directly. If you have multiple different types of VPN users with different security profiles and different connection needs, then you might have multiple concentrators with different endpoints that correspond to appropriate locations inside the network.

To prevent unauthorized wireless access to the network, configuration of remote access protocols to a wireless access point is common. Forcing authentication and verifying authorization comprise a seamless method for performing basic network security for connections in this fashion. These access protocols are covered in Chapter 11.

Wireless Devices

Wireless devices bring additional security concerns. There is, by definition, no physical connection to a wireless device; radio waves or infrared carries the data, allowing anyone within range access to the data. This means that unless you take specific precautions, you have no control over who can see your data. Placing a wireless device behind a firewall does not do any good, because the firewall stops only physically connected traffic from reaching the device. Outside traffic can come literally from the parking lot directly to the wireless device and into the network.

The point of entry from a wireless device to a wired network is performed at a device called a **wireless access point (WAP)**. Wireless access points can support multiple concurrent devices accessing network resources through the network node they create. A typical wireless access point, a Google mesh Wi-Fi access point, is shown here.

Most PCs, laptops, and tablets sold today have built-in wireless, so the addition of wireless is not necessary. In most cases, these devices will determine the type of wireless that one employs in their home, because most people are not likely to update their devices just to use faster wireless as it becomes available.

Modems

Modems were once a slow method of remote connection that was used to connect client workstations to remote services over standard telephone lines. **Modem** is a shortened form of *modulator/demodulator,* converting analog signals to digital, and vice versa. Connecting a digital computer signal to the analog telephone line required one of these devices. Today, the use of the term has expanded to cover devices connected to special digital telephone lines (DSL modems), cable television lines (cable modems), and fiber modems. Although these devices are not actually modems in the true sense of the word, the term has stuck through marketing efforts directed at consumers. Fiber and cable modems offer broadband high-speed connections and the opportunity for continuous connections to the Internet. In most cases, residential connections are terminated with a provider device (modem) that converts the signal into both a wired connection via RJ-45 connections and wireless signal.

Cable modems were designed to share a party line in the terminal signal area, and the cable modem standard, Data Over Cable Service Interface Specification (DOCSIS), was designed to accommodate this concept. DOCSIS includes built-in support for security protocols, including authentication and packet filtering. Although this does not guarantee privacy, it prevents ordinary subscribers from seeing others' traffic without using specialized hardware.

• **Figure 10.6** Modern cable modem

Figure 10.6 shows a modern cable modem. It has an imbedded wireless access point, a Voice over IP (VoIP) connection, a local router, and a DHCP server. The size of the device is fairly large, but it has a built-in lead-acid battery to provide VoIP service when power is out.

> **Tech Tip**
>
> **Cable/Fiber Security**
>
> *The modem equipment provided by the subscription service converts the cable or fiber signal into a standard Ethernet signal that can then be connected to a NIC on the client device. This is still just a direct network connection, with no security device separating the two. The most common security device used in cable/fiber connections is a router that acts as a hardware firewall. With continuous connection to the Internet, changing the device password and other protections are still needed.*

Both cable and fiber services are designed for a continuous connection, which brings up the question of IP address life for a client. Although some services originally used a static IP arrangement, virtually all have now adopted the Dynamic Host Configuration Protocol (DHCP) to manage their address space. A static IP address has the advantage of remaining the same and enabling convenient DNS connections for outside users. Because cable and DSL services are primarily designed for client services, as opposed to host services, this is not a relevant issue. The security issue with a static IP address is that it is a stationary target for hackers. The move to DHCP has not significantly lessened this threat, however, because the typical IP lease on a cable modem DHCP server is for days. This is still relatively stationary, and some form of firewall protection needs to be employed by the user.

Telephony

A **private branch exchange (PBX)** is an extension of the public telephone network into a business. Although typically considered separate entities from data systems, PBXs are frequently interconnected and have security requirements as part of this interconnection, as well as security requirements of their own. PBXs are computer-based switching equipment designed to connect telephones into the local phone system. Basically digital switching systems, they can be compromised from the outside and used by phone hackers (known as *phreakers)* to make phone calls at the business's expense. Although this type of hacking has decreased as the cost of long-distance calling has decreased, it has not gone away, and as several firms learn every year, voicemail boxes and PBXs can be compromised and the long-distance bills can get very high, very fast.

Another problem with PBXs arises when they are interconnected to the data systems, either by corporate connection or by rogue modems in the hands of users. In either case, a path exists for connection to outside data networks and the Internet. Just as a firewall is needed for security on data connections, one is needed for these connections as well. Telecommunications firewalls are a distinct type of firewall designed to protect both the PBX and the data connections. The functionality of a telecommunications firewall is the same as that of a data firewall: it is there to enforce security policies. Telecommunication security policies can be enforced even to cover hours of phone use, to prevent unauthorized long-distance usage through the implementation of access codes and/or restricted service hours.

> **Tech Tip**
>
> **Coexisting Communications**
>
> *Data and voice communications have coexisted in enterprises for decades. Recent connections inside the enterprise of VoIP and traditional private branch exchange solutions increase both functionality and security risks. Specific firewalls to protect against unauthorized traffic over telephony connections are available to counter the increased risk.*

Intrusion Detection Systems

Intrusion detection systems (IDSs) are an important element of infrastructure security. IDSs are designed to detect, log, and respond to unauthorized network or host use, both in real time and after the fact. IDSs are available from a wide selection of vendors and are an essential part of a comprehensive network security program. These systems are implemented using software, but in large networks or systems with significant traffic levels, dedicated hardware is typically required as well. IDSs can be divided into two categories: network-based systems and host-based systems.

> **Cross Check**
>
> **Intrusion Detection**
>
> From a network infrastructure point of view, network-based IDSs can be considered part of infrastructure, whereas host-based IDSs are typically considered part of a comprehensive security program and not necessarily infrastructure. Two primary methods of detection are used: signature-based and anomaly-based. IDSs are covered in detail in Chapter 13.

Network Access Control

Networks comprise connected workstations and servers. Managing security on a network involves managing a wide range of issues, from various connected hardware and the software operating these devices. Assuming that the network is secure, each additional connection involves risk. Managing the endpoints on a case-by-case basis as they connect is a security methodology known as **network access control (NAC)**. NAC is built around the idea that the network should be able to enforce a specific level of endpoint security before it accepts a new connection. The initial vendors were Microsoft and Cisco, but NAC now has a myriad of vendors, with many different solutions providing different levels of "health" checks before allowing a device to join a network.

Agent and Agentless

In *agent*-based solutions, code is stored on the host machine for activation and use at time of connection. Having agents deployed to endpoints can provide very fine-grained levels of scrutiny to the security posture of the endpoint. In recognition that deploying agents to machines can be problematic in some instances, vendors have also developed agentless solutions for NAC. Rather than have the agent wait on the host for activation and use, the agent can operate from within the network itself, rendering the host in effect agentless. In *agentless* solutions, the code resides on the network and is deployed to memory for use in a machine requesting connections, but since it never persists on the host machine, it is referred to as agentless. In most instances, there is no real difference in the performance of agent versus agentless solutions when properly deployed. The real difference comes in the issues of having agents on boxes versus persistent network connections for agentless.

> NAC agents are installed on devices that connect to networks in order to produce secure network environments. With agentless NAC, the NAC code resides not on the connecting devices, but on the network, and it's deployed to memory for use in a machine requesting connection to the network.

Agentless NAC is often implemented in a Microsoft domain through an Active Directory (AD) controller. For example, NAC code verifies devices are in compliance with access policies when a domain is joined by a user or when they log in or log out. Agentless NAC is also often implemented through the use of intrusion prevention systems.

Network Monitoring/Diagnostic

> SNMP, the Simple Network Management Protocol, is a part of the Internet Protocol suite of protocols. It is an open standard, designed for transmission of management functions between devices. Do not confuse this with SMTP, the Simple Mail Transfer Protocol, which is used to transfer mail between machines.

A computer network itself can be considered a large computer system, with performance and operating issues. Just as a computer needs management, monitoring, and fault resolution, so too do networks. SNMP was developed to perform this function across networks. The idea is to enable a central monitoring and control center to maintain, configure, and repair network devices, such as switches and routers, as well as other network services, such as firewalls, IDSs, and remote access servers. SNMP has some security limitations, and many vendors have developed software solutions that sit on top of SNMP to provide better security and better management tool suites.

The concept of a **network operations center (NOC)** comes from the old phone company network days, when central monitoring centers supervised the health of the telephone network and provided interfaces for maintenance and management. This same concept works well with computer networks, and companies with midsize and larger networks employ the same philosophy. The NOC allows operators to observe and interact with the network, using the self-reporting and, in some cases, self-healing nature of network devices to ensure efficient network operation. Although generally a boring operation under normal conditions, when things start to go wrong, as in the case of a virus or worm attack, the NOC can become a busy and stressful place, as operators attempt to return the system to full efficiency while not interrupting existing traffic.

Because networks can be spread out literally around the world, it is not feasible to have a person visit each device for control functions.

Software enables controllers at NOCs to measure the actual performance of network devices and make changes to the configuration and operation of devices remotely. The ability to make remote connections with this level of functionality is both a blessing and a security issue. Although this allows for efficient network operations management, it also provides an opportunity for unauthorized entry into a network. For this reason, a variety of security controls are used, from secondary networks to VPNs and advanced authentication methods with respect to network control connections.

Network monitoring is an ongoing concern for any significant network. In addition to monitoring traffic flow and efficiency, monitoring of security-related events is necessary. IDSs act merely as alarms, indicating the possibility of a breach associated with a specific set of activities. These indications still need to be investigated and an appropriate response needs to be initiated by security personnel. Simple items such as port scans may be ignored by policy, but an actual unauthorized entry into a network router, for instance, would require NOC personnel to take specific actions to limit the potential damage to the system. In any significant network, coordinating system changes, dynamic network traffic levels, potential security incidents, and maintenance activities are daunting tasks requiring numerous personnel working together. Software has been developed to help manage the information flow required to support these tasks. Such software can enable remote administration of devices in a standard fashion so that the control systems can be devised in a hardware vendor–neutral configuration.

SNMP is the main standard embraced by vendors to permit interoperability. Although SNMP has received a lot of security-related attention of late due to various security holes in its implementation, it is still an important part of a security solution associated with network infrastructure. Many useful tools have security issues; the key is to understand the limitations and to use the tools within correct boundaries to limit the risk associated with the vulnerabilities. Blind use of any technology will result in increased risk, and SNMP is no exception. Proper planning, setup, and deployment can limit exposure to vulnerabilities. Continuous auditing and maintenance of systems with the latest patches is a necessary part of operations and is essential to maintaining a secure posture.

> **Tech Tip**
>
> **Virtual IPs**
>
> *In a load-balanced environment, the IP addresses for the target servers of a load balancer will not necessarily match the address associated with the router sending the traffic. Load balancers handle this through the concept of virtual IP addresses, or* virtual IPs, *which allow for multiple systems to be reflected back as a single IP address.*

Out-of-Band Management

Management of a system across the network can be either in-band or out-of-band. In in-band management systems, the management channel is the same channel as the data channel. This has an advantage in physical connection simplicity and a disadvantage that if a problem occurs due to data flows, the management commands may not be able to access the device. For important network devices and services, an out-of-band management channel is recommended. *Out-of-band management* channels are physically separate connections, via separate interfaces that permit the active management of a device even when the data channel is blocked for some reason.

Load Balancers

Certain systems, such as servers, are more critical to business operations and should therefore be the object of fault-tolerance measures. A common technique that is used in fault tolerance is load balancing through the use of a load balancer. **Load balancing** involves the use of devices that move loads across a set of resources in an effort not to overload individual servers. This technique is designed to distribute the processing load over two or more systems. It is used to help improve resource utilization and throughput but also has the added advantage of increasing the fault tolerance of the overall system since a critical process may be split across several systems. Should any one system fail, the others can pick up the processing it was handling. While there may be an impact to overall throughput, the operation does not go down entirely. Load balancing is often utilized for systems handling websites, high-bandwidth file transfers, and large Internet Relay Chat (IRC) networks. Load balancing works by a series of health checks that tell the load balancer which machines are operating and by a scheduling mechanism to spread the work evenly. Load balancing is best for stateless systems, as subsequent requests can be handled by any server, not just the one that processed the previous request.

Load balancers take incoming traffic from one network location and distribute it across multiple network operations. A load balancer must reside in the traffic path between the requestors of a service and the servers that are providing the service. The role of the load balancer is to manage the workloads on multiple systems by distributing the traffic to and from them. To do this, it must be located within the traffic pathway. For reasons of efficiency, load balancers are typically located close to the systems for which they are managing the traffic.

Scheduling

When a load balancer moves loads across a set of resources, it decides which machine gets a request via a *scheduling* algorithm. There are a couple of commonly used scheduling algorithms: affinity-based scheduling and round-robin scheduling.

Affinity

Affinity-based scheduling is designed to keep a host connected to the same server across a session. Some applications, such as web applications, can benefit from affinity-based scheduling. The method used by affinity-based scheduling is to have the load balancer keep track of where it last balanced a particular session and direct all continuing session traffic to the same server. If it is a new connection, the load balancer establishes a new affinity entry and assigns the session to the next server in the available rotation.

Round-Robin

Round-robin and weighted round-robin are scheduling algorithms used for load-balancing strategies.

Round-robin scheduling involves sending each new request to the next server in rotation. All requests are sent to servers in equal amounts, regardless of the server load. Round-robin schemes are frequently modified with a weighting factor, known as weighted round-robin, to take the server load or other criteria into account when assigning the next server.

Active/Active

In an *active/active* scheme, all the load balancers are active, sharing the load-balancing duties. Active/active load balancing can have performance efficiencies, but it is important to watch the overall load. If the overall load cannot be covered by $N - 1$ load balancers (that is, one fails), then the failure of a load balancer will lead to session interruption and traffic loss. Without a standby passive system to recover the lost load, the system will trim the load based on capacity, dropping requests that the system lacks capacity to service.

> Two or more servers work together to distribute the load in an active/active load-balancing configuration. If a server fails, service interruption or traffic loss may result.

Active/Passive

For high-availability solutions, having a single load balancer creates a single point of failure (SPOF). It is common to have multiple load balancers involved in the balancing work. In an *active/passive* scheme, the primary load balancer is actively doing the balancing while the secondary load balancer passively observes and is ready to step in any time the primary system fails.

> All traffic is sent to the active server in an active/passive configuration. If the active server fails, the passive server is promoted to active.

Virtual IP

In a load-balanced environment, the IP addresses for the target servers of a load balancer will not necessarily match the address associated with the router sending the traffic. Load balancers handle this through the concept of virtual IP addresses, or *virtual IPs*, which allow for multiple systems to be reflected back as a single IP address.

Persistence

Persistence is the condition where a system connects to the same target in a load-balanced system. This can be important for maintaining state and integrity of multiple round-trip events. Persistence is achieved through affinity-based scheduling of server assets in load balancing. This is discussed in a section a few sections earlier in this chapter.

Proxies

Proxies serve to manage connections between systems, acting as relays for the traffic. Proxies can function at the circuit level, where they support multiple traffic types, or they can be application-level proxies, which are designed to relay specific application traffic. An HTTP/HTTPS proxy can manage an HTTP/HTTPS conversation, as it understands the type and function of the content. Application-specific proxies can serve as security devices if they are programmed with specific rules designed to provide protection against undesired content.

Though not strictly a security tool, a **proxy server** (or simply *proxy*) can be used to filter out undesirable traffic and prevent employees from accessing potentially hostile websites. A proxy server takes requests from a client system and forwards them to the destination server on behalf of the client, as shown in Figure 10.7. Proxy servers can be completely transparent (these are usually called *gateways* or *tunneling proxies*), or a proxy server can modify the client request before sending it on, or

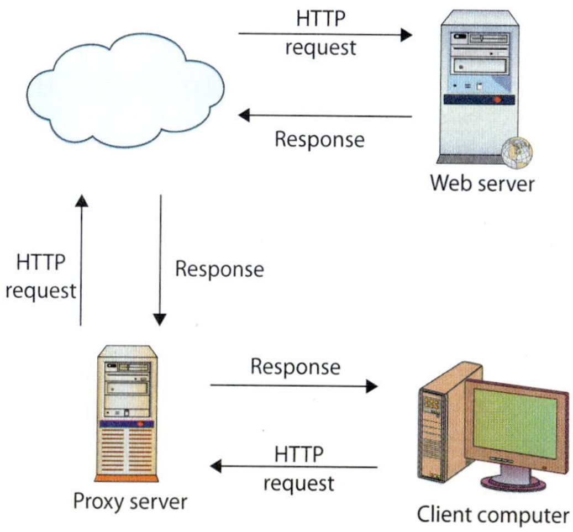

• **Figure 10.7** HTTP proxy handling client requests and web server responses

even serve the client's request without needing to contact the destination server. Several major categories of proxy servers are in use:

- **Anonymizing proxy** An anonymizing proxy is designed to hide information about the requesting system and make a user's web browsing experience "anonymous." This type of proxy service is often used by individuals who are concerned about the amount of personal information being transferred across the Internet and the use of tracking cookies and other mechanisms to track browsing activity.
- **Caching proxy** This type of proxy keeps local copies of popular client requests and is often used in large organizations to reduce bandwidth usage and increase performance. When a request is made, the proxy server first checks to see whether it has a current copy of the requested content in the cache; if it does, it services the client request immediately without having to contact the destination server. If the content is old or the caching proxy does not have a copy of the requested content, the request is forwarded to the destination server.
- **Content-filtering proxy** Content-filtering proxies examine each client request and compare it to an established acceptable use policy (AUP). Requests can usually be filtered in a variety of ways, including by the requested URL, destination system, or domain name or by keywords in the content itself. Content-filtering proxies typically support user-level authentication, so access can be controlled and monitored and activity through the proxy can be logged and analyzed. This type of proxy is very popular in schools, corporate environments, and government networks.
- **Open proxy** An open proxy is essentially a proxy that is available to any Internet user and often has some anonymizing capabilities as well. This type of proxy has been the subject of some controversy, with advocates for Internet privacy and freedom on one side of the argument, and law enforcement, corporations, and government entities on the other side. As open proxies are often used to circumvent corporate proxies, many corporations attempt to block the use of open proxies by their employees.
- **Reverse proxy** A reverse proxy is typically installed on the server side of a network connection, often in front of a group of web servers. The reverse proxy intercepts all incoming web requests and can perform a number of functions, including traffic filtering and shaping, TLS decryption, serving of common static content such as graphics, and load balancing.
- **Forward proxy** A forward proxy operates to forward requests to servers based on a variety of parameters, as described in the other portions of this section. Forward proxies can be used to bypass firewall restrictions, act as a cache server, and change your IP address (more useful before widespread adoption of NAT). Forward proxies can be deployed by attackers to get users to use them for "caching purposes" under the guise of speeding up connections,

when, in fact, they actually slow down the connection and create a man-in-the-middle attack scenario.

- **Web proxy** A web proxy is solely designed to handle web traffic and is sometimes called a *web cache*. Most web proxies are essentially specialized caching proxies.

A *proxy server* is a system or application that acts as a go-between for clients' requests for network services. The client tells the proxy server what it wants and, if the client is authorized to have it, the proxy server connects to the appropriate network service and gets the client what it asked for. Web proxies are the most commonly deployed type of proxy server.

Deploying a proxy solution within a network environment is usually done either by setting up the proxy and requiring all client systems to configure their browsers to use the proxy or by deploying an intercepting proxy that actively intercepts all requests without requiring client-side configuration. As proxies are servers that act as a go-between for clients and other systems, they are designed to act on a client's behalf. This means that the proxies must be in the normal path of network traffic for the system being proxied. As networks become segregated, the proxy placement must be such that it is in the natural flow of the routed traffic for it to intervene on the client's behalf.

From a security perspective, proxies are most useful in their ability to control and filter outbound requests. By limiting the types of content and websites employees can access from corporate systems, many administrators hope to avoid loss of corporate data, hijacked systems, and infections from malicious websites. Administrators also use proxies to enforce corporate AUPs and track the use of corporate resources. Most proxies can be configured to either allow or require individual user authentication—this gives them the ability to log and control activity based on specific users or groups. For example, an organization might want to allow the human resources group to browse Facebook during business hours but not allow the rest of the organization to do so.

Web Security Gateways

Some security vendors combine proxy functions with content-filtering functions to create a product called a **web security gateway**. Web security gateways are intended to address the security threats and pitfalls unique to web-based traffic. Web security gateways typically provide the following capabilities:

- **Real-time malware protection (a.k.a. malware inspection)** The ability to scan all outgoing and incoming web traffic to detect and block undesirable traffic such as malware, spyware, adware, malicious scripts, file-based attacks, and so on
- **Content monitoring** The ability to monitor the content of web traffic being examined to ensure that it complies with organizational policies
- **Productivity monitoring** The ability to measure the types and quantities of web traffic being generated by specific users, groups of users, or the entire organization
- **Data protection and compliance** Scanning web traffic for sensitive or proprietary information being sent outside of the organization as well as the use of social network sites or inappropriate sites

Internet Content Filters

With the dramatic proliferation of Internet traffic and the push to provide Internet access to every desktop, many corporations have implemented content-filtering systems, called **Internet content filters**, to protect them from employees' viewing of inappropriate or illegal content at the workplace and the subsequent complications that occur when such viewing takes place. Internet content filtering is also popular in schools, libraries, homes, government offices, and any other environment where there is a need to limit or restrict access to undesirable content. In addition to filtering undesirable content, such as pornography, some content filters can also filter out malicious activity such as browser hijacking attempts or cross-site scripting (XSS) attacks. In many cases, content filtering is performed with or as a part of a proxy solution, as the content requests can be filtered and serviced by the same device. Content can be filtered in a variety of ways, including via the requested URL, the destination system, the domain name, by keywords in the content itself, and by type of file requested.

The term *Internet content filter,* or just *content filter,* is applied to any device, application, or software package that examines network traffic (especially web traffic) for undesirable or restricted content. A content filter could be a software package loaded on a specific PC or a network appliance capable of filtering an entire organization's web traffic.

Content-filtering systems face many challenges, because the ever-changing Internet makes it difficult to maintain lists of undesirable sites (sometimes called block lists/deny lists or black lists); for example, terms used on a medical site can also be used on a pornographic site, making keyword filtering challenging, and determined users are always seeking ways to bypass proxy filters. To help administrators, most commercial content-filtering solutions provide an update service, much like IDS or antivirus products, that updates keywords and undesirable sites automatically.

Data Loss Prevention

Data loss prevention (DLP) refers to technology employed to detect and prevent transfers of data across an enterprise. Employed at key locations, DLP technology can scan packets for specific data patterns. This technology can be tuned to detect account numbers, secrets, specific markers, or files. When specific data elements are detected, the system can block the transfer. The primary challenge in employing DLP technologies is the placement of the sensor. The DLP sensor needs to be able to observe the data, so if the channel is encrypted, DLP technology can be thwarted.

Unified Threat Management

Many security vendors offer "all-in-one security appliances," which are devices that combine multiple functions into the same hardware appliance. Most commonly these functions are firewall, IDS/IPS, and antivirus/anti-malware, although all-in-one appliances can include VPN capabilities, anti-spam, malicious web traffic filtering, anti-spyware, content filtering, traffic shaping, and so on. All-in-one appliances are often sold as being cheaper, easier to manage, and more efficient than having separate solutions that accomplish each of the functions the all-in-one appliance is capable of performing. A common name for these all-in-one appliances is **unified threat management (UTM)** appliance. Using a UTM solution simplifies the security activity as a single task, under a common software package

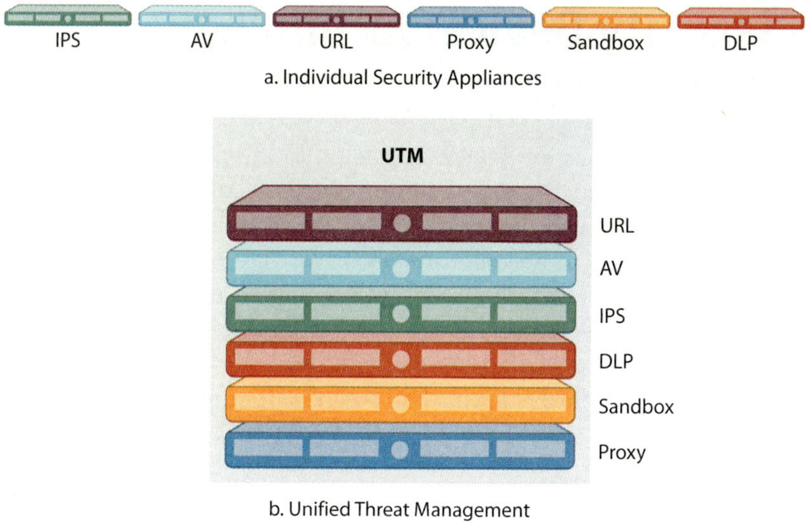

• **Figure 10.8** Unified threat management architecture

for operations. This reduces the learning curve to a single tool rather than a collection of tools. A UTM solution can have better integration and efficiencies in handling network traffic and incidents than a collection of tools connected together.

Figure 10.8 illustrates the advantages of UTM processing. Rather than processing elements in a linear fashion, as shown in 10.8a, the packets are processed in a parallelized fashion, as shown in 10.8b. There is a need to coordinate between the elements, and many modern solutions do this with parallelized hardware.

URL Filtering

URL filters block connections to websites that are in a prohibited list. The use of a UTM appliance, typically backed by a service to keep the list of prohibited websites updated, provides an automated means to block access to sites deemed dangerous or inappropriate. Because of the highly volatile nature of web content, automated enterprise-level protection is needed to ensure a reasonable chance of blocking sources of inappropriate content, malware, and other malicious content.

Content Inspection

Instead of just relying on a URL to determine the acceptability of content, UTM appliances can also inspect the actual content being served. Content inspection is used to filter web requests that return content with specific components, such as names of body parts, music or video content, and other content that is inappropriate for the business environment.

Malware Inspection

Malware is another item that can be detected during network transmission, and UTM appliances can be tuned to detect malware. Network-based malware detection has the advantage of having to update only a single system, as opposed to all machines.

Security Device/Technology Placement

The placement of security devices is related to the purpose of the device and the environment that it requires. Technology placement has similar restrictions; these devices must be in the flow of the network traffic that they use to function. If an enterprise has two Internet connections, with half of the servers going through one and the other half through the other, then at least two of each technology to be deployed between the Internet and the enterprise are needed. As you will see, with different devices, the placement needs are fairly specific and essential for the devices to function.

Sensors

Sensors are devices that capture data and act upon it. There are multiple kinds and placements of sensors. Each type is different, and no single type of sensor can do everything. Sensors can be divided into two types based on placement location: network and host. Network-based sensors can provide coverage but are limited by traffic engineering; they may have issues with encrypted traffic and have limited knowledge of what hosts are doing. Host-based sensors provide more specific and accurate information in relation to what the host machine is seeing and doing, but they are limited to just that host.

Sensors have several different actions they can take: they can report on what is observed, they can use multiple readings to match a pattern and create an event, and they can act based on prescribed rules. Not all sensors can take all actions, and the application of specific sensors is part of a monitoring and control deployment strategy. This deployment must consider network traffic engineering, the scope of action, and other limitations.

Collectors

Collectors are sensors that collect data for processing by other systems. Collectors are subject to the same placement rules and limitations as sensors.

TAPs and Port Mirror

Most enterprise switches have the ability to copy the activity of one or more ports through a Switch Port Analyzer (SPAN) port, also known as a *port mirror*. This traffic can then be sent to a device for analysis. Port mirrors can have issues when traffic levels get heavy because they can exceed the throughput of the device. A 16-port switch, with each port running at 100 Mbps, can have traffic levels of 1.6 GB if all circuits are maxed. With this example, it is easy to see why this technology can have issues in high-traffic environments.

A *TAP* (or *test access point*) is a passive signal-copying mechanism installed between two points on the network. The TAP can copy all packets they receive, rebuilding a copy of all messages. TAPs provide the one distinct advantage of not being overwhelmed by traffic levels, at least not in the process of data collection. The primary disadvantage is that it is a separate piece of hardware and adds to network costs.

Monitoring Services

Network security monitoring (NSM) is the process of collecting and analyzing network data to detect unauthorized activity. NSM is not a way to prevent intrusions, but when deployed inside a network, it can detect where other defenses have failed. It is like having a local security guard patrolling inside a closed building. NSM can be deployed as a service, and many firms have an offering to support monitoring services that give an enterprise a means of detecting unauthorized activity. Having defenses is important but watching to see when those defenses are failing is the purpose of NSM and monitoring services.

For any of the preceding devices to work, it must be situated into the traffic flow that it is intended to interact with. If there are network paths around the device, it will not perform as designed. Understanding the network architecture is important when you're placing devices.

Correlation Engines

Correlation engines take sets of data and match the patterns against known patterns. Should incoming data match one of the stored profiles, the engine can alert or take other actions. Correlation engines are limited by the strength of the match when you factor in time and other variants that create challenges in a busy traffic environment. The placement of correlation engines is subject to the same issues as all other network placements: the traffic you desire to study must pass the sensor feeding the engine. If the traffic is routed around the sensor, the engine will fail.

Filters

Packet *filters* use the process of passing or blocking packets at a network interface based on source and destination addresses, ports, or protocols. Packet filtering is often part of a firewall program for protecting a local network from unwanted traffic, and it's the most basic form of allowing or denying traffic into or out of a network. The filters are local to the traffic being passed, so they must be inline with a system's connection to the network and Internet; otherwise, they will not be able to see traffic to act upon it.

SSL Accelerators

An *SSL accelerator* is used to provide SSL/TLS encryption/decryption at scale, removing the load from web servers. Because of this, it needs to be between the appropriate web servers and the clients they serve (typically Internet facing).

DDoS Mitigator

DDoS mitigators must by nature exist outside the area they are protecting. They act as an umbrella, shielding away the unwanted DDoS packets. As with all of the devices in this section, the DDoS mitigator must reside in the network path of the traffic it is shielding the inner part of the networks from. Because the purpose of the DDoS mitigator is to stop unwanted DDoS traffic, it should be positioned at the very edge of the network, before other devices.

Aggregation Switches

An *aggregation switch* is just a switch that provides connectivity for several other switches. Think of a one-to-many type of device. It's the one switch that many other switches will be connecting to. This also demonstrates where it is placed—it is upstream from the multitudes of devices and takes the place of a router or a much larger switch. Assume you have ten users on each of three floors. You can place a 16-port switch on each floor and then consume three router ports. Now make that ten floors of ten users, and you are now consuming ten ports on your router for the ten floors. An aggregate switch will reduce this to one connection, while providing faster switching between users than the router would. These traffic-management devices are located based on network layout topologies to limit unnecessary router usage.

Tunneling/VPN

Tunneling is a method of packaging packets so that they can traverse a network in a secure, confidential manner. Tunneling involves encapsulating packets within packets, enabling dissimilar protocols to coexist in a single communication stream, as in IP traffic routed over an Asynchronous Transfer Mode (ATM) network. Tunneling also can provide significant measures of security and confidentiality through encryption and encapsulation methods.

Tunneling can also be used for *virtual private network (VPN)* deployment. VPN is technology used to allow two networks to connect securely across an insecure stretch of network. These technologies are achieved with protocols discussed in multiple chapters throughout this book. At this level, understand that these technologies enable two sites, or a worker at a home site, to communicate across unsecure networks, including the Internet, at a much lower risk profile. The two main uses for tunneling/VPN technologies are site-to-site communications and remote access to a network.

The best example of this is a VPN that is established over a public network through the use of a tunnel, as shown in Figure 10.9, connecting a firm's Boston office to its New York City (NYC) office.

Assume, for example, that a company has multiple locations and decides to use the public Internet to connect the networks at these locations. To make these connections secure from outside unauthorized use, the company can employ a VPN connection between the different networks. On each network, an edge device, usually a router or VPN concentrator, connects to another edge device on the other network. Then, using IPSec

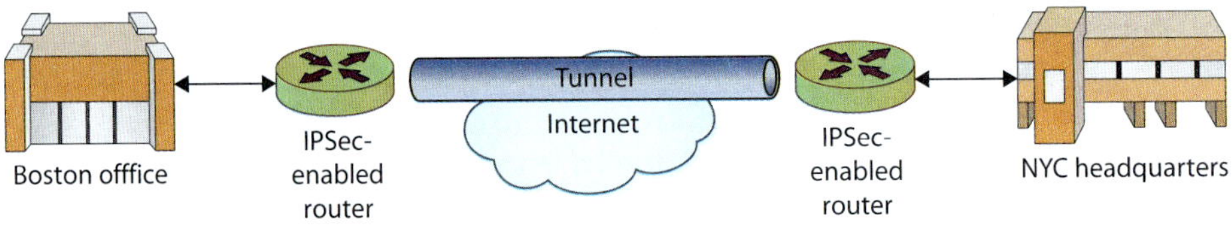

• **Figure 10.9** Tunneling across a public network

protocols, these routers establish a secure, encrypted path between them. This securely encrypted set of packets cannot be read by outside routers; only the addresses of the edge routers are visible. This arrangement acts as a tunnel across the public Internet and establishes a private connection, secure from outside snooping or use.

Because of ease of use, low-cost hardware, and strong security, tunnels and the Internet are a combination that will see more use in the future. IPSec, VPN, and tunnels will become a major set of tools for users requiring secure network connections across public segments of networks. The complete story of an IPSec VPN is more complex, as it uses L2TP to actually create and manage the tunnel; for more information on VPNs and remote access, refer to Chapter 11.

A *VPN concentrator* is a specialized piece of hardware designed to handle the encryption and decryption required for remote, secure access to an organization's network.

Site-to-Site

Site-to-site communication links are network connections that link two or more networks across an intermediary network layer. In almost all cases, this intermediary network is the Internet or some other public network. To secure the traffic that is going from site to site, encryption in the form of either a VPN or a tunnel can be employed. In essence, this makes all of the packets between the endpoints in the two networks unreadable to nodes between the two sites.

Remote Access

Remote access is when a user requires access to a network and its resources but is not able to make a physical connection. Remote access via a tunnel or VPN has the same effect as directly connecting the remote system to the network you are connecting to; it's as if you just plugged a network cable directly into your machine. So, if you do not trust a machine to be directly connected to your network, you should not use a VPN or tunnel, because if you do, that is what you are logically doing.

Storage Area Networks

Storage area networks (SANs) are systems that provide remote storage of data across a network connection. The design of SAN protocols is such that the disk appears to actually be on the client machine as a local drive rather than as attached storage, as in network-attached storage (NAS). This makes the disk visible in disk- and volume-management utilities and enables their functionality. Common SAN protocols include iSCSI and Fibre Channel.

iSCSI

The Internet Small Computer System Interface (iSCSI) is a protocol for IP-based storage. iSCSI can be used to send data over existing network infrastructures, enabling SANs. Positioned as a low-cost alternative to Fibre Channel storage, the only real limitation is one of network bandwidth.

Fibre Channel

Fibre Channel (FC) is a high-speed network technology (with throughput up to 16 Gbps) used to connect storage to computer systems. The FC protocol is a transport protocol similar to the TCP protocol in IP networks. Because it is carried via special cables, one of the drawbacks of FC-based storage is cost.

FCoE

The Fibre Channel over Ethernet (FCoE) protocol encapsulates the FC frames, enabling FC communication over 10-Gigabit Ethernet networks.

Media

The base of communications between devices is the physical layer of the OSI model. This is the domain of the actual connection between devices, whether by wire, fiber, or radio frequency waves. The physical layer separates the definitions and protocols required to transmit the signal physically between boxes from higher-level protocols that deal with the details of the data itself. Four common methods are used to connect equipment at the physical layer:

- Coaxial cable
- Twisted-pair cable
- Fiber optics
- Wireless

Coaxial Cable

Coaxial cable is familiar to many households as a method of connecting televisions to VCRs or to satellite or cable services. It is used because of its high bandwidth and shielding capabilities. Compared to standard twisted-pair lines such as telephone lines, **coaxial cable** (commonly known as *coax*) is much less prone to outside interference. It is also much more expensive to run, both from a cost-per-foot measure and from a cable-dimension measure. Coax costs much more per foot than standard twisted-pair wires and carries only a single circuit for a large wire diameter.

An original design specification for Ethernet connections, coax was used from machine to machine in early Ethernet implementations. The connectors were easy to use and ensured good connections, and the limited distance of most office LANs did not carry a large cost penalty. Today, almost all of this older Ethernet specification has been replaced by faster, cheaper twisted-pair alternatives, and the only place you're likely to see coax in a data network is from the cable box to the cable modem.

Because of its physical nature, it is possible to drill a hole through the outer part of a coax cable and connect to the center connector. This is called a "vampire tap" and is an easy method to get access to the signal and data being transmitted.

UTP/STP

Twisted-pair wires have all but completely replaced coaxial cables in Ethernet networks. Twisted-pair wires use the same technology used by the phone company for the movement of electrical signals. Single pairs of twisted wires reduce electrical crosstalk and electromagnetic interference. Multiple groups of twisted pairs can then be bundled together in common groups and easily wired between devices.

Twisted pairs come in two types: shielded and unshielded. **Shielded twisted-pair (STP)** has a foil shield around the pairs to provide extra shielding from electromagnetic interference. **Unshielded twisted-pair (UTP)** relies on the twist to eliminate interference. UTP has a cost advantage over STP and is usually sufficient for connections, except in very noisy electrical areas.

Twisted-pair lines are categorized by the level of data transmission they can support. Four categories are currently in use:

- **Category 3 (Cat 3)** Minimum for voice and 10Mbps Ethernet.
- **Category 5 (Cat 5/Cat 5e)** For 100Mbps Fast Ethernet. Cat 5e is an enhanced version of the Cat 5 specification to address far-end crosstalk and is suitable for 1000 Mbps.
- **Category 6 (Cat 6/Cat 6a)** For 10-Gigabit Ethernet over short distances. Cat 6a is used for longer (up to 100m) 10Gbps cables.
- **Category 7 (Cat 7)** For 10-Gigabit Ethernet and higher. Cat 7 has been used for 100 GB up to 15 meters.
- **Category 8 (Cat 8)** For 40Gbps up to 30-meter runs. When 10 Gbps is used, a 100-meter run is permissible.

A comparison of the different cables is shown next. Note that UTP is unshielded twisted pair, STP is shielded twisted pair, and S/FTP is shielded/foil twisted pair.

	Cat 3	Cat 5	Cat 5e	Cat 6	Cat 6a	Cat 7	Cat 8
Cable Type	UTP	UTP	UTP	UTP or STP	STP	S/FTP	S/FTP
Speed	10 Mbps	10/100/ 1000 Mbps	10/100/ 1000 Mbps	10/100/ 1000 Mbps	10 Gbps	10+ Gbps	40 Gbps
Bandwidth	16 MHz	100 MHz	100 MHz	250 MHz	500 MHz	600 MHz	2000 MHz

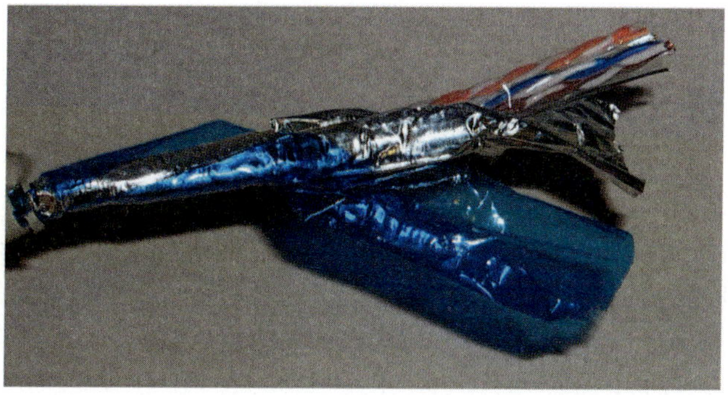

The standard method for connecting twisted-pair cables is via an 8-pin connector, called an RJ-45 connector, which looks like a standard phone jack connector but is slightly larger. One nice aspect of twisted-pair cabling is that it's easy to splice and change connectors. Many a network administrator has made Ethernet cables from stock Cat-6 wire, two connectors, and a crimping tool. This ease of connection is also a security issue; because twisted-pair cables are easy to splice into, rogue connections for sniffing could be made without detection in cable runs. Both coax and fiber are much more difficult to splice because each requires a tap to connect, and taps are easier to detect. With higher levels of speed and shielded connections (Cat 7 and 8), homemade cables are nearly impossible to make, as the terminations have to be done precisely to operate at GHz speeds.

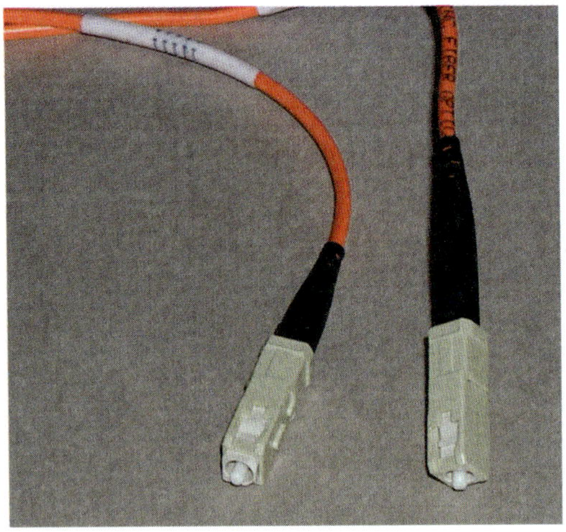

Fiber

Fiber-optic cable uses beams of laser light to connect devices over a thin glass wire. The biggest advantage to fiber is its bandwidth, with transmission capabilities into the terabits per second range. Fiber-optic cable is used to make high-speed connections between servers and is the backbone medium of the Internet and large networks. For all of its speed and bandwidth advantages, fiber has one major drawback—cost.

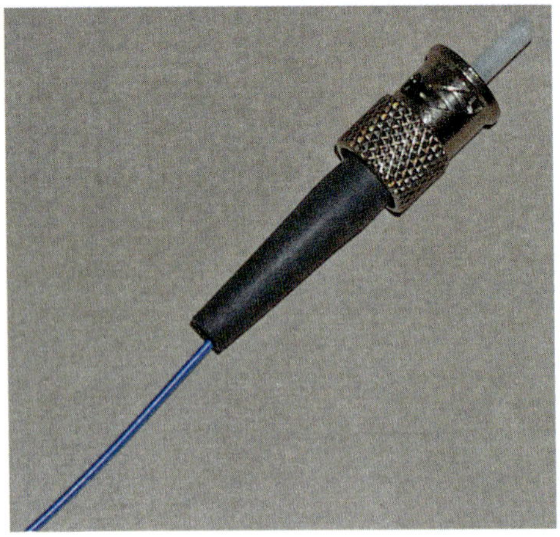

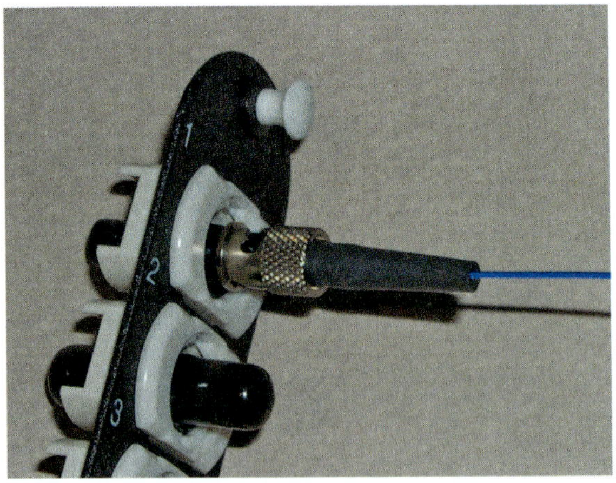

The cost of using fiber is a two-edged sword. When measured by bandwidth, using fiber is cheaper than using competing wired technologies. The length of runs of fiber can be much longer, and the data capacity of fiber is much higher. However, making a connection to fiber is difficult and expensive, and fiber is impossible to splice. Making the precise connection on the end of a fiber-optic line is a highly skilled job and is done by specially trained professionals who maintain a level of proficiency. Once the connector is fitted on the end, several forms of connectors and blocks are used, as shown in the preceding images.

Splicing fiber is practically impossible; the solution is to add connectors and connect through a repeater. This adds to the security of fiber in that unauthorized connections are all but impossible to make. The high cost of connections to fiber and the higher cost of fiber per foot also make it less attractive for the final mile in public networks where users are connected to the public switching systems. For this reason, cable companies use coax and DSL providers use twisted-pair to handle the "last mile" scenario. Although fiber is used to reach the customer location, a modem is used to convert the fiber connection to traditional RJ-45 and wireless methods of networking.

Unguided Media

Electromagnetic waves have been transmitted to convey signals literally since the inception of radio. *Unguided media* is a term used to cover all transmission media not guided by wire, fiber, or other constraints; it includes radio frequency, infrared, and microwave methods. All types of unguided media have one attribute in common: because they are unguided, they can travel to many machines simultaneously. Transmission patterns can be modulated by antennas, but the target machine can be one of many in a reception zone. As such, security principles are even more critical, as they must assume that unauthorized users have access to the signal.

Infrared

Infrared (IR) is a band of electromagnetic energy just beyond the red end of the visible color spectrum. IR has been used in remote-control devices for years. IR made its debut in computer networking as a wireless method to connect to printers. Now that wireless keyboards, wireless mice, and mobile devices exchange data via IR, it seems to be everywhere. IR can also be used to connect devices in a network configuration, but it is slow compared to other wireless technologies. IR cannot penetrate walls but instead bounces off them. Nor can it penetrate other solid objects; therefore, if you stack a few items in front of the transceiver, the signal is lost.

RF/Microwave

The use of radio frequency (RF) waves to carry communication signals goes back to the beginning of the 20th century. RF waves are a common method of communicating in a wireless world. They use a variety of frequency bands, each with special characteristics. The term *microwave* is used to describe a specific portion of the RF spectrum that is used for communication and other tasks, such as cooking.

Point-to-point microwave links have been installed by many network providers to carry communications over long distances and rough terrain. Many different frequencies are used in the microwave bands for many different purposes. Today, home users can use wireless networking throughout their house and enable laptops to surf the Web while they're moved around the house. Corporate users are experiencing the same phenomenon, with wireless networking enabling corporate users to check e-mail on laptops while riding a shuttle bus on a business campus. These wireless solutions are covered in detail in Chapter 12.

Tech Tip

Wireless Options

There are numerous radio-based alternatives for carrying network traffic. They vary in capacity, distance, and other features. Commonly found examples are Wi-Fi, WiMAX, Zigbee, Bluetooth, 900 MHz, and NFC. Understanding the security requirements associated with each is important and is covered in more detail in Chapter 12.

One key feature of microwave communications is that microwave RF energy can penetrate reasonable amounts of building structure. This allows you to connect network devices in separate rooms, and it can remove the constraints on equipment location imposed by fixed wiring. Another key feature is broadcast capability. By its nature, RF energy is unguided and can be received by multiple users simultaneously. Microwaves allow multiple users access in a limited area, and microwave systems are seeing application as the last mile of the Internet in dense metropolitan areas. Point-to-multipoint microwave devices can deliver data communication to all the business users in a downtown metropolitan area through rooftop antennas, reducing the need for expensive building-to-building cables. Just as microwaves carry cell phone and other data communications, the same technologies offer a method to bridge the "last mile" problem.

The "last mile" problem is the connection of individual consumers to a backbone, an expensive proposition because of the sheer number of connections and unshared line at this point in a network. Again, cost is an issue, as transceiver equipment is expensive, but in densely populated areas, such as apartments and office buildings in metropolitan areas, the user density can help defray individual costs. Speed on commercial microwave links can exceed 10 Gbps, so speed is not a problem for connecting multiple users or for high-bandwidth applications.

Removable Media

One concept common to all computer users is data storage. Sometimes storage occurs on a file server and sometimes it occurs on movable media, which can then be transported between machines. Moving storage media represents a security risk from a couple of angles—the first being the potential loss of control over the data on the moving media. Second is the risk of introducing unwanted items, such as a virus or a worm, when the media is attached back to a network. Both of these issues can be remedied through policies and software. The key is to ensure that the policies are enforced and the software is effective. To describe media-specific issues, media can be divided into three categories: magnetic, optical, and electronic.

Removable and transportable media make the physical security of the data a more difficult task. The only solution to this problem is encryption, which is covered in Chapter 5.

Magnetic Media

Magnetic media stores data through the rearrangement of magnetic particles on a nonmagnetic substrate. Common forms included hard drives, floppy disks, zip disks, and magnetic tape. Although the specific format can differ, the basic concept is the same. All these devices share some common characteristics: each has sensitivity to external magnetic fields. Attach a floppy disk to the refrigerator door with a magnet if you want to test the sensitivity. They are also affected by high temperatures, as in fires, and by exposure to water. Today, the only remaining magnetic methods in wide use are mechanical hard drives and tape solutions. And both of these are being replaced by solid state solutions at a fairly significant pace.

Hard Drives

Hard drives used to require large machines in mainframes. Now they are small enough to attach to mobile devices. The concepts remain the same among all of them: a spinning platter rotates the magnetic media beneath heads that read the patterns in the oxide coating. As drives have gotten smaller and rotation speeds have increased, the capacities have also grown. Today, gigabytes of data can be stored in a device slightly larger than a bottle cap. Portable hard drives in the 1TB to 6TB range are now available and affordable.

One of the security controls available to help protect the confidentiality of the data is full drive encryption built into the drive hardware. Using a key that is controlled, through a Trusted Platform Module (TPM) interface, for instance, this technology protects the data if the drive itself is lost or stolen. This may not be important if a thief takes the whole PC, but in larger storage environments, drives are placed in separate boxes and remotely accessed. In the specific case of notebook machines, this layer can be tied to smart card interfaces to provide more security. As this is built into the controller, encryption protocols such as Advanced Encryption Standard (AES) can be performed at full drive speed.

Diskettes

Floppy disks were the computer industry's first attempt at portable magnetic media. The movable medium was placed in a protective sleeve, and the drive remained in the machine. Capacities up to 1.4 MB were achieved, but the fragility of the device as the size increased, as well as USB-based media, has rendered floppies obsolete. Diskettes are part of history now.

Tape

Magnetic tape has held a place in computer centers since the beginning of computing. Its primary use has been bulk offline storage and backup. Tape functions well in this role because of its low cost. The disadvantage of tape is its nature as a serial access medium, making it slower to work with for large quantities of data. Modern tape solutions are built around the Linear Tape Open (LTO) format, also known as the LTO Ultrium format. LTO is a powerful, scalable, adaptable open tape format that is optimized for high capacity, maximum storage density, and performance, with cartridge capacities exceeding 40 TB.

Tapes are still a major concern from a security perspective, as they are used to back up many types of computer systems. The physical protection afforded tapes is of concern because if a tape is stolen, an unauthorized user could establish a network and recover your data on their system—because it's all stored on the tape. Offsite storage is needed for proper disaster recovery protection, but secure offsite storage and transport is what is really needed. This important issue is frequently overlooked in many facilities. The simple solution to maintain control over the data even when you can't control the tape is through encryption. Backup utilities can secure the backups with encryption, but this option is frequently not used, for a variety of reasons. Regardless of the rationale for not encrypting data, once a tape is lost, not using the encryption option becomes a lamented decision.

Optical Media

Optical media involves the use of a laser to read data stored on a physical device. Instead of having a magnetic head that picks up magnetic marks on a disk, a laser picks up deformities embedded in the media containing the information. As with magnetic media, optical media can be read-write, although the read-only version is still more common.

CD-R/DVD

The compact disc (CD) took the music industry by storm, and then it took the computer industry by storm as well. A standard CD holds more than 640 MB of data, in some cases up to 800 MB, and a digital video disc (DVD) can hold almost 5 GB of data single sided, or 8.5 GB dual layer. These devices operate as optical storage, with little marks burned in them to represent 1's and 0's on a microscopic scale. Today, these optical discs are artifacts of days gone by and are found on some older machines, but not in machines built in the last decade.

> **Tech Tip**
>
> **Backup Lifetimes**
>
> *A common misconception is that data backed up onto magnetic media will last for long periods of time. Although once touted as lasting decades, modern micro-encoding methods are proving less durable than expected, sometimes with lifetimes less than ten years. A secondary problem is maintaining operating system access via drivers to legacy equipment. As technology moves forward, finding drivers for ten-plus-year-old tape drives for Windows 10 or the latest version of Linux can prove to be a major hurdle.*

Blu-ray Discs

The latest version of optical disc is the Blu-ray disc. Using a smaller, violet-blue laser, this system can hold significantly more information than a DVD. Blu-ray discs can hold up to 128 GB in four layers. The transfer speed of Blu-ray at more than 48 Mbps is over four times greater than that of DVD systems. Designed for high-definition (HD) video, Blu-ray offers significant storage for data as well.

Electronic Media

The latest form of removable media is electronic memory. Electronic circuits of static memory, which can retain data even without power, fill a niche where high density and small size are needed. Originally used in audio devices and digital cameras, electronic memory comes in a variety of vendor-specific types, such as smart cards, SmartMedia, SD cards, flash cards, memory sticks, and CompactFlash devices. These range from small card-like devices (for example, microSD cards are smaller than a dime and hold up to 512 GB) to USB sticks that hold up to 2 TB. These devices are becoming ubiquitous, with new PCs and netbooks containing built-in slots to read them like any other storage device.

Although they are used primarily for photos and music, these devices could be used to move any digital information from one machine to another. To a machine equipped with a connector port, these devices look like any other file storage location. They can be connected to a system through a special reader or directly via a USB port. In newer PC systems, a USB boot device has replaced the older floppy drive. These devices are small, can hold a significant amount of data (over 1 TB at the time of writing), and are easy to move from machine to machine. Another novel interface is a mouse that has a slot for a memory stick. This dual-purpose device conserves space, conserves USB ports, and is easy to use. The memory stick is placed in the mouse, which can then be used normally. The stick is easily removable and transportable. The mouse works with or without the memory stick; it is just a convenient device to use for a portal.

The advent of large-capacity USB sticks has enabled users to build entire systems, OSs, and tools onto them to ensure the security and veracity of the OS and tools. With the expanding use of virtualization, a user could carry an entire system on a USB stick and boot it using virtually any hardware. With USB 3.2 and its 20Gbps speeds, this is a highly versatile form of memory that enables many new capabilities.

Solid State Hard Drives

With the rise of solid state memory technologies comes a solid state "hard drive." **Solid state drives (SSDs)** have moved into mobile devices, desktops, and even servers. Memory densities are significantly beyond those of physical drives, there are no moving parts to wear out or fail, and SSDs have vastly superior performance specifications. A high-end SSD today can hold 4 TB and operate at nearly 6 Gbps. Figure 10.10 shows a 512GB SSD from a laptop, on a half-height minicard mSATA interface. The only factor that has

• **Figure 10.10** 512GB solid state half-height minicard

slowed the spread of this technology has been cost, but recent cost reductions have made this form of memory a first choice in many systems.

Security Concerns for Transmission Media

The primary security concern for a system administrator has to be preventing physical access to a server by an unauthorized individual. Such access will almost always spell disaster—with direct access and the correct tools, any system can be infiltrated. One of the administrator's next major concerns should be preventing unfettered access to a network connection. Access to switches and routers is almost as bad as direct access to a server, and access to network connections would rank third in terms of worst-case scenarios. Preventing such access is costly, yet the cost of replacing a server because of theft is also costly.

Physical Security Concerns

A balanced approach is the most sensible approach when addressing physical security, and this applies to transmission media as well. Keeping network switch rooms secure and cable runs secure seems obvious, but cases of using janitorial closets for this vital business purpose abound. One of the keys to mounting a successful attack on a network is information. Usernames, passwords, server locations—all of these can be obtained if someone has the ability to observe network traffic in a process called *sniffing*. A sniffer can record all the network traffic, and this data can be mined for accounts, passwords, and traffic content, all of which can be useful to an unauthorized user. One starting point for many intrusions is the insertion of an unauthorized sniffer into the network, with the fruits of its labors driving the remaining unauthorized activities. Many common scenarios exist when unauthorized entry to a network occurs, including these:

- Inserting a node and functionality that is not authorized on the network, such as a sniffer device or unauthorized wireless access point
- Modifying firewall security policies
- Modifying ACLs for firewalls, switches, or routers
- Modifying network devices to echo traffic to an external node

Network devices and transmission media become targets because they are dispersed throughout an organization, and physical security of many dispersed items can be difficult to manage. Although limiting physical access is difficult, it is essential. The least level of skill is still more than sufficient to accomplish unauthorized entry into a network if physical access to the network signals is allowed. This is one factor driving many organizations to use fiber optics because these cables are much more difficult to tap. Although many tricks can be employed with switches and VLANs to increase security, it is still essential that you prevent unauthorized contact with the network equipment.

Cross Check

Physical Infrastructure Security

The best first effort is to secure the actual network equipment to prevent this type of intrusion. As you should remember from Chapter 8, physical access to network infrastructure opens up a myriad of issues, and most of them can be catastrophic with respect to security. Physically securing access to network components is one of the "must dos" of a comprehensive security effort.

Wireless networks make the intruder's task even easier, as they take the network to the users, authorized or not. A technique called *war-driving* involves using a laptop (or other mobile device) and software to find wireless networks from outside the premises. A typical use of war-driving is to locate a wireless network with poor (or no) security and obtain free Internet access, but other uses can be more devastating. A simple solution is to place a firewall between the wireless access point and the rest of the network and authenticate users before allowing entry. Business users use VPN technology to secure their connection to the Internet and other resources, and home users can do the same thing to prevent neighbors from "sharing" their Internet connections. To ensure that unauthorized traffic does not enter your network through a wireless access point, you must either use a firewall with an authentication system or establish a VPN.

Chapter 10 Review

Chapter Summary

After reading this chapter and completing the exercises, you should understand the following aspects of networking and secure infrastructures.

Construct networks using different types of network devices

- Understand the differences between basic network devices, such as hubs, bridges, switches, and routers.
- Networks connect workstations and servers as well as serve as the means of data communication between these elements.
- Understand the security implications of network devices and how to construct a secure network infrastructure.

Understand virtualization concepts

- Type 1 hypervisors run directly on system hardware.
- Type 2 hypervisors run on top of a host operating system.
- Virtualization comes with its own set of issues, including VM sprawl, VM escape, and security implementation and testing issues.

Use basic terminology associated with network functions related to information security

- Understanding and using the correct vocabulary for device names and their relationship to networking are important to a security professional.
- Security appliances add terminology, including specific items for IDS and firewalls.
- Understand port-based security efforts.

Understand security devices employed in a network

- Firewalls act as policy enforcers over network traffic
- Firewalls can be stateless or stateful and have different performance factors based on use.

Enhance security using security devices

- Understand the use of firewalls, next-generation firewalls, and intrusion detection systems.
- Understand the use and placement of load balancers and proxy servers as part of a secure network solution.
- Understand the use of security appliances, such as web security gateways, data loss prevention, and unified threat management.

Understand the placement of security devices

- Sensors, collectors, correlation engines, filters, and other security elements need to be placed at specific locations to be effective.
- TAPs and port mirrors can be employed to collect network data.

Identify the different types of media used to carry network signals

- Guided and unguided media can both carry network traffic.
- Wired technology, from coax cable through twisted-pair Ethernet, provides a cost-effective means of carrying network traffic.
- Fiber technology is used to carry higher bandwidth traffic.
- Unguided media such as infrared and RF (including wireless and Bluetooth) provide short-range network connectivity.

Describe the different types of storage media, including the cloud, used to store information

- There are a wide array of removable media types, from memory sticks to optical discs to portable drives.
- Data storage on removable media, because of increased physical access, creates significant security implications.
- The cloud can represent a realm of storage media.

Key Terms

basic packet filtering *(325)*
bridge *(317)*
coaxial cable *(344)*
collision domain *(317)*
concentrator *(328)*
data loss prevention (DLP) *(338)*
Dynamic Host Configuration Protocol (DHCP) *(320)*
firewall *(322)*
hub *(317)*
hypervisor *(313)*
Internet content filters *(338)*
load balancing *(334)*
MAC filtering *(320)*
modem *(329)*
network access control (NAC) *(331)*
network-attached storage (NAS) *(312)*
network interface card (NIC) *(316)*
network operations center (NOC) *(332)*
next-generation firewall (NGFW) *(327)*
private branch exchange (PBX) *(330)*
proxy server *(335)*
router *(321)*
sandboxing *(316)*
servers *(312)*
shielded twisted-pair (STP) *(345)*
snapshot *(315)*
solid state drives (SSDs) *(351)*
storage area networks (SANs) *(343)*
switch *(318)*
tunneling *(342)*
unified threat management (UTM) *(338)*
unshielded twisted-pair (UTP) *(345)*
virtualization *(313)*
VPN concentrator *(329)*
web security gateway *(337)*
wireless access point (WAP) *(329)*
workstation *(311)*

Key Terms Quiz

Use terms from the Key Terms list to complete the sentences that follow. Don't use the same term more than once. Not all terms will be used.

1. A(n) _______________ routes packets based on IP addresses.
2. Technology used to verify endpoint compliance with security rules before connecting to a network is called _______________.
3. To connect a computer to a network, you use a(n) _______________.
4. A(n) _______________ or _______________ distributes traffic based on MAC addresses.
5. _______________ is quarantining or isolation of a system from its surroundings.
6. _______________ is a name for the typical computer a user uses on a network.
7. A(n) _______________ repeats all data traffic across all connected ports.
8. Cat 6 is an example of _______________ cable.
9. Basic packet filtering occurs at the _______________.
10. A(n) _______________ is an extension of the telephone service into a firm's telecommunications network.

Multiple-Choice Quiz

1. Switches operate at which layer of the OSI model?
   - **A.** Physical layer
   - **B.** Transport layer
   - **C.** Data link layer
   - **D.** Application layer
2. UTP cables are terminated for Ethernet using what type of connector?
   - **A.** A BNC plug
   - **B.** An Ethernet connector
   - **C.** A standard phone jack connector
   - **D.** An RJ-45 connector
3. Coaxial cable carries how many physical channels?
   - **A.** Two
   - **B.** Four
   - **C.** One
   - **D.** None of the above
4. Network access control is associated with which of the following?
   - **A.** NAP
   - **B.** IPSec
   - **C.** IPv6
   - **D.** NAT
5. What is the purpose of twisting the wires in twisted-pair circuits?
   - **A.** To increase speed
   - **B.** To increase bandwidth
   - **C.** To reduce crosstalk
   - **D.** To allow easier tracing
6. What is one of the challenges when managing a large number of VMs in the enterprise?
   - **A.** VM permissions
   - **B.** VM sprawl
   - **C.** VM size
   - **D.** VM locking
7. SNMP is a protocol used for which of the following functions?
   - **A.** Secure e-mail
   - **B.** Secure encryption of network packets
   - **C.** Remote access to user workstations
   - **D.** Remote access to the network infrastructure
8. Firewalls can use which of the following in their operation?
   - **A.** Stateful packet inspection
   - **B.** Port blocking to deny specific services
   - **C.** NAT to hide internal IP addresses
   - **D.** All of the above
9. SMTP is a protocol used for which of the following functions?
   - **A.** E-mail
   - **B.** Secure encryption of network packets
   - **C.** Remote access to user workstations
   - **D.** None of the above
10. USB-based flash memory is characterized by which of the following?
    - **A.** High cost
    - **B.** Low capacity
    - **C.** Slow access
    - **D.** None of the above

Essay Quiz

1. Compare and contrast routers and switches by describing the advantages and disadvantages of each.
2. Describe the common threats to the various types of transmission media in a network.

Lab Projects

• Lab Project 10.1

Configure two PCs and a SOHO-type router to communicate across the network with each other.

• Lab Project 10.2

Demonstrate network connectivity using Windows command-line tools.

chapter 11

Authentication and Remote Access

We should set a national goal of making computers and Internet access available for every American.

—William Jefferson Clinton

In this chapter, you will learn how to

- **Identify the differences among user, group, guest, service accounts, and role management**
- **Implement account policies**
- **Describe methods of account management (SSO, time of day, logical token, SSH keys, smart cards, account expiration, lockout, disablement)**
- **Describe methods of access management (MAC, DAC, RBAC, and ABAC)**
- **Explain authentication methods and the security implications in their use**
- **Examine the use of biometrics technology for authentication**
- **Discuss the methods and protocols for remote access to networks**
- **Identify authentication, authorization, and accounting (AAA) protocols**
- **Implement virtual private networks (VPNs) and their security aspects**

On single-user systems such as PCs, the individual user typically has access to most of the system's resources, processing capability, and stored data. On multiuser systems, such as servers and mainframes, an individual user typically has very limited access to the system and the data stored on that system. An administrator responsible for managing and maintaining the multiuser system has much greater access. So how does the computer system know which users should have access to what data? How does the operating system know what applications a user is allowed to use? There are three steps in the establishment of proper privileges; authentication, authorization, and accounting. These terms are commonly combined and simply referred to as **AAA**.

Authentication is the process of verifying an identity previously established in a computer system. Authentication is commonly performed by matching a set of user-supplied credentials to previously stored credentials on a host machine (for example, an account username and password). Once the user is authenticated, the authorization step takes place. There are a variety of methods of performing this function, each with its advantages and disadvantages. Authentication methods and their advantages and disadvantages are described throughout the chapter.

Remote access is another key issue for multiuser systems in today's world of connected computers. Isolated computers, not connected to networks or the Internet, are rare items these days. Except for some special-purpose machines, most computers need interconnectivity to fulfill their purpose. Remote access enables users outside a network to have network access and privileges as if they were inside the network. Being *outside* a network means that the user is working on a machine that is not physically connected to the network and must therefore establish a connection through a remote means, such as by dialing in, connecting via the Internet, or connecting through a wireless connection.

User, Group, and Role Management

To manage the privileges of many different people effectively on the same system, a mechanism for separating people into distinct entities (that is, *users*) is required, so you can control access on an individual level. At the same time, it's convenient and efficient to be able to lump users together when granting many different people (that is, *groups*) access to a resource at the same time. At other times, it's useful to be able to grant or restrict access based on a person's job or function within the organization (that is, *roles*). While you can manage privileges on the basis of users alone, managing user, group, and role assignments together is far more convenient and efficient.

> **Tech Tip**
>
> **Usernames, Permissions, and Rights**
>
> *A username is a unique alphanumeric identifier used to identify a user to a computer system. Permissions control what a user is allowed to do with objects on a computer system—what files they can open, what printers they can use, and so on. In Windows security models, permissions define the actions a user can perform on an object (open a file, delete a folder, and so on).* **Rights** *define the actions a user can perform on the system itself, such as change the time, adjust auditing levels, and so on. Rights are typically applied to operating system–level tasks.*

User

The term **user** generally applies to any person accessing a computer system. In privilege management, a user is a single individual, such as "John Forthright" or "Sally Jenkins." This is generally the lowest level addressed by privilege management and the most common area for addressing access, rights, and capabilities. When accessing a computer system, each user is generally given a **username**—a unique alphanumeric identifier they will use to identify themselves when logging in to or accessing the system. When developing a scheme for selecting usernames, you should keep in mind that usernames must be unique to each user, but they must also be fairly easy for the user to remember and use.

With some notable exceptions, in general a user who wants to access a computer system must first have a username created for them on the system they want to use. This is usually done by a system administrator, security administrator, or other privileged user, and this is the first step in privilege management—a user should not be allowed to create their own account.

Once the account is created and a username is selected, the administrator can assign specific permissions to that user. **Permissions** control what the user is allowed to do with objects on the system—which files they may access, which programs they may execute, and so on. Whereas PCs typically have only one or two user accounts, larger systems such as servers and mainframes can have hundreds of accounts on the same system. Figure 11.1 shows the Users tab of the Computer Management utility on a Windows

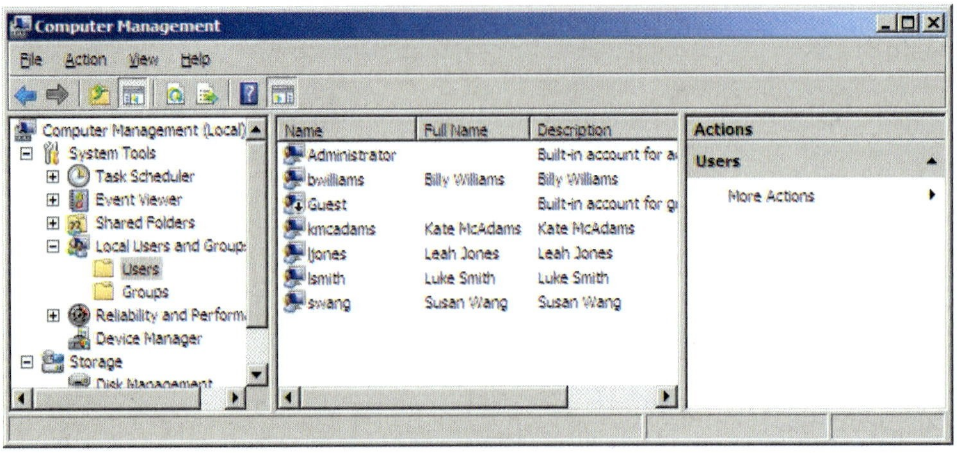

• **Figure 11.1** Users tab on a Windows Server system

Auditing user accounts, group membership, and password strength on a regular basis is an extremely important security control. Many compliance audits focus on the presence or lack of industry-accepted security controls.

Tech Tip

Generic Accounts

Generic accounts *are accounts without a named user behind them. These can be employed for special purposes, such as running services and batch processes, but because they cannot be attributed to an individual, they should not have login capability. It is also important that if they have elevated privileges, their activities should be continually monitored as to what functions they are performing versus what they are expected to be doing. General use of generic accounts should be avoided because of the increased risk associated with no attribution capability.*

Server system. Note that several user accounts have been created on this system, each identified by a unique username.

A few "special" user accounts don't typically match up one-to-one with a real person. These accounts are reserved for special functions and typically have much more access and control over the computer system than the average user account. Two such accounts are the **administrator** account under Windows and the **root** account under Linux. These are called privileged accounts because their privileges are elevated. These accounts are not typically assigned to a specific individual and are restricted, accessed only when the full capabilities of the account are required.

Due to the power possessed by these accounts, and the few, if any, restrictions placed on them, they must be protected with strong passwords that are not easily guessed or obtained. These accounts are also the most common targets of attackers—if the attacker can gain root access or assume the privilege level associated with the root account, they can bypass most access controls and accomplish anything they want on that system.

Another account that falls into the "special" category is the system account used by Windows operating systems. The system account has the same file privileges as the administrator account and is used by the operating system and by services that run under Windows. By default, the system account is granted full control to all files on an NTFS volume. Services and processes that need the capability to log on internally within Windows will use the system account—for example, the DNS Server and DHCP Server services in Windows Server use the Local System account.

Shared and Generic Accounts/Credentials

Shared accounts go against the specific treatise that accounts exist so that user activity can be tracked. This said, there are times when guest accounts are used, especially in situations where the guest access is limited to a defined set of functions and specific tracking is not particularly useful. Sometimes the shared accounts are called *generic accounts* and exist only to provide a specific set of functionalities, like in a PC running in kiosk mode, with a browser limited to specific sites as an information display. Under these circumstances, being able to trace the activity to a user is not particularly useful.

Guest Accounts

Guest accounts are frequently used on corporate networks to provide visitors' access to the Internet and to some common corporate resources, such as projectors, printers in conference rooms, and so on. Again, these types of accounts are restricted in their network capability to a defined set of machines, with a defined set of access, much like a user from the Internet visiting their publicly facing website. As such, logging and tracing activity have little to no use, so the overhead of establishing an account does not make sense.

> **Tech Tip**
>
> **Guest Accounts**
>
> *Guest accounts are granted limited permissions and access. They are used primarily for visitors. It is common practice to disable guest accounts as well as other default accounts when not in use. If guest accounts are by wireless access, it is important to change passwords to prevent the user of the account from returning after the period of authorization.*

> Service accounts run without human intervention and are granted only enough permission to run the services they support.

Service Accounts

Service accounts are accounts that are used to run processes that do not require human intervention to start/stop/administer. From batch jobs that run in a data center, to simple tasks that are run on the enterprise for compliance objectives, the reasons for running them are many, but the need for an accountholder is not really there. One thing you can do with these accounts in Windows systems is to not allow them to log in to the system. This limits some of the attack vectors that can be applied to these accounts. Another security provision is to apply time restrictions for accounts that run batch jobs at night and then monitor when they run. Any service account that has to run in an elevated privilege mode should receive extra monitoring and scrutiny.

> **Tech Tip**
>
> **Onboarding/Offboarding**
>
> ***Onboarding*** *and* ***offboarding*** *involve the bringing of personnel on and off a project or team. During onboarding, proper account relationships need to be managed. New members can be put into the correct groups; then, when offboarded, they can be removed from the groups. This is one way in which groups can be used to manage permissions, which can be very efficient when users move between units and tasks.*

Privileged Accounts

Privileged accounts are any accounts with greater-than-normal user access. Privileged accounts are typically root or admin-level accounts and represent risk in that they are unlimited in their powers. These accounts require regular real-time monitoring, if at all possible, and should always be monitored when operating remotely. There may be reasons why and occasions when system administrators are acting via a remote session, but when they are, the purposes should be known and approved.

Group

Under privilege management, a **group** is a collection of users with some common criteria, such as a need for access to a particular data set or group of applications. A group can consist of one user or hundreds of users, and each user can belong to one or more groups. Figure 11.2 shows a common approach to grouping users—building groups based on job function.

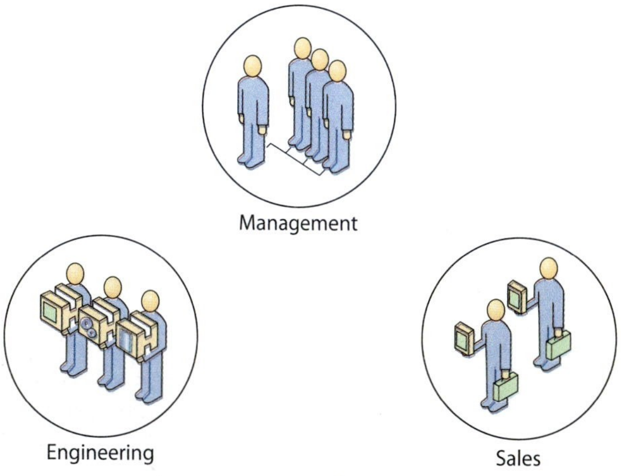

• **Figure 11.2** Logical representation of groups

By assigning membership in a specific group to a user, you make it much easier to control that user's access and privileges. For example, if every member of the engineering department needs access to product development documents, administrators can place all the users in the engineering department in a single group and allow that group to access the necessary documents. Once a group is assigned permissions to access a particular resource, adding a new user to that group will automatically allow that user to access that resource. In effect, the user "inherits" the permissions of the group as soon as they are placed in that group. As Figure 11.3 shows, a computer system can have many different groups, each with its own rights and permissions.

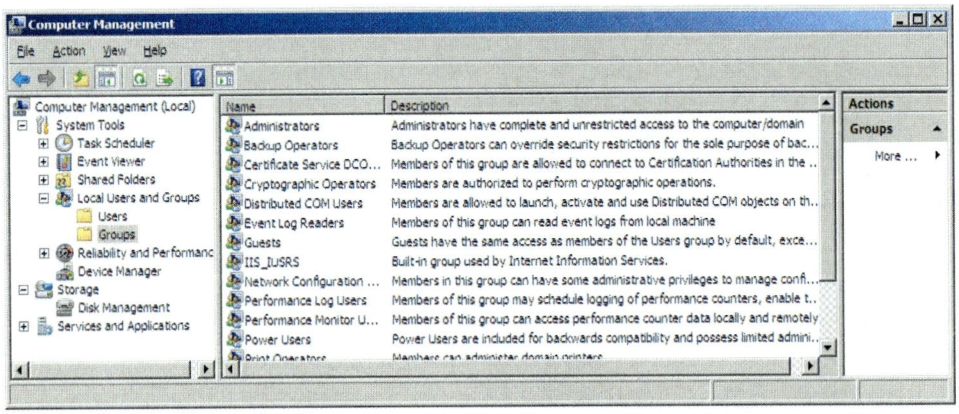

• **Figure 11.3** Groups tab on a Windows Server system

As you can see from the description for the Administrators group in Figure 11.3, this group has complete and unrestricted access to the system. This includes access to all files, applications, and data sets. Anyone who belongs to the Administrators group or is placed in this group will have a great deal of access and control over the system.

Some operating systems, such as Windows, have built-in groups—groups that are already defined within the operating system, such as Administrators, Power Users, and Everyone. The whole concept of groups revolves around making the tasks of assigning and managing permissions easier, and built-in groups certainly help to make these tasks easier. Individual users accounts can be added to built-in groups, allowing administrators to grant permission sets to users quickly and easily without having to specify permissions manually. For example, adding the user account named "bjones" to the Power Users group gives bjones all the permissions assigned to the built-in Power Users group, such as installing drivers, modifying settings, and installing software.

Role

Another common method of managing access and privileges is by roles. A **role** is usually synonymous with a job or set of functions. For example, the role of security admin in Microsoft SQL Server may be applied to someone who is responsible for creating and managing logins, reading error logs, and auditing the application. Security admins need to accomplish specific functions and need access to certain resources that other users do not—for example, they need to be able to create and delete logins, open and read error logs, and so on. In general, anyone serving in the role of security admin needs the same rights and privileges as every other security admin. For simplicity and efficiency, rights and privileges can be assigned to the role security admin, and anyone assigned to fulfill that role automatically has the correct rights and privileges to perform the required tasks.

Account Policies

One of the key elements to guide security professionals in daily tasks is a good set of policies. Many issues are associated with the daily tasks, and leaving a lot of the decisions up to individual workers will rapidly result in conflicting results. Policies are needed for a wide range of elements, from naming conventions to operating rules, such as audit frequency and other specifics. Having these issues resolved as a matter of policy enables security professionals to go about the task of verifying and monitoring systems, rather than trying to adjudicate policy type issues with each user case that comes along.

Account Policy Enforcement

The primary method of account policy enforcement used in most access systems is still one based on passwords. The concepts of each user ID being traceable to a single person's activity and no sharing of passwords and credentials form the foundation of a solid account policy. Passwords need to be managed to provide appropriate levels of protection. They need to be strong enough to resist attack, and yet not too difficult for users to remember. A password policy can act to ensure that the necessary steps are taken to enact a secure password solution, both by users and by the password infrastructure system.

Cross Check

Password Policies

Password policies, along with many other important security policies, are covered in detail in Chapter 3.

Domain Passwords

A **domain password policy** is a password policy for a specific domain. Because these policies are usually associated with the Windows operating system, a domain password policy is implemented and enforced on the **domain controller**, which is a computer that responds to security authentication requests, such as logging in to a computer, for a Windows domain. The domain password policy usually falls under a group policy object (GPO) and has the following elements (see Figure 11.4):

- **Enforce password history** Tells the system how many passwords to remember and does not allow a user to reuse an old password.

- **Maximum password age** Specifies the maximum number of days a password may be used before it must be changed.
- **Minimum password age** Specifies the minimum number of days a password must be used before it can be changed again.
- **Minimum password length** Specifies the minimum number of characters that must be used in a password.
- **Password must meet complexity requirements** Specifies that the password must meet the minimum length requirement and have characters from at least three of the following four groups: English uppercase characters (A through Z), English lowercase characters (a through z), numerals (0 through 9), and non-alphabetic characters (such as !, $, #, and %).
- **Store passwords using reversible encryption** Reversible encryption is a form of encryption that can easily be decrypted and is essentially the same as storing a plaintext version of the password (because it's so easy to reverse the encryption and get the password). This should be used only when applications use protocols that require the user's password for authentication, such as the Challenge-Handshake Authentication Protocol (CHAP).

> New research from NIST indicates that password complexity rules designed to force entropy into passwords do so at the risk of other, less-desirable password behaviors by users, such as writing them down or versioning them with an increasing number element. The latest NIST guidance (Special Publication 800-63B, June 2017) is that long passphrases offer the best protection. Proper practice today is to not rely on passwords alone but rather to use multifactor authentication. Also, users should use password managers to manage the passwords.

> Not only is it essential to ensure every account has a strong password, but it is also essential to disable or delete unnecessary accounts. If your system does not need to support guest or anonymous accounts, then disable them. When user or administrator accounts are no longer needed, remove or disable them. As a best practice, all user accounts should be audited periodically to ensure there are no unnecessary, outdated, or unneeded accounts on your systems.

Domains are logical groups of computers that share a central directory database, known as the Active Directory database for the more recent Windows operating systems. The database contains information about the user accounts and security information for all resources identified within the domain. Each user within the domain is assigned their own unique account (that is, a domain is not a single account shared by multiple users), which is then assigned access to specific resources within the domain. In operating systems that provide domain capabilities, the password policy is set in the root container for the domain and applies to all users within that domain. Setting a password policy for a domain is similar to setting other password policies in that the same critical elements need to be considered (password length, complexity, life, and so on). If a change to one of these elements is desired for a group of users, a new domain needs to be created because the domain is considered a security boundary. In a Windows operating system

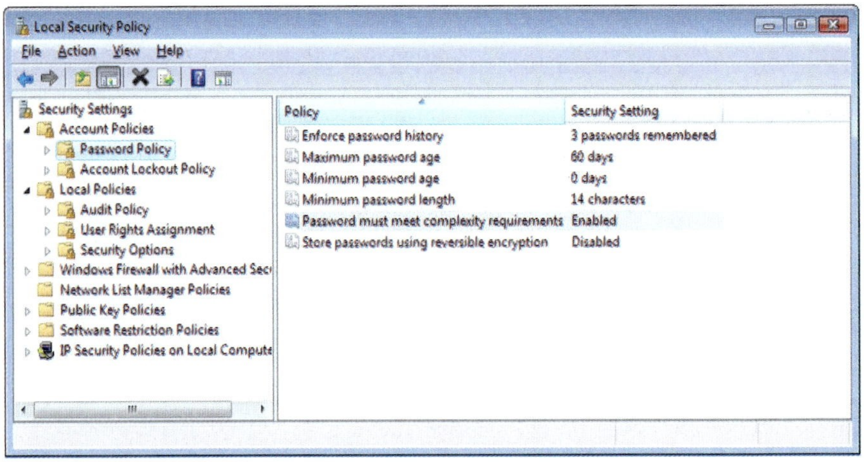

• **Figure 11.4** Password policy options in Windows Local Security Policy

that employs Active Directory, the domain password policy can be set in the Active Directory Users and Computers menu in the Administrative Tools section of the Control Panel.

Tech Tip

Calculating Unique Password Combinations

One of the primary reasons administrators require users to have longer passwords that use upper- and lowercase letters, numbers, and at least one "special" character is to help deter password-guessing attacks. One popular password-guessing technique, called a brute force attack, *uses software to guess every possible password until one matches a user's password. Essentially, a brute force attack tries* a, *then* aa, *then* aaa, *and so on, until it runs out of combinations or gets a password match. Increasing both the pool of possible characters that can be used in the password and the number of characters required in the password can exponentially increase the number of "guesses" a brute force program needs to perform before it runs out of possibilities. For example, if our password policy requires a three-character password that uses only lowercase letters, there are only 17,576 possible passwords (with 26 possible characters, a password that's three characters long equates to 26^3 combinations). Requiring a six-character password increases that number to 308,915,776 possible passwords (26^6). An eight-character password with upper- and lowercase letters, a special symbol, and a number increases the possible passwords to 70^8, or over 576 trillion combinations.*

Precomputed hashes in rainbow tables can also be used to brute-force past shorter passwords. As the length increases, so does the size of the rainbow table.

Single Sign-On

To use a system, users must be able to access it, which they usually do by supplying their user IDs (or usernames) and corresponding passwords. As any security administrator knows, the more systems a particular user has access to, the more passwords that user must have and remember. The natural tendency for users is to select passwords that are easy to remember, or even the same password for use on the multiple systems they access. Wouldn't it be easier for the user simply to log in once and have to remember only a single, good password? This is made possible with a technology called single sign-on.

Single sign-on (SSO) is a form of authentication that involves the transferring of credentials between systems. As more and more systems are combined in daily use, users are forced to have multiple sets of credentials. A user may have to log in to three, four, five, or even more systems every day just to do their job. Single sign-on allows a user to transfer their credentials so that logging in to one system acts to log them in to all of the systems. Once the user has entered a user ID and password, the single sign-on system passes these credentials transparently to other systems so that repeated logons are not required. Put simply, you supply the right username and password once and you have access to all the applications and data you need, without having to log in multiple times and remember many different passwords. From a user standpoint, SSO means you need to remember only one username and one password. From an administration standpoint, SSO can be easier to manage and maintain. From a security

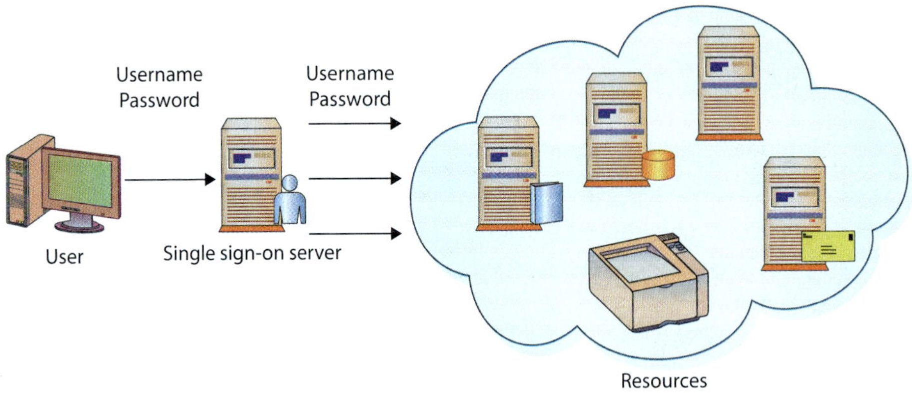

• **Figure 11.5** Single sign-on process

> **Tech Tip**
>
> **Heartbleed**
>
> *In 2014, a vulnerability that could cause user credentials to be exposed was discovered in millions of systems. Called the Heartbleed incident, this resulted in numerous users being told to change their passwords because of potential compromise. Users were also warned of the dangers of reusing passwords across different accounts. Although this makes passwords easier to remember, it also improves guessing chances. What made this whole effort of users protecting their passwords particularly challenging is that the breach was widespread—virtually all Linux systems—and the patching rate was uneven, so people could be suffering multiple exposures over time. After one year, an estimated 40 percent of all compromised systems remained unpatched. This highlights the importance of not reusing passwords across multiple accounts.*

standpoint, SSO can be even more secure, as users who need to remember only one password are less likely to choose something too simple or something so complex they need to write it down. The following is a logical depiction of the SSO process (see Figure 11.5):

1. The user signs in once, providing a username and password to the SSO server.
2. The SSO server provides authentication information to any resource the user accesses during that session. The server interfaces with the other applications and systems—the user does not need to log in to each system individually.

In reality, SSO is usually a little more difficult to implement than vendors would lead you to believe. To be effective and useful, all your applications need to be able to access and use the authentication provided by the SSO process. The more diverse your network, the less likely this is to be the case. If your network, like most, contains different operating systems, custom applications, and a diverse user base, SSO may not even be a viable option.

Credential Management

Credential management refers to the processes, services, and software used to store, manage, and log the use of user credentials. Credential management solutions are typically aimed at assisting end users manage their growing set of passwords. There are credential management products that provide a secure means of storing user credentials and making them available across a wide range of platforms, from local stores to cloud storage locations.

Group Policy

Microsoft Windows systems in an enterprise environment can be managed via **group policy objects (GPOs)**. GPOs act through a set of registry settings that can be managed via the enterprise. A wide range of settings can be managed via GPOs, many of which are related to security, including user credential settings such as password rules.

Standard Naming Convention

Agreeing on a standard naming convention is one of the topics that can bring controversy out of professionals who seem to agree on most things. Having a standard naming convention has pluses in that it enables users to extract meaning from a name. Having servers with "dev," "test," and "prod" as part of their names can prevent inadvertent changes by a user because of the misidentification of an asset. By the same token, calling out privileges (say, appending "SA" to the end of usernames with system administrator privileges) results in two potential problems. First, it alerts adversaries to which accounts are the most valuable. Second, it creates a problem when the person is no longer a member of the system administrators group, as now the account must be renamed.

One aspect that everyone does agree on is the concept of leaving room for the future. The simplest example is in the numbering of accounts. For instance, for e-mail, use first initial plus last name plus a digit for a repeat. Will we ever have more than 10 John Smiths? Well, you might be surprised, as Joan Smiths and Jack Smiths also take from the pool. And the pool is further diluted by the fact that we inactivate old accounts, not reuse them. So plan on having plenty of room ahead for fixing any naming scheme.

Account Maintenance

Account maintenance is not the sexiest job in the security field. But then again, traffic cops have boring lives as well—until you realize that roughly half of all felons are arrested on simple traffic stops. The same is true with account maintenance—no, we aren't catching felons, but we do find errors that otherwise only increase risk and because of their nature are hard to defend against any other way. Account maintenance is the routine screening of all attributes for an account. Is the business purpose for the account still valid—that is, is the user still employed? Is the business process for a system account still occurring? Are the actual permissions associated with the account appropriate for the account holder? Best practice indicates that this be performed in accordance with the risk associated with the profile. System administrators, and other privileged accounts, need greater scrutiny that normal users. Shared accounts, such as guest accounts, also require scrutiny to ensure they are not abused.

For some high-risk situations, such as unauthenticated guest accounts being granted administrator privilege, an automated check can be programmed and run on a regular basis. In Active Directory, it is also possible for the security group to be notified any time a user is granted domain admin privilege. And it is also important to note that the job of determining who has what access is actually one that belongs to the business, not the security group. The business side of the house is where the policy decision on who should have access is determined. The security group merely takes the steps to enforce this decision. Account maintenance is a joint responsibility.

Usage Auditing and Review

As with all security controls, a monitoring component is an important aspect of security controls used to mitigate risk. Logs are the most frequently

Logging and monitoring of failed login attempts provides valuable information during investigations of compromises.

Tech Tip

Account Recertification

User accounts should periodically be recertified as necessary. The process of **account recertification** *can be as simple as a check against current payroll records to ensure all users are still employed, or as intrusive as having users identify themselves again. The latter is highly intrusive but may be warranted for high-risk accounts. The process of recertification ensures that only users needing accounts have accounts in the system.*

used component, and with respect to privileged accounts, logging can be especially important. **Usage auditing and review** is just that: an examination of logs to determine user activity. Reviewing access control logs for root-level accounts is an important element of securing access control methods. Because of the power and potential for misuse, administrative or root-level accounts should be closely monitored. One important element for continuous monitoring of production would be the use of an administrative-level account on a production system.

A strong configuration management environment will include the control of access to production systems by users who can change the environment. Root-level changes in a system tend to be significant changes, and in production systems these changes would be approved in advance. A comparison of all root-level activity against approved changes will assist in the detection of activity that is unauthorized.

Account Audits

Account audits are audits like all other audits—an independent verification that the policies associated with the accounts are being followed. An independent auditor can check all of the elements of policies. Passwords can be checked using a password cracker—if it breaks the password, odds are the user wasn't following the rules. The various restrictions, such as account lockout and reuse, can be checked. An auditor can verify that all the authorized users are still with the firm or in an authorized capacity. Audits work to ensure the implementation of policies is actually working to specification.

Time-of-Day Restrictions

Some organizations need to tightly control certain users, groups, or even roles and limit access to certain resources to specific days and times. Most server-class operating systems enable administrators to implement **time-of-day restrictions** that limit when a user can log in, when certain resources can be accessed, and so on. Time-of-day restrictions are usually specified for individual accounts, as shown in Figure 11.6.

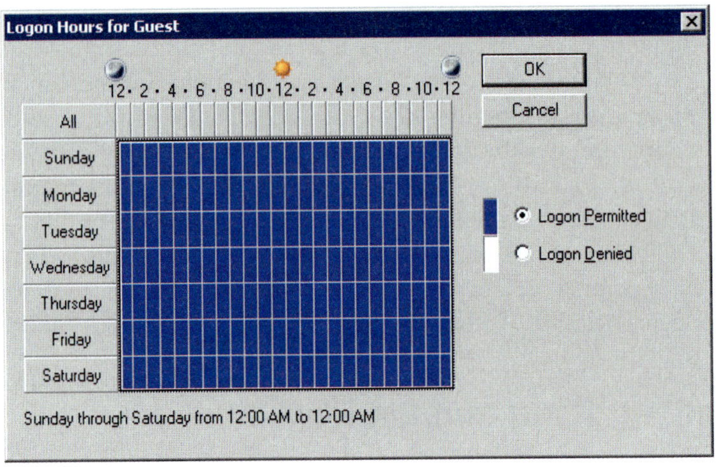

• **Figure 11.6** Logon hours for Guest account

From a security perspective, time-of-day restrictions can be very useful. If a user normally accesses certain resources during normal business hours, an attempt to access these resources outside this time period (either at night or on the weekend) might indicate an attacker has gained access to or is trying to gain access to that account. Specifying time-of-day restrictions can also serve as a mechanism to enforce internal controls of critical or sensitive resources. Obviously, a drawback to enforcing time-of-day restrictions is that it means a user can't go to work outside of normal hours to "catch up" with work tasks. As with all security policies, usability and security must be balanced in this policy decision.

Be careful implementing time-of-day restrictions. Some operating systems give you the option of disconnecting users as soon as their "allowed login time" expires, regardless of what the user is doing at the time. The more commonly used approach is to allow currently logged-in users to stay connected but reject any login attempts that occur outside of allowed hours.

Impossible Travel Time/Risky Login

Correct logins to an account can record many elements of information, including where the login came from. This "where" can be a machine in a network or even a geographic location. Using this metadata, some interesting items can be calculated. Should a login occur from a separate location where a user is already logged in, is it possible for the user to be in two locations at the same time? Likewise, if the second login occurs from a geographically separate location, is there time to actually travel this far in the time between the logins? These are cases of *risky logins* or examples of *impossible travel time.* There are applications that can detect these anomalies and present this information so you can make decisions as to whether the second login should be allowed or not. What should govern these decisions is a policy that specifically addresses these conditions.

Elements of the policy are not simple because, while a remote login from a continent away might be easy to deny, what of the two logins in the same building overlapping? Is it against policy for a user to have one system logged in with the screen locked and then go to a different system? In some high-security instances, this second occurrence might be blocked by policy, whereas in less secure instances, the usability of multiple logins might be allowed. This is why a policy is needed, to coordinate management across all of these differing conditions, not leaving it up to the security technician's discretion as they configure appliances and access control systems.

Account Expiration

In addition to all the other methods of controlling and restricting access, most modern operating systems allow administrators to specify the length of time an account is valid and when it "expires" or is disabled. **Account expiration** is the setting of an ending time for an account's validity. This is a great method for controlling temporary accounts, or accounts for contractors or contract employees. For these accounts, the administrator can specify an expiration date; when the date is reached, the account automatically becomes locked out and cannot be logged in to without administrator intervention. A related action can be taken with accounts that never expire: they can automatically be marked "inactive" and locked out if they have been unused for a specified number of days. Account expiration is similar to password expiration, in that it limits the time window of potential compromise. When an account has expired, it cannot be used unless the expiration deadline is extended.

Tech Tip

Disabling Accounts

An administrator has several options for ending a user's access (for instance, upon termination or offboarding). The best option is to disable the account but leave it in the system. This preserves account permission chains and prevents reuse of a user ID, leading to potential confusion later when examining logs.

Similarly, organizations must define whether accounts are deleted or disabled when no longer needed. Deleting an account removes the account from the system permanently, whereas disabling an account leaves it in place but marks it as unusable. Many organizations disable an account for a period of time after an employee departs (30 or more days) prior to deleting the account. This prevents anyone from using the account and allows administrators to reassign files, forward mail, and "clean up" before taking any permanent actions on the account.

Privileged Access Management

Privilege management is the process of restricting a user's ability to interact with the computer system. Essentially, everything a user can do to or with a computer system falls into the realm of privilege management. Privilege management occurs at many different points within an operating system or even within applications running on a particular operating system.

Privileged accounts are any accounts with greater-than-normal user access. Privileged accounts are typically root- or administrative-level accounts and represent risk in that they are unlimited in their powers. These accounts require regular real-time monitoring, if at all possible, and should always be monitored when operating remotely. Administrators may need to perform tasks via a remote session in certain scenarios, but when they do, they first need to identify the purpose and get approval.

Privileged access management is a combination of the policies, procedures, and technologies for controlling access to and use of elevated or privileged accounts. This enables the organization to log and control privileged access across the entire environment. The primary purpose is to limit the attack surface that these accounts have, and to minimize exposure based on current operational needs and conditions.

Authorization

Authorization is the process of permitting or denying access to a specific resource. Once identity is confirmed via authentication, specific actions can be authorized or denied. Many types of authorization schemes are used, but the purpose is the same: determine whether a given user who has been identified has permissions for a particular object or resource being requested. This functionality is frequently part of the operating system and is transparent to users.

The separation of tasks, from identification to authentication to authorization, has several advantages. Many methods can be used to perform each task, and on many systems several methods are concurrently present for each task. Separation of these tasks into individual elements allows combinations of implementations to work together. Any system or resource, be it hardware (router or workstation) or a software component (database system), that requires authorization can use its own authorization method once authentication has occurred. This makes for efficient and consistent application of these principles.

Accounting is the process of ascribing resource usage by account for the purpose of tracking resource utilization. This is a basic accounting function that is still used by some enterprises. Accounting can include the collection of billing and other detail records. Network access is often a billable function, and a log of how much time, bandwidth, file transfer space, or other resources were used needs to be maintained. Other accounting functions include keeping detailed security logs to maintain an audit trail of tasks being performed.

Access Control

The term **access control** has been used to describe a variety of protection schemes. It sometimes refers to all security features used to prevent unauthorized access to a computer system or network—or even a network resource such as a printer. In this sense, it may be confused with authentication. More properly, access is the ability of a subject (such as an individual or a process running on a computer system) to interact with an object (such as a file or hardware device). Once the individual has verified their identity, access controls regulate what the individual can actually do on the system. Just because a person is granted entry to the system does not mean they should have access to all the data the system contains.

Security Controls and Permissions

If multiple users share a computer system, the system administrator likely needs to control who is allowed to do what when it comes to viewing, using, or changing system resources. Although operating systems vary in how they implement these types of controls, most operating systems use the concepts of permissions and rights to control and safeguard access to resources. As we discussed earlier, *permissions* control what a user is allowed to do with objects on a system, and *rights* define the actions a user can perform on the system itself. Let's examine how the Windows operating systems implement this concept.

The Windows operating systems use the concepts of permissions and rights to control access to files, folders, and information resources. When using the NTFS filesystem, administrators can grant users and groups permission to perform certain tasks as they relate to files, folders, and Registry keys. The basic categories of NTFS permissions are as follows:

- **Full Control** A user/group can change permissions on the folder/file, take ownership if someone else owns the folder/file, delete subfolders and files, and perform actions permitted by all other NTFS folder permissions.
- **Modify** A user/group can view and modify files/folders and their properties, can delete and add files/folders, and can delete properties from or add properties to a file/folder.
- **Read & Execute** A user/group can view the file/folder and can execute scripts and executables, but they cannot make any changes (files/folders are read-only).
- **List Folder Contents** A user/group can list only what is inside the folder (applies to folders only).
- **Read** A user/group can view the contents of the file/folder and the file/folder properties.
- **Write** A user/group can write to the file or folder.

Tech Tip

AAA

Authentication is the process of validating an identity. Authorization is the process of permitting or denying access to resources. Accounting is the process of keeping track of the resources a user accesses. Together, they make up the AAA framework for identity access security.

Tech Tip

Access Control vs. Authentication

It may seem that access control and authentication are two ways to describe the same protection mechanism. This, however, is not the case. Authentication provides a way to verify to the computer who the user is. Once the user has been authenticated, the access controls decide what operations the user can perform. The two go hand-in-hand but are not the same thing.

Permissions can be applied to a specific user or group to control that user or group's ability to view, modify, access, use, or delete resources such as folders and files.

Figure 11.7 shows the permissions on a folder called Data from a Windows Server system. In the top half of the Permissions window are the users and groups that have permissions for this folder. In the bottom half of the window are the permissions assigned to the highlighted user or group.

The Windows operating system also uses user rights or privileges to determine what actions a user or group is allowed to perform or access. These user rights are typically assigned to groups, as it is easier to deal with a few groups than to assign rights to individual users, and they are usually defined in either a group or a local security policy. The list of user rights is quite extensive, but here are a few examples of user rights:

- **Log on locally** Users/groups can attempt to log on to the local system itself.
- **Access this computer from the network** Users/groups can attempt to access this system through the network connection.
- **Manage auditing and security log** Users/groups can view, modify, and delete auditing and security log information.

Rights tend to be actions that deal with accessing the system itself, process control, logging, and so on. Figure 11.8 shows the user rights contained in the Local Security Policy on a Windows system.

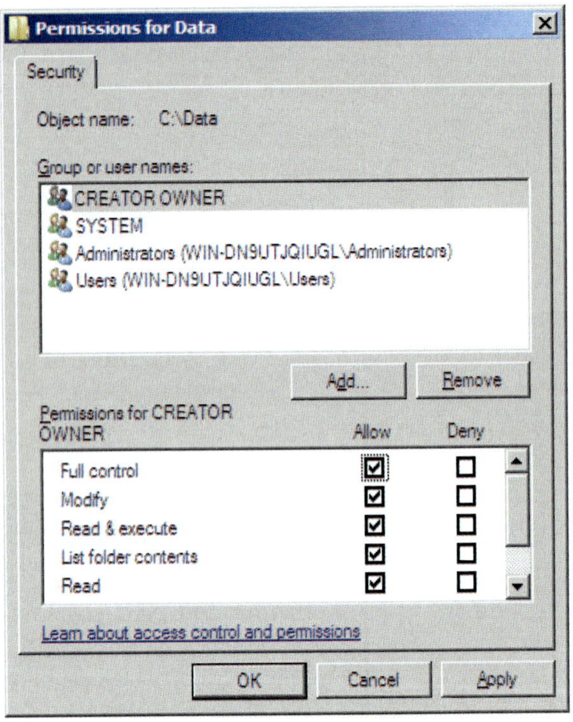

• **Figure 11.7** Permissions for the Data folder

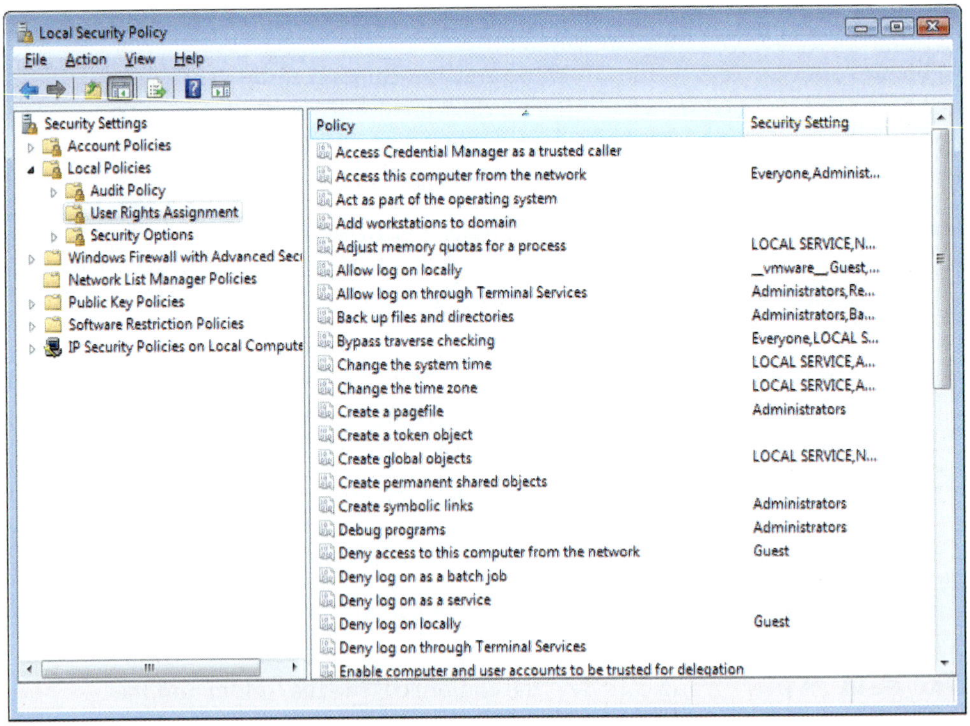

• **Figure 11.8** User Rights Assignment options from Windows Local Security Policy

Folders and files are not the only things that can be safeguarded or controlled using permissions. Even access and use of peripherals such as printers can be controlled using permissions. Figure 11.9 shows the Security tab from a printer attached to a Windows system. Permissions can be assigned to control who can print to the printer, who can manage documents and print jobs sent to the printer, and who can manage the printer itself. With this type of granular control, administrators have a great deal of control over how system resources are used and who uses them.

Under Linux operating systems, file permissions consist of three distinct parts:

- **Owner permissions (read, write, and execute)** The owner of the file
- **Group permissions (read, write, and execute)** The group to which the owner of the file belongs
- **World permissions (read, write, and execute)** Anyone else who is not the owner and does not belong to the group to which the owner of the file belongs

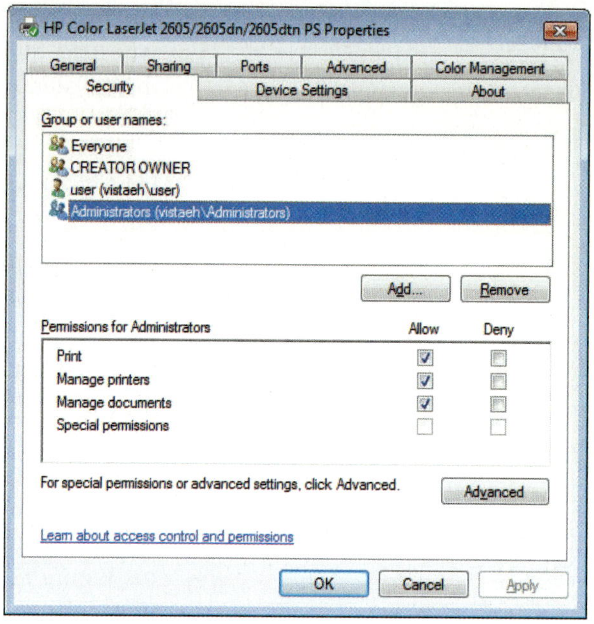

• **Figure 11.9** Security tab showing printer permissions in Windows

Although it is very important to get security settings "right the first time," it is just as important to perform routine audits of security settings such as user accounts, group memberships, file permissions, and so on.

Discretionary access control (DAC) restricts access based on the user's identity or group membership.

For example, suppose a file called *secretdata* has been created by the owner of the file, Luke, who is part of the Engineering group. The owner permissions on the file would reflect Luke's access to the file (as the owner). The group permissions would reflect the access granted to anyone who is part of the Engineering group. The world permissions would represent the access granted to anyone who is not Luke and is not part of the Engineering group.

In Linux, a file's permissions are usually displayed as a series of nine characters, with the first three characters representing the owner's permissions, the second three characters representing the group permissions, and the last three characters representing the permissions for everyone else (that is, for the world). This concept is illustrated in Figure 11.10.

Suppose the file secretdata is owned by Luke with group permissions for Engineering (because Luke is part of the Engineering group), and the permissions on that file are rwx, rw-, and ---, as shown in Figure 11.10. This would mean the following:

- Luke can read, write, and execute the file (rwx).
- Members of the Engineering group can read and write the file but not execute it (rw-).
- The world has no access to the file and can't read, write, or execute it (---).

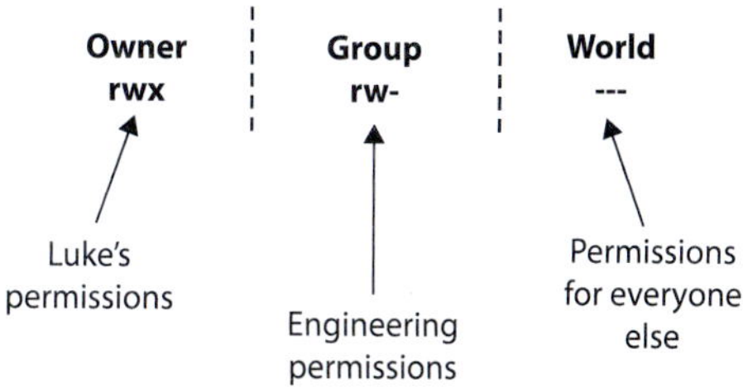

• **Figure 11.10** Discretionary file permissions in the Linux environment

Remember that under the DAC model, the file's owner, Luke, can change the file's permissions any time he wants.

A very important concept to consider when assigning rights and privileges to users is the concept of least privilege. Least privilege requires that users be given the absolute minimum number of rights and privileges required to perform their authorized duties. For example, if a user does not need the ability to install software on their own desktop to perform their job, then don't give them that ability. This reduces the likelihood the user will load malware, insecure software, or unauthorized applications onto their system.

Access Control Lists (ACLs)

The term **access control list (ACL)** is used in more than one manner in the field of computer security. When we discuss routers and firewalls, an ACL is a set of rules used to control traffic flow into or out of an interface or network. When we discuss system resources, such as files and folders, an ACL lists the permissions attached to an object—who is allowed to view, modify, move, or delete that object.

To illustrate this concept, consider an example. Figure 11.11 shows the access control list (permissions) for the Data folder. The user identified as Billy Williams has Read & Execute, List Folder Contents, and Read permissions, meaning this user can open the folder, see what's in the folder, and so on. Figure 11.12 shows the permissions for a user identified as Leah Jones, who has only Read permissions on the same folder.

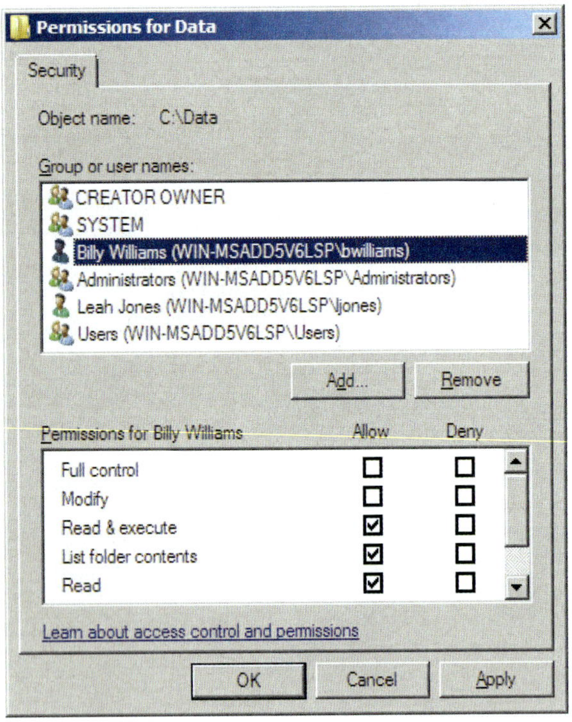

• **Figure 11.11** Permissions for Billy Williams on the Data folder

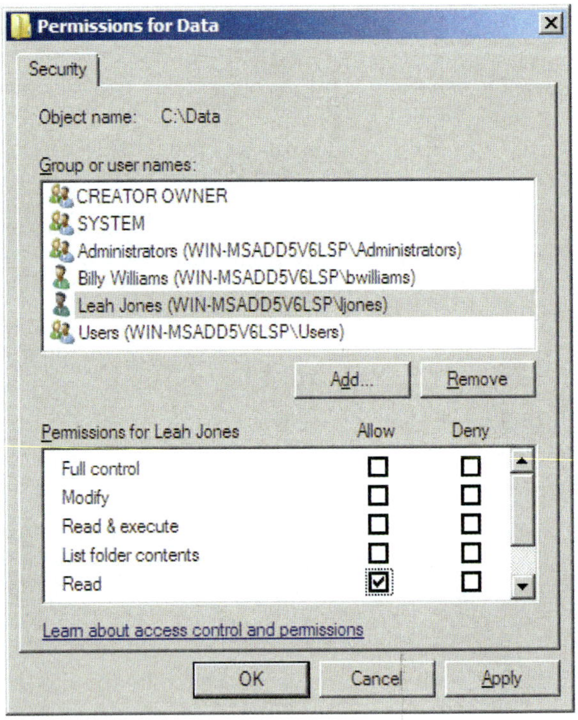

• **Figure 11.12** Permissions for Leah Jones on the Data folder

In computer systems and networks, access controls can be implemented in several ways. An **access control matrix** provides the simplest framework for illustrating the process. An example of an access control matrix is provided in Table 11.1. In this matrix, the system is keeping track of two processes, two files, and one hardware device. Process 1 can read both File 1 and File 2 but can write only to File 1. Process 1 cannot access Process 2, but Process 2 can execute Process 1. Both processes have the ability to write to the printer.

Table 11.1 An Access Control Matrix

	Process 1	Process 2	File 1	File 2	Printer
Process 1	Read, write, execute		Read, write	Read	Write
Process 2	Execute	Read, write, execute	Read, write	Read, write	Write

Although simple to understand, the access control matrix is seldom used in computer systems because it is extremely costly in terms of storage space and processing. Imagine the size of an access control matrix for a large network with hundreds of users and thousands of files.

Mandatory Access Control (MAC)

Mandatory access control (MAC) is the process of controlling access to information based on the sensitivity of that information and whether or not the user is operating at the appropriate sensitivity level and has the authority to access that information. Under a MAC system, each piece of information and every system resource (files, devices, networks, and so on) is labeled with its sensitivity level (such as Public, Engineering Private, Jones Secret, and so on). Users are assigned a clearance level that sets the upper boundary of the information and devices that they are allowed to access.

Mandatory access control restricts access based on the sensitivity of the information and whether or not the user has the authority to access that information.

The access control and sensitivity labels are required in a MAC system. Labels are defined and then assigned to users and resources. Users must then operate within their assigned sensitivity and clearance levels—they don't have the option to modify their own sensitivity levels or the levels of the information resources they create. Due to the complexity involved, MAC is typically run only on systems where security is a top priority, such as Trusted Solaris, OpenBSD, and SELinux.

Tech Tip

MAC Objective

Mandatory access controls are often mentioned in discussions of multilevel security. For multilevel security to be implemented, a mechanism must be present to identify the classification of all users and files. A file identified as Top Secret (that is, it has a label indicating that it is "Top Secret") may be viewed only by individuals with a Top Secret clearance. For this control mechanism to work reliably, all files must be marked with appropriate controls and all user access must be checked. This is the primary goal of MAC.

Figure 11.13 illustrates MAC in operation. The information resource on the left has been labeled "Engineering Secret," meaning only users in the Engineering group operating at the Secret sensitivity level or above can access that resource. The top user is operating at the Secret level but is not a member of Engineering and is denied access to the resource. The middle

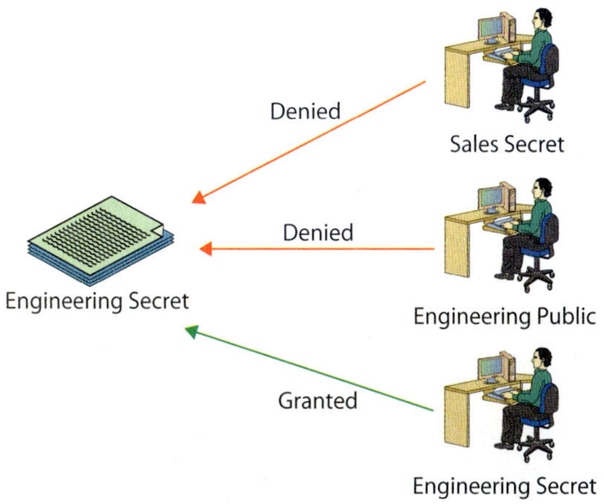

• **Figure 11.13** Logical representation of mandatory access control

user is a member of Engineering but is operating at a Public sensitivity level and is therefore denied access to the resource. The bottom user is a member of Engineering, is operating at a Secret sensitivity level, and is allowed to access the information resource.

Discretionary Access Control (DAC)

Discretionary access control (DAC) is the process of using file permissions and optional ACLs to restrict access to information based on a user's identity or group membership. DAC is the most common access control system and is commonly used in both Linux and Windows operating systems. The "discretionary" part of DAC means that a file or resource owner has the ability to change the permissions on that file or resource.

> **Tech Tip**
>
> **Multilevel Security**
>
> *In the U.S. government, the following security labels are used to classify information and information resources for MAC systems:*
>
> - **Top Secret** *The highest security level and is defined as information that would cause "exceptionally grave damage" to national security if disclosed.*
> - **Secret** *The second highest level and is defined as information that would cause "serious damage" to national security if disclosed.*
> - **Confidential** *The lowest level of classified information and is defined as information that would "damage" national security if disclosed.*
> - **For Official Use Only** *Information that is unclassified but not releasable to public or unauthorized parties. Sometimes called Sensitive But Unclassified (SBU).*
> - **Unclassified** *Not an official classification level.*
>
> *The labels work in a top-down fashion so that an individual holding a Secret clearance would have access to information at the Secret, Confidential, and Unclassified levels. An individual with a Secret clearance would not have access to Top Secret resources because that label is above the highest level of the individual's clearance.*

> As defined by the "Orange Book," a Department of Defense document (in the "rainbow series") that at one time was the standard for describing what constituted a trusted computing system, a *discretionary access control (DAC)* is "a means of restricting access to objects based on the identity of subjects and/or groups to which they belong. The controls are discretionary in the sense that a subject with a certain access permission is capable of passing that permission (perhaps indirectly) on to any other subject (unless restrained by mandatory access control)." This definition is still valid today.

Role-Based Access Control (RBAC)

Access control lists can be cumbersome and can take time to administer properly. **Role-based access control (RBAC)** is the process of managing access and privileges based on the user's assigned roles. RBAC is the access control model that most closely resembles an organization's structure. In this scheme, instead of each user being assigned specific access permissions for the objects associated with the computer system or network, that user is assigned a set of roles that the user may perform. The roles are in turn assigned the access permissions necessary to perform the tasks associated with the role. Users will thus be granted permissions to objects in terms of the specific duties they must perform—not just because of a security classification associated with individual objects.

Under RBAC, you must first determine the activities that must be performed and the resources that must be accessed by specific roles. For example, the role of "securityadmin" in Microsoft SQL Server must be able to create and manage logins, read error logs, and audit the application. Once all the roles are created and the rights and privileges associated with those roles are determined, users can then be assigned one or more roles based on their job functions. When a role is assigned to a specific user, the user gets all the rights and privileges assigned to that role.

Unfortunately, in reality, administrators often find themselves in a position of working in an organization where more than one user has multiple roles or even access to multiple accounts (a situation quite common in smaller organizations). Users with multiple accounts tend to select the same or similar passwords for those accounts, thereby increasing the chance one compromised account can lead to the compromise of other accounts accessed by that user. Where possible, administrators should first eliminate shared or additional accounts for users and then examine the possibility of combining roles or privileges to reduce the "account footprint" of individual users.

> Role-based and rule-based access control can both be abbreviated as RBAC. Standard convention is for RBAC to be used to denote role-based access control. *Role*-based focuses on the user's role (administrator, backup operator, and so on). *Rule*-based focuses on predefined criteria such as time of day (users can only log in between 8 A.M. and 6 P.M.) or type of network traffic (web traffic is allowed to leave the organization).

Rule-Based Access Control

Rule-based access control is yet another method of managing access and privileges (and unfortunately shares the same acronym as role-based access control). In this method, access is either allowed or denied based on a set of predefined rules. Each object has an associated ACL (much like DAC), and when a particular user or group attempts to access the object, the appropriate rule is applied.

A good example for rule-based access control is permitted logon hours. Many operating systems give administrators the ability to control the hours during which users can log in. For example, a bank might allow its employees to log in only between the hours of 8 A.M. and 6 P.M., Monday through Saturday. If a user attempts to log in outside of these hours (3 A.M. on Sunday, for example), then the rule will reject the login attempt regardless of whether the user supplies valid login credentials.

> The ABAC process of authorization evaluates specific rules and policies against attributes associated with a subject or object. ABAC is often used in large enterprises that use a federated structure. It is somewhat more complicated and costly to implement than other access control models.

Attribute-Based Access Control (ABAC)

Attribute-based access control (ABAC) is a new access control schema based on the use of attributes associated with an identity. These can use any type of attributes (user attributes, resource attributes, environment attributes, and so on), such as location, time, activity being requested, and user credentials. An example would be a doctor getting access for a specific patient versus a different patient. ABAC can be represented via the **eXtensible Access Control Markup Language (XACML)**, a standard that implements attribute- and policy-based access control schemes.

Conditional Access

Conditional access is an access control scheme where specific conditions are examined before access is given. Conditions include location when accessing resources, such as if local then grant access; if remote then deny access. The list of conditions can be broad and follows this general form:

If { condition } then { action }

Examples of this would be **If** { client is using legacy authentication } **then** { block access }, **If** { device is not compliant } **then** { block access }, and **If** { User is an Admin } **then** { Enable Multifactor Authentication }. Conditional access can be very useful when an entity has a wide array of different systems with differing access needs.

Identity

Identification is the process of ascribing a computer ID to a specific user, computer, network device, or computer process. The identification process is typically performed only once, when a user ID is issued to a particular user. User identification enables authentication and authorization to form the basis for accountability. For accountability purposes, user IDs should not be shared, and for security purposes, they should not be descriptive of job function. This practice enables you to trace activities to individual users or computer processes so that they can be held responsible for their actions. Identification links the logon ID or user ID to credentials that have been submitted previously to either HR or the IT staff. A required characteristic of user IDs is that they must be unique so that they map back to the credentials presented when the account was established.

Identity Provider (IdP)

The identity provider (IdP) creates, manages, and is responsible for authenticating identity.

The term **identity provider (IdP)** is used to denote a system or service that creates, maintains, and manages identity information. IdPs can range in scale and scope—from operating for a single system to operating across an enterprise. Additionally, they can be operated locally, distributed, or federated, depending on the specific solution. Multiple standards have been employed to achieve these services, including those built on the Security Assertion Markup Language (SAML), OpenID, and OAuth.

Identity Attributes

How would you describe the elements of an identity? Identity attributes are the specific characteristics of an identity—name, department, location, login ID, identification number, e-mail address, and so on—that are used to accurately describe a specific entity. These elements are needed if one is to store identity information in some form of directory, such as an LDAP directory. The particulars of a schema need to be considered to include attributes for people, equipment (servers and devices), and services (apps and programs), as any of these can have an identity in a system. The details of schemas have already been taken care of via Active Directory, various IdPs, and so on, so this is not something that needs to be created; however, it does need to be understood.

Certificates

Certificate-based authentication is a means of proving identity via the presentation of a certificate. Certificates offer a method of establishing authenticity of specific objects such as an individual's public key or downloaded software. A *digital certificate* is a digital file that is sent as an attachment to a message and is used to verify that the message did indeed come from the entity it claims to have come from. Using a digital certificate is a verifiable means of establishing possession of an item (specifically, the certificate). When the certificate is held within a store that prevents tampering or extraction, this becomes a reliable means of identification, especially when combined with an additional factor such as something you know or a biometric. The technical details behind digital certificates are covered in Chapter 7.

Identity Tokens

An access token is a physical object that identifies specific access rights and, in authentication, falls into the "something you have" factor. Your house key, for example, is a basic physical access token that allows you access into your home. Although keys have been used to unlock devices for centuries, they do have several limitations. Keys are paired exclusively with a lock or a set of locks, and they are not easily changed. It is easy to add an authorized user by giving the user a copy of the key, but it is far more difficult to give that user selective access unless that specified area is already set up as a separate key. It is also difficult to take access away from a single key or key holder, which usually requires a rekey of the whole system.

In many businesses, physical access authentication has moved to contactless radio frequency cards and proximity readers. When passed near a card reader, the card sends out a code using radio waves. The reader picks up this code and transmits it to the control panel. The control panel checks the code against the reader from which it is being read and the type of access the card has in its database. The advantages of this kind of token-based system include the fact that any card can be deleted from the system without affecting any other card or the rest of the system. In addition, all doors connected to the system can be segmented in any form or fashion to create multiple access areas, with different permissions for each one. The tokens themselves can also be grouped in multiple ways to provide different access levels to different groups of people. All of the access levels or segmentation of doors can be modified quickly and easily if building space is repurposed. Newer technologies are adding capabilities to the standard token-based systems. Smart cards can also be used to carry identification tokens. The primary drawback of token-based authentication is that only the token is being authenticated. Therefore, the theft of the token could grant anyone who possesses the token access to what the system protects.

The risk of theft of the token can be offset by the use of multifactor authentication described later in this chapter. One of the ways that people have tried to achieve multifactor authentication is to add a biometric factor to the system. A less expensive alternative is to use hardware tokens in a challenge/response authentication process. In this way, the token functions as both a "something you have" and "something you know" authentication mechanism. Several variations on this type of device exist, but they all work on the same basic principles. The device has an LCD screen and may or may not have a numeric keypad. Devices without a keypad will display a password (often just a sequence of numbers) that changes at a constant interval, usually about every 60 seconds. When an individual attempts to log in to a system, they enter their own user ID number and then the number that is displayed on the LCD. These two numbers are either entered separately or concatenated. The user's own ID number is secret, and this prevents someone from using a lost device. The system knows which device the user has and is synchronized with it so that it will know the number that should have been displayed. Since this number is constantly changing, a potential attacker who is able to see the sequence will not be able to use it later, since the code will have changed. Devices with a keypad work in a similar fashion (and may also be designed to function as a simple calculator). The individual who wants to log in to the system will first type their personal identification number into the calculator. They will then attempt to log in. The system will then provide a challenge; the user must enter that challenge into the calculator and press a special function key. The calculator will then determine the correct response and display it. The user provides the response to the system they are attempting to log in to, and the system verifies that this is the correct response. Since each user has a different PIN, two individuals receiving the same challenge will have different responses. The device can also use the date or time as a variable for the response calculation so that the same challenge at different times will yield different responses, even for the same individual.

SSH Keys

SSH keys are access credentials used by the Secure Shell (SSH) protocol. They function like usernames and passwords, but SSH keys are primarily used for automated processes and services. SSH keys are also used in implementing single sign-on (SSO) systems used by system administrators. SSH keys are exchanged using public key cryptography, and the keys themselves are digital keys. The concepts of public key cryptography are covered in Chapter 5.

Smart Cards

Smart cards are devices that store cryptographic tokens associated with an identity. The form factor is commonly a physical card, credit card sized, that contains an embedded chip that has various electronic components to act as a physical carrier of information.

The U.S. federal government has several smart card solutions for identification of personnel. The Personal Identity Verification (PIV) card is a U.S. government smart card that contains the cardholder's credential data used to determine access to federal facilities and information systems. The Common Access Card (CAC) is a smart card used by the U.S. Department of Defense (DoD) for active-duty military, Selected Reserve members, DoD civilians, and eligible contractors. Like the PIV card, it is used for carrying the cardholder's credential data, in the form of a certificate, and to determine access to federal facilities and information systems.

Authentication Methods

Authentication is the process of verifying an identity previously established in a computer system. There are a variety of methods of performing this function, each with its advantages and disadvantages, as detailed in the following sections.

Authentication

Authentication is the process of binding a specific ID to a specific computer connection. Two items need to be presented to cause this binding to occur—the user ID and some "secret" to prove that the user is the valid possessor of the credentials. Historically, three categories of secrets are used to authenticate the identity of a user: what users know, what users have, and what users are. Today, an additional category is used: what users do.

These methods can be used individually or in combination. These controls assume that the identification process has been completed and the identity of the user has been verified. It is the job of authentication mechanisms to ensure that only valid users are admitted. Described another way, authentication is using some mechanism to prove that you are who you claimed to be when the identification process was completed.

The most common method of authentication is the use of a password. For greater security, you can add an element from a separate group, such as a smart card token—something a user has in their possession. Passwords are common because they are one of the simplest forms of authentication, and they use user memory as a prime component. Because of their simplicity, passwords have become ubiquitous across a wide range of authentication systems.

Another method to provide authentication involves the use of something that only valid users should have in their possession. A physical-world example of this would be a simple lock and key. Only those individuals with the correct key will be able to open the lock and thus gain admittance to a house, car, office, or whatever the lock was protecting. A similar method can be used to authenticate users for a computer system or network (though the key may be electronic and could reside on a smart card or similar device). The problem with this technology, however, is that people do lose their keys (or cards), which means not only that the user can't log in to the system but that somebody else who finds the key may then be able to access the system, even though they are not authorized. To address this problem, a combination of the something-you-know and something-you-have methods is often used so that the individual with the key is also required to provide a password or passcode. The key is useless unless the user knows this code.

The third general method to provide authentication involves something that is unique about you. We are accustomed to this concept in our physical world, where our fingerprints or a sample of our DNA can be used to identify us. This same concept can be used to provide authentication in the computer world. The field of authentication that uses something about you or something that you are is known as *biometrics*. A number of different mechanisms can be used to accomplish this type of authentication, such as a fingerprint, iris, retinal, or hand geometry scan. All of these methods obviously require some additional hardware in order to operate. The inclusion of fingerprint readers on mobile computers has become common as the additional hardware has become cost effective.

A new method, based on how users perform an action, such as their walking gait or their typing patterns, has emerged as a source of a personal "signature." While not directly embedded into systems as yet, this is an option that will be coming in the future.

Although the three main approaches to authentication appear to be easy to understand and in most cases easy to implement, authentication is not to be taken lightly because it is such an important component of security. Potential attackers are constantly searching for ways to get past the system's authentication mechanism, and they have employed some fairly ingenious methods to do so. Consequently, security professionals are constantly devising new methods, building on these three basic approaches, to provide authentication mechanisms for computer systems and networks.

• **Figure 11.14** How basic authentication operates

Basic Authentication

Basic authentication is the simplest technique used to manage access control across HTTP. Basic authentication operates by passing information encoded in Base64 form using standard HTTP headers. This is a plaintext method without any pretense of security. Figure 11.14 illustrates the operation of basic authentication.

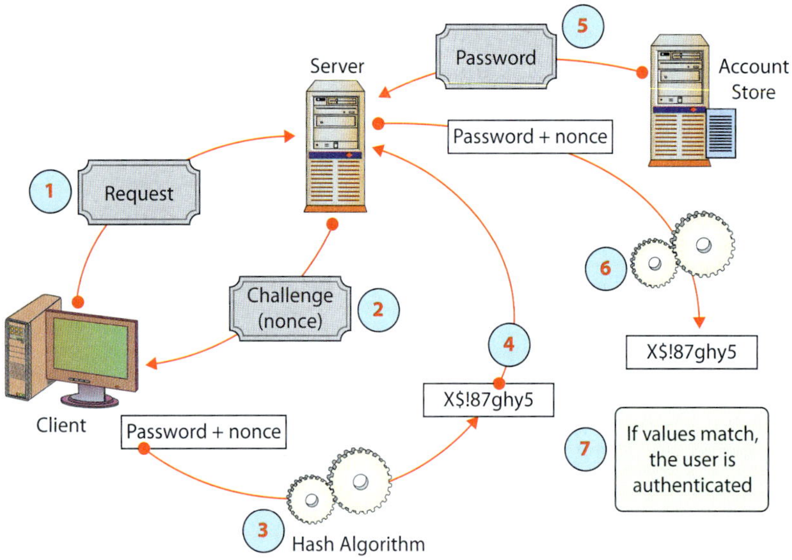

• **Figure 11.15** How digest authentication operates

Digest Authentication

Digest authentication is a method used to negotiate credentials across the Web. Digest authentication uses hash functions and a nonce to improve security over basic authentication. Digest authentication works as follows, as illustrated in Figure 11.15:

1. The client requests login.
2. The server responds with a challenge and provides a nonce.
3. The client hashes the password and nonce.
4. The client returns the hashed password to the server.
5. The server requests the password from a password store.
6. The server hashes the password and nonce.
7. If both hashes match, login is granted.

Digest authentication, although it improves security over basic authentication, does not provide any significant level of security. Passwords are not sent in the clear. Digest authentication is subject to on-path (formally man-in-the-middle) attacks and potentially replay attacks.

> The bottom line for both basic and digest authentication is that these are insecure methods and should not be relied upon for any level of security.

Kerberos

Developed as part of MIT's project Athena, **Kerberos** is a network authentication protocol designed for a client/server environment. The current version is Kerberos 5 release 1.16 and is supported by all major operating systems. Kerberos securely passes a symmetric key over an insecure network using the Needham-Schroeder symmetric key protocol. Kerberos is built around the idea of a trusted third party, termed a **key distribution center (KDC)**, which consists of two logically separate parts: an **authentication server (AS)** and a **ticket-granting server (TGS)**. Kerberos communicates via "tickets" that serve to prove the identity of users.

> Two tickets are used in Kerberos. The first is a *ticket-granting ticket (TGT)* obtained from the authentication server (AS). The TGT is presented to a ticket-granting server (TGS) when access to a server is requested and then a client-to-server ticket is issued, granting access to the server. Typically both the AS and the TGS are logically separate parts of the key distribution center (KDC).

Taking its name from the three-headed dog of Greek mythology, Kerberos is designed to work across the Internet, an inherently insecure environment. Kerberos uses strong encryption so that a client can prove its identity to a server and the server can in turn authenticate itself to the client. A complete Kerberos environment is referred to as a Kerberos *realm*. The Kerberos server contains user IDs and hashed passwords for all users who will have authorizations to realm services. The Kerberos server also has shared secret keys with every server to which it will grant access tickets.

The basis for authentication in a Kerberos environment is the ticket. Tickets are used in a two-step process with the client. The first ticket is a **ticket-granting ticket (TGT)** issued by the AS to a requesting client. The client can then present this ticket to the Kerberos server with a request for a ticket to access a specific server. This **client-to-server ticket** (also called a *service ticket*) is used to gain access to a server's service in the realm. Because the entire session can be encrypted, this eliminates the inherently insecure transmission of items such as a password that can be intercepted on the network. Tickets are timestamped and have a lifetime, so attempting to reuse a ticket will not be successful. Figure 11.16 details Kerberos operations.

Tech Tip

Kerberos Authentication

Kerberos is a third-party authentication service that uses a series of tickets as tokens for authenticating users. The six steps involved are protected using strong cryptography:

- *The user presents their credentials and requests a ticket from the key distribution center (KDC).*
- *The KDC verifies credentials and issues a ticket-granting ticket (TGT).*
- *The user presents a TGT and request for service to the KDC.*
- *The KDC verifies authorization and issues a client-to-server ticket (or service ticket).*
- *The user presents a request and a client-to-server ticket to the desired service.*
- *If the client-to-server ticket is valid, service is granted to the client.*

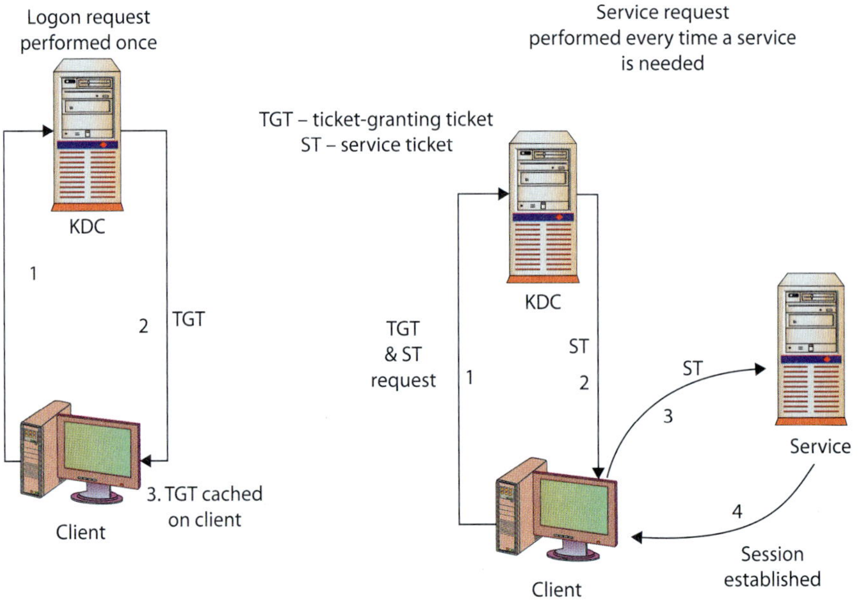

Client Authentication
1. The client sends a cleartext message to the AS requesting services on behalf of the user.
2. The AS checks to see if the client is in its database. If it is, the AS sends back ticket-granting ticket.
3. Once the client receives messages, it decrypts them to obtain the client/TGS session key.

Service Request
1. Using its TGT, client requests a service ticket.
2. Client submits ST to service provider with request.
3. The server provides the requested services to the client.

• **Figure 11.16** Kerberos operations

> Kerberos is a third-party authentication service that uses a series of tickets as tokens for authenticating users. The steps involved are protected using strong cryptography.

To illustrate how the Kerberos authentication service works, think about the common driver's license. You have received a license that you can present to other entities to prove you are who you claim to be. Because other entities trust the state in which the license was issued, they will accept your license as proof of your identity. The state in which the license was issued is analogous to the Kerberos authentication service realm, and the license acts as a client-to-server ticket. It is the trusted entity both sides rely on to provide valid identifications. This analogy is not perfect, because we all probably have heard of individuals who obtained a phony driver's license, but it serves to illustrate the basic idea behind Kerberos.

Mutual Authentication

Mutual authentication describes a process in which each side of an electronic communication verifies the authenticity of the other. We are accustomed to the idea of having to authenticate ourselves to our ISP before we access the Internet, generally through the use of a user ID/password pair, but how do we actually know that we are really communicating with our ISP and not some other system that has somehow inserted itself into our communication (a man-in-the-middle attack)? Mutual authentication provides a mechanism for each side of a client/server relationship to verify the authenticity of the other to address this issue. A common method of performing mutual authentication involves using a secure connection, such as Transport Layer

Security (TLS), to the server and a one-time password generator that then authenticates the client.

Certificates

Certificates are a method of establishing authenticity of specific objects such as an individual's public key or downloaded software. A **digital certificate** is a digital file that is sent as an attachment to a message and is used to verify that the message did indeed come from the entity it claims to have come from.

> **Cross Check**
>
> **Digital Certificates and Digital Signatures**
>
> Kerberos uses tickets to convey messages. Part of the ticket is a certificate that contains the requisite keys. Understanding how certificates convey this vital information is an important part of understanding how Kerberos-based authentication works. Certificates, how they are used, and the protocols associated with PKI were covered in Chapter 7. Refer back to this chapter as needed for more information.

> Mutual TLS–based authentication provides the same functions as normal TLS, with the addition of authentication and nonrepudiation of the client. This second authentication, the authentication of the client, is done in the same manner as the normal server authentication using digital signatures. The client authentication represents the many sides of a many-to-one relationship. Mutual TLS authentication is not commonly used because of the complexity, cost, and logistics associated with managing the multitude of client certificates. This reduces the effectiveness, and most web applications are not designed to require client-side certificates.

Tokens

While the username/password combination has been and continues to be the cheapest and most popular method of controlling access to resources, many organizations look for a more secure and tamper-resistant form of authentication. Usernames and passwords are "something you know" (which can be used by anyone else who knows or discovers the information). A more secure method of authentication is to combine the "something you know" with "something you have." A **token** is an authentication factor that typically takes the form of a physical or logical entity that the user must be in possession of to access their account or certain resources.

A token is a hardware device that can be used in a challenge/response authentication process. In this way, it functions as both a something-you-have and something-you-know authentication mechanism. Several variations on this type of device exist, but they all work on the same basic principles. Tokens are commonly employed in remote authentication schemes because they provide additional surety of the identity of the user, even users who are somewhere else and cannot be observed.

Most tokens are physical tokens that display a series of numbers that changes every 30 to 90 seconds, such as the token pictured in Figure 11.17

> **Tech Tip**
>
> **PIV/CAC/Smart Cards**
>
> *The U.S. federal government has several smart card solutions for identification of personnel. The* **personal identity verification (PIV)** *card is a U.S. government smart card that contains the credential data for the cardholder used to determine access to federal facilities and information systems. The* **Common Access Card (CAC)** *is a smart card identification used by the U.S. Department of Defense (DoD) for active-duty military, selected reserve personnel, DoD civilians, and eligible contractors. Like the PIV card, it is used for carrying the credential data, in the form of a certificate, for the cardholder and is used to determine access to federal facilities and information systems.*

• **Figure 11.17** Token authenticator from Blizzard Entertainment

The use of a token is a common method of using "something you have" for authentication. A token can hold a cryptographic key or act as a one-time password (OTP) generator. It can also be a smart card that holds a cryptographic key (examples include the U.S. military Common Access Card and the Federal Personal Identity Verification [PIV] card). These devices can be safeguarded using a PIN and lockout mechanism to prevent use if stolen.

Understand that tokens represent (1) something you have with respect to authentication and (2) a device that can store more information than you can memorize. This makes them very valuable for access control. The details in the question on the exam will provide the necessary criteria to pick the best token method for the question.

HOTP passwords can remain valid and active for an unknown time period. TOTP passwords are considered more secure because they are valid for short amounts of time and change often.

from Blizzard Entertainment. This sequence of numbers must be entered when the user is attempting to log in or access certain resources. The ever-changing sequence of numbers is synchronized to a remote server such that when the user enters the correct username, password, and matching sequence of numbers, they are allowed to log in. Even if an attacker obtains the username and password, the attacker cannot log in without the matching sequence of numbers. Other physical tokens include Common Access Cards (CACs), USB tokens, smart cards, and PC cards.

Software Tokens

Access tokens may also be implemented in software. **Software tokens** still provide two-factor authentication but don't require the user to have a separate physical device on hand. Some tokens require software clients that store a symmetric key (sometimes called a *seed record*) in a secured location on the user's device (laptop, desktop, tablet, and so on). Other software tokens use public key cryptography. Asymmetric cryptography solutions, such as public key cryptography, often associate a PIN with a specific user's token. To log in or access critical resources, the user must supply the correct PIN. The PIN is stored on a remote server and is used during the authentication process so that if the user presents the right token, but not the right PIN, the user's access can be denied. This helps prevent an attacker from gaining access if they get a copy of or gain access to the software token. The most common form of software token is for identifying a specific device in addition to a user, in that the software token is on the device and the user supplies the rest of the details needed to demonstrate authenticity.

HOTP/TOTP

HMAC-based One-Time Password (HOTP) is an algorithm that can be used to authenticate a user in a system by using an authentication server. (HMAC stands for Hash-based Message Authentication Code.) It is defined in RFC 4226, dated December 2005. The **Time-based One-Time Password (TOTP)** algorithm is a specific implementation of an HOTP that uses a secret key with a current timestamp to generate a one-time password. It is described in RFC 6238, dated May 2011.

Smart Cards

Smart cards can increase physical security because they can carry cryptographic tokens that are too long to remember and have too large a space to guess. Because of the manner in which they are employed and used, copying the number is not a practical option either. Smart cards can find use in a variety of situations where you want to combine something you know (a PIN or password) together with something you have (and can't be duplicated, such as a smart card). Many standard corporate-type laptops come with smart card readers installed, and their use is integrated into the Windows user access system.

Knowledge-Based Authentication

Knowledge-based authentication is a method where the identity of a user is verified via a common set of knowledge. This is a very useful method for verifying the identity of a user without having a stored secret in advance.

The standard methodology associated with authentication is an identity and a common secret that are previously recorded in a system, and then upon later use verified by recall on the user's part and lookup by the system. But what if the user has never accessed the site to establish their identity? How can it be established on the fly, so to speak? Knowledge-based authentication relies on a set of knowledge that, while it may be available to many, is from such a vast set of information that the recall only will work for the user themselves.

A good example is when accessing a site such as a credit bureau to obtain information on yourself. The site has a vast array of knowledge associated with you, and it can see if you can identify an address you have lived at (out of a list of four addresses), a car you owned (out of a list of four cars), a car or mortgage payment amount, or a credit card account. In a timed quiz, to eliminate extensive lookups, the user is presented with a series of multiple-choice options. If they get them all correct, then odds are that they are the person they represent themselves to be. The last time the author went through one of these tests, the range of time for the knowledge covered was greater than 20 years, making the breadth of knowledge to choose from large indeed.

Directory Services

A **directory** is a data storage mechanism similar to a database, but it has several distinct differences designed to provide efficient data-retrieval services compared to standard database mechanisms. A directory is designed and optimized for reading data, offering very fast search and retrieval operations. The types of information stored in a directory tend to be descriptive attribute data. A directory offers a static view of data that can be changed without a complex update transaction. The data is hierarchically described in a tree-like structure, and a network interface for reading is typical. Common uses of directories include e-mail address lists, domain server data, and resource maps of network resources. The *Lightweight Directory Access Protocol (LDAP)* is commonly used to handle user authentication and authorization and to control access to Active Directory (AD) objects.

When integrating with cloud-based systems, you might find managing credentials across the two different domains challenging. Different vendors have created directory-based technologies to address this, such as AWS Directory Service for Microsoft Active Directory, also known as AWS Managed Microsoft AD. This service enables your directory-aware workloads and AWS resources to use a managed Active Directory in the AWS Cloud. Because AWS Managed Microsoft AD is built on the actual Microsoft Active Directory, you can use standard Active Directory administration tools and take advantage of built-in Active Directory features, such as Group Policy and single sign-on (SSO) features.

Federation

Federation, or *identity federation*, defines policies, protocols, and practices to manage identities across systems and organizations. Federation's ultimate goal is to allow users to seamlessly access data or systems across domains. Federation is enabled through the use of industry standards such as Security Assertion Markup Language (SAML). Federated identity access management systems allow users to authenticate and access resources across multiple enterprises using a single credential. But don't confuse this with single sign-on (SSO), which allows users access to multiple resource within a single organization or enterprise.

Attestation

Attestation is the supplying of proof or evidence of some fact. In the case of authentication, attestation can be done by a service that checks the credentials supplied, and if they are correct and match the required values, the service can attest that the entry is valid or correct. Attestation is used throughout cybersecurity whenever a third party or entity verifies an object as valid or an item as correct in value.

Transitive Trust

Security across multiple domains is provided through trust relationships. When trust relationships between domains exist, authentication for each domain trusts the authentication for all other trusted domains. Thus, when an application is authenticated by a domain, its authentication is accepted by all other domains that trust the authenticating domain.

It is important to note that trust relationships apply only to authentication. They do not apply to resource usage, which is an access control issue. Trust relationships allow users to have their identity verified (authentication). The ability to use resources is defined by access control rules. Thus, even though a user is authenticated via the trust relationship, it does not provide access to actually use resources.

> Transitive trust involves three parties: if A trusts B, and B trusts C, then in a transitive trust relationship, A will trust C.

A **transitive trust** relationship means that the trust relationship extended to one domain will be extended to any other domain trusted by that domain. A two-way trust relationship means that two domains trust each other.

Technologies

There are multiple ways to perform authentication, and multiple technologies can be employed to assist in the effort.

Short Message Service (SMS)

The use of *Short Message Service*, or text messaging, in a cell phone provides a second authentication factor that is sent to a preidentified number. The message that is sent provides a code that the user enters into the system. This code typically has an expiration time, as shown in Figure 11.18. This is a way of verifying that the first credential, usually a password, was entered by the person expected—assuming they have control over the cell phone. This is a practical example of multifactor authentication, which is discussed later in this chapter.

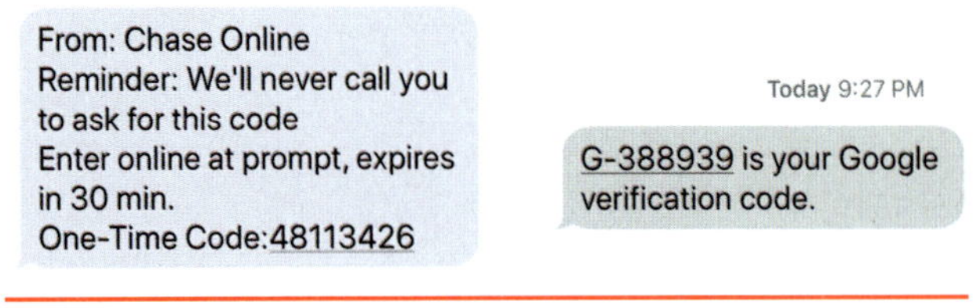

Figure 11.18 Sample SMS verification codes

Trusted Platform Module (TPM)

The **trusted platform module (TPM)** is a hardware solution on the motherboard, one that assists with key generation and storage as well as random number generation. When the encryption keys are stored in the TPM, they are not accessible via normal software channels and are physically separated from the hard drive or other encrypted data locations. This makes the TPM a more secure solution than keeping the keys in the machine's normal storage. A TPM acts as a secure cryptoprocessor. It is a hardware solution that assists with key generation and secure, encrypted storage.

Hardware Security Module (HSM)

A **hardware security module (HSM)** is a device used to manage or store encryption keys. It can also assist in cryptographic operations such as encryption, hashing, or the application of digital signatures. HSMs typically are peripheral devices connected via USB or a network connection. HSMs have tamper-protection mechanisms to prevent physical access to the secrets they protect. Because of their dedicated design, they can offer significant performance advantages over general-purpose computers when it comes to cryptographic operations. When an enterprise has significant levels of cryptographic operations, HSMs can provide throughput efficiencies. Storing private keys anywhere on a networked system is a recipe for loss. HSMs are designed to allow the use of keys without exposing them to the wide range of host-based threats.

Static Codes

Static codes are just that—codes that do not change or are static in nature. There are many use cases where these are essential, cases such as devices without user intervention. Deployed devices that do not have user intervention are widely deployed in many systems. An example would be a smart electric meter, a device that needs to communicate with other systems and authenticate its identity. The use of static codes has a weakness in that, if compromised, the keys are no longer valid. The standard is to use cryptographic protection of all transmission of static codes, making the code unreadable even if the communication channel data is copied.

Authentication Applications

Need a second factor for authentication? We have an app for that. And this is not just a joke, but an increasingly common method of authentication that works by verifying that a user has a given mobile device in their possession. An authentication application functions by accepting user input, and if the user input is correct, it can pass the appropriate credentials to the system requesting authentication. This can be in the form of either a stored digital value or a one-time code in response to a challenge. Authentication applications exist for a variety of platforms—from Android to iOS, Linux, and Windows—and there are multiple vendors for each platform. The use of the application on the device is a second factor of authentication and is part of a multifactor authentication scheme.

Push Notifications

Push notification authentication supports user authentication by pushing a notification directly to an application on the user's device. The user receives the alert that an authentication attempt is taking place, and they can approve or deny the access via the user interface on the application. The push notification itself is not a secret; it is merely a means by which the user can authenticate and approve access. This is an out-of-band communication and demonstrates a second communication channel, thus making account hacking significantly more challenging.

> **Tech Tip**
>
> **Tokens**
>
> *Tokens represent something you have with respect to authentication as well as devices that can store more information than a user can memorize, which makes them very valuable for access control. The details in the scenario preceding a question will provide the necessary criteria to pick the best token method for the question.*

Phone Call

Another form of authenticating a user has an interaction with the system via a phone call. The authentication *phone call* is delivered from the authentication system to a specified phone number, which then can verify that the user is in possession of the actual mobile device.

Smart Card Authentication

A *smart card* (also known as an *integrated circuit card [ICC]* or *chip card*) is a credit card–sized card with embedded integrated circuits that is used to provide identification security authentication. Smart cards can increase physical security because they can carry long cryptographic tokens that are too long to remember and too large a space to guess. Also, because of the manner in which smart cards are employed and used, copying the number is not a practical option. Smart cards can find use in a variety of situations where you want to combine something you know (a PIN or password) with something you have (and can't be duplicated, such as a smart card). Many standard corporate-type laptops come with smart card readers installed, and their use is integrated into the Windows user access system.

Password Vaults

Password vaults are software mechanisms designed to manage the problem of users having multiple passwords for the myriad of different systems. Vaults provide a means of storing the passwords until they are needed, and many password manager programs include additional functionality such as password generation and password handling via a browser. Vaults do represent a single point of failure in that if an attacker gets the password key, or master password, they have access to all of the user's passwords. Cryptographic protections should remedy this, but it also introduces another issue with vaults—what to do when the user loses their master password. Any recovery mechanism would represent a major risk for the system, so in most systems it is incumbent on the user to maintain this information somewhere else as a backup.

Another form of password vault is the systems built into software and operating systems (OSs) to securely hold credentials. Examples of these are the Keychain in macOS and iOS and the Credential Manager in Microsoft Windows. The use of browser-based password storage is much less secure, as numerous utilities exist that can get the passwords out of most of them, making these solutions less secure and an obvious target for attackers. The OS-based Keychain and Credential Manager solutions are much more robust and can limit overall risk.

Biometric Factors

Biometrics factors use the measurements of certain biological features to identify one specific person from other people. These factors are based on parts of the human body that are unique. The most well-known of these unique biological factors is the fingerprint. Fingerprint readers have been available for several years in laptops and other mobile devices, on keyboards, and as standalone USB devices.

Many other biological factors can be used, too, such as the retina or iris of the eye, the geometry of the hand, and the geometry of the face. When these are used for authentication, there is a two-part process: enrollment and then authentication. During enrollment, a computer takes the image of the biological factor and reduces it to a numeric value, called a template. When the user attempts to authenticate, the biometric feature is scanned by the reader, and the computer computes a value in the same fashion as the template and then compares the numeric value being read to the one stored in the database. If they match, access is allowed. Because these physical factors are unique, theoretically only the actual authorized person would be allowed access.

In the real world, however, the theory behind biometrics breaks down. Tokens that have a digital code work very well because everything remains in the digital realm. A computer checks your code, such as 123, against the database; if the computer finds 123 and that number has access, the computer opens the door. Biometrics, however, take an analog signal, such as a fingerprint or a face, and attempt to digitize it, and it is then matched against the digits in the database. The problem with an analog signal is that it might not encode the exact same way twice. For example, if you came to work with a bandage on your chin, would the face-based biometrics grant you access or deny it? Because of this, the templates are more complex in a manner where there can be a probability of match (that is, they use a closeness measurement).

Fingerprint Scanner

Fingerprint scanners are used to measure the unique shape of fingerprints and then change them to a series of numerical values, or a template. Fingerprint readers can be enhanced to ensure that the pattern is a live pattern—one with blood moving or other detectable biological activity. This is to prevent simple spoofing with a mold of the print made of Jell-O. Fingerprint scanners are cheap to produce and have widespread use in mobile devices. One of the challenges of fingerprint scanners is they fail if the user is wearing gloves (such as medical gloves) or has worn-down fingerprints, as is the case for those involved in the sheetrock trade.

Retinal Scanner

Retinal scanners examine blood vessel patterns in the back of the eye. Believed to be unique and unchanging, this is a readily detectable biometric. It does suffer from user acceptance, as it involves a laser scanning the inside of the user's eyeball, which has some psychological issues. This detection is close up, and the user has to be right at the device for it to work. It is also more expensive because of the precision of the detector and the involvement of lasers and users' vision.

Iris Scanner

Iris scanners work in a way similar to retinal scanners in that they use an image of a unique biological measurement (in this case, the pigmentation associated with the iris of the eye). This can be photographed and measured from a distance, removing the psychological impediment of placing one's eye on a scanner. But there are downsides: because the measurement can be taken at a distance, it is easy to measure other people's values, and contact lenses can be constructed that mimic a certain pattern. There are also medical issues such as diseases, which if revealed would be a violation of privacy.

Voice Recognition

Voice recognition is the use of unique tonal qualities and speech patterns to identify a person. Long the subject of sci-fi movies, this biometric has been one of the hardest to develop into a reliable mechanism, primarily because of problems with false acceptance and rejection rates, which will be discussed later in the chapter.

Facial Recognition

Facial recognition was mostly the stuff of sci-fi until it was integrated into various mobile phones. A sensor that recognizes when you move the phone into a position to see your face, coupled with a state of not being logged in, turns on the forward-facing camera, causing the system to look for its enrolled owner. This system has proven to have fairly high discrimination and works fairly well, with only one drawback: another person can move the phone in front of the registered user to unlock it. In essence, another user can activate the unlocking mechanism when the user is unaware. The other minor drawback is that for certain transactions, such as positive identification for financial transactions, the position of the phone on an NFC location, together with the user's face needing to be in a certain orientation with respect to the phone, leads to some awkward positions. In other words, having to put your face in a proper position on the phone to identify you while holding it against the counter-height NFC credit card reader can be awkward.

Vein

A different biometric is the use of blood *vein* patterns to identify a user. Humans have a common vascular system, but the individual elements can vary in size and microstructure, and these fine-grained patterns are believed to be unique. Sensors can measure these patterns and use them to identify a user. Three common vascular pattern locations are used: palms, fingers, and the veins in the retina. This measurement is done via spectral analysis of the tissue, using frequencies that detect the hemoglobin in the blood. These are noninvasive measurements, but they do require close proximity to the user's item under measurement.

Gait Analysis

Gait analysis is the measurement of the pattern expressed by a person as they walk. An analysis of the gait, its length, the speed, and the rate of movement of specific points provides a unique signature that can be recorded and compared to previous samples. Even when not used for authentication, as a previous sample is required, gait analysis can be used to identify a suspect in a group of others, enabling the tracking of individuals in a crowd. From an access control perspective, in high-security situations, a camera can record the gait of incoming personnel and compare it to known values, providing a remote and early additional factor in determining identity.

Biometric Efficacy Rates

Biometric measurements have a level of uncertainty, and thus the efficacy of biometric solutions has been an issue since they were first developed. As each generation of sensor improved the accuracy of the measurements, the errors have been reduced to what is now a manageable level. For biometrics to be effective, they must have both low false positive rates and low false negative rates. The terms *false acceptance rate (FAR)* and *false rejection rate (FRR)* describe the chance that an incorrect user will be falsely accepted or a correct user will be falsely rejected, respectively, as covered in detail in the next sections. These two measures are different, and while a low false rejection rate is important for usability, a low false acceptance rate is more important from a security perspective. Users having to repeat trying to authenticate is bad, but having authentication occur for unauthorized users is worse.

The FIDO Alliance, a leading authentication standards and certification body, has specifications for error rates. FRR should be below 3 percent (no more than three errors in 100 attempts) and FAR should be below 0.01 percent (no more than one error in 10,000 attempts). As in all defense-in-depth scenarios, the backstop is a lockout function where devices will lock after a certain number of failed attempts. This makes the FAR more secure than just the simple percentage

False Positives and False Negatives

Engineers who design systems understand that if a system was set to exact checking, an encoded biometric might never grant access because it might never scan the biometric exactly the same way twice. Therefore, most systems have tried to allow a certain amount of error in the scan, while not allowing too much. This leads to the concepts of false positives and false negatives. A **false positive** is where you receive a positive result for a test, when you should have received a negative result. Thus, a false positive result occurs when a biometric is scanned and allows access to someone who is not authorized—for example, two people who have very similar fingerprints might be recognized as the same person by the computer, which in turn might grant access to the wrong person. A **false negative** occurs when the system denies access to someone who is actually authorized—for example, a user at the hand geometry scanner may have forgotten to wear a ring they usually wear and the computer doesn't recognize their hand and denies them access.

In statistical terms, a false positive is called a type I error, and a false negative is a type II error. When you're working with scientific problems, a type II error is considered to be more serious. In practical systems, the more serious error depends on the circumstances. If you are willing to trade off legitimate access (make authorized users try several times) to keep out unauthorized parties, then type II errors are being avoided at the expense of type I errors. But if legitimate access is not to be denied, even if in error (for example, signing in to prevent the meltdown of the core at a power plant), then type I errors might be prioritized over type II errors. Context and circumstances matter. For example, you need to consider what the biometrics are protecting and what the cost is of each type of failure.

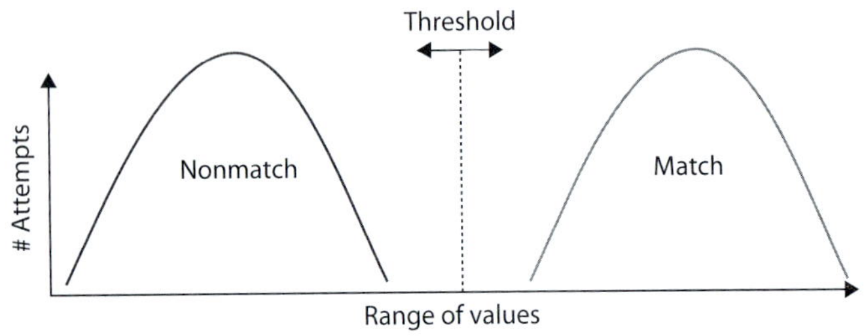

• **Figure 11.19** Ideal probabilities

What is desired is for the system to be able to differentiate the two signals—one being the stored value and the other being the observed value—in such a way that the two curves do not overlap. Figure 11.19 illustrates two probability distributions that do not overlap.

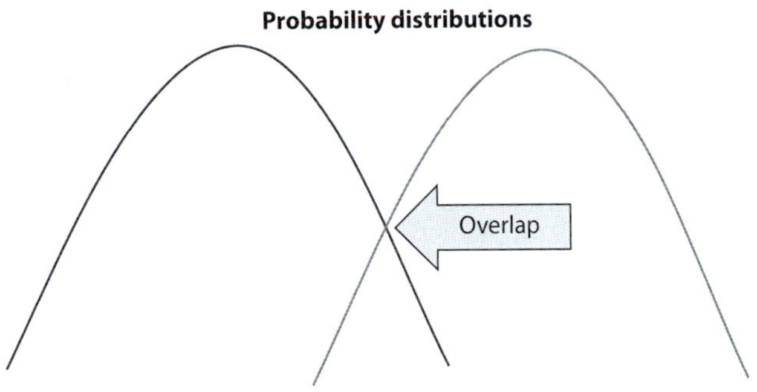

• **Figure 11.20** Overlapping probabilities

For biometric authentication to work properly, and also be trusted, it must minimize the existence of both false positives and false negatives. But biometric systems are seldom that discriminating, and the curves tend to overlap, as shown in Figure 11.20. For detection to work, a balance between exacting and error must be created so that the machines allow a little physical variance—but not too much.

This leads us to acceptance and rejection rates.

False Acceptance Rate

The **false acceptance rate (FAR)** is just that: what level of false positives are going to be allowed in the system. If an unauthorized user is accepted by the system, this is a false acceptance. A false positive is demonstrated by the grayed-out area in Figure 11.21. In this section, the curves overlap, and the decision has been set that at the threshold or better an accept signal will be given. Thus, if you are on the upper end of the nonmatch curve, in the gray area, you will be a false positive. Expressed as probabilities, the false acceptance rate is the probability that the system incorrectly identifies a match between the biometric input and the stored

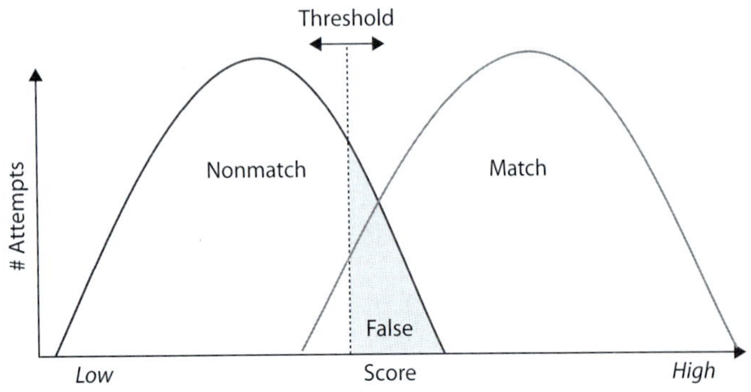

• **Figure 11.21** False acceptance rate

template value. The FAR is calculated by counting the number of unauthorized accesses granted, divided by the total number of access attempts.

When selecting the threshold value, the designer must be cognizant of two factors: one is the rejection of a legitimate biometric, the area on the match curve below the threshold value. The other is the acceptance of a false positive. As you set the threshold higher, you will decrease false positives but increase false negatives (or rejections).

False Rejection Rate

The **false rejection rate (FRR)** is just that: what level of false negatives, or rejections, are going to be allowed in the system. If an authorized user is rejected by the system, this is a false rejection. A false rejection is demonstrated by the grayed-out area in Figure 11.22. In this section, the curves overlap, and the decision has been set that at the threshold or lower a reject signal will be given. Thus, if you are on the lower end of the match curve, in the gray area, you will be rejected, even if you should be a match. Expressed as probabilities, the false rejection rate is the probability that the system incorrectly rejects a legitimate match between the biometric input and the stored template value. The FRR is calculated by counting the number of authorized access attempts that were not granted, divided by the total number of access attempts.

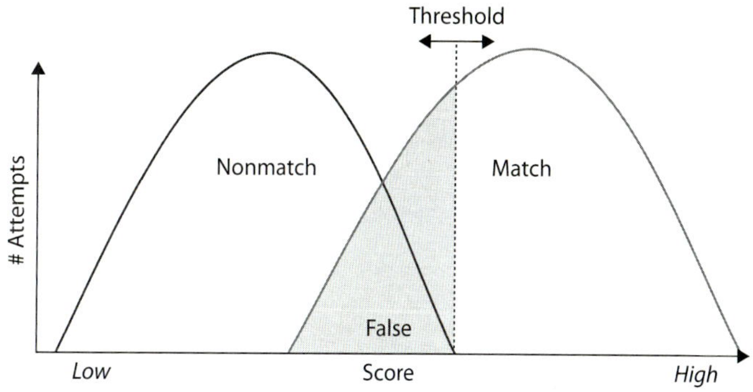

• **Figure 11.22** False rejection rate

When comparing the FAR and the FRR, one realizes that in most cases, whenever the curves overlap, they are related. This brings up the issue of the crossover error rate (see Table 11.2).

Table 11.2 Comparison of Outcomes and Error Terms

User	Outcome	Error Type	Contributes to
Authorized	Access granted	None	N/A
Authorized	Access denied	False negative Type I	False rejection rate (FRR)
Unauthorized	Access granted	False positive Type II	False acceptance rate (FAR)
Unauthorized	Access denied	None	N/A

Crossover Error Rate

The **crossover error rate (CER)**, also known as the *equal error rate (EER)*, is the rate where both accept and reject error rates are equal. This is the desired state for most efficient operation, and it can be managed by manipulating the threshold value used for matching. In practice, the values might not be exactly the same, but they will typically be close to each other. Figure 11.23 demonstrates the relationship between the FAR, FRR, and CER.

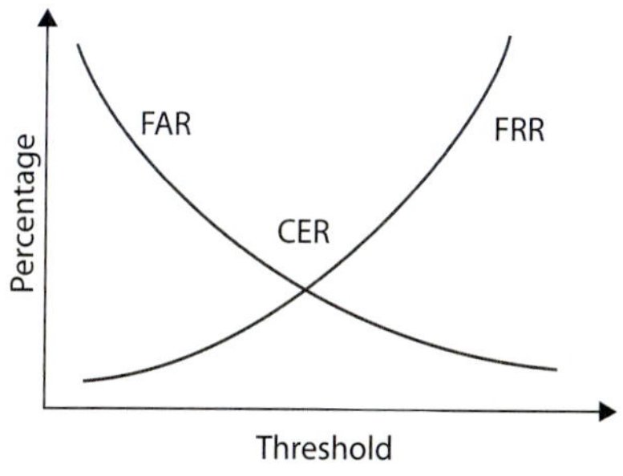

• **Figure 11.23** FRR, FAR, and CER compared

Biometrics Calculation Example

Assume we are using a fingerprint biometric system, and we have 1000 users. During the enrollment stage, five users were unable to enroll (the system could not establish a fingerprint signature/template for them). This means the system has a *failure to enroll rate* (FER) for 0.5 percent. In other words, only 995 users can use the system, and an alternative means needs to be in place for the users who cannot use the system.

During the testing of the 995 users, 50 users were rejected when the system matched their fingerprint against their enrollment fingerprint template.

FAR = (NFA / NIA) * 100%

(NFA = number of false acceptances, and NIA = number of imposter attempts)

FAR = (50/995) * 100

This makes the FRR 5.02 percent.

Also, 25 users out of the 995 users were accepted by the system when the system matched their fingerprint against other users' fingerprint templates.

FRR = (NFR / NEA) * 100%

(NFR = number of failed rejections, and NEA = number of legitimate access attempts)

FRR = (25/995) * 100%

This means the FAR is 2.51 percent.

The lower the FAR and FRR, the better the system, and the ideal situation is setting the thresholds where the FAR and FRR are equal (the crossover error rate).

> Understand how to calculate FAR and FRR, given data. This is an easy calculation, and remember to include those who fail enrollment.

Multifactor Authentication

Multifactor authentication (or multiple-factor authentication) is simply the combination of two or more types of authentication. Five broad categories of authentication can be used: what you are (for example, biometrics), what you have (for instance, tokens), what you know (passwords and other information), somewhere you are (location), and something you do (physical performance). Two-factor authentication combines any two of these before granting access. An example would be a card reader that then turns on a fingerprint scanner—if your fingerprint matches the one on file for the card, you are granted access. Three-factor authentication would combine all three types, such as a smart card reader that asks for a PIN before enabling a retina scanner. If all three correspond to a valid user in the computer database, access is granted.

> Two-factor authentication combines any two methods, matching items such as a token with a biometric. Three-factor authentication combines any three, such as a passcode, a biometric, and a token.

Multifactor authentication methods greatly enhance security by making it very difficult for an attacker to obtain all the correct materials for authentication. They also protect against the risk of stolen tokens, as the attacker must have the correct biometric, password, or both. More important, multifactor authentication enhances the security of biometric systems by protecting against a stolen biometric. Changing the token makes the biometric useless unless the attacker can steal the new token. It also reduces false positives by trying to match the supplied biometric with the one that is associated with the supplied token. This prevents the computer from seeking a match using the entire database of biometrics. Using multiple factors is one of the best ways to ensure proper authentication and access control.

Factors

Factors are the specific elements that comprise an item of proof. These items can be grouped into three classes: something you know (passwords), something you have (token), and something you are (biometrics). Each of these has advantages and disadvantages, as discussed in the following sections.

Something You Know

The most common example of **something you know** is a password. One of the challenges with using something you know as an authentication factor is that it can be "shared" (or duplicated) without you knowing it. Another concern with using something you know is that because of the vast number of different elements a typical user has to remember, they do things to assist with memory, such as repeating passwords, making slight changes to a password, such as incrementing the number from password1 to password2, and writing them down. These are all common methods used to deal with password sprawl, yet they each introduce new vulnerabilities.

Another form of authentication via something you know is identity-driven authentication. In identity-driven authentication, you contact someone to get access, and they respond with a series of challenge questions. Sometimes the questions are based on previously submitted information, and sometimes the questions are based on publicly known information, such as previous addresses, phone numbers, cars purchase/licensed, and so on. Again, the proper respondent will know these answers, whereas an imposter will not. These tests are timed, and if the respondent takes too long (for example, taking the time to perform a lookup), they will fail.

Something You Have

Something you have specifically refers to security tokens and other items that a user can possess physically. One of the challenges with using something you have as an authentication factor is that you have to have it with you whenever you wish to be authenticated, and this can cause issues. It also relies on interfaces that may not be available for some systems, such as mobile devices, although interfaces, such as one-time password (OTP) generators, are device independent. OTP generators create new passwords on demand, against a sequence that is known only to the OTP generator and the OTP element on the system accepting the password.

One of the challenges of something you have is the concept of "something you lost," such as something you left in a briefcase, at home, and so on. Just as leaving behind your key ring with your office key can force a return trip back home to get it, so can leaving a dongle or other security element that is "something you have" in nature. And if something you have becomes something you had stolen, the implications are fairly clear—you don't have access and you have to re-identify yourself to get access again.

Something You Are

Something you are specifically refers to biometrics. One of the challenges with using "something you are" artifacts as authentication factors is that typically they are hard to change; once assigned, they inevitably become immutable, as you can change fingers, but only a limited number of times, and then you run out of changes. Another challenge with biometrics is that cultural or other issues associated with measuring things on a person may exist. For example, people in some cultures object to having their pictures taken. Another example is that physical laborers in some industries tend to lack scannable fingerprints because they are worn down. Some biometrics are not usable in certain environments; for instance, in the case of medical workers, or workers in clean-room environments, their personal protective gear inhibits the use of fingerprint readers and potentially other biometric devices.

Attributes

Attributes are collections of artifacts, like the factors previously presented, but rather than focus on the authentication item, they focus on elements associated with the user. Common attributes include the user's location, their ability to perform a task, or something about the user themselves. These attributes are discussed in the following sections.

Somewhere You Are

One of the more discriminant authentication factors is your location, or **somewhere you are**. When a mobile device is used, GPS can identify where the device is currently located. When you are logged on to a local, wired desktop connection, it shows you are in the building. Both of these can be compared to records to see if you are really there or should be there. If you are badged into your building, and at your desk on a wired PC, then a second connection with a different location would be suspect, as you can only be in one place at a time.

With geofencing, location becomes a big thing for marketing services pushing content to devices when in specific locations. Location services on mobile devices, coupled with geofencing, can alert others when you are in a specific area—not specifically authentication, but leading toward it.

Something You Can Do

Something you can do specifically refers to a physical action that you perform uniquely. An example of this is a signature; the movement of the pen and the two-dimensional output are difficult for others to reproduce. This makes it useful for authentication, but challenges exist in capturing the data, as signature pads are not common peripherals on machines. Gait analysis, presented earlier, is another example of this attribute. Something you can do is one of the harder artifacts to capture without specialized hardware, making it less ubiquitous as a method of authentication.

Something You Exhibit

Something you exhibit is a special case of a biometric. An example would be a brainwave response to seeing a picture. Another example would be the results of a lie detector test. The concept is to present a trigger and measure a response that cannot be faked. As sensors improve, tracking eye movement and sensing other aspects of responses will become forms that can be used to assist in authentication.

Someone You Know

Just as passwords relate to possession of knowledge, **someone you know** relates to a specific memory, but in this case an individual. This is the classic "having someone vouch for you" attribute. Electronically, this can be done via a chain of trust model, and it was commonly used in the past as a result of people signing each other's keys, indicating trust.

> **Tech Tip**
>
> **Securing Remote Connections**
>
> *By using encryption, remote access protocols can securely authenticate and authorize a user according to previously established privilege levels. The authorization phase can keep unauthorized users out, but after that, encryption of the communications channel becomes very important in preventing unauthorized users from breaking in on an authorized session and hijacking an authorized user's credentials. As more and more networks rely on the Internet for connecting remote users, the need for and importance of secure remote access protocols and secure communication channels will continue to grow.*

Remote Access

The process of connecting by remote access involves two elements: a temporary network connection and a series of protocols to negotiate privileges and commands. The temporary network connection can occur via a dial-up service, the Internet, wireless access, or any other method of connecting to a network. Once the connection is made, the primary issue is authenticating the identity of the user and establishing proper privileges for that user. This is accomplished using a combination of protocols and the operating system on the host machine.

When a user connects to the Internet through an ISP, this is similarly a case of remote access—the user is establishing a connection to their ISP's network, and the same security issues apply. The issue of authentication, the matching of user-supplied credentials to previously stored credentials on a host machine, is usually done via a user account name and password. Once the user is authenticated, the authorization step takes place. Remote authentication usually takes the common form of an end user submitting their credentials via an established protocol to a **remote access server (RAS)**, which acts upon those credentials, either granting or denying access.

Access controls define what actions a user can perform or what objects a user is allowed to access. Access controls are built on the foundation of elements designed to facilitate the matching of a user to a process. These elements are identification, authentication, and authorization. A myriad of details and choices are associated with setting up remote access to a network, and to provide for the management of these options, it is important for an organization to have a series of remote access policies and procedures spelling out the details of what is permitted and what is not for a given network.

> **Tech Tip**
>
> **Federation**
>
> **Federated identity management** *is an agreement between multiple enterprises that lets parties use the same identification data to obtain access to the networks of all enterprises in the group. This federation enables access to be managed across multiple systems in common trust levels.*

IEEE 802.1X

IEEE 802.1X is an authentication standard that supports port-based authentication services between a user and an authorization device, such as an edge router. IEEE 802.1X is used by all types of networks, including Ethernet,

One security issue associated with 802.1X is that the authentication occurs only upon initial connection, and another user can insert themselves into the connection by changing packets or using a hub. The secure solution is to pair 802.1X, which authenticates the initial connection, with a VPN or IPSec, which provides persistent security.

Token Ring, and wireless. This standard describes methods used to authenticate a user prior to granting access to a network and the authentication server, such as a RADIUS server. 802.1X acts through an intermediate device, such as an edge switch, enabling ports to carry normal traffic if the connection is properly authenticated. This prevents unauthorized clients from accessing the publicly available ports on a switch, keeping unauthorized users out of a LAN. Until a client has successfully authenticated itself to the device, only Extensible Authentication Protocol over LAN (EAPOL) traffic is passed by the switch.

EAPOL is an encapsulated method of passing EAP messages over 802.1X frames. EAP is a general protocol that can support multiple methods of authentication, including one-time passwords, Kerberos, public keys, and security device methods such as smart cards. Once a client successfully authenticates itself to the 802.1X device, the switch opens ports for normal traffic. At this point, the client can communicate with the system's AAA method, such as a RADIUS server, and authenticate itself to the network.

802.1X is commonly used on wireless access points as a port-based authentication service prior to admission to the wireless network. 802.1X over wireless uses either 802.11i or EAP-based protocols, such as EAP-TLS and PEAP-TLS.

Cross Check

Wireless Remote Access

Wireless is a common method of allowing remote access to a network, as it does not require physical cabling and allows mobile connections. Wireless security, including protocols such as 802.11i and EAP-based solutions, is covered in Chapter 12.

LDAP

The **Lightweight Directory Access Protocol (LDAP)** is commonly used to handle user authentication/authorization as well as control access to Active Directory objects. A client starts an LDAP session by connecting to an LDAP server, called a Directory System Agent (DSA), which by default is on TCP and UDP port 389, or on port 636 for LDAPS (LDAP over SSL).

To enable interoperability, X.500 was created as a standard for directory services. The primary method for accessing an X.500 directory is through the Directory Access Protocol (DAP), a heavyweight protocol that is difficult to implement completely, especially on PCs and more constrained platforms. This led to LDAP, which contains the most commonly used functionality. LDAP can interface with X.500 services and, more importantly, can be used over TCP with significantly less computing resources than a full X.500 implementation. LDAP offers all of the functionality most directories need and is easier and more economical to implement; hence, LDAP has become the Internet standard for directory services. LDAP standards are governed by two separate entities, depending on use: the International Telecommunication Union (ITU) governs the X.500 standard, and LDAP is governed for Internet use by the IETF. Many RFCs apply to LDAP functionality, but some of the most important are RFCs 2251 through 2256 and RFCs 2829 and 2830.

RADIUS

Remote Authentication Dial-In User Service (RADIUS) is an AAA protocol. It was submitted to the Internet Engineering Task Force (IETF) as a series of RFCs: RFC 2058 (RADIUS specification), RFC 2059 (RADIUS accounting standard), and updated RFCs 2865–2869, which are now standard protocols.

RADIUS is designed as a connectionless protocol that uses the User Datagram Protocol (UDP) as its transport layer protocol. Connection type issues, such as timeouts, are handled by the RADIUS application instead of the transport layer. RADIUS utilizes UDP port 1812 for authentication and authorization and UDP port 1813 for accounting functions.

RADIUS is a client/server protocol. The RADIUS client is typically a network access server (NAS). Network access servers act as intermediaries, authenticating clients before allowing them access to a network. RADIUS, RRAS (Microsoft), RAS, and VPN servers can all act as network access servers. The RADIUS server is a process or daemon running on a UNIX or Windows Server machine. Communications between a RADIUS client and RADIUS server are encrypted using a shared secret that is manually configured into each entity and not shared over a connection. Hence, communications between a RADIUS client (typically a NAS) and a RADIUS server are secure, but the communications between a user (typically a PC) and the RADIUS client are subject to compromise. This is important to note, because if the user's machine (the PC) is not the RADIUS client (the NAS), then communications between the PC and the NAS are typically not encrypted and are passed in the clear.

RADIUS Authentication

The RADIUS protocol is designed to allow a RADIUS server to support a wide variety of methods to authenticate a user. When the server is given a username and password, it can support Point-to-Point Protocol (PPP), Password Authentication Protocol (PAP), Challenge-Handshake Authentication Protocol (CHAP), Linux login, and other mechanisms, depending on what was established when the server was set up. A user login authentication consists of a query (Access-Request) from the RADIUS client and a corresponding response (Access-Accept, Access-Challenge, or Access-Reject) from the RADIUS server, as you can see in Figure 11.24. The Access-Challenge response is the initiation of a challenge/response handshake. If the client cannot support challenge/response, it treats the Challenge message as an Access-Reject.

The Access-Request message contains the username, encrypted password, NAS IP address, and port. The message also contains information concerning the type of session the user wants to initiate. Once the RADIUS server receives this information, it searches its database for a match on the username. If a match is not found, either a default profile is loaded or an Access-Reject reply is sent to the user. If the entry is found or the default profile is used, the next phase involves authorization, because in RADIUS these steps are performed in sequence. Figure 11.24 shows the interaction between a user and the RADIUS client and RADIUS server as well as the steps taken to make a connection.

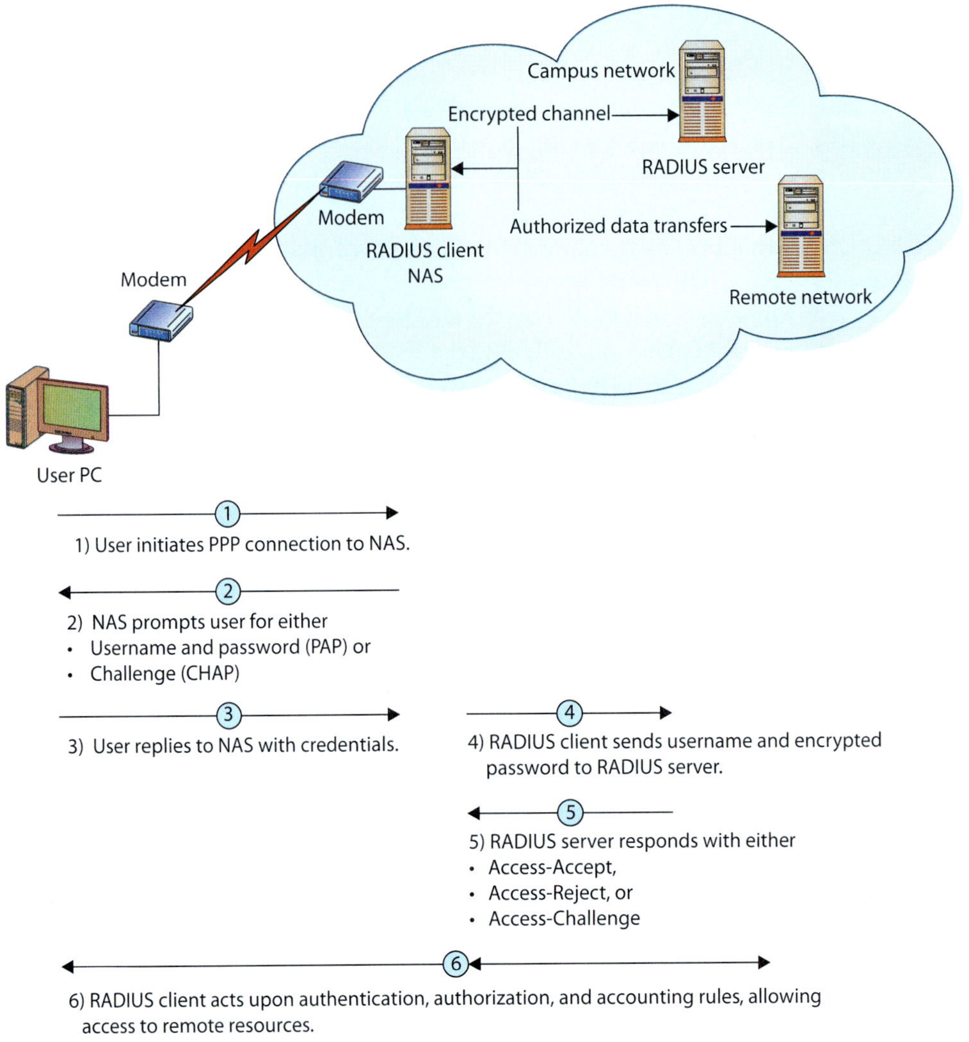

• **Figure 11.24** RADIUS communication sequence

> **Tech Tip**
>
> **Shell Accounts**
>
> *Shell account requests are those that desire command-line access to a server. Once authentication is successfully performed, the client is connected directly to the server so command-line access can occur. Rather than being given a direct IP address on the network, the NAS acts as a pass-through device conveying access.*

RADIUS Authorization

In the RADIUS protocol, the authentication and authorization steps are performed together in response to a single Access-Request message, although they are sequential steps (see Figure 11.24). Once an identity has been established, either known or default, the authorization process determines what parameters are returned to the client. Typical authorization parameters include the service type allowed (shell or framed), the protocols allowed, the IP address to assign to the user (static or dynamic), and the access list to apply or static route to place in the NAS routing table.

These parameters are all defined in the configuration information on the RADIUS client and server during setup. Using this information, the RADIUS server returns an Access-Accept message with these parameters to the RADIUS client.

RADIUS Accounting

The RADIUS accounting function is performed independently of RADIUS authentication and authorization. The accounting function uses a separate

UDP port, 1813 (see Table 11.3 in the "Connection Summary" section at the end of the chapter). The primary functionality of RADIUS accounting was established to support ISPs in their user accounting, and it supports typical accounting functions for time billing and security logging. The RADIUS accounting functions are designed to allow data to be transmitted at the beginning and end of a session, and they can indicate resource utilization, such as time, bandwidth, and so on.

Using UDP transport to a centralized network access server, RADIUS provides client systems authentication and access control within an enterprise network.

Diameter

Diameter is the name of an AAA protocol suite, designated by the IETF to replace the aging RADIUS protocol. Diameter operates in much the same way as RADIUS in a client/server configuration, but it improves upon RADIUS, resolving discovered weaknesses. Diameter is a TCP-based service and has more extensive AAA capabilities. Diameter is also designed for all types of remote access, not just modem pools. As more and more users adopt broadband and other connection methods, these newer services require more options to determine permissible usage properly and to account for and log the usage. Diameter is designed with these needs in mind.

Diameter also has an improved method of encrypting message exchanges to prohibit replay and on-path (formerly known as man-in-the-middle) attacks. Taken all together, Diameter, with its enhanced functionality and security, is an improvement on the proven design of the old RADIUS standard.

TACACS+

The **Terminal Access Controller Access Control System Plus (TACACS+)** protocol is the current generation of the TACACS family. Originally TACACS was developed by BBN Planet Corporation for MILNET, an early military network, but it has been enhanced by Cisco, which has expanded its functionality twice. The original BBN TACACS system provided a combination process of authentication and authorization. Cisco extended this to Extended Terminal Access Controller Access Control System (XTACACS), which provided for separate authentication, authorization, and accounting processes. The current generation, TACACS+, has extended attribute control and accounting processes.

One of the fundamental design aspects is the separation of authentication, authorization, and accounting in this protocol. Although there is a straightforward lineage of these protocols from the original TACACS, TACACS+ is a major revision and is not backward-compatible with previous versions of the protocol series.

TACACS+ uses TCP as its transport protocol, typically operating over TCP port 49. This port is used for the login process and is reserved in RFC 3232, "Assigned Numbers," manifested in a database from the Internet Assigned Numbers Authority (IANA). In the IANA specification, both UDP port 49 and TCP port 49 are reserved for the TACACS+ login host protocol (see Table 11.3 in the "Connection Summary" section at the end of the chapter).

TACACS+ is a client/server protocol, with the client typically being a NAS and the server being a daemon process on a UNIX, Linux, or Windows Server. This is important to note, because if the user's machine (usually a PC) is not the client (usually a NAS), then communications between the PC and NAS are typically not encrypted and are passed in the clear. Communications between a TACACS+ client and TACACS+ server are encrypted using a shared secret that is manually configured into each entity and is not shared over a connection. Hence, communications between a TACACS+ client (typically a NAS) and a TACACS+ server are secure, but the communications between a user (typically a PC) and the TACACS+ client are subject to compromise.

TACACS+ Authentication

TACACS+ allows for arbitrary length and content in the authentication exchange sequence, enabling many different authentication mechanisms to be used with TACACS+ clients. Authentication is optional and is determined as a site-configurable option. When authentication is used, common forms include PPP PAP, PPP CHAP, PPP EAP, token cards, and Kerberos. The authentication process is performed using three different packet types: START, CONTINUE, and REPLY. START and CONTINUE packets originate from the client and are directed to the TACACS+ server. The REPLY packet is used to communicate from the TACACS+ server to the client.

The authentication process is illustrated in Figure 11.25, and it begins with a START message from the client to the server. This message may be in response to an initiation from a PC connected to the TACACS+ client. The START message describes the type of authentication being requested (simple plaintext password, PAP, CHAP, and so on). This START message may also contain additional authentication data, such as a username and password. A START message is also sent as a response to a restart request from the server in a REPLY message. A START message always has its sequence number set to 1.

When a TACACS+ server receives a START message, it sends a REPLY message. This REPLY message indicates whether the authentication is complete or needs to be continued. If the process needs to be continued, the REPLY message also specifies what additional information is needed. The response from a client to a REPLY message requesting additional data is a CONTINUE message. This process continues until the server has all the information needed, and the authentication process concludes with a success or failure.

TACACS+ Authorization

Authorization is defined as the granting of specific permissions based on the privileges held by the account. This generally occurs after authentication, as shown in Figure 11.25, but this is not a firm requirement. A default state of "unknown user" exists before a user is authenticated, and permissions can be determined for an unknown user. As with authentication, authorization is an optional process and may or may not be part of a site-specific operation. When it is used in conjunction with authentication, the authorization process follows the authentication process and uses the confirmed user identity as input in the decision process.

The authorization process is performed using two message types: REQUEST and RESPONSE. The authorization process is performed using an authorization session consisting of a single pair of REQUEST and RESPONSE messages. The client issues an authorization REQUEST message containing a fixed set of fields enumerating the authenticity of the user or

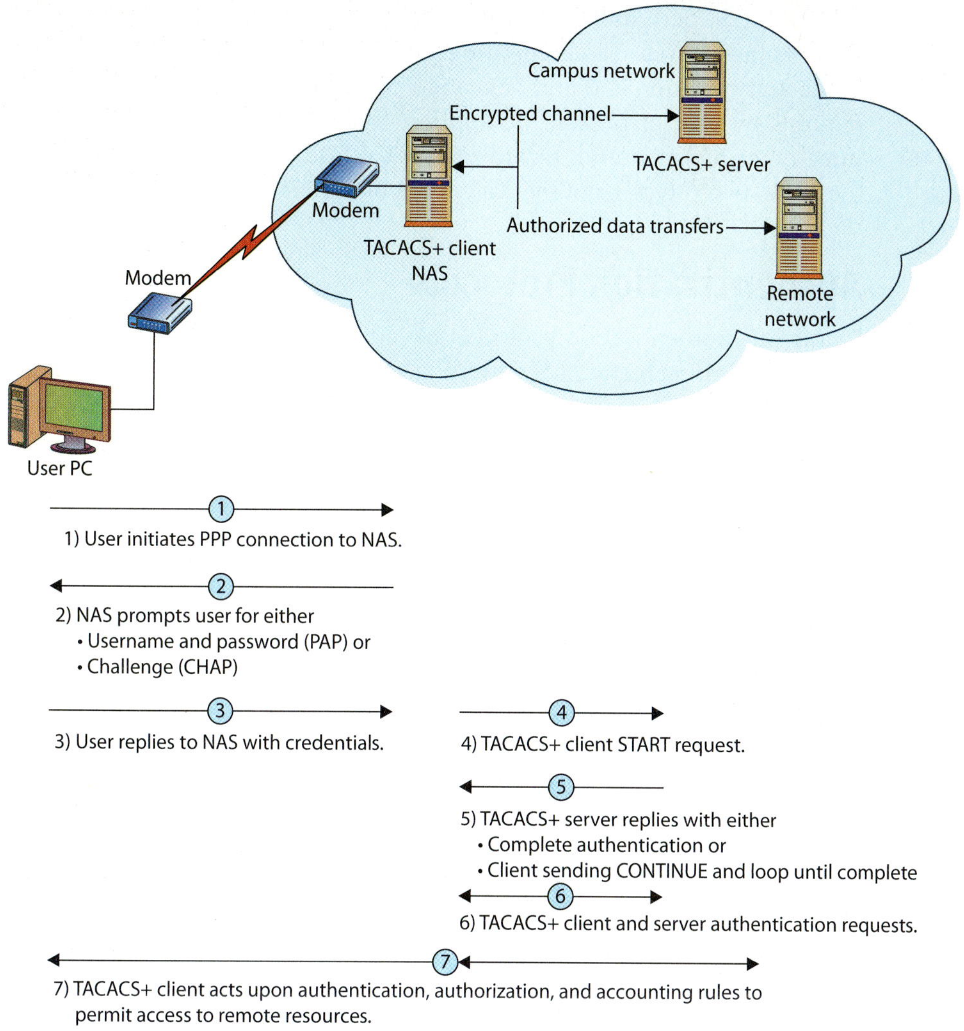

• **Figure 11.25** TACACS+ communication sequence

process requesting permission and a variable set of fields enumerating the services or options for which authorization is being requested.

The RESPONSE message in TACACS+ is not a simple yes or no; it can also include qualifying information, such as a user time limit or IP restrictions. These limitations have important uses, such as enforcing time limits on shell access or enforcing IP access list restrictions for specific user accounts.

TACACS+ Accounting

As with the two previous services, accounting is also an optional function of TACACS+. When utilized, it typically follows the other services. Accounting in TACACS+ is defined as the process of recording what a user or process has done. Accounting can serve two important purposes:

- It can be used to account for services being utilized, possibly for billing purposes.
- It can be used for generating security audit trails.

TACACS+ is a protocol that takes a client/server model approach and handles authentication, authorization, and accounting (AAA) services. It is similar to RADIUS but uses TCP (port 49) as a transport method.

TACACS+ accounting records contain several pieces of information to support these tasks. The accounting process has the information revealed in the authorization and authentication processes, so it can record specific requests by user or process. To support this functionality, TACACS+ has three types of accounting records: START, STOP, and UPDATE. Note that these are record types, not message types as earlier discussed.

Authentication Protocols

Numerous authentication protocols have been developed, used, and discarded in the brief history of computing. Some have come and gone because they did not enjoy market share, others have had security issues, and yet others have been revised and improved in newer versions. It's impractical to cover them all, so only some of the common ones follow.

Tunneling

Layer 2 Tunneling Protocol (L2TP) and Point-to-Point Tunneling Protocol (PPTP) are both OSI Layer 2 tunneling protocols. **Tunneling** is the encapsulation of one packet within another, which allows you to hide the original packet from view or change the nature of the network transport. This can be done for both security and practical reasons.

From a practical perspective, assume that you are using TCP/IP to communicate between two machines. Your message may pass over various networks, such as an Asynchronous Transfer Mode (ATM) network, as it moves from source to destination. Because the ATM protocol can neither read nor understand TCP/IP packets, something must be done to make them passable across the network. By encapsulating a packet as the payload in a separate protocol, so it can be carried across a section of a network, a mechanism called a *tunnel* is created. At each end of the tunnel, called the tunnel *endpoints*, the payload packet is read and understood. As it goes into the tunnel, you can envision your packet being placed in an envelope with the address of the appropriate tunnel endpoint on it. When the envelope arrives at the tunnel endpoint, the original message (the tunnel packet's payload) is re-created, read, and sent to its appropriate next stop. The information being tunneled is understood only at the tunnel endpoints; it is not relevant to intermediate tunnel points because it is only a payload.

L2TP

Layer 2 Tunneling Protocol (L2TP) is also an Internet standard and came from the Layer 2 Forwarding (L2F) protocol, a Cisco initiative designed to address issues with PPTP. Whereas PPTP is designed around PPP and IP networks, L2F (and hence L2TP) is designed for use across all kinds of networks, including ATM and Frame Relay. Additionally, whereas PPTP is designed to be implemented in software at the client device, L2TP was conceived as a hardware implementation using a router or a special-purpose appliance. L2TP can be configured in software and is in Microsoft's Routing and Remote Access Service (RRAS), which uses L2TP to create a VPN.

L2TP works in much the same way as PPTP, but it opens up several items for expansion. For instance, in L2TP, routers can be enabled to concentrate

VPN traffic over higher-bandwidth lines, creating hierarchical networks of VPN traffic that can be more efficiently managed across an enterprise. L2TP also has the ability to use IPSec, providing a higher level of data security. L2TP is also designed to work with established AAA services such as RADIUS and TACACS+ to aid in user authentication, authorization, and accounting.

L2TP is established via UDP port 1701, so this is an essential port to leave open across firewalls supporting L2TP traffic. Microsoft supports L2TP in Windows operating systems, but because of the computing power required, most implementations will use specialized hardware (such as a Cisco router).

PPTP

Microsoft led a consortium of networking companies to extend PPP to enable the creation of virtual private networks (VPNs). The result was the **Point-to-Point Tunneling Protocol (PPTP)**, a network protocol that enables the secure transfer of data from a remote PC to a server by creating a VPN across a TCP/IP network. This remote network connection can also span a public switched telephone network (PSTN) and is thus an economical way of connecting remote dial-in users to a corporate data network. The incorporation of PPTP into the Microsoft Windows product line provides a built-in secure method of remote connection using the operating system, and this has given PPTP a large marketplace footprint.

For most PPTP implementations, three computers are involved: the PPTP client, the NAS, and a PPTP server, as shown in Figure 11.26. The connection between the remote client and the network is established in stages, as illustrated in Figure 11.27. First, the client makes a PPP connection to a NAS, typically an ISP. (In today's world of widely available broadband, if there is already an Internet connection, then there is no need to perform the PPP connection to the ISP.) Once the PPP connection is established, a second connection is made over the PPP connection to the PPTP server. This second connection creates the VPN connection between the remote client and the PPTP server. A typical VPN connection is one in which the user is in a hotel with a wireless Internet connection, connecting to a corporate network. This connection acts as a tunnel for future data transfers. Although these diagrams illustrate a telephone connection, this first link can be virtually any method. Common in hotels today are wired connections to the

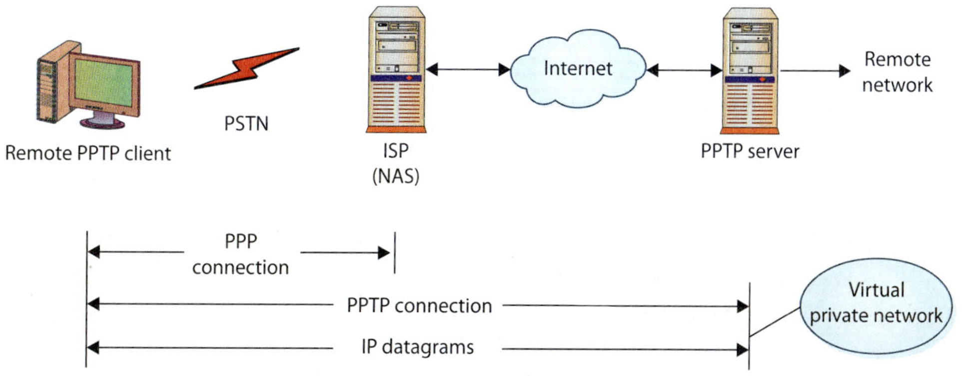

• **Figure 11.26** PPTP communication diagram

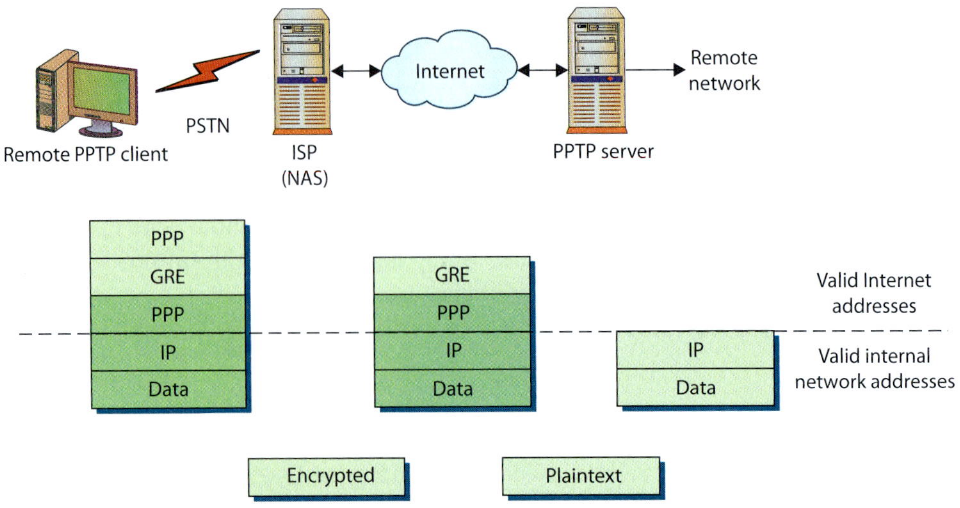

• **Figure 11.27** PPTP message encapsulation during transmission

Internet. These wired connections typically are provided by a local ISP and offer the same services as a phone connection, albeit at a much higher data transfer rate.

PPTP establishes a tunnel from the remote PPTP client to the PPTP server and enables encryption within this tunnel. This provides a secure method of transport. To do this and still enable routing, an intermediate addressing scheme, Generic Routing Encapsulation (GRE), is used.

To establish the connection, PPTP uses communications across TCP port 1723 (see Table 11.3 in the "Connection Summary" section at the end of the chapter), so this port must remain open across the network firewalls for PPTP to be initiated. Although PPTP allows the use of any PPP authentication scheme, CHAP is used when encryption is specified, to provide an appropriate level of security. For the encryption methodology, Microsoft chose the RSA RC4 cipher, with either a 40- or 128-bit session key length, and this is OS driven. Microsoft Point-to-Point Encryption (MPPE) is an extension to PPP that enables VPNs to use PPTP as the tunneling protocol.

> **Tech Tip**
>
> **PPP Functions and Authentication**
>
> *PPP supports three functions:*
>
> - *Encapsulate datagrams across serial links*
> - *Establish, configure, and test links using LCP*
> - *Establish and configure different network protocols using NCP*
>
> *PPP supports three authentication protocols:*
>
> - *Password Authentication Protocol (PAP)*
> - *Challenge-Handshake Authentication Protocol (CHAP)*
> - *Extensible Authentication Protocol (EAP)*

PPP

Point-to-Point Protocol (PPP) is an older, still widely used protocol for establishing dial-in connections over serial lines or Integrated Services Digital Network (ISDN) services. PPP has several authentication mechanisms, including PAP, CHAP, and the Extensible Authentication Protocol (EAP). These protocols are used to authenticate the peer device, not a user of the system. PPP is a standardized Internet encapsulation of IP traffic over point-to-point links, such as serial lines. The authentication process is performed only when the link is established.

EAP

Extensible Authentication Protocol (EAP) is a universal authentication framework defined by RFC 3748 that is frequently used in wireless networks and point-to-point connections. Although EAP is not limited to wireless and can be used for wired authentication, it is most often used in wireless LANs. EAP is discussed in detail in Chapter 12.

CHAP

Challenge-Handshake Authentication Protocol (CHAP) is used to provide authentication across a point-to-point link using PPP. In this protocol, authentication after the link has been established is not mandatory. CHAP is designed to provide authentication periodically through the use of a challenge/response system that is sometimes described as a *three-way handshake*, as illustrated in Figure 11.28. The initial challenge (a randomly generated number) is sent to the client. The client uses a one-way hashing function to calculate what the response should be and then sends this back. The server compares the response to what it calculated the response should be. If they match, communication continues. If the two values don't match, then the connection is terminated. This mechanism relies on a shared secret between the two entities so that the correct values can be calculated.

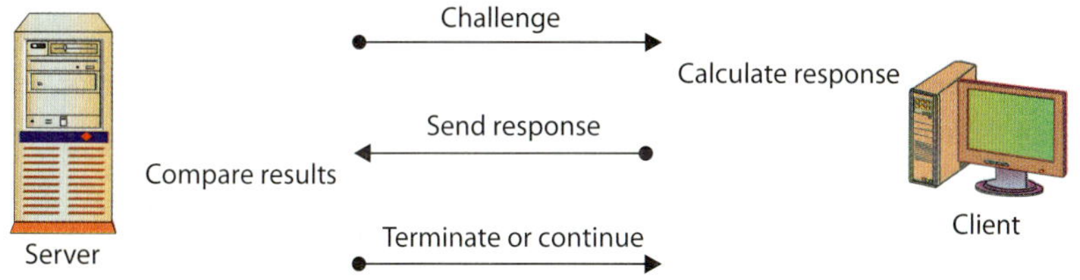

• **Figure 11.28** The CHAP challenge/response sequence

Microsoft has created two versions of CHAP, modified to increase the usability of CHAP across Microsoft's product line. MS-CHAP v1, defined in RFC 2433, has been deprecated and was dropped in Windows Vista. The current standard, MS-CHAP v2, defined in RFC 2759, was introduced with Windows 2000.

NTLM

NT LAN Manager (NTLM) is an authentication protocol designed by Microsoft for use with the Server Message Block (SMB) protocol. SMB is an application-level network protocol primarily used for sharing of files and printers in Windows-based networks. NTLM is the successor to the authentication protocol in Microsoft LAN Manager (LANMAN), an older Microsoft product. Both of these suites have been widely replaced by Microsoft's Kerberos implementation, although NTLM is still used for logon authentication on standalone Windows machines. The current version is NTLM v2, which was introduced with Windows NT 4.0 SP4. NTLM uses an encrypted challenge/response protocol to authenticate a user without sending the user's password over the wire, but the cryptography by today's standards is weak, including MD4. Although Microsoft has adopted the Kerberos protocol for authentication, NTLM v2 is still used in the following situations:

- When authenticating to a server using an IP address
- When authenticating to a server that belongs to a different Active Directory forest
- When authenticating to a server that doesn't belong to a domain
- When no Active Directory domain exists ("workgroup" or "peer-to-peer" connection)

PAP is a cleartext authentication protocol and hence is subject to interception.

PAP

Password Authentication Protocol (PAP) involves a two-way handshake in which the username and password are sent across the link in cleartext. PAP authentication does not provide any protection against playback and line sniffing. PAP is now a deprecated standard.

Telnet

One of the methods to grant remote access to a system is through Telnet. Telnet is the standard terminal-emulation protocol within the TCP/IP protocol series, and it is defined in RFC 854. Telnet allows users to log in remotely and access resources as if the user had a local terminal connection. Telnet is an old protocol and offers little security. Information, including account names and passwords, is passed in cleartext over the TCP/IP connection.

Telnet makes its connection using TCP port 23. As Telnet is implemented on most products using TCP/IP, it is important to control access to Telnet on machines and routers when setting them up. Failure to control access by using firewalls, access lists, and other security methods, or even by disabling the Telnet daemon, is equivalent to leaving an open door for unauthorized users on a system.

SSH

Secure Shell (SSH) is a protocol series designed to facilitate secure network functions across an insecure network. SSH provides direct support for secure remote login, secure file transfer, and secure forwarding of TCP/IP and X Window System traffic. An SSH connection is an encrypted channel, providing for confidentiality and integrity protection. SSH uses TCP port 22. SCP (secure copy) and SFTP (secure FTP) use SSH, so each also uses TCP port 22.

SSH has its origins as a replacement for the insecure Telnet application from the UNIX operating system. An original component of UNIX, Telnet allowed users to connect between systems. Although Telnet is still used today, it has some drawbacks, as discussed in the preceding section. Some enterprising University of California, Berkeley, students subsequently developed the **r-** commands, such as **rlogin**, to permit access based on the user and source system, as opposed to passing passwords. This was not perfect either, however, because when a login was required, it was still passed in the clear. This led to the development of the SSH protocol series, designed to eliminate all of the insecurities associated with Telnet, **r-** commands, and other means of remote access.

SSH opens a secure transport channel between machines by using an SSH daemon on each end. These daemons initiate contact over TCP port 22 and then communicate over higher ports in a secure mode. One of the strengths of SSH is its support for many different encryption protocols. SSH 1.0 started with RSA algorithms, but at the time they were still under patent, and this led to SSH 2.0 with extended support for Triple DES (3DES) and other encryption methods. Today, SSH can be used with a wide range of encryption protocols, including RSA, Blowfish, International Data Encryption Algorithm (IDEA), CAST128, AES256, and others.

The SSH protocol has facilities to encrypt data automatically, provide authentication, and compress data in transit. It can support strong encryption, cryptographic host authentication, and integrity protection.

The authentication services are host based and not user based. If user authentication is desired in a system, it must be set up separately at a higher level in the OSI model. The protocol is designed to be flexible and simple, and it is designed specifically to minimize the number of round trips between systems. The key exchange, public key, symmetric key, message authentication, and hash algorithms are all negotiated at connection time. Individual data-packet integrity is ensured through the use of a message authentication code that is computed from a shared secret, the contents of the packet, and the packet sequence number.

The SSH protocol consists of three major components:

- **Transport layer protocol** Provides server authentication, confidentiality, integrity, and compression
- **User authentication protocol** Authenticates the client to the server
- **Connection protocol** Provides multiplexing of the encrypted tunnel into several logical channels

SSH is very popular in Linux environments, and it is actively used as a method of establishing VPNs across public networks. Because all communications between the two machines are encrypted at the OSI application layer by the two SSH daemons, this leads to the ability to build very secure solutions and even solutions that defy the ability of outside services to monitor. As SSH is a standard protocol series with connection parameters established via TCP port 22, different vendors can build differing solutions that can still interoperate.

Although Windows Server implementations of SSH exist, this has not been a popular protocol in the Windows environment from a server perspective. The development of a wide array of commercial SSH clients for the Windows platform indicates the marketplace strength of interconnection from desktop PCs to Linux-based servers utilizing this protocol. Windows 10 uses OpenSSH as both its default SSH client and server.

> **Tech Tip**
>
> **RDP**
>
> **Remote Desktop Protocol (RDP)** *is a proprietary Microsoft protocol designed to provide a graphical connection to another computer. The computer requesting the connection has RDP client software (built into Windows), and the target uses an RDP server. This software has been available for many versions of Windows and was formerly called Terminal Services. Client and server versions also exist for Linux platforms. RDP uses TCP and UDP ports 3389, so if RDP is desired, these ports need to be open on the firewall.*

SAML

Security Assertion Markup Language (SAML) is a single sign-on (SSO) capability used for web applications to ensure user identities can be shared and are protected. It defines standards for exchanging authentication and authorization data between security domains. It is becoming increasingly important with cloud-based solutions and with Software as a Service (SaaS) applications because it ensures interoperability across identity providers.

SAML is an XML-based protocol that uses security tokens and assertions to pass information about a "principal" (typically an end user) with a SAML authority (an "identity provider," or IdP) and the service provider (SP). The principal requests a service from the SP, which then requests and obtains an identity assertion from the IdP. The SP can then grant access or perform the requested service for the principal.

> By allowing identity providers to pass on credentials to service providers, SAML allows you log in to many different websites using one set of credentials.

OAuth

OAuth (Open Authorization) is an open protocol that allows secure token-based authentication and authorization in a simple and standard method from web, mobile, and desktop applications for authorization on the Internet. OAuth is used by companies such as Google, Facebook, Microsoft, and Twitter to permit users to share information about their accounts with third-party applications or websites. OAuth 1.0 was developed by a Twitter engineer as part of the Twitter **OpenID** implementation. OAuth 2.0 (not backward compatible) has taken off with support from most major web platforms. OAuth's main strength is that it can be used by an external partner site to allow access to protected data without having to reauthenticate the user.

OAuth was created to remove the need for users to share their passwords with third-party applications, instead substituting a token. OAuth 2.0 expanded this into also providing authentication services, so it can eliminate the need for OpenID.

OpenID Connect

OpenID Connect is a simple identity layer on top of the OAuth 2.0 protocol. OpenID Connect allows clients of all types (mobile, JavaScript, and web-based clients) to request and receive information about authenticated sessions and end users. OpenID is about proving who you are, which is the first step in the Authentication-Authorization ladder. To perform authorization, a second process is needed, and OpenID is commonly paired with OAuth 2.0. OpenID was created for federated authentication that lets a third party authenticate your users for you, by using accounts the users already have.

> OpenID and OAuth are typically used together, yet have different purposes. OpenID is used for authentication, whereas OAuth is used for authorization.

Shibboleth

Shibboleth is a service designed to enable single sign-on and federated identity-based authentication and authorization across networks. It began in 2000, has been through several revisions and versions, but has yet to gain any widespread acceptance. Shibboleth is a web-based technology that is built using SAML technologies. Shibboleth uses the HTTP/POST, artifact, and attribute push profiles of SAML, including both Identity Provider (IdP) and Service Provider (SP) components to achieve its goals. As such, it is included by many services that use SAML for identity management.

Secure Token

Within a claims-based identity framework, such as OASIS WS-Trust, security tokens are used. A **secure token** service is responsible for issuing, validating, renewing, and cancelling these security tokens. The tokens issued can then be used to identify the holder of the token to any services that adhere to the WS-Trust standard. Secure tokens solve the problem of authentication across stateless platforms, because user identity must be established with each request. The following outlines the basic five-step process for using tokens:

1. The user requests access with a username and password.
2. The secure token service validates the user's credentials.
3. The secure token service provides a signed token to the client.
4. The client stores that token and sends it along with every request.
5. The server verifies the token and responds with data.

These steps are highly scalable and can be widely distributed and even shared. A user application can use a token for access via another app (for example, allowing someone to validate a login to Twitter via Facebook) because the token is transportable.

FTP/FTPS/SFTP

One of the methods of transferring files between machines is through the use of the File Transfer Protocol (FTP). FTP is a plaintext protocol that operates by communicating over TCP between a client and a server. The client initiates a transfer with an FTP request to the server's TCP port 21. This is the control connection, and this connection remains open over the duration of the file transfer. The actual data transfer occurs on a negotiated data transfer port, typically a high-order port number. FTP was not designed to be a secure method of transferring files. If a secure method is desired, then using FTPS or SFTP is best.

FTPS is the use of FTP over an SSL/TLS secured channel. This can be done either in explicit mode, where an **AUTH TLS** command is issued, or in implicit mode, where the transfer occurs over TCP port 990 for the control channel and TCP port 989 for the data channel. **SFTP** is not FTP per se, but rather a completely separate Secure File Transfer Protocol as defined by an IETF draft, the latest of which, version 6, expired in July of 2007 but has been incorporated into products in the marketplace.

FTP uses TCP port 21 as a control channel and TCP port 20 as a typical active mode data port, as some firewalls are set to block ports above 1024.

It is also possible to run FTP over SSH, as later versions of SSH allow securing of channels such as the FTP control channel; this has also been referred to as Secure FTP, or SFTP. This leaves the data channel unencrypted, a problem that has been solved in version 3.0 of SSH, which supports FTP commands. The challenge of encrypting the FTP data communications is that the mutual port agreement must be opened on the firewall, and for security reasons, high-order ports that are not explicitly defined are typically secured. Because of this challenge, Secure Copy (SCP) is often a more desirable alternative to SFTP when using SSH.

VPNs

A **virtual private network (VPN)** is a secure virtual network built on top of a *physical* network. The security of a VPN lies in the encryption of packet contents between the endpoints that define the VPN. The physical network upon which a VPN is built is typically a public network, such as the Internet. Because the packet contents between VPN endpoints are encrypted, to an outside observer on the public network, the communication is secure, and depending on how the VPN is set up, security can even extend to the two communicating parties' machines.

Virtual private networking is not a protocol but rather a method of using protocols to achieve a specific objective—secure communications—as shown in Figure 11.29. A user who wants to have a secure communication channel with a server across a public network can set up two intermediary devices, called *VPN endpoints*, to accomplish this task. The user can communicate with their endpoint, and the server can communicate with its endpoint. The two endpoints then communicate across the public network. VPN endpoints can be software solutions, routers, or specific servers set up for specific functionality. This implies that VPN services are set up in advance and are not something negotiated on the fly.

VPNs are commonly used for remote access to enterprise networks, providing protection from outside traffic. VPNs can also be used from site to site between network nodes in an overall system with geographic separation.

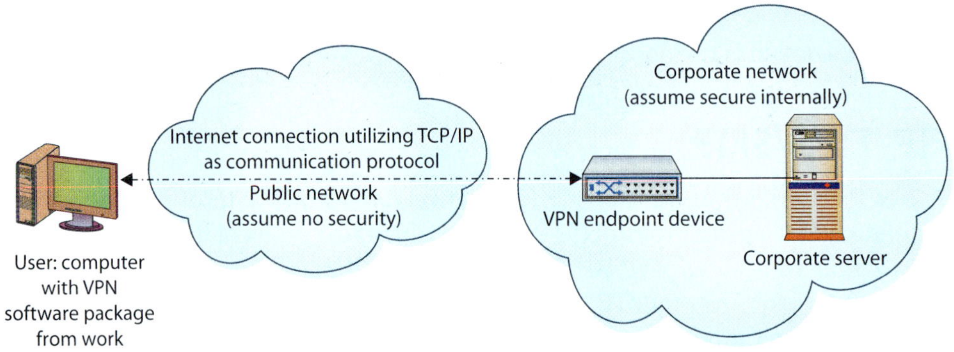

• **Figure 11.29** VPN service over an Internet connection

A typical use of VPN services is a user accessing a corporate data network from a home PC across the Internet. The employee installs VPN software from work on a home PC. This software is already configured to communicate with the corporate network's VPN endpoint; it knows the location, the protocols that will be used, and so on. When the home user wants to connect to the corporate network, they connect to the Internet and then start the VPN software. The user can then log in to the corporate network by using an appropriate authentication and authorization methodology. The sole purpose of the VPN connection is to provide a private connection between the machines, which encrypts any data sent between the home user's PC and the corporate network. Identification, authorization, and all other standard functions are accomplished with the standard mechanisms for the established system.

> **Tech Tip**
>
> **Split Tunnels**
>
> *Split-tunnel is a form of VPN where not all traffic is routed via the VPN. Split tunneling allows multiple connection paths, some via the protected route such as the VPN, whereas other traffic from, say, local network resources, such as printers, is routed via non-VPN paths. A full tunnel solution routes all traffic over the VPN.*

VPNs can use many different protocols to offer a secure method of communicating between endpoints. Common methods of encryption on VPNs include PPTP, IPSec, SSH, and L2TP, all of which are discussed in this chapter. The key is that both endpoints know the protocol and share a secret. All of this necessary information is established when the VPN is set up. At the time of use, the VPN only acts as a private tunnel between the two points and does not constitute a complete security solution.

Vulnerabilities of Remote Access Methods

The primary vulnerability associated with many of these methods of remote access is the passing of critical data in cleartext. Plaintext passing of passwords provides no security if the password is sniffed, and sniffers are easy to use on a network. Even plaintext passing of user IDs gives away information that can be correlated and possibly used by an attacker. Plaintext credential passing is one of the fundamental flaws with Telnet and is why SSH was developed. This is also one of the flaws with RADIUS and TACACS+, as they have a segment unprotected. There are methods for overcoming these limitations, although they require discipline and understanding in setting up a system.

The strength of the encryption algorithm is also a concern. Should a specific algorithm or method prove to be vulnerable, services that rely solely on it are also vulnerable. To get around this dependency, many of the protocols allow numerous encryption methods so that, should one prove vulnerable, a shift to another restores security.

As with any software implementation, there always exists the possibility that a bug could open the system to attack. Bugs have been corrected in most software packages to close holes that made systems vulnerable, and remote access functionality is no exception. This is not a Microsoft-only phenomenon, as one might believe from the popular press. Critical flaws have been found in almost every product, from open system implementations such as OpenSSH to proprietary systems such as Cisco IOS. The important issue is not the presence of software bugs, because as software continues to become more complex, this is an unavoidable issue. The true key is vendor responsiveness to fixing the bugs once they are discovered, and the major players, such as Cisco and Microsoft, have been very responsive in this area.

Tech Tip

Access Violations

The importance of authentication and authorization to a security program cannot be understated. These systems are the foundation of access to system objects, actions, and resources. Should failures occur, it is important to invoke logging and notification so that incident response can be activated if necessary. Access violations can be minor, or they can be significant with respect to risk, but they must be detected and acted upon. In this regard, the authorization system should be linked to logging for all critical items in a system so that actions can be initiated when violations occur.

Preventing Data Loss or Theft

Identity theft and commercial espionage have become very large and lucrative criminal enterprises over the past decade. Hackers are no longer merely content to compromise systems and deface websites. In many attacks performed today, hackers are after intellectual property, business plans, competitive intelligence, personal information, credit card numbers, client records, or any other information that can be sold, traded, or manipulated for profit. This has created a whole industry of technical solutions labeled *data loss prevention (DLP)* solutions.

It can be assumed that a hacker has assumed the identity of an authorized user, and DLP solutions exist to prevent the exfiltration of data regardless of access control restrictions. DLP solutions come in many forms, and each of these solutions has strengths and weaknesses. The best solution is a combination of security elements: some to secure data in storage (encryption) and some in the form of monitoring (proxy devices to monitor data egress for sensitive data), and even NetFlow analytics to identify new bulk data transfer routes.

Database Security

Database security is a concern for many enterprises, as the data in the databases represents valuable information assets. Major database engines have built-in encryption capabilities. This can provide the desired levels of confidentiality and integrity to the contents of the database. The advantage to these encryption schemes is that they can be tailored to the data structure, protecting the essential columns while not impacting columns that are not sensitive. Properly employing database encryption requires that the data schema and its security requirements be designed into the database implementation. The advantages are better protection against any database compromise, and the performance hit is typically negligible with respect to other alternatives.

Cloud vs. On-premises Requirements

Authentication to *cloud versus on-premises requirements* is basically a revisiting of the identity and authentication problem all over again. When establishing either a cloud or on-premises system, you use identity and authentication as the foundation of your security effort. Whether you use an Active Directory methodology or other system to manage identities on premises, when you're establishing a cloud-based system, the options need to be completely reviewed and appropriate choices made based on the use of the cloud in the enterprise. Simple methods include a completely new independent system, although this increases costs and reduces usability when the number of users grows. Solutions such as federated authentication and single sign-on exist, and the proper determination of authentication processes should rest on data criticality and who needs access.

Connection Summary

Many protocols are used for remote access and authentication and related purposes. These methods have their own assigned ports, and these assignments are summarized in Table 11.3.

Table 11.3 Common TCP/UDP Remote Access Networking Port Assignments

TCP Port Number	UDP Port Number	Keyword	Protocol
20		FTP-Data	File Transfer (Default Data)
21		FTP	File Transfer Control
22		SSH	Secure Shell Login
22		SCP	SCP uses SSH
22		SFTP	SFTP uses SSH
23		TELNET	Telnet
25		SMTP	Simple Mail Transfer
37	37	TIME	Time
49	49	TACACS+	TACACS+ login
53	53	DNS	Domain Name Server
65	65	TACACS+	TACACS+ database service
	69	TFTP	Trivial File Transfer Protocol
80		HTTP	Web
88	88	Kerberos	Kerberos
	137	NetBIOS	Name Service
	138	NetBIOS	Datagram Service
139		NetBIOS	NetBIOS
443		HTTPS	HTTPS
500	500	ISAKMP	ISAKMP protocol

(Continued)

Table 11.3 (Continued)

TCP Port Number	UDP Port Number	Keyword	Protocol
512		rexec	
513		rlogin	UNIX rlogin
	513	rwho	UNIX Broadcast Naming Service
514		rsh	UNIX rsh and rep
	514	SYSLOG	UNIX system logs
614	614	SSHELL	SSL Shell
989		FTPS	FTPS (implicit mode) data channel
990		FTPS	FTPS (implicit mode) control channel
	1645	RADIUS	RADIUS: Historical
	1646	RADIUS	RADIUS: Historical
	1701	L2TP	L2TP
1723	1723	PPTP	PPTP
1812	1812	RADIUS	RADIUS authorization
1813	1813	RADIUS-actg	RADIUS accounting

For More Information

SANS Consensus Policy Resource Community – Password Policy www.sans.org/security-resources/policies/general/pdf/password-protection-policy

Chapter 11 Review

Chapter Summary

After reading this chapter and completing the exercises, you should understand the following about privilege management, authentication, and remote access protocols.

Identify the differences among user, group, and role management

- Privilege management is the process of restricting a user's ability to interact with the computer system.
- Privilege management can be based on an individual user basis, on membership in a specific group or groups, or on a function/role.
- Key concepts in privilege management are the ability to restrict and control access to information and information systems.
- One of the methods used to simplify privilege management is single sign-on, which requires a user to authenticate successfully once. The validated credentials and associated rights and privileges are then automatically carried forward when the user accesses other systems or applications.

Implement account policies

- Password policies are sets of rules that help users select, employ, and store strong passwords. Tokens combine "something you have" with "something you know," such as a password or PIN, and can be hardware or software based.
- Passwords should have a limited span and should expire on a scheduled basis.

Describe methods of account management

- Administrators have many different tools at their disposal to control access to computer resources, including password- and account-expiration methods.
- User authentication methods can incorporate several factors, including tokens.
- Users can be limited as to the hours during which they can access resources.
- Resources such as files, folders, and printers can be controlled through permissions or access control lists.
- Permissions can be assigned based on a user's identity or their membership in one or more groups.

Describe methods of access management

- Mandatory access control is based on the sensitivity of the information or process itself.
- Discretionary access control uses file permissions and ACLs to restrict access based on a user's identity or group membership.
- Role-based access control restricts access based on the user's assigned role or roles.
- Rule-based access control restricts access based on a defined set of rules established by the administrator.
- Attribute-based access control evaluates specific rules and policies against attributes associated with a subject or object.

Explain authentication methods and the security implications in their use

- Password-based authentication is still the most widely used because of cost and ubiquity.
- Ticket-based systems, such as Kerberos, form the basis for most modern authentication and credentialing systems.

Examine the use of biometrics technology for authentication

- Numerous biometric factors can be utilized for authentication including fingerprints, retina patterns, iris patterns, voice, face, vein patters, and more.
- Biometric efficacy rates, including false acceptance and false rejection rates, are critical in making biometrics work.
- Multifactor authentication is commonly employed with biometrics.

Discuss the methods and protocols for remote access to networks

- Remote access protocols provide a mechanism to remotely connect clients to networks.
- A wide range of remote access protocols has evolved to support various security and authentication mechanisms.
- Remote access is granted via remote access servers, such as RRAS and RADIUS.

Identify authentication, authorization, and accounting (AAA) protocols

- Authentication is a cornerstone element of security, connecting access to a previously approved user ID.
- Authorization is the process of determining whether an authenticated user has permission.
- Accounting protocols manage connection time and cost records.
- RADIUS and TACACS+ are examples of implementations of AAA.

Implement virtual private networks (VPNs) and their security aspects

- VPNs use protocols to establish a private network over a public network, shielding user communications from outside observation.
- VPNs can be invoked via many different protocol mechanisms and involve either a hardware or software client on each end of the communication channel.

Key Terms

AAA *(358)*
access control *(371)*
access control list (ACL) *(374)*
access control matrix *(374)*
accounting *(370)*
account expiration *(369)*
account maintenance *(367)*
account recertification *(368)*
administrator *(360)*
attestation *(388)*
attribute-based access control (ABAC) *(377)*
authentication *(358)*
authentication server (AS) *(383)*
authorization *(370)*
basic authentication *(382)*
biometric factors *(391)*
certificate *(385)*
Challenge-Handshake Authentication Protocol (CHAP) *(409)*
client-to-server ticket *(383)*
Common Access Card (CAC) *(385)*
conditional access *(377)*
credential management *(366)*
crossover error rate (CER) *(395)*
digest authentication *(382)*
digital certificate *(385)*
directory *(387)*
discretionary access control (DAC) *(376)*
domain controller *(363)*
domain password policy *(363)*
eXtensible Access Control Markup Language (XACML) *(377)*
Extensible Authentication Protocol (EAP) *(408)*
false acceptance rate (FAR) *(394)*
false negative *(394)*
false positive *(393)*
false rejection rate (FRR) *(395)*
federated identity management *(399)*
FTPS *(413)*
gait analysis *(393)*
generic accounts *(360)*
group *(361)*
group policy object (GPO) *(366)*
guest accounts *(361)*
hardware security module (HSM) *(389)*
HMAC-based One-Time Password (HOTP) *(386)*
identification *(378)*
identity provider (IdP) *(378)*
IEEE 802.1X *(399)*
Kerberos *(383)*
key distribution center (KDC) *(383)*
knowledge-based authentication *(386)*
Layer 2 Tunneling Protocol (L2TP) *(406)*
Lightweight Directory Access Protocol (LDAP) *(400)*
mandatory access control (MAC) *(375)*
multifactor authentication *(396)*

- mutual authentication (384)
- OAuth (Open Authorization) (411)
- offboarding (361)
- onboarding (361)
- OpenID (412)
- OpenID Connect (412)
- Password Authentication Protocol (PAP) (410)
- password vaults (390)
- permissions (359)
- personal identity verification (PIV) (385)
- Point-to-Point Protocol (PPP) (408)
- Point-to-Point Tunneling Protocol (PPTP) (407)
- privilege management (370)
- privileged accounts (361)
- remote access server (RAS) (399)
- Remote Authentication Dial-In User Service (RADIUS) (401)
- Remote Desktop Protocol (RDP) (411)
- rights (359)
- role (362)
- role-based access control (RBAC) (376)
- root (360)
- rule-based access control (377)
- Security Assertion Markup Language (SAML) (411)
- secure token (412)
- service accounts (361)
- SFTP (413)
- SSH keys (380)
- single sign-on (SSO) (365)
- shared accounts (360)
- Shibboleth (412)
- smart card (386)
- software tokens (386)
- someone you know (399)
- something you are (398)
- something you can do (398)
- something you exhibit (399)
- something you have (397)
- something you know (397)
- somewhere you are (398)
- static codes (389)
- Terminal Access Controller Access Control System Plus (TACACS+) (403)
- ticket-granting server (TGS) (383)
- ticket-granting ticket (TGT) (383)
- time-based One-Time Password (TOTP) (386)
- Time-of-day restrictions (368)
- token (385)
- transitive trust (388)
- trusted platform module (TPM) (389)
- tunneling (406)
- usage auditing and review (368)
- user (359)
- username (359)
- virtual private network (VPN) (413)

Key Terms Quiz

Use terms from the Key Terms list to complete the sentences that follow. Don't use the same term more than once. Not all terms will be used.

1. _______________ is an authentication model designed around the concept of using tickets for accessing objects.
2. _______________ is designed around the type of tasks people perform.
3. _______________ refers to the condition where trust is extended to another domain that is already trusted.
4. _______________ describes a system where every resource has access rules set for it all of the time.
5. _______________ is an authentication process where the user can enter their user ID (or username) and password and then be able to move from application to application or resource to resource without having to supply further authentication information.
6. _______________ is an algorithm that can be used to authenticate a user in a system by using an authentication server.

7. If your fingerprints fail to let you into a system when they should, this is called a(n) _______________.

8. When both the client and the server authenticate each other, this is called _______________.

9. _______________ is an access control method that would allow you to control access to records only when someone is scheduled to work.

10. Authentication that is sent in plaintext with only Base64 encoding is an example of _______________.

Multiple-Choice Quiz

1. Authentication can be based on what?
   A. Something a user possesses
   B. Something a user knows
   C. Something measured on a user, such as a fingerprint
   D. All of the above

2. You've spent the last week tweaking a fingerprint-scanning solution for your organization. Despite your best efforts, roughly 1 in 50 attempts will fail even if the user is using the correct finger and their fingerprint is in the system. Your supervisor says 1 in 50 is "good enough" and tells you to move onto the next project. Your supervisor just defined which of the following for your fingerprint-scanning system?
   A. False rejection rate
   B. False acceptance rate
   C. Critical threshold
   D. Failure acceptance criteria

3. A ticket-granting server is an important element in which of the following authentication models?
   A. L2TP
   B. RADIUS
   C. PPP
   D. Kerberos

4. What protocol is used for RADIUS?
   A. UDP
   B. NetBIOS
   C. TCP
   D. Proprietary

5. Under which access control system is each piece of information and every system resource (files, devices, networks, and so on) labeled with its sensitivity level?
   A. Discretionary access control
   B. Resource access control
   C. Mandatory access control
   D. Media access control

6. Which of the following algorithms uses a secret key with a current timestamp to generate a one-time password?
   A. Hash-based Message Authentication Code
   B. Date-hashed Message Authorization Password
   C. Time-based One-Time Password
   D. Single sign-on

7. You have to implement an OpenID solution. What is the typical relationship with existing systems?
   A. OpenID is used for authentication, OAuth is used for authorization.
   B. OpenID is used for authorization, OAuth is used for authentication.
   C. OpenID is not compatible with OAuth.
   D. OpenID only works with Kerberos.

8. Elements of Kerberos include which of the following?
   - **A.** Tickets, ticket-granting server, ticket-authorizing agent
   - **B.** Ticket-granting ticket, authentication server, ticket
   - **C.** Services server, Kerberos realm, ticket authenticators
   - **D.** Client-to-server ticket, authentication server ticket, ticket
9. To establish a PPTP connection across a firewall, you must do which of the following?
   - **A.** Do nothing. PPTP does not need to cross firewalls by design.
   - **B.** Do nothing. PPTP traffic is invisible and tunnels past firewalls.
   - **C.** Open a UDP port of choice and assign it to PPTP.
   - **D.** Open TCP port 1723.
10. To establish an L2TP connection across a firewall, you must do which of the following?
    - **A.** Do nothing. L2TP does not cross firewalls by design.
    - **B.** Do nothing. L2TP tunnels past firewalls.
    - **C.** Open a UDP port of choice and assign it to L2TP.
    - **D.** Open UDP port 1701.

Essay Quiz

1. A co-worker with a strong Windows background is having difficulty understanding Linux file permissions. Describe Linux file permissions to him. Compare Linux file permissions to Windows file permissions.
2. How are authentication and authorization alike and how are they different. What is the relationship, if any, between the two?

Lab Projects

• Lab Project 11.1

Using two workstations and some routers, set up a simple VPN. Using Wireshark (a shareware network protocol analyzer, available at https://wireshark.com), observe traffic inside and outside the tunnel to demonstrate protection. Examine the traffic to see what information is available between the machines when tunneling is employed.

• Lab Project 11.2

Using freeSSHd and freeFTPd (both shareware programs, available at www.freesshd.com) and Wireshark, demonstrate the security features of SSH compared to Telnet and FTP. Examine the traffic to see what information is available between the different protocols.

chapter 12

Wireless Security and Mobile Devices

App stores and mobile apps are the greatest hostile code and malware delivery mechanism ever created.

—Winn Schwartau

In this chapter, you will learn how to

- Describe the different wireless systems in use today
- Identify 802.11's security issues and possible solutions
- Learn about wireless configuration and deployment
- Learn about the different types of wireless attacks
- Examine the security of mobile systems

Wireless is increasingly the way people access the Internet. Because wireless access is considered a consumer benefit, many businesses have added wireless access points to lure customers into their shops. With the rollout of fifth-generation (5G) high-speed cellular networks, mobile devices are connected via the Internet for virtually any content type. The massive growth of the Internet of Things (IoT) devices has contributed to this data-rich environment that is made possible by wireless networks.

As wireless use increases, the security of the wireless protocols has become a more important factor in the security of the entire network. As a security professional, you need to understand wireless network applications because of the risks inherent in broadcasting a network signal where anyone can intercept it. Sending unsecured information across public airwaves is tantamount to posting your company's passwords by the front door of the building. This chapter opens with a look at several current wireless protocols and their security features. The chapter finishes with an examination of mobile systems and their security concerns.

Connection Methods and Receivers

Mobile devices, by their mobile nature, require a nonwired means of connection to a network. Typically, this connection on the enterprise side is via the Internet, but on the mobile device side a wide range of options exist for connectivity. Where and how mobile devices connect to a network are manageable by the enterprise in architecting the mobile connection aspect of their wireless network. This section will cover the common methods of connecting, including cellular, Wi-Fi, Bluetooth, NFC, infrared, and USB. The connection methods of point-to-point and point-to-multipoint are also explained. Specialized receivers, such as GPS and RFID, are covered at the end of the section.

Cellular

Cellular connections use mobile telephony circuits, today typically fourth-generation (4G) or LTE in nature, although some 3G services still exist. One of the strengths of cellular is that robust nationwide networks have been deployed, making strong signals available virtually anywhere with reasonable population density. The corresponding weakness is that gaps in cellular service still exist in remote areas.

As this book is being written, the telecommunication world is moving to 5G, the newest form of cellular. This change will occur in densely populated areas first and then move across the globe. 5G is more than just a newer, faster network; it is a redesign to improve network communications through greater throughput, lower latency, better quality-of-service controls, and service differentiations. It is also designed to handle streaming video downloads, standard audio calls, and data transfers from a myriad of smaller Internet of Things devices, all with appropriate service levels. 5G will enable network services that facilitate the move to widespread data connectivity and transfers over the cellular networks. 5G is much more than just a better cellphone; it is the network for the data connectivity era.

Wi-Fi

Wi-Fi refers to the radio communication methods developed under the Wi-Fi Alliance. These systems exist on 2.4GHz and 5GHz frequency spectrums, and networks are constructed by both the enterprise you are associated with and third parties. This communication methodology is ubiquitous with computing platforms and is relatively easy to implement and secure. Securing Wi-Fi networks is covered later in the chapter. In 2021, a new range in the 6GHz spectrum in the U.S. will be used by Wi-Fi 6E devices, offering even greater throughput. As this is a new radio frequency, it will take new hardware to utilize this addition. The hardware is scheduled to be released in 2021.

Bluetooth

Bluetooth is a short-to-medium-range, low-power wireless protocol that transmits in the 2.4GHz band, the same band used for 802.11. The original concept for this short-range (approx. 32 feet) wireless protocol is to transmit data in personal area networks (PANs). Bluetooth transmits and receives data from a variety of devices, the most common being mobile phones, laptops, printers, and audio devices. The mobile phone has driven a lot of Bluetooth growth and has even spread Bluetooth into new cars as a mobile phone hands-free kit. Advances in transmitter power, antenna gain, and operating environment uses have expanded the range up to 3800 meters in some outdoor applications.

Bluetooth has gone through several releases. Version 1.1 was the first commercially successful version, with version 1.2 released in 2007 and correcting some of the problems found in 1.1. Version 1.2 allows speeds up to 721 Kbps and improves resistance to interference. Version 1.2 is backward-compatible with version 1.1. With the rate of advancement and the life of most tech items, Bluetooth 1 series is basically extinct. Bluetooth 2.0 introduced enhanced data rate (EDR), which allows the transmission of up to 3.0 Mbps. Bluetooth 3.0 has the capability to use an 802.11 channel to achieve speeds up to 24 Mbps. The current version is the Bluetooth 4.0 standard, with support for three modes: classic, high speed, and Low Energy.

Tech Tip

Bluetooth Security

Bluetooth should always have discoverable mode turned off unless you're deliberately pairing a device.

Bluetooth 4 introduced a new method to support collecting data from devices that generate data at a very low rate. Some devices, such as medical devices, may only collect and transmit data at low rates. This feature, called Bluetooth Low Energy (BLE), was designed to aggregate data from various sensors, like heart rate monitors, thermometers, and so forth, and it carries the commercial name Bluetooth Smart. Bluetooth 5 continues the improvements of BLE, increasing its data rate and range.

As Bluetooth became popular, people started trying to find holes in it. Bluetooth features easy configuration of devices to allow communication, with no need for network addresses or ports. Bluetooth uses pairing to establish a trust relationship between devices. To establish that trust, the devices advertise capabilities and require a passkey. To help maintain security, most devices require the passkey to be entered into both devices; this prevents a "default passkey" type of attack. The Bluetooth's protocol advertisement of services and pairing properties is where some of the security issues start. Bluetooth should always have discoverable mode turned off unless you're deliberately pairing a device. Table 12.1 displays Bluetooth versions and speeds.

Table 12.1 Bluetooth Versions, Range, and Speed

Bluetooth Version	Maximum Range	Maximum Data Rate
3.0 (Classic)	< 200 feet	25 Mbps
4.x	200 feet/60 meters	25 Mbps
5.x	985 feet/300 meters	50 Mbps

In the Bluetooth 5.x versions, different data rates correspond to differing ranges with higher rates at lower ranges supporting more data rich devices, and lower rates having longer ranges to support lower-data-rate IoT devices. Bluetooth 5 uses a different frequency spectrum, requiring new hardware and limiting backward compatibility, but it is designed for local networks of the future with low power consumption, inexpensive hardware, small implementations, and scalable data rate versus range considerations.

NFC

Near field communication (NFC) is a set of wireless technologies that enables smartphones and other devices to establish radio communication when they are within close proximity to each other—typically a distance of 10 cm (3.9 in) or less. This technology did not see much use until recently when it started being employed to move data between cell phones and in mobile payment systems. NFC is likely to become a high-use technology in the years to come as multiple uses exist for the technology, and the next generation of smartphones is sure to include this as a standard function. Currently, NFC relies to a great degree on its very short range for security, although apps that use it have their own security mechanisms as well.

Infrared

Infrared (IR) is a band of electromagnetic energy just beyond the red end of the visible color spectrum. IR has been used in remote-control devices for years. IR made its debut in computer networking as a wireless method to connect to printers. Now that wireless keyboards, wireless mice, and mobile devices exchange data via IR, it seems to be everywhere. IR can also be used to connect devices in a network configuration, but it is slow compared to other wireless technologies. IR cannot penetrate walls but instead bounces off them. Nor can it penetrate other solid objects; therefore, if you stack a few items in front of the transceiver, the signal is lost. Because IR can be seen by all in range, any desired security must be on top of the base transmission mechanism.

USB

Universal Serial Bus (USB) has become the ubiquitous standard for connecting devices with cables. Mobile phones can transfer data and charge their battery via USB. Laptops, desktops, even servers have USB ports for a variety of data connection needs. Many devices, such as phones, tablets, routers, and IoT devices, also use USB ports, albeit many are moving to the newer smaller USB type C connector. USB ports have greatly expanded users' ability to connect devices to their computers. USB ports automatically recognize a device being plugged into the system and usually work without the user needing to add drivers or configure software. This has spawned a legion of USB devices, from music players to peripherals to storage devices—virtually anything that can consume or deliver data connects via USB.

The most interesting of these devices, for security purposes, are the USB flash memory–based storage devices. USB drive keys, which are basically flash memory with a USB interface in a device typically about the size of your thumb, provide a way to move files easily from computer to computer. When plugged into a USB port, these devices automount and behave like any other drive attached to the computer. Their small size and relatively large capacity, coupled with instant read-write ability, present security problems. They can easily be used by an individual with malicious intent to conceal the removal of files or data from the building or to bring malicious files into the building and onto the company network.

USB connectors come in a wide range of sizes and shapes. For mobile use there is USB mini, USB micro, and now USB Type-C, which is faster and reversible (does not care which side is up). There are also Type-A and Type-B connectors, with different form factors. The original USB provided data rates up to 480 Mbps, with USB 3.0 raising it to 5 Gbps, 3.1 raising it to 10 Gbps, and 3.2 raising it to 20 Gbps. USB 4 provides speeds up to 40 Gbps.

Point-to-Point

Radio signals travel outward from an antenna and eventually are received by a receiving antenna. *Point-to-point* communications are defined as communications with one endpoint on each end. An example would be a single transmitter talking to a single receiver. This terminology transferred to networking, where a communication channel between two entities in isolation is referred to as point-to-point. Examples of point-to-point communications include Bluetooth, where this is mandated by protocol, and USB, where it is mandated by physical connections.

A point-to-point connection is between two devices (one to one) while a point-to-multipoint connection is one (device) to many (devices).

Point-to-Multipoint

Point-to-multipoint communications have multiple receivers for a transmitted signal. When a packet is sent to a broadcast address, it has multiple receivers and is called a point-to-multipoint communication. Most radio-based and networked systems are potentially point-to-multipoint, from a single transmitter to multiple receivers, limited only by protocols.

Global Positioning System (GPS)

The *Global Positioning System (GPS)* is a series of satellites that provide nearly global coverage of highly precise time signals, which when multiple signals are combined can produce precise positional data in all three dimensions. GPS receivers, operating in the 6GHz band, are small, cheap, and have been added to numerous mobile devices, becoming nearly ubiquitous. The ability to have precise time, precise location, and, given differential math, speed has transformed many mobile device capabilities. GPS enables geolocation, geofencing, and a whole host of other capabilities.

RFID

Radio Frequency Identification (RFID) tags are used in a wide range of use cases. From tracking devices to tracking keys, the unique serialization of these remotely sensible devices has made them useful in a wide range of applications. RFID tags come in several different forms and can be classified as either active or passive. Active tags have a power source, whereas passive tags utilize the RF energy transmitted to them for power. RFID tags are used as a means of identification and have the advantage over bar codes in that they do not have to be visible, just within radio wave range—typically centimeters to 200 meters, depending on tag type. RFID tags are used in a range of security situations, including contactless identification systems such as smart cards.

The various mobile device connection methods are conducive to performance-based questions, which means you need to pay attention to the scenario presented and choose the best connection methodology. Consider data rate, purpose, distances, and so forth in picking the best choice.

SATCOM

SATCOM (Satellite Communications) is the use of terrestrial transmitters and receivers and satellites in orbit to transfer the signals. SATCOM can be one-way, as in satellite radio, but for most communications two-way signals are needed. Satellites are expensive, and for high-density urban areas, both cost and line-of-sight issues make SATCOM a more costly option. However, in rural and remote areas as well as mobile areas such as at sea, SATCOM is one of the only options for communications. With the advent of SpaceX's Starlink satellite-based Internet service, the fulfillment of global, affordable communications using satellites may finally happen. It is still too early to know for sure, but in the next couple of years this technology may become commonplace, especially for rural and remote users.

Wireless Protocols

Several different wireless bands are in common use today, the most common of which is the Wi-Fi series, referring to the 802.11 Wireless LAN standards certified by the Wi-Fi Alliance. Another set of bands is **WiMAX**, which refers to the set of 802.16 wireless network standards ratified by the WiMAX Forum. Lastly, there is **Zigbee**, a low-power, personal area networking technology described by the IEEE 802.15.4 series.

IEEE 802.11 is a family of protocols instead of a single specification. Table 12.2 provides a summary of the 802.11 family. The standard launched a range of products (such as wireless routers, an example of which is shown in Figure 12.1) that would open the way to a whole new genre of possibilities for attackers and a new series of headaches for security administrators everywhere. 802.11 was a new standard for sending packetized data traffic over radio waves in the unlicensed 2.4GHz band.

This group of IEEE standards is also called Wi-Fi, which is a certification owned by an industry group, the Wi-Fi Alliance. A device marked as Wi-Fi

• **Figure 12.1** A common wireless router

Certified adheres to the standards of the alliance. As the products matured and became easy to use and affordable, security experts began to deconstruct the limited security that had been built into the standard.

Tech Tip

What Is Wi-Fi 4? Wi-Fi 5? Wi-Fi 6?

For consumers, the IEEE naming scheme for wireless standards is confusing and has details most do not care about. To simplify marketing, the Wi-Fi Alliance has introduced some simpler names: Wi-Fi 4, Wi-Fi 5, and Wi-Fi 6. The main purpose is to make it easier to match endpoints and routers for consumers.

Name	Specification
Wi-Fi 4	802.11n
Wi-Fi 5	802.11ac
Wi-Fi 6	802.11ax

Table 12.2 The IEEE 802.11 Family

Specification	Speed	Frequency Range	Modulation
802.11a	54 Mbps	5.2 GHz	OFDM
802.11b	11 Mbps	2.4 GHz	DSSS
802.11g	11 Mbps/54 Mbps	2.4 GHz	OFDM
802.11i			
802.11n	124–248 Mbps	2.4 GHz/5 GHz	MIMO
802.11ac	150 Mbps–2.6 Gbps	2.4 GHz/5 GHz	MU-MIMO OFDM
802.11ad (WiGig)	7 Gbps	60 GHz	OFDM
802.11af (White-Fi)	25–550 Mbps	< 1 GHz (old TV bands)	
802.11ah	Up to 347 Mbps	< 1 GHz ISM bands	
802.11ax	11 Gbps	2.4 GHz/5 GHz	OFDMA MU-MIMO

Direct-sequence spread spectrum (DSSS) is a modulation type that spreads the traffic sent over the entire bandwidth. It does this by injecting a noise-like signal into the information stream and transmitting the normally narrowband information over the wider band available. The primary reason that spread-spectrum technology is used in 802.11 protocols is to avoid interference on the public 2.4 GHz and 5 GHz bands. **Multiple-input and multiple-output (MIMO)** technology is a method for multiplying the capacity of a radio link using multiple transmission and receiving antennas to exploit multipath propagation. MIMO is a practical technique for sending and receiving more than one data signal simultaneously over the same radio channel by exploiting multipath propagation of the radio waves. **Orthogonal frequency division multiplexing (OFDM)** multiplexes, or separates, the data to be transmitted into smaller chunks and then transmits the chunks on several subchannels. This use of subchannels is what the "frequency division" portion of the name refers to. Both of these techniques, multiplexing and frequency division, are used to avoid interference. *Orthogonal* refers to the manner in which the subchannels are assigned—principally to avoid crosstalk, or interference, with your own channels. The latest versions of the 802.11 series, ax, introduces multi-user versions of OFDM and MIMO. Orthogonal frequency-division multiple access (OFDMA) is a multiuser version of the popular OFDM digital modulation scheme, and MU-MIMO is multiuser MIMO. Both of these were designed to facilitate multiple users in Wi-Fi dense locations, increasing the capacity of 802.11ax signals.

802.11: Individual Standards

The 802.11b protocol provides for multiple-rate Ethernet over 2.4GHz spread-spectrum wireless. The most common layout is a point-to-multipoint environment, with the available bandwidth being shared by all users. The typical range is roughly 100 yards indoors and 300 yards outdoors, line of sight. 802.11a uses a higher band and has a higher bandwidth. It operates in the 5GHz spectrum using OFDM. Supporting rates of up to 54 Mbps, it is the faster brother of 802.11b; however, the higher frequency used by 802.11a shortens the usable range of the devices and makes it incompatible with 802.11b. The 802.11g standard uses portions of both of the other standards: it uses the 2.4GHz band for greater range but uses the OFDM transmission method to achieve the faster 54Mbps data rates. Because it uses the 2.4GHz band, this standard interoperates with the older 802.11b standard. This allows older 802.11g access points (APs) to give access to both "g" and "b" clients.

The 802.11n version improves on the older standards by greatly increasing speed. It has a functional data rate of up to 600 Mbps, gained through the use of wider bands and multiple-input multiple-output (MIMO) processing. MIMO uses multiple antennas and can bond separate channels together to increase data throughput. 802.11ax is the latest in the 5GHz band, with functional data rates up to a theoretical 11+ Gbps using multiple antennas. The 802.11ac standard was ratified in 2014, and chipsets have been available since late 2011. 802.11ac is designed for multimedia streaming and other high-bandwidth operations, the individual channels are twice the width of 802.11n channels, and as many as eight antennas can be deployed in a MU-MIMO form. 802.11ax was designed to use higher-efficiency encoding methods and radio methods to improve the capability over 802.11ac. Called high efficiency wireless by many in marketing, the ax standard is designed for signal dense environments such as major gatherings.

All these protocols operate in bands that are "unlicensed" by the FCC. This means that people operating this equipment do not have to be certified by the FCC, but it also means that the devices could possibly share the band with other devices, such as cordless phones, closed-circuit TV (CCTV) wireless transceivers, and other similar equipment. This other equipment can cause interference with the 802.11 equipment, possibly causing speed degradation.

The 2.4GHz band is commonly used by many household devices that are constantly on, such as cordless phones. It is also the frequency used by microwave ovens to heat food. So if you are having intermittent interference on your Wi-Fi LAN, check to see if the microwave is on.

WEP

The designers of the 802.11 protocol also attempted to maintain confidentiality by introducing **Wired Equivalent Privacy (WEP)**, which uses a cipher to encrypt the data as it is transmitted through the air. WEP has been shown to have an implementation problem that can be exploited to break security. WEP encrypts the data traveling across the network with an **RC4 stream cipher**, attempting to ensure confidentiality. (The details of the RC4 cipher are covered in Chapter 5.) This synchronous method of encryption ensures some method of authentication. The system depends on the client and the AP having a shared secret key, ensuring that only authorized people with the proper key have access to the wireless network. WEP supports two key lengths, 40 and 104 bits, though these are more typically referred to as 64 and 128 bits. In 802.11a and 802.11g, manufacturers extended this to 152-bit WEP keys. This is because in all cases, 24 bits of the overall key length are used for the initialization vector (IV).

Tech Tip

WEP Isn't Equivalent, or Private

Wired Equivalent Privacy (WEP) should not be trusted alone to provide confidentiality. If WEP is the only protocol supported by your AP, place your AP outside the corporate firewall and VPN to add more protection.

The biggest weakness of WEP is that the IV problem exists, regardless of key length, because the IV always remains at 24 bits, and IVs can frequently be repeated due to the limited size. Most APs also have the ability to lock in access only to known MAC addresses, providing a limited authentication capability. Given sniffers' capacity to grab all active MAC addresses on the network, this capability is not very effective. An attacker simply configures their wireless cards to a known-good MAC address.

Current Security Methods

WEP was designed to provide some measure of confidentiality on an 802.11 network, similar to what is found on a wired network, but that has not been the case. Accordingly, the Wi-Fi Alliance developed Wi-Fi Protected Access (WPA) to improve upon WEP. The 802.11i standard is the IEEE standard for security in wireless networks, also known as Wi-Fi Protected Access 2 (WPA2). The 802.11i standard specifies the use of the Temporal Key Integrity Protocol (TKIP) and uses AES with the Counter Mode with CBC-MAC Protocol (in full, the Counter Mode with Cipher Block Chaining–Message Authentication Codes Protocol, or simply CCMP). These two protocols have different functions, but they both serve to enhance security.

TKIP is used for backward compatibility with draft 802.11i implementation and WPA standards, and it works by using a shared secret combined with the card's MAC address to generate a new key, which is mixed with the IV to make per-packet keys that encrypt a single packet using the same RC4 cipher used by traditional WEP. This overcomes the WEP key weakness, as a key is used on only one packet. The other advantage to this method is that it can be retrofitted to current hardware with only a software change, unlike AES and 802.1X. CCMP is actually the mode in which the AES cipher is used to provide message integrity. Unlike TKIP, CCMP requires new hardware to perform the AES encryption. The advances of 802.11i have corrected the weaknesses of WEP.

WPA

The first standard to be used in the market to replace WEP was Wi-Fi Protected Access (WPA). This standard uses the flawed WEP algorithm with the Temporal Key Integrity Protocol (TKIP). WPA also introduced a message integrity check (MIC) that is known by the name Michael.

Whereas WEP uses a 40-bit or 104-bit encryption key that must be manually entered on wireless access points and devices and does not change, TKIP employs a per-packet key, generating a new 128-bit key for each packet. This can generally be accomplished with only a firmware update, enabling a simple solution to the types of attacks that compromise WEP.

WPA also suffers from a lack of forward secrecy protection. If the WPA key is known, as in a public Wi-Fi password, then an attacker can collect all the packets from all of the connections and decrypt those packets later. This is why, when using public Wi-Fi, one should always use a secondary means of protection—either a VPN or a TLS-based solution to protect their content.

TKIP

Temporal Key Integrity Protocol (TKIP) was created as a stopgap security measure to replace the WEP protocol without requiring the replacement of legacy hardware. The breaking of WEP had left Wi-Fi networks without viable link-layer security, and a solution was required for already deployed hardware. TKIP works by mixing a secret root key with the IV before the RC4 encryption. WPA/TKIP uses the same underlying mechanism as WEP, and consequently is vulnerable to a number of similar attacks. TKIP is no longer considered secure and has been deprecated with the release of WPA2.

> TKIP is an integrity check; AES is an encryption algorithm.

Wi-Fi Protected Access 2 (WPA2)

IEEE 802.11i is the standard for security in wireless networks and is also known as **Wi-Fi Protected Access 2 (WPA2)**. It uses 802.1X to provide authentication and uses Advanced Encryption Standard (AES) as the encryption protocol. WPA2 uses the AES block cipher, a significant improvement over WEP and WPA's use of the RC4 stream cipher. WPA2 specifies the use of the Counter Mode with CBC-MAC Protocol (in full, the Counter Mode with Cipher Block Chaining–Message Authentication Codes Protocol, or simply CCMP). CCMP is described later in this chapter.

While WPA2 addressed the flaws in WPA and was the de facto standard for many years on wireless networks that were serious about security, it too fell to a series of issues, leading to the development of WPA3. WPA2 comes with a variety of methods to set up the shared key elements, and those are described later in the chapter. The WPA2-Personal passphrase can be cracked using brute force attacks. Even worse, once a hacker captures the data from the airwaves, the actual password cracking can occur offline on a more powerful, dedicated machine. Any encrypted messages they recorded can then be decrypted later, thus yielding passwords and other sensitive data.

WPA2 comes in two flavors: WPA2-Personal and WPA2-Enterprise. WPA2-Personal is also called WPA2-PSK because it uses authentication based on a pre-shared key (PSK), which allows home users without an enterprise authentication server to manage the keys. To use WPA2-PSK on a network, the router is given the pre-shared key, typically a plain-English passphrase between 8 and 63 characters long. WPA2-Personal then uses TKIP to combine that passphrase with the network Service Set Identifier (SSID) to generate unique encryption keys for each wireless client. WPA2-Enterprise replaces the pre-shared key with IEEE 802.1X, which is discussed in its own section later in this chapter. By eliminating the PSK element, WPA2-Enterprise can create stronger keys, and the information is not subject to capture.

In WPA2, an attacker can record the 4-way handshake between a client and the access point and use this data to crack the password. This will then crack all the keys that have been used or will be used in the future. Because of the ability to break future messages based on past messages, forward secrecy is not provided by WPA2.

WPS

Wi-Fi Protected Setup (WPS) is a network security standard that was created to provide users with an easy method of configuring wireless networks. Designed for home networks and small business networks, this standard involves the use of an eight-digit PIN to configure wireless devices. WPS consists of a series of Extensible Authentication Protocol (EAP) messages and has been shown to be susceptible to brute force attack. A successful attack can reveal the PIN and subsequently the WPA/WPA2 passphrase and allow unauthorized parties to gain access to the network. Currently, the only effective mitigation is to disable WPS.

Setting Up WPA2

If WPS is not safe for use, how does one set up WPA2? To set up WPA2, you need to have several parameters. Figure 12.2 shows the screens for a WPA2 setup in Windows.

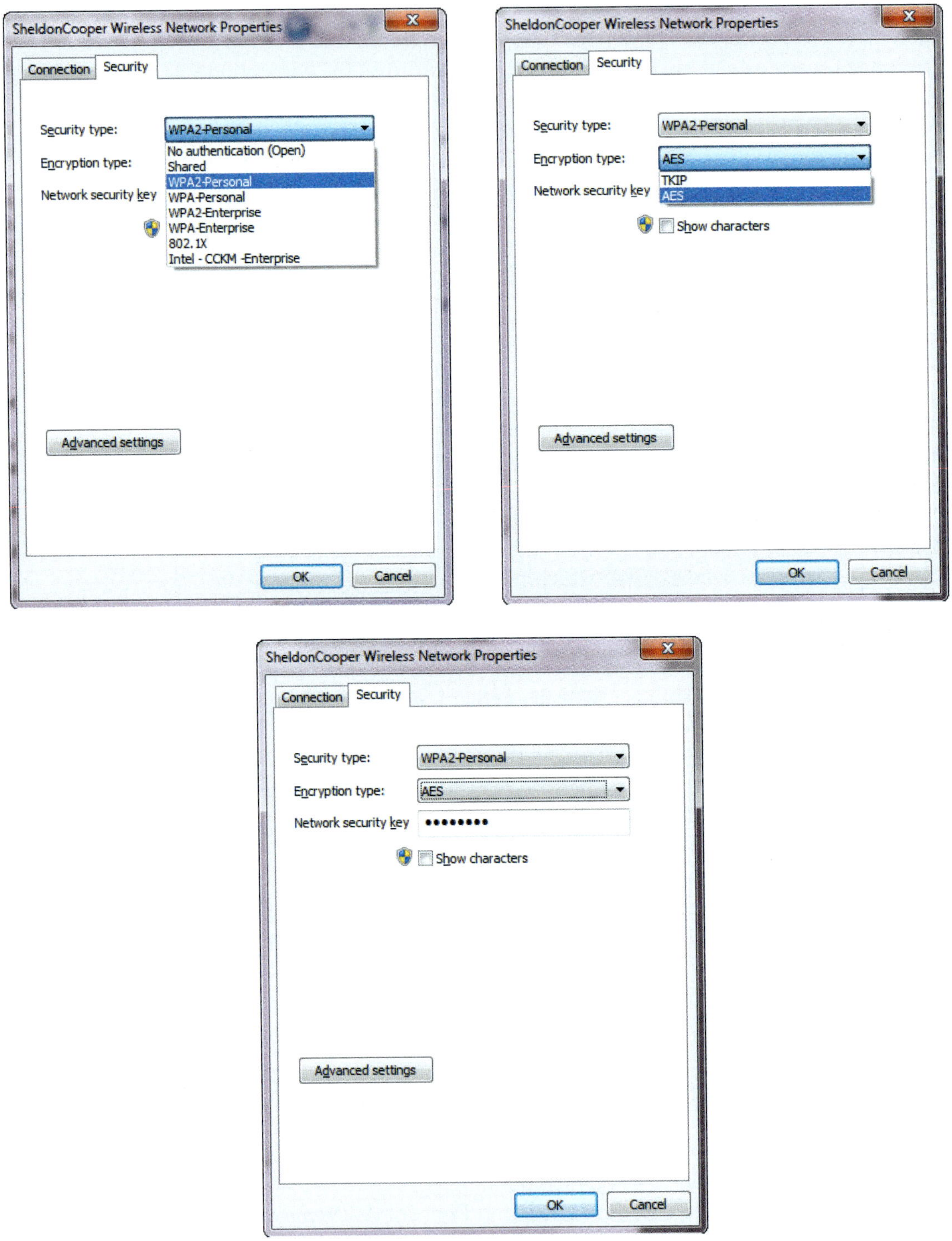

• **Figure 12.2** WPA2 setup options in Windows

The first element is to choose a security framework. When configuring an adapter to connect to an existing network, you need to match the choice of the network. When setting up your own network, you can choose whichever option you prefer. There are many selections, but for security purposes, you should choose WPA2-Personal or WPA2-Enterprise. Both of these require the choice of an encryption type, either TKIP or AES. TKIP has been deprecated, so choose AES. The last element is the choice of the network security key—the secret that is shared by all users. WPA2-Enterprise, which is designed to be used with an 802.1X authentication server that distributes different keys to each user, is typically used in business environments.

PSK vs. Enterprise vs. Open System

When building out a wireless network, you must decide how you are going to employ security on the network. Specifically, the questions need to be addressed with respect to who will be allowed to connect, and what level of protection will be provided in the transmission of data between mobile devices and the access point.

Both WPA and WPA2, discussed in detail earlier in the chapter, have two methods to establish a connection: PSK and Enterprise. *PSK* stands for pre-shared key, which is exactly what it sounds like—a secret that has to be shared between users. A PSK is typically entered as a passphrase of up to 63 characters. This key must be securely shared between users, as it is the basis of the security provided by the protocol. The PSK is converted to a 256-bit key that is then used to secure all communications between the device and access point. PSK has one particular vulnerability: simple and short PSKs are at risk of brute force attempts. Keeping them at least 20 random characters long should mitigate this attack vector. Table 12.3 illustrates the differences between WAP and WPA2.

Table 12.3 WPA and WPA2 Compared

Mode	WPA	WPA2
Enterprise Mode	Authentication: 802.1X EAP Encryption: TKIP/MIC	Authentication: 802.1X EAP Encryption: AES/CCMP
Personal Mode	Authentication: PSK Encryption: TKIP/MIC	Authentication: 802.1X EAP Encryption: TKIP/MIC

In *Enterprise* mode, the devices use IEEE 802.1X and a RADIUS authentication server to enable a connection. This method allows the use of usernames and passwords and provides enterprise-class options such as NAC integration, multiple random keys, and the same PSK for everyone.

In WEP-based systems, there are two options: Open System authentication and shared key authentication. Open System authentication is not truly authentication—it is merely a sharing of a secret key based on the SSID. The process is simple: First, the mobile client matches the SSID with the access point and requests a key (called authentication) to the access point. Then the access point generates an authentication code (the key, as there is no specific authentication of the client), which is a random number intended for use only during that session. The mobile client uses the authentication code and joins the network. The session continues until disassociation either by request or loss of signal.

> In practice, you will encounter the differences between PSK, Enterprise, and Open System authentication.

Wi-Fi Protected Access 3 (WPA3)

Wi-Fi Protected Access 3 (WPA3) is the successor to WPA2. Developed in 2018, it strives to resolve the weaknesses found in WPA2. WPA3 improves the security of the encryption by using Simultaneous Authentication of Equals (SAE) in place of the PSK authentication method used in prior WPA versions. SAE is described in detail later in this chapter. This change allows WPA3-Personal networks to employ simple passphrases that are significantly more time consuming to break than was the case with WPA/WPA2.

WPA3-Enterprise brings a whole host of upgrades, including 192-bit minimum-strength security protocols and cryptographic tools such as the following:

- **Authenticated encryption** 256-bit Galois/Counter Mode Protocol (GCMP-256)
- **Key derivation and confirmation** 384-bit Hashed Message Authentication Mode (HMAC) with Secure Hash Algorithm (HMAC-SHA-384)
- **Key establishment and authentication** Elliptic Curve Diffie-Hellman (ECDH) exchange and Elliptic Curve Digital Signature Algorithm (ECDSA) using a 384-bit elliptic curve
- **Robust management frame protection** 256-bit Broadcast/Multicast Integrity Protocol Galois Message Authentication Code (BIP-GMAC-256)

> WPA2 uses pre-shared keys; WPA3 does not. If SAE is used, it is for WPA3-level authentication. Forward secrecy is only provided by WPA3.

> It is important to see the history of security protocol failures in Wi-Fi to understand the challenges and to help prevent repeating obvious failure modes. This lesson was not heeded in WEP and WAP, forcing a lot of changes to get to WPA3 today.

WPA3 integrates with the back-end enterprise authentication infrastructure, such as a RADIUS server. It can use elliptic curve Diffie-Hellman exchanges and elliptic curve Digital Signature Algorithm (DSA) protocols to provide a method of strong authentication. The WPA3 protocol makes use of a Quick Response (QR) code for users to connect their devices to the "Wi-Fi CERTIFIED Easy Connect" network, which allows them to scan a QR code on a device with their smartphone. WPA3 offers forward secrecy based on its method of encryption; previous messages do not enable future decryption.

Simultaneous Authentication of Equals (SAE)

Simultaneous Authentication of Equals (SAE) is a password-based key exchange method developed for mesh networks. Defined in RFC 7664, it uses the Dragonfly protocol to perform a key exchange and is secure against passive monitoring. SAE is not a new protocol; it has been around for more than a decade, but its incorporation as part of enterprise-level wireless protocols is relatively new. It is well suited for this because it creates a cryptographically strong shared secret for securing other data. Because of its zero-knowledge key generation method, it is resistant to active, passive, and dictionary attacks. As a peer-to-peer protocol, it does not rely on other parties, so it is an alternative to using certificates or a centralized authority for authentication. To configure SAE, you must set the security parameter k to a value of at least 40, per the recommendation in RFC 7664, "Dragonfly Key Exchange," for all groups to prevent timing leaks.

Authentication Protocols

Wireless networks have a need for secure authentication protocols. The following authentication protocols should be understood for the Security+ exam: EAP, PEAP, EAP-FAST, EAP-TLS, EAP-TTLS, IEEE 802.1X, and RADIUS from the RADIUS Federation.

EAP

Extensible Authentication Protocol (EAP) is defined in RFC 2284 (obsoleted by 3748). EAP-TLS relies on Transport Layer Security (TLS), an attempt to standardize the SSL structure to pass credentials. EAP-TTLS (the acronym stands for EAP–Tunneled TLS protocol) is a variant of the EAP-TLS protocol. EAP-TTLS works much the same way as EAP-TLS, with the server authenticating to the client with a certificate, but the protocol tunnels the client side of the authentication, allowing the use of legacy authentication protocols such as Password Authentication Protocol (PAP), Challenge-Handshake Authentication Protocol (CHAP), MS-CHAP, and MS-CHAP v2.

LEAP

Cisco designed a proprietary version of EAP known as Lightweight Extensible Authentication Protocol (LEAP); however, this is being phased out for newer protocols such as PEAP and EAP-TLS. Because it is susceptible to offline password guessing, and because tools are available that actively break LEAP security, this protocol has been deprecated in favor of stronger methods of EAP.

PEAP

PEAP, or Protected EAP, was developed to protect the EAP communication by encapsulating it with TLS. This is an open standard developed jointly by Cisco, Microsoft, and RSA. EAP was designed assuming a secure communication channel. PEAP provides that protection as part of the protocol via a TLS tunnel. PEAP is widely supported by vendors for use over wireless networks.

EAP-FAST

The Wi-Fi Alliance added EAP-FAST to its list of supported protocols for WPA/WPA2 in 2010. **EAP-FAST** is EAP–Flexible Authentication via Secure Tunneling, which is described in RFC-4851 and proposed by Cisco to be a replacement for LEAP, a previous Cisco version of EAP. It offers a lightweight, tunneling protocol to enable authentication. The distinguishing characteristic is the passing of a Protected Access Credential (PAC) that's used to establish a TLS tunnel through which client credentials are verified.

EAP-TLS

The Wi-Fi Alliance also added EAP-TLS to its list of supported protocols for WPA/WPA2 in 2010. **EAP-TLS** is an IETF open standard (RFC 5216) that uses the Transport Layer Security (TLS) protocol to secure the authentication process. This is still considered one of the most secure implementations, primarily because common implementations employ client-side certificates. This means that an attacker must also possess the key for the client-side certificate to break the TLS channel.

You need to know two key elements concerning EAP. First, it is only a framework to secure the authentication process, not an actual encryption method. Second, many variants exist, and understanding the differences between EAP, EAP-FAST, EAP-TLS, and EAP-TTLS is important when using these methods.

EAP-TTLS

The Wi-Fi Alliance also added EAP-TTLS to its list of supported protocols for WPA/WPA2 in 2010. **EAP-TTLS** is an extension of TLS called Tunneled TLS. In EAP-TTLS, the authentication process is protected by the tunnel from man-in-the-middle attacks, and although client certificates can be used, they are not required, making this easier to set up than EAP-TLS for clients without certificates.

Implementing 802.1X

The **IEEE 802.1X** protocol can support a wide variety of authentication methods and also fits well into existing authentication systems such as RADIUS and LDAP. This allows 802.1X to interoperate well with other systems such as VPNs and dial-up RAS. Unlike other authentication methods, such as the Point-to-Point Protocol over Ethernet (PPPoE), 802.1X does not use encapsulation, so the network overhead is much lower. Unfortunately, the protocol is just a framework for providing implementation, so no specifics guarantee strong authentication or key management. Implementations of the protocol vary from vendor to vendor in method of implementation and strength of security, especially when it comes to the difficult test of wireless security.

Three common methods are used to implement 802.1X: EAP-TLS, EAP-TTLS, and EAP-MD5. EAP-TLS relies on TLS, an attempt to standardize the SSL structure to pass credentials. The standard, developed by Microsoft, uses X.509 certificates and offers dynamic WEP key generation. This means that the organization must have the ability to support the public key infrastructure (PKI) in the form of X.509 digital certificates. Also, per-user, per-session dynamically generated WEP keys help prevent anyone from cracking the WEP keys in use, as each user individually has their own WEP key. Even if a user were logged onto the AP and transmitted enough traffic to allow cracking of the WEP key, access would be gained only to that user's traffic. No other user's data would be compromised, and the attacker could not use the WEP key to connect to the AP. This standard authenticates the client to the AP, but it also authenticates the AP to the client, helping to avoid man-in-the-middle attacks. The main problem with the EAP-TLS protocol is that it is designed to work only with Microsoft's Active Directory and Certificate Services; it will not take certificates from other certificate issuers. Thus, a mixed environment would have implementation problems.

As discussed earlier, EAP-TTLS works much the same way as EAP-TLS, with the server authenticating to the client with a certificate, but the protocol tunnels the client side of the authentication, allowing the use of legacy authentication protocols such as Password Authentication Protocol (PAP), Challenge-Handshake Authentication Protocol (CHAP), MS-CHAP, and MS-CHAP v2. This makes the protocol more versatile while still supporting the enhanced security features, such as dynamic WEP key assignment.

RADIUS Federation

Using a series of RADIUS servers in a federated connection has been employed in several worldwide *RADIUS Federation* networks. One example is the EDUROAM project that connects users of education institutions worldwide. The process is relatively simple in concept, although the technical details to maintain the hierarchy of RADIUS servers and routing tables is daunting at worldwide scale. A user packages their credentials at a local access point using a certificate-based tunneling protocol method. The first RADIUS server determines which RADIUS server to send the request to, and from there the user is authenticated via their home RADIUS server and the results passed back, permitting a joining to the network.

Because the credentials must pass multiple different networks, the EAP methods are limited to those with certificates and credentials to prevent loss of credentials during transit. This type of federated identity at global scale demonstrates the power of RADIUS and EAP methods.

Counter Mode/CBC-MAC Protocol (CCMP)

CCMP stands for *Counter Mode with Cipher Block Chaining–Message Authentication Code Protocol* (or *Counter Mode with CBC-MAC Protocol*). CCMP is a data encapsulation encryption mechanism designed for wireless use. CCMP is actually the mode in which the AES cipher is used to provide message integrity. Unlike WPA/TKIP, WPA2/CCMP requires new hardware to perform the AES encryption.

Wireless Systems Configuration

Wireless systems are more than just protocols. Putting up a functional wireless system in a house is as easy as plugging in a wireless access point and connecting. However, in an enterprise, where multiple access points will be needed, the configuration takes significantly more work. Site surveys are needed to determine proper access point and antenna placement, as well as channels and power levels.

Access Point

Wi-Fi *access points* are the point of entry for radio-based network signals into and out of a network. As wireless has become more capable in all aspects of networking, wireless-based networks are replacing cabled or wired solutions. In this scenario, one could consider the access point to be one half of a NIC, with the other half being the wireless card in a host.

Wireless access points can operate in several different modes, depending upon the unit capability and the need of the network. The most common mode, and the one all access points support, is normal mode. This is where the access point provides a point of connection from the wireless network to the wired network. A separate mode, bridged mode, allows an access point to communicate directly with another access point. This allows the extension of a wireless LAN over greater distance. A repeater mode is similar in that it extends the range by working between access points. A bridge mode device allows connections, while a repeater merely acts to extend range.

SSID

The 802.11 protocol designers expected some security concerns and attempted to build provisions into the 802.11 protocol that would ensure adequate security. The 802.11 standard includes attempts at rudimentary authentication and confidentiality controls. Authentication is handled in its most basic form by the 802.11 access point (AP), forcing clients to perform a handshake when attempting to "associate" to the AP.

SSIDs can be set to anything by the person setting up an access point. So, while "FBI Surveillance Van #14" may seem humorous, what about SSIDs with the name of an airport, coffee house, or a hotel? Can you trust them? Because anyone can use any name, the answer is no. So, if you need a secure connection, you should use some form of secure channel such as a VPN for communication security. For even more security, you can carry your own access point and create a wireless channel that you control.

Renaming the SSID and disabling SSID broadcast are not considered to be useful security measures.

Association is the process required before the AP will allow the client to talk across the AP to the network. Association occurs only if the client has all the correct parameters needed in the handshake, among them the **service set identifier (SSID)**. This SSID setting should limit access only to the authorized users of the wireless network. The SSID is a phrase-based mechanism that helps ensure you are connecting to the correct AP. This SSID phrase is transmitted in all the access point's **beacon frames**. The beacon frame is an 802.11 management frame for the network and contains several different fields, such as the timestamp and beacon interval, but most importantly the SSID. This allows attackers to scan for the beacon frame and retrieve the SSID.

Because multiple WLANs can coexist in one place, each WLAN needs a unique name. The **service set identifier (SSID)** is the name of the wireless network. A wireless device can see the SSIDs for all available networks, allowing users to select the desired network. For example, suppose your campus wireless network consists of three SSIDs named Student, Faculty, and Guest. This means that the network administrator has created three WLAN service profiles, and this allows different services to be provided by network. SSIDs can be hidden as well, but as they are used as part of the connection process, hiding the SSID will not stop an attacker, only a casual user.

Multiple overlapping access points present a different problem—how do you differentiate them? The identifier for access points is called the *basic service set identifier (BSSID)*, and it too is included in all packets. By convention, an access point's MAC address is used as the BSSID. When multiple access points are involved, the collective BSSIDs for a given network are referred to as the extended service set (ESS).

Tech Tip

SSID, ESS, BSSID: What's in a Name?

Because wireless networks are not bounded by physical items, it is common to have overlapping wireless networks. It is also common to have wireless networks with repeaters to extend system ranges. This leads to the issue of identifying networks when a wireless device is connecting to different access points. This is why we have SSIDs (names for humans) and BSSIDs (identities for machines, or MAC addresses). Figure 12.3 shows what overlapping networks (named Faculty, Student, Guest) and two overlapping access points would look like from a technical point of view. This example can be extended to 32 networks per AP.

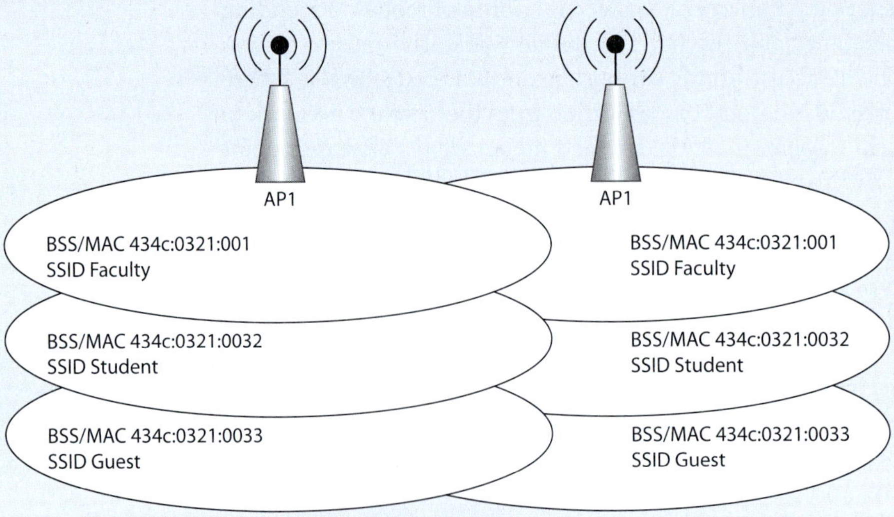

• **Figure 12.3** Wireless SSIDs and BSSIDs illustrated

Fat vs. Thin

Fat (or *thick*) access points refer to standalone access points, whereas *thin* access points refer to controller-based access points. These solutions differ in their handling of common functions such as configuration, encryption, updates, and policy settings. Determining which is more effective requires a closer examination of the differences, as presented in the next section, compared to a site's needs and budget.

Controller Based vs. Standalone

Small *standalone* Wi-Fi access points can have substantial capabilities with respect to authentication, encryption, and even, to a degree, channel management. As the wireless deployment grows in size and complexity, there are some advantages to a *controller-based* access point solution. Controller-based solutions allow for centralized management and control, which can facilitate better channel management for adjacent access points, better load balancing, and easier deployment of patches and firmware updates. From a security standpoint, controller-based solutions offer large advantages in overall network monitoring and security controls. In large-scale environments, controller-based access points can enable network access control based on user identity, thus managing large sets of users in subgroups. Internet access can be blocked for some users (clerks), while internal access can be blocked for others (guests).

Signal Strength

The usability of a wireless signal is directly related to its signal strength. Too weak of a signal, and the connection can drop out or lose data. Signal strength can be influenced by a couple of factors: the transmitting power level and the environment across which the signal is transmitted. In buildings with significant metal in the walls and roofs, additional power may be needed to have sufficient signal strength at the receivers. Wi-Fi power levels can be controlled by the hardware for a variety of reasons. The lower the power used, the less the opportunity for interference. However, if the power levels are too low, then signal strength limits range. Access points can have the power level set either manually or via programmatic control. For most users, power level controls are not very useful, and leaving the unit in default mode is the best option. In complex enterprise setups, with site surveys and planned overlapping zones, this aspect of signal control can be used to increase capacity and control on the network.

Band Selection/Width

Today's wireless environments employ multiple different bands, each with different bandwidths. Band selection may seem trivial, but with 802.11a, b/g, n, ac, and ax radios, the deployment of access points should support the desired bands based on client needs. Multiband radio access points exist and are commonly employed to resolve these issues. Wi-Fi operates over two different frequencies: 2.4 GHz for b/g and n, and 5 GHz for a, n, and ac. 802.11ax also has the ability to be used in the 6 GHz band, under

Wi-Fi 6E, and equipment will be entering the market in 2021 to take advantage of the extended bandwidth.

Antenna Types and Placement

The standard access point is equipped with an omnidirectional antenna. Omnidirectional antennas operate in all directions, making the relative orientation between devices less important. Omnidirectional antennas cover the greatest area per antenna. The weakness occurs in corners and hard-to-reach areas, as well as boundaries of a facility where directional antennas are needed to complete coverage. Figure 12.4 shows a sampling of common Wi-Fi antennas: (a) is a common home wireless router, (b) is a commercial indoor wireless access point, and (c) is an outdoor directional antenna. These can be visible, as shown, or hidden above ceiling tiles.

Because wireless antennas can transmit outside a facility, tuning and placement of antennas can be crucial for security. Adjusting radiated power through the power level controls will assist in keeping wireless signals from being broadcast outside areas under physical access control.

Wireless networking problems caused by weak signal strength can sometimes be solved by installing upgraded Wi-Fi radio antennas on the access points. On business networks, the complexity of multiple access points typically requires a comprehensive site survey to map the Wi-Fi signal strength in and around office buildings. Additional wireless access points can then be strategically placed where needed to resolve dead spots in coverage. For small businesses and homes, where a single access point may be all that is needed, an antenna upgrade may be a simpler and more cost-effective option to fix Wi-Fi signal problems.

Two common forms of upgraded antennas are the Yagi antenna and the panel antenna. An example of a Yagi antenna is shown in Figure 12.4(c). Both Yagi and panel antennas are directional in nature, spreading the RF energy in a more limited field, increasing effective range in one direction while limiting it in others. Panel antennas can provide solid room performance while preventing signal bleed behind the antennas. This works well on the edge of a site, limiting the stray emissions that could be captured offsite. Yagi antennas act more like a rifle, funneling the energy along a beam. This allows much longer communication distances using standard power. This also enables eavesdroppers to capture signals from much greater distances because of the gain provided by the antenna itself.

Tech Tip

MIMO

MIMO is a set of multiple-input and multiple-output antenna technologies where the available antennas are spread over a multitude of independent access points, each having one or multiple antennas. This can enhance the usable bandwidth and data transmission capacity between the access point and user. There are a wide variety of MIMO methods, and this technology, once considered cutting edge or advanced, it is now mainstream. The latest versions of 802.11, specifically the ax version, uses MU-MIMO, or multiuser MIMO. This is designed for high-density locations, such as areas where crowds exist and wireless is desired. This further increases the channel capacities of the radios.

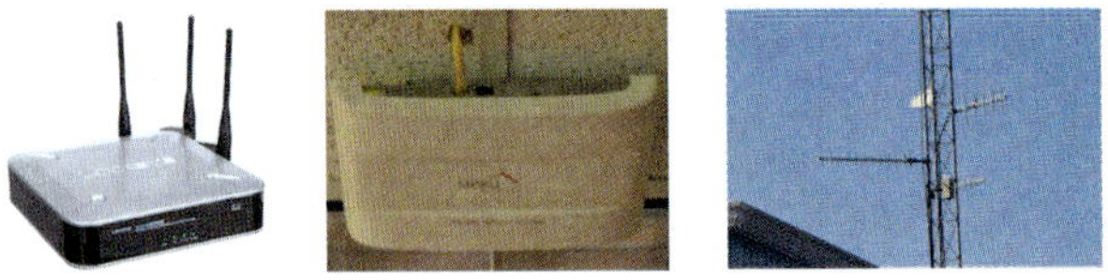

a b c

• **Figure 12.4** Wireless access point antennas

Power-Level Controls

Wi-Fi power levels can be controlled by the hardware for a variety of reasons. The lower the power used, the less the opportunity for interference. However, if the power levels are too low, then signal strength limits range. Access points can have the power level set either manually or via programmatic control. For most users, power-level controls are not very useful, and leaving the unit in default mode is the best option. In complex enterprise setups, with site surveys and planned overlapping zones, this aspect of signal control can be used to increase capacity and control on the network.

Wi-Fi Analyzers

Wi-Fi analyzers provide a means of determining signal strength and channel interference. A Wi-Fi analyzer is an RF device used to measure signal strength and quality. It can determine if the Wi-Fi signal strength is sufficient, and if there are competing devices on a particular channel. This enables an engineer to allocate signals both in strength and channel to improve Wi-Fi performance.

Channel Overlays

Wi-Fi radio signals exist at specific frequencies: 2.4 GHz and 5.0 GHz. Each of these signals is broken into a series of channels, and the actual data transmissions occur across these channels. Wi-Fi versions of IEEE 802.11 (a, b, g, n) work with channel frequencies of 2400 MHz and 2500 MHz, hence the term 2.4 GHz for the system. The 100 MHz in between is split into 14 channels of 20 MHz each. As a result, each channel overlaps with up to four other channels. If you used nearby channels, this overlapping makes wireless network throughput quite poor. For this reason, most 2.4 GHz systems use channels 1, 6, and 11. When multiple access points are in close proximity, there can be issues with competing signals. In an apartment, if you find that your neighbors are using channels 2 and 10, then you would want to switch your devices to 6 to improve signal strength in your channel. Most wireless routers use an auto function to manage this, but in cases where congestion is occurring, learning the distribution of signals via a site survey and partitioning your devices into available channels will improve performance.

Beyond just improving channel overlay issues, the Wi-Fi Alliance has improved system throughput through the use of newer standards, including 802.11ac and 802.11ax. These systems use a set of different encoding mechanisms and frequency allocations to increase throughput in dense Wi-Fi environments such as large public gatherings. These methods are referred to as Wi-Fi 6 or, in the case of 802.11ax specifically, High Efficiency Wireless (HEW).

Wireless Access Point (WAP) Placement

Wireless access point (WAP) placement is seemingly simple. Perform a site survey, determine the optimum placement based on RF signal strength, and you are done. But not so fast. Access points also need power, so the availability of power to the placement can be an issue. Also, if the access point is going to be connected to the network, then availability of a network connection is also a consideration. These issues can actually be more challenging in a home environment because home users are not likely to incur the expense of running dedicated power and network connections to the access point. To help solve this issue in home and small networks, many vendors have mesh-based Wi-Fi extenders that enable Wi-Fi radio frequency (RF) signals to be extended via relays, but this can come at a throughput cost if the network becomes congested with devices.

For security reasons, you should be aware that Wi-Fi signals go through walls, so placing access points where they produce large areas of coverage outside a facility may lead to outsiders accessing your system. Protecting the access point from physical access is also important. Coordinating AP placement with site surveys is important to address issues of poor placement leading to bad coverage, signal bleed, and throughput costs associated with adding too many APs or extenders.

Site Surveys

> Wireless networks are dependent on radio signals to function. It is important to understand that antenna type, placement, and site surveys are used to ensure proper coverage of a site, including areas blocked by walls, interfering signals, and echoes.

When developing a coverage map for a complex building site, you need to take into account a wide variety of factors, particularly walls, interfering sources, and floor plans. A **site survey** involves several steps: mapping the floor plan, testing for RF interference, testing for RF coverage, and analysis of material via software. The software can suggest placement of access points. After deploying the APs, you survey the site again, mapping the results versus those predicted, watching signal strength and signal-to-noise ratios. Figure 12.5 illustrates what a site survey looks like. The different shades indicate signal strength, showing where reception is strong and where it is weak. Site surveys can be used to ensure availability of wireless, especially when it's critical for users to have connections.

Heat Maps

A Wi-Fi *heat map* is a map of wireless signal coverage and strength. Typically, a heat map shows a layout of a room, floor, or facility overlaid by a graphical representation of a wireless signal. Heat maps are created using a Wi-Fi analyzer and software to allow the analysis of Wi-Fi signal strength in the form of a graphical layout. This allows network administrators to find areas of

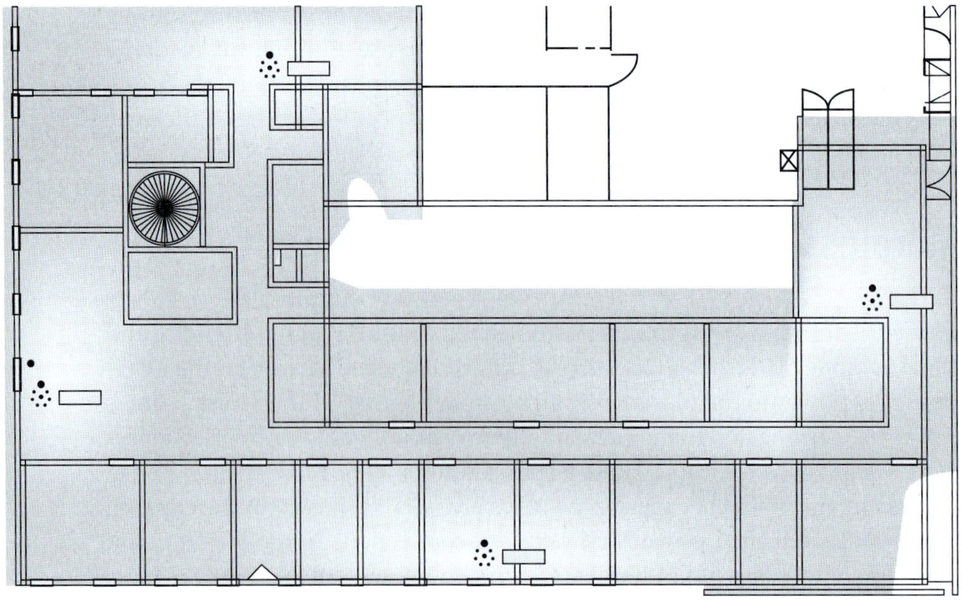

• **Figure 12.5** Example of a site survey

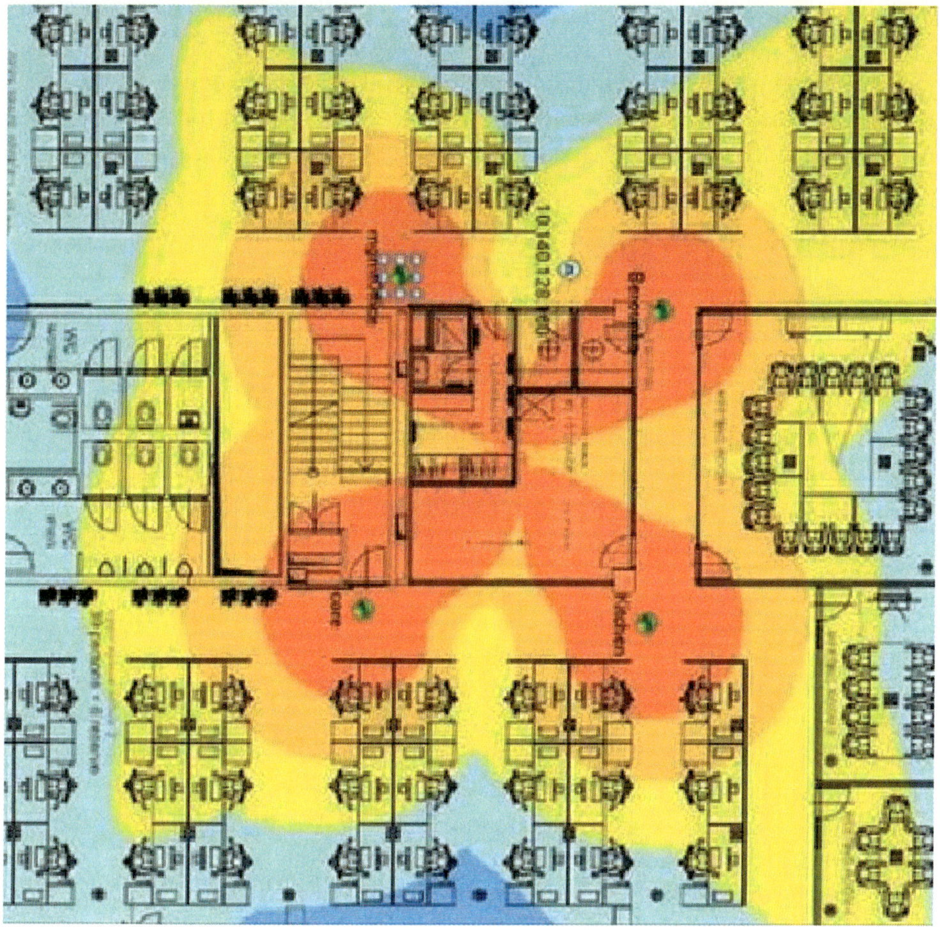

• **Figure 12.6** Example of a Wi-Fi heat map

weak signals and consider alternative access point placement. An example of a heat map is shown in Figure 12.6. The different shades indicate signal strength, showing where reception is strong and where it is weak.

> A site survey is a process for determining Wi-Fi signal strengths; the heat map is one of the outcomes and is part of the survey.

Controller and Access Point Security

Wireless access points are physical connections to your network infrastructure and should be guarded as such. Proper *controller and access point security* provisions include both physical and logical security precautions. The case of logical security has been the main focus of this chapter, keeping unauthorized users from accessing the channels. Physical security is just as important, if not more so, and the actual devices and network connections should be placed in a location that is not readily accessible to an attacker. This is especially true for exterior connections where no one would observe someone physically manipulating the device.

MAC Filtering

MAC filtering is the selective admission of packets based on a list of approved Media Access Control (MAC) addresses. Employed on switches, this method is used to provide a means of machine authentication. In wired networks,

MAC filtering can be employed on wireless access points, but it can be bypassed by attackers observing allowed MAC addresses and spoofing the allowed MAC address for the wireless card.

Captive portals are common in coffee shops, airports, hotels, and stores. The user accepts the offered conditions, views, and advertisements, provides an e-mail address or other authentication requirement, and is granted access to the portal.

this enjoys the protection afforded by the wires, making interception of signals to determine their MAC addresses difficult. In wireless networks, this same mechanism suffers from the fact that an attacker can see the MAC addresses of all traffic to and from the access point, and then can spoof the MAC addresses that are permitted to communicate via the access point.

Captive Portals

Captive portal refers to a specific technique of using an HTTP client to handle authentication on a wireless network. Frequently employed in public hotspots, a captive portal opens a web browser to an authentication page. This occurs before the user is granted admission to the network. The access point uses this simple mechanism by intercepting all packets and returning the web page for login. The actual web server that serves up the authentication page can be in a walled-off section of the network, blocking access to the Internet until the user successfully authenticates.

Securing Public Wi-Fi

Public Wi-Fi is a common perk that some firms provide for their customers and visitors. When providing a Wi-Fi hotspot, even free open-to-the-public Wi-Fi, the firm should make security a concern. One of the issues associated with wireless transmissions is that they are subject to interception by anyone within range of the hotspot. This makes it possible for others to intercept and read the traffic of anyone using the hotspot, unless encryption is used. For this reason, it has become common practice to use wireless security, even when the intent is to open the channel for everyone. Having a default password, even one that everyone knows, will make it so that people cannot observe other traffic.

There is an entire open wireless movement designed around a sharing concept that promotes sharing of the Internet to all. For information, check out https://openwireless.org.

Wireless Attacks

Wireless is a common networking technology that has a substantial number of standards and processes to connect users to networks via a radio signal, freeing machines from wires. As in all software systems, wireless networking is a target for hackers. This is partly because of the simple fact that wireless removes the physical barrier.

Attacking 802.11

Wireless is a popular target for several reasons: the access gained from wireless, the lack of default security, and the wide proliferation of devices. However, other reasons also make it attackable. The first of these is *anonymity*. An attacker can probe your building for wireless access from the street. Then they can log packets to and from the AP without giving any indication that an attempted intrusion is taking place. The attacker will announce their presence only if they attempt to associate to the AP. Even then, an attempted association is recorded only by the MAC address of the wireless card associating to it, and most APs do not have alerting functionality to indicate when users associate to them. This fact gives administrators a very limited view of who is gaining access to the network, if they are even paying attention at all. It gives attackers the ability to seek out and compromise wireless networks with relative impunity.

The second reason is the low cost of the equipment needed. A single wireless access card costing less than $100 can give access to any unsecured AP within driving range. Finally, attacking a wireless network is relatively easy compared to attacking other target hosts. Windows-based tools for locating and sniffing wireless-based networks have turned anyone who can download files from the Internet and has a wireless card into a potential attacker.

Locating wireless networks was originally termed **war-driving**, an adaptation of the term **war-dialing**. War-dialing comes from the 1983 movie *WarGames;* it is the process of dialing a list of phone numbers looking for modem-connected computers. War-drivers drive around with a wireless locater program recording the number of networks found and their locations. This term has evolved along with *war-flying* and *war-walking,* which mean exactly what you expect. **War-chalking** started with people using chalk on sidewalks to mark some of the open wireless networks they found.

> Anonymity also works in another way; once an attacker finds an unsecured AP with wireless access, they can use an essentially untraceable IP address to attempt attacks on other Internet hosts.

The most common tools for an attacker to use are reception-based programs that listen to the beacon frames output by other wireless devices, and programs that promiscuously capture all traffic. A wide variety of programs can assist in troubleshooting wireless networks, and these all work in the same manner, by listening for the beacon frames of APs that are within range of the network interface card (NIC) attached to the computer. When the program receives the frames, it logs all available information about the AP for later analysis. If the computer has a GPS unit attached to it, the program also logs the AP's coordinates. This information can be used to return to the AP or to plot maps of APs in a city. One of the more commonly used tools is Wireshark. Other common tools include the Aircrack-ng suite, Kismet, NetSurveyor, Vistumbler, and NetSpot. Different tools have different specializations; some are better for troubleshooting some issues such as congestion, while others can map signal strengths and assist in site surveys.

> Because wireless antennas can transmit outside a facility, the proper tuning and placement of these antennas can be crucial for security. Adjusting radiated power through these power-level controls will assist in keeping wireless signals from being broadcast outside areas under physical access control.

Once an attacker has located a network, and assuming they cannot directly connect and start active scanning and penetration of the network, the attacker will use the best attack tool there is: a network sniffer. The network sniffer, when combined with a wireless network card it can support, is a powerful attack tool because the shared medium of a wireless network exposes all packets to interception and logging. Popular wireless sniffers are Wireshark and Kismet. Regular sniffers used on wired Ethernet have also been updated to include support for wireless. Sniffers are also important because they allow you to retrieve the MAC addresses of the nodes of the network. APs can be configured to allow access only to pre-specified MAC addresses, and an attacker spoofing the MAC can bypass this feature.

After the limited security functions of a wireless network are broken, the network behaves exactly like a regular Ethernet network and is subject to the exact same vulnerabilities. The host machines that are on or attached to the wireless network are as vulnerable as if they and the attacker were physically connected. Being on the network opens up all machines to vulnerability scanners, Trojan horse programs, virus and worm programs, and traffic interception via sniffer programs. Any unpatched vulnerability on any machine accessible from the wireless segment is now open to compromise.

Replay

A **replay attack** occurs when the attacker captures a portion of a communication between two parties and retransmits it at a later time. For example, an attacker might replay a series of commands and codes used in a financial transaction to cause the transaction to be conducted multiple times. Generally, replay attacks are associated with attempts to circumvent authentication mechanisms, such as the capturing and reuse of a certificate or ticket.

The best method for defending against replay attacks is through the use of encryption and short time frames for legal transactions. Encryption can protect the contents from being understood, and a short time frame for a transaction prevents subsequent use.

The best way to prevent replay attacks is with encryption, cryptographic authentication, and timestamps. If a portion of the certificate or ticket includes a date/time stamp or an expiration date/time, and this portion is also encrypted as part of the ticket or certificate, replaying it at a later time will prove useless because it will be rejected as having expired.

IV

The **initialization vector (IV)** is used in wireless systems as the randomization element at the beginning of a connection. Attacks against the IV aim to determine it, thus finding the repeating key sequence. This was the weakness that led to the fall of WEP and WPA. It is not that the IV is bad; its length was short enough that all the values could be cycled through, forcing a repeat.

The IV is the primary reason for the weaknesses in WEP. The IV is sent in the plaintext part of the message, and because the total keyspace is approximately 16 million keys, the same key will be reused. Once the key has been repeated, an attacker has two ciphertexts encrypted with the same key stream. This allows the attacker to examine the ciphertext and retrieve the key. This attack can be improved by examining only packets that have weak IVs, reducing the number of packets needed to crack the key. Using only weak IV packets, the number of required captured packets is reduced to around four or five million, which can take only a few hours to capture on a fairly busy AP. For a point of reference, this means that equipment with an advertised WEP key of 128 bits can be cracked in less than a day, whereas to crack a normal 128-bit key would take roughly 2,000,000,000,000,000,000 years on a computer able to attempt one trillion keys a second. AirSnort is a modified sniffing program that takes advantage of this weakness to retrieve the WEP keys. The biggest weakness of WEP is that the IV problem exists regardless of key length, because the IV always remains at 24 bits.

Evil Twin

The **evil twin** attack is in essence an attack against the wireless protocol via substitute hardware. This attack uses an access point owned by an attacker that usually has been enhanced with higher-power and higher-gain antennas to look like a better connection to the users and computers attaching to it. By getting users to connect through the evil access point, attackers can more easily analyze traffic and perform man-in-the-middle types of attacks. For simple denial of service (DoS), an attacker could use interference to jam the wireless signal, not allowing any computer to connect to the access point successfully.

Rogue AP

By setting up a **rogue access point (AP)**, an attacker can attempt to get clients to connect to it as if it were authorized and then simply authenticate to the real AP—a simple way to have access to the network and the client's credentials. Rogue APs can act as a man in the middle and easily steal the user's credentials. Enterprises with wireless APs should routinely scan for and remove rogue APs, because users have difficulty avoiding them.

Jamming

Jamming is a form of denial of service, specifically against the radio spectrum aspect of wireless. Just as other DoS attacks can manipulate things behind the scenes, so can jamming on a wireless AP, enabling things such as attachment to a rogue AP.

Bluetooth Attacks

As a wireless method of communication, Bluetooth is open to connection and attack from outside the intended sender and receiver. Several different attack modes have been discovered that can be used against Bluetooth systems. These are discussed later in the chapter.

Bluetooth technology is likely to grow due to the popularity of mobile phones. Software and protocol updates have helped to improve the security of the protocol. Almost all phones now keep Bluetooth turned off by default, and they allow you to make the phone discoverable for only a limited amount of time. User education about security risks is also a large factor in avoiding security breaches.

Bluejacking

Bluejacking is the term used for the sending of unauthorized messages to another Bluetooth device. This involves sending a message as a phonebook contact, as shown here.

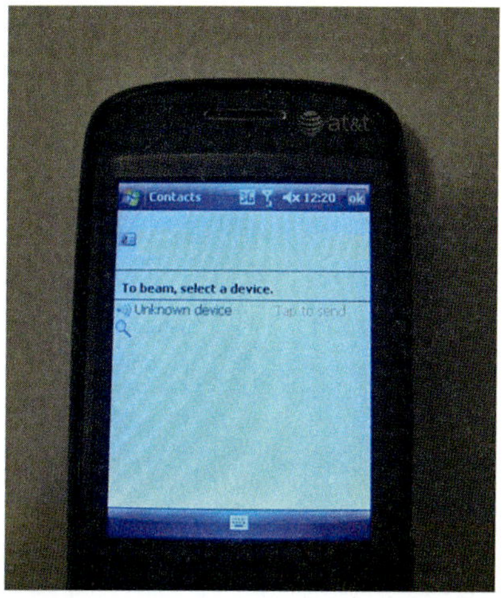

Then the attacker sends the message to the possible recipient via Bluetooth. Originally, this involved sending text messages, but more recent phones can send images or audio as well. A popular variant of this is the transmission of "shock" images, featuring disturbing or crude photos. Because Bluetooth is a short-range protocol, the attack and victim must be within roughly 10 yards of each other. The victim's phone must also have Bluetooth enabled and must be in discoverable mode. On some early phones, this was the default configuration, and while it makes connecting external devices easier, it also allows attacks against the phone. If Bluetooth is turned off, or if the device is set to nondiscoverable, bluejacking can be avoided.

Bluesnarfing

Bluesnarfing is similar to bluejacking in that it uses the same contact transmission protocol. The difference is that instead of sending an unsolicited message to the victim's phone, the attacker copies off the victim's information, which can include e-mails, contact lists, calendars, and anything else that exists on that device. More recent phones with media capabilities can be snarfed for private photos and videos. Bluesnarfing used to require a laptop with a Bluetooth adapter, making it relatively easy to identify a possible attacker, but bluesnarfing applications are now available for mobile devices. Bloover, a combination of Bluetooth and Hoover, is one such application that runs as a Java applet. The majority of Bluetooth phones need to be discoverable for the bluesnarf attack to work, but they do not necessarily need to be paired. In theory, an attacker can also brute-force the device's unique 48-bit name. A program called RedFang attempts to perform this brute force attack by sending all possible names and seeing what gets a response. This approach was addressed in Bluetooth 1.2 with an anonymity mode.

Bluejacking and bluesnarfing are both attacks against Bluetooth. They differ in that bluejacking is the sending of unauthorized data via Bluetooth, whereas bluesnarfing is the unauthorized taking of data over a Bluetooth channel. Understanding this difference is important to ensure you are covering both attacks.

Bluebugging

Bluebugging is a far more serious attack than either bluejacking or bluesnarfing. In bluebugging, the attacker uses Bluetooth to establish a serial connection to the device. This allows access to the full AT command set—GSM phones use AT commands similar to Hayes-compatible modems.

This connection allows full control over the phone, including the placing of calls to any number without the phone owner's knowledge. Fortunately, this attack requires pairing of the devices to complete, and phones initially vulnerable to the attack have updated firmware to correct the problem. To accomplish the attack now, the phone owner would need to surrender their phone and allow an attacker to physically establish the connection.

Bluetooth DoS is the use of Bluetooth technology to perform a denial-of-service attack against another device. In this attack, an attacker repeatedly requests pairing with the victim device. This type of attack does not divulge information or permit access, but it is a nuisance. More importantly, if done repeatedly it can drain a device's battery, or prevent other operations from occurring on the victim's device. As with all Bluetooth attacks, because of the short range involved, all one has to do is leave the area and the attack will cease.

RFID

RFID tags have multiple security concerns; first and foremost, because they are connected via RF energy, physical security is a challenge. Security was recognized as an important issue for RFID tag systems because they form a means of identification and there is a need for authentication and confidentiality of the data transfers. Several standards are associated with securing the RFID data flow, including ISO/IEC 18000 and ISO/IEC 29167 for cryptography methods to support confidentiality, untraceability, tag and reader authentication, and over-the-air privacy, whereas ISO/IEC 20248 specifies a digital signature data structure for use in RFID systems.

Several different attack types can be performed against RFID systems. The first is against the RFID devices themselves—the chips and readers. A second form of attack goes against the communication channel between the device and the reader. The third category of attack is against the reader and back-end system. This last type is more of a standard IT/IS attack, depending on the interfaces used (web, database, and so on) and therefore is not covered any further. Attacks against the communication channel are relatively easy because the radio frequencies are known and devices exist to interface with tags. Two main attacks are replay and eavesdropping. In a replay attack, the RFID information is recorded and then replayed later; in the case of an RFID-based access badge, it could be read in a restaurant from a distance and then replayed at the appropriate entry point to gain entry. In the case of eavesdropping, the data can be collected, monitoring the movement of tags for whatever purpose needed by an unauthorized party. Both of these attacks are easily defeated using the aforementioned security standards.

If eavesdropping is possible, then what about man-in-the-middle attacks? These are certainly possible because they would be a combination of a sniffing (eavesdropping) action, followed by replay (spoofing) attack. This leads to the question as to whether an RFID can be cloned. Again, the answer is yes, if the RFID information is not protected via a cryptographic component.

Disassociation

Disassociation attacks against a wireless system are those attacks designed to disassociate a host from the wireless access point, and from the wireless network. Disassociation attacks stem from the deauthentication frame that is in the IEEE 802.11 (Wi-Fi) standard. The deauthentication frame is designed as a tool to remove unauthorized stations from a Wi-Fi access point, but because of the design of the protocol, they can be implemented by virtually anyone. An attacker only needs to have the MAC address of the intended victim, and then they can send a spoofed message to the access point, specifically spoofing the MAC address of the victim machine. This results in the disconnection of the victim machine, making this attack a form of denial of service.

Disassociation attacks are not typically used alone, but rather in concert with another attack objective. For instance, if you disassociate a connection and then sniff the reconnect, you can steal passwords. After disassociating a machine, the user attempting to reestablish a WPA or WPA2 session will need to repeat the WPA 4-way handshake. This gives the hacker a chance to sniff this event, the first step in gathering needed information for a brute force or dictionary-based WPA password-cracking attack. Forcing users to reconnect gives the attacker a chance to mount a man-in-the-middle attack against content provided during a connection. This has been used by the Wifiphisher tool to collect passwords.

Mobile Device Management Concepts

The concepts of **mobile device management (MDM)** are essential knowledge in today's environment of connected devices. MDM began as a marketing term for a collective set of commonly employed protection elements associated with mobile devices. When viewed as a comprehensive set of security options for mobile devices, an MDM policy should be created and enforced by every corporation. The policy should require the following:

- Device locking with a strong password
- Encryption of data on the device
- Device locking automatically after a certain period of inactivity
- The capability to remotely lock the device if it is lost or stolen
- The capability to wipe the device automatically after a certain number of failed login attempts
- The capability to remotely wipe the device if it is lost or stolen

Password policies should extend to mobile devices, including lockout and, if possible, the automatic wiping of data. Corporate policy for data encryption on mobile devices should be consistent with the policy for data encryption on laptop computers. In other words, if you don't require encryption of portable computers, then should you require it for mobile devices? There is not a uniform answer to this question. Mobile devices are much more mobile in practice than laptops, and more prone to loss. This is ultimately a risk question that management must address: what is the risk and what are the costs of the options employed? This also raises bigger questions: Which devices should have encryption as a basic security protection mechanism? Is it by device type or by user based on what data would be exposed to risk? Fortunately, MDM solutions exist that make the choices manageable.

Mobile device management (MDM) is a marketing term for a collective set of commonly employed protection elements associated with mobile devices.

Application Management

Most mobile device vendors provide some kind of application store for finding and purchasing applications for their mobile devices. The vendors do a reasonable job of making sure that offered applications are approved and don't create an overt security risk. Yet many applications request access to various information stores on the mobile device as part of their business model. Understanding what access is requested and approved upon installation of an app is an important security precaution. These are all potential problems for mobile users concerned over data security and drive the need for a *mobile application management (MAM)* solution. Your company may have to restrict the types of applications that can be downloaded and used on mobile devices. If you need very strong protection, your company can be very proactive and provide an enterprise application store where only company-approved applications are available, with a corresponding policy that apps cannot be obtained from any other source. Another method involves the use of an MDM solution, as discussed in the previous section.

Full Device Encryption (FDE)

Just as laptop computers should employ full disk encryption (FDE) to protect the laptop in case of loss or theft, you may need to consider encryption for mobile devices used by your company's employees. Mobile devices are much more likely to be lost or stolen, so you should consider encrypting data on your devices. More and more, mobile devices are used for accessing and storing business-critical data or other sensitive information. Protecting the information on mobile devices is becoming a business imperative. This is an emerging technology, so you'll need to complete some rigorous market analysis to determine what commercial product meets your needs.

BitLocker is a full disk encryption (FDE) feature included with Microsoft Windows operating systems. It protects data by encrypting entire volumes and has full-featured key management capabilities. BitLocker uses the Advanced Encryption Standard (AES) encryption algorithm by default. BitLocker can manage key recovery even via the Azure cloud deployment of Active Directory services in enterprise deployments.

Content Management

Applications are not the only information moving to mobile devices. Content is moving as well, and organizations need a means of content management for mobile devices. For instance, it might be fine to have, and edit, some types of information on mobile devices, whereas other more sensitive information would be best suited not to be shared to this extent. *Content management* is the set of actions used to control content issues on mobile devices. Most organizations have a data ownership policy that clearly establishes the company ownership rights over data, regardless of the device on which it is shared. However, content management goes a step further, examining what content belongs on what devices and then establishing mechanisms to enforce these rules. Again, MDM solutions exist to assist in this security issue with respect to mobile devices.

Tech Tip

Location Services

Mobile devices by their specific nature are on the move, and hence the location of a device can have significant ramifications with respect to its use. Mobile devices can connect to multiple public Wi-Fi locations, and they can provide users with navigation and other location context-sensitive information, such as a local sale. To enable this functionality, location services are a set of functions that enable, and control, the location information possessed by the device.

Remote Wipe

Today's mobile devices are almost innumerable and are very susceptible to loss and theft. Further, it is unlikely that a lost or stolen device will be recovered, thus making even encrypted data stored on a device more vulnerable to decryption. If the thief can have your device for a long time, they can take all the time they want to try to decrypt your data. Therefore, many companies prefer to just remotely wipe a lost or stolen device. **Remote wiping** a mobile device typically removes data stored on the device and resets the device to factory settings.

Geofencing

Geofencing is the use of GPS and/or RFID technology to create a virtual fence around a particular location, and to detect when devices cross the fence. This enables devices to be recognized by location and have actions taken. Geofencing is used in marketing to send messages to devices that are in a specific area—near a point of sale, or just to count potential customers. Geofencing has been used for remote workers, notifying management when they have arrived at remote work sites. This allows network connections to be enabled for them, for example. The uses of geofencing are truly only limited by one's imagination.

Geolocation

Most mobile devices are now capable of using the Global Positioning System (GPS) for tracking device location. Many apps rely heavily on GPS location, such as device-locating services, mapping applications, traffic-monitoring apps, and apps that locate nearby businesses such as gas stations and restaurants. Such technology can be exploited to track movement and the location of the mobile device, which is referred to as *geolocation*. This tracking can be used to assist in the recovery of lost devices.

Geo-Tagging

Geo-tagging is the posting of location information into a data stream, signifying where the device was when the stream was created. Because many mobile devices include on-board cameras, and the photos/videos they take can divulge information, geo-tagging can make location part of any picture or video, and this information can be associated with anything the camera can image—whiteboards, documents, and even the location of the device when the photo/video was taken.

Posting photos with geo-tags embedded in them has its use, but it can also unexpectedly divulge information users might not want to share. For example, if you use your smartphone to take a photo of your car in the driveway and then post the photo on the Internet in an attempt to sell your car, if geo-tagging is enabled on the smartphone, the location of where the photo was taken is embedded as metadata in the digital photo. Such a posting could inadvertently expose where your home is located. Some social media applications strip out the metadata on a photo before posting, but then they indicate where you posted the photo within the posting itself. There has been much public discussion on this topic, and geo-tagging can be disabled on most mobile devices. It is recommended that it be disabled unless you have a specific reason for having the location information embedded in a photo.

• **Figure 12.7** iOS lock screens

Screen Locks

Most corporate policies regarding mobile devices require the use of the mobile device's **screen-locking** capability. This usually consists of entering a passcode or PIN to unlock the device. It is highly recommended that screen locks be enforced for all mobile devices. Your policy regarding the quality of the passcode should be consistent with your corporate password policy. However, many companies merely enforce the use of screen locking. Thus, users tend to use convenient or easy-to-remember passcodes. Some devices allow complex passcodes. As shown in Figure 12.7, the device screen on the left supports only a simple iOS passcode, limited to four numbers, whereas the device screen on the right supports a passcode of indeterminate length and can contain alphanumeric characters.

Some more advanced forms of screen locks work in conjunction with device wiping. If the passcode is entered incorrectly a specified number of times, the device is automatically wiped. This is one of the security features of BlackBerry that has traditionally made it of interest to security-conscious users. Apple has made this an option on newer iOS devices. Apple also allows remote locking of a device from the user's iCloud account.

> **Tech Tip**
>
> **Mobile Device Security**
>
> *Mobile devices require basic security mechanisms of screen locks, lockouts, device wiping, and encryption to protect sensitive information contained on them.*

Lockout

If a user discovers that they've lost their device, a quick way to protect it is to remotely lock the device as soon as they recognize it has been lost or stolen. Several products are available on the market today to help enterprises manage their devices. Remote lockout is usually the first step taken in securing a mobile device.

Push Notification Services

Push notification services are services that deliver information to mobile devices without a specific request from the device. Push notifications are used a lot in mobile devices to indicate that content has been updated. Push notification methods are typically unique to the platform, with Apple Push Notification service for Apple devices and Android Cloud to Device Messaging as examples. Many other back-end server services have similar methods for updating their content.

Passwords and PINs

Passwords and PINs are common security measures used to protect mobile devices from unauthorized use. These are essential tools and should be used in all cases, and mandated by company policy.

Biometrics

Biometrics is used across a wide range of mobile phones as a means of access control. Many of these devices have less-than-perfect recognition, however, and many security presentations on hacking past the biometric sensor have been shown at conferences. The newest biometric method, facial recognition, is based on a camera image of the user holding their phone. Because it has been shown that these devices can be bypassed, one should consider them to be convenience features, not security features. As facial recognition has gotten better, even the addition of masks as part of the pandemic in 2020 did not stop facial recognition, as the AI-based processing can be trained to ignore the mask. Hence, it is important for management policies to reflect this and not rely on these methods for securing important data.

Context-Aware Authentication

Context-aware authentication is the use of information such as who is the user, what are they requesting, what machine are they using, how are they connected, and so on, to make the authentication decision as to whether to permit the requested resource. The goal is to prevent unauthorized end users, devices, or network connections from being able to access corporate data. This approach can be used to allow an authorized user to access network-based resources from inside the office, but deny access if they are connecting via a public Wi-Fi network.

Containerization

Containerization on mobile devices is just that: dividing the device into a series of containers, with one container holding work-related materials and the other personal materials. The containers can separate apps, data, and virtually everything on the device. Depending on the mobile device management solution employed, remote control over the work container can be possible. This enables a much stronger use case for mixing business and personal data on a single device.

Storage Segmentation

Containerization and storage segmentation are both technologies used to keep personal data separate from corporate data on devices.

On mobile devices, it can be very difficult to keep personal data separate from corporate data. **Storage segmentation** is similar to containerization in that it represents a logical separation of the storage in the unit. Some companies have developed capabilities to create distinct virtual containers to keep personal data separate from corporate data and applications. For devices that are used to handle highly sensitive corporate data, this form of protection is highly recommended.

Asset Control

Because each user can have multiple devices connecting to the corporate network, it is important to implement a viable asset-tracking and inventory-control mechanism. For security and liability reasons, the company needs to know what devices are connecting to its systems and what access has been granted. Just as in IT systems, maintaining a list of approved devices is a critical control.

Device Access Control

The principles of access control for mobile devices need to be managed just like access control from wired or wireless desktops and laptops. This will become more critical as storage in the cloud and Software as a Service (SaaS) become more prevalent. Emerging tablet/mobile device sharing intends to provide the user with a seamless data access experience across many devices. Data access capabilities will continue to evolve to meet this need. Rigorous data access principles need to be applied, and they become even more important with the inclusion of mobile devices as fully functional computing devices. When reviewing possible solutions, it is important that you consider seeking proof of security and procedures rather than relying on marketing brochures.

Removable Storage

Because removable devices can move data outside of the corporate-controlled environment, their security needs must be addressed. Removable devices can bring unprotected or corrupted data into the corporate environment. All removable devices should be scanned by antivirus software upon connection to the corporate environment. Corporate policies should address the copying of data to removable devices. Many mobile devices can be connected via USB to a system and used to store data—and in some cases vast quantities of data. This capability can be used to avoid some implementations of data loss prevention (DLP) mechanisms.

Disabling Unused Features

As with all computing devices, features that are not used or that present a security risk should be disabled. Bluetooth access is particularly problematic. It is best to make Bluetooth connections undiscoverable. However, users will need to enable it to pair with a new headset or car connection, for example. Requiring Bluetooth connections to be undiscoverable is very hard to enforce but should be encouraged as a best practice. Users should receive training as to the risks of Bluetooth—not so they avoid Bluetooth, but so they understand when they should turn it off. Having a mobile device with access to sensitive information carries with it a level of responsibility. Helping users understand this and act accordingly can go a long way toward securing mobile devices.

Mobile Application Security

Devices are not the only concern in the mobile world. Applications that run on the devices also represent security threats to the information that is stored on and processed by the device. Applications are the software elements that can be used to violate security, even when the user is not aware. Many games and utilities offer value to the user, but at the same time they scrape information stores on the device for information.

Application Control

Mobile devices are typically updated through the use of an app store. This store provides the apps and their updates in one convenient location. In devices used on enterprise networks, the security provided by the app store may not meet the requirements of the business. In these circumstances, a separate application, known typically as the Management Device Manager (MDM), can handle device configuration as well as security. The configuration of the MDM solution provides the company with a method of controlling what applications are loaded on the device and thus would potentially become connected to the network and other sensitive systems.

Key and Credential Management

The MDM marketplace is maturing quickly. Key and credential management services are being integrated into most MDM services to ensure that existing strong policies and procedures can be extended to mobile platforms securely. These services include protection of keys for digital signatures and S/MIME encryption and decryption. Keys and credentials are among the highest-value items that can be found on mobile devices, so ensuring protection for them is a key element in mobile device security. The keys and credentials stored on the device can be used by multiple applications. Providing protection of these keys while still maintaining usability of them is an essential element of modern mobile application security.

Authentication

When mobile devices are used to access business networks, authentication becomes an issue. Is the device allowed to access the network? Is the user of the device a network user? If so, how do you authenticate the user? Mobile devices have some advantages in that they can store certificates, which by their very nature are more secure than passwords. This moves the authentication problem to the endpoint, where it relies on passcodes, screen locks, and other mobile device protections. These can be relatively weak unless structured together, including wiping after a limited number of failures. The risk in mobile authentication is that strong credentials stored in the device are protected by the less rigorous passcode and the end user. End users can share their mobile devices, and by proxy unwittingly share their strong corporate authentication codes.

> In light of changing speech due to political correctness, the terms *whitelisting* and *blacklisting* as well as *white hat* and *black hat* are being challenged. The history of these terms goes back to old westerns, where the good guy wore a white hat, and the bad guy wore a black hat; neither is a reference to race. Many are considering the terms *application approved list* and *application block list* (or *deny list*) to replace whitelisting and blacklisting.

Application Whitelisting

As discussed in the "Application Control" section earlier in the chapter, controlling what applications a device can access may be an important element of your company's mobile device policy. The use of application whitelisting and blacklisting enables you to control and block applications available on the mobile device. Whitelisting is the use of a preapproved list of behaviors—only those on the whitelist are allowed. Blacklisting involves using a list of behaviors that are specifically blocked. Blacklisting is great against specific known threats. Whitelisting, when possible, restricts use to only approved functions. The challenge in whitelisting is in the definition of allowed activities. This is usually administered through some type of MDM capability. Application whitelisting can improve security by preventing unapproved applications from being installed and run on the device.

Encryption

Just as the device should be encrypted, thereby protecting all information on the device, applications should be encrypted as well. Just employing encryption for the data store is not sufficient. If the device is fully encrypted, then all apps would have to have access to the data, in essence bypassing the encryption from an app point of view. Apps with sensitive information should control access via their own set of protections. The only way to segregate data within the device is for apps to manage their own data stores through app-specific encryption. This will allow sensitive data to be protected from rogue applications that would leak data if uniform access was allowed.

Transitive Trust/Authentication

Security across multiple domains/platforms is provided through trust relationships. When trust relationships between domains or platforms exist, authentication for each domain trusts the authentication for all other trusted domains. Thus, when an application is authenticated, its authentication is accepted by all other domains/platforms that trust the authenticating domain or platform. Trust relationships can be very complex in mobile devices, and often security aspects aren't properly implemented. Mobile devices tend to be used across numerous systems, including business, personal, public, and private. This greatly expands the risk profile and opportunity for transitive trust–based attacks. As with all other applications, mobile applications should be carefully reviewed to ensure that trust relationships are secure.

Mobile Devices

Mobile devices can bring much to the enterprise in terms of business functionality, but with this increased utility comes additional risks. There are a variety of ways to manage the risk, including the use of encryption and endpoint protections designed for mobile devices. You can use several different methodologies to manage mobile devices, and these are covered in the following sections.

MicroSD Hardware Security Module (HSM)

A *MicroSD HSM* is a hardware security module in a MicroSD form factor. This device allows you a portable means of secure cryptographic key storage for a wide range of keys. These devices come with an application that manages the typical HSM functions associated with keys, including backup, restore, and many PKI functions.

MDM/Unified Endpoint Management (UEM)

MDM software is an application that runs on a mobile device and, when activated, can manage aspects of the device such as connectivity and functions. The purpose of an MDM application is to turn the device into one where the functionality is limited in accordance with the enterprise policy. *Unified endpoint management (UEM)* is an enterprise-level endpoint management solution that can cover all endpoints, from PC to laptops, from phones to other mobile devices, tablets, and even some wearables. The idea behind UEM is to extend the function set from MDM to include all endpoint devices, including bringing more functionality under enterprise control. A UEM can manage the deployment of corporate resources onto an endpoint, providing control over items such as application and resource access, remote control of the device, and monitoring of device activity. MDM and UEM solutions also assist with asset management, including location and tracking.

Distinguishing between MDM, UEM, and MAM applications is by functionality. MAM controls in-house applications on devices. MDM controls the data on the device, segregating it from the general data on the device. UEM is a complete endpoint control solution that works across virtually every form of endpoint, mobile or not.

Mobile Application Management (MAM)

Mobile devices bring a plethora of applications along with the device into an enterprise. While MDM solutions can protect the enterprise from applications installed on a device, there is also a need to manage corporate applications on the device. The deployment, updating, and configuration of applications on devices requires an enterprise solution that is scalable and provides for the installation, updating, and management of in-house applications across a set of mobile devices. *Mobile application management (MAM)* tool suites provide these capabilities in the enterprise.

SEAndroid/SELinux

Security Enhanced Linux (SELinux) is a modified Linux distribution that enforces mandatory access control (MAC) over all processes, even processes running with root/superuser privileges. SELinux has one overarching principle: default denial. This means that anything that is not explicitly allowed is denied. SEAndroid is a version of SELinux used on mobile devices.

Policies for Enforcement and Monitoring

This section covers the topics of corporate policies and mobile device usage in a corporate environment. Your corporate policies regarding mobile devices should be consistent with your existing computer security policies. Your training programs should include instruction on mobile device security. Disciplinary actions should be consistent. Your monitoring programs should be enhanced to include monitoring and control of mobile devices.

Third-party App Stores

Many mobile devices have manufacturer-associated application stores, where applications can be downloaded to the device. From a corporate enterprise point of view, these application stores are *third-party app stores,* as they represent neither the user nor the enterprise in the nature and quantity of their offerings. Currently there are two main app stores: one from Apple and one from Google. The Apple Store is built on a principle of exclusivity, and security is highly enforced on apps. The Google Store has less restrictions, which has translated into some security issues from apps. Managing what applications a user can add to the device is essential because many of these applications can create security risks for the enterprise. This issue becomes significantly more complex with employee-owned devices and access to corporate data stores. There are very few segmentation options for most devices to separate work and personal spaces, so the ability to control this access becomes problematic. For devices with access to sensitive corporate information, a company-owned device is recommended, thus allowing for more stringent control.

Rooting/Jailbreaking

A common hack associated with Apple iOS mobile devices is the jailbreak. **Jailbreaking** is a process by which the user escalates their privilege level, bypassing the operating system's controls and limitations. The user still has the complete functionality of the device, but also has additional capabilities that bypass the OS-imposed user restrictions. There are several schools of thought concerning the utility of jailbreaking, but the important issue from a security point of view is that running any device with enhanced privileges can result in errors that cause more damage, because normal security controls are typically bypassed.

Rooting a device is a process whereby OS controls are bypassed on Android devices. The effect is the same whether the device is rooted or jailbroken: the OS controls designed to constrain operations are no longer in play and the device can do things it was never intended to do, good or bad.

> Rooting is used to bypass OS controls on Android, and jailbreaking is used to escalate privileges and do the same on iOS devices. Both processes stop OS controls from inhibiting user behaviors.

Sideloading

Sideloading is the process of adding apps to a mobile device without using the authorized store associated with the device. Currently, sideloading only works on Android devices because Apple has not enabled any application execution except of those coming through the App Store. Sideloading is an alternative means of instantiating an app on the device without having to have it hosted on the app store. The downside, simply put, is that without the app store screening, one is at greater risk of installing malicious software in the guise of a desired app.

Custom Firmware

Custom firmware is firmware for a device that has been altered from the original factory settings. This firmware can bring added functionality, but it can also result in security holes. The use of custom firmware should only be done on devices without access to critical information.

Carrier Unlocking

Most mobile devices in the U.S. come locked to a carrier, while in other parts of the world they are unlocked, relying on a SIM card for connection and billing information. This is a byproduct of the business market decisions made early in the mobile phone market lifecycle and has remained fairly true to date. If you have a carrier-locked device and you attempt to use a SIM card from another carrier, the phone will not accept it unless you unlock the device. *Carrier unlocking* is the process of telling the device to sever itself from the carrier. This is usually done through the inputting of a special key sequence that unlocks the device.

Firmware OTA Updates

Firmware is, at the end of the day, software. It may be stored in a chip, but like all software, it sometimes requires updating. With mobile devices being literarily everywhere, the scale does not support bringing the device to a central location or connection for updating. **Firmware OTA (over the air) updates** are a solution to this problem. Just as one can add an app, or update an app from the store, it is possible to have a menu option that permits the device firmware to be updated. All major device manufacturers support this model because it is the only real workable solution.

Camera Use

Many mobile devices include on-board cameras, and the photos/videos they take can divulge information. This information can be associated with anything the camera can image—whiteboards, documents, and even the location of the device when the photo/video was taken via geo-tagging. Another challenge presented by mobile devices is the possibility that they will be used for illegal purposes. This can create liability for the company if it is a company-owned device. Despite all the potential legal concerns, possibly the greatest concern of mobile device users is that their personal photos will be lost during a device wipe originated by the company.

SMS/MMS/RCS

Short Message Service (SMS) and **Multimedia Messaging Service (MMS)** are standard protocols used to send messages, including multimedia content in the case of MMS, to and from mobile devices over a cellular network. SMS is limited to short text-only messages of less than 160 characters and is carried over the signaling path of the cellular network when signaling data is not being sent. SMS dates back to the early days of mobile telephony in the 1980s, whereas MMS is a more recent development designed to support multimedia content to and from mobile devices. Because of the content connections that can be sent via MMS in particular, and SMS in certain cases, it is important to at least address these communication channels in relevant policies.

Rich Communication Services (RCS) is a protocol that is currently used alongside SMS and MMS. RCS operates between the mobile device and the carrier. RCS messaging requires RCS-capable apps on both ends of the communication. RCS supports modern methods of communication, like adding user-desired features such as integration with stickers, video, images, groups, and other modern mobile data formats. RCS is intended to eventually replace both SMS and MMS.

External Media

External media refers to any item or device that can store data. From flash drives to hard drives, music players, smartphones, and even smart watches, if it can store data, it is a pathway for data exfiltration. External media can also deliver malware into the enterprise. The risk is evident: these devices can carry data in and out of the enterprise, yet they have become synonymous with today's tech worker. The key is to develop a policy that determines where these devices can exist and where they should be banned, and then follow the plan with monitoring and enforcement.

USB On-The-Go (USB OTG)

Universal Serial Bus is a common method of connecting mobile devices to computers and other host-based platforms. Connecting mobile devices directly to each other required changes to USB connections. Enter **USB OTG (USB On-The-Go)**, an extension of USB technology that facilitates direct connection between USB OTG–enabled mobile devices. USB OTG allows those devices to switch back and forth between the roles of host and device, including deciding who provides power (host) and who consumes power across the interface. USB OTG also allows the connection of USB-based peripherals, such as keyboards, mice, and storage, to mobile devices. Although USB OTG is relatively new, most mobile devices made since 2015 are USB OTG compatible.

Recording Microphone

Many of today's electronic devices—from smartphones to watches, to devices such as the online assistants from Amazon and Google, and even toys—have the ability to record audio information. *Recording microphones* can be used to record conversations and collect sensitive data, and the parties under observation are not even aware of the incident. As with other high-tech gadgets, the key is to determine the policy of where they can be used and the rules for their use.

GPS Tagging

GPS tagging is the addition of GPS information to a file or folder, or other digital item. Adding GPS information to the metadata of a file can enhance value in that it enables site-specific information to be associated with the digital item. This can be a location where a picture was taken, or map coordinates when linking to mapping software. A more extensive coverage of this type of tagging was covered earlier in the chapter under the section heading "Geo-Tagging."

Wi-Fi Direct/Ad Hoc

Wi-Fi typically connects a Wi-Fi device to a network via a wireless access point. Other methods exist—namely, *Wi-Fi Direct* and *Wi-Fi ad hoc*. In Wi-Fi Direct, two Wi-Fi devices connect to each other in a single-hop connection.

In essence, one of the two devices acts as an access point for the other device. The key element is the single-hop nature of a Wi-Fi Direct connection. In the end, Wi-Fi Direct connects only two devices. These two devices can be connected with all of the bells and whistles of modern wireless networking, including WPA2/WPA3.

Wi-Fi Direct uses a couple of services to establish secure connections between devices. The first is Wi-Fi Direct Device and Service Discovery. This protocol provides a way for devices to discover each other based on the services they support before connecting. A device can see all compatible devices in the area and then narrow down the list to only devices that allow a specific service (say, printing) before displaying to the user a list of available printers for pairing. The other method used is WPA2/WPA3. This protocol is used to protect the connections and prevent unauthorized parties from pairing to Wi-Fi Direct devices, or intercepting communications from paired devices.

For Wi-Fi ad hoc, the primary difference is that in the network, multiple devices can communicate with each other, with each device capable of communicating with all other devices.

Tethering

Tethering is the connection of a device to a mobile device that has a means of accessing a network for the purpose of sharing network access. Connecting a mobile phone to a laptop to charge the phone's battery is not tethering. Connecting it so that the laptop can use the phone to connect to the Internet *is* tethering. Tethering introduces new outside-of-the-enterprise, span-of-control network connections; it can act to bridge your enterprise network with the outside network.

> Tethering involves the connection of a device to a mobile device to gain network connectivity. A hotspot can be tethered if the actual device is mobile, but if the device is fixed, it is not tethering.

Hotspot

The term *hotspot* can refer to a specific piece of network equipment, an endpoint for a wireless solution, or, in other respects, the physical area where connectivity is provided. Typically a Wi-Fi endpoint, a hotspot provides a set of users a method of connecting to a network. This can be done for employees, customers, guests, or a combination thereof based on access control mechanisms employed at the endpoint device. A network engineer will refer to a hotspot as the physical equipment that provides services over a specified geographic area, whereas a user will refer to it as a place they can connect to the network.

Payment Methods

Twenty years ago, payment methods were cash, check, and charge. Today, we have new intermediaries; for example, smart devices with NFC linked to credit cards offer a convenient alternative for payments. Although the actual payment is still a credit/debit card charge, the payment pathway is through the digital device. Utilizing the security features of the device, NFC, and biometrics/PIN, this form of payment has some advantages over the other methods because it allows for the addition of specific security measures before the payment method is accessed.

Deployment Models

When determining how to incorporate mobile devices securely within the enterprise, you have a wide range of considerations. How will security be enforced? How will all the policies be enforced? And, ultimately, what devices will be supported in the enterprise? There are a variety of deployment models—from employee-owned devices to corporate-owned devices, with mixtures of the two in between. Each of these models has advantages and disadvantages.

CYOD

CYOD (choose your own device) is very similar to BYOD (bring your own device) in concept: users have a choice in the type of device. In most cases, this choice is constrained to a list of acceptable devices that can be supported in the enterprise. Because the device is corporate owned, CYOD provides greater flexibility in corporate restrictions on device use, in terms of apps, data, updates, and so on.

COPE

COPE (company-issued, personally enabled) is a model where employees are supplied a phone chosen and paid for by the company, but they are given permission to use it for personal activities. The company can decide how much choice and freedom employees get with the personal use of the device. This allows the enterprise to control security functionality while dealing with the employee dissatisfaction associated with the traditional method of supplying devices: corporate-owned business-only (COBO).

Corporate-Owned

Corporate-owned business-only (COBO) is a model in which the business supplies a mobile device for company-only use on the part of the employee. This has the disadvantage of the employee having to carry two devices—one personal and one for work—and then separate functions between the devices based on the purpose of use in each instance. The advantage is that the corporation has complete control over the device and can apply any security controls desired without interference from other device functionality.

BYOD

BYOD (bring your own device) has many advantages in business, and not just from the perspective of device cost. Users tend to prefer having a single device rather than carrying multiple devices. Users also have less of a learning curve on devices they already have an interest in learning. This model is popular in small firms and those employing a lot of temporary workers. The big disadvantage is that employees will not be eager to limit the use of their personal device based on corporate policies, so corporate control will be limited.

> **Tech Tip**
>
> **BYOD Concerns**
>
> *There is a dilemma in the use of BYOD devices that store both personal and enterprise data. Wiping the device usually removes all data, both personal and enterprise. Therefore, if corporate policy requires wiping a lost device, that policy may mean the device's user loses personal photos and data. The software controls for separate data containers—one for business and one for personal—have been proposed but are not a mainstream option yet.*

Data Ownership

BYOD blurs the lines of data ownership because it blurs the lines of device management. If a company owns a smartphone issued to an employee, the company can repossess the phone upon employee termination. This practice may protect company data by keeping the company-issued devices in the hands of employees only. However, a company cannot rely on a simple factory reset before reissuing a device, because factory resetting might not remove all the data on the device. If a device is reissued, it is possible that some of the previous owner's personal information, such as private contacts, still remains on the device. On the other hand, if the employee's device is a personal device that has been used for business purposes, upon termination of the employee, it is likely that some company data remains on the phone despite the company's best efforts to remove its data from the device. If that device is resold or recycled, the company's data might remain on the device and be passed on to the subsequent owner. Keeping business data in separate, MDM-managed containers is one method of dealing with this issue.

Storage Segmentation

Storage segmentation methods are needed whenever a device has multilevel data security types, as in personal and corporate, or corporate and highly sensitive corporate. Having the ability to manage the separate data streams based on their sensitivity is important because of the highly mobile nature of the device. When an enterprise is using BYOD, then it is expected that non-business use will be occurring, making storage segmentation, covered earlier in the chapter, even more important.

Support Ownership

Support costs for mobile devices are an important consideration for corporations. Each device has its own implementation of various functions. While those functions typically are implemented against a specification, software implementations might not fully or properly implement the specification. This can result in increased support calls to your help desk or support organization. It is very difficult for a corporate help desk to be knowledgeable on all aspects of all possible devices that access a corporate network. For example, your support organization must be able to troubleshoot iPhones, Android devices, tablets, and so forth. These devices are updated frequently, new devices are released, and new capabilities are added on a regular basis. Your support organization will need viable knowledge base articles and job aids in order to provide sufficient support for the wide variety of ever-changing devices.

Patch Management

Just as your corporate policy should enforce the prompt update of desktop and laptop computers to help eliminate security vulnerabilities on those platforms, it should also require mobile devices to be kept current with respect to patches. Having the latest applications, operating system, and so on is an important best defense against viruses, malware, and other threats. It is important to recognize that "jailbreaking" or "rooting" your device can remove the manufacturer's security mechanisms and protection against malware and other threats. These devices might also no longer be able to update their applications or OS against known issues. Jailbreaking or rooting is also a method used to bypass security measures associated with the device manufacturer control, and in some locations, this can be illegal. Mobile devices that are jailbroken or rooted should not be trusted on your enterprise network or allowed to access sensitive data.

Antivirus/Anti-malware Management

Just like desktop and laptop computers need protection against viruses and malware, so too do smartphones, tablets, and other mobile devices. It is important that corporate policy and personal usage keep operating systems and applications current. Antivirus and malware protection should be employed as widely as possible and kept up to date against current threats.

Forensics

Mobile device forensics is a rapidly evolving and fast-changing field. Because devices are evolving so quickly, it is difficult to stay current in this field. Solid forensics principles should always be followed. Devices should be properly handled by using RF-shielded bags or containers. Because of the rapid changes in this area, it's best to engage the help of trained forensic specialists to ensure that data isn't contaminated and that the device state and memory are unaltered. If forensics are needed on a device that has both personal and business data, then policies need to be in place to cover the appropriate privacy protections on the personal side of the device.

Privacy

When an employee uses their personal device to perform their work for the company, they may have strong expectations that privacy will be protected by the company. The company policy needs to consider this and address it explicitly. On company-owned devices, it's quite acceptable for the company to reserve the right to access and wipe any company data on the device. The company can thus state that the user can have no expectation of privacy when using a company device. However, when the device is a personal device, the user may feel stronger ownership. Expectations of privacy and data access on personal devices should be included in your company policy.

Onboarding/Offboarding

Most companies and individuals find it relatively easy to connect mobile devices to the corporate network. Often there are no controls around for connecting a device other than having a Microsoft Exchange account. When new employees join a company, the onboarding processes need to include provisions for mobile device responsibilities. It is easy for new employees to bypass security measures if they are not part of the business process of onboarding.

Employee termination needs to be modified to include termination of accounts on mobile devices. It's not uncommon to find terminated employees with accounts or even company devices still connecting to the corporate network months after being terminated. E-mail accounts should be removed promptly as part of the employee termination policy and process. Mobile devices supplied by the company should be collected upon termination. BYOD equipment should have its access to corporate resources terminated as part of the offboarding process. Regular audits for old or unterminated accounts should be performed to ensure prompt deletion of accounts for terminated employees.

Adherence to Corporate Policies

Your corporate policies regarding BYOD devices should be consistent with your existing computer security policies. Your training programs should include instruction on mobile device security. Disciplinary actions should be consistent. Your monitoring programs should be enhanced to include monitoring and control of mobile devices.

BYOD User Acceptance

BYOD inherently creates a conflict between personal and corporate interests. An employee who uses their own device to conduct corporate business inherently feels strong ownership over the device and may resent corporate demands to control corporate information downloaded to the device. On the other hand, the corporation expects that corporate data be properly controlled and protected and thus desires to impose remote wiping or lockout requirements in order to protect corporate data. An individual who loses their personal photos from a special event will likely harbor ill feelings toward the corporation if it wipes their device, including those irreplaceable photos. Your corporate BYOD policy needs to be well defined, approved by the corporate legal department, and clearly communicated to all employees through training.

Architecture/Infrastructure Considerations

Mobile devices consume connections to your corporate IT infrastructure. It is not unusual now for a single individual to be connected to the corporate infrastructure with one or more smartphones, tablets, and laptop or desktop computers. Some infrastructure implementations in the past have not been efficient in their design, sometimes consuming multiple connections for a single device. This can reduce the number of available connections for other end users. It is recommended that load testing be performed to ensure that your design or existing infrastructure can support the potentially large number of connections from multiple devices.

Multiple connections can also create security issues when the system tracks user accounts against multiple connections. Users will need to be aware of this so that they don't inadvertently create incident response situations or find themselves locked out by their own actions. This can be a tricky issue and requires a bit more intelligent design than the traditional philosophy of "one user ID equals one current connection."

Legal Concerns

It should be apparent from the various topics discussed in this chapter that there are many security challenges presented by mobile devices used for corporate business. Because the technology is rapidly changing, it's best to make sure you have a solid legal review of policies. There are both legal and public relation concerns when it comes to mobile devices. Employees who use both company-owned and personal devices have responsibilities when company data is involved. Policies and procedures should be reviewed on a regular basis to stay current with technology.

Another challenge presented by mobile devices is the possibility that they will be used for illegal purposes. This can create liability for the company if the device is company-owned.

> Mobile devices offer many usability advantages across the enterprise, and they can be managed securely with the help of security-conscious users. Security policies can go a long way toward assisting users in understanding their responsibilities associated with mobile devices and sensitive data.

Acceptable Use Policy

Similar to your acceptable use policies for laptops and desktops, your mobile device policies should address acceptable use of mobile or BYOD devices. Authorized usage of corporate devices for personal purposes should be addressed. Disciplinary actions for violation of mobile device policies should be defined. BYOD offers both the company and the user advantages; ramifications should be specifically spelled out, along with the specific user responsibilities.

Virtual Desktop Infrastructure (VDI)

While it seems the deployment models are only associated with phones, this is really not the case, because personal computers can also be external mobile devices requiring connections at times. In the case of laptops, a *virtual desktop infrastructure (VDI)* solution can bring control to the mobile environment associated with non-corporate-owned equipment. The enterprise can set up virtual desktop machines that are fully security compliant and contain all the necessary applications needed by the employee, and then let the employee access the virtual machine via either a virtual connection or a remote desktop connection. This can solve most if not all of the security and application functionality issues associated with mobile devices. It does require an IT staff that is capable of setting up, maintaining, and managing the VDI in the organization, which is not necessarily a small task, depending on the number of instances needed. Interaction with a VDI can be accomplished easily on many of today's mobile devices because of their advanced screens and compute power.

Chapter 12 Review

Chapter Summary

After reading this chapter and completing the exercises, you should understand the following about wireless security and mobile devices.

Describe the different wireless systems in use today

- A wide range of wireless connectivity methods exist today beyond just Wi-Fi, including cellular, Bluetooth, NFC, and satellite-based services.
- 802.11 is the IEEE standard for wireless local area networks. The standard includes several different specifications of 802.11 networks, such as 802.11b, 802.11a, 802.11g, 802.11n, 802.11ac, and 802.11ax.
- Wi-Fi 4, Wi-Fi 5, and Wi-Fi 6 are more than just new marketing names. They are a means to propel better Wi-Fi-based service in more diverse environments.

Identify 802.11's security issues and possible solutions

- 802.11 does not allow physical control of the transport mechanism.
- Wireless transmission of all network data sends frames to all wireless machines, not just a single client, similar to Ethernet hub devices.
- Poor authentication is caused by the SSID being broadcast to anyone listening.
- Multiple encryption methods have been deployed over the years, including WEP (now considered a failure), WPA (deprecated), WPA2, and WPA3.
- A wide range of authentication protocols are supported, including EAP, LEAP, PEAP, EAP-FAST, EAP-TLS, and EAP-TTLS.

Learn about wireless configuration and deployment

- Wireless networks are built using access points and SSIDs.
- Technical selection of antennas, device placement, and deployment management through site surveys and testing are important to ensure coverage.
- Deployment of physical equipment is complemented through the deployment of security technologies, including MAC filtering and captive portals, to the network elements.

Learn about the different types of wireless attacks

- Attacks against protocols include bluejacking, bluesnarfing, and IV attacks.
- Attacks against the wireless system include evil twin, replay, disassociation, and rogue AP attacks.

Examine the security of mobile systems

- Mobile devices have specific security concerns and specific controls to assist in securing them.
- BYOD has its own concerns as well as policies and procedures to manage mobile devices in the enterprise.
- Mobile applications require security, and the issues associated with mobile, apps, and security need to be addressed.
- The range of security issues associated with mobile devices is a superset of normal endpoint concerns, as mobility and device capabilities increase the points of risk.
- Policies are needed to address the unique capabilities and risks associated with the use of mobile devices in the corporate environment.
- Specific mobile solutions exist, including MicroSD HSM, MDM with unified endpoint management, and mobile application management.

Key Terms

beacon frames *(440)*
bluebugging *(450)*
bluejacking *(449)*
bluesnarfing *(450)*
Bluetooth *(425)*
Bluetooth DoS *(450)*
captive portal *(446)*
containerization *(456)*
custom firmware *(461)*
direct-sequence spread spectrum (DSSS) *(430)*
disassociation *(451)*
EAP-FAST *(437)*
EAP-TLS *(437)*
EAP-TTLS *(438)*
evil twin *(448)*
Extensible Authentication Protocol (EAP) *(437)*
firmware OTA updates *(462)*
geo-tagging *(454)*
IEEE 802.1X *(438)*
infrared (IR) *(427)*
initialization vector (IV) *(448)*
jailbreaking *(461)*
jamming *(449)*
MAC filtering *(445)*
mobile device management (MDM) *(452)*
Multimedia Messaging Service (MMS) *(462)*
multiple-input and multiple-output (MIMO) *(430)*
near field communication (NFC) *(427)*
orthogonal frequency division multiplexing (OFDM) *(430)*
PEAP *(437)*
Radio Frequency Identification (RFID) *(428)*
RC4 stream cipher *(431)*
remote wiping *(453)*
replay attack *(448)*
rogue access point *(449)*
rooting *(461)*
screen locking *(454)*
service set identifier (SSID) *(440)*
Short Message Service (SMS) *(462)*
sideloading *(461)*
site survey *(444)*
storage segmentation *(456)*
Temporal Key Integrity Protocol (TKIP) *(432)*
USB OTG (USB On-The-Go) *(463)*
war-chalking *(447)*
war-dialing *(447)*
war-driving *(447)*
Wi-Fi Protected Access 2 (WPA2) *(433)*
Wi-Fi Protected Access 3 (WPA3) *(436)*
WiMAX *(429)*
Wired Equivalent Privacy (WEP) *(431)*
Wireless Application Protocol (WAP) placement *(443)*
Zigbee *(429)*

Key Terms Quiz

Use terms from the Key Terms list to complete the sentences that follow. Don't use the same term more than once. Not all terms will be used.

1. An AP uses _______________ to advertise its existence to potential wireless clients.
2. The _______________ is the part of the RC4 cipher that has a weak implementation in WEP.
3. Two common mobile device security measures are _______________ and _______________.
4. To identify a specific AP and network, one would use the _______________.
5. The 32-character identifier attached to the header of a packet used for authentication to an 802.11 access point is the _______________.
6. _______________ is a feature that can disclose a user's position when sharing photos.
7. 802.11i updates the flawed security protocol called _______________.
8. The standard for wireless local area networks is called _______________.
9. The type of application used to control security across multiple mobile devices in an enterprise is called _______________.
10. 802.11a uses frequencies in the _______________.

Multiple-Choice Quiz

1. Bluebugging can give an attacker what?
   - A. All of your contacts
   - B. The ability to send "shock" photos
   - C. Total control over a mobile phone
   - D. A virus
2. How does 802.11n improve network speed?
   - A. Wider bandwidth
   - B. Higher frequency
   - C. Multiple-input multiple-output (MIMO)
   - D. Both A and C
3. 802.11ax is also called?
   - A. Wi-Fi 4
   - B. Wi-Fi 5
   - C. Wi-Fi 6
   - D. 5G
4. WEP has used an implementation of which of the following encryption algorithms?
   - A. SHA
   - B. ElGamal
   - C. RC4
   - D. Triple-DES
5. What element does not belong in a mobile device security policy in an enterprise employing BYOD?
   - A. Separation of personal and business-related information
   - B. Remote wiping
   - C. Passwords and screen locking
   - D. Mobile device carrier selection
6. What is bluejacking?
   - A. Stealing a person's mobile phone
   - B. Sending an unsolicited message via Bluetooth
   - C. Breaking a WEP key
   - D. Leaving your Bluetooth in discoverable mode
7. While the SSID provides some measure of authentication, why is it not very effective?
   - A. It is dictated by the manufacturer of the access point.
   - B. It is encrypted.
   - C. It is broadcast in every beacon frame.
   - D. SSID is not an authentication function.
8. 802.1X is a protocol for which aspect of Ethernet?
   - A. Authentication
   - B. Speed
   - C. Wireless
   - D. Cabling
9. What is the best way to avoid problems with Bluetooth?
   - A. Keep personal info off your phone.
   - B. Keep Bluetooth discoverability off.
   - C. Buy a new phone often.
   - D. Encryption.
10. Why is attacking wireless networks so popular?
    - A. There are more wireless networks than wired.
    - B. They all run Windows.
    - C. It's easy.
    - D. It's more difficult and more prestigious than other network attacks.

Essay Quiz

1. Produce a report on why sensitive information should not be sent over the Wireless Application Protocol.
2. When you want to start scanning for rogue wireless networks, your supervisor asks you to write a memo detailing the threats of rogue wireless access points. What information would you include in the memo?
3. Write a security policy for company-owned cell phones that use the Bluetooth protocol.
4. Write a memo recommending upgrading your organization's old 802.11b infrastructure to an 802.11ac- or ax-compliant network, and detail the security enhancements.

Lab Projects

• Lab Project 12.1

Set up a wireless scanner on a computer and then use it to find wireless access points. You will need the following:

- A laptop with Windows or Linux installed
- A compatible wireless 802.11 network adapter

Then do the following:

1. Pick an appropriate scanner software package.
2. Install and configure package.
3. Start the program and make sure it sees your wireless adapter.
4. Take the laptop on your normal commute (or drive around your neighborhood) with the software running.
5. Log any access points you detect. If a multi-AP environment is available, record the different APs and values for key identifiers.

• Lab Project 12.2

Attempt to scan the area for Bluetooth devices. You will need a cell phone with Bluetooth installed or a computer with a Bluetooth adapter. Then do the following:

1. If you're using a PC, download BlueScanner from SourceForge at https://sourceforge.net/projects/bluescanner/.
2. Take your phone or computer to a place with many people, such as a café.
3. Start the program and make sure it sees your Bluetooth adapter.
4. Attempt to scan for vulnerable Bluetooth devices.
5. If you're using your phone, tell it to scan for Bluetooth devices. Any devices that you find are running in "discoverable" mode and are potentially exploitable.

chapter 13

Intrusion Detection Systems and Network Security

Our adversaries are very adept at hiding attacks in normal traffic. The only true way to protect our networks is to have an intrusion detection system.

—Robert Jamison, Under Secretary of the National Protection and Programs Directorate at DHS

In this chapter, you will learn how to

- **Apply the appropriate network tools to facilitate network security**
- **Determine the appropriate use of tools to facilitate network security**
- **Apply host-based security applications**

An **intrusion detection system (IDS)** is a security system that detects inappropriate or malicious activity on a computer or network. Most organizations use their own approaches to network security, choosing the layers that make sense for them after they weigh the risks, potential for loss, costs, and manpower requirements.

The foundation for a layered network security approach usually starts with a well-secured system, regardless of the system's function (whether it's a user PC or a corporate e-mail server). A well-secured system uses up-to-date application and operating system patches, requires well-chosen passwords, runs the minimum number of services necessary, and restricts access to available services. On top of that foundation, you can add layers of protective measures such as antivirus products, firewalls, sniffers, and IDSs.

IDSs, which are to the network world what burglar alarms are to the physical world, are some of the more complicated and interesting types of network/data security devices. The main purpose of an IDS is to identify suspicious or malicious activity, note activity that deviates from normal behavior, catalog and classify the activity, and, if possible, respond to the activity.

History of Intrusion Detection Systems

Like much of the network technology we see today, IDSs grew from a need to solve specific problems. Like the Internet itself, the IDS concept came from U.S. Department of Defense–sponsored research. In the early 1970s, the U.S. government and military became increasingly aware of the need to protect the electronic networks that were becoming critical to daily operations. The U.S. government led the evolution of IDSs through work in the U.S. Air Force in the 1990s. In the mid-to-late 1990s, commercial devices began to be marketed, and the development shifted to the commercial sector.

IDS Overview

An IDS is somewhat like a burglar alarm. It watches the activity going on around it and tries to identify undesirable activity. IDSs are typically divided into two main categories, depending on how they monitor activity:

- **Host-based IDS (HIDS)** Examines activity on an individual system, such as a mail server, web server, or individual PC. It is concerned only with an individual system and usually has no visibility into the activity on the network or systems around it.
- **Network-based IDS (NIDS)** Examines activity on the network itself. It has visibility only into the traffic crossing the network link it is monitoring and typically has no idea of what is happening on individual systems.

> Know the differences between host-based and network-based IDSs. A host-based IDS runs on a specific system (server or workstation) and looks at all the activity on that host. A network-based IDS sniffs traffic from the network and sees only activity that occurs on the network.

Whether it is network or host based, an IDS typically consists of several specialized components working together, as illustrated in Figure 13.1. These components are often logical and software based rather than physical and will vary slightly from vendor to vendor and product to product. Typically, an IDS has the following logical components:

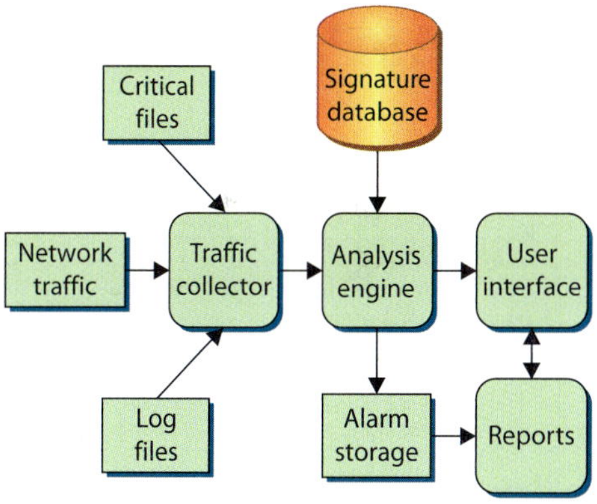

• **Figure 13.1** Logical depiction of IDS components

- **Traffic collector (or sensor)** Collects activity/events for the IDS to examine. On an HIDS, this could be log files, audit logs, or traffic coming to or leaving a specific system. On a NIDS, this is typically a mechanism for copying traffic off the network link—basically functioning as a sniffer. This component is often referred to as a *sensor.*
- **Analysis engine** Examines the collected network traffic and compares it to known patterns of suspicious or malicious activity stored in the signature database. The analysis engine is the "brains" of the IDS.
- **Signature database** A collection of patterns and definitions of known suspicious or malicious activity.
- **User interface and reporting** Interfaces with the human element, providing alerts when appropriate and giving the user a means to interact with and operate the IDS.

Tech Tip

IDS Signatures

An IDS relies heavily on its signature database, just like antivirus products rely on their virus definitions. If an attack is something completely new, an IDS might not recognize the traffic as malicious.

Most IDSs can be tuned to fit a particular environment. Certain signatures can be turned off, telling the IDS not to look for certain types of traffic. For example, if you are operating in a pure UNIX/Linux environment, you may not wish to see Windows-based alarms, as they will not affect your systems. Additionally, the severity of the alarm levels can be adjusted depending on how concerned you are over certain types of traffic. Some IDSs also allow the user to exclude certain patterns of activity from specific hosts. In other words, you can tell the IDS to ignore the fact that some systems generate traffic that looks like malicious activity, because it really isn't.

Let's look at an example to see how all these components work together. Imagine a network intruder is scanning your organization for systems running a web server. The intruder launches a series of network probes against every IP address in your organization. The traffic from the intruder comes into your network and passes through the traffic collector (sensor). The traffic collector forwards the traffic to the analysis engine. The analysis engine examines and categorizes the traffic—it identifies a large number of probes coming from the same outside IP address (the intruder). The analysis engine compares the observed behavior against the signature database and gets a match. The intruder's activity matches a TCP port scan. The intruder is sending probes to many different systems in a short period of time. The analysis engine generates an alarm that is passed off to the user interface and reporting mechanisms. The user interface generates a notification to the administrator (icon, log entry, and so on). The administrator sees the alert and can now decide what to do about the potentially malicious traffic. Alarm storage is simply a repository of alarms the IDS has recorded—most IDS products allow administrators to run customized reports that sift through the collected alarms for items the administrator is searching for, such as all the alarms generated by a specific IP address.

In addition to the network-versus-host distinction, some IDS vendors will further categorize an IDS based on how it performs the detection of suspicious or malicious traffic. The different models used are covered in the next section.

IDS Models

In addition to being divided along the host and network lines, IDSs are often classified according to the detection model they use: anomaly or misuse. For an IDS, a model is a method for examining behavior so that the IDS can determine whether that behavior is "not normal" or in violation of established policies.

Anomaly detection looks for things that are out of the ordinary, such as a user logging in when they're not supposed to or unusually high network traffic into and out of a workstation.

Anomaly detection identifies deviations from normal behavior.

An **anomaly detection model** is the more complicated of the two. In this model, the IDS must know what "normal" behavior on the host or network being protected really is. Once the "normal" behavior baseline is established, the IDS can then go to work identifying deviations from the norm, which are further scrutinized to determine whether or not that activity is malicious. Building the profile of normal activity is usually done by the IDS, with some input from security administrators, and can take days to months. The IDS must be flexible and capable enough to account for things such as new systems, new users, movement of information resources, and other factors, but be sensitive enough to detect a single user illegally switching from one account to another at 3 A.M. on a Saturday.

Anomaly detection was developed to make the system capable of dealing with variations in traffic and better able to determine which activity patterns are malicious. A perfectly functioning anomaly-based system would be able to ignore patterns from legitimate hosts and users but still identify those patterns as suspicious should they come from a potential attacker. Unfortunately, most anomaly-based systems suffer from extremely high false positives, especially during the "break-in" period while the IDS is learning the network. On the other hand, an anomaly-based system is not restricted to a specific signature set and is far more likely to identify a new exploit or attack tool that would go unnoticed by a traditional IDS.

A **misuse detection model** is a little simpler to implement, and therefore it's the more popular of the two models. In a misuse detection model, the IDS looks for suspicious activity or activity that violates specific policies and then reacts as it has been programmed to do. This reaction can be an alarm, e-mail, router reconfiguration, or TCP reset message. Technically, misuse detection is the more efficient model, as it takes fewer resources to operate, does not need to learn what "normal" behavior is, and will generate an alarm whenever a pattern is successfully matched. However, the misuse model's greatest weakness is its reliance on a predefined signature base—any activity, malicious or otherwise, that the misuse-based IDS does not have a signature for will go undetected. Despite that drawback and because it is easier and cheaper to implement, most commercial IDS products are based on the misuse detection model.

Misuse detection looks for things that violate policy, such as a denial-of-service attack launched at your web server or an attacker attempting to brute-force an SSH session.

Some analysts break down IDS models even further into four categories, depending on how the IDS operates and detects malicious traffic (the same models can also be applied to intrusion prevention systems as well—both NIPS and HIPS):

- **Behavior based** This model relies on a collected set of "normal behavior": what should happen on the network and is considered "normal" or "acceptable" traffic. Behavior that does not fit into the "normal" activity categories or patterns is considered suspicious or malicious. This model can potentially detect zero-day or unpublished attacks but carries a high false-positive rate, as any new traffic pattern can be labeled as "suspect."
- **Signature based** This model relies on a predefined set of patterns (called *signatures*). The IDS has to know what behavior is considered "bad" ahead of time before it can identify and act upon suspicious or malicious traffic. Signature-based systems work by matching signatures in the network traffic stream to defined patterns stored in the system. Signature-based systems can be very fast and precise, with low false-positive rates. The weakness of signature-based systems is that they rely on having accurate signature definitions beforehand, and as the number of signatures expand, this creates an issue in scalability.
- **Anomaly based** This model is essentially the same as the behavior-based model. The IDS is first taught what "normal" traffic looks like and then looks for deviations to those "normal" patterns. An anomaly is a deviation from an expected pattern or behavior. Specific anomalies can also be defined, such as Linux commands sent to Windows-based systems and implemented via an AI-based engine to expand the utility of specific definitions.
- **Heuristic** This model uses artificial intelligence to detect intrusions and malicious traffic. A heuristic model is typically implemented through algorithms that help an IDS decide whether or not a traffic pattern is malicious. For example, a URL containing 10 or more repeating instances of the same character may be considered "bad" traffic as a single signature. With a heuristic model, the IDS understands that if having 10 repeating characters is bad, then having 11 is still bad, and having 20 is even worse. This implementation of fuzzy logic allows this model to fall somewhere between the signature-based and behavior-based models.

> **Tech Tip**
>
> **Advanced IDS Rules**
>
> *IDS/IPS make use of an analytics engine that use rules to determine whether or not an event of interest has occurred. These rules may be simple signature-based rules, such as Snort rules, or more complex Bayesian rules associated with heuristic/behavioral systems or anomaly-based systems. Rules are the important part of the NIDS/NIPS capability equation—without an appropriate rule, the system will not detect the desired condition. One of the things that has to be updated when new threats are discovered is a rule to enable their detection.*

Signatures

As you have probably deduced from the discussion so far, one of the critical elements of any good IDS is the signature database—the set of patterns the IDS uses to determine whether or not activity is potentially hostile. Signatures can be very simple or remarkably complicated, depending on the activity they are trying to highlight. In general, signatures can be divided into two main groups, depending on what the signature is looking for: content-based signatures and context-based signatures.

Content-based signatures are generally the simplest. They are designed to examine the content of such things as network packets or log entries. Content-based signatures are typically easy to build and look for simple things, such as a certain string of characters or a certain flag set in a TCP packet. Here are some example content-based signatures:

- **Matching the characters "/etc/passwd" in a Telnet session** On a Linux system, the names of valid user accounts (and sometimes the passwords for those user accounts) are stored in a file called passwd located in the etc directory.
- **Matching the characters "to: decode" in the header of an e-mail message** On certain older versions of sendmail, sending an e-mail message to "decode" would cause the system to execute the contents of the e-mail.

Context-based signatures are generally more complicated, as they are designed to match large patterns of activity and examine how certain types of activity fit into the other activities going on around them. Context-based signatures generally address the question, How does this event compare to other events that have already happened or might happen in the near future? Context-based signatures are more difficult to analyze and take more resources to match, as the IDS must be able to "remember" past events to match certain context signatures. Here are some examples of context-based signatures:

- *Match a potential intruder scanning for open web servers on a specific network.* A potential intruder may use a port scanner to look for any systems accepting connections on port 80. To match this signature, the IDS must analyze all attempted connections to port 80 and then be able to determine which connection attempts are coming from the same source but are going to multiple, different destinations.
- *Identify a Nessus scan.* Nessus is an open source vulnerability scanner that allows security administrators (and potential attackers) to quickly examine systems for vulnerabilities. Depending on the tests chosen, Nessus typically performs the tests in a certain order, one after the other. To be able to determine the presence of a Nessus scan, the IDS must know which tests Nessus runs as well as the typical order in which the tests are run.
- *Identify a ping flood attack.* A single Internet Control Message Protocol (ICMP) packet on its own is generally regarded as harmless, certainly not worthy of an IDS signature. Yet thousands of ICMP packets coming to a single system in a short period of time can have a devastating effect on the receiving system. By flooding a

system with thousands of valid ICMP packets, an attacker can keep a target system so busy it doesn't have time to do anything else—a very effective denial-of-service attack. To identify a ping flood, the IDS must recognize each ICMP packet and keep track of how many ICMP packets different systems have received in the recent past.

To function, the IDS must have a decent signature base with examples of known, undesirable activity that it can use when analyzing traffic or events. Any time an IDS matches current events against a signature, the IDS could be considered successful, as it has correctly matched the current event against a known signature and reacted accordingly (usually with an alarm or alert of some type).

You should note the differences between content-based and context-based signatures. Content-based signatures match specific content, such as a certain string or series of characters (matching the string */etc/passwd* in an FTP session). Context-based signatures match a pattern of activity based on the other activity around it, such as a port scan.

False Positives and False Negatives

Viewed in its simplest form, an IDS is really just looking at activity (be it host based or network based) and matching it against a predefined set of patterns. When it matches activity to a specific pattern, the IDS cannot know the true intent behind that activity—whether it is benign or hostile—and therefore it can react only as it has been programmed to do. In most cases, this means generating an alert that must then be analyzed by a human who tries to determine the intent of the traffic from whatever information is available. When an IDS matches a pattern and generates an alarm for benign traffic, meaning the traffic was not hostile and not a threat, this is called a **false positive**. In other words, the IDS matched a pattern and raised an alarm when it didn't really need to do so. Keep in mind that the IDS can only match patterns and has no ability to determine intent behind the activity, so in some ways this is an unfair label. Technically, the IDS is functioning correctly by matching the pattern, but from a human standpoint this is not information the analyst needed to see, as it does not constitute a threat and does not require intervention.

An IDS is also limited by its signature set—it can match only activity for which it has stored patterns. Hostile activity that does not match an IDS signature and therefore goes undetected is called a **false negative**. In this case, the IDS is not generating any alarms, even though it should be, giving a false sense of security.

To reduce the generation of false positives, most administrators tune the IDS. "Tuning" an IDS is the process of configuring the IDS so that it works in your specific environment—generating alarms for malicious traffic and not generating alarms for traffic that is "normal" for your network. Effectively tuning an IDS can result in significant reductions in false-positive traffic.

Network-Based IDSs

Network-based IDSs (NIDSs) actually came along a few years after host-based systems. After running host-based systems for a while, many organizations grew tired of the time, energy, and expense involved with managing the first generation of these systems—the host-based systems were not centrally managed, there was no easy way to correlate alerts between systems, and false-positive rates were high. The desire for a "better way" grew along with the amount of interconnectivity between systems and, consequently, the amount of malicious activity coming across the networks themselves. This fueled development of a new breed of IDS designed to focus on the source for a great deal of the malicious traffic—the network itself.

Tech Tip

Network Visibility

A network IDS has to be able to see traffic to find the malicious traffic. Encrypted traffic such as SSH and HTTPS sessions must be decrypted before a network IDS can examine them.

• **Figure 13.2** Network perimeters are a little like castles—firewalls and NIDSs form the gates and guards to keep malicious traffic out.

The NIDS integrated very well into the concept of **perimeter security**. More and more companies began to operate their computer security like a castle or military base (see Figure 13.2), with attention and effort focused on securing and controlling the ways in and out—the idea being that if you could restrict and control access at the perimeter, you didn't have to worry as much about activity inside the organization. Even though the idea of a security perimeter is somewhat flawed (many security incidents originate inside the perimeter), it caught on very quickly, as it was easy to understand and devices such as firewalls, bastion hosts, and routers were available to define and secure that perimeter. The best way to secure the perimeter from outside attack is to reject all traffic from external entities, but this is impossible and impractical to do, so security personnel needed a way to let traffic in but still be able to determine whether or not the traffic was malicious. This is the problem that NIDS developers were trying to solve.

As its name suggests, a NIDS focuses on network traffic—the bits and bytes traveling along the cables and wires that interconnect the systems. A NIDS must examine the network traffic as it passes by and be able to analyze traffic according to protocol, type, amount, source, destination, content, traffic already seen, and other factors. This analysis must happen quickly, and the NIDS must be able to handle traffic at whatever speed the network operates to be effective.

NIDSs are typically deployed so that they can monitor traffic in and out of an organization's major links: connections to the Internet, remote offices, partners, and so on. Like host-based systems, NIDSs look for certain activities that typify hostile actions or misuse, such as the following:

- Denial-of-service attacks
- Port scans or sweeps
- Malicious content in the data payload of a packet or packets
- Vulnerability scanning
- Trojans, viruses, or worms
- Tunneling
- Brute force attacks

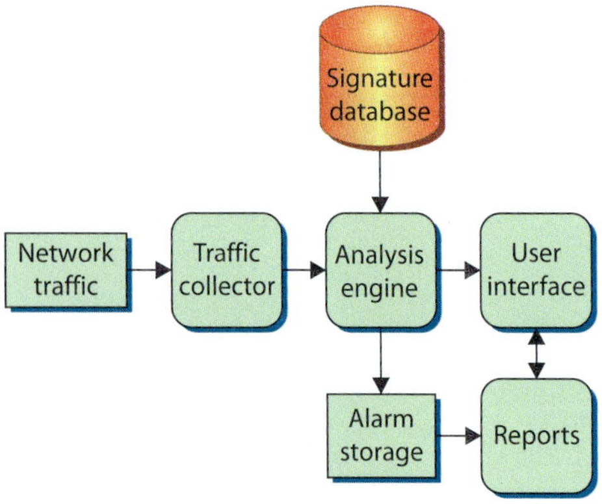

• **Figure 13.3** Network IDS components

In general, most NIDSs operate in a fairly similar fashion. Figure 13.3 shows the logical layout of a NIDS. By considering the function and activity of each component, you can gain some insight into how a NIDS operates.

In the simplest form, a NIDS has the same major components: traffic collector, analysis engine, reports, and a user interface.

In a NIDS, the **traffic collector** is specifically designed to pull traffic from the network. This component usually behaves in much the same way as a network traffic sniffer—it simply pulls every packet it can see off the network to which it is connected. In a NIDS, the traffic collector will logically attach itself to a network interface card (NIC) and instruct the NIC to accept every packet it can. A NIC that accepts and processes every packet, regardless of the packet's origin and destination, is said to be in *promiscuous mode.*

The **analysis engine** in a NIDS serves the same function as its host-based counterpart, with some substantial differences. The network analysis engine must be able to collect packets and examine them individually or, if necessary, reassemble them into an entire traffic session. The patterns and signatures being matched are far more complicated than host-based signatures, so the analysis engine must be able to remember what traffic preceded the traffic currently being analyzed so that it can determine whether or not that traffic fits into a larger pattern of malicious activity. Additionally, the network-based analysis engine must be able to keep up with the flow of traffic on the network, rebuilding network sessions and matching patterns in real time.

Tech Tip

Another Way to Look at NIDSs

In its simplest form, a NIDS is a lot like a motion detector and a video surveillance system rolled into one. The NIDS notes the undesirable activity, generates an alarm, and records what happens.

Cross Check

NIDS and Encrypted Traffic

You learned about encrypted traffic in Chapter 5, so check your memory with these questions. What is SSH? What is a one-time pad? Can you name at least three different algorithms?

The NIDS **signature database** is usually much larger than that of a host-based system. When examining network patterns, the NIDS must be able to recognize traffic targeted at many different applications and operating systems as well as traffic from a wide variety of threats (worms, assessment tools, attack tools, and so on). Some of the signatures themselves can be quite large, as the NIDS must look at network traffic occurring in a specific order over a period of time to match a particular malicious pattern.

Using the lessons learned from early host-based systems, NIDS developers modified the logical component design somewhat to distribute the user interface and reporting functions. Because many companies had more than one network link, they needed an IDS capable of handling multiple links in many different locations. The early IDS vendors solved this dilemma by dividing the components and assigning them to separate entities. The traffic collector, analysis engine, and signature database were bundled into a single entity, usually called a *sensor* or *appliance.* The sensors would report to and be controlled by a central system or master console. This central system, shown in Figure 13.4, consolidated alarms and provided the user interface and reporting functions that allowed users in one location to manage, maintain, and monitor sensors deployed in a variety of remote locations.

By creating separate components designed to work together, the NIDS developers were able to build a more capable and flexible system. With encrypted communications, network sensors could be placed around both local and remote perimeters and

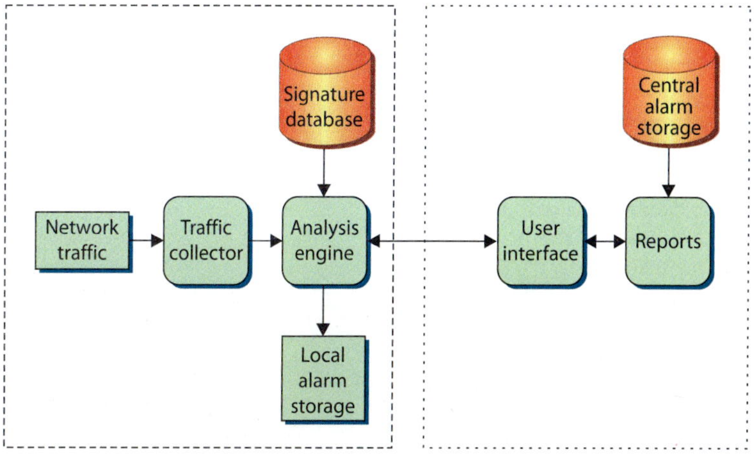

• **Figure 13.4** Distributed network IDS components

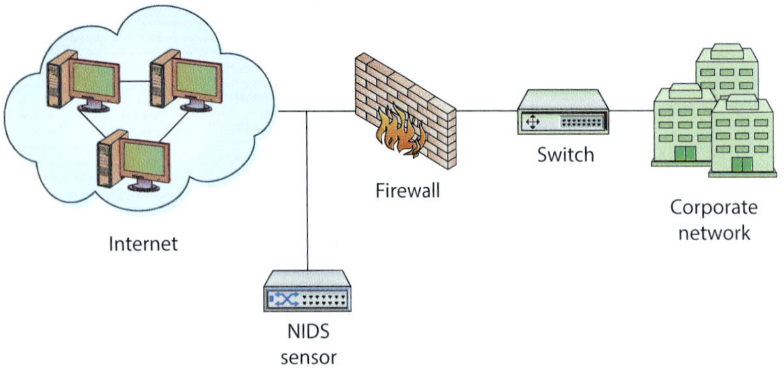

• **Figure 13.5** NIDS sensor placed in front of firewall

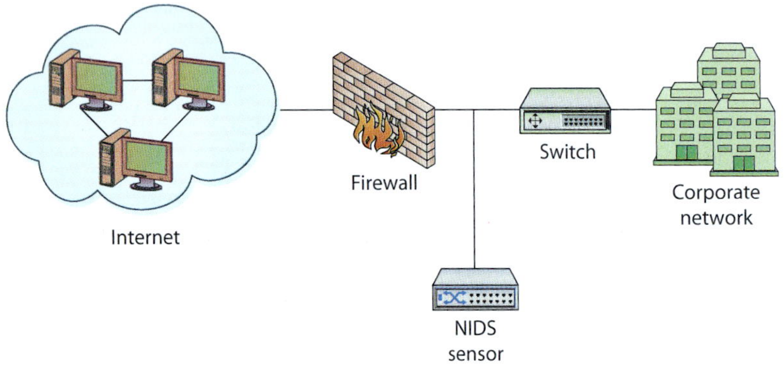

• **Figure 13.6** NIDS sensor placed behind firewall

still be monitored and managed securely from a central location. Placement of the sensors very quickly became an issue for most security personnel, as the sensors obviously had to have visibility of the network traffic in order to analyze it. Because most organizations with NIDSs also had firewalls, the location of the NIDS relative to the firewall had to be considered as well. Placed before the firewall, as shown in Figure 13.5, the NIDS will see all traffic coming in from the Internet, including attacks against the firewall itself. This includes traffic that the firewall stops and does not permit into the corporate network. With this type of deployment, the NIDS sensor will generate a large number of alarms (including alarms for traffic that the firewall would stop). This tends to overwhelm the human operators managing the system.

Placed after the firewall, as shown in Figure 13.6, the NIDS sensor sees and analyzes the traffic that is being passed through the firewall and into the corporate network. Although this does not allow the NIDS to see attacks against the firewall, it generally results in far fewer alarms and is the most popular placement for NIDS sensors.

As you already know, NIDSs examine the network traffic for suspicious or malicious activity. Here are two examples of suspicious traffic to illustrate the operation of a NIDS:

- **Port scan** A port scan is a reconnaissance activity a potential attacker uses to find out information about the systems they want to attack. Using any of a number of tools, the attacker attempts to connect to various services (web, FTP, SMTP, and so on) to see if they exist on the intended target. In normal network traffic, a single user might connect to the FTP service provided on a single system. During a port scan, an attacker may attempt to connect to the FTP service on every system. As the attacker's traffic passes by the IDS, the IDS will notice this pattern of attempting to connect to different services on different systems in a relatively short period of time. When the IDS compares the activity to its signature database, it will very likely match this traffic against the port scanning signature and generate an alarm.
- **Ping of death** Toward the end of 1996, it was discovered that certain operating systems, such as Windows, could be crashed by sending a very large Internet Control Message Protocol (ICMP) echo request packet to them. This is a fairly simple traffic pattern for a NIDS to identify, as it simply has to look for ICMP packets over a certain size.

Port scanning activity is rampant on the Internet. Most organizations with NIDSs see hundreds or thousands of port scan alarms every day from sources around the world. Some administrators reduce the alarm level of port scan alarms or ignore port scanning traffic because there is simply too much traffic to track down and respond to each alarm.

Advantages of a NIDS

A NIDS has certain advantages that make it a good choice for certain situations:

- *Providing IDS coverage requires fewer systems.* With a few well-placed NIDS sensors, you can monitor all the network traffic going in and out of your organization. Fewer sensors usually equates to less overhead and maintenance, meaning you can protect the same number of systems at a lower cost.
- *Deployment, maintenance, and upgrade costs are usually lower.* The fewer systems that have to be managed and maintained to provide IDS coverage, the lower the cost to operate the IDS. Upgrading and maintaining a few sensors is usually much cheaper than upgrading and maintaining hundreds of host-based processes.
- *A NIDS has visibility into all network traffic and can correlate attacks among multiple systems.* Well-placed NIDS sensors can see the "big picture" when it comes to network-based attacks. The network sensors can tell you whether attacks are widespread and unorganized or focused and concentrated on specific systems.

Disadvantages of a NIDS

A NIDS has certain disadvantages:

- *It is ineffective when traffic is encrypted.* When network traffic is encrypted from application to application or system to system, a NIDS sensor will not be able to examine that traffic. With the increasing popularity of encrypted traffic, this is becoming a bigger problem for effective IDS operations.
- *It can't see traffic that does not cross it.* The IDS sensor can examine only traffic crossing the network link it is monitoring. With most IDS sensors being placed on perimeter links, traffic traversing the internal network is never seen.
- *It must be able to handle high volumes of traffic.* As network speeds continue to increase, the network sensors must be able to keep pace and examine the traffic as quickly as it can pass the network. When NIDSs were introduced, 10Mbps networks were the norm. Now 100Mbps and even 1Gbps networks are commonplace. This increase in traffic speeds means IDS sensors must be faster and more powerful than ever before.
- *It doesn't know about activity on the hosts themselves.* NIDSs focus on network traffic. Activity that occurs on the hosts themselves will not be seen by a NIDS.

Active vs. Passive NIDSs

Most NIDSs can be distinguished by how they examine the traffic and whether or not they interact with that traffic. On a *passive* system, the NIDS simply watches the traffic, analyzes it, and generates alarms. It does not interact with the traffic itself in any way, and it does not modify the

Tech Tip

TCP Reset

The most common defensive ability for an active NIDS is to send a TCP reset message. Within TCP, the reset message (RST) essentially tells both sides of the connection to drop the session and stop communicating immediately. While this mechanism was originally developed to cover situations such as systems accidentally receiving communications intended for other systems, the reset message works fairly well for NIDSs, but with one serious drawback: a reset message affects only the current session. Nothing prevents the attacker from coming back and trying again and again. Despite the "temporariness" of this solution, sending a reset message is usually the only defensive measure implemented on NIDS deployments, as the fear of blocking legitimate traffic and disrupting business processes, even for a few moments, often outweighs the perceived benefit of discouraging potential intruders.

defensive posture of the system to react to the traffic. A passive NIDS is very similar to a simple motion sensor—it generates an alarm when it matches a pattern, much as the motion sensor generates an alarm when it sees movement. An *active* NIDS contains all the same components and capabilities of the passive NIDS with one critical addition—the active NIDS can *react* to the traffic it is analyzing. These reactions can range from something simple, such as sending a TCP reset message to interrupt a potential attack and disconnect a session, to something complex, such as dynamically modifying firewall rules to reject all traffic from specific source IP addresses for the next 24 hours.

NIDS Tools

There are numerous examples of NIDS tools in the marketplace, from open source projects to commercial entries. **Snort** has been the de facto standard IDS engine since its creation in 1998. It has a large user base and has set the standard for many IDS elements, including rulesets and formats. Snort rules are the list of activities that Snort will alert on and provide the flexible power behind the IDS platform. Snort rulesets are updated by a large, active community as well as by the Sourcefire Vulnerability Research Team, the company behind Snort. Snort VRT rulesets are available to subscribers and provide such elements as same-day protection for items such as Microsoft patch Tuesday vulnerabilities. These rules are moved to the open community after 30 days.

A newer entrant to the IDS marketplace is **Suricata**. Suricata is an open source IDS that began with grant money from the U.S. government and is maintained by the Open Source Security Foundation (OSIF). Suricata has one advantage over Snort: it supports multithreading, whereas Snort only supports single-threaded operation. Both of these systems are highly flexible and scalable, operating on both Windows and Linux platforms.

Tech Tip

Snort Rules

The basic format for Snort rules is a rule header followed by rule options, as shown here.

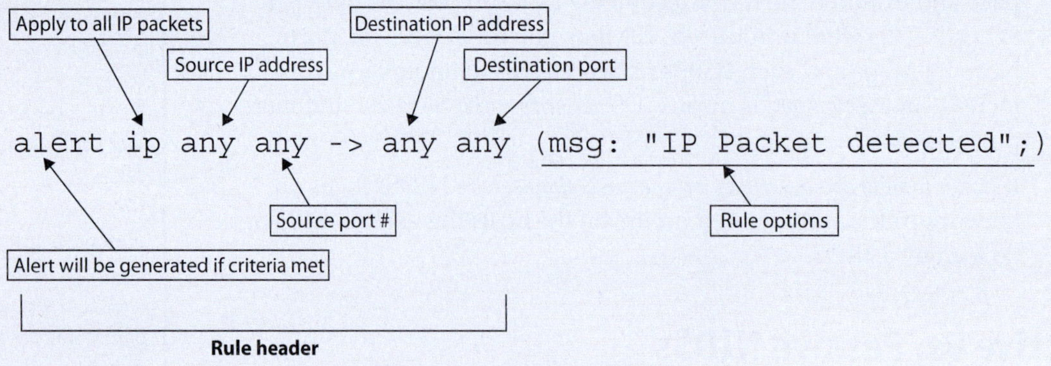


```
alert tcp $TELNET_SERVERS 23 -> $EXTERNAL_NET any (msg:"TELNET
  Attempted SU from wrong group" ; flow:
from_server,established; content:"to su root"; nocase;
  classtype:attempted-admin; sid:715; rev:6;)
```

Host-Based IDSs

The very first IDSs were host based, designed to examine activity only on a specific host. A **host-based IDS (HIDS)** examines log files, audit trails, and network traffic coming into or leaving a specific host. HIDSs can operate in *real time,* looking for activity as it occurs, or in *batch mode,* looking for activity on a periodic basis. Host-based systems are typically self-contained, but many of the newer commercial products have been designed to report to and be managed by a central system. Host-based systems also take local system resources to operate. In other words, an HIDS will use up some of the memory and CPU cycles of the system it is protecting. Early versions of HIDSs ran in batch mode, looking for suspicious activity on an hourly or daily basis, and typically looked only for specific events in the system's log files. As processor speeds increased, later versions of HIDSs looked through the log files in real time and even added the ability to examine the data traffic the host was generating and receiving.

Most HIDSs focus on the log files or audit trails generated by the local operating system. On UNIX systems, the examined logs usually include those created by syslog, such as messages, kernel logs, and error logs. On Windows systems, the examined logs are typically the three event logs: Application, System, and Security. Some HIDSs can cover specific applications, such as FTP or web services, by examining the logs produced by those specific applications or examining the traffic from the services themselves. Within the log files, the HIDS is looking for certain activities that typify hostile actions or misuse, such as the following:

- Logins at odd hours
- Login authentication failures
- Additions of new user accounts
- Modification or access of critical system files
- Modification or removal of binary files (executables)
- Starting or stopping processes
- Privilege escalation
- Use of certain programs

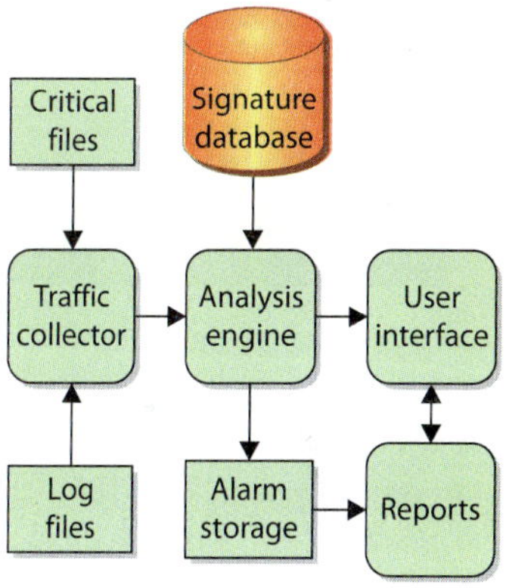

• **Figure 13.7** Host-based IDS components

In general, most HIDSs operate in a very similar fashion. (Figure 13.7 shows the logical layout of an HIDS.) By considering the function and activity of each component, you can gain some insight into how HIDSs operate.

As on any IDS, the *traffic collector* on an HIDS pulls in the information the other components, such as the analysis engine, need to examine. For most HIDSs, the traffic collector pulls data from information the local system has already generated, such as error messages, log files, and system files. The traffic collector is responsible for reading those files, selecting which items are of interest, and forwarding them to the analysis engine. On some HIDSs, the traffic collector also examines specific attributes of critical files, such as file size, date modified, and checksum.

The *analysis engine* is perhaps the most important component of the HIDS, as it must decide what activity is "okay" and what activity is "bad." The analysis engine is a sophisticated decision and pattern-matching

Critical files are those that are vital to the system's operation or overall functionality. They may be program (or binary) files, files containing user accounts and passwords, or even scripts to start or stop system processes. Any unexpected modifications to these files could mean the system has been compromised or modified by an attacker. By monitoring these files, the HIDS can warn users of potentially malicious activity.

mechanism—it looks at the information provided by the traffic collector and tries to match it against known patterns of activity stored in the signature database. If the activity matches a known pattern, the analysis engine can react, usually by issuing an alert or alarm. An analysis engine may also be capable of remembering how the activity it is looking at right now compares to traffic it has already seen or may see in the near future, so that it can match more complicated, multistep malicious activity patterns. An analysis engine must also be capable of examining traffic patterns as quickly as possible, because the longer it takes to match a malicious pattern, the less time the HIDS or human operator has to react to malicious traffic. Most HIDS vendors build a decision tree into their analysis engines to expedite pattern matching.

The *signature database* is a collection of predefined activity patterns that have already been identified and categorized—patterns that typically indicate suspicious or malicious activity. When the analysis engine has an activity or traffic pattern to examine, it compares that pattern to the appropriate signatures in the database. The signature database can contain anywhere from a few to a few thousand signatures, depending on the vendor, type of HIDS, space available on the system to store signatures, and other factors.

The user interface is the visible component of the HIDS—the part that humans interact with. The user interface varies widely, depending on the product and vendor, and could be anything from a detailed GUI to a simple command line. Regardless of the type and complexity, the interface is provided to allow the user to interact with the system: changing parameters, receiving alarms, tuning signatures and response patterns, and so on.

Tech Tip

Decision Trees

In computer systems, a tree *is a data structure, each element of which is attached to one or more structures directly beneath it (the connections are called* branches*). Structures on the end of a branch without any elements below them are called* leaves*. Trees are most often drawn inverted, with the root at the top and all subsequent elements branching down from the root. Trees in which each element has no more than two elements below it are called* binary trees*. In IDSs, a decision tree is used to help the analysis engine quickly examine traffic patterns and eliminate signatures that don't apply to the particular traffic or activity being examined, so that the fewest number of comparisons need to be made. For example, as shown in the illustration, the decision tree may contain a section that divides the activity into one of three subsections based on the origin of the activity (a log entry for an event taken from the system logs, a file change for a modification to a critical file, or a user action for something a user has done).*

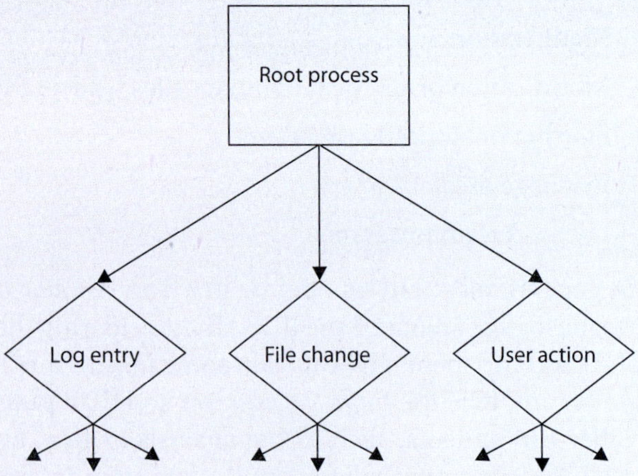

When the analysis engine looks at the activity pattern and starts down the decision tree, it must decide which path to follow. If it is a log entry, the analysis engine can then concentrate on only the signatures that apply to log entries, and it does not need to worry about signatures that apply to file changes or user actions. This type of decision tree allows the analysis engine to function much faster, as it does not have to compare activities to every signature in the database, just the signatures that apply to that particular type of activity. It is important to note that HIDSs can look at both activities occurring on the host itself and the network traffic coming into or leaving the host.

To better understand how an HIDS operates, take a look at the following examples from a UNIX system and a Windows system.

On a UNIX system, the HIDS is likely going to examine any of a number of system logs—basically, large text files containing entries about what is happening on the system. For this example, consider the following lines from the "messages" log on a Red Hat system:

```
Jan 5 18:20:39 jeep su(pam_unix)[32478]: session opened for
    user bob by (uid=0)
Jan 5 18:20:47 jeep su(pam_unix)[32516]: authentication
    failure; logname= uid=502 euid=0 tty= ruser=bob rhost=
    user=root
Jan 5 18:20:53 jeep su(pam_unix)[32517]: authentication
    failure; logname= id=502 euid=0 tty= ruser=bob
    rhost= user=root
Jan 5 18:21:06 jeep su(pam_unix)[32519]: authentication
   failure; logname= uid=502 euid=0 tty= ruser=bob
   rhost= user=root
```

In the first line beginning with "Jan 5," you see a session being opened by a user named *bob*. This usually indicates that whoever owns the account bob has logged in to the system. On the next three lines beginning with "Jan 5," you see authentication failures as bob tries to become *root*—the superuser account that can do anything on the system. In this case, user bob tries three times to become root and fails on each try. This pattern of activity could mean a number of different things—bob could be an admin who has forgotten the password for the root account, bob could be an admin and someone changed the root password without telling him, bob could be a user attempting to guess the root password, or an attacker could have compromised bob's account and is now trying to compromise the root account on the system. In any case, our HIDS will work through its decision tree to determine whether an authentication failure in the message log is something it needs to examine. In this instance, when the HIDS examines these lines in the log, it will note the fact that three of the lines in the log match one of the patterns it has been told to look for (as determined by information from the decision tree and the signature database), and it will react accordingly, usually by generating an alarm or alert of some type that appears on the user interface or in an e-mail, page, or other form of message.

On a Windows system, the HIDS will likely examine the logs generated by the operating system. The three basic types of logs (Application, System, and Security) are similar to the logs on a UNIX system, though the Windows logs are not stored as text files and typically require a utility or application to read them. This example uses the Security log from a Windows system:

```
Audit Failure 5/2/2020 6:47:29 PM Microsoft-Windows-
   Security-Auditing Logon 529
Audit Failure 5/2/2020 6:47:54 PM Microsoft-Windows-
   Security-Auditing Logon 542
Audit Failure 5/2/2020 6:48:22 PM Microsoft-Windows-
   Security-Auditing Logon 578
Audit Success 5/2/2020 6:49:14 PM Microsoft-Windows-
   Security-Auditing Logon 601
```

Tech Tip

Analyst-Driven Log Analysis

Log analysis is the art of translating computer-generated logs into meaningful data. For example, a computer can't always tell you if an administrator-level login at 3 A.M. on a Saturday is definitely a bad thing, but an analyst can. Human analysts can add value through the interpretation of information in context with other sources of information.

In the first three main lines of the Security log, you see an Audit Failure entry for the Logon process. This indicates someone has tried to log in to the system three times and has failed each time (much like our UNIX example), and then succeeded on the fourth try. You won't see the name of the account until you expand the log entry within the Windows Event Viewer tool, but for this example, assume it was the administrator account—the Windows equivalent of the root account. Here again, you see three login failures—if the HIDS has been programmed to look for failed login attempts, it will generate alerts when it examines these log entries.

Advantages of HIDSs

HIDSs have certain advantages that make them a good choice for certain situations:

- *They can be very specific to an operating system and have more detailed signatures.* An HIDS can be very specifically designed to run on a certain operating system or to protect certain applications. This narrow focus lets developers concentrate on the specific things that affect the particular environment they are trying to protect. With this type of focus, the developers can avoid generic alarms and develop much more specific, detailed signatures to identify malicious traffic more accurately.
- *They can reduce false-positive rates.* When running on a specific system, the HIDS process is much more likely to be able to determine whether or not the activity being examined is malicious. By more accurately identifying which activity is "bad," the HIDS will generate fewer false positives (alarms generated when the traffic matches a pattern but is not actually malicious).
- *They can examine data after it has been decrypted.* With security concerns constantly on the rise, many developers are starting to encrypt their network communications. When designed and implemented in the right manner, an HIDS will be able to examine traffic that is unreadable to a network-based IDS. This particular ability is becoming more important each day as more and more websites start to encrypt all of their traffic.
- *They can be very application specific.* On a host level, the IDS can be designed, modified, or tuned to work very well on specific applications without having to analyze or even hold signatures for other applications that are not running on that particular system. Signatures can be built for specific versions of web server software, FTP servers, mail servers, or any other application housed on that host.
- *They can determine whether or not an alarm may impact that specific system.* The ability to determine whether or not a particular activity or pattern will really affect the system being protected assists greatly in reducing the number of generated alarms. Because the HIDS resides on the system, it can verify things such as patch levels, presence of certain files, and system state when it analyzes traffic. By knowing what state the system is in, the HIDS can more accurately determine whether an activity is potentially harmful to the system.

Disadvantages of HIDSs

HIDSs also have certain disadvantages that must be weighed in making the decision of whether to deploy this type of technology:

- *The HIDS must have a process on every system you want to watch.* You must have an HIDS process or application installed on every host you want to watch. To watch 100 systems, then, you would need to deploy 100 HIDSs, or remote agents.
- *The HIDS can have a high cost of ownership and maintenance.* Depending on the specific vendor and application, an HIDS can be fairly costly in terms of time and manpower to maintain. Unless some type of central console is used that allows for the maintenance of remote processes, administrators must maintain each HIDS process individually. Even with a central console, with an HIDS, there will be a high number of processes to maintain, software to update, and parameters to tune.
- *The HIDS uses local system resources.* To function, the HIDS must use CPU cycles and memory from the system it is trying to protect. Whatever resources the HIDS uses are no longer available for the system to perform its other functions. This becomes extremely important on applications such as high-volume web servers, where fewer resources usually means fewer visitors served and the need for more systems to handle expected traffic.
- *The HIDS has a very focused view and cannot relate to activity around it.* The HIDS has a limited view of the world, as it can see activity only on the host it is protecting. It has little to no visibility into traffic around it on the network or events taking place on other hosts. Consequently, an HIDS can tell you only if the system it is running on is under attack.
- *The HIDS, if logging only locally, could be compromised or disabled.* When an HIDS generates alarms, it typically stores the alarm information in a file or database of some sort. If the HIDS stores its generated alarm traffic on the local system, an attacker who is successful in breaking into the system might be able to modify or delete those alarms. This makes it difficult for security personnel to discover the intruder and conduct any type of post-incident investigation. A capable intruder may even be able to turn off the HIDS process completely.

A security best practice is to store or make a copy of log information, especially security-related log information, on a separate system. When a system is compromised, the attacker typically hides their tracks by clearing out any log files on the compromised system. If the log files are only stored locally on the compromised system, you'll know an attacker was present (due to the empty log files) but you won't know what they did or when they did it.

Active vs. Passive HIDSs

Most IDSs can be distinguished by how they examine the activity around them and whether or not they interact with that activity. This is certainly true for HIDSs. On a *passive* system, the HIDS is exactly that—it simply watches the activity, analyzes it, and generates alarms. It does not interact with the activity itself in any way, and it does not modify the defensive posture of the system to react to the traffic. A passive HIDS is similar to a simple motion sensor—it generates an alarm when it matches a pattern, much as the motion sensor generates an alarm when it sees movement.

An *active* IDS will contain all the same components and capabilities of the passive IDS with one critical exception—the active IDS can *react* to the activity it is analyzing. These reactions can range from something simple, such as running a script to turn a process on or off, to something as complex as modifying file permissions, terminating the offending processes, logging off specific users, and reconfiguring local capabilities to prevent specific users from logging in for the next 12 hours.

Resurgence and Advancement of HIDSs

The past few years have seen a strong resurgence in the use of HIDSs. With the great advances in processor power, the introduction of multicore processors, and the increased capacity of hard drives and memory systems, some of the traditional barriers to running an HIDS have been overcome. Combine those advances in technology with the widespread adoption of always-on broadband connections, the rise in the use of telecommuting, and a greater overall awareness of the need for computer security, and HIDSs start to become an attractive and sometimes effective solution for business and home users alike.

Integrated security products can provide a great deal of security-related features in a single package. This is often cheaper and more convenient than purchasing a separate antivirus product, a firewall, and an IDS. However, integrated products are not without potential pitfalls—if one portion of the integrated product fails, the entire protective suite may fail. Symantec's Endpoint Protection and McAfee's Internet Security are examples of integrated, host-based protection products.

The latest generation of HIDSs has introduced new capabilities designed to stop attacks by preventing them from ever executing or accessing protected files in the first place, rather than relying on a specific signature set that only matches known attacks. The more advanced host-based offerings, which most vendors refer to as *host-based intrusion prevention systems (HIPSs)*, combine the following elements into a single package:

- **Integrated system firewall** The firewall component checks all network traffic passing into and out of the host. Users can set rules for what types of traffic they want to allow into or out of their system.
- **Behavioral- and signature-based IDS** This hybrid approach uses signatures to match well-known attacks and generic patterns for catching "zero-day" or unknown attacks for which no signatures exist.
- **Application control** This allows administrators to control how applications are used on the system and whether or not new applications can be installed. Controlling the addition, deletion, or modification of existing software can be a good way to control a system's baseline and prevent malware from being installed.
- **Enterprise management** Some host-based products are installed with an "agent" that allows them to be managed by and report back to a central server. This type of integrated remote management capability is essential in any large-scale deployment of host-based IDS/IPS.
- **Malware detection and prevention** Some HIDSs/HIPSs include scanning and prevention capabilities that address spyware, malware, rootkits, and other malicious software.

When you're examining endpoint security solutions, one of the key differentiators is in what the system detects. There are single-purpose systems, antivirus, anti-malware, and data loss prevention (DLP). Multipurpose systems such as EDR, firewalls, and HIDS/HIPS can look for a variety of types of items. The key to all this is in the definition of the rules for each product.

Intrusion Prevention Systems

An **intrusion prevention system (IPS)** monitors network traffic for malicious or unwanted behavior and can block, reject, or redirect that traffic in real time. Sound familiar? It should: while many vendors will argue that an

IPS is a different animal from an IDS, the truth is that most IPSs are merely expansions of existing IDS capabilities. As a core function, an IPS must be able to monitor for and detect potentially malicious network traffic, which is essentially the same function as an IDS. However, an IPS does not stop at merely monitoring traffic—it must be able to block, reject, or redirect that traffic in real time to be considered a true IPS. It must be able to stop or prevent malicious traffic from having an impact. To qualify as an IDS, a system just needs to see and classify the traffic as malicious. To qualify as an IPS, a system must be able to do something about that traffic. In reality, most products that are called IDSs, including the first commercially available IDS, NetRanger, can interact with and stop malicious traffic, so the distinction between the two is often blurred.

The term *intrusion prevention system* was originally coined by Andrew Plato in marketing literature developed for NetworkICE, a company that was purchased by ISS and is now part of IBM. The term *IPS* has effectively taken the place of the term *active IDS*.

Like IDSs, most IPSs have an internal signature database to compare network traffic against known "bad" traffic patterns. IPSs can perform content-based inspections, looking inside network packets for unique packets, data values, or patterns that match known malicious patterns. Some IPSs can perform protocol inspection, in which the IPS decodes traffic and analyzes it as it would appear to the server receiving it. For example, many IPSs can do HTTP protocol inspection, so they can examine incoming and outgoing HTTP traffic and process it as an HTTP server would. The advantage here is that the IPS can detect and defeat popular evasion techniques such as encoding URLs because the IPS "sees" the traffic in the same way the web server would when it receives and decodes it. The IPS can also detect activity that is abnormal or potentially malicious for that protocol, such as passing an extremely large value (over 10,000 characters) to a login field on a web page.

Unlike a traditional IDS, an IPS must sit inline (in the flow of traffic) to be able to interact effectively with the network traffic. Most IPSs can operate in "stealth mode" and do not require an IP address for the connections they are monitoring. When an IPS detects malicious traffic, it can drop the offending packets, reset incoming or established connections, generate alerts, quarantine traffic to/from specific IP addresses, or even block traffic from offending IP addresses on a temporary or permanent basis. As they are sitting inline, most IPSs can also offer *rate-based monitoring* to detect and mitigate denial-of-service attacks. With rate-based monitoring, the IPS can watch the amount of traffic traversing the network. If the IPS sees too much traffic coming into or going out from a specific system or set of systems, the IPS can intervene and throttle down the traffic to a lower and more acceptable level. Many IPSs perform this function by "learning" what are "normal" network traffic patterns with regard to the number of connections per second, amount of packets per connection, packets coming from or going to specific ports, and so on, and then comparing current traffic rates for network traffic (TCP, UDP, ARP, ICMP, and so on) to those established norms. When a traffic pattern reaches a threshold or varies dramatically from those norms, the IPS can react and intervene as needed.

Tech Tip

Inline Network Devices

Two methods can be employed: an inline sensor *and a* passive sensor*. An inline sensor is one where the data packets actually pass through the device. A failure of an inline sensor would block traffic flow. A passive sensor monitors the traffic via a copying process, so the actual traffic does not flow through or depend on the sensor for connectivity. Some administrators choose to have their firewalls and IPSs fail "closed," meaning that if the devices are not functioning correctly, all traffic is stopped until those devices can be repaired. Inline placement is also required for elements that are designed to interrupt traffic on occasion, such as IPS, where the* P *refers to an active element.*

Like a traditional IDS, the IPS has a potential weakness when dealing with encrypted traffic. Traffic that is encrypted will typically pass by the IPS untouched (provided it does not trigger any non-content-related alarms such as rate-based alarms). To counter this problem, some IPS vendors are including the ability to decrypt Secure Sockets Layer (SSL) sessions for further inspection. To do this, some IPS solutions store copies of any protected

The term *wire speed* refers to the theoretical maximum transmission rate of a cable or other medium and is based on a number of factors, including the properties of the cable itself and the connection protocol in use (in other words, how much data can be pushed through under ideal conditions).

Tech Tip

Detection Controls vs. Prevention Controls

When securing your organization, especially your network perimeter and critical systems, you will likely have to make some choices as to what type of protective measures and controls you need to implement. For example, you may need to decide between detection *controls (capabilities that detect and alert on suspicious or malicious activity) and* prevention *controls (capabilities that stop suspicious or malicious activity). Consider the differences between a traditional IDS and IPS. Although many IDSs have some type of response capability, their real purpose is to watch for activity and then alert when "hostile" activity is noted. On the other hand, an IPS is designed to block, thwart, and prevent that same "hostile" activity.*

Parallel examples in the physical security space would be a camera and a security guard. A camera watches activity and can even generate alerts when motion is detected, but a camera cannot stop an intruder from breaking into a facility and stealing something—it only records and alerts. A security guard, however, has the ability to stop the intruder physically, either before they break into the facility or before they can leave with the stolen goods.

web servers' private keys on the sensor itself. When the IPS sees a session initiation request, it monitors the initial transactions between the server and the client. By using the server's stored private keys, the IPS will be able to determine the session keys negotiated during the SSL session initiation. With the session keys, the IPS can decrypt all future packets passed between server and client during that web session. This gives the IPS the ability to perform content inspection on SSL-encrypted traffic.

You will often see IPSs (and IDSs) advertised and marketed by the amount of traffic they can process without dropping packets or interrupting the flow of network traffic. In reality, a network will never reach its hypothetical maximum transmission rate, or wire speed, due to errors, collisions, retransmissions, and other factors; therefore, a 1Gbps network is not actually capable of passing 1 Gbps of network traffic, even if all the components are rated to handle 1 Gbps. When used in a marketing sense, *wire speed* is the maximum throughput rate the networking or security device equipment can process without impacting that network traffic. For example, a 1Gbps IPS should be able to process, analyze, and protect 1 Gbps of network traffic without impacting traffic flow. IPS vendors often quote their products' capacity as the combined throughput possible for all available ports on the IPS sensor—for example, a 10Gbps sensor may have 12 Gigabit Ethernet ports but is capable of handling only 10 Gbps of network traffic.

Network Security Monitoring

Network security monitoring (NSM) is the collection, analysis, and escalation of indications and warnings to detect and respond to intrusions. Although an IDS will provide an indication of a rule being met or some other aspect, it typically provides a singular event. NSM is a process of collecting a bunch of different indications and then using these points of data and the context from which they are examined to come to a more complete understanding of what is happening.

An example of an IDS alert is when an FTP session is opened on a non-FTP server in the enterprise (assuming you had a rule watching for this). What are you as a security analyst going to do with this information? It is a single point-in-time indication of something that has happened, and it violates the rules, but what do you do? Using NSM, where you have the same indication of the FTP issue, also available (assuming you are capturing and logging the correct data elements) are additional data elements that can be examined. You could go look at the packet that created the alert and then, using this information, along with a tool such as Wireshark, reconstruct the conversation and see what the attacker did. Was this an intentional attack, or did the attacker actually just enter the wrong server IP address?

A Linux distribution specifically aimed at NSM is Security Onion, and it has a whole host of tools preconfigured. Whereas IDS is an important element in detecting bad activity on a system, NSM takes this considerably further, giving you tools and techniques that can provide greater insight into what is happening.

Deception and Disruption Technologies

Deception and disruption have become tools in the defender's arsenal against advanced threats. Because a threat actor has limited information about how a system is architected, the addition of deceptive elements such as honeypots/nets can lead to situations where the adversary is discovered. Once an adversary is discovered, a campaign can be waged against them, including the use of additional deception elements to disrupt the attacker's attack methodology. Deception adds a fake layer to your enterprise by placing decoy assets, fake data, and other artifacts in your enterprise. This fake technology is not part of your enterprise configurations, so no system or person should ever touch something fake unless they are actively seeking something or there is a misconfiguration.

Honeypots and Honeynets

As is often the case, one of the best tools for information security personnel has always been knowledge. To secure and defend a network and the information systems on that network properly, security personnel need to know what they are up against. What types of attacks are being used? What tools and techniques are popular at the moment? How effective is a certain technique? What sort of impact will this tool have on my network? Often this sort of information is passed through white papers, conferences, mailing lists, or even word of mouth. In some cases, the tool developers themselves provide much of the information in the interest of promoting better security for everyone.

Information is also gathered through examination and forensic analysis, often after a major incident has already occurred and information systems are already damaged. One of the most effective techniques for collecting this type of information is to observe activity firsthand—watching an attacker as they probe, navigate, and exploit their way through a network. To accomplish this without exposing critical information systems, security researchers often use something called a honeypot.

A **honeypot**, sometimes called a **digital sandbox**, is an artificial environment where attackers can be contained and observed without putting real systems at risk. A good honeypot appears to an attacker to be a real network consisting of application servers, user systems, network traffic, and so on, but in most cases it's actually made up of one or a few systems running specialized software to simulate the user and network traffic common to most targeted networks. Figure 13.8 illustrates a simple honeypot layout in which a single system is placed on the network to deliberately attract attention from potential attackers.

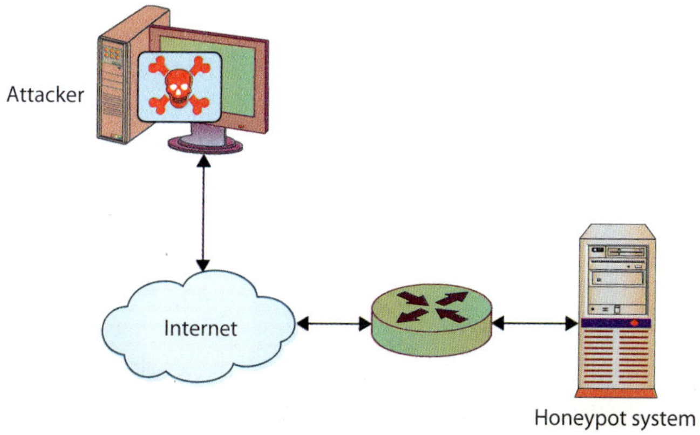

• **Figure 13.8** Logical depiction of a honeypot

Figure 13.8 shows the security researcher's view of the honeypot, while Figure 13.9 shows the attacker's view. The security administrator knows that the honeypot, in this case, actually consists of a single system

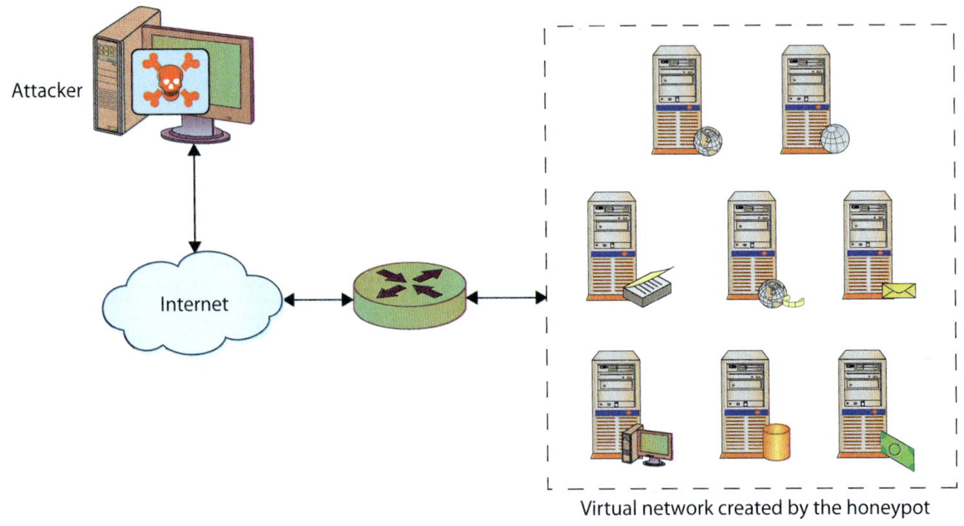

• **Figure 13.9** Virtual network created by the honeypot

running software designed to react to probes, reconnaissance attempts, and exploits as if it were an entire network of systems. When the attacker connects to the honeypot, they are presented with an entire "virtual" network of servers and PCs running a variety of applications. In most cases, the honeypot will appear to be running versions of applications that are known to be vulnerable to specific exploits. All this is designed to provide the attacker with an enticing, hopefully irresistible, target.

A *honeypot* is a system designed to attract potential attackers by pretending to be one or more systems with open network services.

Any time an attacker has been lured into probing or attacking the virtual network, the honeypot records the activity for later analysis: what the attacker does, which systems and applications they concentrate on, what tools are run, how long the attacker stays, and so on. All this information is collected and analyzed in the hopes that it will allow security personnel to better understand and protect against the threats to their systems.

There are many honeypots in use, specializing in everything from wireless to denial-of-service attacks; most are run by research, government, or law enforcement organizations. Why aren't more businesses running honeypots? Quite simply, the time and cost are prohibitive. Honeypots take a lot of time and effort to manage and maintain, and even more effort to sort, analyze, and classify the traffic the honeypot collects. Unless they are developing security tools, most companies focus their limited security efforts on preventing attacks, and in many cases, companies aren't even that concerned with detecting attacks as long as the attacks are blocked, are unsuccessful, and don't affect business operations. Even though honeypots can serve as a valuable resource by luring attackers away from production systems and allowing defenders to identify and thwart potential attackers before they cause any serious damage, the costs and efforts involved deter many companies from using honeypots.

A **honeynet** is a collection of two or more honeypots. Larger, very diverse network environments can deploy multiple honeypots (thus forming a honeynet) when a single honeypot device does not provide enough coverage. Honeynets are often integrated into an organization-wide IDS/IPS because the honeynet can provide relevant information about potential attackers.

Honeyfiles/Honeyrecords

A *honeyfile* is a file that is designed to look like a real file on a server, but the data it possesses is fake. Honeyfiles serve as attractive targets to attackers. A honeyfile acts as a trap for attackers, and the data in the file can contain triggers to alert DLP solutions. Access to the files can be monitored as well. A variation of a honeyfile is a honeyrecord in a database. These records serve the same purpose: they are fake and are never used, but if they are ever copied, you know there is unauthorized activity.

Honeyfiles and honeyrecords can be comingled with legitimate files and records, making their discovery and exploitation more likely. These elements act as tripwires and can be tracked to alert to unauthorized activity.

Fake Telemetry

When you are on a system and you realize there is no other traffic, the first thought is you are no longer in the enterprise network. To prevent a lack of "normal" traffic from being a dead giveaway that you have entered a fake part of the network, fake telemetry is used. *Fake telemetry* is synthetic network traffic that resembles genuine communications, delivered at an appropriate volume to make honeynets and honeypots look real.

> Fake telemetry is a deception technology used to make honeynets and honeypots look real and appealing to would-be attackers.

DNS Sinkhole

A *DNS sinkhole* is a DNS provider that returns specific DNS requests with false results. This results in the requester being sent to the wrong address, usually a nonroutable address. When a computer visits a DNS server to resolve a domain name, the server will give a result, if available; otherwise, it will send the resolution request to a higher-level DNS server for resolution. This means that the higher a DNS sinkhole is in this chain, the more requests it will affect and the more beneficial effect it can provide. A typical DNS sinkhole is a standard DNS server that has been configured to return nonroutable addresses for all domains in the sinkhole list so that every request will result in failure to get access to the real site. Some of the larger botnets have been rendered unusable by top-level domain (TLD) sinkholes that can span the entire Internet. DNS sinkholes are a useful tool for blocking malicious traffic, and they are used to combat bots and other malware that rely on DNS responses to communicate. A famous example of this was the use of a DNS sinkhole to block the WannaCry malware in 2017.

> A DNS sinkhole is a deception and disruption technology that returns specific DNS requests with false results. DNS sinkholes can be used in both destructive and constructive ways. When used in a constructive fashion, a DNS sinkhole prevents users from accessing malicious domains.

Analytics

Big data *analytics* is currently all the rage in the IT industry with claims of how much value can be derived from large data sets. NIDS/NIPS as well as other detection equipment can certainly create large data sets, especially when connected to other data sources such as log files in a SIEM solution. (SIEM is covered next in this chapter.) Using analytics to increase accurate detection of desired events requires planning, testing, and NIDS/NIPS/SIEM solutions that support this level of functionality. In the past, being able to write Snort rules was all that was needed to have a serious NIDS/NIPS solution. Today, it is essential to integrate the data from NIDS/NIPS together with other security data to detect advanced persistent threats (APTs). Analytics is essential today, and tomorrow it will be artificial intelligence (AI) determining how to examine packets.

SIEM

Security information and event management (SIEM) systems are a combination of hardware and software designed to classify and analyze security data from numerous sources. What was once considered to be only for the largest of enterprises, the large number of data sources associated with security have made SIEMs essential in almost all security organizations. There is a wide range of vendor offerings in this space, from virtually free to systems large enough to handle any enterprise, with a budget to match. During an investigation, the SIEM system can provide a host of information concerning a user, what they have done, and so on. The fundamental purpose of a SIEM system is to provide alerts and relevant information to incident response teams that are investigating incidents. If something happens that initiates an investigation, and the SIEM system has no relevant information, then this suggests that the SIEM and its component elements need better tuning to provide meaningful surveillance of the system for potential problems.

SIEMs allow you to identify, visualize, and monitor trends via alerts and a dashboard.

SIEM Dashboards

SIEM dashboards are the windows into the SIEM datastore, a collection of information that can tell you where attacks are occurring and provide a trail of breadcrumbs to show how the attacker got into the network and moved to where they are now. SIEM systems act as the information repository for information surrounding potential and actual intrusions.

Sensors

Sensors are the devices that provide security data into the security data store. Regardless of where that data store is housed, the security information is important for investigators. Sensors don't just happen; they have to be placed in the correct location to collect information. Sensor placement begins with defining collection objectives. A study of where the data flows, where the information of value is in a network, and where adversaries can gain access, coupled with what information you wish to collect, are just some of the factors that go into designing sensor placement. Just as logs can provide a lot of useful information, they also can produce a lot of meaningless data. Sensors are no different. Packet capture sensors can record vital information for an investigation, but they have to be in the correct location (that is, have visibility with respect to the desired packets) while also avoiding common traffic areas where there is a lot of noise. To be properly prepared for future investigations, you need to properly design and place your sensors.

Sensitivity

Sensitivity is the quality of being quick to detect or respond to slight changes, signals, or influences. As the purpose of a SIEM system is to alert operators to changes that indicate significant events, sensitivity to those events is important. The biggest problem with SIEMs and sensitivity is the tradeoff between false positives and false negatives. If you alert on too many possible conditions, you increase false positives and create operator fatigue. Wait for too much data, and you miss some, creating a false negative and an impression that the SIEM system doesn't work. Adjusting the sensitivity until you have the right balance is a tough but important task.

Trends

Trends are a series of data points that indicate a change over time. Trends can be increasing, decreasing, cyclical, or related to variability. What is important is that trends indicate some form of change. Not all forms of change are relevant to the SIEM system's mission, and a key element is in understanding which changes are and which aren't. Some changes are important in a direct fashion, such as failed logins. If the average number of failed logins is 20 per day, and suddenly you are getting 10,000 in an hour, that indicates something has changed. An attacker? A script with an error? It will take some investigation to find. What if those same failures were spread across four users, all system admins? Trends matter, but so does the information behind them. This makes alerting on multiple items with good comprehensive reports more useful than just an alert stating "this number is too high." Context matters.

Alerts

Alerts are the primary method of communication between the SIEM system and operators. When conditions meet the rule requirements, the SIEM system can send an alert. The more information that can be provided in the alert (other related information, the context of the event, and so on), the better the alert. The key isn't to tell a security engineer "something happened, go find out what it is," but rather to steer the engineer in the correct direction with supplemental information that the operator can interpret and then devise a plan to investigate effectively.

Correlation

Correlation is the process of establishing a relationship between two variables. However, as a wise scientist once stated, correlation is not causation, meaning that just because measurements trend together doesn't mean one causes the other. There is frequently another element at play, some variable not being measured. Think about a series of failed logins coming from an IP address that was also rejected at a firewall for scanning activity. Or how about some access control failures, and activity such as a successful login with a different username from same IP address in a short time period? Or a UDP packet with port 67 as the destination port, but the destination address is not one of your DHCP servers? Correlation is a means for a SIEM system to apply rules to combine data sources to fine-tune event detection.

SIEM event correlation logs are extremely useful because they can be used to identify malicious activity across a plethora of network devices and programs. This is data that otherwise may go unnoticed.

Correlation is the connection of events based on some common basis. Things can correlate based on time, based on common events, based on behaviors—the list can go on and on. Although correlation is not necessarily causation, it is still useful to look for patterns and then use these patterns to find future issues before they get to the end of their cycle. Correlation can identify things like suspicious IP addresses based on recent behavior. For instance, a correlation rule can identify port scanning, a behavior that in of itself is not hostile, but also not normal; hence, future activity from that IP would be considered suspect.

Aggregation

One of the key functions of a SIEM solution is the aggregation of security information sources. In this instance, *aggregation* refers to the collecting of information in a central place, in a common format, to facilitate analysis and decision making. The sources that can feed a SIEM solution are many, including system event logs, firewall logs, security application logs, and specific program feeds from security appliances. Having this material in a central location that facilitates easy exploration by a security analyst is very useful during incident response events.

Automated Alerting and Triggers

SIEMs have the ability through a set of rules and the use of analytical engines to identify specific predetermined patterns and either alert or react to them. *Automated alerting* can remove much of the time delays between specific activity and security operations reaction. Consider this like an IDS on steroids, because it can use external information in addition to current traffic information to provide a much richer pattern-matching environment. A *trigger* event, such as the previously mentioned scanning activity, or the generation of *access control list (ACL)* failures in log events, can result in a connection being highlighted on an analyst's workstation, or in some cases, an automated response.

Time Synchronization

Time synchronization is a common problem for computer systems. When multiple systems handle aspects of a particular transaction, having them all have a common time standard is essential if one is going to compare the logs from different systems. This problem becomes even more pronounced when an enterprise has geographically dispersed operations across multiple time zones. Most systems record things in local time, and when multiple time zones are involved, analysts need to be able to work two time readings synchronously: local time and UTC time. UTC is global time and does not have the issues of daylight saving settings, or even different time zones. UTC is in essence a global time zone. Local time is still important to compare events to local activities. SIEMs can handle both time readings simultaneously, using UTC for correlation across the entire enterprise, and local time for local process meaning.

Event Deduplication

In many cases, multiple records related to the same item can be generated. A firewall log may note an event, and the system log file on the system may also note the event. NetFlow data, because of how and where it is generated, is full of duplicate records for the same packet. Having multiple records in a database representing the same event is wasteful of space and processing, and it can skew analytics. To avoid these issues, using a special form of correlation, where records are determined to be duplicates of a specific event, the SIEM can delete all but a single record of an event from the multiple recordset. This *event deduplication* assists security analysts by reducing clutter in a data set that can obscure real events that have meaning. For this to happen, the events need a central store—something a SIEM solution provides.

Understanding how and when you would use a SIEM solution relates to the problems it can help solve. Understanding the need to aggregate information, correlate events, synchronize times, deduplicate records/events, and use all this for automated detection, alerting, and triggers is the key to understanding the value of a SIEM solution.

Logs/WORM

Log files exist across a wide array of sources and have a wide range of locations and details recorded. One of the valuable elements of a SIEM solution is the collection of these disparate data sources into a standardized data structure that can then be employed using database tools to create informative reports. Logs are written once into this SIEM data store, and then can be read many times by different rules and analytical engines for different decision support processes. This *write once read many (WORM)* times concept is commonly employed to achieve operational efficiencies, especially when working with large data sets, such as log files on large systems.

One of the most powerful use cases for SIEM solutions is in the identification of log and event anomalies. In the stream of log and event data, anomalies can be difficult to detect, but upon correlation with other information they can be found. This is the primary purpose of a SIEM solution.

DLP

Data loss prevention (DLP) refers to technology employed to detect and prevent transfers of data across an enterprise. Employed at key locations, DLP technology can scan packets for specific data patterns. This technology can be tuned to detect account numbers, secrets, specific markers, or files. When specific data elements are detected, the system can block the transfer. The primary challenge in employing DLP technologies is the placement of the sensor. The DLP sensor needs to be able observe the data, so if the channel is encrypted, DLP technology can be thwarted.

USB Blocking

USB devices offer a convenient method of connecting external storage to a system and an easy means of moving data between machines. They also provide a means by which data can be infiltrated from a network by an unauthorized party. There are numerous methods of performing *USB blocking*—from the extreme of physically disabling the ports, to software solutions that enable a wide range of controls. Most enterprise-level DLP solutions include a solution for USB devices. Typically this involves preventing the use of USB devices for transferring data to the device without specific authorization codes. This acts as a barrier, allowing USBs to bring data in, but not allow data out.

Cloud-Based DLP

As data moves to the cloud, so does the need for data loss prevention. However, performing *cloud-based* DLP is not as simple as moving the enterprise edge methodology to the cloud. There are several attributes of cloud systems that can result in issues for DLP deployments. Enterprises move data to the cloud for many reasons, but two primary ones are size (cloud data sets can be very large) and availability (cloud-based data can be highly available across the entire globe to multiple parties), and both of these are challenges for DLP solutions. The DLP industry has responded with cloud-based DLP solutions designed to manage these and other cloud-related issues while still affording the enterprise visibility and control over data transfers.

E-mail

E-mail is a common means of communication in the enterprise, and it is common to attach files to an e-mail to provide additional information. Transferring information out of the enterprise by e-mail is a concern for many organizations. Blocking e-mail attachments is not practical given their ubiquity in normal business, so a solution is needed to scan e-mails for unauthorized data transfers. This is a common chore for enterprise-class DLP solutions because they can connect to the mail server and use the same scanning technology used for other network connections.

Tools

Tools are a vital part of any security professional's skill set. You may not be an "assessment professional" who spends most of their career examining networks looking for vulnerabilities, but you can use many of the same tools for internal assessment activities, tracking down infected systems, spotting inappropriate behavior, and so on. Knowing the right tool for the job can be critical to performing effectively.

Protocol Analyzer

A **protocol analyzer** (also known as a *packet sniffer, network analyzer,* or *network sniffer*) is a piece of software or an integrated software/hardware system that can capture and decode network traffic. Protocol analyzers have been popular with system administrators and security professionals for decades because they are such versatile and useful tools for a network environment. From a security perspective, protocol analyzers can be used for a number of activities, such as the following:

- Detecting intrusions or undesirable traffic. (An IDS/IPS must have some type of capture and decode capabilities to be able to look for suspicious/malicious traffic.)
- Capturing traffic during incident response or incident handling.
- Looking for evidence of botnets, Trojans, and infected systems.
- Looking for unusual traffic or traffic exceeding certain thresholds.
- Testing encryption between systems or applications.

From a network administration perspective, protocol analyzers can be used for activities such as these:

- Analyzing network problems
- Detecting misconfigured applications or misbehaving applications
- Gathering and reporting network usage and traffic statistics
- Debugging client/server communications

A sniffer must use a NIC placed in promiscuous (promisc) mode; otherwise, it will not see all the network traffic coming into the NIC.

Regardless of the intended use, a protocol analyzer must be able to see network traffic in order to capture and decode it. A software-based protocol analyzer must be able to place the NIC it is going to use to monitor network traffic in *promiscuous mode* (sometimes called *promisc mode*). Promiscuous mode tells the NIC to process every network packet it sees regardless of the intended destination. Normally, a NIC processes only *broadcast* packets (which go to everyone on that subnet) and packets with the NIC's Media Access Control (MAC) address as the destination address inside the packet. As a sniffer, the analyzer must process every packet crossing the wire, so the ability to place a NIC into promiscuous mode is critical.

With older networking technologies, such as hubs, it was easier to operate a protocol analyzer because the hub broadcasted every packet across every interface, regardless of the destination. With switches now the standard for networking equipment, placing a protocol analyzer becomes more difficult because switches do not broadcast every packet across every port. Although this might make it harder for administrators to sniff the traffic, it also makes it harder for eavesdroppers and potential attackers.

Network Placement

To accommodate protocol analyzers, IDS devices, and IPS devices, most switch manufacturers support **port mirroring** or a Switched Port Analyzer (SPAN) port (discussed in the next section). Depending on the manufacturer and the hardware, a mirrored port will see all the traffic passing through the switch or through a specific virtual LAN (or multiple VLANs), or all the traffic passing through other specific switch ports. The network traffic is essentially copied (or mirrored) to a specific port, which can then support a protocol analyzer.

Another option for traffic capture is to use a **network tap**, a hardware device that can be placed inline on a network connection and that will copy traffic passing through the tap to a second set of interfaces on the tap. Network taps are often used to sniff traffic passing between devices at the network perimeter, such as the traffic passing between a router and a firewall. Many common network taps work by bridging a network connection and passing incoming traffic through one tap port (A) and outgoing traffic through another tap port (B), as shown in Figure 13.10.

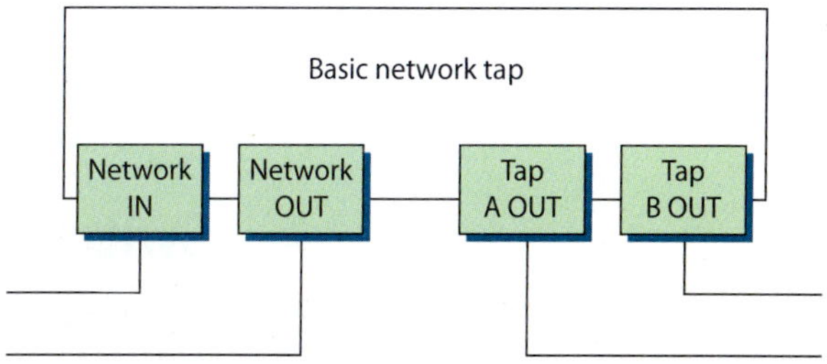

Figure 13.10 A basic network tap

A popular, open source protocol analyzer is Wireshark (www.wireshark.org). Available for both UNIX/Linux and Windows operating systems, Wireshark is a GUI-based protocol analyzer that allows users to capture and decode network traffic on any available network interface in the system on which the software is running (including wireless interfaces), as demonstrated in Figure 13.11. Wireshark has some interesting features, including the ability to "follow the TCP stream," which allows the user to select a single TCP packet and then see all the other packets involved in that TCP conversation.

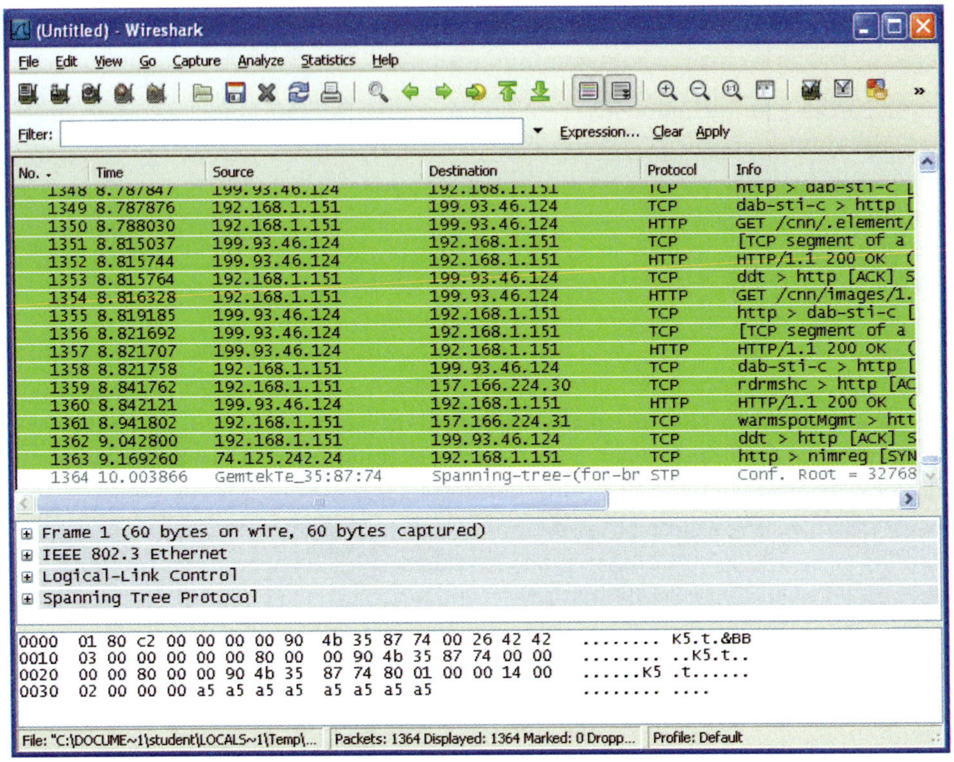

• **Figure 13.11** Wireshark—a popular, open source protocol analyzer

In-Band vs. Out-of-Band NIDS/NIPS

In-band versus out-of-band NIDS/NIPS is similar to the inline-versus-passive issue in an earlier section. An *in-band* NIDS/NIPS is an inline sensor coupled to a NIDS/NIPS that makes its decisions "in band" and enacts changes via the sensor. This has the advantage of high security, but it also has implications related to traffic levels and traffic complexity. In-band solutions work great for protecting network segments that have high-value systems and a limited number of traffic types—for instance, in front of a set of database servers with serious corporate data, where the only types of access would be via database connections.

An *out-of-band* system relies on a passive sensor, or set of passive sensors, and has the ability for greater flexibility in detection across a wider range of traffic types. The disadvantage is the delay in reacting to the positive findings as the traffic has already passed on to the end host.

Switched Port Analyzer

The term **Switched Port Analyzer (SPAN)** is usually associated with Cisco switches—other vendors refer to the same capability as *port mirroring* or *port monitoring*. A SPAN has the ability to copy network traffic passing through one or more ports on a switch or one or more VLANs on a switch and then forward that copied traffic to a port designated for traffic capture and analysis (as shown in Figure 13.12). A SPAN port or mirror port creates the collection point for traffic that will be fed into a protocol analyzer or IDS/IPS. SPAN or mirror ports can usually be configured to monitor traffic passing into interfaces, passing out of interfaces, or passing in both directions. When configuring port mirroring, you need to be aware of the capabilities of the switch you are working with. Can it handle the volume of traffic? Can it successfully mirror all the traffic, or will it end up dropping packets to the SPAN if traffic volume gets too high?

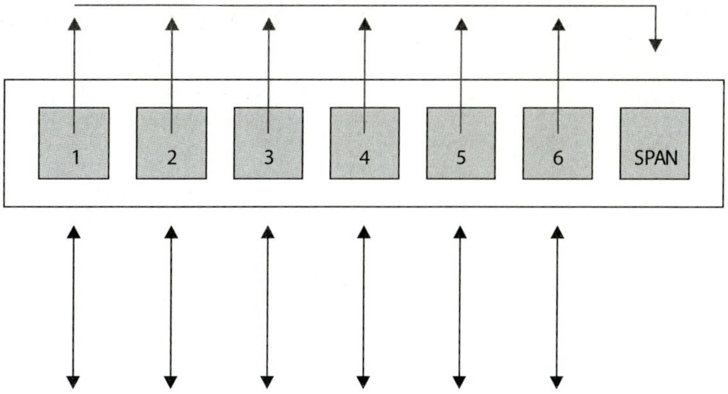

• **Figure 13.12** A SPAN port collects traffic from other ports on a switch.

Port Scanner

A *port scanner* is a tool designed to probe a system or systems for open ports. Its job is to probe for open (or listening) ports and report back to the user which ports are closed, which are filtered, and which are open. Port scanners are available for virtually every operating system and almost every popular mobile computing platform—from tablets to smartphones. Having a good port-scanning tool in your toolset and knowing how to use it can be very beneficial. The good news/bad news about port scanners is that the "bad guys" use them for basically the same reasons the good guys use them. Port scanners can be used to do the following:

- *Search for "live" hosts on a network.* Most port scanners enable you to perform a quick scan using ICMP, TCP, or UDP packets to search for active hosts on a given network or network segment. ICMP is still very popular for this task, but with the default blocking of ICMP v4 in many modern operating systems, such as Windows 10, users are increasingly turning to TCP or UDP scans for these tasks.
- *Search for any open ports on the network.* Port scanners are most often used to identify any open ports on a host, group of hosts, or network. By scanning a large number of ports over a large number of hosts, a port scanner can provide you (or an attacker) with a very good picture of what services are running on which hosts on your network. Scans can be done for the "default" set of popular ports, a large range of ports, or every possible port (from 1 to 65535).
- *Search for specific ports.* Only looking for web servers? Mail servers? Port scanners can also be configured to just look for specific services.
- *Identify services on ports.* Some port scanners can help identify the services running on open ports based on information returned by the service or the port/service assigned (if standards have been followed). For example, a service running on port 80 is likely to be a web server.
- *Look for TCP/UDP services.* Most port scanners can perform scans for both TCP and UDP services, although some tools do not allow you to scan for both protocols at the same time.

As a security professional, you'll use port scanners in much the same way an attacker would: to probe the systems in your network for open services. When you find open services, you'll need to determine if those services should be running at all, if they should be running on the system(s) you found them on, and if you can do anything to limit what connections are allowed to those services. For example, you may want to scan your network for any system accepting connections on TCP port 1433 (Microsoft SQL Server). If you find a system accepting connections on TCP port 1433 in your Sales group, chances are someone has installed something they shouldn't have (or someone installed something for them).

So how does a port scanner actually work? Much will depend on the options you select when configuring your scan, but for the sake of this example, assume you're running a standard TCP connect scan against 192.168.1.20 for ports 1–10000. The scanner will attempt to create a TCP connection to each port in the range 1–10000 on 192.168.1.20. When the scanner sends out that SYN packet, it waits for the responding SYN/ACK. If a SYN/ACK is received, the scanner will attempt to complete the three-way handshake and mark the port as "open." If the sent packet times out or an RST packet is received, the scanner will likely mark that port as "closed." If an "administratively prohibited" message or something similar comes back, the scanner may mark that port as "filtered." When the scan is complete, the scanner will present the results in a summary format—listing the ports that are open, closed, filtered, and so on. By examining the responses from each port, you can typically deduce a bit more information about the system(s) you are scanning, as detailed here:

- **Open** Open ports accept connections. If you can connect to these with a port scanner, the ports are not being filtered at the network level. However, there are instances where you may find a port that is marked as "open" by a port scanner that will immediately drop your connections if you attempt to connect to it in some other manner. For example, port 22 for SSH may appear "open" to a port scanner but will immediately drop your SSH connections. In such a case, the service is likely being filtered by a host-based firewall or a firewall capability within the service itself.
- **Closed** You will typically see this response when the scanned target returns an RST packet.
- **Filtered** You will typically see this response when an "ICMP unreachable" error is returned. This usually indicates that the port is being filtered by a firewall or other device.
- **Additional types** Some port scanners will attempt to further classify responses, such as dropped, blocked, denied, timeout, and so on. These are fairly tool specific, and you should refer to any documentation or help file that accompanies that port scanner for additional information.

In general, you will want to run your scanning efforts multiple times using different options to ensure you get a better picture. A SYN scan may return different results than a NULL scan or FIN scan. You'll want to run both TCP and UDP scans as well. You may need to alter your scanning approach to use multiple techniques at different times of the day/night to ensure complete coverage. The bad guys are doing this against your network right now, so you might as well use the same tools they do to see what they see. Port scanners can also be very useful for testing firewall configurations because the results of the port scans can show you exactly which ports are open, which ones you allow through, which ports are carrying services, and so on.

So how do you defend against port scans? Well, it's tough. Port scans are pretty much a part of the Internet traffic landscape now. Although you can block IP addresses that scan you, most organizations don't because they run the risk of an attacker spoofing source addresses as decoys for other scanning activity. The best defense is to carefully control what traffic you let in and out of your network, using firewalls, network filters, and host filters. Then carefully monitor any traffic that you do allow in.

Passive vs. Active Tools

Tools can be classified as active or passive. *Active tools* interact with a target system in a fashion where their use can be detected. Scanning a network with nmap (Network Mapper) is an active act that can be detected. In the case of nmap, the tool may not be specifically detectable, but its use, the sending of packets, can be detected. When you need to map out your network or look for open services on one or more hosts, a port scanner is probably the most efficient tool for the job. Figure 13.13 shows a screenshot of Zenmap, a cross-platform version of the very popular nmap port scanner available from https://insecure.org.

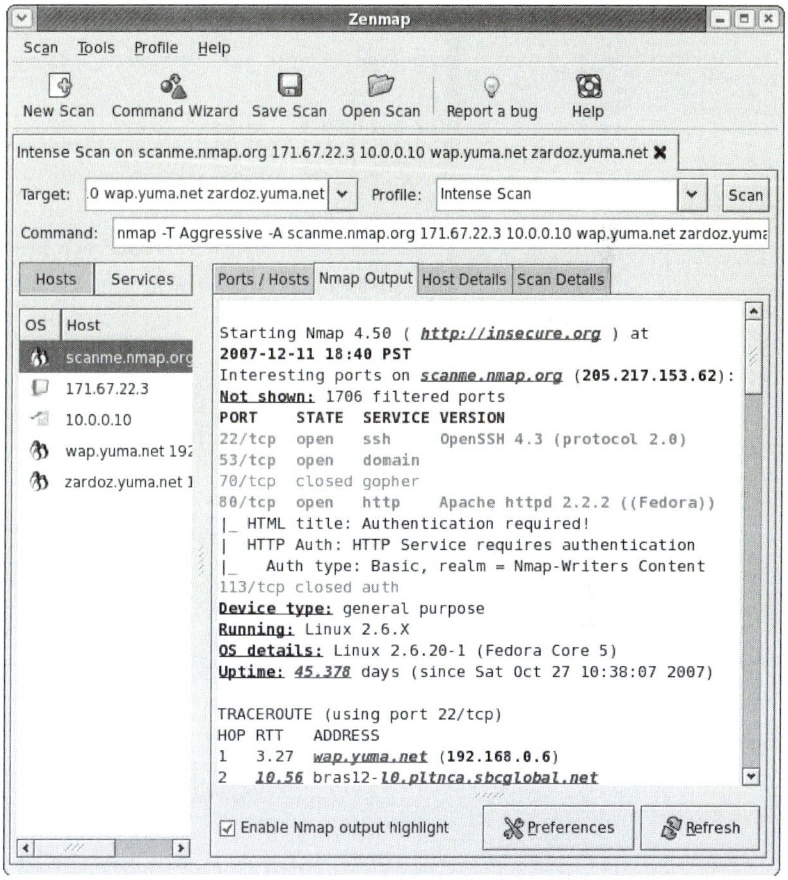

Figure 13.13 Zenmap—a port scanner based on nmap

Passive tools are those that do not interact with the system in a manner that would permit detection, as in sending packets or altering traffic. An example of a passive tool is Tripwire, which can detect changes to a file based on hash values. Another passive example is the OS mapping by analyzing TCP/IP traces with a tool such as Wireshark. Passive sensors can use existing traffic to provide data for analysis.

Passive tools receive traffic only and do nothing to the traffic flow that would permit others to know they are interacting with the network. Active tools modify or send traffic and are thus discoverable by their traffic patterns.

Banner Grabbing

Banner grabbing is a technique used to gather information from a service that publicizes information via a banner. Banners can be used for many things; for example, they can be used to identify services by type, version, and so forth, and they enable administrators to post information, including warnings, to users when they log in. Attackers can use banners to determine what services are running, and typically do for common banner-issuing services such as HTTP, FTP, SMTP, and Telnet. Figure 13.14 shows a couple of banner grabs being performed from a Telnet client against a web server. In this example, Telnet sends information to two different web servers and displays the responses (the banners). The top response is from an Apache instance (Apache/2.0.65) and the bottom is from Microsoft IIS (Microsoft-HTTPAPI/2.0).

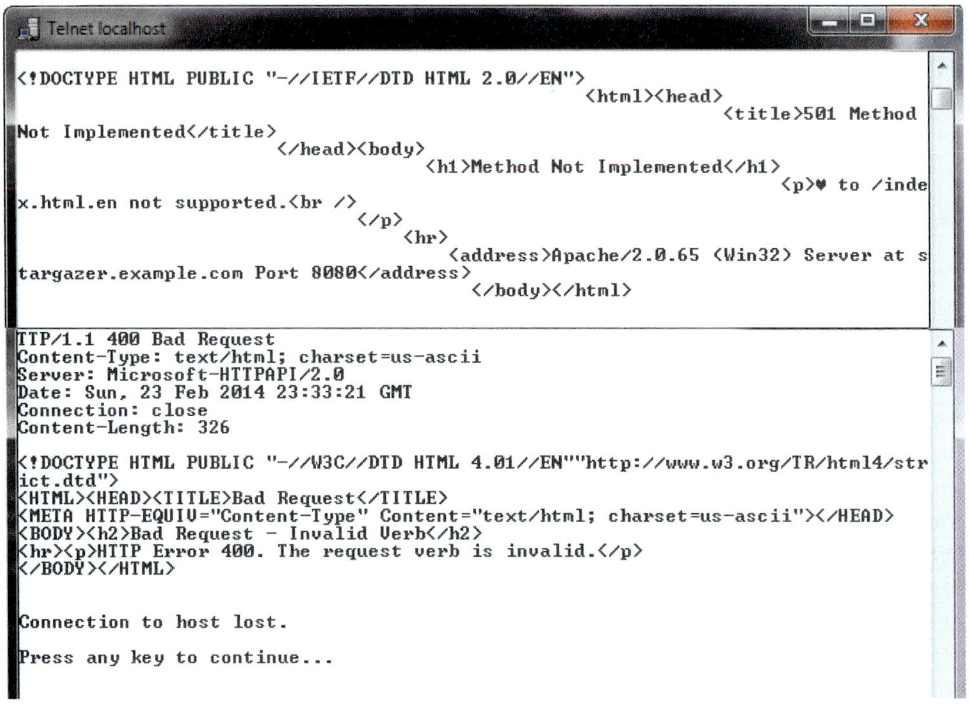

• **Figure 13.14** Banner grabbing using Telnet

Indicators of Compromise

Indicators of compromise (IOCs) are just that—indications that a system has been compromised by unauthorized activity. When a threat actor makes changes to a system—either by direct action, malware, or other exploit—forensic artifacts are left behind in the system. IOCs act as breadcrumbs for investigators, providing little clues that can help identify the presence of an attack on a system. The challenge is in looking for, collecting, and analyzing these bits of information and then determining what they mean for a given system. This is one of the primary tasks for an incident responder—gathering and processing these disparate pieces of data and creating a meaningful picture of the current state of a system.

Fortunately, there are toolsets to aid the investigator in this task. Tools such as Yara can take a set of signatures (also called IOCs) and then scan a system for them, determining whether or not a specific threshold is met, thus indicating a particular infection. Although the specific list will vary based on the system and the specific threat being looked for, here is a common set of IOCs that firms should monitor for:

- Unusual outbound network traffic
- Anomalies in privileged user account activity
- Geographical irregularities in network traffic
- Account log-in red flags
- Increases in database read volumes
- HTML response sizes
- Large numbers of requests for the same file
- Mismatched port-application traffic, including encrypted traffic on plain ports
- Suspicious registry or system file changes
- Unusual DNS requests
- Unexpected patching of systems
- Mobile device profile changes
- Bundles of data in the wrong place
- Web traffic with nonhuman behavior
- Signs of DDoS activity, even if temporary

No single compromise will hit all of these IOCs, but monitoring these items will tend to catch most compromises, because at some point in their lifecycle, the compromises will exhibit one or more of these behaviors. Then, once a compromise is detected, a responder can zero in on the information and fully document the nature and scope of the problem.

As with many other sophisticated systems, IOCs have developed their own internal languages, protocols, and tools. Two major, independent systems for communicating IOC information are available: the OpenIOC and the STIX/TAXII/CybOX system. OpenIOC was developed by Mandiant to facilitate information of IOC data, whereas MITRE, under contract with the U.S. government, developed STIX/TAXII/CybOX. MITRE designed Structured Threat Information Expression (STIX), Trusted Automated Exchange of Indicator Information (TAXII), and Cyber Observable Expression (CybOX) to specifically facilitate automated information sharing between organizations.

Advanced Malware Tools

Advanced malware tools include tools such as Yara, a command-line pattern matcher to look for indicators of compromise in a system. Yara assists security engineers in hunting down malware infections based on artifacts that the malware leaves behind in memory. Another advanced malware tool is a threat prevention platform that analyzes a system and its traffic in real time and alerts engineers to common malware artifacts such as callbacks to external devices.

For More Information

SANS Intrusion Detection FAQ www.sans.org/security-resources/IDFAQ/What-is-nmap.htm

SANS Reading Room—Firewalls & Perimeter Protection www.sans.org/reading_room/whitepapers/firewalls/

The Honeynet Project www.honeynet.org

Fight Spam on the Internet! www.consumer.ftc.gov/articles/0038-spam

Chapter 13 Review

Chapter Summary

After reading this chapter and completing the exercises, you should understand the following facts about intrusion detection systems and network security.

Apply the appropriate network tools to facilitate network security

- Intrusion detection is a mechanism for detecting unexpected or unauthorized activity on computer systems.
- IDSs can be "host based," examining only the activity applicable to a specific system, or "network based," examining network traffic for a large number of systems.
- Protocol analyzers, often called *sniffers,* are tools that capture and decode network traffic.
- Honeypots are specialized forms of intrusion detection that involve setting up simulated hosts and services for attackers to target.
- Honeypots are based on the concept of luring attackers away from legitimate systems by presenting more tempting or interesting systems that, in most cases, appear to be easy targets.

Determine the appropriate use of tools to facilitate network security

- IDSs match patterns known as *signatures* that can be content or context based. Some IDSs are model based and alert an administrator when activity does not match normal patterns (anomaly based) or when it matches known suspicious or malicious patterns (misuse detection).
- Newer versions of IDSs include prevention capabilities that automatically block suspicious or malicious traffic before it reaches its intended destination. Most vendors call these *intrusion prevention systems (IPSs).*
- Analyzers must be able to see and capture network traffic to be effective, and many switch vendors support network analysis through the use of mirroring or SPAN ports.
- Network traffic can also be viewed using a network tap, which is a device for replicating network traffic passing across a physical link.
- By monitoring activity within the honeypot, security personnel are better able to identify potential attackers, along with their tools and capabilities.

Apply host-based security applications

- Host-based IDSs can apply specific context-sensitive rules because of the known host role.
- Host-based IPSs can provide better control over specific attacks because the scope of control is limited to a host.

Key Terms

analysis engine *(481)*
anomaly detection model *(476)*
banner grabbing *(505)*
content-based signature *(478)*
context-based signature *(478)*
digital sandbox *(493)*
false negative *(479)*
false positive *(479)*
honeynet *(494)*
honeypot *(493)*
host-based IDS (HIDS) *(485)*
intrusion detection system (IDS) *(474)*
intrusion prevention system (IPS) *(490)*
misuse detection model *(477)*
network tap *(501)*
network-based IDs (NIDs) *(479)*
perimeter security *(480)*
port mirroring *(501)*
protocol analyzer *(500)*
signature database *(481)*
Snort *(484)*
Suricata *(484)*
Switched Port Analyzer (SPAN) *(502)*
traffic collector *(480)*

Key Terms Quiz

Use terms from the Key Terms list to complete the sentences that follow. Don't use the same term more than once. Not all terms will be used.

1. A(n) _______________ is a piece of software or an integrated software/hardware system that can capture and decode network traffic.
2. When an IDS generates an alarm on "normal" traffic that is actually not malicious or suspicious, that alarm is called a(n) _______________.
3. An attacker scanning a network full of inviting, seemingly vulnerable targets might actually be scanning a(n) _______________, where the attacker's every move can be watched and monitored by security administrators.
4. A(n) _______________ looks at a certain string of characters inside a TCP packet.
5. An IDS that looks for unusual or unexpected behavior is using a(n) _______________.
6. _______________ allows administrators to send all traffic passing through a network switch to a specific port on the switch.
7. Within an IDS, the _______________ examines the collected network traffic and compares it to known patterns of suspicious or malicious activity stored in the signature database.
8. _______________ is a technique whereby a host is queried and identified based on its response to a query.
9. _______________ is a technique for matching an element against a large set of patterns and using activity as a screening element.
10. _______________ is a new entry in the IDS toolset as a replacement for Snort.

Multiple-Choice Quiz

1. What are the two main types of intrusion detection systems?
   - **A.** Network based and host based
   - **B.** Signature based and event based
   - **C.** Active and reactive
   - **D.** Intelligent and passive
2. What are the two main types of IDS signatures?
   - **A.** Network based and file based
   - **B.** Context based and content based
   - **C.** Active and reactive
   - **D.** None of the above
3. Which of the following describes a passive, host-based IDS?
   - **A.** It runs on the local system.
   - **B.** It does not interact with the traffic around it.
   - **C.** It can look at system event and error logs.
   - **D.** All of the above.
4. Which of the following is *not* a capability of network-based IDS?
   - **A.** It can detect denial-of-service attacks.
   - **B.** It can decrypt and read encrypted traffic.
   - **C.** It can decode UDP and TCP packets.
   - **D.** It can be tuned to a particular network environment.
5. An active IDS can do which of the following?
   - **A.** Respond to attacks with TCP resets
   - **B.** Monitor for malicious activity
   - **C.** A and B
   - **D.** None of the above
6. What are honeypots used for?
   - **A.** To attract attackers by simulating systems with open network services
   - **B.** To monitor network usage by employees
   - **C.** To process alarms from other IDSs
   - **D.** To attract customers to e-commerce sites

7. Connecting to a server and sending a request over a known port in an attempt to identify the version of a service is an example of what?
   - **A.** Port sniffing
   - **B.** Protocol analysis
   - **C.** Banner grabbing
   - **D.** TCP reset
8. Preventative intrusion detection systems:
   - **A.** Are cheaper
   - **B.** Are designed to stop malicious activity from occurring
   - **C.** Can only monitor activity
   - **D.** Were the first type of IDS
9. IPS stands for which of the following?
   - **A.** Intrusion processing system
   - **B.** Intrusion prevention sensor
   - **C.** Intrusion prevention system
   - **D.** Interactive protection system
10. What is a protocol analyzer used for?
    - **A.** To troubleshoot network problems
    - **B.** To collect network traffic statistics
    - **C.** To monitor for suspicious traffic
    - **D.** All of the above

Essay Quiz

1. Discuss the differences between an anomaly-based and a misuse-based detection model. Which would you use to protect a corporate network of 10,000 users? Why would you choose that model?
2. Pick three technologies discussed in this chapter and describe how you would deploy them to protect a small business network. Describe the protection each technology provides.

Lab Projects

• Lab Project 13.1

Design three content-based signatures and three context-based signatures for use in an IDS. Name each signature and describe what the signature should look for, including traffic patterns or characters that need to be matched. Describe any activity that could generate a false positive for each signature.

• Lab Project 13.2

Use the Internet to research Snort (an open source IDS). With your instructor's permission, download Snort and install it on your classroom network. Examine the traffic and note any alarms that are generated. Research and note the sources of the alarm traffic. See if you can track down the sources of the alarm traffic and discover why these sources are generating those alarms on your IDS.

chapter 14

System Hardening and Baselines

People can have the Model T in any color—so long as it's black.

—Henry Ford

In this chapter, you will learn how to

- Harden operating systems and network operating systems
- Implement host-level security
- Harden applications
- Establish group policies
- Implement endpoint protections
- Secure alternative environments (SCADA, real-time, and others)

The many uses for systems and operating systems require flexible components that allow users to design, configure, and implement the systems they need. Yet it is this very flexibility that causes some of the biggest weaknesses in computer systems. Computer and operating system developers often build and deliver systems in "default" modes that do little to secure the systems from external attacks. From the view of the developer, this is the most efficient mode of delivery, as there is no way they can anticipate what every user in every situation will need. From the user's view, however, this means a good deal of effort must be put into protecting and securing the system before it is ever placed into service. The process of securing and preparing a system for the production environment is called **hardening**. Unfortunately, many users don't understand the steps necessary to secure their systems effectively, resulting in hundreds of compromised systems every day.

Hardening systems, servers, workstations, networks, and applications is a process of defining the required uses and needs and then aligning security controls to limit a system's desired functionality. Once this is determined, you have a system baseline that you can compare changes to over the course of a system's lifecycle.

Overview of Baselines

The process of establishing a system's operational state is called **baselining**, and the resulting product is a system **baseline** that describes the capabilities of a software system. Once the process has been completed for a particular hardware and software combination, any similar systems can be configured with the same baseline to achieve the same level of application. Uniform baselines are critical in large-scale operations, because maintaining separate configurations and security levels for hundreds or thousands of systems is far too costly.

Constructing a baseline or hardened system is similar for servers, workstations, and network operating systems (NOSs). The specifics may vary, but the objects are the same.

Hardware/Firmware Security

Hardware, in the form of servers, workstations, and even mobile devices, can represent a weakness or vulnerability in the security system associated with an enterprise. While hardware can be easily replaced if lost or stolen, the information that is contained by the devices complicates the security picture. Data or information can be safeguarded from loss by backups, but this does little in the way of protecting it from disclosure to an unauthorized party. There are software measures that can assist in the form of encryption, but these also have drawbacks in the form of scalability and key distribution.

> **Tech Tip**
>
> **Opal**
>
> *FDE and SED began as software-only proprietary solutions, but a hardware-based standard called Opal has been created. Developed by the Trusted Computing Group (TCG), Opal is used for applying hardware-based encryption to mass storage devices, hard drives (rotating media), solid state drives, and optical drives. Having a standard has the advantages of interoperability between vendors and can be OS independent. Having it in hardware improves performance and increases security. The encryption/decryption keys are stored in the hard drive controller and are never loaded into system memory, keeping them safe from attack.*

FDE/SED

Full drive encryption (FDE) and *self-encrypting drives (SED)* are methods of implementing cryptographic protection on hard drives and other similar storage media with the express purpose of protecting the data even if the drive is removed from the machine. Portable machines, such as laptops, have a physical security weakness in that they are relatively easy to steal and then can be attacked offline at the attacker's leisure. The use of modern cryptography, coupled with hardware protection of the keys, makes this vector of attack much more difficult. In essence, both of these methods offer a transparent, seamless manner of encrypting the entire hard drive using keys that are only available to someone who can properly log in to the machine.

TPM

The **Trusted Platform Module (TPM)** is a hardware solution on the motherboard, one that assists with key generation and storage as well as random number generation. When the encryption keys are stored in the TPM, they are not accessible via normal software channels and are physically separated from the hard drive or other encrypted data locations. This makes the TPM a more secure solution than storing the keys on the machine's normal storage.

Hardware Root of Trust

A *hardware root of trust* is the concept that if one has trust in a source's specific security functions, this layer can be used to promote security to higher layers of a system. Because roots of trust are inherently trusted, they must be secure by design. This is usually accomplished by keeping them small and limiting their functionality to a few specific tasks. Many roots of trust are implemented in hardware that is isolated from the OS and the rest of the system so that malware cannot tamper with the functions they provide. Examples of roots of trust include TPM chips in computers and Apple's Secure Enclave coprocessor in its iPhones and iPads. Apple also uses a signed Boot ROM mechanism for all software loading.

HSM

A **hardware security module (HSM)** is a device used to manage or store encryption keys. It can also assist in cryptographic operations such as encryption, hashing, and the application of digital signatures. HSMs are typically peripheral devices, connected via USB or a network connection. HSMs have tamper-protection mechanisms to prevent physical access to the secrets they guard. Because of their dedicated design, they can offer significant performance advantages over general-purpose computers when it comes to cryptographic operations. When an enterprise has significant levels of cryptographic operations, HSMs can provide throughput efficiencies.

> Storing private keys anywhere on a networked system is a recipe for loss. HSMs are designed to allow the use of a key without exposing it to the wide range of host-based threats.

UEFI BIOS

Basic Input/Output System (BIOS) is the firmware that a computer system uses as a connection between the actual hardware and the operating system. BIOS is typically stored on nonvolatile flash memory, which allows for updates, yet persists when the machine is powered off. The purpose behind BIOS is to initialize and test the interfaces to the actual hardware in a system. Once the system is running, the BIOS translates low-level access to the CPU, memory, and hardware devices, making a common interface for the OS to connect to. This facilitates multiple hardware manufacturers and differing configurations against a single OS install.

Unified Extensible Firmware Interface (UEFI) is the current replacement for BIOS. UEFI offers a significant modernization over the decades-old BIOS, including dealing with modern peripherals such as high-capacity storage and high-bandwidth communications. UEFI also has more security designed into it, including provisions for secure booting. One of the key characteristics of the UEFI BIOS as opposed to the legacy BIOS is that UEFI BIOS is designed to work with the hardware platform to ensure that the flash memory that holds the BIOS cannot be changed without the proper cryptographic credentials. This forms a **root of trust** in the contents of the flash memory, specifically in the UEFI BIOS. The key used to sign the BIOS is controlled by the equipment manufacturer, thus preventing unauthorized changes to the BIOS. The BIOS performs a countercheck on all updates prior to loading them, using a private key stored on the BIOS, ensuring all updates are properly signed by the manufacturer. These steps create the root of trust for the system.

Measured Boot

Measured boot is also a method of depending on the root of trust in starting a system, but rather than using signatures to verify subsequent components, a measured boot process hashes the subsequent processes and compares the hash values to known-good values. This has the advantage that it can be extended beyond items covered by the manufacturer, as the signatures come from the manufacturer and thus are limited to only specific items. The known-good hash values must be stored in a secure location, and the Trusted Platform Module (TPM) platform configuration registers (PCRs) comprise the secure location that is used.

Secure Boot and Attestation

One of the challenges in securing an OS is the myriad of drivers and other add-ons that hook into the OS and provide specific added functionality. If these additional programs are not properly vetted before installation, this pathway can provide a means by which malicious software can attack a machine. Also, because these attacks can occur at boot time, at a level below security applications such as antivirus software, they can be very difficult to detect and defeat. UEFI offers a solution to the problem of boot integrity, called **Secure Boot**, which is a mode that when enabled only allows signed drivers and OS loaders to be invoked. Secure Boot requires specific setup steps, but once enabled, it blocks malware that attempts to alter the boot process. Secure Boot enables the *attestation* that the drivers and OS loaders being used have not changed since they were approved for use. Secure Boot is supported by Microsoft Windows and all major versions of Linux.

> Attestation means verifying the authenticity of a platform or device based on a trusted record of evidence. Secure Boot, for example, ensures the system boots into a trusted configuration by having evidence of each step's authenticity verified.

Integrity Measurement

Integrity measurement is the measuring and identification of changes to a specific system away from an expected value. Whether it's the simple changing of data as measured by a hash value or the TPM-based integrity measurement of the system boot process and attestation of trust, the concept is the same: take a known value, store a hash or other keyed value, and then, at the time of concern, recalculate and compare values.

In the case of TPM-mediated systems, where the TPM chip provides a hardware-based root of trust anchor, the TPM system is specifically designed to calculate hashes of a system and store them in a platform configuration register (PRC). This register can be read later and compared to a known, or expected, value, and if they differ, there is a trust violation. Certain BIOSs, UEFIs, and bootloaders can all work with the TPM chip in this manner, providing a means of establishing a trust chain during system boot.

Firmware Version Control

Firmware is present in virtually every system, but in many embedded systems it plays an even more critical role because it may also contain the OS and application. Maintaining strict control measures over the changing of firmware is essential to ensuring the authenticity of the software on a system. **Firmware updates** require extreme quality measures to ensure that errors are not introduced as part of an update process. Updating firmware, although only occasionally necessary, is a very sensitive event, because failure can lead to system malfunction. If an unauthorized party is able to change the firmware of a system, as demonstrated in an attack against ATMs, an adversary can gain complete functional control over a system.

EMI/EMP

Electromagnetic interference (EMI) is an electrical disturbance that affects an electrical circuit. This is due to either electromagnetic induction or radiation emitted from an external source, either of which can induce currents into the small circuits that make up computer systems and cause logic upsets. An *electromagnetic pulse (EMP)* is a burst of current in an electronic device as a result of a current pulse from electromagnetic radiation. EMP can produce damaging current and voltage surges in today's sensitive electronics. The main sources for EMP would be industrial equipment on the same circuit, solar flares, and nuclear bursts high in the atmosphere.

It is important to shield computer systems from circuits with large industrial loads, such as motors. These power sources can have significant noise, including EMI and EMPs that will potentially damage computer equipment. Another source of EMI is fluorescent lights. Be sure any cabling that goes near fluorescent light fixtures is well shielded and grounded.

Supply Chain

Hardware and firmware security is ultimately dependent on the manufacturer for the root of trust. In today's world of global manufacturing with global outsourcing, fully understanding who your manufacturer *supply chain* is and how it changes from device to device, and even between lots, is difficult because many details can be unknown. Who manufactured all the components of the device you are ordering? If you're buying a new PC, where did the hard drive come from? Can the new PC come preloaded with malware? Yes, it has happened.

Supply chain for assembled equipment can be very tricky, because not only do you have to worry about where you get the computer, but also where they get the parts and the software, including who wrote the software and with what libraries. These can be very difficult issues to negotiate if you have very strict rules concerning country of origin.

Operating System and Network Operating System Hardening

The **operating system (OS)** of a computer is the basic software that handles things such as input, output, display, memory management, and all the other highly detailed tasks required to support the user environment and associated applications. Most users are familiar with the Microsoft family of desktop operating systems: Windows 7, Windows 8, and Windows 10.

Indeed, the vast majority of home and business PCs run some version of a Microsoft operating system. Other users may be familiar with macOS, Solaris, or one of the many varieties of the UNIX/Linux operating system.

A **network operating system (NOS)** is an operating system that includes additional functions and capabilities to assist in connecting computers and devices, such as printers, to a local area network (LAN). For most modern operating systems, including Windows Server, Solaris, and Linux, the terms *operating system* and *network operating system* are used interchangeably because they perform all the basic functions and provide enhanced capabilities for connecting to LANs. Network operating system can also apply to the operational software that controls managed switches and routers, such as Cisco's IOS and Juniper's Junos.

> **Tech Tip**
>
> **The Term Operating System**
>
> Operating system *is the commonly accepted term for the software that provides the interface between computer hardware and the user. It is responsible for the management, coordination, and sharing of limited computer resources such as memory and disk space.*

Protection Rings

Protection rings were devised in the Multics operating system in the 1960s to deal with security issues associated with time-sharing operations. Protection rings can be enforced by hardware, software, or a combination of the two, and they serve to act as a means of managing privilege in a hierarchical manner. Ring 0 is the level with the highest privilege and is the element that acts directly with the physical hardware (CPU and memory). Higher levels, with less privilege, must interact through adjoining rings through specific gates in a predefined manner. Use of rings separates elements such as applications from directly interfacing with the hardware without going through the OS and, specifically, the security kernel, as shown here.

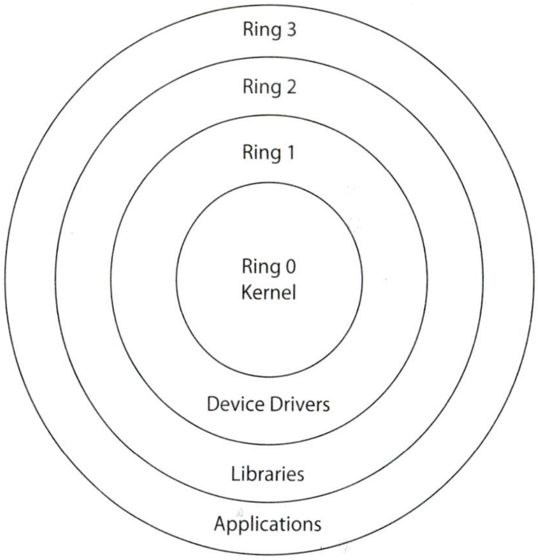

OS Security

The operating system itself is the foundation of system security. The operating system does this through the use of a security kernel. The **security kernel** is also called a **reference monitor** and is the component of the operating system that enforces the security policies of the operating system. The core of the OS is constructed so that all operations must pass through and be moderated by the security kernel, placing it in complete control over the enforcement of rules. Security kernels must exhibit some properties to be relied upon: they must offer complete mediation, as just discussed, and must be tamperproof and verifiable in operation. Because they are part of the OS and are in fact a piece of software, ensuring that security kernels are tamperproof and verifiable is a legitimate concern. Achieving assurance with respect to these attributes is a technical matter that is rooted in the actual construction of the OS and technically beyond the level of this book.

> **Tech Tip**
>
> **Data Execution Prevention**
>
> *Data Execution Prevention (DEP) is a collection of hardware and software technologies to limit the ability of malware to execute in a system. Windows uses DEP to prevent code execution from data pages.*

OS Types

Many different systems have the need for an operating system. Hardware in networks requires an operating system to perform the networking function. Servers and workstations require an OS to act as the interface between applications and the hardware. Specialized systems such as kiosks and appliances, both of which are forms of automated single-purpose systems, require an OS between the application software and hardware.

Network

Network components use a *network* operating system to provide the actual configuration and computation portion of networking. There are many vendors of networking equipment, and each has its own proprietary operating system. Cisco has the largest footprint with its IOS (for Internetworking Operating System). Juniper has Junos, which is built off of a stripped Linux core. As networking moves to software-defined networking (SDN), the concept of a network operating system will become more important and mainstream because it will become a major part of day-to-day operations in the IT enterprise.

Server

Servers require an operating system to bridge the gap between the server hardware and the applications that are being run. Currently, server OSs include Microsoft Windows Server, many flavors of Linux, and more and more VM/hypervisor environments. For performance reasons, Linux has a significant market share in the realm of server OSs, although Windows Server with its Active Directory technology has made significant inroads into market share.

Workstation

The OS on a *workstation* exists to provide a functional working space for a user to interact with the system and its various applications. Because of the high level of user interaction on workstations, it is very common to see Windows in this role. In large enterprises, the ability of Active Directory to manage users, configurations, and settings easily across the entire enterprise has given Windows client workstations an advantage over Linux.

Appliance

Appliances are standalone devices, wired into the network and designed to run an application to perform a specific function on traffic. These systems operate as headless servers, preconfigured with applications that run and perform a wide range of security services on the network traffic they see. For reasons of economics, portability, and functionality, the vast majority of appliances are built on top of a Linux-based system. As these are often customized distributions, keeping them patched becomes a vendor problem because this sort of work is outside the scope or ability of most IT people to properly manage.

Kiosk

Kiosks are standalone machines that typically operate a browser instance on top of a Windows OS. These machines are usually set up to automatically log in to a browser instance that is locked to a website that allows all of the functionality desired. Kiosks are commonly used for interactive customer service applications, such as interactive information sites, menus, and so on. The OS on a kiosk needs to be able to be locked down to minimal function, have elements such as automatic login, and offer an easy way to construct the applications.

Mobile OS

Mobile devices began as phones with limited additional capabilities, but as the Internet and functionality spread to mobile devices, the capabilities of these devices have expanded as well. From smartphones to tablets to wearables, today's mobile system is a computer, with virtually all the compute capability one could ask for—with a phone attached. The two main mobile OSs in the market today are Apple's iOS and Google's Android system.

Trusted Operating System

A **trusted operating system** is one that is designed to allow multilevel security in its operation. This is further defined by its ability to meet a series of criteria required by the U.S. government. Trusted OSs are expensive to create and maintain because any change must typically undergo a recertification process. The most common criteria used to define a trusted OS is the Common Criteria for Information Technology Security Evaluation (abbreviated as Common Criteria, or CC), a harmonized set of security criteria recognized by many nations, including the United States, Canada, Great Britain, most of the EU countries, as well as others. Versions of Windows, Linux, mainframe OSs, and specialty OSs have been qualified to various Common Criteria levels.

The term *trusted operating system* is used to refer to a system that has met a set of criteria and demonstrated correctness to meet requirements of multilevel security. The Common Criteria is one example of a standard used by government bodies to determine compliance to a level of security need.

Patch Management

Patch management is the process used to maintain systems in an up-to-date fashion, including all required patches. Every OS, from Linux to Windows, requires software updates, and each OS has different methods of assisting users in keeping their systems up to date.

In Windows 10 forward, Microsoft has adopted a newer methodology treating the OS as a service and has dramatically updated its servicing model. Windows 10 now has a twice-per-year feature update release schedule, aiming for March and September, with an 18-month servicing timeline for each release. Each of these releases will be serviced for 10 years from the date of release. Microsoft regularly issues patches for its Windows and Office products on a monthly schedule, which has become known as "Patch Tuesday." Patch Tuesday occurs on the second Tuesday of each month. Windows 10 checks for updates about once per day. The typical Windows PC will automatically download these updates via Windows Update by Wednesday afternoon if it's powered on and connected to the Internet. Administrators may choose to delay and test these updates before deploying them to PCs in their organizations.

For critical issues that are currently being exploited, Microsoft will issue out-of-band patches. When these are released, it is best practice to immediately update, as the flaws are being exploited actively by attackers.

For Microsoft cloud-based products like the Office 365 suite, patches are seamless and issued against the cloud-based product and are integrated by users typically upon next use.

How you patch a Linux system depends a great deal on the specific version in use and the patch being applied. In some cases, a patch will consist of a series of manual steps requiring the administrator to replace files, change permissions, and alter directories. In other cases, the patches are executable scripts or utilities that perform the patch actions automatically. Some Linux versions, such as Red Hat, have built-in utilities that handle the patching process. In those cases, the administrator downloads a specifically formatted file that the patching utility then processes to perform any modifications or updates that need to be made.

Regardless of the method you use to update the OS, it is critically important to keep systems up to date. New security advisories come out every day, and while a buffer overflow may be a "potential" problem today, it will almost certainly become a "definite" problem in the near future. Much like the steps taken to baseline and initially secure an OS, keeping every system patched and up to date is critical to protecting the system and the information it contains.

Vendors typically follow a hierarchy for software updates:

- **Hotfix** This term refers to a (usually) small software update designed to address a specific problem, such as a buffer overflow in an application that exposes the system to attacks. Hotfixes are typically developed in reaction to a discovered problem and are produced and released rather quickly.
- **Patch** This term refers to a more formal, larger software update that can address several or many software problems. Patches often contain enhancements or additional capabilities as well as fixes for known bugs. Patches are usually developed over a longer period of time.
- **Service pack** This refers to a large collection of patches and hotfixes rolled into a single, rather large package. Service packs are designed to bring a system up to the latest known-good level all at once, rather than requiring the user or system administrator to download dozens or hundreds of updates separately.

Disabling Unnecessary Ports and Services

Disabling unnecessary ports and services is a simple way to improve system security. This minimalist setup is similar to the "implicit deny" philosophy and can significantly reduce an attack surface.

An important management issue for running a secure system is to identify the specific needs of a system for its proper operation and to enable only items necessary for those functions. *Disabling unnecessary ports and services* prevents their use by unauthorized users and improves system throughput and increases security. Systems have ports and connections that need to be disabled if not in use.

Just as we have a principle of least privilege, we should follow a similar track with least functionality on systems. A system should do what it supposed to do, and only what it is supposed to do. Any additional functionality is an added attack surface for an adversary and offers no additional benefit to the enterprise.

Secure Configurations

Operating systems can be configured in a variety of manners—from completely open with lots of functionality, whether it is needed or not, to stripped to the services needed to perform a particular task. Operating system developers and manufacturers all share a common problem: they cannot possibly anticipate the many different configurations and variations that the user community will require from their products. So, rather than spending countless hours and funds attempting to meet every need, manufacturers provide a "default" installation for their products that usually contains the base OS and some more commonly desirable options, such as drivers, utilities, and enhancements. Because the OS could be used for any of a variety of purposes, and could be placed in any number of logical locations (LAN, screened subnet, WAN, and so on), the manufacturer typically does little to nothing with regard to security. The manufacturer may provide some recommendations or simplified tools and settings to facilitate securing the system, but in general, end users are responsible for securing their own systems. Generally this involves removing unnecessary applications and utilities, disabling unneeded services, setting appropriate permissions on files, and updating the OS and application code to the latest version.

Weak security configurations are a result of many different items, each specific to a particular set of components and operating conditions. The path to avoid weak configurations involves a combination of information sources. One is manufacturer recommendations, another is industry best practices, and the last is testing.

This process of securing an OS is called *hardening*, and it is intended to make the system more resistant to attack, much like armor or steel is hardened to make it less susceptible to breakage or damage. Each OS has its own approach to security, and although the process of hardening is generally the same, different steps must be taken to secure each OS. The process of securing and preparing an OS for the production environment is not trivial; it requires preparation and planning. Unfortunately, many users don't understand the steps necessary to secure their systems effectively, resulting in hundreds of compromised systems every day.

System hardening is the process of preparing and securing a system and involves the removal of all unnecessary software and services.

You must meet several key requirements to ensure that the system hardening processes described in this section achieve their security goals. These are OS independent and should be a normal part of all system maintenance operations:

- The base installation of all OS and application software comes from a trusted source and is verified as correct by using hash values.
- Machines are connected only to a completely trusted network during the installation, hardening, and update processes.
- The base installation includes all current patches and updates for both the OS and applications.
- Current backup images are taken after hardening and updates to facilitate system restoration to a known state.

These steps ensure that you know what is on the machine, can verify its authenticity, and have an established backup version.

Disable Default Accounts/Passwords

Because accounts are necessary for many systems to be established, default accounts with default passwords are a way of life in computing. Whether the account is for the OS or an application, this is a significant security vulnerability if not immediately addressed as part of setting up the system or installing of the application. *Disabling default accounts/passwords* should be such a common practice that there should be no systems with this vulnerability. This is a simple task, and one that must be done. When you cannot disable the default account (and there will be times when disabling is not a viable option), the other alternative is to change the password to a very long one that offers strong resistance to brute force attacks.

> **Tech Tip**
>
> **Configurations**
>
> *Modern software is configuration driven. This means that setting proper configurations is essential for secure operation of the software. Using weak configurations or allowing access to configuration files so attackers can weaken or misconfigure a system is a security failure. Default configurations should be checked to ensure they employ the desired level of security.*

Application Whitelisting/Blacklisting

Applications can be controlled at the OS at the time of start via blacklisting or whitelisting. *Application blacklisting* is essentially noting which applications should not be allowed to run on the machine. This is basically a permanent "ignore" or "call block" type of capability. *Application whitelisting* is the exact opposite: it consists of a list of allowed applications. Each of these approaches has advantages and disadvantages. Blacklisting is difficult to use against dynamic threats, as the identification of a specific application can easily be avoided through minor changes. Whitelisting is easier to employ from the aspect of the identification of applications that are allowed to run—hash values can be used to ensure the executables are not corrupted. The challenge in whitelisting is the number of potential applications that are run on a typical machine. For a single-purpose machine, such as a database server, whitelisting can be relatively easy to employ. For multipurpose machines, it can be more complicated.

> CompTIA updated a number of terms in the most recent exam objectives for CompTIA Security+ and has moved away from using terms like *whitelisting* and *blacklisting* and is now using *allow list* and *block list/deny list*, respectively.

Microsoft has two mechanisms that are part of the OS to control which users can use which applications:

- **Software restrictive policies** Employed via group policies and allow significant control over applications, scripts, and executable files. The primary mode is by machine and not by user account.
- **User account level control** Enforced via AppLocker, which is a service that allows granular control over which users can execute which programs. Through the use of rules, an enterprise can exert significant control over who can access and use installed software.

> Using OS-level restrictions to control what software can be used can prevent users from loading and running unauthorized software. Unauthorized software, whether because of licensing restrictions or because it is not vetted for use, can present risk to the enterprise. Controlling this risk via an enterprise operational control such as whitelisting can simplify compliance and improve baseline security posture.

On a Linux platform, similar capabilities are offered from third-party vendor applications.

Sandboxing

Sandboxing refers to the quarantine or isolation of a system from its surroundings. It has become standard practice for some programs with an increased risk surface to operate within a sandbox, limiting the interaction with the CPU and other processes, such as memory. This works as a means of quarantine, preventing problems from getting out of the sandbox and onto the OS and other applications on a system.

Virtualization can be used as a form of sandboxing with respect to an entire system. You can build a VM, test something inside the VM, and, based on the results, make a decision with regard to stability or whatever concern was present.

Secure Baseline

While the process of establishing software's base state is called *baselining*, and the resulting product is a baseline that describes the capabilities of the software, it is not necessarily secure. To secure the software on a system effectively and consistently, you must take a structured and logical approach. This starts with an examination of the system's intended functions and capabilities to determine what processes and applications will be housed on the system. As a best practice, anything that is not required for operations should be removed or disabled on the system; then, all the appropriate patches, hotfixes, and settings should be applied to protect and secure it. This becomes the system's *secure baseline*.

Software and hardware can be integrally tied when it comes to security, so they must be considered together. Once the process has been completed for a particular hardware and software combination, any similar systems can be configured with the same baseline to achieve the same level and depth of security and protection. Uniform software baselines are critical in large-scale operations, because maintaining separate configurations and security levels for hundreds or thousands of systems is far too costly.

After administrators have finished patching, securing, and preparing a system, they often create an initial baseline configuration. This represents a secure state for the system or network device and a reference point of the software and its configuration. This information establishes a reference that can be used to help keep the system secure by establishing a known-safe configuration. If this initial baseline can be replicated, it can also be used as a template when similar systems and network devices are being deployed.

> **Tech Tip**
>
> **Securing a Workstation**
>
> *Workstations are attractive targets for crackers because they are numerous and can serve as entry points into the network and the data that is commonly the target of an attack. Although* security *is a relative term, following these basic steps will increase workstation security immensely:*
>
> - *Remove unnecessary protocols such as Telnet and NetBIOS.*
> - *Remove unnecessary software.*
> - *Remove modems unless needed and authorized.*
> - *Remove all shares that are not necessary.*
> - *Rename the administrator account, securing it with a strong password.*
> - *Remove or disable the Local Admin account in Windows.*
> - *Disable unnecessary user accounts.*
> - *Disable unnecessary ports and services.*
> - *Install an antivirus program and keep abreast of updates.*
> - *If the floppy drive is not needed, remove or disconnect it.*
> - *Consider disabling USB ports via BIOS/UEFI settings to restrict data movement to USB devices.*
> - *If no corporate firewall exists between the machine and the Internet, install a firewall.*
> - *Keep the operating system (OS) patched and up to date.*
> - *Keep all applications patched and up to date.*
> - *Turn on event logging for determined security elements.*

Machine Hardening

The key management issue behind running a secure server setup is to identify the specific needs of a server for its proper operation and enable only items necessary for those functions. Keeping all other services and users off the system improves system throughput and increases security. Reducing the attack surface area associated with a server reduces the vulnerabilities now and in the future as updates are required.

> **Tech Tip**
>
> **Server Hardening Tips**
>
> *Specific security needs can vary depending on the server's specific use, but at a minimum, the following are beneficial:*
>
> - *Remove unnecessary protocols such as Telnet, NetBIOS, and File Transfer Protocol (FTP).*
> - *Remove unnecessary programs such as Internet Information Services (IIS).*
> - *Remove all shares that are not necessary.*
> - *Rename the administrator account, securing it with a strong password.*
> - *Remove or disable the Local Admin account in Windows.*
> - *Disable unnecessary user accounts.*
> - *Disable unnecessary ports and services.*
> - *Keep the operating system (OS) patched and up to date.*
> - *Keep all applications patched and up to date.*
> - *Turn on event logging for determined security elements.*
> - *Control physical access to servers.*

Once a server has been built and is ready to be placed into operation, the recording of hash values on all of its crucial files will provide valuable information later in case of a question concerning possible system integrity after a detected intrusion. The use of hash values to detect changes was first developed by Gene Kim and Eugene Spafford at Purdue University in 1992. The concept became the product Tripwire, which is now available in commercial and open source forms. The same basic concept is used by many security packages to detect file-level changes.

The primary method of controlling the security impact of a system on a network is to reduce the available attack surface area. Turning off all services that are not needed or permitted by policy will reduce the number of vulnerabilities. Removing methods of connecting additional devices to a workstation to move data—such as optical drives and USB ports—assists in controlling the movement of data into and out of the device. User-level controls, such as limiting e-mail attachment options, screening all attachments at the e-mail server level, and reducing network shares to needed shares only, can be used to limit excessive connectivity that can impact security.

Early versions of home operating systems did not have separate named accounts for separate users. This was seen as a convenience mechanism; after all, who wants the hassle of signing in to the machine? This led to the simple problem that all users could then see, modify, and delete everyone else's content. Content could be separated by using access control mechanisms, but that required configuration of the OS to manage every user's identity. Early versions of many OSs came with literally every option turned on. Again, this was a convenience factor, but it led to systems running processes and services that they never used, thus increasing the attack surface of the host unnecessarily.

Determining the correct settings and implementing them correctly is an important step in securing a host system. The following sections explore the multitude of controls and options that need to be employed properly to achieve a reasonable level of security on a host system.

Hardening Microsoft Operating Systems

Microsoft has spent years working to develop the most secure and securable OS on the market. As a desktop OS, Windows has provided a range of security features for users to secure their systems. Most of these options can be employed via group policies in enterprise setups, making them easily deployable and maintainable across an enterprise.

Here are some of the security capabilities in the Windows environment:

- *User Account Control allows users to operate the system without requiring administrative privileges.* If you've used Windows, you've undoubtedly seen the "Windows needs your permission to continue" pop-ups.
- *Windows Firewall includes an outbound filtering capability.* Windows allows filtering of traffic coming into and leaving the system, which is useful for controlling things like peer-to-peer applications.
- *BitLocker allows encryption of all data on a server, including any data volumes.* This capability is only available in the higher-end distributions of Windows.

- *Windows clients can control applications with AppLocker.* AppLocker allows administrators to configure which applications can be run on a Windows machine within an enterprise environment. This is part of the Microsoft OS.
- *Windows Defender (part of Windows Security) is a built-in malware detection and removal tool.* Windows Defender detects many types of potentially suspicious software and can prompt the user before allowing applications to make potentially malicious changes.

Hardening Windows Server

Windows Server comes with a host of mechanisms that can be deployed to provide a secure platform:

- *BitLocker allows encryption of all data on a server, including any data volumes.* Improved BitLocker functionality now allows administrator-less reboots.
- *Role-based installation of functions and capabilities minimizes the server's footprint.* For example, if a server is going to be a web server, it does not need DNS or SMTP software, and thus those features are no longer installed by default.
- *AppLocker can control which executables can run on a server.* This feature, deployable from a central location and managed enterprise wide, enables administrators to define which applications are allowed to run on each server. This feature reduces malware spread and enables compliance with corporate governance policy.
- *Read-only domain controllers can be created and deployed in high-risk locations, but they can't be modified to add new users, change access levels, and so on.* This new ability to create and deploy "read-only" domain controllers can be very useful in high-threat environments.
- *More-granular password policies allow for different password policies on a group or user basis.* This allows administrators to assign different password policies and requirements for the sales group and the engineering group, for example, if that capability is needed.
- *Websites or web applications can be administered within IIS 10.* This allows administrators quicker and more convenient administration capabilities, such as the ability to turn on or off specific modules through the IIS management interface. For example, removing CGI support from a web application is a quick and simple operation in the Web Server (IIS) role and IIS version 10.
- *The traditional ROM-BIOS has been replaced with Unified Extensible Firmware Interface (UEFI).* The current version is 2.8, which prevents boot code updates without appropriate digital certificates and signatures.
- *The trustworthy and verified boot process has been extended to the entire Windows OS boot code with a feature known as Secure Boot.* UEFI and Secure Boot significantly reduce the risk of malicious code such as rootkits and boot viruses.
- *Early Launch Anti-Malware (ELAM) has been instituted to ensure that only known, digitally signed anti-malware programs can load right after*

Secure Boot finishes (without requiring UEFI or Secure Boot). This permits legitimate anti-malware programs to get into memory and start doing their job before fake antivirus programs or other malicious code can act.

- *DNSSEC is fully integrated.*
- *Data Classification with Rights Management Service is fully integrated so that you can control which users and groups can access which documents based on content or marked classification.*
- *Managed Service Accounts allow for advanced self-maintaining features with extremely long passwords, which automatically reset every 30 days, all under the control of Active Directory in the enterprise.*
- *Credential Guard enables the use of virtualization-based security to isolate credential information, preventing password hashes or Kerberos tickets from being intercepted.* Credential Guard uses an entirely new isolated Local Security Authority (LSA) process, which is not accessible to the rest of the operating system. All binaries used by the isolated LSA are signed with certificates that are validated before they are launched in the protected environment, making pass-the-hash-type attacks completely ineffective.
- *Windows Server 2019 includes Windows Defender Device Guard to ensure that only trusted software can be run on the server.* Using virtualization-based security, this system can limit what binaries can run on the system based on the organization's policy. If anything other than the specified binaries tries to run, Windows OS blocks it and logs the failed attempt so that administrators can see that there has been a potential breach. Windows Defender Device Guard is also integrated with PowerShell so that you can authorize which scripts can run on your system.

> **Tech Tip**
>
> **Virtualization-Based Security**
>
> *In Microsoft Windows Server, both Device Guard and Credential Guard depend on* **Virtual Secure Mode (VSM)**. *One lens to examine security is via segmentation. This forces a separation between programmatic elements. Windows Hyper-V hypervisor separates the hardware of its residing host, and its internal processes, from those of other virtual machines (VMs). VSM is based on this concept and leverages the hypervisor process to secure the server/desktop. Using VSM, specific processes and their associated memory become isolated from the host operating system. This forces malicious code to operate independently of the host OS and the hardware underneath.*

The tools available in each subsequent release of the Windows Server OS are designed to increase the difficulty factor for attackers, eliminating known methods of exploitation. The challenge is in administrating the security functions, although the integration of many of these via Active Directory makes this much more manageable than in the past.

Microsoft Security Compliance Manager

Microsoft provided a tool called Security Compliance Manager (SCM) to assist system and enterprise administrators with the configuration of security options across a wide range of Microsoft platforms. SCM allows administrators to use group policy objects (GPOs) to deploy security configurations across Internet Explorer, the desktop OSs, server OSs, and common applications such as Microsoft Office. Microsoft retired SCM in the summer of 2017 in favor of a new toolset called Desired State Configuration (DSC).

Desired State Configuration (DSC)

Desired State Configuration (DSC) is a PowerShell-based approach to configuration management of a system. Rather than having documentation that describes the security settings for a system and expecting a user to set them, DSC performs the work via PowerShell functions. This makes security configuration a managed-by-code process that brings with it many advantages. Using DSC, it is easier and faster to adopt, implement, maintain, deploy, and share system configuration information. DSC brings the advantages of DevOps to system configuration in the Windows environment. While detailed PowerShell implementations are beyond the scope of this book, the concept of programmable configuration control is not. DSC is more than just PowerShell because DSC configurations separate intent ("what I want to do") from execution ("how I want to do it"). By separating the specifics of deployments, DSC enables multiple environments to be serviced by single DSC implementations that via configuration data can target dev, test, and production environments appropriately.

Microsoft Attack Surface Analyzer

One of the challenges in a modern enterprise is understanding the impact of system changes from the installation or upgrade of an application on a system. To help you overcome that challenge, Microsoft has released the Attack Surface Analyzer (ASA), a free tool that can be deployed on a system before a change and then again after a change to analyze the alterations to various system properties as a result of the change.

Using ASA, developers can view changes in the attack surface resulting from the introduction of their code onto the Windows platform, and system administrators can assess the aggregate attack surface change by the installation of an application. Security auditors can use the tool to evaluate the risk of a particular piece of software installed on the Windows platform. Also, if ASA is deployed in a baseline mode before an incident, security incident responders can potentially use ASA to gain a better understanding of the state of a system's security during an investigation.

Group Policies

Microsoft defines a **group policy** as "an infrastructure used to deliver and apply one or more desired configurations or policy settings to a set of targeted users and computers within an Active Directory environment. This infrastructure consists of a Group Policy engine and multiple client-side extensions (CSEs) responsible for writing specific policy settings on target client computers." Introduced with the Windows 2000 operating system, group policies are a great way to manage and configure systems centrally in an Active Directory environment (Windows NT had policies, but technically not "group policies"). Group policies can also be used to manage users, making these policies valuable tools in any large environment.

Within the Windows environment, group policies can be used to refine, set, or modify a system's Registry settings, auditing and security policies, user environments, logon/logoff scripts, and so on. Policy settings are stored in a **group policy object (GPO)** and are referenced internally by the OS using a **globally unique identifier (GUID)**. A single policy can be linked to a single user, a group of users, a group of machines, or an entire organizational unit (OU), which makes updating common settings on large groups of users or systems much easier. Users and systems can have more than one GPO assigned and active, which can create conflicts between policies that must then be resolved at an attribute level. Group policies can also overwrite local policy settings. Group policies should not be confused with local policies. *Local* policies are created and applied to a specific system (locally), are not user specific (you can't have local policy X for user A and local policy Y for user B), and are overwritten by GPOs. Further confusing some administrators

Tech Tip

Microsoft Security Baselines

A security baseline is a group of Microsoft-recommended configuration settings with an explanation of their security impact. There are over 3000 Group Policy settings for Windows 10, which does not include over 1800 browser settings. So of these 4800-plus settings, only some are security related, and choosing which to set can be a laborious process. Security baselines bring an expert-based consensus view to this task. Microsoft provides a security compliance toolkit to facilitate the application of Microsoft-recommended baselines for a system. The Microsoft Security Compliance Toolkit (SCT) is a set of tools that allows enterprise security administrators to download, analyze, test, edit, and store Microsoft-recommended security configuration baselines for Windows.

Using the toolkit, administrators can compare their current group policy objects (GPOs) with Microsoft-recommended GPO baselines or other baselines. You can also edit them, store them in GPO backup file format, and apply them broadly through Active Directory or individually through local policy. The Security Compliance Toolkit consists of specific baselines based on OS and two tools—the Policy Analyzer tool and the Local Group Policy Object (LGPO) tool.

For further information, see Microsoft Security Compliance Toolkit 1.0 (www.microsoft.com/en-us/download/details.aspx?id=55319).

and users, policies can be applied at the local, site, domain, and OU levels. Policies are applied in hierarchical order—local, then site, then domain, and so on. This means settings in a local policy can be overridden or reversed by settings in the domain policy if there is a conflict between the two policies. If there is no conflict, the policy settings are aggregated.

Try This!

Windows Local Security Policies

Open a command prompt as either administrator or a user with administrator privileges on a Windows system. Type the command **secpol** and press ENTER (this should bring up the Local Security Policy utility). Expand Account Policies on the left side of the Local Security Policy window (which should have a + next to it). Click Password Policy. Look in the right side of the Local Security Policy window. What is the minimum password length? What is the maximum password age in days? Now explore some of the policy settings—but be careful! Changes made to the local security policy can affect the functionality or usability of your system.

Creating GPOs is usually done through either the Group Policy Object Editor, shown in Figure 14.1, or the Group Policy Management Console

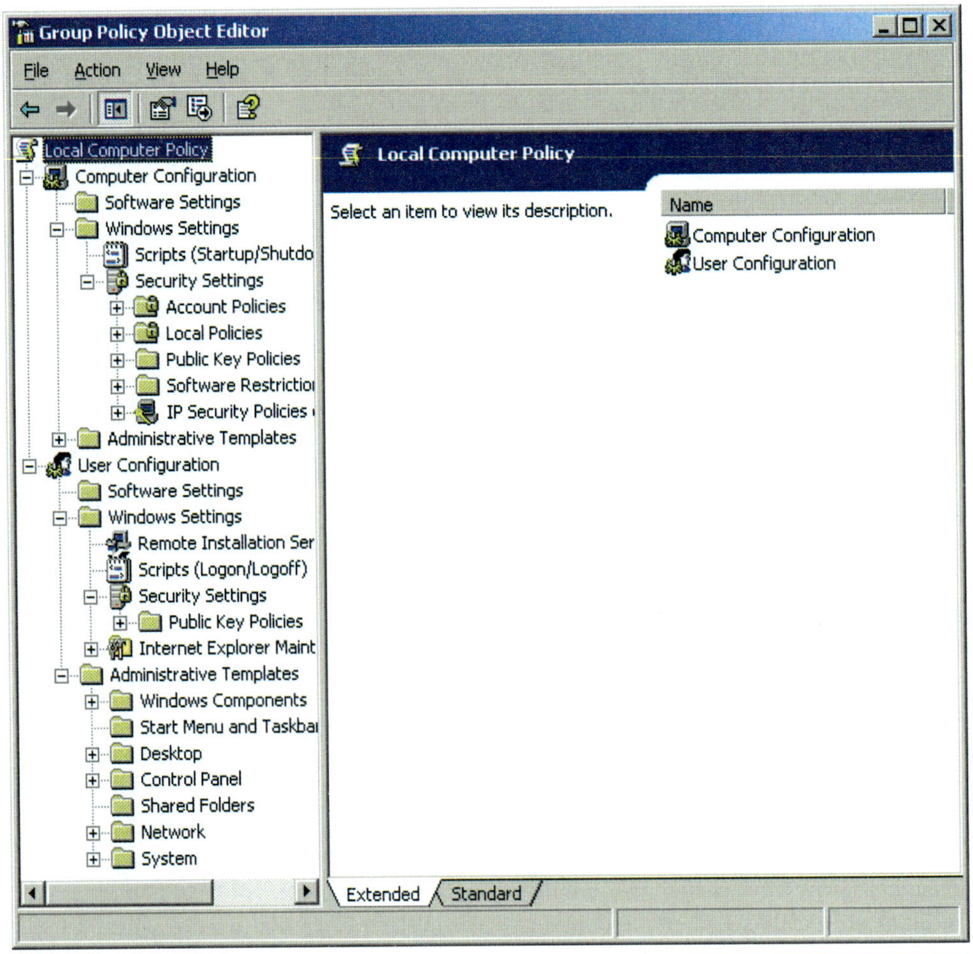

• **Figure 14.1** Group Policy Object Editor

(GPMC). The GPMC is a more powerful GUI-based tool that can summarize GPO settings; simplify security filtering settings; backup, clone, restore, and edit GPOs; and perform other tasks. After creating a GPO, administrators will associate it with the desired targets. After association, group policies operate on a *pull model*, meaning that at a semi-random interval, the Group Policy client will collect and apply any policies associated to the system and the currently logged-on user.

Microsoft group policies can provide many useful options, including the following:

- **Network location awareness** Systems are now "aware" of which network they are connected to and can apply different GPOs as needed. For example, a system can have a very restrictive GPO when connected to a public network and a less restrictive GPO when connected to an internal, trusted network.
- **VPN compatibility** As a side benefit of network location awareness, mobile users who connect through VPNs can receive a GPO update in the background after connecting to the corporate network via VPN.
- **Power management** Power management settings can be configured using GPOs.
- **Device access blocking** Policy settings have been added that allow administrators to restrict user access to USB drives, CD-RW drives, DVD-RW drives, and other removable media.
- **Location-based printing** Users can be assigned to various printers based on their location. As mobile users move, their printer locations can be updated to the closest local printer.

In Windows, policies are applied in hierarchical order. Local policies get applied first, then site policies, then domain policies, and finally OU policies. If a setting from a later policy conflicts with a setting from an earlier policy, the setting from the later policy "wins" and is applied. Keep this in mind when building group policies.

Hardening UNIX- or Linux-Based Operating Systems

Although you do not have the advantage of a single manufacturer for all UNIX operating systems (like you do with Windows operating systems), the concepts behind securing different UNIX- or Linux-based operating systems are similar, regardless of whether the manufacturer is Red Hat or Sun Microsystems. Indeed, the overall tasks involved with hardening all operating systems are remarkably similar.

Establishing General UNIX Baselines

General UNIX baselining follows similar concepts as baselining for Windows OSs: disable unnecessary services, restrict permissions on files and directories, remove unnecessary software, apply patches, remove unnecessary users, and apply password guidelines. Some versions of UNIX provide GUI-based tools for these tasks, while others require administrators to edit configuration files manually. In most cases, anything that can be accomplished through a GUI can be accomplished from the command line or by manually editing configuration files.

Like Windows systems, UNIX systems are easiest to secure and baseline if they are providing a single service or performing a single function, such as acting as a Simple Mail Transfer Protocol (SMTP) server or web server. Prior to performing any software installations or baselining, the administrator should define the purpose of the system and identify all required capabilities and functions. One nice advantage of UNIX systems is that you typically have complete control over what does or does not get installed on the system. During the installation process, the administrator can select which services and applications are placed on the system, offering an opportunity to not install services and applications that will not be required. However, this assumes that the administrator knows and understands the purpose of this system, which is not always the case. In other cases, the function of the system itself may have changed.

Services on a UNIX system (called *daemons*) can be controlled through a number of different mechanisms. As the root user, an administrator can start and stop services manually from the command line or through a GUI tool. The OS can also stop and start services automatically through configuration files (usually contained in the /etc directory). (Note that UNIX systems vary a good deal in this regard, as some use a super-server process, such as inetd, while others have individual configuration files for each network service.) Unlike Windows, UNIX systems can also have different runlevels in which the system can be configured to bring up different services, depending on the runlevel selected.

> **Tech Tip**
>
> **Runlevels**
>
> **Runlevels** *are used to describe the state of init (initialization) and what system services are operating in UNIX systems. For example, runlevel 0 is shutdown. Runlevel 1 is single-user mode (typically for administrative purposes). Runlevels 2 through 5 are user defined (that is, administrators can define what services are running at each level). Runlevel 6 is for reboot.*

Linux Hardening

One of the "strengths" behind Linux is the ability of a sysadmin to fully control all of the features—the ultimate in customizable solutions. This can lead to leaner and faster processing, but it also can lead to security problems. Securing a Linux environment involves a couple different types of operations, as in how a sysadmin operates and how the system is configured. What's more, there are the intricacies of the Linux system itself.

Linux has several separate operating spaces, each with its own characteristics. The application space is where user applications exist and run. These are above the kernel and can be changed while operating by simply restarting the application. The kernel space is integral to the system and can only be changed by rebooting the hardware. Thus, updates to kernel processes require a reboot to finish and become active.

Securing Linux is in many ways like securing any other operating system. Issues such as securing the services, keeping things up to date, and enforcing policies are all the same objectives regardless of the type or version of OS. The differences occur in how one achieves these objectives. Using passwords as an example, there is no centralized method like Active Directory and group policies. Instead, these functions are controlled granularly using commands on the system. It is possible to manage passwords to the same degree as through unified systems; it just takes a bit more work. The same goes for controlling access to administrative or root access accounts. On a running UNIX system, you can see which processes, applications, and services are running by using the process status, or **ps**, command, as shown in Figure 14.2. To stop a running service, you can identify the service by its unique **process identifier (PID)** and then use the **kill** command to stop the service. For example, if you wanted to stop the bluetooth-applet service in Figure 14.2, you would use the command **kill 2443**. To prevent this service from starting again when the system is rebooted, you would have to modify the appropriate runlevels to remove this service, as shown in Figure 14.2, or modify the configuration files that control this service.

Linux is built around the concept of a file—everything is a file. Files are files, as are directories. Devices are files, I/O locations are files, conduits between programs, called *pipes*, are files. Making everything addressable as a file makes permissions easier. Users are *not* files; they are subjects in the subject-object model. Subjects act upon objects according to permissions. Users exist in the singular, and in groups, and permissions are layered between the owner of the object, groups, and single subjects (users). In Linux, a *group* is a name for a list of users; this allows for shorter access control entry (ACE) lists on objects because groups are checked first. When a subject attempts to act upon an object, the security kernel examines the entries for the object's access control entries until it finds a match. If no match is found, the action is not allowed.

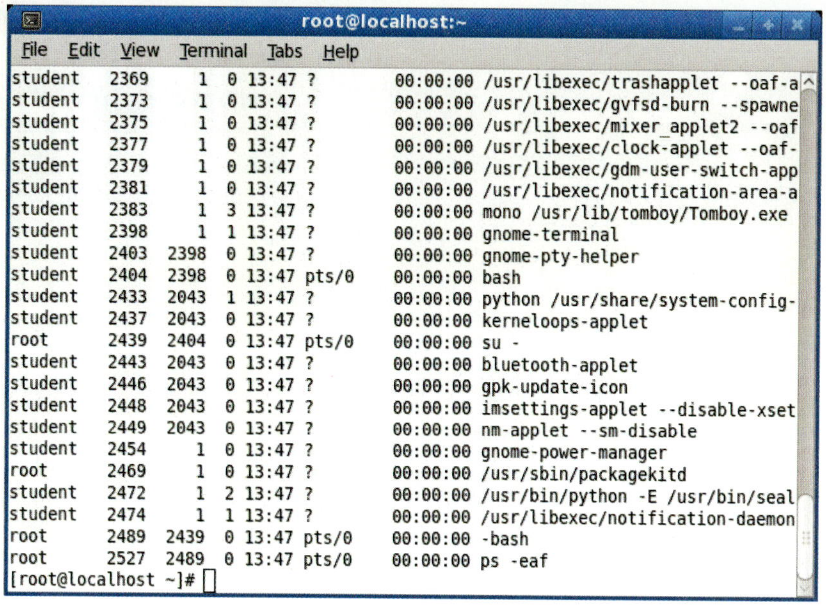

• **Figure 14.2** The **ps** command run on a Fedora system

Permissions on files are expressed in bit patterns, as illustrated in Figures 14.3 and 14.4. Permissions are modified using the **chmod** command and indicating a three-digit number that translates to the appropriate set of read, write, and execute permissions for the item. Figure 14.3 illustrates how the permissions are displayed during a file listing as well as how the relative positions relate to the owner, group, and others. Figure 14.4 illustrates the decoding pattern of the bit structure.

The common patterns frequently used in Linux systems are illustrated in Table 14.1.

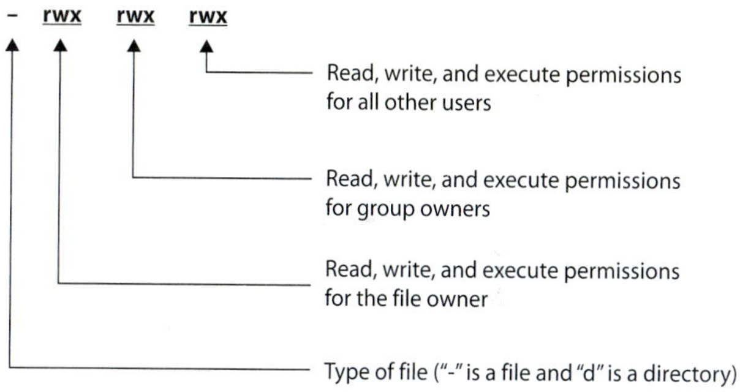

• **Figure 14.3** Linux permissions listing

```
Linux permission settings
are a series of bits

rwx rwx rwx = 111 111 111      rwx = 111 = 7 read, write, execute
rw- rw- rw- = 110 110 110      rw- = 110 = 6 read, write
rwx --- --- = 111 000 000      r-x = 101 = 5 read, execute
                               r-- = 100 = 4 read
chmod 741 → 111 100 001        -wx = 011 = 3 write, execute
            rwx r-- --x        -w- = 010 = 2 write
                               --x = 001 = 1 execute
                               --- = 000 = 0 no permissions
```

• **Figure 14.4** Linux permission bit sequence

Table 14.1 Common Linux File Permissions

Value	Meaning	Use
777	rwx rwx rwx	No restrictions on permissions. Anybody can do anything.
755	rwx r-x r-x	This setting is common for programs that are used by all users. The file's owner may read, write, and execute the file. All others may read and execute the file.
700	rwx --- ---	This setting is useful for programs that only the owner may use and must be kept private from others.
666	rw- rw- rw-	All users may read and write the file.
644	rw- r-- r--	A common setting for data files that everybody may read but only the owner may change.
600	rw- --- ---	A common setting for data files that the owner wants to keep private.

For applications in the user space on a Linux box, setting the correct permissions is extremely important. These permissions are what protect configuration and other settings that enable or disable a lot of functionality—and could, if set erroneously, allow attackers to perform a wide range of attacks, including installing malware that can watch other users. For these reasons and more, Linux can be an awesome system, with great performance and capability. The downside is that it requires significant expertise to do these things securely in today's computing environment.

Directories also use the same nomenclature as files for permissions, but with minor differences. An **r** indicates that the contents can be read. A **w** indicates that the contents can be written, and **x** allows a directory to be entered. Both **r** and **w** have no effect without **x** being set. A setting of 777 indicates that anyone can list and create/delete files in the directory. 755 gives the owner full access, while others may only list the files. 700 restricts access to only the owner.

There are times when a user needs more permissions than their account holds, as in needing root permission to perform a task. Rather than logging in as root, and thus losing their identity in logs and such, the user can use the superuser command, **su**, in order to assume root privilege, provided they have the root password.

Endpoint Protection

Endpoint protection is the concept of extending the security perimeter to the devices that are connecting to the network. A variety of endpoint protection solutions can be employed, including antivirus/anti-malware solutions, endpoint detection and response solutions, data loss prevention solutions, and firewalls. Host-based intrusion detection and prevention solutions can also be deployed at endpoints. Not all endpoints are the same with respect to either capability or the risks from attack, and endpoint solutions should be tailored to take those elements into account.

Antivirus

Antivirus (AV) products attempt to identify, neutralize, or remove malicious programs, macros, and files. These products were initially designed to detect and remove computer viruses, though many of the antivirus products are now bundled with additional security products and features. Most current antivirus software packages provide protection against a wide range of threats, including viruses, worms, trojans, and other malware. Use of an up-to-date antivirus package is essential in the current threat environment.

Although antivirus products have had over two decades to refine their capabilities, the purpose of the antivirus products remains the same: to detect and eliminate computer viruses and malware. Most antivirus products combine the following approaches when scanning for viruses:

- **Signature-based scanning** Much like an intrusion detection system (IDS), the antivirus products scan programs, files, macros, e-mails, and other data for known worms, viruses, and malware. The antivirus product contains a virus dictionary with thousands of known virus signatures that must be frequently updated, as new viruses are discovered daily. This approach will catch known viruses but is limited by the virus dictionary—what it does not know about it cannot catch.
- **Heuristic scanning (or analysis)** Heuristic scanning does not rely on a virus dictionary. Instead, it looks for suspicious behavior—anything that does not fit into a "normal" pattern of behavior for the operating system (OS) and applications running on the system being protected.

As signature-based scanning is a familiar concept, let's examine heuristic scanning in more detail. **Heuristic scanning** typically looks for commands or instructions that are not normally found in application programs, such as attempts to access a reserved memory register. Most antivirus products use either a weight-based system or a rule-based system in their heuristic scanning (more effective products use a combination of both techniques). A *weight-based system* rates every suspicious behavior based on the degree of threat associated with that behavior. If the set threshold is passed based on a single behavior or a combination of behaviors, the antivirus product will treat the process, application, macro, and so on that is performing the behavior(s) as a threat to the system. A *rule-based system* compares activity to a set of rules meant to detect and identify malicious software. If part of the software matches a rule, or if a process, application, macro, and so on performs a behavior that matches a rule, the antivirus software will treat that as a threat to the local system.

Some heuristic products are very advanced and contain capabilities for examining memory usage and addressing, a parser for examining executable code, a logic flow analyzer, and a disassembler/emulator so they can "guess" what the code is designed to do and whether or not it is malicious.

As with IDS/IPS products, encryption and obfuscation pose a problem for antivirus products: anything that cannot be read cannot be matched against current virus dictionaries or activity patterns. To combat the use of encryption in malware and viruses, many heuristic scanners look for

> Heuristic scanning is a method of detecting potentially malicious or "virus-like" behavior by examining what a program or section of code does. Anything that is "suspicious" or potentially "malicious" is closely examined to determine whether or not it is a threat to the system. Using heuristic scanning, an antivirus product attempts to identify new viruses or heavily modified versions of existing viruses before they can damage your system.

encryption and decryption loops. As malware is usually designed to run alone and unattended, if it uses encryption, it must contain all the instructions to encrypt and decrypt itself, as needed. Heuristic scanners look for instructions such as the initialization of a pointer with a valid memory address, manipulation of a counter, or a branch condition based on a counter value. While these actions don't always indicate the presence of an encryption/decryption loop, if the heuristic engine can find a loop, it might be able to decrypt the software in a protected memory space, such as an emulator, and evaluate the software in more detail. Many viruses share common encryption/decryption routines that help antivirus developers.

Current antivirus products are highly configurable, and most offerings will have the following capabilities:

- **Automated updates** Perhaps the most important feature of a good antivirus solution is its ability to keep itself up to date by automatically downloading the latest virus signatures on a frequent basis. This usually requires that the system be connected to the Internet in some fashion and that updates be performed on a daily (or more frequent) basis.
- **Automated scanning** Most antivirus products allow for the scheduling of automated scans so that you can designate when the antivirus product will examine the local system for infected files. These automated scans can typically be scheduled for specific days and times, and the scanning parameters can be configured to specify what drives, directories, and types of files are scanned.
- **Media scanning** Removable media is still a common method for virus and malware propagation, and most antivirus products can be configured to automatically scan optical media, USB drives, memory sticks, or any other types of removable media as soon as they are connected to or accessed by the local system.
- **Manual scanning** Many antivirus products allow the user to scan drives, files, or directories (folders) "on demand."
- **E-mail scanning** E-mail is still a major method of virus and malware propagation. Many antivirus products give users the ability to scan both incoming and outgoing messages as well as any attachments.
- **Resolution** When the antivirus product detects an infected file or application, it can typically perform one of several actions. The antivirus product may quarantine the file, making it inaccessible. It may try to repair the file by removing the infection or offending code, or it may delete the infected file. Most antivirus products allow the user to specify the desired action, and some allow for an escalation in actions, such as cleaning the infected file if possible and quarantining the file if it cannot be cleaned.

Antivirus solutions are typically installed on individual systems (desktops, servers, and even mobile devices), but network-based antivirus capabilities are also available in many commercial gateway products. These gateway products often combine firewall, IDS/IPS, and antivirus capabilities into a single integrated platform. Most organizations will also employ antivirus solutions on e-mail servers, as that continues to be a very popular propagation method for viruses.

The intentions of computer virus writers have changed over the years—from simply wanting to spread a virus in order to be noticed, to creating stealthy botnets as a criminal activity. One method of remaining hidden is to produce viruses that can morph to lower their detection rates by standard antivirus programs. The number of variants for some viruses has increased from less than 10 to greater than 10,000. This explosion in signatures has created two issues: One, users must constantly (sometimes more than daily) update their signature file. Two, and more important, detection methods are having to change as the number of signatures becomes too large to scan quickly. For end users, the bottom line is simple: update signatures automatically, and at least daily.

While the installation of a good antivirus product is still considered a necessary best practice, there is growing concern about the effectiveness of antivirus products against developing threats. Early viruses often exhibited destructive behaviors; they were poorly written and modified files and were less concerned with hiding their presence than they were with propagation. We are seeing an emergence of viruses and malware created by professionals, sometimes financed by criminal organizations or governments, that go to great lengths to hide their presence. These viruses and malware are often used to steal sensitive information or turn the infected PC into part of a larger botnet for use in spamming or attack operations.

Antivirus is an essential security application on all platforms. There are numerous compliance schemes that mandate antivirus deployment, including Payment Card Industry Data Security Standard (PCI DSS) and North American Electric Reliability Council Critical Infrastructure Protections (NERC CIP).

Anti-Malware

In the early days of PC use, threats were limited: most home users were not connected to the Internet 24/7 through broadband connections, and the most common threat was a virus passed from computer to computer via an infected floppy disk (much like the medical definition, a *computer virus* is something that can infect the host and replicate itself). But things have changed dramatically since those early days, and current threats pose a much greater risk than ever before. Automated probes from botnets and worms are not the only threats roaming the Internet—there are viruses and malware spread by e-mail, phishing, infected websites that execute code on your system when you visit them, adware, spyware, and so on. Anti-malware is the name of a product designed to protect your machine from malicious software or malware. Today, most anti-malware solutions are combined with antivirus solutions into a single product. Fortunately, as the threats increase in complexity and capability, so do the products designed to stop them. One of the most dangerous forms of malware is ransomware; it spreads quickly, encrypting a user's files, and locking it until a ransom is paid. For more details on anti-malware products, reread the preceding "Antivirus" section and realize that malware is a different threat than a virus, but the defenses are the same.

Endpoint Detection and Response (EDR)

Endpoint detection and response (EDR) solutions are integrated solutions that combine individual endpoint security functions into a complete package. Having a packaged solution makes updating easier, and frequently these products are designed to integrate into an enterprise-level solution with a centralized management platform. Some of the common EDR components include antivirus, anti-malware, software patching, firewall, and DLP solutions. Unified endpoint management (UEM) is a newer security model that focuses on the managing and securing devices in an enterprise such as desktops, laptops, smartphones, and other devices from a single location.

DLP

Data loss prevention (DLP) solutions serve to prevent sensitive data from leaving the network without notice. What better place to check than at endpoints? Well, it is important to understand what an endpoint is. For e-mail, the endpoint really is the server, and this offers a scalable location against multiple mailboxes. Applying DLP across endpoints to chase items such as USB downloads of data can be an exercise fraught with heavy maintenance of DLP rulesets, heavyweight clients that affect endpoint performance, and a lack of discrimination that can cause productivity issues. This has led to endpoint DLP monitoring, where file activity is reported to centralized systems, and to specialized DLP offerings such as the content DLP being rolled out by Microsoft across the Microsoft 365 environment. These endpoint solutions do not provide complete or comprehensive coverage but taken together can achieve many of the objectives with less cost and complexity.

Next-Generation Firewall (NGFW)

Next-generation firewalls (NGFWs) act by inspecting the actual traffic crossing the firewall—not just looking at the source and destination addresses and ports but also at the actual content being sent. This makes next-generation firewalls a potent player in the hunt for malicious content on the way in and company secrets on the way out. As with all of these rule-driven platforms, the challenge is in maintaining appropriate rulesets that catch the desired bad traffic.

Host-based Intrusion Detection System (HIDS)

Host-based intrusion detection systems (HIDSs) act to detect undesired elements in network traffic to and from the host. Because the intrusion detection system is tied to the host, it can be very specific with respect to threats to the host OS and ignore those that would have no effect. Being deployed at a specific endpoint, it can be tuned to the specifics of the endpoint and endpoint applications, providing greater levels of specific detection. Intrusion detection systems were covered in detail in Chapter 13.

Host-based Intrusion Prevention System (HIPS)

A *host-based intrusion prevention system (HIPS)* is a HIDS with additional components to permit it to respond automatically to a threat condition. The response can be as simple as dropping a packet, up to killing a connection. Intrusion prevention systems were covered in detail in Chapter 13.

Host-based Firewall

Personal firewalls, or *host-based firewalls,* are host-based protective mechanisms that monitor and control traffic passing in to and out of a single system. Designed for the end user, software firewalls often have a configurable security policy that allows the user to determine which traffic is "good" and is allowed to pass and which traffic is "bad" and is blocked. The decision for good versus bad is based on the addresses being passed, both IP address and port combinations. Software firewalls are extremely commonplace—so much so that most modern OSs come with some type of personal firewall included. Having the firewall on the host OS provides the ability to tune the firewall to the usage pattern of the specific endpoint.

Linux-based OSs have had built-in software-based firewalls for a number of years, including TCP Wrapper, ipchains, and iptables (see Figure 14.5).

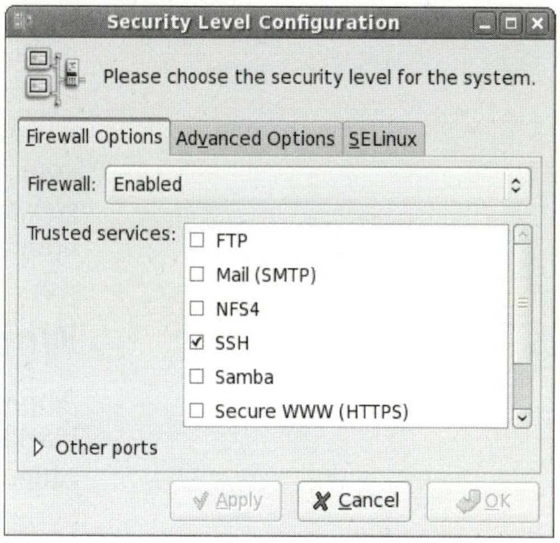

• **Figure 14.5** A Linux firewall

TCP Wrapper is a simple program that limits inbound network connections based on port number, domain, or IP address and is managed with two text files called hosts.allow and hosts.deny. If the inbound connection is coming from a trusted IP address and destined for a port to which it is allowed to connect, then the connection is allowed.

Ipchains is a more advanced, rule-based software firewall that allows for traffic filtering, Network Address Translation (NAT), and redirection. Three configurable "chains" are used for handling network traffic: input, output, and forward. The input chain contains rules for traffic that is coming into the local system. The output chain contains rules for traffic that is leaving the local system. The forward chain contains rules for traffic that was received by the local system but is not destined for the local system. Iptables is the latest evolution of ipchains. Iptables uses the same three chains for policy rules and traffic handling as ipchains, but with iptables each packet is processed only by the appropriate chain. Under ipchains, each packet passes through all three chains for processing. With iptables, incoming packets are processed only by the input chain, and packets leaving the system are processed only by the output chain. This allows for more granular control of network traffic and enhances performance.

In addition to the "free" firewalls that come bundled with OSs, many commercial personal firewall packages are available. Many commercial software firewalls limit inbound and outbound network traffic, block pop-ups, detect adware, block cookies and malicious processes, and scan instant messenger traffic. While you can still purchase or even download a free software-based personal firewall, most commercial vendors are bundling the firewall functionality with additional capabilities such as antivirus and anti-spyware.

Microsoft Windows has had a personal software firewall since Windows XP SP2. Today, Windows Firewall is called Windows Defender Firewall (see Figure 14.6). It is enabled by default and provides warnings when disabled. Windows Defender Firewall is fairly configurable; it can be set up to block all traffic, to make exceptions for traffic you want to allow, and to log rejected traffic for later analysis.

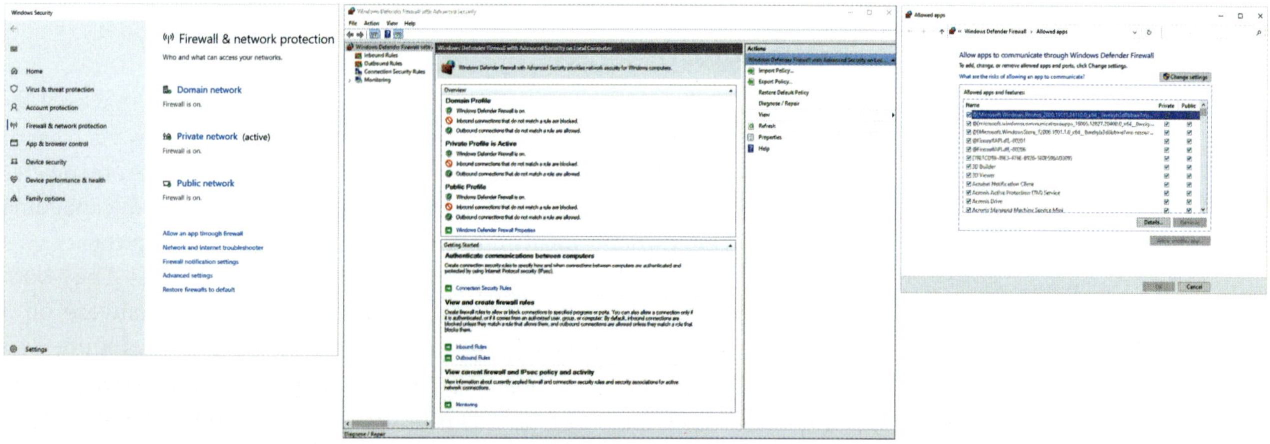

• **Figure 14.6** Windows Defender Firewall is enabled by default.

In Windows 10, Microsoft modified Windows Defender Firewall to make it more capable and configurable. More options were added to allow for more granular control of network traffic as well as the ability to detect when certain components are not behaving as expected. For example, if your Microsoft Outlook client suddenly attempts to connect to a remote web server, Windows Defender Firewall can detect this as a deviation from normal behavior and block the unwanted traffic.

Whitelisting vs. Blacklisting Applications

Applications can be controlled at the OS level when they are started via blacklisting or whitelisting. **Blacklisting** is essentially noting which applications should not be allowed to run on the machine. This is basically a permanent "ignore" or "call block" type of capability. **Whitelisting** is the exact opposite: it consists of a list of allowed applications. Each of these approaches has advantages and disadvantages. Blacklisting is difficult to use against dynamic threats, as the identification of a specific application can easily be avoided through minor changes. Whitelisting is easier to employ from the aspect of the identification of applications that are allowed to run—hash values can be used to ensure the executables are not corrupted. The challenge in whitelisting is the number of potential applications that are run on a typical machine. For a single-purpose machine, such as a database server, whitelisting can be relatively easy to employ. For multipurpose machines, it can be more complicated.

Microsoft has two mechanisms that are part of the OS to control which users can use which applications:

- **Software restrictive policies** Employed via group policies and allow significant control over applications, scripts, and executable files. The primary mode is by machine and not by user account.
- **User account level control** Enforced via AppLocker, which is a service that allows granular control over which users can execute which programs. Through the use of rules, an enterprise can exert significant control over who can access and use installed software.

On a Linux platform, similar capabilities are offered from third-party vendor applications.

AppLocker

AppLocker is a component of Enterprise licenses of Windows that enables administrators to enforce which applications are allowed to run via a set of predefined rules. AppLocker is an adjunct to software restriction policies (SRPs). SRPs required significant administration on a machine-by-machine basis and were difficult to administer across an enterprise. AppLocker was designed so the rules can be distributed and enforced by GPO. They both act to prevent the running of unauthorized software and malware on a machine, but AppLocker is significantly easier to administer. Figure 14.7 shows the AppLocker interface. Some of the features that are enabled via AppLocker are restrictions by user and the ability to run in an audit mode, where results are logged but not enforced, allowing settings to be tested before use.

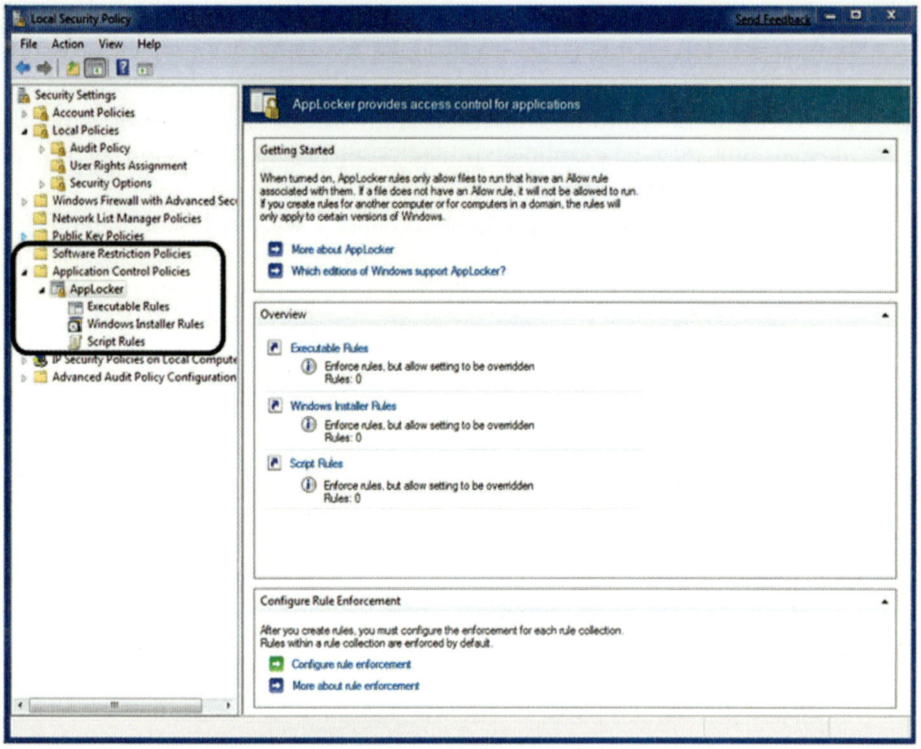

• **Figure 14.7** Microsoft AppLocker interface

Hardware Security

Hardware, in the form of servers, workstations, and even mobile devices, can represent a weakness or vulnerability in the security system associated with an enterprise. While hardware can be easily replaced if lost or stolen, the information that is contained by the devices complicates the security picture. Data or information can be safeguarded from loss by backups, but this does little in the way of protecting it from disclosure to an unauthorized party. There are software measures that can assist in the form of encryption, but these also have drawbacks in the form of scalability and key distribution.

Physical security is an essential element of a security plan. Unauthorized access to hardware and networking components can make many security controls ineffective.

Certain hardware protection mechanisms should be employed to safeguard information in servers, workstations, and mobile devices. Cable locks can be employed on mobile devices to prevent their theft. Locking cabinets and safes can be used to secure portable media, USB drives, and CDs/DVDs. Physical security is covered in more detail in Chapter 8.

Network Hardening

While considering the baseline security of systems, you must consider the role the network connection plays in the overall security profile. The tremendous growth of the Internet and the affordability of multiple PCs and Ethernet networking have resulted in almost every computer being attached to some kind of network, and once computers are attached to a network, they are open to access from any other user on that network. Proper controls over network access must be established on computers by controlling the services that are running and the ports that are opened for network access. In addition to servers and workstations, however, network devices must also be examined: routers, switches, and modems, as well as various other components.

These network devices should be configured with very strict parameters to maintain network security. Like normal computer OSs that need to be patched and updated, the software that runs network infrastructure components needs to be updated regularly. Finally, an outer layer of security should be added by implementing appropriate firewall rules and router ACLs.

Software Updates

Maintaining current vendor patch levels for your software is one of the most important things you can do to maintain security. This is also true for the infrastructure that runs the network. While some equipment is unmanaged and typically has no network presence and few security risks, any managed equipment that is responding on network ports will have some software or firmware controlling it. This software or firmware needs to be updated on a regular basis.

The most common device that connects people to the Internet is the network router. Dozens of brands of routers are available on the market, but Cisco Systems products dominate. The popular Cisco Internetwork Operating System (IOS) runs on more than 70 of Cisco's devices and is installed countless times at countless locations. Its popularity has fueled research into vulnerabilities in the code, and over the past few years quite a few vulnerabilities have been reported. These vulnerabilities can take many forms because routers send and receive several different kinds of traffic, from the standard Telnet remote terminal, to routing information in the form of Routing Information Protocol (RIP) or Open Shortest Path First (OSPF) packets, to Simple Network Management Protocol (SNMP) packets. This highlights the need to update the Cisco IOS software on a regular basis.

Although we focus on Cisco in our discussion, it's important to note that every network device, regardless of the manufacturer, needs to be maintained and patched to remain secure.

Cisco IOS also runs on many of its Ethernet switching products. Like routers, these have capabilities for receiving and processing protocols such as Telnet and SNMP. Smaller network components do not usually run large software suites and typically have smaller software loaded on internal nonvolatile RAM (NVRAM). While the update process for this kind of software is typically called a *firmware update*, this does not change the security implications of keeping it up to date. In the case of a corporate network with several devices, someone must take ownership of updating the devices, and updates must be performed regularly according to security and administration policies.

Device Configuration

As important as it is to keep software up to date, properly configuring network devices is equally, if not more, important. Many network devices, such as routers and switches, now have advanced remote management capabilities, with multiple open ports accepting network connections. Proper configuration is necessary to keep these devices secure. Choosing a good password is very important in maintaining external and internal security, and closing or limiting access to any open ports is also a good step for securing the devices. On the more advanced devices, you must carefully consider what services the device is running, just as with a computer. Here are some general steps to take when securing networking devices:

- *Limit access to only those who need it.* If your networking device allows management via a web interface, SSH, or any other method, limit who can connect to those services. Many networking devices allow you to specify which IP addresses are allowed to connect to those management services.
- *Choose good passwords.* Always change default passwords and follow good password-selection guidelines. If the device supports encryption, ensure passwords are stored in encrypted format on the device.
- *Password-protect the console and remote access.* If the device supports password protection, ensure that all local and remote access capabilities are password protected.
- *Turn off unnecessary services.* If your networking equipment supports Telnet but your organization doesn't need it, turn that service off. It's always a good idea to disable or remove unused services. Your device may also support the use of ACLs to limit access to services such as Telnet and SSH on the device itself.
- *Change the SNMP community strings.* SNMP is widely used to manage networking equipment and typically allows a "public" string, which can typically only read information from a device, and a "private" string, which can often read and write to a device's configuration. Some manufacturers use default or well-known strings (such as "public" for the public string). Therefore, you should always change both the public and private strings if you are using SNMP.

The use of "public" as an SNMP community string is an extremely well-known vulnerability. Any system using an SNMP community string of "public" should have the string changed immediately. The use of older versions of SNMP as well as misconfigurations of SNMP can present a large security hole in a network.

Securing Management Interfaces

Some network security devices will have "management interfaces" that allow for remote management of the devices themselves. Often seen on firewalls, routers, and switches, a management interface allows connections to the device's management application, an SSH service, or even a web-based configuration GUI, which are not allowed on any other interface. Due to this high level of access, management interfaces and management applications must be secured against unauthorized access. They should not be connected to public networks (the Internet) and screened subnets (formerly DMZ). Where possible, access to management interfaces and applications should be restricted within an organization so employees without the proper access rights and privileges cannot even connect to those interfaces and applications.

VLAN Management

A *virtual LAN,* or *VLAN,* is a group of hosts that communicate as if they were on the same broadcast domain. A VLAN is a logical construct that can be used to help control broadcast domains, manage traffic flow, and restrict traffic between organizations, divisions, and so on. Layer 2 switches, by definition, will not bridge IP traffic across VLANs, which gives administrators the ability to segment traffic quite effectively. For example, if multiple departments are connected to the same physical switch, VLANs can be used to segment the traffic such that one department does not see the broadcast traffic from the other departments. By controlling the members of a VLAN, administrators can logically separate network traffic throughout the organization.

Network Segmentation

Network segmentation is the use of network addressing schemes to restrict machine-to-machine communication within specific boundaries. This mechanism uses the network structure and protocols themselves to accomplish a limitation of communication. This mechanism can restrict outside attackers from accessing machines, even if they have stolen credentials, because the network will not connect the attacker's machine to the target machine.

IPv4 vs. IPv6

IPv4 (Internet Protocol version 4) is the de facto communication standard in use on almost every network around the planet. Unfortunately, IPv4 contains some inherent shortcomings and vulnerabilities. In an attempt to address these issues, the Internet Engineering Task Force (IETF) launched an effort to update or replace IPv4; the result is IPv6. Using a new packet format and much larger address space, IPv6 is designed to speed up packet processing by routers and supply 3.4×10^{38} possible addresses (IPv4 uses only 32 bits for addressing; IPv6 uses 128 bits). Additionally, IPv6 has security "built in," with mandatory support for network layer security. Although widely adopted under IPv4, IPSec support is mandatory in IPv6. The issue now is one of conversion. IPv4 and IPv6 networks cannot talk directly to each other and must rely on some type of gateway. Many operating systems and devices currently support dual IP stacks and can run both IPv4 and IPv6. While adoption of IPv6 is proceeding, it is moving slowly and has yet to gain a significant foothold.

If your network is not using IPv6, you should disable IPv6 on all clients and servers to prevent malicious traffic from using this protocol to bypass security devices. This follows the principle of "if you are not using something, disable it."

Tech Tip

Port Scanners

To find out what services are open on a given host or network device, many administrators will use a tool called a port scanner. A port scanner is designed to probe remote systems for open TCP and UDP services. Nmap is a very popular (and free) port scanner (see https://nmap.org).

Application Hardening

Perhaps as important as OS and network hardening is **application hardening**—securing an application against local and Internet-based attacks. Hardening applications is fairly similar to hardening operating systems—you remove the functions or components you don't need, restrict access where you can, and make sure the application is kept up to date with patches. In most cases, the last step in that list is the most important for maintaining application security. After all, applications must be accessible to users; otherwise, they serve no purpose. As most problems with applications tend to be buffer overflows in legitimate user input fields, patching the application is often the only way to secure it from attack.

Application Configuration Baseline

As with operating systems, applications (particularly those providing public services such as web servers and mail servers) will have recommended security and functionality settings. In some cases, vendors will provide those recommended settings, and, in other cases, an outside organization such as NSA, ISSA, or SANS will provide recommended configurations for popular applications. Many large organizations will develop their own *application configuration baseline*—a list of settings, tweaks, and modifications which creates a functional and hopefully secure application for use within the organization. Developing an application baseline and using it any time that application is deployed within the organization helps to ensure a consistent (and hopefully secure) configuration across the organization.

Application Patches

As obvious as this seems, application patches are most likely going to come from the vendor that sells the application. After all, who else has access to the source code? In some cases, such as with Microsoft's IIS, this is the same company that sold the OS that the application runs on. In other cases, such as Apache, the vendor is OS independent and provides an application with versions for many different OSs.

Application patches are likely to come in three varieties: hotfixes, patches, and upgrades. As described for OSs earlier in the chapter, hotfixes are usually small sections of code designed to fix a specific problem. For example, a hotfix may address a buffer overflow in the login routine for an application. Patches are usually collections of fixes, tend to be much larger, and are usually released on a periodic basis or whenever enough problems have been addressed to warrant a patch release. Upgrades are another popular method of patching applications, and they tend to be presented with a more positive spin than patches. Even the term *upgrade* has a positive connotation—you are moving up to a better, more functional, and more secure application. For this reason, many vendors release "upgrades" that consist mainly of fixes rather than new or enhanced functionality.

Some application "patches" contain new or enhanced functions, and some change user-defined settings back to defaults during installation of the patch. If you are deploying an application patch across a large group of users, it is important to understand exactly what that application patch really does. Patches should first be tested in a nonproduction environment before deployment to determine exactly how they affect the system and the network it is connected to.

Patch Management

In the early days of network computing, things were easy—fewer applications existed, vendor patches came out annually or quarterly, and access was restricted to authorized individuals. Updates were few and easy to handle. Now application and OS updates are pushed constantly as vendors struggle to provide new capabilities, fix problems, and address vulnerabilities. Microsoft created "Patch Tuesday" in an effort to condense the update cycle and reduce the effort required to maintain its products and has now gone to continuous patching of its newest OS. As the number of patches continues to rise, many organizations struggle to keep up with patches—which patches should be applied immediately, which are compatible with the current configuration, which will not affect current business operations, and so on. To help cope with this flood of patches, many organizations have adopted *patch management*, the process of planning, testing, and deploying patches in a controlled manner.

Patch management is a disciplined approach to the acquisition, testing, and implementation of OS and application patches and requires a fair amount of resources to implement properly. To implement patch management effectively, you must first have a good inventory of the software used in your environment, including all OSs and applications. Then you must set up a process to monitor for updates to those software packages. Many vendors provide the ability to update their products automatically or to automatically check for updates and inform the user when updates are available.

Keeping track of patch availability is merely the first step; in many environments, patches must be analyzed and tested. Does the patch apply to the software you are running? Does the patch address a vulnerability or critical issue that must be fixed immediately? What is the impact of applying that patch or group of patches? Will it break something else if you apply this patch? To address these issues, it is recommended that you use development or test platforms, where you can carefully analyze and test patches before placing them into a production environment. Although patches are generally "good," they are not always exhaustively tested; some have been known to "break" other products or functions within the product being patched, and others have introduced new vulnerabilities while attempting to address an existing vulnerability. The extent of analysis and testing varies widely from organization to organization. Testing and analysis will also vary depending on the application or OS and the extent of the patch.

> **Tech Tip**
>
> **Production Patching**
>
> *Patching of production systems brings risk in the change process. This risk should be mitigated via a change management process. Change management is covered in detail in Chapter 21. Patching of production systems should follow the enterprise change management process.*

Once a patch has been analyzed and tested, administrators have to determine when to apply the patch. Because many patches require a restart of applications or services or even a reboot of the entire system, most operational environments apply patches only at specific times, to reduce downtime and possible impact and to ensure administrators are available if something goes wrong. Many organizations will also have a rollback plan that allows them to recover the systems back to a known-good configuration prior to the patch, in case the patch has unexpected or undesirable effects. Some organizations require extensive coordination and approval of patches prior to implementation, and some institute "lockout" dates where no patching or system changes (with few exceptions) can be made, to ensure business operations are not disrupted. For example, an e-commerce site might have a lockout between the Thanksgiving and Christmas holidays to ensure the site is always available to holiday shoppers.

With any environment, but especially with larger environments, it can be a challenge to track the update status of every desktop and server in the organization. Documenting and maintaining patch status can be a challenge. However, with a disciplined approach, training, policies, and procedures, even the largest environments can be managed. To assist in their patch-management efforts, many organizations use a patch-management product that automates many of the mundane and manpower-intensive tasks associated with patch management. For example, many patch-management products provide the following:

- Ability to inventory applications and operating systems in use
- Notification of patches that apply to your environment

- Periodic or continual scanning of systems to validate patch status and identify missing patches
- Ability to select which patches to apply and to which systems to apply them
- Ability to push patches to systems on an on-demand or scheduled basis
- Ability to report patch success or failure
- Ability to report patch status on any or all systems in the environment

Patch management solutions can also be useful to satisfy audit or compliance requirements, as they can show a structured approach to patch management, show when and how systems are patched, and provide a detailed accounting of patch status within the organization.

Microsoft provides a free patch management product called Windows Server Update Services (WSUS), shown in Figure 14.8. Using the WSUS product, administrators can manage updates for any compatible Windows-based system in their organization. The WSUS product can be configured to download patches automatically from Microsoft based on a variety of factors (such as OS, product family, criticality, and so on). When updates are downloaded, the administrator can determine whether or not to push out the patches and when to apply them to the systems in their environment. The WSUS product can also help administrators track patch status on their systems, which is a useful and necessary feature.

Tech Tip

Patch Availability

Software vendors update software and eventually end support for older versions. Software that has reached its end of service life can represent a threat to security, as it is no longer being patched against problems as they are discovered. This same outcome can result from a vendor going out of business. Software in these cases should be carefully monitored for increased risk to the enterprise.

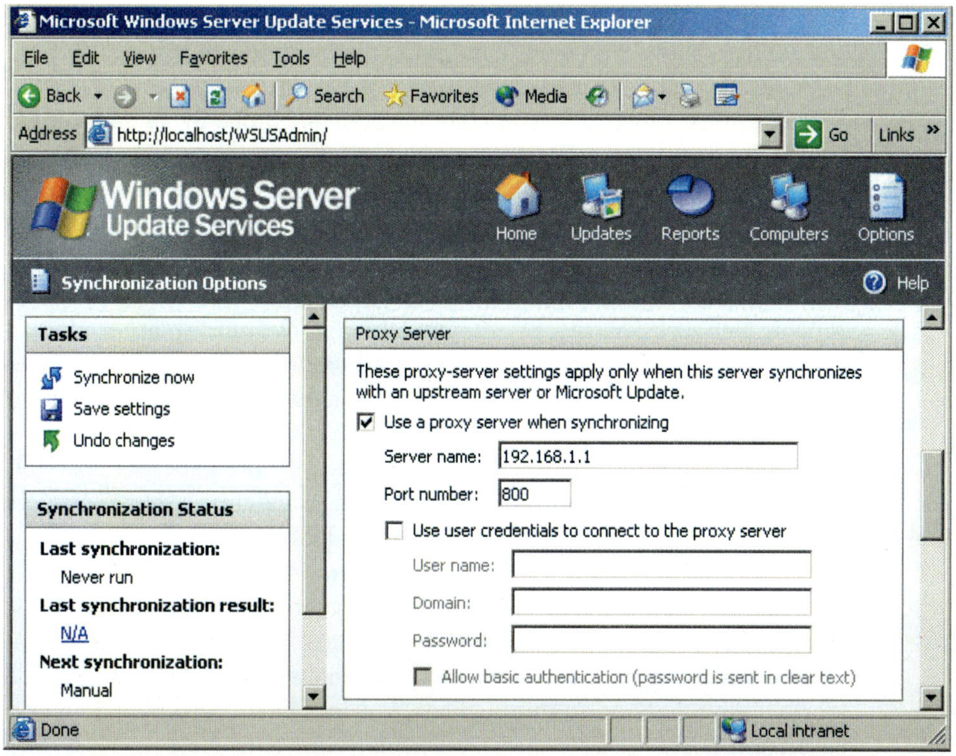

• **Figure 14.8** Windows Server Update Services

Host Software Baselining

To secure, configure, and patch software, administrators must first know what software is installed and running on systems. Maintaining an accurate picture of what operating systems and applications are running inside an organization can be a very labor-intensive task for administrators—especially if individual users have the ability to load software onto their own servers and workstations. To address this issue, many organizations develop *software baselines* for hosts and servers. Sometimes called "default," "gold," or "standard" configurations, a software baseline contains all the approved software that should appear on a desktop or server within the organization. While software baselines can differ slightly due to disparate needs between groups of users, the more "standard" a software baseline becomes, the easier it will be for administrators to secure, patch, and maintain systems within the organization.

Vulnerability Scanner

Due to the number of checks they can perform, network scanners can generate a great deal of traffic and a large number of connections to the systems being examined, so care should be taken to minimize the impact on production systems and production networks.

A vulnerability scanner is a program designed to probe hosts for weaknesses, misconfigurations, old versions of software, and so on. There are essentially three main categories of vulnerability scanners: network, host, and application.

A **network vulnerability scanner** probes a host (or hosts) for issues across its network connections. Typically a network scanner will either contain or use a port scanner to perform an initial assessment of the network to determine which hosts are alive and which services are open on those hosts. Each system and service is then probed. Network scanners are very broad tools that can run potentially thousands of checks, depending on the OS and services being examined. This makes them a very good "broad sweep" for network-visible vulnerabilities.

Network scanners are essentially the equivalent of a Swiss Army knife for assessments. They do lots of tasks and are extremely useful to have around, but they might not be as good as a tool dedicated to examining one specific type of service. However, if you can only run a single tool to examine your network for vulnerabilities, you'll want that tool to be a network vulnerability scanner. Figure 14.9 shows a screenshot of Nessus from Tenable Network Security, a very popular network vulnerability scanner.

Bottom line: If you need to perform a broad sweep for vulnerabilities on one or more hosts across the network, a network vulnerability scanner is the right tool for the job.

Host vulnerability scanners are designed to run on a specific host and look for vulnerabilities and misconfigurations on that host. Host scanners tend to be more specialized because they're looking for issues associated with a specific operating system or set of operating systems.

Selecting the right type of vulnerability scanner isn't that difficult. Just focus on what types of vulnerabilities you need to scan for and how you will be accessing the host/services/applications being scanned. It's also worth noting that to do a thorough job, you will likely need both network-based and host-based scanners—particularly for critical assets. Host- and

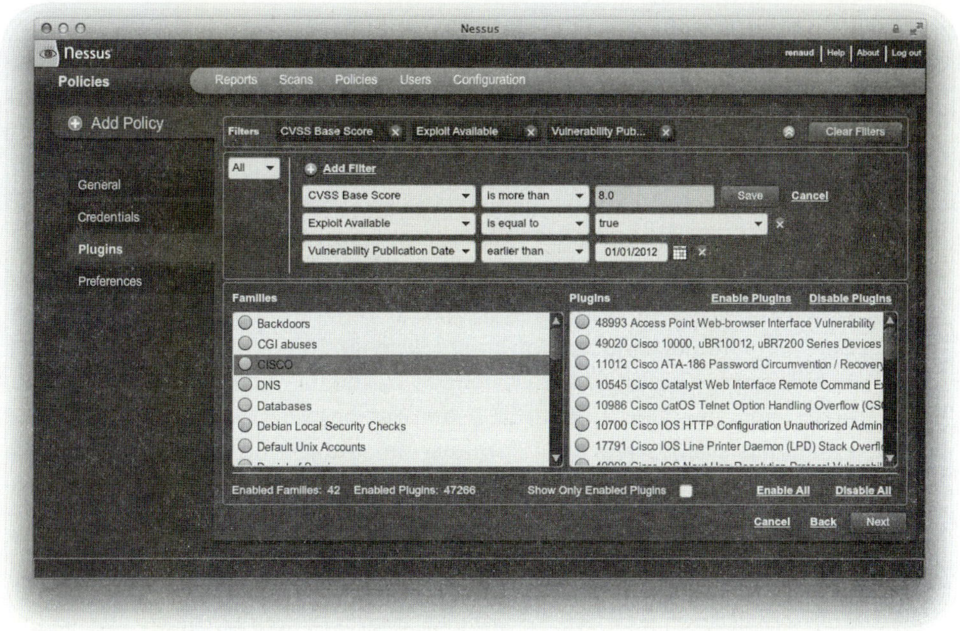

• **Figure 14.9** Nessus—a network vulnerability scanner

network-based scanners perform different tests and provide visibility into different types of vulnerabilities. If you want to ensure the best coverage, you'll need to run both.

Application vulnerability scanners are designed to look for vulnerabilities in applications or certain types of applications. Application scanners are some of the most specialized scanners—even though they contain hundreds or even thousands of checks, they only look for misconfigurations or vulnerabilities in a specific type of application. Arguably the most popular type of application scanners are designed to test for weaknesses and vulnerabilities in web-based applications. Web applications are designed to be visible, interact with users, and accept and process user input—all things that make them attractive targets for attackers.

Data-Based Security Controls

Security controls can be implemented on a host machine for the express purpose of providing data protection on the host. This section explores methods to implement the appropriate controls to ensure data security.

Data Security

Data or information is the most important element to protect in the enterprise. Equipment can be purchased, replaced, and shared without consequence; it is the information that is being processed that has the value. *Data security* refers to the actions taken in the enterprise to secure data, wherever it resides: in transit, at rest, or in use.

Data in Transit

Data has value in the enterprise, but for the enterprise to fully realize the value, data elements need to be shared and moved between systems. Whenever data is *in transit,* being moved from one system to another, it needs to be protected. The most common method of this protection is via encryption. What is important is to ensure that data is always protected in proportion to the degree of risk associated with a data security failure.

Data at Rest

Data at rest refers to data being stored. Data is stored in a variety of formats: in files, in databases, and as structured elements. Whether in ASCII, XML, JavaScript Object Notation (JSON), or a database, and regardless of on what media it is stored, data at rest still requires protection commensurate with its value. Again, as with data in transit, encryption is the best means of protection against unauthorized access or alteration.

Data in Use

Data is processed in applications, is used for various functions, and can be at risk when in system memory or even in the act of processing. Protecting data while *in use* is a much trickier proposition than protecting it in transit or in storage. While encryption can be used in these other situations, it is not practical to perform operations on encrypted data. This means that other means need to be taken to protect the data. Protected memory schemes and address space layout randomization are two tools that can be used to prevent data security failures during processing. Secure coding principles, including the definitive wiping of critical data elements once they are no longer needed, can assist in protecting data in use.

Data Encryption

Data encryption continues to be the best solution for data security. Properly encrypted, the data is not readable by an unauthorized party. There are numerous ways to enact this level of protection on a host machine.

Full Disk

Full disk encryption refers to the act of encrypting an entire partition in one operation. Then, as specific elements are needed, those particular sectors can be decrypted for use. This offers a simple convenience factor and ensures that all of the data is protected. It does come at a performance cost, as the act of decrypting and encrypting takes time. For some high-performance data stores, especially those with latency issues, this performance hit may be critical. Although better performance can be achieved with specialized hardware, as with all security controls there needs to be an evaluation of the risk involved versus the costs.

Database

Major database engines have built-in encryption capabilities. The advantage to these encryption schemes is that they can be tailored to the data structure, protecting the essential columns while not impacting columns that are not sensitive. Properly employing database encryption requires that the data schema and its security requirements be designed into the database implementation. The advantage is in better protection against any database compromise, and the performance hit is typically negligible with respect to other alternatives.

Individual Files

Individual files can also be encrypted in a system. This can be done either at the OS level or via a third-party application. Managing individual file encryption can be tricky, as the problem moves to an encryption key security problem. When using built-in encryption methods with an OS, the key issue is resolved by the OS itself, with a single key being employed and stored with the user credentials. One of the advantages of individual file encryption comes when transferring data to another user. Transporting a single file via an unprotected channel such as e-mail can be done securely with single-file encryption.

USB Encryption

Universal Serial Bus (USB) offers an easy mechanism to connect devices to a computer. It acts as the mechanism of transport between the computer and an external device. When data traverses the USB connection, it typically ends up on a portable device and thus requires an appropriate level of security. Many mechanisms exist, from encryption on the USB device itself, to OS-enabled encryption, to independent encryption before the data is moved. Each of these mechanisms has advantages and disadvantages, and it is ultimately up to the user to choose the best method based on the sensitivity of the data.

Mobile Devices

Mobile device security, covered in detail in Chapter 12, is also essential when critical or sensitive data is transmitted to mobile devices. The protection of mobile devices goes beyond simple encryption of the data, as the device can act as an authorized endpoint for the system, opening up avenues of attack.

Handling Big Data

Big data is the industry buzzword for very large data sets being used in many enterprises. Data sets in the petabyte, exabyte, and even zettabyte range are now being explored in some applications. Data sets of these sizes require special hardware and software to handle them, but this does not alleviate the need for security. Planning for security on this scale requires enterprise-level thinking, but it is worth noting that eventually some subset of the information makes its way to a host machine for use. It is at this point that the data is vulnerable, because whatever protection scheme is in place on the large storage system, the data is outside that realm now. This means that local protection mechanisms, such as provided by Kerberos-based authentication, can be critical in managing this type of protection scheme.

Cloud Storage

Cloud computing is the use of online resources for storage, processing, or both. When data is stored in the cloud, encryption can be used to protect the data, so that what is actually stored is encrypted data. This reduces the risk of data disclosure both in transit to the cloud and back, as well as while in storage.

Storage Area Network

A storage area network (SAN) is a means of storing data across a secondary dedicated network. SANs operate to connect data storage devices as if they were local storage, yet they are separate and can be collections of disks, tapes, and other storage devices. Because the dedicated network is separate from the normal IP network, accessing the SAN requires going through one of the attached machines. This makes SANs a bit more secure than other forms of storage, although loss through a compromised client machine is still a risk.

> **Tech Tip**
>
> **Permissions Issues**
>
> *Permissions are the cornerstone of security, and ACLs are how they are enforced. ACL mistakes and failures result in the improper configuration of permissions—one of the most common errors in security. This is a problem to keep in mind throughout the material in the book. One question that should be forefront in any professional's mind, both in configuring and testing, is "are the permissions being done correctly?"*

Permissions/ACL

Access control lists (ACLs) form one of the foundational bases for security on a machine. ACLs can be used by the operating system to make determinations as to whether or not a user can access a resource. This level of permission restriction offers significant protection of resources and transfers the management of the access control problem to the management of ACLs, which is a smaller and more manageable problem.

Environment

A modern *environment* is separated into multiple areas designed to isolate the functions of development, test, and production. These areas are primarily used to prevent accidents from arising from untested code ending up in production, and they are segregated by access control list and hardware, thus preventing users from accessing multiple different areas of the environment. Special accounts are used to move code between these areas of the environment in order to eliminate issues of crosstalk.

Development

A *development* system is one that is sized, configured, and set up for developers to create applications and systems. The development hardware does not have to scale like production, and it probably does not need to be as responsive for certain transactions. The development platform does need to be of the same type of system, because developing on Windows and deploying to Linux is fraught with difficulties that can be avoided by matching development environments to production in terms of OS type and version. After code is successfully developed, it is moved to a test system.

Test

The *test* environment is one that fairly closely mimics the production environment, with the same versions of software (down to the patch level) and the same sets of permissions, file structures, and so on. The purpose of the test environment is to enable a system to be fully tested prior to being deployed into production. The test environment might not scale like production, but from the viewpoint of a software/hardware footprint, it looks exactly like production.

Staging

The *staging* environment is an optional environment, but it is commonly found when there are multiple production environments. After passing the test, the system moves into staging, where it can be deployed to the different production systems. The primary purpose of staging is as a sandbox after test, so the test system can test the next set while the current set is deployed across the enterprise. One method of deployment is a staged deployment, where software is deployed to part of the enterprise and then paused to watch for unforeseen problems. If none occur, the deployment continues, stage by stage, until all of the production systems are changed. By moving software in this manner, you never lose the old production system until the end of the move, giving you time to judge and catch any unforeseen problems. This also prevents the total loss of production to a failed update.

Production

Production is the environment where the systems work with real data, doing the business that the system is supposed to perform. This is an environment where there are by design virtually no changes, except as approved and tested via the system's change management process.

Automation/Scripting

Automation and *scripting* are valuable tools for system administrators and others to safely and efficiently execute tasks. Although many tasks can be performed by simple command-line execution or through the use of GUI menu operations, the use of scripts has two advantages. First, prewritten and tested scripts remove the chance of error, either a typo or clicking the wrong option. Errors are common and can take significant time to undo; for example, erasing the wrong file or directory can take time to locate and restore from a backup. The second advantage is that scripts can be chained together to provide a means of automating action.

Automation is a major element of an enterprise security program. There is an entire set of protocols, standards, methods, and architectures developed to support automation. The security community has developed automation methods associated with vulnerability management, including the Security Content Automation Protocol (SCAP), Common Vulnerabilities Enumeration (CVE), and more. Details can be found at https://measurablesecurity.mitre.org/.

Automated Courses of Action

Scripts are the best friend of administrators, analysts, investigators, or any professional who values efficient and accurate technical work. Scripts allow you to automate courses of action, with the subsequent steps tested and, when necessary, approved. Scripts and automation are important enough that they are specified in National Institute of Standards and Technology Special Publication 800-53 series, which describes security controls. For instance, under patching, not only is an automated method of determining which systems need patches specified but also that the patching mechanism be automated. *Automated courses of action* reduce errors.

Automated courses of action can save time as well. If, during an investigation, one needs to take an image of a hard drive on a system, calculate hash values, and record all the details in a file for chain of custody, this all can be done in just a few command lines—or with a single script that has been tested and approved for use.

Continuous Monitoring

Continuous monitoring is the term used to describe a system that has monitoring built into it, so rather than monitoring being an external event that may or may not happen, monitoring is an intrinsic aspect of the action. From a big-picture point of view, continuous monitoring is the name used to describe a formal risk assessment process that follows the NIST Risk Management Framework (RMF) methodology. Part of that methodology process is the use of security controls. Continuous monitoring is the operational process by which you can monitor and know if controls are functioning in an effective manner.

As most enterprises have a large number of systems and larger number of security controls, part of an effective continuous monitoring plan is the automated handling of the continuous monitoring status data, to facilitate consumption in a meaningful manner. Automated dashboards and alerts that show out-of-standard conditions allow operators to focus on the parts of the system that need attention rather than staring at literally tons of data.

Configuration Validation

Configuration validation is a challenge as systems age and change over time. When a system is placed into service, its configuration should be validated against security standards, ensuring that the system will do what it is supposed to do, and only what it is supposed to do. No added functionality. All extra ports, services, accounts, and so on are disabled, removed, or turned off. The configuration files, including ACLs for the system, are correct and working as designed.

Over time, as things change, software is patched, and other things are added to or taken away from the server. Updates to the application, the OS, and even other applications on the server change the configuration. Is the configuration still valid? How does one monitor all of their machines to ensure valid configurations? Automated testing is a method that can scale and resolve this issue, making it just another part of the continuous monitoring system. Any other manual method eventually fails because of fluctuating priorities that will result in routine maintenance being deferred.

Templates

Templates are master recipes for the building of objects, be they servers, programs, or even entire systems. Templates contain all of the required configuration options and setup controls enabling the automation of item deployment. You can have multiple templates for a given service, each tailored to different requirements or circumstances. The end result is that you have predefined the setup and deployment options for the item, whether hardware or software. **Security templates** can provide directions for securely provisioning a system.

Templates are what make Infrastructure as a Service (IaaS) possible: you establish a business relationship with an IaaS firm (the time-consuming part), they need to collect billing information, and you need to review a lot of terms and conditions with your legal team. But, then, the part you want is the standing up of some piece of infrastructure (say, for example, a LAMP stack). A LAMP stack is a popular open source web platform that is ideal for running dynamic sites. It is composed of Linux, Apache, MySQL, and PHP/Python/Perl—hence the term LAMP. You want this server to be secured, patched, and have specific accounts for access. You fill out a web form, which uses your information to match to an appropriate template. You specify all the conditions and click the Create button. If you were going to stand this up on your own, it might take days to configure all of these elements from scratch on in-house hardware. Next, the IaaS firm uses templates and master images, and your solution is online within minutes, or even seconds. If you have special needs, it might take a bit longer, but you get the idea: templates allow for the rapid, error-free creation of items such as configurations, the connection of services, testing, and deployment.

Master Image

Master images are premade, fully patched images of systems. A *master image,* in the form of a virtual machine, can be configured and deployed in seconds to replace a system that has become tainted or is untrustworthy because of an incident. Master images provide the true, clean backup of the operating systems, applications, and everything else but the data. When you architect your enterprise to take advantage of master images, you make many administrative tasks easier to automate, easier to perform, and substantially more free of errors. Should an error be found, you have one image to fix and then deploy. Master images work very well for enterprises with multiple desktops, because you can create a master image that can be quickly deployed on new or repaired machines, bringing the systems to an identical and fully patched condition.

Nonpersistence

Nonpersistence is when a change to a system is not permanent. Making a system nonpersistent can be a useful tool when you wish to prevent certain types of malware attacks, for example. A system that has been made nonpersistent is not able to save changes to its configuration, its apps, or anything else. There are utility programs that can freeze a machine from change, in essence making it nonpersistent. This is useful for machines deployed in places where users can invoke changes, download stuff from the Internet, and so on. Nonpersistence offers a means for the enterprise to address these risks, by not letting them happen in the first place. In some respects this is similar to whitelisting, only allowing approved applications to run.

Snapshots

Snapshots are instantaneous save points in time on virtual machines. These allow the virtual machine to be restored to that point in time. This works, because in the end, a VM is just a file on a machine, and setting the file back to a previous version reverts the VM to the state it was in at that time. Snapshots can be very useful in reducing risk, as you can take a snapshot, make a change to the system, and, if the change is bad, revert back to the snapshot like the change had never been made.

Reverting to a Known State

Reverting to a known state is akin to reverting to a snapshot. Many OSs now have the capability to produce a restore point, which is a copy of key files that change upon updates to the OS. If you add a driver or update the OS, and the update results in problems, you can restore the system to the previously saved restore point. This is a very commonly used option in Microsoft Windows, and the system by default creates restore points before it processes updates to the OS, and at set points in time between updates. This gives users the ability to roll back the clock on the OS and restore to an earlier time when they know the problem did not exist. Unlike snapshots, which record everything, this only protects the OS and associated files; it also does not result in the loss of users' files, which is something that does happen with snapshots.

Rolling Back to a Known Configuration

Rolling back to a known configuration is another way of saying "revert to a known state." It was the specific language Microsoft uses with respect to rolling back the Registry values to a known-good configuration on boot. If you make an incorrect configuration change in Windows and now the system won't boot properly, you could select the Last Known Good Configuration option in the boot setup menu and roll back the Registry to the last value that properly completed a boot cycle. Microsoft stores most configuration options in the Registry, and this is a way to revert to a previous set of configuration options for the machine. Microsoft discontinued the direct ability to roll back to the last known-good configuration after Windows 7, and now the only option is to boot into safe mode and diagnose the problem via those menu options.

Live Boot Media

A *live boot media* CD/USB is a device that contains a complete bootable system. These devices are specially formatted so as to be bootable from the media. This allows you a means of booting the device to an external OS source, should the one on the internal drive become unusable. This may be used as a recovery mechanism, although if the internal drive is encrypted, you will need backup keys to access it. This is also a convenient means of booting to a task-specific operating system, such as forensic tools or incident response tools that are separate from the OS on the machine.

Wrappers

TCP wrappers are structures used to enclose or contain some other system. Wrappers have been used in a variety of ways, including to obscure or hide functionality. A trojan horse is a form of wrapper. Wrappers also can be used to encapsulate information, such as in tunneling or VPN solutions. Wrappers can act as a form of channel control, including integrity and authentication information that a normal signal cannot carry. It is common to see wrappers used in alternative environments to prepare communications for IP transmission.

Elasticity

Elasticity is the ability of a system to increase the workload using additional hardware resources—commonly dynamically added on demand—in order to scale out. If the workload increases, you scale by adding more resources; conversely, when demand wanes, you scale back by removing unneeded resources. Elasticity is one of the strengths of cloud environments, as you can configure them to scale up and down, and only pay for the actual resources you use. In a server farm that you own, you pay for the equipment, even when not in use. In an elastic cloud environment, you literally only pay for what you use.

> Elasticity and scalability seem to be the same thing, but they are different. *Elasticity* is related to dynamically scaling a system with workload (scaling out), whereas *scalability* is a design element that enables both scaling up (to more capable hardware) and scaling out (to more instances).

Scalability

Scalability is the ability of the system to accommodate larger workloads through the addition of resources, either by making hardware stronger, scaling up, adding additional nodes, or scaling out. This term is commonly used in server farms and database clusters, as these both can have scale issues with respect to workload.

Distributive Allocation

Distributive allocation is the transparent allocation of requests across a range of resources. When multiple servers are employed to respond to load, distributive allocation handles the assignment of jobs across the servers. When the jobs are stateful, as in database queries, the process ensures that the subsequent requests are returned to the same server to maintain transactional integrity. When the system is stateless, like web servers, other load-balancing routines are used to spread the work.

Alternative Environments

Alternative environments are those that are not traditional computer systems in a common IT environment. This is not to say that these environments are rare; in fact, there are millions of systems, composed of hundreds of millions of devices, all across society. Computers exist in many systems where they perform critical functions specifically tied to a particular system. These alternative systems are frequently static in nature; that is, their software is unchanging over the course of its function. Updates and revisions are few and far between. Although this may seem to run counter to current security practices, it doesn't: because these alternative systems are constrained to a limited, defined set of functionality, the risk from vulnerabilities is limited. Examples of these alternative environments include embedded systems, SCADA (supervisory control and data acquisition) systems, mobile devices, mainframes, game consoles, and in-vehicle computers.

Alternative Environment Methods

Many of the alternative environments can be considered static systems. *Static systems* are those that have a defined scope and purpose and do not regularly change in a dynamic manner, unlike most PC environments. Static systems tend to have closed ecosystems, with complete control over all functionality by a single vendor. A wide range of security techniques can be employed in the management of alternative systems. Network segmentation, security layers, wrappers, and firewalls assist in the securing of the network connections between these systems. Manual updates, firmware control, and control redundancy assist in the security of the device operation.

Peripherals

Peripherals used to be basically dumb devices, with low to no interaction; however, with the low cost of compute power and the desire to program greater functionality, many of these devices have embedded computers in them. This has led to hacking of peripherals and the need to understand the security aspects of peripherals. Items such as wireless keyboards and mice, printers, displays, and storage devices all become sources of risk.

Wireless Keyboards

Wireless keyboards operate via a short range wireless signal between the keyboard and the computer. The main method of connection is either via a USB Bluetooth connector, in essence creating a small personal area network (PAN), or via a 2.4GHz dongle. Wireless keyboards are frequently paired with wireless mice, thus removing those troublesome and annoying cables from the desktop. Because of the wireless connection, the signals to and from the peripherals are subject to interception, and attacks have been made on these devices.

Wireless Mice

Wireless mice are similar in nature to wireless keyboards. They tend to connect as a human interface device (HID) class of USB. This is part of the USB specification and is used for mice and keyboards, simplifying connections, drivers, and interfaces through a common specification.

One of the interesting security problems with wireless mice and keyboards has been the development of the *mousejacking* attack. This is when an attacker performs a man-in-the-middle attack on the wireless interface and can control the mouse and/or intercept the traffic. When this attack first hit the environment, manufacturers had to provide updates to their software interfaces to block this form of attack. Some of the major manufacturers, like Logitech, made this effort for their mainstream product lines, but a lot of mice that are older were never patched. Also, smaller vendors have never addressed the vulnerability, so it still exists.

Displays

Computer displays are primarily connected to machines via a cable to one of several types of display connectors. However, for conferences and other group settings, a wide array of devices today can enable a machine to connect to a display via a wireless network. These devices are available from Apple, Google, and a wide range of A/V companies. The risk of using these devices is simple—who else within range of the wireless signal can watch what you are beaming to the display in the conference room? And would you even know if the signal was intercepted? In a word, you wouldn't. This doesn't mean these devices should not be used in the enterprise, but just that they should not be used for transmitting sensitive data to the screen.

Printers/MFDs

Printers have CPUs and a lot of memory. The primary purpose for this is to offload the printing from the device sending the print job to the print queue. Modern printers now come standard with a bidirectional channel so that you can send a print job to the printer and then the printer can send back information as to job status, printer status, and other items. Multifunction devices (MFDs) are like printers on steroids. They typically combine printing, scanning, and faxing all into a single device. This has become a popular market segment because it reduces costs and device proliferation in the office.

With printers being connected to the network, multiple people can connect and independently print jobs, thus sharing a fairly expensive high-speed duplexing printer. But with the CPU, firmware, and memory comes the risk of an attack vector, and hackers have demonstrated malware passed via a printer. This is not a mainstream issue yet, but it has passed the proof-of-concept phase, and in the future we will need to have software protect us from our printers.

External Storage Devices

The rise of network array storage (NAS) devices moved quickly from the enterprise into form factors that are found in homes. As users have developed large collections of digital videos and music, these external storage devices, running on the home network, solve the storage problem. These devices are typically fairly simple Linux-based appliances, with multiple hard drives in a RAID arrangement. With the rise of ransomware, these devices can spread infections to any and all devices that connect to the network. For this reason, precautions should be taken with respect to always-on connections to storage arrays.

Wi-Fi-Enabled MicroSD Cards

A class of Wi-Fi-enabled MicroSD cards were developed to eliminate the need to move the card from device to device in order to move the data. Primarily designed for digital cameras, these cards became very useful for creating Wi-Fi devices out of devices that had an SD slot. These cards have a tiny computer embedded in them that runs a stripped-down version of Linux. One of the major vendors in this space used a stripped-down version of BusyBox and had no security invoked at all, making the device completely open to hackers.

Phones and Mobile Devices

Mobile devices may seem to be a static environment, one where the OS rarely changes or is rarely updated, but as these devices have become more and more ubiquitous, offering greater capabilities, this is no longer the case. Mobile devices have regular OS software updates, and as users add applications, this makes most mobile devices a complete security challenge. Mobile devices frequently come with Bluetooth connectivity mechanisms. Protection of the devices from attacks against the Bluetooth connection, such as bluejacking and bluesnarfing, is an important mitigation. To protect against unauthorized connections, a Bluetooth device should always have discoverable mode turned off, unless the user is deliberately pairing the device.

Mobile devices are covered in detail in Chapter 12.

Embedded Systems

Embedded systems is the name given to computers that are included as an integral part of a larger system, typically hardwired in. From computer peripherals like printers, to household devices like smart TVs and thermostats, to the car you drive, embedded systems are everywhere. Embedded systems can be as simple as a microcontroller with fully integrated interfaces (a system on a chip) or as complex as the tens of interconnected embedded systems in a modern automobile. Embedded systems are designed with a single control purpose in mind and have virtually no additional functionality, but this does not mean that they are free of risk or security concerns. The vast majority of security exploits involve getting a device or system to do something it is capable of doing, and technically designed to do, even if the resulting functionality was never an intended use of the device or system.

The designers of embedded systems typically are focused on minimizing costs, with security seldom seriously considered as part of either the design or the implementation. Because most embedded systems operate as isolated systems, the risks have not been significant. However, as capabilities have increased, and these devices have become networked together, the risks have increased significantly. For example, smart printers have been hacked as a way into enterprises, and as a way to hide from defenders. And when next-generation automobiles begin to talk to each other, passing traffic and other information between them, and begin to have navigation and other inputs being beamed into systems, the risks will increase and security will become an issue. This has already been seen in the airline industry, where the separation of in-flight Wi-Fi, in-flight entertainment, and cockpit digital flight control networks has become a security issue.

Camera Systems

Digital camera systems have entered the computing world through a couple of different portals. First, there is the world of high-end digital cameras that have networking stacks, image processors, and even 4K video feeds. These are used in enterprises such as the news, where getting the data live without extra processing delays can be important. What is important to note is that most of these devices, although they are networked into other networks, have built-in virtual private networks (VPNs) that are always on, because the content is considered valuable enough to protect as a feature.

The next set of cameras reverses the quantity and quality characteristics. Whereas the high-end devices are fairly small in number, there is a growing segment of video surveillance cameras, including household surveillance, baby monitors, and the like. Hundreds of millions of these devices are sold, and they all have a sensor, a processor, a network stack, and so on. These are part of the Internet of Things (IoT) revolution, where millions of devices connect together either on purpose or by happenstance. It was a network of these devices, along with a default username and password, that led to the Mirai botnet that actually broke the Internet for a while in the fall of 2016. The true root cause was a failure to follow a networking RFC concerning source addressing, coupled with the default username and password and remote configuration, that enabled these devices to be taken over. Two sets of failures, working together, created weeks' worth of problems.

Game Consoles

Computer-based game consoles can be considered a type of embedded system designed for entertainment. The OS in a game console is not there for the user but rather to support the specific application or game. There typically is no user interface to the OS on a game console for a user to interact with; rather, the OS is designed for a sole purpose. With the rise of multifunction entertainment consoles, the attack surface of a gaming console can be fairly large, but it is still constrained by the closed nature of the gaming ecosystem. Updates for the firmware and OS-level software are provided by the console manufacturer. This closed environment offers a reasonable level of risk associated with the security of the systems that are connected. As game consoles become more general in purpose and include features such as web browsing, the risks increase to levels commensurate with any other general computing platform.

Mainframes

Mainframes represent the history of computing, and although many people think they have disappeared, they are still very much alive in enterprise computing. Mainframes are high-performance machines that offer large quantities of memory, computing power, and storage. Mainframes have been used for decades for high-volume transaction systems as well as high-performance computing. The security associated with mainframe systems tends to be built into the operating system on specific-purpose mainframes. Mainframe environments tend to have very strong configuration control mechanisms, and very high levels of stability.

Mainframes have become a cost-effective solution for many high-volume applications because many instances of virtual machines can run on the mainframe hardware. This opens the door for many new security vulnerabilities—not on the mainframe hardware per se, but rather through vulnerabilities in the guest OS in the virtual environment.

SCADA/ICS

SCADA is an acronym for *supervisory control and data acquisition,* a system designed to control automated systems in cyber-physical environments. SCADA systems control manufacturing plants, traffic lights, refineries, energy networks, water plants, building automation and environmental controls, and a host of other systems. SCADA is also known by names such as distributed control systems (DCSs) and industrial control systems (ICSs). The variations depend on the industry and the configuration. Where computers control a physical process directly, a SCADA system likely is involved.

Most SCADA systems involve multiple components networked together to achieve a set of functional objectives. These systems frequently include a human machine interface (HMI), where an operator can exert a form of directive control over the operation of the system under control. SCADA systems historically have been isolated from other systems, but the isolation is decreasing as these systems are being connected across traditional networks to improve business functionality. Many older SCADA systems were air-gapped from the corporate network; that is, they shared no direct network connections. This meant that data flows in and out were handled manually and took time to accomplish. Modern systems remove this constraint, with direct network connections between the SCADA networks and the enterprise IT network. These connections increase the attack surface and the risk to the system, and the more they resemble an IT networked system, the greater the need for security functions.

SCADA systems have been drawn into the security spotlight with the Stuxnet attack on Iranian nuclear facilities, initially reported in 2010. Stuxnet is malware designed to attack a specific SCADA system and cause failures, resulting in plant equipment damage. This attack was complex and well designed, crippling nuclear fuel processing in Iran for a significant period of time. This attack raised awareness of the risks associated with SCADA systems, whether connected to the Internet or not (Stuxnet crossed an air gap to hit its target).

HVAC

Building-automation systems, climate control systems, HVAC (heating, ventilation, and air conditioning) systems, elevator control systems, and alarm systems are just some of the examples of systems that are managed by embedded systems. Although these systems used to be independent and standalone systems, the rise of hyperconnectivity has shown value in integrating them. Having a "smart building" that reduces building resources in accordance with the number and distribution of people inside increases efficiency and reduces costs. Interconnecting these systems and adding in Internet-based central control mechanisms does increase the risk profile from outside attacks.

Smart Devices/IoT

Smart devices and devices that comprise the Internet of Things (IoT) have taken the world's markets by storm—from key fobs that can track things via GPS, to cameras that can provide surveillance, to connected household appliances, TVs, dishwashers, refrigerators, crockpots, and washers and dryers. Anything with a microcontroller now seems to be connected to the Web so that external controls can be used. From the smart controllers from Amazon, the Echo, and its successors, to Google Home, to Microsoft Cortana, artificial intelligence has entered into the mix, enabling even greater functionality. Computer-controlled light switches, LED light bulbs, thermostats, and baby monitors—the smart home is connecting everything. You can carry a key fob that your front door recognizes, unlocking before you get to it. Of course, the security camera saw you first and alerted the system that someone was coming up the driveway. The only thing that can be said with confidence about this revolution is that someone will figure out how and why to connect virtually anything to the network.

All of these devices have a couple of similarities. They all have a network interface, because their connectivity is their purpose as a smart device or a member of the Internet of Things. On that network interface is some form of computer platform. With complete computer functionality now included in a System on a Chip (SoC) platform, which will be covered in a later section, these tiny devices can have a complete working computer for a couple of dollars in cost. The use of a Linux-type kernel as the core engine makes programming easier because the base of programmers is very large. Also, you have something that can be mass-produced and at a relatively low cost. The scaling of the software development over literally millions of units makes costs scalable, and the driving element is functionality. Security or anything else that might impact new expanded functionality has taken a backseat.

Wearable Technologies

Wearable technologies include everything from biometric sensors for measuring heat rate, to step counters for measuring how much one exercises, to smart watches that combine both these functions, and many more. By measuring biometric signals such as pulse rate and body movements, it is possible to track fitness goals and even hours of sleep. These wearable devices are built using very small computers that run a real-time operating system, usually built from a stripped-down Linux kernel.

Home Automation

Home automation is one of the driving factors behind the IoT movement. From programmable smart thermostats, to electrical control devices that replace wall switches and enable voice-operated lights, the home environment is awash with tech. Locks can be operated electronically, allowing you to lock or unlock them remotely from your smartphone. Surveillance cameras connected to your smartphone can tell you when someone is at your door and allow you to talk to them without even being home or opening the door. Appliances can be set up to run when energy costs are lower, or to automatically order more food when you take the last of an item from the pantry or refrigerator. These are not things of a TV show about the future; they are available today and at fairly reasonable prices.

The tech behind these items is the same tech behind a lot of recent advances. This includes a small System on a Chip (a complete computer system with a real-time operating system designed not as a general compute platform but just to drive the needed elements); a network connection (usually wireless); some sensors to measure light, heat, or sound; and an application to integrate the functionality. The security challenge is that most of these devices literally have no security. Poor networking software led to a legion of baby monitors and other home devices becoming part of a large botnet called Mirai, which attacked the Krebs on Security site with a DDoS rate that exceeded 600 Gbps in the fall of 2016.

Special-Purpose Systems

Special-purpose systems are those designed specifically for systems with particular uses, defined by their intended operating environment. Three primary types of special-purpose systems are medical devices, vehicles, and aircraft. Each of these has significant computer system elements providing much of the functionality control for the device, and each of these systems has its own security issues.

Medical Devices

Medical devices comprise a very wide group of devices—from small implantable devices, such as pacemakers, to multi-ton MRI machines. In between are devices that measure things and devices that actually control things, such as infusion pumps. Each of these has several interesting characteristics, the most important of which is that they can have a direct effect on human life. This makes security a function of safety.

Medical devices such as lab equipment and infusion pumps have been running on computerized controls for years. The standard choice has been an embedded Linux kernel that has been stripped of excess functionality and pressed into service in the embedded device. One of the problems with this approach is how one patches this kernel when vulnerabilities are found. Also, as the base system gets updated to a newer version, the embedded system stays trapped on the old version. This requires regression testing for problems, and most manufacturers will not undertake this labor-intensive chore.

Medical devices are manufactured under strict regulatory guidelines that are designed for static systems that do not need patching, updating, or changes. Any change would force a requalification, which is a lengthy, time-consuming, and expensive process. Because of this, these devices tend never to be patched. With the advent of several high-profile vulnerabilities, including Heartbleed and BASH shell attacks, most manufacturers simply recommended that the devices be isolated and never connected to an outside network. In concept, this is fine, but in reality, this can never happen because all the networks in a hospital or medical center are connected.

A recall of nearly a half million pacemakers in 2017 for a software vulnerability that allows a hacker to access and change the performance characteristics of the device is proof of the problem. The good news is that the devices can be updated without being removed, but it will take a doctor's visit to have the new firmware installed.

SoC

System on a Chip (SoC) technologies involve the miniaturization of the various circuits needed for a working computer system. These systems are designed to provide the full functionality of a computing platform on a single chip. This includes networking and graphics display. Some SoC solutions come with memory, and for others the memory is separate. SoCs are very common in the mobile computing market (both phones and tablets) because of their low power consumption and efficient design. Some SoCs have become household names as mobile phone companies have advertised their inclusion in their system (for example, the Snapdragon processor in Android devices). Quad-core and eight-core SoC systems are already in place, and they even have advanced designs such as Quad Plus One, where the fifth processor is slower and designed for simple processes and uses extremely small amounts of power. This way, when the quad cores are not needed, there is no significant energy usage.

The programming of SoC systems can occur at several different levels. Dedicated OSs and applications can be written for them, such as the Android fork of Linux, which is specific to the mobile device marketplace. At the end of the day, because these devices represent computing platforms for billions of devices worldwide, they have become a significant force in the marketplace.

RTOS

Real-time operating systems (RTOSs) are operating systems designed for systems in which the processing must occur in real time and where data cannot be queued or buffered for any significant time. RTOSs are not for general-purpose machines, but are programmed for a specific purpose. They still have to deal with contention, and scheduling algorithms are needed to deal with timing collisions, but in general an RTOS processes each input as it is received, or within a specific time slice defined as the response time.

Most general-purpose computer operating systems are multitasking by design. This includes Windows and Linux. Multitasking systems make poor real-time processors, primarily because of the overhead associated with separating tasks and processes. Windows and Linux may have interrupts, but these are the exception, not the rule, for the processor. RTOS-based software is written in a completely different fashion, designed to emphasize the thread in processing rather than handling multiple threads.

Vehicles

A modern vehicle has hundreds of computers in it, all interconnected on a bus. The CAN bus (controller area network bus) is designed to allow multiple microcontrollers to communicate with each other without a central host computer. As individual microcontrollers were used in automobiles to control the engine, emissions, transmission, breaking, heating, electrical, and other systems, the wiring harnesses used to interconnect everything became a problem. Robert Bosch developed the CAN bus for cars, specifically to address the wiring harness issue, and when it was first deployed in 1986 at BMW, the weight reduction was over 100 pounds.

By 2008, all new U.S. and European cars had to use the CAN bus per SAE (Society of Automotive Engineers) regulations, and with the addition of more and more subsystems, this technology did not require selling to engineers. The CAN bus comes with a reference protocol specification, but recent auto hacking discoveries have revealed several interesting points. First, Toyota claimed in court that the only way to make a car go was to step on the gas pedal, and that software alone won't do it. This claim has been proven false. Second, every automobile manufacturer has interpreted/ignored the reference architecture to varying degrees. Finally, as demonstrated by hackers at DEF CON, it is possible to disable cars on the go, over the Internet, as well as fool around with the entertainment console settings and such.

The bottom line for automobiles and vehicles is that they are composed of multiple computers, all operating semi-autonomously and virtually without any security. The U.S. Department of Transportation is pushing for vehicle-to-vehicle communication so that cars can tell each other when traffic is changing ahead of them. Couple that with the advances in self-driving technology, and you can see how important it is that security become a stronger issue in the industry.

Aircraft/UAV

Aircraft also have a significant computer footprint inside, as most modern jets have what is called an *all-glass cockpit.* The old individual gauges and switches are replaced with a computer display with touchscreen. This enables greater functionality and is more reliable than the older systems. But as with cars, the connecting of all of this equipment onto busses that are then eventually connected to outside networks has led to a lot of security questions within the aviation industry. And, like the medical industry, change is difficult, because the level of regulation and testing precludes ever patching an operating system. This makes for systems that over time will become vulnerable as the base OS is thoroughly explored and every vulnerability mapped and exploited in non-aviation systems—and these use cases can easily be ported to planes.

Recent revelations have shown that the in-flight entertainment systems are separated from flight controls, not by separate networks, but by a firewall. This has led hackers to sound the alarm over aviation computing safety.

Unmanned aerial vehicles (UAVs) represent the next frontier of flight. These machines range from hobbyist devices that cost under $300 to full-size aircraft that can fly across oceans. What makes these systems different from regular aircraft is that the pilot is on the ground, flying the device via remote control. These devices have cameras, sensors, and processors to manage the information; even the simple home hobbyist versions have sophisticated autopilot functions. Because of the remote connection, they are either under direct radio control (rare) or connected via a networked system (much more common).

Industry-Standard Frameworks and Reference Architectures

Industry-standard frameworks and **reference architectures** are conceptual blueprints that define the structure and operation of the IT systems in the enterprise. Just as in an architecture diagram, which provides a blueprint for constructing a building, the enterprise architecture provides the blueprint and roadmap for aligning IT and security with the enterprise's business strategy.

Regulatory

Industries under governmental regulation frequently have an approved set of architectures defined by regulatory bodies. Architectures like the electric industry have the NERC (North American Electric Reliability Corporation) Critical Infrastructure Protection (CIP) standards. This is a set of 14 individual standards that, when taken together, drive a reference framework/architecture for this bulk electric system in North America. Most industries in the U.S. find themselves regulated in one manner or another. When it comes to cybersecurity, more and more regulations are beginning to apply—from privacy, to breach notification, to due diligence and due care provisions. NIST has been careful to promote its Cyber Security Framework (CSF), covered later in this chapter, not as a government-driven "must," stating it is optional.

Nonregulatory

There are some reference architectures that are neither industry specific nor regulatory, but rather technology focused like the NIST / CSA (Cloud Security Alliance) reference architecture for cloud-based systems. In the nonregulatory set is the NIST CSF (Cyber Security Framework), a consensus-created overarching framework to assist enterprises in their cybersecurity programs. The CSF has three main elements: a core, tiers, and profiles. The core is built around five functions: Identify, Protect, Detect, Respond, and Recover. The core then has elements for each of these covering categories of actions, subcategories, and normative references to standards. The tiers are a way of representing an organization's level of achievement—from partial, to risk informed, to repeatable, to adaptive. These tiers are similar to maturity model levels. The profiles section describes the current state of alignment for the elements and the desired state of alignment—a form of gap analysis. The NIST CSF is being mandated for government agencies, but it is completely voluntary in the private sector. This framework has been well received, partly because of its comprehensive nature and partly because of its consensus approach, which created a useable document.

National vs. International

The U.S. federal government has its own cloud-based reference architecture for systems that use the cloud. Called FedRAMP (the Federal Risk and Authorization Management Program), this process is a government-wide program that provides a standardized approach to security assessment, authorization, and continuous monitoring for systems using cloud products and services.

One of the more interesting international frameworks has been the harmonization between the U.S. and the EU with respect to privacy (U.S.) or data protection (EU). The rules and regulations covering privacy issues are so radically different, a special framework was created to harmonize the concepts, allowing the U.S. and EU to effectively do business together. This was referred to as the U.S.–EU Safe Harbor Framework. Changes in EU law, coupled with EU court determinations that the U.S.–EU Safe Harbor Framework is not a valid mechanism to comply with EU data protection requirements when transferring personal data from the European Union to the United States, forced a complete refreshing of the methodology. The new privacy-sharing methodology is called the EU–U.S. Privacy Shield Framework and became effective in the summer of 2016.

Industry-Specific Frameworks

There are several examples of industry-specific frameworks. Although some of these may not seem to be complete frameworks, they provide instructive guidance on how systems should be architected. Some of these frameworks are regulatory based, like the electric industry CIP referenced earlier. Another industry-specific framework is the HITECH CSF (Common Security Framework) for use in the medical industry and enterprises that must address HIPAA/HITECH rules and regulations.

Benchmarks/Secure Configuration Guides

Benchmarks and **secure configuration guides** offer a set of guidance for setting up and operating systems to a secure level that is understood and documented. As each organization may differ, the standard for a benchmark is a consensus-based set of knowledge designed to deliver a reasonable set of security across as wide a base as possible. There are numerous sources for these guides, and three main sources exist for many of these systems. You can get benchmark guides from manufacturers of the software, the government, and an independent organization called Center for Internet Security. Not all systems have benchmarks, nor do all sources cover all systems, but searching for the correct configuration and setup directives can go a long way in establishing security.

The vendor/manufacturer guidance source is easy—pick the vendor for your product. The government sources are a bit more scattered, but two solid sources are the U.S. National Institute of Standards and Technology Computer Security Resource Center's National Vulnerability Database

National Checklist Program (NCP) Repository (https://nvd.nist.gov/ncp/repository) and the U.S. Department of Defense's Defense Information Security Agency's Security Technical Implementation Guides (STIGs). These are detailed step-by-step implementation guides, and a list is available at https://public.cyber.mil/stigs/.

Platform/Vendor-Specific Guides

Setting up secure services is important to enterprises, and some of the best guidance comes from the manufacturer in the form of *platform/vendor-specific guides*. These guides include installation and configuration guidance, and in some cases operational guidance as well.

Web Server

There are many web servers used in enterprises. Web servers offer a connection between users (clients) and enterprise resources (data being provided), and therefore they are prone to adversarial attempts at penetration. Setting up any external-facing application securely is the key to preventing unnecessary risk. Fortunately for web servers, there are several authoritative and proscriptive sources of information available for properly securing the application. In the case of Microsoft's IIS and SharePoint Server, the company provides solid guidance on the proper configuration of the servers. The Apache foundation provides some information for its web server products as well.

Another good source of information is from the Center for Internet Security, as part of its benchmarking guides. The CIS guides provide authoritative, proscriptive guidance developed as part of a consensus effort between consultants, professionals, and others. This guidance has been subjected to and has withstood significant peer review via implementation. CIS guides are available for multiple versions of Apache, Microsoft, and other vendors' products.

Operating System

The operating system (OS) is the interface between the applications that perform the tasks we want done and the actual physical computer hardware. As such, the OS becomes a key component for the secure operation of a system. Comprehensive, proscriptive configuration guides for all major operating systems are available from the manufacturer, or in an easier-to-digest form from CIS, as mentioned earlier, or from the U.S. government through the Department of Defense DISA STIGs (Security Technical Implementation Guides) program.

Application Server

Application servers are the part of the enterprise that handles specific tasks we associate with IT systems. Whether it is an e-mail server, a database server, a messaging platform, or any other server, application servers are where the work happens. Proper configuration of an application server depends to a great degree on the server specifics. Standard application servers, such as e-mail and database servers, have guidance from the manufacturer, CIS, and STIGs. Less-standard servers, such as ones with

Tech Tip

Media Gateways

A specialty application used to connect voice calling systems to IP networks, to enable voice over IP (VOIP), is called a media gateway. These application servers are a blend of hardware and software, part application server, part network infrastructure, and perform the necessary functions to integrate and separate voice and IP signals as required. These systems show the blurring of the lines when separating systems as either application servers or network devices.

An example of a network infrastructure device is an SSL decryptor, a piece of hardware designed to streamline SSL/TLS connections in an enterprise, relieving other servers of this computationally intensive task.

significant customizations (for example, a custom set of applications written in-house for your inventory control operations or order processing) or any other custom middleware, also require proper configuration, but the true vendor in these cases is the in-house builders of the software. Ensuring proper security settings and testing should be part of the build program for these so that they can be integrated into the normal security audit process to ensure continued proper configuration.

Network Infrastructure Devices

Network infrastructure devices are particularly important to properly configure because failures at this level can adversely affect the security of traffic being processed by them. Properly setting up these devices, switches, routers, concentrators, and other specialty devices can be challenging. The criticality of these devices makes them targets, because if a firewall fails, in many cases there are no indications until an investigation finds that it failed to do its job. Ensuring these devices are properly configured and maintained is not a job to gloss over, but one that requires professional attention by properly trained personnel and backed by routine configuration audits to ensure they stay properly configured. With respect to most of these devices, the greatest risk lies in the user configuration of the device via rulesets, and these are specific to each user and cannot be mandated by a manufacturer installation guide. Proper configuration and verification is site specific and many times individual device specific. Without a solid set of policies and procedures to ensure this work is properly maintained, these devices, while they may work, will not perform the services desired.

General-Purpose Guides

The best general-purpose guide to information security is probably the common set of CIS Critical Security Controls, which are 20 best-practice effective security controls. This project, originally known as the SANS Institute Top 20 Security Controls, began as a consensus project out of the U.S. Department of Defense and has over nearly 20 years morphed into the de facto standard for selecting an effective set of security controls. The framework is now maintained by the Center for Internet Security and can be found at https://www.cisecurity.org/cybersecurity-best-practices/.

For More Information

Microsoft's Safety & Security Center https://docs.microsoft.com/en-us/windows/security/

SANS Reading Room: Application and Database Security www.sans.org/reading_room/whitepapers/application/

Chapter 14 Review

Chapter Summary

After reading this chapter and completing the exercises, you should understand the following about hardening systems and baselines.

Harden operating systems and network operating systems

- Security baselines are critical to protecting information systems, particularly those allowing connections from external users.
- The process of establishing a system's security state is called baselining, and the resulting product is a security baseline that allows the system to run safely and securely.
- Hardening is the process by which operating systems, network resources, and applications are secured against possible attacks.
- Securing operating systems consists of removing or disabling unnecessary services, restricting permissions on files and directories, removing unnecessary software (or not installing it in the first place), applying the latest patches, removing unnecessary user accounts, and ensuring strong password guidelines are in place.
- Securing network resources consists of disabling unnecessary functions, restricting access to ports and services, ensuring strong passwords are used, and ensuring the code on the network devices is patched and up to date.
- Securing applications depends heavily on the application involved but typically consists of removing samples and default materials, preventing reconnaissance attempts, and ensuring the software is patched and up to date.

Implement host-level security

- Anti-malware/spyware/virus protections are needed on host machines to prevent malicious code attacks.
- Whitelisting can provide strong protections against malware on key systems.
- Host-based firewalls can provide specific protections from some attacks.

Harden applications

- Patch management is a disciplined approach to the acquisition, testing, and implementation of OS and application patches.
- A hotfix is a single package designed to address a specific, typically security-related problem in an operating system or application.
- A patch is a fix (or collection of fixes) that addresses vulnerabilities or errors in operating systems or applications.
- A service pack is a large collection of fixes, corrections, and enhancements for an operating system, application, or group of applications.

Establish group policies

- Group policies are a method for managing the settings and configurations of many different users and systems in an Active Directory environment.
- Group policies can be used to refine, set, or modify a system's Registry settings, auditing and security policies, user environments, logon/logoff scripts, and so on.
- Security templates are collections of security settings that can be applied to a system. Security templates can contain hundreds of settings that control or modify settings on a system, such as password length, auditing of user actions, and restrictions on network access.

Implement endpoint protections

- Endpoints require protection in the form of anti-malware/antivirus, as well as firewalls and intrusion detection/prevention systems.
- Additional controls that should be examined include DLP solutions and EDR solutions.
- Controlling what software executes is important via whitelisting/blacklisting and specific application controls like AppLocker, Device Guard, and Credential Guard.

Secure alternative environments (SCADA, real-time, and others)

- Alternative environments include process control (SCADA) networks, embedded systems, mobile devices, mainframes, game consoles, transportation systems, and more.
- Alternative environments require security but are not universally equivalent to IT systems, so the specifics can vary tremendously from system to system.

Key Terms

antivirus (AV) *(533)*
application hardening *(542)*
application vulnerability scanner *(547)*
baseline *(513)*
baselining *(513)*
Basic Input/Output System (BIOS) *(514)*
benchmarks *(566)*
blacklisting *(538)*
continuous monitoring *(552)*
Desired State Configuration (DSC) *(526)*
elasticity *(555)*
firmware update *(516)*
globally unique identifier (GUID) *(527)*
group policy *(527)*
group policy object (GPO) *(527)*
hardening *(512)*
hardware security module (HSM) *(514)*
heuristic scanning *(533)*
host vulnerability scanner *(546)*
hotfix *(520)*
industry-standard frameworks *(565)*
measured boot *(515)*
network operating system (NOS) *(517)*
network segmentation *(542)*
network vulnerability scanner *(546)*
operating system (OS) *(516)*
patch *(520)*
patch management *(519)*
process identifier (PID) *(530)*
reference architectures *(565)*
reference monitor *(517)*
root of trust *(514)*
runlevels *(530)*
scalability *(555)*
Secure Boot *(515)*
secure configuration guides *(566)*
security kernel *(517)*
security template *(553)*
service pack *(520)*
TCP Wrapper *(555)*
trusted operating system *(519)*
Trusted Platform Module (TPM) *(513)*
whitelisting *(538)*
Unified Extensible Firmware Interface (UEFI) *(514)*
Virtual Secure Mode (VSM) *(526)*

Key Terms Quiz

Use terms from the Key Terms list to complete the sentences that follow. Don't use the same term more than once. Not all terms will be used.

1. _____________ is the process of establishing a system's security state.
2. Securing and preparing a system for the production environment is called _____________.
3. A(n) _____________ is a small software update designed to address a specific, often urgent, problem.
4. The basic software on a computer that handles input and output is called the _____________.
5. ___________ is the use of the network architecture to limit communication between devices.
6. A(n) _____________ is a bundled set of software updates, fixes, and additional functions contained in a self-installing package.
7. In most UNIX operating systems, each running program is given a unique number called a(n) _____________.
8. When a user or process supplies more data than was expected, a(n) _____________ may occur.
9. _____________ are used to describe the state of init and what system services are operating in UNIX systems.
10. A(n) _____________ is a collection of security settings that can be applied to a system.

Multiple-Choice Quiz

1. A small software update designed to address an urgent or specific problem is called what?
   - A. Hotfix
   - B. Service pack
   - C. Patch
   - D. None of the above
2. In a UNIX operating system, which runlevel describes single-user mode?
   - A. 0
   - B. 6
   - C. 4
   - D. 1
3. TCP wrappers do what?
   - A. Help secure the system by restricting network connections
   - B. Help prioritize network traffic for optimal throughput
   - C. Encrypt outgoing network traffic
   - D. Strip out excess input to defeat buffer overflow attacks
4. File permissions under UNIX consist of what three types?
   - A. Modify, read, and execute
   - B. Read, write, and execute
   - C. Full control, read-only, and run
   - D. Write, read, and open
5. What is the mechanism that allows for centralized management and configuration of computers and remote users in an Active Directory environment called?
   - A. Baseline
   - B. Group policies
   - C. Simple Network Management Protocol
   - D. Security templates
6. What feature in Windows Server 2008 controls access to network resources based on a client computer's identity and compliance with corporate governance policy?
   - A. BitLocker
   - B. Network Access Protection
   - C. inetd
   - D. Process identifiers

7. To stop a particular service or program running on a UNIX operating system, you might use the ______ command.

   A. netstat

   B. ps

   C. kill

   D. inetd

8. Updating the software loaded on nonvolatile RAM is called what?

   A. A buffer overflow

   B. A firmware update

   C. A hotfix

   D. A service pack

9. The shadow file on a UNIX system contains which of the following?

   A. The password associated with a user account

   B. Group policy information

   C. File permissions for system files

   D. Network services started when the system is booted

10. On a UNIX system, if a file has the permissions **rwx r-x rw-**, what permissions does the owner of the file have?

    A. Read only

    B. Read and write

    C. Read, write, and execute

    D. None

Essay Quiz

1. Explain the difference between a hotfix and a service pack, and describe why both are so important.

2. A new administrator needs some help creating a security baseline. Create a checklist/template that covers the basic steps in creating a security baseline to assist them, and explain why each step is important.

Lab Projects

• Lab Project 14.1

Use a lab system running Linux with at least one open service, such as FTP, Telnet, or SMTP. From another lab system, connect to the Linux system and observe your results. Configure TCP wrappers on the Linux system to reject all connection attempts from the other lab system. Try to reconnect and then observe your results. Document your steps and explain how TCP wrappers work.

• Lab Project 14.2

Using a system running Windows, experiment with the Password Policy settings under the Local Security Policy (Settings | Control Panel | Administrative Tools | Local Security Policy). Find the setting for Passwords Must Meet Complexity Requirements and make sure it is disabled. Set the password on the account you are using to **bob**. Now enable the Passwords Must Meet Complexity Requirements settings and attempt to change your password to **jane**. Were you able to change it? Explain why or why not. Set your password to something the system will allow and explain how you selected that password and how it meets the complexity requirements.

chapter 15 Types of Attacks and Malicious Software

If you know the enemy and know yourself, you need not fear the results of a hundred battles.

—Sun Tzu

In this chapter, you will learn how to

- **Identify the different types of malicious software that exist, including viruses, worms, trojan horses, logic bombs, time bombs, and rootkits**
- **Describe the various types of computer and network attacks, including denial of service, spoofing, hijacking, and password guessing**
- **Recognize the different types of password attacks**

Attacks can be made against virtually any layer or level of software, from network protocols to applications. When an attacker finds a vulnerability in a system, they exploit the weakness to attack the system. The effect of an attack depends on the attacker's intent and can result in a wide range of effects, from minor to severe. An attack on one system might not be visible on the user's system because the attack is actually occurring on a different system, and the data the attacker will manipulate on the second system is obtained by attacking the first system.

Avenues of Attack

A computer system is attacked for one of two general reasons: it is specifically targeted by an attacker, or it is a target of opportunity. In the first case, the attacker has chosen the target not because of the hardware or software the organization is running, but for another reason, such as a political reason. For example, an individual in one country might attack a government system in another country to gather secret information. Or the attacker might target an organization as part of a "hacktivist" attack—the attacker could deface the website of a company that sells fur coats, for example, because the attacker believes using animals in this way is unethical. Perpetrating some sort of electronic fraud is another reason a specific system might be targeted for attack. Whatever the reason, the attacker usually begins an attack of this nature before they know which hardware and software the organization uses.

The second type of attack, an attack against a target of opportunity, is launched against a site that has hardware or software that is vulnerable to a specific exploit. The attacker, in this case, is not targeting the organization; they have instead learned of a specific vulnerability and are simply looking for an organization with this vulnerability that they can exploit. This is not to say that an attacker might not be targeting a given sector and looking for a target of opportunity in that sector. For example, an attacker who wants to obtain credit card or other personal information may search for any exploitable company that stores credit card information on its system to accomplish the attack.

Targeted attacks are more difficult and take more time and effort than attacks on a target of opportunity. The latter type of attack simply relies on the fact that, with any piece of widely distributed software, somebody in the organization will not have patched the system like they should have.

Tech Tip

Defense Begins with Eliminating Vulnerabilities

Defense against attacks begins with eliminating vulnerabilities. Vulnerabilities are exploited by attackers to gain access to a system. Minimization of vulnerabilities is one of the foundational elements of defense.

Cross Check

Anatomy of an Attack

Hackers use a process when attacking, and this is covered in detail in Chapter 22.

Minimizing Possible Avenues of Attack

By understanding the steps an attacker can take, you can limit the exposure of your system and minimize the possible avenues an attacker can exploit. Your first step in minimizing possible attacks is to ensure that all patches for the operating system and applications are installed. Many security problems, such as viruses and worms, exploit known vulnerabilities for which patches actually exist. These attacks are successful only because administrators have not taken the appropriate actions to protect their systems.

The next step is to limit the services that are running on the system. As mentioned in earlier chapters, limiting the number of services to those that are absolutely necessary provides two safeguards: it limits the possible avenues of attack (the possible services for which a vulnerability may exist and be exploited), and it reduces the number of services the administrator has to worry about patching in the first place.

> **Cross Check**
>
> **Baseline Analysis and Patching of Systems**
>
> Keeping a system patched and up to date for the operating system and applications is the best defense against exposed vulnerabilities. How up to date is the system you are currently using? How do you know? Chapter 14 covers the topics of baselining and patching of systems in order to understand and remove vulnerabilities. Refer to that chapter for more in-depth information on how to perform these activities.

Another step is to limit public disclosure of private information about your organization and its computing resources. Since the attacker is after this information, don't make it easy to obtain.

Malicious Code

Malicious code refers to software that has been designed for some nefarious purpose. Malicious code can damage a system in many ways, and lead to compromise and risk. Most malware instances attack vulnerabilities in programs or operating systems. This is why patching of vulnerabilities is so important, because it closes the point of entry for most malware. Typically the installation of malicious code is done in such a way that it is not obvious to the authorized users. There are a wide array of different types of malicious software including viruses, trojan horses, logic bombs, spyware, and worms, and ransomware.

Malware can be fairly complex in its construction, with specific features designed to assist malware in avoiding detection. Modern malware can be multipart in construction, where several pieces work together to achieve a desired effect. When malware has multiple different objects that it specifically attacks, it is called *multipartite*. Many types of malware can include a changing encryption layer to resist pattern-matching detection. These are called *polymorphic*. If the malware actually changes the code at the time of infection, this property is called *metamorphic*.

Malware

Malware refers to software that has been designed for some nefarious purpose. Such software can be designed to cause damage to a system, such as by deleting all files, or it can be designed to create a backdoor into the system to grant access to unauthorized individuals. Generally the installation of malware is done so that it is not obvious to the authorized users. Several different types of malicious software can be used, such as viruses, trojan horses, logic bombs, spyware, and worms, and they differ in the ways they are installed and their purposes.

Ransomware

Ransomware is a form of malware that performs some action and extracts a ransom from the user. Ransomware typically encrypts files on a system and then leaves them unusable either permanently, acting as a denial of service, or temporarily until a ransom is paid, thus the name. Ransomware is typically a worm, completely automated, and when targeted as a means of denial of service, the only repair mechanism is to rebuild the system. This can be time consuming and/or impractical in some cases, making this attack mechanism equivalent to the physical destruction of assets. **Crypto-malware** is an early name given to ransomware.

A ransomware threat that first appeared in 2013 was CryptoLocker, a trojan horse that encrypted certain files using RSA public key encryption. When the user attempted to get these files, they were provided with a message instructing them how to purchase the decryption key. Because the system is using 2048-bit RSA encryption, brute force decryption was out of the realm of recovery options. The system was highly automated, and users have a short time window in which to get the private key. Failure to get the key resulted in the loss of the data.

In May of 2017, a cryptoworm form of malware called WannaCry was released, resulting in a ransomware attack that swept across many government computers in Europe, including medical devices in the UK's NHS. This ransomware created havoc by exploiting the EternalBlue vulnerability in Microsoft Windows systems that was exposed by the group known as Shadow Brokers. The U.S. announced in December of 2017 that it believed that the Lazarus Group, which works on behalf of the North Korean government, carried out the WannaCry attack.

A second, similar attack, called NotPetya by Kaspersky Labs, was a crypto-malware attack against Ukrainian assets. This was not a ransomware attack, as there was no operating ransom machinery in place to handle codes. This was a form of file- and system-based denial of service, by which the system was destroyed cryptographically and could no longer function. In January of 2018, the global shipping company Maersk announced that the June 2017 NotPetya malware attack that it experienced resulted in the forced rebuilding of its entire IT infrastructure—over 4000 servers, 45,000 desktops, and all applications. This cost the company over $300 million. Even with a good backup, you could be completely out of luck against this type of attack if it successfully penetrates far enough into your systems.

> **Tech Tip**
>
> **WannaCry and Marcus Hutchins**
>
> *WannaCry was stopped by Marcus Hutchins, a hacker turned white hat (authorized). Marcus found a vulnerability in the WannaCry worm and was able to disable it globally. His story as a hacker is an amazing journey, involving crime, prosecution, and eventually vindication when he stopped WannaCry. This story can be read in* Wired *magazine's treatise at www.wired.com/story/confessions-marcus-hutchins-hacker-who-saved-the-internet/.*

> Ransomware is a form of malware that locks the user out of their files or even the entire device until an online ransom payment is made to restore access. In most cases, the best solution is to have a complete and accurate backup available to recover the lost files.

Trojans

A trojan horse, or simply **trojan**, is a piece of software that appears to do one thing (and may, in fact, actually do that thing) but hides some other functionality. The analogy to the famous story of antiquity is very accurate. In the original case, the object appeared to be a large wooden horse, and in fact it was. At the same time, it hid something much more sinister and dangerous to the occupants of the city of Troy. As long as the horse was left outside the city walls, it could cause no damage to the inhabitants. However, it had to be taken in by the inhabitants of Troy, and it was inside that the hidden purpose was activated. A computer trojan works in much the same way. Unlike a virus, which reproduces by attaching itself to other files or programs, a trojan is a standalone program that must be copied and installed by the user—it must be "brought inside" the system by an authorized user. The challenge for the attacker is enticing the user to copy and run the program. This generally means that the program must be disguised as something that the user would want to run—a special utility or game, for example. Once it has been copied and is inside the system, the trojan will perform its hidden purpose with the user often still unaware of its true nature.

A good example of a trojan is Back Orifice (BO), originally created in 1999 and now offered in several versions. BO can be attached to a number of types of programs. Once it is attached, and once an infected file is run, BO will create a way for unauthorized individuals to take over the system remotely, as if they were sitting at the console. BO is designed to work with Windows-based systems. Many trojans communicate to the outside through a port that the trojan opens, and this is one of the ways trojans can be detected.

> **Tech Tip**
>
> **Famous Trojans**
>
> *There have been many "famous" trojans that have caused significant havoc in systems. Back Orifice (BO), created in 1999, was offered in several versions. BO can be attached to a number of types of programs. Koobface is a trojan that affects Facebook users. Zeus is a financial trojan/malware that has a wide range of functionality.*

Worms

It was once easy to distinguish between a worm and a virus. Recently, with the introduction of new breeds of sophisticated malicious code, the distinction has blurred. **Worms** are pieces of code that attempt to penetrate networks and computer systems. Once a penetration occurs, the worm will create a new copy of itself on the penetrated system. Reproduction of a worm thus does not rely on the attachment of the virus to another piece of code or to a file, which is the definition of a virus.

> Worms act like a virus but also have the ability to travel without human action. They do not need help to spread.

Viruses were generally thought of as a system-based problem, and worms were network-based. If the malicious code is sent throughout a network, it may subsequently be called a worm. The important distinction, however, is whether the code has to attach itself to something else (a virus) or if it can "survive" on its own (a worm).

Some examples of worms that have had high profiles include the Sobig worm of 2003, the SQL Slammer worm of 2003, the 2001 attacks of Code Red and Nimda, and the 2005 Zotob worm that took down CNN Live. Nimda was particularly impressive in that it used five different methods to spread: via e-mail, via open network shares, from browsing infected websites, using the directory traversal vulnerability of Microsoft IIS 4.0/5.0, and most impressively through the use of backdoors left by Code Red II and sadmind worms. Recently, worms have become a tool of choice for ransomware attacks, as they can spread from system to system without operator intervention. The NotPetya worm of 2017 caused an estimated $10 billion in damage.

> **Tech Tip**
>
> **Protection Against Worms**
>
> *How you protect your system against worms depends on the type of worm. Those attached and propagated through e-mail can be avoided by following the same guidelines about not opening files and not running attachments unless you are absolutely sure of their origin and integrity. Protecting against worms involves securing systems and networks against penetration in the same way you would protect your systems against human attackers: install patches, eliminate unused and unnecessary services, enforce good password security, and use firewalls and intrusion detection systems (IDSs). More sophisticated attacks, such as the Samy worm, are almost impossible to avoid.*

Viruses

The best-known type of malicious code is the **virus**. Much has been written about viruses as a result of several high-profile security events that involved them. A virus is a piece of malicious code that replicates by attaching itself to another piece of executable code. When the other executable code is run, the virus also executes and has the opportunity to infect other files and perform any other nefarious actions it was designed to do. The specific way that a virus infects other files, and the type of files it infects, depends on the type of virus. The first viruses created were of two types—boot sector viruses and program viruses.

Boot Sector Virus

A boot sector virus infects the boot sector portion of the bootable media for a system. When a computer is first turned on, a small portion of the operating system is initially loaded from hardware. This small operating system then attempts to load the rest of the operating system from a specific location (sector) on either the USB thumb drive or detachable hard drive. A boot sector virus infects this portion of the drive.

An early example of this type of virus was the Stoned virus, which moved the true Master Boot Record (MBR) from the first to the seventh sector of the first cylinder and replaced the original MBR with the virus code. When the system was turned on and the virus was first executed, it had a one-in-seven chance of displaying a message stating the computer was "stoned." Otherwise, it would not announce itself and would instead attempt to infect other boot sectors. This virus was rather tame in comparison to other viruses of its time, which were often designed to delete the entire hard drive after a period of time in which they would attempt to spread.

Boot sector viruses still exist. NotPetya would overwrite the boot sector, and hackers routinely use this method to modify boot sectors to load drivers used by malware.

Tech Tip

Modern Virus and Worm Threats

Early virus and worm attacks would cause damage to PCs, but they were generally visible to users. Many modern viruses and worms are used to deliver payloads that lead to machines becoming zombies in a botnet, controlled by an attacker. This type of attack is typically invisible to the end user, so as not to alert them to the malware.

Program Virus

A second type of virus is the program virus, which attaches itself to executable files—typically files ending in .exe or .com on Windows-based systems. The virus is attached in such a way that it is executed before the program executes. Most program viruses also hide a nefarious purpose, such as deleting the hard drive data, which is triggered by a specific event, such as a particular date or after a certain number of other files are infected. Like other types of viruses, program viruses are often not detected until after they execute their malicious payload. One method that has been used to detect this sort of virus before it has an opportunity to damage a system is to calculate checksums for commonly used programs or utilities. Should the checksum for an executable ever change, it is quite likely that it is due to a virus infection.

Macro Virus

In the late 1990s, another type of virus appeared that now accounts for the majority of viruses. As systems and operating systems became more powerful, the boot sector virus, which once accounted for most reported infections, became less common. Systems no longer commonly booted from floppies, which were the main method for boot sector viruses to spread. Instead, the proliferation of software that included macro programming languages resulted in a new breed of virus—the macro virus.

The Concept virus was the first known example of this new breed. It appeared to be created to demonstrate the possibility of attaching a virus to a document file, something that had been thought to be impossible before the introduction of software that included powerful macro language capabilities. By this time, however, Microsoft Word documents could include segments of code written in a derivative of Visual Basic. Further development of other applications that allowed macro capability, and enhanced versions of the original macro language, had the side effect of allowing the proliferation of viruses that took advantage of this capability.

This type of virus is so common today that it is considered a security best practice to advise users never to open a document attached to an e-mail if it seems at all suspicious. Many organizations now routinely have their mail servers eliminate any attachments containing Visual Basic macros.

Remember that unlike a traditional virus, which attaches itself to a file, a fileless virus lives in memory and will continue to run until the device is powered down.

Fileless Malware

Most antivirus/anti-malware solutions find malware through monitoring the filesystem for writes and then filter the writes for known signatures. When a piece of malware operates only in memory, never touching the filesystem, it is much harder to detect. This type of attack is called a **fileless malware**, or memory-based attack.

Avoiding Virus Infection

Always being cautious about executing programs or opening documents sent to you is a good security practice. "If you don't know where it came from or where it has been, don't open or run it" should be the basic mantra for all computer users. Another security best practice for protecting against virus infection is to install and run an antivirus program. Since these programs are designed to protect against known viruses, it is also important to maintain an up-to-date listing of virus signatures for your antivirus software. Antivirus software vendors provide this information, and administrators should stay on top of the latest updates to the list of known viruses.

Two advances in virus writing have made it more difficult for antivirus software to detect viruses. These advances are the introduction of *stealth virus* techniques and *polymorphic viruses*. A stealthy virus employs techniques to help evade being detected by antivirus software that uses checksums or other techniques. Polymorphic viruses also attempt to evade detection, but they do so by changing the virus itself (the virus "evolves"). Because the virus changes, signatures for that virus may no longer be valid, and the virus can thus escape detection by antivirus software.

Modern viruses have a whole host of defenses from detection and analysis. Polymorphic viruses change their appearance, making signature matches difficult. Armored viruses resist being reverse-engineered to determine how they operate. Viruses are designed to be quiet, avoid detection, avoid analysis, and still work—they are significant threats.

Armored Virus

When a new form of malware/virus is discovered, antivirus companies and security researchers will decompile the program in an attempt to reverse-engineer its functionality. Much can be determined from reverse engineering, such as where the malware came from, how it works, how it communicates, how it spreads, and so forth. Armoring malware can make the process of determining this information much more difficult, if not impossible. Some malware, such as Zeus, comes encrypted in ways to prevent criminals from stealing the intellectual property of the very malware that they use.

Virus Hoaxes

Viruses have caused so much damage to systems that many Internet users become extremely cautious any time they hear a rumor of a new virus. Many users will not connect to the Internet when they hear about a virus outbreak, just to be sure their machines don't get infected. This has given rise to virus hoaxes, in which word is spread about a new virus and the extreme danger it poses. It may warn users to not read certain files or connect to the Internet.

Hoaxes can actually be even more destructive than just wasting time and bandwidth. Some hoaxes warning of a dangerous virus have included instructions to delete certain files if they're found on the user's system. Unfortunately for those who follow the advice, the files may actually be part of the operating system, and deleting them could keep the system from booting properly. This suggests another good piece of security advice: make sure of the authenticity and accuracy of any virus report before following somebody's advice. Antivirus software vendors are a good source of factual data for this sort of threat as well.

Polymorphic Malware

The detection of malware by anti-malware programs is primarily done through the use of a signature. Files are scanned for sections of code in the executable that act as markers—unique patterns of code that enable detection. Just as the human body creates antigens that match marker proteins, anti-malware programs detect malware through unique markers present in the code of the malware.

Malware writers are aware of this functionality and have adapted methods to defeat it. One of the primary means of avoiding detection by sensors is the use of polymorphic code, which is code that changes on a regular basis. These changes or mutations are designed not to affect the functionality of the code, but rather to mask any signature from detection. **Polymorphic malware** can change its coding after each use, making each replicant different from a detection point of view.

Potentially unwanted programs are a form of malware. The name is one the industry chose because the makers of PUPs claim you read and agreed to their terms as part of a download agreement. It is easy to miss these details when installing programs, and then you have unwanted apps. PUPs can exhibit some very undesired characteristics, such as the following:

- Slowing down your computer
- Displaying a ton of annoying ads
- Adding toolbars that steal space on the browser
- Collecting private information

Potentially Unwanted Programs

Potentially unwanted program (PUP) is a designation used by security companies and antivirus vendors to identify programs that may have adverse effects on a computer's security or privacy. Frequently these involve adware or spyware components and are used for revenue generation purposes.

A common source of PUPs is third-party download sites for downloading apps—even legitimate apps can be bundled by third-party distributers. The use of an anti-malware solution should catch and enable PUPs to be stopped before installation.

Command and Control

Command-and-control servers are used by hackers to control malware that has been launched against targets. Malware infections are seldom a single file on a single machine when an attack occurs in an enterprise. Multiple malware elements, on multiple systems, under various IDs, all working to provide a means for hackers to re-enter a system are commonly found in enterprises. These malware elements also work to exfiltrate stolen data.

Sometime before 2007, the FBI began an anti-botnet operation dubbed Bot Roast. The operation dismantled several botnets and led to several convictions of botnet operators. Other successful anti-botnet operations include the McColo takedown, which decimated Rustock, and coordinated efforts by industry, academia, and law enforcement that have led to the dismantling of BredoLabs, Mariposa, and made significant inroads against Conficker and Zeus.

Botnets

Malware can have a wide range of consequences on a machine, from relatively benign to extremely serious. One form of malware that is seemingly benign to a user is a botnet zombie. Hackers create armies of machines by installing malware agents on the machines, which then are called **zombies**. These collections of machines are called **botnets**. These zombie machines are used to conduct other attacks and to spread spam and other malware. Botnets have grown into networks of over a million nodes and are responsible for tens of millions of spam messages daily.

Bots use a structure by which large legions of infected machines are controlled by a smaller number of command-and-control (C2) servers. These servers are also typically machines owned by someone else, infected with just a different set of malware. The C2 machines allow the bots to be controlled, letting the botnet owner rent out the spam or use it for other evil intent. The C2 aspect is both a strength and a weakness. Attacking the individual bots on machines worldwide is a losing cause since they can number in the millions. Attacking the C2 side and taking these bots down has proven to be an effective method against botnets.

Tech Tip

Famous Botnets

The following are some famous botnets and their current status (as of the end of 2020):

Name	Use	Status
BredoLabs	Spam	Dismantled in 2010
Mariposa	Cyberscamming	Dismantled in 2009, authors in jail
Mirai	DDOS	Still active, authors in jail
Conficker (series)	Malware propagation	Still active
Zeus (series)	Financial crime	Still active
Marino	Spam	Faded, but still active
Rustock	Spam	Dismantled in 2011

Crypto-Malware

The first thought when one sees the term *crypto-malware* is ransomware, but that would be wrong. Crypto-malware is now the name the security industry uses for malware that uses a system's resources to mine cryptocurrency. This is really just a theft-of-services attack, where an attacker is using the CPU cycles of someone else's computer to do the crypto mining.

Logic Bombs

Logic bombs, unlike viruses and Trojans, are a type of malicious software that is deliberately installed, generally by an authorized user. A logic bomb is a piece of code that sits dormant for a period of time until some event invokes its malicious payload. An example of a logic bomb might be a program that is set to load and run automatically, and that periodically checks an organization's payroll or personnel database for a specific employee. If the employee is not found, the malicious payload executes, deleting vital corporate files.

Logic bombs are difficult to detect because they are often installed by authorized users and, in particular, by administrators who are also often responsible for security. This demonstrates the need for a separation of duties and a periodic review of all programs and services that are running on a system. It also illustrates the need to maintain an active backup program so that if your organization loses critical files to this sort of malicious code, it loses only transactions that occurred since the most recent backup and no permanent loss of data results.

If the event invoking the logic bomb is a specific date or time, the program will often be referred to as a *time bomb*. In one famous example, a disgruntled employee left a time bomb in place just prior to being fired from his job. Two weeks later, thousands of client records were deleted. Police were eventually able to track the malicious code to the disgruntled ex-employee, who was prosecuted for his actions. He had hoped that the two weeks that had passed since his dismissal would have caused investigators to assume he could not have been the individual who had caused the deletion of the records.

Spyware

Spyware is software that "spies" on users, recording and reporting on their activities. Typically installed without user knowledge, spyware can perform a wide range of activities. It can record keystrokes (commonly called *keylogging*) when the user logs in to specific websites. It can monitor how a user uses a specific piece of software (for example, monitoring attempts to cheat at games).

Many uses of spyware seem innocuous at first, but the unauthorized monitoring of a system can be abused very easily. In other cases, the spyware is specifically designed to steal information. Many states have passed legislation banning the unapproved installation of software, but many cases of spyware circumvent this issue through complex and confusing end-user license agreements.

Keylogging is one of the holy grails for attackers, because if they can get a keylogger on a machine, the capturing of user-typed credentials is a quick win for the attacker.

Adware

The business of software distribution requires a form of revenue stream to support the cost of development and distribution. One form of revenue stream is advertising. Software that is supported by advertising is called **adware**. Adware comes in many different forms. With legitimate adware, the user is aware of the advertising and agrees to the arrangement in return for free use of the software. This type of adware often offers an alternative, ad-free version for a fee. Adware can also refer to a form of malware that is characterized by software that presents unwanted ads. These ads are sometimes an irritant, and at other times represent an actual security threat. Frequently these ads are in the form of pop-up browser windows, and in some cases they cascade upon any user action.

Keyloggers

As the name suggests, a **keylogger** is a piece of software that logs all the keystrokes a user enters. Keyloggers in their own respect are not necessarily evil—you could even consider Microsoft Word to be a keylogger. What makes a keylogger a malicious piece of software is when its operation is (1) unknown to the user, and (2) not under the user's control. Keyloggers have been marketed for a variety of uses—from surveillance over your children's activity, or the activity of a spouse, to maintaining records of what has been done on a machine. Malicious keyloggers have several specific characteristics: they are frequently hidden from the user's view, even when looking at Task Manager, and they are used against the end user's interests. Hackers use keyloggers to obtain passwords and other sensitive pieces of information, enabling them to use these secrets to act as the user without the user's consent. Keylogger functionality has even been found in legitimate programs, where keystrokes are recorded for "legitimate" purposes and then are stored in a fashion that enables unauthorized users to steal the data.

Remote-Access Trojans (RATs)

A **remote-access trojan (RAT)** is a toolkit designed to provide the capability of covert surveillance and/or the capability to gain unauthorized access to a target system. RATs often mimic the behavior of keyloggers and packet sniffers using the automated collection of keystrokes, usernames, passwords, screenshots, browser history, e-mails, chat logs, and more, but they also do so with a design of intelligence. RATs can also employ malware to infect a system with code that can be used to facilitate the exploitation of a target. Rather than just collect the information, RATs present it to an attacker in a form to facilitate the capability to gain unauthorized access to the target machine. This frequently involves the use of specially configured communication protocols that are set up upon initial infection of the target computer. This backdoor into the target machine can allow an attacker unfettered access, including the ability to monitor user behavior, change computer settings, browse and copy files, access connected systems, and more. RATs are commonly employed by the more skilled threat actors, although there are RATs that are easy enough for even beginners to employ.

A RAT should be considered another form of malware, but rather than just being a program, it has an operator behind it, guiding it to do even more persistent damage. RATs can be delivered via phishing e-mails, watering holes, or any of a myriad of other malware infection vectors. RATs typically involve the creation of hidden file structures on a system and are vulnerable to detection by modern anti-malware programs. There are several major families of RATs, but an exhaustive list would be long and ever increasing. When facing a more skilled adversary, it is not uncommon to find RAT packages that have been modified for specific use, such as the program used in the Ukraine electric grid attack in 2015.

Rootkit

Rootkits are a form of malware that is specifically designed to modify the operation of the operating system in some fashion to facilitate nonstandard functionality. The history of rootkits goes back to the beginning of the UNIX operating system, where rootkits were sets of modified administrative tools. Originally designed to allow a program to take greater control over an operating system's functions when it fails or becomes unresponsive, the technique has evolved and is used in a variety of ways. One high-profile case occurred at Sony BMG Corporation, when rootkit technology was used to provide copy protection technology on some of the company's CDs. Two major issues led to this being a complete debacle for Sony: First, the software modified systems without the users' approval. Second, the software opened a security hole on Windows-based systems, creating an exploitable vulnerability at the rootkit level. This led the Sony case to be labeled as *malware*, which is the most common use of rootkits.

A rootkit can do many things—in fact, it can do virtually anything that the operating system does. Rootkits modify the operating system kernel and supporting functions, changing the nature of the system's operation. Rootkits are designed to avoid, either by subversion or evasion, the security functions of the operating system to avoid detection. Rootkits act as a form of malware that can change thread priorities to boost an application's performance, perform keylogging, act as a sniffer, hide other files from other applications, or create backdoors in the authentication system. The use of rootkit functionality to hide other processes and files enables an attacker to use a portion of a computer without the user or other applications knowing what is happening. This hides the exploit code from antivirus and anti-spyware programs, acting as a cloak of invisibility.

Rootkits can load before the operating system loads, acting as a virtualization layer, as in SubVirt and Blue Pill. Rootkits can exist in firmware, and these have been demonstrated in both video cards and expansion cards. Rootkits can exist as loadable library modules, effectively changing portions of the operating system outside the kernel. Further information on specific rootkits in the wild can be found at www.antirootkit.com.

Once a rootkit is detected, it needs to be removed and cleaned up. Because of the invasive nature of rootkits, and the fact that many aspects of rootkits are not easily detectable, most system administrators don't even attempt to clean up or remove them. It is far easier to use a previously captured clean system image and reimage the machine than to attempt to determine the depth and breadth of the damage and attempt to fix individual files.

Five types of rootkits exist:

- **Firmware** Attacks firmware on a system
- **Virtual** Attacks at the virtual machine level
- **Kernel** Attacks the kernel of the OS
- **Library** Attacks libraries used on a system
- **Application level** Attacks specific applications

Backdoors and Trapdoors

Backdoors were originally (and sometimes still are) nothing more than methods used by software developers to ensure that they can gain access to an application even if something were to happen in the future to prevent normal access methods. An example would be a hard-coded password that could be used to gain access to the program in the event that administrators forget their own system password. The obvious problem with this sort of backdoor (also sometimes referred to as a *trapdoor*) is that, because it is hard-coded, it cannot be removed. Should an attacker learn of the backdoor, all systems running that software would be vulnerable to attack.

The term *backdoor* is also more commonly used to refer to programs that attackers install after gaining unauthorized access to a system to ensure that they can continue to have unrestricted access to the system, even if their initial access method is discovered and blocked. Backdoors can also be installed by authorized individuals inadvertently, should they run software that contains a trojan horse (introduced earlier). A variation on the backdoor is the rootkit, discussed in the previous section, which is established not to gain root access but rather to ensure continued root access.

Common backdoors include Zeus, NetBus, and Back Orifice. Any of these, if running on your system, can allow an attacker remote access to your system—access that allows them to perform any function on your system.

Application-Level Attacks

Attacks against a system can occur at the network level, at the operating system level, at the application level, or at the user level (social engineering). Early attack patterns were against the network, but most of today's attacks are aimed at the applications. This is primarily because this is where the objective of most attacks resides—or in the infamous words of bank robber Willie Sutton, "because that's where the money is." In fact, many of today's attacks on systems are combinations of using vulnerabilities in networks, operating systems, and applications, all as a means to an end to obtain the desired objective of an attack, which is usually some form of data.

Application-level attacks take advantage of several facts associated with computer applications. First, most applications are large programs written by groups of programmers and, by their nature, have errors in design and coding that create vulnerabilities. For a list of typical vulnerabilities, see the Common Vulnerability and Exposures (CVE) list maintained by MITRE (https://cve.mitre.org). Second, even when vulnerabilities are discovered and patched by software vendors, end users are slow to apply patches, as evidenced by the SQL Slammer incident in January of 2003. The vulnerability exploited was a **buffer overflow**, and the vendor supplied a patch six months prior to the outbreak, yet the worm still spread quickly due to the multitude of unpatched systems.

> **Cross Check**
>
> **Application Vulnerabilities**
>
> Applications are a common target of attacks, as attackers have shifted to easier targets as the network and OS have become more hardened. What applications are not up to date on the PC you use every day? How would you know? How would you update them? A more complete examination of common application vulnerabilities is presented in Chapter 19.

Malware Defenses

Malware in all forms—virus, worm, spyware, botnet, and so on—can be defended against by following these simple steps:

- *Use an antivirus/anti-malware program.* Most major-vendor antivirus/anti-malware suites are designed to catch most widespread forms of malware. In some markets, the antivirus software is being referred to as anti-*x* software, indicating that it covers more than viruses. However, because the threat environment changes literally daily, the signature files for the software need regular updates, which most antivirus programs offer to perform automatically.
- *Keep your software up to date.* Many forms of malware achieve their objectives through exploitation of vulnerabilities in software, both in the operating system and applications. Although operating system vulnerabilities were the main source of problems, today

application-level vulnerabilities pose the greatest risk. Unfortunately, while operating system vendors are becoming more and more responsive to patching, most application vendors are not, and some, like Adobe, have very large footprints across most machines.

One of the challenges in keeping a system up to date is keeping track of the software that is on the system and keeping track of all vendor updates. There are several utility programs that one can use for this function across the enterprise. The key element is ensuring coverage across your application base.

> **Tech Tip**
>
> **Defenses Against Malware**
>
> *There are two primary defense mechanisms against malware: backups and updates. Malware acts against vulnerabilities, which are patched by keeping software up to date. One of the primary sources of loss is from the inability to recover something covered by backups.*

Attacking Computer Systems and Networks

From a high-level standpoint, attacks on computer systems and networks can be grouped into two broad categories: attacks on specific software (such as an application or the operating system) and attacks on a specific protocol or service. Attacks on a specific application or operating system are generally possible because of an oversight in the code (and possibly in the testing of that code) or because of a flaw, or bug, in the code (again indicating a lack of thorough testing). Attacks on specific protocols or services are attempts either to take advantage of a specific feature of the protocol or service or to use the protocol or service in a manner for which it was not intended. This section discusses various forms of attacks of which security professionals need to be aware.

Denial-of-Service Attacks

A **denial-of-service (DoS) attack** is an attack designed to prevent a system or service from functioning normally. A DoS attack can exploit a known vulnerability in a specific application or operating system, or it can attack features (or weaknesses) in specific protocols or services. In a DoS attack, the attacker attempts to deny authorized users access either to specific information or to the computer system or network itself. This can be accomplished by crashing the system—taking it offline—or by sending so many requests that the machine is overwhelmed.

> **Tech Tip**
>
> **Resource Exhaustion Attacks**
>
> *Resource exhaustion attacks result in a denial of service as a result of a shortage of required resources. An example is a SYN flood attack, in which excess SYN packets consume all the memory needed to create new connections.*

The purpose of a DoS attack can be simply to prevent access to the target system, or the attack can be used in conjunction with other actions to gain unauthorized access to a computer or network. For example, a **SYN flood** attack can be used to prevent service to a system temporarily in order to take advantage of a trusted relationship that exists between that system and another.

SYN flooding is an example of a DoS attack that takes advantage of the way TCP/IP networks were designed to function, and it can be used to illustrate the basic principles of any DoS attack. SYN flooding uses the TCP three-way handshake that establishes a connection between two systems. Under normal circumstances, the first system sends a SYN packet to the system with which it wants to communicate. The second system responds with a SYN/ACK if it is able to accept the request. When the initial system receives

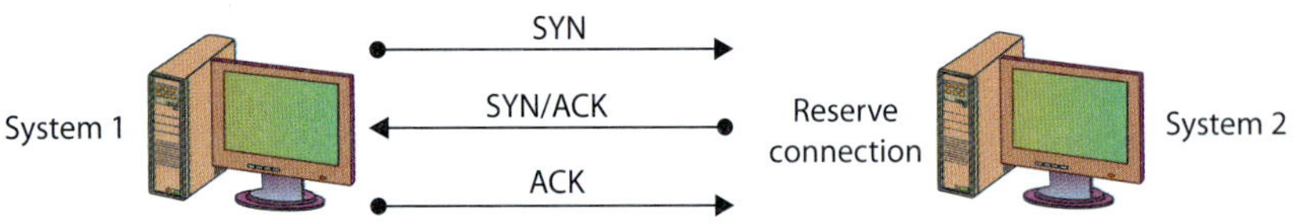

• **Figure 15.1** The TCP three-way handshake

the SYN/ACK from the second system, it responds with an ACK packet, and communication can then proceed. This process is shown in Figure 15.1.

In a SYN flooding attack, the attacker sends fake communication requests to the targeted system. Each of these requests will be answered by the target system, which then waits for the third part of the handshake. Since the requests are fake (a nonexistent IP address is used in the requests, so the target system is responding to a system that doesn't exist), the target will wait for responses that never come, as shown in Figure 15.2. The target system will drop these connections after a specific timeout period, but if the attacker sends requests faster than the timeout period eliminates them, the system will quickly be filled with requests. The number of connections a system can support is finite, so when more requests come in than can be processed, the system will soon be reserving all its connections for fake requests. At this point, any further requests are simply dropped (ignored), and legitimate users who want to connect to the target system will not be able to do so, because use of the system has been denied to them.

A SYN/ACK is actually the SYN packet sent to the first system combined with an ACK packet acknowledging the first system's SYN packet.

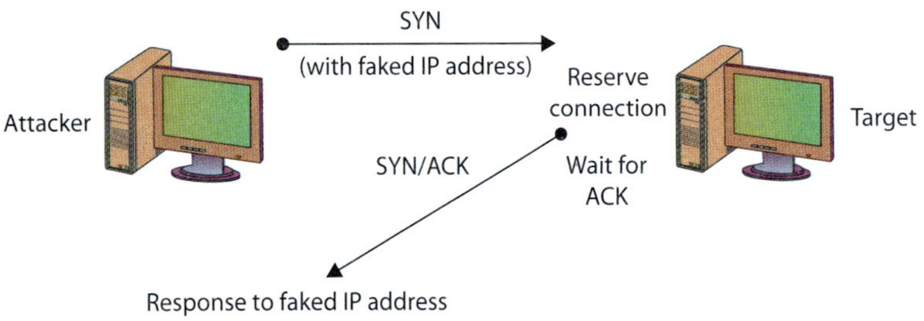

• **Figure 15.2** A SYN flooding–based DoS attack

Another simple DoS attack is the infamous *ping of death (POD),* and it illustrates the other type of attack—one targeted at a specific application or operating system, as opposed to SYN flooding, which targets a protocol. In the POD attack, the attacker sends an Internet Control Message Protocol (ICMP) ping packet equal to, or exceeding, 64 KB. Certain older systems are not able to handle this size of packet, and the system will hang or crash.

Distributed Denial of Service

DoS attacks are conducted using a single attacking system. A DoS attack employing multiple attacking systems is known as a **distributed denial-of-service (DDoS) attack**. The goal of a DDoS attack is also to deny the use of or access to a specific service or system. DDoS attacks were made famous in 2000 with the highly publicized attacks on eBay, CNN, Amazon, and Yahoo!

A *botnet* is a network of machines controlled by a malicious user. Each of these controlled machines is commonly referred to as a *zombie*.

In a DDoS attack, service is denied by overwhelming the target with traffic from many different systems. A network of attack agents (sometimes called *zombies*) is created by the attacker, and upon receiving the attack command from the attacker, the attack agents commence sending a specific type of traffic against the target. If the attack network is large enough, even ordinary web traffic can quickly overwhelm the largest of sites.

Creating a DDoS attack network is not a simple task. The attack agents are not willing agents—they are systems that have been compromised and on which the DDoS attack software has been installed. To compromise these agents, the attacker has to have gained unauthorized access to the system or have tricked authorized users into running a program that installed the attack software. The creation of the attack network may in fact be a multistep process in which the attacker first compromises a few systems and then uses those systems as *handlers* or *masters,* which in turn compromise other systems. Once the network has been created, the agents wait for an attack message, which will include data on the specific target, before launching the attack. One important aspect of a DDoS attack is that with just a few messages to the agents, the attacker can have a flood of messages sent against the targeted system. Figure 15.3 illustrates a DDoS network with agents and handlers.

A final option you should consider that will address several forms of DoS and DDoS attacks is to block ICMP packets at your border, since many attacks rely on ICMP. Blocking ICMP packets at the border devices prevents external ICMP packets from entering your network, and although this may block some functionality, it will leave internal ICMP functionality intact. It is also possible to block specific forms of ICMP; blocking Type 8, for instance, will block ICMP-based ping sweeps. It is worth noting that not all pings occur via ICMP; some tools, such as hping2, use TCP and UDP to carry ping messages.

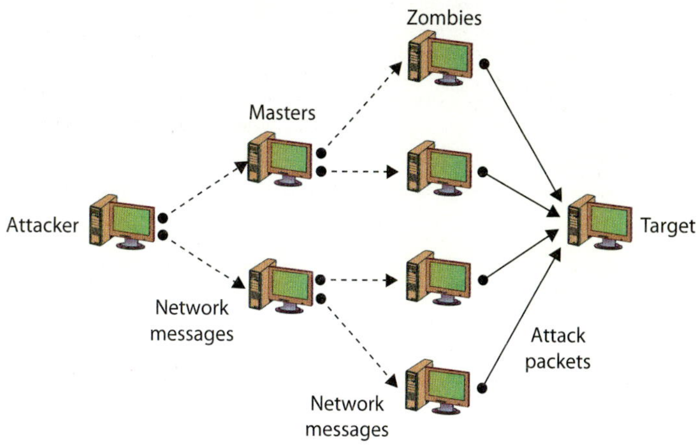

• **Figure 15.3** DDoS attack

> **Tech Tip**
>
> **Edge Blocking of ICMP**
>
> *Blocking ICMP at the edge device of the network will prevent ICMP-based attacks from external sites while still allowing full ICMP functionality for traffic inside the network. Common practice is to block ICMP at the edge of IPv4 networks, although in IPv6, ICMP is a must-carry item and cannot be blocked.*

Smurf Attack

In a specific DoS attack known as a **smurf attack**, the attacker sends a spoofed packet to the broadcast address for a network, which distributes the packet to all systems on that network. Further details are listed in the "IP Address Spoofing" section.

Defending Against DOS-Type Attacks

How can you stop or mitigate the effects of a DoS or DDoS attack? One important precaution is to ensure that you have applied the latest patches and upgrades to your systems and the applications running on them. Once a specific vulnerability is discovered, it does not take long before multiple exploits are written to take advantage of it. Typically you will have a small window of opportunity in which to patch your system between the time the vulnerability is discovered and the time exploits become widely available. A vulnerability can also be discovered by hackers, and exploits provide the first clues that a system has been compromised. Attackers can also reverse-engineer patches to learn what vulnerabilities have been patched, allowing them to attack unpatched systems.

Another approach involves changing the timeout option for TCP connections so that attacks such as the SYN flooding attack are more difficult to perform, because unused connections are dropped more quickly.

For DDoS attacks, much has been written about distributing your own workload across several systems so that any attack against your system would have to target several hosts to be completely successful. While this is effective against some DDoS attacks, if large enough DDoS networks are created (with tens of thousands of zombies, for example), any network, no matter how much the load is distributed, can be successfully attacked. Such an approach also involves additional costs to your organization to establish this distributed environment. Addressing the problem in this manner is actually an attempt to mitigate the effect of the attack rather than preventing or stopping it.

To prevent a DDoS attack, you must either be able to intercept or block the attack messages or keep the DDoS network from being established in the first place. Tools have been developed that will scan your systems, searching for sleeping zombies waiting for an attack signal. Many of the current antivirus/spyware security suite tools will detect known zombie-type infections. The problem with this type of prevention approach, however, is that it is not something you can do to prevent an attack on your network—it is something you can do to keep your network from being used to attack other networks or systems. You have to rely on the community of network administrators to test their own systems to prevent attacks on yours.

War-Dialing and War-Driving

War-dialing is the term used to describe an attacker's attempt to discover unprotected modem connections to computer systems and networks. The term's origin is the 1983 movie *WarGames,* in which the star has his machine systematically call a sequence of phone numbers in an attempt to find a computer connected to a modem. In the case of the movie, the intent was to find a machine with games the attacker could play, though obviously an attacker could have other purposes once access is obtained.

War-dialing was surprisingly successful, mostly because of *rogue modems*—unauthorized modems attached to computers on a network by authorized users. In most cases the reason for attaching the modem is not malicious—an individual may simply want to be able to go home and then connect to the organization's network to continue working. This has become history with the rise of remote desktop technology and ubiquitous Internet connectivity.

Another avenue of attack on computer systems and networks has seen a tremendous increase over the last few years because of the increase in the use of wireless networks. **War-driving** is the unauthorized scanning for and connecting to wireless access points, frequently done while driving near a facility. Wireless networks have some obvious advantages—they free employees from the cable connection to a port on their wall, allowing them to move throughout the building with their laptops and still be connected.

Cross Check

Wireless Vulnerabilities

Wireless systems have their own vulnerabilities unique to the wireless protocols. Wireless systems are becoming very common. If your machine is wireless capable, how many wireless access points can you see from your current location? Securing wireless systems from unauthorized access is an essential element of a comprehensive security program. This material is covered in depth in Chapter 12.

Social Engineering

Social engineering relies on lies and misrepresentation, which an attacker uses to trick an authorized user into providing information or access the attacker would not normally be entitled to. Complete coverage of social engineering attacks can be found in Chapter 4.

Sniffing

The group of protocols that makes up the TCP/IP suite was designed to work in a friendly environment in which everybody who connected to the network used the protocols as they were designed. The abuse of this friendly assumption is illustrated by network-traffic sniffing programs, sometimes referred to as *sniffers*. **Sniffing** is when someone examines all the network traffic that passes their NIC, whether addressed for them or not.

A network sniffer is a software or hardware device that is used to observe traffic as it passes through a network on shared broadcast media. The device can be used to view all traffic, or it can target a specific protocol, service, or even string of characters (looking for logins, for example). Normally, the network device that connects a computer to a network is designed to ignore all traffic that is not destined for that computer. Network sniffers ignore this friendly agreement and observe all traffic on the network, whether destined for that computer or others, as shown in Figure 15.4. Some network sniffers are designed not just to observe all traffic but to modify traffic as well. Network sniffing is more difficult in switched network environments due to the way collision domains are eliminated in full-duplex switching, but certain techniques can be used (spanning ports, ARP poisoning, and attacks forcing a switch to fail and act as a hub) to circumvent this.

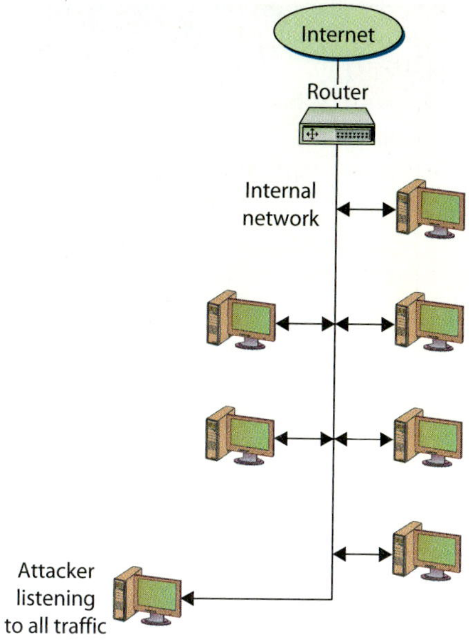

• **Figure 15.4** Network sniffers listen to all network traffic.

> A network interface card (NIC) that is listening to all network traffic and not just its own is said to be in "promiscuous mode."

Network sniffers can be used by network administrators to monitor network performance. They can be used to perform traffic analysis, for example, to determine what type of traffic is most commonly carried on the network and to determine which segments are most active. They can also be used for network bandwidth analysis and to troubleshoot certain problems (such as duplicate MAC addresses).

Network sniffers can also be used by attackers to gather information that can be used in penetration attempts. Information such as an authorized username and password can be viewed and recorded for later use. The contents of e-mail messages can also be viewed as the messages travel across the network. It should be obvious that administrators and security professionals will not want unauthorized network sniffers on their networks because of the security and privacy concerns they introduce. Fortunately, for network sniffers to be most effective, they need to be on the internal network, which generally means that the chances of outsiders using them against you are extremely limited. This is another reason that physical security is an important part of information security in today's environment.

> **Cross Check**
>
> **Physical Access and Security**
>
> One of the challenges in a modern network is getting a connection to a point in the network where your sniffing will result in the discovery of interesting information. Getting access to an open port, or to an equipment room where routers and switches are maintained, is a failure of physical security. Physical security is an important component of a comprehensive information security program. At this point ask yourself, Where can I connect into my company network? Can I get connections near high-value targets such as database servers? Details on physical security measures are covered in Chapter 8.

> **Tech Tip**
>
> **What Is Spoofing?**
>
> *Spoofing is when you assemble packets with false header information to deceive the receiver as to the true address of the sender. This can be done to manipulate return packets in the case of ping sweeps, or to provide anonymity for e-mails.*

Spoofing

Spoofing is nothing more than making data look like it has come from a different source. This is possible in TCP/IP because of the friendly assumptions behind the protocols. When the protocols were developed, it was assumed that individuals who had access to the network layer would be privileged users who could be trusted.

When a packet is sent from one system to another, it includes not only the destination IP address and port but the source IP address as well. You are supposed to fill in the source with your own address, but nothing stops you from filling in another system's address. This is one of the several forms of spoofing.

Spoofing E-mail

In e-mail spoofing, a message is sent with a From address that differs from that of the sending system. This can be easily accomplished in several different ways using several programs. To demonstrate how simple it is to spoof an e-mail address, you can telnet to port 25 (the port associated with e-mail) on a mail server. From there, you can fill in any address for the From and To sections of the message, whether or not the addresses are yours or even actually exist.

You can use several methods to determine whether an e-mail message was sent by the source it claims to have been sent from, but most users do not question their e-mail and will accept as authentic where it appears to have originated. A variation on e-mail spoofing, though not technically spoofing, is for the attacker to acquire a URL similar to the URL they want to spoof so that e-mail sent from their system appears to have come from the official site—until the recipient reads the address carefully. For example, if attackers want to spoof XYZ Corporation, which owns XYZ.com, the attackers might gain access to the URL XYZ.Corp.com. An individual receiving a message from the spoofed corporation site would not normally suspect it to be a spoof but would take it to be official. This same method can be, and has been, used to spoof websites. If, however, the attackers made their spoofed site appear similar to the official one, they could easily convince many potential viewers that they were at the official site. Today, many .com and other domains of common sites, as well as common typos of URLs, are purchased and directed to the legitimate site.

> **Cross Check**
>
> **E-mail Spoofing**
>
> E-mail was created in an era with a different security environment—one where attribution was not even an afterthought. This has led to issues associated with trust regarding e-mails. Full details of securing e-mails are covered in Chapter 17.

IP Address Spoofing

IP is designed to work so that the originators of any IP packet include their own IP address in the From portion of the packet. Although this is the intent, nothing prevents a system from inserting a different address in the From portion of the packet. This is known as *IP address spoofing*. An IP address can be spoofed for several reasons. In a specific DoS attack known as a *smurf attack,* the attacker sends a spoofed packet to the broadcast address for a network, which distributes the packet to all systems on that network. In the smurf attack, the packet sent by the attacker to the broadcast address is an echo request with the From address forged so that it appears another system (the target system) has made the echo request. The normal response of a system to an echo request is an echo reply, and it is used in the ping utility to let a user know whether a remote system is reachable and is responding. In the smurf attack, the request is sent to all systems on the network, so all will respond with an echo reply to the target system, as shown in Figure 15.5. The attacker has sent one packet and has been able to generate as many as 254 responses aimed at the target. Should the attacker send several of these spoofed requests, or send them to several different networks, the target can quickly become overwhelmed with the volume of echo replies it receives.

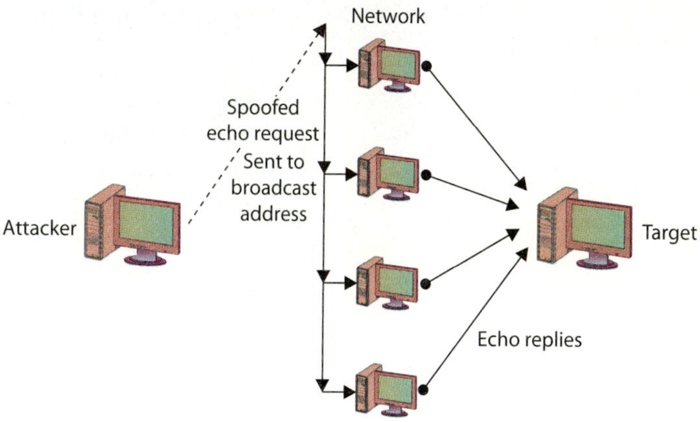

• **Figure 15.5** Spoofing used in a smurf DOS attack

A smurf attack allows an attacker to use a network structure to send large volumes of packets to a victim. By sending ICMP requests to a broadcast IP address, with the victim as the source address, the multitudes of replies will flood the victim system.

Spoofing and Trusted Relationships

Spoofing can also take advantage of a *trusted relationship* between two systems. If two systems are configured to accept the authentication accomplished by each other, an individual logged on to one system might not be forced to go through an authentication process again to access the other system. An attacker can take advantage of this arrangement by sending a packet to one system that appears to have come from a trusted system. Because the trusted relationship is in place, the targeted system may perform the requested task without authentication.

Because a reply will often be sent once a packet is received, the system that is being impersonated could interfere with the attack, since it would receive an acknowledgment for a request it never made. The attacker will often initially launch a DoS attack (such as a SYN flooding attack) to temporarily take out the spoofed system for the period of time that the attacker is exploiting the trusted relationship. Once the attack is completed, the DoS attack on the spoofed system would be terminated, and the system administrators, apart from having a temporarily nonresponsive system, might never notice that the attack occurred. Figure 15.6 illustrates a spoofing attack that includes a SYN flooding attack.

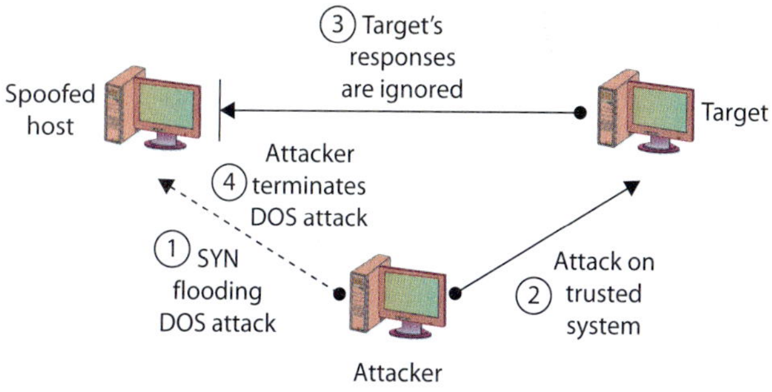

• **Figure 15.6** Spoofing to take advantage of a trusted relationship

Because of this type of attack, administrators are encouraged to strictly limit any trusted relationships between hosts. Firewalls should also be configured to discard any packets from outside of the firewall that have From addresses indicating they originated from inside the network (a situation that should not occur normally and that indicates spoofing is being attempted).

Spoofing and Sequence Numbers

How complicated the spoofing is depends heavily on several factors, including whether the traffic is encrypted and where the attacker is located relative to the target. Spoofing attacks from inside a network, for example, are much easier to perform than attacks from outside of the network, because the inside attacker can observe the traffic to and from the target and can do a better job of formulating the necessary packets.

Formulating the packets is more complicated for external attackers because a sequence number is associated with TCP packets. A **sequence number** is a 32-bit number established by the host that is incremented for each packet sent. Packets are not guaranteed to be received in order, and the sequence number can be used to help reorder packets as they are received and to refer to packets that may have been lost in transmission.

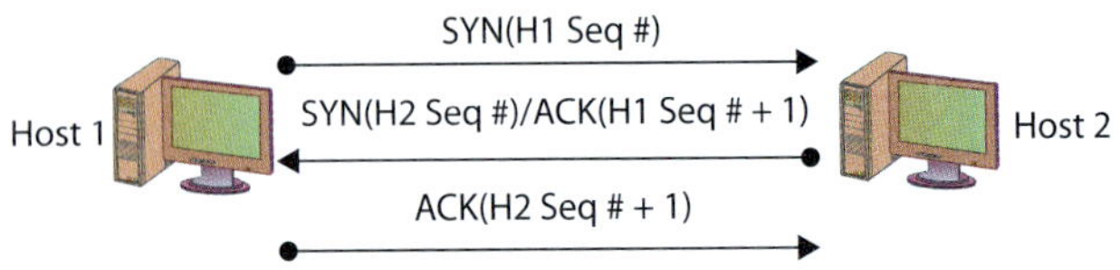

• **Figure 15.7** Three-way handshake with sequence numbers

In the TCP three-way handshake, two sets of sequence numbers are created, as shown in Figure 15.7. The first system chooses a sequence number to send with the original SYN packet. The system receiving this SYN packet acknowledges with a SYN/ACK. It sends an acknowledgment number back, which is based on the first sequence number plus one (that is, it increments the sequence number sent to it by one). It then also creates its own sequence number and sends that along with it. The original system receives the SYN/ACK with the new sequence number. It increments the sequence number by one and uses it as the acknowledgment number in the ACK packet with which it responds.

The difference in the difficulty of attempting a spoofing attack from inside a network and from outside involves determining the sequence number. If the attacker is inside of the network and can observe the traffic with which the target host responds, the attacker can easily see the sequence number the system creates and can respond with the correct sequence number. If the attacker is external to the network and the sequence number the target system generates is not observed, it is next to impossible for the attacker to provide the final ACK with the correct sequence number. Therefore, the attacker has to guess what the sequence number might be.

Sequence numbers are somewhat predictable, based on the operating systems in question. Sequence numbers for each session are not started from the same number, so different packets from different concurrent connections will not have the same sequence numbers. Instead, the sequence number for each new connection is incremented by some large number to keep the numbers from being the same. The sequence number may also be incremented by some large number every second (or some other time period). An external attacker has to determine what values are used for these increments. The attacker can do this by attempting connections at various time intervals to observe how the sequence numbers are incremented. Once the pattern is determined, the attacker can attempt a legitimate connection to determine the current value and then immediately attempt the spoofed connection. The spoofed connection sequence number should be the legitimate connection incremented by the determined value or values.

Sequence numbers are also important in session hijacking, which is discussed in an upcoming section. When an attacker spoofs addresses and imposes their packets in the middle of an existing connection, this is known as an **on-path attack**, although still often referred to as a *man-in-the-middle attack*.

MAC Spoofing

MAC spoofing is the act of changing a MAC address to bypass security checks based on the MAC address. This can work when the return packets are being routed by IP address and can be correctly linked to the correct MAC. Not all MAC spoofing is an attack; small firewall routers have commonly had a MAC clone function, by which the device can clone a MAC, making it seem transparent to other devices such as the cable modem connection.

TCP/IP Hijacking

TCP/IP hijacking and *session hijacking* are terms used to refer to the process of taking control of an already existing session between a client and a server. The advantage to an attacker of hijacking over attempting to penetrate a computer system or network is that the attacker doesn't have to circumvent any authentication mechanisms, because the user has already authenticated and established the session. Once the user has completed the authentication sequence, the attacker can then usurp the session and carry on as if they, not the user, had authenticated with the system. To prevent the user from noticing anything unusual, the attacker can decide to attack the user's system and perform a DoS attack on it, taking it down so that the user, and the system, will not notice the extra traffic that is taking place.

Hijack attacks generally are used against web and Telnet sessions. Sequence numbers as they apply to spoofing also apply to session hijacking, since the hijacker will need to provide the correct sequence number to continue the appropriated sessions.

Man-in-the-Middle Attacks

A **man-in-the-middle attack**, as the name implies, generally occurs when attackers are able to place themselves in the middle of two other hosts that are communicating. Ideally, this is done by ensuring that all communication going to or from the target host is routed through the attacker's host (which can be accomplished if the attacker can compromise the router for the target host). The attacker can then observe all traffic before relaying it and can actually modify or block traffic. To the target host, it appears that communication is occurring normally, since all expected replies are received. Figure 15.8 illustrates this type of attack.

> CompTIA has chosen new names for several terms. Man-in-the-middle attacks has been renamed on-path attacks. For the purpose of the Security+ exam, be cognizant of these names. This book will reference both the historical and new names to assist in transitional learning of the new terms when examined against historical literature.

There are numerous methods of instantiating a man-in-the-middle attack; one of the common methods is via session hijacking. Session hijacking can occur when information such as a cookie is stolen, allowing the attacker to impersonate the legitimate session. This attack can be as a result of a cross-site scripting attack, which tricks a user into executing code resulting in cookie theft. The amount of information that can be obtained in a man-in-the-middle attack will obviously be limited if the communication is encrypted. Even in this case, however, sensitive

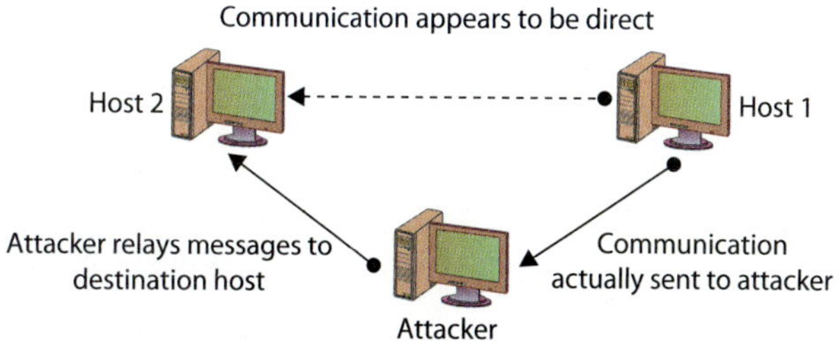

• **Figure 15.8** A man-in-the-middle attack

information can still be obtained, since knowing what communication is being conducted, and between which individuals, may in fact provide information that is valuable in certain circumstances.

Man-in-the-Middle Attacks on Encrypted Traffic

The term *man-in-the-middle attack* is sometimes used to refer to a more specific type of attack—one in which the encrypted traffic issue is addressed. If you wanted to communicate securely with your friend Bob, you might ask him for his public key so you could encrypt your messages to him. You, in turn, would supply Bob with your public key. An attacker can conduct a man-in-the-middle attack by intercepting your request for Bob's public key and the sending of your public key to him. The attacker would replace your public key with their public key, and they would send this on to Bob. The attacker's public key would also be sent to you (by the attacker) instead of Bob's public key. Now when either you or Bob encrypts a message, it will be encrypted using the attacker's public key, enabling the attacker to intercept it, decrypt it, and then send it on by re-encrypting it with the appropriate key for either you or Bob. Each of you thinks you are transmitting messages securely, but in reality your communication has been compromised. Well-designed cryptographic products use techniques such as mutual authentication to avoid this problem.

Cross Check

Encryption

Cryptography and encryption are tools that can solve many of our secrecy problems. The challenges solved through encryption and the new problems associated with the use of encryption require an understanding of the technical details. Public key encryption, discussed in detail in Chapters 5 and 6, uses two keys: a public key, which anybody can use to encrypt or "lock" your message, and a private key, which only you know and which is used to "unlock" or decrypt a message locked with your public key. One of the key challenges associated with the use of public keys and corresponding private keys is determining who has what key values. Do you have your own key pair? If so, do you know the public key value you need to share with others?

Man-in-the-Browser

The **man-in-the-browser (MITB)** attack is a variant of a man-in-the-middle attack. In an MITB attack, the first element is a malware attack that places a trojan element that can act as a proxy on the target machine. This malware changes browser behavior through browser helper objects or extensions. When a user connects to their bank, the malware recognizes the target (a financial transaction) and injects itself in the stream of the conversation. When the user approves a transfer of $150 to pay a utility bill, the malware intercepts the user's keystrokes and modifies them to perform a different transaction. A famous example of an MITB attack is the financial malware Zeus, which targeted financial transactions on users' machines, manipulating and changing them after the user had entered password credentials.

Replay Attacks

A **replay attack** occurs when the attacker captures a portion of a communication between two parties and retransmits it at a later time. For example, an attacker might replay a series of commands and codes used in a financial transaction to cause the transaction to be conducted multiple times. Generally, replay attacks are associated with attempts to circumvent authentication mechanisms, such as the capturing and reuse of a certificate or ticket.

The best way to prevent replay attacks is with encryption, cryptographic authentication, and timestamps. If a portion of the certificate or ticket includes a date/timestamp or an expiration date/time, and this portion is also encrypted as part of the ticket or certificate, then replaying it at a later time will prove useless because it will be rejected as having expired.

The best method for defending against replay attacks is through the use of encryption and short time frames for legal transactions. Encryption can protect the contents from being understood, and a short time frame for a transaction prevents subsequent use.

Transitive Access

Transitive access is a means of attacking a system by violating the trust relationship between machines. A simple example is when servers are well protected and clients are not, and the servers trust the clients. In this case, attacking a client can provide transitive access to the servers.

Trust is an essential part of security. If B trusts A, and C trusts B, then C trusts A. A transitive attack takes advantage of this trust chain by obtaining trust from one element in the chain (for example, through spoofing) and then using that to gain transitive access to another trusted system via the chain of trust.

Scanning Attacks

Scanners can be used to send specifically crafted packets in an attempt to determine TCP/UDP port status. An XMAS scan, named because the alternating bits in the TCP header look like Christmas lights, uses the URG, PSH, and FIN flags to determine TCP port availability. If the port is closed, an RST is returned. If the port is open, there is typically no return. An XMAS scan can help determine OS type and version, based on TCP/IP stack responses, and can also help determine firewall rules. These attacks can also be used to consume system resources, resulting in DoS.

Simple stateless firewalls check for the SYN flag set to prevent SYN floods, and Christmas tree packets are designed not to have SYN set, so they pass right by these devices. Newer security devices such as advanced firewalls can detect these packets, alerting people to the scanning activities.

Tech Tip

XMAS Attack

The XMAS attack, or Christmas attack, comes from a specific set of protocol options. A Christmas tree packet is a packet that has many of its options turned on. The name comes from the observation that these packets are lit up like a Christmas tree. When sent as a scan, a Christmas tree packet has the FIN, URG, and PSH options set. Many OSs implement their compliance with RFC 791, the RFC governing IP packets, in slightly different ways. Their response to the packet can tell the scanner what type of OS is present. Another option is in the case of a DoS attack, where Christmas tree packets can take up significantly greater processing on a router, thus consuming resources.

Attacks on Encryption

Encryption is the process of transforming *plaintext* into an unreadable format known as *ciphertext* using a specific technique or algorithm. Most encryption techniques use some form of key in the encryption process. The key is used in a mathematical process to scramble the original message to arrive at the unreadable ciphertext. Another key (sometimes the same one and sometimes a different one) is used to decrypt or unscramble the ciphertext to re-create the original plaintext. The length of the key often directly relates to the strength of the encryption.

Cryptanalysis is the process of attempting to break a cryptographic system—it is an attack on the specific method used to encrypt the plaintext. Cryptographic systems can be compromised in various ways.

Weak Keys

Certain encryption algorithms may have specific keys that yield poor, or easily decrypted, ciphertext. Imagine an encryption algorithm that consists solely of a single XOR function (an exclusive OR function where two bits are compared and a 1 is returned if either of the original bits, but not both, is a 1), where the key is repeatedly used to XOR with the plaintext. A key where all bits are 0's, for example, would result in ciphertext that is the same as the original plaintext. This would obviously be a weak key for this encryption algorithm. In fact, any key with long strings of 0's would yield portions of the ciphertext that were the same as the plaintext. In this simple example, many keys could be considered weak.

Encryption algorithms used in computer systems and networks are much more complicated than a simple, single XOR function, but some algorithms have still been found to have weak keys that make cryptanalysis easier.

Exhaustive Search of Key Space

Even if the specific algorithm used to encrypt a message is complicated and has not been shown to have weak keys, the key length will still play a significant role in how easy it is to attack the method of encryption. Generally speaking, the longer a key, the harder it will be to attack. Thus, a 40-bit encryption scheme will be easier to attack using a brute force technique (which tests all possible keys, one by one) than a 256-bit based scheme. This is easily demonstrated by imagining a scheme that employs a 2-bit key. Even if the resulting ciphertext were completely unreadable, performing a brute force attack until one key is found that can decrypt the ciphertext would not take long, since only four keys are possible. Every bit that is added to the length of a key doubles the number of keys that have to be tested in a brute force attack on the encryption. It is easy to understand why a scheme utilizing a 40-bit key would be much easier to attack than a scheme that utilizes a 256-bit key.

The bottom line is simple: an exhaustive search of the keyspace will decrypt the message. The strength of the encryption method is related to the sheer size of the keyspace, which with modern algorithms is large enough to provide significant time constraints when using this method to break an encrypted message. Algorithmic complexity is also an issue with respect to brute forcing, and you cannot immediately compare different key lengths from different algorithms and assume relative strength.

Indirect Attacks

One of the most common ways of attacking an encryption system is to find weaknesses in mechanisms surrounding the cryptography. Examples include poor random-number generators, unprotected key exchanges, keys stored on hard drives without sufficient protection, and other general programmatic errors, such as buffer overflows. In attacks that target these types of weaknesses, it is not the cryptographic algorithm itself that is being attacked but rather the implementation of that algorithm in the real world.

Address System Attacks

> The process of using a new domain name for the five-day "test" period and then relinquishing the name, only to repeat the process again—in essence, obtaining a domain name for free—is called *DNS kiting*.

Many aspects of a computer system are controlled by the use of addresses. IP addresses can be manipulated, as shown earlier, and the other address schemes can be manipulated as well. In the summer of 2008, much was made of a serious Domain Name System (DNS) vulnerability that required the simultaneous patching of systems by over 80 vendors. This coordinated effort was to close a technical loophole in the domain name resolution infrastructure that would allow the hijacking and man-in-the-middle attack on the DNS system worldwide.

The DNS system has been the target of other attacks. One attack, **DNS kiting**, is an economic attack against the terms of using a new DNS entry. New DNS purchases are allowed a five-day "test period" during which the name can be relinquished for no fee. Creative users learned to register a name, use it for less than five days, relinquish the name, and then get the name again and begin all over, repeating this cycle many times to use a name without paying for it. Typical registration versus permanent entry ratios of 15:1 occur, and in February of 2007 GoDaddy reported that out of 55.1 million requests only 3.6 million were not canceled.

Another twist on this scheme is the concept of domain name front running, where a registrar places a name on a five-day hold after someone searches for it, and then offers it for sale at a higher price. In January of 2008, Network Solutions was accused of violating the trust as a registrar by forcing people to purchase names from them after they engaged in domain name testing.

Cache Poisoning

Many network activities rely on various addressing schemes to function properly. When you point your web browser at your bank, by typing the bank's URL, your browser consults the system's Domain Name System to turn the words into a numerical address. When a packet is being switched to your machine by the network, a series of address caches is involved. Whether the cache is for the DNS system or the ARP system, it exists for the same reason: efficiency. These caches prevent repeated redundant lookups, saving time for the system. However, they can also be poisoned, sending incorrect information to the end user's application, redirecting traffic, and changing system behaviors.

DNS Poisoning

The DNS system is used to convert a name into an IP address. There is no single DNS system, but rather a hierarchy of DNS servers, from root servers on the backbone of the Internet, to copies at your ISP, your home router, and your local machine, each in the form of a DNS cache. To examine a DNS query for a specific address, you can use the **nslookup** command. Figure 15.9 shows a series of DNS queries executed on a Windows machine. In the first request, the DNS server was with an ISP, whereas on the second request, the DNS server was from a VPN connection. Between the two requests, the network connections were changed, resulting in different DNS lookups. This is a form of DNS poisoning attack.

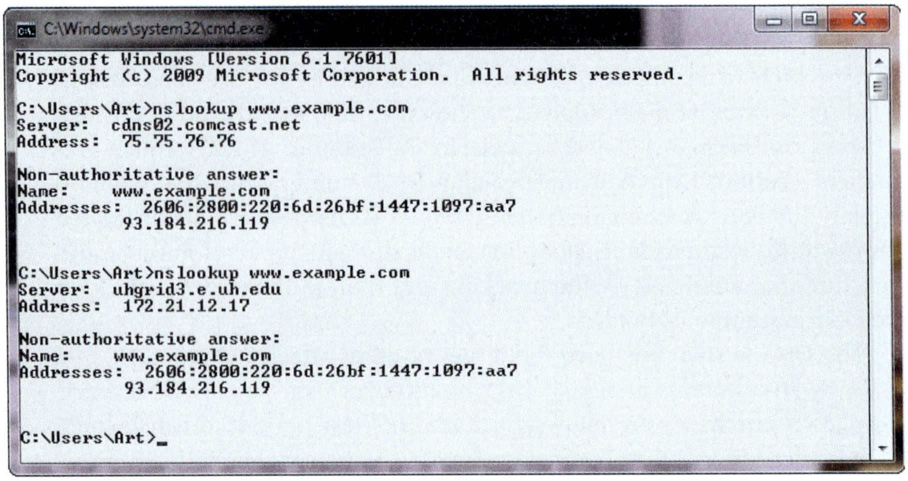

• **Figure 15.9** An **nslookup** of a DNS query

At times, **nslookup** will return a nonauthoritative answer, as shown in Figure 15.10. This typically means the result is from a cache as opposed to a server that has an authoritative answer (that is, one known to be current).

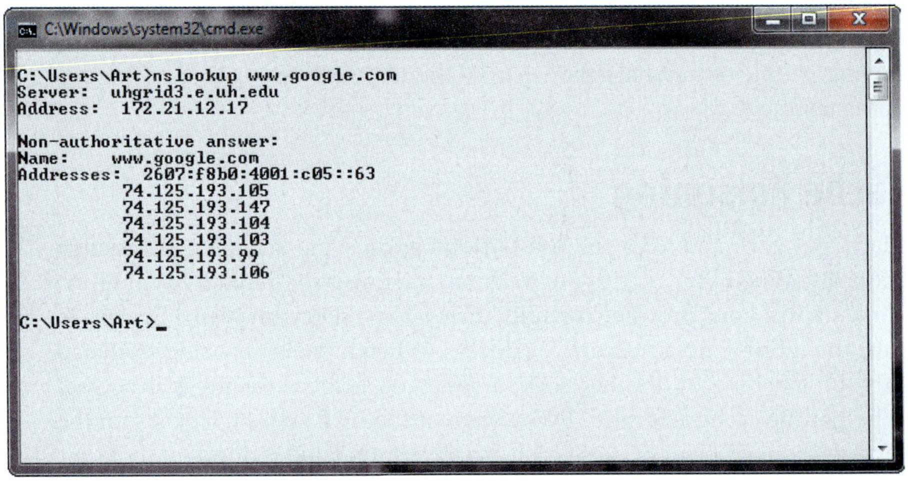

• **Figure 15.10** Cache response to a DNS query

You can use other commands to examine and manipulate the DNS cache on a system. In Windows, the **ipconfig/displaydns** command will show the current DNS cache on a machine. Figure 15.11 shows a small DNS cache. This cache was recently emptied using the **ipconfig/flushdns** command to make it fit on the screen.

Looking at DNS as a complete system shows that there are hierarchical levels from the top (root server) down to the cache in an individual machine. DNS poisoning can occur at any of these levels, with the effect of the poisoning growing wider the higher up it occurs. In 2010, a DNS poisoning event resulted in the "Great Firewall of China" censoring inbound Internet traffic into China from the United States until caches were resolved. Today, after further examination, the attack was shown to be much more complex.

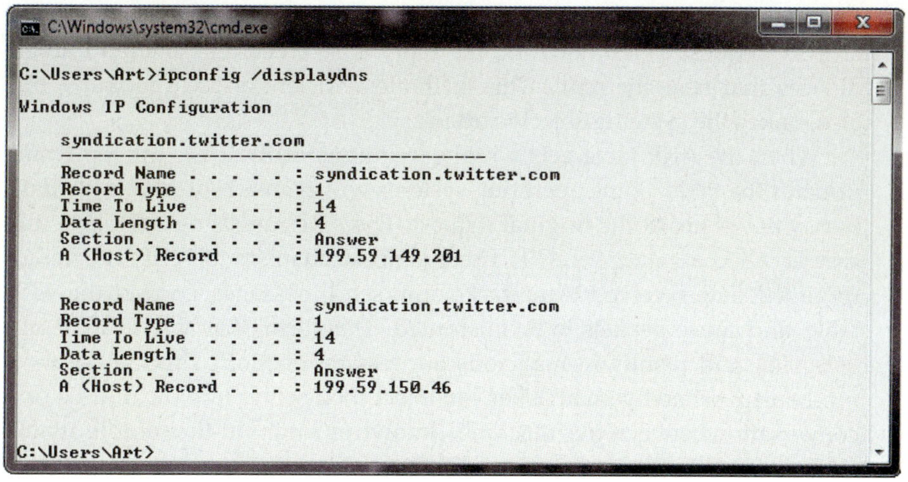

Figure 15.11 Cache response to a DNS table query

The efforts of the Chinese government actively seek to strictly control all aspects of Internet traffic in China.

DNS poisoning is a variant of a larger attack class referred to as *DNS spoofing,* in which an attacker changes a DNS record through any of a multitude of means. There are many ways to perform DNS spoofing, a few of which include compromising a DNS server, the use of the Kaminsky attack, and the use of a false network node advertising a false DNS address. An attacker can even use DNS cache poisoning to result in DNS spoofing. When an upstream DNS cache is poisoned, all of the downstream users will get spoofed DNS records.

Because of the importance of integrity on DNS requests and responses, a project has begun to secure the DNS infrastructure using digital signing of DNS records. This project, initiated by the U.S. government and called Domain Name System Security Extensions (DNSSEC), works by digitally signing records. This is done by adding records to the DNS system, a key, and a signature attesting to the validity of the key. With this information, requestors can be assured that the information they receive is correct. It will take a substantial amount of time (years) for this new system to propagate throughout the entire DNS infrastructure, but in the end, the system will have much greater assurance.

ARP Poisoning

In moving packets between machines, a device sometimes needs to know where to send a packet using the MAC or Layer 2 address. Address Resolution Protocol (ARP) handles this problem through four basic message types:

- **ARP request** "Who has this IP address?"
- **ARP reply** "I have that IP address; my MAC address is…"
- **Reverse ARP request (RARP)** "Who has this MAC address?"
- **RARP reply** "I have that MAC address; my IP address is…"

These messages are used in conjunction with a device's ARP table, where a form of short-term memory associated with these data elements resides.

ARP poisoning involves the altering of the ARP cache on the local system. Using the Windows command prompt (as an administrator), examine the ARP table with the **arp -1** command. The results will be a table showing the IP addresses in the left column and the MAC addresses in the middle. If the table contains two different IP addresses that share the same MAC address, you are probably undergoing an ARP poisoning attack.

The commands are used as a simple form of lookup. When a machine sends an ARP request to the network, the reply is received and entered into all devices that hear the reply. This facilitates efficient address lookups, but also makes the system subject to attack.

When the ARP table gets a reply, it automatically trusts the reply and updates the table. Some operating systems will even accept ARP reply data if they never heard the original request. The ARP message received in this case is called a *gratuitous ARP.* There is no mechanism to verify the veracity of the data received. An attacker can send messages, corrupt the ARP table, and cause packets to be misrouted. This form of attack is called **ARP poisoning** and results in malicious address redirection. This can allow a mechanism whereby an attacker can inject themselves into the middle of a conversation between two machines, known as a man-in-the-middle attack.

Local MAC addresses can also be poisoned in the same manner, although it is called ARP poisoning. This can cause miscommunications locally. Poisoning attacks can be used to steal information, establish man-in-the-middle attacks, and even create DoS opportunities.

Amplification

Certain types of attacks could be considered dependent upon volume, such as denial of service and distributed denial of service. For these attacks to generate a sufficient volume of packets to overwhelm a host, typically a large server, more than a single home PC is required. *Amplification* is a trick whereby the attacker uses a specific protocol aspect to achieve what a single machine cannot by itself. As an example, let's look at the ICMP command **ping**. When you issue an ICMP **ping** command, the machine receiving it provides a **ping** reply packet. What if you send the ICMP request to a network address, in essence to all active hosts within that network? They would all reply with a packet. Now, you could forge the requesting packet so that the reply address is a specific machine. The net effect is that all those machines will reply to the forged address—one machine—with an amplified response.

Domain Hijacking

Domain hijacking is the act of changing the registration of a domain name without the permission of its original registrant. Technically a crime, this act can have devastating consequences because the DNS system will automatically spread the false domain location far and wide. The original owner can request it to be corrected, but that takes time.

Pass-the-Hash Attacks

Pass the hash is a hacking technique where the attacker captures the hash used to authenticate a process. They can then use this hash by injecting it into a process in place of the password. This is a highly technical attack, targeting the Windows authentication process, injecting a copy of the password hash directly into the system. The attacker does not need to know the password but instead can use a captured hash and inject it directly, which will verify correctly, thus granting access. Because this is a very technically specific hack, tools have been developed to facilitate its operation.

Software Exploitation

An attack that takes advantage of bugs or weaknesses in software is referred to as *software exploitation*. These bugs and weaknesses can be the result of poor design, poor testing, or poor coding practices. Software exploitation is covered in Chapter 19.

Client-Side Attacks

The web browser has become the major application for users to engage resources across the Web. The popularity and the utility of this interface has made it a prime target for attackers to gain access and control over a system. A wide variety of attacks can occur via a browser, typically resulting from a failure to validate input properly before use. Unvalidated input can result in a series of injection attacks, header manipulation, and other forms of attack.

Header Manipulations

When Hypertext Transfer Protocol (HTTP) elements are being dynamically generated through the use of user inputs, unvalidated inputs can give attackers an opportunity to change these HTTP elements. When user-supplied information is used in a header, it is possible to deploy a variety of attacks, including cache poisoning, cross-site scripting, cross-user defacement, page hijacking, cookie manipulation, and open redirect.

Typo Squatting/URL Hijacking

Typo squatting is a form of attack that involves capitalizing on common typographical errors. If a user mistypes a URL, then the result should be a 404 error, or "resource not found." However, if an attacker has registered the mistyped URL, the user would land on the attacker's page. This attack pattern is also referred to as either URL hijacking, fake URL, or brandjacking (if the objective is to deceive based on branding).

URL hijacking is a generic name for a wide range of attacks that target the URL. The URL is the primary means by which a user receives web content. If the correct URL is used, you get the desired content. If the URL is tampered with or altered, you can get different content. There is a wide range of URL-based attacks, from malware manipulations, to typo squatting, to ad-based attacks that make the user think they are clicking the correct link. The net result is the same: the user thinks they are asking for content A, but they get content B instead.

There are several reasons why an attacker might pursue this avenue of attack. The most obvious one is to conduct a **phishing** attack. The fake site collects credentials, passing them on to the real site, and then steps out of the conversation to avoid detection once the credentials are obtained. It can also be used to plant drive-by malware on the victim machine. In addition, it can move the packets through an affiliate network, thus earning

> **Tech Tip**
>
> **Mimikatz**
>
> *Mimikatz is a toolset that can provide insight and exploration into Windows security elements, including obtaining Kerberos credentials and creating a "golden ticket," a universal Kerberos ticket. Mimikatz has been included in Metasploit, making it an awesome post-exploitation tool that can enable tremendous attacker functionality on a Windows machine.*

> **Tech Tip**
>
> **All Input Is Evil**
>
> *You can never trust input from a client machine. A client can manipulate the input, the data can be changed in transit, and simple transmission errors can occur. The net result is that inputs can be manipulated, spoofed, or otherwise changed. The bottom line is to never trust input—always verify it before use.*

Drive-by downloads can occur via a couple different mechanisms. It is possible for an ad that is rotated into content on a reputable site to contain a drive-by download. Users don't have control over what ads are presented. A second, more common method is a website that the user gets to either by mistyping a URL or by following a search link without vetting where they are clicking first. Just like cities can have bad neighborhoods, so too does the Internet, and surfing in a bad neighborhood can result in bad outcomes.

A zero-day attack or threat is a computer threat that tries to exploit computer application vulnerabilities that are unknown to others or possibly even the software developer.

Tech Tip

Watering Hole Attacks

Watering hole attacks can occur from even innocent websites. Brian Krebs gives a strong analysis of watering hole attacks on his blog, Krebs on Security, *at https://krebsonsecurity.com/2012/09/espionage-hackers-target-watering-hole-sites.*

click-through revenue based on the typos. There are numerous other forms of attacks that can be perpetrated using a fake URL as a starting point.

Drive-by Download Attack

Browsers are used to navigate the Internet, using HTTP and other protocols to bring files to users' computers. Some of these files are images, some are scripts, and some are text based. Together they form the web pages we see. Users don't ask for each component—it is the job of the browser to identify the needed files and fetch them. A new type of attack takes advantage of this mechanism by initiating a download of malware, regardless of whether a user clicks it. This automated download of materials is referred to as a **drive-by download attack**.

Watering Hole Attack

The most commonly recognized attack vectors are those that are direct to a target. Because of their incoming and direct nature, defenses are crafted to detect and defend against them. But what if the user "asked" for the attack by visiting a website? Just as a hunter waits near a watering hole for animals to come drink, attackers can plant malware at sites where users are likely to frequent. First identified by RSA, **watering hole attacks** involve the infecting of a target website with malware. In some of the cases detected, the infection was constrained to a specific geographical area. These are not simple attacks, yet they can be very effective at delivering malware to specific groups of end users. Watering hole attacks are complex to achieve and appear to be backed by nation-states and other high-resource attackers. In light of the stakes, the typical attack vector will be a **zero-day attack** to further avoid detection.

Clickjacking

Clickjacking is an attack against the design element of a user interface. Clickjacking tricks a web browser user into clicking on something different from what the user perceives, by means of malicious code in the web page. This malicious code can be an overlay, and other means, but the net result is the user thinks they clicked No, but in reality they clicked Yes, and the browser executes the corresponding code. If the attacker modifies a page so that a transparent overlay with invisible clickable elements aligns with the actual elements, then the code that runs when a click occurs can be the attacker's code.

Driver Manipulation

Drivers are pieces of software that sit between the operating system and a peripheral device. In one respect, drivers are a part of the OS; they're an extension. In another respect, drivers are code that is not part of the OS and is developed by firms other than the OS developer.

Shimming

Shimming is the process of putting a layer of code between the driver and the OS. Shimming allows for flexibility and portability because it enables changes between different versions of an OS without modifying the original driver code. Shimming also represents a means by which malicious code can change a driver's behavior without changing the driver itself.

Refactoring

Refactoring is the process of restructuring existing computer code without changing its external behavior. Refactoring is done to improve nonfunctional attributes of the software, such as improving code readability and/or reducing complexity. Refactoring can uncover design flaws that lead to exploitable vulnerabilities, allowing these to be closed without changing the external behavior of the code.

Advanced Persistent Threat

The advanced persistent threat (APT) is a method of attack that primarily focuses on stealth and continuous presence on a system. APT is a very advanced method, requiring a team to maintain access, and typically involves high-value targets. APT typically uses specially crafted attack vectors, coupled with phishing or **spear phishing** for the initial entry. Then techniques are employed to develop backdoors and multiple account access routes. The skill level of the attackers is typically exceedingly high, and their aim is to completely own a system without being detected.

> **Cross Check**
>
> **APT Groups**
>
> Information on different nation-state groups performing APT attacks is covered in detail in Chapter 1.

Once the attackers have completely penetrated a system and gain the ability to read e-mails to watch for reports of detection, they can accomplish their goal of stealing materials. Their long-term objectives are to remain hidden and undetected, while harvesting information over months and years. APT is the attack method of choice for nation-states and industrial espionage.

> **Tech Tip**
>
> **Signs of an APT Attack**
>
> *The following are indications of an APT attack:*
>
> - **Off-hours activity** *If logs demonstrate "normal" activity at times when your workers are at home, this is a sign of compromised accounts. Look for large numbers of occurrences, as APT attackers tend to use multiple accounts.*
> - **Finding multiple backdoor trojans or remote-access trojans** *When security scans begin to find a lot of malware, this can be a sign of an APT.*
> - **Finding unknown files** *APTs tend to bundle exfiltration data and keep it in encrypted form before slowly siphoning it out. Large files of unknown origin can be these bundles.*
> - **Finding spear phishing e-mails and pass-the-hash tools** *These advanced attack methods are indications of an advanced adversary.*
> - **Strange data flows** *This is the most telltale sign. Finding unusual data flows—movement of data outside the normal course of business—indicates leakage.*

Password Attacks

The most common form of authentication is the user ID and password combination. While it is not inherently a poor mechanism for authentication, the combination can be attacked in several ways. All too often, these attacks yield favorable results for the attacker, not as a result of a weakness in the scheme, but usually due to the user not following good password procedures.

Password Guessing

Passwords are secrets that are supposed to be known by only the authorized user. However, people tend to pick things easy to remember and also reuse these secrets. This makes the password guessing attack possible. If a site has

One of the realities of modern data breaches is that your e-mail and password may be lost. Technically, if companies handled passwords correctly, a salted hash of your password would be exposed, but that is for another chapter. If your e-mail and password end up exposed, then what other accounts do you use the same password on? With so many accounts and our limited ability to manage passwords, it is a given that many times passwords are repeated. When a repeated password is exposed, it is up to the user to change the password on other systems. This is a good reason why you shouldn't repeat passwords on sites with direct financial implications.

a leak of password data and users have reused a password, attackers can start with disclosed passwords associated with data breaches and many times can guess a password. This is why the addition of a single number that you change doesn't provide security because attackers will try other numbers.

Poor Password Choices

The least technical of the various password-attack techniques consists of the attacker simply attempting to guess the password of an authorized user of the system or network. It is surprising how often this simple method works, and the reason it does is because people are notorious for picking poor passwords. Users need to select a password that they can remember, so they create simple passwords, such as their birthday, their mother's maiden name, the name of their spouse or one of their children, or even simply their user ID itself. All it takes is for the attacker to obtain a valid user ID (often a simple matter, because organizations tend to use an individual's names in some combination—first letter of their first name combined with their last name, for example) and a little bit of information about the user before guessing can begin.

Spraying

Password *spraying* is an attack that uses a limited number of commonly used passwords and applies them to a large number of accounts. Traditional brute force attacks attempt to gain unauthorized access to a single account by guessing the password. Spraying is the reverse of this, using a limited number of passwords and trying them against all the accounts. This is a useful attack when you don't care which account you get and is fairly successful when given a large set of accounts. Defending against this is important in organizations, because if one account is breached, it is the foothold needed to gain entry.

Dictionary Attack

Another method of determining passwords is to use a password-cracking program that uses a list of dictionary words to try to guess the password, hence the name *dictionary* attack. The words can be used by themselves, or two or more smaller words can be combined to form a single possible password. A number of commercial and public-domain password-cracking programs employ a variety of methods to crack passwords, including using variations on the user ID.

These programs often permit the attacker to create various rules that tell the program how to combine words to form new possible passwords. Users commonly substitute certain numbers for specific letters. If the user wants to use the word *secret* for a password, for example, the letter *e* could be replaced with the number 3, yielding *s3cr3t*. This password will not be found in the dictionary, so a pure dictionary attack would not crack it, but the password is still easy for the user to remember. If a rule were created that tried all words in the dictionary and then tried the same words substituting the number 3 for the letter *e*, however, the password would be cracked.

Rules can also be defined so that the password-cracking program will substitute special characters for other characters or combine words. The ability of the attacker to crack passwords is directly related to the method the user employs to create the password in the first place, as well as the dictionary and rules used.

A dictionary attack involves the use of a lookup table to try and find an answer. With that in mind, repeated use of passwords, coupled with data breaches, provides a set of passwords to try. This is why unique passwords for security-sensitive sites are so important, because a data breach at one firm could cost you all of your accounts, because the attacker's job becomes as simple as looking them up.

Brute Force Attack

If the user has selected a password that is not found in a dictionary, even if simply by substituting various numbers or special characters for letters, then the only way the password can be cracked is for an attacker to attempt a brute force attack, in which the password-cracking program attempts all possible character combinations.

Tech Tip

Password Cracking with GPUs

The following data comes from a 2017 PC running multiple GPUs (8 GeForce GTX 1080 Ti, using hashcat v3.40) dedicated to cracking passwords. Note the differences in speeds based on hashing method. (This is why simple hashes don't provide the protection that newer, stronger methods do.)

Hash Function	Hash Rate	Hash Funtion	Hash Rate
MD5	257 GH/s	SHA1	94.7 GH/s
SHA256	37 GH/s	SHA512	12.2 GH/s
SHA3	9.7 GH/s	RipeMD160	57 GH/s
DES	185.2 GH/s	3DES	5.3 GH/s
NTLMv2	441 GH/s	Kerberos 5	3.4 GH/s
PBKDF2-HMAC-MD5	84 MH/s		
PBKDF2-HMAC-SHA1	38 MH/s		
PBKDF2-HMAC-SHA256	14 MH/s		
PBKDF2-HMAC-SHA512	5 MH/s		
Bcrypt, Blowfish	173 kH/s		
TrueCrypt PBKDF2-HMAC-RipeMD160 + XTS 512 bit 3.2 MH/s			

kH = 1000 hashes, MH = 1 million hashes, and GH = 1 billion hashes

This shows the speed penalties against brute forcing that PBKDF2 and Bcrypt offer. More details on these can be found in Chapter 6. Although newer machines are faster, the relative differences will still hold true.

The length of the password and the size of the set of possible characters in the password will greatly affect the time a brute force attack will take. A few years ago, this method of attack was very time consuming, because

Modern multicore GPUs and large on-chip cache memories have significantly improved the speed of password-cracking programs, making brute force methods practical in many cases. Today, all 10-character passwords can be cracked in less than a month. This is why salting passwords is essential to increase the effective length.

Tech Tip

Offline Password Attacks

Because an attacker who obtains a password file has unlimited time offline to prepare for the online attack, and can prepare without tipping off the target, all passwords should be considered to be vulnerable over extended periods of time. For this reason, even batch passwords (used for system-run batch jobs) should be changed periodically to prevent offline attacks.

it took considerable time to generate all possible combinations. With the increase in computer speed, however, generating password combinations is much faster, making it more feasible to launch brute force attacks against certain computer systems and networks.

A brute force attack on a password can take place at two levels: the attacker can use a password-cracking program to attempt to guess the password directly at a login prompt, or the attacker can first steal a password file, use a password-cracking program to compile a list of possible passwords based on the list of password hashes contained in the password file (offline), and then use that narrower list to attempt to guess the password at the login prompt. The first attack can be made more difficult if the account locks after a few failed login attempts. The second attack can be thwarted if the password file is securely maintained so that others cannot obtain a copy of it.

Offline

Offline brute force attacks can be employed to perform hash comparisons against a stolen password file. This has the challenge of stealing the password file, but if accomplished, it is possible to use high-performance GPU-based parallel machines to try passwords at very high rates and against multiple accounts at the same time.

Online

When the brute force attack occurs in real time against a system, it is frequently being done to attack a single account with multiple examples of passwords. Success or failure is determined by the system under attack, and the attacker either gets in or doesn't. *Online* brute force attacks tend to be very noisy and easy to see by network security monitoring, and they are also limited by system response time and bandwidth.

Hybrid Attack

A hybrid password attack is an attack that combines the preceding dictionary and brute force methods. Most cracking tools have this option built in, first attempting a dictionary attack, and then moving on to brute force methods.

The programs often permit the attacker to create various rules that tell the program how to combine words to form new possible passwords. Users commonly substitute certain numbers for specific letters. If the user wanted to use the word *secret* as a base for a password, for example, they could replace the letter *e* with the number 3, yielding *s3cr3t*. This password will not be found in the dictionary, so a pure dictionary attack would not crack it, but the password is still easy for the user to remember. If the attacker created a rule that instructed the program to try all words in the dictionary and then try the same words substituting the number 3 for the letter *e*, however, the password would be cracked.

Birthday Attack

The **birthday attack** is a special type of brute force attack that gets its name from something known as the *birthday paradox*, which states that in a group of at least 23 people, the chance that two individuals will have the same birthday is greater than 50 percent. Mathematically, the equation is $1.25 \times k^{1/2}$, where k equals the size of the set of possible values, which in the birthday paradox is 365 (the number of possible birthdays). This same phenomenon applies to passwords, with k (number of passwords) being quite a bit larger.

Rainbow Tables

Rainbow tables are precomputed tables or hash values associated with passwords. Using rainbow tables can change the search for a password from a computational problem to a lookup problem. This can tremendously reduce the level of work needed to crack a given password. The best defense against rainbow tables is *salted hashes,* as the addition of a salt value increases the complexity of the problem by making the precomputing process not replicable between systems. A *salt* is merely a random set of characters designed to increase the length of the item being hashed, effectively making rainbow tables too big to compute.

A *salt* is a random set of characters designed to increase the length of the item being hashed. It is an effective defense against rainbow table attacks.

Plaintext/Unencrypted

Passwords that are stored are subject to retrieval. Any time a system can send you a copy of your password, there is a security issue. Plaintext password attacks are those taken against these specific issues. Lest anyone think that this is only a problem from rogue systems or programs, even mainstream systems can fall prey to this trap. Microsoft allows administrators to push out passwords for local accounts via group policy preferences. To protect the passwords, they are encrypted using Advanced Encryption Standard (AES). For reasons of compatibility with other systems, Microsoft published the AES key. See the problem?

In Microsoft Windows systems, Mimikatz is a security tool that can extract Kerberos tickets from memory, and it also possesses the ability to extract plaintext passwords from process dumps of the LSASS process. This means that by using the security tools ProcDump and Mimikatz, one can harvest plaintext passwords from a system.

Chapter 15 Review

Chapter Summary

After reading this chapter and completing the exercises, you should understand the following aspects of attacks and malware.

Identify the different types of malicious software that exist, including viruses, worms, trojan horses, logic bombs, time bombs, and rootkits

- Malware is the common name for a wide range of code used to attack systems.
- Viruses are pieces of malware that require a file to infect a system.
- Worms are pieces of malware that can exist without infecting a file.
- Trojan horses are pieces of malware disguised as something else, something the user wants or finds useful.
- Logic bombs trigger when specific events occur in code, allowing an attack to be timed against an event.
- Time bombs are delayed malware designed to occur after a set period of time or on a specific date.
- Rootkits are pieces of malware designed to alter the lower-level functions of a system in a manner to escape detection.
- Keyloggers capture user entries such as passwords.
- Remote-access trojans provide attackers significant capabilities.

Describe the various types of computer and network attacks, including denial of service, spoofing, hijacking, and password guessing

- Understand how denial-of-service (DoS) and distributed denial-of-service (DDoS) attacks are performed and the defenses against them.
- Both packet headers and e-mail headers can be spoofed to take advantage of the trust users place in these data elements, even when they are not protected from change.
- Understand how session hijacking and on-path (formerly man-in-the-middle) attacks are performed and what the defenses are against these attacks.
- Password systems can have numerous vulnerabilities—some based on the system and some on the choice of password itself.

Recognize the different types of password attacks

- Password guessing is a real thing and takes advantage of predictable patterns.
- Poor password choices can lead to account compromise.
- Common attacks include spraying, dictionary attacks, brute force, and rainbow tables.

Key Terms

adware *(583)*
ARP poisoning *(602)*
backdoor *(585)*
birthday attack *(608)*
botnet *(582)*
buffer overflow *(586)*
clickjacking *(604)*
crypto-malware *(577)*
denial-of-service (DoS) attack *(587)*
distributed denial-of-service (DDoS) attack *(588)*
DNS kiting *(599)*
domain hijacking *(602)*
drive-by download attack *(604)*
fileless malware *(580)*
keylogger *(583)*
logic bomb *(582)*
MAC spoofing *(595)*
malware *(576)*
man in the browser (MITB) *(596)*
on-path/man-in-the-middle attack *(595)*
pass the hash *(602)*
phishing *(603)*

polymorphic malware *(581)*
potentially unwanted program (PUP) *(581)*
rainbow tables *(609)*
ransomware *(577)*
remote-access trojan (RAT) *(584)*
replay attack *(597)*
rootkit *(584)*
sequence number *(594)*
smurf attack *(589)*
sniffing *(591)*
spear phishing *(605)*
spoofing *(592)*
spyware *(583)*
SYN flood *(587)*
TCP/IP hijacking *(595)*
transitive access *(597)*
trojan *(577)*
typo squatting *(603)*
URL hijacking *(603)*
virus *(578)*
war-dialing *(590)*
war-driving *(590)*
watering hole attacks *(604)*
worm *(578)*
zero-day attack *(604)*
zombie *(582)*

Key Terms Quiz

Use terms from the Key Terms list to complete the sentences that follow. Don't use the same term more than once. Not all terms will be used.

1. Changing a source IP address for malicious purpose is an example of _______________.
2. A(n) _______________ is a way back into a machine via an unauthorized channel of access.
3. A malicious proxy could create a(n) _______________ attack.
4. Abusing the TCP handshake in an effort to overuse server resources can be done using a(n) _______________.
5. The main TCP/IP defense against an on-path/man-in-the-middle attack is the use of a(n) _______________.
6. Holding a DNS name without paying is called _______________.
7. When a keylogger is installed as malware, it is referred to as _______________.
8. Rendering a resource useless is called a(n) _______________.
9. An attack designed to match any user's password as opposed to a specific user's password is an example of a(n) _______________.
10. A NIC can be set to promiscuous mode to enable _______________.

Multiple-Choice Quiz

1. A SYN flood is an example of what type of attack?
   - **A.** Malicious code
   - **B.** Denial-of-service attack
   - **C.** On-path/man-in-the-middle attack
   - **D.** Spoofing
2. An attack in which the attacker simply listens for all traffic being transmitted across a network, in the hope of viewing something such as a user ID and password combination, is known as:
   - **A.** An on-path/man-in-the-middle attack
   - **B.** A denial-of-service attack
   - **C.** A sniffing attack
   - **D.** A backdoor attack
3. Which attack takes advantage of a trusted relationship that exists between two systems?
   - **A.** Spoofing
   - **B.** Password guessing
   - **C.** Sniffing
   - **D.** Brute force
4. In what type of attack does an attacker re-send the series of commands and codes used in a financial transaction to cause the transaction to be conducted multiple times?
   - **A.** Spoofing
   - **B.** Man in the middle
   - **C.** Replay
   - **D.** Backdoor
5. Why are rootkits challenging security problems?
   - **A.** They can be invisible to the operating system and end user.
   - **B.** Their true functionality can be cloaked, preventing analysis.
   - **C.** They can do virtually anything an operating system can do.
   - **D.** All of the above.
6. An attack in which an attacker attempts to lie and misrepresent himself in order to gain access to information that can be useful in an attack is known as which of the following?
   - **A.** Social science
   - **B.** Authenticated/white-hat hacking
   - **C.** Social engineering
   - **D.** Social manipulation
7. An attack that is designed to deny a system access to its files and spread across a network causing destruction is called?
   - **A.** Worm
   - **B.** Ransomware
   - **C.** Trojan horse
   - **D.** Remote access trojan
8. What is the best way to minimize possible avenues of attack for your system?
   - **A.** Install a firewall and check the logs daily.
   - **B.** Monitor your intrusion detection system for possible attacks.
   - **C.** Limit the information that can be obtained on your organization and the services that are run by your Internet-visible systems.
   - **D.** Ensure that all patches have been applied for the services that are offered by your system.
9. A war-driving attack is an attempt to exploit what technology?
   - **A.** Fiber-optic networks, whose cables often run alongside roads and bridges
   - **B.** Cellular telephones
   - **C.** The public switched telephone network (PSTN)
   - **D.** Wireless networks
10. Malicious code that is set to execute its payload on a specific date or at a specific time is known as which of the following?
    - **A.** A logic bomb
    - **B.** A trojan horse
    - **C.** A virus
    - **D.** A time bomb

Essay Quiz

1. Compare and contrast port scanning and ping sweeps.
2. What is the best practice to employ to mitigate malware effects on a machine?

Lab Projects

• Lab Project 15.1

Using the Internet, research password-cracking tools. Then, using a tool of choice, examine how easy it is to crack passwords on Windows- and Linux/UNIX-based systems. Create a series of accounts with different complexities of passwords and see how well they fare.

• Lab Project 15.2

Obtain a copy of the nmap scanning tool. Explore the various command-line options to scan networks, fingerprint operating systems, and perform other network-mapping functions.

Note: Students should try these options, but only in a lab environment, not across the Internet from their home ISP.

chapter 16

Security Tools and Techniques

A good tool improves the way you work. A great tool improves the way you think.

—Jeff Duntemann

In this chapter, you will learn how to

- Explore security tools and their use
- Describe security tool suites
- Detail penetration and vulnerability testing methods
- Explore common vulnerabilities that can be discovered using the tools

Having a solid security program is more than just building a correct set of defensive elements. In today's environment, there needs to be a series of testing and investigative elements that assist in the tasks of incident response and threat hunting, not to mention environmental testing. Security tools are an essential part of an enterprise security teams strategy.

Network Reconnaissance and Discovery Tools

A network is like most infrastructure—you never see or care about it until it isn't working. And when you do want to look, how do you do it? A wide range of tools can be used to permit you to see the inner workings of a network, and they are covered in the sections that follow.

tracert/traceroute

The **tracert** command is a Windows command for tracing the route that packets take over the network. The tracert command provides a list of the hosts, switches, and routers in the order in which a packet passes through them, providing a trace of the network route from source to target. As tracert uses Internet Control Message Protocol (ICMP), if ICMP is blocked, tracert will fail to provide information. On Linux and macOS systems, the command with similar functionality is traceroute. Figure 16.1 shows using the tracert command to trace the route from a Windows system on a private network to a Google DNS server.

> The **tracert** and **traceroute** commands display the route a packet takes to a destination, recording the number of hops along the way. These are excellent tools to use to see where a packet may get hung up during transmission.

```
Command Prompt

C:\>tracert 8.8.8.8

Tracing route to dns.google [8.8.8.8]
over a maximum of 30 hops:

  1     4 ms     2 ms     6 ms  192.168.86.1
  2     3 ms     3 ms     3 ms  10.0.0.1
  3    10 ms    11 ms    12 ms  96.120.17.9
  4    11 ms    12 ms    11 ms  ae-251-1204-rur02.northshore.tx.houston.comcast.net [68.85.255.153]
  5    13 ms    11 ms    11 ms  ae-2-rur01.northshore.tx.houston.comcast.net [162.151.135.233]
  6    81 ms    15 ms    14 ms  ae-88-ar01.greenspoint.tx.houston.comcast.net [68.85.244.89]
  7    21 ms   128 ms    22 ms  be-33662-cr02.dallas.tx.ibone.comcast.net [68.86.92.61]
  8    24 ms    20 ms    27 ms  be-3111-pe11.1950stemmons.tx.ibone.comcast.net [96.110.34.82]
  9    24 ms    19 ms   163 ms  75.149.230.70
 10    21 ms    19 ms    19 ms  209.85.247.155
 11   103 ms    18 ms    18 ms  108.170.230.113
 12    20 ms    20 ms    20 ms  dns.google [8.8.8.8]

Trace complete.

C:\>
```

• **Figure 16.1** **tracert** example

nslookup/dig

The Domain Name System (DNS) is used to convert a human-readable domain name into an IP address. This is not a single system but rather a hierarchy of DNS servers—from root servers on the backbone of the Internet, to copies at your Internet service provider (ISP), your home router, and your local machine, each in the form of a DNS cache. To examine a DNS query for a specific address, you can use the **nslookup** command. Figure 16.2 shows a series of DNS queries executed on a Windows machine. In the first request, the DNS server was with an ISP, while the second

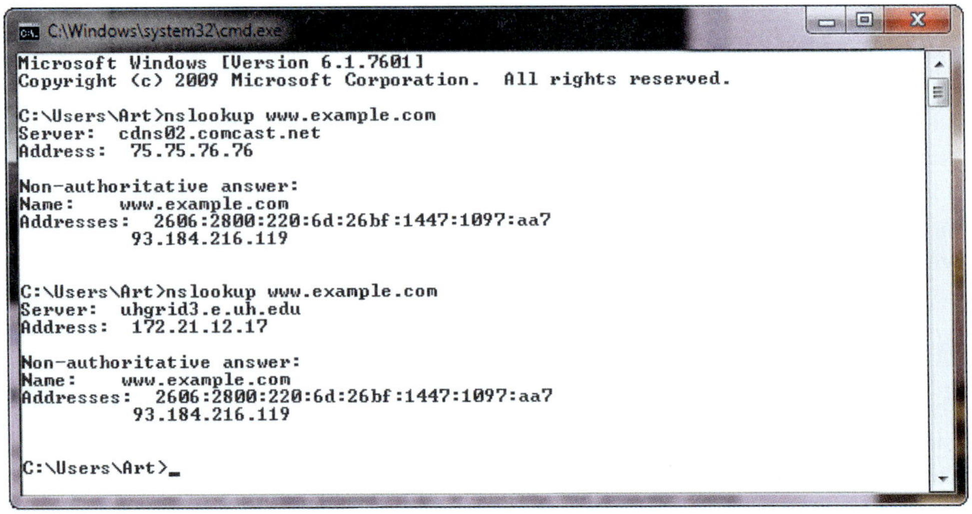

• **Figure 16.2** **nslookup** of a DNS query

request, the DNS server was from a virtual private network (VPN) connection. Between the two requests, the network connections were changed, resulting in different DNS lookups.

At times, nslookup will return a nonauthoritative answer, as shown in Figure 16.3. This typically means the result is from a cache as opposed to a server that has an authoritative (that is, known to be current) answer, such as from a DNS server.

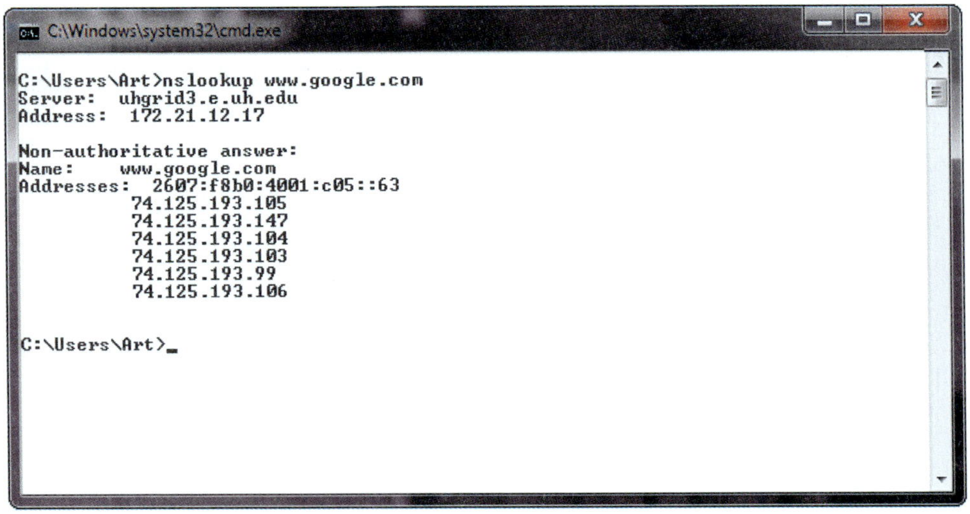

• **Figure 16.3** Cache response to a DNS query

While **nslookup** works on Windows systems, the command **dig**, which stands for Domain Information Groper, works on Linux systems. One difference is that **dig** is designed to return answers in a format that is easy to parse and include in scripts, which is a common trait of Linux command-line utilities.

ipconfig/ifconfig

Both **ipconfig** (for Windows) and **ifconfig** (for Linux) are command-line tools to manipulate the network interfaces on a system. They have the ability to list the interfaces and connection parameters, alter parameters, and release/renew connections. If you are having network connection issues, this is one of the first tools you should use, to verify the network setup of the operating system and its interfaces.

The **ip** command in Linux is used to show and manipulate routing, devices, policy routing, and tunnels. The ipconfig command is an important command for troubleshooting because it displays current TCP/IP configurations on a local system. The command displays adapter information such as MAC address, current IP addresses (both IPv4 and IPv6), subnet mask, default gateway, as well as DNS servers and whether DHCP is enabled. Figure 16.4 shows some of the information available from ipconfig on a Windows machine. This is an important troubleshooting tool because when you can't connect to something, it is the first place to start exploring network connections, as it gives you all of your settings.

```
Command Prompt

Wireless LAN adapter Wireless Network Connection:

   Connection-specific DNS Suffix  . : lan
   Description . . . . . . . . . . . : Intel(R) Dual Band Wireless-AC 7260
   Physical Address. . . . . . . . . : 48-51-B7-B7-7B-77
   DHCP Enabled. . . . . . . . . . . : Yes
   Autoconfiguration Enabled . . . . : Yes
   Link-local IPv6 Address . . . . . : fe80::d452:6002:630c:aeae%4(Preferred)
   IPv4 Address. . . . . . . . . . . : 192.168.86.76(Preferred)
   Subnet Mask . . . . . . . . . . . : 255.255.255.0
   Lease Obtained. . . . . . . . . . : Monday, November 23, 2020 10:12:49 AM
   Lease Expires . . . . . . . . . . : Tuesday, November 24, 2020 10:12:50 AM
   Default Gateway . . . . . . . . . : 192.168.86.1
   DHCP Server . . . . . . . . . . . : 192.168.86.1
   DHCPv6 IAID . . . . . . . . . . . : 357061047
   DHCPv6 Client DUID. . . . . . . . : 00-01-00-01-26-6E-0E-28-48-51-B7-B7-7B-77
   DNS Servers . . . . . . . . . . . : 192.168.86.1
   NetBIOS over Tcpip. . . . . . . . : Enabled
```

• **Figure 16.4** **ipconfig** example

nmap

Nmap is a free, open source port scanning tool developed by Gordon Lyon and has been the standard network mapping utility for Windows and Linux since 1999. The **nmap** command is the command to launch and run the nmap utility. **Nmap** is used to discover what systems are on a network and the open ports and services on those systems. This tool has many other additional functions, such as OS fingerprinting, finding rogue devices, and discovering services and even application versions. It operates via the command line, so it's very scriptable. It also has a GUI interface called Zenmap. **Nmap** works on a wide range of operating systems, including Microsoft Windows, Linux, and macOS. This is one of the top ten tools used by system administrators on a regular basis. The nmap utility includes a scripting engine using the Lua programming language to write, save, and share scripts that can

```
Command Prompt

C:\Users\Art>ping 10.20.0.1

Pinging 10.20.0.1 with 32 bytes of data:
Reply from 10.20.0.1: bytes=32 time=1ms TTL=64
Reply from 10.20.0.1: bytes=32 time=1ms TTL=64
Reply from 10.20.0.1: bytes=32 time=1ms TTL=64
Reply from 10.20.0.1: bytes=32 time=1ms TTL=64

Ping statistics for 10.20.0.1:
    Packets: Sent = 4, Received = 4, Lost = 0 (0% loss),
Approximate round trip times in milli-seconds:
    Minimum = 1ms, Maximum = 1ms, Average = 1ms

C:\Users\Art>_
```

• **Figure 16.5** **ping** command

> The ping command is used to test connectivity between systems.

automate different types of scans. All sorts of tasks can be automated, including regular checks for well-known network infrastructure vulnerabilities.

ping/pathping

The **ping** command sends echo requests to a designated machine to determine if communication is possible. The syntax is **ping** [*options*] ***targetname/address***. The options include items such as name resolution, how many pings, data size, TTL counts, and more. Figure 16.5 shows a ping command on a Windows machine.

Pathping is a TCP/IP-based utility that provides additional data beyond that of a ping command. **Pathping** will first display your path results as if you were using **tracert** or **traceroute**. **Pathping** then calculates loss information, as shown in Figure 16.6.

```
Command Prompt

C:\>pathping 96.120.17.9

Tracing route to 96.120.17.9 over a maximum of 30 hops

  0  Art-PC.lan [192.168.86.76]
  1  192.168.86.1
  2  10.0.0.1
  3  96.120.17.9

Computing statistics for 75 seconds...
            Source to Here   This Node/Link
Hop  RTT    Lost/Sent = Pct  Lost/Sent = Pct  Address
  0                                           Art-PC.lan [192.168.86.76]
                                0/ 100 =  0%   |
  1   14ms     0/ 100 =  0%     0/ 100 =  0%  192.168.86.1
                                0/ 100 =  0%   |
  2   19ms     0/ 100 =  0%     0/ 100 =  0%  10.0.0.1
                                1/ 100 =  1%   |
  3   26ms     1/ 100 =  1%     0/ 100 =  0%  96.120.17.9

Trace complete.

C:\>
```

• **Figure 16.6** **pathping** example

hping

Hping is a TCP/IP packet creation tool that allows a user to craft raw IP, TCP, UDP, and ICMP packets from scratch. This tool provides a means of performing a wide range of network operations; anything that you can do with those protocols can be crafted into a packet. This includes port scanning, crafting ICMP packets, host discovery, and more. The current version is **hping3**, and it is available on most operating systems, including Windows and Linux.

Like all Linux commands, hping can be programmed in BASH scripts to achieve greater functionality. Outputs can also be piped to other commands.

Hping also works with an embedded Tcl scripting functionality, which further extends its usefulness for system administrators. Between the range of options and the native scripting capability, hping offers a wide range of functions, including creating password-protected backdoors that are piped to other services. The power comes from the programmability, the options, and the creative work of system administrators.

netstat

The **netstat** command is used to monitor network connections to and from a system. The following are some examples of how you can use netstat:

- **netstat –a** Lists all active connections and listening ports
- **netstat –at** Lists all active TCP connections
- **netstat –an** Lists all active UDP connections

Many more options are available and useful. The **netstat** command is available on Windows and Linux, but the availability of certain **netstat** command switches and other **netstat** command syntax may differ from operating system to operating system.

The **netstat** command is useful for viewing all listening ports on a computer and determining which connections are active.

netcat (nc)

Netcat is the network utility designed for Linux environments. The netcat utility is the tool of choice in Linux for reading from and writing to network connections using TCP or UDP. Like all Linux command-line utilities, it is designed for scripts and automation. Netcat has a wide range of functions. It acts as a connection to the network and can act as a transmitter or a receiver, and with redirection it can turn virtually any running process into a server. It can listen on a port and pipe the input it receives to the process identified. Netcat has been ported to Windows but is not regularly used in Windows environments.

The actual command to invoke netcat is **nc** ***–options –address***.

IP Scanners

IP scanners do just what the name implies: they scan IP networks and can report on the status of IP addresses. There are a wide range of free and commercial scanning tools, and most come with significantly greater functionality than just reporting on address usage. If all you want are addresses, a variety of simple command-line network discovery tools can provide those answers. For instance, if you only want to scan your local LAN, **arp – a** will do just that. If you want more functionality, you can use the nmap program covered earlier in the chapter. Another solution is Nessus, a commercial offering covered later in the chapter.

arp

The **arp** command is designed to interface with the operating system's Address Resolution Protocol (ARP) caches on a system. In moving packets between machines, a device sometimes needs to know where to send a packet using the MAC or layer 2 address. ARP handles this problem through four basic message types:

- **ARP request** "Who has this IP address?"
- **ARP reply** "I have that IP address; my MAC address is…"
- **Reverse ARP (RARP) request** "Who has this MAC address?"
- **RARP reply** "I have that MAC address; my IP address is…"

These messages are used in conjunction with a device's ARP table, where a form of short-term memory associated with these data elements resides. The commands are used as a simple form of lookup. When a machine sends an ARP request to the network, the reply is received and entered into all devices that hear the reply. This facilitates efficient address lookups but also makes the system subject to attack.

The **arp** command allows a system administrator the ability to see and manipulate the ARP cache on a system. This way, the system administrator can see if entries have been spoofed or if other problems, such as errors, occur.

route

The **route** command works in Linux and Windows systems to provide information on current routing parameters and to manipulate these parameters. In addition to listing the current routing table, it has the ability to modify the table. Figure 16.7 shows three examples of the route command on a Linux system. The first is a simple display of the kernel IP routing table. The second shows a similar result using the ip command. The last is the use of the ip command to get the details of the local table with destination addresses that are assigned to localhost.

```
root@kali-lab: ~
File  Edit  View  Search  Terminal  Help
root@kali-lab:~# route
Kernel IP routing table
Destination     Gateway         Genmask         Flags Metric Ref    Use Iface
default         gateway         0.0.0.0         UG    100    0        0 eth0
192.168.116.0   0.0.0.0         255.255.255.0   U     100    0        0 eth0
root@kali-lab:~# ip route
default via 192.168.116.2 dev eth0 proto static metric 100
192.168.116.0/24 dev eth0 proto kernel scope link src 192.168.116.128 metric 100

root@kali-lab:~# ip route show table local
broadcast 127.0.0.0 dev lo proto kernel scope link src 127.0.0.1
local 127.0.0.0/8 dev lo proto kernel scope host src 127.0.0.1
local 127.0.0.1 dev lo proto kernel scope host src 127.0.0.1
broadcast 127.255.255.255 dev lo proto kernel scope link src 127.0.0.1
broadcast 192.168.116.0 dev eth0 proto kernel scope link src 192.168.116.128
local 192.168.116.128 dev eth0 proto kernel scope host src 192.168.116.128
broadcast 192.168.116.255 dev eth0 proto kernel scope link src 192.168.116.128
root@kali-lab:~#
```

• **Figure 16.7** The **route** and **ip** commands in Linux

curl

Curl is a tool designed to transfer data to or from a server, without user interaction. It supports a long list of protocols (DICT, FILE, FTP, FTPS, Gopher,

HTTP, HTTPS, IMAP, IMAPS, LDAP, LDAPS, MQTT, POP3, POP3S, RTMP, RTMPS, RTSP, SCP, SFTP, SMB, SMBS, SMTP, SMTPS, Telnet, and TFTP) and acts like a Swiss army knife for interacting with a server. Originally designed to interact with URLs, curl has expanded into a jack-of-all-trades supporting numerous protocols. It works on both Linux and Windows systems, although the command options are slightly different.

Here's a simple example of using **curl** to simulate a GET request for a website URL:

```
curl https://www.example.com
```

theHarvester

theHarvester is a Python-based program designed to assist penetration testers in the gathering of information during the reconnaissance portion of a penetration test. This is a useful tool for exploring what is publicly available about your organization on the Web, and it can provide information on employees, e-mails, and subdomains using different public sources such as search engines, PGP key servers, and Shodan databases. Designed for Linux and included as part of Kali and other penetration testing distributions, theHarvester is shown in Figure 16.8 searching for the first 500 e-mails from the domain kali.org using Google.

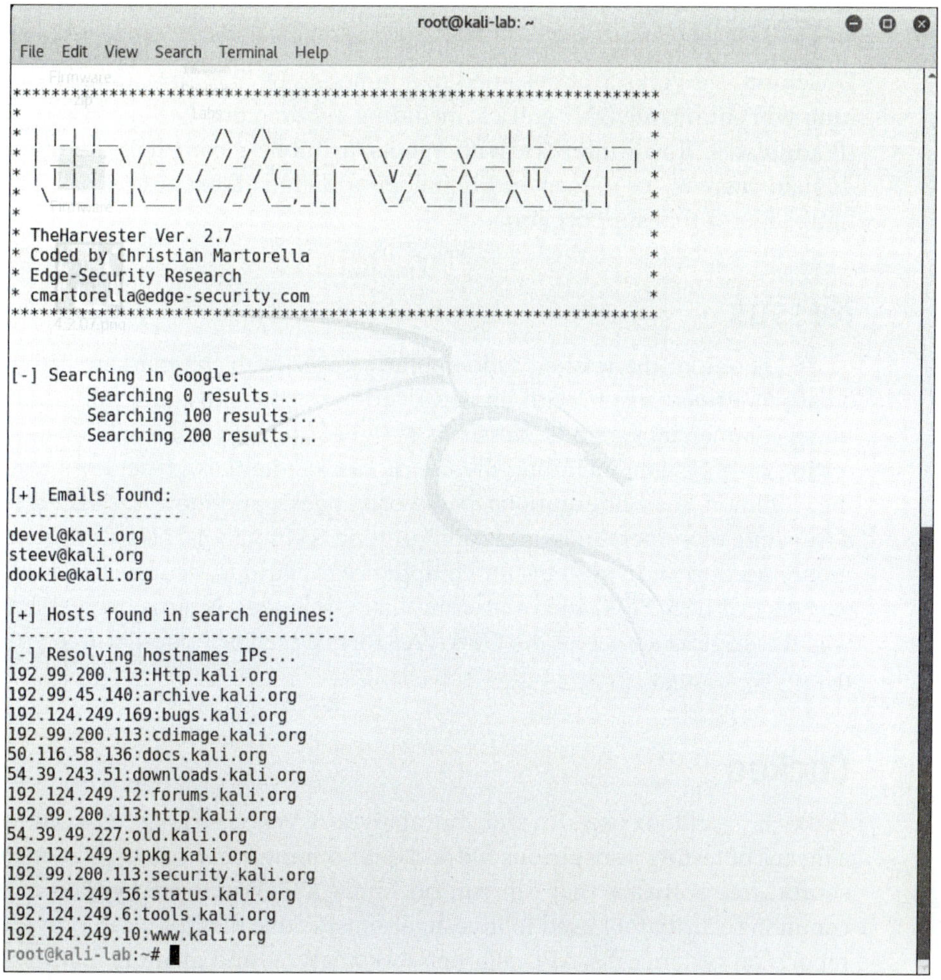

Figure 16.8 theHarvester

sn1per

Sn1per is a Linux-based tool used by penetration testers. Sn1per is an automated scanner designed to collect a large amount of information while scanning for vulnerabilities. It runs a series of automated scripts to enumerate servers, open ports, and vulnerabilities, and it's designed to integrate with the penetration testing tool Metasploit. Sn1per goes further than just scanning; it can also brute-force open ports, brute-force subdomains and DNS systems, scan web applications for common vulnerabilities, and run targeted nmap scripts against open ports as well as targeted Metasploit scans and exploit modules. This tool suite comes as a free community edition, with limited scope, as well as an unlimited professional version for corporations and penetration testers.

scanless

Scanless is a command-line utility to interface with websites that can perform port scans as part of a penetration test. When you use this tool, the source IP address for the scan is the website, not your testing machine. Written in Python, with a simple interface, scanless anonymizes your port scans.

dnsenum

DNS enumeration can be used to collect information such as usernames and IP addresses of targeted systems.

Dnsenum is a Perl script designed to enumerate DNS information. **Dnsenum** will enumerate DNS entries, including subdomains, MX records, and IP addresses. It can interface with Whois, a public record that identifies domain owners, to gather additional information. **Dnsenum** works on Linux distros that support Perl.

Nessus

Nessus is one of the leading vulnerability scanners in the marketplace. It comes in a free version, with limited IP address capability, and fully functional commercial versions. Nessus is designed to perform a wide range of testing on a system, including the use of user credentials, patch level testing, common misconfigurations, password attacks, and more. Designed as a full suite of vulnerability and configuration testing tools, Nessus is commonly used to audit systems for compliance to various security standards such as PCI DSS, SOX, and other compliance schemes. Nessus free version was the original source of the OpenVAS fork, which is a popular free vulnerability scanner.

Cuckoo

Cuckoo is a sandbox used for malware analysis. Cuckoo is designed to allow a means of testing a suspicious file and determining what it does. It is open source, free software that can run on Linux and Windows. Cuckoo is a common security tool used to investigate suspicious files, as it can provide reports on system calls, API calls, network analysis, and memory analysis.

File Manipulation Tools

In computer systems, most information can be represented as a file. Files are files, as are directories and even entire storage systems. The concept of a file is the basic interface to information. Because of this, file manipulation tools have the ability to manage a lot of tasks. As many operations are scripted, the ability to manipulate a file, returning specific elements or records, has great utility. This section looks at a bunch of tools used to manipulate files in Linux systems.

head

Head is a utility designed to return the first lines of a file. A common option is the number of lines one wishes to return. For example, **head -5** returns the first five lines of a file.

tail

Tail is a utility designed to return the last lines of a file. A common option is the number of lines one wishes to return. For example, **tail -5** returns the last five lines of a file.

cat

Cat is a Linux command, short for concatenate, that can be used to create and manipulate files. It can display the contents of a file, handle multiple files, and can be used to input data from stdin, which is a stream of input, to a file if the file does not exist. Here is an example:

```
# cat textfile.txt
```

The **cat** command can be piped through **more** or **less** to limit scrolling of long files:

```
# cat textfile.txt | more
```

If you need line numbers in the output, you can add the **-n** option. The output can be piped through various other Linux commands, providing significant manipulation capability. For instance, you can combine four files and sort the output into a fifth file, like so:

```
# cat textfile1.txt textfile2.txt textfile3.txt textfile4.txt
| sort > textfile5.txt
```

grep

Grep is a Linux utility that can perform pattern-matching searches on file contents. The name grep comes from "Globally search for Regular Expression and Print the matching lines." **Grep** dates back to the beginning of the UNIX OS and was written by Ken Thompson. Today, the uses of **grep** are many. It can count the number of matches, and it can find lines with matching expressions, either case sensitive or case insensitive. It can use anchors (matching based on beginning or ending of a word), wildcards, and negative searches (finding lines that do not contain a specified element), and it works with other tools through the redirection of inputs and outputs.

Grep has many options, including the use of regular expressions to perform matching. Here's a sampling of the more common options:

```
grep [options] pattern [files]
Options Description
-c : This prints only a count of the lines that match a pattern
-h : Display the matched lines, but do not display the filenames.
-i : Ignores, case for matching
-l : Displays list of a filenames only.
-n : Display the matched lines and their line numbers.
-v : This prints out all the lines that do not matches the pattern
-w : Match whole word
-o : Print only the matched parts of a matching line, with each such
part on a separate output line.
```

There are many other options, including the display of lines before and after matches. To get a full feel of the breadth of options, consult the **man** page for **grep**.

chmod

Chmod is the Linux command used to change access permissions of a file. The general form of the command is

```
chmod <options> <permissions> <filename>
```

Permissions can be entered either in symbols or octal numbers. Let's assume we want to set the following permissions: The user can read, write, and execute the file. Members of the group can read and execute it, and all others may only read it. In this case, we can use either of the following two commands, which are identical in function:

```
chmod u=rwx,g=rx,o=r <filename>
chmod 754 <filename>
```

The octal notation works as follows: 4 stands for "read," 2 stands for "write," 1 stands for "execute," and 0 stands for "no permission." Thus, for the user, 7 is the combination of permissions 4+2+1 (read, write, and execute). For the group, 5 is 4+0+1 (read, no write, and execute), and for all others, 4 is 4+0+0 (read, no write, and no execute).

logger

The Linux command **logger** is how you can add log file information to /var/log/syslog. The **logger** command works from the command line, from scripts, or from other files, thus providing a versatile means of making log entries. The syntax is simple:

```
logger <message to put in the log>
```

This command will put the text in the option into the syslog file.

Shell and Script Environments

One of the more powerful aspects of the Linux environment is the ability to create shell scripts. By combining a series of functions, and through the use of redirecting inputs and outputs, one can do significant data manipulation. Take a PCAP file for instance. Let's assume you need to extract specific data elements. You want only ping (echo) replies to a specific IP address. And for those records, you only want 1 byte in the data section. Using a series of commands in a shell script, you can create a dissector that takes the PCAP, reads it with tcpdump, extracts the fields, and then writes the desired elements to a file. You could do this with Python as well, and with some tools, you can get partway there. Bottom line: there is a lot you can do using the OS shell and scripts.

SSH

SSH (Secure Shell) is a cryptographically secured means of communicating to and managing a network over an unsecured connection. It was originally designed as a replacement for the plaintext protocols of Telnet and other tools. When remotely accessing a system, it is important not to use a plaintext communication channel, as that would expose information such as passwords and other sensitive items to interception.

> SSH is a cryptographically secured means of communicating and managing a network. SSH uses port 22 and is the secure replacement for Telnet.

PowerShell

PowerShell is a Microsoft Windows–based task automation and configuration management framework, consisting of a command-line shell and scripting language. PowerShell is built on top of the .NET Common Language Runtime (CLR) and accepts and returns .NET objects. The commands used in PowerShell are called cmdlets, and they can be combined to process complex tasks. PowerShell can be run from a PowerShell Console prompt, or through the Windows PowerShell Integrated Scripting Environment (ISE), which is a host application for Windows PowerShell. The following example finds all executables within the Program Files folder that were last modified after October 1, 2020, and that are neither smaller than 1 MB nor larger than 10 MB:

```
Get-ChildItem -Path $env:ProgramFiles -Recurse -Include *.exe |
Where-Object -FilterScript {($_.LastWriteTime -gt '2020-10-01') -and
($_.Length -ge 1mb) -and ($_.Length -le 10mb)} | out-host -paging
```

> PowerShell is a powerful command-line scripting interface. PowerShell files use the .ps1 file extension.

Because the Microsoft Windows object model is included, as well as numerous cmdlets designed to perform specific data access operations, PowerShell is an extremely powerful tool for managing Windows systems in an enterprise. With its latest release, PowerShell has been modified to run on multiple platforms, including Windows, macOS, and Linux.

Python

Python is a computer language commonly used for scripting and data analysis tasks facing system administrators and security personnel. Python is a full-fledged computer language. It supports objects, functional programming, and garbage collection, and most importantly has a very large range of libraries that can be used to bring functionality to a program. The downside is that it is interpreted, so speed is not a strong attribute. However, usability is high, and coupled with the library support, Python is a must-learn language for most security professionals.

Python is a general-purpose computer programming language that uses the file extension .py.

OpenSSL

OpenSSL is a general-purpose cryptography library that offers a wide range of cryptographic functions on Windows and Linux systems. Designed to be a full-featured toolkit for the Transport Layer Security (TLS) and Secure Sockets Layer (SSL) protocols, it provides so much more for real-world daily challenges. OpenSSL can perform the following tasks in either scripts or programs, offering access to cryptographic functions without having to develop the code:

- Work with RSA and ECDSA keys
- Create certificate signing requests (CSRs)
- Verify CSRs
- Create certificates
- Generate self-signed certificates
- Convert between encoding formats (PEM, DER) and container formats (PKCS12, PKCS7)
- Check certificate revocation status
- And more

One can view OpenSSL as a Swiss army knife for all things involving cryptography functions.

Packet Capture and Replay Tools

Computers communicate and exchange data via network connections by way of packets. Software tools that enable the capturing, editing, and replaying of the packet streams can be very useful for a security professional. Whether you're testing a system or diagnosing a problem, having the ability to observe exactly what is flowing between machines and being able to edit the flows is of great utility. The tools in this section provide this capability. They can operate either on live network traffic or recorded traffic in the form of packet capture (PCAP) files.

tcpreplay

Tcpreplay is the name for both a tool and a suite of tools. As a suite, tcpreplay is a group of free, open source utilities for editing and replaying previously captured network traffic. As a tool, it specifically replays a PCAP file on a network. Originally designed as an incident response tool, tcpreplay has utility in a wide range of circumstances where network packets are used.

It can be used to test all manner of security systems through the use of crafted PCAP files to trip certain controls. It is also used to test online services such as web servers. If you have a need to send network packets to another machine, tcpreplay suite has your answer.

tcpdump

The **tcpdump** utility is designed to analyze network packets either from a network connection or a recorded file. You also can use tcpdump to create files of packet captures, called PCAP files, and perform filtering between input and output, making it a valuable tool to lessen data loads on other tools. For example, if you have a complete packet capture file that has hundreds of millions of records, but you are only interested in one server's connections, you can make a copy of the PCAP file containing only the packets associated with the server of interest. This file will be smaller and easier to analyze with other tools.

Wireshark

Wireshark is the gold standard for graphical analysis of network protocols. With dissectors that allow the analysis of virtually any network protocol, this tool can allow you to examine individual packets, monitor conversations, carve out files, and more. When it comes to examining packets, Wireshark is the tool. When it comes to using this functionality in a scripting environment, **TShark** provides the same processing in a scriptable form, producing a wide range of outputs, depending on the options set. Wireshark has the ability to capture live traffic, or it can use recorded packets from other sources.

When you're examining packets, the differentiator is what do you need to do. Wireshark allows easy exploration. Tcpdump captures packets into PCAP files, and tcpreplay has a suite of editing tools.

Forensic Tools

Digital forensics is the use of specific methods to determine who did what on a system at a specific time, or some variant of this question. Computers have a wide range of artifacts that can be analyzed to make these determinations. There are tools to collect these artifacts as well as tools used to analyze the data collected. In this section, we examine some of the primary tools used in these efforts. Digital forensic processes and procedures are covered in detail in Chapter 23. This is just an examination of some of the tools used.

dd

Data dump (**dd**) is a Linux command-line utility used to convert and copy files. On Linux systems, virtually everything is represented in storage as a file, and **dd** can read and/or write from/to these files, provided that function is implemented in the respective drivers. As a result, dd can be used for tasks such as backing up the boot sector of a hard drive, obtaining a fixed amount of random data, or copying (backing up) entire disks. The dd program can also perform conversions on the data as it is copied, including byte order swapping and conversion to and from the ASCII and EBCDIC text encodings. **dd** has the ability to copy everything, back up/restore a partition, and create/restore an image of an entire disk. Some common examples follow.

Here's how to back up an entire hard disk:

```
# dd if = /dev/sda of = /dev/sdb
```

Here, **if** represents input file and **of** represents output file. Therefore, the exact copy of /dev/sda will be available in /dev/sdb. If there are any errors, the preceding command will fail. If you give the parameter **conv=noerror**, it will continue to copy if there are read errors. Note that input file and output file should be checked very carefully because mistakes can overwrite data, causing you to lose all your data.

Here's how to create an image of a hard disk:

```
# dd if = /dev/hda of = ~/hdadisk.img
```

When doing a forensics data capture, rather than taking a backup of the hard disk, you should create an image file of the hard disk and save it on another storage device. There are many advantages to backing up your data to a disk image—one being the ease of use. Image files contain all the information on the associated source, including unused and previously used space.

memdump

Linux has a utility program called memory dumper, or **memdump**. This program dumps system memory to the standard output stream, skipping over any holes in memory maps. By default, the program dumps the contents of physical memory (/dev/mem). The output from **memdump** is in the form of a raw dump. Because running **memdump** uses memory, it is important to send the output to a location that is off the host machine being copied, using a tool such as **nc**.

WinHex

WinHex is a hexadecimal file editor. This tool is very useful in forensically investigating files, and it provides a whole host of forensic functions such as the ability to read almost any file, display contents of the file, convert between character sets and encoding, perform hash verification functions, and compare files. As a native file reader/hex editor, it can examine specific application files without invoking the application and changing the data. WinHex is a commercial program that is part of the X-Ways forensic suite, which is a comprehensive set of digital forensic tools.

FTK Imager

FTK Imager is the company AccessData's answer to dd. FTK Imager is a commercial program, free for use, and is designed to capture an image of a hard drive (or other device) in a forensic fashion. Forensic duplications are bit-by-bit copies, supported by hashes to demonstrate that the copy and the original are exact duplicates in all ways. As with all forensically sound collection tools, FTK Imager retains the filesystem metadata (and the file path) and creates a log of the files copied. This process does not change file access attributes. FTK Imager is part of the larger, and commercial, FTK suite of forensic tools.

Autopsy

Autopsy is the open source answer for digital forensic tool suites. This suite, developed by Brian Carrier, has evolved over that past couple decades into a community-supported open source project that can perform virtually all digital forensic functions. It runs on Windows and offers a comprehensive set of tools that can enable network-based collaboration and automated, intuitive workflows. It has tools to support hard drives, removable devices, and smartphones. It supports MD5 hash creation and lookup, deleted file carving, EXIF data extraction from JPEG images, indexed keyword searches, extension mismatch detections, e-mail message extractions, and artifact extractions from web browsers.

It has case management tools to support the functions of case analysis and reporting, including managing timelines.

Tool Suites

A variety of toolsets are used by security professionals that can also be used for malicious purposes. These toolsets are used by penetration testers when testing the security posture of a system, but the same tools in the hands of an adversary can be used for malicious purposes.

Metasploit

Metasploit is a framework that enables attackers to exploit systems (bypass controls) and inject payloads (attack code). Metasploit is widely distributed, powerful, and one of the most popular tools used by attackers. When new vulnerabilities are discovered in systems, Metasploit exploit modules are quickly created in the community, making this the go-to tool for most professionals.

Kali

Kali is a Linux distribution that is preloaded with many security tools primarily designed for penetration testing. The current version is called Kali Linux 2021.1. It's regularly updated by the development team and includes a whole host of preconfigured, preloaded tools, including Metasploit, Social-Engineering Toolkit, and others. It can be found at https://kali.org.

Parrot OS

Parrot OS is a GNU/Linux distribution based on Debian and designed with tools for penetration testing and incident response operations. It has tools to support a wide range of cyber security operations, from penetration testing to digital forensics and reverse engineering of malware. This is a free distribution and is available at https://parrotsec.org.

Security Onion

Security Onion is a Linux distribution that is preloaded with many security tools primarily designed for use during incident response, threat hunting, enterprise security monitoring, and log management. It includes TheHive, Playbook and Sigma, Fleet and osquery, CyberChef, Elasticsearch, Logstash, Kibana, Suricata, Zeek, Wazuh, and many other security tools. It can also be configured as a collector and used in an enterprise to automate the collection and processing of information.

Social-Engineering Toolkit

The **Social-Engineering Toolkit (SET)** is a set of tools that can be used to target attacks at the people using systems. It has applets that can be used to create phishing e-mails, Java attack code, and other social engineering–type attacks. The SET is included in BackTrack/Kali and other distributions.

Cobalt Strike

Cobalt Strike is a powerful application that can replicate advanced threats and assist in the execution of targeted attacks on systems. Cobalt Strike expands the Armitage tool's capabilities, adding advanced attack methods.

Core Impact

Core Impact is an expensive commercial suite of penetration test tools. It has a wide spectrum of tools and proven attack capabilities across an enterprise. Although it's expensive, the level of automation and integration makes this a powerful suite of tools.

Burp Suite

Burp Suite began as a port scanner tool with limited additional functionality in the arena of intercepting proxies, web application scanning, and web-based content. Burp Suite is a commercial tool, but it is reasonably priced, well liked, and highly utilized in the pen-testing marketplace.

Penetration Testing

Understanding a system's risk exposure is not, in actuality, a simple task. Using a series of tests, one can determine an estimate of the risk that a system has to the enterprise. Vulnerability tests detail the known vulnerabilities and the degree to which they are exposed. It is important to note that zero-day vulnerabilities will not be known, and the risk from them still remains unknown. A second form of testing, penetration testing, is used to simulate an adversary to see whether the controls in place perform to the desired level.

A penetration test (or pen test) simulates an attack from a malicious outsider, probing your network and systems for a way in (often any way in). Pen tests are often the most aggressive form of security testing and can take on many forms, depending on what is considered "in" or "out" of scope. For example, some pen tests simply seek to find a way into the network—any way in. This can range from an attack across network links to social engineering to having a tester physically break into the building. Other pen tests are limited—only attacks across network links are allowed, with no physical attacks.

Regardless of the scope and allowed methods, the goal of a pen test is the same: to determine whether an attacker can bypass your security and access your systems. Unlike a vulnerability assessment, which typically just catalogs vulnerabilities, a pen test attempts to exploit vulnerabilities to see how much access a vulnerability allows. Penetration tests are useful in the following ways:

- They can show relationships between a series of "low-risk" items that can be sequentially exploited to gain access (making them a "high-risk" item in the aggregate).
- They can be used to test the training of employees, the effectiveness of your security measures, and the ability of your staff to detect and respond to potential attackers.
- They can often identify and test vulnerabilities that are difficult or even impossible to detect with traditional scanning tools.

An effective penetration test offers several critical elements. First, it focuses on the most commonly employed threat vectors seen in the current threat environment. Using zero-day exploits that no one else has does not help an organization understand its security defenses against the existing threat environment. It is important to mimic real-world attackers if that is what the company wants to test its defenses against. The second critical element is to focus on real-world attacker objectives, such as getting to and stealing intellectual property. Just bypassing defenses but not obtaining the attacker's objectives, again, does not provide a full exercise of security capabilities. The objective is to measure actual risk under real-world conditions.

Penetration Testing Authorization

Penetration tests are used by organizations that want a real-world test of their security. Unlike actual attacks, penetration tests are conducted with the knowledge of the organization, although some types of penetration tests occur without the knowledge of the employees and departments being tested.

Obtaining *penetration testing authorization* is the first step in penetration testing. This permission step is the time that the testing team, in advance, obtains permission from the system owner to perform the penetration test. The penetration test authorization document is a key element in the communication plan for the test. Penetration tests are typically used to verify threats or to test security controls. They do this by bypassing security controls and exploiting vulnerabilities using a variety of tools and techniques, including the attack methods discussed earlier in this book. Social engineering, malware, and vulnerability exploit tools are all fair game when it comes to penetration testing. Penetration tests actively test security controls by bypassing them and exploiting vulnerabilities, and this helps to verify that a risk exists.

Reconnaissance

After the penetration test is planned, **reconnaissance** is the first step in performing a penetration test. The objective of reconnaissance is to obtain an understanding of the system and its components that someone wants to attack. Multiple methods can be employed to achieve this objective, and in most cases, multiple methods will be employed to ensure good coverage of the systems and to find the potential vulnerabilities that may be present. There are two classifications for reconnaissance activities: active and passive. *Active reconnaissance* testing involves tools that actually interact with the network and systems in a manner that their use can be observed. Active reconnaissance can provide a lot of useful information; you just need to be aware that this may alert defenders to the impending attack. *Passive reconnaissance* is the use of tools that do not provide information to the network or systems under investigation. Google hacking is a prime example; Google and other third parties such as Shodan allow you to gather information without sending packets to a system where they could be observed.

Passive vs. Active Tools

Tools can be classified as active or passive. *Active tools* interact with a target system in a fashion where their use can be detected. Scanning a network with nmap (Network Mapper) is an active act that can be detected. In the case of nmap, the tool may not be specifically detectable, but its use, the sending of packets, can be detected. When you need to map out your network or look for open services on one or more hosts, a port scanner is probably the most efficient tool for the job. *Passive tools* are those that do not interact with the system in a manner that would permit detection through sending packets or altering traffic. An example of a passive tool is Tripwire, which can detect changes to a file based on hash values. Another passive example is OS mapping by analyzing TCP/IP traces with a tool such as Wireshark. Passive sensors can use existing traffic to provide data for analysis.

Pivoting

Pivoting is a key method used by a pen tester or attacker to move across a network. The first step is the attacker obtaining a presence on a machine; let's call it machine A. The attacker then remotely, through this machine, examines the network again, using machine A's IP address. This enables an attacker to see sections of networks that were not observable from the previous position. Performing a *pivot* is not easy because the attacker not only must establish access to machine A but also must move their tools to machine A and control those tools remotely from another machine, all while not being detected. This activity, also referred to as *traversing* a network, is one place where defenders can observe the attacker's activity. When an attacker traverses the network, network security monitoring tools will detect the activity as unusual with respect to both the account being utilized and the actual traversing activity.

Initial Exploitation

A key element of a penetration test is the actual exploitation of a vulnerability. Exploiting the vulnerabilities encountered serves two purposes. First, it demonstrates the level of risk that is actually present. Second, it demonstrates the viability of the mechanism of the attack vector. During a penetration test, the exploitation activity stops short of destructive activity. The *initial exploitation* is the first step because just being able to demonstrate that a vulnerability is present and exploitable does not demonstrate that the objective of the penetration test is achievable. In many cases, multiple methods, including pivoting (network traversal) and escalation of privilege to perform activities with administrator privileges, are used to achieve the final desired effect.

Persistence

Persistence is one of the key elements of a whole class of attacks referred to as *advanced persistent threats (APTs)*. APTs place two elements at the forefront of all activity: invisibility from defenders and persistence. APT actors tend to be patient and use techniques that make it difficult to remove them once they have gained a foothold. Persistence can be achieved via a wide range of mechanisms—from agents that beacon back out to malicious accounts, to vulnerabilities introduced to enable reinfection.

Escalation of Privilege

Escalation of privilege is the movement to an account that enables root or higher-level privilege. Typically this occurs when a normal user account exploits a vulnerability on a process that is operating with root privilege, and as a result of the specific exploit, the attacker assumes the privileges of the exploited process at the root level. Once this level of privilege is achieved, additional steps are taken to provide a persistent access back to the privileged level. With root access, things such as log changes and other changes are possible, expanding the ability of the attacker to achieve their objective and to remove information, such as logs that could lead to detection of the attack.

Vulnerability Testing

Vulnerability tests are used to scan for specific vulnerabilities or weaknesses. These weaknesses, if left unguarded, can result in loss. Obtaining *vulnerability testing authorization* from management before commencing the test is the step designed to prevent avoidable accidents. Just as it is important to obtain authorization for penetration tests, it is important to obtain permission for penetration tests in the active machines. This permission is usually a multiperson process and involves explaining the risk of these tests and their purpose to the people running the system. The vulnerability tests are then analyzed with respect to how the security controls respond and notify management of the adequacy of the defenses in place.

Vulnerability Scanning Concepts

One valuable method that can help administrators secure their systems is vulnerability scanning, which is the process of examining your systems and network devices for holes, weaknesses, and issues and then finding them before a potential attacker does. Specialized tools called *vulnerability scanners* are designed to help administrators discover and address vulnerabilities. But there is much more to vulnerability scanning than simply running tools and examining the results—administrators must be able to analyze any discovered vulnerabilities and determine their severity, how to address them if needed, and whether any business processes will be affected by potential fixes. Vulnerability scanning can also help administrators identify common misconfigurations in account setup, patch level, applications, and operating systems. Most organizations look at vulnerability scanning as an ongoing process because it is not enough to scan systems once and assume they will be secure from that point on.

Vulnerability scanning is also used to examine services on computer systems for known vulnerabilities in software. This is basically a simple process of determining the specific version of a software program and then looking up the known vulnerabilities. The Common Vulnerabilities and Exposures (CVE) database (https://cve.mitre.org/cve/) can be used as a repository; it has recorded over 145,000 specific vulnerabilities. This makes the task more than just a manual one; numerous software programs can be used to perform this function.

> False positives and false negatives depend on the results of the test and the true outcome. If you test for something, get a positive indication, but the indication is wrong, that is a false positive. If you test for something, do not get an indication, but the results should have been true, this is a false negative.

False Positives

Any system that uses a measurement of some attribute to detect some other condition can be subject to errors. When a measurement is used as part of a decision process, external factors can introduce errors. In turn, these errors can influence a measurement to a condition that creates an error in the final number. When a measurement is used in a decision process, the possibility of errors and their influence must be part of the decision process. For example, when a restaurant cooks a steak to a medium temperature, the easiest way to determine if the steak is cooked correctly would be to cut it open and look. But this can't be done in the kitchen, so other measures are used, such as time, temperature, and so on. When the customer cuts into the steak is the moment of truth, because then the actual condition is revealed.

> A false positive occurs when expected or normal behavior is wrongly identified as malicious. The detection of a failed login followed by a successful login being labeled as malicious, when the activity was caused by a user making a mistake after recently changing their password, is an example of a false positive.

Two types of errors are involved: false positive and false negative. The choice of the terms *positive* and *negative* relate to the result of the test. If you are using nmap as a tool to test an operating system, it will report the operating system as a specific type (say, Windows 10). If this result is incorrect, then this is a **false positive** error if you were counting on the result to be true.

False Negatives

False negative results are the opposite of false positive results. If you test something and it comes back negative, but it was in fact positive, then the result is a false negative. For example, if you scan ports to find any open ones and you miss a port that is open because the scanner could not detect it being open, and you do not run a test because of this false result, you are suffering from a false negative error.

> When an intrusion detection system (IDS) does not generate an alert from a malware attack, this is a false negative.

Log Reviews

A properly configured log system can provide tremendous insight into what has happened on a computer system. The key is in proper configuration so that you capture the events you want without adding extraneous data. That being said, a log system is a potential treasure trove of useful information to someone attacking a system. It will have information on systems, account names, what has worked for access, and what hasn't. *Log reviews* can provide information as to security incidents, policy violations (or attempted policy violations), and other abnormal conditions that require further analysis.

Credentialed vs. Non-Credentialed

Vulnerability scans can be performed with and without credentials. Performing a scan without credentials can provide some information as to the state of a service and whether or not it might be vulnerable. This is the view of a true outsider on the network. It can be done quickly, in an automated fashion, across large segments of a network. However, without credentials, it is not possible to see the detail that a login provides. Credentialed vulnerability scans can look deeper into a host and return more accurate and critical risk information. Frequently these scans are used together. First, a **non-credentialed scan** is performed across large network segments using automated tools. Then, based on these preliminary results, more detailed **credentialed scans** are run on machines with the most promise for vulnerabilities.

> Credentialed scans are more involved, requiring credentials and extra steps to log in to a system, whereas non-credentialed scans can be done more quickly across multiple machines using automation. Credentialed scans can reveal additional information over non-credentialed scans.

Intrusive vs. Non-Intrusive

Vulnerability scans can be intrusive or non-intrusive to the system being scanned. A non-intrusive scan is typically a simple scan of open ports and services, whereas an intrusive scan attempts to leverage potential vulnerabilities through an exploit to demonstrate the vulnerabilities. This intrusion can result in system crashes and is therefore referred to as intrusive.

Applications

Applications are the software programs that perform data processing on the information in a system. Being the operational element with respect to the data, as well as the typical means of interfacing between users and the data, applications are common targets of attackers. Vulnerability scans assess the strength of a deployed application against the desired performance of the system when being attacked. Application vulnerabilities represent some of the riskier problems in the enterprise because the applications are necessary, and there are fewer methods to handle miscommunications of data the higher up the stack one goes.

Web Applications

Web applications are just applications that are accessible across the Web. This method of accessibility brings convenience and greater potential exposure to unauthorized activity. All the details of standard applications still apply, but the placing of the system on the Web adds additional burdens on the system to prevent unauthorized access and keep web-based risks under control. From a vulnerability scan perspective, a web application is like an invitation to explore how well it is secured. At greatest risk are homegrown web applications because they seldom have the level of input protections needed for a hostile web environment.

Network

The network is the element that connects all the computing systems together, carrying data between the systems and users. The network can also be used in vulnerability scanning to access connected systems. The most common vulnerability scans are performed across the network in a sweep, where all systems are scanned, mapped, and enumerated per the ports and services. This information can then be used to further target specific scans of individual systems in a more detailed fashion, using credentials and potentially intrusive operations.

Common Vulnerabilities and Exposures (CVE)/Common Vulnerability Scoring System (CVSS)

The **Common Vulnerabilities and Exposures (CVE)** enumeration is a list of known vulnerabilities in software systems. Each vulnerability in the list has an identification number, a description, and reference. This list is the basis for most vulnerability scanner systems, as the scanners determine the software version and look up known or reported vulnerabilities. The **Common Vulnerability Scoring System (CVSS)** is a scoring system to determine how risky a vulnerability can be to a system. The CVSS score ranges from 0 to 10. As the CVSS score increases, so does the severity of risk from the vulnerability. Although the CVSS can't take into account where the vulnerability is in an enterprise, it can help determine severity using metrics such as whether it's easy to exploit, whether it requires user intervention, what level of privilege is required, and so on. Together, these two sets of information can provide a lot of data on the potential risk associated with a specific software system.

CVSS scores and their associated risk severity are as follows:

Risk Rating	CVSS Score
Critical	9.0–10
High	7.0–8.9
Medium	4.0–6.9
Low	0.1–3.9

The Common Vulnerabilities and Exposures (CVE) is a list of known vulnerabilities, each with an identification number, description, and reference. The Common Vulnerability Scoring System (CVSS) determines how risky a vulnerability can be to a system. The CVSS score ranges from 0 to 10. As it increases, so does the severity of risk from the vulnerability.

Configuration Review

System configurations play a significant role in system security. Misconfigurations leave a system in a more vulnerable state, sometimes even causing security controls to be bypassed completely. Verification of system configurations is an important vulnerability check item; if you find a misconfiguration, the chances are high that it exposes a vulnerability. Configuration reviews are important enough that they should be automated and performed on a regular basis. There are protocols and standards for measuring and validating configurations. The Common Configuration Enumeration (CCE) and Common Platform Enumeration (CPE) guides, as part of the National Vulnerability Database (NVD) maintained by NIST, are places to start for details.

Passively Test Security Controls

When an automated vulnerability scanner is used to examine a system for vulnerabilities, one of the side effects is the passive testing of the security controls. This is referred to as *passive testing* because the target of the vulnerability scanner is the system, not the controls. If the security controls are effective, then the vulnerability scan may not properly identify the vulnerability. If the security control prevents a vulnerability from being attacked, then it may not be exploitable.

Identify Vulnerability

Vulnerabilities are known entities; otherwise, the scanners would not have the ability to scan for them. When a scanner finds a vulnerability present in a system, it makes a log of the fact. In the end, an enumeration of the vulnerabilities that were discovered is part of the vulnerability analysis report.

Identify Lack of Security Controls

If a vulnerability is exposed to the vulnerability scanner, then a security control is needed to prevent the vulnerability from being exploited. As vulnerabilities are discovered, the specific environment of each vulnerability is documented. As the security vulnerabilities are all known in advance, the system should have controls in place to protect against exploitation. Part of the function of the vulnerability scan is to learn where controls are missing or are ineffective.

Identify Common Misconfigurations

One source of failure with respect to vulnerabilities is in the misconfiguration of a system. Common misconfigurations include access control failures

> **Tech Tip**
>
> **Misconfiguration Testing**
>
> *One of the key objectives of testing and penetration testing is to discover misconfigurations or weak configurations. Misconfigurations and/or weak configurations represent vulnerabilities in systems that can increase risk to the system. Discovering them so that appropriate mitigations can be employed is an essential security process.*

and failure to protect configuration parameters. Vulnerability scanners can be programmed to test for these specific conditions and report on them.

False Results

Tools are not perfect. Sometimes they will erroneously report things as an issue when they really are not a problem, and other times they won't report an issue at all. As previously discussed, a *false positive* is an incorrect finding—something that is incorrectly reported as a vulnerability. The scanner tells you there is a problem when in reality nothing is wrong. A *false negative* is when the scanner fails to report a vulnerability that actually does exist; the scanner simply missed the problem or didn't report it as a problem.

System Testing

Systems can be tested in a variety of manners. One method of describing the test capabilities relates to the information given to the tester. Testers can have varying levels of detail, from complete knowledge of a system and how it works to zero knowledge. These differing levels of testing are referred to as white box, gray box, and black box testing.

Black Box Testing

Black box testing is a testing technique where testers have no knowledge of the internal workings of the software they are testing. They treat the entire software package as a "black box"—they put input in and look at the output. They have no visibility into how the data is processed inside the application, only the output that comes back to them. Test cases for black box testing are typically constructed around intended functionality (what the software is supposed to do) and focus on providing both valid and invalid inputs. Black box software testing techniques are useful for examining any web-based application. Web-based applications are typically subjected to a barrage of valid, invalid, malformed, and malicious input from the moment they are exposed to public traffic.

White Box Testing

White box testing is almost the polar opposite of black box testing. Sometimes called clear-box testing, white box techniques test the internal structures and processing within an application for bugs, vulnerabilities, and so on. A white box tester will have detailed knowledge of the application they are examining—they'll develop test cases designed to exercise each path, decision tree, input field, and processing routine of the application. White box testing is often used to test paths within an application (if X, then go do this; if Y, then go do that), data flows, decision trees, and so on.

Gray Box Testing

What happens when you mix a bit of black box testing and a bit of white box testing? You get gray box testing. In a gray box test, the testers typically have some knowledge of the software, network, or systems they are testing. For this reason, gray box testing can be efficient and effective because testers can often quickly eliminate entire testing paths, test cases, and toolsets and can rule out things that simply won't work and are not worth trying.

Pen Testing vs. Vulnerability Scanning

Penetration testing is the examination of a system for vulnerabilities that can be exploited. The key is exploitation. There may be vulnerabilities in a system. In fact, one of the early steps in penetration testing is the examination for vulnerabilities, but the differentiation comes in the follow-on steps, which examine the system in terms of exploitability.

Auditing

Auditing, in the financial community, is done to verify the accuracy and integrity of financial records. Many standards have been established in the financial community about how to record and report a company's financial status correctly. In the computer security world, **auditing** serves a similar function. It is a process of assessing the security state of an organization compared against an established standard.

The important elements here are the standards. Organizations from different communities may have widely different standards, and any audit will need to consider the appropriate elements for the specific community. Audits differ from security or vulnerability assessments in that assessments measure the security posture of the organization but may do so without any mandated standards against which to compare them. In a security assessment, general security "best practices" can be used, but they may lack the regulatory teeth that standards often provide. Penetration tests can also be encountered—these tests are conducted against an organization to determine whether any holes in the organization's security can be found. The goal of the penetration test is to penetrate the security rather than measure it against some standard. Penetration tests are often viewed as *white hat hacking* in that the methods used often mirror those that attackers (often called *black hats*) might use.

> CompTIA updated a number of terms in the most recent exam objectives for CompTIA Security+ and has moved away from using terms like *white hat* and *black hat* for attackers and is now using *authorized* and *unauthorized* instead. Originally these terms referred to the cowboy movies of the late 1950s, where the good guy wore a white hat and the bad guy wore a black hat, which in the era of monochrome (black-and-white) TV made them immediately recognizable.

You should conduct some form of security audit or assessment on a regular basis. Your organization might spend quite a bit on security, and it is important to measure how effective the efforts have been. In certain communities, audits can be regulated on a periodic basis with very specific standards that must be measured against. Even if your organization is not part of such a community, periodic assessments are important.

Many particulars can be evaluated during an assessment, but at a minimum, the security perimeter (with all of its components, including host-based security) should be examined, as well as the organization's policies, procedures, and guidelines governing security. Employee training is another aspect that should be studied, since employees are the targets of social engineering and password-guessing attacks.

Security audits, assessments, and penetration tests are a big business, and a number of organizations can perform them for you. The costs of these vary widely depending on the extent of the tests you want, the background of the company you are contracting with, and the size of the organization to be tested.

A powerful mechanism for detecting security incidents is the use of security logs. For logs to be effective, however, they require monitoring. Monitoring of event logs can provide information concerning the events that have been logged. This requires making decisions in advance about the

One of the key management principles involves the measurement of a process. When referring to security, until it is measured, one should take answers with a grain of salt. Logging information is only good if you examine the logs and analyze them. Security controls work, but auditing their use provides assurance of their protection.

items to be logged. Logging too many items uses a lot of space and increases the workload for personnel who are assigned the task of reading those logs. The same is true for security, access, audit, and application-specific logs. The bottom line is that, although logs are valuable, preparation is needed to determine the correct items to log and the mechanisms by which logs are reviewed. Security information event management (SIEM) software can assist in log file analysis.

Performing Routine Audits

As part of any good security program, administrators must perform periodic audits to ensure things are "as they should be" with regard to users, systems, policies, and procedures. Installing and configuring security mechanisms is important, but they must be reviewed on a regularly scheduled basis to ensure they are effective, up to date, and serving their intended function. Here are some examples of items, but by no means a complete list, that should be audited on a regular basis:

- **User access** Administrators should review which users are accessing the systems, when they are doing so, what resources they are using, and so on. Administrators should look closely for users accessing resources improperly or accessing legitimate resources at unusual times.
- **User rights** When a user changes jobs or responsibilities, they will likely need to be assigned different access permissions; they may gain access to new resources and lose access to others. To ensure that users have access only to the resources and capabilities they need for their current positions, all user rights should be audited periodically.
- **Storage** Many organizations have policies governing what can be stored on "company" resources and how much space can be used by a given user or group. Periodic audits help to ensure that no undesirable or illegal materials exist on organizational resources.
- **Retention** In some organizations, how long a particular document or record is stored can be as important as what is being stored. A record's retention policy helps to define what is stored, how it is stored, how long it is stored, and how it is disposed of when the time comes. Periodic audits help to ensure that records or documents are removed when they are no longer needed.
- **Firewall rules** Periodic audits of firewall rules are important to ensure the firewall is filtering traffic as desired and to help ensure that "temporary" rules do not end up as permanent additions to the ruleset.

Vulnerabilities

Vulnerabilities are weaknesses in systems that can be exploited by attackers. Tools are the pathway to discovering the vulnerabilities in your systems. Finding them and patching them before an adversary finds them is important. This section lists some of the common vulnerabilities that attackers try to exploit.

Cloud-based vs. On-premises Vulnerabilities

Cloud computing has been described by pundits as computing on someone else's computer, and to a degree there is truth in that statement. As vulnerabilities exist in all systems, then regardless of whether a system is *on premises* or *cloud based,* it will always have potential vulnerabilities. With on-premises vulnerabilities, the enterprise has unfettered access to the infrastructure elements, making the discovery and remediation of vulnerabilities a problem defined by scope and resources. With the cloud, the economies of scale and standardized environments give cloud providers an advantage in the scope and resource side of the equation. What is lacking in vulnerability management from the enterprise point of view is a lack of visibility into the infrastructure element itself, as this is under the purview of the cloud provider.

Data can be stored locally on premises or remotely in the cloud. It is important to remember that no matter where data is stored, there will always be potential vulnerabilities that exist.

Zero Day

Zero day is a term used to define vulnerabilities that are newly discovered and not yet addressed by a patch. Most vulnerabilities exist in an unknown state until discovered by a researcher or developer. If a researcher or developer discovers a vulnerability but does not share the information, then this vulnerability can be exploited without the vendor's ability to fix it, because for all practical knowledge, the issue is unknown except to the person who found it. From the time of discovery until a fix or patch is made available, the vulnerability goes by the name "zero day," indicating that it has not been addressed yet. The most frightening thing about a zero-day threat is the unknown factor—its capability and effect on risk are unknown because it is unknown. Although there are no patches for zero-day vulnerabilities, you can use compensating controls to mitigate the risk.

Zero-day threats have become a common topic in the news and are a likely target for exam questions. Keep in mind that defenses exist, such as compensating controls, which are controls that mitigate the risk indirectly; for example, a compensating control may block the path to the vulnerability rather than directly address the vulnerability.

Weak Configurations

Most systems have significant configuration options that administrators can adjust to enable or disable functionality based on usage. When a system suffers from misconfiguration or *weak configuration,* it may not achieve all of the desired performance or security objectives. Configuring a database server to build a complete replica of all actions as a backup system can result in a system that is bogged down and not capable of proper responses when usage is high. Similarly, old options, such as support for legacy protocols, can lead to vulnerabilities. Misconfiguration can result from omissions as well, such as when the administrator does not change default credentials, which is equivalent to having no credentials at all, thus leaving the system vulnerable. This form of vulnerability provides a means for an attacker to gain entry or advance their level of privilege, and because this can happen on components with a wide span of control, such as routers and switches, in some cases an attacker can effectively gain total ownership of an enterprise.

Open Permissions

Permissions is the term used to describe the range of activities permitted on an object by an actor in a system. Having properly configured permissions is one of the defenses that can be employed in the enterprise. Managing permissions can be tedious, and as the size of the enterprise grows, the scale of permissions requires automation to manage. When permissions are not properly set, the condition of *open permissions* exists. The risk associated with an open permission is context dependent, as for some items, unauthorized access leads to little or no risk, whereas in other systems it can be catastrophic. The vulnerability of open permissions is equivalent to no access control for an item, and this needs to be monitored in accordance with the relative risk of the element in the enterprise.

Strong configurations include secure root (Linux) and Administrator (Windows) accounts. Without securing these accounts, anything they are connected to, including processes and services, is exposed to vulnerabilities.

Unsecure Root Accounts

Unsecure root accounts are like leaving master keys to the enterprise outside on the curb. Root accounts have access to everything and the ability to do virtually any activity on a network. All root accounts should be monitored, and all accesses should be verified as correct. One method of protecting high-value accounts such as root accounts is through access control vaults, where credentials are checked out before use. This prevents unauthorized activity using these accounts.

Errors

Errors are the condition where something has gone wrong. Every system will experience errors, and the key to managing this condition is in establishing error trapping and responses. How a system handles errors is everything, because unhandled errors are eventually handled at some level, and the higher up through a system an error goes, the less likely it will be handled correctly. One of the biggest weaknesses exploited by attackers is improper input validations. Whether against a program input, an API, or any other interface, inserting bad information that causes an error and forces a program into a non-normal operating state can result in an exploitable vulnerability. Trapping and handling errors can reduce the possibility of an error becoming exploitable.

Errors should be trapped by the program and appropriate log files generated. For example, web server logs include common error logs, customized logs, and W3C logs. W3C logs are web server logs that focus on recording specific web-related events. The Windows System log records operating system error messages. Windows can be configured to log records of success and failure of login attempts and other audited events. The Windows Application log records events related to local system applications.

Weak Encryption

Cryptographic errors come from several common causes. One typical mistake is choosing to develop your own cryptographic algorithm. Development of a secure cryptographic algorithm is far from an easy task, and even when it's attempted by experts, weaknesses can be discovered that make the algorithm unusable. Cryptographic algorithms become trusted only after years of scrutiny and repelling attacks, so any new algorithms would take years to join the trusted set. If you instead decide to rely on secret algorithms, be warned that secret or proprietary algorithms have never provided the desired level of protection. A similar mistake to attempting to develop your own cryptographic algorithm is to attempt to write your own implementation of a known cryptographic algorithm. Errors in coding implementations are common and lead to weak implementations of secure algorithms that are vulnerable to bypass. Do not fall prey to creating a weak implementation; instead, use a proven, vetted cryptographic library.

The second major cause of cryptographic weakness, or weak encryption, is the employment of deprecated or weak cryptographic algorithms. Weak cipher suites are those that at one time were considered secure but are no longer considered secure. As the ability to use ever faster hardware has enabled attackers to defeat some cryptographic methods, the older, weaker methods have been replaced by newer, stronger ones. Failure to use the newer, stronger methods can result in weakness. A common example of this is SSL; all versions of SSL are now considered deprecated and should not be used. Everyone should switch their systems to TLS-based solutions.

The impact of cryptographic failures is fairly easy to understand: whatever protection that was provided is no longer there, even if it is essential for the security of the system.

Unsecure Protocols

Another important weak configuration to guard against in the enterprise is *unsecure protocols*. One of the most common protocols used, HTTP, is by its own nature unsecure. Adding TLS to HTTP, using HTTPS, is a simple configuration change that should be enforced everywhere. But what about all the other protocol stacks that come prebuilt in OSs and are just waiting to become a vulnerability, such as FTP, Telnet, and SNMP? Improperly secured communication protocols and services and unsecure credentials increase the risk of unauthorized access to the enterprise. Network infrastructure devices can include routers, switches, access points, gateways, proxies, and firewalls. When infrastructure systems are deployed, these devices remain online for years, and many of them are rarely rebooted, patched, or upgraded.

Default Settings

Default settings can be a security risk unless they were created with security in mind. Older operating systems used to have everything enabled by default. Old versions of some systems had hidden administrator accounts, and Microsoft's SQL Server used to have a blank system administrator password by default. Today, most vendors have cleaned these issues up, setting default values with security in mind. But when you instantiate something in your enterprise, it is then yours. Therefore, you should make the settings what you need and only what you need, and you should create these settings as the default configuration baseline. This way, the settings and their security implications are understood. Not taking these steps leaves too many unknowns within an enterprise.

Open Ports and Services

For a service to respond to a request, its port must be open for communication. Having *open ports* is like having doors in a building. Even a bank vault has a door. Having excess *open services* only leads to pathways into your systems that must be protected. Disabling unnecessary services, closing ports, and using firewalls to prevent communications except on approved channels creates a barrier to entry by unauthorized users. Many services run with elevated privileges by default, and malware takes advantage of this. Security professionals should make every effort to audit services and disable any that aren't required.

Improper or Weak Patch Management

All systems need patches periodically as errors and vulnerabilities are discovered and vendors issue software fixes to these vulnerabilities. One of the important takeaways from patching is that once a supplier patches their software, hackers can reverse engineer the vulnerability from the patch. Therefore, once the patch is released, attackers learn where to attack. To manage the risk associated with patch management vulnerabilities, it is important to establish a strong patch management program that covers all systems and all software. The literature of security failures is full of examples where the missing of a system or two was all it took for an attacker to get into the system. Having an *improper or weak patch management* system is an open invitation to having vulnerabilities exploited. This makes patch management one of the essential security controls and one that there should be no excuses as to why it was not implemented.

To minimize the risks associated with applying patches to production systems, it is recommended that the enterprise change control process be used. Because patches can be time sensitive, it is important to have defined periods of time when patches must be installed as well as an automated means of determining what patches are needed, where they are needed, and status of the current patch level by target location.

Firmware

Firmware is just another form of software with one noted distinction: it is stored in hardware to be present when the system boots up. However, it is still software, with all the baggage of software—bugs, vulnerabilities, patch requirements, updates, and so on. With firmware being part of the system itself, always present, it is frequently missed when considering how to keep software up to date. This goes for manufacturers as well. If you are looking at a system that has firmware, reasonable questions to ask as part of your research before selection include, How is the firmware updated? How often? And how are updates distributed? The lifecycle, vulnerabilities, and maintenance issues associated with firmware mirror those of software. Patching firmware is an often-neglected issue, and this can lead to vulnerabilities, especially given the typical lifetime of some equipment.

> Updates and patching are used to ensure software and firmware are up to date and secure. Manufacturers of hardware often provide updates for firmware, and it is the organization's responsibility to ensure firmware updates are applied.

Operating System (OS)

Operating system (OS) patch management was a chore years ago, with patches coming haphazardly over time, each requiring manual intervention.

Today, major operating systems can patch themselves, and with a little automation, the tracking and management of patches is easy. There are only a couple of steps to get this right. First, have a patch management policy, and make it patch everything and track all patches. Second, follow up on that policy. There are excuses about not being able to patch for a wide range of reasons, but a properly executed patch management strategy overcomes all of those risks. Worried about a patch breaking a crucial system? If it is a crucial system, you have more than one, right? Patch one system, test to see if it still works, and then patch the rest.

The list of enterprises that missed a patch that then became the pathway for an attacker is long. Attackers have it easy when it comes to testing whether you have patched—they try to exploit the known vulnerability, and if it works, they know you haven't patched and they have gained access.

Applications

Applications are the programs that comprise the functional aspect of the enterprise. From server-based elements such as web servers and database servers, to desktop applications like Microsoft Office, applications are the tools that handle the data and add value to the system. Applications, like all software, require updating and patching to fix vulnerabilities and bugs. The challenge with application patching across an enterprise is in the tracking of all of the applications used, including even small, seemingly meaningless programs that are installed on desktops. Not only does the enterprise have to keep track of all the applications it has, but it has to determine which ones have updates and when. Some major software vendors make this process easy, but the myriad of additional vendors make the task of knowing what needs updating, when and where, a real challenge. There are applications designed to manage this aspect, and it is highly recommended that enterprises use patch-tracking software that can identify when patches are available and install them.

Legacy Platforms

Legacy platforms is the term used to describe systems that are no longer being marketed or supported. They are also considered old, which in IT terms can be as little as a few years. Legacy systems represent an interesting vulnerability because, by being in the legacy category, they are no longer supported, so if new problems are discovered, the only fix is a compensating control. Having systems that can't be patched is a risk, but like all risks, it must be measured and weighed against the costs of change. In a properly architected secure environment, the risk of legacy vulnerabilities is partially covered by the compensating controls that make executing those vulnerabilities extremely hard if not impossible.

Chapter 16 Review

Chapter Summary

After reading this chapter and completing the exercises, you should understand the following about security tools and techniques.

Explore security tools and their use

- A wide range of tools can be used to explore networks via reconnaissance and discovery.
- File manipulation tools can be used to manage data.
- Shell and scripting environments provide the power to automate tool usage.
- Tools can be used for packet capture, analysis, and replay.
- Specific tools are used during computer forensic investigations.

Describe security tool suites

- Tool suites group tools together to facilitate usability on a standard platform.
- Tool suites exist for penetration testing, incident response, and forensics purposes.

Detail penetration and vulnerability testing methods

- Penetration testing is designed to mimic real-world threats to examine the security posture.
- Vulnerability testing is designed to test systems for known vulnerabilities.
- False positive and false negative results are real and add issues to making solid decisions.

Explore common vulnerabilities that can be discovered using the tools

- Vulnerabilities are the doors attackers use to enter systems.
- Testing for vulnerabilities is important to determine the security risk a system has.

Key Terms

arp *(619)*
auditing *(639)*
Autopsy *(629)*
black box testing *(638)*
cat *(623)*
chmod *(624)*
Common Vulnerabilities and Exposures (CVE) *(636)*
Common Vulnerability Scoring System (CVSS) *(636)*
credentialed scan *(635)*
cuckoo *(622)*
curl *(620)*
dd *(627)*
escalation of privilege *(633)*
false negative *(635)*
false positive *(634)*
grep *(623)*
head *(623)*
hping *(618)*
ifconfig *(617)*
ipconfig *(617)*
Kali *(629)*
Nessus *(622)*
netcat (nc) *(619)*
netstat *(619)*
nmap *(617)*
non-credentialed scan *(635)*
nslookup *(615)*
OpenSSL *(626)*
Parrot OS *(629)*
pathping *(618)*
persistence *(633)*
ping *(618)*
pivoting *(632)*
PowerShell *(625)*

reconnaissance *(632)*
route *(620)*
Security Onion *(630)*
Social-Engineering Toolkit (SET) *(630)*
SSH *(625)*
tail *(623)*
tcpdump *(627)*
tcpreplay *(626)*
tracert *(615)*
TShark *(627)*
white box testing *(638)*
Wireshark *(627)*
zero day *(641)*

Key Terms Quiz

Use terms from the Key Terms list to complete the sentences that follow. Don't use the same term more than once. Not all terms will be used.

1. If you wish to find a file containing a particular text pattern, you could use _______________.
2. The command _______________ can return the first few lines of a file.
3. The utility used to read and write across network connections on Linux is _______________.
4. ________ is a sandbox program designed to analyze malicious software, separating the software from direct connection to the OS.
5. The _______________ enumeration is a list of known vulnerabilities in software systems.
6. The tool _______________ is designed to transfer data to or from a server, without user interaction.
7. On Linux, the tool _______________ is used to copy files, directories, and even entire disks, including making backups.
8. If you wish to use Wireshark in a script, the command is _______________.
9. The command _______________ replays a set of packets on a network.
10. To collect packets into a file, you would use _______________.

Multiple-Choice Quiz

1. To secure communications during remote access of a system, you can use which of the following tools?
   - **A.** OpenSSL
   - **B.** SSH
   - **C.** dd
   - **D.** tcpdump
2. Which of the following is not a packet capture/analysis tool?
   - **A.** Wireshark
   - **B.** tcpreplay
   - **C.** tcpdump
   - **D.** dd
3. To capture an image of the memory in a running system, you can use which of the following?
   - **A.** grep
   - **B.** dumpmem
   - **C.** memdump
   - **D.** logger
4. Which tools are used in IP address investigations? (Choose all that apply.)
   - **A.** tracert
   - **B.** theHarvester
   - **C.** dnsenum
   - **D.** chmod

5. To search through a system to find files containing a phrase, what would be the best tool to use?
   - **A.** curl
   - **B.** logger
   - **C.** chmod
   - **D.** grep
6. What does chmod do?
   - **A.** Sets permission on a file
   - **B.** Initiates a change modification entry in a log file
   - **C.** Cryptographically hashes a file
   - **D.** Lists the files in a working directory
7. You need to analyze previously collected packet data on a network, including editing some of the data. Which is the best tool to use?
   - **A.** tcpreplay
   - **B.** tcpdump
   - **C.** netstat
   - **D.** Wireshark
8. Which of these tools is used in penetration testing? (Choose all that apply.)
   - **A.** nmap
   - **B.** Nessus
   - **C.** scanless
   - **D.** theHarvester
9. To automate system administration across an enterprise Windows network, including using Windows objects, the best choice would be which of the following?
   - **A.** BASH scripting
   - **B.** Python
   - **C.** Wireshark
   - **D.** PowerShell
10. You think a file is malware. What is the first tool you should invoke?
    - **A.** Cuckoo
    - **B.** WinHex
    - **C.** OpenSSL
    - **D.** Autopsy

Essay Quiz

1. Which set of tools would you employ for incident response activities? Give examples and common distros if available.
2. What are the top ten Linux commands one should understand, and what do they do? Provide an example usage for each one.

Lab Project

• Lab Project 16.1

Obtain Security Onion distro for use in a VM and then perform the following steps:

1. Instantiate Security Onion in a VM.
2. Update the tools in Security Onion.
3. Run Setup from the desktop to configure Security Onion.
4. Capture some traffic and test the tools.

chapter 17

Web Components, E-mail, and Instant Messaging

The "free" distribution of unwelcome or misleading messages to thousands of people is an annoying and sometimes destructive use of the Internet's unprecedented efficiency.

—Bill Gates, *New York Times*, 1998

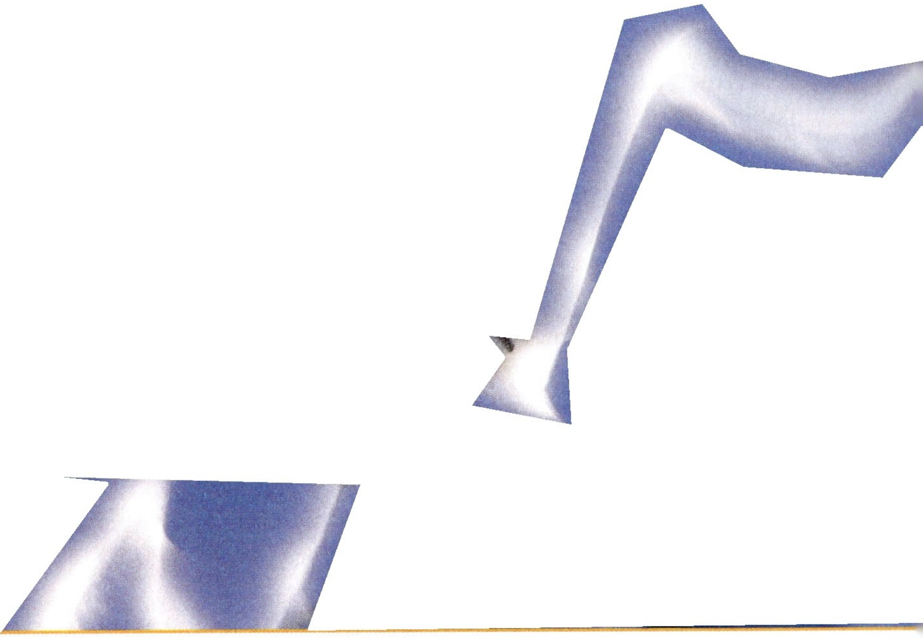

In this chapter, you will learn how to

- Describe the functioning of the TLS protocol suite
- Explain web applications, plug-ins, and associated security issues
- Describe secure file transfer options
- Explain directory usage for data retrieval
- Explain scripting and other Internet functions that present security concerns
- Use cookies to maintain parameters between web pages
- Examine web-based application security issues
- Describe security issues associated with e-mail
- Implement security practices for e-mail
- Detail the security issues of instant messaging protocols

The World Wide Web was invented by Tim Berners-Lee to give physicists a convenient method of exchanging information. What began in 1990 as a physics tool in the European Laboratory for Particle Physics (CERN, the acronym for the original French name) has grown into a complex system used by millions of computer users for a range of tasks, from e-commerce to e-mail, chatting, games, and even the original intended use—file and information sharing. Before the Web, plenty of methods were used to perform these tasks, and they were already widespread in use. File Transfer Protocol (FTP) was used to move files, and Telnet allowed users access to other machines. What was missing was the common architecture brought by Berners-Lee: first, a common addressing scheme built around the concept of a **Uniform Resource Locator (URL)** and, second, the concept of linking documents to other documents via URLs through the **Hypertext Markup Language (HTML)**.

E-mail is one of the most popular applications on company networks. With over 4.3 billion e-mail users, more than 260 billion e-mails per year, and the average worker getting over 120 e-mails a day, the usage numbers are staggering. The split between business and personal e-mail is 55 percent to 45 percent, respectively. The total amount of spam is unknown, but even after extensive filtering, spam averages nearly 10 percent of inbox traffic.

Current Web Components and Concerns

The usefulness of the Web is due not just to browsers, but also to web components that enable services for end users through their browser interfaces. These components use a wide range of protocols and services to deliver the desired content. From a security perspective, they offer users an easy-to-use, secure method of conducting data transfers over the Internet. Many protocols have been developed to deliver this content, although for most users, the browser handles the details.

From a systems point of view, many security concerns have arisen, but they can be grouped into three main tasks:

- Securing a server that delivers content to users over the Web
- Securing the transport of information between users and servers over the Web
- Securing the user's computer from attack over a web connection

This chapter presents the components used on the Web to request and deliver information securely over the Internet. It also covers web-mediated communication, such as e-mails and instant messages.

Web Protocols

When two people communicate, several things must happen for the communication to be effective: they must use a language that both parties understand, and they must correctly use the language—that is, structure and syntax—to express their thoughts. The mode of communication is a separate entity entirely, because the previous statements are important in both spoken and written forms of communication. The same requirements are present with respect to computer communications, and they are addressed through *protocols,* which are agreed-upon sets of rules that allow different vendors to produce hardware and software that can interoperate with hardware and software developed by other vendors. Because of the worldwide nature of the Internet, protocols are very important and form the basis by which all the separate parts can work together. The specific instantiation of protocols is done through hardware and software components. The majority of this chapter concentrates on protocols related to the Internet as instantiated by software components.

Encryption (SSL and TLS)

Secure Sockets Layer (SSL) was a general-purpose protocol developed by Netscape for managing the encryption of information being transmitted over the Internet. It began as a competitive feature to drive sales of Netscape's web server product, which could then send information securely to end users. This early vision of securing the transmission channel between the web server and the browser became an Internet standard. Today the term SSL is almost ubiquitous with respect to e-commerce—all browsers supported it, as did web servers, and virtually all e-commerce websites used this method to protect sensitive financial information in transit between web servers and browsers. However, when speaking nowadays about SSL, we are generally referring to the TLS protocol. Today, SSL is completely deprecated. It has internal vulnerabilities and has been completely breached by multiple tools and attack methods, and thus has been replaced everywhere by TLS.

All versions of SSL have been shown to be vulnerable to breach. This means the entire SSL suite is now no longer considered secure. SSL v3 fell to the POODLE attack in 2014, leaving only TLS as a secure method. It is important that both clients and web servers as well as other applications be updated to only use TLS in the future.

The **Internet Engineering Task Force (IETF)** embraced SSL in 1996 through a series of RFCs and named the group of RFCs **Transport Layer Security (TLS)**. Starting with SSL 3.0, in 1999, the IETF issued RFC 2246, "TLS Protocol Version 1.0," followed by RFC 2712, which added Kerberos authentication, and then RFCs 2817 and 2818, which extended TLS to HTTP version 1.1 (HTTP/1.1). Although SSL has been through several versions, TLS begins with an equivalency to SSL 3.0. Because SSL has had all versions deprecated, only TLS remains secure, and wherever the term SSL is found in this book, it refers to TLS.

Tech Tip

TLS, Not SSL

Just know that TLS should be used in place of SSL for all instances. To use the TLS protocol effectively between a client and a server, an agreement must be reached on which protocol to use, which is done via the TLS handshake process. The process begins with a client request for a secure connection and a server's response. After a few exchanges, a secure channel is formed between the client and server. The SSL protocol is no longer secure, and today versions of TLS remain the only option.

TLS is a series of functions that exists in the Open System Interconnection (OSI) model between the application layer and the transport and network layers. The goal of the Transmission Control Protocol (TCP) is to send an unauthenticated, error-free stream of information between two computers. TLS adds message integrity and authentication functionality to TCP through the use of cryptographic methods. Because cryptographic methods are an ever-evolving field, and because both parties must agree on an implementation method, TLS has embraced an open, extensible, and adaptable method to allow flexibility and strength. When two programs initiate a TLS connection, one of their first tasks is to compare available protocols and agree on an appropriate common cryptographic protocol for use in this particular communication. Because TLS can use separate algorithms and methods for encryption, authentication, and data integrity, each of these is negotiated and determined depending on need at the beginning of a communication.

How TLS Works

TLS uses a wide range of cryptographic protocols. At the initiation of the protocol, the questions asked and answered are which TLS version and which cryptographic algorithm will be used. For the client and server to communicate, both sides must agree on a commonly held version of the protocol (TLS v1.2 or v1.3). Commonly available cryptographic algorithms include Diffie-Hellman, AES, and AEAD. The next step is to exchange certificates and keys, as necessary, to enable authentication.

Just as all versions of SSL have been deprecated, the first two versions of TLS, v1 and v1.1, have been deprecated and should not be used.

Tech Tip

TLS Handshake

The following steps, depicted in the following illustration, establish a TLS-secured channel:

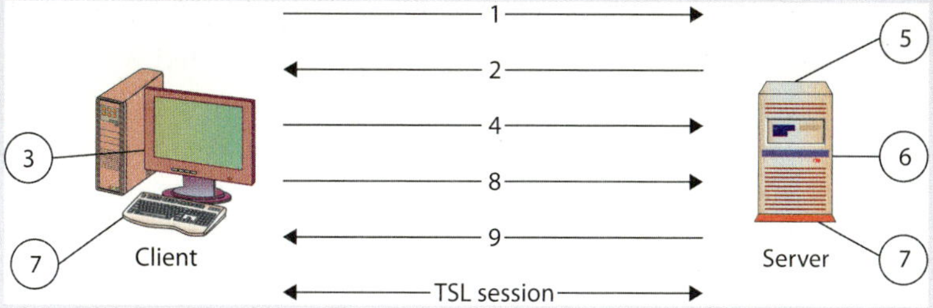

1. *The client sends to the server the client's TLS version number, cipher settings, and session-specific data.*
2. *The server sends to the client the server's TLS version number, cipher settings, session-specific data, and its own certificate. If the resource requested requires client authentication, the server requests the client's certificate.*
3. *The client authenticates the server using the information it has received. If the server cannot be authenticated, the user is warned of the problem and informed that an encrypted and authenticated connection cannot be established.*
4. *The client encrypts a seed value with the server's public key (from the certificate in step 2) and sends it to the server. If the server requested client authentication, the client also sends the client certificate.*
5. *If the server requested client authentication, the server attempts to authenticate the client certificate. If the client certificate cannot be authenticated, the session ends.*
6. *The server uses its private key to decrypt the secret and then performs a series of steps (which the client also performs) to generate a master secret. The required steps depend on the cryptographic method used for key exchange.*
7. *Both the client and the server use the master secret to generate the session key, which is a symmetric key used to encrypt and decrypt information exchanged during the TLS session.*
8. *The client sends a message informing the server that future messages from the client will be encrypted with the session key. It then sends a separate (encrypted) message indicating that the client portion of the handshake is finished.*
9. *The server sends a message informing the client that future messages from the server will be encrypted with the session key. It then sends a separate (encrypted) message indicating that the server portion of the handshake is finished.*
10. *The TLS handshake is now complete and the session can begin.*

As this exchange illustrates, new TLS connections require two roundtrips to complete a full handshake. Two methods are available to reduce this to one roundtrip: False Start and Session Resumption.

False Start is a TLS protocol extension that allows the client and server to start transmitting encrypted application data when the handshake is only partially complete. Once the ChangeCipherSpec and Finished messages are sent, without waiting for the other side to do the same, each side can begin with encrypted packets. This works because both parties know the key, and the remainder of the handshake is to confirm no one has tampered with the channel. This reduces handshake overhead for new TLS connections to one roundtrip, a significant savings at scale.

If the TLS client has previously communicated with the server, an "abbreviated handshake" can be used, which involves the client indicating to the server, in the ClientHello message, that it still remembers the negotiated cipher suite and keys from the previous connection and is able to reuse them. If the server has the same information, the abbreviated handshake, which requires one roundtrip, can be used. This also allows the client and server to reduce the CPU overhead by reusing the previously negotiated parameters for the secure session rather than recomputing new ones.

> **Tech Tip**
>
> **Certificates**
>
> *A certificate is merely a standard set of formatted data that represents the authenticity of the public key associated with the signer. Details of certificates and PKI elements to support their use are covered in Chapter 6, and you are encouraged to brush up on these details if needed.*

Once authentication is established, the channel is secured with symmetric key cryptographic methods and hashes—typically AES for symmetric key and SHA-256 for the hash functions.

At this point, the authenticity of the server and possibly the client has been established, and the channel is protected by encryption against eavesdropping. Each packet is encrypted using the symmetric key before transfer across the network, and then it's decrypted by the receiver. All of this work requires CPU time; hence, TLS connections require significantly more overhead than unprotected connections. Establishing connections is particularly time consuming, so even stateless web connections are held in a stateful fashion when secured via SSL/TLS, to avoid repeating the handshake process for each request. This makes some web server functionality more difficult, such as implementing web farms, and requires that either a TLS appliance be used before the web server to maintain state or the TLS state information be maintained in a directory-type service accessible by all of the web farm servers. Either method requires additional infrastructure and equipment. However, to enable secure e-commerce and other private data transactions over the Internet, this is a cost-effective method to establish a specific level of necessary security.

The use of certificates could present a lot of data and complication to a user. Fortunately, browsers have incorporated much of this desired functionality into a seamless operation. Once you have decided always to accept code from XYZ Corporation, subsequent certificate checks are handled by the browser. In the Chrome browser, the details for a certificate are found under the Security tab on the DevTools page, as shown in Figure 17.1.

Once a communication is in the TLS channel, it is very difficult to defeat the TLS protocol. Before data enters the secured channel, however, defeat is possible. A Trojan program that copies keystrokes and echoes them to another TCP/IP address in parallel with the intended communication can defeat TLS, for example, provided that the Trojan program copies the data prior to TLS encapsulation. This type of attack has occurred and has been

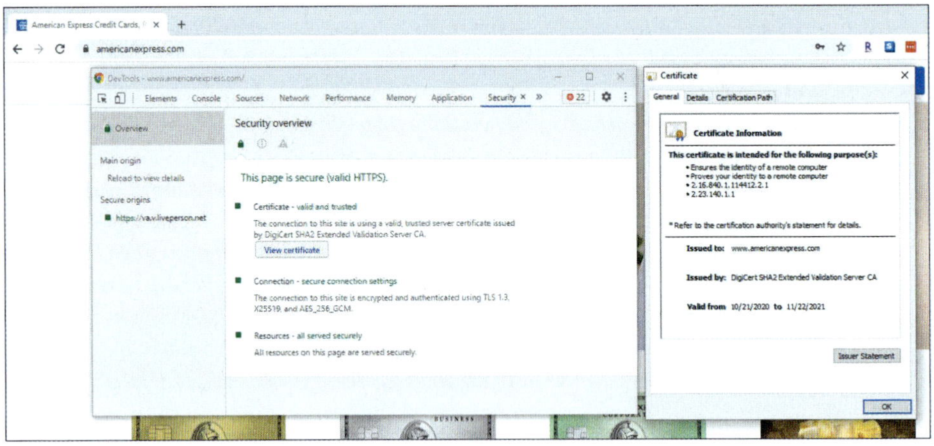

• **Figure 17.1** Viewing a certificate in Chrome browser

used to steal passwords and other sensitive material from users, performing the theft as the user actually types in the data.

> **Tech Tip**
>
> **TLS Proxy Attack**
>
> *TLS-based security is not foolproof. It can be defeated, as in the case of a proxy-based attack. During the handshake, the following steps could occur, as shown in the following illustration:*
>
> 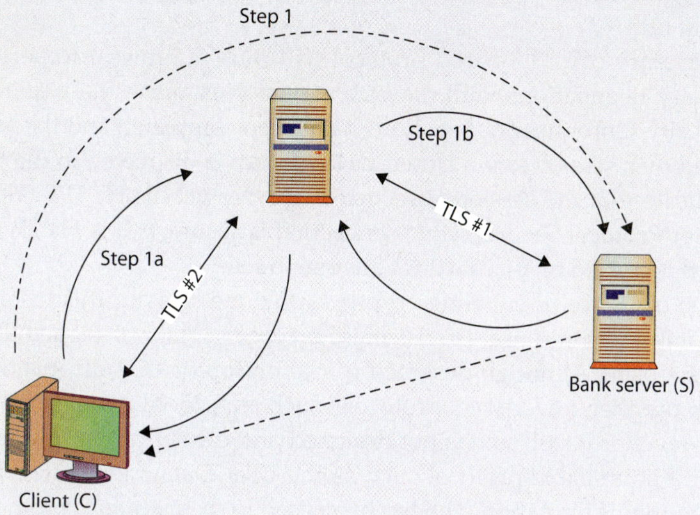
>
>
> 1. *The client (C) initiates a TLS session with their bank server (S) through a proxy (P).*
> 2. *P acts by echoing the information sent to it by C (step 1a) to S (step 1b), imitating C to S, and establishing a secure channel between P and S (TLS #1).*
> 3. *P creates a second secure channel to C (TLS #2) using information received from S, pretending to be S.*
> 4. *The user assumes that the dotted lines occur—a secure channel to the bank directly—when the client actually has only a secure channel to the proxy. In fact, the proxy has the secure channel to the bank, and as far as the bank is concerned, the proxy is the client and using the client's credentials. For a proxy that is not completely trusted, this could be a nightmare for the client.*
>
> *The advent of high-assurance certificates prevents the proxy from imitating the bank because it cannot give the correct set of credentials back to the client to complete the high-assurance handshake. Mutual authentication is also designed to prevent this, as the proxy cannot simultaneously imitate both sides of the handshake. Mutual authentication is rarely used because there is the issue of maintaining client certificates that are trusted to a server—a challenge for broad-reach sites like financial institutions and e-commerce sites.*

The Web (HTTP and HTTPS)

The Hypertext Transfer Protocol (HTTP) is used for the transfer of hyperlinked data over the Internet, from web servers to browsers. When a user types a URL such as http://www.example.com into a browser, the http://

portion indicates that the desired method of data transfer is HTTP. Although it was initially created just for HTML pages, today many protocols deliver content over this connection protocol. HTTP traffic takes place over TCP port 80 by default, and this port is typically left open on firewalls because of the extensive use of HTTP.

One of the primary drivers behind the development of TLS was the desire to hide the complexities of cryptography from end users. When a TLS-enabled browser is used, this can be done simply by requesting a secure connection from a web server instead of a nonsecure connection. With respect to HTTP connections, this is as simple as using https:// in place of http://.

The entry of a TLS-based protocol will cause a browser to perform the necessary negotiations with the web server to establish the required level of security. Once these negotiations have been completed and the session is secured by a session key, a closed padlock icon is displayed in the URL bar to indicate that the session is secure. If the protocol is HTTPS (Hypertext Transfer Protocol Secure), your connection is secure; if it is HTTP, the connection is carried by plaintext for anyone to see.

The objective of enabling cryptographic methods in this fashion is to make it easy for end users to use these protocols. TLS is designed to be protocol agnostic. Although designed to run on top of TCP/IP, it can operate on top of other, lower-level protocols, such as X.25. TLS requires a reliable lower-level protocol, so it is not designed and cannot properly function on top of a nonreliable protocol such as the User Datagram Protocol (UDP). Even with this limitation, TLS has been used to secure many common TCP/IP-based services, as shown in Table 17.1.

Table 17.1 SSL/TLS-Protected Services

Protocol	TCP Port	Use
HTTPS	443	SSL/TLS-secured HTTP traffic
SSMTP	465	SSL/TLS-secured SMTP for mail sending
SPOP3 (SecurePOP3)	995	SSL/TLS-secured POP3 for mail receiving
sNEWS	563	SSL/TLS-secured Usenet news
SSL = LDAP	636	SSL/TLS-secured LDAP services

HTTPS Everywhere

When websites were first deployed, providing HTTPS was a resource cost issue, because it took processor cycles to encrypt all the connections. Today, with a variety of encryption technologies available, managing the resources for HTTPS connections is much easier, and a case has been made by many in security that all web connections should be HTTPS. This has resulted in the HTTPS Everywhere movement (www.eff.org/https-everywhere/), spearheaded by the Electronic Frontier Foundation (EFF).

If websites everywhere would turn off HTTP in favor of using only HTTPS (with TLS in light of SSL vulnerabilities), this would not solve all the security problems, but it would raise the bar substantially for many attacks, making most of them impossible. HTTPS Everywhere would go a long way for privacy because it would prevent data snooping. It would also prevent many man-in-the-middle attacks, such as SSL stripping.

Because not all sites are HTTPS yet, the EFF has developed a plug-in for browsers called HTTPS Everywhere. This plug-in helps the browser maintain an HTTPS connection and warns when it is not present.

HTTP Strict Transport Security

HTTP Strict Transport Security (HSTS) is an IETF standard and a mechanism for enforcing rules to prevent browsers from downgrading security when accessing a site. The policy states that when a web server provides an HTTP response header field named "Strict-Transport-Security," the user agent shall comply by not issuing insecure requests. The header field has a time period associated with it, set in the header, during which the policy is in effect.

HSTS was created in response to a series of attack profiles, the most critical being the SSL stripping man-in-the-middle attacks first publicly introduced by Moxie Marlinspike. The **SSL stripping attack** works on both SSL and TLS by transparently converting the secure HTTPS connection into a plain HTTP connection, removing the transport layer encryption protections. Although an observant user might notice the drop in security, by then the damage may have been done, and this relies on users knowing whether or not a page should be secure. No warnings are presented to the user during the downgrade process, which makes the attack fairly subtle to all but the most vigilant. Marlinspike's sslstrip tool fully automates the attack and is available on the Web.

Try This!

Sniff Your Own Connections!

Determining what level of protection you have when surfing the Web is easy. Use a packet-sniffing tool like Wireshark to record your own communications. Because HTTPS ends at your browser, the packet capture mechanism should reflect the same experience an outsider will see if sniffing your traffic. By examining the packets, you can see if traffic is encrypted, which traffic is encrypted, and what is visible to outsiders.

Directory Services (DAP and LDAP)

A *directory* is a data storage mechanism similar to a database, but it has several distinct differences designed to provide efficient data retrieval services compared to standard database mechanisms. A directory is designed and optimized for reading data, offering very fast search and retrieval operations. The types of information stored in a directory tend to be descriptive attribute data. A directory offers a static view of data that can be changed without a complex update transaction. The data is hierarchically described in a treelike structure, and a network interface for reading is typical.

Because directories are optimized for read operations, they are frequently employed where data retrieval is desired. Common uses of directories include e-mail address lists, domain server data, and resource maps of network resources.

To enable interoperability, **X.500** was created as a standard for directory services. The primary method for accessing an X.500 directory is through the Directory Access Protocol (DAP), a heavyweight protocol that is difficult to implement completely, especially on PCs and more constrained platforms. This led to the **Lightweight Directory Access Protocol (LDAP)**, which contains the most commonly used functionality. LDAP can interface with X.500 services, and, most importantly, LDAP can be used over TCP with significantly less computing resources than a full X.500 implementation. LDAP offers all the functionality most directories need and is easier and more economical to implement; hence, LDAP has become the Internet standard for directory services. TLS provides several important functions to LDAP services. It can establish the identity of a data source through the use of certificates, and it can also provide for the integrity and confidentiality of the data being presented from an LDAP source. Because LDAP and TLS are two separate independent protocols, interoperability is more a function of correct setup than anything else. To achieve LDAP over SSL/TLS, the typical setup is to establish a TLS connection and then open an LDAP connection over the protected channel. To do this requires that both the client and the server be enabled for SSL/TLS. In the case of the client, most browsers are already enabled. In the case of an LDAP server, this specific function must be enabled by a system administrator. Because this setup initially is complicated, it's definitely a task for a competent system administrator.

Once an LDAP server is set up to function over a TLS connection, it operates as it always has. The LDAP server responds to specific queries with the data returned from a node in the search. The TLS functionality is transparent to the data flow from the user's perspective. From the outside, TLS prevents observation of the data request and response, thus ensuring confidentiality.

Lightweight Directory Access Protocol (LDAP) is a directory services protocol for use on IP networks. By default, LDAP traffic is unsecured. LDAP over SSL (LDAPS) is a method to secure LDAP by enabling communication over SSL/TLS. LDAPS uses port 636.

File Transfer (FTP and SFTP)

One of the original intended uses of the Internet was to transfer files from one machine to another in a simple, secure, and reliable fashion, which was needed by scientific researchers. Today, file transfers represent downloads of music content, reports, and other data sets from other computer systems to a PC-based client. Until 1995, the majority of Internet traffic was file transfers. With all of this need, a protocol was necessary so that two computers could agree on how to send and receive data. As such, FTP is one of the older protocols.

FTP

File Transfer Protocol (FTP) is an application-level protocol that operates over a wide range of lower-level protocols. FTP is embedded in most operating systems and provides a method of transferring files from a sender to a receiver. Most FTP implementations are designed to operate both ways, sending and receiving, and can enable remote file operations over a TCP/IP connection. FTP clients are used to initiate transactions, and FTP servers are used to respond to transaction requests. The actual request can be either to upload (send data from client to server) or to download (send data from server to client).

Clients for FTP on a PC can range from application programs, to the command-line FTP programs in Windows, to most browsers. To open an FTP data store in a browser, you can enter **ftp://*url*** in the browser's address field to indicate that you want to see the data associated with the URL via an FTP session—the browser handles the details.

Tech Tip

FTP Is Not Secure

FTP is a plaintext protocol. User credentials used for logins are sent as plaintext across the network. File transfers via FTP can be either binary or in text mode, but in either case, they are in plaintext across the network. If confidentiality of a transfer is desired, then a secure channel should be used for the transfer. If integrity is a concern, a more complex method of transfer will be required, to support digital hashes and signatures.

Blind FTP (Anonymous FTP)

To access resources on a computer, an account must be used to allow the operating system–level authorization function to work. In the case of an FTP server, you may not wish to control who gets the information, so a standard account called *anonymous* exists. This allows unlimited public access to the files and is commonly used when you want to have unlimited distribution. On a server, access permissions can be established to allow only downloading, only uploading, or both downloading and uploading, depending on the system's function.

Because FTP servers can present a security risk, they are typically not permitted on workstations and are disabled on servers without need for this functionality.

> Because FTP can be used to allow anyone access to upload files to a server, it is considered a security risk and is commonly implemented on specialized servers isolated from other critical functions.

SFTP

FTP operates in a plaintext mode, so an eavesdropper can observe the data being passed. If confidential transfer is required, Secure FTP (SFTP) combines both the Secure Shell (SSH) protocol and FTP to accomplish this task. SFTP operates as an application program that encodes both the commands and the data being passed and requires SFTP to be on both the client and the server. SFTP is not interoperable with standard FTP—the encrypted commands cannot be read by the standard FTP server program. To establish SFTP data transfers, the server must be enabled with the SFTP program, and then clients can access the server, provided they have the correct credentials. One of the first SFTP operations is the same as that of FTP: an identification function that uses a username and an authorization function that uses a password. There is no anonymous SFTP account by definition, so access is established and controlled from the server using standard access control lists (ACLs), IDs, and passwords.

FTPS

FTPS is the implementation of FTP over an SSL/TLS-secured channel. This supports complete FTP compatibility, yet provides the encryption protections enabled by SSL/TLS. FTPS commonly runs on port 990 but can also run on port 21. When FTPS runs on port 990, it is referred to as *implicit FTPS* because the use of port 990 implies a secure connection. Conversely, FTPS running on port 21 is an *explicit FTPS* connection. When a client connects to an FTPS server on port 990, the assumption is that the client intends to perform SSL/TLS. Therefore, the TLS handshake begins with the session. FTP clients who connect on port 21 and intend to use TLS for security will need to take an extra step to explicitly state their intentions by sending an AUTH SSL or AUTH TLS command to the server. Once the server receives this command, the two parties perform a TLS handshake and enable a secure channel.

Vulnerabilities

Modern encryption technology can provide significant levels of privacy, up to military-grade secrecy. The use of protocols such as TLS provides a convenient method for end users to use cryptography without having to understand how it works. This can result in complacency—the impression that once TLS is enabled, the user is safe, but this is not necessarily the case. If a Trojan program is recording keystrokes and sending the information to another unauthorized user, for example, TLS cannot prevent the security breach. If the user is connecting to an untrustworthy site, the mere fact that the connection is secure does not prevent the other site from running a scam.

> TLS is not a guarantee of security. All TLS can do is secure the transport link between the computer and the server. A number of vulnerabilities can still affect the security of the system. A keylogger on the client can copy the secrets before they go to the TLS-protected link. Malware on either end of the secure communication can copy and/or alter transmissions outside the secure link.

Using TLS and other encryption methods will not guard against your credit card information being "lost" by a company with which you do business. Protecting the communication channel is important, but it's not enough. Many of the security failures that result in data breaches are due to internal security failures within the company; they do not occur during data transfer to the firm. So even with secure web controls, data can be lost after being stored in a company database.

The key to understanding what is protected and where it is protected is to understand what these protocols can and cannot do. The TLS suite can protect data in transit, but not on either end in storage. It can authenticate users and servers, provided that the certificate mechanisms are established and used by both parties. Properly set up and used, TLS can provide a very secure method of authentication, followed by confidentiality in data transfers and data integrity checking. But again, all of this occurs during transit, and the protection ends once the data is stored.

Code-Based Vulnerabilities

The ability to connect many machines together to transfer data is what makes the Internet so functional for so many users. Browsers enable much of this functionality, and as the types of data have grown on the Internet, browser functionality has grown as well. But not all functions can be anticipated or included in each browser release, so the idea of extending browser functions through plug-ins became a standard. Browsers can perform many types of data transfer, and in some cases, additional helper programs, or plug-ins, can increase functionality for specific types of data transfers. In other cases, separate application programs may be called by a browser to handle the data being transferred. Common examples of these plug-ins and programs include Shockwave and Flash plug-ins, Windows Media Player, and Adobe Acrobat (both plug-in and standalone). The richness that enables the desired functionality of the Internet has also spawned some additional types of interfaces in the form of ActiveX components and Java applets.

In essence, all of these are pieces of code that can be written by third parties, distributed via the Internet, and run on your PC. If the code does what the user wants, the user is happy. But the opportunity exists for these applications or plug-ins to include malicious code that performs actions not desired by the end user. Malicious code designed to operate within a web browser environment is a major tool for computer crackers to use to obtain unauthorized access to computer systems. Whether delivered by HTML-based e-mail, by getting a user to visit a website, or even delivery via an ad server, the result is the same: malware performs malicious tasks in the browser environment.

Cross Check

Dangers of Software Vulnerabilities

Errors in software lead to vulnerabilities associated with the code being run. These vulnerabilities are exploited by hackers to perform malicious activity on a machine. These errors are frequently related to web-enabled programs, as the Internet provides a useful conduit for hackers to achieve access to a system. The problem of code vulnerabilities—from buffer overflows, to arithmetic overflows, to cross-site request forgeries, cross-site scripting, and injection attacks—is a serious issue that has many faces. It is noted in this chapter because web components are involved, but full details on the severity of and steps to mitigate this issue appear in Chapter 19. The next time you provide input to a web-based application, think of what malicious activity you could perform on the server in question.

Java

Java is a computer language invented by Sun Microsystems as an alternative to Microsoft's development languages. Designed to be platform independent and based on C, Java offers a low learning curve and a way of implementing programs across an enterprise, independent of platform. Java is now owned and managed by Oracle and is one of the leading object-oriented programming languages.

Most browsers initially adopted a security policy, restricting Java functionality on a client unless the program was loaded directly from the client's hard drive. Although this solved many problems initially, it also severely limited functionality. Today, browsers allow much more specific granularity on security for Java, based on security zones and user settings.

> Java is designed for safety, reducing the opportunity for system crashes. Java can still be used to perform malicious activities, and the fact that many users falsely believe it is safe increases its usefulness to attackers.

> Java and JavaScript are completely separate entities. JavaScript cannot be used to create applets or standalone applications. JavaScript resides inside HTML documents and can provide levels of interactivity to web pages that are not achievable with simple HTML. Java is used to create applications that run in a virtual machine or browser. JavaScript code is run on a browser only. JavaScript is not part of the Java environment.

JavaScript

JavaScript is a scripting language developed by Netscape and designed to be operated within a browser instance. JavaScript works through the browser environment. The primary purpose of JavaScript is to enable features such as the validation of forms before they are submitted to the server. Enterprising programmers found many other uses for JavaScript, such as manipulating the browser history files, which is now prohibited by design. JavaScript actually runs within the browser, and the code is executed by the browser itself. Control of JavaScript functions in Chrome is found under Settings | Privacy and Security | Site Settings | Content (JavaScript), as shown in Figure 17.2.

Although JavaScript was designed not to be able to access files or network resources directly, except through the browser functions, it has not proven to be as secure as desired. This fault traces back to a similar fault in the Java language, where security was added on, without the benefit of a comprehensive security model. So, although designers put thought and common sense into the design of JavaScript, the lack of a comprehensive security model left some security holes. For instance, a form could submit itself via e-mail to an undisclosed recipient for the purpose of eavesdropping, spamming, or causing other problems—imagine your machine sending death threat e-mails to high-level government officials from a rogue JavaScript implementation.

Further, most browsers do not have a mechanism to halt a running script, short of aborting the browser instance—and even this might not be possible if the browser has stopped responding to commands. Malicious JavaScripts can do many things, including opening two new windows every time you close one, each with the code to open two more. There is no way out of this one, short of killing the browser process from the operating system.

JavaScripts can also trick users into thinking they are communicating with one entity when in fact they are communicating with another. For example, a window may open asking whether you want to download and execute the new update from "http://www.microsoft.com.../update.exe," and what is covered by the ellipsis (...) is actually "/attacker.org/," and you assume this is a Microsoft address that is cut short by space restrictions on the display.

> Many websites may have behaviors that users deem less than desirable, such as popping open additional windows, either on top (pop-up) or underneath (pop-under). To prevent these behaviors, a class of applet referred to as a pop-up blocker may be employed. Although they may block some desired pop-ups, most pop-up blockers have settings to allow pop-ups only on selected sites. The use of a pop-up blocker assists in retaining strict control over browser behavior and enhances security for the user.

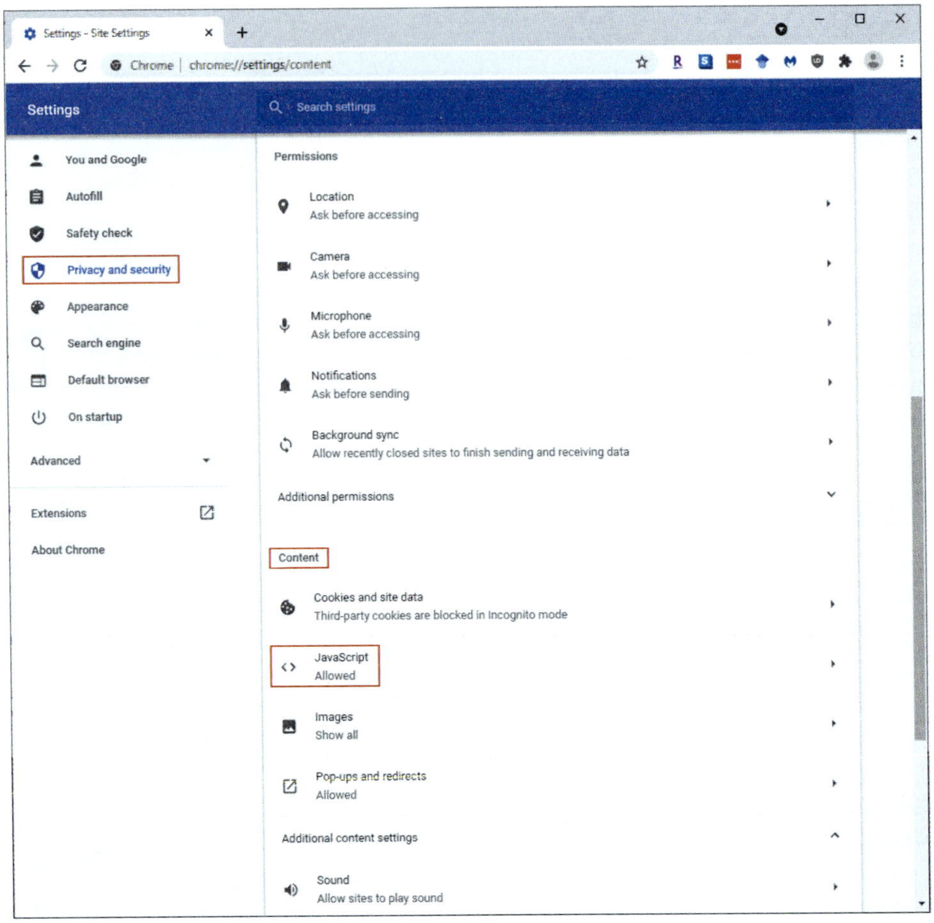

• **Figure 17.2** JavaScript configuration settings in Chrome

As a browser scripting language, JavaScript is here to stay. Its widespread popularity for developing applets such as animated clocks, mortgage calculators, and simple games will overcome its buggy nature and poor level of security.

Securing the Browser

A great deal of debate concerns the relative security issue of browser extensions versus the rich user interaction they provide. There is no doubt that the richness of the environment offered by various browser extension mechanisms can add to the user experience, but as is the case in most coding situations, added features means weaker security, all other things being constant. If nothing else, a development team must spend some portion of its time on secure development practices—time that some developers and marketers would prefer to spend on new features.

There is a wide range of activities one can do to increase browser security—from blocking scripts to invoking newer privacy-enhancing browsers such as the Brave browser. The Brave browser, built on top of the Chrome engine, gives users significant control over selected elements during browsing, including ads, trackers, and other elements used by servers as part of the browsing experience. Flat out blocking everything results in an unusable browsing experience in many cases, but offering control to the user over which elements are allowed provides balance, resulting in a secure browsing experience for the user.

> A man-in-the-browser (MITB) attack is a Trojan that infects web browser components such as browser plug-ins and other helper objects. MITB attacks are particularly dangerous because everything occurs at the application level on the user's system.

Server-Side Scripts

The Common Gateway Interface (CGI) has been replaced in many websites through **server-side scripting** technologies such as Java, **Active Server Pages (ASP)**, **ASP.NET**, and **PHP**. All these technologies operate in much the same fashion as CGI: they allow programs to be run outside the web server and to return data to the web server to be served to end users via a web page. The term *server-side script* is actually a misnomer, as the "script" is actually an executable program that's either interpreted or run in a virtual machine. Each of these newer technologies has advantages and disadvantages, but all of them have stronger security models than CGI. With these security models come reduced functionality and, because each is based on a different language, a steeper learning curve. Still, the need for adherence to programming fundamentals exists in these technologies—code must be well designed and well written to avoid the same vulnerabilities that exist in all forms of code. Buffer overflows are still an issue. Changing languages or technologies does not eliminate the basic security problems associated with incorporating open-ended user input into code. Understanding and qualifying user responses before blindly using them programmatically is essential to the security of a system.

Cookies

> Cookies come in two types: session and persistent. Session cookies last only during a web browsing session with a website. Persistent cookies are stored on the user's hard drive and last until an expiration date.

Cookies are small chunks of ASCII text passed within an HTTP stream to store data temporarily in a web browser instance. Invented by Netscape, cookies pass back and forth between web server and browser and act as a mechanism to maintain state in a stateless world. *State* is a term that describes the dependence on previous actions. By definition, HTTP traffic served by a web server is *stateless*—each request is completely independent of all previous requests, and the server has no memory of previous requests. This dramatically simplifies the function of a web server, but it also significantly complicates the task of providing anything but the most basic functionality in a site. Cookies were developed to bridge this gap. Cookies are passed along with HTTP data through a Set-Cookie message in the header portion of an HTTP message.

A cookie is actually a series of name-value pairs stored in memory within a browser instance. The specification for cookies established several specific name-value pairs for defined purposes. Additional name-value pairs may be defined at will by a developer. The specified set of name-value pairs includes the following:

- **Expires** This field specifies when the cookie expires. If no value exists, the cookie is good only during the current browser session and will not be persisted to the user's hard drive. Should a value be given, the cookie will be written to the user's machine and persisted until this datetime value occurs.

- **Domain** Specifies the domain where the cookie is used. Cookies were designed as memory-resident objects, but because the user or data can cause a browser to move between domains—say, from comedy.net to jokes.org—some mechanism needs to tell the browser which cookies belong to which domains.
- **Path** This name-value pair further resolves the applicability of the cookie into a specific path within a domain. If path = /directory, the cookie will be sent only for requests within /directory on the given domain. This allows a level of granular control over the information being passed between the browser and server, and it limits unnecessary data exchanges.
- **Secure** The presence of the keyword **[secure]** in a cookie indicates that it is to be used only when connected in a TLS session. This does not indicate any other form of security, as cookies are stored in plaintext on the client machine. Cookie management on a browser is normally an invisible process, but most browsers have methods for users to examine and manipulate cookies on the client side. Chrome users can examine, delete, and block individual cookies through the interface shown in Figure 17.3.

So what good are cookies? Disable cookies in your browser and go to some common sites that you visit, and you'll quickly learn the usefulness of

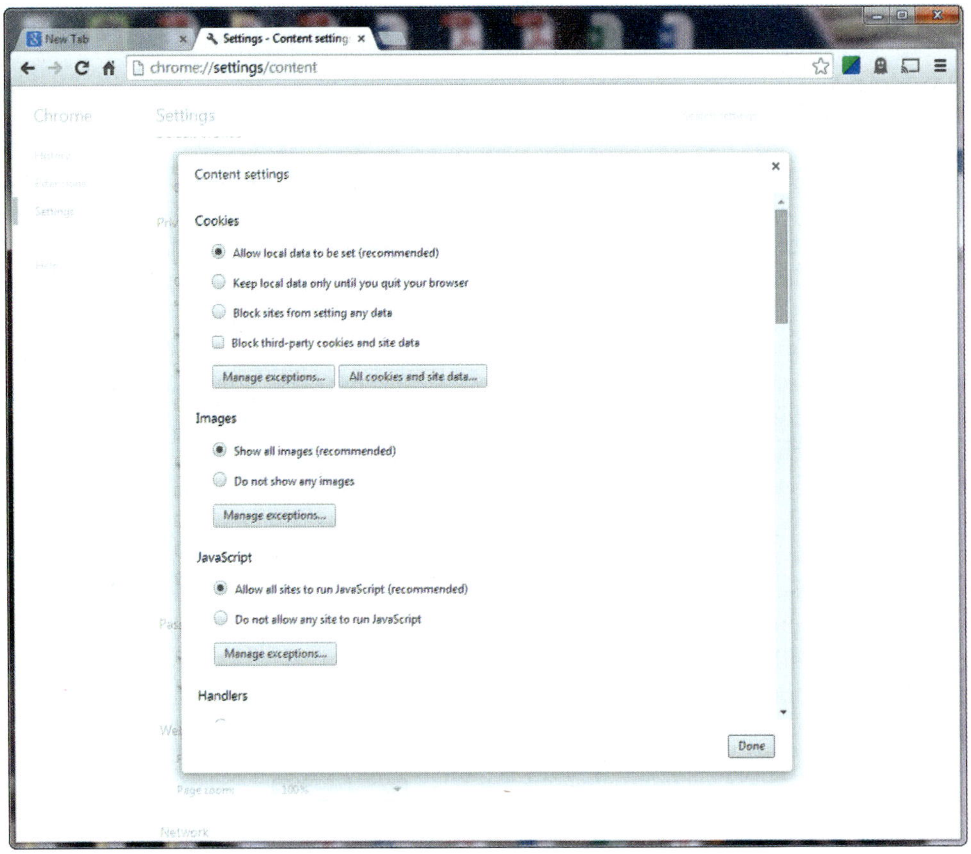

• **Figure 17.3** Chrome cookie management

cookies. Cookies store a variety of information, from customer IDs to data about previous visits. Because cookies are stored on a user's machine in a form that will allow simple manipulation, they must always be considered suspect and are not suitable for use as a security mechanism. They can, however, allow the browser to provide crucial pieces of information to a web server. Advertisers can use them to control which ads you are shown, based on previous ads you have viewed. Specific sites can use cookies to pass state information between pages, enabling functionality at the user's desired levels. Cookies can also remember your ZIP code for a weather site, your ID for a stock tracker site, the items in your shopping cart—these are all typical cookie uses. In the final analysis, cookies are a part of the daily web experience; they are here to stay and are useful if not used improperly (such as to store security data and to provide ID and authentication).

Disabling Cookies

If the user disables cookies in a browser, this type of information will not be available for the web server to use. IETF RFC 2109 describes the HTTP state-management system (cookies) and specifies the following specific cookie functions to be enabled in browsers:

- The ability to turn on and off cookie usage
- An indicator as to whether cookies are in use
- A means of specifying cookie domain values and lifetimes

Several of these functions have already been discussed, but to surf cookie-free requires more than a simple step. Telling a browser to stop accepting cookies is a setup option available through an Options menu, but this has no effect on cookies already received and stored on the system. To prevent the browser from sending cookies already received, the user must delete the cookies from the system. This bulk operation is easily performed, and then the browser can run cookie-free. Several third-party tools enable an even finer granularity of cookie control.

> With new EU privacy rules, and the use of cookies as a tracking mechanism, sites have had to ask permission before invoking cookies for tracking. You will see this all over the web as it is easier to ask all, than to try and identify the specific EU affected customers.

Browser Plug-Ins

The addition of browser scripting components allows a browser to change how it handles data, tremendously increasing its functionality as a user interface. However, all data types and all desired functionality cannot be offered through these programming technologies. Plug-ins are used to fill the gaps.

Plug-ins are small application programs that increase a browser's ability to handle new data types and add new functionality. Adobe has developed Acrobat Reader, a plug-in that enables a browser to read and display Portable Document Format (PDF) files directly in a browser. PDF files offer platform independence for printed documents and are usable across a wide array of platforms—they are a compact way to provide printed information.

With Microsoft's newer browser, Edge, comes a new method of adding functionality. **Browser extensions** is the name for add-ons to Edge, and they are found in the Microsoft app store, accessible from all Microsoft

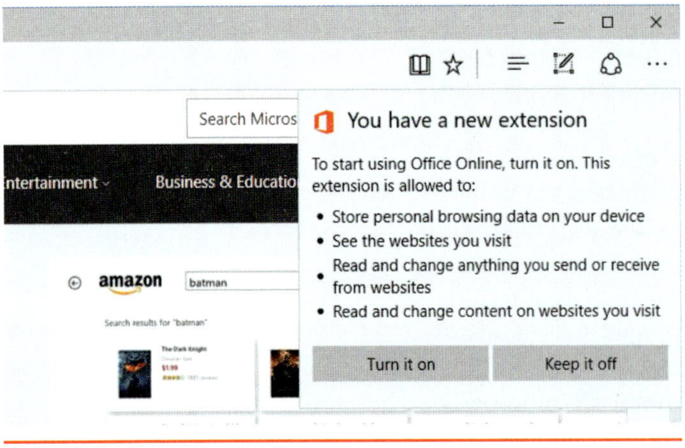

Figure 17.4 Browser extensions in Microsoft Edge

platforms. Figure 17.4 shows the addition of a new extension in the Microsoft Edge browser.

The combination of a development environment for developers and plug-in-enabled browsers that can display the content has caused these technologies to see widespread use. The result is a tremendous increase in visual richness in web communications, and this, in turn, has made the Web more popular and has increased usage in various demographic segments.

Until recently, these plug-ins have had a remarkable safety record. As Flash-based content grew more popular, crackers have examined the Flash plug-ins and software, determined vulnerabilities, and developed exploit code to use against the Flash protocol. Adobe has patched the issue, but because Apple has decided not to use Flash on its iPhones and iPads, the death of Flash is on the horizon.

The move of add-ons to curated environments like Microsoft's app store also provides a means for controlling malicious content. The safety record is unknown and based on previous systematic attempts to curate content for safety, it is fairly safe to say that the record will not be 100 percent safe, as errors will creep in due to complacent moderators.

> **Tech Tip**
>
> **Browser Malware**
>
> *The circumvention of browser functionality is a common form of malware. Browser malware exploits security vulnerabilities in the browser itself, its extensions, and plug-ins.*

Malicious Add-Ons

Add-ons are distributed pieces of code that allow extra functionality to be added to an existing program. An example of these are **browser helper objects (BHOs)**, which provide a means of creating a plug-in module that is loaded with Internet Explorer as well as a means of adding capability to the browser. The functionality can be significant, as in the case of the Adobe Acrobat BHO, which allows PDFs to be rendered in the browser. A BHO has unrestricted access to the Internet Explorer event model and can perform actions such as capturing keystrokes.

Other programs can have add-ons that utilize the permissions given the master program. You should only use add-ons from trusted sources, and you need to understand the level of interaction risk they pose.

Code Signing

To enable security and consumer confidence in downloaded programs, Microsoft developed **Authenticode**, a system that uses digital signatures and allows Windows users to determine who produced a specific piece of code and whether or not the code has been altered. As in the case of Java, safety and security are different things, and Authenticode promotes neither in reality. Authenticode provides limited accountability at the time of download and provides reasonable assurance that the code has not been changed since the time of signing. Authenticode does not identify whether a piece of code will cause damage to a system, nor does it regulate how code is used, so a perfectly safe program under one set of circumstances may be malicious if used improperly. As with a notary's signature, recourse is very limited—if code is signed by a terrorist organization and the code ruins your machine, all Authenticode did was make it seem legitimate. It is still incumbent upon the users to know from whom they are getting code and to determine whether or not they trust that organization.

Critics of Authenticode and other code-signing techniques are not against code signing, because this is a universally recognized good thing. What the critics argue is that code signing is not a panacea for security issues and that marketing it as doing more than it really does is irresponsible. Understanding the nuances of security is important in today's highly technical world, and leaving the explanations to marketing departments is not the ideal solution.

Code signing was an attempt to bring the security of shrink-wrapped software to software downloaded from the Internet. Code signing works by adding a digital signature and a digital certificate to a program file to demonstrate file integrity and authenticity. The certificate identifies the author, and the digital signature contains a hash value that covers the code, certificate, and signature to prove integrity, and this establishes the integrity of the code and publisher via a standard browser certificate check. The purpose of a company signing the code is to state that it considers the code it created to be safe, and it is stating that the code will not do any harm to the system (to the company's knowledge). The digital signature also tells the user that the stated company is, indeed, the creator of the code.

The ability to use a certificate to sign an applet or a control allows the identity of the author of a control or applet to be established. This has many benefits. For instance, if a user trusts content from a particular vendor, such as Microsoft, the user can trust controls that are signed by Microsoft. This signing of a piece of code does not do anything other than identify the code's manufacturer and guarantee that the code has not been modified since it was signed.

A signed applet can be hijacked as easily as a graphic or any other file. The two ways an attacker could hijack a signed control are by inline access and by copying the file in its entirety and republishing it. **Inlining** is using an embedded control from another site with or without the other site's permission. Republishing a signed control is done much like stealing a GIF or JPEG image—a copy of the file is maintained on the unauthorized site and served from there instead of from the original location. If a signed control cannot be modified, why be concerned with these thefts, apart from the issue of intellectual property? The primary security concern comes from how the control is used. A cracker may be able to use a control in an unintended fashion, resulting in file loss or buffer overflow—conditions that weaken a system and can allow exploitation of other vulnerabilities. A common programming activity is cleaning up installation files from a computer's hard drive after successfully installing a software package. If a signed control is used for this task and permission has already been granted, then improperly using the control could result in the wrong set of files being deleted. The control will still function as designed, but the issue becomes who it is used by and how. These are concerns not addressed simply by signing a control or applet.

Application-Based Weaknesses

Web browsers are not the only aspect of software being abused by crackers. The application software written to run on servers and serve up the content for users is also a target. Web application security is a fairly hot topic in security circles, as it has become a prime target for professional crackers. Criminal hackers typically are after some form of financial reward, whether from stolen data, stolen identity, or some form of extortion. Attacking web-based applications has proven to be a lucrative venture for several reasons. First, the target is a rich environment, as company after company has developed a customer-facing web presence, often including custom-coded functionality that permits customer access to back-end systems for legitimate business purposes. Second, building these custom applications to high levels of security is a difficult if not impossible feat, especially given the corporate pressure on delivery time and cost.

> **Cross Check**
>
> **Common Application Vulnerabilities**
>
> Certain application vulnerabilities are commonly used by hackers to attack websites, including injection attacks, cross-site request forgeries, cross-site scripting attacks, and numeric attacks. These attacks use the browser's ability to submit input to a back-end server program, and they take advantage of coding errors on the back-end system, enabling behavior outside the desired program response. These errors are covered in more detail in Chapter 19, as they are fundamentally programming errors on the server side.

The same programmatic errors that plague operating systems, such as buffer overflows, can cause havoc with web-based systems. However, web-based systems have a new history of rich customer interactions, including the collection of information from the customer and dynamically using customer-supplied information to modify the user experience. This makes the customer a part of the application, and when proper controls are not in place, problems such as the MySpace-based Samy worm can occur. Different types of errors are commonly observed in the deployment of web applications, and these have been categorized into six logical groupings of vulnerabilities: authentication, authorization, logical attacks, information disclosure, command execution, and client-side attacks. A total of 24 different types of vulnerabilities have been classified by the Web Application Security Consortium (WASC), an international organization that establishes best practices for web application security.

The changing nature of the web-based vulnerabilities is demonstrated by the changing of the OWASP Top Ten list of web application vulnerabilities from year to year. The Open Web Application Security Project, or OWASP for short, is a worldwide free and open community focused on improving the security of application software. OWASP publishes a series of Top Ten vulnerability lists highlighting the current state-of-the-art threats facing web application developers. OWASP maintains a website (www.owasp.org) with significant resources to help firms build better software and eliminate these common and pervasive problems. The true challenge in this area is not just about coding, but also about developing an understanding of the nature of web applications and the difficulty of using user-supplied inputs for crucial aspects of a rich, user-experience-based web application. The programming errors included in the OWASP Top Ten list have plagued some of the largest sites and those with arguably the best talent, including Amazon, eBay, and Google.

Session Hijacking

For communication across the Web, it is common to create a session to control communication flows. Sessions can be established and controlled using a variety of methods, including TLS and cookies. It is important to securely implement the setup and teardown of a session, because if one party ends the communication without properly tearing down the communication session, an interloper can take over the session, continue after one of the parties has left, and impersonate that party. If you log in to your bank to conduct transactions, but allow a session hijacker in, then the hijacker can continue banking after you leave, using your account. This is one of the reasons it is so important to log off of banking and financial sites, rather than just closing the browser.

There are numerous methods of session hijacking, from man-in-the-middle attacks to sidejacking and browser takeovers. Sidejacking is the use of packet sniffing to steal a session cookie. Securing only the logon process and then switching back to standard HTTP can enable this attack methodology.

The best defenses are to use encryption correctly (TLS, not SSL) and to log out of and close applications when done. When you're using a browser with multiple tabs open, it is best to close the entire browser instance, not just the tab in question.

Client-Side Attacks

The web browser has become the major application for users to engage resources across the Web. The popularity and the utility of this interface have made the web browser a prime target for attackers to gain access and control over a system. A wide variety of attacks can occur via a browser, typically resulting from a failure to properly validate input before use. Unvalidated input can result in a series of injection attacks, header manipulation, and other forms of attack.

Cross-Site Scripting

A cross-site scripting attack is a code injection attack in which an attacker sends code in response to an input request. This code is then rendered by the web server, resulting in the execution of the code by the web server. Cross-site scripting attacks take advantage of a few common elements in web-based systems. Cross-site scripting is covered in detail in Chapter 19.

Header Manipulations

When HTTP is being dynamically generated through the use of user inputs, unvalidated inputs can give attackers an opportunity to change HTTP

A wide variety of attack vectors can be used against a client machine, including cache poisoning, cross-site scripting, cross-user defacement, page hijacking, cookie manipulation, and open redirect. Chapter 19 discusses attack vectors in detail.

elements. When user-supplied information is used in a header, it is possible to create a variety of attacks, including cache poisoning, cross-site scripting, cross-user defacement, page hijacking, cookie manipulation, and open redirect.

Autofill and Hidden Fields

Autofill is a browser mechanism designed to make it easier for users to submit common data to web pages. The mechanics of how this is done varies from browser to browser, but the basic idea is that you identify what you wish to autofill and the browser prepopulates known fields by name for you. This is a convenience factor but can also be a risk if the fields it is populating are hidden. Not all browsers will autofill hidden fields, but those that do can be giving away items such as your e-mail address, phone number, house address, credit card details, and so on—all based on previous entries and without you noticing because the fields are hidden.

Web 2.0 and Security

A relatively new phenomenon known as Web 2.0 has swept the Internet. Web 2.0 is a collection of technologies designed to make websites more useful for users. From newer languages and protocols, such as JSON and AJAX, to user-provided content, to social networking sites and user-created mashups, the Internet has changed dramatically from its static HTML roots. A wide range of security issues are associated with this new level of deployed functionality.

The new languages and protocols add significant layers of complexity to a website's design, and errors can have significant consequences. Early efforts by Google to add Web 2.0 functionality to its applications created holes that allowed hackers access to a logged-in user's Gmail account and password. Google has fixed these errors, but they illustrate the dangers of rushing into new functionality without adequate testing. The fine details of Web 2.0 security concerns are far too numerous to detail here—in fact, they could comprise their own book. The important thing to remember is that the foundations of security apply the same way in Web 2.0 as they do elsewhere. In fact, with more capability and greater complexity comes a greater need for strong foundational security efforts, and Web 2.0 is no exception.

Tech Tip

E-mail and Firewalls

For e-mail applications to work with e-mail servers, they need to communicate across specific channels. To ensure communication, TCP ports 25, 110, and 143 must be open on clients that need to connect to mail servers. This is for SMTP, POP3, and IMAP, respectively.

How E-mail Works

E-mail started with mailbox programs on early time-sharing machines, allowing researchers to leave messages for others using the same machine. The first intermachine e-mail was sent in 1972, and a new era in person-to-person communication was launched. E-mail proliferated, but it remained unsecured, only partly because most e-mail is sent in plaintext, providing no privacy in its default form. Current e-mail in its use is not different from its earlier versions; it's still a simple way to send a relatively short text message to another user. Users' dependence on e-mail has grown with the number of people accessing the Internet.

Internet e-mail depends on three primary protocols: SMTP, POP3, and IMAP. **Simple Mail Transfer Protocol (SMTP)** is the method by which mail is sent to the server as well as from server to server. SMTP by default uses TCP port 25. POP3 stands for Post Office Protocol version 3, which by default uses TCP port 110. POP3 is a method by which a client computer may connect to a server and download new messages. POP3 has been partly replaced by IMAP, or Internet Message Access Protocol, which uses TCP port 143 by default. IMAP is similar to POP3 in that it allows the client to retrieve messages from the server, but IMAP typically works in greater synchronization; for example, e-mails are left on the server until the client deletes them in the client, at which time IMAP instructs the server to delete them. As e-mail services became more standardized, the methods of transmission became easier to attack because they were not strange proprietary protocols. Also, as the world became more connected, there were many more available targets for the malware and commercial e-mails.

Secure versions of the common communication protocols exist via the STARTTLS method. STARTTLS is a means of using Transport Layer Security (TLS) to secure a communication channel for text-based communication protocols. Table 17.2 shows the port assignments associated with STARTTLS.

Table 17.2 STARTTLS Port Assignments

Protocol	Purpose	Normal Port	TLS Variant	TLS Port
SMTP	Send e-mail	25/587	SMTPS	465 (legacy)
POP3	Retrieve e-mail	110	POP3S	995
IMAP	Read e-mail	143	IMAPS	993

E-mail appears to be a client-to-client communication, between sender and receiver. In reality, a lot of steps are involved, as shown in Figure 17.5 and described here:

1. A user composes and sends an e-mail from the user's client machine.
2. The e-mail is sent to the client's e-mail server. In an Internet service provider (ISP) environment, this could be via the ISP. In the case of web mail, it is the mail service (Gmail, Hotmail/Live, and so on). In a corporate environment, it is the corporate mail server.
3. a. The receiving e-mail server scans the e-mail for viruses, malware, and other threats.

   b. The mail server uses DNS to obtain the recipient e-mail server address via an MX record.
4. The mail server prepares the e-mail for transit across the Internet to the recipient's mail server.
5. The e-mail is routed across the Internet.
6. The receiving e-mail server scans the e-mail for viruses, malware, and other threats.
7. The e-mail is passed to the recipient's in-box, where it can be read.

This list of steps leaves out a lot of details, but it provides the main steps in e-mail transference. The steps are remarkably similar for instant

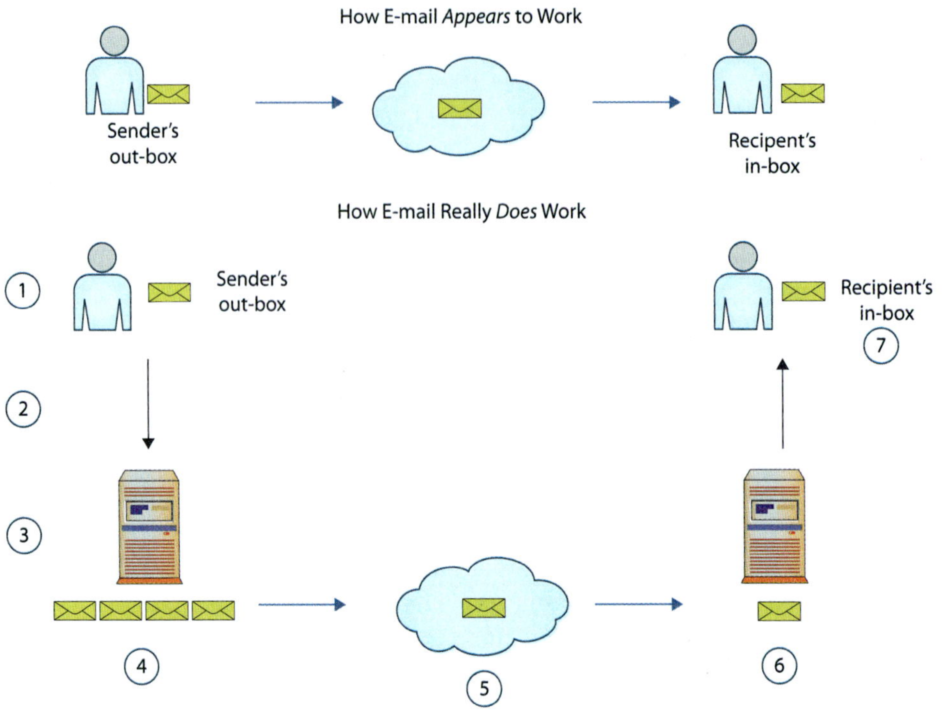

• **Figure 17.5** How e-mail works

messaging applications as well. Rather than in-boxes and e-mail as a medium, the instant messaging apps deliver the text messages directly to the screen of the app.

In technical terms, the application on the sender's machine is referred to as a **mail user agent (MUA)**, and the mail server is a **mail transfer agent (MTA)**. The recipient's mail server is referred to as a **mail delivery agent (MDA)**. These terms are used when discussing mail transfers to provide accuracy in the conversation. For communication from the MUA to the MTA, SMTP (port 25) is used, and communication from MTA to MTA is also SMTP. The protocol used for communication from the MDA to the MUA on the recipient machine is typically POP3/IMAP.

E-mail Structure

E-mail is structured in two elements: a header and the body. The entire message is sent via plain ASCII text, with attachments included using Base64 encoding. The e-mail header provides information for the handling of the e-mail between MUAs, MTAs, and MDAs. The following is a sample e-mail header:

```
Received: from smtp4.cc.uh.edu (129.7.234.211) by xFENode3B.mail.example.
net (129.7.40.150) with Microsoft SMTP Server id 8.2.255.0; Sat, 10 Apr 2021
18:54:42 -0500
Received: from smtp4.cc.uh.edu (smtp4.example.net [127.0.0.1]) by localhost
(Postfix) with SMTP id BC4DA1E004A for <waconklin@example.com>; Sat, 10 Apr
2021 18:53:55 -0500 (CDT)
Received: from nm22.bullet.mail.ne1.yahoo.com (nm22.bullet.mail.ne1.yahoo.com
```

```
 [98.138.90.85]) by smtp4.example.net (Postfix) with ESMTP id  538C31E0034 for
<waconklin@example.com>; Sat, 10 Apr 2021
 18:53:55 -0500 (CDT)
DKIM-Signature: v=1; a=rsa-sha256; c=relaxed/relaxed;
d=yahoo.com; s=s2048;
 t=1428796434; bh=esKcEn6Pe1DHaDx/5lqarnNbc5vZAFO5+z93Xt/06S0=;
h=Date:From:Reply-To:To:In-Reply-To:References:Subject:From:Subject;
b=OQTvNETmW6KKGn/cWXsQd43khwTbwsGpRFhpwB0iCopROLVxabwPryOB/6RpSb37JC5IYTxYrDjr
slDhaSBj1381Y8ior9CS83YyV3JnRzk6F+YrDQDUXAuG5vbhDo9lKUX0pNa/R4rdvK47T6uO9
2k7wf1++egSLATDeId5ccUFUZLBQpxBJx6WtLJbI6eValGPQLgLCNdhedkgGBEugp+Yfc0xDr97
5euYFsxwLDS36pi88etIkMso0FDbQLsGfk3SneIkm+o5wSDq7lAsWk3NX4p+yFjW16V
7OjQSg2Xf6KnNt9gUh9v98U+WW/Crwlq110xUHL1FjiP6oNsGkw==
Received: from [98.138.100.112] by nm22.bullet.mail.ne1.yahoo.com
with NNFMP;
 10 Apr 2021 23:53:54 -0000
Received: from [98.138.89.173] by tm103.bullet.mail.ne1.yahoo.com
with NNFMP;
 10 Apr 2021 23:53:53 -0000

Received: from [127.0.0.1] by omp1029.mail.ne1.yahoo.com with NNFMP;
10 Apr 2021 23:53:53 -0000
X-Yahoo-Newman-Property: ymail-5
X-Yahoo-Newman-Id: 880223.99814.bm@omp1029.mail.ne1.yahoo.com
X-YMail-OSG: NKvYQJkVM1kWuLmyDvNnFXECaMumy9LBgfZhcKRiubzkoq9_NVdEUqlT7hMlkOv
1oWFqcbcyiJwpOTgEmUZIsGX2ZpKSfNrUUzmQ3.ksRewbg9xRVVDqnQbdJksIfeePVCUGNJ26elD
Ts4mEjfkzWPGKiXkxmy8iNhDzszw0RmJpDOrRDymsdTE3ObnKA83ZXSj9w0CwXnkJ_UtmVSWtyl0
NLDv8KRSPl0IaW8APZeaAmmTKPO06z.8jJg.GOGWAZbonqsm_zXvMjcfmmQ8wd8PBOh2pFqzvwvn
cfwHL3.iDmOzcNBYrF5mNfbmdaoHAztYxA8edB2kFqN3vje3VJPkoPOCiOhq_c_wFIs8E6W02VjK
0gCJRLAPEwyo30kyz_QDyGgfpfv4GAXrz9bQet8sy_e2ztRyVnj9GDu.DHSYnU5TaTLzvRhMQO3p
082zOb2Qm_4Miilk36RzypHRAEWh_GlTxr3sRloz1RhsioTgMYqksk0E_7P2bBJOJb3HsTyG2o_i
swOuz7CIt8U67Fe1IlDoPsU5hJj8DXHlSK_pGUl3j

Received: by 98.138.105.206; Sat, 10 Apr 2021 23:53:53 +0000
Date: Sat, 10 Apr 2021 23:53:52 +0000
From: Sender Name SenderName@yahoo.com
Reply-To: Sender Name SenderName@yahoo.com
To: "Conklin, Wm. Arthur" waconklin@example.com
Message-ID: 517184424.1041513.1428796432644.JavaMail.yahoo@mail.yahoo.com
In-Reply-To: 9AF24FE2BE34BC42A10F1DE75C05D8871652896780@EXSERVER3.example.com
References: 9AF24FE2BE34BC42A10F1DE75C05D8871652896780@EXSERVER3.example.com
Subject: Re: Homework Lab 2
MIME-Version: 1.0
Content-Type: multipart/mixed;
        boundary="----=_Part_1041512_683422731.1428796432643"
X-PMX-Version: 6.0.3.2322014, Antispam-Engine: 2.7.2.2107409, Antispam-Data:
2021.4.10.234523
X-PerlMx-Spam: Gauge=IIIIIIII, Probability=8%, Report='
HTML_50_70 0.1, HTML_NO_HTTP 0.1, BODYTEXTH_SIZE_10000_LESS 0,
BODYTEXTP_SIZE_3000_LESS 0, BODY_SIZE_10000_PLUS 0, DKIM_SIGNATURE 0,
ECARD_KNOWN_DOMAINS 0, REFERENCES 0, WEBMAIL_SOURCE 0, __ANY_URI 0,
__BOUNCE_CHALLENGE_SUBJ 0, __BOUNCE_NDR_SUBJ_EXEMPT 0, __C230066_P1_5 0,
Return-Path: SenderName@yahoo.com
```

The specific elements shown in this header will be examined throughout this chapter. What is important to note is that the format of the message and its attachments are in plaintext.

MIME

When a message has an attachment, the protocol used to deliver the message is **Multipurpose Internet Mail Extensions (MIME)**. This protocol allows the exchange of different kinds of data across text-based e-mail systems. When MIME is used, it is marked in the header of the e-mail, along with supporting elements to facilitate decoding. The following is an excerpt from a header that has MIME elements:

```
Content-Type: multipart/alternative;
 boundary="------------040905030006040404060008"
This is a multi-part message in MIME format.
--------------040905030006040404060008
Content-Type: text/plain; charset=UTF-8; format=flowed
Content-Transfer-Encoding: 7bit
**Poster found in a Texas Gun Shop: ****
--------------040905030006040404060008
Content-Type: multipart/related;
 boundary="------------090502030607030308090400"
--------------090502030607030308090400
Content-Type: text/html; charset=UTF-8
Content-Transfer-Encoding: 8bit
<!DOCTYPE html PUBLIC "-//W3C//DTD HTML 4.01 Transitional//EN">
<html>
<head>
</head>
<body bgcolor="#ffffff" text="#000000">
<HTML E-MAIL message goes here>
</body>
</html>
--------------090502030607030308090400
Content-Type: image/jpeg
Content-Transfer-Encoding: base64
Content-ID: <part1.00060501.01000908@example.com>
/9j/4AAQSkZJRgABAQAAAQABAAD/2wBDAAUDBAQEAwUEBAQFBQUGBwwIBwcHBw8LCwkMEQ8S
EhEPERETFhwXExQaFRERGCEYGh0dHx8fExciJCIeJBweHx7/2wBDAQUFBQcGBw4ICA4eFBEU
Hh4eHh4eHh4eHh4eHh4eHh4eHh4eHh4eHh4eHh4eHh4eHh4eHh4eHh4eHh4eHh4eHh7/wAAR
CAJYAaQDASIAAhEBAxEB/8QAHwAAAQUBAQEBAQEAAAAAAAAAAAECAwQFBgcICQoL/8QAtRAA
AgEDAwIEAwUFBAQAAAF9AQIDAAQRBRIhMUEGE1FhByJxFDKBkaEII0KxwRVS0fAkM2JyggkK
BAcFBAQAAQJ3AAECAxEEBSExBhJBUQdhcRMiMoEIFEKRobHBCSMzUvAVYnLRChYk
NOEl8RcYGRomJygpKjU2Nzg5OkNERUZHSElKU1RVVldYWVpjZGVmZ2hpanN0dXZ3eHl6goOE
hYaHiImKkpOUlZaXmJmaoqOkpaanqKmqsrO0tba3uLm6wsPExcbHyMnK0tPU1dbX2Nna4uPk
5ebn6Onq8vP09fb3+Pn6/9oADAMBAAIRAxEAPwD46nml8+T96/3j/EfWo/Om/wCesn/fRpZ/
+PiT/fP86ioAk86b/nrJ/wB9Gjzpv+esn/fRqOigCTzpv+esn/fRo86b/nrJ/wB9Go6KAJPO
m/56yf8AfRo86b/nrJ/30ajooAk86b/nrJ/30aPOm/56yf8AfRqOigCTzpv+esn/AH0aPOm/
56yf99Go6KAJPOm/56yf99Gjzpv+esn/AH0ajooAk86b/nrJ/wB9Gjzpv+esn/fRqOigCTzp
```

The e-mail text has been replaced with <HTML E-MAIL message goes here> and the JPEG image is truncated, but the structure of the sample shows how content can be encoded and included in an e-mail.

Security of E-mail

E-mail can be used to move a variety of threats across the network. From spam, to viruses, to advanced malware in spear-phishing attacks, e-mail can act as a transmission medium. Spam is the most common attack but is now just a nuisance; the majority of spam is now mostly cleaned up by mail server filters and software.

The **e-mail hoax** has become another regular occurrence; Internet-based urban legends are spread through e-mail, with users forwarding them in seemingly endless loops around the globe. And, of course, people still haven't found a good way to block ubiquitous spam e-mails (a sampling of which is shown in Figure 17.6), despite the remarkable advance of every other technology.

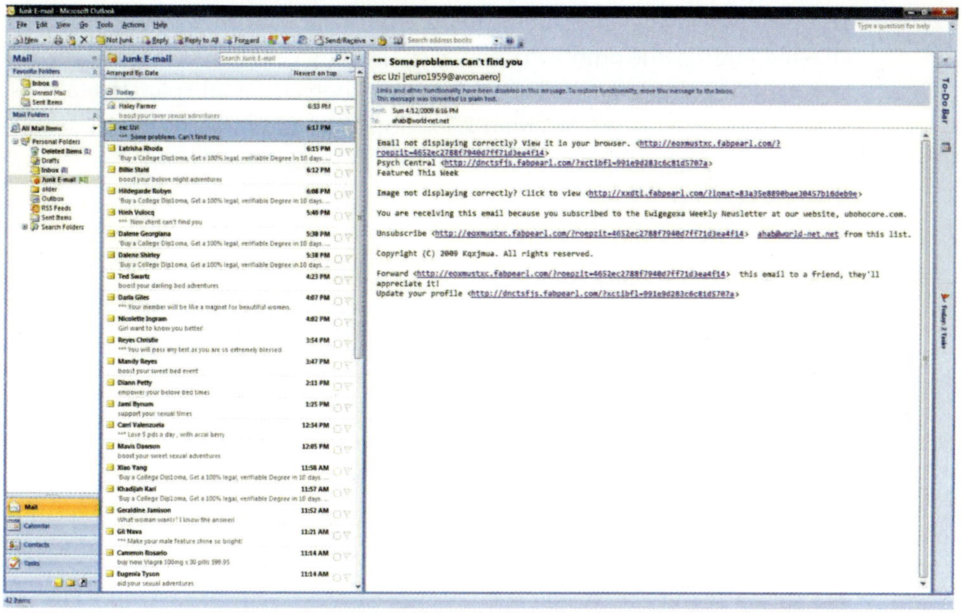

• **Figure 17.6** A typical list of spam e-mails

E-mail security is ultimately the responsibility of users themselves, because they are the ones who will actually be sending and receiving the messages. However, security administrators can give users the tools they need to fight malware, spam, and hoaxes. Secure/Multipurpose Internet Mail Extensions (S/MIME) and Pretty Good Privacy (PGP) are two popular methods used for encrypting e-mail, as discussed later in the chapter. Server-based and desktop-based virus protection can help against malicious code, and spam filters attempt to block all **unsolicited commercial e-mail**, also called **spam**. E-mail users need to be educated about security as well, however, because the popularity and functionality of e-mail is only going to increase with time.

Instant messaging (IM), while not part of the e-mail system, is similar to e-mail in many respects, particularly in the sense that it is commonly plaintext and can transmit files. IM's handling of files opens the application to virus exploitation just like e-mail.

Spam

Spam is the industry trade name for unsolicited e-mails. There are a variety of reasons that spam is sent. For one, it is low to no cost to send. Also, about 3 percent of users click the links in spam, so bottom line, it works. Spam can be sent by legitimate companies, using a shotgun approach to drive sales. This is generally seen as annoying and is avoided by most companies with images to protect. Currently, the most common types of spam in the U.S. are pharmacy/healthcare spam and dating spam. Spam is also used by criminals to send malware, to get users to click items they normally wouldn't, or to set a user up for a scam or fraudulent attack. There are entire **botnets** whose sole purpose is to spread spam for these causes, such as the Marina Botnet, Kraken, and Conficker.

Although spam levels are extreme, comprising as much as 60 percent of all e-mail traffic, the number of actual spam sources is remarkably lower. As few as 100 spammers account for nearly 80 percent of all spam. Details as to who these characters are, their ISPs, domains, and other technical details are publicized by the Spamhaus project (www.spamhaus.org/statistics/spammers/).

Malicious Code

> ⚠ Viruses and worms both can carry malicious payloads and cause damage. The difference is in how they are transmitted: viruses require a file to infect, whereas worms can exist independently of a file.

Viruses and worms are popular programs because they make themselves popular. When viruses were constrained to only one computer, they attempted to spread by attaching themselves to every executable program that they could find. This worked out very well for the viruses, because they could piggyback onto a floppy disk with a program that was being transferred to another computer. The virus would then infect the next computer, and the next computer after that. While often successful, virus propagation was slow, and floppies could be scanned for viruses.

The advent of computer networks was a computer virus writer's dream, allowing viruses to attempt to infect every network share to which the computer was attached. This extended the virus's reach from a set of machines that might share a floppy disk to every machine on the network. Because the e-mail protocol permits users to attach files to e-mail messages, as shown in Figure 17.7, viruses can travel by e-mail from one local network to another, anywhere on the Internet. This changed the nature of virus programs—they once were localized but now could spread virtually everywhere. E-mail gave the virus a global reach.

When active content was designed for the Web, in the form of Java and ActiveX scripts, these scripts were interpreted and run by the web browser. E-mail programs also would run these scripts, and that's when the trouble began. Some e-mail programs, most notably Microsoft Outlook, use a

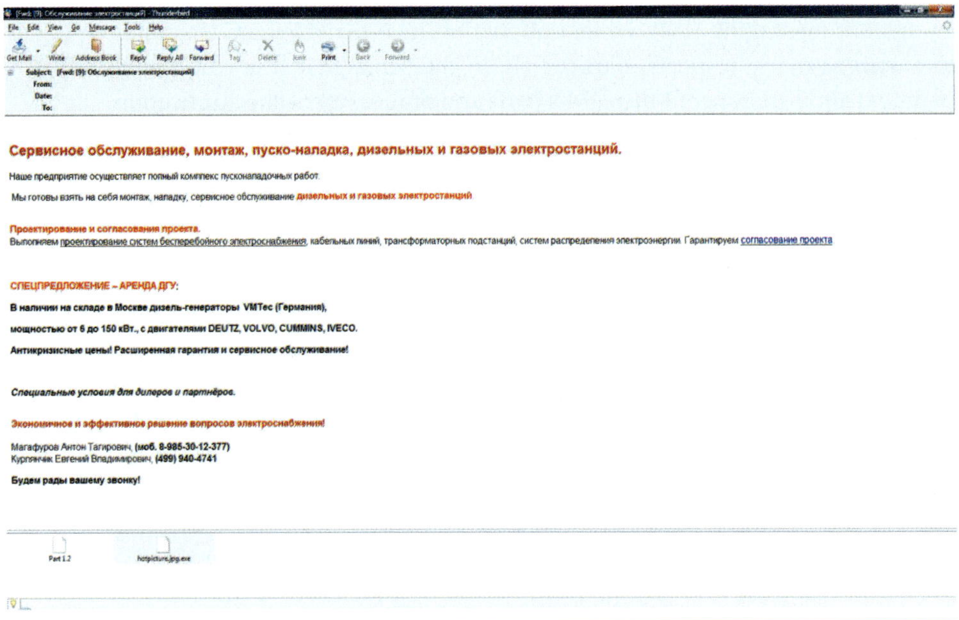

• **Figure 17.7** Viruses commonly spread through e-mail attachments.

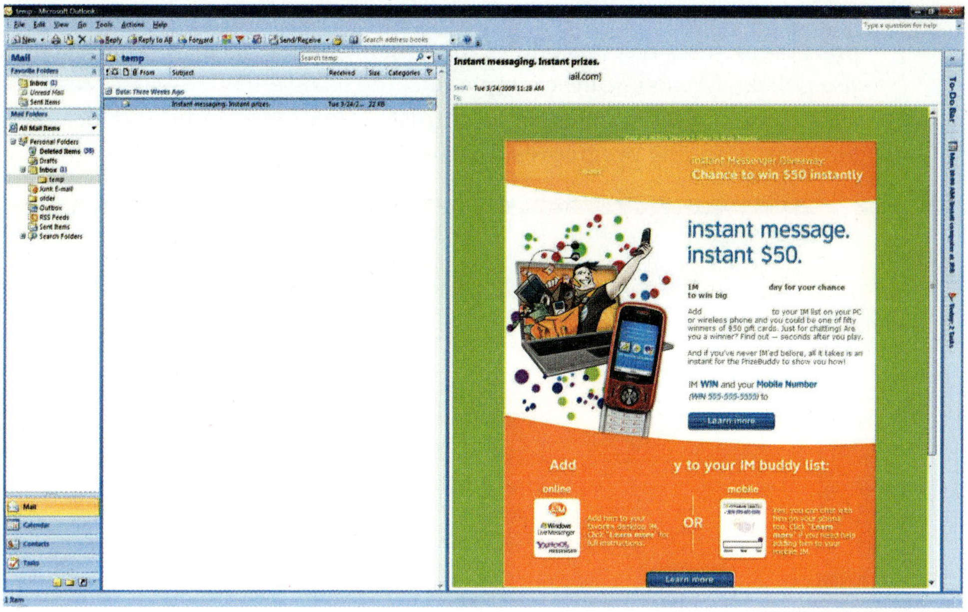

• **Figure 17.8** The preview pane on the right can execute code in e-mails without them being opened.

preview pane, which allows users to read e-mails without opening them in the full screen (see Figure 17.8).

Unfortunately, this preview still activates all the content in the e-mail message, and because Outlook supports Visual Basic scripting, it is vulnerable to e-mail worms. A user doesn't need to run the program or even open the e-mail to activate the worm—simply previewing the e-mail in the preview pane can launch the malicious content. This form of automatic execution was the primary reason for the spread of the ILOVEYOU worm.

All malware is a security threat, with the several different types having different countermeasures. The antivirus systems we have used for years have progressed to try and stop all forms of malicious software, but they are not a panacea. Worm prevention also relies on patch management of the operating system and applications. Viruses are launched by users, and because one of the most common transfer methods for viruses is through e-mail, the people using the e-mail system create the front line of defense against viruses. In addition to antivirus scanning of user systems, and possibly an e-mail virus filter, users need to be educated about the dangers of viruses.

Although the great majority of users are now aware of viruses and the damage they can cause, more education may be needed to instruct them on the specific things that need to be addressed when a virus is received via e-mail. These can vary from organization to organization and from e-mail software to e-mail software; however, some useful examples of good practices involve examining all e-mails for a known source as well as a known destination, especially if the e-mails have attachments. Strange files or unexpected attachments should always be checked with an antivirus program before execution. Users also need to know that some viruses can be executed simply by opening the e-mail or viewing it in the preview pane. Education and proper administration is also useful in configuring the e-mail software to be as virus resistant as possible—turning off scripting

Tech Tip

HTML E-mail

HTML e-mail can carry embedded instructions to download or run scripts that can be launched from the preview pane in some e-mail programs, without requiring that the user actively launch the attached program.

Tech Tip

E-mail Hygiene

All e-mail should be scanned for malware, spam, and other unwanted items before it truly enters the e-mail system in an organization. This reduces risk and also reduces the costs of backup. With spam comprising the majority of received e-mails, not having to back it up saves a lot of space.

support and the preview pane are good examples. Many organizations outline specific user responsibilities for e-mail, similar to network acceptable use policies (AUPs). Some examples include using e-mail resources responsibly, avoiding the installation of untrusted programs, and using localized antivirus scanning programs such as AVG.

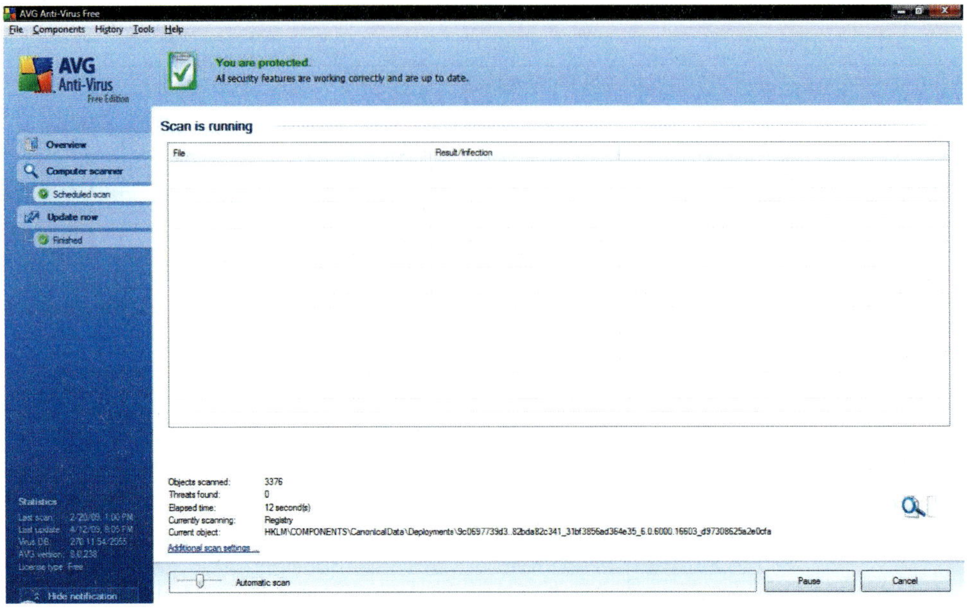

Another protection is to carefully create virus-scanning procedures. If possible, perform virus scans on every e-mail as it comes into the company's e-mail server. This is actually the one place that spam may prove useful. The explosion in spam mail has driven the adoption of e-mail-filtering gateways designed to greatly reduce spam messages. These specialized e-mail servers have evolved to attempt to protect against virus threats as well as spam. Some users will also attempt to retrieve e-mail offsite from a normal ISP account, which can bypass the server-based virus protection, so every machine should also be protected with a host-based virus protection program that scans all files on a regular basis and performs checks of files upon their execution. Although these steps will not eliminate the security risks of malicious code in e-mail, they will limit infection and help to keep the problem to manageable levels.

Hoax E-mails

> ⚠ Forwarding hoax e-mails and other jokes, funny movies, and non-work-related e-mails at work can be a violation of your company's acceptable use policy and result in disciplinary actions.

E-mail hoaxes are mostly a nuisance, but they do cost everyone, not only in the time wasted by receiving and reading the e-mails, but also in the Internet bandwidth and server processing time they take up. E-mail hoaxes are global urban legends, perpetually traveling from one e-mail account to the next, and most have a common theme of some story you must tell ten other people about right away for good luck or because of some virus that will harm your friends unless you tell them immediately. Hoaxes are similar to chain letters, but instead of promising a reward, the story in the e-mail is typically what produces the action.

Hoaxes have been circling the Internet for many years, and many websites are dedicated to debunking them, such as Snopes.com (see Figure 17.9).

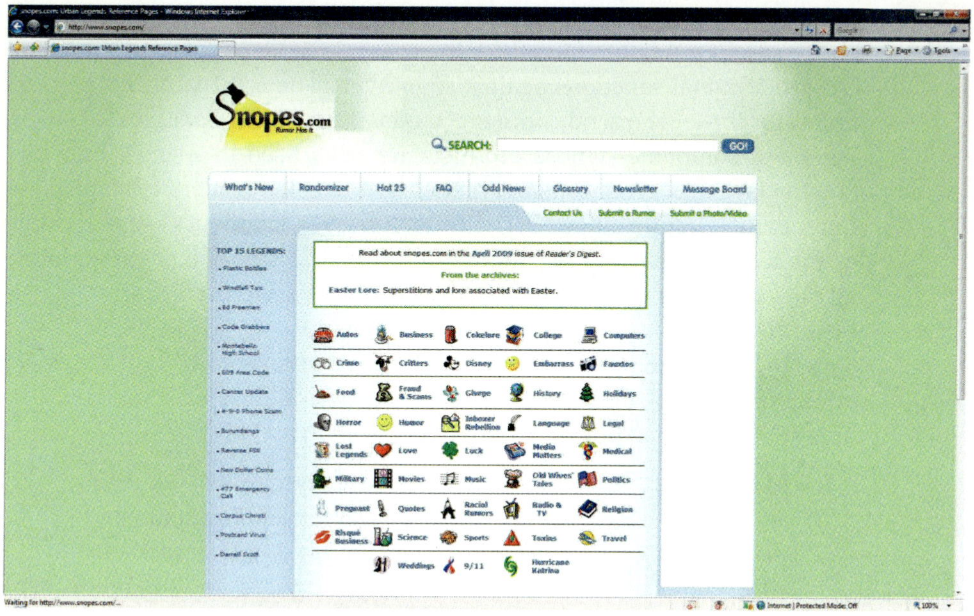

• **Figure 17.9** Snopes is an online reference for urban legends common in hoax e-mails.

The most important thing to do in this case is educate e-mail users: they should be familiar with a hoax or two before they go online, and they should know how to search the Internet for hoax information. Users need to apply the same common sense on the Internet that they would in real life: if it sounds too outlandish to be true, it probably is a fabrication. The goal of education about hoaxes should be to change user behavior to delete the hoax e-mail and not send it on.

Mail Gateway

E-mail is one of the reasons for connecting networks together, and *mail gateways* can act as solutions to handle mail-specific traffic issues. Mail gateways are used to process e-mail packets on a network, providing a wide range of e-mail-related services. From filtering spam, to managing data loss, to handling the encryption needs, mail gateways are combinations of hardware and software optimized to perform these tasks in the enterprise.

Spam Filter

The bane of users and system administrators everywhere, *spam* is essentially unsolicited or undesired bulk electronic messages. While typically applied to e-mail, spam can be transmitted via text message to phones and mobile devices, as postings to Internet forums, and by other means. If you've ever used an e-mail account, chances are you've received spam. Enter the issue of *spam filtering*, the identification and removal of spam traffic from an e-mail stream.

From a productivity and security standpoint, spam costs businesses and users billions of dollars each year, and it is such a widespread problem that the U.S. Congress passed the CAN-SPAM Act of 2003 to empower the Federal Trade Commission to enforce the act and the Department of Justice to enforce criminal sanctions against spammers. The act establishes requirements for those who send commercial e-mail, spells out penalties for spammers and companies whose products are advertised in spam if they violate the law, and gives consumers the right to ask e-mailers to stop spamming them. Despite all our best efforts, however, spam just keeps coming; as the technologies and techniques developed to stop the spam get more advanced and complex, so do the tools and techniques used to send out the unsolicited messages.

Here are a few of the more popular methods used to fight the spam epidemic; most of these techniques are used to filter e-mail but could be applied to other mediums as well:

- **Blacklisting** Blacklisting is essentially noting which domains and source addresses have a reputation for sending spam and then rejecting messages coming from those domains and source addresses. This is basically a permanent "ignore" or "call block" type of capability. Several organizations and a few commercial companies provide lists of known spammers.
- **Content or keyword filtering** Similar to Internet content filtering, this method filters e-mail messages for undesirable content or indications of spam. Much like content filtering of web content, filtering e-mail based on something like keywords can cause unexpected results, as certain terms can be used in both legitimate and spam e-mail. Most content-filtering techniques use regular expression matching for keyword filtering.
- **Trusted servers** The opposite of blacklisting, a trusted server list includes SMTP servers that are being "trusted" not to forward spam.
- **Delay-based filtering** Some Simple Mail Transfer Protocol (SMTP) servers are configured to insert a deliberate pause between the opening of a connection and the sending of the SMTP server's welcome banner. Some spam-generating programs do not wait for that greeting banner, and any system that immediately starts sending data as soon as the connection is opened is treated as a spam generator and dropped by the SMTP server.
- **PTR and reverse DNS checks** Some e-mail filters check the origin domain of an e-mail sender. Checking the reverse lookup reference from the DNS (the PTR record entry) can assist in determining the validity of the e-mail. If the reverse checks show the mail is coming from a dial-up user, home-based broadband, or a dynamically assigned address, or has a generic or missing domain, then the filter rejects it because these are common sources of spam messages.
- **Callback verification** As many spam messages use forged "from" addresses, some filters attempt to validate the "from" address of incoming e-mail. The receiving server can contact the sending server in an attempt to validate the sending address, but this is not always effective, as spoofed addresses are sometimes valid e-mail addresses that can be verified.

- **Statistical content filtering** Statistical filtering is much like a document classification system. Users mark received messages as either spam or legitimate mail and the filtering system learns from the user's input. The more messages that are seen and classified as spam, the better the filtering software should get at intercepting incoming spam. Spammers counteract many filtering technologies by inserting random words and characters into the messages, making it difficult for content filters to identify patterns common to spam.
- **Rule-based filtering** Rule-based filtering is a simple technique that merely looks for matches in certain fields or keywords. For example, a rule-based filtering system may look for any message with the words "get rich" in the subject line of the incoming message. Many popular e-mail clients have the ability to implement rule-based filtering.
- **Egress filtering** Some organizations perform spam filtering on e-mail leaving their organization as well, and this is called egress filtering. The same types of anti-spam techniques can be used to validate and filter outgoing e-mail in an effort to combat spam.
- **Hybrid filtering** Most commercial anti-spam methods use hybrid filtering, or a combination of several different techniques to fight spam. For example, a filtering solution may take each incoming message and match it against known spammers, then against a rule-based filter, then against a content filter, and finally against a statistical-based filter. If the message passes all filtering stages, it will be treated as a legitimate message; otherwise, it is rejected as spam.

Much spam filtering is done at the network or SMTP server level. It's more efficient to scan all incoming and outgoing messages with a centralized solution than it is to deploy individual solutions on user desktops throughout the organization. E-mail is essentially a proxied service by default: messages generally come into and go out of an organization's mail server. (Users don't typically connect to remote SMTP servers to send and receive messages, but they can.) Anti-spam solutions are available in the form of software that is loaded on the SMTP server itself or on a secondary server that processes messages either before they reach the SMTP server or after the messages are processed by the SMTP server. Anti-spam solutions are also available in appliance form, where the software and hardware are a single integrated solution. Many centralized anti-spam methods allow individual users to customize spam filtering for their specific in-box, specifying their own filter rules and criteria for evaluating inbound e-mail.

The central issue with spam is that, despite all the effort placed into building effective spam-filtering programs, spammers continue to create new methods for flooding in-boxes. Spam-filtering solutions are good but are far from perfect and continue to fight the constant challenge of allowing in legitimate messages while keeping the spam out. The lack of central control over Internet traffic also makes anti-spam efforts more difficult. Different countries have different laws and regulations governing e-mail, which range from draconian to nonexistent. For the foreseeable future, spam will continue to be a burden to administrators and users alike.

Recent efforts to remove specific language usages has suggested the new terms "allow list" and "block list/deny list" to replace "whitelisting" and "blacklisting," respectively.

Tech Tip

Controlling Port 25 on Mail Servers

SMTP authentication forces the users who use your server to obtain permission to send mail by first supplying a username and password. This helps to prevent open relay and abuse of your server and is highly recommended when your mail server has a routed IP address. This ensures that only known accounts can use your server's SMTP to send e-mail.

The number of connections to an SMTP server should be limited based on the specifications of the server hardware (memory, NIC bandwidth, CPU, and so on) and its nominal load per day. Limiting connections is useful to mitigate spam floods and denial-of-service (DoS) attacks that target your network infrastructure.

Mail Relaying

> **Tech Tip**
>
> **Open Relays**
>
> *Configure mail relay options carefully to avoid being an open relay. All mail servers have an option where you can specify which domains or IP addresses your mail server will relay mail for. It's very important to configure your mail relay parameter to be very restrictive so that your server does not become a gateway for spamming others, possibly resulting in your server getting blacklisted.*

One of the steps that the majority of system administrators running Internet e-mail servers have taken to reduce spam, and which is also a good e-mail security principle, is to shut down mail relaying. Port scanning occurs across all hosts all the time, typically with a single host scanning large subnets for a single port, and some of these people could be attempting to send spam e-mail. When they scan for TCP port 25, they are looking for SMTP servers, and once they find a host that is an **open relay** (a mail server that will accept mail from anyone), they can use that host to send as many commercial e-mails as possible. The reason that they look for an open relay is that spammers typically do not want the e-mails traced back to them. **Mail relaying** is similar to dropping a letter off at a post office instead of letting the postal carrier pick it up at your mailbox. On the Internet, that consists of sending e-mail from a separate IP address, making it more difficult for the mail to be traced back to you. SMTP server software is typically configured to accept mail only from specific hosts or domains. All SMTP software can and should be configured to accept only mail from known hosts, or to known mailboxes; this closes down mail relaying and helps to reduce spam.

Since it may not be possible to close all mail relays, and because some spammers will mail from their own mail servers, software must be used to combat spam at the recipient's end. Spam can be filtered at two places: at the host itself and at the server. Filtering spam at the host level is done by the e-mail client software and usually employs basic pattern matching, focusing on the sender, subject, or text of the e-mail. This fairly effective system uses an inordinate amount of bandwidth and processing power on the host computer, however. These problems can be solved by filtering spam at the mail server level. Many companies offer a dedicated appliance designed as a specialty e-mail server with the primary task of filtering spam. This server typically uses a combination of techniques listed here. It also implements an internal database to allow more granular filtering based on spam the appliance has already seen.

> **Try This!**
>
> **Testing Your Mail Server for Open Relay**
>
> Make note of your e-mail server settings, and then try to send regular SMTP mail when you are on a different network, such as the Wi-Fi network at a coffee shop or other similar open access Internet connection. You should get an error refusing relaying. If the mail goes through, that server might have a misconfiguration.

Greylisting

Another technique for combatting spam is known as *greylisting*. When an e-mail is received, it is bounced as a temporary rejection. SMTP servers that are compliant with RFC 5321 will wait a configurable amount of time and attempt retransmission of the message. Obviously, spammers will not retry sending of any messages, so spam is reduced.

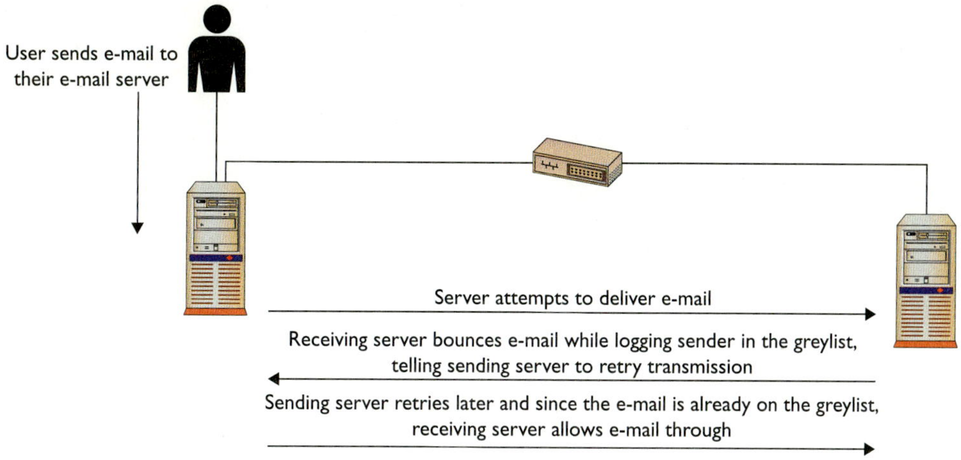

All the techniques we have discussed for dealing with spam have advantages and disadvantages, and most people will run some combination of techniques to attempt to filter as much spam as possible while not rejecting legitimate messages.

A side benefit of filtering spam at the receiving server is reduced e-mail. In enterprises, performing backups of information is a significant task. Backups are size dependent, both in cost and time, and reducing e-mail by eliminating spam can have significant impacts on e-mail backups. Spam reduction will also have a significant impact on the e-discovery process, as it reduces the quantity of material that needs to be searched. *E-discovery* is short for electronic discovery, the electronic component of a legal discovery process. The discovery process is court mandated and, when applied to a corporate environment, can cause the shutdown of corporate operations until the process is complete. For this reason, anything that makes the process easier or faster will benefit the corporation.

> **Tech Tip**
>
> **Activate Reverse DNS to Block Bogus Senders**
>
> *Messaging systems use DNS lookups to verify the existence of e-mail domains before accepting a message. A reverse DNS lookup is an option for fighting off bogus mail senders, as it verifies the sender's address before accepting the e-mail. Reverse DNS lookup acts by having SMTP verify that the sender's IP address matches both the host and domain names that were submitted by the SMTP client in the EHLO/HELO command. This works by blocking messages that fail the address-matching test, suggesting that they did not come from where they say they came from.*

Spam URI Real-time Block Lists

Spam URI Real-time Block Lists (SURBLs) detect unwanted e-mail based on invalid or malicious links within a message. Using an SURBL filter is a valuable tool to protect users from malware and phishing attacks. Not all mail servers support SURBL, but this technology shows promise in the fight against malware and phishing.

There are multiple methods of blocking lookup resources, through a method referred to as *blacklists* or *block lists*. A **Real-time Blackhole List (RBL)** is a list of e-mail servers that are known for allowing spam, or have open relays, and enable bad e-mail behaviors.

Sender Policy Framework (SPF)

Sender Policy Framework (SPF) validates the originating address of the e-mail. This is the originating mail server. SPF has been widely adopted by the major service providers, including Gmail, Hotmail, AOL, and Yahoo!, and

> **Tech Tip**
>
> **How SPF Works**
>
> *SPF works by using the SPF record, a small piece of text that is stored in the Domain Name Service (DNS) record of your domain name. Because only domain name owners, or other authorized parties, can alter DNS records, this is hard for a spammer to alter. The SPF record explains which servers are allowed to send e-mail from your domain. When a system receives e-mail, it looks up the SPF record and checks it against the details of the server that sent the message. If they match, the mail is kept; otherwise, it is usually trashed or put in the spam folder.*

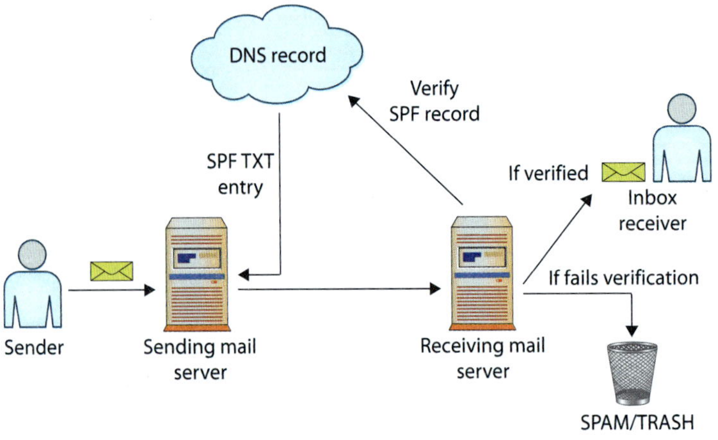

• **Figure 17.10** How SPF works

works using DNS records of the sender and acts at the time of sending (see Figure 17.10).

Sender ID Framework

Microsoft offers another server-based solution to spam, called the *Sender ID Framework (SIDF)*. SIDF attempts to authenticate messages by checking the sender's domain name against a list of IP addresses authorized to send e-mail by the domain name listed. Sender ID works similarly to SPF, and works via a Sender ID TXT record in your DNS. Sender ID has not had a lot of uptake other than by Bell Canada, so in most cases it is of limited use.

DomainKeys Identified Mail

DomainKeys Identified Mail (DKIM) is an e-mail validation system employed to detect e-mail spoofing. DKIM operates by providing a mechanism to allow receiving MTAs to check that incoming mail is authorized and that the e-mail (including attachments) has not been modified during transport. It does this through a digital signature included with the message that can be validated by the recipient using the signer's public key published in the DNS. DKIM is the result of the merging of two previous methods: DomainKeys and Identified Internet Mail. DKIM is the basis for a series of IETF standards-track specifications and is used by AOL, Gmail, and Yahoo! Mail. Any mail from these organizations should carry a DKIM signature.

The following is an example of the DKIM information that appears in an e-mail header:

```
DKIM-Signature: v=1; a=rsa-sha256; d=example.net; s=brisbane;
     c=relaxed/simple; q=dns/txt; l=1234; t=1117574938; x=1118006938;
     h=from:to:subject:date:keywords:keywords;
     bh=MTIzNDU2Nzg5MDEyMzQ1Njc4OTAxMjM0NTY3ODkwMTI=;
     b=dzdVyOfAKCdLXdJOc9G2q8LoXSlEniSbav+yuU4zGeeruD00lszZVoG4ZHRNiYzR
```

The two signatures, b and bh, relate as follows:

- **b** The actual digital signature of the contents (headers and body) of the mail message
- **bh** The body hash

DLP

Data loss prevention (DLP) is also an issue for outgoing mail. Two options are available: either use an integrated DLP solution that scans both outgoing traffic and mail or use a separate standalone system. A separate standalone system has the disadvantage that one must maintain two separate DLP keyword lists. Most enterprise-level DLP solutions have built-in gateway methods for integration with mail servers to facilitate outgoing mail scanning. This allows for the checking of outgoing mail traffic against the same list of keywords that other outgoing traffic is scanned against.

Mail Encryption

The e-mail concerns discussed so far in this chapter are all global issues involving security, but e-mail suffers from a more important security problem—the lack of confidentiality, or, as it is sometimes referred to, privacy. As with many Internet applications, e-mail has always been a plaintext protocol. When many people first got onto the Internet, they heard a standard lecture about not sending anything through e-mail that they wouldn't want posted on a public bulletin board. Part of the reason for this was that e-mail is sent with the cleartext of the message exposed to anyone who is sniffing the network. Any attacker at a choke point in the network could read all e-mail passing through that network segment.

Some tools can be used to solve this problem by using encryption on the e-mail's content. The first method is S/MIME and the second is PGP.

S/MIME

Secure/Multipurpose Internet Mail Extensions (S/MIME) is a *secure* implementation of the MIME protocol specification. MIME was created to allow Internet e-mail to support new and more creative features. The original e-mail RFC specified only text e-mail, so any nontext data had to be handled by a new specification—MIME. MIME handles audio files, images, applications, and multipart e-mails. MIME allows e-mail to handle multiple types of content in a message, including file transfers. Every time you send a file as an e-mail attachment, you are using MIME. S/MIME takes this content and specifies a framework for encrypting the message as a MIME attachment.

Cross Check

X.509 Certificates

In Chapter 7, you learned about X.509 certificate standards. Why is it important to have a standardized certificate format?

S/MIME was developed by RSA Data Security and uses the X.509 format for certificates. The original specification supported both 40-bit RC2 and 3DES for symmetric encryption, and it has been extended to use AES, as 3DES has been effectively retired. The protocol can affect the message in one of two ways: the host mail program can encode the message with

S/MIME, or the server can act as the processing agent, encrypting all messages between servers.

The host-based operation starts when the user clicks Send; the mail agent then encodes the message using the generated symmetric key. Next, the symmetric key is encoded with the remote user's public key for confidentiality or is signed with the local user's private key for authentication/nonrepudiation. This enables the remote user to decode the symmetric key and then decrypt the actual content of the message. Of course, all of this is handled by the user's mail program, requiring the user simply to tell the program to decode the message. If the message is signed by the sender, it will be signed with the sender's public key, guaranteeing the source of the message. The reason that both symmetric and asymmetric encryption are used in the mail is to increase the speed of encryption and decryption. Because encryption is based on difficult mathematical problems, it takes time to encrypt and decrypt. To speed this up, the more difficult process, asymmetric encryption, is used only to encrypt a relatively small amount of data, the symmetric key. The symmetric key is then used to encrypt the rest of the message.

The S/MIME process of encrypting e-mails provides integrity, privacy, and, if the message is signed, authentication. Several popular e-mail programs support S/MIME, including the popular Microsoft products Outlook and Windows Mail. They both manage S/MIME keys and functions through the E-mail Security screen, shown in Figure 17.11. This figure shows the different settings that can be used to encrypt messages and use

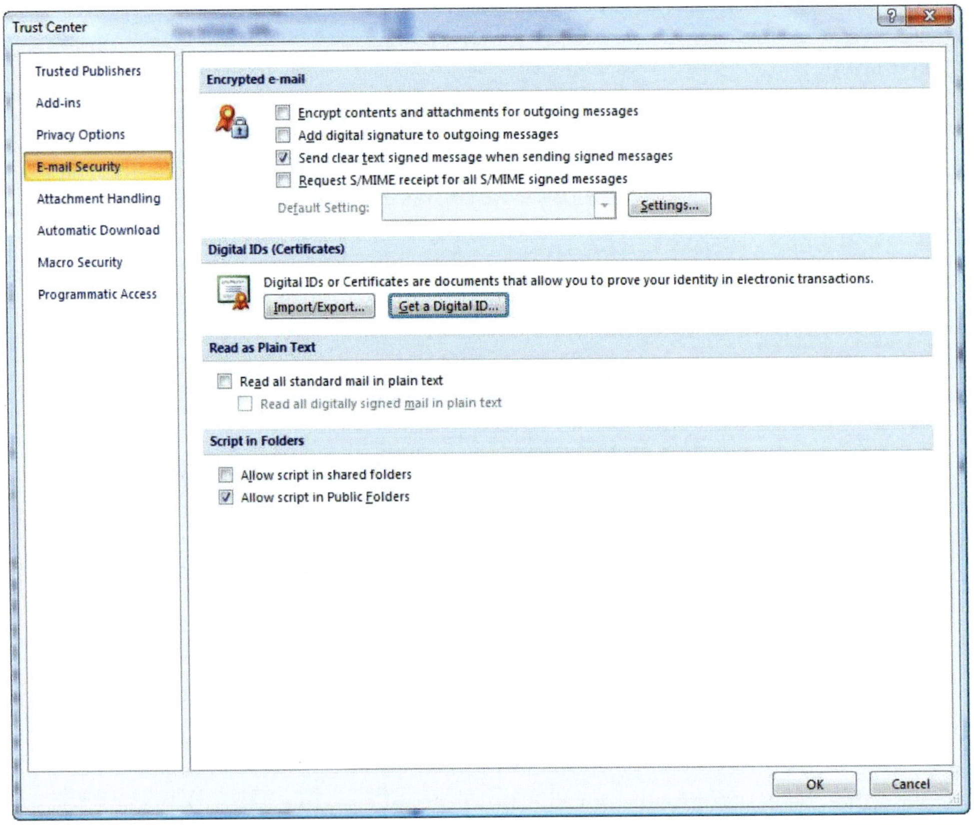

• **Figure 17.11** S/MIME options in Outlook

X.509 digital certificates. This allows interoperability with web certificates, and trusted authorities are available to issue the certificates. Trusted authorities are needed to ensure the senders are who they claim to be—an important part of authentication. In Windows Mail, the window is simpler (see Figure 17.12), but the same functions of key management and secure e-mail operation are available.

While S/MIME is a good and versatile protocol for securing e-mail, its implementation can be problematic. S/MIME allows the user to select low-strength (40-bit) encryption, which means a user can send a message that is thought to be secure but that can be more easily decoded than messages sent with 3DES encryption. Also, as with any protocol, bugs can exist in the software itself. Just because an application is designed for security does not mean that it, itself, is secure. Despite its potential flaws, however, S/MIME is a tremendous leap in security over regular e-mail.

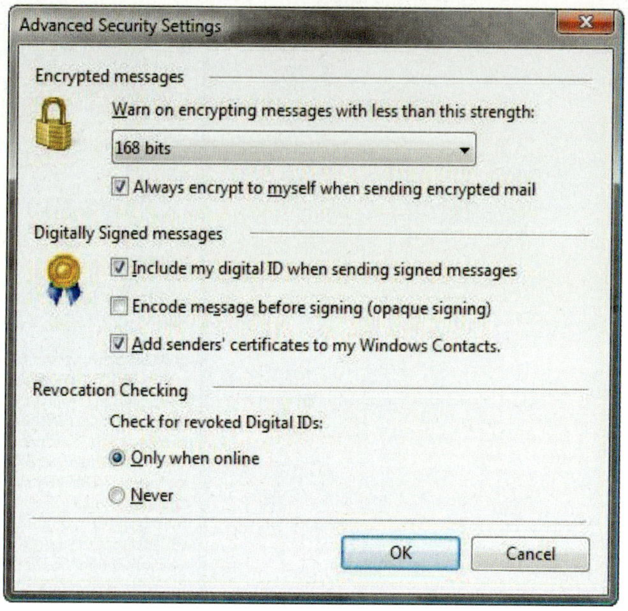

• **Figure 17.12** S/MIME options in Windows Mail

PGP

Pretty Good Privacy (PGP) implements e-mail security in a similar fashion to S/MIME, but PGP uses completely different protocols. The basic framework is the same: The user sends the e-mail, and the mail agent applies encryption as specified in the mail program's programming. The content is encrypted with the generated symmetric key, and that key is encrypted with the public key of the recipient of the e-mail for confidentiality. The sender can also choose to sign the mail with a private key, allowing the recipient to authenticate the sender. Currently, PGP supports the public key infrastructure (PKI) provided by multiple vendors, including X.509 certificates and Lightweight Directory Access Protocol (LDAP) key sources such as Microsoft's Active Directory.

In Figure 17.13, you can see how PGP manages keys locally in its own software. This is where you store not only your local keys, but also any keys that were received from other users. A free key server is available for storing PGP public keys. PGP can generate its own keys using either Diffie-Hellman or RSA, and it can then transmit the public keys to the PGP LDAP server so other PGP users can search for and locate your public key to communicate with you. This key server is convenient, as each person using PGP for communications does not have to implement a server to handle key management. For the actual encryption of the e-mail content itself, PGP supports International Data Encryption Algorithm (IDEA), 3DES, and Carlisle Adams and Stafford Tavares (CAST) for symmetric encryption. PGP provides pretty good security against brute force attacks by using a 3DES key length of 168 bits, an IDEA key

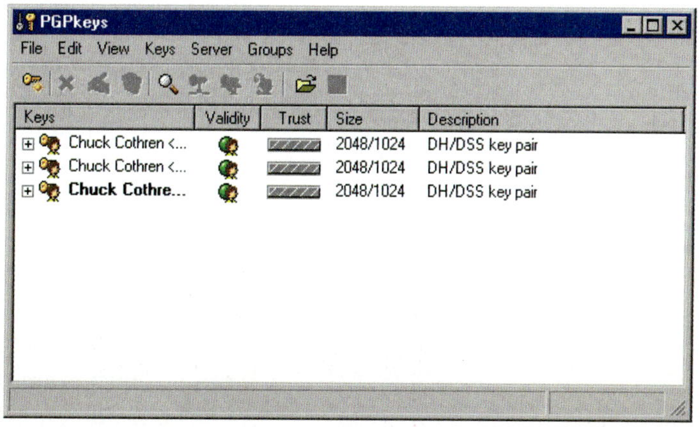

• **Figure 17.13** PGP key management

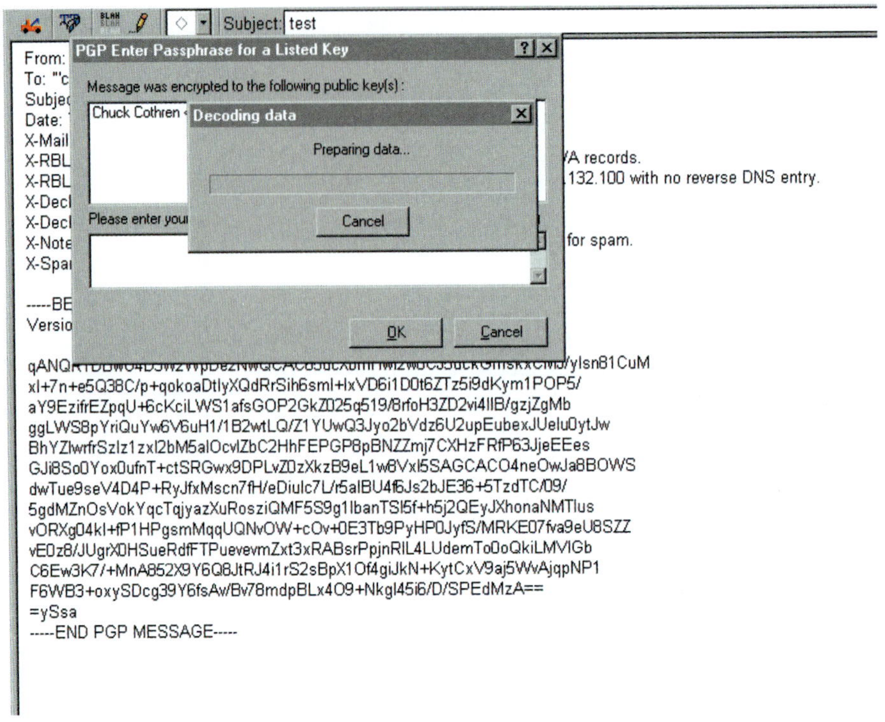

• **Figure 17.14** Decoding a PGP-encoded message

length of 128 bits, and a CAST key length of 128 bits. All of these algorithms are difficult to brute-force with existing hardware, requiring well over a million years to break the code. Although this is not a promise of future security against brute force attacks, the security is reasonable for today.

PGP has plug-ins for many popular e-mail programs, including Outlook and Mozilla's Thunderbird. These plug-ins handle the encryption and decryption behind the scenes, and all the user must do is enter the encryption key's passphrase to ensure that they are the owner of the key. In Figure 17.14, you can see the string of encrypted text that makes up the MIME attachment. This text includes the encrypted content of the message and the encrypted symmetric key. You can also see that the program does not decrypt the message upon receipt; it waits until instructed to decrypt it. PGP also stores encrypted messages in the encrypted format, as does S/MIME. This is important because it provides end-to-end security for the message.

Like S/MIME, PGP is not problem free. You must be diligent about keeping the software up to date and fully patched, because vulnerabilities are occasionally found. For example, a buffer overflow was found in the way PGP was handled in Outlook, causing the overwriting of heap memory and leading to possible malicious code execution. There is also a lot of discussion about the way PGP handles key recovery, or key escrow. PGP uses what's called an *Additional Decryption Key (ADK)*, which is basically an additional public key stacked upon the original public key. An ADK, in theory, would give the proper organization a private key that would be used to retrieve the secret messages. In practice, the ADK is not always controlled by a properly authorized organization, and the danger exists for someone to add an ADK and then distribute it to the world. This creates a situation in which other users will be sending messages that they believe can be read only by the first party, but that can actually be read by the third party who modified the key. These are just examples of the current vulnerabilities in the product, showing that PGP is just a tool, not the ultimate answer to security.

Instant Messaging

Instant messaging (IM) is another technology that has seen a change in recent years. Gone are the old services of AOL Instant Messenger, and in are messaging apps that are connected to a social media app (for example, Facebook Messenger), connected to a smart device (for example, a messaging app on a phone), or provide security (for example, Wire).

IM programs are designed to attach to a server, or a network of servers, and allow you to talk with other people on the same network of servers in near real time. The nature of this type of communication opens several holes in a system's security. One of the common issues is that the IM application will tell other users when a user is online.

Popular IM clients were not implemented with security in mind. All support sending files as attachments, few currently support encryption, and currently none have a virus scanner built into the file-sharing utility. This has created a market for a secure IM system, and several have sprung up to serve IM on the mobile device marketplace. One is called Wire, and its opening screen can be seen here.

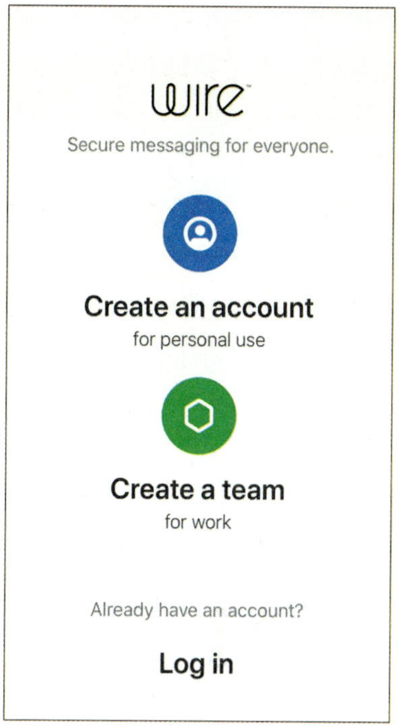

Modern Instant Messaging Systems

Instant messaging is an application that can increase productivity by saving communication time, but it's not without risks. The protocol sends messages in plaintext and thus fails to preserve their confidentiality. It also enables the sharing of files between clients, thus allowing a backdoor access method for files. There are some methods to minimize security risks, but more development efforts are required before IM is ready to be implemented in a secure fashion. The best ways in which to protect yourself on an IM network are similar to those for almost all Internet applications: avoid communication with unknown persons, avoid running any program you are unsure of, and do not write anything you wouldn't want posted with your name on it.

Instant messaging also plays a role in today's social media–driven world. Many very popular "messaging systems" are in use today, such as Snapchat, Instagram, Jabber, Tumblr, WhatsApp, and more. These are instant sharing systems that allow user bases to share files, pictures, and videos among users. Each of these systems has large numbers of users and literally billions of transferred items every year. As the social aspect of the Web grows, so do the instant sharing systems connecting users in social webs. Apple has its own messaging service, as does Android, and apps exist for a wide range of different "messaging" systems.

Any list of messaging apps will become outdated rather rapidly, but at the time this book went to press, the list included the following:

- Discord
- Facebook Messenger

- Instagram
- Skype
- Slack
- Snapchat
- Tumblr
- WeChat

The main security threat on most of these apps is information disclosure. Because they can be used from mobile devices outside of an enterprise network, there is the possibility for information to be captured and released across these platforms. For this reason, one of the security policies of high-security facilities is to not allow personal devices.

As the workforce has grown younger, new technologies have entered the workspace. Slack, shown next, is one such example. Slack is a messaging app that works to provide work teams with communication and file-sharing capabilities in real time within the enterprise.

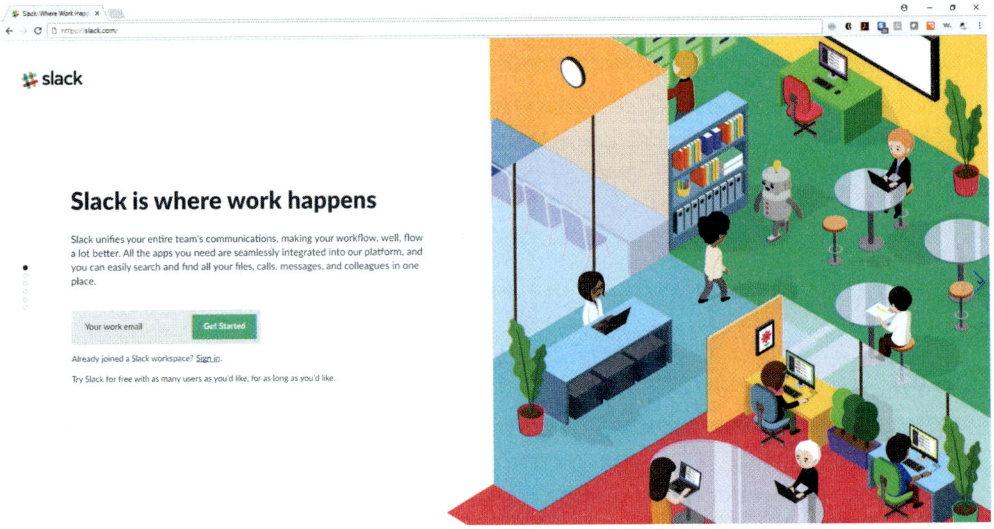

Chapter 17 Review

Chapter Summary

After reading this chapter and completing the exercises, you should understand the following about web components, e-mail, and IM security.

Describe the functioning of the TLS protocol suite

- TLS uses a combination of symmetric and asymmetric cryptographic methods to secure traffic.
- Before a TLS session can be secured, a handshake occurs to exchange cryptographic information and keys.

Explain web applications, plug-ins, and associated security issues

- Web browsers have mechanisms to enable plug-in programs to manage applications such as Flash objects and videos.
- Plug-ins that block pop-up windows and phishing sites can improve end-user security by permitting greater control over browser functionality.

Describe secure file transfer options

- FTP operations occur in plaintext, allowing anyone who sees the traffic to read it.
- SFTP combines the file transfer application with the Secure Shell (SSH) application to provide for a means of confidential FTP operations.

Explain directory usage for data retrieval

- LDAP is a protocol describing interaction with directory services.
- Directory services are data structures optimized for retrieval and are commonly used where data is read many times more than written, such as ACLs.

Explain scripting and other Internet functions that present security concerns

- Scripts are pieces of code that can execute within the browser environment.
- Some scripts or code elements can be called from the server side.

Use cookies to maintain parameters between web pages

- Cookies are small text files used to maintain state between web pages.
- Cookies can be set to persistent (last for a defined time period) or session (expire when the session is closed).

Examine web-based application security issues

- As more applications move to a browser environment to ease programmatic deployment, it makes it easier for users to work with a familiar user environment.
- Browsers have become powerful programming environments that perform many actions behind the scenes for a user, and malicious programmers can exploit this hidden functionality to perform actions on a user's PC without the user's obvious consent.

Describe security issues associated with e-mail

- Malicious code is code that performs something harmful to the computer it runs on. Malicious code is often sent through e-mail.
- Viruses are pieces of malicious code that require user action to spread.
- Worms are pieces of malicious code that use automated methods to spread.
- Spam, or unsolicited commercial e-mail, is e-mail that is sent to you without you requesting it, attempting to sell you something. It is the electronic equivalent of a telemarketing call.
- Hoax e-mails are e-mails that travel from user to user because of the compelling story contained in them.

Implement security practices for e-mail

- Protecting your e-mail system from virus code requires several measures:
    - Don't execute any attachment from an unknown source.

- Use antivirus programs that run on the server to filter all e-mails.
- Use client-side antivirus programs to catch any viruses that might come from web-based e-mail accounts.

- Keeping all software up to date helps to prevent worm propagation.
- Server-side filtering software and the application of Spam Blackhole Lists help limit the amount of unsolicited e-mail.
- E-mail encryption is a great way to protect the privacy of communication since e-mail is a cleartext medium.
- PGP, or Pretty Good Privacy, is a good specific application for e-mail encryption.
- S/MIME, or Secure/Multipurpose Internet Mail Extension, is the e-mail protocol that allows encryption applications to work.
- Antivirus software is important to protect against malware.

Detail the security issues of instant messaging protocols

- The most popular IM programs all send messages in the clear, without native encryption built into the default clients.
- All the IM clients need to attach to a server to communicate. Therefore, when attached to the server, they announce the source IP of a particular user.
- Instant messaging can also be used to transfer files. This activity typically bypasses any security built into the network, especially mail server virus protections.

Key Terms

Active Server Pages (ASP) *(663)*
ASP.NET *(663)*
Authenticode *(666)*
botnet *(675)*
browser extension *(665)*
browser helper objects (BHOs) *(666)*
code signing *(667)*
cookie *(663)*
DomainKeys Identified Mail (DKIM) *(684)*
e-mail *(670)*
e-mail hoax *(674)*
File Transfer Protocol (FTP) *(658)*
Hypertext Markup Language (HTML) *(650)*
inlining *(667)*
instant messaging (IM) *(689)*
Internet Engineering Task Force (IETF) *(652)*
Java *(661)*
JavaScript *(661)*
Lightweight Directory Access Protocol (LDAP) *(657)*
mail delivery agent (MDA) *(672)*
mail relaying *(682)*
mail transfer agent (MTA) *(672)*
mail user agent (MUA) *(672)*
Multipurpose Internet Mail Extensions (MIME) *(673)*
open relay *(682)*
PHP *(663)*
plug-in *(665)*
Pretty Good Privacy (PGP) *(687)*
Real-time Blackhole List (RBL) *(683)*
Secure/Multipurpose Internet Mail Extensions (S/MIME) *(685)*
Secure Sockets Layer (SSL) *(652)*
Sender Policy Framework (SPF) *(683)*
server-side scripting *(663)*
Simple Mail Transfer Protocol (SMTP) *(671)*
spam *(675)*
SSL stripping attack *(657)*
Transport Layer Security (TLS) *(652)*
Uniform Resource Locator (URL) *(650)*
unsolicited commercial e-mail *(675)*
X.500 *(657)*

Key Terms Quiz

Use terms from the Key Terms list to complete the sentences that follow. Don't use the same term more than once. Not all terms will be used.

1. Spam is the popular term for _______________.
2. _______________ is a method for detecting e-mail spoofing.
3. A large source of spam is zombie computers that are part of a(n) _______________.
4. _______________ is the protocol used to add attachments to an e-mail.
5. A(n) _______________ is a compilation of servers that are blocked because they have been known to send spam.
6. _______________ allows outside users to send e-mail via your mail servers—a risky practice to allow.
7. _______________ is a protocol for verifying e-mail addresses using DNS records to reduce spam.
8. A(n) _______________ is a small application program that increases a browser's ability to handle new data types and add new functionality.
9. _______________ can have the same virus risks as e-mail.
10. The most prevalent protocol that e-mail is sent by is _______________.

Multiple-Choice Quiz

1. What is one of the biggest reasons spam is prevalent today?
   - **A.** Criminals use zombie botnets.
   - **B.** Regular mail is too slow.
   - **C.** Spam is popular among recipients.
   - **D.** Spam is sent from the government.
2. What does the keyword **[secure]** in a cookie do?
   - **A.** It causes the system to encrypt its contents.
   - **B.** It prevents the cookie from passing over HTTP connections.
   - **C.** It tells the browser that the cookie is a security upgrade.
   - **D.** None of the above.
3. Why is an open e-mail relay bad?
   - **A.** It allows anyone to remotely control the server.
   - **B.** It makes the e-mail server reboot once a day.
   - **C.** No e-mail will go through.
   - **D.** It will allow anyone to send spam through the server.
4. Security for JavaScript is established by whom?
   - **A.** The developer at the time of code development.
   - **B.** The user at the time of code usage.
   - **C.** The user through browser preferences.
   - **D.** Security for JavaScript is not necessary—the Java language is secure by design.
5. What is code signing used to do?
   - **A.** Allow authors to take artistic credit for their hard work
   - **B.** Provide a method to demonstrate code integrity
   - **C.** Guarantee code functionality
   - **D.** Prevent copyright infringement by code copying
6. Why are instant messaging protocols dangerous for file transfer?
   - **A.** They bypass server-based virus protections.
   - **B.** File sharing is never dangerous.
   - **C.** They allow everyone you chat with to view all your files.
   - **D.** You'll end up receiving many spam files.

7. Why do PGP and S/MIME need public key cryptography?
   - **A.** Public keys are necessary to determine whether the e-mail is encrypted.
   - **B.** The public key is necessary to encrypt the symmetric key.
   - **C.** The public key unlocks the password to the e-mail.
   - **D.** The public key is useless and gives a false sense of privacy.
8. Why is HTML e-mail dangerous?
   - **A.** It can't be read by some e-mail clients.
   - **B.** It sends the content of your e-mails to web pages.
   - **C.** It can allow the launching of malicious code from the preview pane.
   - **D.** It is the only way spam can be sent.
9. If they are both text protocols, why is instant messaging traffic riskier than e-mail?
   - **A.** More viruses are coded for IM.
   - **B.** IM has no business purpose.
   - **C.** IM traffic has to travel outside of the organization to a server.
   - **D.** Emoticons.
10. TLS provides which of the following functionalities?
   - **A.** Data integrity services
   - **B.** Authentication services
   - **C.** Data confidentiality services
   - **D.** All of the above

Essay Quiz

1. How would you implement a successful spam-filtering policy?
2. Draft a memo describing malware risks to the common user and what the user can do to avoid infection.

Lab Projects

• Lab Project 17.1

Show that instant messaging is an insecure protocol. You will need a lab computer with Windows installed, an IM program, and a sniffer. Do the following:

1. If you need to install an IM program, download either Google Chat or Flock from the Internet.
2. Run the Installer program.
3. Generate a username and password and log in.
4. Start the sniffer program and set it to capture all traffic.
5. Start a chat session with a partner in the class.
6. Decode the sniff trace to view the cleartext messages of the chat.

• Lab Project 17.2

Find at least ten pieces of spam mail from any account, whether it be home, work, school, or somewhere else. Using the e-mail headers, and any website that might provide information, attempt to trace the spam mail back to its original source.

You will need the following materials:

1. Collect the e-mails and view the e-mail header information in your e-mail program.
2. Find the "Received:" field in the headers and write down as many DNS names or IP addresses as you can. Also look for common details in the header elements of the different messages, such as the same e-mail servers and spammers.
3. Using the Internet, research the physical locations of the IP addresses.
4. Report the different locations from which your spam e-mail originated. What did you learn about tracing e-mail and spam?

chapter 18

Cloud Computing

Cloud is about how you do computing, not where you do computing.

—Paul Maritz, CEO VMware

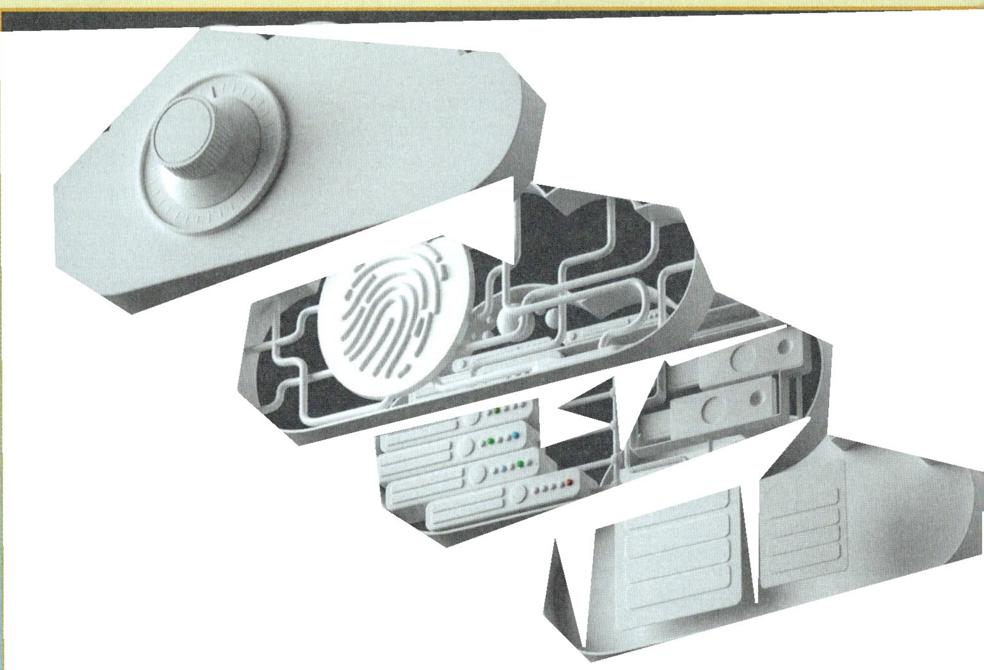

In this chapter, you will learn how to

- Explore cloud security controls
- Compare and contrast cloud security solutions
- Learn about cloud native controls versus third-party solutions
- Explore virtualization

Cloud computing is becoming more and more prevalent because of multiple business factors. It has many economic and technical advantages over traditional IT in many use cases, but that is not to say it comes without problems. Securing cloud systems is in one respect no different from securing a traditional IT system: protect the data from unauthorized reading and manipulation. However, the tools, techniques, and procedures vary greatly from standard IT, and while clouds can be secure, it is by the application of the correct set of security controls, not by happenstance.

Cloud Computing

Cloud computing is a common term used to describe computer services provided over a network. These computing services are computing, storage, applications, and services that are offered via the Internet Protocol. One of the characteristics of cloud computing is transparency to the end user. This improves usability of this form of service provisioning. Cloud computing offers much to the user: improvements in performance, scalability, flexibility, security, and reliability, among other items. These improvements are a direct result of the specific attributes associated with how cloud services are implemented.

Security is a particular challenge when data and computation are handled by a remote party, as in cloud computing. The specific challenge is how does one allow data outside their enterprise and yet remain in control over how the data is used, and the common answer is encryption. When data is properly encrypted before it leaves the enterprise, external storage can still be performed securely.

There are many different *cloud deployment models*. Clouds can be created by many entities, both internal and external to an organization. Many commercial cloud services are available from a variety of firms, ranging from Google and Amazon to smaller, local providers. Internally, an organization's own services can replicate the advantages of cloud computing while improving the utility of limited resources. The promise of cloud computing is improved utility and is marketed under the concepts of Platform as a Service (PaaS), Software as a Service (SaaS), and Infrastructure as a Service (IaaS).

There are pros and cons to cloud-based computing. And for each use, the economic factors may differ (issues of cost, contracts, and so on). However, for someone standing up a test project for which they might not want to incur hardware costs associated with buying servers that may live beyond the test project, then "renting" space in the cloud makes sense. When multiple sites are involved and the issues of distributing data and backup solutions are a concern, cloud services offer advantages. However, with less control comes other costs, such as forensics, incident response, archiving data, long-term contracts, and network connectivity. For each case, a business analysis must be performed to determine the correct choice between cloud options and on-premises computing.

Cloud Characteristics

NIST defines cloud computing as a system that enables ubiquitous, convenient, on-demand network access to a shared pool of configurable computing resources that can be rapidly provisioned and released with minimal management effort or service provider interaction. Five essential characteristics are associated with the cloud model: on-demand self-service, broad network access, resource pooling, rapid elasticity and scalability, and measured service.

On-Demand Self-Service

A cloud customer can unilaterally provision computing capabilities, such as server time and network storage, as needed automatically, without requiring human interaction with each service provider as provided under the terms of the cloud service agreement.

Broad Network Access

Cloud capabilities are available over the network and accessed through standard mechanisms that promote use by heterogeneous thin- or thick-client platforms. Reliance on standard network protocols and methods enable a level of architectural flexibility in accessing the cloud capabilities.

Resource Pooling

The cloud provider's computing resources are pooled to serve multiple consumers using a multitenant model, with different physical and virtual resources dynamically assigned and reassigned according to customer demand. This enables the first characteristic, self-service, and the next, rapid elasticity and scalability. There is a sense of location independence in that the cloud is accessed via the network. Examples of resources that can be pooled include storage, processing, memory, and network bandwidth.

Rapid Elasticity and Scalability

Cloud capabilities can be elastically provisioned and released, in some cases automatically, to match resources commensurate with demand. For example, a spike in web traffic may increase workloads, requiring more resources. This is also called *horizontal scaling,* or scaling in or out. Scalability refers to the ability to increase workload with a given set of hardware resources. This is also called *vertical scaling,* or scaling up or down. Vertical scaling can involve more or less CPU power, RAM, and/or network bandwidth. To the customer, the capabilities available for provisioning often appear to be unlimited and can be appropriated in any quantity at any time.

Measured Service

Cloud systems control and optimize resource use by leveraging a metering capability at some level of abstraction appropriate to the type of service (for example, storage, processing, bandwidth, and active user accounts). This can be done automatically via cloud-side automation, adjusting as necessary per the cloud service agreement. Resource usage can be monitored, controlled, and reported, providing transparency for both the provider and customer of the utilized service.

Cloud Computing Service Models

Clouds can be created by many entities, both internal and external to an organization. Commercial cloud services are already available and offered by a variety of firms, as large as Google and Amazon and as small as local providers. Internal services can replicate the advantages of cloud computing while improving the utility of limited resources. The promise of cloud computing is improved utility and, as such, is marketed under the concepts of Infrastructure as a Service, Platform as a Service, Software as a Service, and Anything as a Service.

Infrastructure as a Service (IaaS)

Infrastructure as a Service (IaaS) is a marketing term used to describe cloud-based systems that are delivered as a virtual solution for computing. Rather than firms needing to build data centers, IaaS allows them to contract for utility computing, as needed. IaaS is specifically marketed on a pay-per-use basis, scalable directly with need.

Platform as a Service (PaaS)

Platform as a Service (PaaS) is a marketing term used to describe the offering of a computing platform in the cloud. Multiple sets of software working together to provide services, such as database services, can be delivered via the cloud as a platform. PaaS offerings generally focus on security and scalability, both of which are characteristics that fit with cloud and platform needs.

Software as a Service (SaaS)

Software as a Service (SaaS) is the offering of software to end users from within the cloud. Rather than installing software on client machines, SaaS acts as software on demand, where the software runs from the cloud. This has a couple advantages: updates can be seamless to end users, and integration between components can be enhanced. Common examples of SaaS are products offered via the Web as subscription services, such as Microsoft Office 365 and Adobe Creative Suite.

> Be sure you understand the differences between the cloud computing service models Platform as a Service, Software as a Service, Infrastructure as a Service, and Anything as a Service.

Anything as a Service (XaaS)

With the growth of cloud services, applications, storage, and processing, the scale provided by cloud vendors has opened up new offerings that are collectively called **Anything as a Service (XaaS)**. The wrapping of the previously mentioned SaaS and IaaS components into a particular service (say, Disaster Recovery as a Service) creates a new marketable item.

Level of Control in the Hosting Models

One way to examine the differences between the cloud models and on-premises computing is to look at who controls what aspect of the model. In Figure 18.1, you can see that the level of control over the systems goes

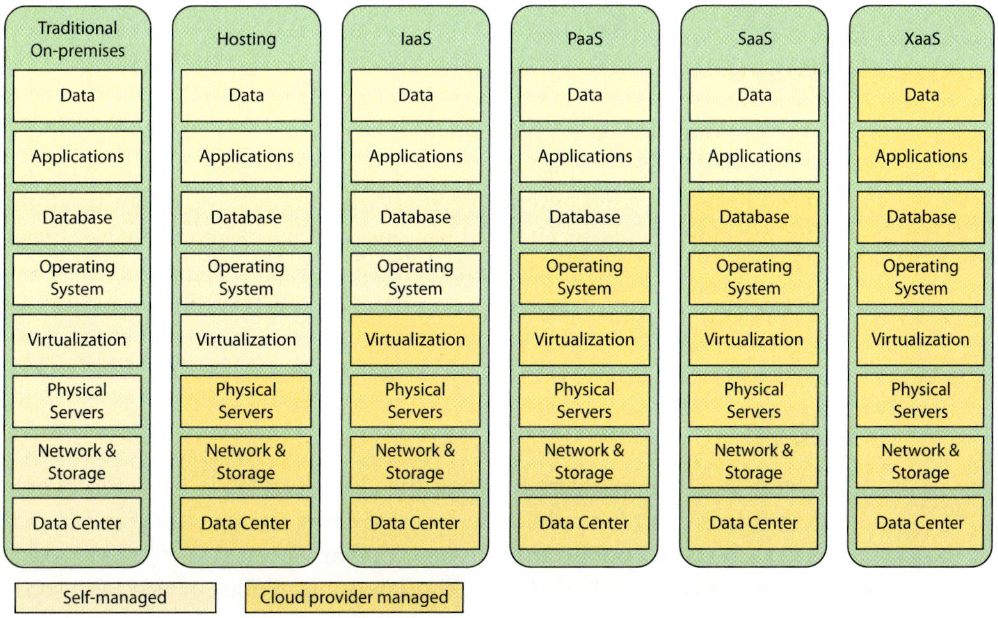

• **Figure 18.1** Comparison of the level of control in the various hosting models

from complete self-control in on-premises computing to complete vendor control in XaaS.

Infrastructure as Code

Infrastructure as code is the use of machine-readable definition files as well as code to manage and provision computer systems. By making the process of management programmable, there are significant scalability and flexibility advantages. Rather than having to manage physical hardware configurations using interactive configuration tools, infrastructure as code allows for this to be done programmatically. A good example of this is in the design of software-defined networking.

Services Integration

Services integration is the connection of infrastructure and software elements to provide specific services to a business entity. Connecting processing, storage, databases, web, communications, and other functions into an integrated comprehensive solution is the goal of most IT organizations. Cloud-based infrastructure is the ideal environment to achieve this goal. Through predesigned scripts, the cloud provider can manage services integration in a much more scalable fashion than individual businesses. For a business, each integration is a one-off creation, whereas the cloud services provider can capitalize on the reproducibility of doing the same integrations for many customers. With this scale and experience comes cost savings and reliability.

Cloud Types

Depending on the size and particular needs of an organization, there are four basic types of cloud: public, private, hybrid, and community.

Private

If your organization is highly sensitive to sharing resources, you might want to consider the use of a private cloud. **Private clouds** are essentially reserved resources used only for your organization—your own little cloud within the cloud. This service will be considerably more expensive, but it should also carry less exposure and should enable your organization to better define the security, processing, and handling of data that occurs within your cloud.

Public

The term **public cloud** refers to when the cloud service is rendered over a system that is open for public use. In most cases, there is little operational difference between public and private cloud architectures, but the security ramifications can be substantial. Although public cloud services will separate users with security restrictions, the depth and level of these restrictions, by definition, will be significantly less in a public cloud.

Hybrid

A **hybrid cloud** structure is one where elements are combined from private, public, and community cloud structures. When examining a hybrid structure, you need to remain cognizant that operationally these differing environments may not actually be joined, but rather used together. Sensitive information can be stored in the private cloud and issue-related information can be stored in the community cloud, all of which is accessed by an application. This makes the overall system a hybrid cloud system.

Community

A **community cloud** system is one where several organizations with a common interest share a cloud environment for the specific purposes of the shared endeavor. For example, local public entities and key local firms may share a community cloud dedicated to serving the interests of community initiatives. This can be an attractive cost-sharing mechanism for specific data-sharing initiatives.

Be sure to understand and recognize the different cloud systems—private, public, hybrid, and community.

On-premises vs. Hosted vs. Cloud

Systems can exist in a wide array of places—from on premises, to hosted, to in the cloud. **On-premises** means the system resides locally in the building of the organization. Whether it's a virtual machine (VM), storage, or even a service, if the solution is locally hosted and maintained, it is referred to as "on-premises." The advantage is that the organization has total control of the system and generally has high connectivity to it. The disadvantage is that it requires local resources and is not necessarily easy to scale. Off-premises or hosted services refers to having the services hosted somewhere else, commonly in a shared environment. Using a third party for hosted services provides you a set cost based on the amount of those services you use. This has cost advantages, especially when scale is included—does it make sense to have all the local infrastructure, including personnel, for a small, informational-only website? Of course not; you would have that website hosted. Storage works the opposite with scale. Small-scale storage needs are easily met in-house, whereas large-scale storage needs are typically either hosted or in the cloud.

On-premises means the system is on your site. *Off-premises* means it is somewhere else—a specific location. The phrase "in the cloud" refers to having the system distributed across a remotely accessible infrastructure via a network, with specific cloud characteristics, such as scalability and so on. This is true for both on- and off-premises.

Cloud Service Providers

Cloud service providers (CSPs) come in many sizes and shapes, with a myriad of different offerings, price points, and service levels. There are the mega-cloud providers, Amazon, Google, Microsoft, and Oracle, which have virtually no limit to the size they can scale to when needed. There are smaller firms, with some offering reselling from the larger clouds and others hosting their own data centers. Each of these has a business offering, and the challenge is determining which offering best fits the needs of your project or company. Many issues have to be resolved around which services are being provided and which are not, as well as price points and contractual terms. One important thing to remember: if something isn't in the contract, it won't be done. Take security items, for example: if you want the cloud provider to offer specific security functionality, it must be in the package you subscribe to; otherwise, you won't receive this functionality.

Transit Gateway

A **transit gateway** is a network connection that is used to interconnect virtual private clouds (VPCs) and on-premises networks. Using transit gateways, organizations can define and control communication between resources on the cloud provider's network and their own infrastructure. Transit gateways are unique to each provider and are commonly implemented to support the administration of the provider's cloud environment.

Cloud Security Controls

Cloud security controls are a shared issue—one that is shared between the user and the cloud provider. Depending on your terms of service with your cloud provider, you will share responsibilities for software updates, access control, encryption, and other key security controls. Figure 18.1 previously illustrated the differing levels of shared responsibility in various cloud models. What is important to remember is to define the requirements up front and have them written into the service agreement with the cloud provider, because unless they are part of the package, they will not occur.

High Availability Across Zones

Cloud computing environments can be configured to provide nearly full-time availability (that is, a high availability system). This is done using redundant hardware and software that make the system available despite individual element failures. When something experiences an error or failure, the failover process moves the processing performed by the failed component to the backup component elsewhere in the cloud. This process is transparent to users as much as possible, creating an image of a high availability system to users. Architecting these failover components across zones provides *high availability across zones*. As with all cloud security issues, the details are in your terms of service with your cloud provider; you cannot just assume the system will be high availability. It must be specified in your terms and architected in by the provider.

Zones can be used for replication and provide load balancing as well as high availability.

Resource Policies

When you are specifying the details of a cloud engagement, how much processing power, what apps, what security requirements, how much storage, and access control are all resources. Cloud-based resources are controlled via a set of policies. This is basically your authorization model projected into the cloud space. Management of these items is done via *resource policies*. Each cloud service provider has a different manner of allowing you to interact with their menu of services, but in the end, you are specifying the resource policies you want applied to your account. Through resource policies you can define what, where, or how resources are provisioned. This allows your organization to set restrictions, manage the resources, and manage cloud costs.

The integration between the enterprise identity access management (IAM) system and the cloud-based IAM system is a configuration element of utmost importance when setting up the cloud environment. The policies set the permissions for the cloud objects. Once the resource policies from the enterprise are extended into the cloud environment and set up, they must be maintained. The level of integration between the cloud-based IAM system and the enterprise-based IAM system will determine the level of work required for regular maintenance activities.

Secrets Management

Data that is in the cloud is still data that is on a server and is therefore, by definition, remotely accessible. Hence, it is important to secure the data using encryption. A common mistake is to leave data unencrypted on the cloud. It seems hardly a week goes by without a report of unencrypted data being exposed from a cloud instance. Fingers always point to the cloud provider, but in most cases the blame is on the end user. Cloud providers offer encryption tools and management services, yet too many companies don't implement them, which sets the scene for a data breach.

Secrets management is the term used to denote the policies and procedures employed to connect the IAM systems of the enterprise and the cloud to enable communication with the data. Storing sensitive data, or in most cases virtually any data, in the cloud without putting in place appropriate controls to prevent access to the data is irresponsible and dangerous. Encryption is a failsafe—even if security configurations fail and the data falls into the hands of an unauthorized party, the data can't be read or used without the keys. It is important to maintain control of the encryption keys. The security of the keys, which can be done outside the primary cloud instance and elsewhere in the enterprise, is how the secrecy is managed.

Secrets management is an important aspect of maintaining cloud security. The secrets used for system-to-system access should be maintained separately from other configuration data and handled according to the strictest principles of confidentiality because these secrets allow access to the data in the cloud.

> Use of a secrets manager can enable secrets management by providing a central trusted storage location for certificates, passwords, and even application programming interface (API) keys.

Integration and Auditing

The integration of the appropriate level and quantity of security controls is a subject that is always being audited. Are the controls appropriate? Are they placed and used correctly? Most importantly, are they effective? These are standard IT audit elements in the enterprise. The moving of computing resources to the cloud does not change the need or intent of audit functions.

Cloud computing audits have become a standard as enterprises are realizing that unique cloud-based risks exist with their data being hosted by other organizations. To address these risks, organizations are using specific cloud computing audits to gain assurance and to understand the risk of their information being lost or released to unauthorized parties. These cloud-specific audits have two sets of requirements: one being an understanding of the cloud security environment as deployed, and the second being related to the data security requirements. The result is that cloud computing audits can be in different forms, such as SOC 1 and SOC 2 reporting, HITRUST, PCI, and FedRAMP. For each one of these data-specific security frameworks, additional details are based on the specifics of the cloud environment and the specifics of the security controls employed by both the enterprise and the cloud vendor.

Storage

Cloud-based data *storage* was one of the first uses of cloud computing. Security requirements related to storage in the cloud environment are actually based on the same fundamentals as in the enterprise environment. Permissions to access and modify data need to be defined, set, and enforced. A means to protect data from unauthorized access is generally needed, and encryption is the key answer, just as it is in the enterprise. The replication of data across multiple different systems as part of the cloud deployment and the aspects of high availability elements of a cloud environment can complicate the securing of data.

Permissions

Permissions for data access and modifications are handled in the same manner as in an on-premises IT environment. Identity access management (IAM) systems are employed to manage the details of who can do what with each object. The key to managing this in the cloud is the integration of the on-premises IAM system with the cloud-based IAM system.

Encryption

Encryption of data in the cloud is one of the foundational elements to securing one's data when it is on another system. Data should be encrypted when stored in the cloud, and the keys should be maintained by the enterprise, not the cloud provider. Keys should be managed in accordance with the same level of security afforded keys in the enterprise.

Replication

Data may replicate across the cloud as part of a variety of cloud-based activities. From shared environments to high availability systems, including their backup systems, data in the cloud can seem to be fluid, moving across multiple physical systems. This level of replication is yet another reason that data should be encrypted for security. The act of replicating data across multiple systems is part of the resiliency of the cloud, in that single points of failure will not have the same effects that occur in the standard IT enterprise. Therefore, this is one of the advantages of the cloud.

High Availability

High availability storage works in the same manner as high availability systems described earlier in the chapter. Having multiple different physical systems working together to ensure your data is redundantly and resiliently stored is one of the cloud's advantages. What's more, the cloud-based

IAM system can use encryption protections to keep your data secret, while high availability keeps it available.

Network

Cloud-based systems are made up of machines connected using a network. Typically this network is under the control of the cloud service provider (CSP). While you may be given network information, including addresses, the networks you see might actually be encapsulated on top of another network that is maintained by the service provider. In this fashion, many cloud service providers offer a virtual network that delivers the required functions without providing direct access to the actual network environment.

Virtual Networks

Most networking in cloud environments is via a virtual network operating in an overlay on top of a physical network. The *virtual network* can be used and manipulated by users, whereas the actual network underneath cannot. This gives the cloud service provider the ability to manage and service network functionality independent of the cloud instance with respect to a user. The virtual network technology used in cloud environments can include software-defined networking (SDN) and network function virtualization (NFV) as elements that make it easier to perform the desired networking tasks in the cloud.

Public and Private Subnets

Just as in traditional IT systems, there is typically a need for public-facing subnets, where the public/Internet can interact with servers, such as mail servers, web servers, and the like. There is also a need for private subnets, where access is limited to specific addresses, preventing direct access to secrets such as datastores and other important information assets. The cloud comes with the capability of using both public-facing and private subnets; in other words, just because something is "in the cloud" does not change the business architecture of some having machines connected to the Internet and some not. Now, being "in the cloud" means that, in one respect, the Internet is used for all access. However, in the case of private subnets, the cloud-based IAM system can determine who is authorized to access which parts of the cloud's virtual network.

Segmentation

Segmentation is the network process of separating network elements into segments and regulating traffic between the segments. The presence of a segmented network creates security barriers for unauthorized accessors through the inspection of packets as they move from one segment to another. This can be done in a multitude of ways—via MAC tables, IP addresses, and even tunnels, with devices such as firewalls and secure web gateways inspecting at each connection. The ultimate in segmentation is the zero-trust environment, where microsegmentation is used to continually invoke the verification of permissions and controls. All of these can be performed in a cloud network. Also, as with the other controls already presented, the details are in the service level agreement (SLA) with the cloud service provider.

API Inspection and Integration

APIs are software interfaces that allow various software components to communicate with each other. This is true in the cloud just as it is in the traditional IT enterprise. Because of the nature of cloud environments, accepting virtually all of requests across the Web, there is a need for verifying information before it can be used. One key element in this solution is presented later in the chapter—the next-generation secure web gateway. This system analyzes information transfers at the application layer to verify authenticity and correctness.

Cloud security controls provide the same functionality as normal network security controls; they just do it in a different environment. The cloud is not a system without controls.

Content inspection refers to the examination of the contents of a request to an API by applying rules to determine whether a request is legitimate and should be accepted. As APIs act to integrate one application to another, errors in one application can be propagated to other components, thus creating bigger issues. The use of API content inspection is an active measure to prevent errors from propagating through a system and causing trouble.

Compute

The cloud has become a service operation where applications can be deployed, providing a form of cloud-based computing. The *compute* aspects of a cloud system have the same security issues as a traditional IT system; in other words, the fact that a compute element is in the cloud does not make it any more or less secure. What has to happen is that security requirements need to be addressed as data comes and goes from the compute element.

Security Groups

Security groups are composed of the set of rules and policies associated with a cloud instance. These rules can be network rules, such as rules for passing a firewall, or they can be IAM rules with respect to who can access or interact with an object on the system. Security groups are handled differently by each cloud service provider, but in the end they provide a means of managing permissions in a limited granularity mode. Different providers have different limits, but in the end the objective is to place users into groups rather than to perform individual checks for every access request. This is done to manage scalability, which is one of the foundational elements of cloud computing.

Dynamic Resource Allocation

A cloud-based system has certain hallmark characteristics besides just being on another computer. Among these characteristics is providing scalable, reliable computing in a cost-efficient manner. Having a system whose resources can grow and shrink as the compute requirements change, without the need to buy new servers, expand systems, and so on, is one of the primary advantages of the cloud. Cloud service providers offer more than just bare hardware. One of the values associated with the cloud is its ability to grow as the load increases and to shrink (thus saving costs) as the load decreases. Cloud service providers manage this using *dynamic resource allocation* software that monitors the levels of performance. In accordance with the service agreement, they can act to increase resources incrementally as needed.

Instance Awareness

Just as enterprises have moved to the cloud, so too have attackers. Command-and-control networks can be spun up in cloud environments, just as they are on real enterprise hardware. This creates a situation where a cloud is communicating with another cloud, and how does the first cloud understand if the second cloud is legit? **Instance awareness** is the name of a capability that must be enabled on firewalls, secure web gateways, and cloud access security brokers (CASBs) to determine if the next system in a communication chain is legitimate or not. Take a cloud-enabled service such as Google Drive, Microsoft OneDrive, or Box, or any other cloud-based storage. Do you block them all? Or do you determine by instance which are legit and which are not? This is a relatively new and advanced feature, but one that is becoming increasingly important to prevent data disclosures and other issues from integrating cloud apps with unauthorized endpoints.

Virtual Private Cloud (VPC) Endpoint

A **virtual private cloud endpoint** allows connections to and from a virtual private cloud instance. VPC endpoints are virtual elements that can scale. They are also redundant and typically highly available. A VPC endpoint provides a means to connect a VPC to other resources without going out over the Internet. View it as a secure tunnel to directly access other cloud-based resources without exposing the traffic to other parties. VPC endpoints can be programmable to enable integration with IAM and other security solutions, enabling cross-cloud connections securely.

> A VPC endpoint provides a means to connect a VPC to other resources without going out over the Internet. In other words, you don't need additional VPN connection technologies or even an Internet gateway.

Container Security

Container security is the process of implementing security tools and policies to ensure your container is running as intended. Container technology allows applications and their dependencies to be packaged together into one operational element. This element, also commonly called a *manifest*, can be version-controlled, deployed, replicated, and managed across an environment. Containers can contain all the necessary OS elements for an application to run; they can be considered self-contained compute platforms. Security can be designed into the containers, as well as enforced in the environment in which the containers run. Running containers in cloud-based environments is a common occurrence because the ease of managing and deploying the containers fits the cloud model well. Most cloud providers have container-friendly environments that enable the necessary cloud environment security controls as well as allow the container to make its own security decisions within the container.

> Cloud-based computing has requirements to define who can do what (security groups) and what can happen and when (dynamic resource allocation) as well as to manage the security of embedded entities such as containers. Some of these controls are the same (security groups and containers) while other controls are unique to the cloud environment (dynamic resource allocations).

Security as a Service

Just as one can get Software as a Service or Infrastructure as a Service, one can contract with a security firm for **Security as a Service**, which is the outsourcing of security functions to a vendor that has advantages in scale, costs, or speed. Security is a complex, wide-ranging cornucopia of technical specialties, all working together to provide appropriate risk reductions in today's enterprise. This means there are technical people, management, specialized hardware and software, and fairly complex operations, both routine and in response to incidents. Any or all of this can be outsourced to a security vendor, and firms routinely examine vendors for solutions where the business economics make outsourcing attractive.

Several types of items are delivered as a service—software, infrastructure, platforms, cloud access, and security—each with a specific deliverable and value proposition.

Different security vendors offer different specializations—from network security to web application security, e-mail security, incident response services, and even infrastructure updates. These can all be managed from a third party. Depending on architecture, needs, and scale, these third-party vendors can oftentimes offer a compelling economic advantage for part of a security solution.

Managed Security Service Provider (MSSP)

A managed service provider (MSP) is a company that remotely manages a customer's IT infrastructure. A **managed security service provider (MSSP)** does the same thing as a third party that manages security services. For each of these services, the devil is in the details. The scope of the engagement, what is in the details of the contract, is what is being provided by the third party, and nothing else. For example, if you don't have managing backups as part of the contract, either you do it yourself or you have to modify the contract. Managed services provide the strength of a large firm but at a fraction of the cost that a small firm would have to pay to get that scale. So, obviously, there are advantages. However, the downside is flexibility, as there is no room for change without renegotiating the contract for services.

Cloud Security Solutions

Cloud security solutions are similar to traditional IT security solutions in one simple way: there is no easy, magic solution. Security is achieved through multiple actions designed to ensure the security policies are being followed. Whether in the cloud or in an on-premises environment, security requires multiple activities, with metrics, reporting, management, and auditing to ensure effectiveness. With respect to the cloud, some specific elements need to be considered, mostly in interfacing existing enterprise IT security efforts with the methods employed in the cloud instance.

Cloud Access Security Broker (CASB)

Cloud access security brokers (CASBs) are integrated suites of tools or services offered as Security as a Service, or third-party managed security service providers (MSSPs), focused on cloud security. CASB vendors provide a range of security services designed to protect cloud infrastructure and data. CASBs act as security policy enforcement points between cloud service providers and their customers to enact enterprise security policies as the cloud-based resources are utilized.

A CASB is a security policy enforcement point that is placed between cloud service consumers and cloud service providers to manage enterprise security policies as cloud-based resources are accessed. A CASB can be an on-premises or cloud-based item; the key is that it exists between the cloud provider and customer connection, thus enabling it to mediate all access. Enterprises use CASB vendors to address cloud service risks, enforce security policies, and comply with regulations. A CASB solution works wherever the cloud services are located, even when they are beyond the enterprise perimeter and out of the direct control of enterprise operations. CASBs work at both the bulk and microscopic scale. They can be configured to block some types of access like a sledgehammer, while also operating as a scalpel, trimming only specific elements. They do require an investment in the development of appropriate strategies in the form of data policies that can be enforced as data moves to and from the cloud.

A CASB is a security policy enforcement point that is placed between cloud service consumers and cloud service providers to manage enterprise security policies as cloud-based resources are accessed.

Application Security

When applications are provided by the cloud, application security is part of the equation. Again, this immediately becomes an issue of potentially shared responsibility based on the cloud deployment model chosen. If the customer has the responsibilities for securing the applications, then the issues are the same as in the enterprise, with the added twist of maintaining software on a different platform—the cloud. Access to the application for updating as well as auditing and other security elements must be considered and factored into the business decision behind the model choice.

If the cloud service provider is responsible, there can be economies of scale, and the providers have the convenience of having their own admins maintain the applications. However, with that comes the cost, and the issues of auditing to ensure it is being done correctly. At the end of the day, the concept of what needs to be done with respect to application security does not change just because it is in the cloud. What does change is who becomes responsible for it and how it is accomplished in the remote environment. As with other elements of potential shared responsibilities, this is something that needs to be determined before the cloud agreement is signed; if it is not in the agreement, then it is solely on the user to provide the responses.

Firewall Considerations in a Cloud Environment

Firewalls are needed in cloud environments in the same manner they are needed in traditional IT environments. In cloud computing, the network perimeter has essentially disappeared; it is a series of services running outside the traditional IT environment and connected via the Internet. To the cloud, the user's physical location and the device they're using no longer matter. The cloud needs a firewall blocking all unauthorized connections to the cloud instance. In some cases, this is built into the cloud environment; in others, it is up to the enterprise or cloud customer to provide this functionality.

Cost

The first question on every manager's mind is *cost*—what will this cost me? There are cloud environments that are barebones and cheap, but they also don't come with any built-in security functionality, such as a firewall, leaving it up to the customer to provide. Therefore, this needs to be included in the cost comparisons to cloud environments with built-in firewall functionality. The cost of a firewall is not just in the procurement but also the deployment and operation. And all of these factors need to be included, not only for firewalls around the cloud perimeter, but internal firewalls used for segmentation as well.

Need for Segmentation

As previously discussed, segmentation can provide additional opportunities for security checks between critical elements of a system. Take the database servers that hold the crown jewels of a corporation's data, be that intellectual property (IP), business information, customer records; each enterprise has its own flavor, but all have critical records that the loss of or disclosure of would be a serious problem. Segmenting off this element of the network and only allowing access to a small set of defined users at the local segment is a strong security protection against attackers traversing your network. It can also act to keep malware and ransomware from hitting these critical resources. Firewalls are used to create the segments, and the need for them must be managed as part of the requirements package for designing and creating the cloud environment.

Open Systems Interconnection (OSI) Layers

The Open Systems Interconnection (OSI) layers act as a means of describing the different levels of communication across a network. From the physical layer (layer 1) to the network layer (layer 3) is the standard realm of networking. Layer 4, the transport layer, is where TCP and UDP function, and through level 7, the application layer, is where applications work. This is relevant with respect to firewalls because most modern application-level attacks do not occur at layers 1–3, but rather happen in layers 4–7. This makes traditional IT firewalls inadequately prepared to see and stop most modern attacks. Modern next-generation firewalls and secure web gateways operate higher in the OSI model, including up to the application layer, to make access decisions. These devices are more powerful and require significantly more information and effort to effectively use, but with integrated security orchestration, automation, and response (SOAR) frameworks and systems, they are becoming valuable components in the security system. As the cloud networking is a virtualized function, many of the old network-based attacks will not function on the cloud network, but the need is still there for the higher-level detection of the next-generation devices. These are the typical firewall and security appliances that are considered essential in cloud environments.

Modern next-generation firewalls and secure web gateways operate higher in the OSI model, using application layer data to make access decisions.

Cloud-native Controls vs. Third-party Solutions

When one is looking at cloud security automation and orchestration tools, there are two sources. First is the set provided by the cloud service provider. These cloud-native controls vary by provider and by specific offering that an enterprise subscribes to as part of the user agreement and service license. Third-party tools also exist that the customer can license and deploy in the cloud environment. The decision is one that should be based on a comprehensive review of requirements, including both capabilities and cost of ownership. This is not a simple binary A-or-B choice; there is much detail to consider. How will each integrate with the existing security environment? How will the operation be handled, and who will have to learn what tools to achieve the objectives? This is a complete review of the people, processes, and technologies, because any of the three can make or break either of these deployments.

Virtualization

Virtualization technology is used to enable a computer to have more than one OS present and, in many cases, operating at the same time. Virtualization is an abstraction of the OS layer, creating the ability to host multiple OSs on a single piece of hardware. To enable virtualization, a hypervisor is employed. A **hypervisor** is a low-level program that allows multiple operating systems to run concurrently on a single host computer. Hypervisors use a thin layer of code to allocate resources in real time. The hypervisor acts as the traffic cop that controls I/O and memory management. One of the major advantages of virtualization is the separation of the software and the hardware, creating a barrier that can improve many system functions, including security. The underlying hardware is referred to as the host machine, and on it is a host OS. Either the host OS has built-in hypervisor capability or an application is needed to provide the hypervisor function to manage the virtual machines (VMs). The virtual machines are typically referred to as guest OSs. Two types of hypervisors exist: Type I and Type II.

> A hypervisor is the interface between a virtual machine and the host machine hardware. Hypervisors comprise the layer that enables virtualization.

Type I

Type I hypervisors run directly on the system hardware. They are referred to as native, bare-metal, or embedded hypervisors in typical vendor literature. Type I hypervisors are designed for speed and efficiency, as they do not have to operate through another OS layer. Examples of Type I hypervisors include KVM (Kernel-based Virtual Machine, a Linux implementation), Xen (Citrix Linux implementation), Microsoft Windows Server Hyper-V (a headless version of the Windows OS core), and VMware's vSphere/ESXi platforms. All of these Type I hypervisors are designed for the high-end server market in enterprises and are designed to allow multiple VMs on a single set of server hardware. These platforms come with management tool sets to facilitate VM management in the enterprise.

Type II

Type II hypervisors run on top of a host operating system. In the beginning of the virtualization movement, Type II hypervisors were the most popular. Administrators could buy the VM software and install it on a server they already had running. Typical Type II hypervisors include Oracle's VirtualBox and VMware's VMware Player. These are designed for limited numbers of VMs, typically running in a desktop or small server environment.

Virtual Machine (VM) Sprawl Avoidance

Sprawl is the uncontrolled spreading and disorganization caused by lack of an organizational structure when many similar elements require management. Just as you can lose track of a file in a large file directory and have to hunt for it, you can lose track of a VM among many others that have been created. VMs basically are files that contain a copy of a working machine's disk and memory structures. Creating a new VM is a simple process. If an organization has only a couple of VMs, keeping track of them is relatively easy. But as the number of VMs grows rapidly over time, sprawl can set in. VM sprawl is a symptom of a disorganized structure. An organization needs to implement **VM sprawl** avoidance through policy. It can avoid VM sprawl through naming conventions and proper storage architectures so that the files are in the correct directory/folder, making finding the correct VM easy and efficient. But as in any filing system, it works only if everyone routinely follows the established policies and procedures to ensure that proper VM naming and filing are performed.

One of the strongest business cases for an integrated VM management tool such as ESXi Server from VMware is its ability to enable administrators to manage VMs and avoid sprawl. Being able to locate and use resources when required is an element of security, specifically availability, and sprawl causes availability issues.

VM Escape Protection

When multiple VMs are operating on a single hardware platform, one concern is **VM escape**, which is where software, either malware or an attacker, escapes from one VM to the underlying OS. Once the VM escape occurs, the attacker can attack the underlying OS or resurface in a different VM. When you examine the problem from a logical point of view, both VMs use the same RAM, the same processors, and so forth; the difference is one of timing and specific combinations. While the VM system is designed to provide protection, as with all things of larger scale, the devil is in the details. Large-scale VM environments have specific modules designed to detect escape and provide *VM escape protection* to other modules.

VM sprawl and VM escape are different and each pose specific issues to the deployment environment.

VDI/VDE

Virtual desktop infrastructure (VDI) and **virtual desktop environment (VDE)** are terms used to describe the hosting of a desktop environment on a central server. There are several advantages to this desktop environment. From a user perspective, their "machine" and all of its data are persisted in the server environment. This means that a user can move from machine to machine and have a singular environment following them around. And because the end-user devices are just simple doors back to the server instance of the user's desktop, the computing requirements at the edge point are considerably lower and can be performed on older machines. Users can utilize a wide range of machines, even mobile phones, to access their desktop and get their work finished. Security can be a very large advantage of VDI/VDE. Because all data, even when being processed, resides on servers inside the enterprise, there is nothing to compromise if a device is lost.

Fog Computing

Cloud computing has been described by pundits as using someone else's computer. If this is the case, then fog computing is using someone else's computers. **Fog computing** is a distributed form of cloud computing, in which the workload is performed on a distributed, decentralized architecture. Originally developed by Cisco, fog computing moves some of the work into the local space to manage latency issues, with the cloud being less synchronous. In this form, it is similar to edge computing, which is described in the next section.

Fog computing is an architecture where devices mediate processing between local hardware and remote servers. It regulates which information is sent to the cloud and which is processed locally, with the results sent to the user immediately and to the cloud with its latency. One can view fog computing as using intelligent gateways that handle immediate needs while managing the cloud's more efficient data storage and processing. This makes fog computing an adjunct to cloud, not a replacement.

Edge Computing

Edge computing refers to computing performed at the edge of a network. Edge computing has been driven by network vendors who have processing power on the network and want new markets rather than just relying on existing markets. Edge computing is similar to fog computing in that it is an adjunct to existing computing architectures—one that is designed for speed. The true growth in edge computing has occurred with the Internet of Things (IoT) revolution. This is because edge computing relies on what one defines as "the edge," coupled with the level of processing needed. In many environments, the actual edge is not as large as one might think, and what some would call edge computing is better accomplished using fog computing. But when you look at a system such as IoT, where virtually every device may be an edge, then the issue of where to do computing comes into play—on the tiny IoT device with limited resources or at the nearest device with computing power. This has led networking companies to create devices that can manage the data flow and do the computing on the way.

> Edge computing brings processing closer to the edge of the network, which optimizes web applications and IoT devices.

Thin Client

A thin client is a lightweight computer, with limited resources, whose primary purpose is to communicate with another machine. Thin clients can be very economical when they are used to connect to more powerful systems. Rather than having 32 GB of memory, a top-level processor, a high-end graphics card, and a large storage device on every desktop, where most of the power goes unused, the thin client allows access to a server where the appropriate resources are available and can be shared. With cloud computing and virtualization, where processing, storage, and even the apps themselves exist on servers in the cloud, what is needed is a device that connects to that power and acts as an input/output device.

Containers

Virtualization enables multiple OS instances to coexist on a single hardware platform. The concept of containers is similar, but rather than having multiple independent OSs, a container holds the portions of an OS that it needs separate from the kernel. Therefore, multiple containers can share an OS, yet have separate memory, CPU, and storage threads, guaranteeing that they will not interact with other containers. This allows multiple instances of an application or different applications to share a host OS with virtually no overhead. This also allows portability of the application to a degree separate from the OS stack. Multiple major container platforms exist, such as Docker. Rather than adopt a specific industry solution, the industry has coalesced around a standard form called the Open Container Initiative (OCI), designed to enable standardization and the market stability of the environment. Different vendors in the container space have slightly different terminologies, so you need to check with your specific implementation by vendor to understand the exact definition of container and cell in their environment.

You can think of containers as the evolution of the VM concept to the application space. A container consists of an entire runtime environment bundled into one package: an application, including all its dependencies, libraries, and other binaries, and the configuration files needed to run it. This eliminates the differences between development, test, and production environments, as the differences are in the container as a standard solution. By containerizing the application platform, including its dependencies, any differences in OS distributions, libraries, and underlying infrastructure are abstracted away and rendered moot.

Containers are a form of operating system virtualization. They are a packaged-up combination of code and dependencies that help applications run quickly in different computing environments.

Microservices/API

An application programming interface (API) is a means for specifying how one interacts with a piece of software. Let's use a web service as an example: if it uses the Representational State Transfer (REST) API, then the defined interface is a set of four actions expressed in HTTP:

- **GET** Get a single item or a collection.
- **POST** Add an item to a collection.
- **PUT** Edit an item that already exists in a collection.
- **DELETE** Delete an item in a collection.

Microservices is a different architectural style. Rather than defining the inputs and outputs, microservices divide a system into a series of small modules that can be coupled together to produce a complete system. Each of the modules in a microservices architecture is designed to be lightweight, with simple interfaces and structurally complete. This allows for more rapid development and maintenance of code.

Serverless Architecture

When an infrastructure is established "on premises," the unit of computing power is a server. To set up e-mail, you set up a server. To set up a website, you set up a server. The same issues exist for storage: Need storage? Buy disks. Yes, these disks can all be shared, but in the end, computing is servers, and storage is disks. With the cloud, this all changes. The cloud is like the ultimate shared resource, and with many large providers, you don't specify servers or disks; instead, you specify capacity. The provider then spins up the required resources. This **serverless architecture** simplifies a lot of things and adds significant capabilities. By specifying the resources needed in terms of processing power, the cloud provider can spin up the necessary resources. Because you are in essence renting from a large pool of resources, this gives you the ability to have surge capacity, where for a period of time you increase capacity for some specific upturn in usage. One of the operational advantages of this is that cloud providers can make these changes via automated scripts that can occur almost instantaneously, as opposed to the on-premises problem of procurement and configuration. This architecture also supports service integration, thus expanding the utility of computing to the business.

Serverless architecture is a way to develop and run applications and services without owning and managing an infrastructure. Servers are still used, but they are owned and managed "off-premises."

Chapter 18 Review

Chapter Summary

After reading this chapter and completing the exercises, you should understand the following about cloud computing and virtualization concepts.

Explore cloud security controls

- Cloud computing is characterized by the capabilities of on-demand self-service, resource pooling, rapid elasticity and scalability, and measured service.
- Cloud deployments use security controls just like normal IT deployments.

Compare and contrast cloud security solutions

- Cloud computing service models include IaaS, PaaS, SaaS, and XaaS.
- Clouds models can be on-premises, hosted, private, public, community, or hybrid.

Learn about cloud native controls versus third-party solutions

- Transit gateways connect clouds to customers.
- The connection between a cloud and a user is managed by a CASB.

Explore virtualization

- VMs come in two types: Type I (on bare metal) and Type II (on a host OS).
- Enterprise VM deployments at scale can result in VM sprawl.
- Software can leave a VM and cross to other VMs via VM escape mechanisms.
- Containers are a means of managing apps like VMs.

Key Terms

Anything as a Service (XaaS) *(699)*
cloud access security brokers (CASBs) *(708)*
cloud computing *(697)*
cloud service providers (CSPs) *(701)*
community cloud *(701)*
container security *(707)*
edge computing *(713)*
fog computing *(713)*
high availability *(704)*
hybrid cloud *(701)*
hypervisor *(711)*
Infrastructure as a Service (IaaS) *(698)*
infrastructure as code *(700)*
instance awareness *(707)*
managed security service provider (MSSP) *(708)*
on-premises *(701)*
Platform as a Service (PaaS) *(699)*
private cloud *(700)*
public cloud *(700)*
secrets management *(703)*
Security as a Service *(707)*
serverless architecture *(715)*
Software as a Service (SaaS) *(699)*
transit gateway *(702)*
Type I hypervisors *(711)*
Type II hypervisors *(711)*
virtual desktop environment (VDE) *(712)*
virtual desktop infrastructure (VDI) *(712)*
virtual private cloud endpoint *(707)*
virtualization *(711)*
VM escape *(712)*
VM sprawl *(712)*

Key Terms Quiz

Use terms from the Key Terms list to complete the sentences that follow. Don't use the same term more than once. Not all terms will be used.

1. _______________ is a distributed form of cloud computing, where the workload is performed on a distributed, decentralized architecture.
2. A(n) _______________ allows connections to and from a virtual private cloud instance.
3. A(n) _______________ structure is one where elements are combined from private, public, and community cloud structures.
4. A(n) _______________ is a network connection that is used to interconnect virtual private clouds (VPCs) and on-premises networks.
5. Specifying compute requirements in terms of resources needed (for example, processing power and storage) is an example of _______________.
6. _______________ is the infrastructure needed to enable the hosting of a desktop environment on a central server.
7. _______________ is the term used to denote the policies and procedures employed to connect the IAM systems of the enterprise and the cloud to enable communication with the data.
8. _______________ is the term used to describe the offering of a computing platform in the cloud.
9. When software, either malware or an attacker, escapes from one VM to the underlying OS, this is referred to as _______________.
10. The name of a capability that must be enabled on firewalls, secure web gateways, and cloud access security brokers (CASBs) to determine if the next system in a communication chain is legitimate or not is called _______________.

Multiple-Choice Quiz

1. The policies and procedures employed to connect the IAM systems of the enterprise and the cloud to enable communication with the data is referred to as what?
   - **A.** API inspection and integration
   - **B.** Secrets management
   - **C.** Dynamic resource allocation
   - **D.** Container security
2. You have deployed a network of Internet-connected sensors across a wide geographic area. These sensors are small, low-power IoT devices, and you need to perform temperature conversions and collect the data into a database. The calculations would be best managed by which architecture?
   - **A.** Fog computing
   - **B.** Edge computing
   - **C.** Thin client
   - **D.** Decentralized database in the cloud
3. Resource policies involve all of the following except?
   - **A.** Permissions
   - **B.** IAM
   - **C.** Cost
   - **D.** Access
4. Why is VM sprawl an issue?
   - **A.** VM sprawl uses too many resources on parallel functions.
   - **B.** The more virtual machines in use, the harder it is to migrate a VM to a live server.
   - **C.** Virtual machines are so easy to create, so you end up with hundreds of small servers only performing a single function.
   - **D.** When servers are no longer physical, it can be difficult to locate a specific machine.

5. Which of the following is a security policy enforcement point placed between cloud service consumers and cloud service providers to manage enterprise security policies as cloud-based resources are accessed?

   A. SWG

   B. VPC endpoint

   C. CASB

   D. Resource policies

6. You are planning to move some applications to the cloud, including your organization's accounting application, which is highly customized and does not scale well. Which cloud deployment model is best for this application?

   A. SaaS

   B. PaaS

   C. IaaS

   D. None of the above

7. Which is the most critical element in understanding your current cloud security posture?

   A. Cloud service agreement

   B. Networking security controls

   C. Encryption

   D. Application security

8. One of the primary resources in use at your organization is a standard database that many applications tie into. Which cloud deployment model is best for this kind of application?

   A. SaaS

   B. PaaS

   C. IaaS

   D. None of the above

9. Which cloud deployment model has the fewest security controls?

   A. Private

   B. Public

   C. Hybrid

   D. Community

10. What is the primary downside of a private cloud model?

   A. Restrictive access rules

   B. Cost

   C. Scalability

   D. Lack of vendor support

Essay Quiz

1. Compare and contrast VMs and containers.
2. What are the defining characteristics of cloud computing? What does it enable in the enterprise? How and when is it advantageous over standalone servers?

Lab Projects

• Lab Project 18.1

Experiment with virtual computing. Using a virtual machine solution (Virtual Box, VMware, or some other method), create a series of three virtual machines and connect them together using the virtual networking method provided by the VM vendor. Then experiment with using one machine as a source, another as the target (for example, web browser and web server or FTP client and server), with the third machine monitoring the activity via Wireshark and other network monitoring tools.

• Lab Project 18.2

Obtain a free account from one of the cloud service providers (Amazon, Oracle, or Microsoft) and create an instance of a data store and service in the cloud. Then explore how you connect and how things operate. How do you manage the instance, provisioning, security, and so on?

Chapter 19 Secure Software Development

Security Features != Secure Features

—Michael Howard, Microsoft Corporation

In this chapter, you will learn how to

- Describe how secure coding can be incorporated into the software development process
- List the major types of coding errors and their root causes
- Describe good software development practices and explain how they impact application security
- Describe how using a software development process enforces security inclusion in a project
- Use application-hardening techniques

Software engineering is the systematic development of software to fulfill a variety of needs, such as business, recreational, scientific, and educational functions, which are just a few of the many areas where software comes in handy. Regardless of the type of software, there is a universal requirement that software applications work properly, perform the desired functions, and perform them in the correct fashion. The functionality of software ranges from spreadsheets that accurately add figures to pacemakers that stimulate the heart. Developers know that functional specifications must be met for the software to be satisfactory. Software engineering, then, fits as many requirements as possible into the project management schedule timeline. But with analysts and developers working overtime to get as many functional elements correct as possible, the issue of nonfunctional requirements often gets pushed to the back burner or neglected entirely.

Security has been described as a nonfunctional requirement. This places it into a category of secondary importance for many developers. Their view is that if timelines, schedules, and budgets are all in the green, then maybe there will be time to devote to security programming.

The Software Engineering Process

This chapter contains many details of how to test for exploitable vulnerabilities in software. Do not perform or attempt these steps outside of systems for which you either are the owner or have explicit permission from the owner. Otherwise, you may find yourself being accused of hacking and possibly even facing legal charges.

Software does not build itself. This is good news for software designers, analysts, programmers, and the like, because the complexity of designing and building software enables them to engage in well-paying careers. To achieve continued success in this difficult work environment, software engineering processes have been developed. Rather than just sitting down and starting to write code at the onset of a project, software engineers use a complete development process. There are several major categories of software engineering processes. The waterfall model, the spiral model, and the evolutionary model are major examples. Within each of these major categories are numerous variations, and each group then personalizes the process to its project requirements and team capabilities.

Traditionally, security is an add-on item that is incorporated into a system after the functional requirements have been met. It is not an integral part of the software development lifecycle process. This places it at odds with both functional and lifecycle process requirements. The resolution to all of these issues is relatively simple: incorporate security into the process model and build it into the product along with each functional requirement. The challenge is in how to accomplish this goal. There are two separate and required elements needed to achieve this objective: first, the inclusion of security requirements and measures in the specific process model being used, and, second, the use of secure coding methods to prevent opportunities to introduce security failures into the software's design.

Process Models

There are several major software engineering process models, each with slightly different steps and sequences, yet they all have many similar items. The **waterfall model** is characterized by a multistep process in which steps follow each other in a linear, one-way fashion, like water in a waterfall. The **spiral model** has steps in phases that execute in a spiral fashion, repeating at different levels with each revolution of the model. The **agile model** is characterized by iterative development, where requirements and solutions evolve through an ongoing collaboration between self-organizing cross-functional teams. The **evolutionary model** is an iterative model designed to enable the construction of increasingly complex versions of a project. There are numerous other models and derivations in use today. The details of these process models are outside the scope of this book, and most of the detail is not significantly relevant to the issue of security. From a secure coding perspective, a **secure development lifecycle (SDL) model** is essential to success.

From requirements to system architecture to coding to testing, security is an embedded property in all aspects of the process. There are several specific items of significance with respect to security. Four primary items of interest, regardless of the particular model or methodology employed in software creation, are the requirements, design, coding, and testing phases. These (and other) phases are described in the following section.

Secure Development Lifecycle

There may be as many different software engineering methods as there are software engineering groups, but an analysis of these methods indicates that most share common elements from which an understanding of a universal methodology can be obtained. For decades, secure coding—that is, creating code that does what it is supposed to do and only what it is supposed to do—has not been high on the radar for most organizations. The past decade of explosive connectivity and the rise of malware and hackers have increased awareness of this issue significantly. A recent alliance of several major software firms concerned with secure coding principles revealed several interesting patterns. First, they were all attacking the problem using different methodologies yet in surprisingly similar fashions. Second, they found a series of principles that appears to be related to success in this endeavor.

First, recognition of the need to include secure coding principles into the development process is a common element among all firms. Microsoft has been very open and vocal about its implementation of its SDL and has published significant volumes of information surrounding its genesis and evolution (https://www.microsoft.com/en-us/sdl/default.aspx).

The Software Assurance Forum for Excellence in Code (SAFECode) is an organization formed by some of the leading software development firms with the objective of advancing software assurance through better development methods. SAFECode (www.safecode.org) members include EMC, Microsoft, and Intel. An examination of SAFECode members' processes reveals an assertion that secure coding must be treated as an issue that exists throughout the development process and cannot be effectively treated at a few checkpoints with checklists. Regardless of the software development process used, the first step down the path to secure coding is to infuse the process with secure coding principles.

Threat Modeling and Attack Surface Area Minimization

Two important tools have come from the secure coding revolution: attack surface area minimization and threat modeling.

Attack surface area minimization is a strategy to reduce the places where code can be attacked. *Threat modeling* is the process of analyzing threats and their potential effects on software in a finely detailed fashion. The output of the threat model process is a compilation of threats and how they interact with the software. This information is communicated across the design and coding team so that potential weaknesses can be mitigated before the software is released.

Step by Step

Threat Modeling Steps

Follow the steps are used to conduct threat modeling:

Step 1 *Define scope.* Communicate what is in scope and out of scope with respect to the threat modeling effort. This includes both attacks and software components.

Step 2 *Enumerate assets.* List all the component parts of the software being examined.

Step 3 *Decompose assets.* Break the software into small subsystems composed of inputs and outputs. This is to simplify data flow analysis and to capture internal entry points.

Step 4 *Enumerate threats.* List all the threats to the software.

Step 5 *Classify threats.* Classify the threats by their mode of operation.

Step 6 *Associate threats to assets.* Connect specific threats and modes to specific software subsystems.

Step 7 *Score and rank threats.* Score each specific threat–asset pair and then rank them from most dangerous to least dangerous.

Step 8 *Create threat trees.* Create a graphical representation of the required elements for an attack vector.

Step 9 *Determine and score mitigation.* Score the mitigation efforts associated with each attack vector.

Requirements Phase

The **requirements phase** should define the specific security requirements if there is any expectation of them being designed into the project. Regardless of the methodology employed, the process is all about completing the requirements. Secure coding does not refer to adding security functionality into a piece of software. Security functionality is a standalone requirement. The objective of the secure coding process is to properly implement this and all other requirements so that the resultant software performs as desired and only as desired.

The requirements process is a key component of security in software development. Security-related items enumerated during the requirements process are visible throughout the rest of the software development process. They can be architected into the systems and subsystems, addressed during coding, and tested. For the subsequent steps to be effective, the security requirements need to be both specific and positive. Requirements such as

> **Tech Tip**
>
> **Common Secure Coding Requirements**
>
> *Common secure coding requirements include the following:*
>
> - *Analysis of security and privacy risk*
> - *Authentication and password management*
> - *Audit logging and analysis*
> - *Authorization and role management*
> - *Code integrity and validation testing*
> - *Cryptography and key management*
> - *Data validation and sanitization*
> - *Network and data security*
> - *Ongoing education and awareness*
> - *Team staffing requirements*
> - *Third-party component analysis*

"make secure code" or "no insecure code" are nonspecific and not helpful in the overall process. Specific requirements such as "prevent unhandled buffer overflows and unhandled input exceptions" can be specifically coded for in each piece of code.

During the requirements activity, it is essential that the project/program manager and any business leaders who set schedules and allocate resources are aware of the need and requirements of the secure development process. The cost of adding security at a later time rises exponentially, with the most expensive form being the common release-and-patch process used by many firms. The development of both functional and nonfunctional security requirements occurs in tandem with other requirements through the development of use cases, analysis of customer inputs, implementation of company policies, and compliance with industry best practices. Depending on the nature of a particular module, special attention may be focused on sensitive issues such as personally identifiable information (PII), sensitive data, and intellectual property data.

One of the outputs of the requirements phase is a security document that helps guide the remaining aspects of the development process, ensuring that secure code requirements are being addressed. These requirements can be infused into design, coding, and testing, thus ensuring they are addressed throughout the development process.

Design Phase

Coding without designing first is like building a house without using plans. This might work fine on small projects, but as the scope grows, so do complexity and the opportunity for failure. Designing a software project is a multifaceted process. Just as there are many ways to build a house, there are many ways to build a program. Design is a process involving trade-offs and choices, and the criteria used during the design decisions can have lasting impacts on program construction. Two major secure coding principles can be applied during the design phase that can have a large influence on the code quality. The first of these is the concept of *minimizing the attack surface area*. Reducing the avenues of attack available to a hacker can have obvious benefits. Minimizing the attack surface area is a concept that tends to run counter to the way software has been designed—most designs come as a result of incremental accumulation, adding features and functions without regard to maintainability. The second is to perform a risk analysis of the design to include threats and mitigations.

Coding Phase

The point at which the design is implemented is the coding step in the software development process. The act of instantiating an idea into code is a point where an error can enter the process. These errors are of two types: the failure to include desired functionality and the inclusion of undesired behavior in the code. Testing for the first type of error is relatively easy if the requirements are enumerated in a previous phase of the process.

Testing for the inclusion of undesired behavior is significantly more difficult. Testing for an *unknown* is a virtually impossible task. What makes this possible at all is the concept of testing for categories of previously determined errors. Several classes of common errors have been observed. Enumerations of known software weaknesses and vulnerabilities have been compiled and published as **Common Weakness Enumeration (CWE)** and **Common Vulnerabilities and Exposures (CVE)** by the MITRE Corporation, a government-funded research group (www.mitre.org). These enumerations have enabled significant advancement in the development of methods to reduce code vulnerabilities. Both CVE and CWE are vendor- and language-neutral methods of describing errors. These enumerations allow a common vocabulary for communication about weaknesses and vulnerabilities. This common vocabulary has also led to the development of automated tools to manage the tracking of these issues.

There are many common coding errors, but some of the primary and most damaging are least privilege violations and cryptographic failures. Language-specific failures are another common source of vulnerabilities.

There are several ways to go about searching for coding errors that lead to vulnerabilities in software. One method is by manual code inspection. Developers can be trained to "not make mistakes," but this approach has not proven successful. This has led to the development of a class of tools designed to analyze code for potential defects.

Static code-analysis tools can be used to analyze software for coding errors that can lead to known types of vulnerabilities and weaknesses. Sophisticated static code analyzers can examine codebases to find function calls of unsafe libraries, potential buffer-overflow conditions, and numerous other conditions. Currently, CWE describes more than 750 different weaknesses—far too many for developer memory and direct knowledge. In light of this and because some weaknesses are more prevalent than others, MITRE has collaborated with SANS to develop the **CWE/SANS Top 25 Most Dangerous Software Errors** list. One of the ideas behind the Top 25 list is that it can be updated periodically as the threat landscape changes. Explore the current listing at http://cwe.mitre.org/top25/.

The two main enumerations of common software errors are the Top 25 list maintained by MITRE and the **Open Web Application Security Project (OWASP)** Top Ten list for web applications. Depending on the type of application being evaluated, these lists provide a solid starting point for security analysis of known error types. MITRE is the repository of the industry-standard list for standard programs, and OWASP is for web applications. As the causes of common errors do not change quickly, these lists are not updated every year.

Least Privilege One of the central paradigms of security is the notion of running a process with the least required privilege. **Least privilege** requires that the developer understand what privileges are needed specifically for an application to execute and access all its necessary resources. Obviously, from a developer point of view, it would be easier to use administrative-level permission for all tasks, which removes access controls from the equation, but this also removes the very protections that access-level controls are designed to provide. The other end of the spectrum is software designed for operating systems without any built-in security, such as early versions of Windows and some mainframe OSs, where security comes in the form of an application package. When migrating these applications to platforms, the issue of access controls arises.

As developers increasingly are tasked with incorporating security into their work, the natural tendency is to code around this "new" security

Developers who do development and testing on an integrated environment on their own PC—that is, they have a web server and/or database engine on their PC—can produce code that works fine on their machine, where unified account permissions exist (and where they are frequently the administrator). When this code is transitioned to a distributed environment, permissions can become an issue. The proper method is to manage permissions appropriately on the developer box from the beginning.

When software fails because of an exploited vulnerability, the hacker typically achieves whatever level of privilege that the application had prior to the exploit occurrence. If an application always operates with root-level privilege, this will be passed on to the hacker as well.

requirement, developing in the same fashion as before, as if security is not an issue. This is commonly manifested as a program that runs only under an administrative-level account or runs as a service utilizing the SYSTEM account for permissions in Windows. Both of these are bad practices that reduce security, introduce hard-to-fix errors, and produce code that is harder to maintain and extend.

The key principle in designing and coding software with respect to access-level controls is to plan and understand the nature of the software's interaction with the operating system and system resources. Whenever the software accesses a file, a system component, or another program, the issue of appropriate access control needs to be addressed. And although the simple practice of just giving everything root or administrative access may solve this immediate problem, it creates much bigger security issues that will be much less apparent in the future. An example is when a program runs correctly when initiated from an administrator account but fails when run under normal user privileges. The actual failure may stem from a privilege issue, but the point of failure in the code may be many procedures away and diagnosing these types of failures is a difficult and time-consuming operation.

The bottom line is actually simple: Determine what needs to be accessed and what the appropriate level of permission is and then use that level in design and implementation. Repeat this for every item accessed. In the end, it is rare that administrative access is needed for many functions. Once the application is designed, the whole process will need to be repeated with the installation procedure because, frequently, installing software will need a higher level of access than needed for executing the software. Design and implementation details must be determined with respect to required permission levels, not to a higher level such as administrative root access just for convenience.

The cost of failure to heed the principle of least privilege can be twofold. First, you have expensive, time-consuming access-violation errors that are hard to track down and correct. Second, you face a problem when an exploit is found that allows some other program to use portions of your code in an unauthorized fashion. A prime example is the sendmail exploit in the UNIX environment. Because sendmail requires root-level access for some functions, the sendmail exploit inserts foreign code into the process stream, thereupon executing its code at root-level access because the sendmail process thread itself has root-level access. In this case, sendmail needs the root-level access, but this exploit illustrates that the risk is real and will be exploited once found. Proper design can, in many cases, eliminate the need for such high-access privilege levels.

Cryptographic Failures Hailed as a solution for all problems, cryptography has as much chance of being the ultimate cure-all as did the tonics sold by traveling salesmen of a different era. There is no such thing as a universal solution, yet there are some versatile tools that provide a wide range of protections. Cryptography falls into this "useful tool" category. Proper use of cryptography can provide a wealth of programmatic functionality—from authentication and confidentiality to integrity and nonrepudiation. These are valuable tools, and many programs rely on proper cryptographic implementation for important functionality. The need for this functionality in an application tempts programmers to roll their own cryptographic functions. This is a task fraught with opportunity for catastrophic error.

Cryptographic errors come from several common causes. One typical mistake is choosing to develop your own cryptographic algorithm. Developing a secure cryptographic algorithm is far from an easy task, and even when done by experts, weaknesses can occur that make the algorithms unusable. Cryptographic algorithms become trusted after years of scrutiny and attacks, and any new algorithms would take years to join the trusted set. If you instead decide to rest on secrecy, be warned that secret or proprietary algorithms have never provided the desired level of protection. One of the axioms of cryptography is that there is no security through obscurity.

Deciding to use a trusted algorithm is a proper start, but several major errors can still occur. The first is an error in instantiating the algorithm. An easy way to avoid this type of error is to use a library function that has already been properly tested. Sources of these library functions abound, and they provide an economical solution to this functionality's needs. Once you have an algorithm and have chosen a particular instantiation, the next item needed is the random number to generate a random key. Cryptographic functions use an algorithm and a key, the latter being a digital number.

The generation of a real random number is not a trivial task. Computers are machines that are renowned for reproducing the same output when given the same input, so generating a pure, nonreproducible random number is a challenge. Functions for producing random numbers are built into the libraries of most programming languages, but these are pseudorandom number generators, and although the distribution of output numbers appears random, they generate a reproducible sequence. Given the same input, a second run of the function will produce the same sequence of "random" numbers. Determining the seed and random sequence and using this knowledge to "break" a cryptographic function has been used more than once to bypass the security. This method was used to subvert an early version of Netscape's SSL implementation. Using a number that is **cryptographically random**—suitable for an encryption function—resolves this problem. Again, the use of trusted library functions designed and tested for generating such numbers is the proper methodology.

Now you have a good algorithm and a good random number—so where can you go wrong? Well, storing private keys in areas where they can be recovered by an unauthorized person is the next worry. Poor key management has failed many a cryptographic implementation. A famous example of getting cryptographic keys from an executable and using them to break a cryptographic scheme is the case of hackers using this exploit to break DVD encryption and develop the DeCSS program. Tools have been developed that can search code for "random" keys and extract the key from the code or running process. The bottom line is simple: do not hard-code secret keys in your code. They can, and will, be discovered. Keys should be generated and then passed by reference, minimizing the travel of copies across a network or application. Storing them in memory in a noncontiguous fashion is also important to prevent external detection. Again, trusted cryptographic library functions come to the rescue.

Tech Tip

Use Only Approved Cryptographic Functions

Always use vetted and approved libraries for all cryptographic work. Never create your own cryptographic functions, even when using known algorithms. For example, the .NET Framework has a number of cryptography classes that developers can call upon to perform encryption services.

Never hard-code secret keys into codebases. Hackers can use disassemblers and various code differential tools to dissect your code and find static information.

You might have deduced by this point that the term *library function* has become a common theme in this section. This is not an accident. In fact, this is probably one of the best pieces of advice from this chapter: use commercially proven functions for cryptographic functionality.

> **Tech Tip**
>
> **Deprecated C Functions**
>
> *Microsoft recommends that the following function families be deprecated/removed:*
>
> - ***strcpy()** and **strncpy()***
> - ***strcat()** and **strncat()***
> - ***scanf()***
> - ***sprint()***
> - ***gets()***
> - ***memcpy(), CopyMemory(), and RtlCopyMemory()***

Language-Specific Failures Modern programming languages are built around libraries that permit reuse and that speed up the development process. The development of many library calls and functions was done without regard to secure coding implications, and this has led to issues related to specific library functions. As will be shown later in the chapter, **strcpy()** has had its fair share of involvement in buffer overflows and should be avoided. Developing and maintaining a series of **deprecated functions** and prohibiting their use in new code, while removing them from old code when possible, is a proven path toward more secure code.

Banned functions are easily handled via automated code reviews during the check-in process. The challenge is in garnering the developer awareness as to their potential dangers and the value of safer coding practices.

Testing Phase

If the requirements phase marks the beginning of the generation of security in code, then the **testing phase** marks the other boundary. Although there are additional functions after testing, no one wants a user to validate errors in code. Errors discovered after the code has shipped are the most expensive to fix, regardless of the severity. Employing **use cases** to compare program responses to known inputs and then comparing the output to the desired output is a proven method of testing software. The design of use cases to test specific functional requirements occurs based on the requirements determined in the requirements phase. Providing additional security-related use cases is the process-driven way of ensuring that security specifics are also tested.

The testing phase is the last opportunity to determine that the software performs properly before the end user experiences problems. Errors found in testing are late in the development process, but at least they are still learned about internally, before the end customer suffers. Testing can occur at each level of development: module, subsystem, system, and completed application. The sooner errors are discovered and corrected, the lower the cost and the lesser the impact will be to project schedules. This makes testing an essential step in the process of developing good programs.

Testing for security requires a much broader series of tests than functional testing does. Misuse cases can be formulated to verify that vulnerabilities cannot be exploited. *Fuzz testing* (also known as *fuzzing*) uses random inputs to check for exploitable buffer overflows. Code reviews by design and development teams are used to verify that security elements such as input and output validation are functional because these are the best defenses against a wide range of attacks, including cross-site scripting and cross-site request forgeries. Code walkthroughs begin with design reviews, architecture examinations, unit testing, subsystem testing, and, ultimately, complete system testing.

Testing includes **white-box testing**, where the test team has access to the design and coding elements; **black-box testing**, where the team does not have access; and **gray-box testing**, where the test team has more information than in black-box testing but not as much as in white-box testing. These modes of testing are used for different objectives; for example, fuzz testing works perfectly fine regardless of the type of testing, whereas certain types of penetration tests are better in a white-box testing environment. Testing is also performed on the production code to verify that error handling and exception reporting, which may provide detailed diagnostic information during development, are squelched to prevent information release during error conditions.

Final code can be subjected to *penetration tests,* designed specifically to test configuration, security controls, and common defenses such as input and output validation and error handling. Penetration testing can explore the functionality and whether specific security controls can be bypassed. Using the attack surface analysis information, penetration testers can emulate adversaries and attempt a wide range of known attack vectors to verify that the known methods of attack are all mitigated.

One of the most powerful tools that can be used in testing is fuzzing, the systematic application of a series of malformed inputs to test how the program responds.

Deployment Phase

Although not considered by many to be part of the software development process, the **deployment phase** is the release of new changes to production. The ultimate success or failure of the development process is measured in production, so this should not be a dismissed phase. Code should not be released to a production environment until it has passed all the necessary steps required before release. These steps include the necessary program reviews established by the defined process. The development process does not stop here either, because after deployment there is still an ongoing maintenance phase.

Maintenance Phase

The **maintenance phase** begins when the software moves to production. In a perfect world, everything would be perfect—there would be no compatibility issues, no bugs, no need to issue patches or fixes, and the only need for new releases would be for new features. But the world isn't perfect, and software certainly isn't, and errors and vulnerabilities will be discovered. A key element in a secure development process is the triaging and handling of errors when they are found. Both in the development process and after release. The maintenance phase has a primary activity of collecting and managing issues associated with software releases. Bugs and vulnerabilities need to be classified, and if determined to be essential for immediate fixing, the patch process is managed via this phase.

Environments

Most organizations have multiple, separate computing *environments* designed to provide isolation between the functions of development, test, staging, and production. The primary purpose of having these separate environments is to prevent security incidents arising from untested code ending up in the production environment. The hardware of these environments is segregated and access control lists are used to prevent users from accessing more than one environment at a time. Moving code between environments requires a special account that can access both, minimizing issues of cross-contamination.

Development

The *development environment* is sized, configured, and set up for developers to develop applications and systems. Unlike production hardware, the development hardware does not have to be scalable, and it probably does not need to be as responsive for given transactions. The development platform does need to use the same OS type and version as used in the production environment; for example, developing on Windows and deploying to Linux is fraught with difficulties that can be avoided by matching the environments in terms of OS type and version. After code is successfully developed, it is moved to a test system.

Test

The **test environment** fairly closely mimics the production environment—same versions of software, down to patch levels, same sets of permissions, same file structures, and so forth. The purpose of the test environment is to test a system fully prior to deploying it into production to ensure that it is bug-free and will not disrupt the production environment. The test environment may not scale like production, but from a software/hardware footprint, it will look exactly like production. This is important to ensure that system-specific settings are tested in an environment identical to that in which they will be run.

Staging

The **staging environment** is an optional environment, but it is commonly used when an organization has multiple production environments. After passing testing, the system moves into staging, from where it can be deployed to the different production systems. The primary purpose of staging is to serve as a sandbox after testing, so the test system can test the next set, while the current set is deployed across the enterprise. One method of deployment is a staged deployment, where software is deployed to part of the enterprise and then a pause occurs to watch for unseen problems. If none occur, the deployment continues, stage by stage, until all of the production systems are changed. By moving software in this manner, you never lose the old production system until the end of the move, giving you time to monitor and catch any unforeseen problems. This also prevents the total loss of production to a failed update.

Production

The **production environment** is where the systems work with real data, doing the business that the system is intended to perform. This is an environment where, by design, very few changes occur, and those that do must first be approved and tested via the system's change management process.

Secure Coding Concepts

Application security begins with code that is secure and free of vulnerabilities. Unfortunately, all code has weaknesses and vulnerabilities, so instantiating the code in a manner that has effective defenses to prevent the exploitation of vulnerabilities can maintain a desired level of security. Proper handling of configurations, errors and exceptions, and inputs can assist in the creation of a secure application. Testing the application throughout the system lifecycle can determine the actual security risk profile of a system.

There are numerous individual elements in the secure development lifecycle that can assist a team in developing secure code. Correct secure development lifecycle processes, such as input validation, proper error and exception handling, and cross-site scripting and cross-site request forgery mitigations, can improve the security of code. Process elements such as security testing, fuzzing, and patch management also help to ensure applications meet a desired risk profile.

Error and Exception Handling

Every application will encounter errors and exceptions that need to be handled in a secure manner. One attack methodology includes forcing errors to move an application from normal operation to exception handling. During an exception, it is common practice to record/report the condition, including supporting information such as the data that resulted in the error. This information can be invaluable in diagnosing the cause of the error condition. The challenge is in where this information is captured. The best method is to capture it in a log file, where it can be secured by an access control list (ACL). The worst case is when it is echoed to the user. Echoing error condition details to users can provide valuable information to attackers when they cause errors on purpose.

> All errors and exceptions should be trapped and handled in the generating routine.

Improper exception handling can lead to a wide range of disclosures. Errors associated with Structured Query Language (SQL) statements can disclose data structures and data elements. Remote procedure call (RPC) errors can give up sensitive information such as filenames, paths, and server names. Programmatic errors can give up line numbers that an exception occurred on, the method that was invoked, and information such as stack elements.

Input and Output Validation

With the move to web-based applications, common errors have shifted from buffer overflows to input-handling issues. Users have the ability to manipulate input, so it is up to the developer to handle the input appropriately to prevent malicious entries from having an effect. Buffer overflows could be considered a class of improper input, but newer attacks include canonicalization attacks and arithmetic attacks. Probably the most important defensive mechanism that can be employed is input validation. Considering all inputs to be hostile until properly validated can mitigate many attacks based on common vulnerabilities. This is a challenge because the validation efforts need to occur after all parsers have completed manipulating input streams, a common function in web-based applications using Unicode and other international character sets.

Consider all input to be hostile. Input validation is one of the most important secure coding techniques employed, mitigating a wide array of potential vulnerabilities. Failure to properly validate input is the leading cause of vulnerabilities.

Input validation is especially well suited for the following vulnerabilities: buffer overflow, reliance on untrusted inputs in a security decision, cross-site scripting, cross-site request forgery, path traversal, and incorrect calculation of buffer size. Input validation may seem suitable for various injection attacks, but given the complexity of the input and the ramifications from legal but improper input streams, this method falls short for most injection attacks. What can work is a form of recognition and whitelisting approach, where the input is validated and then parsed into a standard structure that is then executed. This restricts the attack surface to not only legal inputs but also expected inputs.

Tech Tip

Pointer Dereference

Some computer languages use a construct referred to as a pointer, which is a element that refers to the memory location that holds a variable as opposed to the value in the memory location. To get the value at the memory location denoted by a pointer variable, one must dereference the pointer. The act of pointer dereference *now changes the meaning of the object to the contents of the memory location, not the memory location as identified by the pointer. Pointers can be very powerful and allow fast operations across a wide range of structures. But they can also be dangerous, as mistakes in their use can lead to unexpected consequences. When a programmer uses user inputs in concert with pointers, for example, this lets the user pick a place in an array and use a pointer to reference the value. Mistakes in the input validation can lead to errors in pointer dereference, which may or may not trigger an error, as the location will contain data and it will be returned.*

In today's computing environment, a wide range of character sets is used. Unicode allows multilanguage support. Character code sets allow multilanguage capability. Various encoding schemes, such as hex encoding, are supported to allow diverse inputs. The net result of all these input methods is that there are numerous ways to create the same input to a program. *Canonicalization* is the process by which application programs manipulate strings to a base form, creating a foundational representation of the input. A **canonicalization error** arises from the fact that inputs to a web application may be processed by multiple applications, such as the web server, application server, and database server, each with its own parsers to resolve appropriate canonicalization issues. Where this is an issue relates to the form of the input string at the time of error checking. If the error-checking routine occurs prior to resolution to canonical form, then issues may be missed. The string representing */../*, used in directory traversal attacks, can be obscured by encoding and hence missed by a character string match before an application parser manipulates it to canonical form.

The first line of defense is to write solid code. Regardless of the language used, or the source of outside input, prudent programming practice is to treat all input from outside a function as hostile. Validate all inputs as if they were hostile and an attempt to force a buffer overflow. Accept the notion that although during development everyone may be on the same team, be conscientious, and be compliant with design rules, future maintainers may not be as robust.

Normalization

Normalization is an initial step in the input validation process. Specifically, it is the process of creating the canonical form, or simplest form, of a string before processing. Strings can be encoded using Unicode and other encoding methods. This makes byte-by-byte comparisons meaningless when trying to test user input of strings. Checking to see whether the string is "rose" can be difficult when "A Rose is a rose is a r%6fse." The process of normalization converts all of these instances to "rose," where it can then be screened as valid input.

Different libraries exist to assist developers in performing this part of input validation. Developers should always normalize their inputs prior to validation steps to remove Unicode and other encoding issues. Per the Unicode standard, "When implementations keep strings in a normalized form, they can be assured that equivalent strings have a unique binary representation."

Tech Tip

A Rose is a rose is a r%6fse

Canonical form *refers to simplest form and, because of the many encoding schemes in use, can be a complex issue. Characters can be encoded in ASCII, Unicode, hex, UTF-8, or even combinations of these. So, if the attacker desires to obfuscate a response, then several things can happen.*

By URL-encoding URL strings, it may be possible to circumvent filter security systems and IDS. For example, the URL

```
http://www.myweb.com/cgi?file=/etc/passwd
```

can be written as

```
http://www.myweb.com/cgi?file=/
%2F%65%74%63%2F%70%61%73%73%77%64
```

Double encoding can complicate the matter even further. For example, the round 1 decoding

```
scripts/..%255c../winnt
```

becomes

```
scripts/..%5c../winnt
(%25 = "%" Character)
```

And the round 2 decoding

```
scripts/..%5c../winnt
```

becomes

```
scripts/..\../winnt
```

The bottom line is simple: know that encoding can be used and plan for it when designing input verification mechanisms. Expect encoded transmissions to be used to attempt to bypass security mechanisms.

A second, and equally important, line of defense is proper string handling. String handling is a common event in programs, and string-handling functions are the source of a large number of known buffer-overflow vulnerabilities. Using **strncpy()** in place of **strcpy()** is a possible method of improving security because **strncpy()** requires an input length for the number of characters to be copied. This simple function call replacement can ultimately fail, however, because Unicode and other encoding methods can make character counts meaningless. Resolving this issue requires new library calls and much closer attention to how input strings, and subsequently output strings, can be abused. Proper use of functions to achieve program objectives is essential to prevent unintended effects such as buffer overflows. Using the **gets()** function can probably never be totally safe since it reads from the stdin stream until a linefeed or carriage return. In most cases, there is no way to predetermine whether the input is going to overflow the buffer. A better solution is to use a C++ stream object or the

fgets() function. The function **fgets()** requires an input buffer length and hence avoids the overflow. Simply replace

```
{
     char buf[512];
     gets( buf ); ←if buf is > 512 bytes, overflow will occur
/*      The rest of your code ... */
}
```

with this:

```
{
     char buf[512];
     fgets( buf, sizeof(buf), stdin );
     /* ... the rest of your code ... */
}
```

Output validation is just as important in many cases as input validation. If querying a database for a username and password match, the expected forms of the output of the match function should be either one match or none. If the record count is used to indicate the level of match, which is a common practice, then a value other than 0 or 1 would be an error. Defensive coding using output validation would not act on values greater than 1 because these are clearly an error and should be treated as a failure.

Bug Tracking

Bug tracking is a foundational element in secure development. All bugs are enumerated, classified, and tracked. If the classification of a bug exceeds a set level, then it must be resolved before the code advances to the next level of development. Bugs are classified based on the risk the vulnerability exposes. Microsoft uses these four levels:

- **Critical** A security vulnerability having the highest potential for damage
- **Important** A security vulnerability having significant potential for damage, but less than Critical
- **Moderate** A security vulnerability having moderate potential for damage, but less than Important
- **Low** A security vulnerability having low potential for damage

Examples of Critical vulnerabilities include those that without warning to the user can result in remote exploit involving elevation of privilege. Critical is really reserved for the most significant risks. As an example of the distinction between Critical and Important, a vulnerability that would lead to a machine failure requiring reinstallation of software would only score Important. The key difference is that the user would know of this penetration and risk, whereas for a Critical vulnerability, the user may never know that it occurred.

The tracking of errors serves several purposes. First, from a management perspective, what is measured is managed, both by management and by those involved. Over time, fewer errors will occur if the workforce knows they are being tracked, are taken seriously, and represent an issue with the product. Second, since not all errors are immediately correctable, this enables future correction when a module is rewritten. Zero defects in code is like zero defects in quality; it's not an achievable objective. But this does not mean that constant improvement of the process cannot dramatically reduce the error rates. Evidence from firms involved in SAFECode support this because they are reaping the benefits of lower error rates and reduced development costs from lower levels of corrective work.

Application Attacks

Attacks against a system can occur at the network level, at the operating system level, at the application level, and at the user level (social engineering). Early attack patterns were against the network, but most of today's attacks are aimed at the applications, primarily because that is where the objective of most attacks resides—in the infamous words of bank robber Willie Sutton, "because that's where the money is." In fact, many of today's attacks on systems use combinations of vulnerabilities in networks, operating systems, and applications—all a means to an end to obtain the desired objective of an attack, which is usually some form of data.

Application-level attacks take advantage of several facts associated with computer applications. First, most applications are large programs written by groups of programmers and by their nature have errors in design and coding that create vulnerabilities. For a list of typical vulnerabilities, see the Common Vulnerabilities and Exposures list maintained by MITRE (http://cve.mitre.org). Second, even when vulnerabilities are discovered and patched by software vendors, end users are slow to apply patches, as evidenced by the SQL Slammer incident in January 2003. The vulnerability exploited was a buffer overflow, and the vendor supplied a patch six months prior to the outbreak, yet the worm still spread quickly because of the multitude of unpatched systems.

> Cross-site scripting is abbreviated as XSS to distinguish it from Cascading Style Sheets (CSS).

Cross-Site Scripting

Cross-site scripting (XSS) is one of the most common web attack methodologies.

A *cross-site scripting attack* is a code injection attack in which an attacker sends code in response to an input request. This code is then rendered by the web server, resulting in the execution of the code by the web server. Cross-site scripting attacks take advantage of a few common elements in web-based systems. First is the common failure to perform complete input validation. XSS sends a script in response to an input request, even when the script is not the expected or authorized input type. Second is the nature of web-based systems to dynamically self-create output. Web-based systems are frequently collections of images, text, scripts, and more, which are presented by a web server to a browser that interprets and renders. XSS attacks can exploit the dynamically self-created output by executing a script in the client browser that receives the altered output.

The cause of the vulnerability is weak user input validation. If input is not validated properly, an attacker can include a script in their input and have it rendered as part of the web process. There are several different types of XSS attacks, distinguished by the effect of the script:

- **Nonpersistent XSS attack** The injected script is not persisted or stored but rather is immediately executed and passed back via the web server.
- **Persistent XSS attack** The script is permanently stored on the web server or some back-end storage. This allows the script to be used against others who log in to the system.
- **DOM-based XSS attack** The script is executed in the browser via the Document Object Model (DOM) process as opposed to the web server.

Cross-site scripting attacks can result in a wide range of consequences, and in some cases, the list can be anything that a clever scripter can devise. Common uses that have been seen in the wild include the following:

- Stealing authentication information from a web application
- Hijacking a session
- Deploying hostile content
- Changing user settings, including future users
- Impersonating a user
- Phishing or stealing sensitive information

Input validation, also commonly known as data validation, is the structured and proper testing of any input that is supplied by an application or user. Input validation prevents improperly formed (malformed) data from entering a system.

Controls to defend against XSS attacks include the use of anti-XSS libraries to strip scripts from the input sequences. Various other ways to mitigate XSS attacks include limiting types of uploads and screening the size of uploads, whitelisting inputs, and so on, but attempting to remove scripts from inputs can be a tricky task. Well-designed anti-XSS input library functions have proven to be the best defense. Cross-site scripting vulnerabilities are easily tested for and should be part of the test plan for every application. Testing a variety of encoded and unencoded inputs for scripting vulnerability is an essential test element.

Injections

Using input to a function without validation has already been shown to be risky behavior. Another issue with unvalidated input is the case of **code injection**. Rather than the input being appropriate for the function, this code injection changes the function in an unintended way. A **SQL injection** attack is a form of code injection aimed at any SQL-based database, regardless of vendor.

The primary method of defense against this type of vulnerability is similar to that for buffer overflows: validate all inputs. But rather than validating toward just length, you need to validate inputs for content. Imagine a web page that asks for user input and then uses that input to build a subsequent page. Now imagine that the user puts the text for a JavaScript function in the middle of their input sequence, along with a call to the script. Now, the generated web page has an added JavaScript function that is called when displayed. Passing the user input through an **HTMLencode** function before use can prevent such attacks.

Again, good programming practice goes a long way toward preventing these types of vulnerabilities. This places the burden not just on the programmers but also on the process of training programmers, the software engineering process that reviews code, and the testing process to catch programming errors. This is much more than a single-person responsibility; everyone involved in the software development process needs to be aware of the types and causes of these errors, and safeguards need to be in place to prevent their propagation.

SQL Injection

A SQL injection attack is a form of code injection aimed at any SQL-based database, regardless of vendor. An example of this type of attack is where the function takes the user-provided inputs for username and password and substitutes them into a **where** clause of a SQL statement with the express purpose of changing the **where** clause into one that gives a false answer to the query.

Assume the desired SQL statement is as follows:

```
select count(*) from users_table where username = 'JDoe' and
password = 'newpass'
```

The values JDoe and newpass are provided by the user and are simply inserted into the string sequence. Though seemingly safe functionally, this can be easily corrupted by using the following sequence:

```
' or 1=1 –
```

This changes the **where** clause to one that returns all records, as shown here:

```
select count(*) from users_table where username = 'JDoe' and
password = '' or 1=1 –'
```

The addition of the **or** clause, with an always-true statement and the beginning of a comment line to block the trailing single quote, alters the SQL statement to one in which the **where** clause is rendered inoperable.

Stored procedures are precompiled methods implemented within a database engine. Stored procedures act as a secure coding mechanism because they offer an isolation of user input from the actual SQL statements being executed. This is the primary defense mechanism against SQL injection attacks—in other words, separation of user input from the SQL statements. User-supplied input data is essential in interactive applications that use databases; these types of applications allow the user to define the specificity of search, match, and so on. But what cannot happen is to allow a user to write the actual SQL code that is executed. There are too many things that could go wrong, there is too much power to allow a user to directly wield it, and eliminating SQL injection attacks by "fixing" input has never worked.

All major database engines support stored procedures. Stored procedures have a performance advantage over other forms of data access. The downside is that stored procedures are written in another language, SQL, and typically need a database programmer to implement the more complex ones.

Both whitelisting and input validation are helpful at preventing SQL injection attacks. But the gold standard to protect from SQL injection is the use of stored procedures.

Tech Tip

Testing for SQL Injection Vulnerability

There are two main steps associated with testing for SQL injection vulnerability. The first one needs to confirm that the system is at all vulnerable. This can be done using various inputs to test whether an input variable can be used to manipulate the SQL command. The following are common test vectors used:

' or 1=1—

" or 1=1—

or 1=1—

' or 'a'='a

" or "a"="a

') or ('a'='a

Note that the use of single or double quotes is SQL implementation dependent because there are syntactic differences between the major database engines.

The second step is to use the error message information to attempt to perform an actual exploit against the database.

> **Tech Tip**
>
> **DLL Injection**
>
> *Dynamic link libraries (DLLs) are pieces of code that can add functionality to a program through the inclusion of library routines linked at runtime.* DLL injection *is the process of adding to a program at runtime a DLL that has a specific vulnerability of function that can be capitalized upon by an attacker. A good example of this is Microsoft Office, a suite of programs that use DLLs loaded at runtime. Adding an "evil" DLL in the correct directory, or via a registry key, can result in additional functionality being incurred.*

LDAP Injection

LDAP-based systems are also subject to injection attacks. When an application constructs an LDAP request based on user input, a failure to validate the input can lead to bad LDAP requests. Just as SQL injection can be used to execute arbitrary commands in a database, the LDAP injection can do the same in a directory system. Something as simple as a wildcard character (*) in a search box can return results that would normally be beyond the scope of a query. Proper input validation is important before passing the request to an LDAP engine.

XML Injection

XML can be tampered with via injection as well. XML injections can be used to manipulate an XML-based system. As XML is nearly ubiquitous in the web application world, this form of attack has a wide range of targets.

Directory Traversal/Command Injection

A directory traversal attack is when an attacker uses special inputs to circumvent the directory tree structure of the file system. Adding encoded symbols for "../.." in an unvalidated input box can result in the parser resolving the encoding to the traversal code, bypassing many detection elements, and passing the input to the file system. The program then executes the commands in a different location than designed. When combined with a command injection, the input can result in the execution of code in an unauthorized manner. Classified as input validation errors, these can be difficult to detect without doing code walkthroughs and specifically looking for them. This illustrates the usefulness of the Top 25 Most Dangerous Software Errors checklist during code reviews because it alerts developers to this issue during development.

Directory traversals can be masked by using the encoding of input streams. If the security check is done before the string is decoded by the system parser, then recognition of the attack form may be impaired. There are many ways to represent a particular input form, the simplest of which is the canonical form (introduced earlier in the "A Rose is a rose is a r%6fse" Tech Tip). Parsers are used to render the canonical form for the OS, but these embedded parsers may act after input validation, making it more difficult to detect certain attacks from just matching a string.

Buffer Overflow

If there's one item that could be labeled as the "most wanted" in coding security, it would be the **buffer overflow**. The CERT/CC at Carnegie Mellon University estimates that nearly half of all exploits of computer programs stem historically from some form of buffer overflow. Finding a vaccine to buffer overflows would stamp out half of these security-related incidents by type, and probably 90 percent by volume. The Morris finger worm in 1988 was an exploit of an overflow, as were more recent big-name events such as Code Red and Slammer. The generic classification of buffer overflows includes many variants, such as static buffer overruns, indexing errors, format string bugs, Unicode and ANSI buffer size mismatches, and heap overruns.

The concept behind these vulnerabilities is relatively simple. The input buffer that is used to hold program input is overwritten with data that is larger than the buffer can hold. The root cause of this vulnerability is a mixture of two things: poor programming practice and programming language weaknesses. For example, what would happen if a program that asks for a seven- to ten-character phone number instead receives a string of 150 characters? Many programs will provide some error checking to ensure that this will not cause a problem. Some programs, however, cannot handle this error, and the extra characters continue to fill memory, overwriting other portions of the program. This can result in a number of problems, including causing the program to abort or the system to crash. Under certain circumstances, the program can execute a command supplied by the attacker. Buffer overflows typically inherit the level of privilege enjoyed by the program being exploited. This is why programs that use root-level access are so dangerous when exploited with a buffer overflow, as the code that will execute does so with root-level access.

Programming languages such as C were designed for space and performance constraints. Many functions in C, like **gets()**, are unsafe in that they will permit unsafe operations, such as unbounded string manipulation into fixed buffer locations. The C language also permits direct memory access via pointers, a functionality that provides a lot of programming power but carries with it the burden of proper safeguards being provided by the programmer.

Buffer overflows are input validation attacks, designed to take advantage of input routines that do not validate the length of inputs. Surprisingly simple to resolve, all that is required is the validation of all input lengths prior to writing to memory. This can be done in a variety of manners, including the use of safe library functions for inputs. This is one of the vulnerabilities that has been shown to be solvable, and in fact the prevalence is declining substantially among major security-conscious software firms.

> Buffer overflows can occur in any code, and code that runs with privilege has an even greater risk profile. In 2014, a buffer overflow in the OpenSSL library, called Heartbleed, left hundreds of thousands of systems vulnerable and exposed critical data for millions of users worldwide.

Integer Overflow

An *integer overflow* is a programming error condition that occurs when a program attempts to store a numeric value, which is an integer, in a variable that is too small to hold it. The results vary by language and numeric type. In some cases, the value saturates the variable, assuming the maximum value for the defined type and no more. In other cases, especially with signed integers, it can roll over into a negative value because the most significant bit is usually reserved for the sign of the number. This can create significant logic errors in a program.

Integer overflows are easily tested for, and static code analyzers (covered later) can point out where they are likely to occur. Given this, there are no excuses for having these errors end up in production code.

Cross-Site Request Forgery

Cross-site request forgery (XSRF) attacks utilize unintended behaviors that are proper in defined use but are performed under circumstances outside the authorized use. This is an example of the "confused deputy" problem—a class of problems where one entity mistakenly performs an action on behalf of another. An XSRF attack relies upon several conditions to be effective. It is performed against sites that have an authenticated user and exploits the sites' trust in a previous authentication event. Then, by tricking a user's browser into sending an HTTP request to the target site, the trust is exploited. Assume your bank allows you to log in and perform financial transactions but does not validate the authentication for each subsequent transaction. If a user is logged in and has not closed their browser, then an action in another browser tab could send a hidden request to the bank, resulting in a transaction that appears to be authorized but in fact was not done by the user.

Many different mitigation techniques can be employed—from limiting authentication times to cookie expiration to managing some specific elements of a web page like header checking. The strongest method is the use of random XSRF tokens in form submissions. Subsequent requests cannot work because the token was not set in advance. Testing for XSRF takes a bit more planning than for other injection-type attacks, but this, too, can be accomplished as part of the design process.

The term *I days* refers to vulnerabilities that are good forever (infinite) because they are caused by design errors and thus are almost impossible to mitigate directly.

Tech Tip

0, N, and I Day Vulnerabilities

Zero days, or 0 days (also called "oh days"), represent a set of vulnerabilities that are known to an attacker but not to the software developer, and hence are not being looked at to remediate.

N days *is the term used to describe vulnerabilities that are known in general but not known to the affected users. A vendor may have been warned about a vulnerability, but until it is patched and each customer has addressed it, the clock keeps running. This requires communication between the software vendor and its customers to get them to install the patches and protect their systems. Many famous worms have used vulnerabilities that are months past discovery but not fixed.*

I days *are infinite days, or vulnerabilities that are known, not fixed, and no plan or method to fix them exists. These vulnerabilities require an outside compensating control to manage.*

All vulnerabilities begin when the code is released. These categories merely describe their relationship with the vendor with respect to discovery.

Zero Day

Zero day is a term used to define vulnerabilities that are newly discovered and not yet addressed by a patch. Most vulnerabilities exist in an unknown state until discovered by a researcher or the developer. If a researcher or developer discovers a vulnerability but does not share the information, then this vulnerability can be exploited without a vendor's ability to fix it because for all practical knowledge the issue is unknown, except to the person who found it. From the time of discovery until a fix or patch is made available, the vulnerability goes by the name *zero day,* indicating that it has not been addressed yet. The most frightening thing about zero days is the unknown factor—their capability and effect on risk are unknown.

Attachments

Attachments can also be used as an attack vector. If a user inputs a graphics file (for instance, a JPEG file) and that file is altered to contain executable code such as Java, then when the image is rendered, the code is executed. This can enable a wide range of attacks.

Locally Shared Objects

Locally shared objects (LSOs) are pieces of data that are stored on a user's machine to save information from an application, such as a game. Frequently these are cookies used by Adobe Flash, called *Flash cookies,* and can store information such as user preferences. As these can be manipulated outside of the application, they can represent a security or privacy threat.

Adobe Flash is being retired at the end of 2020 and will no longer function. Locally shared objects still exist and still present risk.

Client-Side Attacks

The web browser has become the major application for users to engage resources across the Web. Web-based attacks are covered in detail in Chapter 17.

Arbitrary/Remote Code Execution

One of the risks involved in taking user input and using it to create a command to be executed on a system is arbitrary or remote code execution. This attack involves an attacker preparing an input statement that changes the form or function of a prepared statement. A form of command injection, this attack can allow a user to insert arbitrary code and then remotely execute it on a system. This is a form of input validation failure because users should not have the ability to change the way a program interacts with the host OS outside of a set of defined and approved methods.

Open Vulnerability and Assessment Language

MITRE has done extensive research into software vulnerabilities. To enable collaboration between the many different parties involved in software development and maintenance, MITRE has developed a taxonomy of vulnerabilities, the Common Vulnerabilities and Exposures list, as mentioned earlier in the chapter. This is just one of the many related enumerations that MITRE has developed in an effort to make machine-readable data exchanges to facilitate system management across large enterprises. The CVE list led to efforts such as the development of the Open Vulnerability and Assessment Language (OVAL). OVAL comprises two main elements: an XML-based machine-readable language for describing vulnerabilities and a repository (see http://oval.mitre.org).

> CVE provides security personnel with a common language to use when discussing vulnerabilities. If one is discussing a specific vulnerability in the Flash object that allows an arbitrary execution of code, then using the nomenclature CVE-2005-2628 records the specifics of the vulnerability and ensures everyone is discussing the same problem.

In addition to the CVE and OVAL efforts, MITRE has developed a wide range of enumerations and standards designed to ease the automation of security management at the lowest levels across an enterprise. Additional efforts include the following:

- Common Attack Pattern Enumeration and Classification (CAPEC)
- Extensible Configuration Checklist Description Format (XCCDF)
- Security Content Automation Protocol (SCAP)
- Common Configuration Enumeration (CCE)
- Common Platform Enumeration (CPE)
- Common Weakness Enumeration (CWE)
- Common Event Expression (CEE)
- Common Result Format (CRF)

The Common Weakness Enumeration is important for secure development in that it enumerates common patterns of development that lead to weakness and potential vulnerabilities. Additional information can be obtained from the MITRE Making Security Measurable website at http://measurablesecurity.mitre.org.

Application Hardening

Application hardening works in the same fashion as system hardening (discussed in Chapter 14). The first step is the removal of unnecessary components or options. The second step is the proper configuration of the system as it is implemented. Every update or patch can lead to changes to these conditions, and they should be confirmed after every update.

The primary tools used to ensure a hardened system are a secure application configuration baseline and a patch management process. When properly employed, these tools can lead to the most secure system.

Application Configuration Baseline

A *baseline* is the set of proper settings for a computer system. An *application configuration baseline* outlines the proper settings and configurations for an application or set of applications. These settings include many elements, from application settings to security settings. Protection of the settings is crucial, and the most common mechanisms used to protect them include access control lists and protected directories. The documentation of the desired settings is an important security document, assisting administrators in ensuring that proper configurations are maintained across updates.

Application Patch Management

Patch management might be referred to as *update management, configuration management,* or *change management.* Although these terms are not strictly synonyms, they might be used interchangeably on the exam.

Application patch management is a fundamental component of application and system hardening. The objective is to be running the most secure version of an application, and with few exceptions, that would be the most current version of software, including patches. Most updates and patches include fixing security issues and closing vulnerabilities. Current patching is a requirement of many compliance schemes as well.

Patching does not always go as planned, and some patches may result in problems in production systems. A formal system of patch management is needed to test and implement patches in a change-controlled manner.

NoSQL Databases vs. SQL Databases

Current programming trends include topics such as whether to use SQL databases or NoSQL databases. SQL databases are those that use Structured Query Language to manipulate items that are referenced in a relational manner in the form of tables. *NoSQL* refers to data stores that employ neither SQL nor relational table structures. Each system has its strengths and weaknesses, and both can be used for a wide range of data storage needs.

SQL databases are by far the most common, with implementations by IBM, Microsoft, and Oracle being the major players. NoSQL databases tend to be custom-built using low-level languages and lack many of the standards of existing databases. This has not stopped the growth of NoSQL databases in large-scale, well-resourced environments.

The important factor in accessing data in a secure fashion is in the correct employment of programming structures and frameworks to abstract the access process. Methods such as inline SQL generation coupled with input validation errors are recipes for disaster in the form of SQL injection attacks.

Server-Side vs. Client-Side Validation

In a modern client/server environment, data can be checked for compliance with input/output requirements either on the server or on the client. There are advantages to verifying data elements on a client before sending them to the server (namely, efficiency). Doing checks on the client saves a round trip, and its delays, before a user can be alerted to a problem. This can improve the usability of software interfaces.

The client is not a suitable place to perform any critical value checks or security checks. The reasons for this are twofold. First, the client can change anything after the check. Second, the data can be altered while in transit or at an intermediary proxy. For all checks that are essential, either for business reasons or for security, the verification steps should be performed on the server side, where the data is free from unauthorized alterations. Input validation checks can be safely performed only on the server side.

> All input validation should be performed on the server side of the client/server relationship, where it is free from outside influence and change. This is the only way to guarantee appropriate screening of inputs.

Code Signing

An important factor in ensuring that software is genuine and has not been altered is a method of testing the software integrity. With software being updated across the Web, how can one be sure that the code received is genuine and has not been tampered with? The answer comes from the application of digital signatures to the code, a process known as *code signing*.

Code signing involves applying a digital signature to code, providing a mechanism where the end user can verify the code integrity. In addition to verifying the integrity of the code, digital signatures provide evidence as to the source of the software. Code signing rests upon the established public key infrastructure. To use code signing, a developer will need a key pair. For this key to be recognized by the end user, it needs to be signed by a recognized certificate authority.

Encryption

Encryption is one of the elements where secure coding techniques have some unique guidance: "never roll your own crypto." This doesn't just mean you should not write your own cryptographic algorithms but means you should not implement standard algorithms by yourself. Vetted, proven cryptographic libraries exist for all major languages, and the use of these libraries is considered best practice. There are a variety of interrelated rationales for this directive, but the simple explanation is that crypto is almost impossible to invent and very hard to implement correctly. This means to have usable secure encryption in your program, you need to adopt proven algorithms and utilize proven codebases.

Obfuscation/Camouflage

Obfuscation or **camouflage** is the hiding of obvious meaning from observation. While obscurity is not considered adequate security under most circumstances, adding obfuscation or camouflage to a system to make it harder for an attacker to understand and exploit is a good thing. Numbering your e-mail servers email1, email2, email3, and so on tells an attacker what namespace to explore. Removing or hiding these hints makes the work harder and offers another layer of protection.

This works well for data names and other exposed elements that have to be exposed to the outside. Where this does not work well is in the construction of code. Obfuscated code, or code that is hard or even nearly impossible to read, is a ticking time bomb. The day will come when someone will need to read the code, figure out how it works so it can be modified, or determine why it is not working. If programmers have issues reading and understanding the code, including how it functions and what it is supposed to do, how can they contribute to its maintenance?

Code Reuse/Dead Code

Modern software development includes the extensive reuse of components. From component libraries to common functions across multiple components, there is significant opportunity to reduce development costs through **code reuse**. This can also simplify a system through the reuse of known elements. The downside of massive reuse is associated with a monoculture environment, which is where a failure has a larger footprint because of all the places where it is involved.

> The use of legacy code in current projects should not exempt that code from security reviews. All code should receive the same scrutiny, especially legacy code that may have been developed prior to the adoption of software development lifecycle (SDLC) processes.

During the design phase, decisions should be made as to the appropriate level of reuse. For some complex functions, such as in cryptography, reuse is the preferred path. In other cases, where the lineage of a component cannot be established, the risk of use may outweigh the benefit. Additionally, the inclusion of previous code, sometimes referred to as *legacy code*, can reduce development efforts and risk.

Dead code is code that while it may be executed, the results that it obtains are never used elsewhere in the program. There are compiler options that can remove dead code, called *dead code elimination*, but these must be used with care. Assume you have a section of code that you put in specifically to set a secret value to all zeros. The logic is as follows: generate a secret key, use the secret key, set the secret key to zero. You set the secret key to zero to remove the key from memory and keep it from being stolen. But along comes the dead code removal routine. It sees you set the value of secretkey == 0, but then you never use it again. So, the compiler, in optimizing your code, removes your protection step.

Memory Management

Memory management encompasses the actions used to control and coordinate computer memory, assigning memory to variables and reclaiming it when no longer being used. Errors in memory management can result in a program that has a memory leak, and it can grow over time, consuming more and more resources. The routine to clean up memory that has been allocated in a program but is no longer needed is called *garbage collection*. In the C and C++ programming languages where there is no automatic garbage collector, the programmer must allocate and free memory explicitly. One of the advantages of newer programming languages such as Java, C#, Python, and Ruby is that they provide automatic memory management with garbage collection. This may not be as efficient as specifically coding in C, but it is significantly less error prone.

Use of Third-Party Libraries and SDKs

Programming today is to a great extent an exercise in using *third-party libraries* and *software development kits (SDKs)*. This is because once code has been debugged and proven to work, rewriting it is generally not a valuable use of time. Also, some fairly complex routines, such as encryption, have vetted, proven library sets that remove a lot of risk from programming these functions.

Software developers use packaged sets of software programs and tools called SDKs to create apps for specific vender platforms.

Data Exposure

Data exposure is the loss of control over data from a system during operations. Data must be protected during storage, during communication, and even at times during use. It is up to the programming team to chart the flow of data through a system and ensure it is protected from exposure throughout the process. Data can be lost to unauthorized parties (a failure of confidentiality) and, equally dangerous, can be changed by an unauthorized party (a failure of integrity).

Code Quality and Testing

When coding operations commence, tools and techniques can be used to assist in the assessment of the security level of the code under development. Code can be analyzed either statically or dynamically to find weaknesses and vulnerabilities. Manual code reviews by the development team can provide benefits both to the code and to the team. *Code quality* does not end with development because the code needs to be delivered and installed both intact and correctly on the target system.

Code analysis is a term used to describe the processes to inspect code for weaknesses and vulnerabilities. It can be divided into two forms: static and dynamic. Static analysis involves examining the code without execution. Dynamic analysis involves executing the code as part of the testing. Both static and dynamic analyses are typically done with tools, which are much better at the detailed analysis steps needed for any but the smallest code samples.

Code analysis can be performed at virtually any level of development—from unit level to subsystem to system to complete application. The higher the level, the greater the test space and more complex the analysis. When the analysis is done by teams of humans reading the code, typically at the smaller unit level, it is referred to as *code review*. Code analysis should be done at every level of development because the sooner that weaknesses and vulnerabilities are discovered, the easier they are to fix. Issues found in design are cheaper to fix than those found in coding, which are cheaper than those found in final testing—and all of these are cheaper than fixing errors once the software has been deployed.

Static Code Analyzers

Static code analysis is when the code is examined without being executed. This analysis can be performed on both source and object codebases. The term *source code* is typically used to designate the high-level language code, although technically source code is the original codebase in any form, from high language to machine code. Static analysis can be performed by humans or tools, with humans limited to the high-level language, while tools can be used against virtually any form of codebase.

Static code analysis is frequently performed using automated tools. These tools are given a variety of names but are commonly called *static code analyzers* or *source code analyzers*. Sometimes, extra phrases such as binary scanners or bytecode scanners are used to differentiate the tools. Static tools use a variety of mechanisms to search for weaknesses and vulnerabilities. Automated tools can provide advantages when checking syntax, approving function/library calls, and examining rules and semantics associated with logic and calls. They can catch elements a human could overlook.

Dynamic Analysis (Fuzzing)

Dynamic analysis is performed while the software is executed, either on a target or on an emulated system. The system is fed specific test inputs designed to produce specific forms of behaviors. Dynamic analysis can be particularly important on systems such as embedded systems, where a high degree of operational autonomy is expected. As a case in point, the failure to perform adequate testing of software on the Ariane rocket program led to the loss of an Ariane 5 booster during takeoff. Subsequent analysis showed that if proper testing had been performed, the error conditions could have been detected and corrected without the loss of the flight vehicle.

Dynamic analysis requires specialized automation to perform specific testing. There are dynamic test suites designed to monitor operations for programs that have a high degree of parallel functions. There are thread-checking routines to ensure multicore processors and software applications are managing threads correctly. There are programs designed to detect race conditions and memory-addressing errors.

Fuzzing (or fuzz testing) is a brute force method of addressing input validation issues and vulnerabilities. The basis for fuzzing a program is the application of large numbers of inputs to determine which ones cause faults and which ones might be vulnerable to exploitation. Fuzz testing can be applied to anywhere data is exchanged to verify that input validation is being performed properly. Network protocols can be fuzzed, file protocols can be fuzzed, and web protocols can be fuzzed. The vast majority of browser errors are found via fuzzing. Fuzzing has been used by hackers for years to find potentially exploitable buffer overflows, without any specific knowledge of the coding. Fuzz testing works perfectly fine regardless of the type of testing—white box or black box. Fuzzing serves as a best practice for finding unexpected input validation errors.

A tester can use a fuzzing framework to automate numerous input sequences. In examining whether a function can fall prey to a buffer overflow, a tester can run numerous inputs, testing lengths and ultimate payload-delivery options. If a particular input string results in a crash that can be exploited, the tester would then examine this input in detail. Fuzzing is still relatively new to the development scene but is rapidly maturing and will soon be on nearly equal footing with other automated code-checking tools.

Fuzz testing works by sending a multitude of input signals and seeing how the program handles them. Specifically, malformed inputs can be used to vary parser operation and check for memory leaks, buffer overflows, and a wide range of input validation issues. There are several ways to classify fuzz testing. One set of categories is smart and dumb, indicating the type of logic used in creating the input values. Smart testing uses knowledge of what could go wrong and malforms the inputs using this knowledge. Dumb testing just uses random inputs. Other terms used to describe fuzzers are generation-based and mutation-based.

Fuzz testing is a staple of SDLC-based testing, finding a wide range of errors with a single test method. This method is widely used by hackers to look for vulnerabilities.

Generation-based fuzz testing uses the specifications of input streams to determine the data streams that are to be used in testing. Mutation-based fuzzers take known-good traffic and mutate it in specific ways to create new input streams for testing. Each of these has its advantages, and the typical fuzzing environment involves both used together.

Stress Testing

The typical objective in performance testing is not to find specific bugs but rather to determine bottlenecks and performance factors for the systems under test. These tests are frequently referred to as *load testing* and *stress testing*. Load testing involves running the system under a controlled speed environment, whereas stress testing takes the system past this operating point to see how it responds to overload conditions. Part of the set of requirements for the software under development should be the expected service levels from the software. Typically, these are expressed in a service level agreement (SLA).

Sandboxing

Sandboxing is a term for the execution of computer code in an environment designed to isolate the code from direct contact with the target system. Sandboxes are used to execute untrusted code, code from guests, and unverified programs. Sandboxes work as a form of virtual machine (VM) and can mediate a wide range of system interactions, including memory access, network access, and access to other programs, the file system, and devices. The level of protection offered by a sandbox depends on the level of isolation and mediation offered.

Model Verification

Ensuring the code does what it is supposed to do, called *verification*, is more complex than just running the program and looking for runtime errors. The program results for a given set of inputs need to match the expected results per the system model. For instance, if you're applying a simple mathematical operation, is the calculation correct? This is simple on a case-by-case basis, but when a program has many interdependent calculations, then verifying the result matches the desired design model can be a fairly complex task.

Validation and *verification* are terms used to describe this testing. Validation is the process of checking whether the program specification captures the requirements from the customer, whereas verification is the process of checking that the software developed meets the model specification. Performing *model verification testing* is important because this is the assurance that the code as developed meets the design requirements.

Compiled Code vs. Runtime Code

Compiled code is code that is written in one language and then run through a **compiler** and transformed into executable code that can be run on a system. Compilers can do many things to optimize code and create smaller, faster running programs on the actual hardware. But compilers have problems with dynamic code that wants to change at runtime. Interpreters create *runtime code* that can be executed via an interpreter engine, like a Java virtual machine (JVM), on a computer system. Although they are viewed as slower, there are times when interpreters excel. To run a program with a compiler, one must take the source program, compile it into the target program, and then load and execute the target program. These steps must all occur and can take time. Conversely, an interpreter manages the conversion of the high-level code into the machine code on the fly, removing the compile steps. Therefore, although an interpreter may be slow at running the code, if a lot of changes are happening that force recompiles, it can be faster.

In today's world there are both compilers and interpreters for most languages so that the correct tool can be used for the correct situation. There are also systems such as just-in-time compilers and bytecode interpreters that blur the traditional categorizations of compilers and interpreters.

Software Diversity

Software is not a single product; there are many different forms, and these can be characterized by a wide range of differentiators. Software can be categorized by elements such as platform (PC, server, mobile, IoT device, cloud), programming language, interface (web, API, messaging, direct connections), purpose, and a whole host of other factors. One can say that each project in the end is unique. However, the fact that someone can point to why their software is different or special does not diminish the fact that it is a series of instructions for a computer to operate on, and that based on design decisions, coding decisions, and environment decisions, it can and will have vulnerabilities that could enable an attacker to do things that are not desired outcomes. Hence, all software needs security. Having a proper security process as part of the development process is important to reduce vulnerabilities and manage security issues as they are uncovered.

Another key aspect of **software diversity** is the issue of monoculture avoidance. As many systems in an enterprise have common elements, such as the operating system, key libraries, and so on, there exists the possibility for common vulnerabilities to affect many components. As a consequence of software systems sharing common vulnerabilities, there's an increased susceptibility to malware and other attacks with common methods. The primary method of beating this systemic risk is through software diversity—that is, having different components with different software elements.

Compiler

Compilers take computer programs written in one language and convert them to a set of codes that can run on a specific set of hardware. Modern compilers can take high-level code that is platform agnostic and convert it to machine language code that actually can run on a given platform. In the process of doing this transformation, compilers can manage various aspects of a program, including memory, code efficiency, and more.

Binary

Ultimately, in the end, all digital computer systems are *binary machines*, which operate in one of two states: on (1) or off (0). Grouping these signals together, the 1's and the 0's into words, with larger memory and processing structures, is what makes computers capable of doing their work. But one interesting aspect of all of this is reproducibility. On two identical computers running the exact same code, the signals and memory structures will be identical because that is how computers work. This leads to another form of important diversity: randomization. Although all computer memory is a collection of 1's and 0's, how they are arranged has implications. Having two machines, or more, with completely identical memory layouts again provides attackers a reproducible target. This has led to defenses that include randomizing memory layouts—yes, to a pattern, but the pattern is specific to each boot of the machine and is only known to the machine.

Binary diversity is the creation of identically functioning binary images, but with different specific instantiations. Having different locations for memory variables, different pointer offsets, and different layouts in computer memory can be done today and yet completely preserve functionality. For an attacker trying to bypass controls and inject something directly into memory, this type of defense makes that even more difficult.

Taking binary diversity to the extreme, one can run a set of multiple variants simultaneously in a multi-variant execution environment (MVEE). The system then unifies input/outputs and monitors the operation, enabling detection of when variants diverge in behavior. This indicates abnormal behavior and enables the system to react and recover from the bad result stream.

Secure DevOps

DevOps is a combination of development and operations—in other words, a blending of tasks performed by a company's application development and systems operations teams. DevOps emphasizes communication and collaboration between product management, software development, and operations professionals to facilitate continuous development, continuous integration, continuous delivery, and continuous monitoring processes.

Automation/Scripting

Automation through **scripting** and other programmable means has great utility in software development. The use of these technology-backed methods has led to a field of development known as DevOps.

One of the key elements of DevOps is automation. DevOps relies on automation for much of its efficiencies. *Security automation* can provide the same gains in efficiency that automation has in DevOps. Automating routine and extensive processes allows fewer resources to cover more environment in a more effective and efficient manner. Automation removes manual labor costs, especially skilled cybersecurity personnel. Rather than replacing the personnel with scripts, the use of automation allows the personnel to spend their time doing value-added work in analysis.

DevOps can be considered the anti-waterfall model because rather than going from phase to phase, in DevOps, when small changes are ready, they advance. This leads to many small incremental changes but less time between updates and less time to fix or change things. Secure DevOps is the addition of security steps to the DevOps process. Just as you can add security steps to the waterfall model, or any other software development model, you can add them to DevOps as well, resulting in a secure DevOps outcome.

Continuous Monitoring

Continuous monitoring is the term used to describe the technologies and processes employed to enable rapid detection of compliance issues and security risks. More than just a buzzword, continuous monitoring is one of the most important tools available for risk management. Automation and scripts are commonly used as part of a continuous monitoring framework, as they can provide 24/7/365 monitoring of processes and conditions, feeding alerts into the organization's monitoring system for review and action by security personnel.

Continuous Validation

Continuous validation is the extension of testing to support the continuous process of software development that occurs in DevOps. As code is changed in the DevOps process, the new code must be tested with the existing codebase to ensure functionality and stability. Making this part of the continuous development process is essential to keeping development on a timely trajectory.

Continuous Integration

Continuous integration is the DevOps manner of continually updating and improving the production codebase. By using high levels of automation and automated back-out routines as safety nets, continuous integration allows for testing and updating even minor changes without a lot of overhead. This means that rather than several large updates, with many integrated and many potentially cross-purpose update elements, all squeezed into a single big package, a whole series of smaller single-purpose integrations is run. This means that when testing, you have isolated the changes to a small manageable number, without the significance of multiple potential interactions. This reduces both isolated and interaction errors that are time-consuming to chase.

Continuous Delivery

Continuous delivery is a natural extension of continuous integration so that you can quickly release new changes to production in a sustainable way. Continuous delivery relies on automated testing and is an automated release process that enables the delivery of updates when they are complete, at any point of time, as opposed to a fixed release schedule. When code is ready to be released to production, continuous delivery is the automation of that step, but still under specific operator control.

> Continuous deployment goes one step further than continuous delivery; every change that passes all stages of your production pipeline is automatically released to customers.

Continuous Deployment

Continuous deployment is continuous delivery on autopilot. It goes one step further than continuous delivery in that the release is automatic. With this practice, every change that passes all stages of your production pipeline is released to production. There's no human intervention, and when all gates are met (that is, no failed tests), continuous deployment automatically sends the code to production.

> Understanding how DevOps interacts with and can be supported by a secure development lifecycle is important. Understanding the major methods such as immutable systems and continuous integration and where they can be employed effectively is important.

Infrastructure as Code

Infrastructure as Code is a key attribute of enabling best practices in DevOps. Developers become more involved in defining system configuration, and the Ops teams get more involved in the actual development process. The objective is not to write applications and toss them over a wall to implementers (the Ops team) and expect them to make the apps work in the environment. As systems have become larger, more complex, and more inter-related, connecting developers to implementers has created an environment of Infrastructure as Code, which is a version of Infrastructure as a Service.

Elasticity

Elasticity is the characteristic that something is capable of change without breaking. One of the strengths of cloud computing is its elasticity. One can add or subtract resources in a cloud environment almost automatically without issue. Elasticity in software works in the same fashion—how resilient is the software to changes in its environment, while remaining secure? For software to be elastic, it needs to be able to run under a variety of different conditions. Legacy software that runs in a single thread, while easier to write, is not elastic. When single-threaded software gets employed in a VM environment of multiple processors or in a cloud environment, its performance is limited to a single thread. Multithreaded software can scale and adapt better, but this also increases its complexity, bringing in issues such as race conditions. For scalability to be stable and sustainable, the software needs to be elastic.

Scalability

Scalability is the characteristic of a software system to process higher workloads on its current resources (scale up) or on additional resources (scale out) without interruption. Scalability is important in web systems, databases, application engines, and cloud systems. Workloads can vary, and cloud/container systems can add processing and storage, but the software must be capable of addressing the changes in an environment. While this seems obvious, the devil is in the details. Timing loops can affect the ability of software to run on faster hardware, as the system can only run as fast as its slowest link. Scaling out to multiple machines brings in issues of synchronization and coordination. All of these issues can be solved, but this has to happen during design and development, not after delivery.

Version Control and Change Management

Programs are developed, released, and used, and then changes are desired, either to alter functionality, to fix errors, or to improve performance. This leads to multiple versions of programs. **Version control** is as simple as tracking which version of a program is being worked on, whether in dev, test, or production. Versioning tends to use primary numbers to indicate major releases and uses numbers after a decimal point to indicate minor changes.

Having the availability of multiple versions brings into focus the issue of *change management*. How does a firm manage which versions are currently being used, and how does the firm coordinate changes as they are released by a manufacturer? In traditional software publishing, a new version requires a new install and fairly significant testing because the level of change can be drastic and call into question issues of compatibility, functionality, and even correctness. DevOps has turned the tables on this by introducing the idea that developers and production can work together and create in essence a series of micro-releases so that any real problems are associated with single changes and are not bogged down by interactions between multiple module changes.

Whether you are in the traditional camp or are operating in the DevOps world, you still need a change management process that ensures all changes in production are authorized, properly tested, and, if they fail, rolled back. You also need to maintain current and accurate documentation.

Baselining

Baselining is the process of determining a standard set of functionality and performance. This is a metrics-driven item, where later changes can be compared to the baseline for performance and other figures. If a change improves the baseline elements in a positive fashion, a new baseline can be established. If the new values are of lesser quality, then a decision can be made as to whether to accept the changes or change the baseline. It is through baselining that performance degradation and feature creep are countered by the management team. If a new feature impacts performance enough, then the new feature might be withheld.

Immutable Systems

An **immutable system** is one that, once deployed, is never modified, patched, or upgraded. If a patch or update is required, the system is merely replaced with a new, updated one. In a typical system (one that is mutable or changeable and that is patched and updated before deployment), it is extremely difficult to conclusively know whether or not future changes to the system are authorized and whether or not they are correctly applied. Linux makes this determination especially difficult. On a Linux system, the binaries and libraries are scattered over many directories: /boot, /bin, /usr/bin, /lib, /usr/lib, /opt/bin, /usr/local/bin, and many more. Configuration files are similarly scattered over /etc, /opt/etc, /usr/local/etc, /usr/lib, and so on. These directories have some files that should never be modified and others that are regularly updated. When the system update services run, they often create temporary files in these directories as well. Consequently, it is difficult to lock down all these directories and perform authorized system and software updates at the same time. Immutable systems resolve these issues.

Provisioning and Deprovisioning

Provisioning is the process of assigning permissions or authorities to objects. Users can be provisioned into groups, and computer processes or threads can be provisioned to higher levels of authority when executing. **Deprovisioning** is the removal of permissions or authorities. In secure coding, the practice is to provision a thread to an elevated execution permission level (for example, root) only during the time that the administrative permissions are needed. After those steps have passed, the thread can be deprovisioned back to a lower access level. This combination lowers the period of time an application is at an increased level of authority, reducing the risk exposure should the program get hijacked or hacked.

Integrity Measurement

Integrity is defined in security as a determination that data has no unauthorized changes. In a software development and deployment environment, this is a very important issue, because even little changes can cause huge issues and can be very difficult to detect. **Integrity measurement** is the set of processes used to insure that the source code repositories are free of unauthorized changes. Maintaining control over a codebase means that two things are happening. First, you have control over the copies in such a way that people are only working on a legitimate codebase. Nothing ruins a day faster than learning your all-day programming session was performed on a set of code that is not being updated—you worked on the wrong copy. While not as disastrous as painting the wrong house (you don't have to paint it back), the work is in essence lost. When code is undergoing constant change from multiple authors, this is not as simple as it seems, and some form of version control is required. The second thing that has to be maintained is a log of the changes and a method of identifying the versions. The version control system that you use should keep track of the versions, but to clearly identify a set of code requires a different tool. Hash algorithms create a unique hash value for each unique item being operated on, and codebases are digital objects. Maintaining a directory of hash values that denote the different versions of the codebase is how integrity controls are annotated to the code. If you have any version of the code, you can hash it and look up in the version table to see which version you have. This is superior to using meta-labels in the code because labels can be changed, but the hash is tied to the code. When code is released for deployment, it is typically signed digitally, and the hash value ensures users that the code has not been changed.

For More Information

SAFECode www.safecode.org

DHS Build Security In https://buildsecurityin.us-cert.gov

Microsoft SDL www.microsoft.com/sdl

CVE http://cve.mitre.org

CWE http://cwe.mitre.org

CWE/SANS Top 25 http://cwe.mitre.org/top25/index.html

Chapter 19 Review

Chapter Summary

After reading this chapter and completing the exercises, you should understand the following about security issues related to software development.

Describe how secure coding can be incorporated into the software development process

- The requirements phase is the most important part of the software engineering process since it outlines the project's future requirements, thus defining its scope and limitations.
- The use of an enhanced lifecycle development process that includes security elements will build security into the product.
- Understanding the different environments, including development, test, staging, and production, is important for understanding the context in which a developer is working.

List the major types of coding errors and their root causes

- The most common coding error is a failure to validate inputs.
- Code injection errors can result in undesired code execution, as defined by the end user.
- Input validation is the best method of ensuring against buffer overflows and code injection errors.

Describe good software development practices and explain how they impact application security

- Early testing helps resolve errors at an earlier stage and results in cleaner code.
- Security-related use cases can be employed to test for specific security requirements.
- Fuzz testing can find a wide range of errors.

Describe how using a software development process enforces security inclusion in a project

- Security is built into the software by including security concerns and reviews throughout the software development process.
- Regardless of the specific software engineering process model used, security can be included in the normal process by being input as a requirement.

Use application-hardening techniques

- The first step in application hardening is to determine the application configuration baseline.
- Applications as well as the OS require patching, and proper enterprise application patch management is important.
- All validations of client-to-server data need to be done on the server side because this is the security-controllable side of the communication.
- The use of automation and scripting can reduce errors, improve process flow, and speed up development efforts.
- The use of continuous processes, including monitoring, validation, and integration, can improve quality and security of system development efforts.
- The use of DevOps can improve secure development processes.

Key Terms

agile model *(721)*
automation *(750)*
black-box testing *(728)*
buffer overflow *(738)*
bug tracking *(734)*
canonicalization error *(732)*
code injection *(736)*
code reuse *(744)*
Common Vulnerabilities and Exposures (CVE) *(725)*
Common Weakness Enumeration (CWE) *(725)*
compiler *(748)*
continuous delivery *(751)*
continuous deployment *(751)*
continuous integration *(751)*
continuous monitoring *(750)*
continuous validation *(750)*
cryptographically random *(727)*
CWE/SANS Top 25 Most Dangerous Software Errors *(725)*
data exposure *(745)*
dead code *(744)*
deployment phase *(729)*
deprecated functions *(728)*
deprovisioning *(753)*
DevOps *(749)*
elasticity *(751)*
evolutionary model *(721)*
fuzzing *(746)*
gray-box testing *(729)*
immutable system *(753)*
integrity measurement *(754)*
least privilege *(725)*
maintenance phase *(729)*
normalization *(732)*
obfuscation/camouflage *(744)*
Open Web Application Security Project (OWASP) *(725)*
production environment *(730)*
provisioning *(753)*
requirements phase *(723)*
scalability *(752)*
scripting *(750)*
secure development lifecycle (SDL) model *(721)*
software diversity *(749)*
spiral model *(721)*
SQL injection *(736)*
staging environment *(730)*
stored procedures *(737)*
test environment *(730)*
testing phase *(728)*
use cases *(728)*
version control *(752)*
waterfall model *(721)*
white-box testing *(728)*
zero day *(740)*

Key Terms Quiz

Use terms from the Key Terms list to complete the sentences that follow. Don't use the same term more than once. Not all terms will be used.

1. The _______________ is a linear software engineering model with no repeating steps.
2. A(n) _______________ causes an application to malfunction because of a misrepresented name for a resource.
3. CWE-20: Improper Input Validation refers to a(n) _______________.
4. Using a series of malformed inputs to test for conditions such as buffer overflows is called _______________.
5. Modifying a SQL statement through false input to a function is an example of _______________.
6. Using an administrator-level account for all functions is a violation of the principle of _______________.
7. The _______________ is the first opportunity to address security functionality during a project.
8. The banning of _______________ helps improve code quality by using safer library calls.
9. A(n) _______________ is a vulnerability that has been discovered by hackers but not by the developers of the software.
10. A number that is suitable for an encryption function is called _______________.

Multiple-Choice Quiz

1. Problems in which phase will specifically stop continuous deployment, but not necessarily continuous delivery?
   - **A.** Continuous integration
   - **B.** Continuous monitoring
   - **C.** Continuous validation
   - **D.** Continuous development
2. Which of the following is *not* involved with a code injection error?
   - **A.** SQL statement building
   - **B.** Input validation
   - **C.** JavaScript
   - **D.** A pointer in the C language
3. Input validation is important to prevent what?
   - **A.** Buffer overflow
   - **B.** Index sequence error
   - **C.** Operator overload error
   - **D.** Unhandled exception
4. It's most important to define security requirements during _______________.
   - **A.** testing
   - **B.** use case development
   - **C.** code walkthroughs
   - **D.** the requirements phase of the project
5. The largest class of errors in software engineering can be attributed to which of the following?
   - **A.** Poor testing
   - **B.** Privilege violations
   - **C.** Improper input validation
   - **D.** Canonicalization errors
6. Least privilege applies to _______________________.
   - **A.** only the application code
   - **B.** calls to operating system objects only
   - **C.** all resource requests from applications to other entities
   - **D.** applications under named user accounts

7. Common cryptographic failures include which of the following?
   - **A.** Use of cryptographically random numbers
   - **B.** Cryptographic sequence failures
   - **C.** Poor encryption protocols
   - **D.** Canonicalization errors
8. When is testing best accomplished?
   - **A.** After all code is finished
   - **B.** As early as possible in the process
   - **C.** After all elements are complete (code complete)
   - **D.** During the design phase
9. Code review by a second party is helpful to do what?
   - **A.** Increase the creativity of the junior programmer
   - **B.** Reduce cost, making for a better, cheaper method of testing
   - **C.** Catch errors early in the programming process
   - **D.** Ensure all modules work together
10. Which of the following is one of the most fundamental rules to good coding practice?
    - **A.** Code once, test twice.
    - **B.** Validate all inputs.
    - **C.** Don't use pointers.
    - **D.** Use obscure coding practices so viruses cannot live in the code.

Essay Quiz

1. Describe the relationship of the requirements phase, testing phase, and use cases with respect to software engineering development and secure code.
2. Develop a list of five security-related issues to be put into a requirements document as part of a secure coding initiative.
3. Choose two requirements from the previous question and describe use cases that would validate them in the testing phase.
4. You have been asked by your manager to develop a worksheet for code walkthroughs (another name for structured code reviews). This worksheet should include a list of common errors to look for during the examination, acting as a memory aid. You want to leave a lasting impression on the team as a new college graduate. Outline what you would include on the worksheet related to security.

Lab Projects

• Lab Project 19.1

Learn the specific software engineering process model used at a local firm (or you may be able to research a company online or find one in a software engineering textbook at a library). Examine where security is built (or could be built) into the model. Provide an overview of the strengths and opportunities of the model with respect to designing secure code.

• Lab Project 19.2

Develop an example of a SQL injection statement for a web page inquiry. List the web page inputs, what the projected back-end SQL is, and how it can be changed.

chapter 20

Risk Management

The revolutionary idea that defines the boundary between modern times and the past is the mastery of risk: the notion that the future is more than a whim of the gods and that men and women are not passive before nature. Until human beings discovered a way across that boundary, the future was the mirror of the past or the murky domain of oracles and soothsayers who held a monopoly over knowledge of anticipated events.

—Peter Bernstein

In this chapter, you will learn how to

- Use risk management tools and principles to manage risk effectively
- Explore risk mitigation strategies
- Describe risk models
- Explain the differences between qualitative and quantitative risk assessment
- Use risk management tools
- Examine risk management best practices

Risk management can best be described as a decision-making process. In the simplest terms, when you manage risk, you determine what could happen to your business, you assess the impact if it were to happen, and you decide what you could do to control that impact as much as you or your management deems necessary. You then decide to act or not to act, and, finally, you evaluate the results of your decision. The process may be iterative, as industry best practices clearly indicate that an important aspect of effectively managing risk is to consider it an ongoing process.

An Overview of Risk Management

Risk management is an essential element of management from the enterprise level down to the individual project. Risk management encompasses all the actions taken to reduce complexity, increase objectivity, and identify important decision factors. There has been, and will continue to be, discussion about the complexity of risk management and whether it is worth the effort. Businesses must take risks to retain their competitive edge, however, and as a result, risk management must occur as part of managing any business, program, or project.

Risk management is about making a business profitable, not about buying insurance.

Risk management is both a skill and a task that is performed by all managers, either deliberately or intuitively. It can be simple or complex, depending on the size of the project or business and the amount of risk inherent in an activity. Every manager, at all levels, must learn to manage risk. The required skills can be learned.

Organizations should exercise due diligence in managing cybersecurity and privacy risk. This can be accomplished, in part, by establishing a comprehensive risk management program. The second part involves executing the program and, finally, verifying the effectiveness of the elements via an assessment. Exercising due diligence and implementing a robust and comprehensive cybersecurity and privacy risk management program can greatly assist in compliance with applicable laws, regulations, and stakeholder expectations. Risk management begins with the selection of a framework and the development of risk management processes. These steps are essential in developing, implementing, and maintaining the protection measures necessary to address the risks and the threats to organizational operations and assets. Mature organizations include cybersecurity and privacy risks as part of an all-hazards risk management approach—one that addresses all known risks with appropriate levels of control.

Employing effective risk-based processes, procedures, methods, and technologies ensures that the organization and its information-handling systems have the necessary trustworthiness and resiliency to support the business functions while meeting the expectations of stakeholders, as well as complying with legal and regulatory guidance.

Example of Risk Management at the International Banking Level

The Basel Committee on Banking Supervision is composed of government central-bank governors from around the world. This body created a basic, global risk management framework for market and credit risk. It implemented internationally a flat 8 percent capital charge to banks to manage bank risks. In layman's terms, this means that for every $100 a bank makes in loans, it must possess $8 in reserve to be used in the event of financial difficulties. However, if banks can show they have very strong risk-mitigation procedures and controls in place, that capital charge can be reduced to as low as $0.37 (0.37 percent). If a bank has poor procedures and controls, that capital charge can be as high as $45 (45 percent) for every $100 the bank loans out. See www.bis.org/bcbs/ for source documentation regarding the Basel Committee.

This example shows that risk management can be and is used at high levels—the remainder of this chapter focuses on smaller implementations and demonstrates that risk management is used in many aspects of business conduct.

Risk Management Vocabulary

You need to understand a number of key terms to manage risk successfully. Some of these terms are defined here because they are used throughout the chapter. This list is somewhat ordered according to the organization of this chapter. More comprehensive definitions and other pertinent terms are listed alphabetically in the glossary at the end of this book.

Risk **Risk** is the possibility of suffering harm or loss.

Risk Management **Risk management** is the overall decision-making process of identifying threats and vulnerabilities and their potential impacts, determining the costs to mitigate such events, and deciding what actions are cost effective for controlling these risks.

Risk Assessment **Risk assessment** is the process of analyzing an environment to identify the risks (threats and vulnerabilities) and mitigating actions to determine (either quantitatively or qualitatively) the impact of an event that would affect a project, program, or business. It's also referred to as **risk analysis**.

Asset An **asset** is any resource or information an organization needs to conduct its business.

Threat A **threat** is any circumstance or event with the potential to cause harm to an asset. For example, a malicious hacker might choose to hack your system by using readily available hacking tools.

Threat Actor A **threat actor** (agent) is the entity behind a threat.

Threat Vector A **threat vector** is a method used to effect a threat—for example, malware (threat) that is delivered via a watering-hole attack (vector).

Vulnerability A **vulnerability** is any characteristic of an asset that can be exploited by a threat to cause harm. A vulnerability can also be the result of a lack of security controls or weaknesses in controls. Your system has a security vulnerability, for example, if you have not installed patches to fix a cross-site scripting (XSS) error on your web site.

Impact **Impact** is the loss (or harm) resulting when a threat exploits a vulnerability. A malicious hacker (threat agent) uses an XSS tool (threat vector) to hack your unpatched web site (the vulnerability), stealing credit card information (threat) that is then used fraudulently. The credit card company pursues legal recourse against your company to recover the losses from the credit card fraud (the impact).

Control A **control** is a measure taken to detect, prevent, or mitigate the risk associated with a threat. It is also called a **countermeasure** or **safeguard**.

Qualitative Risk Assessment **Qualitative risk assessment** is the process of subjectively determining the impact of an event that affects a project, program, or business. Completing the assessment usually involves the use of expert judgment, experience, or group consensus.

> The distinction between qualitative and quantitative risk assessment will be more apparent as you read the section "Qualitative vs. Quantitative Risk Assessment" later in the chapter.

Quantitative Risk Assessment **Quantitative risk assessment** is the process of objectively determining the impact of an event that affects a project, program, or business. Completing the assessment usually involves the use of metrics and models.

Mitigate The term **mitigate** refers to taking action to reduce the likelihood of a threat occurring and/or to reduce the impact if a threat does occur.

Single Loss Expectancy **Single loss expectancy (SLE)** is the monetary loss or impact of each occurrence of a threat exploiting a vulnerability.

Exposure Factor **Exposure factor (EF)** is a measure of the magnitude of loss of an asset. It is used in the calculation of single loss expectancy.

Annualized Rate of Occurrence **Annualized rate of occurrence (ARO)** is the frequency with which an event is expected to occur on an annualized basis.

Annualized Loss Expectancy **Annualized loss expectancy (ALE)** is how much a loss is expected to cost per year.

Systematic Risk **Systematic risk** is the chance of loss that is predictable under relatively stable circumstances. Examples such as fire, wind, and flood produce losses that, in the aggregate over time, can be accurately predicted despite short-term fluctuations. Systematic risk can be diversified away, which gives managers a level of control that can be employed.

Unsystematic Risk **Unsystematic risk** is the chance of loss that is unpredictable in the aggregate because it results from forces difficult to predict. Examples include, but are not limited to, recession, unemployment, epidemics, war-related events, and so forth. Unsystematic risk cannot be mitigated via diversification, limiting management responses.

Hazard A **hazard** is a circumstance that increases the likelihood or probable severity of a loss. For example, running systems without antivirus is a hazard because it increases the probability of loss due to malware.

Moral Hazard **Moral hazard** is an economic term describing a situation in which one party gets involved in a risky event knowing that it is protected against the risk and the other party will incur the cost.

Externality **Externality** is an economics term for a cost (or benefit) that is imposed on a third party who did not agree to incur the risk.

Force Majeure **Force majeure** is a legal concept for a situation where there is an occurrence of an event which is outside the reasonable control of a party and which prevents that party from performing its obligations under a contract.

What Is Risk Management?

> **Tech Tip**
>
> **Risk Management Applies to All Business Processes**
>
> *Even human resource management has an effect on risk management in a firm. For example, risk management theory used to posit that older workers were more likely to create liabilities. Recent studies have shown that as employees age, they have lower absenteeism, are more productive, and have higher levels of job satisfaction. Their greatest risk is longer recovery time from accidents, so companies are finding ways to prevent accidents to manage that risk.*

Three definitions relating to risk management reveal why it is sometimes considered difficult to understand:

- The dictionary defines *risk* as the possibility of suffering harm or loss.
- Carnegie Mellon University's Software Engineering Institute (SEI) defines *continuous risk management* as "processes, methods, and tools for managing risks in a project. It provides a disciplined environment for proactive decision-making to 1) assess continuously what could go wrong (risks); 2) determine which risks are important to deal with; and 3) implement strategies to deal with those risks" (SEI, *Continuous Risk Management Guidebook* [Pittsburgh, PA: Carnegie Mellon University, 1996], 22).
- The Information Systems Audit and Control Association (ISACA) says, "In modern business terms, risk management is the process of identifying vulnerabilities and threats to an organization's resources and assets and deciding what countermeasures, if any, to take to reduce the level of risk to an acceptable level based on the value of the asset to the organization" (ISACA, *Certified Information Systems Auditor (CISA) Review Manual, 2002* [Rolling Meadows, IL: ISACA, 2002], 344).

These three definitions show that risk management is based on what can go wrong and what action should be taken, if any. Figure 20.1 provides a macro-level view of how to manage risk.

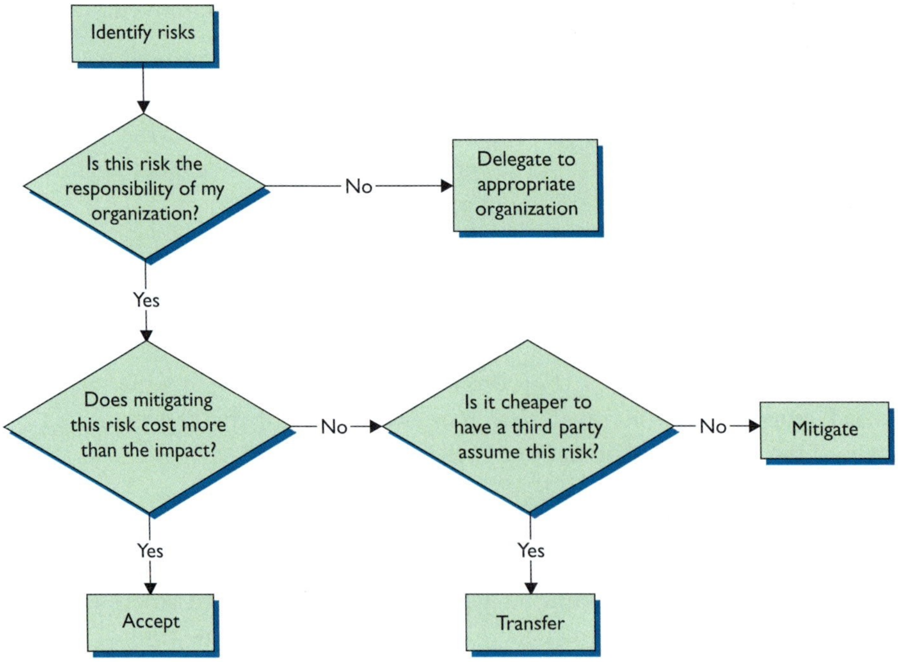

• **Figure 20.1** A planning decision flowchart for risk management

Risk Management Culture

Organizations have a culture associated with their operation. Frequently, this culture is set and driven by the activities of senior management personnel. The risk management culture of an organization can have an effect upon actions being taken by others. Table 20.1 illustrates the symptoms and results associated with risk management culture.

Table 20.1 Characteristics of Risk Management Culture

	Management Styles		
	Pathological	**Bureaucratic**	**Enlightened**
Situational Awareness	Don't want to know	May not find out	Actively seek
Communication Style	Messengers shot	Heard if it arrives	Messengers rewarded
Responsibility	Shirked or blamed	Compartmentalized	Shared
Failures Are	Punished	Local repairs only	Source of reforms
Ideas/Solutions	Discouraged	Beget problems	Welcomed

Risk Response Techniques

The presence of risks in a system is an absolute—they cannot be removed or eliminated. Actions can be taken to change the effects that a risk poses to a system, but the risk itself doesn't really change, no matter what actions are taken to mitigate that risk. A high risk will always be a high risk. However, actions can be taken to reduce the impact of that risk if it occurs. A limited number of strategies can be used to manage risk. The risk can be *avoided, transferred, mitigated,* or *accepted.*

Avoiding the risk can be accomplished in many ways. Although threats cannot be removed from the environment, the exposure can be altered. Not deploying a module that increases risk is one manner of risk avoidance.

Another possible action to manage risk is to transfer that risk. A common method of transferring risk is to purchase insurance. Insurance allows risk to be transferred to a third party that manages specific types of risk for multiple parties, thus reducing the individual cost. Another common example of risk transfer is the protection against fraud that consumers have on their credit cards. The risk is transferred to another party, so people can use the card in confidence.

Risk can also be mitigated through the application of controls that reduce the impact of an attack. Controls can alert operators so that the level of exposure is reduced through process intervention. When an action occurs that is outside the accepted risk profile, a second set of rules can be applied, such as calling the customer for verification before committing a transaction. Controls such as these can act to reduce the risk associated with potential high-risk operations.

In addition to mitigating risk or transferring risk, it may be acceptable for a manager to accept risk; in other words, despite the potential cost of a given risk and its associated probability, the manager of the organization will accept responsibility for the risk if it does happen. For example, a manager may choose to allow a programmer to make "emergency" changes to a production system (in violation of good separation of duties and the change management process) because the system cannot go down during a given

> **Tech Tip**
>
> **Risk Responses**
>
> *Four things can be done to respond to risk: accept, transfer, avoid, and mitigate. Whatever risk is not transferred, mitigated, or avoided is referred to as* residual risk *and by definition is accepted.*

period of time. The manager accepts that the risk of the programmer possibly making unauthorized changes is outweighed by the high-availability requirement of that system. However, there should always be some additional controls, such as a management review or a standardized approval process, to ensure the assumed risk is adequately managed.

Understand that risk cannot be completely eliminated. A risk that remains after implementing controls is a residual risk. In this step, you further evaluate residual risks to identify where additional controls are required to reduce risk even more. As stated earlier, the risk management process is iterative.

Risk Management Frameworks

A risk management framework provides a structure for the risk management strategy and guides the creation of the proper guidelines with steps to follow to provide for a comprehensive coverage of the risk environment. There is a wide array of risk management frameworks, and different consultancies will each have its own variation. Most of these are derived from one of the common risk management frameworks, such as NIST Risk Management Framework (NIST RMF), COSO (Committee of Sponsoring Organizations) Enterprise Risk Management Framework, ISO 3100 Standard Framework, or FAIR (Factor Analysis of Information Risk). Numerous other frameworks also have cybersecurity risk implications or are industry specific, including the following:

- **Payment Card Industry Data Security Standard (PCI DSS)** Governs the way credit and debit card information is handled.
- **ISO 27001** The international standard that describes best practice for implementing an information security management system (ISMS).
- **NIST Framework for Improving Critical Infrastructure Security** A cybersecurity framework that provides a common taxonomy and mechanism for organizations to manage their cybersecurity risk associated with critical infrastructure deployments.
- **Control Objectives for Information and Related Technologies (COBIT)** A cybersecurity framework that integrates a business's best aspects to its IT security, governance, and management.
- **Health Information Trust Alliance (HITRUST)** A cybersecurity framework that addresses the various measures for enhancing security and covers the Health Insurance Portability and Accountability Act (HIPAA).
- **Federal Risk and Authorization Management Program (FedRAMP)** A framework designed for government agencies to evaluate cyber threats and risks to the different infrastructure platforms, as well as cloud-based services and software solutions.
- **General Data Protection Regulation (GDPR)** The latest framework to secure personally identifiable information belonging to European citizens in the European Union (EU).

- **North American Electric Reliability Corporation Critical Infrastructure Protection (NERC CIP)** A cybersecurity framework that contains standards for protecting the bulk electric system.

Picking the correct framework(s) for your organization will depend on several factors, including industry, services you offer, the risk environment you are in, and more. One thing is clear: not having a framework will put you at a distinct disadvantage. One of the things an organization should get from its framework is a standardized and well-documented methodology for the following:

- Executing cybersecurity strategies using a range of security controls and best practices
- Conducting risk assessments that evaluate business priorities and identify gaps in cybersecurity controls
- Performing risk analysis on existing control gaps
- Measuring and scoring cybersecurity program maturity
- Prioritizing future cybersecurity investment based on risk analysis

Security Controls

Security controls are the mechanisms employed to minimize exposure to risk and mitigate the effects of loss. Using the security attributes of confidentiality, integrity, and **availability** associated with data, it is incumbent upon the security team to determine the appropriate set of controls to achieve the security objectives.

Just as security controls play a role in information security, the proper application of controls can assist in the risk management associated with physical security. Controls can be of a variety of types, as described in this chapter. The different categories of controls do not act as a taxonomy because there are overlapping descriptions and some control categories come from third-party policies and procedures.

One of the best references for security controls is NIST SP 800-53, currently in its fifth revision (see https://nvlpubs.nist.gov/nistpubs/SpecialPublications/NIST.SP.800-53r5.pdf). This document explains the use of controls and contains a catalog of hundreds of controls and modifiers, as well as a methodology of applying these controls based on a risk assessment of the asset being protected.

Controls should not just be chosen at random; rather, a design set of controls with purposeful aim toward actual threats and risk should be developed. A solid explanation of this is covered in NIST SP 800-53B, "Control Baselines for Information Systems and Organizations." The objective is to determine the correct control baseline. A **control baseline** is the set of controls employed to address the level of risk an enterprise faces. Once this set is identified, the controls can be tailored to the specifics of the risk by the system and the risk level associated with the specific system.

The process of building a control baseline begins with a determination of the information criticality and sensitivity associated with the system. This is known as a security categorization, using levels such as High, Moderate, and Low with respect to a loss of confidentiality, integrity, or availability. The results of the security categorization are used to guide and inform the selection of security control baselines to protect systems and information. Once the baseline is constructed, it must be tailored to address specific instances and levels of risk for each system. The process can be summed up with the following steps:

- Identifying and designating common controls
- Applying scoping considerations where required
- Supplementing baselines controls with control enhancements, as needed
- Assigning values to organization-defined control parameters (from SP 800-53 controls) to provide specific details, including providing specification information for control implementation
- Adding further controls where needed
- Specifying compensating controls, if needed

The use of the risk management and control concepts from NIST SP 800-53B and NIST SP 800-53 can be employed in virtually any organization of any size or industry.

Categories

Three categories of security controls are specified in a variety of defining documents, and these categories have become the de facto standard for the cybersecurity industry. The use of *categories* separates the controls into groups based on what the control uses as its lever: managerial activity, operational activity, or technical control. Each of these is described in the following sections. For some controls, it is possible they have aspects that span more than one category.

Managerial

The NIST SP 800 series refers to managerial controls as *management* controls.

Managerial controls are those that are based on overall risk management. These security controls focus on the management of risk or the management of the cybersecurity system. An example of a managerial control would be the use of periodic security risk assessments to provide feedback to senior management on the current risk posture. Table 20.2 lists the managerial controls.

Table 20.2 Managerial Controls

NIST Control Family	Identifier
Risk Assessment	RA
Planning	PL
System and Services Acquisition	SA
Certification, Accreditation, and Security Assessments	CA
*Program Management	PM
*PII Processing and Transparency	PT
*Supply Chain Risk Management	SR

The last three items in the table are new entries that entered the NIST publications with SP 800-53 R5.

Operational

An *operational* control is a policy or procedure used to limit security risk. These security controls are primarily implemented and executed by people, as opposed to systems. Instructions to guards are an example of an operational control. Table 20.3 lists the operational controls.

Table 20.3 Operational Controls

NIST Control Family	Identifier
Personnel Security	PS
Physical and Environmental Protection	PE
Contingency Planning	CP
Configuration Management	CM
Maintenance	MA
System and Information Integrity	SI
Media Protection	MP
Incident Response	IR
Awareness and Training	AT

Per the footnote in the publication on page 8, "Of the 20 control families in NIST SP 800-53, 17 are aligned with the minimum security requirements in [FIPS 200]. The Program Management (PM), PII Processing and Transparency (PT), and Supply Chain Risk Management (SR) families address enterprise-level program management, privacy, and supply chain risk considerations pertaining to federal mandates emergent since [FIPS 200]."

Technical

A *technical* control uses some form of technology to address a physical security issue. These security controls are primarily implemented and executed by the information system through mechanisms contained in its hardware, software, or firmware components. Biometrics is an example of a technical control. Table 20.4 lists the technical controls.

The main difference between operational and technical controls is that operational controls are those that people initiate and follow, whereas technical controls are typically automated and involve a machine to execute.

Table 20.4 Technical Controls

NIST Control Family	Identifier
Identification and Authentication	IA
Access Control	AC
Audit and Accountability	AU
System and Communications Protection	SC

Control Types

Controls can also be categorized by **control type**. The cybersecurity industry recognizes several different control types, and while these categories can be descriptive, they are not a taxonomy because they are not necessarily exclusive. Controls can fit into multiple types, depending on deployment and use. A door lock is an example of both a physical control and a preventative control.

Deterrent

A *deterrent* control acts to influence the attacker by reducing the likelihood of success. An example would be laws and regulations that increase punishment. Note that a deterrent control must be one that has to be known to a person for it to be effective. If it is unknown, it cannot deter. An example of this is a physical control, such as a CCTV or a warning sign. If a potential intruder does not see this control, it cannot deter the intruder.

Preventive

A *preventative* control is one that prevents specific actions from occurring; for example, an access control vestibule (formerly known as a mantrap) prevents tailgating. Preventative controls act before an event, preventing it from advancing. Unlike a deterrent control (which in itself also acts as a preventative control), a control classified as preventative does not have to be known by a person in order to be effective (for example, a firewall rule).

Detective

A **detective** control is one that facilitates the detection of a physical security breach. Detective controls act during an event, alerting operators to specific conditions. Alarms are common examples of detective controls.

Corrective

Corrective controls are used post-event, in an effort to minimize the extent of damage. Backups are a prime example of a corrective control because they can facilitate rapid resumption of operations.

The three descriptors of controls—technical, administrative, and physical—are separate from the other descriptors and can be used independently of them. It is possible to have a control that is a technical physical preventative control (a door lock).

Compensating

A **compensating** control is one that is used to meet a requirement when the requirement cannot be directly met. Fire suppression systems do not stop fire damage, but if properly employed, they can mitigate or limit the level of damage from fire.

Physical

A **physical** control is one that prevents specific physical actions from occurring; for example, an access control vestibule prevents tailgating. Physical controls prevent specific human interaction with a system and are primarily designed to prevent accidental operation of something. Physical controls act before an event, preventing it from actually occurring. Using covers over critical buttons is one example, as is a big red "STOP" button, positioned so it is easily reachable. The former stops inadvertent activation, while the latter facilitates easy activation in an emergency.

Tech Tip

Transferring Risk

One possible action to manage risk is to transfer that risk. The most common method of transferring risk is to purchase insurance. Cybersecurity insurance, for example, allows some level of risk to be transferred to a third party that manages specific types of risk for multiple parties, thus reducing the individual cost. Note that transferring risk usually applies to financial aspects of risk; it normally does not apply to legal accountability or responsibility.

Business Risks

No comprehensive identification of all risks in a business environment is possible. In today's technology-dependent business environment, risk is often simplistically divided into two areas: business risk and, a major subset, technology risk.

Examples of Business Risks

The following are some of the most common business risks:

- **Treasury management** Management of company holdings in bonds, futures, currencies, and so on
- **Revenue management** Management of consumer behavior and the generation of revenue
- **Contract management** Management of contracts with customers, vendors, partners, and so on
- **Fraud** Deliberate deception made for personal gain, to obtain property or services, and so on
- **Environmental risk management** Management of risks associated with factors that affect the environment
- **Regulatory risk management** Management of risks arising from new or existing regulations
- **Business continuity management** Management of risks associated with recovering and restoring business functions after a disaster or major disruption occurs
- **Technology** Management of risks associated with technology in its many forms

It is important that you understand that technology itself is a business risk. Hence, it must be managed along with other risks. Today, technology risks are so important they should be considered separately.

Examples of Technology Risks

The following are some of the most common technology risks:

- **Security and privacy** The risks associated with protecting personal, private, or confidential information
- **Information technology operations** The risks associated with the day-to-day operation of information technology systems
- **Business systems control and effectiveness** The risks associated with manual and automated controls that safeguard company assets and resources
- **Business continuity management** The risks associated with the technology and processes to be used in the event of a disaster or major disruption
- **Information systems testing** The risks associated with testing processes and procedures of information systems
- **Reliability and performance management** The risks associated with meeting reliability and performance agreements and measures
- **Information technology asset management** The risks associated with safeguarding information technology physical assets
- **Project risk management** The risks associated with managing information technology projects
- **Change management** The risks associated with managing configurations and changes (see Chapter 21)

Tech Tip

Risk According to the Basel Committee

The Basel Committee referenced earlier in the chapter has defined three types of risk specifically to address international banking:

- ***Market risk*** *Risk of losses due to fluctuation of market prices*
- ***Credit risk*** *Risk of default of outstanding loans*
- ***Operational risk*** *Risk from disruption by people, systems, processes, or disasters*

Business Impact Analysis

Business impact analysis (BIA) is the name often used to describe a document created by addressing the questions associated with sources of risk and the steps taken to mitigate them in the enterprise. The BIA also outlines what the loss of any of your critical functions will mean to the organization. A range of terms and concepts is used in describing and understanding the nature and role of risk in the business environment, as explored in this section.

Mission-Essential Functions

When examining business functions, you should also be aware of identifying vulnerable business processes. These are processes that have external inputs that could be less trustworthy and subject to manipulation.

When examining risk and impacts to a business, it is important to separate *mission-essential functions* from other business functions. In most businesses, the vast majority of daily functions, although important, are not mission essential. Mission-essential functions are those that, should they not occur or should they be performed improperly, the mission of the organization will be directly affected. The reason that identifying these functions is vital for risk management is simple: this is where you spend the majority of your effort, protecting the functions that are essential. Other functions may need protection, but their impairment will not cause the immediate impact that a mission-essential function would.

Identification of Critical Systems

A part of identifying mission-essential functions is identifying the systems and data that support the functions. *Identification of critical systems* enables the security team to properly prioritize defenses to protect the systems and data in a manner commensurate with the associated risk.

Single Point of Failure

A key principle of security is defense in depth. This layered approach to security is designed to eliminate any specific single points of failure. A *single point of failure* is any aspect that, if triggered, could result in the failure of the system. Redundancies have costs, but if the alternative cost is failure, then levels of redundancy are acceptable. For mission-essential systems, single points of failure are items that need to be called to management's attention, with full explanation of the risk and costs associated with them. There may be times that dealing with the single point of failure is not possible or practical, but everyone should understand the nature of the situation and resultant risk profile.

Impact

Risk is the chance of something not working as planned. *Impact* is the cost associated with a realized risk. Impact can be in many forms, including human life (as in injury or death), property loss, safety, financial loss, and loss of reputation. Losses are seldom absolute; they can come in all sizes and combinations. Different levels of risk can result in different levels of impact. Sometimes external events can affect the impact. If everyone in the industry has been experiencing a specific type of loss and your firm had time and warning to mitigate it but didn't, the environment defined by these outside factors may well indeed increase the impact to your firm from this type of event.

Data Loss

Data loss is when an organization actually loses information. Files can be deleted, overwritten, or even misplaced. Ransomware is the most dangerous form of data loss because it is driven by outside forces and its very nature is to make the data unavailable to the enterprise until a ransom is paid. Hardware failure is another source of data loss. The primary defense for data loss is a solid backup program that can restore lost data.

Data Breaches

Data breaches are the release of data to unauthorized parties. Attackers that infiltrate a system are frequently looking to steal information such as personally identifiable information (PII), financial data, corporate data with value on the open market, and intellectual property. Having a data breach can be a legal issue, a financial issue, a reputation issue, or any combination of these issues, depending on the type and scope of the breach. Strong access controls, encryption of data at rest, and data loss prevention (DLP) elements can lessen the impact. Encryption is the strongest control because a breach of encrypted data without the key isn't actually a breach.

Data Exfiltration

Data is a unique asset in many ways. One of the more relevant ways it is unique is in the fact that it can be copied, and then stolen, without affecting the original data. Stealing data becomes an exercise in data exfiltration or taking the copy out of the enterprise. Just as when a thief steals anything, the true theft only occurs when they escape with the item. *Data exfiltration* is the exporting of stolen data from an enterprise. Data exfiltration impact is related to the data being stolen. If it is intellectual property, then the impact can be directly to the bottom line. Loss of intellectual property can result in loss of future sales.

The loss of customer data can have impacts to reputation as well as direct financial impacts via regulatory penalties. Major data breaches have cost companies hundreds of millions of dollars in penalties, fines, and court settlements.

Identity Theft

Identity theft is a crime where someone uses information on another party to impersonate them. This is a secondary impact once data is exfiltrated. The loss of data can come from commercial systems and even home systems, and the results are the same: people can lose money, property, and time cleaning up an identity theft claim. The impact of data exfiltration that includes personally identifiable information (PII) can be significant in terms of regulatory costs. Recent major breaches have had substantial regulatory fines and legal costs associated with the loss of PII. The most expensive type of record to lose was customer PII records, which were involved in around

80 percent of breaches in the Verizon breach report. This is not just a big company financial issue. With the average cost of each lost record being roughly $150, it makes even small breaches of 1000 records a potential problem for smaller businesses.

Financial

At the end of the day, risk is measured in *financial* terms, and the impact from vulnerabilities can be expressed in financial terms as well. While it is sometimes difficult to directly trace each issue to a financial figure, there have been numerous examples where the results are easy to connect to the financials. A German steel mill was destroyed by attackers, Sony lost a movie release to North Korean hackers, Equifax paid out nearly $2 billion in response to its 2017 breach—these are all costs that are easily attributed to the direct impact of a cyber attack.

Here's a list of items that can contribute to the financial costs of a cyber attack:

- Costs associated with investigating and fixing enterprise systems
- Lost orders/revenue due to system downtime
- Fines for regulatory noncompliance on privacy laws
- Attorney fees from lawsuits
- Ransom payments made for ransomware
- Losses due to stolen intellectual property
- Share price decline and market capitalization loss

Most of the financial numbers seen in the press are skewed by the large settlements of big companies with big losses, but the effect on small to medium-sized enterprises is even more dramatic. An average cybersecurity loss can cost a small to medium-sized business $400,000. For many businesses, that number is large enough to destroy them.

Reputation

Reputation impact as a result of a cyber attack comes in two main forms: loss of customer confidence and, in cases where skilled workforce is involved, a competitive field loss of key employees. If your customer base has questions about your ability to fulfill orders and manage their information, or just has a general loss of confidence in company management, then your customers may go to a competitor. This is true of businesses that have consumer-based customers as well as businesses with corporate-based customers.

Companies that have highly skilled workforce members that are in short supply also have to be concerned with their reputation in the eyes of their employees. After all, who wants to work for a company that embarrasses them due to news stories about management failures that result in cybersecurity losses? Every tech worker wants Google or Apple on their resume, but no one in cybersecurity wants to talk about working for a firm like Equifax, where mismanagement of IT resources caused one of the costliest breaches in history. Having workers quit because they don't trust their company and finding replacements for highly skilled personnel when the company is in a reputational crisis is not a position management ever wants to find itself in.

Availability Loss

The CIA triad is confidentiality, integrity, and availability. Availability is defined as resources being available for authorized users when they are supposed to be available. When the impact of a cyber attack affects infrastructure elements, either by system damage, data loss, or loss of systems during recovery efforts, the effect is one that results in the loss of system capability. If this loss in capability is high enough, the system will stop processing records. For some firms, this is survivable for relatively short periods of time. For others, the downtime translates directly into lost revenue, and in some cases costs associated with service level agreements (SLAs) being broken. The loss of availability on the part of any system will have an impact on the enterprise; otherwise, why have the system? Determining the actual scale of an availability loss is simple in some transactional systems and more complicated in others, but at the end of the day, a firm invests business resources into its IT systems to facilitate business operations, not interrupt them.

Life

Some IT systems are involved in medicine, and failures of these systems can and has resulted in injury and death to patients. Other machines in industrial settings can have similar impacts. Injury and loss of life are outcomes that backups cannot address and can result in consequences beyond recovery.

Property

Property damage can be the result of unmitigated risk. This includes damage to company-owned property, damage to the property of others, and even environmental damage from toxic releases in industrial settings. One example is the Shamoon malware that destroyed the computing resources of Saudi Aramco to the point that the company had to buy replacement equipment because reimaging to a clean state was neither a guaranteed nor a timely solution.

Safety

Safety is the level of concern one places on the well-being of people. In a manufacturing environment, with moving equipment and machines that can present a danger to workers, government regulations drive specific actions to mitigate risk and make the workplace as safe as possible. Computers are becoming more involved in all aspects of businesses, and they can impact safety. Unsafe conditions that are the result of computer issues will face the same regulatory wrath that unsafe factories have caused in manufacturing—namely, fines and criminal complaints.

Third-party Risks

The enterprise computing environment is full of third parties, and their risks become enterprise risks. Common *third-party risks* that are often overlooked are issues of vendor management, system integration, and lack of vendor support. These are all related in the fact that when you chose a vendor as part of your enterprise solution, it made sense at that time. But over time, enterprises change, vendors change, capabilities and needs change, and what was once a good fit might not be at a future point in time. Keeping systems optimized is not a simple task, and many times later conditions will result in different decisions with regard to third parties and their risks.

Supply chains seldom stop with the next hop, and in technology those chains can be long and complex. With these supply chains come risks from elements such as outsourced code development, maintenance of systems, and, in the world of cloud systems, data storage on another party's computer.

Remember that supply chain concerns and lack of vendor support are concerns directly related to third-party risks and management.

With respect to third-party software running in the enterprise, it is important to have an inventory of what the software is, by version, and where it is used. This assists the security team in monitoring for vulnerabilities through sources like the Common Vulnerabilities and Exposures (CVE) database. This list will also help in determining risk levels as software reaches its end of life (EOL) or end of service life (EOSL).

Vendor Management

A vendor or supplier is a firm that has a business relationship with the enterprise. In most cases, this relationship in the enterprise is one of many customers. While the voice of the customer is important, the voice of a single customer is almost never heard. The challenge of *vendor management* is in determining one's own needs and then finding the vendors that offer the best value proposition against those needs. This is more than just selecting and buying a product for most components in an enterprise; issues of support, system lifetime, and maintenance all play a role in the long-term value of a vendor and their products. Mapping the needs and managing the multidimensional problem of determining the best fit and then maintaining that relationship over time are essential in the ever-changing enterprise environment.

System Integration

Enterprises are composed of many different components that all work together to process the information that flows through the enterprise. Different components serve different functions, but in the end, they have to work together. *System integration* is the connecting of these components, each representing a portion of the system into a complete functioning unit. System integration is an area where vulnerabilities can exist, as the pieces can have gaps in their integration or capabilities that do not manifest per the desired specification. System integration is coupled with configuration management because the configurations of the individual pieces can affect how the system as a whole functions. Any deviations from design specifications represent an opportunity for risk.

Lack of Vendor Support

Lack of vendor support can become an issue at several different levels. The most obvious scenario is when the original manufacturer of the item, be it hardware or software, no longer offers support. When an item reaches its end of life (EOL) from the original manufacturer's standpoint, this signifies the finality of its life under almost all circumstances. After the manufacturer stops supporting an item, options to keep it up to date with patches and fixes seldom exist. At this point, an organization that continues to use the product assumes all of the risk associated with issues uncovered after the product has entered EOL status, and the options to address these risks are limited to compensating controls.

Another scenario in which lack of vendor support arises is when the system in question is implemented by a third-party vendor and that vendor either no longer supports the configuration or is no longer in business. The underlying technology may still be supported by the original manufacturers, but the lack of support for the middleware provided by the third-party implementer raises questions as to whether the underlying products can be updated or patched. This places the testing burden on the end user, and in many cases the end user does not have the knowledge or skills necessary to conduct thorough regression testing.

Do not be confused! *End of life (EOL)* is the term used to denote that something has reached the end of its "useful life." *End of service life (EOSL)* or *end of support* is when the manufacturer quits selling an item. In most cases, the manufacturer no longer provides maintenance services or updates.

A system can have vulnerabilities related to its age. Whether the system is composed of old parts, as in an embedded system, or has become an end-of-life legacy system, the lack of vendor support can result in the owner's inability to address many newly discovered issues.

Supply Chain

Supply chain risk is caused by vulnerabilities that lie within the supply chain. Whether these vulnerabilities are in the actual supply chain itself or a product coming from a third party, the results are the same—a level of increased risk. As we saw in 2020 as a result of the pandemic, global supply chains can be interrupted by external events that then go on to cause issues for firms that depend on the supply chain functioning efficiently. Delays of product launches, updates, and milestones can all occur when parts, components, or software elements are not delivered on time.

A supply chain attack typically occurs at the weakest security link in the supply chain, and this is common during the manufacturing process or even in the product delivery phase.

Outsourced Code Development

Code can be one of the greatest sources of vulnerabilities and risk in an enterprise. Code is embedded in so many aspects of the enterprise—from the equipment to the business processes, to the applications that make things run, to the infrastructure it all runs on. Code is the glue that holds it all together. However, when code is buried in the processes, and that code was developed by a third party, often using third-party code fragments, the chain of risk becomes long and difficult to manage. The risk isn't just in the fact that the code is outsourced, but actually in the fact that the visibility and control over these risks becomes harder to manage with every step away from the source.

Creating code that is both maintainable and secure is not a simple task. It is important to have conditions in contracts requiring appropriate development measures be in place for third-party code, including the rights to inspect and verify security functionality. Items such as backdoors, either placed intentionally or left from a testing process, typically require access to the source code to find and remove. Ensuring third-party developers have appropriately secure coding practices and having their code reviewed by independent testers and placed in escrow for safekeeping are considered best practices.

Data Storage

Data storage is an important aspect of every enterprise, and it is typically distributed throughout the enterprise in different capacities and configurations. If all data was in a single location, then data storage management, including backup and recovery functions, would be easy to manage. As data storage is distributed across the enterprise into multiple enclaves with differing requirements and criticalities, the management of data storage becomes more difficult. Ensuring the correct access controls and security protections, such as backups, is important for all data stores, and when gaps in these controls emerge, this creates vulnerabilities. If attackers can manipulate data stores, then they can affect enterprise operations. To ensure all data is protected from becoming a vulnerability to the system, having a standardized data storage policy and checklist is good practice in the enterprise. Elements can be varied based on criticality of the data store, but following a standard procedure will reduce the chances of gaps existing from oversight or errors.

Risk Mitigation Strategies

Risk mitigation strategies are the action plans developed after a thorough evaluation of the possible threats, hazards, and risks associated with business operations. These strategies are employed to lessen the risks associated with operations. The focus of risk mitigation strategies is to reduce the effects of threats and hazards. Common mitigation strategies include change management, incident management, user rights and permission reviews, audits, and technology controls.

Change Management

Change management has its roots in system engineering and looks at the overall view of systems components and processes. Configuration management applies to a lower level of detail—specifically, the actual configuration of components, such as hosts, devices, and so forth. Configuration management might be considered a subset of change management, but they are not the same thing. Most of today's software and hardware change management practices derive from long-standing system engineering configuration management practices. Computer hardware and software development have also evolved to the point that proper management structure and controls must exist to ensure the products operate as planned. It is normal for an enterprise to have a change control board to approve all production changes and ensure the change management procedures are followed before changes are introduced to a system.

Configuration control is the process of controlling changes to items that have been baselined. Configuration control ensures that only approved changes to a baseline are allowed to be implemented. It is easy to understand why a software system, such as a web-based order-entry system, should not be changed without proper testing and control. Otherwise, the system might stop functioning at a critical time. Configuration control is a key step that provides valuable insight to managers. If a system is being changed and configuration control is being observed, managers and others concerned will be better informed. This ensures proper use of assets and avoids unnecessary downtime because of the installation of unapproved changes.

Change management ensures proper procedures are followed when modifying the IT infrastructure.

Incident Management

When an incident occurs, having an incident response management methodology is a key risk mitigation strategy. Incident response and incident management are essential security functions and are covered in detail in Chapter 22.

User Rights and Permissions Reviews

The review of user rights and permissions is one of the more powerful security controls, but the strength of this control depends on it being kept up to date and properly maintained. Ensuring that the list of users and associated rights is complete and up to date is a challenging task in anything bigger than the smallest of enterprises. A compensating control that can assist in keeping the lists of user rights current is a set of periodic audits of the user base and associated permissions.

Data Loss or Theft

Data is the primary target of most attackers. The value of the data can vary, making some data more valuable and hence more at risk of theft. Data can also be lost through a variety of mechanisms, with hardware failure, operator error, and system errors being common causes. Regardless of the cause of loss, an organization can take various actions to mitigate the effects of the loss. Backups lead the list of actions because backups can provide the ultimate in protection against loss.

To prevent theft, a variety of controls can be employed. Some are risk mitigation steps, such as data minimization, which is the act of not storing what isn't needed. If it must be stored and has value, then technologies such as data loss prevention can be used to provide a means of protection. Simple security controls such as firewalls and network segmentation can also act to make data theft more difficult.

Risk Management Models

Risk management concepts are fundamentally the same despite their definitions, and they require similar skills, tools, and methodologies. Several models can be used for managing risk through its various phases. Two models are presented here: the first can be applied to managing risks in general, and the second is tailored for managing risk in software projects.

> **Tech Tip**
>
> **Key Performance Indicators and Key Risk Indicators**
>
> A key performance indicator (KPI) *is a measurable value that demonstrates how effectively a key business objective is being met.* A key risk indicator (KRI) *is a measure used in management to indicate how risky an activity is to the enterprise. Together these metrics provide management information essential for efficient operations. KPIs and KRIs are used to monitor the performance of systems and processes and are critical to effective risk management. If you can't measure it, you have to rely on more subjective evaluation methods.*

General Risk Management Model

The following five steps can be used in virtually any risk management process. Following these steps will lead to an orderly process of analyzing and mitigating risks.

Step 1: Asset Identification

Identify and classify the assets, systems, and processes that need protection because they are vulnerable to threats. Use a classification that fits your business. This classification leads to the ability to prioritize assets, systems, and processes and to evaluate the costs of addressing the associated risks. Assets can include the following:

- Inventory
- Buildings
- Cash
- Information and data
- Hardware
- Software
- Services
- Documents
- Personnel
- Brand recognition
- Organization reputation
- Goodwill

Step 2: Threat Assessment

After identifying the assets, you identify both the possible threats and the possible vulnerabilities associated with each asset and the likelihood of their occurrence. Threats can be defined as any circumstance or event with the potential to cause harm to an asset. Common classes of threats include the following (with examples):

- **Natural disasters** These are hurricanes, earthquakes, lightning, and so on.
- **Man-made disasters** Examples are an earthen dam failure, such as the 1976 Teton Dam failure in Idaho; a car accident that destroys a municipal power distribution transformer; and the 1973 explosion of a railcar containing propane gas in Kingman, Arizona.
- **Internal vs. external** Internal threats include disgruntled employees, well-meaning employees who make mistakes, and other employees who have an accident. External threats come from outside the organization and by definition begin without access to the system.
- **Terrorism** Examples are the 2001 destruction of the World Trade Center and the 1995 gas attack on the Shinjuku train station in Tokyo.
- **Errors** An example is an employee not following safety or configuration management procedures.
- **Malicious damage or attacks** This could be a disgruntled employee purposely corrupting data files.
- **Fraud** This could be an employee falsifying travel expenses or vendor invoices and payments.

- **Theft** This could be an employee stealing from the loading dock a laptop computer after it has been inventoried but not properly secured.
- **Equipment or software failure** This could be an error in the calculation of a company-wide bonus overpaying employees.

Vulnerabilities are characteristics of resources that can be exploited by a threat to cause harm. Common classes of vulnerabilities include the following (with examples):

- **Unprotected facilities** Company offices with no security officer present or no card-entry system
- **Unprotected computer systems** A server temporarily connected to the network before being properly configured/secured
- **Unprotected data** Not installing critical security patches to eliminate application security vulnerabilities
- **Insufficient procedures and controls** Allowing an accounts payable clerk to create vendors in the accounting system, enter invoices, and authorize check payments
- **Insufficient or unqualified personnel** A junior employee not sufficiently securing a server because of a lack of training

Step 3: Impact Determination and Quantification

An impact is the loss created when a threat exploits a vulnerability. When a threat is realized, it creates impact. Impacts can be either tangible or intangible. A **tangible impact** results in financial loss or physical damage. For an **intangible impact**, assigning a financial value to the impact can be difficult. For example, in a manufacturing facility, storing and using flammable chemicals creates a risk of fire to the facility. The vulnerability is that flammable chemicals are stored there. The threat would be that a person could cause a fire by mishandling the chemicals (either intentionally or unintentionally). A tangible impact would be the loss incurred (say, $500,000) if a person ignites the chemicals and fire then destroys part of the facility. An example of an intangible impact would be the loss of goodwill or brand damage caused by the impression that the company doesn't safely protect its employees or the surrounding geographic area.

Tangible impacts include

- Direct loss of money
- Endangerment of staff or customers
- Loss of business opportunity
- Reduction in operational efficiency or performance
- Interruption of a business activity

Intangible impacts include

- Breach of legislation or regulatory requirements
- Loss of reputation or goodwill (brand damage)
- Breach of confidence

Step 4: Control Design and Evaluation

In this step, you determine which controls to put in place to mitigate the risks. Controls (also called *countermeasures* or *safeguards*) are designed to

Tech Tip

Business Dependencies

An area often overlooked in risk assessment is the need to address business dependencies—each organization must assess risks caused by other organizations with which it interacts. This occurs when the organization is either a consumer of or a supplier to other organizations (or both). For example, if a company is dependent on products produced by a laboratory, then the company must determine the impact of the laboratory not delivering the product when needed. Likewise, an organization must assess risks that can occur when it is the supplier to some other company dependent on its products.

The steps in the general risk management model should allow you to identify the steps in any risk management process.

control risk by reducing vulnerabilities to an acceptable level. (For use in this text, the terms *control, countermeasure,* and *safeguard* are considered synonymous and are used interchangeably.)

Controls can be actions, devices, or procedures. As discussed earlier, they can be deterrent, preventive, detective, or corrective in how they act.

Step 5: Residual Risk Management

Understand that risk cannot be completely eliminated. A risk that remains after implementing controls is termed a **residual risk**. In this step, you further evaluate residual risks to identify where additional controls are required to reduce risk even more. This leads us to the earlier statement that the risk management process is iterative.

Software Engineering Institute Model

In an approach tailored for managing risk in software projects, SEI uses the following paradigm (SEI, *Continuous Risk Management Guidebook* [Pittsburgh, PA: Carnegie Mellon University, 1996], 23). Although the terminology varies slightly from the previous model, the relationships are apparent, and either model can be applied wherever risk management is used.

1. **Identify** Look for risks before they become problems.
2. **Analyze** Convert the data gathered into information that can be used to make decisions. Evaluate the impact, probability, and timeframe of the risks. Classify and prioritize each of the risks.
3. **Plan** Review and evaluate the risks and decide what actions to take to mitigate them. Implement those mitigating actions.
4. **Track** Monitor the risks and the mitigation plans. Trends may provide information to activate plans and contingencies. Review periodically to measure progress and identify new risks.
5. **Control** Make corrections for deviations from the risk mitigation plans. Correct products and processes as required. Changes in business procedures may require adjustments in plans or actions, as do faulty plans and risks that become problems.

Tech Tip

Can All Risks Be Identified?

It is important to note that not all risks need to be mitigated or controlled; however, as many risks as possible should be identified and reviewed. Those deemed to have potential impact should be mitigated by countermeasures.

NIST Risk Models

NIST has several informative risk models that can be applied to an enterprise. NIST has published several Special Publications (SPs) associated with risk management. SP 800-39, "Managing Information Security Risk: Organization, Mission, and Information System View," presents several key insights:

- Establish a relationship between aggregated risk from information systems and mission/business success.
- Encourage senior leaders to recognize the importance of managing information security risk within the organization.
- Help those with system-level security responsibilities understand how system-level issues affect the organization/mission as a whole.

SP 800-39 does this through the use of a model, illustrated in Figure 20.2. This model has two distinct levels of analysis that work together as one in describing risk management actions.

The first level of analysis is represented by four elements: Frame, Assess, Respond, and Monitor. The second level is related to the tiers represented in the hierarchical triangles: Organization, Mission/Business Processes, and Information Systems.

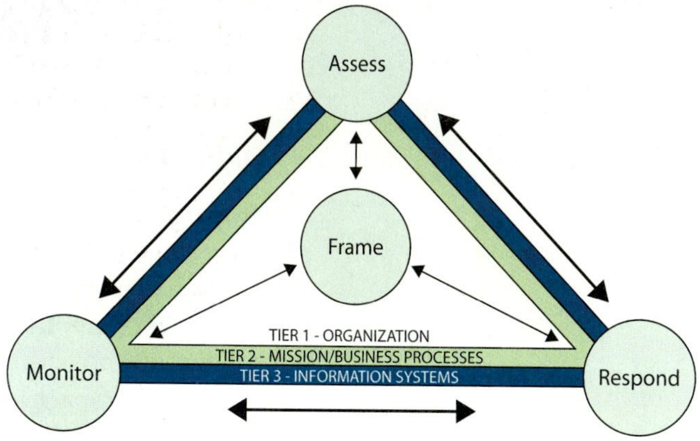

• **Figure 20.2** NIST risk management process applied across the tiers

The Frame element represents the organization's risk framing that establishes the context and provides a common perspective on how the organization manages risk. Risk framing is central to the model, as illustrated by the arrows to the other elements. Its principal output is a risk management strategy that addresses how the organization assesses risk, responds to risk, and monitors risk. The three tiers represent the different distinct layers in an organization that are associated with risk. Tier 1, representing the executive function, is where the risk framing occurs. At Tier 2, the mission and business process layer, the risk management functions of assess, respond, and monitor occur. Tier 3 is the information system layer where activities of risk management are manifested in the systems of the organization.

This explanation is not completely correct. All steps of the risk management and assessment process can occur at all three layers; you can assess risk at Tier 1 (business or mission risk), Tier 2 (programmatic and cross-functional or aggregate system risk), and Tier 3 (system-level risk).

Model Application

The three model examples define steps that can be used in any general or software risk management process. These risk management principles can be applied to any project, program, or business activity, no matter how simple or complex. Figure 20.3 shows how risk management can be applied across the continuum and that the complexity of risk management generally increases with the size of the project, program, or business to be managed.

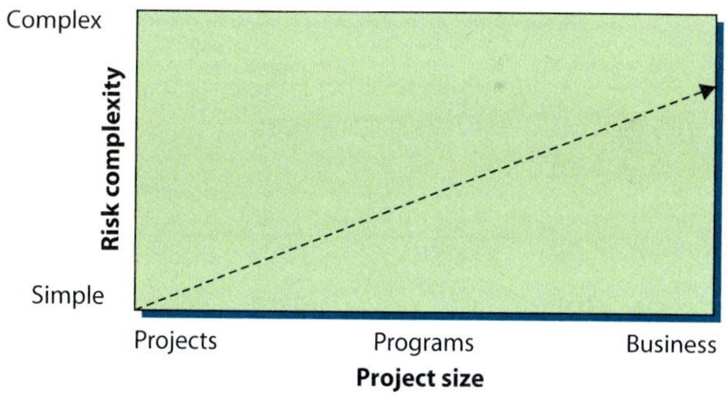

• **Figure 20.3** Risk complexity versus project size

Risk Assessment

Risk assessment is a process with many different aspects, as risk can be assessed from multiple perspectives and levels, as well as via different methodologies. Risk can be assessed using quantitative methods, where specific values are assigned, or qualitative methods, where relative levels are considered. Risk can be assessed across the breadth of an organization via a risk assessment methodology that emphasizes the policies and procedures, examining for missing elements or gaps. Vulnerability assessments can be conducted to examine for specific vulnerabilities testing systems for specific mitigation ability. Red team exercises and penetration exercises are used to test systems against specific threat type environments.

Qualitatively Assessing Risk

Qualitative risk analysis allows expert judgment and experience to assume a prominent role. To assess risk qualitatively, you compare the impact of the threat with the probability of occurrence and assign an impact level and probability level to the risk. For example, if a threat has a high impact and a high probability of occurring, the risk exposure is high and probably requires some action to reduce this threat (pale green box in Figure 20.4). Conversely, if the impact is low with a low probability, the risk exposure is low, and no action may be required to reduce the likelihood of the occurrence or impact of this threat (white box in Figure 20.4). Figure 20.4 shows an example of a *binary assessment,* where only two outcomes are possible each for impact and probability. Either it will have an impact or it will not (or it will have a high or low impact), and it will occur or it won't (or it will have a high probability of occurring or a low probability of occurring).

In reality, a few threats can usually be identified as presenting high-risk exposure, and a few threats present low-risk exposure. The threats that fall somewhere between (pale blue boxes in Figure 20.4) will have to be evaluated by judgment and management experience.

Impact	High impact/Low probability	High impact/High probability
	Low impact/Low probability	Low impact/High probability
	Probability	

• **Figure 20.4** Binary assessment

If the analysis is more complex, requiring three levels of analysis, such as low-medium-high or green-yellow-red, then nine combinations are possible, as shown in Figure 20.5. Again, the pale green boxes probably require action, the white boxes may or may not require action, and the pale blue boxes require judgment. (Note that for brevity, in Figure 20.5 the first term in each box refers to the magnitude of the impact, and the second term refers to the probability of the threat occurring.)

Impact	High Low	High Medium	High High
	Medium Low	Medium Medium	Medium High
	Low Low	Low Medium	Low High
	Probability		

• **Figure 20.5** Three levels of analysis

Other levels of complexity are possible. With five levels of analysis, 25 values of risk exposure are possible. In this case, the possible values of impact and probability could take on the values very low, low, medium, high, or very high. Also, note that the matrix does not have to be symmetrical. For example, if the probability is assessed with three values (low, medium, high) and the impact has five values (very low, low, medium, high, very high), the analysis would be as shown in Figure 20.6. (Again, note that the first term in each box refers to the impact, and the second term in each box refers to the probability of occurrence.)

Impact	Very high Low	Very high Medium	Very high High
	High Low	High Medium	High High
	Medium Low	Medium Medium	Medium High
	Low Low	Low Medium	Low High
	Very low Low	Very low Medium	Very low High
	Probability		

• **Figure 20.6** A three-by-five level analysis

So far, the examples have focused on assessing likelihood versus impact. Qualitative risk assessment can be adapted to a variety of attributes and situations in combination with each other. For example, Figure 20.7 shows the comparison of some specific risks that have been identified during a security assessment. The assessment identified the risk areas listed in the first column (weak intranet security, high number of modems, Internet attack vulnerabilities, and weak incident detection and response mechanism). The

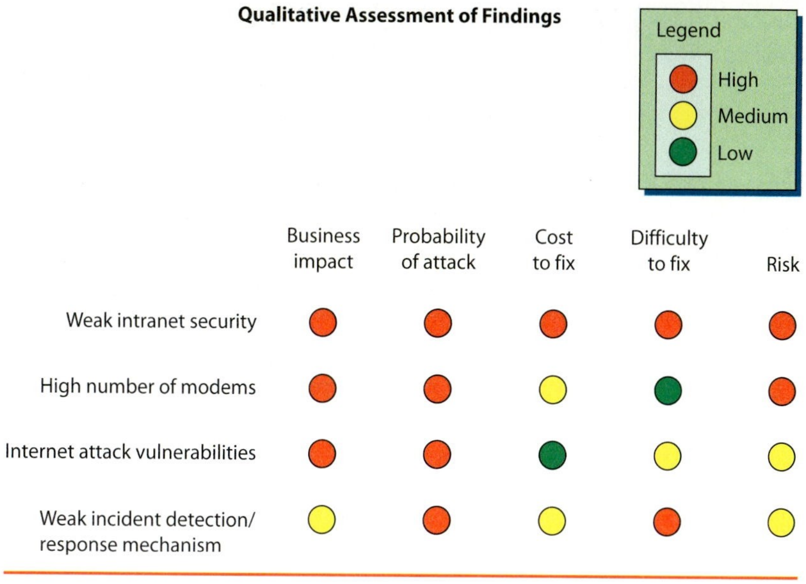

• **Figure 20.7** Example of a combination assessment

assessment also identified various potential impacts, listed across the top (business impact, probability of attack, cost to fix, and difficulty to fix). Each of the impacts has been assessed as low, medium, or high—depicted using green, yellow, and red, respectively. Each of the risk areas has been assessed with respect to each of the potential impacts, and an overall risk assessment has been determined in the last column.

Risk Matrix/Heat Map

A *risk matrix/heat map* is used to visually display the results of a qualitative risk analysis. This method allows expert judgment and experience to assume a prominent role in the risk assessment process and is easier than trying to define an exact number for each element of risk. To assess risk qualitatively, you first determine the likelihood of a threat occurring and also the consequence should it occur. You then take the value of each, multiply them together to get the risk value. For a 5×5 risk matrix/heat map, as shown in Figure 20.8, one uses simple numbers from 1 to 5 for each of

Likelihood						
Likelihood	Almost Certain (5)	Moderate 5	Major 10	Major 15	Critical 20	Critical 25
	Likely (4)	Minor 4	Moderate 8	Major 12	Major 16	Critical 20
	Possible (3)	Minor 3	Moderate 6	Moderate 9	Major 12	Major 15
	Unlikely (2)	Minor 2	Minor 4	Moderate 6	Moderate 8	Major 10
	Rare (1)	Minor 1	Minor 2	Minor 3	Minor 4	Moderate 5
		Inconsequential (1)	Minor (2)	Moderate (3)	Major (4)	Critical (5)
		Consequence				

• **Figure 20.8** Risk Matrix/Heat Map

the axes, and this yields risk values from 1 to 25. These values can then be classified as minor, moderate, major, or critical.

Quantitatively Assessing Risk

Whereas qualitative risk assessment relies on judgment and experience, quantitative risk assessment applies historical information and trends to attempt to predict future performance. This type of risk assessment is highly dependent on historical data, and gathering such data can be difficult. Quantitative risk assessment can also rely heavily on models that provide decision-making information in the form of quantitative metrics, which attempt to measure risk levels across a common scale.

It is important to understand that key assumptions underlie any model, and different models will produce different results even when given the same input data. Although significant research and development have been invested in improving and refining the various risk analysis models, expert judgment and experience must still be considered an essential part of any risk assessment process. Models can never replace judgment and experience, but they can significantly enhance the decision-making process.

Adding Objectivity to a Qualitative Assessment

It is possible to move a qualitative assessment toward being more quantitative. Making a qualitative assessment more detailed can be as simple as assigning numeric values to one of the tables shown in Figures 20.4 through 20.7. For example, the impacts listed in Figure 20.7 can be prioritized from highest to lowest and then weighted, as shown in Table 20.5, with business impact weighted the most and difficulty to fix weighted the least. This is a semiquantitative method and may use numerical values for the sake of convenience to ease computation and provide a more defined answer, but it is still considered a qualitative method.

Table 20.5 Adding Weights and Definitions to the Potential Impacts

Impact	Explanation	Weight
Business impact	If exploited, what is the business impact?	4
Probability of attack	How likely is a potential attacker to try this technique or attack?	3
Cost to fix	How much will it cost in dollars and resources to correct this vulnerability?	2
Difficulty to fix	How hard is this to fix from a technical standpoint?	1

Next, values can be assigned to reflect how each risk was assessed. Figure 20.7 can thus be made more objective by assigning a value to each color that represents an assessment. For example, a red assessment indicates many critical, unresolved issues, and this will be given an assessment value of 3. Green means few issues are unresolved, so it is given a value of 1. Table 20.6 shows values that can be assigned for an assessment using red, yellow, and green.

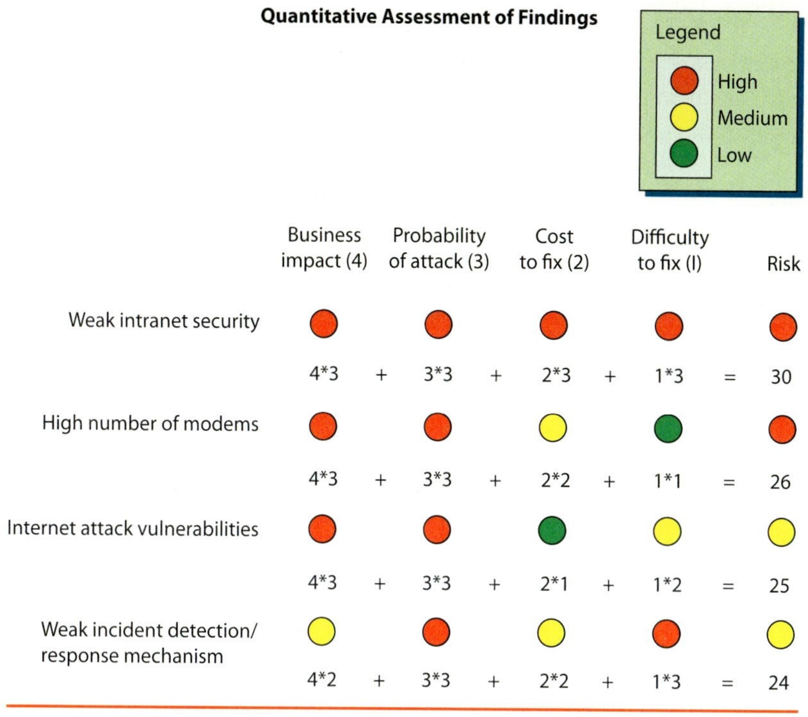

• **Figure 20.9** Final quantitative assessment of the findings

The last step is to calculate an overall risk value for each risk area (each row in Figure 20.7) by multiplying the weights depicted in Table 20.5 by the assessed values from Table 20.6 and summing the products.

$$\text{Risk} = W_1 * V_1 + W_2 * V_2 + \ldots W_4 * V_4$$

The risk calculation and final risk value for each risk area listed in Figure 20.7 have been incorporated into Figure 20.9. The assessed areas can then be ordered from highest to lowest based on the calculated risk value to aid management in focusing on the risk areas with the greatest potential impact.

You can also add more information via an assignment of values, such as shown in Table 20.6.

Table 20.6 Adding Values to Assessments

Assessment	Explanation	Value
Red	Many critical, unresolved issues	3
Yellow	Some critical, unresolved issues	2
Green	Few unresolved issues	1

Risk Calculation

More complex models permit a variety of analyses based on statistical and mathematical models. A common method is the calculation of the annualized loss expectancy (ALE). Calculating the ALE creates a monetary value of the impact. This calculation begins by calculating a single loss expectancy.

Asset Value

The *asset value (AV)* is the amount of money it would take to replace an asset. This term is used with the exposure factor, a measure of how much of an asset is at risk, to determine the single loss expectancy.

Exposure Factor

The *exposure factor (EF)* is a measure of the magnitude of loss of an asset. The exposure factor is the percentage of an asset's value that is at risk. In some cases, if the risk is realized, the asset is lost; in other cases, it may be impaired. If you have one web server and it breaks, you have 100 percent EF. If you have a farm of five web servers and two of them break, the EF is 40 percent.

For example, to calculate the exposure factor, assume the asset value of a small office building and its contents is $2 million. Also assume that this building houses the call center for a business, and the complete loss of the center would take away about half of the capability of the company. Therefore, the exposure factor is 50 percent.

SLE

The *single loss expectancy (SLE)* is the value of a loss expected from a single event. The SLE is calculated using the following formula:

SLE = asset value (AV) × exposure factor (EF)

For our office building example, the SLE is

$2 million × 0.5 = $1 million

ARO

The **annualized rate of occurrence (ARO)** is a representation of the frequency of the event, measured in a standard year. If the event is expected to occur once in 20 years, then the ARO is 1/20. Typically the ARO is defined by historical data, either from a company's own experience or from industry surveys. Continuing our example, assume that a fire at this business's location is expected to occur about once in 20 years. Given this information, the ALE is

$1 million × 1/20 = $50,000

Try This!

Calculate SLE, ARO, and ALE

A company owns five warehouses throughout the United States, each of which is valued at $1 million and contributes equally to the company's capacity. Try calculating the SLE, ARO, and ALE for its warehouse located in the Mountain West, where the probability of an earthquake is once every 500 years.

The solution is SLE = $1 million × 1.0; ARO = 1/500; ALE = $1 million/500, or $2000.

ALE

The *annualized loss expectancy (ALE)* is then calculated simply by multiplying the SLE by the likelihood or number of times the event is expected to occur in a year, which is called the annualized rate of occurrence:

$$ALE = SLE \times ARO$$

The ALE determines a threshold for evaluating the cost/benefit ratio of a given countermeasure. Therefore, a countermeasure to protect this business adequately should cost no more than the calculated ALE of $50,000 per year.

The examples in this chapter have been simplistic, but they demonstrate the concepts of both qualitative and quantitative risk analysis. More complex algorithms and software packages are available for accomplishing risk analyses, but these examples suffice for the purposes of this text.

Risk Register

A **risk register** is a list of the risks associated with a system. It also can contain additional information associated with the risk element, such as the category to group like risks, probability of occurrence, impact to the organization, mitigation factors, and other data. There is no standardized form. The Project Management Institute has one format, and other sources have different formats. The reference document ISO 73:2009, "Risk Management—Vocabulary," defines a risk register to be a "record of information about identified risks." Note that the NIST Risk Management Framework refers to this document as a "Plan of Actions and Milestones" and includes target dates for resolution, as well as resources and responsible personnel required.

Likelihood of Occurrence

The *likelihood of occurrence* is the chance a particular risk will occur. This measure can be qualitative or quantitative. For qualitative measures, it is typically defined on an annual basis to allow use of the measurement with respect to other annualized measures. If defined quantitatively, it is used to create rank order outcomes.

Impact

The *impact* of an event is a measure of the actual loss when a threat exploits a vulnerability. Federal Information Processing Standards (FIPS) 199 defines three levels of impact using the terms *high*, *moderate*, and *low*. The impact needs to be defined in terms of the context of each organization because what is high for some firms may be low for much larger firms. The common method is to define the impact levels in terms of important business criteria. Impacts can be in terms of cost (dollars), performance (service level agreement [SLA] or other requirements), schedule (deliverables), or any other important item. Impact can also be categorized in terms of the information security attribute that is relevant to the problem: confidentiality, integrity, or availability.

Supply Chain Assessment

The analysis of risk in a supply chain has become an important issue in our connected society. One needs to consider not just the risk associated with a system but the risk embedded in a system as a result of its creation, which includes risks from the supply chain associated with elements inside a system. For instance, if a system has critical components that are not replaceable except from a single source, what happens if that source quits making the component? The term *supply chain assessment* describes the process where these risks are determined and explored.

Qualitative vs. Quantitative Risk Assessment

It is recognized throughout industry that it is *impossible* to conduct risk management that is purely *quantitative.* Usually risk management includes both qualitative and quantitative elements, requiring both analysis and judgment or experience. In contrast to quantitative assessment, it is *possible* to accomplish *purely qualitative* risk management. It is easy to see that it is impossible to define and quantitatively measure all factors that exist in a given risk assessment. It is also easy to see that a risk assessment that measures no factors quantitatively but measures them all qualitatively is possible.

The decision of whether to use qualitative versus quantitative risk management depends on the criticality of the project, the resources available, and the management style. The decision will be influenced by the degree to which the fundamental risk management metrics, such as asset value, exposure factor, and threat frequency, can be quantitatively defined.

Tools

Many tools can be used to enhance the risk management process. The following tools can be used during the various phases of risk assessment to add objectivity and structure to the process. Understanding the details of each of these tools is not necessary for the CompTIA Security+ exam, but understanding what they can be used for is important. You can find more information on these tools in any good project management book.

- **Affinity grouping** A method of identifying items that are related and then identifying the principle that ties them together.
- **Baseline identification and analysis** The process of establishing a baseline set of risks. It produces a "snapshot" of all the identified risks at a given point in time.
- **Cause-and-effect analysis** Identifying relationships between a risk and the factors that can cause it. This is usually accomplished using *fishbone diagrams* developed by Dr. Kaoru Ishikawa, former professor of engineering at the Science University of Tokyo.
- **Cost/benefit analysis** A straightforward method for comparing cost estimates with the benefits of a mitigation strategy.

- **Gantt charts** A management tool for diagramming schedules, events, and activity duration.
- **Interrelationship digraphs** A method for identifying cause-and-effect relationships by clearly defining the problem to be solved, identifying the key elements of the problem, and then describing the relationships between each of the key elements.
- **Pareto charts** A histogram that ranks the categories in a chart from most frequent to least frequent, thus facilitating risk prioritization.
- **Program evaluation and review technique (PERT) charts** A diagram depicting interdependencies between project activities, showing the sequence and duration of each activity. When complete, the chart shows the time necessary to complete the project and the activities that determine that time (the critical path).
- **Risk management plan** A comprehensive plan documenting how risks will be managed on a given project. It contains processes, activities, milestones, organizations, responsibilities, and details of each major risk management activity and how it is to be accomplished. It is an integral part of the project management plan.

Tech Tip

Risks Really Don't Change, But They Can Be Mitigated

One final thought to keep in mind is that the threats themselves are independent of your actions, no matter what actions are taken to mitigate the associated risk. A high threat environment will always be a high risk and will require more mitigation than a lower one. However, actions can be taken to reduce the likelihood of the risk and the impact of that risk if it occurs. Over time, risks may be fluid as new threats come into focus and older ones retreat, with the issues of likelihood and potential impact changing. A new web system using a different technology (for example, eliminating Flash elements) will have a different risk profile than the older system.

Cost-Effectiveness Modeling

Cost-effectiveness modeling assumes you are incurring a cost and focuses on the question of what the value of that cost is. This is a rational means of economic analysis used to determine the utility of a specific strategy. It is a nearly foregone conclusion you will be spending resources on security; it's just a question of what you get for your money.

The *total cost of ownership (TCO)* is the set of all costs—including everything from capital costs to operational and exception-handling costs—associated with a technology. There are a lot of arguments over how to calculate TCO, typically to favor one solution over another, but that is not important in this instance. It is important to note the differences between normal operational costs and exception handling. Exception handling is always more expensive.

The objective in risk management is to have a set of overlapping controls such that the TCO is minimized. This means that the solution has a measured effectiveness across the risk spectrum. This is where the compliance-versus-security debate becomes interesting. You establish compliance rules for a variety of reasons, but once established, their future effectiveness depends on the assumption that the same risk environment exists as when they were created. Should the risk, the value, or the impact change over time, the cost effectiveness of the compliance-directed control can shift, frequently in a negative fashion.

Risk Management Best Practices

Best practices are the best defenses that an organization can employ in any activity. One manner of examining best practices is to ensure that the business has the set of best practices to cover its operational responsibilities.

At a deeper level, the details of these practices need to themselves be best practices if you are to get the best level of protection. At a minimum, risk mitigation best practices include business continuity, high availability, fault tolerance, and disaster recovery concepts.

None of these operates in isolation. In fact, they are all interconnected, sharing elements as they all work together to achieve a common purpose: the security of the data in the enterprise, which is measured in terms of risk exposure. Key elements of best practices include understanding the vulnerabilities, understanding the threat vectors and likelihoods of occurrence, and the use of mitigation techniques to reduce residual risk to manageable levels.

System Vulnerabilities

Vulnerabilities are characteristics of an asset that can be exploited by a threat to cause harm. All systems have bugs or errors. Not all errors or bugs are vulnerabilities. For an error or bug to be classified as a vulnerability, it must be exploitable, meaning an attacker must be able to use the bug to cause a desired result. Three elements are needed for a vulnerability to occur:

- The system must have a flaw.
- The flaw must be accessible by an attacker.
- The attacker must possess the ability to exploit the flaw.

Vulnerabilities can be fixed, removed, and mitigated. They are part of any system and represent weaknesses that may be exploited.

Vulnerabilities can exist in many levels and from many causes. From design errors, to coding errors, to unintended (and untested) combinations in complex systems, there are numerous forms of vulnerabilities. Vulnerabilities can exist in software, hardware, and procedures. Whether in the underlying system, in a security control designed to protect the system, or in the procedures employed in the operational use of the system, the result is the same: a vulnerability represents an exploitable weakness that increases the level of risk associated with the system.

Threat Vectors

A threat is any circumstance or event with the potential to cause harm to an asset. For example, a malicious hacker might choose to hack your system by using readily available hacking tools. Threats can be classified in groups, with the term *threat vector* describing the elements of these groups. A threat vector is the path or tool used by an attacker to attack a target. There is a wide range of threat vectors a security professional needs to understand:

- The Web (fake sites, session hijacking, malware, watering hole attacks, and so on)
- Unsecured wireless hotspots
- Mobile devices (iOS/Android)
- USB (removable) media
- E-mail (links, attachments, and malware)
- Social engineering (deceptions, hoaxes, scams, and fraud)

This list is merely a sample of threat vectors. From a defensive point of view, it is important not to become fixated on specific threats but rather to pay attention to the threat vectors. If a user visits a web site that has malicious code, then the nature of the code, although important from a technical viewpoint in one respect, is not the primary concern. The primary issue is the malicious site because it is the threat vector.

Probability/Threat Likelihood

The probability or likelihood of an event is a measure of how often it is expected to occur. From a qualitative assessment, using terms such as *frequent*, *occasionally*, *rare*, and the quantitative measure ARO, the purpose is to allow scaling based on frequency of an event. Determining the specific probabilities of security events with any accuracy is a nearly impossible feat. What is important in the use of probabilities and likelihoods is the relationship they have with respect to determining relative risk. Just as an insurance company cannot tell you when you will have an accident, no one can predict when a security event will occur. What can be determined is that over some course of time—say, the next year—a significant number of users will click malicious links in e-mails. The threat likelihood of different types of attacks will change over time. Years ago, web defacements were all the rage. Today, spear phishing and ransomware are more prevalent.

When risk is examined, the probability or threat likelihood plays a significant role in the determination of risk and mitigation options. In many cases, the likelihood is treated as certain, and for repeat attacks, this may be appropriate, but it certainly is not universally true.

The use of insurance-type actuarial models for risk determination is useful when risks are independent, such as in auto accidents. However, controls need to be added when a factor becomes less independent, such as a bad driver. In cybersecurity, once an attack is successful, it is repeatedly employed against a victim, breaking any form of independence and making the probability equal to 1. This lessens the true usefulness of the insurance-type actuarial models in cybersecurity practice.

Risks Associated with Cloud Computing and Virtualization

When examining a complex system such as a cloud or virtual computing environment from a risk perspective, several basic considerations always need to be observed. First, the fact that a system is either in the cloud or virtualized does not change how risk works. Risk is everywhere, and changing a system to a new environment does not change the fact that there are risks. Second, complexity can increase risk exposure.

There are specific risks associated with both virtualization and cloud environments. Having data and computing occur in environments that are not under the direct control of the data owner adds both a layer of complexity and a degree of risk. The potential for issues with confidentiality, integrity, and availability increases with the loss of direct control over the environment. The virtualization and cloud layers also present new avenues of attack into a system.

Security is a particular challenge when data and computation are handled by a remote party, as in cloud computing. The specific challenge is how to allow data outside your enterprise and yet remain in control over the use of the data. The common answer is encryption. Through the proper use of encryption of data before it leaves the enterprise, external storage can still be performed securely by properly employing cryptographic elements. The security requirements associated with confidentiality, integrity, and availability remain the responsibility of the data owner, and measures must be taken to ensure that these requirements are met, regardless of the location or usage associated with the data. Another level of protections is through the use of service level agreements (SLAs) with the cloud vendor, although these frequently cannot offer much remedy in the event of data loss.

Additional References

NIST SP 800-53, "Security and Privacy Controls for Information Systems and Organizations," https://nvlpubs.nist.gov/nistpubs/SpecialPublications/NIST.SP.800-53r5.pdf

NIST SP 800-53B, "Control Baselines for Information Systems and Organizations," https://nvlpubs.nist.gov/nistpubs/SpecialPublications/NIST.SP.800-53B.pdf

Chapter 20 Review

Chapter Summary

After reading this chapter and completing the exercises, you should understand the following about risk management.

Use risk management tools and principles to manage risk effectively

- Risk management is a key management process that must be used at every level, whether managing a project, a program, or an enterprise.
- Risk management is also a strategic tool to more effectively manage increasingly sophisticated, diverse, and geographically expansive business opportunities.
- Common business risks include fraud and management of treasury, revenue, contracts, environment, regulatory issues, business continuity, and technology.
- Technology risks include security and privacy, information technology operations, business systems control and effectiveness, information systems testing, and management of business continuity, reliability and performance, information technology assets, project risk, and change.

Explore risk mitigation strategies

- Many business processes can be used to mitigate specific forms of risk. These tools include change and incident management, user rights and permission reviews, routine system audits, and the use of technological controls to prevent or alert on data loss.

Describe risk models

- A general model for managing risk includes asset identification, threat assessment, impact determination and quantification, control design and evaluation, and residual risk management.
- The SEI model for managing risk includes these steps: identify, analyze, plan, track, and control.

Explain the differences between qualitative and quantitative risk assessment

- Both qualitative and quantitative risk assessment approaches must be used to manage risk effectively, and a number of approaches were presented in this chapter.
- Qualitative risk assessment relies on expert judgment and experience by comparing the impact of a threat with the probability of it occurring.
- Qualitative risk assessment can be a simple binary assessment weighing high or low impact against high or low probability. Additional levels can be used to increase the comprehensiveness of the analysis. The well-known red-yellow-green stoplight mechanism is qualitative in nature and is easily understood.
- Quantitative risk assessment applies historical information and trends to assess risk. Models are often used to provide information to decision-makers.
- A common quantitative approach calculates the annualized loss expectancy from the single loss expectancy and the annualized rate of occurrence ($ALE = SLE \times ARO$).
- It is important to understand that it is impossible to conduct a purely quantitative risk assessment, but it is possible to conduct a purely qualitative risk assessment.

Use risk management tools

- Numerous tools can be used to add credibility and rigor to the risk assessment process.
- Risk assessment tools help identify relationships, causes, and effects. They assist in prioritizing decisions and facilitate effective management of the risk management process.

Examine risk management best practices

- Explore business continuity concepts.
- Explore the relationships between vulnerabilities, threat vectors, probabilities, and threat likelihoods as they apply to risk management.
- Understand the differences between risk avoidance, transference, acceptance, mitigation, and deterrence.

Key Terms

annualized loss expectancy (ALE) *(763)*
annualized rate of occurrence (ARO) *(788)*
asset *(762)*
availability *(767)*
business impact analysis (BIA) *(772)*
compensating *(770)*
configuration control *(778)*
control *(763)*
control baseline *(767)*
control type *(769)*
corrective *(770)*
countermeasure *(763)*
detective *(770)*
exposure factor *(763)*
externality *(763)*
force majeure *(763)*
hazard *(763)*
impact *(762)*
intangible impact *(781)*
mitigate *(763)*
moral hazard *(763)*
physical *(770)*
qualitative risk assessment *(763)*
quantitative risk assessment *(763)*
residual risk *(782)*
risk *(762)*
risk analysis *(762)*
risk assessment *(762)*
risk management *(762)*
risk register *(789)*
safeguard *(763)*
security controls *(767)*
single loss expectancy (SLE) *(763)*
systematic risk *(763)*
tangible impact *(781)*
threat *(762)*
threat actor *(762)*
threat vector *(762)*
unsystematic risk *(763)*
vulnerability *(762)*

Key Terms Quiz

Use terms from the Key Terms list to complete the sentences that follow. Don't use the same term more than once. Not all terms will be used.

1. Asset value × exposure factor = _______________.
2. A control may also be called a(n) _______________ or a(n) _______________.
3. When a threat exploits a vulnerability, you experience a(n) _______________.
4. Single loss expectancy × annualized rate of occurrence = _______________.
5. If you reduce the likelihood of a threat occurring, you _______________ the risk.
6. The _______________ measures the magnitude of the loss of an asset.
7. Risk analysis is synonymous with _______________.
8. Any circumstance or event with the potential to cause harm to an asset is a(n) _______________.
9. A characteristic of an asset that can be exploited by a threat to cause harm is its _______________.
10. A(n) _______________ is a circumstance that increases the likelihood or probable severity of a loss.

Multiple-Choice Quiz

1. Which of the following correctly defines qualitative risk management?
   - **A.** The process of objectively determining the impact of an event that affects a project, program, or business
   - **B.** The process of subjectively determining the impact of an event that affects a project, program, or business
   - **C.** The loss that results when a vulnerability is exploited by a threat
   - **D.** To reduce the likelihood of a threat occurring
2. Which of the following correctly defines risk?
   - **A.** The risk still remaining after an iteration of risk management
   - **B.** The loss that results when a vulnerability is exploited by a threat
   - **C.** Any circumstance or event with the potential to cause harm to an asset
   - **D.** The possibility of suffering harm or loss
3. Single loss expectancy (SLE) can best be defined by which of the following equations?
   - **A.** SLE = annualized loss expectancy × annualized rate of occurrence
   - **B.** SLE = asset value × exposure factor
   - **C.** SLE = asset value × annualized rate of occurrence
   - **D.** SLE = annualized loss expectancy × exposure factor
4. Which of the following correctly defines annualized rate of occurrence?
   - **A.** How much an event is expected to cost per year
   - **B.** A measure of the magnitude of loss of an asset
   - **C.** On an annualized basis, the frequency with which an event is expected to occur
   - **D.** The resources or information an organization needs to conduct its business

For questions 5 and 6, assume the following: The asset value of a small distribution warehouse is $5 million, and this warehouse serves as a backup facility. Its complete destruction by a disaster would take away about 1/5 of the capability of the business. Also assume that this sort of disaster is expected to occur about once every 50 years.

5. Which of the following is the calculated single loss expectancy (SLE)?
   - **A.** SLE = $25 million
   - **B.** SLE = $1 million
   - **C.** SLE = $2.5 million
   - **D.** SLE = $5 million
6. Which of the following is the calculated annualized loss expectancy (ALE)?
   - **A.** ALE = $50,000
   - **B.** ALE = $1 million
   - **C.** ALE = $20,000
   - **D.** ALE = $50 million
7. When discussing qualitative risk assessment versus quantitative risk assessment, which of the following is true?
   - **A.** It is impossible to conduct a purely quantitative risk assessment, and it is impossible to conduct a purely qualitative risk assessment.
   - **B.** It is possible to conduct a purely quantitative risk assessment, but it is impossible to conduct a purely qualitative risk assessment.
   - **C.** It is impossible to conduct a purely quantitative risk assessment, but it is possible to conduct a purely qualitative risk assessment.
   - **D.** It is possible to conduct a purely quantitative risk assessment, and it is possible to conduct a purely qualitative risk assessment.

8. Which of the following correctly defines residual risk?
   - **A.** The risk still remaining after an iteration of risk management
   - **B.** The possibility of suffering a loss
   - **C.** The result of a vulnerability being exploited by a threat that results in a loss
   - **D.** Characteristics of an asset that can be exploited by a threat to cause harm
9. Which of the following statements about risk is true?
   - **A.** A manager can accept the risk, which will reduce the risk.
   - **B.** The risk itself doesn't really change. However, actions can be taken to reduce the impact of the risk.
   - **C.** A manager can transfer the risk, which will reduce the risk.
   - **D.** A manager can take steps to increase the risk.
10. Which security control is a policy or procedure used to limit physical security risk?
   - **A.** Physical
   - **B.** Technical
   - **C.** Operational
   - **D.** Corrective

Essay Quiz

1. You are drafting an e-mail to your risk management team members to explain the difference between tangible assets and intangible assets. Relate potential threats and risk to tangible and intangible impacts. Write a short paragraph that explains the difference and include two examples of each.
2. You have been tasked with initiating a risk management program for your company. The CEO has just asked you to succinctly explain the relationship between impact, threat, and vulnerability. Think quickly on your feet and give a single sentence that explains the relationship.
3. Your CEO now says, "You've mentioned that risks always exist. If I take enough measures, can't I eliminate the risks?" Explain why risks always exist.
4. You are explaining your risk management plan to a new team member just brought on as part of a college internship program. The intern asks, "With respect to impact, what does a threat do to a risk?" How would you answer?
5. The intern mentioned in the previous question now asks you to compare and contrast accepting risk, transferring risk, and mitigating risk. What's your response?

Lab Projects

• Lab Project 20.1

The asset value of a distribution center (located in the midwestern United States) and its inventory is $10 million. It is one of two identical facilities (the other is in the southwestern United States). Its complete destruction by a disaster would thus take away half of the capability of the business. Also assume that this sort of disaster is expected to occur about once every 100 years. From this, calculate the annualized loss expectancy.

• Lab Project 20.2

You have just completed a qualitative threat assessment of the computer security of your organization, with the impacts and probabilities of occurrence as follows. Properly place the threats in a three-by-three table similar to that shown in Figure 20.5. Which of the threats should you take action on, which should you monitor, and which ones may not need your immediate attention?

Threat	Impact	Probability of Occurrence
Virus attacks	High	High
Internet hacks	Medium	High
Disgruntled employee hacks	High	Medium
Weak incidence response mechanisms	Medium	Medium
Theft of information by a trusted third-party contractor	Low	Medium
Competitor hacks	High	Low
Inadvertent release of noncritical information	Low	Low

chapter 21

Business Continuity, Disaster Recovery, and Change Management

It is not the strongest of the species that survive, nor the most intelligent, but the one most responsive to change.

—CHARLES DARWIN

In this chapter, you will learn how to

- Operational disruptions can and will occur in systems
- Describe the various ways backups are conducted and stored
- Use change management as an important enterprise management tool
- Institute the key concept of separation of duties
- Identify the essential elements of change management
- Implement change management
- Use the concepts of the Capability Maturity Model Integration
- Implement secure systems design for a given scenario

It is well recognized that today's computer systems are extremely complex, and it is obvious that inventory management systems for large international enterprises such as Walmart and Home Depot are probably as complex as an aircraft or skyscraper. Prominent operating systems such as Windows and UNIX/Linux are also very complex, as are computer processors on a chip. Many of today's web-based applications are extremely complex as well. For example, today's web-based applications typically consist of flash content on web sites interacting with remote databases through a variety of services or service-oriented architectures hosted on web servers located anywhere in the world.

You wouldn't think of constructing an aircraft, large building, computer chip, or automobile in the informal manner sometimes used to develop and operate computer systems of equal complexity. Computer systems have grown to be so complex and mission-critical that enterprises cannot afford to develop and maintain them in an ad hoc manner.

Change management procedures can add structure and control to the development and management of large software systems as they move from development to implementation and during operation. In this chapter, change management refers to a standard methodology for performing and recording changes during software development and system operation. The methodology defines steps that ensure that system changes are required by the organization and are properly authorized, documented, tested, and approved by management. In many conversations, the term **configuration management** is considered synonymous with change management and, in a more limited manner, version control or release control.

The term change management is often applied to the management of changes in the business environment, typically as a result of business process reengineering or quality enhancement efforts. The term change management as used in this chapter is directly related to managing and controlling software development, maintenance, and system operation. Configuration management is the application of change management principles to the configuration of both software and hardware.

The objective of all systems is to perform for a specific purpose, and IT systems are no different. By design, IT systems support a wide range of business functions. These business functions change over time, requiring the necessary adjustment to the IT system, and these changes are carefully orchestrated via change control. But how do you handle a unplanned change to the system? A disaster, an outage from a supplier, a pandemic that keeps workers at home? These business interruptions call for a flexible system that has the ability to change in a responsive way. This is the basis of business continuity planning, disaster recovery plans, and continuity of operations planning.

Business Continuity

Keeping an organization running when an event occurs that disrupts operations is not accomplished spontaneously but requires advance planning and periodically exercising those plans to ensure they will work. A term that is often used when discussing the issue of continued organizational operations is *business continuity (BC)*.

There are many risk management best practices associated with business continuity. The topics of planning, business impact analysis, identification of critical systems and components, single points of failure, and more are detailed in the following sections.

> Although the terms *disaster recovery plan (DRP)* and *business continuity plan (BCP)* may be used synonymously in small firms, in large firms there is a difference in focus between the two plans. The focus of the BCP is on continued operation of a business, albeit at a reduced level or through different means during some period of time. The DRP is focused specifically on recovering from a disaster. In many cases, both of these functions happen at the same time, and hence they are frequently combined in small firms and in many discussions. The DRP is part of the larger BCP process.

Business Continuity Plans

As with most operational issues, planning is a foundational element to success. This is true in business continuity, and the **business continuity plan (BCP)** represents the planning and advance policy decisions to ensure the business continuity objectives are achieved during a time of obvious turmoil. You might wonder what the difference is between a disaster recovery plan and a business continuity plan. After all, isn't the purpose of disaster recovery the continued operation of the organization or business during a period of disruption? Many times, these two terms are used synonymously, and for many organizations there may be no major difference between them. There are, however, real differences between a BCP and a DRP, one of which is the focus.

The focus of a BCP is the continued operation of the essential elements of the business or organization. Business continuity is not about operations as normal but rather about trimmed-down, essential operations only. In a BCP, you will see a more significant emphasis placed on the limited number of critical systems the organization needs to operate. The BCP will describe the functions that are most critical, based on a previously conducted business impact analysis (BIA), and will describe the order in which functions should be returned to operation. The BCP describes what is needed in order for the business to continue to operate in the short term, even if all requirements are not met and risk profiles are changed.

The focus of a DRP is on recovering and rebuilding the organization after a disaster has occurred. The recovery's goal is the complete operation of all elements of the business. The DRP is part of the larger picture, while the BCP is a tactical necessity until operations can be restored. A major focus of the DRP is the protection of human life, meaning evacuation plans and system shutdown procedures should be addressed. In fact, the safety of employees should be a theme throughout a DRP.

Business Impact Analysis

Business impact analysis (BIA) is the term used to describe the document that details the specific impact of elements on a business operation (this may also be referred to as a *business impact assessment*). A BIA outlines what the loss of any of your critical functions will mean to the organization. The BIA is a foundational document used to establish a wide range of priorities, including the system backups and restoration that are needed to maintain continuity of operation. While each person may consider their individual tasks to be important, the BIA is a business-level analysis of the criticality of all elements with respect to the business as a whole. The BIA will take into account the increased risk from minimal operations and is designed to determine and justify what is essentially critical for a business to survive versus what someone may state or wish.

Conducting a BIA is a critical part of developing your BCP. This assessment will allow you to focus on the most critical elements of your organization. These critical elements are the ones that you want to ensure are recovered first, and this priority should be reflected in your BCP and subset DRP.

Identification of Critical Systems and Components

A foundational element of a security plan is an understanding of the criticality of systems, the data, and the components. Identifying the critical systems and components is one of the first steps an organization needs to undertake in designing the set of security controls. As the systems evolve and change, the continued identification of the critical systems needs to occur, keeping the information up to date and current.

Removing Single Points of Failure

A key security methodology is to attempt to avoid a single point of failure in critical functions within an organization. When developing your BCP, you should be on the lookout for areas in which a critical function relies on a single item (such as switches, routers, firewalls, power supplies, software, or data) that if lost would stop this critical function. When these points are identified, think about how each of these possible single points of failure can be eliminated (or mitigated).

In addition to the internal resources you need to consider when evaluating your business functions, there are many resources external to your organization that can impact the operation of your business. You must look beyond hardware, software, and data to consider how the loss of various critical infrastructures can also impact business operations.

Risk Assessment

The principles of risk assessment can be applied to business continuity planning. Determining the sources and magnitudes of risks is necessary in all business operations, including business continuity planning. More detailed analysis of risk is presented in Chapter 20.

Succession Planning

Business continuity planning is more than just ensuring that hardware is available and operational. The people who operate and maintain the system are also important, and in the event of a disruptive event, the availability of key personnel is as important as hardware for successful business continuity operations. The development of a succession plan that identifies key personnel and develops qualified personnel for key functions is a critical part of a successful BCP.

> Business continuity is not only about hardware; plans need to include people as well. Succession planning is a proactive plan for personnel substitutions in the event that the primary person is not available to fulfill their assigned duties.

After-Action Reports

Just as lessons learned are a key element of incident response processes, the *after-action reports* associated with invoking continuity of operations provide insight into two functions. First is the level of operations upon transfer. Is all of the desired capability up and running? The second question addresses how the actual change from normal operations to those supported by the continuity systems occurred.

Failover

Failover is the process of moving from a normal operational capability to the continuity of operations version of the business. The speed and flexibility depend on the business type—from seamless for a lot of financial sites, to one where A is turned off and someone goes and turns B on, with some period of no service between. Simple transparent failovers can be achieved through architecture and technology choices, but they must be designed into the system.

Separate from failover, which occurs whenever the problem occurs, is the switch back to the original system. Once a system is fixed, resolving whatever caused the outage, there is a need to move back to the original production system. This "failback" mechanism, by definition, is harder to perform as primary keys and indexes are not easily transferred back. The return to operations is a complicated process, but the good news is that it can be performed at a time of the organization's choosing, unlike the problem that initiated the initial shift of operations to continuity procedures.

Backups

A key element in any business continuity/disaster recovery plan is the availability of backups. This is true not only because of the possibility of a disaster but also because hardware and storage media will periodically fail, resulting in the loss or corruption of critical data. An organization might also find backups critical when security measures have failed and an individual has gained access to important information that may have become corrupted or at the very least can't be trusted. Data backup is thus a critical element in these plans, as well as in normal operation. The following are several factors to consider in an organization's data backup strategy:

- How frequently should backups be conducted?
- How extensive do the backups need to be?
- What is the process for conducting backups?
- Who is responsible for ensuring backups are created?
- Where will the backups be stored?
- How long will backups be kept?
- How many copies will be maintained?

Keep in mind that the purpose of a backup is to provide valid, uncorrupted data in the event of corruption or loss of the original file or the media where the data was stored. Depending on the type of organization, legal requirements for maintaining backups can also affect how it is accomplished.

> **Tech Tip**
>
> **Backups Are a Key Responsibility for Administrators**
>
> *One of the most important tools a security administrator has is a backup. While backups will not prevent a security event (or natural disaster) from occurring, they often can save an organization from a catastrophe by allowing it to quickly return to full operation after an event occurs. Conducting frequent backups and having a viable backup and recovery plan are two of the most important responsibilities of a security administrator.*

What Needs to Be Backed Up

Backups commonly comprise the data that an organization relies on to conduct its daily operations. While this is certainly essential, a good backup plan will consider more than just the data; it will include any application programs needed to process the data and the operating system and utilities that the hardware platform requires to run the applications. Obviously, the application programs and operating system will change much less frequently than the data itself, so the frequency with which these items need to be backed up is considerably different. This should be reflected in the organization's backup plan and strategy.

The business continuity/disaster recovery plan should also address other items related to backups. Personnel, equipment, and electrical power must also be part of the plan. Somebody needs to understand the operation of the critical hardware and software used by the organization. If the disaster that destroyed the original copy of the data and the original systems also results in the loss of the only personnel who know how to process the data, having backup data will not be enough to restore normal operations for the organization. Similarly, if the data requires specific software to be run on a specific hardware platform, then having the data without the application program or required hardware will also not be sufficient.

> **Tech Tip**
>
> **Implementing the Right Type of Backup**
>
> *Carefully consider the type of backup that you want to conduct. With the size of today's PC hard drives, a complete backup of the entire hard drive can take a considerable amount of time. Implement the type of backup you need and check for software tools that can help you in establishing a viable backup schedule.*

Strategies for Backups

The process for creating a backup copy of data and software requires more thought than simply stating "copy all required files." The size of the resulting backup must be considered, as well as the time required to conduct the backup. Both of these will affect details such as how frequently the backup will occur and the type of storage medium that will be used for the backup. Other considerations include who will be responsible for conducting the backup, where the backups will be stored, and how long they should be maintained. Short-term storage for accidentally deleted files that users need to have restored should probably be close at hand. Longer-term storage for backups that may be several months or even years old should occur in a different facility. It should be evident by now that even something that sounds as simple as maintaining backup copies of essential data requires careful consideration and planning.

Types of Backups

The amount of data that will be backed up, and the time it takes to accomplish this, has a direct bearing on the type of backup that should be performed. Table 21.1 outlines the four basic types of backups that can be conducted, the amount of space required for each, and the ease of restoration using each strategy.

Tech Tip

The Archive Bit

The archive bit is used to indicate whether a file has (1) or has not (0) changed since the last backup. The bit is set (changed to 1) if the file is modified, or in some cases, if the file is copied, the new copy of the file has its archive bit set. The bit is reset (changed to 0) when the file is backed up. The archive bit can be used to determine which files need to be backed up when using a method such as the differential backup method.

Table 21.1 Backup Types and Characteristics

	Full	Differential	Incremental	Delta
Amount of Space	Large	Medium	Medium	Small
Restoration	Simple	Simple	Involved	Complex

The values for each of the strategies in Table 21.1 are highly variable depending on your specific environment. The more frequently files are changed between backups, the more these strategies will look alike. What each strategy entails bears further explanation.

Full

The easiest type of backup to understand is the **full backup**. In a full backup, all files and software are copied onto the storage media. Restoration from a full backup is similarly straightforward—you must copy all the files back onto the system. This process can take a considerable amount of time. Consider the size of even the average home PC today, for which storage is measured in tens or hundreds of gigabytes. Copying this amount of data takes time. In a full backup, the archive bit is cleared.

Differential

In a **differential backup**, only the files that have changed since the last full backup was completed are backed up. This also implies that periodically a full backup needs to be accomplished. The frequency of the full backup versus the interim differential backups depends on your organization and needs to be part of your defined strategy. Restoration from a differential backup requires two steps: the last full backup first needs to be loaded, and then the last differential backup performed can be applied to update the files that have been changed since the full backup was conducted. Again,

> **Tech Tip**
>
> **Incremental vs. Differential Backups**
>
> *Both incremental and differential backups begin with a full backup. An incremental backup only includes the data that has changed since the previous backup, including the last incremental. A differential backup contains all of the data that has changed since the last full backup. The advantage that differential backups have over incremental is shorter restore times. The advantage of the incremental backup is shorter backup times. To restore a differential backup, you restore the full backup and the latest differential backup: two events. To restore an incremental system, you restore the full and then all the incremental backups in order.*

this is not a difficult process, but it does take some time. The amount of time to accomplish the periodic differential backup, however, is much less than that for a full backup, and this is one of the advantages of this method. Obviously, if a lot of time has passed between differential backups or if most files in your environment change frequently, then the differential backup does not differ much from a full backup. It should also be obvious that to accomplish the differential backup, the system needs to have a method to determine which files have been changed since some given point in time. The archive bit is not cleared in a differential backup since the key for a differential is to back up all files that have changed since the last full backup.

Delta

Finally, the goal of the **delta backup** is to back up as little information as possible each time you perform a backup. As with the other strategies, an occasional full backup must be accomplished. After that, when a delta backup is conducted at specific intervals, only the portions of the files that have been changed will be stored. The advantage of this is easy to illustrate. If your organization maintains a large database with thousands of records comprising several hundred megabytes of data, the entire database would be copied in the previous backup types even if only one record has changed. For a delta backup, only the actual record that changed would be stored. The disadvantage of this method is that restoration is a complex process because it requires more than just loading a file (or several files). It requires that application software be run to update the records in the files that have been changed.

There are some newer backup methods that are similar to delta backups in that they minimize what is backed up. There are real-time and near-real-time backup strategies, such as journaling, transactional backups, and electronic vaulting, that can provide protection against loss in real-time environments. Implementing these methods into an overall backup strategy can increase options and flexibility during times of recovery.

Snapshots

Snapshots refer to copies of virtual machines. One of the advantages of a virtual machine over a physical machine is the ease with which the virtual machine can be backed up and restored. A snapshot is a copy of a virtual machine at a specific point in time. This is done by copying the files that store the VM. The ability to revert to an earlier snapshot is as easy as pushing a button and waiting for the machine to be restored via a change of the files.

Each type of backup has advantages and disadvantages. Which type is best for your organization depends on the amount of data you routinely process and store, how frequently the data changes, how often you expect to have to restore from a backup, and a number of other factors. The type you select will shape your overall backup strategy and processes.

Backup Frequency and Retention

The type of backup strategy an organization employs is often affected by how frequently the organization conducts the backup activity. The usefulness of a backup is directly related to how many changes have occurred since the backup was created, and this is obviously affected by how often backups are created. The longer it has been since the backup was created, the more changes that likely will have occurred. There is no easy answer, however, to how frequently an organization should perform backups. Every organization should consider how long it can survive without current data from which to operate. It can then determine how long it will take to restore from backups, using various methods, and decide how frequently backups need to occur. This sounds simple, but it is a serious, complex decision to make.

Related to the frequency question is the issue of how long backups should be maintained. Is it sufficient to simply maintain a single backup from which to restore data? Security professionals will tell you no; multiple backups should be maintained for a variety of reasons. If the reason for restoring from the backup is the discovery of an intruder in the system, it is important to restore the system to its pre-intrusion state. If the intruder has been in the system for several months before being discovered and backups are taken weekly, it will not be possible to restore to a pre-intrusion state if only one backup is maintained. This would mean that all data and system files would be suspect and may not be reliable. If multiple backups were maintained, at various intervals, then it is easier to return to a point before the intrusion (or before the security or operational event that is necessitating the restoration) occurred.

There are several strategies or approaches to backup retention. One common and easy-to-remember strategy is the "rule of three," in which the three most recent backups are kept. When a new backup is created, the oldest backup is overwritten. Another strategy is to keep the most recent copy of backups for various time intervals. For example, you might keep the latest daily, weekly, monthly, quarterly, and yearly backups. Note that in certain environments, regulatory issues may prescribe a specific frequency and retention period, so it is important to know your organization's requirements when determining how often you will create a backup and how long you will keep it.

If you are not in an environment for which regulatory issues dictate the frequency and retention for backups, your goal will be to optimize the frequency. In determining the optimal backup frequency, two major costs need to be considered: the cost of the backup strategy you choose and the cost of recovery if you do not implement this backup strategy (that is, if no backups were created). You must also factor into this equation the probability that the backup will be needed on any given day. The two figures to consider then are these:

Alternative 1: (probability the backup is needed) × (cost of restoring with no backup)
Alternative 2: (probability the backup isn't needed) × (cost of the backup strategy)

The first of these two figures, alternative 1, can be considered the probable loss you can expect if your organization has no backup. The second figure, alternative 2, can be considered the amount you are willing to spend to ensure that you can restore, should a problem occur (think of this as backup insurance—the cost of an insurance policy that may never be used but that you are willing to pay for, just in case). For example, if the probability of a backup being needed is 10 percent and the cost of restoring with no backup is $100,000, then the first equation would yield a figure of $10,000. This can

Tech Tip

Determining How Long to Maintain Backups

Determining the length of time that you retain your backups should not be based on the frequency of your backups. The more often you conduct backup operations, the more data you will have. You might be tempted to trim the number of backups retained to keep storage costs down, but you need to evaluate how long you need to retain backups based on your operational environment and then keep the appropriate number of backups.

be compared with the alternative, which would be a 90 percent chance the backup is not needed multiplied by the cost of implementing your backup strategy (of taking and maintaining the backups), which is, say, $10,000 annually. The second equation yields a figure of $9,000. In this example, the cost of maintaining the backup is less than the cost of not having backups, so the former would be the better choice. While conceptually this is an easy trade-off to understand, in reality it is often difficult to accurately determine the probability of a backup being needed.

Fortunately, the figures for the potential loss if there is no backup are generally so much greater than the cost of maintaining a backup that a mistake in judging the probability will not matter—it just makes too much sense to maintain backups. This example also uses a straight comparison based solely on the cost of the process of restoring with and without a backup strategy. What needs to be included in the cost of both of these is the loss that occurs while the asset is not available as it is being restored—in essence, a measurement of the value of the asset itself.

To optimize your backup strategy, you need to determine the correct balance between these two figures. Obviously, you do not want to spend more in your backup strategy than you face losing should you not have a backup plan at all. When working with these two calculations, you have to remember that this is a cost-avoidance exercise. The organization is not going to increase revenues with its backup strategy. The goal is to minimize the potential loss due to some catastrophic event by creating a backup strategy that will address your organization's needs.

> **Tech Tip**
>
> **Onsite Backup Storage**
>
> *One of the most frequent errors committed with backups is to store all backups onsite. While this greatly simplifies the process, it means that all data is stored in the same facility. Should a natural disaster occur (such as a fire or hurricane), you could lose not only your primary data storage devices but your backups as well. You need to use an offsite location to store at least some of your backups.*

When you're calculating the cost of the backup strategy, consider the following:

- The cost of the backup media required for a single backup
- The storage costs for the backup media based on the retention policy
- The labor costs associated with performing a single backup
- The frequency with which backups are created

All of these considerations can be used to arrive at an annual cost for implementing your chosen backup strategy, and this figure can then be used as previously described.

> **Tech Tip**
>
> **Long-Term Backup Storage**
>
> *An easy factor to overlook when upgrading systems is whether long-term backups will still be usable. You need to ensure that the type of media utilized for your long-term storage is compatible with the hardware you are upgrading to. Otherwise, you may find yourself in a situation in which you need to restore data, and you have the data, but you don't have any way to restore it.*

Storage of Backups

An important element to factor into the cost of the backup strategy is the expense of storing the backups. This is affected by many variables, including the number and size of the backups as well as the need for quick restoration. This can be further complicated by keeping hot, warm, and cold sites synchronized. Backup storage is more than just figuring out where to keep tapes, but rather becomes part of business continuity, disaster recovery, and overall risk strategies.

Issues with Long-Term Storage of Backups

Depending on the media used for an organization's backups, degradation of the media is a distinct possibility and needs to be considered. Magnetic media degrades over time (measured in years). In addition, tapes can be used a limited number of times before the surface begins to flake off. Magnetic media should thus be rotated and tested to ensure that it is still usable.

You should also consider advances in technology. The media you used to store your data years ago may now be considered obsolete (floppy disks, for example). Software applications also evolve, and the media may be present but may not be compatible with current versions of the software. This may mean that you need to maintain backup copies of both hardware and software in order to recover from older backup media.

Another issue is security related. If the file you stored was encrypted for security purposes, does anybody in the company remember the password to decrypt the file to restore the data? More than one employee in the company should know the key to decrypt the files, and this information should be passed along to another person when a critical employee with that information leaves, is terminated, or dies.

Geographic Considerations

An important element to factor into the cost of the backup strategy is the location of storing the backups. A simple strategy might be to store all your backups together for quick and easy recovery actions. This is not, however, a good idea. Suppose the catastrophic event that necessitated the restoration of backed-up data was a fire that destroyed the computer system the data was processed on. In this case, any backups that were stored in the same facility might also be lost in the same fire.

The solution is to keep copies of backups in separate locations. The most recent copy can be stored locally because it is the most likely to be needed, while other copies can be kept at other locations. Depending on the level of security your organization desires, the storage facility itself could be reinforced against possible threats in your area (such as tornados or floods). A more recent advance is online backup services. A number of third-party companies offer high-speed connections for storing data in a separate facility. Transmitting the backup data via network connections alleviates some other issues with the physical movement of more traditional storage media, such as the care during transportation (tapes do not fare well in direct sunlight, for example) or the time that it takes to transport the tapes.

Location Selection Picking a storage location has several key considerations. First is physical safety. Because of the importance of maintaining proper environmental conditions that are safe from outside harm, this can limit locations. Heating, ventilating, and air conditioning (HVAC) can be a consideration, as well as issues such as potential flooding and theft. The ability to move the backups in and out of storage is also a concern. Again, the cloud and modern-day networks come to the rescue; with today's high-speed networks, reasonably priced storage, encryption technologies, and the ability to store backups in a redundant array across multiple sites, the cloud is an ideal solution.

Offsite Backups *Offsite backups* are just that—backups that are stored in a separate location from the system being backed up. This can be important when an issue affects a larger area than a single room. A building fire, a hurricane, or a tornado could occur and typically affect a larger area than a single room or building. Having backups offsite alleviates the risk of losing them. In today's high-speed network world with cloud services, storing backups in the cloud is an option that can resolve many of the risks associated with backup availability.

Distance The distance associated with an offsite backup is a logistic problem. If you need to restore a system and the backup is stored hours away by car, this can increase the recovery time. The physical movement of backup tapes has been alleviated in many systems through networks that move the data at the speed of the network.

Legal Implications When planning an offsite backup, you must consider the legal implications of where the data is being stored. Different jurisdictions have different laws, rules, and regulations concerning core tools such as encryption. Understanding how these affect data backup storage plans is critical to prevent downstream problems.

Data Sovereignty *Data sovereignty* is a relatively new phenomenon, but in the past couple of years several countries have enacted laws stating that certain types of data must be stored within their boundaries. In today's multinational economy, with the Internet not knowing borders, this has become a problem. Several high-tech firms have changed their business strategies and offerings in order to comply with data sovereignty rules and regulations. For example, LinkedIn, a business social network site, recently was told by Russian authorities that all data on Russian citizens needed to be kept on servers in Russia. LinkedIn made the business decision that the cost was not worth the benefit and has since abandoned the Russian market.

Alternative Sites

An issue related to the location of backup storage is where the restoration services will be conducted. Determining when or if an alternative site is needed should be included in recovery and continuity plans. If the organization has suffered physical damage to a facility, having offsite storage of data is only part of the solution. This data will need to be processed somewhere, which means that computing facilities similar to those used in normal operations are required. There are a number of ways to approach this problem, including hot sites, warm sites, cold sites, and mobile backup sites.

Try This!

Research Alternative Processing Sites

There is an industry built upon providing alternative processing sites in case of a disaster of some sort. Using the Internet or other resources, determine what resources are available in your area for hot, warm, and cold sites. Do you live in an area in which a lot of these services are offered? Do other areas of the country have more alternative processing sites available? What makes where you live a better or worse place for alternative sites?

Hot Site

A **hot site** is a fully configured environment, similar to the normal operating environment, that can be operational immediately or within a few hours, depending on its configuration and the needs of the organization.

Warm Site

A **warm site** is partially configured, usually having the peripherals and software but perhaps not the more expensive main processing computer. It is designed to be operational within a few days.

Cold Site

A **cold site** will have the basic environmental controls necessary to operate but few of the computing components necessary for processing. Getting a cold site operational may take weeks.

Table 21.2 compares hot, warm, and cold sites.

> Alternative sites are differentiated in whether data is available or not at each location. For example, a hot site has duplicate data or a near-ready backup of the original site. A cold site has no current or backup copies of the original site data. A warm site has backups, but they are typically several days or weeks old.

Table 21.2 Comparison of Hot, Warm, and Cold Sites

	Cost	Speed to Recover	Complexity
Hot	High	Fastest	Lowest
Warm	Moderate	Medium	Moderate
Cold	Low	Slowest	Highest

Shared alternate sites may also be considered. These sites can be designed to handle the needs of different organizations in the event of an emergency. The hope is that the disaster will affect only one organization at a time. The benefit of this method is that the cost of the site can be shared among organizations. Two similar organizations located close to each other should not share the same alternative site because there is a greater chance that they would both need it at the same time.

All of these options can come with a considerable price tag, which makes another option, mutual aid agreements, a possible alternative. With a **mutual aid agreement**, similar organizations agree to assume the processing for the other party in the event a disaster occurs. This is sometimes referred to as a *reciprocal site*. The obvious assumptions here are that both organizations will not be hit by the same disaster and both have similar processing environments. If these two assumptions are correct, then a mutual aid agreement should be considered. Such an arrangement may not be legally enforceable, even if it is in writing, and organizations must consider this when developing their disaster plans. In addition, if the organization that the mutual aid agreement is made with is hit by the same disaster, then both organizations will be in trouble. Additional contingencies need to be planned for, even if a mutual aid agreement is made with another organization. There are also the obvious security concerns that must be considered when having another organization assume your organization's processing.

Order of Restoration

When restoring more than a single machine, you have multiple considerations in the order of restoration. Part of the planning is to decide on the *order of restoration*—in other words, which systems go first, second, and ultimately last. There are a couple of distinct factors to consider. First are dependencies. Any system that is dependent on another for proper operation might as well wait until the prerequisite services are up and running. The second factor is criticality to the enterprise. The most critical service should be brought back up first.

Utilities

The interruption of power is a common issue during a disaster. Computers and networks obviously require power to operate, so emergency power must be available in the event of any disruption of operations. For short-term interruptions, such as what might occur as the result of an electrical storm, uninterruptible power supplies (UPSs) may suffice. These devices contain a battery that provides steady power for short periods of time—enough to keep a system running should power be lost for only a few minutes and enough time to allow administrators to gracefully halt the system or network. For continued operations that extend beyond a few minutes, another source of power will be required. Generally this is provided by a backup emergency generator.

While backup generators are frequently used to provide power during an emergency, they are not a simple, maintenance-free solution. Generators need to be tested on a regular basis, and they can easily become strained if they are required to power too much equipment. If your organization is going to rely on an emergency generator for backup power, you must ensure that the system has reserve capacity beyond the anticipated load for the unanticipated loads that will undoubtedly be placed on it.

Generators also take time to start up, so power to your organization will most likely be lost, even if only briefly, until the generators kick in. This means you should also use a UPS to allow for a smooth transition to backup power. Generators are also expensive and require fuel. Be sure to locate the generator high if flooding is possible, and don't forget the need to deliver fuel to it; otherwise, you may find yourself hauling cans of fuel up a number of stairs.

When determining the need for backup power, don't forget to factor in environmental conditions. Running computer systems in a room with no air conditioning in the middle of the summer can result in an extremely uncomfortable environment for all to work in. Mobile backup sites, generally using trailers, often rely on generators for their power but also factor in the requirement for environmental controls.

Power is not the only essential utility for operations. Depending on the type of disaster that has occurred, telephone and Internet communication may also be lost, and wireless services may not be available. Planning for redundant means of communication (such as using both land lines and wireless) can help with most outages, but for large disasters, your backup plans should include the option to continue operations from a completely different location while waiting for communications in your area to be restored. Telecommunication carriers have their own emergency equipment and are fairly efficient at restoring communications, but it may take a few days.

Secure Recovery

Several companies offer recovery services, including power, communications, and technical support that your organization may need if its operations are disrupted. These companies advertise secure recovery sites or offices from which your organization can again begin to operate in a secure environment. Secure recovery is also advertised by other organizations that provide services that can remotely (over the Internet, for example) provide restoration services for critical files and data.

In both cases—the actual physical suites and the remote service—security is an important element. During a disaster, your data does not become any less important, and you will want to make sure you maintain the security (in terms of confidentiality and integrity, for example) of your data. As in other aspects of security, the decision to employ these services should be made based on a calculation of the benefits weighed against the potential loss if alternative means are used.

Continuity of Operations Planning (COOP)

Ensuring continuity of operations is a business imperative, as it has been shown that businesses that cannot quickly recover from a disruption have a real chance of never recovering and going out of business. The overall goal of **continuity of operations planning (COOP)** is to determine which subset of normal operations needs to be continued during periods of disruption. Continuity of operations planning involves developing a comprehensive plan to enact during a situation where normal operations are interrupted. This includes identifying critical assets (including key personnel), critical systems, and interdependencies as well as ensuring their availability during a disruption.

Developing a continuity of operations plan is a joint effort between the business and the IT team. The business understands which functions are critical for continuity of operations and which functions can be suspended. The IT team understands how this translates into equipment, data, and services and can establish the correct IT functions. Senior management will have to make the major decisions as to balancing risk versus cost versus criticality when examining hot, warm, or cold site strategies.

The COOP is focused on continuing business operations, whereas the BCP is focused on returning a business to functioning profitably, even if at a reduced level or capacity. Government agencies, where service is essential and costs can be dealt with later, focus on COOP, whereas many businesses have to focus on DRP and BCP.

Disaster Recovery

Many types of disasters, whether natural or caused by people, can disrupt your organization's operations for some length of time. Such disasters are unlike threats that intentionally target your computer systems and networks, such as industrial espionage, hacking, attacks from disgruntled employees, and insider threats, because the events that cause the disruption are not specifically aimed at your organization. Although both disasters and intentional threats must be considered important in planning for disaster recovery, the purpose of this section is to focus on recovering from disasters.

How long your organization's operations are disrupted depends in part on how prepared it is for a disaster and what plans are in place to mitigate the effects of a disaster. Any of the events in Table 21.3 could cause a disruption in operations.

Disasters can be caused by nature (for example, fires, earthquakes, and floods) or can be the result of some manmade event (such as war or a terrorist attack). The plans an organization develops to address a disaster need to recognize both of these possibilities. While many of the elements in a disaster recovery plan will be similar for both natural and manmade events, some differences might exist. For example, the most recent backup tapes available can be used to recover data after a natural disaster. If, on the other hand, the event was a loss of all data as a result of a computer virus that wiped your system, restoring from the most recent backup tapes might result in the reinfection of your system if the virus had been dormant for a planned period of time. In this case, recovery might entail restoring some files from earlier backups.

Table 21.3 Common Causes of Disasters

Fire	Flood	Tornado	Hurricane
Electrical storm	Earthquake	Political unrest/riot	Blizzard
Gas leak/explosion	Chemical spill	Terrorism	War

Fortunately, these types of events do not happen frequently in any one location. It is more likely that business operations will be interrupted because of employee error (such as accidental corruption of a database or unplugging a system to plug in a vacuum cleaner—an event that has occurred at more than one organization). A good disaster recovery plan will prepare your organization for any type of organizational disruption.

Disaster Recovery Plans/Process

No matter what event you are worried about—whether natural or manmade and whether targeted at your organization or more random—you can make preparations to lessen the impact on your organization and the length of time that your organization will be out of operation. A **disaster recovery plan (DRP)** is critical for effective disaster recovery efforts. A DRP defines the data and resources necessary and the steps required to restore critical organizational processes.

Consider what your organization needs to perform its mission. This information provides the beginning of a DRP since it tells you what needs to be quickly restored. When considering resources, don't forget to include both the *physical resources* (such as computer hardware and software) and the *personnel* (the people who know how to run the systems that process your critical data).

To begin creating your DRP, first identify all critical functions for your organization and then answer the following questions for each of these critical functions:

- Who is responsible for the operation of this function?
- What do these individuals need to perform the function?
- When should this function be accomplished relative to other functions?
- Where will this function be performed?
- How is this function performed (what is the process)?
- Why is this function so important or critical to the organization?

The terms *business impact assessment* and *business impact analysis* are used interchangeably in the industry.

By answering these questions, you can create an initial draft of your organization's DRP. The name often used to describe the document created by addressing these questions is a *business impact analysis (BIA)*. Both the disaster recovery plan and the business impact analysis, of course, will need to be approved by management, and it is essential that they buy into the plan—otherwise your efforts will more than likely fail. The old adage "Those who fail to plan, plan to fail" certainly applies in this situation.

A good DRP must include the processes and procedures needed to restore your organization to proper functioning and to ensure continued operation. What specific steps will be required to restore operations?

These processes should be documented and, where possible and feasible, reviewed and exercised on a periodic basis. Having a plan with step-by-step procedures that nobody knows how to follow does nothing to ensure the continued operation of the organization. Exercising your DRP and processes before a disaster occurs provides you with the opportunity to discover flaws or weaknesses in the plan when there is still time to modify and correct them. It also provides an opportunity for key figures in the plan to practice what they will be expected to accomplish.

It is often informative to determine what category your various business functions fall into. You may find that certain functions currently being conducted are not essential to your operations and could be eliminated. In this way, preparing for a security event may actually help you streamline your operational processes.

Categories of Business Functions

In developing your disaster recovery plan or the business impact analysis, you may find it useful to categorize the various functions your organization performs, such as shown in Table 21.4. This categorization is based on how critical or important the function is to your business operation and how long your organization can last without the function. Those functions that are the most critical will be restored first, and your DRP should reflect this. If the function doesn't fall into any of the first four categories, then it is not really needed, and the organization should seriously consider whether it can be eliminated altogether.

If a disaster has occurred and has destroyed all or part of your facility, the DRP portion of the business continuity plan will address the building or acquisition of a new facility. The DRP can also include details related to the long-term recovery of the organization.

However you view these two plans, an organization that is not able to quickly restore business functions after an operational interruption is an organization that will most likely suffer an unrecoverable loss and may cease to exist.

The difference between a disaster recovery plan and business continuity plan is that the business continuity plan will be used to ensure that your operations continue in the face of whatever event has occurred that has caused a disruption in operations.

Table 21.4 DRP Considerations

Category	Level of the Function's Need	How Long Can the Organization Last Without the Function?
Critical	Absolutely essential for operations. Without the function, the basic mission of the organization cannot occur.	The function is needed immediately. The organization cannot function without it.
Necessary for normal processing	Required for normal processing, but the organization can live without it for a short period of time.	The organization can live without the function for at most 30 days before the organization is severely impacted.
Desirable	Not needed for normal processing but enhances the organization's ability to conduct its mission efficiently.	The organization can live without the function for more than 30 days, but it is a function that will eventually need to be accomplished when normal operations are restored.
Optional	Nice to have but does not affect the operation of the organization.	The function is not essential, and no subsequent processing will be required to restore it.
Consider eliminating	No discernible purpose for the function.	The function has no impact on the organization; it is not needed for any organizational purpose.

IT Contingency Planning

Important parts of any organization today are the information technology (IT) processes and assets. Without computers and networks, most organizations could not operate. As a result, it is imperative that a business continuity plan include IT contingency planning. Because of the nature of the Internet and the threats that come from it, an organization's IT assets will likely face some level of disruption before the organization suffers from a disruption due to a natural disaster. Events such as viruses, worms, computer intruders, and denial-of-service attacks could result in an organization losing part or all of its computing resources without warning. Consequently, the IT contingency plans are more likely to be needed than the other aspects of a business continuity plan. These plans should account for disruptions caused by any of the security threats discussed throughout this book as well as disasters or simple system failures.

Test, Exercise, and Rehearse

An organization should practice its DRP periodically. The time to find out whether it has flaws is not when an actual event occurs and the recovery of data and information means the continued existence of the organization. The DRP should be tested to ensure that it is sufficient and that all key individuals know their roles in the specific plan. The security plan determines whether the organization's plan and the individuals involved perform as they should during a simulated security incident.

A test implies a "grade" will be applied to the outcome. Did the organization's plan and the individuals involved perform as they should? Was the organization able to recover and continue to operate within the predefined tolerances set by management? If the answer is no, then during the follow-up evaluation of the exercise, the failures should be identified and addressed. Was it simply a matter of untrained or uninformed individuals, or was there a technological failure that necessitates a change in hardware, software, and procedures?

Whereas a test implies a "grade," an exercise can be conducted without the stigma of a pass/fail grade being attached. *Security exercises* are conducted to provide the opportunity for all parties to practice the procedures that have been established to respond to a security incident. It is important to perform as many of the recovery functions as possible, without impacting ongoing operations, to ensure that the procedures and technologies will work in a real incident. You may want to periodically rehearse portions of the recovery plan, particularly those aspects that either are potentially more disruptive to actual operations or require more frequent practice because of their importance or degree of difficulty.

Additionally, there are different formats for exercises with varying degrees of impact on the organization. The most basic is a checklist walkthrough in which individuals go through a recovery checklist to ensure that they understand what to do should the plan be invoked and confirm that all necessary equipment (hardware and software) is available. This type of exercise normally does not reveal "holes" in a plan but will show where discrepancies exist in the preparation for the plan. To examine the completeness of a plan, a different type of exercise needs to be conducted. The simplest is a tabletop exercise in which participants sit around a table with a facilitator who supplies information related to the "incident" and the processes that are being examined. Another type of exercise is a functional test in which certain aspects of a plan are tested to see how well they work (and how well prepared personnel are). At the most extreme are full operational exercises designed to actually interrupt services in order to verify that all aspects of a plan are in place and sufficient to respond to the type of incident being simulated.

> Exercises are an often-overlooked aspect of security. Many organizations do not believe that they have the time to spend on such events, but the question to ask is whether they can afford to *not* conduct these exercises, as they ensure the organization has a viable plan to recover from disasters and that operations can continue. Make sure you understand what is involved in these critical tests of your organization's plans.

Tabletop Exercises

Exercising operational plans is an effort that can take on many different forms. For senior decision-makers, the point of action is more typically a desk or a conference room, with their method being meetings and decisions. A common form of exercising operational plans for senior management is the tabletop exercise. Members of the senior management team, or elements of it, are gathered together and presented a scenario. They can walk through their decision-making steps, communicate with others, and go through the motions of the exercise in the pattern in which they would likely be involved. The scenario is presented at a level to test the responsiveness of their decisions and decision-making process. Because the event is frequently run in a conference room, around a table, the name *tabletop exercise* has come to define this form of exercise.

Recovery Time Objective and Recovery Point Objective

The term **recovery time objective (RTO)** is used to describe the target time that is set for resuming operations after an incident. This is a period of time that is defined by the business, based on the needs of the enterprise. A shorter RTO results in higher costs because it requires greater coordination and resources. This term is commonly used in business continuity and disaster recovery operations.

Recovery point objective (RPO), a totally different concept from RTO, is the time period representing the maximum period of acceptable data loss. The RPO determines the frequency of backup operations necessary to prevent unacceptable levels of data loss. A simple example of establishing an RPO is to answer the following questions: How much data can you afford to lose? How much rework is tolerable?

RTP and RPO are seemingly related but in actuality measure different things entirely. The RTO serves the purpose of defining the requirements for business continuity, whereas the RPO deals with backup frequency. It is possible to have an RTO of 1 day and an RPO of 1 hour or to have an RTO of 1 hour and an RPO of 1 day. The determining factors are the needs of the business.

> Although recovery time objective and recovery point objective seem to be the same or similar, they are very different. The RTO serves the purpose of defining the requirements for business continuity, whereas the RPO deals with backup frequency.

Why Change Management?

To manage the system development and maintenance processes effectively, you need discipline and structure to help conserve resources and enhance effectiveness. Change management, like risk management, is often considered expensive, nonproductive, unnecessary, and confusing—an impediment to progress. However, like risk management, change management can be scaled to control and manage the development and maintenance of systems effectively.

> **Cross Check**
>
> **Risk Management and Change Management Are Essential Business Processes**
>
> Chapter 20 presented risk management as an essential decision-making process. In much the same way, change management is an essential practice for managing a system during its entire lifecycle, from development through deployment and operation, until it is taken out of service. What security-specific risk-based questions should be asked during change management reviews?

Change management should be used in all phases of a system's life: development, testing, quality assurance (QA), and production. Short development cycles have not changed the need for an appropriate amount of management control over software development, maintenance, and operation. In fact, short turnaround times make change management more necessary, because once a system goes active in today's services-based environments, it often cannot be taken offline to correct errors—it must stay up and online, or else business will be lost and brand recognition damaged. In today's volatile stock market, for example, even small indicators of lagging performance can have dramatic impacts on a company's stock value.

The following scenarios exemplify the need for appropriate change management policy and for procedures over software, hardware, and data:

- *The developers can't find the latest version of the production source code.* Change management practices support versioning of software changes.
- *A bug corrected a few months ago mysteriously reappears.* Proper change management ensures developers always use the most recently changed source code.
- *Fielded software was working fine yesterday but does not work properly today.* Good change management controls have access to previously modified modules so that previously corrected errors aren't reintroduced into the system.
- *Development team members overwrote each other's changes.* Today's change management tools support collaborative development.
- *A programmer spent several hours changing the wrong version of the software.* Change management tools support viable management of previous software versions.
- *New tax rates stored in a table have been overwritten with last year's tax rates.* Change control prevents inadvertent overwriting of critical reference data.
- *A network administrator inadvertently brought down a server because he incorrectly punched down the wrong wires.* Just like a blueprint shows key electrical paths, data center connection paths can be version controlled.

- *A newly installed server is hacked soon after installation because it was improperly configured.* Network and system administrators use change management to ensure configurations consistently meet security standards.

Try This!

Scope of Change Management

See if you can explain why each of the following should be placed under an appropriate change management process:

- Web pages
- Service packs
- Security patches
- Third-party software releases
- Test data and test scripts
- Parameter files
- Scripts, stored procedures, or job control language–type programs
- Customized vendor code
- Source code of any kind
- Applications

Just about anyone with more than a year's experience in software development or system operations can relate to at least one of the preceding scenarios. However, each of these scenarios can be controlled, and impacts mitigated, through proper change management procedures.

The Sarbanes-Oxley Act of 2002, officially titled the Public Company Accounting Reform and Investor Protection Act of 2002, was enacted July 30, 2002, to help ensure management establishes viable governance environments and control structures to ensure accuracy of financial reporting. Section 404 outlines the requirements most applicable to information technology. Change management is an essential part of creating a viable governance and control structure and is critical to compliance with the Sarbanes-Oxley Act.

The Key Concept: Separation of Duties

A foundation for change management is the recognition that involving more than one individual in a process can reduce risk. Good business control practices require that duties be assigned to individuals in such a way that no one individual can control all phases of a process or the processing and recording of a transaction. This is called **separation of duties** (also called *segregation of duties*). It is an important means by which errors and fraudulent or malicious acts can be discouraged and prevented. Separation

Tech Tip

Types of Changes

The ITIL v3 Glossary of Terms, Definitions and Acronyms (www.axelos.com/glossaries-of-terms) defines the following types of changes (with examples added in parentheses):

- **Change** *"The addition, modification or removal of anything that could have an effect on IT Services." (For example, modification to a module to implement a new capability.)*
- **Standard change** *"A preapproved change that is low risk, relatively common and follows a procedure or work instruction." (For example, each month Finance must make a small rounding adjustment to reconcile the General Ledger to account for foreign currency calculations.)*
- **Emergency change** *"A change that must be introduced as soon as possible." (For example, to resolve a major incident or implement a security patch. The change management process will normally have a specific procedure for handling emergency changes.)*

See www.axelos.com/best-practice-solutions/itil.aspx for more information.

of duties can be applied in many organizational scenarios because it establishes a basis for accountability and control. Proper separation of duties can safeguard enterprise assets and protect against risks. The specific segregation of duties should be documented, monitored, and enforced.

A well-understood business example of separation of duties is in the management and payment of vendor invoices. If a person can create a vendor in the finance system, enter invoices for payment, and then authorize a payment check to be written, it is apparent that fraud could be perpetrated because the person could write a check to himself for services never performed. Separating duties by requiring one person to create the vendors and another person to enter invoices and write checks makes it more difficult for someone to defraud an employer.

Information technology (IT) organizations should design, implement, monitor, and enforce appropriate separation of duties for the enterprise's information systems and processes. Today's computer systems are rapidly evolving into an increasingly decentralized and networked computer infrastructure. In the absence of adequate IT controls, such rapid growth may allow exploitation of large amounts of enterprise information in a short time. Further, the knowledge of computer operations held by IT staff is significantly greater than that of an average user, and this knowledge could be abused for malicious purposes.

Some of the best practices for ensuring proper separation of duties in an IT organization are as follows:

- Separation of duties between development, testing, QA, and production should be documented in written procedures and implemented by software or manual processes.
- The activities of program developers and program testers should be conducted on "test" data only. They should be restricted from accessing "live" production data. This will assist in ensuring an independent and objective testing environment without jeopardizing the confidentiality and integrity of production data.
- End users or computer operations personnel should not have direct access to program source code. This control helps lessen the opportunity of exploiting software weaknesses or introducing malicious code (or code that has not been properly tested) into the production environment either intentionally or unintentionally.
- Functions of creating, installing, and administrating software programs should be assigned to different individuals. For example, since developers create and enhance programs, they should not be able to install these programs on the production system. Likewise, database administrators should not be program developers on database systems they administer.
- All accesses and privileges to systems, software, or data should be granted based on the principle of least privilege, which gives users no more privileges than are necessary to perform their jobs. Access privileges should be reviewed regularly to ensure that individuals who no longer require access have had their access removed.

- Formal change management policy and procedures should be enforced throughout the enterprise. Any changes in hardware and software components (including emergency changes) that are implemented after the system has been placed into production must go through the approved formal change management mechanism.

Managers at all levels should review existing and planned processes and systems to ensure proper separation of duties. Smaller business entities may not have the resources to implement all of the preceding practices fully, but other control mechanisms, including hiring qualified personnel, bonding contractors, and using training, monitoring, and evaluation practices, can reduce any organization's exposure to risk. The establishment of such practices can ensure that enterprise assets are properly safeguarded and can also greatly reduce error and the potential for fraudulent or malicious activities.

Change management practices implement and enforce separation of duties by adding structure and management oversight to the software development and system operation processes. Change management techniques can ensure that only correct and authorized changes, as approved by management or other authorities, are allowed to be made, following a defined process.

> **Tech Tip**
>
> **Steps to Implement Separation of Duties**
>
> 1. *Identify an indispensable function that is potentially subject to abuse.*
> 2. *Divide the function into separate steps, each containing a small part of the power that enables the function to be abused.*
> 3. *Assign each step to a different person or organization.*

Elements of Change Management

Change management has its roots in system engineering, where it is commonly referred to as *configuration management.* Most of today's software and hardware change management practices derive from long-standing system engineering configuration management practices. Computer hardware and software development have evolved to the point that proper management structure and controls must exist to ensure the products operate as planned. Issues such as the Heartbleed and Shellshock incidents, as detailed in Chapter 15, illustrate the need to understand configurations and change.

> **Tech Tip**
>
> **Change Management**
>
> *The ITIL v3 Glossary defines change management as "The process responsible for controlling the lifecycle of all changes. The primary objective of change management is to enable beneficial changes to be made, with minimum disruption to IT services." See www.axelos.com/glossaries-of-terms.*

Change management and configuration management use different terms for their various phases, but they all fit into the four general phases defined under configuration management:

- Configuration identification
- Configuration control
- Configuration status accounting
- Configuration auditing

Configuration identification is the process of identifying which assets need to be managed and controlled. These assets could be software modules, test cases or scripts, table or parameter values, servers, major subsystems, or entire systems. The idea is that, depending on the size and complexity of the system, an appropriate set of data and software (or other assets) must be identified and properly managed. These identified assets are called **configuration items** or **computer software configuration items**.

Related to configuration identification, and the result of it, is the definition of a baseline. A **baseline** serves as a foundation for comparison or

Large enterprise application systems require viable change management systems. For example, SAP has its own change management system called the Transport Management System (TMS). Third-party software such as Phire Architect (https://phireinc.com/) and Stat for PeopleSoft (www.quest.com/products/stat-peoplesoft/) provide change management applications for Oracle's PeopleSoft and E-Business Suite.

It is important that you understand that even though all servers may be initially configured to the same baseline, individual applications might require a system-specific configuration to run properly. Change management actually facilitates system-specific configuration in that all exceptions from the standard configuration are documented. All people involved in managing and operating these systems will have documentation to help them quickly understand why a particular system is configured in a unique way.

measurement. It provides the necessary visibility to control change. For example, a software baseline defines the software system as it is built and running at a point in time. As another example, network security best practices clearly state that any large organization should build its servers to a standard build configuration to enhance overall network security. The servers are the configuration items, and the standard build is the server baseline.

Configuration control is the process of controlling changes to items that have been baselined. Configuration control ensures that only approved changes to a baseline are allowed to be implemented. It is easy to understand why a software system, such as a web-based order entry system, should not be changed without proper testing and control—otherwise, the system might stop functioning at a critical time. Configuration control is a key step that provides valuable insight to managers. If a system is being changed, and configuration control is being observed, managers and others concerned will be better informed. This ensures proper use of assets and avoids unnecessary downtime due to the installation of unapproved changes.

Configuration status accounting consists of the procedures for tracking and maintaining data relative to each configuration item in the baseline. It is closely related to configuration control. Status accounting involves gathering and maintaining information relative to each configuration item. For example, it documents what changes have been requested; what changes have been made, when, and for what reason; who authorized those changes; who performed the changes; and what other configuration items or systems were affected by the changes.

Returning to our example of servers being baselined, if the operating system of those servers is found to have a security flaw, then the baseline can be consulted to determine which servers are vulnerable to this particular security flaw. Those systems with this weakness can be updated (and only those that need to be updated). Configuration control and configuration status accounting help ensure that systems are more consistently managed and, ultimately in this case, the organization's network security is maintained. It is easy to imagine the state of an organization that has not built all servers to a common baseline and has not properly controlled its systems' configurations. It would be very difficult to know the configuration of individual servers, and security could quickly become weak.

Configuration auditing is the process of verifying that the configuration items are built and maintained according to the requirements, standards, or contractual agreements. It is similar to how audits in the financial world are used to ensure that generally accepted accounting principles and practices are adhered to and that financial statements properly reflect the financial status of the enterprise. Configuration audits ensure that policies and procedures are being followed, that all configuration items (including hardware and software) are being properly maintained, and that existing documentation accurately reflects the status of the systems in operation.

Configuration auditing takes on two forms: functional and physical. A *functional configuration audit* verifies that the configuration item performs as defined by the documentation of the system requirements. A *physical configuration audit* confirms that all configuration items to be included in a release, install, change, or upgrade are actually included, and that no additional items are included—no more, no less.

Implementing Change Management

Change management requires some structure and discipline in order to be effective. The change management function is scalable from small to enterprise-level projects. Figure 21.1 illustrates a sample software change management flow appropriate for medium to large projects. It can be adapted to small organizations by having the developer perform work only on their workstation (never on the production system) and having the system administrator serve in the buildmaster function. The buildmaster is usually an independent person responsible for compiling and incorporating changed software into an executable image.

Figure 21.1 shows that developers never have access to the production system or data. It also demonstrates proper separation of duties between developers, QA and test personnel, and production. It implies that a distinct separation exists between the development, testing and QA, and production environments. This workflow is for changes that have a major impact on production or the customer's business process. For minor changes that have minimal risk or impact on business processes, some of the steps may be omitted.

The change management workflow proceeds as follows:

1. The developer checks out source code from the code-control tool archive to the development system.
2. The developer modifies the code and conducts unit testing of the changed modules.
3. The developer checks the modified code into the code-control tool archive.
4. The developer notifies the buildmaster that changes are ready for a new build and testing/QA.
5. The buildmaster creates a build incorporating the modified code and compiles the code.

> **Tech Tip**
>
> **Release Management**
>
> *The ITIL v3 Glossary defines release management as "The process responsible for planning, scheduling and controlling the movement of releases to test and live environments. The primary objective of release management is to ensure that the integrity of the live environment is protected and that the correct components are released." See www.axelos.com/glossaries-of-terms.*

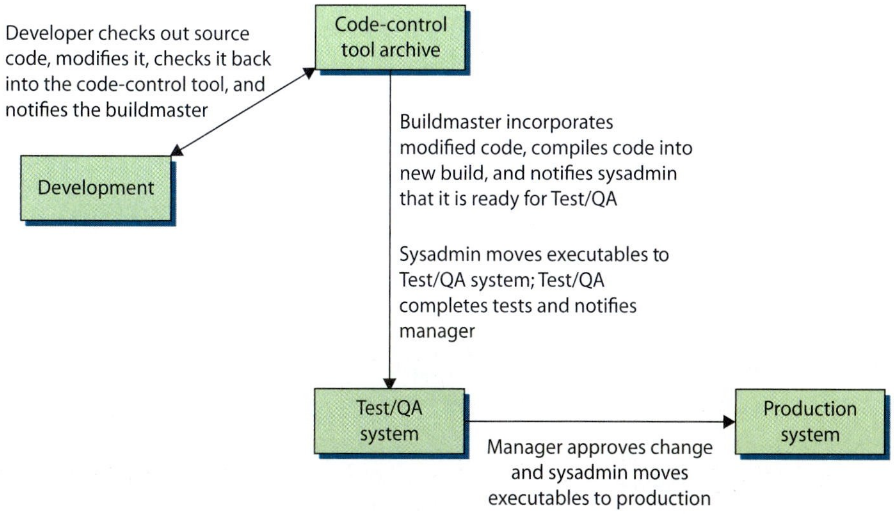

• **Figure 21.1** Software change control workflow

> **Tech Tip**
>
> **Identifying Separation of Duties**
>
> *Using Figure 21.1, observe the separation of duties between development, test/QA, and production. The functions of creating, installing, and administrating are assigned to different individuals. Note also appropriate management review and approval. This implementation also ensures that no compiler is necessary on the production system. Indeed, compilers should not be allowed to exist on the production system.*

6. The buildmaster notifies the system administrator that the executable image is ready for testing/QA.
7. The system administrator moves the executables to the test/QA system.
8. QA tests the new executables. If the tests are passed, test/QA notifies the manager. If tests fail, the process starts over.
9. Upon manager approval, the system administrator moves the executable to the production system.

Backout Plan

One of the key elements of a change plan is a comprehensive **backout plan**. If, in the course of a planned change activity in production, a problem occurs that prevents going forward, it is essential to have a backout plan to restore the system to its previous operating condition. A common element in many operating system updates is the inability to go back to a previous version. This is fine provided that the update goes perfectly, but if for some reason it fails, what then? For a personal device, there may be some inconvenience. For a server in production, this can have significant business implications. The ultimate in backout plans is the restoration of a complete backup of the system. Backups can be time consuming and difficult in some environments, but the spread of virtualization into the enterprise provides many more options in configuration management and backout plans.

The Purpose of a Change Control Board

To oversee the change management process, most organizations establish a **change control board (CCB)**. In practice, a CCB not only facilitates adequate management oversight but also facilitates better coordination between projects. The CCB convenes on a regular basis, usually weekly or monthly, and can meet on an emergency or as-needed basis as well. Figure 21.2 shows the process for implementing and properly controlling hardware or software during changes. The CCB uses standard documents, such as change

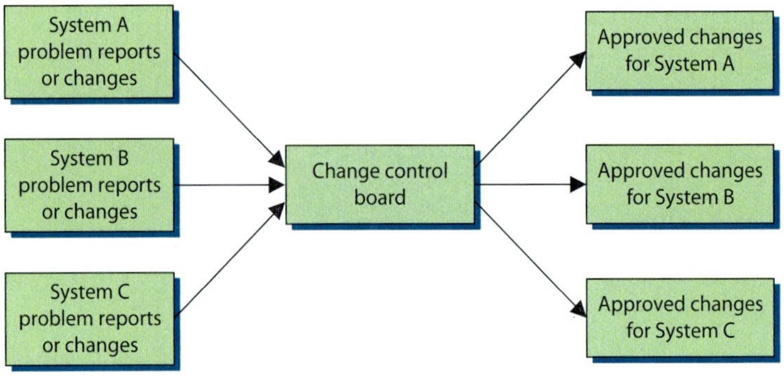

• **Figure 21.2** Change control board process

requests, in concert with business schedules and other elements of operational data, with a focus on system stability. The CCB also ensures that all elements of the change policy have been complied with before approving changes to production systems.

The CCB's membership should consist of development project managers, network administrators, system administrators, test/QA managers, an information security manager, an operations center manager, and a help desk manager. Others can be added as necessary, depending on the size and complexity of the organization.

A **system problem report (SPR)** is used to track changes through the CCB. The SPR documents changes or corrections to a system. It reflects who requested the change and why, what analysis must be done and by whom, and how the change was corrected or implemented. Figure 21.3 shows a sample SPR. Most large enterprises cannot rely on a paper-based SPR process and instead use one of the many software systems available to perform change management functions. Although this example shows a paper-based SPR, it contains all the elements of change management: it describes the problem and who reported it, it outlines resolution of the problem, and it documents approval of the change.

Figure 21.4 shows the entire change management process and its relationship to incident management and release management.

Tech Tip

Incident Management

The ITIL v3 Glossary defines incident management as "The process responsible for managing the lifecycle of all incidents. The primary objective of incident management is to return the IT service to users as quickly as possible."

Code Integrity

One key benefit of adequate change management is the assurance of code consistency and integrity. Whenever a modified program is moved to the production source-code library, the executable version should also be moved to the production system. Automated change management systems greatly simplify this process and are therefore better controls for ensuring executable and source-code integrity. Remember that at no time should the user or application developer have access to production source and executable code libraries in the production environment.

Finally, in today's networked environment, the integrity of the executable code is critical. A common hacking technique is to replace key system executable code with modified code that contains backdoors, allowing unauthorized access or functions to be performed. Executable code integrity can be verified using host-based intrusion detection systems (HIDSs). These systems create and maintain a database of the size and content of executable modules. Conceptually,

SYSTEM PROBLEM REPORT (SPR)

❑ Error SPR Number:____________

❑ Improvement Originator:____________

---------------------------- **Problem** ----------------------------

System Affected:____________

Related Systems:____________

Classification: Problem Description:____________

❑ Software

❑ Hardware

❑ Documentation

❑ Comment

Analysis Assigned to:____________

---------------------------- **Analysis** ----------------------------

(Prepared by responsible software design organization) Date Received:____________

Classification: Explanation:

❑ Design

❑ Coding

❑ Documentation

❑ Environment

Signatures

Analyst:__________ Date:________ Originator:__________ Date:________

---------------------------- **Correction** ----------------------------

Brief Description of Work and List of Modules Changed:

____

Documentation Changed:

____

Signatures

Developer:__________ Date:________ Manager:__________ Date:________

• **Figure 21.3** Sample system problem report

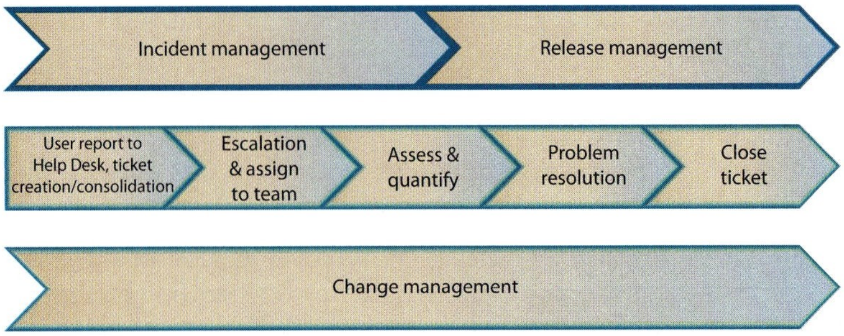

• **Figure 21.4** Change, incident, and release management

this is usually done by performing some kind of hashing or sophisticated checksum operation on the executable modules and storing the results in a database. The operation is performed on a regular schedule against the executable modules, and the results are compared to the database to identify any unauthorized changes that may have occurred to the executable modules.

The Capability Maturity Model Integration

An important set of process models is the **Capability Maturity Model Integration (CMMI)** series developed at Carnegie Mellon University's Software Engineering Institute (SEI). SEI has created three capability maturity model integrations that replace the older Capability Maturity Model (CMM): the Capability Maturity Model Integration for Acquisition (CMMI-ACQ), the Capability Maturity Model Integration for Development (CMMI-DEV), and the Capability Maturity Model Integration for Services (CMMI-SVC). CMMI-DEV is representative of the three models. One of the fundamental concepts of CMMI-DEV is configuration or change management, which provides organizations with the ability to improve their software and other processes by providing an evolutionary path from ad hoc processes to disciplined management processes.

The CMMI-DEV defines five maturity levels:

- **Level 1: Initial** At maturity level 1, processes are generally ad hoc and chaotic. The organization does not provide a stable environment to support processes.
- **Level 2: Managed** At maturity level 2, processes are planned and executed in accordance with policy. The projects employ skilled people who have adequate resources to produce controlled outputs; involve relevant stakeholders; are monitored, controlled, and reviewed; and are evaluated for adherence to their process descriptions.
- **Level 3: Defined** At maturity level 3, processes are well characterized and understood, and they are described in standards, procedures, tools, and methods. These standard processes are used to establish consistency across the organization.

- **Level 4: Quantitatively Managed** At maturity level 4, the organization establishes quantitative objectives for quality and process performance and uses them as criteria in managing projects. Quantitative objectives are based on the needs of the customer, end users, organization, and process implementers. Quality and process performance is understood in statistical terms and is managed throughout the life of projects.
- **Level 5: Optimizing** At maturity level 5, an organization continually improves its processes based on a quantitative understanding of its business objectives and performance needs. The organization uses a quantitative approach to understanding the variation inherent in the process and the causes of process outcomes.

Change management is a key process to implementing the CMMI-DEV in an organization. For example, if an organization is at CMMI-DEV level 1, it probably has minimal formal change management processes in place. At level 3, an organization has a defined change management process that is followed consistently. At level 5, the change management process is a routine, quantitatively evaluated part of improving software products and implementing innovative ideas across the organization. For an organization to manage software development, operation, and maintenance, it should have effective change management processes in place.

Change management is an essential management tool and control mechanism. The concept of segregation of duties ensures that no single individual or organization possesses too much control in a process, thus helping to prevent errors and fraudulent or malicious acts. The elements of change management—configuration identification, configuration control, configuration status accounting, and configuration auditing—coupled with a defined process and a change control board, will provide management with proper oversight of the software lifecycle. Once such a process and management oversight exist, the company can use CMMI-DEV to move from ad hoc activities to a disciplined software management process.

Environment

Within a modern *environment*, there are multiple, separate environments designed to isolate the functions of development, test, and production. These are primarily to prevent accidents arising from untested code ending up in production. These environments are segregated by access control list as well as hardware, preventing users from accessing multiple different levels of the environment. For moving the code between environments, special accounts that can access both are used, thus eliminating issues of crosstalk.

Development

The *development* system is one that is sized, configured, and set up for developers to develop applications and systems. The development hardware does not have to scale like production, and it probably does not need to be as responsive for given transactions. The development platform does need to be of the same type of system, because developing on Windows and then deploying to Linux is fraught with difficulties that can be avoided by matching development environments to production in terms of OS type and version. After code is successfully developed, it is moved to a test system.

Test

The *test* environment is one that fairly closely mimics the production environment, with the same versions of software, down to patch levels, and the same sets of permissions, file structures, and so on. The purpose of the test environment is to enable a system to be fully tested prior to being deployed into production. The test environment may not scale like production, but from the perspective of the software/hardware footprint, it will look exactly like production.

Staging

The *staging* environment is an optional environment, but it is commonly found when there are multiple production environments. After passing testing, the system moves into staging, from where it can be deployed to the different production systems. The primary purpose of staging is as a sandbox after testing so the test system can test the next set while the current set is deployed across the enterprise. One method of deployment is a staged deployment, where software is deployed to part of the enterprise and then the process is paused to watch for unforeseen problems. If none occur, the deployment process continues, stage by stage, until all of the production systems are changed. By moving software in this manner, you never lose the old production system until the end of the move, giving you time to judge and catch any unforeseen problems. This also prevents the total loss of production to a failed update.

Production

Production is the environment where the systems work with real data, doing the business that the system is supposed to perform. This is an environment where there are by design virtually no changes, except as approved and tested via the system's change management process.

Secure Baseline

To secure the software on a system effectively and consistently, you must take a structured and logical approach. This starts with an examination of the system's intended functions and capabilities to determine what processes and applications will be housed on the system. As a best practice, anything that is not required for operations should be removed or disabled on the system; then, all the appropriate patches, hotfixes, and settings should be applied to protect and secure it. This becomes the system's *secure baseline*.

This process of establishing software's base security state is called *baselining,* and the resulting product is a security *baseline* that allows the software to run safely and securely. Software and hardware can be tied integrally when it comes to security, so they must be considered together. Once the process has been completed for a particular hardware and software combination, any similar systems can be configured with the same baseline to achieve the same level and depth of security and protection. Uniform software baselines are critical in large-scale operations, because maintaining separate configurations and security levels for hundreds or thousands of systems is far too costly.

After administrators have finished patching, securing, and preparing a system, they often create an initial baseline configuration. This represents a secure state for the system or network device and a reference point for the software and its configuration. This information establishes a reference that can be used to help keep the system secure by establishing a known-safe configuration. If this initial baseline can be replicated, it can also be used as a template when similar systems and network devices are deployed.

Sandboxing

Sandboxing refers to the quarantine or isolation of a system from its surroundings. It has become standard practice for some programs with an increased risk surface to operate within a sandbox, limiting the interaction with the CPU and other processes such as memory. This works as a means of quarantine, preventing problems from getting out of the sandbox and onto the OS and other applications on a system.

Virtualization can be used as a form of sandboxing with respect to an entire system. You can build a VM, test something inside the VM, and, based on the results, make a decision with regard to stability or whatever concern was present.

Integrity Measurement

Integrity measurement is the measuring and identification of changes to a specific system away from an expected value. From the simple changing of data as measured by a hash value to the TPM-based integrity measurement of the system boot process and attestation of trust, the concept is the same. Take a known value, perform a storage of a hash or other keyed value, and then at the time of concern, recalculate and compare the two values.

In the case of a TPM-mediated system, where the Trusted Platform Module (TPM) chip provides a hardware-based root of trust anchor, the system is specifically designed to calculate hashes of a system and store them in a Platform Configuration Register (PRC). This register can be read later and compared to a known, or expected, value, and if they differ, there is a trust violation. Certain BIOSs, UEFIs, and boot loaders can all work with the TPM chip in this manner, providing a means of establishing a trust chain during system boot.

Chapter 21 Review

Chapter Summary

After reading this chapter and completing the exercises, you should understand the following about change management.

Operational disruptions can and will occur in systems

- A business continuity plan (BCP) involves planning and advanced policy decisions to ensure the business continuity objectives are achieved during a time of disruption.
- Continuity of operations planning (COOP) involves the steps taken to determine which subset of normal operations needs to be continued during periods of disruption.
- The disaster recovery plan (DRP) defines the data and resources necessary and the steps required to restore critical organizational processes.

Describe the various ways backups are conducted and stored

- Backups should include not only the organization's critical data but critical software as well.
- Backups may be conducted by backing up all files (full backup), only the files that have changed since the last full backup (differential backup), only the files that have changed since the last full or differential backup (incremental backup), or only the portion of the files that has changed since the last delta or full backup (delta backup).
- Backups should be stored onsite for quick access, if needed, as well as offsite in case a disaster destroys the primary facility, its processing equipment, and the backups that are stored onsite.

Use change management as an important enterprise management tool

- Change management should be used in all phases of the software lifecycle.
- Change management can be scaled to effectively control and manage software development and maintenance.
- Change management can prevent some of the most common software development and maintenance problems.

Institute the key concept of separation of duties

- Separation of duties ensures that no single individual or organization possesses too much control in a process.
- Separation of duties helps prevent errors and fraudulent or malicious acts.
- Separation of duties establishes a basis for accountability and control.
- Separation of duties can help safeguard enterprise assets and protect against risks.

Identify the essential elements of change management

- Configuration identification identifies assets that need to be controlled.
- Configuration control keeps track of changes to configuration items that have been baselined.
- Configuration status accounting tracks each configuration item in the baseline.
- Configuration auditing verifies that the configuration items are built and maintained appropriately.

Implement change management

- A standardized process and a change control board provide management with proper oversight and control of the software development lifecycle.
- A good change management process will exhibit good separation of duties and have clearly defined roles, responsibilities, and approvals.
- An effective change control board facilitates good management oversight and coordination between projects.

Use the concepts of the Capability Maturity Model Integration

- Once proper management oversight exists, the company will be able to use CMMI in order to move from ad hoc activities to a disciplined software management process.
- CMMI relies heavily on change management to provide organizations with the capability to improve their software processes.

Implement secure systems design for a given scenario

- Examine the environments of development, test, staging, and production and how they are used to build out secure environments.
- Sandboxing is a means of separating a system from the surrounding environment.

Key Terms

backout plan *(824)*
baseline *(821)*
business continuity plan (BCP) *(801)*
business impact analysis (BIA) *(802)*
Capability Maturity Model Integration (CMMI) *(826)*
change control board (CCB) *(824)*
change management *(801)*
cold site *(811)*
computer software configuration items *(821)*
configuration auditing *(822)*
configuration control *(822)*
configuration identification *(821)*
configuration items *(821)*
configuration management *(801)*
configuration status accounting *(822)*
continuity of operations planning (COOP) *(813)*
delta backup *(806)*
differential backup *(805)*
disaster recovery plan (DRP) *(814)*
full backup *(805)*
hot site *(810)*
mutual aid agreement *(811)*
recovery point objective (RPO) *(817)*
recovery time objective (RTO) *(817)*
separation of duties *(819)*
system problem report (SPR) *(825)*
warm site *(811)*

Key Terms Quiz

Use terms from the Key Terms list to complete the sentences that follow. Don't use the same term more than once. Not all terms will be used.

1. ______________ is the maximum period of time in terms of data loss that is acceptable during an outage.
2. A ______________ is a partially configured backup processing facility that usually has the peripherals and software but perhaps not the more expensive main processing computer.
3. ______________ is the process of assigning responsibilities to different individuals such that no single individual can commit fraudulent or malicious actions.
4. Determining what data and processes are needed to restore critical processes is called a ______________.
5. A ______________ describes a system as it is built and functioning at a point in time.
6. A backup that includes only the files that have changed since the last full backup was completed is called a ______________.
7. The process of verifying that configuration items are built and maintained according to requirements, standards, or contractual agreements is called a ______________.
8. The document used by the change control board to track changes to software is called a ______________.
9. When you identify which assets need to be managed and controlled, you are performing ______________.
10. ______________ is the process of controlling changes to items that have been baselined.

Multiple-Choice Quiz

1. Why should developers and testers avoid using "live" production data to perform various testing activities?
   - **A.** The use of "live" production data ensures a full and realistic test database.
   - **B.** The use of "live" production data can jeopardize the confidentiality and integrity of the production data.
   - **C.** The use of "live" production data ensures an independent and objective test environment.
   - **D.** Developers and testers should be allowed to use "live" production data for reasons of efficiency.
2. What is the purpose of establishing software change management procedures?
   - **A.** To ensure continuity of business operations in the event of a natural disaster
   - **B.** To add structure and control to the development of software systems
   - **C.** To ensure changes in business operations caused by a management restructuring are properly controlled
   - **D.** To identify threats, vulnerabilities, and mitigating actions that could impact an enterprise

3. A good backup plan will include which of the following?
   A. The critical data needed for the organization to operate
   B. Any software that is required to process the organization's data
   C. Specific hardware to run the software or to process the data
   D. All of the above
4. Which of the following does *not* adhere to the principle of separation of duties?
   A. Software development, testing, quality assurance, and production should be assigned to the same individuals.
   B. Software developers should not have access to production data and source-code files.
   C. Software developers and testers should be restricted from accessing "live" production data.
   D. The functions of creating, installing, and administrating software programs should be assigned to different individuals.
5. What is configuration auditing?
   A. The process of controlling changes to items that have been baselined
   B. The process of identifying which assets need to be managed and controlled
   C. The process of verifying that the configuration items are built and maintained properly
   D. The procedures for tracking and maintaining data relative to each configuration item in the baseline
6. In which backup strategy are only those portions of the files and software that have changed since the last backup backed up?
   A. Full
   B. Differential
   C. Incremental
   D. Delta
7. What is configuration control?
   A. The process of controlling changes to items that have been baselined
   B. The process of identifying which assets need to be managed and controlled
   C. The process of verifying that the configuration items are built and maintained properly
   D. The procedures for tracking and maintaining data relative to each configuration item in the baseline
8. What is configuration identification?
   A. The process of verifying that the configuration items are built and maintained properly
   B. The procedure for tracking and maintaining data relative to each configuration item in the baseline
   C. The process of controlling changes to items that have been baselined
   D. The process of identifying which assets need to be managed and controlled

9. Which of the following is the name for a partially configured environment that has the peripherals and software that the normal processing facility contains and that can be operational within a few days?
   - **A.** Hot site
   - **B.** Warm site
   - **C.** Online storage system
   - **D.** Backup storage facility

10. What is the purpose of a change control board (CCB)?
   - **A.** To facilitate management oversight and better project coordination
   - **B.** To identify which assets need to be managed and controlled
   - **C.** To establish software processes that are structured enough that success with one project can be repeated for another similar project
   - **D.** To track and maintain data relative to each configuration item in the baseline

Essay Quiz

1. Write a paragraph outlining the differences between a disaster recovery plan and a business continuity plan. Is one more important than the other?
2. Write a brief description of the different backup strategies. Include a discussion of which of these strategies requires the greatest amount of storage space to conduct and which of the strategies involves the most complicated restoration scheme.
3. Explain why the change management principles discussed in this chapter should be used when managing operating system patches.

Lab Projects

• Lab Project 21.1

Using a typical IT organization from a medium-sized company (100 developers, managers, and support personnel), describe the purpose, organization, and responsibilities of a change control board appropriate for this organization.

• Lab Project 21.2

You are the IT staff auditor for the company mentioned in the first lab project. You have reviewed the change control board processes and found they have instituted the following change management process. Describe two major control weaknesses in this particular change management process. What would you do to correct these control weaknesses?

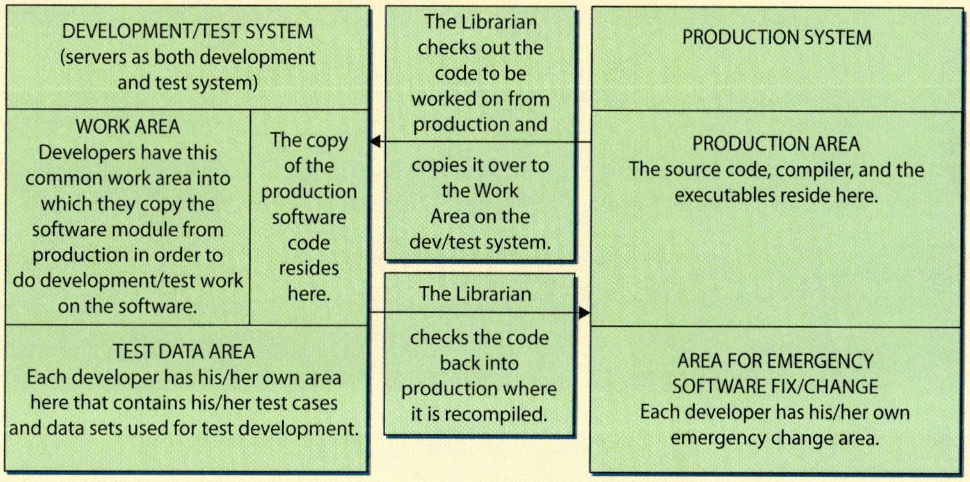

chapter 22

Incident Response

Bad guys will follow the rules of your network to accomplish their mission.

—Ron Schaffer, SANS Incident Detection Summit

In this chapter, you will learn how to

- Understand attack frameworks
- Understand threat intelligence
- Understand the foundations of incident response processes
- Implement the detailed steps of an incident response process
- Understand the data sources available for personnel to employ in incident response
- Describe standards and best practices involved in incident response

Incident response is becoming the new norm in security operations. The reality is that keeping adversaries off your network and preventing unauthorized activity is not going to provide the level of security your enterprise requires. This means the system needs to be able to operate in a state of compromise yet still achieve the desired security objectives. Your mindset has to change from preventing intrusion and attack to preventing loss.

This chapter explores the use of an incident response function to achieve the goals of minimizing loss under all operating conditions. This will mean a shift in focus and a change in priorities as well as security strategy. These efforts can succeed only on top of a solid foundation of security fundamentals as presented earlier in the book, so this is not a starting place but rather the next step in the evolution of defense.

Foundations of Incident Response

An *incident* is any event in an information system or network where the results are different than normal. Incident response is not just an information security operation. Incident response is an effort that involves the entire business. The security team may form a nucleus of the effort, but the key tasks are performed by many parts of the business.

> A successful incident response effort requires two components: knowledge of one's own systems and knowledge of the adversary. The ancient warrior/philosopher Sun Tzu explains it well in *The Art of War*: "If you know the enemy and know yourself, you need not fear the result of a hundred battles. If you know yourself but not the enemy, for every victory gained you will also suffer a defeat. If you know neither the enemy nor yourself, you will succumb in every battle."

Incident response is a term used to describe the steps an organization performs in response to any situation determined to be abnormal in the operation of a computer system. The causes of incidents are many, from the environment (storms) to errors on the part of users to unauthorized actions by unauthorized users, to name a few. Although the causes may be many, the results can be sorted into classes. A low-impact incident may not result in any significant risk exposure, so no action other than repairing the broken system is needed. A moderate-risk incident will require greater scrutiny and response efforts, and a high-level risk exposure incident will require the greatest scrutiny. To manage incidents when they occur, a table of guidelines for the incident response team needs to be created to assist in determining the level of response.

Two major elements play a role in determining the level of response. Information criticality is the primary determinant, and this comes from the data classification and the quantity of data involved. **Information criticality** is defined as the relative importance of specific information to the business. Information criticality is a key measure used in the prioritization of actions throughout the incident response process. The loss of one administrator password is less serious than the loss of all of them. The second major element involves a business decision on how this incident plays into current business operations. A series of breaches, whether minor or not, indicates a pattern that can have public relations and regulatory issues.

Once an incident happens, it is time to react, and proper reaction requires a game plan. Contrary to what many want to believe, there are no magic silver bullets to kill the security monsters. A solid, well-rehearsed incident response plan is required. This plan is custom-tailored to the information criticalities, the actual hardware and software architectures, and the people. Like all large, complex projects, the challenges rapidly become organizational in nature—budget, manpower, resources, and commitment.

Incident Management

Having an incident response management methodology is a key risk mitigation strategy. One of the steps that should be taken to establish a plan to handle business interruptions as a result of a cyber event of some sort is the establishment of a **computer incident response team (CIRT)** or a **computer emergency response team (CERT)**.

> CERT is a trademark of Carnegie Mellon and is frequently used in some situations, such as the US-CERT.

The organization's CIRT will conduct the investigation into the incident and make the recommendations on how to proceed. The CIRT should consist of not only permanent members but also ad hoc members who may be called upon to address special needs, depending on the nature of the incident. In addition to individuals with a technical background, the CIRT should include nontechnical personnel to provide guidance on ways to handle media attention, legal issues that may arise, and management issues regarding the continued operation of the organization. The CIRT should be created, and team members should be identified before an incident occurs. Policies and procedures for conducting an investigation should also be worked out in advance of an incident occurring. It is also advisable to have the team periodically meet to review these procedures.

Goals of Incident Response

The goals of an incident response process are multidimensional in nature:

- Confirm or dispel incident
- Promote accurate information accumulation and dissemination
- Establish controls for evidence
- Protect privacy rights
- Minimize disruption to operations
- Allow for legal/civil recourse
- Provide accurate reports/recommendations

Incident response depends upon accurate information. Without it, the chance of following data in the wrong direction is a possibility, as is missing crucial information and only finding dead ends. The preceding goals are essential for the viability of an incident response process and the desired outcomes.

Attack Frameworks

Attack frameworks provide a roadmap of the types of actions and sequence of actions used when attacking a system. Frameworks bring a sense of structure and order to the multidimensional problem associated with defending a variety of systems against multiple different types of attackers with various objectives. The objective of using a framework is to improve post-compromise detection of adversaries in enterprises by providing guidance on where an adversary's actions may be observable and where one can take specific actions. Organizations can use frameworks to identify holes in defenses and prioritize them based on the risk associated with actions an adversary is likely to take. Three different frameworks are described in the following sections: the MITRE ATT&CK framework, the Diamond Model of Intrusion Analysis, and the Cyber Kill Chain.

Anatomy of an Attack

Attackers have a method by which they attack a system. Although the specifics may differ from event to event, there are some steps that are commonly employed. There are also numerous types of attacks—from old-school hacking to the new advanced persistent threat (APT) attack. The differences are subtle and are related to the objectives of each form of attack.

Old School

Attacks are not a new phenomenon in enterprise security, and a historical examination of large numbers of attacks shows some common methods. The following are the traditional steps:

> **Tech Tip**
>
> **Using nmap to Fingerprint an Operating System**
>
> *To use nmap to fingerprint an operating system, use the* **–O** *option:*
>
> ```
> nmap -O -v
> scanme.nmap.org
> ```
>
> *This command performs a scan of interesting ports on the target (scanme.nmap.org) and attempts to identify the operating system. The* **–v** *option indicates that you want verbose output.*

1. Footprinting
2. Scanning
3. Enumeration
4. Gaining access
5. Escalating privileges
6. Pilfering
7. Creating backdoors
8. Covering tracks
9. Denial of service (DOS)

Footprinting is the determination of the boundaries of a target space. There are numerous sources of information, including websites, DNS records, and IP address registrations. Understanding the boundaries assists an attacker in knowing what is in their target range and what isn't. *Scanning* is the examination of machines to determine what operating systems, services, and vulnerabilities exist. The *enumeration* step is a listing of the systems and vulnerabilities to build an attack game plan. The first actual incursion is *gaining access* to an account on the system, almost always as an ordinary user, as higher-privilege accounts are harder to target.

The next step is to gain access to a higher-privilege account by *escalating privileges*. From a higher-privilege account, the range of accessible activities is greater, including *pilfering* files, creating *backdoors* so you can return, and *covering your tracks* by erasing logs. The step of DOS is commonly used as a technique to block specific services (think DNS) while an attacker injects their own response, misdirecting the victim process. The detail associated with each step may vary from hack to hack, but in most cases, these steps are employed in this manner to achieve an objective.

Advanced Persistent Threat

A relatively new attack phenomenon is the **advanced persistent threat (APT)**, which is an attack that always maintains a primary focus on remaining in the network, operating undetected, and having multiple ways in and out. APTs began with nation-state attackers, but the utility of the long-term attack has proven valuable, and many sophisticated attacks have moved to this route. Most APTs begin via a phishing or spear phishing attack, which establishes a foothold in the system under attack. From this foothold, the attack methodology is similar to the traditional attack method described in the previous section, but additional emphasis is placed on the steps needed to maintain a presence on a network, as shown here:

1. Define target
2. Research target
3. Select tools

4. Test for detection
5. Initial intrusion
6. Establish outbound connection
7. Obtain credentials
8. Expand access
9. Strengthen foothold
10. Cover tracks
11. Exfiltrate data

The initial intrusion is usually performed via social engineering (spear phishing), over e-mail, using zero-day custom malware. Another popular infection method is the use of a watering hole attack, planting the malware on a website that the victim employees will likely visit. The use of custom malware makes detecting the attack by antivirus/malware programs a near impossibility. After the attackers gain access, they attempt to expand access and strengthen the foothold. This is done by planting **remote-access trojan (RAT)** software in the victim's network, creating network backdoors and tunnels that allow stealth access to its infrastructure.

The next steps, obtaining credentials and escalating privileges, are performed through the use of exploits and password cracking. The true objective is to acquire administrator privileges over a victim's computer and ultimately expand it to Windows domain administrator accounts. One of the hallmarks of an APT attack is the emphasis on maintaining a presence on the system to ensure continued control over access channels and credentials acquired in previous steps. A common technique used is lateral movement across a network. Moving laterally allows an attacker to expand control to other workstations, servers, and infrastructure elements and perform data harvesting on them. Attackers also perform internal reconnaissance, collecting information on surrounding infrastructure, trust relationships, and information concerning the Windows domain structure.

> **Tech Tip**
>
> **APT Attack Model**
>
> *The computer security investigative firm Mandiant (now a division of FireEye) was one of the pioneers in the use of incident response techniques against APT-style attacks. They published a model of an APT attack to use as a guide, listed here:*
>
> 1. *Initial compromise*
> 2. *Establish foothold*
> 3. *Escalate privileges*
> 4. *Internal reconnaissance*
> 5. *Move laterally*
> 6. *Maintain presence*
> 7. *Complete mission*
>
> *The key step is step 5, moving laterally.* **Lateral movement** *is where the adversary traverses your network, using multiple accounts, and does so to discover material worth stealing as well as to avoid being locked out by normal operational changes. This is one element that can be leveraged to help slow down, detect, and defeat APT attacks. Blocking lateral movement can defeat APT-style attacks from spreading through a network and can limit their stealth.*

Cyber Kill Chain

The **Cyber Kill Chain** is a model developed by Lockheed Martin as a military form of engagement framework. This model has a series of distinct steps that an attacker uses during a cyberattack—from the early reconnaissance stages to the exfiltration of data. The use of the Cyber Kill Chain helps us understand and combat different forms of attack—from ransomware, to security breaches, and even advanced persistent threats (APTs).

The Cyber Kill Chain, shown in Figure 22.1, has slightly different steps depending on whose version you use, but the most common implementations include the following ones:

1. **Reconnaissance** Research and identify targets.
2. **Weaponization** Exploit vulnerabilities to enter.
3. **Delivery** Deliver the payload (evil content).
4. **Exploitation** Begin the payload attack on the system and gain entry.

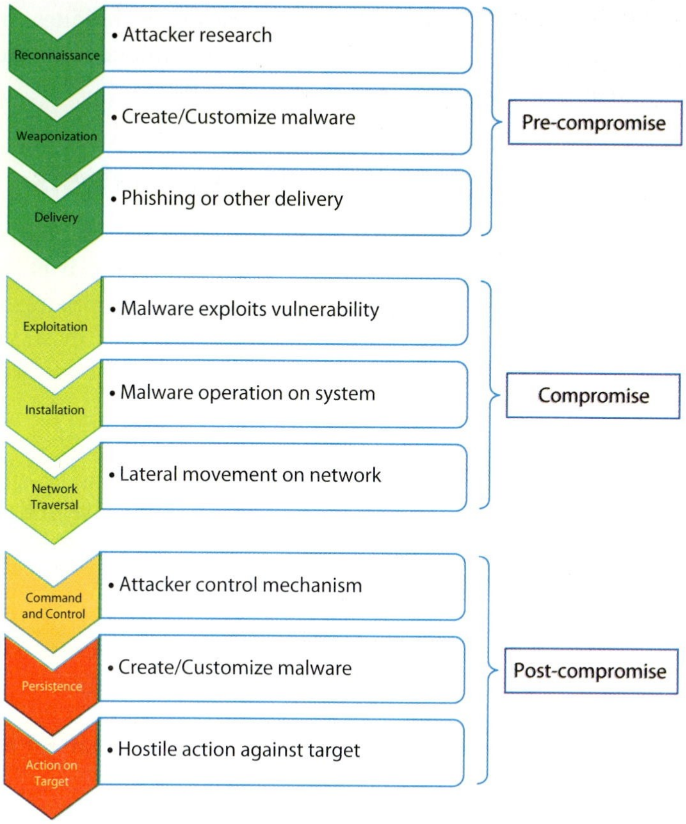

• **Figure 22.1** Cyber Kill Chain

5. **Installation** Implement backdoors, persistent access, bots, and so on.
6. **Command and control** Communicate to outside servers for control purposes.
7. **Action on objective** Obtain the objective of the attack (for example, steal intellectual property).

By understanding the progression of an attack, defenders can choose their point of defense, which enables them to react to an attack with a plan and a purpose.

> Developed by Lockheed Martin, the Cyber Kill Chain is a framework used to defend against the chain of events an attacker takes, from the beginning of an attack to the end of an attack.

MITRE ATT&CK

The **MITRE ATT&CK framework** is a comprehensive matrix of attack elements, including the tactics and techniques used by attackers on a system. This framework can be used by threat hunters, red teamers, and defenders to better classify attacks and understand the sequential steps an adversary will be taking when attacking a system. This framework enables personnel to plan and defend, even during an attack, and it acts as a useful tool in assessing an organization's risk.

The MITRE ATT&CK framework has a fairly simple design, with the top row of the matrix covering activities such as initial access, execution, persistence, privilege escalation, defense evasion, credential access, discovery, lateral movement, collection, command and control, exfiltration, and

The MITRE ATT&CK framework is a knowledgebase of various real-world observations and attack techniques. It is often used by organizations for threat modeling.

impact. Under each of these activities is a series of techniques and sub-techniques. Taken together, this matrix paints a comprehensive picture of paths through an organization's IT enterprise.

The Diamond Model of Intrusion Analysis

The **Diamond Model of Intrusion Analysis** is a cognitive model used by the threat intelligence community to describe a specific event. It is based on the notion that an event has four characteristics, each comprising a corner of the diamond, as shown in Figure 22.2. Taken together, these elements describe an event. The four nodes that make up an event are adversary, infrastructure, capabilities, and victim. The adversary node is a description of the attacker and their data, including anything you know about them (e-mails, names, locations, handles, and so on). The infrastructure node is a description of what is being used in the attack, such as IP addresses, domain names, e-mail addresses, and so on. The victim node is the target, and the capabilities node is a description of what is being used (malware, stolen certificates/credentials, tools, exploits, and so on). As an example, a completed diamond could take the following form:

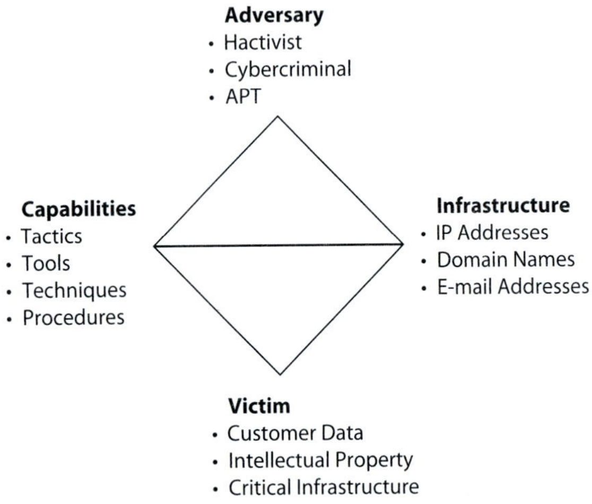

• **Figure 22.2** Diamond Model of Intrusion Analysis

1. **Adversary** Whois is used to get an e-mail for the registrant—the possible attacker.
2. **Infrastructure** The C2 domain name resolves to an IP address.
3. **Capabilities** The response teams finds the C2 server domain name.
4. **Victim** A victim discovers malware and launches an incident response.

The Diamond Model enables intrusion analysis by placing malicious activity at four points of the diamond: adversary, infrastructure, capabilities, and victim.

Threat Intelligence

A major tool for defenders who are hunting attackers is threat intelligence. As presented in Chapter 1, **threat intelligence** is the actionable information about malicious actors, their tools, infrastructure, and methods. Incident response is a game of resource management. No firm has the resources to protect everything against all threats or investigate all possible hostile actions; attempting to do so would result in wasted efforts. A key decision is where to apply incident response resources in response to an incident. A combination of threat intelligence combined with the concept of the kill chain (the attacker's most likely path) and you have a means to prioritize actions against most meaningful threats.

Threat Hunting

Threat hunting is an iterative process of proactively searching out threats inside the network. Several different models can be employed for threat hunting, but one of the most effective is based on creating a hypothesis and then examining that hypothesis. This act provides a level of scope to the hunt—rather than looking for anything in a sea of mostly normal, one is looking for specific items. A typical hypothesis would be something like "an adversary is using stolen credentials to mimic authorized users during nonworking hours." This hypothesis is concise and can be tested by examining a set of logs for specific activities during nonworking hours.

The objective of threat hunting is to use current knowledge of what adversaries are doing to firms, and check to see if that is happening on your network. This can increase detection of malicious activity beyond the typical incident-type triggers. A complete explanation of threat hunting can be found in the whitepaper "A Practical Model for Conducting Cyber Threat Hunting," by Dan Gunter and Marc Seitz (https://www.sans.org/reading-room/whitepapers/threathunting/practical-model-conducting-cyber-threat-hunting-38710).

Security Orchestration, Automation, and Response (SOAR)

Security operations in an enterprise environment have a lot of moving parts. From a top-level view, you have vulnerability management, threat intelligence, incident response, and automated security operations. All of these operate off of data—data that comes from a myriad of network appliances, intrusion detection systems, firewalls, and other security devices. This data is typically fed into a security information and event management (SIEM) system that can collect, aggregate, and apply pattern matching to the volumes of data. Alerts can then be processed by security personnel. However, this is far from complete integration. **Security orchestration, automation, and response (SOAR)** systems take SIEM data as well as data from other sources and assists in the creation of runbooks and playbooks.

Security administrators can create a series of runbooks and playbooks that can be used in response to a wide range of incident response activities. The details behind runbooks and playbooks are covered next. Combinations of runbooks and playbooks can be used to document different security processes and can provide users with approved procedures for orchestrating even the most complex security workflows. SOAR software integrates all of these elements into manageable solutions for the security operations center personnel, combining both raw and processed data into actionable steps based on approved procedures.

> SOAR systems are extremely valuable when it comes to incident mitigation of severe threats because they can automate data gathering and initiate threat response.

Runbooks

A **runbook** consists of a series of action-based conditional steps to perform specific actions associated with security automation. These actions might involve data harvesting and enrichment, threat containment, alerts and notifications, and other automatable elements of a security operations process. The primary purpose of a runbook is to accelerate the incident response process by automating a series of approved steps and processes. Runbooks typically are focused on the systems and services and how they are actively managed.

Playbooks

A **playbook** is a set of approved steps and actions required to successfully respond to a specific incident or threat. Playbooks are commonly

A runbook typically focuses on technical aspects of computer systems or networks. A playbook is more comprehensive and has more of a people/general business focus.

instantiated as itemized checklists, with all pertinent data prefilled in—systems, team members, actions, and so on. Playbooks provide a simple step-by-step, top-down approach to the orchestration of activities of the security team. They can include a wide range of requirements—technical requirements, personnel requirements, and legal or regulatory requirements—all in a preapproved form that alleviates spur-of-the-moment scrambling when the clock is ticking on an active event.

Incident Response Process

Incident response is the set of actions security personnel perform in response to a wide range of triggering events. These actions are vast and varied because they have to deal with a wide range of causes and consequences. Through the use of a structured framework, coupled with properly prepared processes, incident response becomes a manageable task. Without proper preparation, this task can quickly become impossible or intractably expensive.

Incident response is the new business cultural norm in information security. The key is to design the procedures to include appropriate business personnel, not keep it as a pure information security endeavor. The challenges are many, including the aspect of timing as the activities quickly become a case of one group of professionals pursuing another.

For the elements of incident response process, it is important to know the names, the topics contained, and the order in which they are performed, as understanding the basic flow is important if one is to contribute to the response. The steps are as follows: preparation, identification, containment, eradication, recovery, and lessons learned.

Incident response is a multistep process with several component elements. The first is organization preparation, followed by system preparation. An initial detection is followed by initial response and then isolation, investigation, recovery, and reporting. There are additional process steps of follow-up and lessons learned, each of which is presented in the following sections. Incident response is a key element of a security posture and must involve many different aspects of the business to properly respond. This is best built upon the foundation of a comprehensive **incident response policy** that details the roles and responsibilities of the organizational elements with respect to the process elements detailed in this chapter.

Tech Tip

Incident Response Defined

NIST Special Publication 800-61 defines an incident as the act of violating an explicit or implied security policy. This violation can be intentional, incidental, or accidental, with causes being wide and varied in nature. These include but are not limited to the following:

- *Attempts (either failed or successful) to gain unauthorized access to a system or its data*
- *Unwanted disruption or denial of service*
- *The unauthorized use of a system for the processing or storage of data*
- *Changes to system hardware, firmware, or software characteristics without the owner's knowledge, instruction, or consent*
- *Environmental changes that result in data loss or destruction*
- *Accidental actions that result in data loss or destruction*

Incident response activities at times are closely related to other IT activities involving IT operations. Incident response activities can be similar to disaster recovery and business continuity operations. Incident response activities are not performed in a vacuum but rather are integrally connected to many operational procedures, and this connection is key to overall system efficiency.

Preparation

Preparation is the phase of incident response that occurs before a specific incident. Preparation includes all the tasks needed to be organized and ready to respond to an incident. Incident response is the set of actions security personnel perform in response to a wide range of triggering events. These actions are varied, as they have to deal with a wide range of causes and consequences. The organization needs to establish the steps to be taken when an incident is discovered (or suspected); determine points of contact; train all employees and security professionals so they understand the steps to take and who to call; establish an incident response team; acquire the equipment necessary to detect, contain, and recover from an incident; establish the procedures and guidelines for the use of the equipment obtained; and train those who will use the equipment. Through the use of a structured framework coupled with properly prepared processes, incident response becomes a manageable task. Without proper preparation, this task can quickly become impossible or intractably expensive. Successful handling of an incident is a direct result of proper preparation.

> The old adage that "those who fail to prepare, prepare to fail" certainly applies to incident response. Without preparation, an organization's response to a security incident will be haphazard and ineffective. Establishing the processes and procedures to follow in advance of an event is critical.

Organization Preparation

Preparing an organization requires an incident response plan, both for the initial effort and for the maintenance of that effort. Over time, the organization shifts based on business objectives, personnel change, business efforts and focus change, new programs, and new capabilities; virtually any change can necessitate shifts in the incident response activities. At a minimum, the following items should be addressed and periodically reviewed in terms of incident response preparation:

- Develop and maintain comprehensive incident response policies and procedures
- Establish and maintain an incident response team
- Obtain top-level management support
    - Agree to ground rules/rules of engagement
    - Develop scenarios and responses
- Develop and maintain an incident response toolkit
    - System plans and diagrams
    - Network architectures
    - Critical asset lists
- Practice response procedures
    - Fire drills
    - Scenarios ("Who do you call?")

> **Tech Tip**
>
> **Preparing for Incident Detection**
>
> *To ensure that discovering incidents is not an ad hoc, hit-or-miss proposition, the organization needs to establish procedures that describe the process administrators must follow to monitor for possible security events. The tools for accomplishing this task are identified during the preparation phase, as well as any required training. The procedures governing the monitoring tools used should be established as part of the specific guidelines governing the use of the tools but should include references to the incident response policy.*

System Preparation

Systems require preparation for effective incident response efforts. Incident responders are dependent upon documentation for understanding hardware, software, and network layouts. Understanding how access control is employed, including specifics across all systems, is key when determining who can do what—a common incident response question. Understanding the logging methodology and architecture will make incident response data retrieval easier. All of these questions should be addressed in planning of diagrams, access control, and logging, to ensure that these critical security elements are capturing the correct information before an incident.

Having lists of critical files and their hash values, all stored offline, can make system investigation a more efficient process. In the end, when you are architecting a system, taking the time to plan for incident response processes will be crucial to a successful response once an incident occurs. Preparing systems for incident response is similar to preparing them for maintainability, so these efforts can yield regular dividends to the system owners. Determining the steps to isolate specific machines and services can be a complex endeavor and is one best accomplished before an incident, through the preparation phase.

Researching Vulnerabilities

After the hacker has a list of software running on the systems, they will start researching the Internet for vulnerabilities associated with that software. Numerous websites provide information on vulnerabilities in specific programs and operating systems. Understanding how hackers navigate systems is important because system administrators and security personnel can use the same steps to research potential vulnerabilities before a hacker strikes. This information is valuable to administrators who need to know what problems exist and how to patch them.

Incident Response Team

Establishing an incident response team is an essential step in the preparation phase. Although the initial response to an incident may be handled by an individual, such as a system administrator, the complete handling of an incident typically takes an entire team. An incident response team is a group of people who prepare for and respond to any emergency incident, such as a natural disaster or an interruption of business operations. A computer security incident response team in an organization typically includes key skilled members who bring a wide range of skills to bear in the response effort. Incident response teams are common in corporations as well as in public service organizations.

Incident response team members ideally are trained and prepared to fulfill the roles required by the specific situation (for example, to serve as incident commander in the event of a large-scale public emergency). Incident response teams are frequently dynamically sized to the scale and nature of an incident, and as the size of an incident grows and as more resources are drawn into the event, the command of the situation may shift through several phases. In a small-scale event, or in the case of a small firm, usually only a volunteer or ad hoc team may exist to respond. In cases where the incident spreads beyond the local control of the incident response team, higher-level resources through industry groups and government groups exist to assist in the incident. Advanced preparation in the form of contacting and establishing working relations with higher-level groups is an important preparation step.

The incident response team is a critical part of the incident response plan. Team membership will vary depending on the type of incident or suspected incident but may include the following members:

- Team lead
- Network/security analyst
- Internal and external subject matter experts (SMEs)
- Legal counsel
- Public affairs officer
- Security office contact

> **Tech Tip**
>
> **Incident Response Team Questions**
>
> *Well-executed plans are often well tested; when and how often do you test your response plans? How will your team operate undetected in an environment owned by the adversary? Do you have a backup, separate e-mail system that is external to the enterprise solution? Is it encrypted?*

In determining the specific makeup of the team for a specific incident, there are some general points to think about. The team needs a leader, preferably a higher-level manager who has the ability to obtain cooperation from employees as needed. It also needs a computer or network security analyst, since the assumption is that the team will be responding to a computer security incident. Specialists may be added to the team for specific hardware or software platforms as needed. The organization's legal counsel should be part of the team on at least a part-time or as-needed basis. The public affairs office should also be available on an as-needed basis, because it is responsible for formulating the public response should a security incident become public. The organization's security office should also be kept informed. It should designate a point of contact for the team in case criminal activity is suspected. In this case, care must be taken to preserve evidence should the organization decide to push for prosecution of the individuals.

This is by no means a complete list because each organization is different and needs to evaluate what the best mixture is for its own response team. Whatever the decision, the composition of the team, and how and when it will be formed, needs to be clearly addressed in the preparation phase of the incident response policy.

To function in a timely and efficient manner, ideally a team has already defined a protocol or set of actions to perform to mitigate the negative effects of most common forms of an incident. One key and often-overlooked member of the incident response team is the business. It may be an IT system being investigated, but the data, processes, and value all belong to the business, and the business is the element that understands the risk and value of what is under attack. Having key, knowledgeable business members on the incident response team is a necessity to ensure that the security actions remain aligned with the business goals and objectives of the organization.

Incident Response Plan

An **incident response plan** is documentation associated with the steps an organization performs in response to any situation determined to be abnormal in the operation of a computer system. The value of the plan lies in its ability to facilitate execution of the required response steps. Although individual causes may vary, there is a defined response methodology in the plan, and this guides responders to the correct actions. A well-documented and approved plan also assists in providing the necessary management permissions in advance, as opposed to lengthy decision cycles when the heat of an attack is on.

Two major elements play a role in determining the level of response. Information criticality is the primary determinant, and this comes from the data classification and the quantity of data involved. The loss of one administrator password is less serious than the loss of all of them, for example. The second factor involves a business decision on how this incident plays into current business operations. A series of breaches, whether minor or not, indicates a pattern that can have public relations and regulatory issues.

Documented Incident Types/Category Definitions

To assist in the planning of responses and to group the myriad possible incidents into a manageable set of categories, one step of the incident response planning process is to define incident types/categories. *Documented incident types/category definitions* provide planners and responders with a set number of preplanned scripts that can be applied quickly, minimizing repetitive approvals and process flows. Examples of categories are interruption of a service, malicious communication, data exfiltration, malware delivery, phishing attack, and so on. This list should be customized to meet the IT needs of each firm.

Roles and Responsibilities

It's critical to define the *roles and responsibilities* of the incident response team members. These roles and responsibilities may vary slightly based on the identified categories, but defining them before an incident occurs empowers the team to perform the necessary tasks during the time-sensitive aspects of an incident. Permissions to cut connections, change servers, or start/stop services are common examples of predefined actions that are best defined in advance to prevent time-consuming approvals during an actual incident.

Reporting Requirements/Escalation

Planning the desired **reporting requirements**, including escalation steps, is an important part of the operational plan for an incident. Who will speak about the incident and to whom? How does the information flow? Who needs to be involved? When does the issue escalate to higher levels of management? These are all questions best handled in the calm of a pre-incident planning meeting where the procedures are crafted rather than determined on the fly as an incident is occurring.

Cyber-Incident Response Teams

Typically more than one person will respond to an incident. Defining the cyber-incident response team, including identifying key membership and backup members, is a task that needs to be done prior to an incident occurring. Once a response begins, trying to find personnel to do tasks only slows down the function and in many cases makes it unmanageable. The planning aspect of incident response needs to define who is on the team, whether it's a dedicated team or a group of situational volunteers, and what their duties are.

Exercise

You don't really know how well a plan is crafted until it is tested. **Exercises** come in many forms and functions, and doing a tabletop exercise where planning and preparation steps are tested is an important final step in the planning process.

Incident Identification/Detection

An **incident** is defined as a situation that departs from normal, routine operations. What differentiates an incident from an incident that requires a formal response from the incident response team is an important triage step performed at the beginning of the discovery of an abnormal condition. A single failed login is technically an incident, but if it is followed by a correct login, then it is not of any consequence. In fact, this could even be considered as normal. However, having 10,000 failed attempts on a system, or failures across a large number of accounts, is distinctly different and may be worthy of further investigation.

Detection

Of course, an incident response team can't begin an investigation until a suspected incident has been detected. At that point, the detection phase of the incident response policy kicks in. One of the first jobs of the incident response team is to determine whether an actual security incident has occurred. Many things can be misinterpreted as a possible security incident. For example, a software bug in an application may cause a user to lose a file, and the user may blame this on a virus or similar malicious software. The incident response team must investigate each reported incident and treat it as a potential security incident until it can determine whether it is or isn't. This means that your organization will want to respond initially with a limited response team before wasting a lot of time having the full team respond. This is the initial step to take when a report is received that a possible incident has been detected.

Security incidents can take a variety of forms, and who discovers the incident will vary as well. One of the groups most likely to discover an incident is the team of network and security administrators that runs devices such as the organization's firewalls and intrusion detection systems.

Another common incident is a virus. Several packages are available that can help an organization detect potential virus activity or other malicious code. Administrators will often be the ones to notice something is amiss, but so might an average user who has been hit by the virus.

Social engineering is a common technique used by potential intruders to acquire information that may be useful in gaining access to computer systems, networks, or the physical facilities that house them. Anybody in the organization can be the target of a social engineering attack, so all employees need to know what to be looking for regarding this type of attack. In fact, the target might not even be one of your organization's employees—it could be a contractor, such as somebody on the custodial staff or nighttime

Detecting that a security event is occurring or has occurred is not necessarily an easy matter. In certain situations, such as the activation of a malicious payload for a virus or worm that deletes critical files, it will be obvious that an event has occurred. In other situations, such as where an individual has penetrated your system and has been slowly copying critical files without changing or destroying anything, the event may take a lot longer to detect. Often, the first indication that a security event has occurred might be a user or administrator noticing that something is "funny" about the system or its response.

security staff. Whatever the type of security incident suspected, and no matter who suspects it, a reporting procedure needs to be in place for the employees to use when an incident is detected. Everybody needs to know who to call should they suspect something, and everybody needs to know what to do. A common technique is to develop a reporting template that can be supplied to an individual who suspects an incident so that the necessary information is gathered in a timely manner.

Identification

As discussed previously, an incident is defined as any situation that departs from normal, routine operations. Whether an incident is important or not is the first point of decision as part of an incident response process. The act of **identification** is coming to a decision that the information related to the incident is worthy of further investigation by the IR team and, in addition, what aspects of the IR team are needed to respond. For example, an e-mail incident may require different response team members than an attack on web services or Active Directory (AD).

A key first step is in the processing of information and the determination of whether to invoke incident response processes. Incident information can come from a wide range of sources, including logs, employees, help desk calls, system monitoring, security devices, and more. The challenge is to detect that something other than simple common errors that are routine is occurring. When evidence accumulates, or in some cases specific items such as security device logs indicate a potential incident, the next step is to escalate the situation to the incident response team.

Tech Tip

Initial Response Errors

Mistakes such as these are common during initial response:

- *Failure to document findings appropriately*
- *Failure to notify or provide accurate information to decision-makers*
- *Failure to record and control access to digital evidence*
- *Waiting too long before reporting*
- *Underestimating the scope of evidence that may be found*

Initial Response

Although there is no such thing as a typical incident, for any incident there is a series of questions that can be answered to form a proper **initial response**. Regardless of the source, the following items are important to determine during an initial response:

- Current time and date
- Who/what is reporting the incident
- Nature of the incident
- When the incident occurred
- Hardware/software involved
- Point of contact for involved personnel

The purpose of an initial response is to begin the incident response action and place it on a proper pathway toward success. The initial response must support the goals of the information security program. If something is critical, treating it as routine would be a mistake, so triage with respect to information criticality is important. The initial response must also be aligned with the business practices and objectives. Triage with respect to current business imperatives and conditions is important. The initial response actions need to be designed to comply with administrative and legal policies as well as to support decisions with regard to civil, administrative, or criminal investigations/actions. For these purposes, maintaining a forensically sound process from the beginning is important. It is also important that the information is delivered accurately and expeditiously to the appropriate decision-makers so that future actions can be timely. One of the greatest tools to achieve all of these goals is a simple and efficient process, so establishing fewer steps that are clear and clean is preferred. Complexity in the initial response process only leads to issues later because of delays, confusion, and incomplete information.

First Responder

A cyber first responder must do as much as possible to control damage or loss of evidence. Obviously, as time passes, evidence can be tampered with or destroyed. Look around on the desk, on the Rolodex, under the keyboard, in desktop storage areas, and on cubicle bulletin boards for any information that might be relevant. Secure optical discs, flash memory cards, USB drives, tapes, and other removable media. Request copies of logs as soon as possible. Most ISPs will protect logs that could be subpoenaed. Take photos (some localities require the use of Polaroid photos because they are more difficult to modify without obvious tampering) or video. Include photos of operating computer screens and hardware components from multiple angles. Be sure to photograph internal components before removing them for analysis. The first responder can do much to prevent damage or can cause significant loss by digitally altering evidence, even inadvertently. Collecting data should be done in a forensically sound nature (see Chapter 23 for details), and be sure to pay attention to recording time values so time offsets can be calculated.

> **Tech Tip**
>
> **Common Technical Errors**
>
> *Common technical mistakes during initial response include the following:*
>
> - *Altering time/date stamps on evidence systems*
> - *"Killing" rogue processes*
> - *Patching the system*
> - *Not recording the steps taken on the system*
> - *Not acting passively*
>
> *Any of these activities can alter the state of the system making the investigation more difficult, if not impossible.*

Containment/Incident Isolation

Once the incident response team has determined that an incident has occurred and requires a response, the first step is to contain the incident and prevent it from spreading. If this is a virus or worm that is attacking database servers, then the protection of uninfected servers is paramount. **Containment** is the set of actions taken to constrain the incident to the minimal number of machines. This preserves as much of production as possible and ultimately makes handling the incident easier. This can be complex because in many cases to contain the problem, one has to fully understand the problem, its root cause, and the vulnerabilities involved.

Containment and Eradication

Once the incident response team has determined that an incident most likely has occurred, it must attempt to quickly contain the problem. At this point or soon after containment begins, depending on the severity of the incident, management needs to decide whether the organization intends to prosecute the individual who has caused the incident (in which case collection and preservation of evidence is necessary) or simply wants to restore operations as quickly as possible without regard to possibly destroying evidence. In certain circumstances, management might not have a choice, such as if specific regulations or laws require it to report particular incidents. If management makes the decision to prosecute, specific procedures need to be followed in handling potential evidence. Individuals trained in forensics should be used in this case.

The incident response team must decide how to address containment as soon as it has determined that an actual incident has occurred. If an intruder is still connected to the organization's system, one response is to disconnect from the Internet until the system can be restored and vulnerabilities can be patched. This, however, means that your organization is not accessible to customers over the Internet during that time, which may result in lost revenue. Another response might be to stay connected and attempt to determine the origin of the intruder. A decision will need to be made as to which is more important for your organization. Your incident response policy should identify who is authorized to make this decision.

Other possible containment activities might include adding filtering rules or modifying existing rules on firewalls, routers, and intrusion detection systems; updating antivirus software; and removing specific pieces of hardware or halting specific software applications. If an intruder has gained access through a specific account, disabling or removing that account may also be necessary.

Tech Tip

Incident Response Team and Connection to SOC

In many organizations, a group called the Security Operations Center (SOC) exists to manage potential security incidents. Security monitoring controls across the enterprise forward information to the SOC for aggregation, assignment, and handling. The personnel in the SOC are set up in a series of tiers to efficiently handle issues requiring escalation:

- *Tier 1: Alert Analyst (monitors alerts and if needed escalates after analysis)*
- *Tier 2: Incident Responder (performs investigations and remediation)*
- *Tier 3: Subject Matter Experts (typically few in number, handle the tough cases)*

Once the immediate problems have been contained, the incident response team needs to address the cause of the incident. If the incident is the result of a vulnerability that was not patched, the patch must be obtained, tested, and applied. Accounts may need to be disabled or passwords may need to be changed. Complete reloading of the operating system might be necessary if the intruder has been in the system for an unknown length of time or has modified system files. Determining when an intruder first gained access to your system or network is critical in determining how far back to go in restoring the system or network.

Quarantine

One method of isolating a machine is through a quarantine process. **Quarantine** is a process of isolating an object from its surroundings, preventing normal access methods. The machine may be allowed to run, but its connection to other machines is broken in a manner to prevent the spread of infection. Quarantine can be accomplished through a variety of mechanisms, including the erection of firewalls restricting communication between machines. This can be a fairly complex process, but if properly configured in advance, the limitations of the quarantine operation can allow the machine to continue to run for diagnostic purposes, even if it no longer processes a workload.

Device Removal

A more extreme response is device removal. In the event that a machine becomes compromised, it is simply removed from production and replaced. When device removal entails the physical change of hardware, this is a resource-intensive operation. The reimaging of a machine can be a time-consuming and difficult endeavor. The advent of virtual machines (VMs) changes this entirely, as the provisioning of virtual images on hardware can be accomplished in a much quicker fashion.

Escalation and Notification

One key decision point in initial response is that of escalation. When a threshold of information becomes known to an operator and the operator decides to escalate the situation, the incident response process moves to a notification and escalation phase. Not all incidents are of the same risk profile, and incident response efforts should map to the actual risk level associated with the incident. When the incident response team is notified of a potential incident, its first steps are to confirm the existence, scope, and magnitude of the event and then respond accordingly. This is typically done through a two-step escalation process, where a minimal quick-response team begins and then adds members as necessitated by the issue.

Assessing the risk associated with an incident is an important first step. If the characteristics of an incident include a large number of packets destined for different services on a machine (an attack commonly referred to as a port scan), then the actions needed are different from those needed to respond to a large number of packets destined to a single machine service. Port scans are common, and to a degree relatively harmless, whereas port flooding can result in denial of service. Determining the specific downstream risks is important in prioritizing response actions.

Strategy Formulation

The response to an incident will be highly dependent upon the particular circumstances of the intrusion. There are many paths one can take in the steps associated with an incident; the challenge is in choosing the best steps in each case. During the preparation stage, a wide range of scenarios can be examined, allowing time to formulate strategies. Even after an incident response team has planned a series of strategies to respond to various scenarios, determining how to employ those preplanned strategies to proper effect still depends on the circumstances of a particular incident. A variety of factors should be considered in the planning and deployment of strategies, including, but not limited to, the following:

- How critical are the impacted systems?
- How sensitive is the data?
- What is the potential overall dollar loss involved/rate of loss?
- How much downtime can be tolerated?

Tech Tip

Playbooks

Playbooks are a set of step-by-step approved practices to aid analysts in beginning an investigation and/or responding to an uncommon event. Designed with checklists, and structured to match the automated systems data flows, playbooks reduce the cognitive load necessary to manage an incident. And because they have been planned and approved in advance, they alleviate the spur-of-the-moment scrambling when the clock is ticking on an active event. Playbooks are the best practice solution to managing incidents.

- Who are the perpetrators?
- What is the skill level of the attacker?
- Does the incident have adverse publicity potential?

These pieces of information provide boundaries for the upcoming investigations. There are still numerous issues that need to be determined with respect to the upcoming investigation. Addressing these issues helps provide focal points during the investigation.

- Restore normal operations
  - Offline recovery?
  - Online recovery?
- Determine public relations play
  - "To spin or not to spin?"
- Determine probable attacker
  - Internal: Handle internally or prosecute?
  - External: Prosecute?
  - Involve law enforcement?
- Determine type of attack
  - DoS, theft, vandalism, policy violation?
  - Ongoing intrusion?
  - Pivoting?
- Classify victim system
  - Critical server/application?
  - Number of users?
  - What other systems are affected?

Using the answers to these questions helps the team determine the necessary steps in the upcoming investigation phase. Although it is impossible to account for all circumstances, this level of strategy can greatly assist in scoping the work ahead during the investigation phase.

Tech Tip

Investigation Best Practice

The first rule of incident response investigations is "Do no harm." If the investigation itself causes issues for the business, how is this different from a business perspective than the original attack vector? In fact, in advanced threats, the attackers take great care not to impact the system or business operations in any way that could lead to their discovery. It is important for the response team to exercise extreme caution and to do no harm, lest they make future investigations impractical or deemed to be not worth pursuing.

Investigation

The true investigation phase of an incident is a multistep, multiparty event. With the exception of very simple events, most incidents will involve multiple machines and potentially impact the business in multiple ways.

The primary objective of the investigative phase is to make the following determinations:

- What happened
- What systems are affected
- What was compromised
- What was the vulnerability
- Who did it (if possible to determine)
- What are the recovery/remediation options

Although the list appears daunting, this is where the real work of incident response occurs. It will take a team effort; partly because of workload, partly because of specialized skills, and partly because the entire effort is being performed in a race against time.

Duplication

Duplication of drives is a common forensics process. It is important to have accurate copies and associated hash values so that any analysis is performed under proper conditions. Forensic disk duplication is necessary to ensure all data, including metadata, is properly captured and analyzed as part of the overall process.

Network Monitoring

To monitor network flow data, including who is talking to whom, one source of information is NetFlow data. NetFlow is a protocol/standard for the collection of network metadata on the flows of network traffic. NetFlow is now an IETF standard and allows for unidirectional captures of communication metadata. NetFlow can identify both common and unique data flows, and in the case of incident response, typically the new and unique NetFlow patterns are of most interest to incident responders.

> **Tech Tip**
>
> **NetFlow Data**
>
> *A flow is unidirectional, so bidirectional flow would be recorded as two separate flows. NetFlow data is defined by these seven unique keys:*
>
> - *Source IP address*
> - *Destination IP address*
> - *Source port*
> - *Destination port*
> - *Layer 3 protocol*
> - *TOS byte (DSCP)*
> - *Input interface (ifIndex)*

Eradication

Once a problem has been contained to a set footprint, the next step is eradication. **Eradication** involves removing the problem, and in today's complex system environment, this may mean rebuilding a clean machine. A key part of operational eradication is the prevention of reinfection. Presumably, the system that existed before the problem occurred would be prone to a repeat infection; thus, this needs to be specifically guarded against. One of the strongest value propositions for virtual machines is the ability to rebuild quickly, making the eradication step relatively easy.

Recovery

After the issue has been eradicated, the recovery process begins. At this point, the investigation is complete and documented. **Recovery** is the returning of the asset into the business function. Eradication, the previous step, removed the problem, but in most cases the eradicated system will be isolated. The recovery process includes the steps necessary to return the systems and applications to operational status.

Recovery is an important step in all incidents. One of the first rules is to not trust a system that has been compromised, and this includes all aspects of an operating system. Whether there is known destruction or not, the safe path is one where the recovery step includes reconstruction of affected machines. Recovery efforts from an incident involve several specific elements. First, the cause of the incident needs to be determined and resolved. This is done through an incident response mechanism. Attempting to recover before the cause is known and corrected will commonly result in a continuation of the problem. Second, the data, if sensitive and subject to misuse, needs to be examined in the context of how it was lost, who would have access, and what business measures need to be taken to mitigate specific business damage as a result of the release. This may involve the changing of business plans if the release makes them suspect or subject to adverse impacts.

Recovery can be a two-step process. First, the essential business functions can be recovered, enabling business operations to resume. The second step is the complete restoration of all services and operations. Because of the difficulty and uncertainty involved in repairing systems, most best practices today involve reconstituting the underlying system and then transferring the operational data. Staging the recovery operations in a prioritized fashion allows a graceful return to an operating condition.

Restoration can be done in a wide variety of ways. For many systems, the reconstitution of a clean operating system can restore a system. This type of restoration requires a significant amount of preparation. Having a clean version of each of your assets provides for this type of restoration effort. Recovery sounds simple, but in large-scale incidents, the number of machines can be significant. Add to this the chance of reinfection as machines are restored. This means that simply replacing the machine with a clean machine is not sufficient; rather, the replacement needs protection against reinfection.

There are many different incident response processes in the information security space. For the CompTIA Security+ exam, you should know the steps of their process:

- Preparation
- Identification
- Containment
- Eradication
- Recovery
- Lessons learned

The other challenge in large-scale recovery events is the sequencing of the effort. When there are many machines to be restored and the restoration process takes time and resources, scheduling is essential. Setting up a prioritized schedule is one of the steps that needs to be considered in the planning process. The time to do this type of planning is before the hectic pace of an incident occurs.

A key aspect in many incidents is that of external communications. Having a communications expert who is familiar with dealing with the press and has the language nuances necessary to convey the correct information and not inflame the situation is essential to the success of any communication plan. Many firms attempt to use their legal counsel for this, but generally speaking, the legally precise language used by an attorney is not useful from a PR standpoint, and a more nuanced communicator may provide a better image. In many cases of crisis management, it is not the crisis that determines the final costs but the reaction to and communication of details after the initial crisis.

Reporting

After the system has been restored, the incident response team creates a report of the incident. Detailing what was discovered, how it was discovered, what was done, and the results, this report acts as a corporate memory and can be used for future incidents. Having a knowledge base of previous incidents and the actions used is a valuable resource because it is in the context of the particular enterprise. These reports also allow a mechanism to close the loop with management over the incident and, most importantly, provide a road map of the actions that can be used in the future to prevent events of identical or similar nature.

Part of the report will be recommendations, if appropriate, to change existing policies and procedures, including disaster recovery and business continuity. The similarity in objectives makes a natural overlap, and the cross-pollination between these operations is important to make all processes as efficient as possible.

Lessons Learned

A post-mortem session should collect **lessons learned** and assign action items to correct weaknesses and to suggest ways to improve. There is a famous quote about those who fail to learn from history are destined to repeat it. The lessons learned portion serves two distinct lesson sets. The first determines what went wrong and allowed the incident to occur in the first place. The second is that a failure to block this means a sure repeat.

Once the excitement of the incident is over and operations have been restored to their pre-incident state, it is time to take care of a few last items. Senior-level management must be informed about what occurred and what was done to address it. An after-action report should be created to outline what happened and how it was addressed. Recommendations for improving processes and policies should be incorporated so that a repeat incident will not occur. If prosecution of the individual responsible is desired, additional time will be spent helping law enforcement agencies and possibly testifying in court. Training material may also need to be developed or modified as part of the new or modified policies and procedures.

In the reporting process, a critical assessment of what went right, what went wrong, what can be improved, and what should be continued is prepared as a form of lessons learned. This is a critical part of self-improvement and is not meant to place blame but rather to assist in future prevention. Having things go wrong in a complex environment is part of normal operations; having repeat failures that are preventable is not. The key to the lessons learned section of the report is to make the necessary changes so that a repeat event will not occur. Because many incidents are a result of attackers using known methods, once the attack patterns are known in an enterprise and methods exist to mitigate them, then it is the task of the entire enterprise to take the necessary actions to mitigate future events.

Incident Response Team

The *computer (cyber) incident response team (CIRT)* is composed of the personnel who are designated to respond to an incident. The incident response plan should identify the membership and backup members, prior to an incident occurring. Once an incidence response begins, trying to find personnel to perform tasks only slows down the function, and in many cases would make it unmanageable. Whether it's a dedicated team or a group of situational volunteers, the planning aspect of incident response needs to address the topic of who is on the team and what their duties are.

Management needs to appoint the team members and ensure that they have time to be prepared for service. The team leader is typically a member of management who fully understands both the enterprise IT environment and IR process because their job is to lead the team with respect to the process. Subject matter experts (SMEs) on the various systems that are involved provide the actual working portion of the team, often in concert with operational IT personnel for each system. The team is responsible for all phases of the incident response process, which was covered previously in the chapter.

A critical step in the incident response planning process is to define the roles and responsibilities of the incident response team members. These roles and responsibilities may vary slightly based on the identified categories of incident, but defining them before an incident occurs empowers the team to perform the necessary tasks during the time-sensitive aspects of an incident. Permissions to cut connections, change servers, and start/stop services are common examples of actions that are best defined in advance to prevent time-consuming approvals during an actual incident.

Several specific roles are unique to all IR teams: the team leader, the team communicator, and an appropriate bevy of SMEs. The team leader manages the overall IR process, so they need to be a member of management so they can navigate the corporate chain of command. The team communicator is the spokesperson for the team to all other groups, inside and outside the company. IR team members are typically SMEs, and their time is valuable and should be spent on task. The team communicator shields these members from the time-consuming press interview portion as much as possible.

Exercises

One really doesn't know how well a plan is crafted until it is tested. Exercises come in many forms and functions, and doing a tabletop exercise where the planning and preparation steps are tested is an important final step in the planning process. Having a process and a team assembled is not enough unless the team has practiced the process on the systems of the enterprise.

Tabletop

As previously mentioned in the chapter, a *tabletop exercise* is one that is designed for the participants to walk through all the steps of a process, ensuring all elements are covered and that the plan does not forget a key dataset or person. This is typically a fairly high-level review, designed to uncover missing or poorly covered elements and gaps in communications, both between people and systems. This tabletop exercise is a critical final step because it validates the planning covered the needed elements. The steps in the exercise should be performed by the principal leaders of the business and IT functions to ensure that all steps are correct. Although this will take time from senior members, given the criticality of this business process, as it is being done for operations determined to be vital to the business, it hardly seems like overkill.

This exercise aspect is not a one-time thing; it should be repeated after major changes to systems that impact the continuity of the operations plan or other major changes such as personnel turnover. As such, major corporations regularly exercise these types of systems on a predetermined schedule, rotating through day and night shifts, primary and backup personnel, and various systems.

Walkthroughs

Walkthroughs examine the actual steps that take place associated with a process, procedure, or event. Walkthroughs are in essence a second set of eyes, where one party either explains or demonstrates the steps to perform a task while a second person observes. The observer's job is to examine the activity for compliance with applicable policies and directives. Is the task being accomplished correctly in terms of the process? Are the proper controls, processes, and procedures being followed? Walkthroughs can be done on elements such as computer code, where the person who wrote the code shows it to others on the team and walks them through the program, line by line. Explaining how it works and showing how it is coded allows for others to examine both syntax and process flow and provide valuable feedback on the code before it is implemented in a project. Having a supervisor observe the process for any function enables an independent determination as to whether their actions are in line with corporate security policies. Because the person doing the work relies upon training and repetitive practice, a periodic walkthrough provides evidence that proper procedures are actually being followed. Walkthroughs are commonly used by audit personnel to ensure proper processes are being followed.

Simulations

A *simulation* is an approximation of the operation of a process or system that is designed to represent the actual system operations over a period of time. The simulation can be used in place of systems or elements that are not practical to replicate during an exercise, such as a complex element like a chemical plant or a time-consuming activity like a backup operation. Simulations are used in exercises to provide context for the participants without the expense associated with the use of a real system.

The different types of exercise elements, tabletop exercises, walkthroughs, and simulations can be used together as part of an exercise package.

Stakeholder Management

Stakeholders are the parties that have an interest in a process or the outcome of a process. Stakeholders can be internal or external to an organization. With respect to incident response scenarios, all levels of management and many different business functions can be involved internally, including corporate, legal, communications, liaisons with regulators, customer support elements, and the operations personnel. Externally, there can be issues that involve vendors and customers, and there may be reporting requirements to regulators and other outside groups. With this wide range of involved parties, having a structure to manage communication with the various stakeholders is important to keep them properly informed and to separate the communication tasks from the operational tasks associated with responding to the incident. Having a *stakeholder management* process, including defined personnel roles and responsibilities, is essential for the management of the stakeholders and their relationships during incidents.

Communication Plan

Planning the desired reporting requirements, including escalation steps, is an important part of the operational plan for an incident. Who will talk for the incident response team and to whom, and what will they say? How does the information flow? Who needs to be involved? When does the issue escalate to higher levels of management? These are all questions best handled in the calm of a pre-incident planning meeting, where the procedures are crafted, rather than on the fly as an incident is occurring. A *communication plan* as part of the incident response effort that answers the preceding questions and defines responsibilities for communication is a key element to be developed during the preparation phase.

Reporting requirements can refer to industry, regulatory, and statutory requirements in addition to internal communications. Understanding the reporting requirements to external entities is part of the responsibility of the communications lead on the team. Having the correct information in the hands of the correct people at the correct time is an essential part of reporting, and a prime responsibility of the communications lead on the team.

Data Sources

A modern enterprise has many data sources that can aid in the proper running of the enterprise. Some of these sources contain normal operational data that represents a normal baseline. Other data elements indicate a departure from normal conditions. Collecting all of this data, and then processing it to determine normal and abnormal elements is done through the use of tools such as a security information and event management (SIEM) system or a security orchestration, automation, and response (SOAR) system. These systems assist the SOC personnel in managing the flow of data into streams that provide for the investigation of abnormal conditions.

Log Files

Log files are a primary source of information during an investigation. Software can record in log files a wide range of information as it is operating. From self-health checks, to error-related data, to operational metadata supporting the events that are happening on a system, all this data ends up in log files. These log files act as a historical record of what happened on a system. Log files require configuration because if you don't log an event when it happens, you can't go back in time to capture it. By the same token, logging everything creates too much data—data that must be waded through during an investigation. The key is balance: record what you need to know to make determinations—no more, no less.

Network

Networks are filled with equipment that can provide valuable log information. Firewalls, routers, load balancers, and switches can provide a wealth of information as to what is happening on the network. *Network logs* tend to have a duplication issue, as packets can traverse several devices, giving multiple, nearly identical records. Removing duplicate as well as extraneous data is the challenge with network logging, but the payoff can be big because proper logging can make tracing attackers easier.

System

Virtually every operating system creates *system logs*. These logs can provide a very detailed history of what actions were performed on a system. Login records that indicate failed logins can be important, but so can entries that show login success. Multiple failures followed by a success can be suspicious, especially when the number of failures and timing precludes a human operator typing. What about access permission failures? These can indicate an attempt to perform unauthorized activity. What about access successes? Logging these would swamp the database with a large number of irrelevant records. This is one of the challenges of logging things on a system—which logs produce meaningful answers and which just produce noise? Also, realize that the decision to log has to happen before an event occurs; in other words, you can't go back and have a do-over if you fail to log a crucial piece of evidence.

Application

Application logs are generated by the applications themselves as they run. Some applications provide extensive logging; others minimal or even no logging. Some applications allow configuration of what is logged; others do not. Many server applications—web servers, mail servers, and database servers—have extensive logging capability, including which user performed which action and when. Other systems merely log when they start and stop operations and may log errors.

Security

Security logs are logs kept by the OS for metadata associated with security operations. In Microsoft Windows, literally hundreds of different events can be configured to write to the Security log—system starting, system shutting down, permission failures, logins, failed logins, changing the system time, a new process creation, scheduled task changes, and more. These logs can be important, but to be important they need to be tuned to collect the information needed. In Windows, this is typically done through group policy objects. The driving force for what needs to be recorded is the system's audit policy, a statement about what records need to be kept.

The Windows Event Viewer is used to look at Windows logs. The System log displays information related to the operating system. The Application log provides data related to applications that are run on the system. The Security log provides information regarding the success and failure of attempted logins as well as security-related audit events.

Web

Web servers respond to specific, formatted requests for resources with responses, whether in the form of a web page or an error—and all of this activity can be logged. Web servers are specifically deployed to do this task, but they are also targets of attacks—attacks that try to run malicious scripts, perform DDoS attacks, perform injection and cross-site scripting attacks, and more. Web log files can help identify when these activities are occurring.

DNS

DNS logs, when enabled, can contain a record for every query and response. This can be a treasure trove of information for an investigator because it can reveal malware calling out to its command-and-control server, or data transfers to non-company locations. Analysis of DNS logs can show IP addresses and domain names that your systems should be communicating with as well as ones they shouldn't be communicating with. In cases where an attacker or malware is doing the communication, these communication channels may be next to invisible on the network, but the DNS system, as part of the network architecture, can log the activity. This is one of the reasons why DNS logs are some of the most valuable logs to import into a SIEM system.

Authentication

Authentication logs contain information about successful and failed authentication attempts. The most common source of authentication log information comes from the system's security logs, but additional sources exist as well. With the expansion of multifactor authentication services, applications that manage second factors also have logs. These logs are important, as they can show anomalies such as proper primary login data but failed second-factor data, indicating that the primary authentication information may have been disclosed.

Dump Files

Dump files are copies of what was in memory at a point in time—typically a point when some failure occurred. Dump files can be created by the operating system (OS) when the OS crashes, and these files can be analyzed to determine the cause of the crash. Dump files can also be created by several utilities and then shipped off to a third party for analysis when an application is not behaving correctly. Dump files can contain a wide range of sensitive information, including passwords, cryptographic keys, and more. Care should be taken when handling dump files, and especially when sharing them for analysis. Several security vendors have tools that assist in the securing of sensitive information in dump files, but the risk of secret disclosure is still present. Because of the size and complexity involved in interpreting dump files, they are not a common investigative tool, except for narrow investigations such as why a system is crashing.

Attackers, on the other hand, love to get dump files and peruse them; therefore, setting systems to not persist dump files is common to prevent hackers from crashing a server and then coming back to get the subsequent dump file.

VoIP and Call Managers

Voice over IP (VoIP) solutions and *call manager* applications enable a wide range of audio and video communication services over the Internet. These systems can log a variety of data, including call information such as the number called (to and from), time of the call, and duration of the call. These records are called call detail records (CDRs). When combined with video and audio systems using VoIP, these logs can be enhanced with information as to how the information was encoded, including the codecs involved and the resolutions.

Session Initiation Protocol (SIP) Traffic

The Session Initiation Protocol (SIP) is a text-based protocol used for signaling voice, video, and messaging applications over IP. SIP provides information for initiating, maintaining, and terminating real-time sessions. *SIP traffic* logs are typically in the SIP Common Log Format (CLF), which mimics web server logs and captures the details associated with a communication (such as to and from).

Syslog/Rsyslog/Syslog-ng

Syslog stands for System Logging Protocol and is a standard protocol used in Linux systems to send system log or event messages to a specific server, called a syslog server. *Rsyslog* is an open source variant of syslog that follows the syslog specifications but also provides additional features such as content-based filtering. *Syslog-ng* is another open source implementation of the syslog standard. Syslog-ng also extends the original syslog model with elements such as content filtering. A primary advantage of syslog-ng over syslog and rsyslog is that it can tag, classify, and correlate in real time, which can improve SIEM performance. For Linux-based systems, these implementations are the de facto standard for managing log files. As log files are one of the primary artifact sources, investigations make significant use of log files and syslog-captured data to build histories of what actually happened on a system.

> Syslog, rsyslog, and syslog-ng all move data into log files on a log server. Rsyslog and syslog-ng both extend the original syslog standard by adding capabilities such as content filtering, log enrichment, and correlation of data elements into higher-level events.

Journalctl

On Linux systems, the initial daemon that launches the system is called systemd. When systemd creates log files, it does so through the systemd-journald service. Journalctl is the command that is used to view these logs. To see the various command options for journalctl, you should consult the man pages on the system. Here is an example of a journalctl command to view logs for a given system service:

```
journalctl -u ssh
```

> You should understand the differences between journalctl and syslog. Journalctl is the command to examine logs on a server. Syslog (and the variants rsyslog and syslog-ng) is used to move logs to a log server and sometimes to manipulate the log file entries in transit.

NXLog

NXLog is a multiplatform log management tool designed to assist in the use of log data during investigations. This tool suite is capable of handling syslog-type data as well as other log formats, including Microsoft Windows. It has advanced capabilities to enrich log files through context-based lookups, correlations, and rule-based enrichments. NXLog has connectors to most major applications and can act as a log collector, forwarder, aggregator, and investigative tool for searching through log data. As logs are one of the most used data sources in investigations, tools such as NXLog can enable investigators to identify security issues, policy violations, and operational problems in systems.

Bandwidth Monitors

Bandwidth monitors are utilities designed to measure network bandwidth utilization over time. Bandwidth monitors can provide information as to how much bandwidth is being utilized, by service type, and how much remains. Bandwidth monitors can log this information over time and provide a historical record of network congestion problems, including by type of traffic in quality of service–enforced networks.

NetFlow/sFlow

NetFlow and *sFlow* are protocols designed to capture information about packet flows (that is, a sequence of related packets) as they traverse a network. NetFlow is a proprietary standard from Cisco. Flow data is generated by the network devices themselves, including routers and switches. The data that is collected and shipped off to data collectors is a simple set of metadata—source and destination IP addresses, source and destination ports, if any (ICMP, for example, doesn't use ports), and the protocol. NetFlow does this for all packets, while sFlow (sampled flow) does a statistical sampling. On high-throughput networks, NetFlow can generate large quantities of data—data that requires de-duplication. However, having all that data will catch the rare security event packets. sFlow is more suited for statistical traffic monitoring. Cisco added statistical monitoring to NetFlow on its high-end infrastructure routers to deal with the traffic volumes.

> Both NetFlow and sFlow collect packets from routers and switches. NetFlow data can be useful in intrusion investigations. sFlow is used primarily for traffic management, although it will help with DDoS attacks.

IPFIX

Internet Protocol Flow Information Export (IPFIX) is an IETF protocol that's the answer to the proprietary Cisco NetFlow standard. IPFIX is based on NetFlow version 9 and is highly configurable using a series of templates. The primary purpose of IPFIX is to provide a central monitoring station with information about the state of the network. IPFIX is a push-based protocol, where the sender sends the reports and receives no response from the receiver.

Metadata

Metadata is data about data. A file entry on a storage system has the file contents plus metadata, including the filename, creation, access, and update timestamps, size, and more. Microsoft Word files have the document contents and additional fields of associated metadata. JPEGs have the same fields of metadata, including the location of the capture and the device used to create the images. Tons of metadata exists on a system, and in many cases individual elements of metadata need to be correlated with other metadata to determine activities. Take, for example, when a USB is inserted into a system. This creates metadata, but for what user? Separate metadata can tell you who was logged in at that time. Collecting, analyzing, and correlating metadata are all part of almost every investigation.

Remember that everything digital contains metadata, and correlating metadata is a part of almost every investigation.

E-Mail

E-mail is half metadata, half message. For short messages, the metadata can be larger than the message itself. E-mail metadata is in the header of the e-mail and includes routing information, the sender, receiver, timestamps, subject, and other information associated with the delivery of the message. The header of an e-mail includes information for the handling of the e-mail between mail user agents (MUAs), mail transfer agents (MTAs), and mail delivery agents (MDAs), as well as a host of other details. The entire message is sent via plain ASCII text, with attachments included using Base64 encoding. The e-mail header provides all of the information associated with an e-mail as it moves from sender to receiver. E-mail is covered in depth in Chapter 17.

Mobile

Mobile devices generate, store, and transmit metadata. Common fields include when a call or text was made, whether it was an incoming or outgoing transmission, the duration of the call or the text message's length (in characters), and the phone numbers of the senders and recipients. Note that the message or audio signal is not part of the metadata, but how much can you get from the metadata alone? More than meets the eye. For example, numbers can be looked up, providing the identities of senders and receivers (such as a conversation with the doctor's office, followed by a call from a pharmacy).

Other sources of metadata include things like Wi-Fi access points connected to, GPS data in application logs, whether the device has a camera, and EXIF data (discussed later in the "File" section).

Web

The Web provides a means of moving information between browsers and servers. There are a variety of protocols involved and a variety of sources of metadata. The web pages themselves are full of metadata, and browsers store different metadata covering what pages were accessed and when. Browser metadata is a commonly used source of forensic information, because entries of what and when a browser has accessed data can be important. Did a user go to a specific web page? Did they use a web-based e-mail client, exposing actual e-mail information as well as the fact they used e-mail? How long were they on a site? If a user hits a site that displays an image tagged by one of the security appliances, did they stay on that page or immediately go to a different site? There can be a wealth of user behavior information with respect to web browsing.

File

File metadata comes in two flavors: system and application. The filesystem uses metadata to keep track of the filename as well as the timestamps associated with last access, creation, and last write. The system metadata will include items needed by the OS, such as ownership information, parent object, permissions, and security descriptors.

Application metadata in a file is part of the file data field and is used by the application. For instance, a Microsoft Word document contains a lot of metadata, including fields for author, company, number of times edited, last print time, and so on. Currently, Word has over 90 fields of metadata that can be used/modified by a user. A JPEG file, on the other hand, has metadata that's typically expressed in the form of EXIF data. The Exchangeable image file (EXIF) format is a standard that defines the formats of image, audio, and metadata tags used by cameras, phones, and other digital recording devices. Common EXIF metadata can include the following:

- The original filename
- Capture and last edited date and timestamps (with varying precision)
- GPS location coordinates (degrees of latitude and longitude)
- A small thumbnail of the original image
- The author's name and copyright details
- Compass heading
- Device information, including manufacturer and model
- Capture information, including lens type, focal range, aperture, shutter speed, and flash settings

> Metadata is a very valuable source of information during an investigation. Understanding what type of information and detail are present in each major category is important.

EXIF data exists to assist applications that use these files and can be modified independently of the file contents.

Data Collection Models

A plethora of data is available in a system for collection and use. For this to be useful, investigators have to have a sense of what is available and over what time frames. Two models used to document and provide a basis of understanding are the collection inventory matrix (CIM) and the collection management framework (CMF).

Collection Inventory Matrix

The **collection inventory matrix (CIM)** is a simple method used to sort your data sources with respect to a specific investigation or threat hunt. A CIM is a simple matrix with data sources listed as rows, and the columns can indicate what they cover, as in enterprise, business unite, enclaves, and so on. At the intersection of a row and column is a simple qualitative measure of something, like have you used them before? Are they easy or hard? Do you have access? Other commonly used differentiators include automated/not automated, level of completeness, and authority to collect (do you need special permission to access/use?). The purpose is to allow quick sorting when chasing your hypothesis; this is a form for prioritizing the sources. Once the matrix is populated, you can apply the typical heat map colors (red, yellow, green) for high, medium, and low to make an easy-to-use chart of what can help your current hunt/incident.

Collection Management Framework

The **collection management framework (CMF)** is the tool used to maintain a record of what information sources you have available as well as data about those resources. Again, the rows are the different information sources, and probably arranged in some fashion that helps you navigate the rows, either by type or by location. The columns are the descriptors about the data sources, and these can vary from company to company. Some of the common descriptors include what, where, who controls, how long it is stored, what it is good for (what part of the kill chain does it apply to?), and so on. The idea is to have a catalog of what data is available to you that can help you shape your threat hunting and incident response actions. Assume you found that 10 days ago, a suspicious e-mail delivered a payload. You suspect a C2 server was employed by the actor. How long will your DNS logs help you? If the DNS logs are for 60 days, then yes. But what if a forensic investigation shows you a 90-day-old attack? They're not as helpful anymore. Understanding the data sources, what they cover, for how long, and so on, is very helpful to people doing the investigations. Because this information really doesn't change much over time, having it ahead of time as opposed to figuring it out as you go speeds up investigations and removes a lot of frustrations.

Standards and Best Practices

Many options are available to a team when planning and performing processes and procedures. For assistance in choosing a path, the team can consult both standards and best practices in the proper development of processes. From government sources to industry sources, there are many opportunities to gather ideas and methods, even from fellow firms.

State of Compromise

The new standard of information security involves living in a state of compromise, where you should always expect that adversaries are active in your networks. It is unrealistic to expect that you can keep attackers out of your network. Operating in a state of compromise does not mean that you must suffer significant losses. A working assumption when planning for, responding to, and managing the overall incident response process is that the systems are compromised and that prevention cannot be the only means of defense.

NIST

The National Institute of Standards and Technology, a U.S. governmental entity under the Department of Commerce, produces a wide range of Special Publications (SPs) in the area of computer security. Grouped into several different categories, the most relevant SPs for incident response come from the Special Publications 800 series:

- SP 800-61 Rev. 2: Computer Security Incident Handling Guide
- SP 800-126 Rev. 2: NIST Security Content Automation Protocol (SCAP)
- SP 800-137: Information Security Continuous Monitoring for Federal Information Systems and Organizations
- NIST SP 800-36: Guide to Selecting Information Technology Security Products
- NIST SP 800-40 Rev. 3: Guide to Enterprise Patch Management Technologies
- NIST SP 800-51 Rev. 1: Guide to Using Vulnerability Naming Schemes [CVE/CCE]

Department of Justice

In April 2015, the U.S. Department of Justice's Cybersecurity Unit released a best-practices document titled "Best Practices for Victim Response and Reporting of Cyber Incidents." This document identifies steps to take before a cyber incident, the steps to take during an incident response action, a list of actions not to take, and what to do after the incident. The URL for the document can be found in the "For More Information" section at the end of the chapter.

Tech Tip

What Not to Do as Part of Incident Response

The U.S. Department of Justice has two specific recommended steps for what not *to do as part of an incident response action:*

- *Do not use the compromised system to communicate.*
- *Do not hack into or damage another network or system.*

The victim organization should always assume that any communications across affected machines will be compromised. This eavesdropping action is standard hacker behavior, and if you tip off your actions, they can be countered before you regain control of your system. Hacking, even retaliatory hacking, is illegal, and given the difficulty in attribution, attempts to respond by hacking the hacker may accidently result in hacking an innocent third-party machine.

Indicators of Compromise

An **indicator of compromise (IOC)** is an artifact left behind from computer intrusion activity. Detecting IOCs is a quick way to jump-start a response element. Originated by the security firm Mandiant, IOCs have spread in usage to a wide range of firms. IOCs act as a tripwire for responders. An IOC can be tied to a specific observable event, which then can be traced to related events, and to stateful events such as Registry keys. One of the biggest challenges in incident response is getting on the trail of an attacker, and IOCs provide a means of getting on the trail.

Tech Tip

Common Indicators of Compromise

Here are some common indicators of compromise:

- ***Unusual outbound traffic*** *This probably is the clearest indicator that data is going where it shouldn't.*
- ***Geographical irregularities*** *Communications going to countries for which no business ties exist is another key indicator that data is going where it shouldn't.*
- ***Unusual login activity*** *Failed logins, login failures to nonexistent accounts, and so forth, indicate compromise.*
- ***Anomalous usage patterns for privileged accounts*** *Changes in patterns of when administrators typically operate and what they typically access indicate compromise.*
- ***Changes in database access patterns*** *This indicates hackers are searching for data or reading it to collect large quantities.*
- ***Automated web traffic*** *Timing can show some requests are scripts, not humans.*
- ***Change in HTML response sizes*** *SQL injection can result in large HTML response sizes.*
- ***Large numbers of requests for specific files*** *Numerous requests for specific files, such as join.php, may indicate automated attack patterns.*
- ***Mismatched port to application traffic*** *This is a common method of attempting to hide activity.*
- ***Unusual DNS requests*** *Command-and-control server traffic often uses unusual DNS requests.*
- ***Unusual Registry changes*** *Unusual changes are indications of abnormal changes to a system state.*
- ***Unexpected patching*** *Some hackers/malware will patch to prevent other hackers from entering a target.*
- ***Bundles of data/files in wrong place*** *Large aggregations of data, frequently encrypted, may be files being prepared for exfiltration.*
- ***Changes to mobile device profiles*** *Mobile is the new perimeter, and changes may indicate malware.*
- ***DDoS/DoS attacks*** *Denial of service is used as a tool to provide smokescreen or distraction.*

There are several standards associated with IOCs, but the three main ones are Cyber Observable Expression (CybOX), a method of information sharing developed by MITRE; OpenIOC, an open source initiative established by Mandiant that is designed to facilitate rapid communication of specific threat information associated with known threats; and the Incident Object Description Exchange Format (IODEF), an XML format specified in RFC 5070 for conveying incident information between response teams, both internally and externally with respect to organizations. The "For More Information" section at the end of the chapter provides URLs for all three standards.

Security Measure Implementation

All data that is stored is subject to breach or compromise. Given this assumption, the question becomes, what is the best mitigation strategy to reduce the risk associated with breach or compromise? Data requires protection in each of the three states of the data lifecycle: in storage, in transit, and during processing. The level of risk in each state differs because of several factors.

- **Time** Data tends to spend more time in storage and hence is subject to breach or compromise over longer time periods.
- **Quantity** Data in storage tends to offer a greater quantity to breach or compromise than data in transit, and data in processing offers even less. If records are being compromised while being processed, then only records being processed are subjected to risk.
- **Access** Different protection mechanisms exist in each of the domains, and this has a direct effect on the risk associated with breach or compromise. Operating systems tend to have very tight controls to prevent cross-process data issues such as error and contamination.

The next aspect of risk during processing is within process access to the data, and a variety of attack techniques address this channel specifically. Data in transit is subject to breach or compromise from a variety of network-level attacks and vulnerabilities. Some of these are under the control of the enterprise, and some are not.

One primary mitigation step is **data minimization**. Data minimization efforts can play a key role in both operational efficiency and security. One of the first rules associated with data is this: Don't keep what you don't need. A simple example of this is the case of spam remediation. If spam is separated from e-mail before it hits a mailbox, one can assert that it is not mail and not subject to storage, backup, or data retention issues. As spam can comprise greater than 50 percent of incoming mail, spam remediation can dramatically improve operational efficiency in terms of both speed and cost.

This same principle holds true for other forms of information. When credit card transactions are processed, certain data elements are required for the actual transaction, but once the transaction is approved, they have no further business value. Storing this information provides no business value, yet it does represent a risk in the case of a data breach. Data storage should be governed not by what you can store but by the business need to store. What is not stored is not subject to breach, and minimizing storage to only what is supported by the business need reduces risk and cost to the enterprise.

> Data breaches may not be preventable, but they can be mitigated through minimization and encryption efforts.

Minimization efforts begin before data even hits a system, let alone a breach. During system design, the appropriate security controls are determined and deployed, with periodic audits to ensure compliance. These controls are based on the sensitivity of the information being protected. One tool that can be used to assist in the selection of controls is a data classification scheme. Not all data is equally important, nor is it equally damaging in the event of loss. Developing and deploying a data classification scheme can assist in preventative planning efforts when designing security for data elements.

Making Security Measurable

MITRE, working together with partners from government, industry, and academia, has created a set of techniques (called Making Security Measurable) to improve the measurability of security. This is a comprehensive effort, including registries of specific baseline data, standardized languages for the accurate communication of security information, and formats and standardized processes to facilitate accurate and timely communications.

The entirety of the project is beyond the scope of this text, but Table 22.1 lists some of the common items by category, a few of which are described next in a bit more detail.

Table 22.1 Sample Elements of Making Security Measurable

Language/Format	Registry	Standardized Processes
Open Vulnerability and Assessment Language (OVAL)	Common Vulnerabilities and Exposures (CVE) list	NIST Security Content Automation Protocol (SCAP)
Malware Attribute Enumeration and Characterization (MAEC)	Common Weakness Enumeration (CWE)	Information Security Continuous Monitoring for Federal Information Systems and Organizations (NIST SP 800-137)
Cyber Observable Expression (CybOX)	Open Vulnerability and Assessment Language (OVAL) Repository	Guide to Selecting Information Technology Security Products (NIST SP 800-36)
Structured Threat Information Expression (STIX)	Common Attack Pattern Enumeration and Classification (CAPEC)	Guide to Enterprise Patch Management Technologies (NIST SP 800-40, Rev. 3)
Trusted Automated Exchange of Indicator Information (TAXII)		Guide to Using Vulnerability Naming Schemes (CVE/CCE) (NIST SP 800-51, Rev. 1)

STIX and TAXII

MITRE has continued its efforts in the process of making security measurable and adding automation to the mix. **Structured Threat Information Expression (STIX)** is a structured language for cyberthreat intelligence information. MITRE created **Trusted Automated Exchange of Indicator Information (TAXII)** as the main transport mechanism for cyberthreat information represented by STIX. TAXII services allow organizations to share cyberthreat information in a secure and automated manner.

CybOX

Cyber Observable Expression (CybOX) is a standardized schema for the communication of observed data from the operational domain. Designed to streamline communications associated with incidents, CybOX provides a means of communicating key elements, including event management, incident management, and more, in an effort to improve interoperability, consistency, and efficiency.

Retention Policies

Data retention is the storage of data records. One of the first steps in understanding data retention in an organization is the determination of what records require storage and for how long. Among the many reasons for retaining data, some of the most common are for the purposes of billing and accounting, contractual obligation, warranty history, and compliance with local, state, and national government regulations, such as IRS rules. Maintaining data stores for longer than is required is a source of risk, as is not storing the information long enough. Some information is subject to regulations requiring lengthy data retention, such as PHI for workers who have been exposed to specific hazards. Some data elements, such as the card verification code (CVC/CV2) element in a credit card transaction, are never stored as part of a transaction record. They are used for approval and destroyed to prevent loss after the transaction is concluded.

Data retention policies differ by organization. However, some information such as PHI may be subject to regulations requiring specific data retention rules.

Failure to maintain the data in a secure state can also be a retention issue, as is not retaining it. In some cases, destruction of data, specifically data subject to legal hold in a legal matter, can result in adverse court findings and sanctions. Even if the data destruction is unintentional or inadvertent, it is still subject to sanction, as the firm had a responsibility to protect it. Legal hold can add significant complexity to data retention efforts, as it forces almost separate storage of the data until the legal issues are resolved. Once data is on the legal hold track, its retention clock does not expire until the hold is lifted. This makes identifying, labeling, and maintaining the data subject to a legal hold an added dimension to normal storage considerations.

For More Information

CybOX https://cybox.mitre.org/

The DOJ's "Best Practices for Victim Response and Reporting of Cyber Incidents" www.justice.gov/criminal-ccips/file/1096971/download

Incident Object Description Exchange Format (IODEF) https://tools.ietf.org/html/rfc5070

Making Security Measurable https://makingsecuritymeasurable.mitre.org/

Open IOC Framework https://cyware.com/educational-guides/cyber-threat-intelligence/what-is-open-indicators-of-compromise-openioc-framework-ed9d

Chapter 22 Review

Chapter Summary

After reading this chapter and completing the exercises, you should understand the following about incident response.

Understand attack frameworks

- There are several key attack frameworks an IR person needs to understand, including APT, Cyber Kill Chain, and the MITRE ATT&CK model.
- The Diamond Model of Intrusion Analysis helps responders classify different attacks.

Understand threat intelligence

- Threat intelligence is understanding what threats are likely for the enterprise.
- Threat hunting is a proactive examination of a system looking for specific threats.

Understand the foundations of incident response processes

- The role of incident management is the control of a coordinated and comprehensive response to an incident.
- Learn the anatomy of an attack—both old versions and newer APT-style attacks.
- The goals of incident response in an organization are to restore systems to functioning order and prevent future risk.

Implement the detailed steps of an incident response process

- The major steps in the incident response process are preparation, incident identification, initial response, incident isolation, strategy formulation, investigation, recovery, reporting, and follow-up.
- Develop a detailed understanding of the components of each of the steps.
- Understand the linkages and interconnections between key process steps.

Understand the data sources available for personnel to employ in incident response

- Enterprises have a wide range of data sources available for use in incident response, including log files from a wide range of sources.
- Understanding where data sources are and how they can be used is critical for incident responders.
- Metadata is another source of valuable information for IR personnel, and it comes from items such as e-mail, mobile devices, the Web, and file metadata.
- There are two main data collection models: the collection inventory matrix and the collection management framework.

Describe standards and best practices involved in incident response

- Modern systems should expect to exist in a state of compromise and have policies and processes designed to operate under these conditions.
- The U.S. government, including NIST and the Department of Justice, has published useful guidance.
- Indicators of compromise provide early-warning triggers for incident response investigators.
- Taking actions against an incident in progress can be planned using a Cyber Kill Chain philosophy.
- The "Making Security Measurable" material from MITRE can assist in the incident response process.

Key Terms

advanced persistent threat (APT) *(839)*
collection inventory matrix (CIM) *(866)*
collection management framework (CMF) *(867)*
computer emergency response team (CERT) *(837)*
computer incident response team (CIRT) *(837)*
containment *(851)*
Cyber Kill Chain *(840)*
Cyber Observable Expression (CybOX) *(871)*
data minimization *(870)*
Diamond Model of Intrusion Analysis *(842)*
eradication *(855)*
exercises *(849)*

footprinting *(839)*
identification *(850)*
incident *(849)*
incident response *(837)*
incident response plan *(847)*
incident response policy *(844)*
indicator of compromise (IOC) *(868)*
information criticality *(837)*
initial response *(850)*
lateral movement *(840)*
lessons learned *(857)*
MITRE ATT&CK framework *(841)*
playbook *(843)*
preparation *(845)*
quarantine *(852)*
recovery *(855)*
remote-access trojan (RAT) *(840)*
reporting requirements *(848)*
runbook *(843)*
security orchestration, automation, and response (SOAR) *(843)*
Structured Threat Information Expression (STIX) *(871)*
syslog *(863)*
threat hunting *(842)*
threat intelligence *(842)*
Trusted Automated Exchange of Indicator Information (TAXII) *(871)*

Key Terms Quiz

Use terms from the Key Terms list to complete the sentences that follow. Don't use the same term more than once. Not all terms will be used.

1. A(n) ______________ is any event in an information system or network where the results are different than normal.
2. When the attackers are focused on maintaining a presence during an incident, the type of attack is typically called a(n) ______________.
3. The determination of boundaries during an attack is a process called ______________.
4. The steps an organization performs in response to any situation determined to be abnormal in the operation of a computer system are called ______________.
5. One methodology for planning incident response defenses is known as ______________.
6. A(n) ______________ is an artifact that can be used to detect the presence of an attack.
7. The document that contains all the information about various data sources available to incident responders is referred to as the ______________.
8. ______________ is a proactive approach to finding an attacker in a network.
9. A key measure used to prioritize incident response actions is ______________.
10. ______________ and ______________ are used to communicate cyberthreat information between organizations.

Multiple-Choice Quiz

1. Which of the following is not an indicator of compromise (IOC)?
   - **A.** Unusual outbound traffic
   - **B.** Increase in traffic over port 80
   - **C.** Traffic to unusual foreign IP addresses
   - **D.** Discovery of large encrypted data blocks that you don't know the purpose of
2. A sysadmin thinks a machine is under attack, so he logs in as root and attempts to see what is happening on the machine. Which common technical mistake is most likely to occur?
   - **A.** The alteration of date/time stamps on files and objects in the system
   - **B.** Failure to recognize the attacker by process ID
   - **C.** Erasure of logs associated with an attack
   - **D.** The cutting of a network connection between an attacker and the current machine

3. What is the last step of the incident response process?
   A. Reconstitution
   B. Recovery
   C. Follow-up
   D. Lessons learned
4. Which of the following are critical elements in an incident response toolkit? (Choose all that apply.)
   A. Accurate network diagram
   B. Findings of last penetration test report
   C. List of critical data/systems
   D. Phone list of people on-call by area
5. Your organization experienced an APT hack in the past and is interested in preventing a reoccurrence. What step of the attack path is the best step at which to combat APT-style attacks?
   A. Escalate privilege
   B. Establish foothold
   C. Lateral movement
   D. Initial compromise
6. The goals of an incident response process include all of the following except which one?
   A. Confirm or dispel an incident occurrence.
   B. Minimize security expenditures.
   C. Protect privacy rights.
   D. Minimize system disruption.
7. During an initial response to an incident, which of the following is most important?
   A. Who or what is reporting the incident
   B. The time of the report
   C. Who takes the initial report
   D. Accurate information
8. When determining the level of risk of exposure for data in storage, in transit, or during processing, which of the following is not a factor?
   A. Time
   B. Quantity
   C. Data type
   D. Access
9. What is the most useful tool to determine the next steps when investigating a common incident, like malware on a server?
   A. Runbook
   B. SIEM data
   C. Playbook
   D. Security orchestration, automation, and response (SOAR)
10. Which of the following activities should you not do during an incident response investigation associated with an APT?
    A. Use the corporate e-mail system to communicate.
    B. Determine system time offsets.
    C. Use only qualified and trusted tools.
    D. Create an off-network site for data collection.

Essay Quiz

1. The chief financial officer (CFO) sees you in the lunch room. Knowing that you are leading the company's incident response initiative, she comes over to your table and asks if you have time to answer a question. You are surprised but say yes. Her question is simple and to the point: "Can you explain this incident response thing to me, in nontechnical terms, so I can respond appropriately at the next board meeting in the discussion?" In response, you offer to prepare a written outline for the CFO. In one page, outline the major points that need to be addressed and give examples in language suitable for the audience.
2. Explain the relationship between the anatomy of a hack and indicators of compromise.

chapter 23

Computer Forensics

"How often have I said to you that when you have eliminated the impossible, whatever remains, however improbable, must be the truth?"

—Sir Arthur Conan Doyle, from *The Sign of the Four*

In this chapter, you will learn how to

- Explore the basics of digital forensics
- Identify the rules and types of evidence
- Collect and preserve evidence
- Maintain a viable chain of custody
- Investigate a computer crime or policy violation
- Examine system artifacts
- Develop forensic policies and procedures
- Examine the policies and procedures associated with e-discovery

Computer forensics is certainly a popular buzzword in computer security. This chapter addresses the key aspects of computer forensics in preparation for the CompTIA Security+ certification exam. It is not intended to be a treatise on the topic or a legal tutorial regarding the presentation of evidence in a court of law. This material is only an introduction to the topic, and before anyone enters into forensic work or practice, much additional study is necessary. The principles presented in this chapter are of value in conducting any investigative processes, including internal or external audit procedures, but the many nuances of handling legal cases are far beyond the scope of this text.

The term **forensics** relates to the application of scientific knowledge to legal problems. Specifically, computer forensics involves the preservation, identification, documentation, and interpretation of computer data. In today's practice, computer forensics can be performed for these three purposes:

- Investigating and analyzing computer systems as related to a violation of law
- Investigating and analyzing computer systems for compliance with an organization's policies
- Responding to a request for digital evidence (e-discovery)

> **Cross Check**
>
> **Incident Response**
>
> Incident response and associated policies and procedures are covered in Chapter 22.

Forensics is often associated with incident response, which is the procedure used to respond to an abnormal condition in a system. There is a subtle difference, however. Incident response is about corrective action—returning the system to a normal operational state—whereas forensics is about figuring out what happened.

If an unauthorized person accesses a system, that person likely has violated the law. However, a company employee who performs similar acts (accessing data remotely) may or may not violate laws—the determination of which depends on many factors, including specific authorizations and job duties. Someone can violate corporate policies while acting lawfully with respect to computer laws. It is worth noting that knowingly exceeding one's authorizations with respect to system access is a violation of the law.

Any of these situations could ultimately result in legal action and may require legal disclosure. Therefore, it is important to note that computer forensic actions may, at some point in time, deal with legal violations, and investigations could go to court proceedings. As a potential first responder, you should always seek legal counsel. Also seek legal counsel ahead of time as you develop and implement corporate policies and procedures. It is extremely important to understand that even minor procedural missteps can have significant legal consequences. The rule to follow is simple: always assume that the material will be used in a court of law and thus must be handled in a perfectly proper manner at all times. This further means that when dealing with forensics, you must ensure that all steps are performed by qualified forensic examiners.

Evidence

Evidence consists of the documents, verbal statements, and material objects that are admissible in a court of law. Evidence is critical to convincing management, juries, judges, or other authorities that some kind of violation has occurred. The submission of evidence is challenging, but it is even more challenging when computers are used because the people involved may not be technically educated and thus may not fully understand what has happened.

Computer evidence presents yet more challenges because the data itself cannot be experienced with the physical senses—that is, you can see printed characters, but you can't see the bits where that data is stored. Bits of data are merely magnetic pulses on a disk or some other storage technology. Therefore, data must always be evaluated through some kind of "filter" rather than sensed directly. This is often of concern to auditors because good auditing techniques recommend accessing the original data or a version that is as close as possible to the original data.

Types of Evidence

All evidence is not created equal. Some evidence is stronger and better than other evidence. Several types of evidence can be germane, as listed here:

- **Direct evidence** This is oral testimony that proves a specific fact (such as an eyewitness's statement). The knowledge of the facts is obtained through the five senses of the witness, with no inferences or presumptions.
- **Real evidence** Also known as associative or physical evidence, this includes tangible objects that prove or disprove a fact. Physical evidence links the suspect to the scene of a crime.
- **Documentary evidence** This is evidence in the form of business records, printouts, manuals, and the like. Much of the evidence relating to computer crimes is documentary evidence.
- **Demonstrative evidence** This type of evidence is used to aid the jury and can be in the form of a model, experiment, chart, and so on, offered to prove that an event occurred.

The digital forensic process is a technically demanding one, with no room for errors. The most common cause of evidence from an investigation being excluded from court proceedings is *spoliation*, the unauthorized alteration of digital evidence. If the forensic process is less than perfect, spoliation is assumed. The best guidance is (1) always perform forensics as if you are going to court with the evidence, and (2) if you do not have qualified digital forensic investigators in house, do nothing to the device/media—let a professional handle it.

Standards for Evidence

Evidence in U.S. federal court cases is governed by a series of legal precedents, the most notable of which is the Daubert standard. Three U.S. Supreme Court cases articulate the Daubert standard and shape how materials are entered into evidence. Four specific elements are associated with the admission of scientific expert testimony. This is important with respect to digital forensics because the form of the evidence means that it can rarely speak for itself; rather, it must be interpreted by an expert and presented to the court.

The first element is that the judge is the gatekeeper. Materials are not considered evidence until declared so by the judge. This is to ensure that experts are determined to be experts before the court relies upon their judgment. A second element consists of reliability and relevance. The trial judge is to determine that the expert's testimony is relevant to the proceedings at hand and that the expert's methods are reliable with respect to the material being attested to. The third element is that expert knowledge should be based on science—specifically, science that is based on the scientific method with a replicable methodology. The final element relates to this scientific methodology, stating that it must be based on proven science, subjected to peer review, with a known error rate or potential error rate and consensus among the scientific community that the methodology is generally accepted. After these elements are satisfied, the judge can admit the expert's testimony as evidence.

These factors all relate to a U.S. federal court decision and therefore are binding only in the U.S. federal judiciary, but the test is recognized and applied in similar form at many levels of jurisdiction. The bottom line is simple: the data can't speak for itself, and experts who can interpret the data operate under strict guidelines with respect to conduct, qualifications, principles, and methods.

To be credible, especially if evidence will be used in court proceedings or in corporate disciplinary actions that could be challenged legally, evidence must meet these three standards:

- **Sufficient evidence** It must be convincing or measure up without question.
- **Competent evidence** It must be legally qualified and reliable.
- **Relevant evidence** It must be material to the case or have a bearing on the matter at hand.

Tech Tip

Evidence Control Mental Checklist

Keep these questions in mind as you collect evidence:

- *Who collected the evidence?*
- *How was it collected?*
- *Where was it collected?*
- *Who has had possession of the evidence?*
- *How was it protected and stored?*
- *When was it removed from storage? Why? Who took possession?*

Three Rules Regarding Evidence

An item can become evidence when it is admitted by a judge in a case. These three rules guide the use of evidence with regard to its use in court proceedings:

- **Best evidence rule** Courts prefer original evidence rather than a copy to ensure that no alteration of the evidence (whether intentional or unintentional) has occurred. In some instances, an evidence duplicate can be accepted, such as when the original is lost or destroyed by acts of God or in the normal course of business. A duplicate is also acceptable when a third party beyond the court's subpoena power possesses the original.
- **Exclusionary rule** The Fourth Amendment to the U.S. Constitution precludes illegal search and seizure. Therefore, any evidence collected in violation of the Fourth Amendment is not admissible as evidence. Additionally, if evidence is collected in violation of the Electronic Communications Privacy Act (ECPA) or other related provisions of the U.S. Code, it may not be admissible to a court. For example, if no policy exists regarding the company's intent to monitor network traffic or systems electronically and the employee has not acknowledged this policy by signing an agreement, sniffing the employee's network traffic could be a violation of the ECPA.
- **Hearsay rule** Hearsay is secondhand evidence—evidence offered by the witness that is not based on the personal knowledge of the witness but is being offered to prove the truth of the matter asserted. Typically, computer-generated evidence is considered hearsay evidence because the maker of the evidence (the computer) cannot be interrogated. There are exceptions being made where items such as logs and headers (computer-generated materials) are being accepted in court. There are exceptions, but they rarely apply to digital evidence.

The laws mentioned here are U.S. laws. Other countries and jurisdictions may have similar laws that would need to be considered in a similar manner.

Chain of Custody

Evidence, once collected, must be properly controlled to prevent tampering. The **chain of custody** accounts for all people who handled or had access to the evidence. The chain of custody shows who obtained the evidence, when and where it was obtained, where it was stored, and who had control or possession of the evidence for the entire time since the evidence was obtained.

The following are the critical steps in a chain of custody:

1. Record each item collected as evidence.
2. Record who collected the evidence, along with the date and time it was collected or recorded.
3. Write a description of the evidence in the documentation.
4. Put the evidence in containers and tag the containers with the case number, the name of the person who collected it, and the date and time it was collected or put in the container.
5. Record all message digest (hash) values in the documentation.
6. Securely transport the evidence to a protected storage facility.
7. Obtain a signature from the person who accepts the evidence at this storage facility.
8. Provide controls to prevent access to and compromise of the evidence while it is being stored.
9. Securely transport the evidence to court for proceedings.

Never analyze the seized evidence directly. The original evidence must be secured and protected with a chain of custody. It should never be subjected to a forensic examination due to the fragile nature of digital evidence. A forensic copy, however, can be examined and, if something goes wrong, discarded, and the copy process can be repeated. A good forensics process will prove that the forensic copy is identical to the original at the start and at the end of the examination. From a practical standpoint, investigators usually make multiple forensic copies and perform their analysis in parallel on the multiple copies.

Tags

As previously discussed, a chain of custody document records all accesses to evidence from time of collection until destruction. But how does one refer to a specific piece of evidence, especially if it is hardware containing data, such as a USB drive? This is done though tags. Physical serialized **tags** are attached to each item, and the tag number is used to identify a specific item. Frequently the items are then stored in antistatic bags to protect them from damage.

Forensic Process

Forensics is the use of scientific methods in the analysis of matters in connection with crime or other legal matters. Because of the connection to law, it is an exacting process, with no room for error. In digital forensics, the issue of alteration becomes paramount because changing 1s to 0s does not leave a trace in many situations. Because of the issue of contamination or spoliation of evidence, detailed processes are used in the processing of information.

From a high-level point of view, multiple steps are employed in a digital forensic investigation:

1. **Identification** Recognize an incident from indicators and determine its type and scope. This is not explicitly within the field of forensics but is significant because it impacts other steps. What tools

were used? How many systems are involved? How much data is to be copied? These questions all have ramifications on the successful outcome of a forensic process.

2. **Preparation** Prepare tools, techniques, and search warrants and monitor authorizations and management support.
3. **Approach/strategy** Dynamically formulate an approach based on potential impact on bystanders and the specific technology in question. The goal of the strategy should be to maximize the collection of untainted evidence while minimizing impact to the victim or owner.
4. **Preservation** Isolate, secure, and preserve the state of physical and digital evidence. This includes preventing people from using the digital device or allowing other electromagnetic devices to be used within a certain proximity. Proper preservation is essential to prevent alteration of the source.
5. **Collection** Record the physical scene and duplicate digital evidence using standardized and accepted procedures. This is where a digital camera and microphone are vital tools for capturing details—serial numbers, layouts, and so forth—quickly and definitively.
6. **Examination** In-depth, systematic search of evidence relating to the suspected crime. This step occurs later, in a lab, and focuses on identifying and locating potential specific evidence elements, possibly within unconventional locations. It is important to construct detailed documentation for analysis, documenting the metadata and data values that may be relevant to the issues at hand in the investigation.
7. **Analysis** Determine significance, reconstruct fragments of data, and draw conclusions based on the elements of evidence found. The data itself cannot tell a story, and in this step the investigator weaves the elements into a picture, ideally the only one that can be supported. Although the intuition is to prove guilt, the skilled and seasoned investigator focuses on painting the picture that the data describes, regardless of outcome, and making it comprehensive and complete so that it will stand up to challenge. Multiple people with different skill sets may be needed to complete the picture.
8. **Presentation** Summarize and provide an explanation of the conclusions. The results should be written in layperson's terms using abstracted terminology. If you cannot explain the information to a nontechnical layperson, then you do not understand it well enough to complete this aspect. All abstracted terminology should reference the specific details of the case.
9. **Returning evidence** Ensure physical and digital property is returned to its proper owner and determine how and what criminal evidence must be removed. (For example, hardware may be returned, but images of child pornography would be removed.) This is not an explicit step of forensic investigation, and most models that address how to seize evidence rarely address this aspect. But at the end of the day, the job is not done until all aspects are finished, and this includes this level of cleanup activity.

A digital camera is great for recording a scene and information. Screenshots of active monitor images may be obtained as well. Pictures can detail elements such as serial number plates, machines, drives, cable connections, and more. Photographs are truly worth a thousand words.

When information or objects are presented to management or admitted to court to support a claim, that information or those objects can be considered as evidence or documentation supporting your investigative efforts. Senior management will always ask a lot of questions—second- and third-order questions that you need to be able to answer quickly. Likewise, in a court, credibility is critical. Therefore, evidence must be properly acquired, identified, protected against tampering, transported, and stored.

Data Recovery

Data recovery in a digital forensics sense is associated with determining the relevant information for the issue at hand—simply stated, recover the evidence associated with an act. But what if the act is not precisely known? For example, suppose a sales manager for a company quits and goes to work with a competitor. Because she is a sales manager, she has had access to sensitive information that would benefit the new employer. But how do you know whether she took sensitive information with her? And even if she did, how do you determine for purposes of recovery which information she took, and where to look for it? Since forensics software has yet to invent a "Find Evidence" button, and there is no field in any computer protocol to tell investigators this is the data they are looking for, the act of recovering the necessary information can be a significant challenge. What's more, with today's multiterabyte drives, the volumes of data can be daunting.

Acquiring Evidence

When an incident occurs, you will need to collect data and information to facilitate your investigation. If someone is committing a crime or intentionally violating a company policy, she will likely try to hide her tracks. Therefore, you should collect as much information as soon as you can. In today's highly networked world, evidence can be found not only on the workstation or laptop computer but also on company-owned file servers, security appliances, and servers located with the Internet service provider (ISP).

Tech Tip

When Is Evidence Really Evidence?

Evidence is the term used in legal system for when an exhibit is produced in court and is accepted by the court. Technically, the use of the word evidence *throughout this chapter is in error, because what is being collected is a series of exhibits that may be presented to the court for consideration. For an exhibit to be admitted, it must pass a test of* **admissibility**. *Although many criteria can apply, in the case of digital exhibits, careful attention is paid to the entire pedigree, from time of creation, to collection, analysis, and preparation as an exhibit. If at any point in this cycle there is a chance that the element could have changed, it will be objected to and likely be ruled inadmissible. This is why adherence to perfection is important in the evidentiary chain.*

In the process of acquiring evidence, one must do as much as possible to prevent damage or loss of evidence. Photographs can be used to document the scene, but the crucial item is in the acquisition of digital information.

Most interactions with digital media involve reading and writing data, and any written changes during acquisition can destroy critical elements.

Try This!

Find and Create a Tool

Microsoft produced a forensic tool for law enforcement called Computer Online Forensics Evidence Extractor (COFEE) that can be used to collect a wide range of data from a suspect machine. Restricted by license to law enforcement, it was out of reach for most investigators, until it was published by WikiLeaks. An examination of how it functions provides useful information, and many of its functions can be readily copied by investigators. COFEE is a wrapper for a whole host of utilities—think Sysinternals and more—all integrated by script. This automated process can be re-created by any competent forensic investigator. Automated scripts and tools reduce errors and increase effectiveness.

File timestamps may be of use during the analysis phase. To correlate file timestamps to actual time, it is important to know the time offset between the system clock and real time. Recording the time offset while the system is live is critical if the system clock is different from the actual time. This information is lost if the machine is powered off.

When an incident occurs and the computer being used is going to be secured, you must consider two questions: should it be turned off, and should it be disconnected from the network? Forensic professionals debate the reasons for turning a computer on or turning it off. Some state that the plug should be pulled in order to freeze the current state of the computer. However, this results in the loss of any data associated with an attack in progress from the machine. Any data in RAM will also be lost. Further, it may corrupt the computer's filesystem and could call into question the validity of your findings.

Imaging or dumping the physical memory (RAM) of a computer system can help identify evidence that is not available on a hard drive. This is especially appropriate for rootkits, for which evidence on the hard drive is hard to find. Once the memory is imaged, you can use a hex editor to analyze the image offline on another system. (Memory-dumping tools and hex editors are available on the Internet.) Note that dumping memory is more applicable for investigative work where court proceedings will not be pursued. If a case is likely to end up in court, do not dump memory without first seeking legal advice to confirm that live analysis of the memory is acceptable; otherwise, the defendant will easily be able to dispute the claim that evidence was not tampered with.

On the other hand, it is possible for the computer criminal to leave behind a software bomb that you don't know about, and any commands you execute, including shutting down or restarting the system, could destroy or modify files, information, or evidence. The criminal may have anticipated such an investigation and altered some of the system's binary files.

Further, if the computer being analyzed is a server, it is unlikely management will support taking it offline and shutting it down for investigation. So, from an investigative perspective, either course may be correct or incorrect, depending on the circumstances surrounding the incident. What is most important is that you are deliberate in your work, you document your actions, and you can explain why you took the actions you performed.

Many investigative methods are used. Figure 23.1 shows the continuum of investigative methods from simple to more rigorous.

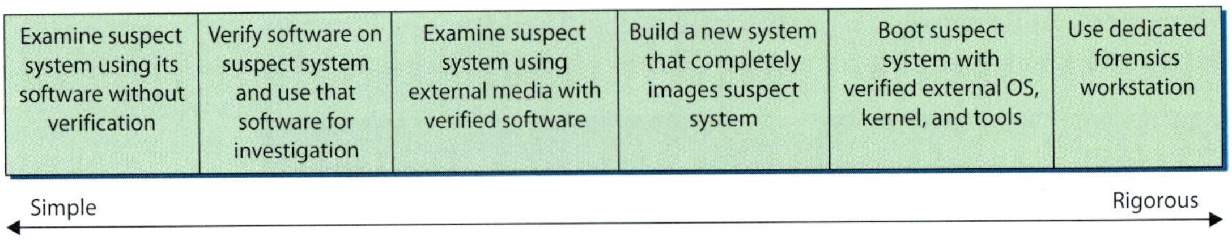

• **Figure 23.1** Investigative method rigor

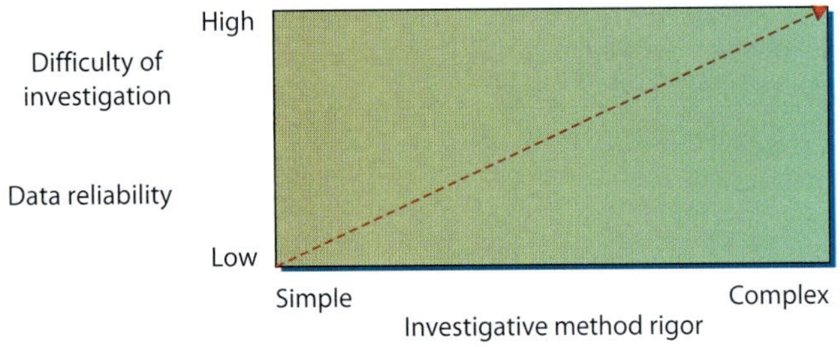

• **Figure 23.2** Required rigor of the investigative method versus both data reliability and the difficulty of investigation

> **Tech Tip**
>
> **Data Volatility**
>
> *Here are some sources listed from the most volatile to the most persistent:*
>
> - *CPU storage (registers/cache)*
> - *System storage (RAM, routing tables, ARP cache, process tables, kernel stats)*
> - *Data on fixed media (complete image)*
> - *Removable media*
> - *Output/hardcopy*

Figure 23.2 shows the relationship between the complexity of your investigation and both the reliability of your forensic data and the difficulty of investigation.

Order of Volatility

There are many sources of data in a computer system, and if the machine is running, some of these sources can be volatile. Things such as the state of the CPU and its registers are always changing, as are memory and even storage. These elements tend to change at different rates, and you should pay attention to the **order of volatility** so that collection priority is devoted where it can matter.

The collection of electronic data can be a difficult task. In some cases, such as volatile data, there may be only one chance to collect it, after which it becomes lost forever. Volatile information locations such as the RAM change constantly, and data collection should occur in the *order of volatility* or lifetime of the data.

The following is the order of volatility of digital information in a system:

1. CPU, cache, and register contents (collect first)
2. Routing tables, ARP cache, process tables, kernel statistics
3. Live network connections and data flows
4. Memory (RAM)
5. Temporary filesystem/swap space
6. Data on hard disk
7. Remotely logged data
8. Data stored on archival media/backups (collect last)

When you're collecting digital evidence, it is important to use the proper techniques and tools. Some of the key tasks are using write blockers when making forensic copies, hashing and verifying hash matches, documenting handling and storage, and protecting media from environmental change factors. Of particular note is that the data present on a system can be a function of both the filesystem and the hardware being employed. A physical hard disk drive will persist data longer than a solid state drive. Additionally, the newer filesystems with journaling and shadow copies can have longer persistence of information than older systems such as File Allocation Table (FAT) systems. Raw disk blocks can be recovered in some filesystems long after data has been rewritten or erased because of the nature of how the filesystems manage the data.

Understanding the order of volatility of digital information in a system is an important issue, for once violated, information can be lost forever. This is not an academic exercise; this information is used in every investigation.

Capture System Image

Capturing a system image of a system is more than just copying the hard drive. Information also exists in the RAM and may be preserved in the files used for hibernation. Having a process that can copy the RAM image as well as the hard drives in a coordinated manner, preserving the evidence, is important in many investigations. Investigations involving malware or rootkits will depend upon this type of data collection if they are to be effective. As previously mentioned in this chapter, this level of data collection has many issues, both technical and procedural. Ensuring a plan is developed and understood before execution is critical to avoid missing elements or spoiling the data.

The other system image is that of the internal storage devices. Making forensic duplicates of all partitions is a key step in preserving evidence. A forensic copy is a bit-by-bit copy and has supporting integrity checks in the form of hashes. The proper practice is to use a write blocker when making a forensic copy of a drive. This device allows a disk to be read but prevents any writing actions to the drive, guaranteeing that the copy operation does not change the original media. Once a forensic copy is created, working copies from the master forensic copy can be created for analysis and sharing with other investigators. The use of hash values provides a means of demonstrating that all of the copies are true to each other and the original.

A digital forensic copy can only be made with specific methods designed to perform bit-by-bit copying of the files' free and slack space, making a verifiably true copy of the medium as demonstrated by hash values.

Network Traffic and Logs

An important source of information in an investigation can be the network activity associated with a device. There can be a lot of useful information in the network logs associated with the network infrastructure. The level and breadth of this information are determined by the scope of the investigation. While the best data would be from that of a live network forensic collection process, in most cases this type of data will not be available. There are many other sources of network forensic data, including firewall and IDS logs, network flow data, and event logs on key servers and services.

Capture Video

A convenient method of capturing significant information at the time of collection is video capture. Videos allow high-bandwidth data collection that can show what was connected to what, how things were laid out, desktops, and so forth. A picture can be worth a thousand words, so take the time to document everything with pictures. Pictures of serial numbers and network and USB connections can prove invaluable later in the forensics process. Complete documentation is a must in every forensics process, and photographs can assist greatly in capturing details that would otherwise take a long time and be prone to transcription error.

Another source of video data is in the closed-circuit television (CCTV) cameras that are used for security, both in industry and in growing numbers of homes. This is digital information like all other digital information; it can be copied and manipulated and needs to be preserved in the same manner as other digital information.

A digital camera is great for recording a scene and information. Screenshots of active monitor images may be obtained as well. Pictures can detail elements such as serial number plates, machines, drives, cables connections, and more. Photographs are truly worth a thousand words.

Understanding time elements for forensics is important. Pay attention to time zones and the specific details in the question.

Social media has created a "marketplace" for people to share videos, and this has led to a dramatic increase in user-created video content, commonly from smartphones. These videos are uploaded to social media platforms and shared with others. The process of uploading the videos can remove a lot of metadata that would be useful from a forensics point of view, but they are still used in legal proceedings under the aspect of the evidence speaking for itself. As AI-generated deep fakes become more advanced, this will have to change. For example, a video of you delivering a speech can be faked with fairly high fidelity, resulting in "evidence" of you giving a speech you never gave. Again, this will make metadata and traceability more important.

Record Time Offset

Files and events logged on a computer will have timestamp markings that are based on the clock time on the machine itself. It is a mistake to assume that this clock is accurate. To allow the correlation of timestamp data from records inside the computer with any external event, it is necessary to know any time offset between the machine clock and the actual time.

Tech Tip

Record Time Offset

A common data element needed later in the forensics process is an accurate system time with respect to an accurate external time source. A **record time offset** *is calculated by measuring system time with an external clock such as a Network Time Protocol (NTP) server. This can be lost if the system is powered down, so it is best collected while the system is still running. Another form of time offset is the difference between local time zones and UTC. As discussed earlier, with most time records being in UTC, conversion to local time zones may be necessary to make sense of some records.*

Take Hashes

If files, logs, and other information are going to be captured and used for evidence, you need to ensure that the data isn't modified. In most cases, a tool that implements a hashing algorithm to create message digests is used.

A **hashing algorithm** performs a function similar to the familiar parity bits, checksum, and cyclic redundancy check (CRC). It applies mathematical operations to a data stream (or file) to calculate some number (the **hash**) that is unique based on the information contained in the data stream (or file). If a subsequent hash created on the same data stream results in a different hash value, it usually means that the data stream was changed.

The mathematics behind hashing algorithms has been researched extensively, and although it is possible that two different data streams could produce the same message digest, it is very improbable. This is an area of cryptography that has been rigorously reviewed, and the mathematics behind Message Digest 5 (MD5) and Secure Hash Algorithm (SHA) are sound. In 2005, weaknesses were discovered in the MD5 and SHA implementations, leading the National Institute of Standards and Technology

(NIST) to announce a competition to find a new cryptographic hashing algorithm, named SHA-3. Although MD5 is still used, best practice is to use the SHA-2 series and then SHA-3 once it becomes integrated into tools.

The hash tool is applied to each file or log, and the message digest value is noted in the investigation documentation. It is a good practice to write the logs to a write-once media such as a CD-ROM. If the case actually goes to trial, the investigator may need to run the tool on the files or logs again to show that they have not been altered in any way.

Hashing is used throughout digital forensics to measure integrity between copies of data. Checksums do not have the specificity of hashes, so hashes are the primary tool.

Screenshots

Particular attention should be paid to the state of what is on the screen at the time of evidence collection. The information on a video screen is lost once the system changes or power is removed. Taking *screenshots,* using a digital camera or smartphone camera, can provide documentation as to what was on the screen at the time of collection. Because you cannot trust the system internals themselves to be free of tampering, do not use internal screenshot capture methods.

Checksums are mathematical algorithms that produce a check digit based on an incoming stream. Designed for error testing across small data sets, they have advantages and disadvantages. For example, for error checking, they are fast and can detect a single bit error. However, they miss larger numbers of errors as the effect cancels out. Thus, checksums serve no real purpose in digital forensics. If two checksums are different, the incoming data streams are different. If the checksums are the same, you might still have different data streams.

Witness Interviews

Remember that witness credibility is extremely important. It is easy to imagine how quickly credibility can be damaged if the witness is asked "Did you lock the filesystem?" and can't answer affirmatively. The same is true if the witness is asked "When you imaged this disk drive, did you use a new system?" and can't answer that the destination disk was new or had been completely formatted using a low-level format before data was copied to it. Witness preparation can be critical in a case, even for technical experts.

You should never examine a system with the utilities provided by that system. You should always use utilities that have been verified as correct and uncorrupted. Even better, use a *forensic workstation,* a computer system specifically designed to perform computer forensic activities. Do not open any files or start any applications. If possible, document the current memory and swap files, running processes, and open files. Disconnect the system from the network and immediately contact senior management. Unless you have appropriate forensic training and experience, consider calling in a professional.

Identifying Evidence

Evidence must be properly marked as it is collected so that it can be identified as a particular piece of evidence gathered at the scene. Properly label and store evidence, and make sure the labels can't be easily removed. Keep an evidence control log book identifying each piece of evidence (in case the label is removed); the people who discovered it; the case number; the date, time, and location of the discovery; and the reason for collection. Keep a log of all staff hours and expenses. This information should be specific enough for recollection later in court. It is important to log other identifying marks, such as device make, model, serial number, cable configuration or type, and so on. Note any type of damage to the piece of evidence.

Being methodical is extremely important when identifying evidence. Do not collect evidence by yourself—have a second person who can serve as a witness to your actions. Keep logs of your actions both during seizure and during analysis and storage. A sample log, providing the minimum contents of an evidence control log book entry, is shown here:

Item Description	Investigator	Case #	Date	Time	Location	Reason
Dell Latitude laptop computer, 7730, serial number 6RKC1G0	Smith	C-25	10 May 2020	1325 MST	Room 312 safe	Safekeeping

Protecting Evidence

Evidence must be properly acquired, identified, protected against tampering, transported, and stored. Digital evidence has one huge glaring issue: it can change and not leave a record of the change. The fact that the outcome of a case can hinge on information that can be argued as being not static leads to the crucial element of preservation. From the initial step in the forensics process, the most important issue must always be the **preservation** of the data. There is no recovery from data that has been changed, so from the beginning safeguards must be in place. There are several key steps that assist the forensic investigator in avoiding data spoilage. First, when data is collected, a solid chain of custody is maintained until the case is completed and the materials are released or destroyed. Second, when a forensic copy of the data is obtained, a hash is collected as well to allow for the verification of integrity. All analysis is done on forensic copies of the original data collection, not on the master copy itself. Also, each copy is verified before and after testing with hash values compared to the original set to demonstrate integrity.

Third-party investigators are commonly used in civil matters. When doing digital forensics for a civil litigation–based case, it is important to consult with the retaining counsel concerning the level of detail and records desired. In civil litigation, anything written will be requested to be disclosed during pretrial discovery. This can provide strategy disclosure beyond what is desired by counsel. The alternative is to keep minimal required records as determined by counsel.

Protect evidence from electromagnetic or mechanical damage. Ensure that evidence is not tampered with, damaged, or compromised by the procedures used during the investigation. This helps avoid potential liability problems later. Protect evidence from extremes in heat and cold, humidity, water, magnetic fields, and vibration. Use static-free evidence-protection gloves as opposed to standard latex gloves. Seal the evidence in a proper container with evidence tape, and mark it with your initials, date, and case number. For example, if a mobile phone with advanced capabilities is seized, it should be properly secured in a hard container designed to prevent accidentally pressing the keys during transit and storage. If the phone is to remain turned on for analysis, radio frequency isolation bags that attenuate the device's radio signal should be used. This will prevent remote wiping, locking, or disabling of the device.

Tech Tip

Protecting Evidence

Any and all collected digital evidence needs to be protected from a wide range of potential losses—environmental, theft, actual loss, alteration, physical or electrical damage, or even the perception of the possibility of loss occurring. In any legal proceeding, whether criminal or civil, the other party will always examine the storage conditions and, if less than perfect, place the burden on the person storing it to prove that it is still intact. This is just one reason why recording hash values upon collection is so important.

This process adds a lot of work and time to an investigation, but it yields one crucial element: repudiation of any claim that the data was changed/tampered/damaged in any way. Should a hash value vary, the action is simple: discard the copy, make a new copy, and begin again. This process shows the courts two key things: process rigor to protect the integrity of the data, and traceability via hash values to demonstrate the integrity of the data and the analysis results derived from the data.

Transporting Evidence

Properly log all evidence in and out of controlled storage. Use proper packing techniques, such as placing components in static-free bags, using foam packing material, and using cardboard boxes. Be especially cautious while transporting evidence to ensure custody of evidence is maintained and the evidence isn't damaged or tampered with.

Storing Evidence

Store the evidence in an evidence room that has low traffic, restricted access, camera monitoring, and entry-logging capabilities. Store components in static-free bags, foam packing material, and cardboard boxes, and inside metal tamper-resistant cabinets or safes whenever possible. Many of today's electronics are sensitive to environmental factors. It is important for storage areas to have environmental controls to protect devices from temperature and humidity changes. It is also prudent to have environmental-monitoring devices to ensure that temperature and humidity remain within safe ranges for electronic devices.

Conducting the Investigation

When analyzing computer storage components, you must use extreme caution. A copy of the system should be analyzed—never the original system, because that will have to serve as evidence. A system specially designed for forensic examination, known as a *forensic workstation,* can be used. Forensic workstations typically contain hard drive bays, write blockers, analysis software, and other devices to safely image and protect computer forensic data. Analysis should be done in a controlled environment with physical security and controlled access.

Never analyze the seized system directly. Always make multiple images of the device and analyze a copy.

Tech Tip

Tools of the Trade

The following are the tools of the forensics trade:

- ***Disk wipe utilities*** *Tools to completely delete files and overwrite contents*
- ***File viewers*** *Text and image viewers*
- ***Forensic programs*** *Tools to analyze disk space, file content, system configuration, and so on*
- ***Forensic workstations*** *Specialized workstations containing hardware, software, and component interface capabilities to perform computer forensic activities*
- ***Hard drive tools*** *Partition-viewing utilities, bootable CDs*
- ***Unerase tools*** *Tools to reverse file deletions*

One of the key elements to preserving the chain of custody, protecting evidence, and having copies of data for analysis is the concept of digital forensic duplication of data. A digital forensic copy is a carefully controlled copy that has every bit the same as the original. Not just files, but all data structures associated with the device, including unused space, are copied in a digital forensic image copy, every bit, bit by bit. Making this type of copy is not something done with normal file utilities; specialty programs are required.

It is also important not to interface with the digital media using the host system because all filesystems both read and write to the storage media as part of their normal operation, thus altering the media. This type of alteration changes information, potentially damaging the trace evidence needed in the investigation. For this reason, a **write blocker** is commonly used to connect the media to the investigator's computer. Figure 23.3 shows a kit that contains both write blockers and a forensic duplicator.

When conducting a digital forensic investigation, consider local laws. Many states require that independent investigators be licensed private investigators. If you are working as an analyst on in-house systems, the laws may have differing levels of applicability. Before consulting, it is best to investigate the need of a license.

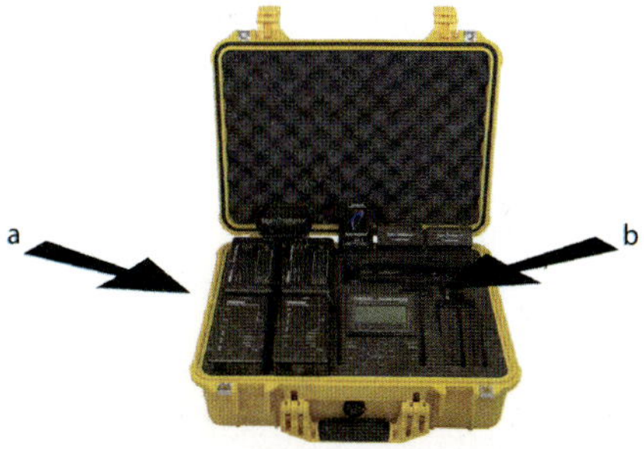

Figure 23.3 (a) Write blocker devices and (b) forensic duplicator device

It is common for forensic duplicator devices to have additional features to assist an investigator, such as making multiple copies at once and calculating hash values for the device and the duplicate. Capturing the hash values for all items is an essential first step in handling any digital evidence.

> **Tech Tip**
>
> **Forensics-Based Drive Imaging**
>
> *When a forensic investigation on a series of computers is needed to determine facts in a computer investigation, a variety of methods can be used to discover and recover the evidence. For example, if a developer group is being investigated, the investigator could look at each machine and find the specific evidence that is being sought. The problem with this approach is that in the process of doing the investigation, the other developers in the area become aware and have a chance to destroy critical evidence. For this reason, and to minimize disruption to a team, many times the investigation begins with a large-scale forensic duplication effort. The steps are remarkably simple and well-practiced by many investigative firms, as shown here:*
>
> 1. *Document the scope of the machines being investigated, noting the number of drives and sizes.*
> 2. *Send in a team after hours to do the duplication.*
> 3. *Open each machine, disconnect the hard drives, and attach external cables.*
> 4. *Duplicate each drive using a forensic duplication procedure that makes a complete image of the hard drive on a separate media source.*
> 5. *Reassemble the machines, leaving no evidence that the duplication was performed.*
>
> *The forensic images are then examined one by one at a later time, away from inquisitive and prying eyes.*

Message Digest and Hash

If files, logs, and other information are going to be captured and used for evidence, you need to ensure that the data isn't modified. In most cases, a tool that implements a hashing algorithm to create message digests is used.

> **Cross Check**
>
> **Hash Algorithms and Forensics**
>
> Hash algorithms offer digital forensics the ability to "bag and tag" evidence. Although it does not protect the evidence from tampering, it provides clear proof of whether data has been changed. This is an important issue to resolve, given how easy it is to change digital data and the fact that typically no trace is left of the change. You can find a complete review of hashing algorithms in Chapter 5. The important question regarding hashes and forensics is this: how and where do you record hash values to protect their integrity as part of the investigative process?

The hash tool is applied to each file or log, and the message digest value is noted in the investigation documentation. It is a good practice to write the logs to a write-once media such as CD-ROM. When the case actually goes to trial, the investigator may need to run the tool on the files or logs again to show that they have not been altered in any way since being obtained.

> The number of files stored on today's hard drives can be large—literally hundreds of thousands of files. Obviously this is far too many for the investigator to directly analyze. However, by matching the message digests for files installed by the most popular software products to the message digests of files on the drive being analyzed, the investigator can avoid analyzing approximately 90 percent of the files because he can assume they are unmodified. The National Software Reference Library (NSRL) collects software from various sources and incorporates file profiles into a Reference Data Set available for download as a service. See www.nsrl.nist.gov.

Analysis

After successfully imaging the drives to be analyzed and calculating and storing the message digests, the investigator can begin the analysis. The details of the investigation will depend on the particulars of the incident being investigated. However, in general, the following steps will be involved:

1. Check the Recycle Bin for deleted files.
2. Check the web browser history files and address bar histories.
3. Check the web browser cookie files. Different web browsers store cookies in different places.
4. Check the Temporary Internet Files folders.
5. Search files for suspect character strings. To conserve valuable time, be wise in the choice of words you search for, choosing *confidential*, *sensitive*, *sex*, or other explicit words and phrases related to your investigation.
6. Search the slack and free space for suspect character strings, as described previously.

> The CAINE Computer Forensics Linux Live distro and SANS Investigative Forensic Toolkit (SIFT) are just two examples of the many tools you can use to perform computer forensic activities.

Timelines of Sequence of Events

Digital forensic investigations begin with a scope—a charge of what is of interest and should be investigated. In a modern computer environment, asking for everything that happened is a scope that is impossible to fulfill, because just booting up a machine can result in hundreds of events, in literally seconds. Once a scope is defined, it inevitably includes a time element, typically something in the order of "between a beginning date and time and an ending date and time, for user XYZ, examine with respect to (insert what is interesting here—keywords, specific types of actions, and so on)." With this information as the boundaries, it is common to produce a *timeline of specific events* that fall within the scope and time boundaries. This timeline will have the specifics, including the metadata to document it, demonstrating the sequence of events as recorded by the computer. The sequence can be very important because it provides key clues as to what actually happened, even when there is not a direct artifact. For instance, if the first time a USB drive was attached to a system, as recorded metadata in the registry, is after the time a file was last touched, then that file is probably not being transported on the USB with a later time of use. User logins and logoffs also help determine sequencing and operations. If a user is accused of performing a certain transaction on a network resource at a specific time

> **Tech Tip**
>
> **Cleanup: Possible Remediation Actions After an Attack**
>
> *Here's a list of things you'll need to do to restore your system after you've responded to an incident and completed your initial investigation:*
>
> - *Place the system behind a firewall.*
> - *Reload the OS.*
> - *Run scanners.*
> - *Install security software.*
> - *Remove unneeded services and applications.*
> - *Apply patches.*
> - *Restore the system from backup.*

and date, but their PC shows they were not logged in, then either they used another machine or something else is happening, such as the account is being hijacked. Building a timeline of activities from multiple perspectives can provide a lot of useful information as to what did happen, what could happen, and what makes no sense (because more data is needed).

Provenance

Provenance is a reference to the origin of data. In the case of digital forensics, it is not enough to present a specific data element as "proof"; one must also show where it came from. Provenance is specific, as in where on a file structure and where on a device, and in most cases there will be multiple representations, as in where the file resides in the file structure with respect to the OS (logical) and its location on a physical drive in sectors (physical). Provenance involves metadata, which can include timestamps, access control information, and a host of other data that can assist in determining which user performed which action at what time with respect to the object. In most cases, there is not a single location for this evidence; like the timeline, it must be constructed from several different artifacts.

Recovery

In a digital forensics sense, recovery is associated with determining the relevant information for the issue at hand. As presented in the earlier example, suppose a sales manager quits and goes to work for a competitor. Since the employee had access to sensitive information that would benefit the new employer, does this change the situation or raise questions? What would you be specifically looking for in the analysis? Analysis works by examining hypotheses, which are specific statements that can be disproved. In other words, what data provides information pertinent to the case at hand? Since forensics software has yet to invent a Find Evidence button, the act of determining what to analyze to demonstrate a hypothesis can be be a significant challenge. If the question is, did person X move a specific file to an external drive, then if your analysis shows the evidence that this movement occurred, hypothesis proven. If not, you can't say it didn't happen, only that there is no evidence to support the statement.

Asking a forensic investigator to tell you everything that happened on a 1TB drive is asking for the impossible. The number of events, files, and processes that occur as a normal part of computing leads to thousands of events for every logon/logoff cycle. Finding a specific activity is not like looking for a needle in a haystack; it is like looking for a needle in all the fields of Kansas. However, there are ways to trim down the work, such as creating timelines to indicate when the suspected activity happened, using keywords to see what strings of information make a record relevant, and looking for specific activities. When you can specify specific activities and those activities have logs associated with their occurrence, you can begin to build a solid data set.

This leads to the idea of active logging. Ideally, you want to minimize logging so when you have to use logs, the event you are interested in stands out without being hidden in a sea of irrelevant log items. Before the problem occurs, if the company sets up logging for specific events in the preparation phase, such as copying sensitive files, then later if questions arise as to whether the event happened or not, a log file exists to provide the information. Active logging is covered in more detail later in the chapter.

Strategic Intelligence/Counterintelligence Gathering

Strategic intelligence is the use of all resources to make determinations. This can make a large difference in whether a firm is prepared for threats. The same idea fits into digital forensics. Strategic intelligence can provide information that limits the scope of an investigation to a manageable level. If you have an idea of specific acts you want to have demonstrable evidence of either happening or not happening, you can build a strategic intelligence data set on the information. Where is it, what is it, and what is allowed/not allowed? These are all pieces of information that, when arranged and analyzed, can lead to a data logging plan to help support forensic event capture. What about things such as adding and removing data wiping programs? The list is long, but just like strategic threat intelligence, it is manageable, and when worked on in concert with other firms and professionals, a meaningful plan can emerge.

Counterintelligence gathering is the act of gathering information specifically targeting the strategic intelligence effort of another entity. Knowing what people are looking at and what information they are obtaining can provide information into their motives and potential future actions.

Active Logging

When you have an idea of what information you will want to examine, you can make an active logging plan that ensures the information is logged when it occurs and, if at all possible, is logged in a location that prevents alteration. **Active logging** is determined during the preparation phase, and when it comes time for recovery, the advance planning pays off in the production of evidence.

Track Man-Hours

Demonstrating the efforts and tasks performed in the forensics process may become an issue in court and other proceedings. Having the ability to demonstrate who did what, when they did it, and how long it took can establish that the steps were taken per the processes employed. Having solid accounting data on man-hours and other expenses can provide corroborating evidence as to the actions performed.

Reports

Reports are the official description of the forensic data. Reports can have a variety of elements—from pure descriptive information, such as machine/device identifiers (make, model and serial number), to information on the data, including size and hash values. Reports can also have specific elements that are derived from this information, such as a timeline, an analysis of keywords, specific artifacts, and present or missing items. An expert can opine on what these elements mean or can mean with respect to the system. For instance, if timestamps are significantly different, the expert may note that the difference exists. From a professional perspective, it is important for the forensics investigator to stick to just what the information can show and not add any commentary. For example, if the timestamp data has been tampered with, this is a provable fact, but then opining on who did it is more speculation and may result in the expert being called out on this in court. Experts who stray from the provable can be reprimanded by the judge, and being stricken from a case is a black mark that will call into question one's opinions both now and in the future. As such, reports tend to be very sanitized, and the lawyers add color to the case later.

Host Forensics

Host forensics refers to the analysis of a specific system. Host forensics includes a wide range of elements, such as the analysis of filesystems and artifacts of the operating system. These elements often are specific to individual systems and operating systems, such as Linux or Windows.

Filesystems

When a user deletes a file, the file is not actually deleted. Instead, a pointer in a file allocation table is deleted. This pointer was used by the operating system to track down the file when it was referenced, and the act of "deleting" the file merely removes the pointer and marks the cluster (or clusters) holding the file as available for the operating system to use. The actual data originally stored on the disk remains on the disk (until that space is used again); it just isn't recognized as a coherent file by the operating system.

Partitions

Physical memory storage devices can be divided into a series of containers; each of these containers is called a **partition**. A partition is a logical storage unit that is subsequently used by an operating system. Systems can have multiple partitions for a wide variety of reasons, ranging from hosting multiple operating systems to performance-maximizing efforts to protection efforts. The broad issue of partition operation and management is outside the scope of this chapter, but this is a critical topic to understand and examine when looking at a system forensically.

Free Space

Since a deleted file is not actually completely erased or overwritten, it sits on the hard disk until the operating system needs to use that space for another file or application. Sometimes the second file that is saved in the same area does not occupy as many clusters as the first file, so a fragment of the original file is left over.

The cluster that holds the fragment of the original file is referred to as **free space** because the operating system has marked it as usable when needed. As soon as the operating system stores something else in this cluster, it is considered allocated. The unallocated clusters still contain the original data until the operating system overwrites them. Looking at the free space might reveal information left over from files the user thought were deleted from the drive.

Slack Space

Another place that should be reviewed is **slack space**, which is different from free space. When a file is saved to a hard drive or other storage medium, the operating system allocates space in blocks of a predefined size, called *clusters.* Even if your file contains only ten characters, the operating system will allocate a full cluster—with space left over in the cluster. This is slack space.

It is possible for a user to hide malicious code, tools, or clues in slack space, as well as in the free space. You may also find information in slack space from files that previously occupied that same cluster. Therefore, an investigator should review slack space using utilities that can display the information stored in these areas.

Hidden Files

There are numerous ways to hide data on a system. One method is to hide files by setting the hidden attribute, which limits the listing of them by standard file utilities. Devised so that system files that should not be directly manipulated are hidden from easy view, this concept raises a broader question with respect to forensics: how can a user hide information from easy accessibility?

There is a wide range of methods for hiding files, and any attempt to list them would be long and subject to continual change. The major ones typically encountered include changing a file extension, encryption, streams, and storage on other partitions. You already learned about partitions—it is obvious that a forensic investigation should find, enumerate, and explore all partitions. Streams will be covered in the next section. Encrypted data, by its very nature, is hidden from view. Without the key, modern encryption methods resist any brute force attempts to determine the contents. It is important to find encrypted data stores and document the locations for later use by legal counsel.

Changing a file's extension does not actually alter the contents or usability of a file. It merely breaks the automated runtime association manager that determines what executable is associated with the file type to properly handle it. The challenge of how to handle file types goes back to the early days of computers, when the magic number method was created. The term **magic number** describes a series of digits near the beginning of the file that provides information about the file format. In some cases, the magic number can be read by humans; for example, GIF87a or GIF89a indicates both Graphics Interchange Format (GIF) and the specification. Other file types are less obvious, such as a Tagged Image File Format (TIFF) file on an Intel platform, which is II followed by 42 as a 2-byte integer (49 49 2A 00).

Most integrated forensic tool suites handle file identification via magic number and are thus able to find hidden videos, pictures, and other items.

The other thing these tools can do is complete searches across the entire storage structure for strings, and this can find many "hidden" items.

Streams

Streams is a short name for *alternate data streams,* a specific data structure associated with NTFS in Windows. The normal location for data in an NTFS-based system is in the data stream, a location identified by a record in the master file table (MFT) called $DATA:, which is technically an unnamed data stream. Alternate data streams have names and are identified by $DATA:*StreamName,* where *StreamName* is the name of the stream being used. Streams can be used to hide information; although the information is still present, most of the normal file utilities do not deal with streams, so it will not be seen. Forensic tool suites have tools that can search for, report on, and analyze stream data on Windows systems.

Artifacts

Artifacts are the principal data element used in forensics. They are connected to how the computer manages data to perform a task. Understanding the artifacts of a particular system is important in the digital forensics process.

Artifacts are the key element in modern digital forensics. Most of the items used to demonstrate a specific action as occurring fall into one of two categories: metadata or OS artifact. Metadata examples include items like registry entries, timestamps, and sizes. OS artifacts include things like prefetch files, jump list artifacts such as most frequently used (MFU) and most recently used (MRU), shellbags, link files, and more. The metadata artifacts are items that the OS uses to perform its duties, while most of the OS artifacts are related to improving performance. Keeping a cache of links to most recently used files will speed up activity if the user returns to previous work, a common task. Also, deletion of the work (a file) does not delete the associated artifacts. Hence, artifacts can live on after a file is gone, leaving proof that the file existed.

Swap/Pagefile

The **swap** or **pagefile** is a structure on a system's disk to provide temporary storage for memory needs that exceed a system's RAM capacity. The operating system has provisions to manage the RAM and pagefile, keeping in RAM what is immediately needed and moving excess to the pagefile when RAM is full. This causes a performance hit, and with the reasonable cost of RAM, most systems avoid this with sufficient RAM. Capturing the pagefile in a forensics investigation is important any time the RAM is captured, as it is an extension of the RAM.

Firmware

Firmware is a set of software that is associated with a physical device. Firmware exists for almost every electronic device, not just computers. It can even be found in things like USB devices. Firmware can be of interest in a forensics investigation when the malfunctioning of a device is an issue, as malware has targeted firmware. As such, it takes a very specialized set of tools and equipment to analyze, as firmware is not readily accessible to outside users.

Snapshot

A **snapshot** is a picture of a particular moment in time. Snapshots are common in virtual machines, providing a point in time to which the machine can be recovered to. Operating systems also have adopted this technology for some of their information: a point-in-time recovery point to assist in fixing problems from updates or changes to the system. These captures of points in time can be useful to a forensic investigator, as they allow a means of looking at specific content at an earlier point of time. The scope of what is covered by a snapshot can vary between different systems, and this may limit usefulness.

Cache

Caches are temporary storage locations used for commonly used items, designed to speed up processing. Caches exist all over in computer systems and are performance-enhancing items. Caches exist for files, for memory, and for artifacts; they exist for fast retrieval of items that the OS expects. As such, they are inherently relevant to something that has been done and is likely to be done again, and they can serve as evidence of things that have been done.

Windows Metadata

Microsoft Windows–based systems have a wide range of artifacts with forensic value. Before examining some of these artifacts, it is important to understand why they exist. The vast majority of artifacts exist for the purpose of improving the user experience. Tracking what users do and have done and making that information available to the operating system to improve future use is one of the primary reasons for the information; its forensic value is secondary.

Registry Analysis

The first and foremost Windows artifact is the system Registry, which acts a database repository of a whole host of information and provides a one-stop shop for a wide range of Windows forensic artifacts—what applications have been installed, user activity, activity associated with external devices, and more. Although the specific artifacts needed in an investigation differ based on the scope of the investigation, it is safe to assume that metadata recorded by the Windows operating system will serve a useful purpose in the investigation, especially since the Registry is stored by user and therefore the activity recorded in the Registry is attributable to a user.

The list of artifacts stored by the Registry is extremely long, but one of the major types is the **event logs** of a wide range of system and security information. There is also a wide range of file activity artifacts that can be analyzed, including analysis of shellbags, which provides evidence of folder opening. LNK files and most recently used (MRU) elements can point to filesystem activity. A wide range of date/time stamps on files, even deleted files, can be present for examination. There are specific toolsets designed to forensically explore the Registry and retrieve the desired artifacts from this voluminous store.

Tech Tip

Windows USB Analysis

Windows records a wide array of information on each USB device used in the system, including the following:

- *Vendor/make/version and possibly unique serial number*
- *Volume name and serial number*
- *Last drive letter assigned*
- *MountPoints2, a registry entry that stores the last drive mapping per user*
- *Username of the user who used the USB device*
- *Time of first USB device connection*
- *Time of last USB device connection*
- *Time of last USB device removal*

As mentioned before and will be mentioned again, Windows forensic analysis is no different from any other forensic analysis with respect to forensic procedures. Skill and proficiency in forensic procedures is the most important issue when analyzing a system because damage may make the use of the information impossible.

Linux Metadata

Linux systems have their own sets of artifacts. From a forensics perspective, Linux systems differ from Windows systems in these three main ways:

- **No registry** Program data is stored in scattered locations.
- **Different filesystem** A multitude of different filesystems are used, each with different attributes.
- **Plaintext abounds** Files and data tend to be in plaintext, which impacts searching.

The lack of a registry to hold system and program information does not mean that the information is not there; it just means that it is distributed. The same is true of filesystems. Rather than offering only two filesystem structures (NTFS and FAT), Linux comes with a whole host of different forms. Each of these has quirks, such as no file creation dates in many of them and the zeroing of metadata when files are deleted, thus resulting in forensic challenges.

When it comes to performing forensics on a Linux system, the value of a good sysadmin cannot be understated. Many of the artifacts of activity on a Linux system are scattered to various local locations, and a good sysadmin can assist in locating and recovering the essential elements for analysis. This is not a license for a sysadmin to begin performing forensic activities, however. The same rules and procedural requirements listed earlier still apply, and in most cases these necessitate the use of forensically trained professionals.

Timestamps

Timestamps are specific metadata entries used as artifacts in a computer system investigation. While a log entry may have one, some items can have multiple timestamps, stored in multiple locations. In NTFS, there are three common file times (Creation, Modification, and Accessed) and one metadata time (MFT Change). These four timestamps are stored in two places: one with the $File_Name attribute, and one with $Standard_Info. And if that isn't enough confusion, the two different attributes are updated differently, meaning they may differ. This is important to forensic investigations because timestamps can be changed on systems, and this can lead to erroneous conclusions. Tampering with timestamps is challenging given that most tools do not handle all timestamps in the same way, which can lead to evidence of tampering.

Time is measured differently in Linux and Windows. Linux uses the concept of Epoch time—the number of seconds that have elapsed since January 1, 1970 (midnight UTC/GMT), not counting leap seconds. It is stored as a signed 32-bit number, enabling times before January 1, 1970, as well as after. The system clock has a resolution of a second, although there are timer elements that allow down to nanosecond timing measurements. Microsoft Windows uses a 64-bit value that represents the elapsed time since 12:00 A.M. January 1, 1601 Coordinated Universal Time (UTC), with a resolution of 100-nanosecond intervals. Note that both systems use UTC as a base, and most storage of time elements is done in UTC, with conversions to local time happening upon reading a value.

One of the challenges for all timestamp usage is inconsistency in the OS in keeping values up to date. While Microsoft Windows has a plethora of different timestamps to look at, there is great inconsistency on many of these values being updated by the OS or an application. The primary reason for this revolves around performance, as most timestamps are mere artifacts and are not important in many standard OS functions. Not maintaining the timestamps, or not maintaining all copies of timestamps, can improve the performance of some operations.

> **Tech Tip**
>
> **SSD Forensics**
>
> *The advent of solid state drives brings substantial improvements in performance. It also brings new issues with respect to forensics. Because of the way the solid state drives work, they are "leveled" periodically to maintain wear across the memory. This results in data being rewritten, and elements that are no longer valid are lost. Thus, a lot of the "standard" artifacts that would be found in a magnetic memory system are not preserved in solid state drives. As these drives are becoming common in systems, forensic analysts have to take all of these technical issues into consideration when attempting to reconstruct what happened.*

Device Forensics

Device forensics is the application of digital forensic principles to devices—mobile phones, tablets, the endless list of devices that comprise the "Internet of Things," and more. The fact that it is a device does not change the principles pertaining to collecting and handling evidence. All of the forensic principles still apply and are just as important. What does change are the tools and processes employed to retrieve and analyze the data. This is because the filesystems, data structures, operating systems, and artifacts are different from those in the world of servers and PCs.

Network Forensics

Network forensics consists of capturing, recording, and analyzing network events to discover the source of network problems or security incidents. Examining networks in a forensic fashion introduces several challenges. First is scale. The scale of a network is related to the number of nodes and the speed of traffic. Second is the issue of volume. Packet capture is not technically difficult, but it can necessitate large quantities of storage. And although storage is relatively cheap, large numbers of packets can be difficult to sort through and analyze. Because of these issues, network forensics becomes an issue of specificity; if you know what target and what protocols you are looking for, you can selectively capture and analyze the traffic for those segments and have data that is useful. But therein lies the other challenge. Network data is temporal. It exists while the packet is in transit, and then it is gone, forever. Metadata such as NetFlow data can provide some information, but it does not contain any content of the data being transmitted.

As a general-purpose tool, network forensics is nearly impossible because of the scale issues. But in specific situations, such as in front of high-value targets that have limited data movement, it can prove to be valuable. It can also be valuable in troubleshooting ongoing incidents and problems in the network.

The same rules apply to network forensics as apply to all other forensic collection efforts. Preserving the integrity of the data is paramount, and maintaining control over the data is always a challenge. Forensic rules (admissibility, chain of custody, and so on) do not change because the source of data has changed.

Legal Hold

In the U.S. legal system, legal precedent requires that potentially relevant information must be preserved at the instant a party "reasonably anticipates" litigation or another type of formal dispute. Although this sounds technical, it is fairly simple: once you realize you need to preserve evidence, you must use a **legal hold**, or **litigation hold**, process by which you properly preserve any and all digital evidence related to a potential case. This event is usually triggered by one firm issuing a litigation hold request to another. Once this notice is received, the receiving firm is required to maintain in complete, unaltered form (both in data and metadata) any and all information related to the issue at hand. This means that ordinary data retention policies no longer are in effect and that even alterations to metadata can be considered to be a violation of the hold request, and if the court believes this can materially affect the ability of a jury to make a decision, the jury can be instructed to consider the act as hiding evidence. Major awards have been decided based on failure to retain information.

Understanding the consequences of legal hold on record retention is important, and legal holds supersede any standard corporate policy or procedure.

Where does this information reside? It resides everywhere, including e-mail, office documents, network shares, mobile phones, tablets, and databases. Just think of everywhere the information is shared; all copies need to be produced unaltered, often years after the document was created. Finding and managing all of this information falls under a topic called **e-discovery**, which is a branch of digital forensics dealing with identifying, managing, and preserving digital information that is subject to legal hold.

E-discovery

Electronic discovery, or *e-discovery*, is the term used for the document and data production requirements as part of legal discovery in civil litigation. When a civil lawsuit is filed, under court approval, a firm can be compelled to turn over specific data from systems pursuant to the legal issue at hand. Electronic information is considered to be the same as paper documents in some respects and completely different in others. The evidentiary value can be identical. The fragility can be substantial—electronic records can be changed without leaving a trace. Electronic documents can also have metadata associated with them, such as who edited the document, previous version information, and more.

One of the pressing challenges in today's enterprise record store is the maintenance of the volumes of electronic information. Keeping track of the information stores based on a wide range of search terms is essential to comply with e-discovery requests. It is common for systems to use forensic processes and tools to perform e-discovery searches.

Reference Model

EDRM, a coalition of consumers and providers focused on improving e-discovery and information governance, has created a reference model for e-discovery. The Electronic Discovery Reference Model, shown in Figure 23.4, provides a framework for organizations to prepare for e-discovery. The major steps of the framework are thoroughly described on the EDRM website (http://edrm.net). Additional resources available from EDRM include XML schemas, glossaries, metrics, and more.

Big Data

It may seem that big data is all the rage in business today, but in reality it is simply a description of the times. We have created large data stores in most enterprises as a byproduct of cheap storage and the ubiquity of the Internet. Big data is an issue in e-discovery as well. The cataloging, storage, and maintenance of corporate records often become big data issues. This facilitates the use of big data methods in many cases. This is an area of rapid development, both for forensics and for e-discovery, as data volumes continue to grow exponentially.

Cloud

The cloud has become a resource for enterprise IT systems, and as such it is intimately involved in both e-discovery and forensics. Having data that may or may not be directly accessed by the tools of e-discovery and forensics can complicate the needed processes. An additional complication is the legal issues associated with the contracts between the organization and the cloud

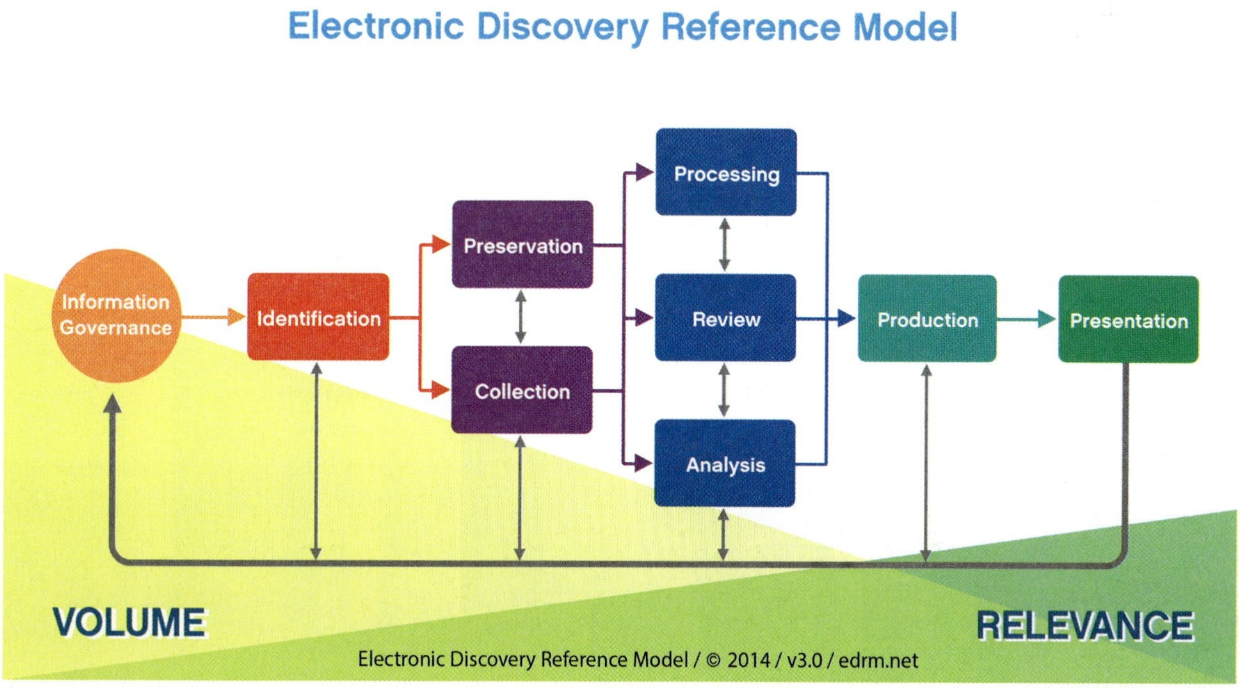

• **Figure 23.4** Electronic Discovery Reference Model (courtesy of EDRM, EDRM.net)

provider. As both forensics and e-discovery are secondary processes from a business perspective, they may or may not be addressed in a standard cloud agreement. Because these processes can become important—and if they do, it may be too late to contractually address them—it behooves an organization to prepare by addressing them in cloud agreements with third parties. The topic of cloud computing is covered in detail in Chapter 18.

Right to Audit Clauses

Audits are the mechanism used to verify that systems are performing to their designed levels of purpose, security, and efficiency. The ability to audit involves access to a system and the data. When the information is stored or processed in the cloud, users need the ability to audit the cloud provider. The level and scope of the audit can vary given the dynamic natures of both the cloud and the regulatory environment, but one thing does not vary. The only rights the customer has are detailed in the service level agreements/contracts with the cloud provider. This makes the **right to audit clause** a critical requirement of any service level agreement, and its specificity needs to match the operational and regulatory scope of the cloud engagement.

Regulatory/Jurisdiction

Whether **on premises** or in the **cloud**, there will be cases where regulatory or law enforcement actions raise jurisdictional issues. If you have your software development data in the cloud, and the servers/storage elements are in a foreign country, whose laws will apply? It is important to consult with the company legal counsel to understand the ramifications of data location with respect to forensics and subsequent data use.

Chapter 23 Review

Chapter Summary

After reading this chapter and completing the exercises, you should understand the following about incident response and forensics.

Explore the basics of digital forensics

- Digital forensics is the collection of processes and procedures used to prepare digital information for use in legal or administrative proceedings.
- Because of the importance of veracity and the fragility of digital data to integrity violations that cannot be detected, it is imperative that processes be complete and comprehensive.

Identify the rules and types of evidence

- Evidence must meet the three standards of being sufficient, competent, and relevant if it is to be used in legal proceedings.
- There are four different types of evidence: direct, real, documentary, and demonstrative.
- There are three rules regarding evidence: the best evidence rule, the exclusionary rule, and the hearsay rule.

Collect and preserve evidence

- Evidence must be properly collected, protected, and controlled to be of value during court or disciplinary activities.
- When acquiring evidence, one must be deliberate to ensure evidence is not damaged and operations are not negatively impacted.
- Evidence must be properly marked so that it can be readily identified as that particular piece of evidence gathered at the scene.
- Evidence must be protected so that it is not tampered with, damaged, or compromised.
- Evidence should be transported cautiously to ensure custody of the evidence is maintained and the evidence itself is not tampered with or damaged.
- Evidence should be stored in properly controlled areas and conditions.
- When conducting an investigation on computer components, one must be deliberate and cautious to ensure evidence is not damaged.

Maintain a viable chain of custody

- A chain of custody that accounts for all persons who handled or have access to the evidence must be maintained to prevent evidence tampering or damage.

Investigate a computer crime or policy violation

- Information can be recorded and possibly hidden in various ways on a computer. Sometimes information will be hidden in either the free space or the slack space of the computer's disk drive.
- Free space is the space (clusters) on a storage medium that is available for the operating system to use.
- Slack space is the unused space on a disk drive created when a file is smaller than the allocated unit of storage, such as a cluster.
- The use of a message digest or hashing algorithm is essential to ensure that information stored on a computer's disk drives has not been changed.
- If the information in the data stream or file is changed, a different message digest will result, indicating the file has been tampered with.
- Forensic analysis of data stored on a hard drive can begin once the drive has been imaged and message digests of important files have been calculated and stored.
- Analysis typically involves investigating the Recycle Bin, web browser and address bar history files, cookie files, temporary Internet file folders, suspect files, and free space and slack space.
- Experience and knowledge are your most valuable tools available when performing computer forensic activities.

Examine system artifacts

- Different systems can have different artifacts based on the operating system and equipment employed.
- Windows and Linux systems have many similar artifacts, although they are located in different areas and preserved in different ways.

Develop forensic policies and procedures

- The overarching principle for all digital forensic investigations is proper procedures. Any deviation from proper procedures can permanently alter evidence and render information unusable in follow-on procedures, whether criminal, civil, or administrative. Ensuring proper procedures by trained professionals is essential from the first aspect of an investigation.

Examine the policies and procedures associated with e-discovery

- E-discovery is the term used for the document and data production requirements as part of legal discovery in civil litigation.
- The Electronic Discovery Reference Model provides a framework for organizations to prepare for e-discovery.

Key Terms

active logging *(893)*
admissibility *(882)*
artifacts *(896)*
best evidence rule *(879)*
cache *(897)*
chain of custody *(880)*
checksums *(887)*
competent evidence *(879)*
counterintelligence gathering *(893)*
data recovery *(882)*
demonstrative evidence *(878)*
device forensics *(899)*
direct evidence *(878)*
documentary evidence *(878)*
e-discovery *(900)*
event logs *(897)*
evidence *(877)*
exclusionary rule *(879)*
firmware *(896)*
forensics *(877)*
free space *(895)*
hash *(886)*
hashing algorithm *(886)*
hearsay rule *(879)*
host forensics *(894)*
legal hold *(900)*
litigation hold *(900)*
magic number *(895)*
network forensics *(899)*
on-premises vs. cloud *(902)*
order of volatility *(884)*
partition *(894)*
preservation *(888)*
provenance *(892)*
real evidence *(878)*
record time offset *(886)*
relevant evidence *(879)*
reports *(893)*
right to audit clause *(902)*
slack space *(895)*
snapshot *(897)*
strategic intelligence *(893)*
stream *(896)*
sufficient evidence *(879)*
swap/pagefile *(896)*
tags *(880)*
timestamps *(898)*
write blocker *(889)*

Key Terms Quiz

Use terms from the Key Terms list to complete the sentences that follow. Don't use the same term more than once. Not all terms will be used.

1. Evidence collected in violation of the Fourth Amendment of the U.S. Constitution, the Electronic Communications Privacy Act (ECPA), or other aspects of the U.S. Code may not be admissible to a court under the terms of the ______________.
2. Evidence that is legally qualified and reliable is ______________.
3. Documents, verbal statements, and material objects admissible in a court of law are called ______________.
4. The rule whereby courts prefer original evidence rather than a copy to ensure that no alteration of the evidence (whether intentional or unintentional) has occurred is termed the ______________.
5. To understand time values relative to other systems in a network, one should ______________.
6. ______________ consists of the preservation, identification, documentation, and interpretation of computer data to be used in legal proceedings.
7. ______________ is evidence that is material to the case or has a bearing on the matter at hand.
8. ______________ is the unused space on a disk drive when a file is smaller than the allocated unit of storage.
9. ______________ is oral testimony or other evidence that proves a specific fact (such as an eyewitness's statement, fingerprint, photo, and so on). The knowledge of the facts is obtained through the five senses of the witness. There are no inferences or presumptions.
10. ______________ consists of the remaining sectors of a previously allocated file that are available for the operating system to use.

Multiple-Choice Quiz

1. What is the order of collecting evidence at a scene?
   - **A.** Take a picture of the screen, RAM, copy USBs, copy hard disk, live network connections
   - **B.** RAM, live network connections, temporary swap space, data on hard disk(s)
   - **C.** Hard disk, RAM, any USBs
   - **D.** ARP cache, live network connections, RAM, hard disk
2. Which of the following correctly defines evidence as being relevant?
   - **A.** The evidence is material to the case or has a bearing on the matter at hand.
   - **B.** The evidence is presented in the form of business records, printouts, or other items.
   - **C.** The evidence is convincing or measures up without question.
   - **D.** The evidence is legally qualified and reliable.
3. Which of the following correctly defines documentary evidence?
   - **A.** The evidence is presented in the form of business records, printouts, manuals, and other items.
   - **B.** The knowledge of the facts is obtained through the five senses of the witness.
   - **C.** The evidence is used to aid the jury and may be in the form of a model, experiment, chart, or other item and be offered to prove an event occurred.
   - **D.** Physical evidence that links the suspect to the scene of a crime.

4. Which of the following correctly defines real evidence?
   - **A.** The evidence is convincing or measures up without question.
   - **B.** The evidence is material to the case or has a bearing on the matter at hand.
   - **C.** The evidence is used to aid the jury and may be in the form of a model, experiment, chart, or other item and be offered to prove an event occurred.
   - **D.** Tangible objects that prove or disprove a fact.
5. Which of the following is the least rigorous investigative method?
   - **A.** Using a dedicated forensic workstation
   - **B.** Verifying software on a suspect system and using that software for the investigation
   - **C.** Examining the suspect system using its software without verification
   - **D.** Booting the suspect system with a verified external OS kernel and tools
6. Which of the following correctly defines slack space?
   - **A.** The space on a disk drive that is occupied by the boot sector
   - **B.** The space located at the beginning of a partition
   - **C.** The remaining sectors of a previously allocated file that are available for the operating system to use
   - **D.** The unused space on a disk drive when a file is smaller than the allocated unit of storage
7. Which of the following correctly describes the minimum contents of an evidence control log book?
   - **A.** Description, Investigator, Case #, Date, Time, Location, Reason
   - **B.** Description, Investigator, Case #, Date, Location, Reason
   - **C.** Description, Case #, Date, Time, Location, Reason
   - **D.** Description, Coroner, Case #, Date, Time, Location, Reason
8. Which of the following correctly describes the chain of custody for evidence?
   - **A.** The evidence is convincing or measures up without question.
   - **B.** It accounts for all persons who handled or had access to a specific item of evidence.
   - **C.** Description, Investigator, Case #, Date, Time, Location, Reason.
   - **D.** The evidence is legally qualified and reliable.
9. Which of the following correctly defines the exclusionary rule?
   - **A.** Any evidence collected in violation of the Fourth Amendment is not admissible as evidence.
   - **B.** The evidence consists of tangible objects that prove or disprove a fact.
   - **C.** The knowledge of the facts is obtained through the five senses of the witness.
   - **D.** The evidence is used to aid the jury and may be in the form of a model, experiment, chart, or the like, offered to prove an event occurred.
10. Which of the following correctly defines free space?
    - **A.** The unused space on a disk drive when a file is smaller than the allocated unit of storage (such as a sector).
    - **B.** The space on a disk drive that is occupied by the boot sector.
    - **C.** The space located at the beginning of a partition.
    - **D.** The remaining sectors of a previously allocated file that are available for the operating system to use.

11. A judge has issued an order for all e-mail to be preserved, and that order is in effect. Which of the following statements is correct?
   A. You can delete old e-mail after the standard retention period.
   B. You should have legal determine which records must be saved.
   C. You should continue archiving all e-mail.
   D. You can delete the e-mail after making a copy to save for e-discovery.
12. You have been tasked with assisting in the forensic investigation of an incident relating to employee misconduct. The employee's supervisor believes evidence of this misconduct can be found on the employee's assigned workstation. Which of the following choices *best* describes what should be done?
   A. Create a timeline of events related to the scope.
   B. Copy the user profile to reduce the search space.
   C. Sign in as the user and search through their recent efforts.
   D. Examine log file entries under the user's profile.

Essay Quiz

1. A supervisor has brought to your office a confiscated computer that was allegedly used to view inappropriate material. He has asked you to look for evidence to support this allegation. Because you work for a small company, you do not have an extra computer you can dedicate to your analysis. How would you boot the system and begin forensic analysis? Provide a reason for your method.
2. Explain why you should always search the free space and slack space if you suspect a person has deliberately deleted files or information on a workstation that you are analyzing.
3. You have been asked by management to secure the laptop computer of an individual who was just dismissed from the company under unfavorable circumstances. Pretend that your own computer is the laptop that has been secured. Make the first entry in your log book and describe how you would start this incident off correctly by properly protecting and securing the evidence.

Lab Projects

• Lab Project 23.1

Use an MD5 or SHA-1 algorithm to obtain the hash value for a file of your choice. Record the hash value. Change the file with a word processor or text editor. Obtain the hash value for the modified file. Compare the results.

• Lab Project 23.2

To understand what information is stored on your computer, examine the contents of the Temporary Internet Files folders. Review the filenames and examine the contents of a few of the files. Describe how this information could be used as evidence of a crime.

chapter 24

Legal Issues and Ethics

If you have ten thousand regulations you destroy all respect for the law.

—Winston Churchill

In this chapter, you will learn how to

- **Explain the laws and rules concerning importing and exporting encryption software**
- **Identify the laws that govern computer access and trespass**
- **Identify the laws that govern encryption and digital rights management**
- **Describe the laws that govern digital signatures**
- **Explore ethical issues associated with information security**

Computer security is no different from any other subject in our society; as technological changes result in conflicts, laws are enacted to enable desired behaviors and prohibit undesired behaviors. The one substantial difference between this aspect of our society and others is that the speed of advancement in the information systems world, as driven by business, computer network connectivity, and the Internet, is much greater than in the legal system of compromise and lawmaking. In some cases, laws have been overly restrictive, limiting business options, such as in the area of importing and exporting encryption technology. In other cases, legislation has been slow in coming, and this fact has stymied business initiatives, such as in digital signatures. And in some areas, legislation has been both too fast and too slow, as in the case of privacy laws. One thing is certain: you will never satisfy everyone with a law, but it does delineate the rules of the game.

The cyber-law environment has not been fully defined by the courts. Laws have been enacted, but until they have been fully tested and explored by cases in court, the exact limits are somewhat unknown. This makes some aspects of interpretation more challenging, but the vast majority of the legal environment is known well enough that effective policies can be enacted to navigate this environment properly. Policies and procedures are tools you use to ensure understanding and compliance with laws and regulations affecting cyberspace.

Cybercrime

One of the many ways to examine cybercrime is to study how the computer is involved in the criminal act. Three types of computer crimes commonly occur: computer-assisted crime, computer-targeted crime, and computer-incidental crime. The differentiating factor is in how the computer is specifically involved from the criminal's point of view. Just as crime is not a new phenomenon, neither is the use of computers, and cybercrime has a history of several decades.

> There are three forms of computer involvement in criminal activity:
> - The computer as a tool of a crime
> - The computer as a victim of a crime
> - The computer that is incidental to a crime

What is new is how computers are involved in criminal activities. The days of simple teenage hacking activities from a bedroom have been replaced by organized crime–controlled botnets (groups of computers commandeered by a malicious hacker) and acts designed to attack specific targets. The legal system has been slow to react, and law enforcement has been hampered by its own challenges in responding to the new threats posed by high-tech crime.

What comes to mind when most people think about cybercrime is a computer that is targeted and attacked by an intruder. The criminal attempts to benefit from some form of unauthorized activity associated with a computer. In the 1980s and '90s, cybercrime was mainly virus and worm attacks, each exacting some form of damage, yet the gain for the criminal was usually negligible. Enter the 21st century, with new forms of malware, rootkits, and targeted attacks; criminals can now target individual users and their bank accounts. In the current environment, it is easy to predict where this form of attack will occur—if money is involved, a criminal will attempt to obtain a cut. A common method of criminal activity is computer-based fraud. Advertising on the Internet is big business, and hence the "new" crime of **click fraud** is now a concern. Click fraud involves a piece of malware that defrauds the advertising revenue counter engine through fraudulent user clicks.

eBay, the leader in the Internet auction space, and PayPal are frequent targets of fraud. Whether the fraud occurs by fraudulent listing, fraudulent bidding, or outright stealing of merchandise, the results are the same: a crime is committed. As users move toward online banking and stock trading, so moves the criminal element. Malware designed to install a keystroke logger and then watch for bank/brokerage logins is common on the Internet. Once the attacker finds the targets, they can begin looting accounts. The risk of getting caught and prosecuted is exceedingly low. Walk into a bank in the United States and rob it, and the odds are better than 95 percent that you will be doing time in federal prison after the FBI hunts you down and

> **Tech Tip**
>
> **FBI Priorities**
>
> *In the post-9/11 environment, federal law enforcement priorities shifted toward terrorism. During the reassessment of national law enforcement priorities, cyber-related crimes increased in importance, moving to number three on the FBI priority list. Currently, the priorities for the FBI (per https://www.fbi.gov/about/mission) are as follows:*
>
> 1. *Protect the United States from terrorist attack.*
> 2. *Protect the United States against foreign intelligence operations and espionage.*
> 3. *Protect the United States against cyber-based attacks and high-technology crimes.*
> 4. *Combat public corruption at all levels.*
> 5. *Protect civil rights.*
> 6. *Combat transnational/national criminal organizations and enterprises.*
> 7. *Combat major white-collar crime.*
> 8. *Combat significant violent crime.*

slaps the cuffs on your wrists. Do the same crime via a computer, and the odds are even better for the opposite outcome: less than 1 percent of these attackers are caught and prosecuted.

The low risk of being caught is one of the reasons that criminals are turning to computer crime. Just as computers have become easy for ordinary people to use, the trend continues for the criminal element. Today's cybercriminals use computers as tools to steal intellectual property or other valuable data and then subsequently market these materials through underground online forums. Using the computer to physically isolate the criminal from the direct event of the crime has made the investigation and prosecution of these crimes much more challenging for authorities.

The last way computers are involved with criminal activities is through incidental involvement. Back in 1931, the U.S. government used accounting records and tax laws to convict Al Capone of tax evasion. Today, similar records are kept on computers. Computers are also used to traffic child pornography and engage in other illicit activities—these computers act more as storage devices than as actual tools to enable the crime. Because child pornography existed before computers made its distribution easier, the computer is actually incidental to the crime itself.

With the three forms of computer involvement in criminal activities, multiplied by the myriad of ways a criminal can use a computer to steal or defraud, added to the indirect connection mediated by the computer and the Internet, computer crime of the 21st century is a complex problem indeed. Technical issues are associated with all the protocols and architectures. A major legal issue is the education of the entire legal system as to the serious nature of computer crimes. All these factors are further complicated by the use of the Internet to separate the criminal and their victim geographically. Imagine this defense: "Your honor, as shown by my client's electronic monitoring bracelet, he was in his apartment in California when this crime occurred. The victim claims that the money was removed from his local bank in New York City. Now, last time I checked, New York City was a long way from Los Angeles, so how could my client have robbed the bank?"

U.S. Law Enforcement Encryption Debate

A debate arose in the 1990s concerning encryption policy that led to laws concerning the export of encryption technology and government access to keys. A project called the Clipper chip was conceived to provide cryptography yet maintain the ability of the government to decrypt messages. But this all died with the rapid rise of e-commerce and the need for SSL.

The debate has been raised again with the widespread use of mobile devices, due to them having more computing power than most enterprises had in the '90s. And with this digital power comes end-to-end encryption of data and devices. Law enforcement can seize devices yet still be unable to get to the data. Due to need, law enforcement and the government have attempted to get laws passed to allow their access. Currently, the debate rages on in the U.S., but the UK and Australia have both passed legislation giving the government access to user data via either a backdoor, tools, or keys. This debate will not be resolved soon. For the best analysis of the technical implications, read "Keys Under the Doormats: Mandating

Insecurity by Requiring Government Access to all Data and Communications" (https://dspace.mit.edu/bitstream/handle/1721.1/97690/MIT-CSAIL-TR-2015-026.pdf). This is a 2015 report from many of the best cryptographers in the world and is regarded as a seminal work in applied cryptography.

Common Internet Crime Schemes

To find crime, just follow the money. In the United States, the FBI and the National White Collar Crime Center (NW3C) have joined forces in developing the Internet Crime Complaint Center (IC3), an online clearinghouse that communicates issues associated with cybercrime. The IC3 website has several useful links, including the following:

- For industry alerts, go to https://www.ic3.gov/Home/IndustryAlerts.
- For consumer alerts, go to https://www.ic3.gov/Home/ConsumerAlertsChoice.
- To file a complaint, go to https://www.ic3.gov/Home/ComplaintChoice.

Sources of Laws

In the United States, three primary sources of laws and regulations affect our lives and govern our actions. A **statutory law** is passed by a legislative branch of government, be it the U.S. Congress or a local city council. Another source of laws and regulations is administrative bodies given power by other legislation. The power of government-sponsored agencies, such as the Environmental Protection Agency (EPA), the Federal Aviation Administration (FAA), the Federal Communication Commission (FCC), and others, lies in their ability to enforce behaviors through administrative rule making, or **administrative law**. The last source of law in the United States is **common law**, or **case law**, which is based on previous events or precedent. This source of law comes from the judicial branch of government: judges decide on the applicability of laws and regulations.

Three types of laws are commonly associated with cybercrime: statutory law, administrative law, and common law (also called case law).

All three sources have an involvement in computer security. Specific statutory laws, such as the Computer Fraud and Abuse Act (CFAA), govern behavior. The CFAA is designed to deal with cases of interstate computer fraud and cases of accessing national security information. The law has been amended several times to keep pace with technology. The primary charge from CFAA is typically one of accessing without authority, or exceeding authority on, a system involved with interstate commerce or national security. Administratively, the FCC and Federal Trade Commission (FTC) have made their presence felt in the Internet arena with respect to issues such as intellectual property theft and fraud. Common law cases are now working their ways through the judicial system, cementing the issues of computers and crimes into the system of precedents and constitutional basis of laws.

Computer Trespass

With the advent of global network connections and the rise of the Internet as a method of connecting computers between homes, businesses, and governments across the globe, a new type of criminal trespass can now be committed. **Computer trespass** is the unauthorized entry into a computer system via any means, including remote network connections. These crimes have introduced a new area of law that has both national and international consequences. For crimes that are committed within a country's borders, national laws apply. For cross-border crimes, international laws and international treaties are the norm. Computer-based trespass can occur even if countries do not share a physical border.

Computer trespass is treated as a crime in many countries. National laws against computer trespass exist in many countries, including Canada, the United States, and the member states of the European Union (EU). These laws vary by country, but they all have similar provisions defining the unauthorized entry into and use of computer resources for criminal activities. Whether called *computer mischief,* as in Canada, or *computer trespass,* as in the United States, unauthorized entry and use of computer resources is treated as a crime with significant punishments. With the globalization of the computer network infrastructure, or the Internet, issues that cross national boundaries have arisen and will continue to grow in prominence. Some of these issues are dealt with through the application of national laws upon request of another government. In the future, an international treaty may pave the way for closer cooperation.

Computer trespass is a convenient catchall law that can be used to prosecute cybercriminals when evidence of other criminal behavior, such as online fraud, identity theft, and so forth, is too weak to achieve a conviction.

Convention on Cybercrime

The Convention on Cybercrime is the first international treaty on crimes committed via the Internet and other computer networks. The convention is the product of four years of work by the Council of Europe (CoE), but also by the United States, Canada, Japan, and other non-CoE countries. The convention has been ratified and came into force in July 2004, and by September 2006, 15 member nations had also ratified it. The United States ratified it in the summer of 2006, with it entering into force in the United States in January 2007.

One of the main objectives of the Convention, set out in the preamble, is "to pursue, as a matter of priority, a common criminal policy aimed at the protection of society against cybercrime, *inter alia,* by adopting appropriate legislation and fostering international cooperation." This has become an important issue with the globalization of network communication. The ability to create a virus anywhere in the world and escape prosecution because of the lack of local laws has become a global concern.

The convention deals particularly with infringements of copyright, computer-related fraud, child pornography, and violations of network security. It also contains a series of powers and procedures covering, for instance, searches of computer networks and data interception. It has been supplemented by an additional protocol making any publication of racist and xenophobic propaganda via computer networks a criminal offense. This supplemental addition is in the process of separate ratification.

One of the challenges of enacting elements such as this convention is the varying legal and constitutional structures from country to country. Simple statements such as a ban on child pornography, although clearly desirable, can run into complicating issues, such as constitutional protections of free speech in the United States. Because of such issues, this well-intended joint agreement will have variations across the political boundaries of the world.

Significant U.S. Laws

The United States has been a leader in the development and use of computer technology. As such, it has a longer history associated with computers as well as with cybercrime. Because legal systems tend to be reactive and move slowly, this leadership position has translated into one from a legal perspective as well. The one advantage of this legal leadership position is the concept that once an item is identified and handled by the legal system in one jurisdiction, subsequent adoption in other jurisdictions is typically quicker.

Electronic Communications Privacy Act (ECPA)

The **Electronic Communications Privacy Act (ECPA)** of 1986 was passed by Congress and signed by President Reagan to address a myriad of legal privacy issues that resulted from the increasing use of computers and other technology specific to telecommunications. Sections of this law address e-mail, cellular communications, workplace privacy, and a host of other issues related to communicating electronically. Section I was designed to modify federal wiretap statutes to include electronic communications. Section II, known as the **Stored Communications Act (SCA)**, was designed to establish criminal sanctions for unauthorized access to stored electronic records and communications. Section III covers pen registers and tap and trace issues. Tap and trace information is related to who is communicating with whom, and when. Pen register data is the conversation information.

A major provision of ECPA was the prohibition against an employer's monitoring an employee's computer usage, including e-mail, unless consent is obtained (for example, clicking Yes on a warning banner is considered consent). Other legal provisions protect electronic communications from wiretap and outside eavesdropping, as users are assumed to have a reasonable expectation of privacy and afforded protection under the Fourth Amendment to the Constitution. It is of note that these constitutional protections only apply to searches and seizures by U.S. government agencies and law enforcement (federal, state, or local jurisdiction), but do not apply to private individuals or employers.

Cross Check

Cybercrime and Privacy

Cybercrime and privacy are concepts that are frequently interconnected. Identity theft is one of the fastest-rising crimes. How does using your personal computer to access the Internet increase your risk in today's world? Can you list a dozen specific risks you are personally exposed to? Privacy issues, being a significant topic in their own right, are covered in Chapter 25.

A common practice with respect to computer access today is the use of a warning banner. These banners are typically displayed whenever a network connection occurs and serve four main purposes. First, from a legal standpoint, they establish the level of expected privacy (usually none on a business system). Second, they serve notice to end users of the intent to conduct real-time monitoring from a business standpoint. Real-time monitoring can be conducted for security reasons, business reasons, or technical network performance reasons. Third, they obtain the user's consent to monitoring. The key is that the banner tells users that their connection to the network signals their consent to monitoring. Consent can also be obtained to look at files and records. In the case of government systems, consent is needed to prevent direct application of the Fourth Amendment. And the last reason is that the warning banner can establish the system or network administrator's common authority to consent to a law enforcement search.

Computer Fraud and Abuse Act (1986)

The **Computer Fraud and Abuse Act (CFAA)** of 1986—amended in 1994 and 1996, in 2001 by the USA PATRIOT Act, and in 2008 by the Identity Theft Enforcement and Restitution Act—serves as the current foundation for criminalizing unauthorized access to computer systems. CFAA makes it a crime to knowingly access a computer that is either considered a government computer or used in interstate commerce, or to use a computer in a crime that is interstate in nature, which in today's Internet-connected age can be almost any machine. The act sets financial thresholds for defining a criminal act, which were lowered by the PATRIOT Act, but in light of today's investigation costs, these are easily met. The act also makes it a crime to knowingly transmit a program, code, or command that results in damage. Trafficking in passwords or similar access information is also criminalized. This is a wide-sweeping act, but the challenge of proving a case still exists.

> **Tech Tip**
>
> **Header Manipulation**
>
> *Falsifying header information is a serious violation of the CAN-SPAM Act. This can be considered an indicator of criminal or malicious intent and can bring the attention of other law enforcement agencies besides the FTC.*

Controlling the Assault of Non-Solicited Pornography and Marketing Act of 2003 (CAN-SPAM)

The CAN-SPAM Act was an attempt by the U.S. government to regulate commercial e-mail by establishing national guidelines and giving the FTC enforcement powers. The objective of the legislation was to curb unsolicited commercial e-mail, or *spam*. The act has applicability to mobile phones as well. Heralded as action to curb the rise of spam, since its enactment, the act has a very poor record.

CAN-SPAM allows unsolicited commercial e-mail as long as it adheres to three rules of compliance:

- **Unsubscribe** It must include an obvious opt-out provision to allow users to unsubscribe, with these requests being honored within ten days.
- **Content** The content must be clear and not deceptive. Adult content must be clearly labeled, and subject lines must be clear and accurate.
- **Sending behavior** The sender must not use harvested e-mail addresses, falsify headers, or use open relays.

CAN-SPAM makes specific exemptions for e-mail pertaining to religious messages, political messages, and national security messages. The law also blocks people who receive spam from suing spammers and restricts states from enacting and enforcing stronger antispam statutes. The law does permit ISPs to sue spammers, and this has been used by some major ISPs to pursue cases against large-scale spam operations. Major firms such as AOL have considered the law useful in their battle against spam. Regarded largely as ineffective, statistics have shown that very few prosecutions have been pursued by the FTC. The act permits both criminal charges against individuals and civil charges against entities involved in suspected spamming operations.

USA PATRIOT Act

The USA PATRIOT Act of 2001, passed in response to the September 11 terrorist attacks on the World Trade Center in New York City and the Pentagon building in Arlington, Virginia, substantially changed the levels of checks and balances in laws related to privacy in the United States. This law extends the tap and trace provisions of existing wiretap statutes to the Internet and mandates certain technological modifications at ISPs to facilitate electronic wiretaps on the Internet and for ISPs to cooperate with the government to aid monitoring. The act also permits the Justice Department to proceed with its rollout of the Carnivore program, an eavesdropping program for the Internet. Much controversy exists over Carnivore, but until it's changed, the PATRIOT Act mandates that ISPs cooperate and facilitate monitoring. In recent actions, the name Carnivore has been retired, but the right of the government to eavesdrop and monitor communications continues to be a hot topic and one where actions continue. The PATRIOT Act also permits federal law enforcement personnel to investigate computer trespass (intrusions) and enacts civil penalties for trespassers.

> **Tech Tip**
>
> **Computer Misuse**
>
> *Two major laws, ECPA and CFAA (as amended), provide wide-sweeping tools for law enforcement to convict people who hack into computers or use them to steal information. Both laws have been strengthened and provide significant federal penalties. These laws are commonly used to convict criminals of computer misuse, even when other charges may have applied.*

Gramm-Leach-Bliley Act (GLBA)

In November 1999, President Clinton signed the **Gramm-Leach-Bliley Act (GLBA)**, a major piece of legislation affecting the financial industry that includes significant privacy provisions for individuals. The key privacy tenets enacted in GLBA include the establishment of an opt-out method for individuals to maintain some control over the use of the information provided in a business transaction with a member of the financial community. GLBA is enacted through a series of rules governed by state law, federal law, securities law, and federal rules. These rules cover a wider range of financial institutions—from banks and thrifts, to insurance companies, to securities dealers. Some internal information sharing is required under the Fair Credit Reporting Act (FCRA) between affiliated companies, but GLBA ended sharing to external third-party firms.

Sarbanes-Oxley Act (SOX)

In the wake of several high-profile corporate accounting/financial scandals in the United States, the federal government in 2002 passed sweeping legislation, the **Sarbanes-Oxley Act (SOX)**, overhauling the financial accounting standards for publicly traded firms in the United States. These changes were comprehensive, touching most aspects of business in one way or another. With respect to information security, one of the most prominent changes was the provision of **Section 404** controls, which specify that all processes associated with the financial reporting of a firm must be controlled and audited on a regular basis. Since the majority of firms use computerized systems, this places internal auditors into the IT shops, verifying that the systems have adequate controls to ensure the integrity and accuracy of financial reporting. These controls have resulted in controversy over the cost of maintaining them versus the risk of not using them.

Section 404 requires firms to establish a control-based framework designed to detect or prevent fraud that would result in misstatement of financials. In simple terms, these controls should detect insider activity that would defraud the firm. This has significant impacts on the internal security controls, because a system administrator with root-level access could perform many if not all tasks associated with fraud and would have the ability to alter logs and cover their tracks. Likewise, certain levels of power users of financial accounting programs would also have significant capability to alter records.

Privacy Laws

A wide range of privacy laws are relevant to computers. There are laws for healthcare (HIPAA) and education records (FERPA), as well as other types of records, including video rental records. These laws are described in detail in Chapter 25.

Payment Card Industry Data Security Standard (PCI DSS)

The payment card industry, including the powerhouses of MasterCard and Visa, through its PCI Security Standards Council, designed a private-sector initiative to protect payment card information between banks and merchants. The **Payment Card Industry Data Security Standard (PCI DSS)** is a set of contractual rules governing how credit card data is to be protected (see the Tech Tip sidebar "PCI DSS Objectives and Requirements"). The current version is 3.2, which was released in April 2016. A new release of PCI DSS version 4.0 is expected in mid-2021, but with the pandemic of 2020, this date may slip. This is a voluntary, private-sector initiative that is proscriptive in its security guidance. PCI DSS rules apply to any organization that processes, stores, or transmits cardholder data or provides services that control or could impact the security of cardholder data or the card holder data environment. Merchants and vendors can choose not to adopt these measures, but the standard has a steep price for noncompliance; the transaction fee for noncompliant vendors can be significantly higher, fines up to $500,000 can be levied, and in extreme cases the ability to process credit cards can be revoked.

Tech Tip

PCI DSS Objectives and Requirements

PCI DSS v3 includes six control objectives containing a total of 12 requirements:

1. *Build and Maintain a Secure Network*

   Requirement 1 *Install and maintain a firewall configuration to protect cardholder data.*

   Requirement 2 *Do not use vendor-supplied defaults for system passwords and other security parameters.*

2. *Protect Cardholder Data*

   Requirement 3 *Protect stored cardholder data.*

   Requirement 4 *Encrypt transmission of cardholder data across open, public networks.*

3. *Maintain a Vulnerability Management Program*

   Requirement 5 *Protect all systems against malware and regularly update antivirus software or programs.*

   Requirement 6 *Develop and maintain secure systems and applications.*

4. *Implement Strong Access Control Measures*

   Requirement 7 *Restrict access to cardholder data by business need-to-know.*

   Requirement 8 *Identify and authenticate access to system components.*

   Requirement 9 *Restrict physical access to cardholder data.*

5. *Regularly Monitor and Test Networks*

   Requirement 10 *Track and monitor all access to network resources and cardholder data.*

   Requirement 11 *Regularly test security systems and processes.*

6. *Maintain an Information Security Policy*

   Requirement 12 *Maintain a policy that addresses information security for all personnel.*

The Payment Card Industry Data Security Standard (PCI DSS) protects customer credit card information and is designed to reduce fraud. The standard has a steep penalty for noncompliance.

PCI DSS has two defined types of information: cardholder data and sensitive authentication data. The protection requirements established for these elements are detailed in Table 24.1.

Table 24.1 PCI DSS Data Retention Guidelines

		Data Element	Storage Permitted	Render Stored Data Unreadable
Account Data	Cardholder Data	Primary Account Number (PAN)	Yes	Yes
		Cardholder Name	Yes	No
		Service Code	Yes	No
		Expiration Date	Yes	No
	Sensitive Authentication Data	Full Track Data	No	Cannot store per Requirement 3.2
		CAV2 / CVC2 / CVV2 / CID	No	Cannot store per Requirement 3.2
		PIN / PIN Block	No	Cannot store per Requirement 3.2

Import/Export Encryption Restrictions

Encryption technology has been controlled by governments for a variety of reasons. The level of control varies from outright banning to little or no regulation. The reasons behind the control vary as well, and control over import and export is a vital method of maintaining a level of control over encryption technology in general. The majority of the laws and restrictions are centered on the use of cryptography, which was until recently used mainly for military purposes. The advent of commercial transactions and network communications over public networks such as the Internet has expanded the use of cryptographic methods to include securing of network communications. As is the case in most rapidly changing technologies, the practice moves faster than law. Many countries still have laws that are outmoded in terms of e-commerce and the Internet. Over time, these laws will be changed to serve these new uses in a way consistent with each country's needs.

> **Tech Tip**
>
> **Wassenaar Arrangement**
>
> *The United States updated its encryption export regulations to provide treatment consistent with regulations adopted by the European Union (EU), easing export and re-export restrictions among the EU member states and Argentina, Australia, Canada, Croatia, Japan, New Zealand, Norway, Republic of Korea, Russia, South Africa, Switzerland, Turkey, Ukraine, and the United States. The member nations of the* **Wassenaar Arrangement** *agreed to remove key-length restrictions on encryption hardware and software that is subject to certain reasonable levels of encryption strength. This action effectively removed "mass-market" encryption products from the list of dual-use items controlled by the Wassenaar Arrangement. The latest update to the Wassenaar agreement came in December of 2019, with updates to the list of dual-use goods and technologies and munitions lists.*

U.S. Law

Export controls on commercial encryption products are administered by the Bureau of Industry and Security (BIS) in the U.S. Department of Commerce. The responsibility for export control and jurisdiction was transferred from the State Department to the Commerce Department in 1996 and updated on June 6, 2002. Rules governing exports of encryption are found in the Export Administration Regulations (EAR), 15 C.F.R. Parts 730–774. Sections 740.13, 740.17, and 742.15 are the principal references for the export of encryption items.

Violation of encryption export regulations is a serious matter and is not an issue to take lightly. Until recently, encryption protection was accorded the same level of attention as the export of weapons for war. With the rise of the Internet, widespread personal computing, and the need for secure connections for e-commerce, this position has relaxed somewhat.

The U.S. encryption export control policy continues to rest on three principles: review of encryption products prior to sale, streamlined post-export reporting, and license review of certain exports of strong encryption to foreign government end users. The current set of U.S. rules requires notification to the BIS for export in all cases, but the restrictions are significantly lessened for mass-market products, as defined by all of the following:

- They are generally available to the public by being sold, without restriction, from stock at retail selling points by any of these means:
  - Over-the-counter transactions
  - Mail-order transactions
  - Electronic transactions
  - Telephone call transactions
- The cryptographic functionality cannot easily be changed by the user.
- They are designed for installation by the user without further substantial support by the supplier.
- When necessary, details of the items are accessible and will be provided, upon request, to the appropriate authority in the exporter's country in order to ascertain compliance with export regulations.

> Mass-market commodities and software employing a key length greater than 64 bits for the symmetric algorithm must be reviewed in accordance with BIS regulations. Restrictions on exports by U.S. persons to terrorist-supporting states, as determined by the U.S. Department of State (currently Iran, Sudan, and Syria), their nationals, and other sanctioned entities are not changed by this rule.

As you can see, this is a very technical area, with significant rules and significant penalties for infractions. The best rule is that whenever you are faced with a situation involving the export of encryption-containing software, first consult an expert and get the appropriate permission or a statement that permission is not required. This is one case where it is better to be safe than sorry.

> **Tech Tip**
>
> **Cryptographic Use Restrictions**
>
> *In addition to the export controls on cryptography, significant laws prohibit the use and possession of cryptographic technology. In China, a license from the state is required for cryptographic use. In some other countries, including Russia, Pakistan, Venezuela, and Singapore, tight restrictions apply to cryptographic uses. France relinquished tight state control over the possession of the technology in 1999. One of the driving points behind France's action is the fact that more and more of the Internet technologies have built-in cryptography.*

Non-U.S. Laws

Export control rules for encryption technologies fall under the Wassenaar Arrangement, an international arrangement on export controls for conventional arms and dual-use goods and technologies (see the Tech Tip sidebar "Wassenaar Arrangement"). The Wassenaar Arrangement was established to contribute to regional and international security and stability by promoting transparency and greater responsibility in transfers of conventional arms and dual-use goods and technologies, thus preventing destabilizing accumulations. Participating states, of which the United States is one of 41, will seek, through their own national policies and laws, to ensure that transfers of these items do not contribute to the development or enhancement of military capabilities that undermine these goals, and are not diverted to support such capabilities.

Many nations have more restrictive policies than those agreed upon as part of the Wassenaar Arrangement. Australia, New Zealand, United States, France, and Russia go further than is required under Wassenaar and restrict general-purpose cryptographic software as dual-use goods through national laws. The Wassenaar Arrangement has had a significant impact on cryptography export controls, and there seems little doubt that some of the nations represented will seek to use the next round to move toward a more repressive cryptography export control regime based on their own national laws. There are ongoing campaigns to attempt to influence other members of the agreement toward less-restrictive rules or, in some cases, no rules. These lobbying efforts are based on e-commerce and privacy arguments.

Digital rights management, secure USB solutions, digital signatures, and Secure Sockets Layer–secured connections are examples of common behind-the-scenes use of cryptographic technologies. In 2007, the United Kingdom passed a new law mandating that when requested by UK authorities, either police or military, encryption keys must be provided to permit decryption of information associated with a terror or criminal investigation. Failure to deliver either the keys or decrypted data can result in an automatic prison sentence of two to five years. Although this seems reasonable, it has been argued that such actions will drive certain financial entities offshore, as the rule applies only to data housed in the United Kingdom. As for deterrence, the two-year sentence may be lighter than a conviction for trafficking in child pornography; hence, the law has not been as useful as was envisioned. Similar questions have been raised over recent laws in Australia which permit the government to force companies to decrypt data when requested. Although these questions are still open, the effect of them is beginning to become evident as LinkedIn is no longer available in Russia because the service owner chose not to comply with Russia's local storage requirements.

Digital Signature Laws

Whether a ring and wax seal, a stamp, or a scrawl indicating a name, signatures have been used to affix a sign of one's approval for centuries. As communications have moved into the digital realm, signatures need to evolve with the new medium, and hence digital signatures were invented. Using elements of cryptography to establish integrity and nonrepudiation, digital signature schemes can actually offer more functionality than their predecessors in the paper-based world.

U.S. Digital Signature Laws

On October 1, 2000, the Electronic Signatures in Global and National Commerce Act (commonly called the E-Sign law) went into effect in the United States. This law implements a simple principle: a signature, contract, or other record may not be denied legal effect, validity, or enforceability solely because it is in electronic form. Another source of law on digital signatures is the Uniform Electronic Transactions Act (UETA), which was developed by the National Conference of Commissioners on Uniform State Laws (NCCUSL) and has been adopted in all but four states—Georgia, Illinois, New York, and Washington—which have adopted a non-uniform version of UETA. The current situation, 20 years later, is that UETA and E-Sign are still not aligned. Both have an effect on the use of digital signatures, and while there are technical differences, vendors have been able to craft systems that comply with both sets of directives, making digital signatures legal and growing in popularity. The pandemic of 2020 probably did more to increase use of digital signatures than any legislation.

The E-Sign Act sets forth protections for consumers engaging in transactions with financial institutions. The E-Sign Act requires financial institutions to do the following:

- Obtain the consumer's affirmative consent to the use of electronic records.
- Inform the consumer of any hardware or software requirements for accessing the electronic records.
- Provide a clear and conspicuous statement indicating
  (i) the consumer has a right to have a record provided in paper or non-electronic form,
  (ii) how the consumer can exercise that right, and
  (iii) details on any fees associated with obtaining the record in paper or non-electronic form.
- Maintain electronic records in such a way that they are retrievable and accessible to all parties who are legally entitled to access them.

Many states have adopted digital signature laws, the first being Utah in 1995. The Utah law, which has been used as a model by several other states, confirms the legal status of digital signatures as valid signatures, provides for use of state-licensed certification authorities, endorses the use of public key encryption technology, and authorizes online databases called repositories, where public keys would be available. The Utah act specifies a negligence standard regarding private encryption keys and places no limit on liability. Thus, if a criminal uses a consumer's private key to commit fraud, the consumer is financially responsible for that fraud, unless the consumer can prove that they used reasonable care in safeguarding the private key. Consumers assume a duty of care when they adopt the use of digital signatures for their transactions, not unlike the care required for PINs on debit cards.

From a practical standpoint, the existence of the E-Sign law and UETA has enabled e-commerce transactions to proceed, and the resolution of the technical details via court actions will probably have little effect on consumers beyond the need to exercise reasonable care over their signature keys. For the most part, software will handle these issues for the typical user.

With the broad movement of people to isolate during the pandemic of 2020, digital signature adoption has become widespread for many transactions. Financial institutions, mortgages, auto lenders, and many other institutions have adopted the use of electronic signatures to replace direct contact with customers.

UN Digital Signature Laws

The United Nations has a mandate to further harmonize international trade. With this in mind, the UN General Assembly adopted in 1996 the United Nations Commission on International Trade Law (UNCITRAL) Model Law on Electronic Commerce (MLEC). To implement specific technical aspects of this model law, more work on electronic signatures was needed. The General Assembly then adopted in 2001 the UNCITRAL Model Law on Electronic Signatures (MLES). These model laws have become the basis for many national and international efforts in this area.

Canadian Digital Signature Laws

Canada was an early leader in the use of digital signatures. Singapore, Canada, and the U.S. state of Pennsylvania were the first governments to have digitally signed an interstate contract. This contract, digitally signed in 1998, concerned the establishment of a Global Learning Consortium between the three governments (source: *Krypto Digest* Vol. 1, No. 749, June 11, 1998). Canada went on to adopt a national model bill for electronic signatures to promote e-commerce. This bill, the Uniform Electronic Commerce Act (UECA), allows the use of electronic signatures in communications with the government. The law contains general provisions for the equivalence between traditional and electronic signatures (source: Bloomberg *BNA ECLR,* May 27, 1998, p. 700) and is modeled after the UNCITRAL Model Law on E-Commerce (source: Bloomberg *BNA ECLR,* September 13, 2000, p. 918). The UECA is similar to Bill C-54, the **Personal Information Protection and Electronic Documents Act (PIPEDA)**, in authorizing governments to use electronic technology to deliver services and communicate with citizens. PIPEDA provides for electronic equivalents to paper-based documents and signatures, including using a stylus on a tablet touchscreen to write a signature by hand and capture it in electronic form.

Individual Canadian provinces have passed similar legislation defining digital signature provisions for e-commerce and government use. These laws are modeled after the UNCITRAL Model Law on E-Commerce to enable widespread use of e-commerce transactions. These laws have also modified the methods of interactions between the citizens and the government, enabling electronic communication in addition to previous forms.

European Laws

The European Commission adopted a Communication on Digital Signatures and Encryption titled "Ensuring Security and Trust in Electronic

Communication—Towards a European Framework for Digital Signatures and Encryption." This communication states that a common framework at the EU level is urgently needed to stimulate "the free circulation of digital signature related products and services within the Internal market" and "the development of new economic activities linked to electronic commerce" as well as "to facilitate the use of digital signatures across national borders." Community legislation should address common legal requirements for certificate authorities, legal recognition of digital signatures, and international cooperation. This communication was debated, and a common position was presented to the member nations for incorporation into national laws.

On May 4, 2000, the European Parliament and Council approved the common position adopted by the council. In June 2000, the final version, the Electronic Commerce Directive (2000/31/EC), was adopted. The directive has been implemented by member states. To implement the articles contained in the directive, member states had to remove barriers, such as legal form requirements, to electronic contracting, leading to uniform digital signature laws across the EU. Electronic signatures are widely used throughout the EU. The use of electronic signatures is regulated by Regulation (EU) No 910/2014 of the European Parliament and of the Council of 23 July 2014 on electronic identification and trust services for electronic transactions in the internal markets of the EU.

> **Tech Tip**
>
> **Digital Copies and Copyright**
>
> *The ability of anyone with a PC to make a perfect copy of digital media led to industry fears that individual piracy actions could cause major economic issues in the recording industry. To protect the rights of the recording artists and the economic health of the industry as a whole, the music and video recording industry lobbied the U.S. Congress for protection, which was granted under the Digital Millennium Copyright Act (DMCA) on October 20, 1998.*

> **Tech Tip**
>
> **DMCA Research Exemption Requirements**
>
> *The DMCA has specific exemptions for research, provided four elements are satisfied:*
>
> - *The person lawfully obtained the encrypted copy, phonorecord, performance, or display of the published work.*
> - *Such act is necessary to conduct such encryption research.*
> - *The person made a good faith effort to obtain authorization before the circumvention.*
> - *Such act does not constitute infringement under this title or a violation of applicable law other than this section, including section 1030 of title 18 and those provisions of title 18 amended by the Computer Fraud and Abuse Act of 1986.*

Digital Rights Management

The ability to make flawless copies of digital media has led to another "new" legal issue. For years, the music and video industry has relied on technology to protect its rights with respect to intellectual property. It has been illegal for decades to copy information, such as music and videos, protected by copyright. Even with the law, people have for years made copies of music and videos to share, thus violating the law. Until the advent of digital copies (see Tech Tip sidebar "Digital Copies and Copyright"), this did not represent a significant economic impact in the eyes of the industry, as the copies were of lesser quality and people would pay for original quality in sufficient numbers to keep the economics of the industry healthy. As a result, legal action against piracy was typically limited to large-scale duplication and sale efforts, commonly performed overseas and subsequently shipped to the United States as counterfeit items.

The primary statute enacted in the United States to bring copyright legal concerns up to date with the digital world is the **Digital Millennium Copyright Act (DMCA)**. The DMCA states its purpose as follows: "To amend title 17, United States Code, to implement the World Intellectual Property Organization Copyright Treaty and Performances and Phonograms Treaty, and for other purposes." The majority of this law was well crafted, but one section has drawn considerable comment and criticism. A section of the law makes it illegal to develop, produce, and trade any device or mechanism designed to circumvent technological controls used in copy protection.

Although, on the surface, this seems a reasonable requirement, the methods used in most cases are cryptographic in nature, and this provision had the ability to eliminate and/or severely limit research into encryption and the strengths and weaknesses of specific methods. A DMCA provision, section 1201(g), was included to provide for specific relief and allow exemptions for legitimate research (see the Tech Tip sidebar "DMCA Research Exemption Requirements"). With this section, the law garnered industry support from several organizations, such as the Software & Information Industry Association (SIIA), Recording Industry Association of America (RIAA), and Motion Picture Association of America (MPAA). Based on these inputs, the U.S. Copyright Office issued support for the DMCA in a required report to the U.S. Congress. This seemed to settle the issues until the RIAA threatened to sue an academic research team headed by Professor Edward Felten from Princeton University. The issue behind the suit was the potential publication of results demonstrating that several copy protection methods were flawed in their application. This research came in response to an industry-sponsored challenge to break the methods. After breaking the methods developed and published by the industry, Felten and his team prepared to publish their findings. The RIAA objected and threatened a suit under provisions of the DMCA. After several years of litigation and support of Felten by the Electronic Frontier Foundation (EFF), the case was eventually resolved in the academic team's favor, although no case law to prevent further industry-led threats was developed.

One of the controversial issues associated with DMCA is the issue of takedown notices. Carriers such as YouTube are granted protection from content violation, provided they remove the content when requested with a takedown order. The publishing industry uses scanners and automated systems to issue takedown notices, and these sometimes go awry (see the sidebar on the Mars Rover mishap). The issue of fair use is one that is not delineated by bright-line regulations, making the system one that sides with the takedown requestor unless the content poster takes them to court.

Mars Rover Crashed by DMCA

NASA maintains a YouTube channel where it posts videos of space events, such as the landing of the rover *Curiosity* on the surface of Mars. The content was developed by NASA with U.S. taxpayer money, yet it was served a takedown notice by Scripps Howard News Service. The issue was remedied, but taxpayers lost early coverage and had to pay the legal bills to fight for their own content. This happens on a regular basis to the NASA channel, and although the law has provisions for prosecuting false takedowns, they are rarely used.

Exemptions are scattered throughout the DMCA, although many were created during various deliberations on the act and do not make sense when the act is viewed in whole. The effect of these exemptions upon people in the software and technology industry is not clear, and until restrained by case law, the DMCA gives large firms with deep legal pockets a potent weapon to use against parties who disclose flaws in encryption technologies used in various products. Actions have already been initiated against individuals and organizations who have reported security holes in products. This will be an active area of legal contention, as the real issues behind digital rights management have yet to be truly resolved.

Ethics

Ethics has been a subject of study by philosophers for centuries. It might be surprising to note that ethics associated with computer systems has a history dating back to the beginning of the computing age. The first examination of cybercrime occurred in the late 1960s, when the professional conduct of computer professionals was examined with respect to their activities in the workplace. If we consider ethical behavior to be consistent with that of existing social norms, it can be fairly easy to see what is considered right and wrong. But with the globalization of commerce, and the globalization of communications via the Internet, questions are raised on what is the appropriate social norm. Cultural issues can have wide-ranging effects on this, and although the idea of an appropriate code of conduct for the world is appealing, it is as yet an unachieved objective.

The issue of globalization has significant local effects. If a user wishes to express free speech via the Internet, is this protected behavior or criminal behavior? Different locales have different sets of laws to deal with items such as free speech, with some recognizing the right, and others prohibiting it. With the globalization of business, what are the appropriate controls for intellectual property when some regions support this right, while others do not even recognize intellectual property as something of value, but rather something owned by the collective of society? The challenge in today's business environment is to establish and communicate a code of ethics so that everyone associated with an enterprise can understand the standards of expected performance.

A great source of background information on all things associated with computer security is the SANS Institute, which published a set of IT ethical guidelines ("IT Code of Ethics") in April 2004 (see www.sans.org/security-resources/ethics.php).

Tech Tip

IT Code of Ethics

The SANS Institute's "IT Code of Ethics," Version 1.0,[1] April 24, 2004:

I will strive to know myself and be honest about my capability.

- *I will strive for technical excellence in the IT profession by maintaining and enhancing my own knowledge and skills. I acknowledge that there are many free resources available on the Internet and affordable books and that the lack of my employer's training budget is not an excuse nor limits my ability to stay current in IT.*
- *When possible I will demonstrate my performance capability with my skills via projects, leadership, and/or accredited educational programs and will encourage others to do so as well.*
- *I will not hesitate to seek assistance or guidance when faced with a task beyond my abilities or experience. I will embrace other professionals' advice and learn from their experiences and mistakes. I will treat this as an opportunity to learn new techniques and approaches. When the situation arises that my assistance is called upon, I will respond willingly to share my knowledge with others.*
- *I will strive to convey any knowledge (specialist or otherwise) that I have gained to others so everyone gains the benefit of each other's knowledge.*

(Continued)

Tech Tip

- *I will teach the willing and empower others with Industry Best Practices (IBP). I will offer my knowledge to show others how to become security professionals in their own right. I will strive to be perceived as and be an honest and trustworthy employee.*
- *I will not advance private interests at the expense of end users, colleagues, or my employer.*
- *I will not abuse my power. I will use my technical knowledge, user rights, and permissions only to fulfill my responsibilities to my employer.*
- *I will avoid and be alert to any circumstances or actions that might lead to conflicts of interest or the perception of conflicts of interest. If such circumstance occurs, I will notify my employer or business partners.*
- *I will not steal property, time, or resources.*
- *I will reject bribery or kickbacks and will report such illegal activity.*
- *I will report on the illegal activities of myself and others without respect to the punishments involved. I will not tolerate those who lie, steal, or cheat as a means of success in IT.*

I will conduct my business in a manner that assures the IT profession is considered one of integrity and professionalism.

- *I will not injure others, their property, reputation, or employment by false or malicious action.*
- *I will not use availability and access to information for personal gains through corporate espionage.*
- *I distinguish between advocacy and engineering. I will not present analysis and opinion as fact.*
- *I will adhere to Industry Best Practices (IBP) for system design, rollout, hardening, and testing.*
- *I am obligated to report all system vulnerabilities that might result in significant damage.*
- *I respect intellectual property and will be careful to give credit for other's work. I will never steal or misuse copyrighted, patented material, trade secrets, or any other intangible asset.*
- *I will accurately document my setup procedures and any modifications I have done to equipment. This will ensure that others will be informed of procedures and changes I've made.*

I respect privacy and confidentiality.

- *I respect the privacy of my co-workers' information. I will not peruse or examine their information including data, files, records, or network traffic except as defined by the appointed roles, the organization's acceptable use policy, as approved by Human Resources, and without the permission of the end user.*
- *I will obtain permission before probing systems on a network for vulnerabilities.*
- *I respect the right to confidentiality with my employers, clients, and users except as dictated by applicable law. I respect human dignity.*
- *I treasure and will defend equality, justice, and respect for others.*
- *I will not participate in any form of discrimination, whether due to race, color, national origin, ancestry, sex, sexual orientation, gender/sexual identity, or expression, marital status, creed, religion, age, disability, veteran's status, or political ideology.*

Chapter 24 Review

Chapter Summary

After reading this chapter and completing the exercises, you should understand the following regarding the basics of legal and ethical considerations associated with information security.

Explain the laws and rules concerning importing and exporting encryption software

- Import and export of high-strength cryptographic software are controlled in many countries, including the United States.
- Possession of encryption programs or encrypted data can be a crime in many countries.
- The Wassenaar Arrangement is an international agreement between countries concerning the import/export of cryptographic software and has enabled mass-marketed products to generally flow across borders.

Identify the laws that govern computer access and trespass

- Gaining unauthorized access, by whatever means, including using someone else's credentials, is computer trespass.
- Exceeding granted authority is also computer trespass.
- Many nations have versions of computer trespass or misuse statutes, although the terminology varies greatly among countries.

Identify the laws that govern encryption and digital rights management

- Encryption technology is used to protect digital rights management and prevent unauthorized use.
- Circumventing technological controls used to protect intellectual property is a violation of the DMCA.
- In some countries, carrying encrypted data can result in authorities demanding the keys or threatening prosecution for failure to disclose the keys.

Describe the laws that govern digital signatures

- Digital signatures have the same legal status as written signatures.
- Digital signatures use PINs or other "secrets" that require end-user safeguarding to be protected from fraud.

Explore ethical issues associated with information security

- Ethics is the social-moral environment in which a person makes decisions.
- Ethics can vary by socio-cultural factors and groups.

Key Terms

administrative law *(911)*
case law *(911)*
click fraud *(909)*
common law *(911)*
Computer Fraud and Abuse Act (CFAA) *(914)*
computer trespass *(912)*
Digital Millennium Copyright Act (DMCA) *(922)*
Electronic Communications Privacy Act (ECPA) *(913)*
Gramm-Leach-Bliley Act (GLBA) *(915)*
Payment Card Industry Data Security Standard (PCI DSS) *(916)*
Personal Information Protection and Electronic Documents Act (PIPEDA) *(921)*
Sarbanes-Oxley Act (SOX) *(916)*
Section 404 *(916)*
statutory law *(911)*
Stored Communications Act (SCA) *(913)*
Wassenaar Arrangement *(918)*

Key Terms Quiz

Use terms from the Key Terms list to complete the sentences that follow. Don't use the same term more than once. Not all terms will be used.

1. IT controls were mandated in public companies by _______________, part of the Sarbanes-Oxley Act.
2. The contractual set of rules governing credit card security is the _______________.
3. A catchall law to prosecute hackers is the statute on _______________.
4. The _______________ is the primary U.S. federal law on computer intrusion and misuse.
5. The power of government-sponsored agencies lies in _______________.
6. A(n) _______________ is passed by a legislative branch of government.
7. _______________ comes from the judicial branch of government.

Multiple-Choice Quiz

1. Your Social Security number and other associated facts kept by your bank are protected by what law against disclosure?

   A. The Social Security Act of 1934

   B. The USA PATRIOT Act of 2001

   C. The Gramm-Leach-Bliley Act

   D. HIPAA

2. Breaking into another computer system in the United States, even if you do not cause any damage, is regulated by what law?

   A. State law, as the damage is minimal

   B. Federal law under the Identity Theft and Assumption Deterrence Act

   C. Federal law under the Electronic Communications Privacy Act (ECPA) of 1986

   D. Federal law under the USA PATRIOT Act of 2001

3. Export of encryption programs is regulated by which entity?

   A. U.S. State Department

   B. U.S. Commerce Department

   C. U.S. Department of Defense

   D. National Security Agency

4. For the FBI to install and operate Carnivore (or subsequent tool) on an ISP's network, what is required?

   A. A court order specifying specific items being searched for

   B. An official request from the FBI

   C. An impact statement to assess recoverable costs to the ISP

   D. A written request from an ISP to investigate a computer trespass incident

5. True or false? A sysadmin who is reading employee e-mail to look for evidence of someone stealing company passwords is protected by the company-owned equipment exemption on eavesdropping.

   A. False, there is no "company-owned exemption."

   B. True, provided they have their manager's approval.

   C. True, provided they have senior management permission in writing.

   D. True, if it is in their job description.

6. True or false? Writing viruses and releasing them across the Internet is a violation of law.

   A. Always true. All countries have reciprocal agreements under international law.

   B. Partially true. Depends on the laws in the country of origin.

   C. False. Computer security laws do not cross international boundaries.

   D. Partially true. Depends on the specific countries involved, both of the virus author and the recipient.

7. Publication of flaws in encryption used for copy protection is a potential violation of which of the following?
   - **A.** HIPAA
   - **B.** U.S. Commerce Department regulations
   - **C.** DMCA
   - **D.** National Security Agency regulations
8. Circumventing technological controls to prevent reverse engineering is a violation of which of the following?
   - **A.** HIPAA
   - **B.** DMCA
   - **C.** ECPA
   - **D.** All of the above
9. Logging in as your boss to fix your time records is:
   - **A.** OK, if you are accurately reporting your time
   - **B.** One of the obscure elements of DMCA
   - **C.** A violation of the Separation of Duties Law
   - **D.** A form of computer trespass
10. You are arrested as a result of your hacking activities, and investigators find you have been breaking password files and sharing them across the Internet. Which law have you violated?
    - **A.** CFAA
    - **B.** ECPA
    - **C.** DMCA
    - **D.** HIPAA

Essay Quiz

1. You are being hired as the director of IT for a small firm that does retail trade business, and you will be the source of knowledge for all things IT, including security and legal regulations. Outline the legal elements you would want to have policy covering and include how you would disseminate this information.
2. You have just been hired as a system administrator for a small college. The college's servers are used for database storage and a website that serves the college community. Describe the laws that will potentially impact your job with respect to computer security. What actions will you take to ensure compliance with laws and regulations?

chapter 25

Privacy

They who would give up an essential liberty for temporary security, deserve neither liberty or security.

—Benjamin Franklin

In this chapter, you will learn how to

- Examine concepts of privacy
- Compare and contrast privacy policies and laws of different jurisdictions
- Describe approaches individuals, organizations, and governments have taken to protect privacy
- Describe issues associated with technology and privacy
- Explain the concept of personally identifiable information (PII)

Privacy can be defined as the power to control what others know about you and what they can do with that information. In the computer age, personal information forms the basis for many decisions, from credit card transactions for purchasing goods to the ability to buy an airplane ticket and fly. Although it is theoretically possible to live an almost anonymous existence today, the price for doing so is high—from higher prices at the grocery store (no frequent shopper discount), to higher credit costs, to challenges with air travel, opening bank accounts, and seeking employment.

Data Handling

Information is an important item in today's society. From instant credit, to digital access to a wide range of information via the Internet, to electronic service portals such as e-commerce sites, e-government sites, and so on, our daily lives have become intertwined with privacy issues. Information has become a valuable entity because it is an enabler of many functions. The creation of an information-centric economy is as dramatic a revolution as the adoption of money to act as an economic utility, simplifying bartering. This revolution and reliance on information imbues information with value, creating the need to protect it.

Privacy is the right to control information about you and what others can do with that information.

Data retention is the determination of what records require storage and for how long. There are several reasons for retaining data: billing and accounting, contractual, warranty, and local, state, and national government rules are some of the obvious. Maintaining data stores for longer than is required is a source of risk, as is not storing the information long enough. Some information, like protected health information (PHI) for workers in some industries or workers who have been exposed to specific hazards, can have very long retention periods.

Failure to maintain the data in a secure state can be a retention issue, as is not retaining it. In some cases, destruction of data, specifically data subject to legal hold in a legal matter, can result in adverse court findings and sanctions. Legal hold can add significant complexity to data retention efforts because it forces almost a separate store of the data until the legal issues are resolved, because once data is on the legal hold track, its retention clock does not expire. This makes determining, labeling, and maintaining data associated with legal hold an added dimension for normal storage times.

Organizational Consequences of Privacy Breaches

When a company loses data that it has stored on its network, the term used is *data breach.* Data breaches have become an almost daily news item, and the result is that people are becoming desensitized to their occurrence. Data breaches act as a means of notification that security efforts have failed.

Verizon publishes an annual data breach report that examines the types and causes of data breaches over the previous calendar year. These results are presented in multiple forms, by attribution to attack type, attacker type, industry, geographic region, company size, and more, providing a significant level of detailed analysis into the incidents. This report is a framework of what actually happened to real companies with real security programs, or in spite of their security programs. It is an extremely valuable collection of data that can provide guidance with respect to current threat environments and results of actual attacks and errors.

Reputation Damage

Reputation damage is a form of damage against a firm's brand. Customers exert a choice when they engage in a commerce transaction, and businesses spend a lot of time and resources on building brands that facilitate the purchase decision toward their firms. Having to notify all customers of a breach/disclosure event is truly damaging to a firm's brands. An online computer vendor, Egghead, suffered a breach/disclosure event near the holiday shopping season, and it saw sales dry up in that critical period, resulting in bankruptcy shortly thereafter.

Target Corporation continues to be the example of record for costly breaches, with a breach in 2013 that cost hundreds of millions in dollars and cost multiple senior executives their jobs. In 2017, Yahoo! had a breach involving three billion accounts, and this led to delays and a $350 million dollar price reduction during its acquisition. Facebook joined this club with its Cambridge Analytica scandal of 2018, where it failed to protect the personal information of its users. Facebook also faced legal and regulatory oversight inquiries as well as triggered EU data protection directive responses.

Identity Theft

Identity theft occurs when a criminal, using stolen information, assumes the identity of another individual to obtain and use credit in the victim's name. If the data disclosure results in loss of customer personal information, regulations may hold a firm responsible for sharing in the risk of identity theft for the victims. The usual response on the part of a company is to purchase an identity theft protection service policy for the affected individuals of a breach. This can cost over $50 per person affected, making a breach of a million records a costly issue.

Fines

Regulatory agencies, such as the Federal Trade Commission (FTC), have the ability to levy fines when regulations are not followed. These fines are not minor. In the EU, General Data Protection Regulation (GDPR) fines can be 4 percent of a firm's revenue, and fines in the hundreds of millions of euros have been levied. In the U.S., Equifax was fined nearly $700 million to be paid in restitution to users affected by their data breach.

IP Theft

One of the primary targets of an attacker on a system is intellectual property. *IP theft* is a major organizational consequence when it occurs, because when it occurs, the damage may not become evident until the material is used by a competitor. In organizations with significant levels of IP, it is one of the most important items to be protected against loss. Years of investment, and more years of potential sales and profits, can vanish quickly if IP is stolen and used actively against a firm.

Be aware that organizational consequences of data privacy breaches can result in reputational damage, identify theft, fines, or IP theft.

Data Sensitivity Labeling and Handling

Effective data classification programs include **data sensitivity labeling**, which enables personnel handling the data to know whether it is sensitive and to understand the levels of protection required. When the data is inside an information-processing system, the protections should be designed into the system. But when the data leaves this cocoon of protection, whether by printing, downloading, or copying, it becomes necessary to ensure continued protection by other means. This is where data labeling assists users in fulfilling their responsibilities. Training to ensure that labeling occurs and that it is used and followed is important for users whose roles can be impacted by this material.

Training plays an important role in ensuring proper data handling and disposal. Personnel are intimately involved in several specific tasks associated with data handling and data destruction/disposal; if properly trained, they can act as a security control. Untrained or inadequately trained personnel will not be a productive security control and, in fact, can be a source of potential compromise.

A key component of IT security is the protection of the information processed and stored on the computer systems and network. Organizations deal with many different types of information, and they need to recognize that not all information is of equal importance or sensitivity. This requires classification of information into various categories, each with its own requirements for its handling. Factors that affect the classification of specific information include its value to the organization (what will be the impact to the organization if it loses this information?), its age, and laws or regulations that govern its protection. The most widely known system of classification of information is that implemented by the U.S. government (including the military), which classifies information into categories such as *Confidential, Secret,* and *Top Secret.* Businesses have similar desires to protect information and often use categories such as *Publicly Releasable, Proprietary, Company Confidential,* and *For Internal Use Only.* Each policy for the classification of information should describe how it should be protected, who may have access to it, who has the authority to release it and how, and how it should be destroyed. All employees of the organization should be trained in the procedures for handling the information that they are authorized to access.

Public

Public data is data that can be seen by the public and has no needed protections with respect to confidentiality. It is important to protect the integrity of public data, lest one communicate incorrect data as being true. Public-facing web pages, press releases, corporate statements—these are examples of public data that still needs protection, but specifically with respect to integrity.

Private

Data is labeled private if its disclosure to an unauthorized party would potentially cause harm or disruption to the organization. Passwords could be considered private. The term *private data* is usually associated with personal data belonging to a person and less often with corporate entities. The level of damage typically associated with private data is lower than confidential but still significant to the organization.

Sensitive

Sensitive data is a generalized term that typically represents data classified as restricted from general or public release. This term is often used interchangeably with confidential data.

Confidential

Data is labeled confidential if its disclosure to an unauthorized party would potentially cause serious harm to the organization. This data should be defined by policy, and that policy should include details regarding who has the authority to release the data. Common examples of confidential data include pricing and cost data, customer data, internal business plans, and so on, as the release of these could result in significant loss to the firm.

Critical

Data is labeled critical if its disclosure to an unauthorized party would potentially cause extreme harm to the organization. This data should be defined by policy, and that policy should include details regarding who has the authority to release the data. Common examples of critical data include trade secrets, proprietary software code, and new product designs, as the release of these could result in significant loss to the firm. The level of damage from a critical data release would be extreme, material to the business, and could result in the highest levels of loss.

> The difference between critical and confidential data lies in the level of potential damage should the information be released.

Proprietary

Proprietary data is data that is restricted to a company because of potential competitive use. If a company has data that could be used by a competitor for any particular reason (say, internal costs and pricing data), then it needs to be labeled and handled in a manner to protect it from release to competitors. Proprietary data may be shared with a third party that is not a competitor, but in labeling the data "proprietary," you alert the party you have shared the data with that it is not to be shared further.

Personally Identifiable Information (PII)

When information is about a person, failure to protect it can have specific consequences. Business secrets are protected through trade secret laws, government information is protected through laws concerning national security, and privacy laws protect information associated with people. A set

Data Controller

The *data controller* is the person responsible for managing how and why data is going to be used by the organization. In the era of GDPR and other privacy laws and regulations, this is a critical position because, under GDPR and other privacy laws, the data controller is the position responsible for protecting the privacy and rights of the data's subject, such as the user of a website. Whether the data is primary data or data from a third party, the data controller remains the point of responsibility for specifying how data is going to be used and processed either internally or externally. There can be multiple data controllers in an organization, with responsibilities over different sets of data.

> In the European Union (EU), General Data Protection Regulation (GDPR) classifies the data controller as the data manager. In other words, the data controller manages the data.

With respect to data with privacy implications, under most privacy regulations and GDPR, the data controller is responsible for deciding the following:

- What data is collected
- Where and how it is used
- With whom and how data is shared
- How long the data is kept and how it is disposed at end of life (EOL)

Data Processor

The **data processor** is the entity that processes data given to it by the data controller. Data processors do not own the data, nor do they control it. Their role is the manipulation of the data as part of business processes. Data processors can be personnel or systems; an example of a system is the use of Google Analytics to manipulate certain elements of data, making them useful for business analysts.

With respect to data with privacy implications, under most privacy regulations and GDPR, data processors are responsible for the following:

- Developing and implementing IT processes and systems that manage personal data
- Implementing security measures that would safeguard personal data
- Using tools and strategies to properly handle personal data

Data Custodian/Steward

Data custodians or **stewards** are the parties responsible for the day-to-day caretaking of data. The data owner sets the relevant policies, and the steward or custodian ensures these policies are followed.

Data Privacy Officer

The **data privacy officer (DPO)** is the C-level executive who is responsible for establishing and enforcing data privacy policy and addressing legal and compliance issues. Data minimization initiatives are also the responsibility of the data privacy officer. Storing data that does not have any real business value only increases the odds of disclosure. The data privacy officer is responsible for determining the gap between a company's privacy practices and the required actions to close the gap to an approved level. This is called a privacy impact analysis.

The data privacy officer is responsible for ensuring legal compliance with data privacy regulations.

The data privacy officer also plays an important role if information on European customers is involved because the EU has strict data protection (privacy) rules. The privacy officer who is accountable for the protection of consumer data from the EU must ensure compliance with EU regulations.

Data Destruction and Media Sanitization

When data is no longer being used, whether it is on old printouts, old systems being discarded, or broken equipment, it is important to destroy the data before losing physical control over the media it is on. Many criminals have learned the value of dumpster diving to discover information that can be used in identity theft, social engineering, and other malicious activities. An organization must concern itself not only with paper trash, but also the information stored on discarded objects such as computers. Several government organizations have been embarrassed when old computers sold to salvagers proved to contain sensitive documents on their hard drives. It is critical for every organization to have a strong disposal and destruction policy and related procedures. This section covers *data destruction and media sanitization* methods.

Data/Information Lifecycle

Data/information has a lifecycle—a beginning, a middle, and, at some point, an end. Understanding the lifecycle of information assets—from the point of collection, use, and storage as well as how the assets are shared, protected, and ultimately destroyed—is important if one is to properly handle the information. Not all information has the same time periods, or even steps, associated with it, so lifecycles are unique to different information sources and elements. The lifecycle forms a foundation upon which information management resides.

Burning

Burning is considered one of the gold-standard methods of data destruction. Once the storage media is rendered into a form that can be destroyed by fire, the chemical processes of fire are irreversible and render the data lost forever. The typical method is to shred the material, even plastic disks and hard drives (including SSDs), and then put the shred in an incinerator and oxidize the material back to base chemical forms. When the material is completely combusted, the information that was on it is gone.

Shredding

Shredding is physical destruction by tearing an item into many small pieces, which can then be mixed, making reassembly difficult if not impossible.

Important papers should be shredded, and *important* in this case means anything that might be useful to a potential intruder or dumpster diver. It is amazing what intruders can do with what appears to be innocent pieces of information. Shredders come in all sizes, from little desktop models that can handle a few pages at a time, or a single CD/DVD, to industrial versions that can handle even phone books and multiple discs at the same time. The ultimate in industrial shredders can even shred hard disk drives, metal case and all. Many document destruction companies have larger shredders on trucks that they bring to their clients location and do on-site shredding on a regular schedule.

Pulping

Pulping is a process by which paper fibers are suspended in a liquid and recombined into new paper. If you have data records on paper, and you shred the paper, the pulping process removes the ink by bleaching, and recombines all the shred into new paper, completely destroying the physical layout of the old paper.

Pulverizing

Pulverizing is a physical process of destruction using excessive physical force to break an item into unusable pieces. Pulverizers are used on items like hard disk drives, destroying the platters in a manner that they cannot be reconstructed. A more modern method of pulverizing the data itself is the use of encryption. The data on the drive is encrypted and the key itself is destroyed. This renders the data nonrecoverable based on the encryption strength. This method has unique advantages of scale; a small business can pulverize its own data, whereas it would either need expensive equipment or a third party to pulverize the few disks it needs to destroy each year.

Degaussing

A safer method for destroying files on magnetic storage devices (that is, magnetic tape and hard drives) is to destroy the data magnetically, using a strong magnetic field to degauss the media. *Degaussing* realigns the magnetic particles, removing the organized structure that represented the data. This effectively destroys all data on the media. Several commercial degaussers are available for this purpose.

Purging

Data **purging** is a term commonly used to describe methods that permanently erase and remove data from a storage space. The key phrase is "remove data," for unlike deletion, which just destroys the data, purging is designed to open up the storage space for reuse. A circular buffer is a great example of an automatic purge mechanism. It stores a given number of data elements and then the space is reused. A circular buffer that holds 64 MB, once full, overwrites the oldest material as new material is added to the buffer.

Wiping

Wiping data is the process of rewriting the storage media with a series of patterns of 1's and 0's. This is not done once, but multiple times to ensure that every trace of the original data has been eliminated. There are data-wiping protocols for various security levels of data, with three, seven, or even 35 passes. Of particular note are solid-state drives, as these devices use a different storage methodology and require special utilities to ensure that all the sectors are wiped.

Data wiping is nondestructive to the media, unlike pulping and shredding, and this makes it ideal for another purpose. Media sanitization is the clearing of previous data off of a media device before the device is reused. Wiping can be used to sanitize a storage device, making it clean before use. This can be important to remove old trace data that will later show up in free and unused space.

U.S. Privacy Laws

Identity privacy and the establishment of identity theft crimes is governed by the Identity Theft and Assumption Deterrence Act, which makes it a violation of federal law to knowingly use another's identity. The collection of information necessary to do this is also governed by the Gramm-Leach-Bliley Act (GLBA), which makes it illegal for someone to gather identity information on another person under false pretenses. In the education area, privacy laws have existed for years. See "Family Education Records and Privacy Act (FERPA)," later in the chapter.

Tech Tip

Major Elements of the Privacy Act

The Privacy Act has numerous required elements and definitions. Among other things, the major elements require federal agencies to do the following:

- *Publish in the Federal Register a notice of each system of records that it maintains, including information about the type of records maintained, the purposes for which they are used, and the categories of individuals on whom they are maintained.*
- *Maintain only such information about an individual as required by law, or is needed to perform a statutory duty.*
- *Maintain information in a timely, accurate, relevant, secure, and complete form.*
- *Inform individuals about access to PII upon inquiry.*
- *Notify individuals from whom it requests information as to what authorizes it to request the information, whether disclosure is mandatory or voluntary, the purpose for which the information may be used, and penalties for not providing the requested information.*
- *Establish appropriate physical, technical, and administrative safeguards for the information that is collected and used.*

Additional elements can be found by examining provisions of the act itself, although it is drafted in legislative form and requires extensive cross-referencing and interpretation.

Two major privacy initiatives followed from the U.S. government: the Privacy Act of 1974 and the Freedom of Information Act of 1996.

Fair Information Practice Principles (FIPPs)

In the United States, the Federal Trade Commission has a significant role in addressing privacy concerns. The core principles the FTC uses are referred to as the **Fair Information Practice Principles (FIPPs)**. The FIPPS and their components, as detailed in OMB Circular A-130, are as follows:

- **Access and Amendment** Agencies should provide individuals with appropriate access to PII and appropriate opportunity to correct or amend PII.
- **Accountability** Agencies should be accountable for complying with these principles and applicable privacy requirements, and should appropriately monitor, audit, and document compliance. Agencies should also clearly define the roles and responsibilities with respect to PII for all employees and contractors and should provide appropriate training to all employees and contractors who have access to PII.
- **Authority** Agencies should only create, collect, use, process, store, maintain, disseminate, or disclose PII if they have authority to do so, and should identify this authority in the appropriate notice.
- **Minimization** Agencies should only create, collect, use, process, store, maintain, disseminate, or disclose PII that is directly relevant and necessary to accomplish a legally authorized purpose, and should only maintain PII for as long as is necessary to accomplish the purpose.
- **Quality and Integrity** Agencies should create, collect, use, process, store, maintain, disseminate, or disclose PII with such accuracy, relevance, timeliness, and completeness as is reasonably necessary to ensure fairness to the individual.
- **Individual Participation** Agencies should involve the individual in the process of using PII and, to the extent practicable, seek individual consent for the creation, collection, use, processing, storage, maintenance, dissemination, or disclosure of PII. Agencies should also establish procedures to receive and address individuals' privacy-related complaints and inquiries.
- **Purpose Specification and Use Limitation** Agencies should provide notice of the specific purpose for which PII is collected and should only use, process, store, maintain, disseminate, or disclose PII for a purpose that is explained in the notice and is compatible with the purpose for which the PII was collected, or that is otherwise legally authorized.
- **Security** Agencies should establish administrative, technical, and physical safeguards to protect PII commensurate with the risk and magnitude of the harm that would result from its unauthorized access, use, modification, loss, destruction, dissemination, or disclosure.
- **Transparency** Agencies should be transparent about information policies and practices with respect to PII, and should provide clear and accessible notice regarding the creation, collection, use, processing, storage, maintenance, dissemination, and disclosure of PII.

Privacy Act of 1974

The **Privacy Act of 1974** was an omnibus act designed to affect the entire federal information landscape. This act has many provisions that apply across the entire federal government, with only minor exceptions for national security (classified information), law enforcement, and investigative provisions. This act has been amended numerous times, and you can find current, detailed information at the Electronic Privacy Information Center (EPIC) website, https://epic.org/privacy/laws/privacy_act.html.

Freedom of Information Act (FOIA)

The **Freedom of Information Act (FOIA)** of 1996 is one of the most widely used privacy acts in the United States, so much so that its acronym, FOIA (pronounced "foya"), has reached common use. FOIA was designed to enable public access to U.S. government records, and "public" includes the press, which purportedly acts on the public's behalf and widely uses FOIA to obtain information. FOIA carries a presumption of disclosure; the burden is on the government, not the requesting party, to substantiate why information cannot be released. Upon receiving a written request, agencies of the U.S. government are required to disclose those records, unless they can be lawfully withheld from disclosure under one of nine specific exemptions in FOIA. The right of access is ultimately enforceable through the federal court system. The nine specific exemptions, listed in Section 552 of U.S. Code Title 5, fall within the following general categories:

1. National security and foreign policy information
2. Internal personnel rules and practices of an agency
3. Information specifically exempted by statute
4. Confidential business information
5. Inter- or intra-agency communication that is subject to deliberative process, litigation, and other privileges
6. Information that, if disclosed, would constitute a clearly unwarranted invasion of personal privacy
7. Law enforcement records that implicate one of a set of enumerated concerns
8. Agency information from financial institutions
9. Geological and geophysical information concerning wells

> FOIA is frequently used and generates a tremendous amount of work for many federal agencies, resulting in delays to requests. This in itself is a testament to its effectiveness.

Record availability under FOIA is less of an issue than is the backlog of requests. To defray some of the costs associated with record requests, and to prevent numerous trivial requests, agencies are allowed to charge for research time and duplication costs. These costs vary by agency, but are typically nominal, in the range of \$8.00 to \$45.00 per hour for search/review fees and \$.10 to \$.35 per page for duplication. Agencies are not allowed to demand a requester to make an advance payment unless the agency estimates that the fee is likely to exceed \$250 or the requester previously failed to pay proper fees. For many uses, the first 100 pages are free, and under some circumstances the fees can be waived.

Family Education Records and Privacy Act (FERPA)

Student records have significant protections under the Family Education Records and Privacy Act of 1974, which includes significant restrictions on information sharing. FERPA operates on an opt-in basis, as the student must approve the disclosure of information prior to the actual disclosure. FERPA was designed to provide limited control to students over their education records. The law allows students to have access to their education records, an opportunity to seek to have the records amended, and some control over the disclosure of information from the records to third parties. For example, if the parent of a student who is 18 or older inquires about the student's schedule, grades, or other academic issues, the student has to give permission before the school can communicate with the parent, even if the parent is paying for the education.

FERPA is designed to protect the privacy of student information. At the K–12 school level, students are typically too young to have legal standing associated with exercising their rights, so FERPA recognizes the parents as part of the protected party. FERPA provides parents with the right to inspect and review their children's education records, the right to seek to amend information in the records they believe to be inaccurate, misleading, or an invasion of privacy, and the right to consent to the disclosure of PII from their children's education records. When a student turns 18 years old or enters a postsecondary institution at any age, these rights under FERPA transfer from the student's parents to the student.

U.S. Computer Fraud and Abuse Act (CFAA)

The U.S. Computer Fraud and Abuse Act (as amended in 1994, 1996, 2001, and 2008) and privacy laws such as the EU GDPR have several specific objectives, but one of the main ones is to prevent unauthorized parties from having access to information they should not have access to. Fraudulent access, or even exceeding one's authorized access, is defined as a crime and can be punished. Although the CFAA is intended for broader purposes, it can be used to protect privacy related to computer records through its enforcement of violations of authorized access.

U.S. Children's Online Privacy Protection Act (COPPA)

Children lack the mental capacity to make responsible decisions concerning the release of PII. The U.S. Children's Online Privacy Protection Act of 1998 (COPPA) specifically addresses this privacy issue with respect to children accessing and potentially releasing information on the Internet. Any website that collects information from children (ages 13 and under), even simple web forms to allow follow-up communications and so forth, is covered by this law. Before information can be collected and used, parental permission needs to be obtained. This act requires that sites obtain parental

Websites that are collecting information from children under the age of 13 are required to comply with the Children's Online Privacy Protection Act (COPPA). The U.S. FTC provides an informational website on COPPA and compliance issues at www.ftc.gov/tips-advice/business-center/privacy-and-security/children%27s-privacy.

permission, post a privacy policy detailing specifics concerning information collected from children, and describe how the children's information will be used.

Video Privacy Protection Act (VPPA)

Considered by many privacy advocates to be the strongest U.S. privacy law, the Video Privacy Protection Act of 1988 provides civil remedies against unauthorized disclosure of personal information concerning video tape rentals and, by extension, DVDs and games as well. This is a federal statute, crafted in response to media searches of rental records associated with Judge Bork when he was nominated to the U.S. Supreme Court. Congress, upset with the liberal release of information, reacted with legislation, drafted by Senator Leahy, who noted during the floor debate that new privacy protections are necessary in "an era of interactive television cables, the growth of computer checking and check-out counters, of security systems and telephones, all lodged together in computers...." (S. Rep. No. 100-599, 100th Cong., 2nd Sess. at 6 [1988]).

This statute, civil in nature, provides for civil penalties of up to $2500 per occurrence, as well as other civil remedies. The statute provides the protections by default, thus requiring a video rental company to obtain the renter's consent to opt out of the protections if the company wants to disclose personal information about rentals. Exemptions exist for issues associated with the normal course of business for the video rental company as well as for responding to warrants, subpoenas, and other legal requests. This law does not supersede state laws, of which there are several.

Many states have enacted laws providing both wider and greater protections than the federal VPPA statute. For example, Connecticut and Maryland laws brand video rental records as confidential, and therefore not subject to sale, while California, Delaware, Iowa, Louisiana, New York, and Rhode Island have adopted state statutes providing protection of privacy with respect to video rental records. Michigan's video privacy law is as sweeping as its broad super-DMCA state statute. This state law specifically protects records of book purchases, rentals, and borrowing as well as video rentals.

Health Insurance Portability and Accountability Act (HIPAA)

Medical and health information also has privacy implications, which is why the U.S. Congress enacted the **Health Insurance Portability and Accountability Act (HIPAA)** of 1996. HIPAA calls for sweeping changes in the way health and medical data is stored, exchanged, and used. From a privacy perspective, significant restrictions of data transfers to ensure privacy are included in HIPAA, including security standards and electronic signature provisions. HIPAA security standards mandate a uniform level of protections regarding all health information that pertains to an individual and is housed or transmitted electronically. The standards mandate safeguards for physical storage, maintenance, transmission, and access to individuals' health information. HIPAA mandates that organizations that use electronic signatures have to meet standards ensuring information integrity, signer authentication, and nonrepudiation. These standards leave to industry the task of specifying the technical solutions and mandate compliance only to significant levels of protection as provided by the rules being released by industry.

HIPAA's language is built on the concepts of **protected health information (PHI)** and **Notice of Privacy Practices (NPP)**. HIPAA describes "covered entities," including medical facilities, billing facilities, and insurance (third-party payer) facilities. Patients are to have access to their PHI and an expectation of appropriate privacy and security associated with medical records. HIPAA mandates a series of administrative, technical, and physical security safeguards for information, including elements such as staff training and awareness, as well as specific levels of safeguards for PHI when in use, stored, or in transit between facilities.

Tech Tip

Protected Health Information (PHI)

HIPAA regulations define protected health information (PHI) as "any information, whether oral or recorded in any form or medium" that "[i]s created or received by a health care provider, health plan, public health authority, employer, life insurer, school or university, or health care clearinghouse" and "[r]elates to the past, present, or future physical or mental health or condition of an individual; the provision of health care to an individual; or the past, present, or future payment for the provision of health care to an individual."

Cross Check

Notice of Privacy Practices

Visit your local doctor's office, hospital, or clinic and ask for their Notice of Privacy Practices (NPP). This notice to patients details what information will be collected and the uses and safeguards that are applied. These can be fairly lengthy and detailed documents, and in many cases are in a booklet form.

In 2009, as part of the American Recovery and Reinvestment Act of 2009, the Health Information Technology for Economic and Clinical Health Act (HITECH Act) was passed into law. Although the primary purpose of the HITECH Act was to provide stimulus money for the adoption of electronic medical records (EMR) systems at all levels of the healthcare system, it also contained new security and privacy provisions to add teeth to those already in HIPAA. HIPAA protections were confined to the direct medical profession and did not cover entities such as health information exchanges and other "business associates" engaged in the collection and use of PHI. Under HITECH, business associates will be required to implement the same security safeguards and restrictions on uses and disclosures, to protect individually identifiable health information, as covered entities under HIPAA. It also subjects business associates to the same potential civil and criminal liability for breaches as covered entities. HITECH also specifies that the U.S. Department of Health and Human Services (HHS) is now required to conduct periodic audits of covered entities and business associates.

Tech Tip

HIPAA Penalties

HIPAA civil penalties for willful neglect are increased under the HITECH Act. These penalties can extend up to $250,000, and repeat/uncorrected violations can extend up to $1.5 million. Under HIPAA and the HITECH Act, an individual cannot bring a cause of action against a provider. The laws specify that a state attorney general can bring an action on behalf of state residents.

Gramm-Leach-Bliley Act (GLBA)

In the financial arena, GLBA introduced the U.S. consumer to privacy notices, requiring firms to disclose what they collect, how they protect the information, and with whom they will share it. Annual notices are required as well as the option for consumers to opt out of the data sharing. The primary concept behind U.S. privacy laws in the financial arena is that consumers be allowed to opt out. This was strengthened in GLBA to include specific wording and notifications as well as requiring firms to appoint a privacy officer. Most U.S. consumers have witnessed the results of GLBA, every year receiving privacy notices from their banks and credit card companies. These notices are one of the visible effects of GLBA on changing the role of privacy associated with financial information.

California Senate Bill 1386 (SB 1386)

California Senate Bill 1386 (SB 1386) was a landmark law concerning information disclosures. It mandates that Californians be notified whenever PII is lost or disclosed. Since the passage of SB 1386, numerous other states have modeled legislation on this bill, and although national legislation has been blocked by political procedural moves, it will eventually be passed. The current list of U.S. states and territories that require disclosure notices is up to 49, with only Alabama, New Mexico, and South Dakota without bills. Each of these disclosure notice laws is different, making the case for a unifying federal statute compelling, but currently it is low on the priority lists of most politicians.

U.S. Banking Rules and Regulations

Banking has always had an element of PII associated with it, from who has deposits to who has loans. As the scale of operations increased, both in numbers of customers and products, the importance of information for processing grew. Checks became a utility instrument to convey information associated with funds transferred between parties. As a check was basically a promise to pay, in the form of directions to a bank, occasionally the check was not honored and a merchant had to track down the party to demand payment. Thus, it became industry practice to write additional information on a check to assist a firm in later tracking down the drafting party. This information included items such as address, work phone number, a credit card number, and so on. This led to the co-location of information about an individual, and this information was used at times to perform the crime of **identity theft**. To combat this and prevent the gathering of this type of information, a series of banking and financial regulations were issued by the U.S. government to prohibit this form of information collection. Other regulations addressed items such as credit card numbers being printed on receipts, mandating only the last five digits be exposed.

Payment Card Industry Data Security Standard (PCI DSS)

As described in Chapter 24, the major credit card firms, such as MasterCard, Visa, American Express, and Discover, designed a private-sector initiative to deal with privacy issues associated with credit card transaction information. PCI DSS is a standard that provides guidance on what elements of a credit card transaction need protection and the level of expected protection. PCI DSS is not a law, but rather a contractual regulation, enforced through a series of fines and fees associated with performing business in this space. PCI DSS was a reaction to two phenomena: data disclosures and identity theft.

Fair Credit Reporting Act (FCRA)

The Fair Credit Reporting Act of 1999 brought significant privacy protections to the consumer credit reporting agencies (CRAs). This act requires that the agencies provide consumers notice of their rights and responsibilities. The agencies are required to perform timely investigations on inaccuracies reported by consumers. The agencies are also required to notify the other CRAs when consumers close accounts. The act also has technical issues associated with data integrity, data destruction, data retention, and consumer and third-party access to data. The details of FCRA proved to be insufficient with respect to several aspects of identity theft, and in 2003, the Fair and Accurate Credit Transactions Act (FACTA) was passed, modifying and expanding on the privacy and security provisions of FCRA.

> **Tech Tip**
>
> **FACTA and Credit Card Receipts**
>
> *One of the provisions of FACTA compels businesses to protect credit card information on receipts. Before FACTA, it was common for receipts to show entire credit card numbers as well as additional information. Today, receipts can display only the last five digits of the card number and cannot include the card expiration date. These rules went into effect in 2005, and merchants had one year to comply.*

Fair and Accurate Credit Transactions Act (FACTA)

The Fair and Accurate Credit Transactions Act of 2003 was passed to enact stronger protections for consumer information from identity theft, errors, and omissions. FACTA amended portions of FCRA to improve the accuracy of customer records in consumer reporting agencies, to improve timely resolution of consumer complaints concerning inaccuracies, and to make businesses take reasonable steps to protect information that can lead to identity theft.

FACTA also had other "disposal rules" associated with consumer information. FACTA mandates that information that is no longer needed must be properly disposed of, by either burning, pulverizing, or shredding. Any electronic information must be irreversibly destroyed or erased. Should third-party firms be used for disposal, the rules still pertain to the original contracting party, so third parties should be selected with care and monitored for compliance.

> **Tech Tip**
>
> **FTC Disposal Rule**
>
> *The FTC's* **Disposal Rule** *applies to consumer reporting agencies as well as to any individuals and businesses that use consumer reports, such as lenders, insurers, employers, and landlords.*

> **Tech Tip**
>
> **Red Flag Rules**
>
> *The FTC has adopted a set of* **red flag rules** *that are invoked to assist entities in determining when extra precautions must be taken concerning PII records. The following are some examples of* **red flags** *that should prompt an organization to initiate additional, specific data handling steps to protect data:*
>
> - *Change of address request. This is a common tool for identity thieves, and as such, firms should provide protection steps to verify change-of-address requests.*
> - *Sudden use of an account that has been inactive for a long time, or radical changes in use of any account.*
> - *A suspicious address or phone number. Many fraudulent addresses and numbers are known, and repeated applications should be quickly noted and stopped.*
> - *Request for credit on a consumer account that has a credit freeze on a credit reporting record.*
>
> *Additional information is available from the FTC at www.ftc.gov/tips-advice/business-center/guidance/fighting-identity-theft-red-flags-rule-how-guide-business.*
>
> *Whenever a red flag issue occurs, the business must have special procedures in place to ensure that the event is not fraudulent. Calling the customer and verifying information before taking action is one example of this type of additional action.*

International Privacy Laws

Privacy is not a U.S.-centric phenomenon, but it does have strong cultural biases. Legal protections for privacy tend to follow the socio-cultural norms by geography; hence, there are different policies in European nations than in the United States. In the United States, the primary path to privacy is via **opt-out**, whereas in Europe and other countries, it is via **opt-in**. What this means is that the fundamental nature of control shifts. In the U.S., a consumer must notify a firm that they wish to block the sharing of personal information; otherwise, the firm has permission by default. In the EU, sharing is blocked unless the customer specifically opts in to allow it. The Far East has significantly different cultural norms with respect to individualism versus collectivism, and this is seen in their privacy laws as well. Their legal systems reflect these cultural norms as well. Even in countries with common borders, distinct differences exist, such as the United States and Canada; Canadian laws and customs have strong roots to their UK history, and in many cases follow European ideals as opposed to U.S. ones. One of the primary sources of intellectual and political thought on privacy has been the Organization for Economic Co-operation and Development (OECD). This multinational entity has for decades conducted multilateral discussions and policy formation on a wide range of topics, including privacy.

OECD Fair Information Practices

OECD Fair Information Practices are the foundational element for many worldwide privacy practices. Dating to 1980, Fair Information Practices are a set of principles and practices that set out how an information-based society may approach information handling, storage, management, and flows with a view toward maintaining fairness, privacy, and security. Members of the OECD recognized that information was a critical resource in a rapidly evolving global technology environment, and that proper handling of this resource was critical for long-term sustainability of growth.

Tech Tip

OECD's Privacy Code

OECD's privacy code was developed to help "harmonise national privacy legislation and, while upholding such human rights, [to] at the same time prevent interruptions in international flows of data. [The Guidelines] represent a consensus on basic principles which can be built into existing national legislation, or serve as a basis for legislation in those countries which do not yet have it." (Source: "OECD Guidelines on the Protection of Privacy and Transborder Flows of Personal Data," www.oecd.org/sti/ieconomy/oecdguidelinesontheprotectionofprivacyandtransborderflowsofpersonaldata.htm.)

European Laws

The EU has developed a comprehensive concept of privacy, which is administered via a set of statutes known as **data protection**. These privacy statutes cover all personal data, whether collected and used by government or by private firms. These laws are administered by state and national data protection agencies in each country. With the advent of the EU, this common comprehensiveness stands in distinct contrast to the patchwork of laws in the United States.

Privacy laws in Europe are built around the concept that privacy is a fundamental human right that demands protection through government administration. When the EU was formed, many laws were harmonized across the original 15 member nations, and data privacy was among those standardized. The initial harmonization related to privacy was the Data Protection Directive, adopted by EU members, which has a provision allowing the European Commission to block transfers of personal data to any country outside the EU that has been determined to lack adequate data protection policies. The impetus for the EU directive is to establish the regulatory framework to enable the movement of personal data from one country to another, while at the same time ensuring that privacy protection is "adequate" in the country to which the data is sent. This can be seen as a direct result of early United States Department of Health, Education, and Welfare (HEW) task force and OECD directions. If the recipient country has not established a minimum standard of data protection, it is expected that the transfer of data will be prohibited.

General Data Protection Regulation (GDPR)

Two factors led to what can only be seen as a complete rewrite of EU data protection regulations. In light of the Snowden revelations, the EU began a new round of examining data protection when shared with the U.S. and others. This brought Safe Harbor provisions into the spotlight as the EU wanted to renegotiate stronger protections. Then, the European Court of Justice invalidated the Safe Harbor provisions. This led the way to the passage of the **General Data Protection Regulation (GDPR)**, which went into effect in May of 2018.

The GDPR ushers in a brand-new world with respect to data protection and privacy. With global trade being important to all countries, and the fact that trade rests upon information transfers, including those of personal data, the ability to transfer data, including personal data, between parties becomes important to trade. Enshrined in the Charter of Fundamental Rights of the EU is the fundamental right to the protection of personal data, including when such data elements are transferred outside the EU. Recognizing that, the new set of regulations is more expansive and restrictive, making the Safe Harbor provisions obsolete. For all firms that wish to trade with the EU, there is now a set of privacy regulations that will require specific programs to address the requirements.

The GDPR brings many changes, one being the appointment of a data protection officer (DPO). This role may be filled by an employee or a third-party service provider (for example, consulting or law firm), and it must be a direct report to the highest management level. The DPO should operate with significant independence, and provisions in the GDPR restrict control over the DPO by management.

The GDPR specifies requirements regarding consent, and they are significantly more robust than previous regulations. Consent requirements are also delineated for specific circumstances:

- Informed/affirmative consent to data processing. Specifically, "a statement or a clear affirmative action" from the data subject must be "freely given, specific, informed and unambiguous."

Tech Tip

GDPR

The GDPR requires significant consideration, including the following:

- *Assessing personal data flows from the EU to the U.S. to define the scale and scope of the cross-border privacy-compliance challenge*
- *Assessing readiness to meet model clauses, remediate gaps, and organize audit artifacts of compliance with the clauses*
- *Updating privacy programs to ensure they are capable of passing an EU regulator audit*
- *Conducting EU data-breach notification stress tests*
- *Monitoring changes in EU support for model contracts and binding corporate rules*

- Explicit consent to process special categories of data. Explicit consent is required for "special categories" of data, such as genetic data, biometric data, and data concerning sexual orientation.
- Explicit parental consent for children's personal data.
- Consent must be specific to each data-processing operation, and the data subject can withdraw consent at any time.

> **Tech Tip**
>
> **Encryption and Privacy**
>
> *Encryption has long been held by governments to be a technology associated with the military. As such, different governments have regulated it in different manners. The U.S. government has greatly reduced controls over encryption in the past decade. Other countries, such as Great Britain, have enacted statutes that compel users to turn over encryption keys when asked by authorities. Countries such as France, Malaysia, and China still tightly control and license end-user use of encryption technologies. The primary driver for Phil Zimmerman to create Pretty Good Privacy (PGP) was the need for privacy in countries where the government was considered a threat to civil liberties.*

The GDPR provides protections for new individual rights, and these may force firms to adopt new policies to address these requirements. The rights include the Right to Information, Right to Access, Right to Rectification, Right to Restrict Processing, Right to Object, Right to Erasure, and Right to Data Portability. Each of these rights is clearly defined with technical specifics in the GDPR. The GDPR also recognizes the risks of international data transfer to other parties and has added specific requirements that data protection issues be addressed by means of appropriate safeguards, including binding corporate rules (BCRs), model contract clauses (MCCs), also known as standard contractual clauses (SCCs), and legally binding documents. These instruments must be enforceable between public authorities or bodies, as well as all who handle data.

The differences in approach between the U.S. and the EU with respect to data protection led the EU to issue expressions of concern about the adequacy of data protection in the United States, a move that could have paved the way to the blocking of data transfers. This has forced U.S. and other international companies to adapt their privacy protections to at least align with the GDPR for EU customers.

Another major difference between U.S. and European regulation lies in where the right of control is exercised. In European directives, the right of control over privacy is balanced in such a way as to favor consumers. Rather than having to pay to opt out, as with unlisted phone numbers in the United States, consumers have such services for free. Rather than users having to opt out at all, the default privacy setting is deemed to be the highest level of data privacy, and users have to opt in to share information. This default setting is a cornerstone of the European Union's Directive on Protection of Personal Data and is enforced through national laws in all member nations.

Canadian Law

Like many European countries, Canada has a centralized form of privacy legislation that applies to every organization that collects, uses, or discloses personal information, including information about employees. These regulations stem from the **Personal Information Protection and Electronic Data Act (PIPEDA)**, which requires that personal information be collected and used only for appropriate purposes. Individuals must be notified as to why the information is requested and how it will be used. The act has safeguards associated with storage, use, reuse, and retention.

To ensure leadership in the field of privacy issues, Canada has a national-level privacy commissioner, and each province has a provincial privacy commissioner. These commissioners act as advocates on behalf of individuals and have used legal actions to enforce the privacy provisions associated with PIPEDA to protect personal information.

Asian Laws

Japan has the Personal Information Protection Law, which requires protection of personal information used by the Japanese government, third parties, and the public sector. The Japanese law has provisions where the government entity must specify the purpose for which information is being collected, specify the safeguards applied, and, when permitted, discontinue use of the information upon request.

Hong Kong has an office of the Privacy Commissioner for Personal Data (PCPD), a statutory body entrusted with the task of protecting personal data privacy of individuals and to ensure compliances with the Personal Data (Privacy) Ordinance in Hong Kong. One main task of the Commissioner is public education, creating greater awareness of privacy issues and the need to comply with the Personal Data Ordinance.

China has had a long reputation of poor privacy practices. Some of this comes from the cultural bias toward collectivism, and some comes from the long-standing government tradition of surveillance. News of the Chinese government eavesdropping on Skype and other Internet-related communications has heightened this concern. China's constitution has provisions for privacy protections for the citizens. Even so, issues have come in the area of enforcement and penalties as well as privacy items that have been far from uniform in their judicial history.

Privacy-Enhancing Technologies

One principal connection between information security and privacy is that without information security, you cannot have privacy. If privacy is defined as the ability to control information about oneself, then the aspects of confidentiality, integrity, and availability from information security become critical elements of privacy. Just as technology has enabled many privacy-impacting issues, technology also offers the means in many cases to protect privacy. An application or tool that assists in such protection is called a **privacy-enhancing technology (PET)**.

Encryption is at the top of the list of PETs for protecting privacy and anonymity. As noted earlier, one of the driving factors behind Phil Zimmerman's invention of PGP was the desire to enable people living in repressive cultures to communicate safely and freely. Encryption can keep secrets secret, and it's a prime choice for protecting information at any stage in its lifecycle. The development of Tor routing to permit anonymous communications, coupled with high-assurance, low-cost cryptography, has made many web interactions securable and safe from eavesdropping.

Other PETs include small application programs called **cookie cutters** that are designed to prevent the transfer of cookies between browsers and web servers. Some cookie cutters block all cookies, while others can be configured to selectively block certain cookies. Some cookie cutters also block the sending of HTTP headers that might reveal personal information but might not be necessary to access a website, as well as block banner ads, pop-up windows, animated graphics, or other unwanted web elements. Some related PET tools are designed specifically to look for invisible images that set cookies (called web beacons or web bugs). Other PETs are available to PC users, including encryption programs that allow users to encrypt and protect their own data, even on USB keys.

Data Minimization

Data minimization is one of the most powerful privacy-enhancing technologies. In a nutshell, it involves not keeping what you don't need. Limiting the collection of personal information to that which is directly relevant and necessary to accomplish a specified purpose still allows the transactions to be accomplished, but it also reduces risk from future breaches and disclosures by not keeping "excess" data. In the EU, privacy rules are built around the idea that individuals own the rights to the reuse of their data, and unless they grant it to a company, the right to store and reuse the data beyond the immediate transaction is prohibited. This serves several purposes, but one important outcome is that when a breach/disclosure event occurs, the reach of the PII loss is limited.

While you may need to have a reasonable amount of PII to process and ship an order, once that process has concluded, do you need the data? There may be a need for a reasonable period for returns, warranty claims, and so on, but once that period has passed, destroying unneeded PII removes it from the chance of disclosure.

Data Masking

> Data masking hides personal or sensitive data but does not render it unusable.

Data masking involves the hiding of data by substituting altered values. A mirror version of a database is created, and data modification techniques such as character shuffling, encryption, and word or character substitution are applied to change the data. Another form is to physically redact elements by substituting a symbol such as * or x. This is seen on credit card receipts, where the majority of the digits are removed in this fashion. Data masking makes reverse engineering or detection impossible.

Tokenization

> Tokenization assigns a random value that can be reversed or traced back to the original data.

Tokenization is the use of a random value to take the place of a data element that has traceable meaning. A good example of this is when you have a credit card approval, you do not need to keep a record of the card number, the cardholder's name, or any of the sensitive data concerning the card verification code (CVC) because the transaction agent returns an approval code, which is a unique token to that transaction. You can store this approval code, the token, in your system, and if there comes a time you need to reference the original transaction, this token provides you with complete traceability to it and yet, if disclosed to an outside party, reveals nothing.

Tokens are used all the time in data transmission systems involving commerce because they protect the sensitive information from being reused or shared, yet they maintain the desired nonrepudiation characteristics of the event. Tokenization is not an encryption step because encrypted data can be decrypted. By substituting a nonrelated random value, tokenization breaks the ability for any outside entity to "reverse" the action because there is no connection.

Anonymization

Data anonymization is the process of protecting private or sensitive information by removing identifiers that connect the stored data to an individual. Separating the PII elements such as names, Social Security numbers, and addresses from the remaining data through a data anonymization process retains the usefulness of the data but keeps the connection to the source anonymous. Data anonymization is easier said than done, because data exists in many places in many forms. This permits data aggregators to collect multiple instances and then, through algorithms and pattern matching, de-anonymize the data through multiple cross-references against multiple sources.

Pseudo-Anonymization

Pseudo-anonymization is a de-identification method that replaces private identifiers with fake identifiers or pseudonyms (for example, replacing the value of the name identifier "Mark Sands" with "John Doe"). Not all uniquely identifying fields are changed because some, such as date of birth, may need to be preserved to maintain statistical accuracy. Noise can be added to some fields to remove direct connections, but maintaining the approximate value; for example, randomly adding or subtracting three days to/from the actual date of birth preserves the age but de-identifies to the original record. Pseudo-anonymization preserves statistical accuracy and data integrity, allowing the modified data to be used for training, development, testing, and analytics while protecting data privacy.

> **Tech Tip**
>
> **Privacy Compliance Steps**
>
> *To ensure that an organization complies with the numerous privacy requirements and regulations, a structured approach to privacy planning and policies is recommended:*
>
> 1. *Identify the role in the organization that will be responsible for compliance and oversight.*
> 2. *Document all applicable laws and regulations, industry standards, and contract requirements.*
> 3. *Identify any industry best practices.*
> 4. *Perform a privacy impact assessment (PIA) and a risk assessment.*
> 5. *Map the identified risks to compliance requirements.*
> 6. *Create a unified risk mitigation plan.*

Privacy Policies

One of the direct outcomes of the legal statutes associated with privacy has been the development of a need for corporate privacy policies associated with data collection. With a myriad of government agencies involved, each with a specific mandate to "assist" in the protection effort associated with PII, one can ask, what is the best path for an industry member? If your organization needs PII to perform its tasks, obtaining and using it is fine in most cases, but you must ensure that everyone in the organization complies with the laws, rules, and regulations associated with these government agencies. Policies and procedures are the best way to ensure uniform compliance across an organization. The development of a **privacy policy** is an essential foundational element of a company's privacy stance.

Terms of Agreement

The legal description of *terms of agreement* (commonly known as *terms and conditions*) is a set of items that both parties agree upon before some joint activity. This is used all the time with any external-facing interface, where you have the responding party agree to a published terms of agreement document before granting them access or processing their data elements.

A typical terms of agreement document includes the terms, the rules, the guidelines of acceptable behavior, and other useful sections to which users must agree in order to use or access an IT resource, such as website, a mobile app, an order placement page, and so on. Important items in the terms of agreement document include legal terms, governing law, agreement to operating rules, what services are offered and under what business conditions, liabilities, remedies for disagreements (for example, arbitration), and business terms such as the right to cancel, refunds, service level agreements, and so on. This becomes a license that binds the parties to the terms the business wishes to enforce.

Privacy Notice

A *privacy notice* is an exterior-facing statement that describes how the organization collects, uses, retains, and discloses personal information. Privacy notices are also referred to as privacy statements or fair processing statements. Special privacy notices are also mandated by specific privacy laws, and a common example of those is the cookies disclosure statement seen on websites that use cookies. The common elements of a privacy notice include the following:

- When you collect personal information
- Why you collect personal information
- What information is collected
- How the information will be protected
- When the information can or will be shared
- Who to contact and where questions should be directed concerning the notice
- How to opt out or opt in
- An effective date of the document

> The key concept to note is that a privacy policy is internally focused, telling employees what they may do with personal information, whereas a privacy notice is externally facing, telling customers, regulators, and other stakeholders what the organization does with personal information.

An example of a web cookie notice would be, "We use cookies to deliver our online services. Details of the cookies and other tracking technologies we use and instructions on how to disable them are set out in our Cookies Policy. By using this website, you consent to our use of cookies."

Privacy Impact Assessment

A **privacy impact assessment (PIA)** is a structured approach to determining the gap between desired privacy performance and actual privacy performance. A PIA is an analysis of how PII is handled through business processes and an assessment of risks to the PII during storage, use, and communication. A PIA provides a means to assess the effectiveness of a process relative to compliance requirements and identify issues that need to be addressed. A PIA is structured with a series of defined steps to ensure a comprehensive review of privacy provisions.

The following steps comprise a high-level methodology and approach for conducting a PIA:

1. *Establish PIA scope.* Determine the departments involved and the appropriate representatives. Determine which applications and business processes need to be assessed. Determine applicable laws and regulations associated with the business and privacy concerns.
2. *Identify key stakeholders.* Identify all business units that use PII. Examine staff functions such as HR, Legal, IT, Purchasing, and Quality Control.
3. *Document all contact with PII:*
   - PII collection, access, use, sharing, and disposal
   - Processes and procedures, policies, safeguards, data-flow diagrams, and any other risk assessment data
   - Website policies, contracts, HR, and administrative for other PII
4. *Review legal and regulatory requirements, including any upstream contracts.* The sources are many, but some commonly overlooked issues are agreements with suppliers and customers over information sharing rights.
5. *Document gaps and potential issues between requirements and practices.* All gaps and issues should be mapped against where the issue was discovered and the basis (requirement or regulation) that the gap maps to.
6. *Review findings with key stakeholders to determine accuracy and clarify any issues.* Before the final report is written, any issues or possible miscommunications should be clarified with the appropriate stakeholders to ensure a fair and accurate report.
7. *Create a final report for management.*

In late 2020, and into 2021, Apple entered into the privacy world with a bold and strong statement supporting users' right to privacy. The company backed these words with changes to its operating systems for the iPhone and iPad tablets to significantly reduce the information shared via apps. This has created a battle between Apple and the marketing giants of Facebook and Google, but Apple seems to be firm in its resolve that technology should support privacy. For more information, see https://time.com/collection/davos-2019/5502591/tim-cook-data-privacy/.

Web Privacy Issues

The Internet acts as a large information-sharing domain and, as such, can be a conduit for the transference of information among many parties. The Web offers much in the form of communication between machines, people, and systems, and this same exchange of information can be associated with privacy based on the content of the information and the reason for the exchange.

Cookies

Cookies are small bits of text that are stored on a user's machine and sent to specific websites when the user visits these sites. Cookies can store many different things, from tokens that provide a reference to a database server behind the web server to assist in maintaining state through an application, to the contents of a shopping cart. Cookies can also hold data directly, in which case there are possible privacy implications. When a cookie holds a token number that is meaningless to outsiders but meaningful to a back-end server, then the loss of the cookie represents no loss at all. When the cookie text contains meaningful information, then the loss can result in privacy issues. For instance, when a cookie contains a long number that has no meaning except to the database server, then the number has no PII. But if the cookie contains text, such as a ship-to address for an order, this can represent PII and can result in a privacy violation. It is common to encode the data in cookies, but Base64 encoding is not encryption and can be decoded by anyone, thus providing no confidentiality.

Cookies provide the useful service of allowing state to be maintained in the stateless process of web serving (see "Cookies" in Chapter 17). But because of the potential for PII leakage, many users have sworn off cookies. This leads to issues on numerous websites, because when properly implemented, cookies pose no privacy danger and can greatly enhance website usefulness.

The bottom line for cookies is fairly clear: Done correctly, they do not represent a security or privacy issue. Done incorrectly, they can be a disaster. A simple rule solves most problems with cookies: never store data directly on a cookie; instead, store a reference to another web application that permits the correct actions to occur based on the key value.

Privacy in Practice

With privacy being defined as the power to control what others know about you and what they can do with that information, there remains the question of what you can do to exercise that control. Information is needed to obtain services, and in many cases the information is reused, often for additional and secondary purposes. Users agree to these uses through acceptance of a firm's privacy policy.

Shared information still requires control, and in this case the control function has shifted to the party that obtained the information. They may store it for future use, for record purposes, or for other uses. If they fail to adequately protect the information from loss or disclosure, then the owner no longer has authorized the uses it may be employed in. Data disclosures and information thefts both result in unauthorized use of information. Users can take actions to protect their information and to mitigate risk from unauthorized sharing and use of their information.

User Actions

Users have to share information for a variety of legitimate purposes. Information has value, both to the authorized user and to those who would steal the information and use it for unauthorized purposes. If users are going to control their information, they have to take certain precautions. This is where security and privacy intersect at an operational level. Security functionality enables control and thus enables privacy functionality.

One aspect of maintaining control over information is in the proper security precautions presented throughout the book, so they will not be repeated here. A second level of actions can be employed by users to maintain knowledge over their information uses. The value of information is in its use, and in many cases, this use can be tracked. The two main types of information that have immediate value are financial and medical. Financial information, such as credit card information, identity information, and banking information, can be used by criminals to steal from others. Many times the use of identity or financial information will show up on the systems of record associated with the information. This is why it is important to actually read bank statements and verify charges.

In the same vein, one should periodically examine their credit report, looking for unauthorized credit requests or accounts. Periodic checks of healthcare insurance accounts and reports are essential for the same reason. Just because you have paid all your copays, you shouldn't shred unopened envelopes from the insurance company. If someone else is using your information, you may be authorizing their use of your stolen information by not alerting the insurance company to the misuse.

Users should periodically, as in annually, request copies of their credit bureau reports and examine them for unauthorized activity. Likewise, users should periodically check their healthcare insurers, looking for unauthorized activity there as well. These checks do not take much time and provide a means to prevent long-term penetration of identities.

Data Breaches

When a company loses data that it has stored on its network, the term used is *data breach*. Data breaches have become an almost daily news item, and the result is that people are becoming desensitized to their occurrence. Data breaches act as means of notification that security efforts have failed. Verizon regularly publishes a data breach investigation report, examining the root causes behind hundreds of breach events. In the Verizon Data Breach Investigations report, Verizon found that breaches can be described by the following distinct patterns:

- Point-of-sale (POS) intrusions
- Web app attacks
- Insider and privilege misuse
- Physical theft and loss
- Miscellaneous errors (misdelivery, misconfiguration, user errors)
- Crimeware
- Payment card skimmers
- Denial of service
- Cyber espionage

In 2020, the report found that 70 percent of breaches were caused by outsiders, 86 percent of the breaches were financially motivated, 43 percent of breaches were attacks on web applications (more than double the previous year), and 27 percent of malware incidents were attributed to ransomware.

Data breaches continue to plague firms. Here are some recent major breaches and the number of records they affected:

- **Equifax** 143,000,000 records
- **Friend Finder Network** 412,000,000 records
- **River City Media** 1,370,000,000 records
- **Spambot** 700,000,000 records
- **Philippine Commission on Elections** 550,000,000 records
- **Uber** 57,000,000 records

There are many additional breaches, varying in size and in data sensitivity. While the large numbers of e-mail addresses capture the headlines, the release of all Swedish car registrations in the entire country is missed because of the limited numbers of cars in Sweden, yet the impact for Swedes could be significant. For further reference and additional information, see www.informationisbeautiful.net/visualizations/worlds-biggest-data-breaches-hacks/.

For More Information

Rebecca Herold, Privacy Professor

Monthly Privacy Professor tips www.privacyguidance.com/eTips.html

Blog www.privacyguidance.com/blog/

Videos www.privacyguidance.com/eMy_Videos.html

Data Breaches

Information Is Beautiful (visualizations) www.informationisbeautiful.net/visualizations/worlds-biggest-data-breaches-hacks/

Verizon data breach investigations report https://enterprise.verizon.com/resources/reports/dbir/

Chapter 25 Review

Chapter Summary

After reading this chapter and completing the exercises, you should understand the following aspects of privacy.

Examine concepts of privacy

- Privacy is the power to control what others know about you and what they can do with that information.
- The concept of privacy does not translate directly to information about a business because it is not about a person.

Compare and contrast privacy policies and laws of different jurisdictions

- Numerous U.S. federal statutes have privacy provisions, including FERPA, VPPA, GLBA, HIPAA, and so on.
- The number of state and local laws that address privacy issues is limited.
- A wide array of international laws address privacy issues, including those of the EU, Canada, and other nations.

Describe approaches individuals, organizations, and governments have taken to protect privacy

- Policies drive corporate actions, and privacy policies are required by several statutes and are essential to ensure compliance with the myriad of mandated actions.
- Cookies represent a useful tool to maintain state when surfing the Web, but if used incorrectly, they can represent a risk to security and privacy.
- Data sensitivity labels are used to identify the types of data sensitivity.
- Assignment of duties to data owners, controllers, custodians/stewards, processors, and privacy officers is done by management.

Describe issues associated with technology and privacy

- A direct relationship exists between information security and privacy—one cannot have privacy without security.
- Privacy-enhancing technologies (PETs) are used in the technological battle to preserve anonymity and privacy.

Explain the concept of personally identifiable information (PII)

- Specific constituent elements of PII need to be protected.
- Corporate responsibilities associated with PII include the need to protect PII appropriately when in storage, use, or transmission.

Key Terms

choice *(935)*
consent *(935)*
cookie cutters *(951)*
cookies *(955)*
data custodian *(937)*
data owner *(936)*
data privacy officer (DPO) *(937)*
data processor *(937)*
data protection *(948)*
data retention *(931)*
data roles *(936)*
data sensitivity labeling *(933)*
data steward *(937)*
Disposal Rule *(947)*
Fair Information Practice Principles (FIPPs) *(941)*
Freedom of Information Act (FOIA) *(942)*
General Data Protection Regulation (GDPR) *(949)*
Health Insurance Portability and Accountability Act (HIPAA) *(944)*
identity theft *(946)*

notice *(935)*
Notice of Privacy Practices (NPP) *(945)*
opt-in *(948)*
opt-out *(948)*
Personal Information Protection and Electronic Data Act (PIPEDA) *(950)*
personally identifiable information (PII) *(935)*
privacy *(930)*
Privacy Act of 1974 *(942)*
privacy-enhancing technology (PET) *(951)*
privacy impact assessment (PIA) *(954)*
privacy policy *(953)*
proprietary data *(934)*
protected health information (PHI) *(945)*
pulping *(939)*
pulverizing *(939)*
purging *(939)*
red flag *(947)*
red flag rules *(947)*
sensitive data *(934)*

Key Terms Quiz

Use terms from the Key Terms list to complete the sentences that follow. Don't use the same term more than once. Not all terms will be used.

1. In the United States, the standard methodology for consumers with respect to privacy is to _______________, whereas in the EU it is to _______________.
2. _______________ is the right to control information about oneself.
3. The FTC mandates firms' use of _______________ procedures to identify instances where additional privacy measures are warranted.
4. The newer set of privacy rules and regulations in the EU are referred to as the _______________.
5. Data that can be used to identify a specific individual is referred to as _______________.
6. Programs used to control the use of _______________ during web browsing are referred to as __________.
7. The major U.S. privacy statutes are the _____________ and the _______________.
8. Medical information in the United States is protected via the _______________.
9. Many privacy regulations have specified that firms provide an annual _______________ to customers.
10. To evaluate the privacy risks in a firm, a(n) _______________ can be performed.

Multiple-Choice Quiz

1. HIPAA requires which of the following controls for medical records?

   A. Encryption of all data

   B. Technical safeguards

   C. Physical controls

   D. Administrative, technical, and physical controls

2. Which of the following is not PII?

   A. Customer name

   B. Customer ID number

   C. Customer Social Security number or taxpayer identification number

   D. Customer birth date

3. A privacy impact assessment:

   A. Determines the gap between a company's privacy practices and required actions

   B. Determines the damage caused by a breach of privacy

   C. Determines what companies hold information on a specific person

   D. Is a corporate procedure to safeguard PII

4. Which of the following should trigger a response under the red flag rule?

   A. All credit requests for people under 25 or over 75

   B. Any new customer credit request, except for name changes due to marriage

   C. Request for credit from a customer who has a history of late payments and poor credit

   D. Request for credit from a customer with a credit freeze on their credit reporting record

5. Which of the following is an acceptable PII disposal procedure?

   A. Shredding

   B. Burning

   C. Electronic destruction per military data destruction standards

   D. All of the above

6. Key elements of GDPR include which of the following?

   A. Conducting EU data-breach notification stress tests

   B. Appointing a data protection officer reporting directly to top-level management of the firm

   C. Right to Erasure

   D. All of the above

7. European privacy laws are built upon which of the following?

   A. General Data Protection Regulations

   B. Personal Information Protection and Electronic Data Act (PIPEDA)

   C. Safe Harbor principles

   D. Common law practices

8. In the United States, company responses to data disclosures of PII are regulated by which of the following?

   A. Federal law, the Privacy Act

   B. A series of state statutes

   C. Contractual agreements with banks and credit card processors

   D. The Gramm-Leach-Bliley Act (GLBA)

9. What is/are the primary factor(s) behind data-sharing compliance between U.S. and European companies?

   A. U.S. firms adopting provisions of the GDPR

   B. Safe Harbor provisions

   C. U.S. FTC enforcement actions

   D. All of the above

10. Privacy is defined as:

    A. One's ability to control information about oneself

    B. Being able to keep one's information secret

    C. Making data-sharing illegal without consumer consent

    D. Something that is outmoded in the Internet age

Essay Quiz

1. Privacy and technology often clash, especially when technology allows data collection that has secondary uses. In the case of automotive technology, black boxes to collect operational data are being installed in new cars in the United States. What are the privacy implications, and what protections exist?
2. Privacy policies are found all over the Web. Pick three websites with privacy policies and compare and contrast them. What do they include and what is missing?
3. The EU has dramatically changed its privacy infrastructure and requirements as a result of several events, including court cases, the Snowden revelations, and government activism. Examine the new world of data privacy regulations under the GDPR and then compare and contrast this to both the U.S. system and the previous EU system.

Lab Project

• Lab Project 25.1

Privacy-enhancing technologies can do much to protect a user's information and/or maintain anonymity when using the Web. Research onion routing and the Tor project. What do these things do? How do they work?

appendix A

CompTIA Security+ Exam Objectives: SY0-601

Official Exam Domains and Objectives	Chapter
1.0 Threats, Attacks, and Vulnerabilities	
1.1 Compare and contrast different types of social engineering techniques.	4
1.2 Given a scenario, analyze potential indicators to determine the type of attack.	8, 15
1.3 Given a scenario, analyze potential indicators associated with application attacks.	19
1.4 Given a scenario, analyze potential indicators associated with network attacks.	12, 15, 16
1.5 Explain different threat actors, vectors, and intelligence sources.	1, 3, 16
1.6 Explain the security concerns associated with various types of vulnerabilities.	15, 16
1.7 Summarize the techniques used in security assessments.	20
1.8 Explain the techniques used in penetration testing.	16
2.0 Architecture and Design	
2.1 Explain the importance of security concepts in an enterprise environment.	14
2.2 Summarize virtualization and cloud computing concepts.	18
2.3 Summarize secure application development, deployment, and automation concepts.	19
2.4 Summarize authentication and authorization design concepts.	11
2.5 Given a scenario, implement cybersecurity resilience.	10
2.6 Explain the security implications of embedded and specialized systems.	10
2.7 Explain the importance of physical security controls.	8
2.8 Summarize the basics of cryptographic concepts.	5, 6
3.0 Implementation	
3.1 Given a scenario, implement secure protocols.	6
3.2 Given a scenario, implement host or application security solutions.	14
3.3 Given a scenario, implement secure network designs.	13, 19
3.4 Given a scenario, install and configure wireless security settings.	9
3.5 Given a scenario, implement secure mobile solutions.	12
3.6 Given a scenario, apply cybersecurity solutions to the cloud.	18
3.7 Given a scenario, implement identity and account management controls.	11
3.8 Given a scenario, implement authentication and authorization solutions.	11
3.9 Given a scenario, implement public key infrastructure.	7
4.0 Operations and Incident Response	
4.1 Given a scenario, use the appropriate tool to assess organizational security.	16
4.2 Summarize the importance of policies, processes, and procedures for incident response.	22
4.3 Given an incident, utilize appropriate data sources to support an investigation.	22
4.4 Given an incident, apply mitigation techniques or controls to secure an environment.	15, 18, 19, 22
4.5 Explain the key aspects of digital forensics.	23

Official Exam Domains and Objectives	Chapter
5.0 Governance, Risk, and Compliance	
5.1 Compare and contrast various types of controls.	20
5.2 Explain the importance of applicable regulations, standards, or frameworks that impact organizational security posture.	24
5.3 Explain the importance of policies to organizational security.	3
5.4 Summarize risk management processes and concepts.	20, 21
5.5 Explain privacy and sensitive data concepts in relation to security.	25

Note: There are chapters that are not mapped directly to CompTIA Security+ objectives in the table above. This is the result of two issues. One, some material supports a complete description of cybersecurity, and hence covers issues not directly related in CompTIA Security+ objectives but that are still valid and important for a comprehensive coverage of the principles of cybersecurity. Second, some chapters provide background and context to the understanding of specific cybersecurity fundamentals.

appendix B

About the Online Content

This book comes complete with TotalTester Online customizable practice exam software with 250 practice exam questions.

System Requirements

The current and previous major versions of the following desktop browsers are recommended and supported: Chrome, Microsoft Edge, Firefox, and Safari. These browsers update frequently, and sometimes an update may cause compatibility issues with the TotalTester Online or other content hosted on the Training Hub. If you run into a problem using one of these browsers, please try using another until the problem is resolved.

Your Total Seminars Training Hub Account

To get access to the online content you will need to create an account on the Total Seminars Training Hub. Registration is free, and you will be able to track all your online content using your account. You may also opt in if you wish to receive marketing information from McGraw Hill or Total Seminars, but this is not required for you to gain access to the online content.

Privacy Notice

McGraw Hill values your privacy. Please be sure to read the Privacy Notice available during registration to see how the information you have provided will be used. You may view our Corporate Customer Privacy Policy by visiting the McGraw Hill Privacy Center. Visit the **mheducation.com** site and click **Privacy** at the bottom of the page.

Single User License Terms and Conditions

Online access to the digital content included with this book is governed by the McGraw Hill License Agreement outlined next. By using this digital content you agree to the terms of that license.

Access To register and activate your Total Seminars Training Hub account, simply follow these easy steps.

1. Go to this URL: **hub.totalsem.com/mheclaim**
2. To register and create a new Training Hub account, enter your e-mail address, name, and password on the **Register** tab. No further personal information (such as credit card number) is required to create an account.

   If you already have a Total Seminars Training Hub account, enter your e-mail address and password on the **Log in** tab.
3. Enter your Product Key: **`h66s-zxvd-xdtd`**
4. Click to accept the user license terms.
5. For new users, click the **Register and Claim** button to create your account. For existing users, click the **Log in and Claim** button.

   You will be taken to the Training Hub and have access to the content for this book.

Duration of License Access to your online content through the Total Seminars Training Hub will expire one year from the date the publisher declares the book out of print.

Your purchase of this McGraw Hill product, including its access code, through a retail store is subject to the refund policy of that store.

The Content is a copyrighted work of McGraw Hill, and McGraw Hill reserves all rights in and to the Content. The Work is © 2022 by McGraw Hill.

Restrictions on Transfer The user is receiving only a limited right to use the Content for the user's own internal and personal use, dependent on purchase and continued ownership of this book. The user may not reproduce, forward, modify, create derivative works based upon, transmit, distribute, disseminate, sell, publish, or sublicense the Content or in any way commingle the Content with other third-party content without McGraw Hill's consent.

Limited Warranty The McGraw Hill Content is provided on an "as is" basis. Neither McGraw Hill nor its licensors make any guarantees or warranties of any kind, either express or implied, including, but not limited to, implied warranties of merchantability or fitness for a particular purpose or use as to any McGraw Hill Content or the information therein or any warranties as to the accuracy, completeness, correctness, or results to be obtained from, accessing or using the McGraw Hill Content, or any material referenced in such Content or any information entered into licensee's product by users or other persons and/or any material available on or that can be accessed through the licensee's product (including via any hyperlink or otherwise) or as to non-infringement of third-party rights. Any warranties of any kind, whether express or implied, are disclaimed. Any material or data obtained through use of the McGraw Hill Content is at your own discretion and risk and user understands that it will be solely responsible for any resulting damage to its computer system or loss of data.

Neither McGraw Hill nor its licensors shall be liable to any subscriber or to any user or anyone else for any inaccuracy, delay, interruption in service, error or omission, regardless of cause, or for any damage resulting therefrom.

In no event will McGraw Hill or its licensors be liable for any indirect, special or consequential damages, including but not limited to, lost time, lost money, lost profits or good will, whether in contract, tort, strict liability or otherwise, and whether or not such damages are foreseen or unforeseen with respect to any use of the McGraw Hill Content.

TotalTester Online

TotalTester Online provides you with a simulation of the CompTIA Security+ exam. Exams can be taken in Practice Mode or Exam Mode. Practice Mode provides an assistance window with hints, references to the book, explanations of the correct and incorrect answers, and the option to check your answer as you take the test. Exam Mode provides a simulation of the actual exam. The number of questions, the types of questions, and the time allowed are intended to be an accurate representation of the exam environment. The option to customize your quiz allows you to create custom exams from selected domains or chapters, and you can further customize the number of questions and time allowed.

To take a test, follow the instructions provided in the previous section to register and activate your Total Seminars Training Hub account. When you register you will be taken to the Total Seminars Training Hub. From the

Training Hub Home page, click **CompTIA Security+ Certification** in the Study drop-down menu at the top of the page and then select **Principles of Computer Security 6e TotalTester**, or make the same selection from the list of Your Topics on the Home page. You can then select the option to customize your quiz and begin testing yourself in Practice Mode or Exam Mode. All exams provide an overall grade and a grade broken down by domain.

Technical Support

For questions regarding the TotalTester or operation of the Training Hub, visit **www.totalsem.com** or e-mail **support@totalsem.com**.

For questions regarding book content, visit **www.mheducation.com/customerservice**.

GLOSSARY

***-property** Pronounced "star property," this aspect of the Bell-LaPadula security model is commonly referred to as the "no-write-down" rule because it doesn't allow a user to write to a file with a lower security classification, thus preserving confidentiality.

3DES Triple DES encryption—three rounds of DES encryption used to improve security. Has been largely replaced by AES encryption.

802.11 A family of standards that describe network protocols for wireless devices.

802.1X An IEEE standard for performing authentication over networks.

AAA *See* authentication, authorization, and accounting.

ABAC *See* attribute-based access control.

Abstract Syntax Notation One (ASN.1) An interface description language for defining data structures that is used in telecommunications and computer networking asset resources and information an organization needs to conduct its business.

acceptable use policy (AUP) A policy that communicates to users what specific uses of computer resources are permitted.

access A subject's ability to perform specific operations on an object such as a file. Typical access levels include read, write, execute, and delete.

access control Mechanisms or methods used to determine what access permissions subjects (such as users) have for specific objects (such as files).

access control list (ACL) A list associated with an object (such as a file) that identifies what level of access each subject (such as a user) has as well as what they can do to the object (such as read, write, or execute).

access point (AP) Shorthand for wireless access point, the device that allows devices to connect to a wireless network.

access tokens A token device used for access control—an example of something you have.

Active Directory (AD) The directory service portion of the Windows operating system that stores information about network-based entities (such as applications, files, printers, and people) and provides a structured, consistent way to name, describe, locate, access, and manage these resources.

Active Server Pages (ASP) An older server-side scripting framework for web servers introduced by Microsoft. Replaced by ASP.NET in 2002.

ActiveX A deprecated Microsoft technology that facilitates rich Internet applications and thus extends and enhances the functionality of Microsoft Internet Explorer. Like Java, ActiveX enables the development of interactive content. When an ActiveX-aware browser encounters a web page that includes an unsupported feature, it can automatically install the appropriate application so the feature can be used.

AD *See* Active Directory.

Address Resolution Protocol (ARP) A protocol in the TCP/IP suite specification used to map an IP address to a Media Access Control (MAC) address.

Address Space Layout Randomization (ASLR) A memory-protection process employed by operating systems where the memory space is block randomized to guard against targeted injections from buffer-overflow attacks.

Advanced Encryption Standard (AES) The current U.S. government standard for symmetric encryption, widely used in all sectors.

Advanced Encryption Standard 256-bit An implementation of AES using a 256-bit key.

advanced persistent threat (APT) A threat vector whose main objective is to remain on the system stealthily, with data exfiltration as a secondary task.

Adversarial Tactics, Techniques, and Common Knowledge (ATT&CK) A framework developed by MITRE for describing the methods used by attackers.

adware Advertising-supported software that automatically plays, displays, or downloads advertisements after the software is installed or while the application is being used.

AEAD *See* Authenticated Encryption with Associated Data.

AES *See* Advanced Encryption Standard.

AES256 *See* Advanced Encryption Standard 256-bit.

agile model A software development mode built around the idea of many small iterations that continually yield a "finished" product at the completion of each iteration.

AH *See* Authentication Header.

AI Acronym for artificial intelligence.

air gap The forced separation of networks, resulting in a "gap" between systems. Communications across an air gap require a manual effort to move data from one network to another, as no network connection exists between the two networks.

AIS *See* Automated Indicator Sharing.

algorithm A step-by-step procedure—typically an established computation for solving a problem within a set number of steps.

amplification An act of leveraging technology to increase the volume of an attack, such as pinging a network address to get all attached devices to respond.

annualized loss expectancy (ALE) How much an event is expected to cost the business per year, given the dollar cost of the loss and how often it is likely to occur. ALE = single loss expectancy (SLE) × annualized rate of occurrence (ARO).

annualized rate of occurrence (ARO) The frequency with which an event is expected to occur on an annualized basis.

anomaly Something that does not fit into an expected pattern.

anti-spam Technology used to combat unsolicited junk e-mail, or spam.

antivirus (AV) A software program designed to detect, mitigate, or remove malware and viruses from a system or network.

AP *See* access point.

application A program or group of programs designed to provide specific user functions, such as a word processor or web server.

application hardening The steps taken to harden an application by mitigating vulnerabilities and reducing the exploitable surface.

application programming interface (API) A set of instructions as to how to interface with a computer program so that developers can access defined interfaces in a program.

application service provider (ASP) A company that offers entities access over the Internet to applications and services.

application vulnerability scanner Technology used to scan applications for potential vulnerabilities and weaknesses.

APT *See* advanced persistent threat.

ARP *See* Address Resolution Protocol.

ARP backscatter The use of ARP scanning against a gateway device to detect the presence of a device behind the gateway or router.

ARP poisoning An attack on the ARP table where values are changed to result in misdirected traffic.

ASLR *See* Address Space Layout Randomization.

ASN.1 *See* Abstract Syntax Notation One.

asset A resource or information that an organization needs to conduct its business.

asset value (AV) The value of an asset that is at risk.

asymmetric encryption Also called public key cryptography. A data encryption system that uses two mathematically derived keys to encrypt and decrypt a message—a public key, available to everyone, and a private key, available only to the owner of the key.

ATT&CK *See* Adversarial Tactics, Techniques, and Common Knowledge.

attribute-based access control (ABAC) An access control mechanism that grants access based on attributes of a user.

audit trail A set of records or events, generally organized chronologically, that records what activity has occurred on a system. These records (often computer files) are often used in an attempt to re-create what took place when a security incident occurred, and they can also be used to detect possible intruders.

auditability The property of an item that makes it available for verification upon inspection.

auditing Actions or processes used to verify the assigned privileges and rights of a user, or any capabilities used to create and maintain a record showing who accessed a particular system and what actions they performed.

Authenticated Encryption with Associated Data (AEAD) A method of encryption that allows a recipient to check the integrity of both the encrypted and unencrypted information in a message.

authentication The process by which a subject's (such as a user's) identity is verified.

authentication, authorization, and accounting (AAA) Three common functions performed upon system login. Authentication and authorization almost always occur, with accounting being somewhat less common. Authentication and authorization are parts of the access control system.

Authentication Header (AH) A portion of the IPSec security protocol that provides authentication services and replay-detection ability. AH can be used either by itself or with Encapsulating Security Payload (ESP). Refer to RFC 2402.

Automated Indicator Sharing (AIS) The use of STIX and TAXII to share threat information between systems.

authentication server (AS) A server used to perform authentication tasks.

Authenticode Microsoft code-signing technology used to provide integrity and attribution on software.

authority revocation list (ARL) A list of authorities that have had their certificates revoked.

authorization The function of determining what is permitted for an authorized user.

AutoPlay Technology employed to launch appropriate applications and play or display content on removable media when the media is mounted or inserted.

AV *See* antivirus or asset value.

availability Part of the "CIA" of security. Applies to hardware, software, and data, specifically meaning that each of these should be present and accessible when the subject (the user) wants to access or use them.

backdoor A hidden method used to gain access to a computer system, network, or application. Often used by software developers to ensure unrestricted access to the systems they create. Synonymous with *trapdoor*.

backout planning The part of a configuration change plan where steps are devised to undo a change, even when not complete, to restore a system back to the previous operating condition.

backup Refers to copying and storing data in a secondary location, separate from the original, to preserve the data in the event that the original is lost, corrupted, or destroyed.

baseline A system or software as it is built and functioning at a specific point in time. Serves as a foundation for comparison or measurement, providing the necessary visibility to control change.

BASH *See* Bourne Again Shell.

Basic Input/Output System (BIOS) A firmware element of a computer system that provides the interface between hardware and system software with respect to devices and peripherals. BIOS has been replaced by Unified Extensible Firmware Interface (UEFI), a more complex and capable system.

Basic Service Set Identifier (BSSID) ID of an access point (AP) in a WLAN, typically the AP's MAC address.

BCP *See* business continuity plan.

beacon frames A series of frames used in Wi-Fi (802.11) to establish the presence of a wireless network device.

Bell-LaPadula security model A computer security model built around the property of confidentiality and characterized by no-read-up and no-write-down rules.

best evidence rule A legal principle that supports a true copy as equivalent to the original.

BGP *See* Border Gateway Protocol.

BIA *See* business impact analysis.

Biba security model An information security model built around the property of integrity and characterized by no-write-up and no-read-down rules.

biometrics Used to verify an individual's identity to the system or network using something unique about the individual, such as a fingerprint, for the verification process. Examples include fingerprints, retinal scans, hand and facial geometry, and voice analysis.

BIOS *See* Basic Input/Output System.

birthday attack An attack methodology based on combinations rather than linear probability. In a room of 30 people, for example, one doesn't have to match a specific birthday but rather have any two birthdays in the room match, making the problem a combinatorial match, which is much more likely.

blacklisting The term used to describe the exclusion of items based on their being on a list (blacklist). The term has recently been updated/replaced by CompTIA Security+ with *block list/deny list.*

black-box testing A form of testing where the tester has no knowledge of the inner workings of a mechanism. The term has recently been updated/replaced by CompTIA Security+ with *unknown environment testing.*

block cipher A cipher that operates on discrete blocks of data.

Blowfish A free implementation of a symmetric block cipher, developed by Bruce Schneier as a drop-in replacement for DES and IDEA. It has a variable-bit-length scheme from 32 to 448 bits, resulting in varying levels of security.

blue team A team composed of defenders in an exercise.

bluebugging The use of a Bluetooth-enabled device to eavesdrop on another person's conversation using that person's Bluetooth phone as a transmitter. The bluebug application silently causes a Bluetooth device to make a phone call to another device, causing the phone to act as a transmitter and allowing the listener to eavesdrop on the victim's conversation in real life.

bluejacking The sending of unsolicited messages over Bluetooth to Bluetooth-enabled devices such as mobile phones, tablets, and laptop computers.

bluesnarfing The unauthorized access of information from a Bluetooth-enabled device through a Bluetooth connection, often between mobile phones, desktops, laptops, and tablets.

Border Gateway Protocol (BGP) The interdomain routing protocol implemented in Internet Protocol (IP) networks to enable routing between autonomous systems.

botnet A collection of software robots, or *bots,* that run autonomously and automatically and, commonly, invisibly in the background. The term is most often associated with malicious software, but it can also refer to the network of computers using distributed computing software.

Bourne Again Shell (BASH) A command language interpreter for Linux systems.

bridge A network device that separates traffic into separate collision domains at the data link layer (Layer 2) of the Open System Interconnection (OSI) model.

bridge protocol data unit (BPDU) A BPDU is a type of data message exchanged across switches within an extended LAN that uses a Spanning Tree Protocol (STP) topology.

bring your own device (BYOD) A term used to describe an environment where users bring their personally owned devices into the enterprise and integrate them into business systems.

BSSID *See* Basic Service Set Identifier.

buffer overflow A specific type of software coding error that enables user input to overflow the allocated storage area and corrupt a running program.

bug bounty A program or campaign where a business or entity pays white-hat hackers to discover new vulnerabilities and disclose them to the company only.

Bureau of Industry and Security (BIS) In the U.S. Department of Commerce, the BIS is the department responsible for export administration regulations that cover encryption technology in the United States.

bus topology A network layout in which a common line (the bus) connects devices.

business availability center (BAC) A software platform that allows the enterprise to optimize the availability, performance, and effectiveness of business services and applications.

business continuity plan (BCP) The plan a business develops to continue critical operations in the event of a major disruption.

business impact analysis (BIA) An analysis of the impact to the business of a specific event.

business partnership agreement (BPA) A written agreement defining the terms and conditions of a business partnership.

BYOD *See* bring your own device.

CA *See* certificate authority.

CA certificate A digital certificate identifying the keys used by a certificate authority (CA).

cache The temporary storage of information before use, typically used to speed up systems. In an Internet context, cache refers to the storage of commonly accessed web pages, graphic files, and other content locally on a user's PC or a web server. The cache helps to minimize download time and preserve bandwidth for frequently accessed websites, and it helps reduce the load on a web server.

Capability Maturity Model (CMM) A structured methodology helping organizations improve the maturity of their software processes by providing an evolutionary path from ad hoc processes to disciplined software management processes. Developed at Carnegie Mellon University's Software Engineering Institute (SEI).

Capability Maturity Model Integration (CMMI) A trademarked process improvement methodology for software engineering. Developed at Carnegie Mellon University's Software Engineering Institute (SEI).

CAPTCHA Completely Automated Public Turing Test to Tell Computers and Humans Apart (CAPTCHA). Software designed to pose tests that require human ability to resolve, preventing robots from filling in and submitting web pages.

captive portal A website used to validate credentials before allowing access to a network connection.

card cloning The process of copying an electronic ID card.

CASB *See* Cloud Access Security Broker.

CBC *See* Cipher Block Chaining.

centralized management A type of privilege management that brings the authority and responsibility for managing and maintaining rights and privileges into a single group, location, or area.

CERT *See* Computer Emergency Response Team.

certificate A cryptographically signed object that contains an identity and a public key associated with this identity. The certificate can be used to establish identity, analogous to a notarized written document.

certificate authority (CA) An entity responsible for issuing and revoking certificates. CAs are typically not associated with the company requiring the certificate, although they exist for internal company use as well (such as Microsoft). This term is also applied to server software that provides these services. The term *certificate authority* is used interchangeably with *certification authority*.

Certificate Enrollment Protocol (CEP) Originally developed by VeriSign for Cisco Systems to support certificate issuance, distribution, and revocation using existing technologies.

certificate path An enumeration of the chain of trust from one certificate to another tracing back to a trusted root.

certificate repository A storage location for certificates on a system so that they can be reused.

certificate revocation list (CRL) A digitally signed object that lists all of the current but revoked certificates issued by a given certification authority. This allows users to verify whether a certificate is currently valid even if it has not expired. A CRL is analogous to a list of stolen charge card numbers that allows stores to reject bad credit cards.

certificate server A server—part of a PKI system—that handles digital certificates.

certificate signing request (CSR) A message sent from an applicant to a certificate authority in order to apply for a digital identity certificate.

certification practices statement (CPS) A document that describes the policy for issuing digital certificates from a CA.

chain of custody Rules for documenting, handling, and safeguarding evidence to ensure no unanticipated changes are made to the evidence.

Challenge Handshake Authentication Protocol (CHAP) Used to provide authentication across point-to-point links using the Point-to-Point Protocol (PPP).

change (configuration) management A standard methodology for performing and recording changes during software development and operation.

change control board (CCB) A body that oversees the change management process and enables management to oversee and coordinate projects.

channel service unit (CSU) A device used to link local area networks (LANs) into a wide area network (WAN) using telecommunications carrier services.

CHAP *See* Challenge Handshake Authentication Protocol.

chief security officer (CSO) The person appointed to oversee security functions in an enterprise.

chief technology officer (CTO) The person appointed to oversee scientific technology functions in an enterprise.

choose your own device (CYOD) A mobile device deployment methodology where each person chooses their own device type.

CIA of security Refers to confidentiality, integrity, and availability—the basic functions of any security system.

cipher A cryptographic system that accepts plaintext input and then outputs ciphertext according to its internal algorithm and key.

Cipher Block Chaining (CBC) A method of adding randomization to blocks, where each block of plaintext is XORed with the previous ciphertext block before being encrypted.

cipher feedback (CFB) A method to make a block cipher into a self-synchronizing stream cipher.

ciphertext The output of an encryption algorithm—the encrypted data.

CIRT *See* Computer Emergency Response Team.

Clark-Wilson security model A security model that uses transactions and a differentiation of constrained data items (CDIs) and unconstrained data items (UDIs).

clickjacking An attack against a user interface where the user clicks something without knowing it, triggering a browser action unbeknownst to the user at the time.

closed circuit television (CCTV) A private television system usually hardwired in security applications to record visual information.

Cloud Access Security Broker (CASB) A security policy enforcement mechanism between cloud users and providers.

cloud computing The automatic provisioning of computational resources on demand across a network.

cloud service provider (CSP) A company that offers cloud-based network services, infrastructure, or business applications.

CMS *See* content management system.

CN *See* Common Name.

coaxial cable A network cable that consists of a solid copper center core conductor and a physical spacer to the outer conductor, which is wrapped around it. Commonly used in video systems.

code injection An attack where unauthorized executable code is injected via an interface in an attempt to get it to run on a system.

code signing The application of digital signature technology to software for the purposes of integrity and authentication control.

codecs A system that provides coding and decoding services, used in multimedia streaming.

cold aisle The cooler side of the HVAC-supplied airflow across a server farm. A function designed to address the heat generated by a server.

cold site An inexpensive form of backup site that does not include a current set of data at all times. A cold site takes longer to get the operational system back up, but it is considerably less expensive than a warm or hot site.

collision Used in the analysis of hashing cryptography, a collision is the outcome situation that occurs when a hash algorithm will produce the same hash value from two different sets of data.

collision attack An attack on a hash function in which a specific input is generated to produce a hash function output that matches another input.

collision domain An area of shared traffic in a network where packets from different conversations can collide.

command and control (C2) A set of servers used by attackers to send commands to botnets and receive information back from them.

Common Access Card (CAC) A smart card used to access U.S. federal computer systems. Also acts as an ID card.

Common Gateway Interface (CGI) An older, outdated technology used for server-side execution of programs on websites.

Common Name (CN) A characteristic field within a Distinguished Name (DN).

Common Vulnerabilities and Exposures (CVE) An enumeration of publicly known vulnerabilities. Each vulnerability has a description, ID, and reference number.

Common Vulnerability Scoring System (CVSS) A framework for scoring, on a scale from 0 to 10, the severity of a vulnerability.

Common Weakness Enumeration (CWE) A structured language (XML) schema used to describe known weakness patterns in software that can result in vulnerabilities.

complete mediation The principle that protection mechanisms should cover every access to every object.

Computer Emergency Response Team (CERT) The group responsible for investigating and responding to security breaches, viruses, and other potentially catastrophic incidents. Also known as a Computer Incident Response Team (CIRT).

computer security In general terms, the methods, techniques, and tools used to ensure that a computer system is secure.

computer software configuration item *See* configuration item.

concentrator A device used to manage multiple, similar networking operations, such as providing a VPN endpoint for multiple VPNs.

confidentiality Part of the CIA of security, confidentiality refers to the security principle that states that information should not be disclosed to unauthorized individuals.

configuration auditing The process of verifying that configuration items are built and maintained according to requirements, standards, or contractual agreements.

configuration control The process of controlling changes to items that have been baselined.

configuration identification The process of identifying which assets need to be managed and controlled.

configuration item Data and software (or other assets) that are identified and managed as part of the software change management process. Also known as *computer software configuration item*.

configuration status accounting Procedures for tracking and maintaining data relative to each configuration item in the baseline.

content management system (CMS) A management system to manage the content for a specific system, such as a website.

content protection The protection of the header and data portion of a user datagram.

context protection The protection of the header of a user datagram.

contingency planning (CP) The act of creating processes and procedures that are used under special conditions (contingencies).

continuity of operations planning (COOP) The creation of plans related to continuing essential business operations.

control A measure taken to detect, prevent, or mitigate the risk associated with a threat.

controller area network (CAN) A bus standard for use in vehicles to connect microcontrollers.

cookie Information stored on a user's computer by a web server to maintain the state of the connection to the web server. Used primarily so preferences or previously used information can be recalled on future requests to the server.

COOP *See* continuity of operations planning.

corporate owned, personally enabled (COPE) A form of mobile device ownership/management where the company provides employees with mobile devices and allows them to use the devices as if they owned them.

corrective action report (CAR) A report used to document the corrective actions taken on a system.

Counter Mode (CTM) Turns a block cipher into a stream cipher.

Counter Mode with Cipher Block Chaining–Message Authentication Code Protocol (CCMP) An enhanced data cryptographic encapsulation mechanism based on the Counter Mode with CBC-MAC from AES, designed for use over wireless LANs.

countermeasure *See* security controls.

cracking A term used by some to refer to malicious hacking, in which an individual attempts to gain unauthorized access to computer systems or networks. *See also* hacking.

CRC *See* cyclic redundancy check.

credential harvesting The process of stealing or obtaining credentials used to attack a system.

critical infrastructure Infrastructure whose loss or impairment would have severe repercussions on society.

CRL *See* certificate revocation list.

cross-certification certificate A certificate used to establish trust between separate PKIs.

crossover error rate (CER) The point at which the false rejection rate (FRR) and false acceptance rate (FAR) are equal in a system.

cross-site request forgery (CSRF or XSRF) A method of attacking a system by sending malicious input to the system and relying on the parsers and execution elements to perform the requested actions, thus instantiating the attack. XSRF exploits the trust a site has in the user's browser.

cross-site scripting (XSS) A method of attacking a system by sending script commands to the system input and relying on the parsers and execution elements to perform the requested scripted actions, thus instantiating the attack. XSS exploits the trust a user has for the site.

cryptanalysis The process of attempting to break a cryptographic system.

cryptographically random A random number that is derived from a nondeterministic source, thus knowing one random number provides no insight into the next.

cryptography The art of secret writing that enables an individual to hide the contents of a message or file from all but the intended recipient.

crypto-malware Malware that uses cryptography to encrypt files for ransom.

CSO *See* chief security officer.

CTO *See* chief technology officer.

CTR *See* Counter Mode (CTM)—an alternative abbreviation.

CVE *See* Common Vulnerabilities and Exposures.

CVSS *See* Common Vulnerability Scoring System.

Cyber Observable eXpression (CybOX) A structured language (XML) for describing cybersecurity events at a granular level.

cyclic redundancy check (CRC) An error detection technique that uses a series of two 8-bit block check characters to represent an entire block of data. These block check characters are incorporated into the transmission frame and then checked at the receiving end.

DAC *See* discretionary access control.

dark web A section of the world wide web that is specifically set up to not be indexed by the major indexing services.

data aggregation A methodology of collecting information through the aggregation of separate pieces and analyzing the effect of their collection.

data encryption key (DEK) An encryption key whose function it is to encrypt and decrypt data.

Data Encryption Standard (DES) A private key encryption algorithm adopted by the U.S. government as a standard for the protection of sensitive but unclassified information. Commonly used in 3DES, where three rounds are applied to provide greater security.

data execution prevention (DEP) A security feature of an OS that can be driven by software, hardware, or both, designed to prevent the execution of code from blocks of data in memory.

data loss prevention (DLP) Technology, processes, and procedures designed to detect when unauthorized removal of data from a system occurs. DLP is typically active, preventing the loss either by blocking the transfer or dropping the connection.

data protection officer (DPO) The person in charge of privacy/data protection in the European Union (EU) under General Data Protection Regulation (GDPR).

data service unit *See* channel service unit.

datagram A packet of data that can be transmitted over a packet-switched system in a connectionless mode.

decision tree A data structure in which each element is attached to one or more structures directly beneath it.

default deny The use of an overarching rule where, if not explicitly permitted, permission will be denied.

delta backup A type of backup that preserves only the blocks that have changed since the last full backup.

demilitarized zone (DMZ) A network segment that exists in a semi-protected zone between the Internet and the inner, secure trusted network. The term has recently been updated/replaced by CompTIA Security+ with *screened subnet*.

denial-of-service (DoS) attack An attack in which actions are taken to deprive authorized individuals from accessing a system, its resources, the data it stores or processes, or the network to which it is connected.

Destination Network Address Translation (DNAT) A one-to-one static translation from a public destination address to a private address.

DES *See* Data Encryption Standard.

DHCP *See* Dynamic Host Configuration Protocol.

Diameter The base protocol that is intended to provide an authentication, authorization, and accounting (AAA) framework for applications such as network access or IP mobility. Diameter is a draft IETF proposal that evolved from RADIUS.

differential backup A type of backup that preserves only changes since the last full backup.

differential cryptanalysis A form of cryptanalysis that uses different inputs to study how outputs change in a structured manner.

Diffie-Hellman A cryptographic method of establishing a shared key over an insecure medium in a secure fashion.

Diffie-Hellman Ephemeral (DHE) A cryptographic method of establishing a shared key over an insecure medium in a secure fashion using a temporary key to enable perfect forward secrecy.

diffusion The principle that the statistical analysis of plaintext and ciphertext results in a form of dispersion, rendering one structurally independent of the other. In plain terms, a change in one character of plaintext should result in multiple changes in the ciphertext in a manner that changes in ciphertext do not reveal information as to the structure of the plaintext.

digital certificate *See* certificate.

digital forensics and investigation response (DFIR) Another name for the incident response process.

digital rights management (DRM) The control of user activities associated with a digital object via technological means.

digital sandbox The isolation of a program and its supporting elements from common operating system functions.

digital signature A cryptography-based artifact that is a key component of a public key infrastructure (PKI) implementation. A digital signature can be used to prove identity because it is created with the private key portion of a public/private key pair. A recipient can decrypt the signature and, by doing so, receive the assurance that the data must have come from the sender and has not changed.

Digital Signature Algorithm (DSA) A U.S. government standard for implementing digital signatures.

direct-sequence spread spectrum (DSSS) A method of distributing a communication over multiple frequencies to avoid interference and detection.

disassociation An attack on a wireless network whereby the attacker sends a de-authentication frame in a wireless connection to break an existing connection.

disaster recovery plan (DRP) A written plan developed to address how an organization will react to a natural or manmade disaster in order to ensure business continuity. Related to the concept of a business continuity plan (BCP).

discretionary access control (DAC) An access control mechanism in which the owner of an object (such as a file) can decide which other subjects (such as other users) may have access to the object as well as what access (read, write, execute) these subjects can have.

Distinguished Encoding Rules (DER) A method of providing exactly one way to represent any ASN.1 value as an octet string.

Distinguished Name (DN) The name that distinguishes an entry in a naming system.

distributed denial-of-service (DDoS) attack A special type of DoS attack in which the attacker elicits the generally unwilling support of other systems to launch a many-against-one attack.

diversity of defense The approach of creating dissimilar security layers so that an intruder who is able to breach one layer will be faced with an entirely different set of defenses at the next layer.

DLL injection An attack that uses the injection of a DLL onto a system, altering the processing of a program by, in essence, recoding it.

DMZ *See* demilitarized zone.

DNS *See* Domain Name System/Server.

DNS kiting The creation and use of a DNS record during the payment grace period without paying for it.

DNS poisoning The changing of data in a DNS table to cause misaddressing of packets.

DNS sinkhole The use of the DNS system responses to prevent connections to unauthorized addresses.

DNSSEC *See* Domain Name System/Service Security Extensions.

domain hijacking The act of changing the registration of a domain name without the permission of its original registrant.

Domain Message Authentication Reporting and Conformance (DMARC) An e-mail authentication, policy, and reporting protocol.

Domain Name System/Server (DNS) The service that translates an Internet domain name (such as www.mheducation.com) into an IP address.

Domain Name System/Service Security Extensions (DNSSEC) The extension of DNS using cryptographically signed requests and answers.

DomainKeys Identified Mail (DKIM) An authentication system for e-mail designed to detect the spoofing of e-mail addresses.

drive-by download attack An attack on an innocent victim machine where content is downloaded without the user's knowledge.

driver manipulation The altering of drivers to cause malicious effects to an OS.

DRP *See* disaster recovery plan.

DSSS *See* direct-sequence spread spectrum.

due care The standard used to determine the degree of care that a reasonable person would exercise under similar circumstances.

due diligence The reasonable steps a person or entity would take in order to satisfy legal or contractual requirements—commonly used when buying or selling something of significant value.

dumpster diving The practice of searching through trash to discover material that has been thrown away that is sensitive, yet not destroyed or shredded.

Dynamic Host Configuration Protocol (DHCP) An Internet Engineering Task Force (IETF) Internet Protocol (IP) specification for automatically allocating IP addresses and other configuration information based on network adapter addresses. It enables address pooling and allocation and simplifies TCP/IP installation and administration.

dynamic link library (DLL) A shared library function used in the Microsoft Windows environment.

EAP *See* Extensible Authentication Protocol.

economy of mechanism The principle that designs should be small and simple.

electromagnetic interference (EMI) The disruption or interference of electronics due to an electromagnetic field.

electromagnetic pulse (EMP) The disruption or interference of electronics due to a sudden, intense electromagnetic field in the form of a spike or pulse.

Electronic Code Book (ECB) A block cipher mode where the message is divided into blocks, and each block is encrypted separately.

electronic serial number (ESN) A unique identification number embedded by manufacturers on a microchip in wireless phones.

elite hacker A hacker who has the skill level necessary to discover and exploit new vulnerabilities.

elliptic curve cryptography (ECC) A method of public key cryptography based on the algebraic structure of elliptic curves over finite fields.

Elliptic Curve Diffie-Hellman Ephemeral (ECDHE) A cryptographic method using ECC to establish a shared key over an insecure medium in a secure fashion using a temporary key to enable perfect forward secrecy.

Elliptic Curve Digital Signature Algorithm (ECDSA) A cryptographic method using ECC to create a digital signature.

Encapsulating Security Payload (ESP) A portion of the IPSec implementation that provides for data confidentiality with optional authentication and replay-detection services. ESP completely encapsulates user data in the datagram and can be used either by itself or in conjunction with Authentication Headers for varying degrees of IPSec services.

enclave A section of a network that serves a specific purpose and is isolated by protocols from other parts of a network.

Encrypted File System (EFS) A security feature of Windows, from Windows 2000 onward, that enables the transparent encryption/decryption of files on the system.

encryption The reversible process of rendering data unreadable through the use of an algorithm and a key.

end of life (EOL) A term used to denote that something has reached the end of its "useful life."

end of service life (EOSL) A term used to denote when the manufacturer quits selling an item. In most cases, the manufacturer no longer provides maintenance services or updates.

entropy The measure of uncertainty associated with a series of values. Perfect entropy equates to complete randomness, such that given any string of bits, there is no computation to improve guessing the next bit in the sequence.

ephemeral keys Cryptographic keys that are used only once after they are generated.

escalation auditing The process of looking for an increase in privileges, such as when an ordinary user obtains administrator-level privileges.

ESSID *See* Extended Service Set Identifier.

Ethernet The common name for the IEEE 802.3 standard method of packet communication between two nodes at Layer 2 (data link layer).

evidence The documents, verbal statements, and material objects admissible in a court of law.

evil twin An attack involving an attacker-owned router in a wireless system, configured to match a legitimate router.

eXclusive OR (XOR) Bitwise function commonly used in cryptography.

exposure factor (EF) A measure of the magnitude of loss of an asset. Used in the calculation of single loss expectancy (SLE).

Extended Service Set Identifier (ESSID) The collection of all the BSSIDs on a WLAN; practically the same as the SSID.

eXtensible Access Control Markup Language (XACML) An open standard XML-based language used to describe access control.

Extensible Authentication Protocol (EAP) A universal authentication framework used in wireless networks and point-to-point connections. It is defined in RFC 3748 and has been updated by RFC 5247.

Extensible Markup Language (XML) A text-based, human-readable data markup language.

fail-safe defaults The principle that when a system fails, the default failure state will be a safe state by design.

false acceptance rate (FAR) The rate of false positives acceptable to the system.

false negative The term used when a system makes an error and misses reporting the existence of an item that should have been detected.

false positive The term used when a security system makes an error and incorrectly reports the existence of a searched-for object. Examples include an intrusion detection system that misidentifies benign traffic as hostile, an antivirus program that reports the existence of a virus in software that actually is not infected, and a biometric system that allows system access to an unauthorized individual.

false rejection rate (FRR) The acceptable level of legitimate users rejected by the system.

fake telemetry The use of fake traffic on a honeynet to make it look real to an attacker.

fault tolerance The characteristics of a system that permit it to operate even when subcomponents of the overall system fail.

FDE *See* full disk encryption.

FHSS *See* frequency-hopping spread spectrum.

field programmable gate array (FPGA) A programmable logic circuit instantiation in hardware.

File Transfer Protocol (FTP) An application layer protocol used to transfer files over a network connection.

File Transfer Protocol Secure (FTPS) An application layer protocol used to transfer files over a network connection that uses FTP over an SSL or TLS connection.

fileless virus A piece of malware that does not instantiate via being written to a filesystem, making it harder to detect.

filesystem access control list (FACL) The implementation of access controls as part of a filesystem.

firewall A network device used to segregate traffic based on rules.

flood guard A network device that blocks flooding-type DoS/DDoS attacks and is frequently part of an IDS/IPS.

footprinting The steps a tester uses to determine the range and scope of a system.

forensics (or computer forensics) The preservation, identification, documentation, and interpretation of computer data for use in legal proceedings.

FPGA *See* field programmable gate array.

free space Sectors on a storage medium that are available for the operating system to use.

frequency-hopping spread spectrum (FHSS) A method of distributing a communication over multiple frequencies over time to avoid interference and detection.

full backup A complete backup of all files and structures of a system to another location.

full disk encryption (FDE) The application of encryption to an entire disk, protecting all of the contents in one container.

fuzzing The use of large quantities of data to test an interface/application against security vulnerabilities. (Also known as *fuzz testing*.)

Galois Counter Mode (GCM) A mode of operation for symmetric key cryptographic block ciphers that has been widely adopted because it can be parallelized to increase efficiency and performance.

General Data Protection Regulation (GDPR) European Union (EU) rules on data privacy.

Generic Routing Encapsulation (GRE) A tunneling protocol designed to encapsulate a wide variety of network layer packets inside IP tunneling packets.

geo-tagging The metadata that contains location-specific information attached to other data elements.

Global Positioning System (GPS) A satellite-based form of location services and time standardization.

globally unique identifier (GUID) A unique reference number used as an identifier of an item in a system.

Gnu Privacy Guard (GPG) An application program that follows the OpenPGP standard for encryption.

GPG *See* Gnu Privacy Guard.

GPO *See* Group Policy object.

graphic processing unit (GPU) A chip designed to manage graphics functions in a system.

grey-box testing A form of testing where the tester has limited or partial knowledge of the inner workings of a system. The term has recently been updated/replaced by CompTIA Security+ with *partially known environment testing.*

group policy The mechanism that allows for centralized management and configuration of computers and remote users in a Microsoft Active Directory (AD) environment.

Group Policy object (GPO) Stores the group policy settings in a Microsoft Active Directory (AD) environment.

hacker A person who attacks other systems or performs hacking activities.

hacking The term used by the media to refer to the process of gaining unauthorized access to computer systems and networks. The term has also been used to refer to the process of delving deep into the code and protocols used in computer systems and networks. *See also* cracking.

hacktivist A hacker who uses their skills for political purposes.

hard disk drive (HDD) A mechanical device used for the storing of digital data in magnetic form.

hardening The process of strengthening a host's level of security by performing specific system preparations.

hardware security module (HSM) A physical device used to protect but still allow the use of cryptographic keys. It is separate from the host machine.

hash A form of encryption that creates a digest of the data put into the algorithm. These algorithms are referred to as one-way algorithms because there is no feasible way to decrypt what has been encrypted.

hash value *See* message digest.

hashed message authentication code (HMAC) The use of a cryptographic hash function and a message authentication code to ensure the integrity and authenticity of a message.

hazard A situation that increases risk.

HDD *See* hard disk drive.

heating, ventilation, air conditioning (HVAC) The systems used to heat and cool air in a building or structure.

HIDS *See* host-based intrusion detection system.

hierarchical trust model A trust model that has levels or tiers of an ascending nature.

high availability (HA) A system design to provide ensured availability.

highly structured threat A threat that is backed by the time and resources to allow virtually any form of attack.

HIPS *See* host-based intrusion prevention system.

HMAC-based one-time password (HOTP) A method of producing one-time passwords using HMAC functions.

homomorphic cryptography A form of cryptosystem where operations can be performed directly on encrypted data.

honeynet A network version of a honeypot, or a set of honeypots networked together.

honeypot A computer system or portion of a network that has been set up to attract potential intruders, in the hope that they will leave the other systems alone. Since there are no legitimate users of this system, any attempt to access it is an indication of unauthorized activity and provides an easy mechanism to spot attacks.

host-based intrusion detection system (HIDS) A system that looks for computer intrusions by monitoring activity on one or more individual PCs or servers.

host-based intrusion prevention system (HIPS) A system that automatically responds to computer intrusions by monitoring activity on one or more individual PCs or servers and responding based on a ruleset.

host security Security functionality that is present on a host system.

hot aisle The warmer side of the airflow delivered via the cooling system for a server rack, after the processor heat has been removed.

hot site A backup site that is fully configured with equipment and data and is ready to immediately accept transfer of operational processing in the event of failure on the operational system.

hotfix A set of updates designed to fix a specific problem.

HSM *See* hardware security module.

hub A network device used to connect devices at the physical layer (Layer 1) of the OSI model.

hybrid trust model A combination of trust models, including mesh, hierarchical, and network.

Hypertext Markup Language (HTML) A protocol used to mark up text for use across HTTP.

Hypertext Transfer Protocol (HTTP) A protocol for transferring material across the Internet that contains links to additional material. HTTP uses port 80.

Hypertext Transfer Protocol over SSL/TLS (HTTPS) A protocol for transferring material across the Internet that contains links to additional material carried over a secure tunnel via SSL or TLS. HTTPS uses port 443.

IAAS *See* Infrastructure as a Service.

IAM *See* identity and access management.

ICMP *See* Internet Control Message Protocol.

ICS *See* industrial control system.

IDEA *See* International Data Encryption Algorithm.

identification (ID) The first step in the authentication process where the user establishes a secret with the authentication system and is bound to a user ID.

identity and access management (IAM) The policies and procedures used to manage access control.

identity provider (IdP) A system that creates, maintains, and manages identity information, including authentication services.

IEEE *See* Institute of Electrical and Electronics Engineers.

IEEE 802.11 A family of standards that describe network protocols for wireless devices.

IEEE 802.1X An IEEE standard for performing authentication over networks.

IETF *See* Internet Engineering Task Force.

IKE *See* Internet Key Exchange.

impact The result of a vulnerability being exploited by a threat, resulting in a loss.

impersonation A social engineering technique that can occur in person, over a phone, or online, where the attacker assumes a role that is recognized by the person being attacked, and in assuming that role, the attacker uses the potential victim's biases against their better judgment to follow procedures.

implicit deny The philosophy that all actions are prohibited unless specifically authorized.

incident A situation that is different from normal for a specific circumstance.

incident response The process of responding to, containing, analyzing, and recovering from a computer-related incident.

incident response plan (IRP) The plan used in responding to, containing, analyzing, and recovering from a computer-related incident.

incremental backup A backup model where files that have changed since the last full or incremental backup are backed up.

indicators of compromise (IOCs) A set of values that, if found in memory or file storage, indicate a specific compromise event.

industrial control system (ICS) The term used to describe the hardware and software that controls cyber-physical systems.

information criticality An assessment of the value of specific elements of information and the systems that handle it.

information security Often used synonymously with computer security, but places the emphasis on the protection of the information that the system processes and stores, instead of on the hardware and software that constitute the system.

information warfare The use of information security techniques, both offensive and defensive, when combating an opponent.

infrared (IR) A set of wavelengths past the red end of the visible spectrum used as a communication medium.

Infrastructure as a Service (IaaS) The automatic, on-demand provisioning of infrastructure elements, operating as a service; a common element of cloud computing.

initialization vector (IV) A data value used to seed a cryptographic algorithm, providing for a measure of randomness.

instant messaging (IM) A text-based method of communicating over the Internet.

Institute of Electrical and Electronics Engineers (IEEE) A nonprofit, technical, professional institute associated with computer research, standards, and conferences.

intangible asset An asset for which a monetary equivalent is difficult or impossible to determine. Examples are brand recognition and goodwill.

integer overflow An error condition caused by the mismatch between a variable's assigned storage size and the size of the value being manipulated.

integrity Part of the CIA of security; the security principle requiring that information is not modified except by individuals authorized to do so.

interconnection security agreement (ISA) An agreement between parties to establish procedures for mutual cooperation and coordination between them with respect to security requirements associated with their joint project.

intermediate distribution frame (IDF) The free-standing or wall-mounted rack or special area for managing and interconnecting the telecommunications cable between end-user devices and the main distribution frame (MDF).

internal segmentation firewall (ISFW) A firewall positioned in the network to provide segmentation of sections of a network.

International Data Encryption Algorithm (IDEA) A symmetric encryption algorithm used in a variety of systems for bulk encryption services.

Internet Assigned Numbers Authority (IANA) The central coordinator for the assignment of unique parameter values for Internet protocols. The IANA is chartered by the Internet Society (ISOC) to act as the clearinghouse to assign and coordinate the use of numerous Internet protocol parameters.

Internet Control Message Protocol (ICMP) One of the core protocols of the TCP/IP protocol suite, used for error reporting and status messages.

Internet Engineering Task Force (IETF) A large international community of network designers, operators, vendors, and researchers, open to any interested individual concerned with the evolution of Internet architecture and the smooth operation of the Internet. The actual technical work of the IETF is done in its working groups, which are organized by topic into several areas (such as routing, transport, and security). Much of the work is handled via mailing lists, with meetings held three times per year.

Internet Key Exchange (IKE) A standard key exchange protocol used on the Internet; an implementation of the Diffie-Hellmann algorithm.

Internet Message Access Protocol version 4 (IMAP4) One of two common Internet standard protocols for e-mail retrieval (the other being POP3).

Internet of Things (IoT) The networking of large numbers of devices via the Internet to achieve a business purpose.

Internet Protocol (IP) The network layer protocol used by the Internet for routing packets across a network.

Internet Protocol Security (IPSec) A protocol used to secure IP packets during transmission across a network. IPSec offers authentication, integrity, and confidentiality services and uses Authentication Headers (AH) and Encapsulating Security Payload (ESP) to accomplish this functionality.

Internet Relay Chat (IRC) An application layer protocol that facilitates communication in the form of text across the Internet.

Internet Security Association and Key Management Protocol (ISAKMP) A protocol framework that defines the mechanics of implementing a key exchange protocol and negotiation of a security policy.

Internet service provider (ISP) A telecommunications firm that provides access to the Internet.

intrusion detection system (IDS) A system to identify suspicious, malicious, or undesirable activity that indicates a breach in computer security.

intrusion prevention system (IPS) A system for identifying suspicious, malicious, or undesirable activity that indicates a breach in computer security and responding automatically without specific human interaction.

IOCs *See* indicators of compromise.

IPSec *See* Internet Protocol Security.

ISA *See* interconnection security agreement.

IT contingency plan (ITCP) The plan used to manage contingency operations in an IT environment.

jailbreaking The process of breaking iOS security features designed to limit interactions with the system itself. Commonly performed on iPhones to unlock features or break locks to carriers.

Kerberos A network authentication protocol designed by MIT for use in client/server environments that eliminates the insecurities caused by passwords being stored or transmitted in plaintext across the network.

key In cryptography, a sequence of characters or bits used by an algorithm to encrypt or decrypt a message.

key archiving The processes and procedures to make a secure backup of cryptographic keys.

key distribution center (KDC) A component of the Kerberos system for authentication that manages the secure distribution of keys.

key encryption key (KEK) An encryption key whose function it is to encrypt and decrypt the data encryption key (DEK).

key escrow The process of placing a copy of cryptographic keys with a trusted third party for backup purposes.

key recovery A process by which lost keys can be recovered from a stored secret.

key stretching A mechanism that takes what would be weak keys and "stretches" them to make the system more secure against brute force attacks.

keyspace The entire set of all possible keys for a specific encryption algorithm.

lateral movement The actions of an attacker as they move between machines and accounts.

Layer 2 Tunneling Protocol (L2TP) A Cisco switching protocol that operates at the data link layer.

layered security The arrangement of multiple layers of defense; a form of defense in depth.

LDAP *See* Lightweight Directory Access Protocol.

least common mechanism The principle that protection mechanisms should be shared to the least degree possible among users.

least privilege A security principle in which a user is provided with the minimum set of rights and privileges needed to perform their required functions. The goal is to limit the potential damage that any user can cause.

lightweight cryptography Cryptosystems designed for use in low-power, low-computation systems.

Lightweight Directory Access Protocol (LDAP) An application protocol used to access directory services across a TCP/IP network.

Lightweight Extensible Authentication Protocol (LEAP) A version of EAP developed by Cisco prior to 802.11i to push 802.1X and WEP adoption.

linear cryptanalysis The use of linear functions to approximate a cryptographic function as a means of analysis.

load balancer A network device that distributes computing across multiple computers.

local area network (LAN) A grouping of computers in a network structure confined to a limited area and using specific protocols such as Ethernet for OSI Layer 2 traffic addressing.

local registration authority A registration authority (RA) that is part of a local unit or enterprise. It is typically only useful within the enterprise, but in many cases this can be sufficient.

Local Security Authority Subsystem Service (LSASS) The process in Microsoft Windows operating systems that is responsible for enforcing the security policy on the system.

log aggregation The collection of logs into a common structure for analysis.

logic bomb A form of malicious code or software that is triggered by a specific event or condition. *See also* time bomb.

loop protection The requirement to prevent bridge loops at the Layer 2 level, which is typically resolved using the Spanning Tree algorithm on switch devices.

Low-Water-Mark policy An integrity-based information security model derived from the Bell-LaPadula model.

LSASS *See* Local Security Authority Subsystem Service.

MAC *See* mandatory access control, Media Access Control, *or* message authentication code.

MAC filtering The use of Layer 2 MAC addresses to filter traffic to only authorized NIC cards.

machine learning (ML) A form of artificial intelligence where machine algorithms learn by examining test cases and solutions.

main distribution frame (MDF) Telephony equipment that connects customer equipment to subscriber carrier equipment.

malware A class of software designed to cause harm.

man-in-the-browser attack (MITB) A man-in-the-middle/on-path attack involving browser helper objects and browsers to conduct the attack.

man-in-the-middle attack (MITM) Any attack that attempts to use a network node as the intermediary between two other nodes. Each of the endpoint nodes thinks it is talking directly to the other, but each is actually talking to the intermediary.

managed security service provider (MSSP) A third party that manages the security aspects of a system under some form of service agreement.

managed service provider (MSP) A third party that manages aspects of a system under some form of service agreement.

mandatory access control (MAC) An access control mechanism in which the security mechanism controls access to all objects (files), and individual subjects (processes or users) cannot change that access.

master boot record (MBR) A strip of data on a hard drive in Windows systems meant to result in specific initial functions or identification.

maximum transmission unit (MTU) A measure of the largest payload that a particular protocol can carry in a single packet in a specific instance.

MD5 Message Digest 5, a hashing algorithm and a specific method of producing a message digest. As a result of major security flaws in MD5, the NIST recommends using SHA-256 instead.

mean time between failures (MTBF) The statistically determined period of time between failures of the system.

mean time to failure (MTTF) The statistically determined time to the next failure.

mean time to repair/recover (MTTR) A common measure of how long it takes to repair a given failure. This is the average time, and may or may not include the time needed to obtain parts.

Measurement Systems Analysis (MSA) An assessment of the measurement process to determine sensitivities and error sources.

Media Access Control (MAC) A protocol used in the data link layer for local network addressing.

memorandum of agreement (MOA) A document executed between two parties that defines some form of agreement.

memorandum of understanding (MOU) A document executed between two parties that defines some form of agreement.

message authentication code (MAC) A short piece of data used to authenticate a message. *See* hashed message authentication code.

message digest The result of applying a hash function to data. Sometimes also called a hash value. *See* hash.

metropolitan area network (MAN) A collection of networks interconnected in a metropolitan area and usually connected to the Internet.

Microsoft Challenge Handshake Authentication Protocol (MS-CHAP) A Microsoft-developed variant of the Challenge Handshake Authentication Protocol (CHAP).

mitigation Action taken to reduce the likelihood of a threat occurring.

mobile device management (MDM) An application designed to bring enterprise-level functionality onto a mobile device, including security functionality and data segregation.

Monitoring as a Service (MaaS) The use of a third party to provide security monitoring services.

MS-CHAP *See* Microsoft Challenge Handshake Authentication Protocol.

MTBF *See* mean time between failures.

MTTF *See* mean time to failure.

MTTR *See* mean time to repair/recover.

multifactor authentication (MFA) The use of more than one different factor for authenticating a user to a system.

multifunction device (MFD) A device, such as a printer, with multiple functions, such as printing and scanning.

Multimedia Message Service (MMS) A standard way to send multimedia messages to and from mobile phones over a cellular network.

multiple encryption The use of multiple layers of encryption to improve encryption strength.

Multiprotocol Label Switching (MPLS) MPLS is a deterministic routing methodology that is carrier supplied to more efficiently handle different traffic types across the WAN.

Multipurpose Internet Mail Extensions (MIME) A standard that describes how to encode and attach nontextual elements in an e-mail.

NAC *See* network access control.

NAP *See* Network Access Protection.

NAT *See* Network Address Translation.

National Institute of Standards and Technology (NIST) A U.S. government physical science and nonregulatory agency responsible for standards and technology.

NDA *See* nondisclosure agreement.

near field communication (NFC) A set of standards and protocols for establishing a communication link over very short distances. Used in mobile devices.

network access control (NAC) An approach to endpoint security that involves monitoring and remediating endpoint security issues before allowing an object to connect to a network.

Network Access Protection (NAP) A Microsoft approach to network access control.

Network Address Translation (NAT) A method of readdressing packets in a network at a gateway point to enable the use of local, nonroutable IP addresses over a public network such as the Internet.

Network Admission Control (NAC) A Cisco technology approach for generic network access control.

network-attached storage (NAS) The addition of storage to a system via a network connection.

network-based intrusion detection system (NIDS) A system for examining network traffic to identify suspicious, malicious, or undesirable behavior.

network-based intrusion prevention system (NIPS) A system that examines network traffic and automatically responds to computer intrusions.

Network Basic Input/Output System (NetBIOS) A system that provides communication services across a local area network.

network card interface (NIC) teaming The connection of multiple NIC cards together for bandwidth managing purposes.

network forensics The application of digital forensics processes to network traffic.

network function virtualization (NFV) The use of virtualization technologies to virtualize network infrastructure.

network interface card (NIC) A piece of hardware designed to connect machines at the physical layer (Layer 1) of the OSI model.

network operating system (NOS) An operating system that includes additional functions and capabilities to assist in connecting computers and devices, such as printers, to a local area network.

network operations center (NOC) A control point from where network performance can be monitored and managed.

network segmentation The separation of a network into separate addressable segments to limit network traffic traversal to areas of limited scope.

network tap A connection to a network that allows sampling, duplication, and collection of traffic.

Network Time Protocol (NTP) A protocol for the transmission of time synchronization packets over a network.

network vulnerability scanner The application of vulnerability scanning to network devices to search for vulnerabilities at the network level.

New Technology File System (NTFS) A proprietary filesystem developed by Microsoft, introduced in 1993, that supports a wide variety of file operations on servers, PCs, and media.

New Technology LANMAN (NTLM) A deprecated security suite from Microsoft that provides authentication, integrity, and confidentiality for users. Because it does not support current cryptographic methods, it is no longer recommended for use.

next-generation access control (NGAC) One of the primary methods of implementing attribute-based access control (ABAC). The other method is XACML.

next-generation firewall (NGFW) A firewall programmed to use higher levels of a message than just addresses and ports to make a decision.

next-generation secure web gateway (NG-SWG) A solution designed to filter unwanted web traffic from a user-initiated session to enforce policy compliance.

NFC *See* near field communication.

NFV *See* network function virtualization.

NIC *See* network interface card.

NIST *See* National Institute of Standards and Technology.

nondisclosure agreement (NDA) A legal contract between parties detailing the restrictions and requirements borne by each party with respect to confidentiality issues pertaining to information to be shared.

nonrepudiation The ability to verify that an operation has been performed by a particular person or account. This is a system property that prevents the parties to a transaction from subsequently denying involvement in the transaction.

null session The way in which Microsoft Windows represents an unauthenticated connection.

Oakley protocol A key exchange protocol that defines how to acquire authenticated keying material based on the Diffie-Hellman key exchange algorithm.

object identifier (OID) A standardized identifier mechanism for naming any object.

object reuse Assignment of a previously used medium to a subject. The security implication is that before it is provided to the subject, any data present from a previous user must be cleared.

on-path attack An attack in which the attacker intercepts material in a communication path to affect the attack. CompTIA Security+ uses this term in place of *man-in-the-middle attack* and *man-in-the-browser attack.*

On-the-Go (OTG) *See* Universal Serial Bus (USB) On-The-Go (OTG).

one-time pad (OTP) An unbreakable encryption scheme in which a series of nonrepeating, random bits is used once as a key to encrypt a message. Since each pad is used only once, no pattern can be established and traditional cryptanalysis techniques are not effective.

Online Certificate Status Protocol (OCSP) A protocol used to request the revocation status of a digital certificate. This is an alternative to certificate revocation lists.

Open Authorization (OAuth) An open standard for token-based authentication and authorization on the Internet.

open design The principle that protection mechanisms should not depend on secrecy of design for security.

open relay A mail server that receives and forwards mail from outside sources.

open source intelligence (OSINT) Security information derived from sources available to the public.

Open Vulnerability and Assessment Language (OVAL) An XML-based standard for the communication of security information between tools and services.

Open Web Application Security Project (OWASP) A non-profit foundation dedicated to improving security in web applications.

operating system (OS) The basic software that handles input, output, display, memory management, and all the other highly detailed tasks required to support the user environment and associated applications.

operational model of computer security The use of a model that structures security activities into prevention, detection, and response.

operational technology (OT) The name for an IT system used in an industrial setting to control physical processes.

opt in The primary privacy standard in the European Union (EU), where a party must opt in to sharing; otherwise, the default option is not to share the information or give permission for other use.

opt out The primary privacy standard in the U.S., where a party must opt out of sharing; otherwise, the default option is to share the information and give permission for other use.

Orange Book The name commonly used to refer to the now outdated Department of Defense Trusted Computer Security Evaluation Criteria (TCSEC).

OVAL *See* Open Vulnerability and Assessment Language.

over the air (OTA) Refers to performing an action wirelessly.

P12 *See* PKCS #12

P2P *See* peer-to-peer.

PAC *See* Proxy Auto-Configuration.

Packet Capture (PCAP) The methods and files associated with the capture of network traffic in the form of text files.

Padding Oracle on Downgraded Legacy Encryption (POODLE) A vulnerability in SSL 3.0 that can be exploited.

PAM *See* Pluggable Authentication Modules.

pan-tilt-zoom (PTZ) A term used to describe a video camera that supports remote directional and zoom control.

PAP *See* Password Authentication Protocol.

pass-the-hash attack An attack where the credentials are passed in hashed form to convince an object that permission has been granted.

password A string of characters used to prove an individual's identity to a system or object. Used in conjunction with a user ID, a password is the most common method of authentication. The password should be kept secret by the individual who owns it.

Password Authentication Protocol (PAP) A simple protocol used to authenticate a user to a network access server.

Password-Based Key Derivation Function 2 (PBKDF2) A key derivation function that is part of the RSA Laboratories Public Key Cryptography Standards, published as IETF RFC 2898.

patch A replacement set of code designed to correct problems or vulnerabilities in existing software.

Payment Card Industry Data Security Standard (PCI DSS) A contractual data security standard initiated by the credit card industry to cover cardholder data.

PBX *See* private branch exchange.

peer-to-peer (P2P) A network connection methodology involving direct connection from peer to peer.

peer-to-peer trust model A trust model built on actual peer-to-peer connection and communication to establish trust.

penetration testing A security test in which an attempt is made to circumvent security controls in order to discover vulnerabilities and weaknesses. Also called a pen test.

perfect forward security (PFS) A property of a cryptographic system whereby the loss of one key does not compromise material encrypted before or after its use.

permissions Authorized actions a subject can perform on an object. *See also* access control.

personal electronic device (PED) A term used to describe an electronic device, owned by the user and brought into the enterprise, that uses enterprise data. This includes laptops, tablets, and mobile phones, to name a few.

personal exchange format (PFX) A file format used when exporting certificates. Also called PKCS #12.

personal health information (PHI) Information related to a person's medical records, including financial, identification, and medical data.

personal identification number (PIN) A number that is secret, known only to the user to establish identity.

Personal Identity Verification (PIV) Policies, procedures, hardware, and software used to securely identify federal workers.

personally identifiable information (PII) Information that can be used to identify a single person.

pharming The use of a fake website to steal a user's credentials using social engineering techniques.

phishing The use of social engineering to trick a user into responding to something such as an e-mail to instantiate a malware-based attack.

phreaking Used in the media to refer to the hacking of computer systems and networks associated with the phone company. *See also* cracking.

physical security The policies, procedures, and actions taken to regulate actual physical access to and the environment of computing equipment.

PID *See* process identifier.

piggybacking A social engineering technique that involves following a credentialed person through a checkpoint to prevent having to present credentials—in other words, following someone through a door that requires a badge to open, effectively using the other person's badge for entry.

PII *See* personally identifiable information.

ping sweep The use of a series of ICMP ping messages to map out a network.

pivoting The process of moving to a new machine and rescanning the network for newly accessible machines.

PKCS #12 A commonly used member of the family of standards called Public Key Cryptography Standards (PKCS), published by RSA Laboratories.

plain old telephone service (POTS) The term used to describe the old analog phone service and later the "landline" digital phone service.

plaintext In cryptography, a piece of data that is not encrypted. It can also mean the data input into an encryption algorithm that would output ciphertext.

Platform as a Service (PaaS) A third-party offering that allows customers to build, operate, and manage applications without having to manage the underlying infrastructure.

Pluggable Authentication Modules (PAM) A mechanism used in Linux systems to integrate low-level authentication methods into an API.

Point-to-Point Protocol (PPP) The Internet standard for transmission of IP packets over a serial line, as in a dial-up connection to an ISP.

Point-to-Point Protocol Extensible Authentication Protocol (PPP EAP) A PPP extension that provides support for additional authentication methods within PPP.

Point-to-Point Protocol Password Authentication Protocol (PPP PAP) A PPP extension that provides support for password authentication methods over PPP.

Point-to-Point Tunneling Protocol (PPTP) The use of generic routing encapsulation over PPP to create a methodology used for virtual private networking.

Port Address Translation (PAT) The manipulation of port information in an IP datagram at a point in the network to map ports in a fashion similar to Network Address Translation's change of network address.

port scan The examination of TCP and UDP ports to determine which are open and what services are running.

Post Office Protocol (POP) A standardized format for the exchange of e-mail.

potentially unwanted program (PUP) A software program you likely didn't want installed on your computer. PUPs are common in bundled systems.

power distribution unit (PDU) A system to manage power distribution to multiple components, like in a rack mount system.

PowerShell A scripting model for Microsoft Windows with full access to the OS object model.

pre-shared key (PSK) A shared secret that has been previously shared between parties and is used to establish a secure channel.

Pretty Good Privacy (PGP) A popular encryption program that has the ability to encrypt and digitally sign e-mail and files.

preventative intrusion detection A system that detects hostile actions or network activities and prevents them from impacting information systems.

privacy Protecting an individual's personal information from those not authorized to see it.

Privacy-enhanced Electronic Mail (PEM) Internet standard that provides for secure exchange of e-mail using cryptographic functions.

privacy-enhancing technology Cryptographic protection mechanisms employed to ensure the privacy of information.

privacy impact assessment (PIA) The process and procedure of determining the privacy impact and subsequent risk of data elements and their use in the enterprise.

private branch exchange (PBX) A telephone exchange that serves a specific business or entity.

privilege auditing The process of checking the rights and privileges assigned to a specific account or group of accounts.

privilege escalation The step in an attack where an attacker increases their privilege, preferably to administrator or root level.

privilege management The process of restricting a user's ability to interact with the computer system.

process identifier (PID) A unique identifier for a process thread in the operating system kernel.

Protected Extensible Authentication Protocol (PEAP) A protected version of EAP developed by Cisco, Microsoft, and RSA Security that functions by encapsulating the EAP frames in a TLS tunnel.

protected health information (PHI) Information that can disclose health-related items for an individual that must be protected in the system. Similar to personally identifiable information (PII) but related to health.

protocol analyzer A tool used by network personnel to identify packets and header information during network transit. The primary use is in troubleshooting network communication issues.

Proxy Auto-Configuration (PAC) A method of automating the connection of web browsers to appropriate proxy services to retrieve a specific URL.

proxy server A server that acts as a proxy for individual requests and is used for performance and security purposes in a scalable fashion.

PSK *See* pre-shared key.

psychological acceptability The principle that protection mechanisms should not impact users, and if they do, the impact should be minimal.

PTZ *See* pan-tilt-zoom.

public key cryptography *See* asymmetric encryption.

Public Key Cryptography Standards (PKCS) A series of standards covering aspects of the implementation of public key cryptography.

public key infrastructure (PKI) Infrastructure for binding a public key to a known user through a trusted intermediary, typically a certificate authority.

PUP *See* potentially unwanted program.

purple team A team composed of red (offense) and blue (defense) members working together.

qualitative risk assessment The process of subjectively determining the impact of an event that affects a project, program, or business. It involves the use of expert judgment, experience, or group consensus to complete the assessment.

Quality of Service (QoS) The use of technology to manage data traffic, reduce packet loss, and control latency and jitter on a network.

quantitative risk assessment The process of objectively determining the impact of an event that affects a project, program, or business. It usually involves the use of metrics and models to complete the assessment.

RADIUS Remote Authentication Dial-In User Service. A standard protocol for providing authentication services that is commonly used in dial-up, wireless, and PPP environments.

RAID *See* Redundant Array of Inexpensive Disks.

rainbow tables A precomputed set of hash tables for matching passwords by searching rather than computing each on the fly. The use of salts makes this type of attack infeasible.

ransomware Malware that encrypts sensitive files and offers their return for a ransom.

rapid application development (RAD) A software development methodology that favors the use of rapid prototypes and changes as opposed to extensive advanced planning.

RAS *See* Remote-Access Service/Server.

RAT *See* remote-access trojan.

RBAC *See* rule-based access control *or* role-based access control.

RC4 stream cipher A stream cipher used in Transport Layer Security (TLS) and Wired Equivalent Privacy (WEP).

Real-time Blackhole List (RBL) A system that uses DNS information to detect and dump spam e-mails.

real-time operating system (RTOS) An operating system designed to work in a real-time environment.

Real-time Transport Protocol (RTP) A protocol for a standardized packet format used to carry audio and video traffic over IP networks.

Recovery Agent (RA) In Microsoft Windows environments, the entity authorized by the system to use a public key recovery certificate to decrypt other users' files using a special private key function associated with the Encrypted File System (EFS).

recovery point objective (RPO) The amount of data a business is willing to place at risk. It is determined by the amount of time a business has to restore a process before an unacceptable amount of data loss results from a disruption.

recovery time objective (RTO) The amount of time a business has to restore a process before unacceptable outcomes result from a disruption.

red team A team that mimics an adversary during an exercise.

Redundant Array of Inexpensive Disks (RAID) The use of an array of disks arranged in a single unit of storage for increasing storage capacity, redundancy, and performance characteristics.

refactoring The process of restructuring existing computer code without changing its external behavior to improve nonfunctional attributes of the software, such as improving code readability and/or reducing complexity.

reference monitor A non-bypassable element of the kernel that processes and enforces all security interactions, including subject-object accesses.

registration authority (RA) Part of the PKI system responsible for establishing registration parameters during the creation of a certificate.

Remote-Access Service/Server (RAS) A combination of hardware and software used to enable remote access to a network.

remote-access trojan (RAT) A set of malware designed to exploit a system providing remote access.

remotely triggered black hole (RTBH) A popular and effective filtering technique for the mitigation of denial-of-service attacks.

replay attack The reusing of data during an attack to cause a system to respond based on previous acts.

repudiation The act of denying that a message was either sent or received.

residual risk Risks remaining after an iteration of risk management.

return on investment (ROI) A measure of the effectiveness of the use of capital.

reverse social engineering A social engineering attack pattern where the attacker pre-positions themselves to be the person you call when you think you are being attacked. Because you call them, your level of trust is higher.

RFID Radio frequency identification. A technology used for remote identification via radio waves.

Ring policy Part of the Biba security model, this is a policy that allows any subject to read any object without regard to the object's level of integrity and without lowering the subject's integrity level.

RIPEMD A hash function developed in Belgium. The acronym expands to RACE Integrity Primitives Evaluation Message Digest, but this name is rarely used. The current version is RIPEMD-160.

risk The possibility of suffering a loss.

risk assessment or risk analysis The process of analyzing an environment to identify the threats, vulnerabilities, and mitigating actions to determine (either quantitatively or qualitatively) the impact of an event affecting a project, program, or business.

risk management Overall decision-making process of identifying threats and vulnerabilities and their potential impacts, determining the costs to mitigate such events, and deciding what cost-effective actions can be taken to control these risks.

Rivest, Shamir, Adleman (RSA) The names of the three men who developed a public key cryptographic system and the company they founded to commercialize the system.

rogue access point An unauthorized access point inserted into a network for allowing unauthorized wireless access.

role-based access control (RBAC) An access control mechanism in which, instead of the users being assigned specific access permissions for the objects associated with the computer system or network, a set of roles the user may perform is assigned to each user.

rootkit A form of malware that modifies the OS in a system to change the behavior of the system.

router A network device that operates at the network layer (Layer 3) of the OSI model.

RTP *See* Real-time Transport Protocol.

rule-based access control (RBAC) An access control mechanism based on rules.

runlevels In UNIX and Linux systems, runlevels indicate the type of state the system is in, from 0 (halted) to 6 (rebooting). Lower runlevels indicate maintenance conditions with fewer services running, whereas higher runlevels are normal operating conditions. Each UNIX variant employs the concept in the same manner, but the specifics for each runlevel can differ.

S/MIME *See* Secure/Multipurpose Internet Mail Extensions.

safeguard *See* security controls.

SaaS *See* Software as a Service.

SAML *See* Security Assertion Markup Language.

SAN *See* storage area network.

sandboxing The concept of isolating a system and specific processes from the OS in order to provide specific levels of security.

SCADA *See* supervisory control and data acquisition.

SCEP *See* Simple Certificate Enrollment Protocol.

script kiddie A hacker with little true technical skill and hence who uses only scripts that someone else developed.

SDK *See* software development kit.

SDLC *See* software development lifecycle.

SDLM *See* software development lifecycle methodology.

SDN *See* software-defined networking.

SDP *See* Service Delivery Platform.

SDV *See* Software-Defined Visibility.

Secure Copy Protocol (SCP) A network protocol that supports secure file transfers.

secure development lifecycle (SDL) model A process model that includes security function considerations as part of the build process of software in an effort to reduce attack surfaces and vulnerabilities.

Secure FTP A method of secure file transfer that involves the tunneling of FTP through an SSH connection. This is different from SFTP, which is the Secure Shell File Transfer Protocol.

Secure Hash Algorithm (SHA) A hash algorithm used to hash block data. The first version is SHA-1, with subsequent versions detailing the hash digest length: SHA-256, SHA-384, and SHA-512.

Secure Hypertext Transfer Protocol (SHTTP) An alternative to HTTPS in which only the transmitted pages and POST fields are encrypted. Rendered moot, by and large, by widespread adoption of HTTPS.

Secure Key Exchange Mechanism for Internet (SKEMI) A protocol and standard for key exchange across the Internet.

Secure/Multipurpose Internet Mail Extensions (S/MIME) An encrypted implementation of the MIME protocol specification.

Secure Real-time Transport Protocol (SRTP) A secure version of the standard protocol for a standardized packet format used to carry audio and video traffic over IP networks.

Secure Shell (SSH) A set of protocols for establishing a secure remote connection to a computer. This protocol requires a client on each end of the connection and can use a variety of encryption protocols. SSH uses port 22.

Secure Shell File Transfer Protocol (SFTP) A secure file transfer subsystem associated with Secure Shell (SSH).

Secure Sockets Layer (SSL) An encrypting layer between the session and transport layers of the OSI model designed to encrypt above the transport layer, enabling secure sessions between hosts. SSL has been replaced by TLS.

secure web gateway (SWG) *See* next-generation secure web gateway.

Security Assertion Markup Language (SAML) An XML-based standard for exchanging authentication and authorization data.

security association (SA) An instance of security policy and keying material applied to a specific data flow. Both IKE and IPSec use SAs, although these SAs are independent of one another. IPSec SAs are unidirectional and are unique in each security protocol, whereas IKE SAs are bidirectional. A set of SAs is needed for a protected data pipe, one per direction per protocol. SAs are uniquely identified by destination (IPSec endpoint) address, security protocol (AH or ESP), and security parameter index (SPI).

security baseline The end result of the process of establishing an information system's security state. It is a known-good configuration resistant to attacks and information theft.

Security Content Automation Protocol (SCAP) A method of using specific protocols and data exchanges to automate the determination of vulnerability management, measurement, and policy compliance across a system or set of systems.

security controls A group of technical, management, or operational policies and procedures designed to implement specific security functionality. Access controls are an example of a security control.

security information and event management (SIEM) The name used for a broad range of technological solutions to the collection and analysis of security-related information across the enterprise.

security kernel *See* reference monitor.

security operations center (SOC) The grouping of security operations in an enterprise.

security orchestration, automation, and response (SOAR) A system designed to facilitate responses in incident response situations.

security through obscurity An approach to security using the mechanism of hiding information to protect it.

segregation or separation of duties A basic control that prevents or detects errors and irregularities by assigning job responsibilities for increased risk tasks to different individuals so that no single individual can commit fraudulent or malicious actions.

self-encrypting drive (SED) A data drive that has built-in encryption capability on the drive control itself.

Sender Policy Framework (SPF) An e-mail validation system designed to detect e-mail spoofing by verifying that incoming mail comes from a host authorized by that domain's administrators.

sequence number A number within a TCP segment for maintaining the correct order of TCP segments sent and received and thus conversation integrity.

Server Message Block (SMB) The Internet standard protocol used by Microsoft Windows to share files, printers, and serial ports.

server-side scripting The processing of scripts on the server side of an Internet connection to prevent client tampering with the process.

Service Delivery Platform (SDP) A set of components that provides a service delivery architecture (service creation, session control, and protocols) for a service delivered to a customer or other system.

service level agreement (SLA) An agreement between parties concerning the expected or contracted uptime associated with a system.

Service Set Identifier (SSID) Identifies a specific 802.11 wireless network. It transmits information about the access point to which the wireless client is connecting.

session hijacking An attack against a communication session by injecting packets into the middle of the communication session.

shadow file The file that stores the encrypted password in a system.

shielded twisted pair (STP) A physical network connection consisting of two wires twisted and covered with a shield to prevent interference.

shift cipher A cipher that operates by substitution, the replacement of one character for another.

shimming The process of putting a layer of code between the driver and the OS to allow flexibility and portability.

Short Message Service (SMS) A form of text messaging over phone and mobile phone circuits that allows up to 160-character messages to be carried over signaling channels.

shoulder surfing Stealing of credentials by looking over someone's shoulder while they type them into a system.

signature database A collection of activity patterns that have already been identified and categorized and that typically indicate suspicious or malicious activity.

SIM *See* Subscriber Identity Module.

Simple Certificate Enrollment Protocol (SCEP) A protocol used in PKI for enrollment and other services.

Simple Mail Transfer Protocol (SMTP) The standard Internet protocol used to transfer e-mail between hosts.

Simple Mail Transfer Protocol Secure (SMTPS) The secure version of the standard Internet protocol used to transfer e-mail between hosts.

Simple Network Management Protocol (SNMP) A standard protocol used to remotely manage network devices across a network.

Simple Object Access Protocol (SOAP) An XML-based specification for exchanging information associated with web services.

Simple Security Rule The principle that states complexity makes security more difficult and hence simplicity is valued.

single loss expectancy (SLE) Monetary loss or impact of each occurrence of a threat. SLE = asset value (AV) × exposure factor (EF).

single point of failure (SPoF) A single system component whose failure can result in system failure.

single sign-on (SSO) An authentication process by which the user can enter a single user ID and password and then move from application to application or resource to resource without having to supply further authentication information.

slack space Unused space on a disk drive created when a file is smaller than the allocated unit of storage (such as a sector).

Small Computer System Interface (SCSI) A protocol for data transfer to and from a machine.

SMB *See* Server Message Block.

SMS *See* Short Message Service.

smurf attack A method of generating significant numbers of packets for a DoS attack.

sniffer A software or hardware device used to observe network traffic as it passes through a network on a shared broadcast media.

sniffing The use of a software or hardware device (sniffer) to observe network traffic as it passes through a network on a shared broadcast media.

SOAR *See* security orchestration, automation, and response.

SOC *See* security operations center.

SoC *See* system on a chip.

social engineering The art of deceiving another person so that they reveal confidential information. This is often accomplished by posing as an individual who should be entitled to have access to the information.

Software as a Service (SaaS) The provisioning of software as a service, commonly known as on-demand software.

software-defined networking (SDN) The use of software to act as a control layer separate from the data layer in a network to manage traffic.

Software-Defined Visibility (SDV) A framework that enables visibility into network operations and functions.

software development kit (SDK) A set of tools and processes used to interface with a larger system element when one is programming changes to an environment.

software development lifecycle (SDLC) The processes and procedures employed to develop software.

software development lifecycle methodology (SDLM) The processes and procedures employed to develop software. Sometimes also called *secure development lifecycle model* when security is part of the development process.

solid-state drive (SSD) A mass storage device, such as a hard drive, that is composed of electronic memory as opposed to a physical device of spinning platters.

SONET *See* Synchronous Optical Network Technologies.

spam E-mail that is not requested by the recipient and is typically of a commercial nature. Also known as unsolicited commercial e-mail (UCE).

spam filter A security appliance designed to remove spam at the network layer before it enters e-mail servers.

spear phishing A phishing attack aimed at a specific individual.

spim Spam sent over an instant messaging channel.

spoofing Making data appear to have originated from another source so as to hide the true origin from the recipient.

spraying An attack method where multiple entries are tried, such as password spraying, where common passwords are tried against accounts.

spyware Malware designed to spy on a user, typically recording information such as keystrokes for passwords.

SQL injection An attack against a SQL engine parser designed to perform unauthorized database activities.

SSD *See* solid-state drive.

SSID *See* Service Set Identifier.

SSL *See* Secure Sockets Layer.

SSL stripping attack A specific type of on-path/man-in-the-middle attack against SSL.

SSO *See* single sign-on.

steganography The use of cryptography to hide communications.

storage area network (SAN) A dedicated network that provides access to data storage.

STP *See* shielded twisted pair.

stream cipher An encryption process used against a stream of information, even bit by bit, as opposed to operations performed on blocks.

Structured Exception Handler (SEH) The process used to handle exceptions in the Windows OS core functions.

Structured Query Language (SQL) A language used in relational database queries.

Structured Query Language Inject (SQLi) An attack against an interface using SQL.

structured threat A threat that has reasonable financial backing and can last for a few days or more. The organizational elements allow for greater time to penetrate and attack a system.

Structured Threat Information eXpression (STIX) A framework for passing threat information across automated interfaces.

Subject Alternative Name (SAN) A field on a certificate that identifies alternative names for the entity to which the certificate applies.

subnet mask The information that tells a device how to interpret the network and host portions of an IP address.

subnetting The creation of a network within a network by manipulating how an IP address is split into network and host portions.

Subscriber Identity Module (SIM) An integrated circuit or hardware element that securely stores the International Mobile Subscriber Identity (IMSI) and the related key used to identify and authenticate subscribers on mobile telephones.

substitution The switching of one value for another in cryptography while maintaining element order.

supervisory control and data acquisition (SCADA) A generic term used to describe the industrial control system networks that interconnect infrastructure elements (such as manufacturing plants, oil and gas pipelines, power generation and distribution systems, and so on) and computer systems.

switch A network device that operates at the data link layer (Layer 2) of the OSI model.

switched port analyzer (SPAN) A technology employed that can duplicate individual channels crossing a switch to another circuit.

symmetric encryption Encryption that needs all parties to have a copy of the key, sometimes called a shared secret. The single key is used for both encryption and decryption.

SYN flood A method of performing DoS by exhausting TCP connection resources through partially opening connections and letting them time out.

Synchronous Optical Network Technologies (SONET) A set of standards used for data transfers over optical networks.

systematic risk A form of risk that can be managed by diversification.

system on a chip (SoC) The integration of complete system functions on a single chip in order to simplify construction of devices.

tailgating The act of following an authorized person through a doorway without using one's own credentials. Can be mitigated with an access control vestibule.

TACACS+ *See* Terminal Access Controller Access Control System Plus.

tactics, techniques, and procedures (TTPs) The methods used by an adversary, organized in a fashion to assist in identification and defense.

tangible asset An asset for which a monetary equivalent can be determined. Examples are inventory, buildings, cash, hardware, software, and so on.

TAXII *See* Trusted Automated eXchange of Intelligence Information.

TCP Wrappers A host-based networking ACL system that's used in some Linux systems to filter network access to Internet Protocol servers.

TCP/IP hijacking An attack where the attacker intercepts and hijacks an established TCP connection.

Telnet An insecure network protocol used to provide cleartext bidirectional communication over TCP. Replaced most often by Secure Shell (SSH).

TEMPEST The U.S. military's name for the field associated with electromagnetic eavesdropping on signals emitted by electronic equipment. *See also* Van Eck phenomenon.

Temporal Key Integrity Protocol (TKIP) A security protocol used in 802.11 wireless networks.

Terminal Access Controller Access Control System Plus (TACACS+) A remote authentication system that uses the TACACS+ protocol, defined in RFC 1492, and TCP port 49.

threat Any circumstance or event with the potential to cause harm to an asset.

threat actor The party behind a threat, although it may be a non-person, as in an environmental issue.

threat vector The method by which a threat actor introduces a specific threat.

three-way handshake A means of ensuring information transference through a three-step data exchange. Used to initiate a TCP connection.

ticket-granting server (TGS) The portion of the Kerberos authentication system that issues tickets in response to legitimate requests.

ticket-granting ticket (TGT) A part of the Kerberos authentication system that is used to prove identity when requesting service tickets.

time-based one-time password (TOTP) A password that is used once and is only valid during a specific time period.

time bomb A form of logic bomb in which the triggering event is a date or specific time. *See also* logic bomb.

TKIP *See* Temporal Key Integrity Protocol.

token A hardware device that can be used in a challenge-response authentication process.

Transaction Signature (TSIG) A protocol used as a means of authenticating dynamic DNS records during DNS updates.

Transmission Control Protocol/Internet Protocol (TCP/IP) A connection-oriented protocol for communication over IP networks.

Transport Layer Security (TLS) A replacement for SSL that is currently being used to secure communications between servers and browsers.

trapdoor *See* backdoor.

Trivial File Transfer Protocol (TFTP) A simplified version of FTP used for low-overhead file transfers using UDP port 69.

trojan horse A form of malicious code that appears to provide one service (and may indeed provide that service) but that also hides another purpose. This hidden purpose often has a malicious intent. This code may also be simply referred to as a *trojan*.

trunking The process of spanning a single VLAN across multiple switches.

Trusted Automated eXchange of Intelligence Information (TAXII) A transport framework for STIX data communication.

trusted OS An OS that can provide appropriate levels of security and has mechanisms to provide assurance of security function.

Trusted Platform Module (TPM) A hardware chip to enable trusted computing platform operations.

TTPs *See* tactics, techniques, and procedures.

tunneling The process of packaging packets so that they can traverse a network in a secure, confidential manner.

typo squatting An attack form that involves capitalizing on common typographical errors at the URL level, hoping the browser user will not notice they end up on a different site.

unified endpoint management (UEM) The aggregation of multiple products into a single system on an endpoint for efficiency purposes.

Unified Extensible Firmware Interface (UEFI) A specification that defines the interface between an OS and the hardware firmware. This is a replacement to BIOS.

unified threat management (UTM) The aggregation of multiple network security products into a single appliance for efficiency purposes.

Uniform Resource Identifier (URI) A set of characters used to identify the name of a resource in a computer system. A URL is a form of URI.

uninterruptible power supply (UPS) A source of power (generally a battery) designed to provide uninterrupted power to a computer system in the event of a temporary loss of power.

Universal Resource Locator (URL) A specific character string used to point to a specific item across the Internet.

Universal Serial Bus (USB) An industry-standard protocol for communication over a cable to peripherals via a standard set of connectors.

Universal Serial Bus On-the-Go (USB OTG) A standardized specification that allows a device to read data from a USB device without requiring a PC.

unmanned aerial vehicle (UAV) A remotely piloted flying vehicle.

unshielded twisted pair (UTP) A physical connection consisting of a pair of twisted wires forming a circuit.

unstructured threat A threat that has no significant resources or ability—typically an individual with limited skill.

unsystematic risk Risk that cannot be mitigated by diversification. Unsystematic risks can result in loss across all types of risk controls.

usage auditing The process of recording who did what and when on an information system.

user acceptance testing (UAT) The application of acceptance-testing criteria to determine fitness for use according to end-user requirements.

User and Entity Behavioral Analytics (UEBA) A security process that uses user behavior patterns to determine anomalies.

User Datagram Protocol (UDP) A protocol in the TCP/IP protocol suite for the transport layer that does not sequence packets—it is "fire and forget" in nature.

user ID A unique alphanumeric identifier that specifies individuals who are logging in or accessing a system.

UTP *See* unshielded twisted pair.

vampire tap A tap that connects to a network line without cutting the connection.

Van Eck phenomenon Electromagnetic eavesdropping through the interception of electronic signals emitted by electrical equipment. *See also* TEMPEST.

Variable-Length Subnet Masking (VLSM) The process of using variable-length subnets to create subnets within subnets.

video teleconferencing (VTC) A business process of using video signals to carry audio and visual signals between separate locations, thus allowing participants to meet virtually instead of traveling to a physical location. Modern videoconferencing equipment can provide very realistic connectivity when lighting and backgrounds are controlled.

Vigenère cipher A polyalphabetic substitution cipher that depends on a password.

virtual desktop environment (VDE) The use of virtualization technology to host desktop systems on a centralized server.

virtual desktop infrastructure (VDI) The use of servers to host virtual desktops by moving the processing to the server and using the desktop machine as merely a display terminal. VDI offers operating efficiencies as well as cost and security benefits.

virtual local area network (VLAN) A broadcast domain inside a switched system.

virtual machine (VM) A form of a containerized operating system that allows a system to be run on top of another OS.

virtual machine (VM) sprawl avoidance The processes and procedures employed to keep sets of VMs properly documented and stored, to prevent the loss of machines due to misfiling of the data.

virtual machine (VM) escape protection Mechanisms employed to prevent processes from escaping the VM process into other VM processes or the host process.

virtual private cloud (VPC) A cloud instance that is virtually isolated by the provider.

virtual private network (VPN) An encrypted network connection across another network, offering a private communication channel across a public medium.

virus A form of malicious code or software that attaches itself to other pieces of code in order to replicate. Viruses may contain a payload, which is a portion of the code that is designed to execute when a certain condition is met (such as on a certain date). This payload is often malicious in nature.

vishing A form of social engineering attack over voice lines (VoIP).

Visual Basic for Applications (VBA) A Microsoft specification for using Visual Basic in applications such as the Office Suite. Microsoft declared this a legacy methodology in 2006.

Voice over IP (VoIP) The packetized transmission of voice signals (telephony) over Internet Protocol.

vulnerability A weakness in an asset that can be exploited by a threat to cause harm.

WAP *See* Wireless Application Protocol.

war-dialing An attacker's attempt to gain unauthorized access to a computer system or network by discovering unprotected connections to the system/network through the telephone system and modems.

war-driving The attempt by an attacker to discover unprotected wireless networks by wandering (or driving) around with a wireless device, looking for available wireless access points.

warm site A backup site, off premises, that has hardware but is not configured with data and will take some time to switch over to.

Wassenaar Arrangement A set of rules and regulations concerning dual-use technologies, including cryptography. These rules are related to arms trading and similar national security concerns and impact some cybersecurity elements.

watering hole attack The infecting of a specific target website—one that users trust and go to on a regular basis—with malware.

web application firewall (WAF) A firewall that operates at the application level, specifically designed to protect web applications by examining requests at the application stack level.

WEP *See* Wired Equivalent Privacy.

whaling A phishing attack targeted against a high-value target like a corporate officer or system administrator.

white-box testing A form of testing where the tester has knowledge of the inner workings of a system. The term has recently been updated by CompTIA for Security+ to be *known environment testing.*

whitelisting A listing of items to be allowed by specific inclusion. This term has been updated by CompTIA for Security+ to be *application approved list.* Whitelisting is the opposite of blacklisting, or application block/deny list.

wide area network (WAN) A network that spans a large geographic region.

Wi-Fi Protected Access (WPA/WPA2/WPA3) A modern protocol to secure wireless communications using a subset of the 802.11i standard. WPA3 is the latest specification in this series.

Wi-Fi Protected Setup (WPS) A network security standard that allows easy setup of a wireless home network.

Wired Equivalent Privacy (WEP) An encryption scheme used to attempt to provide confidentiality and data integrity on earlier 802.11 networks.

wireless access point (WAP) A network access device that facilitates the connection of wireless devices to a network.

Wireless Application Protocol (WAP) A protocol for transmitting data to small handheld devices such as cellular phones.

wireless intrusion detection system (WIDS) An intrusion detection system established to cover a wireless network.

wireless intrusion prevention system (WIPS) An intrusion prevention system established to cover a wireless network.

Wireless Transport Layer Security (WTLS) The encryption protocol used on WAP networks.

worm An independent piece of malicious code or software that self-replicates. Unlike a virus, it does not need to be attached to another piece of code. A worm replicates by breaking into another system and making a copy of itself on this new system. A worm can contain a destructive payload but it is not required.

write blocker A specific interface for storage media that does not permit writing to occur to the device. This allows copies to be made without altering the device.

write once read many (WORM) A data storage technology where things are written once (permanent) and then can be read many times, as in optical disks.

X.509 The standard format for digital certificates.

XaaS An abbreviation for Anything as a Service.

XML *See* Extensible Markup Language.

XOR Bitwise exclusive OR, an operation commonly used in cryptography.

XSRF *See* cross-site request forgery.

XSS *See* cross-site scripting.

zero day A vulnerability for which there is no previous knowledge.

zombie A machine that is at least partially under the control of a botnet.

INDEX

A

B

C

D

E

F

G

H

I

J

K

L

M

N

O

P

Q

R

S

T

U

V

W

X

Y

Z